EARLY SETTLERS OF MISSISSIPPI AS TAKEN FROM LAND CLAIMS IN THE MISSISSIPPI TERRITORY

By
Walter Lowrie
Editor, the *American State Papers*, Vol. I

Book Publishers

Southern Historical Press, Inc.
Greenville, South Carolina

Please direct all correspondence and orders to:

www.southernhistoricalpress.com
or
SOUTHERN HISTORICAL PRESS, Inc.
PO Box 1267
375 West Broad Street
Greenville, SC   29601
southernhistoricalpress@gmail.com

Originally published: Washington, DC, 1834
New Material Copyright 1986
    By: Southern Historical Press, Inc.
ISBN #0-89308-583-9
All rights Reserved.
Printed in the United States of America

AMERICAN STATE PAPERS.

PUBLIC LANDS.

VOLUME I.

DOCUMENTS,

LEGISLATIVE AND EXECUTIVE,

OF THE

Congress of the United States,

IN RELATION TO

THE PUBLIC LANDS,

FROM THE FIRST SESSION OF THE FIRST CONGRESS TO THE FIRST SESSION OF THE
TWENTY-THIRD CONGRESS :

MARCH 4, 1789, TO JUNE 15, 1834.

SELECTED AND EDITED,

UNDER THE AUTHORITY OF THE SENATE OF THE UNITED STATES,

BY WALTER LOWRIE,

SECRETARY OF THE SENATE.

VOLUME I.

FROM MARCH 4th, 1789, TO FEBRUARY 27th, 1809.

WASHINGTON:

PRINTED BY DUFF GREEN.

1834.

PUBLISHER'S PREFACE

When the *American State Papers* were first issued between 1834 and 1860, two different editions were published, one by the Duff Green Company Publishers and the other, and the most widely used, was that done by Gales & Seaton Publishers. Both series contained essentially the same information; the Duff Green series appeared in six volumes, and the Gales & Seaton edition appeared in eight volumes. As well as your publisher has been able to determine, the Gales & Seaton edition was limited to 750 sets, which heightens the problem of their obscurity and their importance to the general public.

Southern Historical Press has taken Volumes I and II of the Duff Green edition and has lifted out for publication those continuous sections that deal with the Land Grants and Claims for the present states of Louisiana, Mississippi and Missouri. It should be noted by the reader that the other volumes of both series of these land papers contain additional information pertaining to land grants and claims in these three states.

Southern Historical Press plans to reprint, with full-name indexes, the entire eight volumes of the Gales & Seaton edition of the *American State Papers — Land Grants and Claims, 1789-1837.*

Concerning Pagination

Please note that the pagination of these three books is the original pagination from Volumes I and II of the Duff Green series. We did not attempt to renumber the pages starting with page one and continuing to the last page of each book, and the full-name index at the back of each volume reflects these *original* page numbers.

AMERICAN STATE PAPERS, PUBLIC LANDS:
An Overview of the Series

By Elizabeth Shown Mills, C.G., F.A.S.G.

The story of America's *land* is the story of the American people. The hunger for *land* populated American shores and drove the settlers westward. *Land* was the American dream: a piece for every man, every family — *land* each could fertilize with his or her own sweat and pass to their own sons.

It was the abundance of land — for farming, for hunting, for mining — that brought the British and the German to the Atlantic Seaboards; the French and the Spanish to the Gulf; Canadians, British, French, and Poles to the Mississippi Valley and the Great Lakes. For land, they challenged the Native American wherever they found him. To keep their land, the Indian nations fought back, then bargained, before finally conceding defeat.

American State Papers, Public Lands Series documents the melding of these peoples on the first great frontiers of the new United States: the Old Southwest and the Old Northwest. *ASP-PL* is, beyond a doubt, the most neglected source — the most *important* neglected source — of data on ethnic settlement and migration within trans-Appalachian America. It also serves as a vital finding aid to rich stores of public land claim files within the National Archives. In overall importance, *ASP-PL* stands second to none but the Draper Papers.

Between 1832 and 1861, the United States Congress selected and published a series of 38 volumes, some 35,000 pages, of congressional documents, chosen for their importance to "the legislative and documentary history of the United States." (*ASP-Foreign Relations*, vol. V, p. vii.) Those records chosen for inclusion in *American State Papers: Documents Legislative and Executive of the Congress of the United States* were grouped into ten classes (*Foreign Relations, Indian Affairs, Finance, Commerce & Navigation, Military Affairs, Naval Affairs, Post Office, Public Lands, Claims,* and *Miscellaneous*), with one to eight volumes per group.

ASP-PL represents the largest class of this now rare series, offering 1,570 documents spanning some 7,728 pages, within 8 volumes. The number of Americans discussed is mind-boggling — 80,000-100,000 would be a conservative estimate of the men and women included in this rich fund of biographical data. The scope of the material which *ASP-PL* makes available to professional and family historians is of both wide range and momentous import. As a sampling:

- Settlements of the United Brethren in Ohio, 1826
- Colonial French, British, and Spanish land grants in the Gulf States throughout the 1700s and early 1800s
- Settlement of exiled supporters of Napoleon in Alabama's Vine and Olive Colony, 1825 (where records subsequent were destroyed by local officials —

on the premise that "no one could read those things anyway, since they're all written in a foreign language"!)

- Lead mining in Missouri, Illinois, and Michigan, ca. 1810-30
- Petitions for bounty land by Revolutionary soldiers of Virginia, and patriot refugees from Canada and Nova Scotia
- Early plats (designating land and lot owners) of such cities as Detroit, Green Bay, Peoria, Cahokia, and Kaskaskia (whose "old town" now lies under the Mississippi River)
- Requests of Polish exiles, deported by the emperor of Austria, to settle in Illinois or Michigan
- Choctaw Land Claimants (full and mixed-blood, as well as white countrymen) under the Treaty of Dancing Rabbit Creek, 1830
- Creek and Cherokee Reservees after the settlement of the War of 1812
- North Carolina payments to Indian reservees, in exchange for their abandonment of their lands
- Similar documents for the Potowatomie, Quapaw, Catawba, Wyandots and other tribes

Thirteen states are directly, and abundantly, treated in *ASP-PL*

Alabama	Indiana	Mississippi
Arkansas	Iowa	Missouri
Florida	Louisiana	Ohio
Illinois	Michigan	Wisconsin
	Minnesota	

At least nine others are less directly treated to an extent worth noting:

Georgia	Pennsylvania	Tennessee
New York	Rhode Island	Vermont
North Carolina	South Carolina	Virginia

Historical studies of the Old Southwest suffer immensely from the underuse of grassroots level resources — caused, in part, by haphazard recordkeeping, by courthouse fires, and by too-little awareness of the value of such materials. The eight volumes of *American State Papers, Public Lands* offers viable substitutes for destroyed or nonexisting records and an extremely convenient source of biographical data and local-oriented documents, all available to the scholar without travel.

Introduction to the Three Volumes on Louisiana, Mississippi and Missouri

These Land Grants are the public record of transactions presented to Congress relating uniquely to settlement of Public Domain between 1789–1837. Types of claims to land on Public Domain are primarily: preemption rights; homestead settlements; military bounty lands and militia claims.

Those persons who presented their claims before Congress receive extensive treatment only in the *State Papers*. Nearly 80,000 diverse claims to land in early America which are treated in this 8-volume series give such valuable genealogical/historical data as: ages of claimants; previous places of habitation; names of children, wives, and other relatives; exact location of claims; and the time period of "cultivation and habitation."

LOUISIANA AND MISSOURI

Louisiana is a major focal point for land grants and claims in the *State Papers*. When the Louisiana Purchase took place in 1803, only two territories were immediately formed—the Louisiana and Orleans territories. An act of Congress in 1812 provided that the territory heretofore called Louisiana should hereafter be called Missouri. The southern portion of the territory of Missouri became the Territory of Arkansas in 1819, and the northern portion became the state of Missouri in 1821. The Territory of Orleans became the state of Louisiana in 1812.

In these records the original proprietor is named, by whom the land is presently being claimed, reason for change of title (purchase or inheritance), nature and extent of claim, and, if the claim was disallowed, the reasons for disallowance.

MISSISSIPPI

Mississippi was formed from land ceded to the United States by South Carolina and Georgia. Part of the British Province of West Florida and part of the land ceded by the French made up the rest of the Territory of Mississippi in 1798. The Territory of Alabama was formed from the Territory of Mississippi in 1812. In 1817 statehood was granted to Mississippi.

The genealogical worth of the foregoing paragraph is evident. The present claimant and original claimant are given in addition to their location; from where the patent was derived; if claim was rejected an explanation was given, plus the exact period of known settlement. Also included are those settling under preemption rights without authority to settle from any governments. The location and nature of claim are listed, both the period of cultivation and habitation, plus the date of first settlement and the parish where these people are located.

EARLY SETTLERS
OF MISSISSIPPI
AS TAKEN FROM
LAND CLAIMS
IN THE
MISSISSIPPI TERRITORY

PRE-EMPTION TITLES IN THE MISSISSIPPI TERRITORY.

COMMUNICATED TO THE HOUSE OF REPRESENTATIVES NOVEMBER 21, 1808.

Mr. JEREMIAH MORROW, from the Committee on the Public Lands, to whom was referred the memorial* of the House of Representatives of the Mississippi territory, made the following report:

The memorial presents three subjects for consideration:

1st. The expediency of giving a right to pre-emption to persons for lands settled on, and improved subsequent to, the 3d of March, 1807.

2d. The expediency of extending the time for making the first payment on pre-emption rights, granted under an act of the last session of Congress; and

3d. A remonstrance against a bill introduced the last session of Congress for establishing a federal court in that territory.

It is stated in the memorial, in favor of the first proposition, that a great number of persons, many of whom are heads of families, have emigrated to that territory within the last twelve months, under an expectation that, on their arrival, lands of the United States might be procured by purchase; but the sales being protracted, and the lands not likely to be exposed to sale within a short time, they were constrained either to settle on the lands of the United States, or seek a residence within the Spanish lines.

The committee do not impute to these settlers the improper intention of violating the laws of their country, but are of opinion that, to give a right of pre-emption to persons who have settled on the lands of the United States contrary to law, would be indirectly rewarding a direct violation of those laws, would be offering an inducement to future intrusion, and be giving support to a practice liable to many abuses, and which, if encouraged, must destroy all competition in the public sales, and eventually defeat the object of drawing a revenue from the sale of lands.

The considerations adduced by the memorial, in support of the second proposition, are, the difficulty or impossibility of commanding money for their produce, owing to the stagnation of commerce, and the consequent inability of the claimants to make their first payment at the time directed by law.

The committee are not insensible to their situation; but, when they consider that most of these claimants

emigrated to that territory with the declared intention of becoming purchasers of public lands, that many of them may have had possession since early in the year 1803, and none of them but must have cultivated and actually inhabited the tracts which they respectively claim before the 3d of March, 1807; if public lands had been open for sale, and they had made purchase at the time of their respective settlements, the first payment under the law must have become due long before the time fixed by the law giving them a right of pre-emption; that they have already had a longer term for making their first payment, from the time of filing the notice of their claim, than other purchasers have from the time of their contracts; and that these claimants have had the selection of the best lands and most eligible situations, without any competition in the market; they cannot recommend an extension of the time of payment. Another consideration, which had influence with the committee in estimating the merits of the claim for indulgence, was the public convenience. Perhaps public convenience ought not to be opposed to a claim of strict right; but, in a case like the present, they think it should, in some measure, be consulted. The 1st of January next is the time fixed by law for making the first payment on the pre-emption claims. By proclamation, the public sales of the lands in that territory (with some exceptions) are to commence in the same month. If the time for making the first payment on pre-emptions should be extended beyond the period fixed for the public sales, then any lands which should become forfeited by the claimant's failure to make payment could not be sold until a public sale, for these particular tracts were directed by proclamation.

The third subject of the memorial, viz., the establishment of a federal court in that territory, the committee have not taken into consideration, as there is not now any proposition or bill having that in view before Congress.

The committee, therefore, recommend to the House the adoption of the following resolutions:

1st. *Resolved*, That a right of pre-emption ought not to be given to persons who have settled on the public lands, for land which they cultivate and inhabit.

2d. *Resolved*, That it is inexpedient to extend the time for making the first payment on pre-emption claims granted under an act of the last session of Congress.

* See Memorial, No. 152.

LAND CLAIMS IN THE MISSISSIPPI TERRITORY.

COMMUNICATED TO THE HOUSE OF REPRESENTATIVES JANUARY 5, 1809.

TREASURY DEPARTMENT, *January* 2, 1809.

SIR: I have the honor, in conformity with the several provisions of the laws providing for the sale of public lands south of the State of Tennessee, to transmit the transcripts of decisions received from the commissioners appointed to settle claims to lands in the Mississippi territory, in the following cases, viz.:

A. British patents disallowed by the commissioners west of Pearl river; the claimants not being residents.

a. British patents disallowed by the commissioners east of Pearl river, for the same reason.

A. 2. British patents filed with the commissioners

west of Pearl river, under the fifth section of the act of the 2d March, 1805.

B. Claims disallowed, as antedated, by the commissioners west of Pearl river.

D. British and Spanish warrants, or orders of survey, disallowed by the commissioners west of Pearl river.

d. Spanish warrants, or orders of survey, disallowed by the commissioners east of Pearl river.

I have the honor to be, with great respect,

Your obedient servant,

ALBERT GALLATIN.

To the Honorable the SPEAKER
of the House of Representatives.

MISSISSIPPI TERRITORY,
TOWN OF WASHINGTON, *July* 3, 1807.

SIR: The Board of Commissioners west of Pearl river, established by a law of Congress regulating the grants of land, and providing for the disposal of the lands of the United States south of the State of Tennessee, respectfully report:

That, having finished the business assigned them, so far as related to decisions, on the 15th ultimo proceeded to the execution of that part of their duty required by the seventh section of the said act, and find that it is not practicable to comply with the requisitions thereof, to the extent originally contemplated: because a survey of the lands has not, as yet, been made and returned, agreeably to the act aforesaid, by which the Board can know and ascertain the British claims required to be reported, and their conflictions with other claims, and also their present situation. They, therefore, are under the necessity of submitting the following, as the only report which, at this time, can be made, to wit:

The annexed abstract, marked (A) contains all the claims to lands held under " British grants, legally and fully executed, which have been duly recorded, the title of which is not confirmed to the holders thereof.

The conditions annexed to those grants are numerous, and may be classed under four heads: those denominated mandamus grants, those to officers of the army and navy, and those to any other description of persons; the conditions of which vary, as will be seen by a reference to a copy of each, which is contained in the annexed sheets, numbered 1, 2, 3, and 4.

As to the performance of any of the conditions of those grants, no evidence has been given or offered to the Board relative thereto: in fact, they seem to have been considered more as matter of form than substance, and to have become obsolete.

Abstract (B) contains such claims as have been disallowed by the Board, on suspicion of their being antedated; but to be reported to the Secretary of the Treasury, in conformity to the third section of an act supplementary to the before recited law.

Abstract (C) contains claims of minors, founded on warrants of survey, &c. and disallowed by the Board, and also required to be reported by the ninth section of said supplemental act. As to the circumstances which occasioned the issuing these warrants, and the validity attached to them, the commissioners observe that it seems to have been the policy of the Spanish Government to guard against monopolies of landed property: hence, it frequently happened that, in allotting lands to men with numerous families of children, certain portions were granted to their children, or some of them, in their own right, which, by the Spanish laws, had the same validity as if granted to persons of full age; that, under this character of title, the parties were in the habit of considering themselves as secure as if they had gone on to perfect their rights to complete patent, and especially as the powers of the Spanish Government to revoke the complete as well as the incomplete titles were the same; added to which, it was very expensive, by reason of the extortion and high fees of the Spanish officers, for the poor, or common class of people, to carry their claims through all the grades of title.

THOMAS RODNEY,
ROBERT WILLIAMS,
THOMAS H. WILLIAMS.

True copy from the journal of the board of Commissioners.

THOMAS H. WILLIAMS.

CONDITIONS.

1. Let a patent be prepared and engrossed, to pass the great seal of this province, importing His Majesty's most gracious grant unto Captain Amos Ogden, his heirs and assigns, of a plantation or tract of land, containing twenty five thousand acres, situate southwesterly about twenty-one miles from the old Natchez fort, bounded southerly by a creek called Homochitto creek, and about one-quarter of a mile east of a tract of one thousand acres, granted to Colin Graham, Esq. on said creek, about half a mile south from land granted to Junis Hooper, on a creek called Second creek, and on the other side by vacant land; together with all rights, members, privileges, and appurtenances to the same, being or in anywise belonging, upon the following terms, conditions, and reservations, viz.: That the said Amos Ogden do settle the said lands with foreign Protestants,

or persons that shall be brought from His Majesty's other colonies in North America, within ten years from the date of the grant, in the proportion of one person for every hundred acres. That if one-third of the land is not settled with foreign Protestants, or persons that shall be brought from His Majesty's other colonies in North America, in the above mentioned proportion, within three years from the date of the grant, the whole to be forfeited to His Majesty, his heirs and successors. That such part of the whole tract as is not settled with foreign Protestants, or persons that shall be brought from His Majesty's other colonies in North America, at the expiration of ten years from the date of the grant, do revert to His Majesty, his heirs, and successors. That an annual quit-rent of one halfpenny sterling per acre be reserved to His Majesty, his heirs, and successors, payable on the feast of St. Michael in every year, to commence and become payable upon one-half of the said land, on the feast of St. Michael which shall first happen after the expiration of five years from the date of the grant, and to be payable on every ensuing feast of St. Michael, or within fourteen days after: and the whole quantity to be subject in like manner to the like quit-rents, at the expiration of ten years. That there be a reservation in the said grant to His Majesty, his heirs, and successors, of all those parts of the land which the surveyor shall, upon the return of the survey, report to be proper for erecting fortifications, public wharfs, and naval yards, or for other military purposes. That there be a reservation to His Majesty, his heirs, and successors, of all mines of gold, silver, copper, lead, and coals. That, if any part of the land shall appear, by the surveyor's report, to be well adapted to the growth of hemp or flax, it shall be a condition of the grant that the grantee shall sow, and continue annually to cultivate, a due proportion of the land, not less than one acre in every thousand, with that beneficial article of produce; the same terms, conditions, and reservations above mentioned being conformable to His Majesty's order in council to me directed, bearing date the thirteenth day of May, in the year of our Lord one thousand seven hundred and sixty-seven, and with the other usual clauses, reservations, provisoes, restrictions, and limitations, as contained in His Majesty's instructions; and, for so doing, this shall be your sufficient warrant.

2. To have and to hold the said tract of land, and all and singular the premises hereby granted, with the appurtenances, unto the said Daniel Clark, his heirs, and assigns, forever, in free and common soccage, yielding and paying unto us, our heirs, and successors, or to the Receiver General of our quit-rents for the time being, or to such other officer as shall be appointed to receive the same, a quit-rent of one halfpenny sterling per acre, at the feast of St. Michael every year, the first payment to commence on the said feast of St. Michael, which shall first happen after the expiration of ten years from the date hereof, or within fourteen days after the said feast, annually: Provided, always, and this present grant is upon condition, nevertheless, that the said Daniel Clark, his heirs, and assigns, shall and do, within three years after the expiration of the term of ten years aforesaid, for every fifty acres of plantable land hereby granted, clear and cultivate three acres, at least, in that part thereof which he or they shall judge most convenient and advantageous, or else do clear and drain three acres of swampy or sunken ground, or do drain three acres of marsh, if any such shall be contained therein; and shall further, within the time aforesaid, put and keep upon every fifty acres thereof, accounted barren, three neat cattle, and continue the same thereon, until three acres, for every fifty acres, be fully cleared and improved: and if it shall so happen that there be no part of the said tract of land fit for cultivation within the time aforesaid, without manuring and improving the same, if the said Daniel Clark, his heirs, and assigns, shall, within three years after the expiration of the ten years, as aforesaid, erect on some part of the said tract of land one good dwelling-house, to contain at least twenty feet in length, and sixteen feet in breadth, and put on his said land the like number of three neat cattle, as aforesaid, for every fifty acres therein contained; or otherwise, if any part of the said tract of land shall be stony or rocky ground, not fit for culture or pasture, shall and do, within three years, as aforesaid, besides erecting the said house, begin to employ thereon, and continue to work, for three years, then next ensuing, in digging any stone quarry or mine, one good and able hand for every hundred acres thereof, it shall be accounted a sufficient cultivation and improvement: Provided, also, that every three acres which shall be cleared and worked, or cleared and drained, as aforesaid, shall

further be accounted a sufficient seating, planting, cultivation, and improvement, to save forever from forfeiture fifty acres of land in any part of the tract hereby granted; and the said Daniel Clark, his heirs, and assigns, shall be at liberty to withdraw his or their stock, or to forbear working in any quarry or mine, in proportion to such cultivation and improvements aforesaid, as shall be made upon the plantable lands, swampy, sunken grounds, or marshes therein contained: Provided, also, that this grant shall be duly registered in the Register's Office of this province, within six months from the date hereof; and, also, that a docket thereof shall be entered in the Auditor's Office within the same time, if any such establishment shall take place in this province: Provided, always, that the said Daniel Clark, his heirs, and assigns, at any time hereafter, having seated, planted, cultivated, and improved the said tract, or any part thereof, according to the directions and conditions above mentioned, may make proof of such seating, planting, cultivation, and improvement, in the general court, or in the court of the county district or precinct where the said land lieth, and have such proof certified to the Register's Office, and there entered with the record of this grant, a copy of which, duly attested, shall be admitted on any trial to prove the seating and planting of said land: Provided, always, nevertheless, that if the said Daniel Clark, his heirs and assigns, do not in all things fully comply with, and fulfil, the respective directions and conditions herein set forth, for the proper cultivation of the said land, within the time herein above limited for the completion thereof; or if the said Daniel Clark, his heirs, or assigns, shall not pay to us, our heirs, and successors, or to the Receiver General of our quit-rents, or to the proper officer appointed to receive the same, the said quit-rent of one halfpenny sterling per acre, on the said feast of St. Michael, or within fourteen days after, annually, for every acre contained in this grant, that then, and in either of these cases, respectively, this grant shall be void, any thing herein contained to the contrary notwithstanding; and the said lands, tenements, hereditaments, and premises hereby specified, and every part and parcel thereof, shall revert to us, our heirs and successors, fully and absolutely, as if the same had never been granted.

3. To have and to hold the said tract of land, and all and singular the premises hereby granted, with the appurtenances, unto the said Christopher Guice, his heirs, and assigns, forever, in free and common soccage, yielding and paying unto us, our heirs, and successors, or to the Receiver General of our quit-rents for the time being, or to such other officer as shall be appointed to receive the same quit-rent of one halfpenny per acre, at the feast of St. Michael, every year, the first payment to commence on the said feast of St. Michael which shall first happen after the expiration of two years from the date hereof, or within fourteen days after the feast, annually: Provided, always, and this present grant is upon condition, nevertheless, that the said Christopher Guice, his heirs, or assigns, shall and do, within three years after the date hereof, for every fifty acres of plantable land hereby granted, clear and cultivate three acres, at least, in that part thereof which he or they shall judge most convenient and advantageous, or else do clear and drain three acres of swampy or sunken ground, or do drain three acres of marsh, if any such shall be contained therein, and shall further, within the time aforesaid, put and keep upon every fifty acres thereof accounted barren, three neat cattle, and continue the same thereon, until three acres, for every fifty acres, be fully cleared and improved; and if it shall so happen that there be no part of the said tract of land fit for present cultivation, without manuring and improving the same, if the said Christopher Guice, his heirs, or assigns, shall, within three years from the date hereof, erect on some part of the said tract of land one good dwelling-house, to contain at least twenty feet in length and sixteen feet in breadth, and put on his said land the like number of three neat cattle as aforesaid, on every fifty acres therein contained; or, otherwise, if any part of the said tract of land shall be stony or rocky ground, not fit for culture or pasture, shall and do, within three years, as aforesaid, besides erecting the said house, begin to employ thereon, and continue to work fourteen years then next ensuing, in digging any stone quarry or mine, one good and able hand for every hundred acres thereof,

it shall be accounted a sufficient cultivation and improvement: Provided, also, that every three acres which shall be cleared and worked, or cleared and drained as aforesaid, shall further be accounted a sufficient seating, planting, cultivation, and improvement, to save forever from forfeiture fifty acres of land, in any part of the tract hereby granted: And the said Christopher Guice, his heirs, and assigns, shall be at liberty to withdraw his or their stock, or to forbear working in any quarry or mine, in proportion to such cultivation and improvements aforesaid, as shall be made upon the plantable lands, swamps, sunken grounds, or marshes therein: Provided, also, that this grant shall be duly registered in the Register's office of this province, within six months from the date thereof, and, also, that a docket thereof shall be entered in the Auditor's Office, within the same time, if such establishment shall take place in this province: Provided, always, that the said Christopher Guice, his heirs, and assigns, at any time hereafter having seated, planted, cultivated, and improved the said land, or any part thereof, according to the directions and conditions above mentioned, may make proof of such seating, planting, cultivation, and improvement in the general court, or in the court of the county, district, or province where the said land lieth, and have such proof certified to the Register's Office, and there entered with the record of this grant, a copy of which, duly attested, shall be admitted on trial, to prove the seating and planting of the said land: Provided, always, nevertheless, that if the said Christopher Guice, his heirs, and assigns, do not in all things fully comply with and fulfil the respective directions and conditions herein above set forth, for the proper cultivation of the said land, within the time herein above limited for the completion thereof; or if the said Christopher Guice, his heirs, and assigns, shall not pay to us, our heirs, and successors, or to the Receiver General of our quit-rents, or to the proper officer appointed to receive the same, the said quit-rent of one halfpenny sterling per acre, on the said feast of St. Michael, or within fourteen days after, annually, for every acre contained in this grant; that then, and in either of these cases, respectively, this grant shall be void, any thing contained herein to the contrary notwithstanding: and the said lands, tenements, hereditaments, and premises hereby specified, and every part or parcel thereof, shall revert to us, our heirs, and successors, fully and absolutely, as if the same had never been granted.

4. To have and to hold the said tract of land, and all and singular the premises hereby granted, with the appurtenances, unto the said William Bay, his heirs, and assigns, forever, in free and common soccage, yielding and paying unto us, our heirs, and successors, or to the Receiver General of our quit-rents for the time being, or to such other officer as shall be appointed to receive the same, a quit-rent of one halfpenny sterling per acre, at the feast of St. Michael every year; the first payment to commence on the said feast of St. Michael which shall first happen after the expiration of ten years from the date hereof, or within fourteen days after the said feast, annually: Provided, always, and this present grant is upon condition, nevertheless, that this grant shall be duly registered in the Register's Office of this province, within six months from the date hereof; and, also, that a docket thereof shall be entered in the Auditor's Office, within the same time, if such establishment shall take place in this province: And provided; also, that if the said William Bay, his heirs, and assigns, do not in all things fully comply with and fulfil the conditions herein above set forth for the registering of this grant, within the time herein above limited for the completion thereof, or if the said William Bay, his heirs, or assigns, shall not pay to us, our heirs, and successors, or to the Receiver General of our quit-rents, or to the proper officer appointed to receive the same, the said quit-rent of one halfpenny sterling per acre, on the said feast of St. Michael, or within fourteen days after, annually, for every acre contained in this grant; that then, and in either of these cases, respectively, this grant shall be void, any thing herein contained to the contrary notwithstanding; and the said lands, tenements, hereditaments, and premises hereby specified, and every part and parcel thereof, shall revert to us, our heirs, and successors, fully and absolutely, as if the same had never been granted.

ABSTRACT A.—*Non-resident British Grants.*

Register's Number.	Names of the present Claimants.	Names of the original Grantees or Claimants.	Quantity.	Situation.	Date of the patent.
31	Elihu Hall Bay	Elihu Hall Bay,	1,100	On the river Homochitto,	September 27, 1773.
32	Ditto,	William Garnier,	4,800	On the waters of river Homochitto,	May 28, 1779.
33	Ditto,	William Grant,	1,000	River Mississippi,	May 6, 1776.
34	Ditto,	Ditto,	1,000	Walnut hills,-	Ditto.
35	Ditto,	Doctor John Lorimer,	2,000	Ditto,	Ditto.
40	Ditto,	John Smith,	600	On Cole's creek,	July 22, 1769.
216	Ditto,	James Barbour,	250	On Seconl creek,	September 13, 1775.
38	Ditto,	Amos Ogden,	1,575	On the river Homochitto,	October 27, 1772.
39	Ditto,	Ditto,	1,500	On Buffalo creek,	May 6, 1774.
36	Ditto,	Thaddeus Lyman,	1,050	On the Bayou Pierre,	February 2, 1775.
37	Ditto,	Ditto,	1,050	Ditto,	Ditto,
1,493	Elihu Hall Bay and Robert J. Turnbull,	James Marcus Prevost,	750	On the river Mississippi,	July 14, 1778.
1,494	Alexander Macullagh,	William Ray,	1,100	Ditto,	November 22, 1776.
19	Ditto,	William Fricker,	500	On Buffalo creek,	November 8, 1777.
20	Ditto,	John Southwell,	1,000	On the waters of Buffalo creek, -	August 2, 1773.
21	Ditto,	Patrick Kelly,	200	On Boyd's or Cole's creek,	September 2, 1779.
217	Ditto,	William Grant,	1,000	On the river Mississippi,	October 2, 1778.
1,566	William McCaleb and Francis Bremarr,	James M. Prevost,	750	Ditto,	March 24, 1777.
120		William Marshall,	600	On the waters of Fairchild's creek,	August 2, 1773.
119	The legal representatives of John Southwell,	John Southwell,	900	On Buffalo creek, -	February 28, 1778.
1,489		John Stephenson,	1,200	On Boyd's or Cole's creek,	July 24, 1772.
691	The legal representatives of John Scott,	John Scott,	1,000	On the river Mississippi,	May 6, 1776.
592	Thomas James,	Thomas James,	200	Ditto,	September 8, 1775.
593	Ditto,	Susanna Jacobs,	500	Ditto,	August 15, 1777.
598	Ditto,	Thomas James,	1,000	On the Bayou Pierre,	April 26, 1779.
599	James Hughes,	James Hughes,	550	On St. Catharine's creek,	November 30, 1776.
688	Ditto,	Ditto,	300	On Boy's or Cole's creek,	March 30, 1778.
761	Oliver Pollock,	Jeremiah German,	1,000	On Second creek,	January 10, 1777.
762	Augustine Prevost,	Augustine Prevost,	1,000	On Cole's creek,	December 31, 1776.
763	Ditto,	Ditto,	5,000	On Sandy creek,	September 15, 1777.
764	Ditto,	Ditto,	1,000	On Cole's creek,	March 30, 1778.
765	Ditto,	Ditto,	200	On the Bayou Fonica,	March 30, 1778.
1,078	William Collins,	William Collins,	3,000	On Cole's creek,	September 22, 1775.
1,136	The legal representatives of Robert Farmer, dec.	Robert Farmer,		On the waters of Cole's creek,	December 6, 1768.
1,755	The legal representatives of Robert Callender, deceased,	Robert Callender,	2,000	On Sandy creek,	April 29, 1777.
1,892	The legal representatives of Thomas Durham,	John Blommart,	2,000	At Loftus cliffs,	July 22, 1769.
1,896	Richard Barry,	Richard Barry,	50	On the waters of Fairchild's creek,	July 22, 1769.
1,897	William Mills,	William Mills,	1,000	On Cole's creek,	March 26, 1774.
1,898	The legal representatives of David Hodge, dec.	James Rumsey,	600	Ditto,	July 24, 1772.
1,899	James Amoss,	James Amos,		Loftus cliffs,-	
1,900	The legal representatives of Sylvester and James Fanning,	Sylvester and James Fanning,	2,000	Near Loftus cliffs,	December 15, 1768.
1,901	The legal representatives of David Hodge, dec.	John Sommers,	2,000	Buffalo creek,	January 30, 1778.

ABSTRACT A—Continued.

Register's Number.	Names of the present Claimants.	Names of the original Grantees or Claimants.	Quantity.	Situation.	Date of the patent.
1,902	The legal representatives of David Hodge, deceased,	Andrew Ransford,	1,250	On the river Mississippi,	May 12, 1773.
1,903	Richard Freeman Pearne,	Richard Freeman Pearne,	50	On Cole's creek,	July 22, 1769.
1,904	The legal representatives of David Hodge, deceased,	-	-	-	-
1,906	Edward Todd,	Frederick Haldermand,	2,000	On the river Mobile,	January 17, 1770.
1,953	The legal representatives of Daniel Ward, deceased,	Alexander McIntosh,	500	Pedit Gulph creek,	March 6, 1670.
1,954	Ditto,	Daniel Ward,	1,500	On the river Mississippi,	November 24, 1768.
1,967	Joshua Ward,	William Fricker,	500	On the waters of Cole's creek,	November 8, 1777.
775	Joseph W. A. Lloyd,	Joshua Ward,	600	On the river Mississippi,	November 24, 1768.
909	Philip Alston,	James Barbour,	250	On Second creek,	September 13, 1775.
975	Ann Carr,	Thomas Fry,	200	On Petit Gulph creek,	July 7, 1775.
974	William Godley,	John Firby,	1,000	On Cole's creek,	September 22, 1779.
1,139	Rhea and Cochran,	William Godley,	250	On the river Mississippi,	October 21, 1771.
1,331	Elijah Cushing,	Thomas Hutchins,	400	On the river Homochitto,	October 21, 1774.
1,364	John Ogden,	Ephraim Thornell,	100	On Second creek,	November 12, 1778.
1,491	David Waugh's heirs,	Amos Ogden,	3,000	On the river Homochitto,	May 6, 1774.
1,492	The legal representatives of Thomas Hardy, deceased,	David Waugh,	1,000	On St. Catharine's creek,	March 11, 1777.
1,877	Solomon Alston,	Thomas Hardy,	500	On the river Mississippi,	July 4, 1769.
1,879	Absalom Hooper,	John Alston,	450	Near Natchez,	June 16, 1777.
1,915	Jacob Winfree,	Absalom Hooper,	250	On Second creek,	September 21, 1772.
1,937	The legal representatives of Sir George Brydges Rodney, deceased,	Jacob Winfree,	1,000	Ditto,	July 7, 1773.
986	James Ferguson, for the use of Benjamin Farrar,	Sir George Brydges Rodney,	5,000	On the river Mississippi,	May 27, ——
992	Edward Evan and James Jones,	James Ferguson,	600	On Second creek,	September 21, 1772.
1,094	Daniel Hughes, agent for William Johnson,	Thaddeus Lyman,	666⅔	On the Bayou Pierre,	February 2, 1775.
1,244	The legal representatives of Joseph King, deceased,	James Barbour,	500	On Second creek,	September 13, 1775.
1,363	The legal representatives of Amos Ogden,	Amos Ogden,	1,000	On the river Homochitto,	October 27, 1772.
1,649	Tench Cox,	Ditto,	4,500	Ditto,	October 27, 1772.
976	The legal representatives of Thomas Wadsworth, deceased,	Thaddeus Lyman,	333⅓	On the Bayou Pierre,	February 2, 1775.
977	Samuel Holliday,	William Marshall,	2,000	On the river Homochitto,	June 5, 1778.
1,844	John Armstreet,	Amos Ogden,	1,000	On the waters of the river Homochitto,	October 27, 1772.
2,027	Thomas Hutchins, Jun.	William Garnier,	200	Ditto,	May 28, 1773.
2,034	Lorenzo Dow,	Thomas Hutchins, senior,	200	On the river Homochitto,	October 21, 1774.
2,033	Ditto,	Joseph Jackson,	500	Briar creek,	July 24, 1778.
		Ditto,	100	Ditto,	July 21, 1778.

a.

The Commissioners appointed east of Pearl river, "for ascertaining the rights of persons claiming the benefit of the articles of agreement and cession between the United States and the State of Georgia, or of the three first sections," of an act entitled "An act regulating the grants of land, and providing for the disposal of the lands of the United States south of the State of Tennessee," pursuant to the requirements of the 7th section of said act, report:

British grants legally and fully executed, and duly recorded, in conformity to the provisions of said act, and not confirmed to the holders thereof under the articles of agreement and cession above mentioned.

Name of the original grantee.	Name of the present claimant.	No. of acres granted.	Date of the grant.	Present situation of the land.	Conditions annexed to the grants.	Evidence exhibited of the fulfilment of the conditions.	Remarks.
John McIntosh,	Heirs of John McIntosh,	500	1775, Sept. 12	It is covered by a certificate issued by the Board to Ann Lawrence, legal representative of Moses Moore, in virtue of a Spanish warrant or order of survey.	To have and to hold the said tract of land, and all and singular the premises hereby granted, with the appurtenances, unto the said John McIntosh, his heirs and assigns, forever, in free and common soccage, yielding and paying unto us, our heirs and successors, or to the Receiver General of our quit-rents for the time being, or to such other officer as shall be appointed to receive the same, a quit-rent of one half-penny sterling per acre, at the feast of St. Michael every year; the first payment to commence on the said feast of St. Michael which shall first happen after the expiration of two years from the date hereof, or within fourteen days after the said feast, annually: Provided always, and the present grant is upon condition nevertheless, that the said John McIntosh, his heirs and assigns, shall and do, within three years from the date hereof, for every fifty acres of plantable land granted, clear and cultivate three acres at least in that part thereof which he or they shall judge most convenient and advantageous, or else to clear and draw three acres of swampy or sunken ground, or to drain three acres of marsh, if any such shall be contained therein; and shall further, within the time aforesaid, put and keep upon every fifty acres thereof, accounted barren, three neat cattle, and continue the same thereon until three acres for every fifty acres be fully cleared and improved; and if it shall so happen that there be no part of the said tract of land fit for present cultivation without manuring and improving the same, if the said John McIntosh, his heirs and assigns, shall, within three years from the date hereof, erect on some part of the said tract of land one good dwelling house, to contain at least twenty feet in length and sixteen feet in breadth; and his said land the like number of three neat cattle as aforesaid, on every fifty acres therein contained; or, otherwise, if any part of the said tract of land shall be stony or rocky ground, not fit for culture or pasture, shall and do within three years as aforesaid, besides erecting the said house, begin to employ thereon, and continue to work for three years the next ensuing, in digging any stone quarry or mine, one good and able hand for every hundred acres thereof; it shall be accounted a sufficient cultivation and improvement: Provided also, that every three acres which shall be cleared and worked, or cleared and drained as aforesaid, shall further be accounted a sufficient seating, planting, cultivation, and improvement, to save forever from forfeiture fifty acres of land in any part of the	It appears from the endorsement on the grant, that it was duly registered in the Register's office. John M°Grew, Esquire, testified that John McIntosh had land cleared, and negroes working on said land in the year 1780, or 1781, and that it was said that the land was cultivated at that time for account of John McIntosh. Thos. Bassett deposed "that he knew that said land was inhabited and cultivated at the time the British held this country, by his, McIntosh's, negroes and overseers."	

a—Continued.

Name of the original grantee.	Name of the present claimant.	Date of the grant.	No. of acres granted.	Present situation of the land.	Conditions annexed to the grants.	Evidence exhibited of the fulfilment of the conditions.	Remarks.
					tract granted. And the said John McIntosh, his heirs and assigns, shall be at liberty to withdraw his or their stock, or to forbear working in any quarry or mine, in proportion to such cultivation and improvements aforesaid, as shall be made upon the plantable lands, swamps, sunken grounds, or marshes therein contained: Provided, also, that this grant shall be duly registered in the Register's office of this province, within six months from the date hereof; and, also, that a docket thereof shall be entered in the Auditor's office within the same time, if such establishment shall take place in this province: Provided, always, that the said John McIntosh, his heirs and assigns, at any time hereafter, having seated, planted, cultivated, and improved the said land, or any part thereof, according to the directions and conditions above mentioned, may make proof of such seating, planting, cultivation, and improvement in the general court, or in the court of the county, district, or precinct where the land lieth; and have such proof certified to the Register's office, and there entered with the record of this grant, a copy of which, duly attested, shall be admitted on trial, to prove the seating and planting of the said land: Provided always, nevertheless, that if the said John McIntosh, his heirs and assigns, do not in all things fully comply with, and fulfil the respective directions and conditions herein above set forth, for the proper cultivation of the said land within the time herein above limited for the cultivation thereof; or if the said John McIntosh, his heirs or assigns, shall not pay to us, our heirs and successors, or to the Receiver General of our quit-rents, or to the proper officer appointed to receive the same, the said quit-rent of one halfpenny sterling per acre, on the feast of St. Michael, or within fourteen days after, annually, for every acre contained in the grant; that then, and in either of these cases, respectively, this grant shall be void, any thing herein contained to the contrary notwithstanding; and the said lands, tenements, hereditaments, and premises hereby specified, and every part and parcel thereof, shall revert to us, our heirs and successors, fully and absolutely, as if the same had never been granted.		
Abraham Little,	Francis Coleman,	1778 Feb. 16.	100	It is covered in part by a donation certificate issued by the Board in favor of John McGrew, sen.	Conditions same as the preceding.		It appears from the endorsement on the grant, that it was duly registered in the Register's office, and docketed in the Auditor's office. No evidence of the fulfilment of the other conditions of the grant.

By whom claimed	In favor of	Date	Quantity	Certificate	Conditions	Remarks
Robert Farmer,	Heirs of Robert Farmer,	1778. August 6,	1,000	It is covered by the following certificates of pre-emption issued by the Board: one in the name of Rawleigh Green; one in the name of Peter Cartwright; one in the name of John Pickering; one in the name of Jos. Westmoreland; and a donation certificate in the name of Clark McGrew.	Conditions same as the preceding.	Same as the next preceding.
Robert Farmer,	Heirs of Robert Farmer,	August 6,	800	It is covered in part by a pre-emption certificate issued by the Board in the name of Chas. Cassiter.	Conditions same as the preceding.	Same as the next preceding.
Peter De Forge,	Heirs of Peter De Forge,	1779. April 16,	100	Not known.	Conditions same as the preceding.	Same as the next preceding.
Allen Grant,	Theodore Gilliard,	Oct. 4,	100	Not known.	Conditions same as the preceding.	Same as the next preceding.
John Sutherland,	Elihu Hall Bay	Oct. 22,	500	It is covered in part by the following certificates issued by the Board: a pre-emption certificate in the name of Peter Malone; a pre-emption certificate in the name of Edward Lt. Wailes; and a certificate in virtue of a Spanish warrant, or order of survey, in the name of John Baker.	Conditions same as the preceding, except that the payment of the quit-rent commences within ten years after the feast of St. Michael which may first happen after the date of the grant, instead of two years, as in the preceding cases.	Same as the next preceding.
Wm. Fradgely,	Elihu Hall Bay,	1776. March 13,	27	It is covered by a certificate issued by the Board in favor of John Johnston, in virtue of a Spanish warrant, or order of survey.	Conditions same as the preceding.	Same as the next preceding.

a—Continued.

Name of the original grantee.	Name of the present claimant.	Date of the grant.	No. of acres granted.	Present situation of the land.	Conditions annexed to the grants.	Evidence exhibited of the fulfilment of the conditions.	Remarks.
Wm. Fradgely,	Elihu Hall Bay,	1776. March 13,	173	It is covered by a certificate issued by the Board in favor of Ann Lawrence, representative of Moses Moore, in virtue of a Spanish warrant, or order of survey, and a certificate in virtue of a Spanish warrant in the name of Cornelius Rain.	Conditions same as the preceding.	Same as the next preceding.	
George Burdon,	George Burdon,	1779. August 17,	200	Not known.	Conditions same as the preceding.	Same as the next preceding.	
George Burdon,	George Burdon,	August 17,	800	Not known.	Conditions same as the preceding.	Same as the next preceding.	
Alex. Macullagh,	Alex. Macullagh, nephew and heir,	1778. April 6,	200	It is covered by a certificate issued by the Board in favor of Daniel Johnson, under a Spanish warrant, or order of survey.	Conditions same as the preceding.	Same as the next preceding.	
William Clark,	Samuel Mims,	August 6,	350	It is inhabited and cultivated by Samuel Mims. No other claim exhibited therefor.	To have and to hold the said tract of land, and all and singular the premises hereby granted, with the appurtenances, unto the said Wm. Clark, his heirs and assigns, forever, in free and common soccage; yielding and paying unto us, our heirs and successors, or to the Receiver General of our quit-rents for the time being, or to such other officer as shall be appointed to receive the same, a quit-rent of one half-penny sterling per acre, at the feast of St. Michael, every year; the first payment to commence on the said feast of St. Michael which shall first happen after the expiration of ten years from the date hereof, or within fourteen days after the said feast, annually: Provided, always, and this present grant is upon condition, nevertheless, that this grant shall be duly registered in the Register's Office of this province, within six months from the date hereof; and also, that a docket thereof shall be entered in the Auditor's Office within the same time, if such establishment shall take place in this province: And provided, also, that if the said Wm. Clarke, his heirs and assigns, do not in all things fully comply with the condition herein	Same as the next preceding.	It has been stated in proof to us, that Samuel Mims, the present claimant, has been in the continued and peaceable possession, cultivation, and habitation of this land for the last eighteen or twenty years, either as the tenant of William Clark, the original grantee, or as a purchaser under said Clark; but we were of opinion, that the

Grantee	Claimant	Date	No.	Claim details	Conditions	Remarks
William Clark,	Samuel Mims,	1778, Aug. 6,	174	Same as the next preceding,	above set forth for the registering of this grant, within the time herein above limited for the completion thereof; or if the said William Clark, his heirs or assigns, shall not pay to us, our heirs and successors, or to the Receiver General of our quit-rents, or to the proper officer appointed to receive the same, the said quit-rent of one halfpenny sterling per acre, on the said feast of St. Michael, or within fourteen days after, annually, for every acre contained in this grant; that then, and in either of these cases, respectively, this grant shall be void, any thing herein contained to the contrary notwithstanding; and the said lands, tenements, hereditaments, and premises, hereby specified, and every part and parcel thereof, shall revert to us, our heirs and successors, fully and absolutely as if the same had never been granted.	chain of title from Clark to Mims, is incomplete. See journal 2, page 436. We had no evidence that William Clark was resident within the ceded territory on the 27th day of Oct'r, 1795. There has been no other claim for this land, or any part of it, presented to us.
John Lott, jun.	Wm. Vardiman,	Feb. 16,	300	It is covered by a certificate issued by the Board in the name of James Caller, in virtue of a Spanish warrant, and a donation certificate in the name of Noah Kenner Hutson, in the occupancy of William Vardiman, the holder of the British grant.	Conditions the same as the next preceding, Conditions same as the next preceding.	Same as the next preceding, Same as the next preceding.
William Wall,	James Hoggatt,	Mar. 20,	250	It is covered by a certificate issued by the Board in the name of Jno. Caller, in virtue of a Spanish warrant.	Conditions same as the next preceding,	It appears from the endorsements on this grant, that it was duly registered in the Register's office, and docketed in the Auditor's office. John McGrew, Esq. deposed "that James Hoggatt lived on the land in the year 1780, and that said Hoggatt had a plantation and barn on said place." Thomas Bassett testified "that he knew that James Hoggatt lived on the land in the year 1789, or before that time."

a—Continued.

Name of the original grantee.	Name of the present claimant.	Date of the grant.	No. of acres granted.	Present situation of the land.	Conditions annexed to the grants.	Evidence exhibited of the fulfilment of the conditions.	Remarks.
Charles Walker,	Francis Coleman,	1777. Jan. 27,	500	It is covered by a certificate issued by the Board in the name of Jno. Baker, in virtue of a Spanish warrant, and a donation certificate in the name of John McGrew, sen.	Conditions same as the next preceding.	It appears from the endorsement on this grant that it was duly registered in the Register's office. John McGrew, sen. deposed "that he knew that Charles Walker settled upon this land in or about the year 1778, built a house, and made two or three crops thereon; and he believed had cleared and under cultivation within the limits of the grant, about forty acres.	

BOARD OF COMMISSIONERS, *East of Pearl River, September 14,* 1805.

RO. C. NICHOLAS,
JOSEPH CHAMBERS, } *Commissioners.*

SIR:—This report is respectfully submitted by your most obedient servants,

The honorable ALBERT GALLATIN, ESQ., *Secretary of the Treasury.*

A 2.

ABSTRACT of British Claims entered with the Register of the Land Office west of Pearl River, under the fifth section of an act entitled "An act further to amend an act entitled "An act regulating the grants of land, and providing for the disposal of the lands of the United States south of the State of Tennessee.

Register's No.	Name of the present claimant.	Name of the original grantee or claimant.	Quantity in acres.	Situation.	Date of the Patent.
2083	Thomas Davy	Weston Varlo	1,000	On the waters of the Bayou Pierre,	The original patents to Weston Varlo for these three tracts have never been filed in this office; deeds of lease and release being the only evidence of title exhibited.
2084	Do.	Do.	1,000	Do.	27th September, 1773.
2085	Do.	Do.	500	do.	17th October, 1774.
2086	Do.	David Dickson	1,000	On the river Homochitto,	24th March, 1777.—Part of a grant of 1000 acres. The residue of the
2087	William Wilton,	William Wilton	500	do.	tract is claimed by William McCaleb and F. Bremarr, by whom the
2088	Do.	William Marshall	400	On Fairchild's creek,	original patent was filed, under the act of 1803, and reported by the Commissioners, and numbered 190.
2089	Do.	James Barbut	200	On Second creek,	13th September, 1775.—The original patent is for 1000 acres, filed by E. H. Bay and J. A. W. Lloyd. See Commissioner's Nos. 216 and 775. This land is also claimed by William Johnson: see No. 1024. Deeds of conveyance, however, for the quantity here claimed, have been filed by the present claimant.
2090	Do.	William Fricker	500	On Cole's creek,	8th November, 1777.—The original patent for 2000 acres, filed by A. Macullagh and Daniel Ward's heirs: See Nos. 19 and 1954, who claim one moiety of the entire tract: there appears to be 500 acres for which no claim has been set up.
2091	The legal representatives of Wm. Clark	Daniel Ryan	400	On Briar creek,	23d April, 1777.—No conveyance from the patentee produced.
2092	do.	William Clark	576	On the river Alabama,	22d October, 1779.
2093	do.	James Peterkin	500	On the river Pascagola,	29th December, 1778.—No conveyance from the patentee produced.
2094	Anthony Francis Halderman	Frederick Halderman	500	Near the Natchez,	The above three tracts lie in the district east of Pearl river. There are no papers filed in these three claims. Halderman's attorney
2095	Do.	Do.	500	Do.	has presented unauthenticated plots of the land, stated to be copies from the original plots of the Surveyor General.
2096	Do.	Do.		On the river Mississippi,	
2097	John Peck	Thaddeus Lyman	6,500	On the Bayou Pierre,	2d February, 1775.—Part of Lyman's mandamus, which was confiscated by the Spanish Government, and has been confirmed to the present settlers in possession, by the Board of Commissioners.
2098	The legal representatives of the Earl of Eglinton.	Earl of Eglinton	20,000	Near the Natchez,	A transcript from the British records, stating that a grant had issued to the Earl of Eglinton for this land, is the only evidence of title exhibited. This was presented by John McCaleb, in behalf of the heirs, but no power of attorney, or other document, proving him to be invested with authority to act, was ever shown. The land is entirely covered by Spanish patents, being one of the most flourishing settlements in this district.
			34,076		

The foregoing is a list of all the claims filed in this office, under the fifth section of the act of the 2d March, 1805.

THO. H. WILLIAMS, *Register of the Land Office.*

LAND OFFICE, WEST OF PEARL RIVER, *July 26, 1808.*

B.

Abstract of Spanish Grants disallowed, on suspicion of being antedated.

Register's Number.	Names of the present Claimants.	Names of the original Grantees or Claimants.	Quantity in arpents.	Situation.	Date of patents.
507	The legal representatives of Wm. Vousdan, dec.	William Vousdan	2,000	On the Bayou Sara	August 30, 1793.
1,400	Robert Moore	Robert Moore	1,000	On the Bayou Sara	December 26, 1795.
1,425	James Moore, in right of his wife Maria	Maria Whittle	700	On the Bayou Sara	June 18, 1795.
1,753	Thomas Burling	Thomas Burling	1,000	On the Bayou Sara	June 18, 1795.
1,420	James Moore	James Moore	1,000	On the Bayou Sara	December 26, 1795.
1,368	Samuel P. Moore, Jas. Moore, and Rob. Moore	Sarah Scott	1,000	On the Bayou Sara	March 22, 1795.
1,370	Samuel P. Moore, Jas. Moore, and Rob. Moore	William Moore	1,000	On the Bayou Sara	March 22, 1795.
1,579	William Scott	William Scott	1,000	On the Bayou Sara	March 20, 1795.
1,097	Abijah Hunt	James White	1,300	On Well's creek	January 20, 1795.
394	Nicholas G. Ridgley	James White	625	On Well's creek	January 20, 1795.
1,657	Edward Evans	James White	280	On Well's creek	January 20, 1795.
1,637	Henry Garvey	Henry Garvey	200	On Well's creek	January 25, 1795.
1,638	Henry Garvey	Henry Garvey	330	River Homochitto	January 26, 1795.
1,111	Abijah Hunt	William Lewis	500	On the Bayou Sara	March 20, 1795.
1,141	Margaret Thompson	Margaret Thompson	1,000	On the Bayou Pierre	December 2, 1797.
1,142	The legal representatives of Jacintha Vidal, dec.	Jacintha Gallagher	1,000	On the Bayou Pierre	December 2, 1797.
1,140	Thomas Thompson	Thomas Thompson	800	On the Bayou Pierre	December 2, 1797.
1,403	Nicholas Kemplin	Nicholas Kemplin	400	On the Bayou Sara	March 22, 1795.
1,728	William Dunbar	William Dunbar	Lot No. 3	Of square No. 26, in the city of Natchez.	December 5, 1794.

D.

Report of Claims founded on British and Spanish Warrants of Survey within the District west of Pearl River, disallowed by the Board of Commissioners; made in pursuance of the fourth section of an act entitled "An act concerning the sales of the lands of the United States, and for other purposes," passed March 31, 1808.

Register's No.	Claimant's name.	Name of the original claimant.	Situation.	Quantity.	Title.		Remarks, &c.
					Whence derived.	Date.	
4 25	William Conway Thomas Green	Maurice Conway Thomas Green	Buffalo creek Near Natchez	800f. 100f.	Spanish Do	Oct. 1, 1788 Sept. 1, 1782	No evidence offered. This land was regranted by the Spanish Government, and a patent issued to Peter Piernas, February 24, 1783. The claim was confirmed by the Board to Robert Cochran, assignee of the patentee. Tho. M. Green says, "that he was present, and saw the Spanish surveyor run the two first lines the length and breadth of said land, beginning at a stake, a made corner. The surveyor marked the name of the claimant in initials on one of the corner trees, and delivered possession of the land to the claimant; and then the said deponent left the ground. The said deponent says, that the said Tho. Green was twenty-one years of age, and the head of a family, on the 1st September, 1782." William Barland says, "that he was present, to wit, in the fall of 1782, when the survey of said land was about to be run. He saw the stake and a made corner stuck in the ground, and saw the surveyor start; and then he went away. The next day he attended, and saw the survey finished." The said deponent further says, that he understood, by common report, that the Spanish commandant had rented, or had obtained leave of said Thomas Green to use said land as a pasture; and the said deponent saw the Spanish troops putting a fence round said premises for said commandant. A few days after the said survey was made the same surveyor run out a tract of land for said witness, and made one of said Thomas Green's lines a boundary for this deponent's line." Palser Shilling says, "that he was in the surveyor's office, where they showed him the plan or plot of the tract of land in question, included in a general map of the lands granted or surveyed in this country by the Spanish Government. This deponent further says, that he knows that the said Thomas Green and all his slaves, property, and papers were seized upon by the Spanish commandant, and sent to New Orleans; and that it was a general practice with said commandant to seize upon papers in particular, and to select and destroy such as he thought proper." Stephen Minor says, "that the claimant was the head of a family at the date of the warrant; that he never inhabited or cultivated this land; that, on the arrival of Peter Piernas, Lieutenant Governor under the Spanish Government, at Natchez, on or about the year 1784, he requested the witness to apply to the claimant to let him have a part of the land in question, to make a pasture for his horses, who consented, and a parcel thereon was fenced in accordingly by the said Piernas, and used as such; and the witness saw the surveyor general, Charles Trudeau, go out with the claimant to survey the said tract of land, and believes he did survey it for the said Green."
49	Heirs of R. Cloyd	Robert Cloyd	Bayou Pierre	1,000f.	Do	Mar. 14, 1794*	

* This warrant was issued by the local governor of the district, and not by the governor-general of the province. Catura Wallis says, "that soon after the grant was obtained, the grantee died, and left a wife and five small children." The witness heard his wife complain, at the time of his decease, that he had made a small improvement on the land, and that she was left unable to continue it. Harrison Person says, "that, about two years ago, (October, 1803,) the claimant sent for the witness to get him to endeavor to save this land for her; and proposed to him, that, if he could save it, he should have one-half of it, or, that if he chose to purchase, he might have the whole for five hundred dollars. The witness took time to consider of said proposition, and, before he returned to her again, she had received a better offer from Thomas Evans, who lived nigh the premises, and refused to comply with the offer she had made to the witness, and required a return of the petition or title papers, which the witness returned about ten days afterwards. In the course of the conversation between the witness and the claimant, she acknowledged that no improvement had been made on the premises." Cyrus Hamilton says, "that Robert Cloyd landed in the Mississippi territory in the year 1796, some time about the month of July; and the witness does not know that he was ever in the country before, as the witness lived in the territory before and after that period, and never knew him, or heard of him, before that time."

D—Continued.

Register's No.	Claimant's name.	Name of the original claimant.	Situation.	Quantity.	Whence derived.	Title. Date.	Remarks, &c.
110 121	Heirs of J. Bernard, Benjamin Dorsey,	Joseph Bernard, Benjamin Dorsey,	Buffalo creek, Homochitto river,	240f. 500f.	Spanish, Do.	Mar. 28, 1794 -	Bennet Truly says, "that Joseph Bernard was the head of a family at the date of the warrant." No warrant produced. "This land was sold by Dorsey to Winifred Ryon, on the 9th January, 1797, and confirmed to her as *a donation* by the commissioners.
161	Everard Green,	Everard Green,	Cole's creek,	650f.	Feb. 10, 1792		Thomas M. Green says, "that the claimant was twenty-one years of age, not at the date of the warrant, but the fore part of the year 1797; that the tract of land in question is swamp land and joins a tract of the claimant which is cultivated, but which has no timber, or not enough to support it; and that the present land was procured for the purpose of supplying timber to the tract cultivated, and has been used as such ever since."
259	Thomas Foster, Patent Aug. 20, 1817	Thomas Foster, Abraham Taylor,	Buffalo creek,	800f.	Do.	Mar. 14, 1793	Reuben Gibson says, "that the claimant resided in the Mississippi territory on the 27th October, 1795, and that he was the head of a family at the date of the warrant."
285	Abraham Taylor,		Homochitto river,	505f.	Do.	Mar. 28, 1794	Joseph King says, "that the claimant was the head of a family, at the date of the warrant, of a wife and seven or eight children."
303 339	Jacob Harman, Job Corey,	Jacob Harman, Job Corey,	Will's creek, Cole's creek,	500f. 400	Do. British,	Jan. 24, 1789 -	No evidence offered. The original warrant was not produced, but, "a certificate under the hand of Luke Collins, that he surveyed the land in question, in virtue of a warrant under the British Government; certificate dated at Opelousas in 1803." Waterman Crane says, "that he knows that Luke Collins was a deputy surveyor two or three years under the British Government of West Florida. The witness also says, that the claimant was the head of a family in the year 1774, and was an actual settler in the Mississippi territory on the 27th day of October, 1795."
346	Alexander Montgomery,	Solomon Whitley,	Homochitto river,	400f.	Spanish,	May 5, 1790	Prosper King says, "that Solomon Whitley was the head of a family at the date of the warrant, and the claimant began to inhabit and cultivate the premises in the year 1798, by his hands, and afterwards by Richard Crozier, for him; and they cleared and cultivated about five acres, and built a dwelling-house, and did nothing more." See act of Congress passed on the 3d March, 1823, "for the relief of the heirs and representatives of Alexander Montgomery, deceased," giving to the heirs and representatives of Montgomery the right to locate other land in lieu of that embraced in this order of survey.
347	Alexander Montgomery,	Alexander Montgomery,	Buffalo creek,	800f.	Do.	July 9, 1789	Prosper King says, "that the claimant was twenty-one years of age at the date of the warrant, and was a resident in the Mississippi territory on the 27th October, 1795." The claimant made a small improvement, and built a cabin on the premises, in the year 1797."
368	David Corey,	David Corey,	Homochitto river,	500f.	Do.	April 7, 1794	John McCoy says, "that the warrantee was under the age of twenty-one years on the 7th April, 1794; that he was born and raised in this territory, and resided in it on the 27th day of October, 1795, and ever since; that the land in question was never inhabited or cultivated until the year 1801, in which year the witness, and another hand with him, went on the land with the claimant, and cleared away half an acre of cane, and cut logs for a house; and nothing more has been done upon it that the witness knows of."
407 442	T. & V. Fortner, Prosper King,	John Peters, Prosper King,	Big Black, Homochitto river,	240f. 800f.	Do. Do.	Ap'l 26, 1790 Mar. 2, 1795	No evidence adduced. Alexander Montgomery says, "that the claimant was twenty-one years of age at the date of the warrant; and, in the year 1797, the witness was on the premises, and saw a small improvement, and a large stock of horses and cattle, but how long the improvement was made before that time he knows not."
468	Daniel Burnet,	James Steuart,	Bayou Pierre,	200f.	Do.	-	No warrant produced, but a certificate of survey and a plot by William Dunbar, district surveyor, dated 16th November, 1794. Stephen Minor says, "that James Steuart was one of the men that composed the company of dragoons under the command of Richard King, and was entitled to the two hundred arpents for his services, and believes that the grants were generally issued to the company, as a number of them were lodged in the hands of the witness, some of which were

No.	Claimant	Original warrantee	Location	Amount		Date	Remarks
534	John Stampley	Hugh Matthews	River Big Black	300f.	Spanish	Feb. 24, 1795	Richard King says, "that he commanded the company of horse above mentioned, and that James Steuart was one of the company, and was entitled to the two hundred arpents aforesaid; that he received a grant from Governor Gayoso for the same, which the witness supposes is lost, with a number of others that were lodged with Stephen Minor, and that the warrants were stolen out of the house, among which might have been the grant belonging or issued to Steuart." Adam Lanehart says, "that Hugh Matthews was the head of a family at the date of the warrant, or order of survey, and that the has been an actual settler in the Mississippi territory ever since, and before that time."
567	*A. Montgomery	J. Montgomery	River Homochitto	300f.	Spanish	April 26, 1790	Prosper King says, "that John Montgomery was the head of a family at the date of the warrant; and the claimant made a small improvement on the premises in the year 1798."
577	James Williams	Henry Willis	Bayou Sara	800f.	Spanish	May 23, 1791	The land was sold by Sanders to Henry Willis in 1791; and Willis, on the 24th September, 1794, devised these two tracts, with others, to his wife, now Sarah F. Chotard, and his son, Lewis Willis, who died; whereupon, his mother became possessed of his part of the property, who, together with her husband, John Chotard La Place, conveyed, by deed, to the claimant, 1st September, 1803. William McIntosh says, "that Henry Willis, in the year 1792, was an actual settler in the Mississippi territory, who left the country, with the permission of the Spanish Government, on necessary business, with the intention of returning; that Willis and Sanders (the original warrantees) were heads of families at the date of the warrants." Mary Conner says, "that Henry Willis, when he went to the State of Georgia, about the year 1791, left papers of considerable value, and also horses and cattle, his right to which has not been disputed by any person, in the possession of Mrs. Ann Savage, who also paid several debts for the said Willis during his absence; and further saith, that when she was in Georgia, in the year 1796, and in the neighborhood in which Willis resided after he left this country, she understood that he had prepared to return to this country as soon as he could go to Charleston in South Carolina, and return; at which place, she understood, he died in the year 1794." Abram Ellis says, "that shortly before Henry Willis left this country, he applied to him for payment, and was informed by him that Mrs. Savage would pay it for him, and that she was to attend to his business during his absence; and also, that the said Willis informed him that he intended to return to this country." William Conner says, "that all the patents of the lands in the Mississippi territory, of Henry Willis, deceased, now claimed by James Williams, as purchaser under the said Henry Willis, were among the papers of Mrs. Savage when her papers came into the hands of the witness, in the year 1798; also several other papers of the said Henry Willis, which showed that Mrs. Savage paid large sums of money towards the consideration money of the said lands during the absence of the said Henry Willis from this territory."
578	James Williams	James Sanders	Bayou Sara	500f.	Spanish	July 5, 1789	
581	Peter Presler	John O'Connor	Cole's creek	400f.	Spanish	April 26, 1790	No evidence. William Atchison says, "that Elias Bonnell was upwards of twenty-one years of age at the date of the warrant, and that he, the witness, surveyed the land in question about the year 1791."
586	John Foster	Elias Bonnell	River Homochitto	152l.	Spanish	May 5, 1790	
625	Heirs of G. Cochran	George Cochran	Bayou Pierre	200f.	Spanish	Jan. 18, 1793	No evidence. William Thomas says, "that Martin Carney was twenty-one years of age at the date of the warrant, and inhabited the land before and at the date of the warrant, by living in a house he had built, but never cultivated it, and then sold it to the claimant; and there has never been any cultivation or habitation of it since Carney sold it." (13th March, 1797.)
624	Heirs of G. Cochran	Martin Carney	Cole's creek	240f.	Spanish	Oct. 30, 1790	
690	Henry Roach	Henry Roach	Buffalo creek	1,038f.	Spanish	-	No order of survey has been produced, and the only evidence that such a document ever existed is contained in a certificate signed in 1803 by William Atchison, formerly a deputy surveyor, stating, in substance, that he had surveyed the land in question for the claimant by virtue of an order from Manuel Gayoso, in 1793, (who was then the Governor of this district,) that every person should adopt the swamp in front of their land. William Roach says, "that the land in question is swamp land, on the Buffalo creek, near the mouth, and that the claimant lived on bluff land adjoining it in the year 1787, and for twelve or fourteen years following; that during the whole time the claimant got boards, shingles, and rails off the premises in question : no other use was ever made of it, except for getting timber."

* The act of Congress, passed on the 3d of March, 1822, "For the relief of the heirs and representatives of Alex. Montgomery, dec'd," authorizes them to locate other lands in lieu of those contained in this order of survey.

D—Continued.

Register's No.	Claimant's name.	Name of original claimant.	Situation.	Quantity.	Title. Whence derived.	Title. Date.	Remarks, &c.
711	P. & R. King	Justus King	Homochitto river	500	British	-	No order of survey produced. Caleb King says, "that he believes that Justus King, deceased, who was his brother, had a British warrant for five hundred acres, and he believes he surveyed the land in question under the said warrant, but it has never been settled or improved. After the land was surveyed, Justus King was driven away from that part of the country by an Indian war, but resided in the territory until he died, and was the head of a family at the date of the warrant." Nathan Swayze says, " that he was present at the surveying of the land in question by one Samuel Lewis, a lawful surveyor under the British Government, in the year 1776, but it never was inhabited or cultivated, owing, to danger from the Indians, who drove off people from that part of the country ; but that Justus King lived in the territory until he died, which was about six years ago." (1798.)
712 713 714	Stephen Swayze Nathan Swayze Neh. Carter	Stephen Swayze Samuel Swayze Nehemiah Carter	Homochitto river Homochitto river Boyd's creek	200 500 1,200	British British British	Nov. 21, 1798	No warrant produced, nor any other evidence offered in support of these claims. John Gaskins says, "that the claimant resided in the Mississippi territory on the 27th October, 1795, and was above twenty-one years of age at the date of the warrant;" Anthony Hutchins says, "that the claimant was an inhabitant of the Mississippi territory at the date of the warrant of survey, and has continued to be so ever since."
739	John Henderson	Wm. Henderson	Thompson's creek	1,000f.	British	Mar. 16, 1777	John Boll says," that William Henderson was twenty-one years of age at the date of the warrant ; and that the claimant was an actual settler in the Mississippi territory before the 27th of October, 1795, and has been ever since, but the premises have not been inhabited or cultivated."
746	Heirs of Charles Boardman	Charles Boardman	Fairchild's creek	226f.	Spanish	-	No order of survey produced ; but a certificate from William Aichison, without date, stating " that he had surveyed the same by an order from Charles Trudeau to William Dunbar."
747	Heirs of Charles Boardman	Charles Boardman	Fairchild's creek	282f.	Spanish	-	No warrant produced, nor any other evidence, except " an order from the Surveyor General of the Spanish Government, directed to William Dunbar, requesting him to survey the land between Boardman's claim and Fairchild's creek, dated 19th November, 1791; also, a certificate from William Dunbar, that he had surveyed the land in favor of Charles Boardman, dated 2d June, 1793."
752	Isaac Gaillard	John McCoy	Homochitto river	300f.	Spanish	Mar. 28, 1794	Alexander McKay says, "that John McKay, the patentee, was the head of a family at the date of the warrant; and the witness helped him to build a cabin on the premises in the year 1796; and they completed it, and cut down cane and saplings on a small spot of ground where the house stood, and then the witness went away, and knows nothing further about the place."
766	Heirs of Garret Rapalje	Garret Rapalje	River Mississippi	1,000f.	Spanish	April 26, 1790	John Shackler says, "that in 1791 he went up with Governor Gayoso to the Walnut hills when he went to settle a garrison there, when he saw an old field adjoining the Rapalje bayou and the Mississippi, below the bayou aforesaid; on which field there was then a cabin uninhabited; there was some ground on the field broken up, and looked like potato hills, as if potatoes had been planted there; that he understood by the Governor and Col. Girault, that Garret Rapalje built the cabin, but said that he should not have it. The witness has seen Garret Rapalje often at the Walnut hills; has heard him say the settlement aforesaid was his, and he should try to get it, but never saw him exercise any ownership on the premises now claimed : some years after-

No.	Claimant	Grantee	Location	Quantity	Nation	Date	Remarks
777	Jos. W. A. Lloyd	Wm. Vardiman	Will's creek	500f.	Spanish	Sept. 28, 1794	wards he heard from others that Garret Rapalje was gone to the States for his family, and died there; that he knows four of his sons, to wit, George, Isaac, Jacques, and Garret; Jacques was in this country in the year 1789, and continued here until he died, in 1797; George came in 1796, and this has been his place of residence ever since; Isaac was here, and several times back and forward to the Walnut hills before his father, Garret, went away; Garret, the younger, has lived, and does live, below the line. The heirs aforesaid have never been in possession of the premises claimed that the witness knows of." John Girault, a witness introduced by Elihu Hall Bay, a conflicting claimant, says, "that, early in the year 1791, he attended Governor Gayoso on a visit to the Walnut hills, to view the place where the Governor intended to erect a fortification; that, on their arrival at Watkin's creek, they found a small cabin on the lower side of it, where they encamped all night; after the Governor had been informed that the cabin was erected by Garret Rapalje, he appeared surprised that Rapalje should have persisted in erecting it after being forbidden by him; the Governor then took possession of it in the name of the King, and wrote on one side of the joists, 'Casa Gayoso;' there was no person at or about the place, nor any appearance of recent cultivation, but there was an old field which the witness took to be the settlement of Watkins, as he, the witness, had been there in 1775, and, from information, understood that Watkins lived there at that time. In the latter part of the month of March following, the Governor returned to erect the fortification he had before proposed, and, on the 1st of April, arrived at the same cabin, which was still uninhabited, and stopped and dined there; that a number of artificers were present for the purpose of erecting the fort, among whom was John Shackler. Afterwards Rapalje made application to permit him to return and inhabit the house, which the Governor positively refused; the witness knows that several other applications were made to settle the Walnut hills, which were also refused; the witness was frequently at the Walnut hills afterwards, and never saw Rapalje or any of his family, inhabiting or cultivating the tenement; but the witness does not know, of his own knowledge, whether Rapalje cultivated the premises or not, but rather thinks he did not."
778 787	Jos. W. A. Lloyd Thomas Percy	Anthony Calvit Thomas Percy	Homochitto river Bayou Sara	200f. 800f.	Spanish Spanish	Jan. 18, 1793 Ap'l 11, 1789	Joshua Howard says, " that William Vardiman was a resident in the Mississippi territory on the 27th October, 1795, and was twenty-one years of age at the date of the warrant." No evidence. John Collins says, " that the claimant was a resident in the Mississippi territory on the 27th October, 1795."
809	John Ellis	Thomas Green	Thompson's creek	800f.	Spanish	Feb. 24, 1795	Bennet Truly says, " that Thomas Green was an actual settler in the Mississippi territory on the 27th October, 1795, and that he was then the head of a family." Ferdinand L. Claiborne says, " that he paid for the claimant, Col. John Ellis, to Col. Thomas Green, two thousand dollars, being the consideration money for a tract of land lying on the bayou Sara, which the said John Ellis had purchased of the said Green, which tract contained eight hundred arpents."
810	Robert Dunbar	Francis Jones	Cole's creek	400f.	Spanish	June 6, 1790	John Roberts says, " that Francis Jones came into the country in the year 1788, to look for land, and procured a warrant of survey from the Spanish Government, and left it in the hands of Henry Green, to have it laid and surveyed, who did the same on the land now claimed; in the mean time, to wit, in the fall of 1788, Jones went to the States to fetch his family, and brought them to the neighborhood, and went on the land with his negroes in May, 1798, and began improving, and cleared trees and cane off of about four or five acres, and prepared timber for a house, and then sold it to Ferguson, Wooley, & Co., who sold to the claimant." Henry Green's deposition: " I do certify, that, in the year 1789, to the best of my recollection, Francis Jones petitioned to the Spanish Government for a certain tract of land, containing four hundred arpents, joining the land I now cultivate; the abovementioned tract was granted to the said Jones, and surveyed by my direction in the year 1791, as agent for Mr. Jones, and kept in possession for said Jones by me, as his agent, until 1798, when said Jones removed to the country, took possession, and improved, and planted fruit trees on said tract." William Thomas says, " that the premises in question were improved either in the year 1790 or 1791, but the witness does not recollect by whom, nor whether the improvement was continued, not having been that way since."

D—Continued.

Ref'r's No.	Claimant's name.	Name of original claimant.	Situation.	Quantity.	Title. Whence derived.	Title. Date.	Remarks, &c.
813	Robert Dunbar	Robert Dunbar	Bayou Pierre	250	British	Feb. 12, 1778.	Benjamin Beall says, "that the claimant was an actual settler, and the head of a family, in the Mississippi territory, in the year 1781, to the best of his knowledge and belief, and was previous to that time." James Truly says, "that Robert Dunbar was an actual settler in the Mississippi territory on and before the date of the warrant, to wit, on the 12th February, 1788, and was then the head of a family; that the said order of survey did not come to the hands of the said Robert, in consequence, as he believes, of the war which prevailed at that time between the British and Spanish Governments, until about the summer of 1803, when it was found among the papers of one Richard Harrison, after his death: said Dunbar being entitled to so much land, as a head right, under the British Government, and expecting a confirmation of his title, disposed of it to said Harrison, and gave his obligation to said Harrison to confirm the same to him when the titles should be fully completed. This deponent further says, that one Philip Barber, the uncle and co-partner in trade of the said Harrison, was taken by the Spaniards on his way from Pensacola to this country, about the year 1778, and, with his papers, was carried to New Orleans; and that this deponent believes the above mentioned warrant of survey to have been among them, as he, this deponent, afterwards found it in a trunk of the said Harrison, after his death, with other papers of a like description." No warrant produced.
882	John Crunkleton	James Crunkleton	Bayou Pierre	640	British		Patrick Cogan says, "he has been acquainted fourteen years with the land in question, and seven years with the claimant. The land, when he was first acquainted with it, appeared to have been formerly settled by some person; and he understood, in the neighborhood, that it belonged to the father of the claimant, and that he formerly resided on it. He understood, also, that the father left the country on account of war in it between the Indians and Spaniards, or at least on account of public troubles." Zachariah Kirkland says, "that, about two years ago, the claimant came to him and offered him lands for sale on James's creek, which he believes to be the land now claimed; that the claimant then showed him a part of a British warrant granted to his father, the other part being lost, but knows not what land it was for; that he has heard John Staybraker say, that he had been at the house of the claimant's father, when he lived upon the land in question."
888	George Matthews	Adam Cloud	Bayou Sara	1,000f.	Spanish		Joseph Dyson says, "that a certain Thomas James went to Pensacola, in the year 1778, to get a warrant for James Symmons, and another for James Crunkleton, the father of the claimant; and, after said Thomas James returned, he saw the warrant in Crunkleton's hands, which he understood was for the land in question, and that Crunkleton settled on the land immediately, and cultivated it for about two years, and then went to the States on account of the rebellion here. In about three or four years, Crunkleton returned with an intention to settle on the land again, but was taken sick and died. The present claimant, immediately after he got married, settled on the land in question, as the witness believes, and has continued to inhabit and cultivate the same ever since; that it is the same place his father formerly settled on as before mentioned, and there are about six acres or more cleared, and a dwelling house and out-houses." On cross-examination, he does not know what quantity of land the warrant called for. Stated to be lost. No warrant produced.

No.	Claimant	Grantee / Settler	Location	Amount	Nation	Date	Remarks
889	George Matthews	Adam Cloud	Cole's creek	500f.	Spanish	Mar. 30, 1790	John Girault says, "that Adam Cloud moved on the land with his family in the year 1789, or 1790, and cultivated it for two or three years following, and then moved off. The witness does not know whether Adam Cloud resided in the Mississippi territory on the 27th October, 1795. Cloud was sent out of the territory by order of the Spanish Government, and left Colonel Forman as his attorney."
924	William Clare	William Clare	Cole's creek	240f.	do.	—	No warrant produced; but a survey made by William Thomas, dated 20th February, 1795, by an order of William Dunbar, dated February 13, 1795. Henry Stampley says, " that the claimant was about twenty years of age at the date of the survey. About four years ago, (1801,) the claimant cleared and cultivated about six acres, and made a crop on it, and has done nothing since that the witness knows of."
937 1,372	Catherine Surget Charles Surget	Peter Surget Charles Surget,	Feliciana creek Feliciana creek	800f. 500f.	do. do.	Nov. 13, 1794 Dec. 13, 1794	William Atchison says, "that Peter Surget and Charles Surget severally inhabited and cultivated these two tracts on the 27th October, 1795, and that the former was the head of a family, and the latter twenty-one years of age at the date of the warrant." Samuel Stockett says, "that, in the year 1802, in the month of March, he came to this country for the purpose of settling, and intended doing so on vacant land, by which intention he had occasion to travel over the land claimed as above stated, and that there was no settlement, or appearance of cultivation, on any part of the above tract; after which, he, this deponent, returned to the State of Tennessee, and came back in the fall following 1802, and traversed said tracts, with other lands, and still discovered no settlement on the said tract; but in consequence of seeing some old marked lines, he did not settle on said lands." Isaac Johnson says, "that he is well acquainted with the land in question, (to wit: No. 1,372;) that he came to this country in the year 1800, and that he went over this tract, and another tract adjoining to, and belonging to the brother of the claimant, (to wit: No. 937,) with an intention of purchasing. In the year 1800, at the time he called on Mr. Surget to make a purchase of it, Mr. Surget informed him that a part of the lands, containing thirteen hundred acres, belonged to him, and a part to his brother; that these two tracts were in one survey, one of eight hundred arpents, and the other of five hundred arpents, but that there were two rights for them. On his return to this country, in the year 1801, he went over these two tracts, and observed the lines, and three or four corner trees marked with the name of Surget; that he travelled over the greater part, if not all the lands in these two tracts, in the spring of 1801, and that there was not then the least evidence of any improvement or cultivation, as the witness observed, on either of the tracts." Moses Starnes says, "that he is acquainted with the premises in question, as he has been frequently over them. In February, 1801, he moved to this country, and settled within a mile or a mile and a half of the premises. He very often travelled over the tract of five hundred arpents, and another tract adjoining thereto, which was claimed by the Surgets, and which he understood were all one claim; that he believes there are not one hundred yards square of both these tracts that he has not travelled over. At the time this deponent first went over these tracts of land, in March 1801, and to the present day, he never discovered the least evidence of an improvement or cultivation on either of the tracts. The only evidence which he discovered, was some marked corner trees, which marks appeared not to be more than two or three years standing." William Atchison, the evidence whose testimony has been previously stated in these claims, being present before the Board, disavows the evidence formerly given, and says that the lands were never inhabited or cultivated as heretofore stated.
958	Ann Brashears	Ann Brashears	Bayou Pierre	300f.	do.	—	No warrant was produced, but a certificate by William Vousdan that a survey was made on the 11th November, 1788. William Thomas says, " that the claimant obtained a warrant from the Spanish Government for eight hundred arpents, upwards of fourteen years ago; that the witness acted as deputy surveyor to William Vousdan, who was surveyor for this district at that time; and, in virtue of said warrant or order, surveyed a tract of land of eight hundred arpents, on the north side of the north fork of the bayou Pierre, which survey included a place called the White Ground Lick, near to which a certain Benjamin Foy resided in what is called a camp, near the centre of the land; that the present claim of three hundred arpents is included in the

D—Continued.

Register's No.	Claimant's name.	Name of original claimant.	Situation.	Quantity.	Title. Whence derived.	Title. Date.	Remarks, &c.
965	Isaac Johnson	Jemima Morgan	Cole's creek	350	British	—	survey of eight hundred arpents before mentioned; and the witness knows nothing further of the claim, nor why Vousdan did not return the whole survey". John Girault says, "that after William Vousdan resigned, William Dunbar was appointed the surveyor of Natchez district by the Spanish Government, and that he, the witness, acting as deputy surveyor under him, surveyed a tract of land, by order of the Spanish Government, of three hundred and twenty arpents, for the above mentioned Benjamin Foy, within the survey of eight hundred arpents aforesaid; that the said Foy, being interpreter to the Spanish Government, was favored by them, and had a grant for five hundred arpents, as the witness understood; but, as Mrs. Brashears had a prior right, he agreed to take only three hundred and twenty arpents out of the eight hundred arpents aforesaid, which the witness surveyed for him as aforesaid, and left the residue for Mrs. Brashears; that said survey was made on the upper end of said eight hundred acre tract". Major Stephen Minor says, "that he, the witness, knows that a warrant of survey issued from the Spanish Government to the claimant for eight hundred arpents, about fourteen or fifteen years ago," (1790.)
972	John Holt	Joseph Sharp	Cole's creek	640f.	Spanish	—	No warrant produced. Robert Miller says, "that a small improvement or clearing was made on the premises by the hands of William Erwine in 1795, and Jemima Morgan was of age in 1779." The only evidence produced is a petition by Joseph Sharp for six hundred arpents, dated 17th November, 1795, which appears not to have been presented to the Spanish Governor, as there is no decree on it. There is also a plot and survey, made in September, 1796, by Silas L. Paine, but no authority mentioned by which it was done.
1,001	John Ellis	William Wikoff	Bayou Sara	800f.	Spanish	Ap'l 15, 1789	William Atchison says, "that he surveyed the land in question for the claimant by the request of William Wikoff, who said he had sold it to the claimant; and the witness says that Wikoff was of age at the date of the warrant, and the land was not at that time inhabited or cultivated, and has not been so since that he knows of."
1,090	A. Hunt and W. G. Forman	Richard Devall	Mississippi river	1,500f.	Spanish	Jan. 12, 1789	No evidence offered.
1,203	Samuel C. Young	Alex'der Pannill	Bayou Sara	500f.	Spanish	Feb. 27, '95	Jeremiah Routh says, "that Ithmer Andrews was above twenty-one years of age at the date of the warrant, and was, together with the inhabitants, driven out of that part of the country by the Indians."
1,204	Samuel C. Young	David Pannill	Bayou Sara	500f.	Spanish	Feb. 27, '95	
1,239	Elijah Cushing	Ithmer Andrews	Big Black	100	British	Nov. 19, 1778	
1,245	R. and P. King	Justus King	Homochitto river	100	British	—	No warrant produced. Caleb King says, "that he was present, and carried the chain when this land was surveyed by one Samuel Lewis, a lawful surveyor, which was in the year 1776, and believes it was done under a warrant from the British Government of West Florida; that Justus King was living on the land with his family at the time the survey was run, and continued on it at least three years afterwards, and then was driven off by the Indians, and never resided on it again. After this it was included in a survey to James Kirk, under a grant of the Spanish Government to him, which prevented King's returning to it. The grant to Kirk has been confirmed by the commissioners.
1,273	Robert Starke	Robert Starke	Bayou Sara	2,000f.	Spanish	Dec. 29, 1791	This land was regranted by the Spanish Government to James Mather, and a patent issued, which was confirmed by the commissioners. Moses Johnson says, "that, in 1791 or 1792, he cultivated

No.	Claimant	Original grantee	Location	Quantity	Nation	Date	Remarks
1276	Heirs of T. Tyler	Charles Bachelet	Apple Island	2,065f.	Spanish	Dec. 1, 1786	the premises for the claimant with his negroes, and made two crops for the claimant; and, within the time he was cultivating the premises, the land was surveyed for the claimant by William Atchison, deputy surveyor under the Spanish Government. When the witness left the place it was in the possession of the claimant, and there was a crop of two or three hundred barrels of corn on the premises. The claimant was the head of a family at the date of the warrant." Matthew McCulloch says, "that, in the summer of the year 1794, he was present when Governor Gayoso and the claimant were conversing about the land in question, and heard the claimant say to Governor Gayoso that he would give up his then settlement on the land, if he, the Governor, would give him another piece of land which he had found; that the Governor turned round to Mr. Mather, who was present, and said, that, as he had been applying for land, this was a fine tract, and he might have it; whereupon, the claimant said, 'Governor, observe, I do not mean to relinquish my settlement unless you give me the land which I found for it,' which was situated in the bayou Sara settlement. The Governor turned round to the claimant, and said to him he was a 'discontented old man.'" Thomas Calvit says, "that he believes Robert Stark, claimant, was a resident in the Mississippi territory on the 27th October, 1795." This land was sold at public sale, and purchased by Arthur Cobb, January 24, 1789, who sold it to Thomas Tyler, October 13, 1803. George Fitzgerald says, "that he knew Arthur Cobb to be a resident in the Mississippi territory before the year 1795, and believes he continued to be so until the year 1799, as he, the witness, was at his house, near the Spanish line of West Florida, at this time, where he was then living with his family." William Kirkwood says, "that in the year 1788, and before then, the premises in question were inhabited and cultivated by one Howard, for the use of the original grantee, Charles Bachelot; that, in that year, the whole island was overflowed, and Howard was obliged to move off; and that the owners annually put stock on it, but no person inhabited it after the great flood till Tyler purchased it; and afterwards Tyler built a cabin, and put a man in it to take care of his stock."
1978	Bennet Truly	Richard Trivilian	Bayou Pierre	336f.	Spanish	-	No warrant produced, but a certificate from William Dunbar, deputy surveyor, dated 10th March, 1795, stating that the land had been surveyed by virtue of a decree, or order of survey, from the Governor General.
1279	Bennet Truly	Edward Rose	Bayou Pierre	400f.	Spanish	Feb. 24, 1795	Do.
1290	Step. Henderson	Wm. Vardiman	Homochitto river	300f.	Spanish	Sep. 28, 1794	No evidence.
1330	William Norris	Wm. Norris	Homochitto river	200f.	Spanish	Jan. 18, 1793	John Searcy says, "that the claimant was twenty-one years of age at the date of the warrant; that, in the fall of the year 1795, the claimant left the territory, and moved into the Opelousas country, and has remained there ever since; and there never was any improvement made on the premises till the year 1803, when James Willis cleared three or four acres, and planted it in corn, but the witness does not know whether on account of the claimant or not; neither does the witness know when the land was surveyed, or by what authority."
1345	Nath. Tomlinson, in right of his wife, Elizabeth	Elizabeth Baker	Second creek	80f.	Spanish	April 26, 1790	Benjamin Newman says, "that Elizabeth Baker was of age at the date of the warrant, and that neither of the claimants ever inhabited or cultivated the land. Samuel Hutchins says, "that, fifteen or sixteen years ago, ('91 or '92) he was on the premises in question, at the house of David Mitchell, who told this witness that he was making an improvement on the land for Mrs. Baker, now the wife of this claimant; and that, some time afterwards, Mrs. Baker told the witness that Mitchell did improve the land for her. The witness also says, that, some short time afterwards, he applied in person to the surveyor for a certificate from him of the land now in question, being vacant, who told this witness that he could not give him one, as he had, some time prior to that, given one to Mrs. Baker for the premises."
1352	Israel Leonard	Abraham Knapp	River Big Black	100	British	Nov. 19, 1779	No evidence.
1354	Caleb King	Caleb King	River Homochitto	300	British	Aug. 4, 1779	Nathan Swayze says, "that the claimant was the head of a family at the date of the warrant, and inhabited and cultivated this land in 1776, and continued on it until he was driven off by the Indians, in or about the year 1780. The Spaniards afterwards took possession of the country, and granted a tract of land to James Kirk, who included the land in question in his survey; and that no person has resided on it or cultivated it since the claimant, King, left it." Kirk's patent has been confirmed by the commissioners.

D—Continued.

Register's No.	Claimant's name.	Name of original claimant.	Situation.	Quantity.	Title.		Remarks, &c.
					Whence derived.	Date.	
1358	Maurice Custard	E. McKimm	River Big Black	600f.	Spanish	Feb. 24, 1795	Jephtha Higdon says, "that he knows the land in question; that it was surveyed in the year 1790, by William Thomas, for William Calvit, who built a house thereon, and planted some peach stones. The witness does not know that any person lived in the house. The land is situated in the Walnut bottom, on the road to the Walnut hills, adjoining lands of Daniel Burnet and William Brocus. The witness and James Spain carried the chain at the time of surveying."
1360 1338 1449 1471	Arthur Patterson James Burnet Heirs of W. Scott Joshua Howard	Josiah Flowers James Burnet Wm. Scott Joshua Howard	Bayou Pierre Big Black River Homochitto Second creek	400 1,180 400f. 200	British Spanish Spanish British	Nov. 19, 1779 Mar. 23, 1795 May 31, 1787 -	No evidence. Do. Do. No warrant produced, but a copy of the survey, from the field book of Luke Collins, formerly a deputy surveyor, which was proven to be the hand-writing of said Luke Collins, dated the 28th of April, 1800; also, a receipt for the surveying fees, dated 23d January, 1777. Henry Phipps says "that he carried one end of the chain when the land in question was surveyed. That the claimant, with his family, settled on the land previous to its being surveyed; that the witness lived with him at that time; and that the claimant continued to inhabit and cultivate it for three years after it was surveyed. The witness further says, that, in the latter part of the year 1779, the claimant left the premises in question, being dissatisfied with the Spanish Government."
1501	John Smith	Richard Winn	Bayou Pierre	240f.	Spanish		No warrant produced, nor any other evidence offered in support of his claim, except a certificate of William Dunbar, dated 14th July, 1790, stating that he had surveyed the land for Richard Winn, and given a plot thereof; but does not mention by what authority.
1522	Heirs of Joseph Voucheré	Joseph Voucheré	River Homochitto	600f.	Spanish	-	The only evidence produced is a certificate of William Vousdan, dated 28th of October, 1788, stating that he had surveyed the land for Joseph Voucheré, but names no authority for doing it.
1524 1528	David Ferguson William Thomas	James Dealy William Thomas	Bayou Sara Bayou Pierre	320f. 600f.	Spanish Spanish	Jan. 17, 1793 Febru'y, 1795	No evidence. James Truly says, that the claimant was an actual settler in the Mississippi territory on the 27th October, 1795."
1531 1537	David Ferguson Heirs of George Cochran	James Carroll Ralph Humphreys	Bayou Sara Bayou Pierre	280f. 169f.	Spanish Spanish	Dec. 19, 1793 -	No evidence. No warrant produced. It is stated to be a part of a warrant for six hundred arpents, granted to Ralph Humphreys, dated 29th of January, 1789. William Smith says, "that R. Humphreys was the head of a family at the date of the warrant, and cultivated the land in question in the year 1789 or 1790. There was then a cabin on it, and ten or twelve acres of cleared ground, which he purchased of Reuben White: the two following years it was cultivated by a certain Benjamin Grubb, for the use of the grantee. No further cultivation was made on it till sold to the claimant, George W. Humphreys, son and heir of the grantee, who sold to the claimant, was a resident in the Mississippi territory on the 27th October, 1795."
1568	Daniel Burnet	Thomas Smith	Bayou Pierre	240f.	Spanish	Feb. 9, 1790	Richard King says, "that Thomas Smith was a resident in the Mississippi territory on the 27th of October, 1795."
1574 1597 1619 1620 1691	H'rs of D. Mygatt George Cochran Joseph Walker John Walker Peter Walker, Jr.	Daniel Mygatt George Cochran Joseph Walker John Walker Peter Walker, Jr.	Bayou Pierre River Homochitto Beaver creek Beaver creek Beaver creek	100 300f. 500f. 500f. 500f.	British Spanish Spanish Spanish Spanish	Nov. 19, 1779 Dec. 29, 1791 -	No evidence. Do. The warrants in neither of those claims were produced. Certificates from William Atchison, dated in March, 1795, stating that the claims, severally, were surveyed, in virtue of warrants from the Spanish Government, dated 30th of January, 1795, were exhibited. William Atchison says, "that there has been no cultivation on either of the tracts that he knows of; that Joseph

No.	Claimant	Assignee	Location	Quantity	Nation	Date	Remarks
1641	Thomas Carter	Thomas Carter	Cole's creek	—	British	Nov. 19, 1779	Walker was of age at the date of the warrant, and was a resident in the Mississippi territory on the 27th October, 1795.
1642	Henry Day	Benjamin Day	River Big Black	1,400	do	Nov. 19, 1778	No warrant produced, and the quantity claimed not mentioned.
1643	Do.	Henry Dwight	Do.	1,100	Spanish	June 6, 1795	No evidence.
1658	James Cole	James Cole	Lot No. 4, square No. 12	Natchez	Spanish		Ditto. Ditto.
1741	William Dunbar	William Dunbar	Thompson's creek	1,200	British	Sept. 16, 1777	Thomas Regar says, " that the grantee was twenty-one years of age at the date of the warrant; and, that some time early in the fall of the year 1795, the claimant had timber hauled to build a house, on the lot in question, and took the witness upon the lot to show him, and to get him to assist in building the house; that, soon afterwards, the claimant was ordered to the Chickasaw bluffs, by the Spanish Government, and from thence he went to the States, and did not return until the year 1798."
1742	David Roberts	David Roberts	River Big Black	240f.	Spanish	April 26, 1790	This lot was regranted by the Spanish Government, and confirmed by the commissioners.
1760	John Burnet, Jr.	John Burnet, Jr.	Bayou Sara	130f.	do	July 9, 1782	No evidence.
1762	Neille & Beauvais	John Cammack	Bayou Sara	400f.	do	Feb. 27, 1795	Ditto. Ditto.
1775	Heirs of S. Crane	Silas Crane	River Homochitto	300	British	Nov. 19, 1778	Ditto.
1780	Francis Brezina	Francis Brezina	Do.	2,000f.	Spanish	—	Richard King says, " that he, the witness, understood that the land in question was surveyed in the year 1778 or 1779, by Samuel Lewis, then a deputy surveyor under the British Government, but that no settlement has been made on it by the claimants, or any person for them that he knows of."
1794	Frederick Mann	Frederick Mann	Bayou Sara	600f.	do	—	No warrant produced, nor any evidence offered. No evidence of title produced, except a petition by the claimant to the Governor General, dated 31st January, 1795, with a recommendation thereon for five hundred arpents, by Gov. Gayoso.
1797	Ebenezer Rees	James McGill	Bayou Pierre	500f.	do	—	No warrant produced.
1799	Do.	Ezina Baker	Homochitto river	500f.	do	Feb. 24, 1795	No evidence.
1800	Silas L. Payne	Joseph King	Bayou Pierre	240f.	do	Apr. 26, 1790	Ditto.
1805	Daniel Finnan	Daniel Finnan	Do.	240f.	do	do	Ditto.
1806	Jacob Stampley	Jacob Stampley	Homochitto river	200f.	do	Jan. 18, 1793	Ditto.
1810	Ebenezer Rees	Jesse Lum	Bayou Pierre	200f.	do	do	Ditto.
1807	Do.	Joseph Sticker	Bayou Sara	400f.	do	Jan. 27, 1790	Ditto.
	Do.	Robert Davis	Thompson's creek	800f.	do	—	
1816	Do.	Ebenezer Rees	Bayou Sara	1,000f.	do	—	No warrant produced, nor other evidence of title, except a petition of Robert Davis to the Governor General, dated 9th January, 1795, and a recommendation thereon by Governor Gayoso.
1819	Jeremiah Bryan	Jeremiah Bryan	Buffalo creek	800f.	do	Nov. 8, 1788	No warrant produced, nor other evidence of title, except a petition from the claimant to the Governor General, dated 1st January, 1795, and a recommendation thereon by Manuel Gayoso, Governor of Natchez, dated 2d January, 1795.
1829	Heirs of T. Tyler	Thomas Tyler	Bayou Pierre	1,000f.	do	—	No evidence.
1855	Bennet Truly	Hugh Logan	Do.	240f.	do	April 7, 1791	No warrant produced, nor other evidence of title, except a petition to the Governor General, dated the 7th of April, 1795, with Governor Gayoso's recommendation thereon, and a certificate of William Dunbar, with a plot, dated 7th April, 1795.
1856	Do.	Bennet Truly	Bayou Sara	200f.	do	Jan. 3, 1787	No evidence.
1857	Heirs of William Ferguson	Wm. Williams	Cole's creek	500	British	Apr. 21, 1776	Ditto.
1869	Peter B. Bruin	Peter B. Bruin	Bayou Pierre	500f.	Spanish	June 15, 1795	Ditto.
1883	Robert Smith	Robert Smith	Do.	200f.	do	Jan. 18, 1793	Ditto.
1885	Winthrop Sargent	Maria Williams	Lots No. 1 and 3, square No. 5	Natchez	do	Sept. 30, 1795	Ditto.
1895	Sarah Davis	S. Coleby & others	Bayou Pierre	400	British	Feb. 21, 1778	Vincent Fortner says, "that the claimant was about eighteen years of age at the date of the warrant; and began to cultivate the premises in the year 1799, and has continued to do so ever since, but has never lived on them, being a single man, until lately, but is now married and about to move on the premises; and there are about seven acres cleared, and a dwelling-house and one out-house."
1917	Thomas Fortner	Thomas Fortner	River Big Black	240f.	Spanish	Apr. 26, 1790	Ditto. Ditto.

D—Continued.

Register's No.	Claimant's name	Name of original claimant	Situation	Quantity	Title — Where derived	Title — Date	Remarks, &c.
1925	Samuel Brooks	William Silkrigs	Mississippi river	200	British	-	No warrant produced, but a certificate of a survey made the 21st August, 1777; and a certificate of William Vousdan, formerly a deputy surveyor, dated in 1801, Anthony Hutchins says, "that the signature to the abovementioned certificate is the hand-writing of William Vousdan, who, on the 21st of August, 1777, was a deputy surveyor for this district, under the British Government of West Florida; and that Silkrigs was twenty-one years of age, and upwards, at the date of the survey." John Girault says, "that William Silkrigs was an actual settler in the Mississippi territory, on the 27th October, 1795." William Silkrigs, sworn on the *voire dire*, says, "that he is in no instance interested in this claim at present; that he, the witness, in the year 1777, began to improve this land, and built him a house, and cleared and fenced in about three acres; and the next year lived as overseer to one of his neighbors, yet cultivated a crop on the same place, and gathered it in, and hauled it to the house of the person where he lived, and then went off and staid about two months, and returned to his land again, and the Americans took him as a prisoner, and carried him down the river in the year 1779, and remained with the Americans some time, and was afterwards retaken by the British. By this time the Indians had plundered his place, and was thereby prevented from returning to it, and he continued down in the settled parts of the country, and continued there until lately, and obtained a Spanish grant in Adams county; that he, the witness, had a British warrant for the land in question; that under that warrant Mr. Vousdan surveyed the land; that he, the witness, sent the warrant and survey to Pensacola to get a patent, but they never were returned; and that the premises were surveyed in the month of August, 1777; the witness says he was twenty-one years of age in the year 1774."
1926	P. McDermot	P. McDermot	Bayou Tunica	440f.	Spanish	Jan. 18, 1793	Narsworthy Hunter says, "that this land was first settled in the year 1796 by the claimant, when he built a small cabin and cleared half an acre, and cultivated it in corn, and nothing more has been done on the premises since that time, that the witness knows of. The witness does not know the age of the grantee or patentee, but, from his appearance, thought he was not twenty-one years of age in 1793." Palser Shilling says, "that the claimant, when he first came to this country, which he thinks was in the year 1790, he came to the house of the witness to undertake to build a mill for him, and that he then appeared to be a man grown, and was acting for himself, and the witness thinks he was two or three-and-twenty years of age at that time." Patrick Foley says: "that the claimant was upwards of twenty-one years of age at the date of the warrant, and the witness believes he was a resident in the Mississippi territory on and before the 27th October, 1795."
1927	John Choate	John Choate	Second creek	100	British	-	No warrant produced, but a certificate from Luke Collins, dated 26th June, 1776, stating that he had surveyed the same in pursuance of an order from Elias Dunford, surveyor general of West Florida.
1928	John Choate	John Choate	Second creek	100	British	-	No warrants produced, nor any other evidence of title offered.
1929		Sarah Choate	St. Catherine's creek	500f.	Spanish	-	
1959	Samuel Brooks	Wm. Hubbard	Bayou Pierre	100	British	Aug. 4, 1779	No warrants produced, nor any other evidence of title offered. James Harman says, "that the original claimant says upwards of twenty-one years of age at the date of the warrant, and had a wife and ten children in the year 1774."

No.	Claimant	In favour of	Situation	Quantity	Authority	Date	Remarks
1968	R. S. Blackburn	R. S. Blackburn	Mississippi river	3,000f.	Spanish	–	William Silkrigs says, "that Hubbard, at the time of his decease, gave him all his papers and rights; that he afterwards got the abovementioned warrant and other papers out of the Spanish office, where they had been lodged, and that he sold the warrant to the claimant, and is not now interested in the claim, either one way or the other. The reason why no settlement was made on the land was because the Spaniards shortly after took the country: it being a soldier's right, Hubbard dare not survey the land. Hubbard was an old, infirm, poor man, and his wife and children were never in this country."
1969	John Lewis	John Lewis	Do.	2,000f.	do.	–	No warrants produced, nor any other evidence produced in support of these claims.
1972	R. S. Blackburn	R. S. Blackburn	Do.	3,000f.	do.	–	Do.
1988	John Girault	John St. Germain	Do.	1,000f.	do.	–	Do.
1989	Do.	Henry Bachelot	Do.	600f.	do.	Dec. 16, 1785	No evidence.
1990	Do.	Hugh Logan	Cole's creek	240f.	do.	Mar. 22, 1785	Do.
2008	James Frazier	James Frazier	Tombigbee river	1,600f.	do.	April 7, 1791	No warrant produced.
2013	Sol. H. Wisdom	Sol. H. Wisdom	Lot No. 1, of sq. No. 13	Natchez	do.	Oct. 3, 1795	This lot was regranted by the Spanish Government, and a patent issued, which was confirmed by the commissioners, to James Moor.
2022	Christ. Connelly	Tomasina Lord	Lot No. 1, of sq. No. 19	Natchez	do.	–	John Girault says, "that the claimant was a resident in the Mississippi territory on the 27th October, 1795, and was the head of a family at the date of the warrant." This lot was regranted, and a patent issued to William Dunbar, which has been confirmed by the commissioners.
2028	Heirs of Peter Walker	Peter Walker	Buffalo creek	800f.	do.	–	No warrant produced. William Atchison says, "that he is well acquainted with the premises in question, and also Elijah Bunch, (of whom Walker purchased;) that, about the year 1793 or 1794, Bunch obtained leave, either written or verbal, from the Spanish Governor Gayoso, to go and settle the land in question, and he did so; and the Governor desired the witness, who was a deputy surveyor, not to trouble him, and Bunch continued to inhabit and cultivate it until he contracted to sell it to the claimant, which was in 1797 or 1798. The witness surveyed it for Walker about the time the contract was made, and he understood that it had never been surveyed before, but that Walker purchased Bunch's improvement, and surveyed the land under a warrant to himself.
2035	William Foster	William Foster	Petty creek	240f.	do.	May 26, 1790	No evidence.
2036	Francis Irvine	Francis Irvine	Homochitto river	240f.	do.	April 26, 1790	Do.
2037	James Stoddard	James Stoddard	Do.	400f.	do.	do	Do.
2038	Isaac Lathrop	Isaac Lathrop	Do.	240f.	do.	do	Do.
2039	Peter Martin	Peter Martin	Cole's creek	240f.	do.	do	Do.
2040	Jacob Stephen	Jacob Stephen	Do.	240f.	do.	do	Do.
2041	John Sinclair	John Sinclair	Do.	240f.	do.	do	Do.
2043	Henry Quirk	Henry Quirk	Bayou Pierre	240f.	do.	do	Do.
2044	William Ivers	William Ivers	Do.	240f.	do.	do	Do.
2045	William Estell	William Estell	Do.	240f.	do.	do	Do.
2046	Lambert de Selle	Patrick Quinn	Homochitto river	300f.	do.	Nov. 25, 1789	Do.
2047	Patrick Quinn	Ephraim Story	Bayou Pierre	240f.	do.	April 26, 1790	Do.
2048	Ephraim Story	Jacob Paul	River Big Black	300f.	do.	Dec. 18, 1789	Do.
2049	Jacob Paul	Edmund Falson	Bayou Pierre	240f.	do.	Nov. 25, 1789	Do.
2050	Edmund Falson	Samuel Porter	Buffalo creek	300f.	do.	June 30, 1789	Do.
2051	Samuel Porter	Adam Pickles	Cole's creek	240f.	do.	April 7, 1791	Do.
2052	Adam Pickles	Hezek. Harman	Do.	400f.	do.	Mar. 2, 1793	Do.
2053	Hezek. Harman	Gabriel Fuzelier	Bayou Pierre	300f.	do.	Jan. 16, 1789	Do.
2055	Gabriel Fuzelier	Samuel Young	River Homochitto	400f.	do.	do	Do.
2056	Samuel Young	Peter Bissardon	Willing's Bayou	240f.	do.	Nov. 25, 1789	Do.
2057	Peter Bissardon	Lot in Natchez			do.	Feb. 2, 1787	Do.
	P. C. Pegroux	P. C. Pegroux	Homochitto river	1,600f.	do.	June 14, 1796	Do.

D—Continued.

Register's No.	Claimant's name.	Name of original claimant.	Situation.	Quantity.	Title. Whence derived.	Title. Date.	Remarks, &c.
1367	Heirs of Hyram Swayze	Hyram Swayze	Near Natchez.	164	Spanish	Jan. 18, 1793	This warrant was granted by Governor Gayoso, and not by the Governor General. Richard King, says, "that the grantee was twenty-one years of age at the date of the warrant, and the land was granted him as a bounty for military services. The claimants resided in the Mississippi territory on the 27th October, 1795. Hiram Swayze lived on or near the land in question from the year 1789 until he died, which was some time in the year 1794." Prosper King says, "that Hyram Swayze inhabited and cultivated the land in question at the time of his death, and his family continued to live on it, and cultivated for about two years afterwards." This land was regranted, and a patent issued, which has been confirmed by the commissioners.

LAND OFFICE, WEST OF PEARL RIVER, *October* 1, 1808.

THO. H. WILLIAMS, *Register.*

Claims founded on Spanish Patents legally and fully executed, but not confirmed by the Board of Commissioners, the claimants being non-residents on the 27th day of October, 1795.

Register's Number.	Claimant's names.	Names of original claimants.	Situation.	Quantity.	Date of Patent.	Remarks, &c.
56	Samuel Young	Samuel Young	Bayou Sara	480	April —, 1790	Regranted, and confirmed by the commissioners.
365	Charles Forget	John Vidal	Lot in the city of Natchez	-	March 12, 1795	
497	John Bisland	James and Evan Jones	Fairchild's creek	500	June 22, 1791	
615	Heirs of George Cochran	John Perry	Bayou Pierre	1,000	October 20, 1788	
623	Do.	Peter Belly	Mississippi river	630	June 1, 1792	
1045	William Brown	William Brown	Bayou Pierre	250	April 1, 1789	
1055	Daniel Hickey	Daniel Hickey	Sandy creek	1,200	March 10, 1789	
1205	Samuel C. Young	John Pannill	Bayou Sara	800	June 20, 1795	
1206	Do.	Joseph Pannill	Do.	1,000	Do.	
1230	William Lintot	Hubbard Rowell	Do.	850	May 6, 1791	
1430	James Moore	George Proffit	Sandy creek	800	March 15, 1789	
1545	William Conway	William Conway	Buffalo creek	800	June —, 1787	
1735	Robert Dow	Robert Dow	Cole's creek	1,000	May 16, 1791	
1764	Neille and Beauvais	William Collins	Feliciana creek	500	April 10, 1795	
1939	James Kennedy	James Kennedy	Buffalo creek	1,600	June 9, 1787	Regranted, and confirmed by the commissioners.
1951	Do.		Near Loftus cliffs	1,000	December 4, 1787	
1966	Stephen Ploché	Stephen Ploché	Charles creek	1,600	March 3, 1789	
2003	George Pollock	Furzelier de la Clare	River Homochitto	1,100	August 8, 1789	
2010	Claudio Baugaud	Claudio Baugaud	Lake of the Cross	1,000	March 6, 1789	
2014	Do.	Do.	Do.	1,034	August 30, 1794	
				17,144		

LAND OFFICE, WEST OF PEARL RIVER, *October 1, 1808.*

THO. H. WILLIAMS, *Register.*

d.

A Report of claims east of *Pearl river*, founded on British or Spanish warrants, or orders of survey, not confirmed by former laws regulating the grants of land in the Mississippi territory, which have been regularly filed with the Register of the Land Office for said district.

Notice. Number presented.	Number.	By whom claimed.	Names of the original grantees or claimants.	Quantity claim'd in acres or arpents.	Situation.	Whence derived.	Date of patent, warrant, or order of survey.	Commissioners' descriptions.
1804. February 2	1	Alex. McCullagh	Alex. McCullagh	200	Tombigbee river	British patent	April 6, 1778	Rejected.
" 8	2	Otto V. T. Barbaree	Robert Farmer	1,000	Do.	Do.	Aug. 6, 1778	Do.
" 8	3	Do.	Do.	800	Do.	Do.	do	Do.
" 23	7	William Vardeman	John Lott, Jr.	300	Do.	Do.	Feb. 16, 1778	Do.
" 25	24	Heirs of John McIntosh	John McIntosh	500	Do.	Do.	Sept. 12, 1775	Do.
March 30	53	Cornelius McCurtin	Cornelius McCurtin	480	Do.	Span. warrant of survey	Jan'y 6, 1794	Do.
" 19	74	Samuel Mims	John Turnbull	1,600	Do.	Do.	July 31, 1787	Do.
" 20	80	James Frasier	James Frasier	1,600	Do.	Do.	do	Do.
" 20	84	Young Gains	Young Gains	780	Do.	Do.	Oct. 22, 1787	Do.
" 21	94	Anthony Epaho	John Turnbull	500	Do.	Do.	July 31, 1787	Do.
" 19	102	Francisco Foutinella	Francisco Foutinella	800	Do.	Do.	June 16, 1795	Do.
" 23	103	Heirs of Peter Frouillet	Peter Frouillet	800	Do.	Do.	Feb. 9, 1788	Do.
" 24	107	John Baker	John Baker	1,600	Do.	Spanish permit	Jan. 9, 1787	Do.
" 24	114	Elihu Hall Bay	William Fradgley	173	Do.	British patent	Mar. 13, 1776	Do.
" 24	115	Do.	Do.	27	Do.	Do.	do	Do.
" 12	116	Do.	John Sutherland	500	Do.	Do.	Oct. 22, 1779	Do.
" 12	117	Heirs of Aug. Rochan	Augustin Rochan	225	Do.	Do.	Dec. 4, 1779	Do.
" 26	118	Do.	Do.	550	Do.	Do.	June 16, 1777	Do.
" 26	119	Francis Coleman	Charles Walker	500	Do.	Do.	Jan. 27, 1777	Do.
" 16	120	Do.	Abraham Little	100	Do.	Do.	Feb. 16, 1778	Do.
" 14	121	James Hoggatt	William Wall	250	Do.	Do.	Mar. 20, 1778	Do.
" 26	122	Joshua Howard	Arthur Moore	334	Do.	Do.		Do.
" 30	123	Robert Abrahams	Robert Abrahams	500	Do.	Do.		Do.
" 31	181	Seth Dean	Charles Walker	2,000	Mobile river	British warrant of survey	Dec. 15, 1778	Do.
" 31	182	Do.	Francis Juzan	1,000	Waters Tombigbee river	British patent	April 3, 1770	Do.
" 30	183	Do.	John Dawson	150	Do.	British patent	- -	Do.
	194	Benjamin King	William Jackson	350	Tombigbee river		- -	Do.

d—Continued.

CLAIMS EAST OF TOMBIGBEE RIVER.

Notice. Number presented.	Claim. No.	By whom claimed.	Names of original grantees or claimants.	Quantity claim'd in acres or arpents.	Situation.	Title. Whence derived.	Date of patent, warrant, or order of survey.	Commissioners' description.
1804, Mar. 19	4	Otto V. T. Barbaree	Peter Deforge	520	Tensaw river	Lease and release	Nov. 1, 1768	Rejected.
"	5	Ditto	Francis Darau	542	Ditto	Mesne conveyance	June 11, 1764	Ditto.
"	7	Samuel Mims	Samuel Mims	982	Alabama river	Spanish warrant of survey	Feb. 27, 1787	Withdrawn by the claimant.
"	8	Heirs of Wm. Powell	William Powell	800	Tombigbee river	Ditto	June 10, 1795	Rejected. It was not received by the Board, being on Indian land.
"	9	Gerald Byrne	Peter Biverest	—	Tensaw river	Bill of sale	June 12, 1792	Not received by the Board, being within Spanish boundary.
" 20	13	John Morris	John Morris	400	Tombigbee river	Spanish warrant of survey	Oct. 22, 1787	Not received by the Board, being on Indian land.
" 21	14	Hardy Perry	Hardy Perry	800	Ditto	Ditto	Feb. 9, 1778	Ditto. ditto.
" 21	15	Anthony Aspaho	John Turnbull	800	Ditto	Ditto	Jan. 14, 1790	Rejected.
" 20	18	Narciso Broutin	Narciso Broutin	400	Ditto	Ditto	Sept. 14, 1787	Withdrawn.
" 19	23	John Johnson	John Johnson	800	Ditto	Ditto	June 10, 1795	Not received by the Board, being on Indian land.
" 23	97	Pitiagad Jurzan	Peter Jurzan	558	Mobile river	Ditto	—	Withdrawn.
" 31	35	Thomas Malone	Thomas Malone	—	Tombigbee river	Ditto	1797	Not received by the Board, being on Indian land.
"	56	Young Gains	Young Gains	800	Ditto	Ditto	June 10, 1795	Ditto, ditto.
"	60	John Baker	John Baker	—	Ditto	British patent	Aug. 6, 1778	Ditto, ditto.
"	67	Samuel Mims	William Clark	350	Alabama river	Ditto	Ap'l 16, 1779	Rejected.
"	68	Heirs of Peter Deforge	Peter Deforge	108	Waters of Tensaw r.	Ditto	Oct. 13, 1779	Ditto.
"	69	Ditto	Ditto	250	Tensaw river	Ditto		Not received by the Board, being within the Spanish boundary.
April 4	70	Theodore Gillard	Allen Grant	100	Briar creek	Ditto	Oct. 4, 1779	Rejected.
"	71	George Burdon	George Burdon	260	Escambia river	Ditto	Jan. 29, 1780	Not received by the Board, being within the Spanish boundary.
"	72	Theodore Gillard	Joseph Lamb	200	Ditto	Ditto	Mar. 2, 1779	Ditto, ditto.
"	73	George Burdon	George Burdon	800	Briar creek	Ditto	Aug. 17, 1779	Rejected.
"	74	Ditto	Ditto	200	Ditto	Ditto	Ditto	Ditto.
"	75	Theodore Gillard	Francis Lewis	300	Escambia river	Ditto	June 16, 1777	Not received by the Board, being within the Spanish boundary.
"	76	Ditto	Charles Ward	500	Ditto	Ditto	Mar. 2, 1779	Ditto, ditto.
"	77	Ditto	Ditto	500	Ditto	Ditto	March, 1779	Ditto, ditto.
June 11	83	Joseph Stiggins	Joseph Stiggins	800	Tensaw lake	Spanish warrant of survey	Feb. 9, 1788	Rejected.
"	89	Abijah Hunt	Augustin Rochan	1000	Mobile river	Deed of conveyance	Dec. 16, 1801	Ditto.
April 30	90	Heir of Al. McCullagh	Thomas Underwood	500	Alabama river	Ditto	Jan. 1, 1779	Ditto.

[The following additional papers are furnished by the General Land Office.]

Registers of the Land Office east of Pearl river—containing

A. Register of certificates granted on British and Spanish patents.
B. Register of certificates on which patents may issue, without any payment of purchase money.
C. Register of certificates on which patents may issue without any payment of purchase money, but not until a judicial decision shall have been obtained against the conflicting British claims.
D. Register of pre-emption certificates.
E. Register of pre-emption certificates on which patents may not issue until a judicial decision shall have been obtained against the conflicting British claims.
F. Register of British patents on which no certificates have issued.
N. Register of claims, presented December, 1805.

A.

Certificates grounded on British and Spanish patents.

Commissioners' certificates.			Recorded.		Claim.					Title.
When entered.	No.	Date.	Vol.	Page	To whom granted.	Name of the original grantee.	Quantity allowed. Acres.	Situation.	Whence derived.	Date of patent.
1805, Aug. 14	4	1805, Aug. 7	1	66	The lawful heirs of Tho. Bassett, dec'd, on application of Thos. Bassett, administrator of Nath. Bassett	Thomas Bassett, deceased -	750	West margin of Tombigbee -	British	Destroyed in the fire at New Orleans, in 1794.
"	3	"	1	68	Heirs of Thomas Bassett, dec'd	Thomas Bassett, deceased -	1050	West margin of Tombigbee -	British	Destroyed as above.
" Sept. 3	5	"	1	126	Heirs of Maria Josepia Narbone, deceased.	- - - -	80	Both sides of the west channel of Mobile -	French	} Sale, and uninterrupted possession since.
"	2	"	1	128	Heirs of Augustine Rochon, dec.	Augustine Rochon, deceased -	550	West bank of Tombigbee -	British	1777, June 16.
"	1	"	1	129	Heirs of Augustine Rochon, dec.	Augustine Rochon, deceased -	225	West bank of Tombigbee -	British	1779, December 4.
" 14	6	" 28	1	157	Richard, Caleb, and Joseph Carpenter, or their heirs or devisees	Richard, Caleb, & Joseph Carpenter - -	1000	East margin of the Alabama -	British	1769, July 22.

73

B.

Certificates on which Patents may issue without any payment of purchase money.

When entered.	No.	Date.	Recorded Vol.	Recorded Page	To whom granted.	Name of the original grantee or claimant.	Quantity allowed.	Situation.	Whence derived.	Date of order of survey or settlement.
1805, Aug. 8	35	1805, Aug.	1	2	Benjamin Harrison	Jacob Miller	640	West side of Tombigbee	Occupancy	1797.
" Aug. "	29	" "	1	4	Wiley Barker	Daniel Barker	640*	Do.	Do.	1797.
"	11	" "	1	6	James Denley	Daniel Ward	1,000	West margin of Tombigbee	Spanish	1787, October 22.
"	14	" "	1	9	James Denley	Solomon Johnson	280	West side of Tombigbee	Do.	1795, June 10.
"	38	" "	1	10	Ephraim Barker	Ephraim Barker	640	West margin of Tombigbee	Occupancy	1797.
"	13	" "	1	11	James Denley	James Denley	400	Do.	Spanish	1787, October 23.
"	54	Aug. 1	1	13	Adam Hollinger	Adam Hollinger	1,000	East margin of Tombigbee	Spanish	1795, January 30.
"	43	Aug. 7	1	16	Richard Hawkins	Richard Hawkins	640	West side of Mobile river	Occupancy	1797.
"	58	Aug. 1	1	17	Joseph Bates	Joseph Bates	1,000†	East margin of Tombigbee	Spanish	1797.
"	53	" "	1	23	Natt Christmas	Michael Hartly	640	Fork of Tombigbee and Alabama	Occupancy	1797.
"	44	Aug. 7	1	25	Young Gaines	Dominique Olive	800	West margin of Tombigbee	Spanish	1795, August 18.
Aug. 9	6	" "	1	26	Heirs of James McGrew	James McGrew	400	do.	Spanish	1788, March 15.
Aug. 10	42	Aug. 1	1	29	Heirs of William Burke	Thomas Jones	640†	do.	Do.	1788, February 9.
"	58	" "	1	31	John Weekley	James Farr	639	East margin of Tensaw lake	Occupancy	1797.
"	55	" "	1	32	Benjamin Hooven	Benjamin Hooven	566‖	East margin of Alabama	Do.	1797.
"	56	" "	1	34	George Weekley	George Weekley	640	East margin of Stedham's lake	Do.	1797.
"	57	" "	1	35	George Weekley	Michael Skipper	§	West margin of Alabama	Spanish	1788, February 9.
Aug. 12	63	" "	1	43	Joseph Stiggins	John Johnson	800	East margin of Tensaw lake	Do.	1789, February 9.
"	60	" "	1	44	Joseph Thompson	Joseph Thompson	640	East margin of Hollow creek	Occupancy	1797.
"	20	" "	1	46	Moses Stedham	Moses Stedham	698	Margin of Stedham's lake	Do.	1797.
"	59	" "	1	47	Samuel Mims	Samuel Mims	640	South margin of the Cut-off	Do.	1797.
"	61	" "	1	49	Joseph Thompson	Adam Hollinger	730	West margin of the Alabama	Spanish	1787, October 22.
"	67	" "	1	51	Simeon Wilks	James Proctor	640	East side of Mobile river	Occupancy	1797.
"	66	" "	1	52	Reuben Dyer	Reuben Dyer	640	Margin of the Tensaw river	Do.	1797.
"	65	" "	1	53	Samuel Frend	Samuel Frend	640	East side of Mobile river	Do.	1797.
"	64	" "	1	55	John Randon	John Randon	301	West margin of Alabama	Do.	1797.
"	68	" "	1	58	Joseph Stiggins	Joseph Stiggins	635	Margin of Tensaw lake	Do.	1797.
Aug. 14	4	Aug. 7	1	60	Nicholas Perkins	Thomas Wheat	306	West margin of Tombigbee	Spanish	1787, October 22.
"	25	" "	1	61	Howel Dupree	William Hillis	613	West margin of Mobile river	Occupancy	1797.
"	3	" "	1	63	Nicholas Perkins	Daniel Johnson	200	West margin of Tombigbee	Spanish	1787, October 22.
"	39	" "	1	64	Heirs of Godfrey Helverson	Godfrey Helverson	640	West bank of Mobile river	Occupancy	1797.
"	16	" "	1	65	Thomas Bates	Thomas Bates	698	West margin of Tombigbee	Do.	1797.
"	5	" "	1	69	Heirs of O. Sullivan, dec'd, on application of J. Hinson, adm'r of O. Sullivan, dec'd	Owen Sullivan, deceased		Do.	Spanish	1795, June 10.
Aug. 15	18	" "	1	73	Heirs of James Copelen, deceased	James Copelen, deceased	400	West margin of Three River lake	Occupancy	1797.
Aug. 16	40	" "	1	74	George Brewer, Jr.	George Brewer, Jr.	640	West margin of Tombigbee river	Do.	1797.
"	19	" "	1	75	James Griffin	James Griffin	639	West side of Tombigbee	Do.	1797.
"	47	" "	1	77	George Brewer, Jr.	Valentine Dubroca	640	West margin of Tombigbee	Spanish	1787, October 22.
"	2	" "	1	78	Heirs of William Powell, deceased	William Powell, deceased	800	do.	Do.	1795, June 10.

No.	Claimant	In right of whom claimed	Situation	Quantity (acres)	Nature of claim	Date
80	George Brewer, jr.	James Watkins	West side of Tombigbee	630	Occupancy	1797.
82	Thomas Carson	John Jacob Abner	West margin of Tombigbee	640	Do	1797.
85	John Mills	John Mills	West margin of Alabama	¶	Do	1797.
86	Abraham Walker	Abraham Walker	East margin of Hollow creek	630	Do	1797.
88	Francis Killingworth	William Mills	East margin of Pine log creek	640	Do	1797.
89	Lemuel Henry	John Linder, sen.	Tensaw lake and Alabama	491	Spanish	1788, June 3.
91	Heirs of John Linder, jr.	John Linder, jr.	Do do	800**	Do	1788, June 3.
94	Simon Andry	Simon Andry	East bank of west channel Mobile	48	Do	1793, Feb'y 2.
96	Joseph Chastang	Joseph Chastang	West bank of the Mobile river	640	Occupancy	1797.
97	Doctor John Chastang	Doctor John Chastang	West margin of Tombigbee	480	Spanish	1795, Jan'y 30.
98	Doctor John Chastang	John Talley	do	480	Do	1787, Nov'r 27.
99	John Chastang	John Chastang	West side of west channel Mobile	1,938	Do	1795, Jan'y 18.
102	Simon Andry	Simon Andry	West margin of Mobile river	480	Do	1787, May 14.
103	William McDaniel	George Philips	Major's creek, east side of Mobile	632	Occupancy	1797.
104	Isaac Ryan	Isaac Ryan	Basset's creek	640	Do	1797.
105	Josiah Fletcher	Josiah Fletcher	West margin of Alabama	††	Do	1797.
109	John Bapt. Trennier	John Bapt. Trennier	West margin of Mobile river	327	Spanish	1787, Sept. 1.
111	John Bapt. Trennier	John Bapt. Trennier	East bank of west channel Mobile	1,000	Do	1790, Oct. 14.
112	Thomas Malone	John Arnot	West margin of Tombigbee	480	Do	1787, July 2.
114	Heirs of Dominique De Olive	Dominique De Olive	East margin of Mobile river	1,200	Do	1794, Dec. 6.
120	Richard Coleman	Richard Coleman	East margin of Tensaw lake	634	Occupancy	1797.
123	Joseph Campbell	Augustine Rochon	East margin of Mobile	400	Spanish	1794, March 9.
124	Joseph Campbell	Louisa Rochon	do	400	Do	1794, March 9.
134	Frances Steel	Frances Steel	Tensaw lake	640	Occupancy	1797.
137	Narciso Broutin	Narciso Broutin	East margin of Mobile river	800	Spanish	1794, Jan. 10.
138	The heirs of Michael Milton	Michael Milton	South margin of Tensaw lake	611	Occupancy	1797.
139	William Buford	Conrad Selhoof	East margin of Tensaw river	800	Spanish	1788, Feb. 9.
142	William and John Pierce	Jeremiah Philips	West margin of Alabama	640	Occupancy	1797.
143	John Brewer	Charles Arbon Demoy	West margin of Tombigbee	800	Spanish	1787, Oct. 22.
144	John Brewer	John Brewer	West side of Tombigbee	640	Occupancy	1797.
145	Daniel Johnson	William Burke	Margin of Three River lake	320	Occupancy	1797.
147	William Webber	William Webber	East side of the Mobile	640	Do	1797.
148	Francis Boykin	Adam Hollinger	West margin of Tombigbee	800	Spanish	1795, June 10.
150	Heirs of Matthew Bilbo, deceased	Matthew Bilbo, deceased	Island in the Tombigbee	401	Occupancy	1797.
154	Hardy Wooton	William Hunt	West side of Tombigbee	615	Do	1797.
156	Richard Lee	Jordan Morgan	do	640	Do	1797.
158	Richard Barrow	Richard Barrow	West bank of Mobile river	640	Do	1797.
160	James Mills	John Linder, sen.	West side of the Mobile	640	Spanish	1788, June 3.
163	Nathan Blackwell	Gabriel Burrows	West margin of Tombigbee	299	Occupancy	1797.
171	Ann Lawrence	Ann Lawrence	do	375	Do	1797.
175	John F. McGrew and Clarke McGrew	Julian De Castro	do	640	Spanish	1795, June 10.
179	James Cockaram	Samuel Lyons	Waters of Rice creek	445	Occupancy	1797.
180	James Callier	Joseph Campbell	East margin of Mobile river	400	Do	1797.
181	James Callier	Jesse Bryant & H'ry Snelgrove	West margin of Tombigbee	640	Do	1797.
207	Anna Munger	Anna Munger	do	573	Do	1797.
208	Hiram Munger	Hiram Munger	West side of Tombigbee	504	Do	1797.
210	Sampson Munger	Sampson Munger	do	634	Do	1797.

* If the lines include too much.
† If included within the lines.
‡ If included in the lines.
|| If included by the lines.
§ The quantity included in the lines, not exceeding six hund'ed and forty acres.
¶ Whatever may be included in the lines, not exceeding six hundred and forty acres.
** If included in the lines.
†† Whatever the lines may include, not exceeding six hundred and forty acres.

C.

Certificates on which Patents may issue without any payment of purchase money, but not until a judicial decision shall have been obtained against the conflicting British claims.

Commissioners' certificate.					Claim.			Title.		Adverse British claims.		
When entered.	Number	Date.	Recorded. Vol.	Page.	Name of original grantee or cla't.	Quantity allowed. Acres.	Situation.	Whence derived.	Date of order of survey or settlement.	Name of claimant.	Name of original grantee or claimant.	Register P'r. Page
1805, August 8	6	1805, August 7	1	14	Wilford Hoggatt	800	West margin of Tombigbee	Spanish	1788, Feb. 9	James Hoggatt	William Wall	6
" 10	8	" "	1	28	John Johnson	400	Do	Do	1795, June 10	E. Hall Bay	Wm. Fradgely	6
" 28	4	" "	1	108	John Baker	400	Do	Do	1787, July 2	{E. Hall Bay {Franc. Coleman	{John Southerland {Charles Walker	6
Sept. 14	5	" "	1	146	Daniel Johnson	800	Do	Do	1795, June 10	Alexander McCullagh	Alr. McCullagh	6
" 16	1	" "	1	159	Anthony Hoggatt	732	Do	Do	1788, Feb. 9	William Vardeman	John Lott, jr.	6
" 26	3	" "	1	170	Moses Moore	800	Do	Do	1787, Oct. 22	{Heirs of J. McIntosh {Elihu Hall Bay	{John McIntosh {Wm. Fradgely	6
" 28	2	" 24	1	176	Clark McGrew	640	On Taula creek	Occupancy	-	Otto V. T. Barbarie	Robert Farmer	6
Oct. 7	9	" 7	1	189	Cornelius Rain	400	West margin of Tombigbee	Spanish	1795, June 10	Elihu Hall Bay	Wm. Fradgely	6
" 8	4	" "	1	194	Henry Nail	329	Do	Occupancy	-	William Vardeman	John Lott, jr.	6
" Nov. 14	7	" 24	1	218	J. McGrew, sen.	640	Do	Do	-	{Franc. Coleman {Franc. Coleman	{Abraham Little {Charles Walker	6

D.

Pre-emption Certificates.

Commissioners' certificate.					Claim.				
When entered.	No.	Date.	Recorded. Vol.	Page.	To whom granted.	Name of original settler.	Quantity allowed. Acres.	Situation.	Page.
1805. August 8	66	1805. August	7	1	Solomon Wheat	Solomon Wheat	100	West side of Tombigbee	1
" " 8	8	"	"	7	Edward Creighton	Benjamin King	100	West margin of Tombigbee	1
" "	23	"	"	19	Natt Christmas	Natt Christmas	270	Do do	2
" "	14	"	"	20	Adam Hollinger	Adam Hollinger	640	Do do	3
" 10	65	"	1	21	Jordan Morgan	Jordan Morgan	640	Do do	3
" "	48	"	7	37	Cornelius Dunn	Cornelius Dunn	252	South margin of Hollow creek	4
" "	18	"	"	38	James Morgan	John Burney	320	West side of Tombigbee	4
" "	54	"	1	40	John Dease	John Dease	139	East side of Bilbo's creek	5
" 12	29	"	1	41	William Weekley	William Weekley	133	East side of Mobile river	5
" "	70	"	7	57	Benjamin Stedham	Benjamin Stedham	253	West margin of Alabama	6
" 14	55	"	7	71	Heirs of Emanuel Chaney, deceased	Levin Hainsworth	388	West side of Tombigbee river	6
" 17	39	"	17	93	William Rogers	William Rogers	24	West margin of Tombigbee	7
" 21	57	"	7	101	Simon Andry	Simon Andry	320	West bank of Mobile	7
" 24	13	"	24	107	Figures Lewis	Figures Lewis	197	West margin of Three River lake	8
" 29	73	"	22	115	Ransom Harwell	Ransom Harwell	320	West side of Tombigbee	8
" "	38	"	"	117	Thomas Malone	Thomas Malone	320	West margin of Tombigbee	9
September 2	71	"	7	121	John and Tandy Walker	John and Tandy Walker	160	Laura's creek	9
" 3	41	"	24	130	Wilson Carman	Wilson Carman	160	West bank of the Mobile	10
" "	63	"	"	133	Richard Brashear	Patrick Brewer	160	West side of Tombigbee	10
" "	72	"	1	134	William Murrel	William Murrel	160	Do do	11
" 4	24	"	7	135	Simpson Whaley	Simpson Whaley	100	West margin of Barrow's lake	11
" 9	74	"	24	139	Elisha Simmons	Elisha Simmons	160	West margin of Tombigbee	12
" 14	52	"	7	149	George Farrar	George Farrar	320	West side of Tombigbee	12
" "	44	"	"	151	Thomas Sullivan	Thomas Sullivan	240	Do do	13
" "	43	"	"	152	Thomas Sullivan, jr.	Thomas Sullivan, jr.	190	West margin of Tombigbee	13
" "	13	"	24	155	Wyche Watley	Wyche Watley	156	West side of Tombigbee	13
" 18	46	"	7	161	William Hunt	William Hunt	160	Do do	14
" "	59	"	"	161	John Gordon	John Gordon	113	Do do	14
" 23	2	"	"	163	William McGrew	William McGrew	638	Waters of Tolla creek	15
" "	10	"	"	164	Adam Scott	Adam Scott	100	Margin of Barrow's lake	15
" 24	47	"	"	165	William H. Hargrave	Stephen Williams	320	West side of Tombigbee	16
" 25	69	"	17	166	Edwin Lewis	Edwin Lewis	160	West margin of Tombigbee	16
" "	20	"	29	167	Edwin Lewis	William Green	160	Tolla and Fulsom's creek	17
" "	19	"	"	168	Edwin Lewis	Cole and McClendon	160	South margin of Tolla	17
" "	36	"	7	169	Robert Sorrel, sen.	Robert Sorrell, sen.	320	On Little Bassett's creek	18
" 26	51	"	"	172	John Wamack	John Wamack	240	West side of Tombigbee	18
" "	31	"	"	173	Isaac Stanley	Isaac Stanley	100	Do do	19

D—Continued.

Commissioners' certificates.						Claim.			
When entered.	No.	Date.	Recorded. Vol.	Recorded. Page	To whom granted.	Name of original settler.	Quantity allowed. (Acres.)	Situation.	Page.
1805. September 27	30	1805. August 7	1	174	Patrick Donelly	Patrick Donelly	390	Waters of Little Bassett's creek	19
" 28	1	" 22	1	177	John Flood McGrew	John Flood McGrew	320	West side of Tombigbee	20
" 30	63	" 7	1	180	James Callier	Joseph Anderson	640	West bank of Tombigbee	20
"	64	"	1	182		Isabella Trouillett	640	West bank of the Mobile	21
"	21	"	1	183	Micajah Wall	Micajah Wall	320	West side of Tombigbee	21
October 1	33	"	1	184	Joseph Wilson	Joseph Dunbar	640	West margin of Tombighee	22
" 2	16	" 22	1	185	William Williams	William Williams	101	Do do	22
" 5	58	" 7	1	186	Sanford McClendon	Sanford McClendon	100	West side of Tombigbee	23
" 7	61	" 24	1	187	William Gilliam	John Clark -	102	Do do	23
"	32	" 7	1	188	Zachariah Landrum	Zachariah Landrum	114	Do do	23
" 24	7	"	1	191	Thomas Goodwin	Hiram Munger	120	Do do	24
" 7	40	"	1	193	John Kannady	John Kannady	640	West margin of Tombighee	24
" 8	6	" 22	1	196	George Robins	Zadoc Brashear	220	Do do	25
"	15	" 17	1	199	James Huckaby	James Huckaby	467	South margin of Tolla creek	25
" 11	5	" 22	1	200	Francis Stringer	Francis Stringer	160	West side of Tombigbee	26
" 14	34	" 22	1	201	Matthew Shaw	Matthew Shaw	333	West margin of Tombighee	26
"	3	" 7	1	203	Sterling Dupree	Emanuel Cheney	320	Do do	27
" 18	12	" 24	1	204	Edward Gatland	Edward Gatland	320	West margin of the Mobile	27
" 26	60	" 7	1	206	Thomas Goodwin	David Kannady	286	Margin of Ryan's lake	28
" 29	9	"	1	211	Sanders Rea -	Sanders Rea -	160	West side of Tombigbee	29
November 4	49	"	1	212	William Morgan	William Morgan	320	Do do	29
"	37	"	1	214	Priscilla Miles	Priscilla Miles	160	Do do	30
" 6	68	" 22	1	215	Hezekiah Carter	Hezekiah Carter	60	Do do	30
"	22	" 7	1	216	Benjamin Few -	Benjamin Few -	640	West margin of Tombighee	31
" 19	45	" 22	1	220	John Dunn -	John Dunn -	320	Do do	31

E.

Pre-emption Certificates on which Patents may not issue until a judicial decision shall have been obtained against the conflicting British claims.

| Commissioners' certificate. | | | | | Claim. | | | | | | |
When entered.	No.	Date.	Recorded. Vol.	Page	To whom granted.	Name of the original settler.	Quantity allowed.	Situation.	Name of claimant.	Name of original grantee or claimant.	Register. Page
1805. August 16	1	1805. August 16	1	83	Peter Malone -	John Woods -	Acres. 320	West side of Tombigbee	Elihu Hall Bay	John Southerland -	6
August 29	3	August 17	1	118	Edward Lloyd Wailes -	John Baker -	480	Do. do.	Elihu Hall Bay	John Southerland -	6
September 26	7	August 7	1	173	Charles Casseter -	Charles Casseter -	100	Do. do.	Otto V. T. Barbarie -	Robert Farmer -	6
October 8	2	August 22	1	197	Joseph Westmoreland -	Lewis Crane -	197	West margin of Tombigbee	Otto V. T. Barbarie	Robert Farmer -	6

F.

British Patents on which no certificates have been issued by the Commissioners.

By whom claimed.	British claim — Name of original grantee.	Quantity. (Acres)	Situation.	Date of patent.	Name of claimant.	Adverse claim — Name of original grantee or claimant.	Quantity claimed by individuals.	Quantity vacant.	Certificate registered — No.	Book.	Page.
Alexander McCullagh	Alexander McCullagh	900	Tombigbee	April 6, 1778	Daniel Johnson	Daniel Johnson			5	C	3
Otto V. T. Barbarie	Robert Farmer	1,000	Same	Aug. 6, 1778	Charles Casseter	Charles Casseter			7	E	5
Same	Same	800	Same		Jos. Westmoreland; Clarke M'Grew	Lewis Crane; Clarke M'Grew			2; 2	E; C	5; 3
William Vardeman	John Lott, Jr.	300	Same	Feb. 16, 1778	James Callier; N. Kenner Hutson	Anthony Hoggatt; Henry Nail			1; 4	C; C	3; 3
Heirs of John McIntosh	John McIntosh	500	Same	Sept. 12, 1775	Ann Lawrence	Moses Moore			3	C	3
Elihu Hall Bay	William Fradgely	173	Same	Mar. 13, 1776	John Johnson; Ann Lawrence	John Johnson; Moses Moore			8; 9	C	3
Same	Same	27	Same	Mar. 13, 1776	Cornelius Rain	Cornelius Rain					
Same	John Southerland	500	Same	Oct. 29, 1779	Peter Malone; Ed. Lloyd Wailes; John Baker	John Woods; John Baker; Same			1; 3; 4	E	5
Francis Coleman	Charles Walker	500	Same	Jan. 27, 1777	John M'Grew, Sen.	John M'Grew, Sen.			7	C	3
Same	Abraham Little	100	Same	Feb. 16, 1778	John Callier	Wilford Hoggatt			6	C	3
James Hoggatt	William Wall	250	Same.	Mar. 20, 1778							
Joshua Howard	Arthur Moore	394	Same.								
Seth Dean	Charles Walker	2,000	Same.	April 3, 1770							
Same	John Dawson	150	Same.	Aug. 6, 1778							
Samuel Mims	William Clarke	174	Alabama	Aug. 6, 1778							
Same	Same	350	Same	April 16, 1779							
Heirs of Peter De Forge	Peter De Forge	108	Waters of Tensaw river	Oct. 13, 1779							
Same	Allen Grant	250	Tensaw river	Oct. 4, 1779							
Theodore Gilliard	George Burdon	100	Brier creek	Jan. 29, 1780							
George Burdon	George Burdon	260	Escambia, below the southern boundary.								
Theodore Gilliard	Joseph Lamb	900	Same	Mar. 2, 1779							
George Burdon	George Burdon	800	Brier creek	Aug. 17, 1779							
Same	Same	200	Same	Aug. 17, 1779							
Theodore Gilliard	Francis Lewis	300	Escambia, below the southern boundary.	Jan. 16, 1777							
Same	Charles Ward	500	Same	Mar. 2, 1779							
Same	Same	50	Same	March, 1779							

N. B. This table is very imperfect; nor is it possible that it should be otherwise, until surveys have been made for the express purpose of ascertaining the extent of the interferences.

N.

Claims presented.

When presented	No.	By whom claimed	Name of original grantee or claimant	Quantity claim'd in acres or arpents	Situation	Whence derived	Date of patent, order of survey, or settlement	Recorded, vol. I. Page	What	Entered in register Letter	Page	Under what title allowed	Letter	Page
1804, Febr'y 2	1	Alex. McCullagh	Alex. McCullagh	200	Tombigbee	British patent	April 6, 1778	1	Rejected	F	6			
" 8	2	Otto V. T. Barbarie	Robert Farmer	1,000	Same	Same	Aug. 6, 1778	6	Rejected	F	6			
" 8	3	Same	Same	800	Same	Same	-	13	Rejected	F	11			
" 13	4	Isaac Ryan	Isaac Ryan	635	Bassett's creek	Occupancy	1797	19	Allowed	B	4			
" 14	5	James Morgan	John Burney	320⅝	House's Mill creek	Pre-emption	Mar. 3, 1803	20	Allowed	D				
" 22	6	Rich. S. Bryan, and Geo. Brewer, Sen.	Rich. S. Bryan, and G. Brewer, Sen.	319	Tolla creek	Same	Mar. 3, 1803	21	Allowed					
" 23	7	William Vardeman	John Lott, Jr.	300 9/10	Tombigbee	British patent	Feb. 16, 1778	23	Rejected	F	6			
" 27	8	William Morgan	William Morgan	319 4/10	Waters of Bassett's creek	Pre-emption	Mar. 3, 1803	38	Allowed	D	14			
" 28	9	James Griffin	James Griffin	618	Smith's creek	Occupancy	1797	39	Allowed	B	10			
" 29	11	Edward Gatlen	Edward Gatlen	306	Mobile river	Pre-emption	Mar. 3, 1803	41	Allowed	B	14			
" 29	13	Sterling Dupree	Enanuel Chaney	495	Tombigbee	Occupancy	1797	42	Allowed	I	12	Pre-emption	D	14
March 3	14	Nathan Blackwell	Nathaniel Blackwell	640	Same	Same	1797	44	Allowed	B				
" 3	15	Edward Young	Edward Young	488	Same	Same	1797	46	Rejected					
" 3	16	Daniel Young	Daniel Young	640	Fulsom's creek	Same	1797	48	Rejected					
" 3	17	William McGrew	William McGrew	638	Waters of Tolla creek	Same	1797	49	Rejected					
" 3	18	Levin Hainsworth	L. Hainsworth	396	Waters of Sintee-bogee	Pre-emption	Mar. 3, 1803	50	Rejected	D	13	Pre-emption	D	13
" 3	19	Elisha Simmons	Elisha Simmons	454	Tombigbee	Same	Mar. 3, 1803	52	Allowed	D	13			
" 3	20	Edwin Lewis	Debois McClindon	175	Fulsom's creek	Same	Mar. 3, 1803	53	Allowed	D	13			
" 3	21	Edwin Lewis	William Green	400	Tolla creek	Same	Mar. 3, 1803	55	Allowed	D	13			
" 3	22	Edwin Lewis	William Green	640	Same	Same	Mar. 3, 1803	57	Allowed					
" 3	23	Edwin Lewis	Henry Nail	640	Tombigbee	Occupancy	1797	63	Rejected					
Febr'y 25	24	Heirs of J. McIntosh	John McIntosh	500	Same	British patent	Sept. 12, 1775	64	Rejected	D	6	Pre-emption	D	6
March 3	25	William Rogers	William Rogers	388	Same	Pre-emption	Mar. 3, 1803	72	Rejected					
" 6	26	George Robbins	Zadoc Brashear	640	Mobile river	Occupancy	1797	73	Rejected	B	10			
" 7	27	Heirs of G. Helverston	Godfrey Helverston	640	Same	Same	1797	76	Allowed	B	12			
" 7	28	Richard Barrow	Richard Barrow	640	Same	Same	1797	78	Allowed	D	6	Pre-emption	D	6
" 9	29	John Dease	John Dease	50	Bilbo's creek	Pre-emption	Mar. 3, 1803	80	Allowed	B	10			
" 13	30	Solomon Johnson	Solomon Johnson	640	Waters of Johnson's creek	Occupancy	1797	81	Allowed	B	14			
" 13	31	James Callier	Jesse Bryant	573	Tombigbee	Same	1797	83	Allowed	B	12	Pre-emption	D	14
" 14	32	Matthew Shaw	Matthew Shaw	333	Same	Pre-emption	Mar. 3, 1803	86	Allowed	B	14			
" 15	33	Hiram Munger	Solomon Wheat	640	Sunflower creek	Occupancy	1797	87	Allowed	B	12			
" 15	34	Ephraim Barker	Ephraim Barker	640	Tombigbee	Same	1797	90	Allowed	B	2			
" 15	35	Sampson Munger	Sampson Munger	634	Waters of Tombigbee	Same	1797	91	Allowed	B	1			
" 15	36	Solomon Wheat	Hiram Munger	257	Same	Same	1797	93	Rejected					

N—Continued.

No.	By whom claimed.	Name of original grantee or claimant.	Quantity claim'd in acres or arpents.	Situation.	Whence derived.	Date of patent, order of survey, or settlement.	Recorded, vol. I.	What.	Entered in register. (Letter)	Entered in register. (Page)	Under what title allowed.	Entered in register. (Letter)	Entered in register. (Page)
37	G. Brewer, Jr. att'y for the heirs of W. Brewer, deceased	William Brewer	594	Tombigbee	Occupancy	1797	94	Rejected	B	10			
38	Thomas Carson	John J. Abner	649	Same	Same	1797	97	Allowed	B	10	Pre-emption	D	13
39	Micajah Wall	Micajah Wall	390	Waters of Smith's creek	Pre-emption	March 3, 1803	100	Allowed	D	13			
40	James Callier	Joseph Anderson	567	Tombigbee	Occupancy	1797	101	Rejected	B	12			
41	James Scott	Gabriel Burroughs	375	Waters of Tombigbee	Same	1797	106	Allowed	B	10			
42	Howell Dupree	William Hillis	613	Mobile river	Same	1797	108	Allowed	B	10			
43	O. Sullivant's heirs	Owen Sullivant	400	Tombigbee	Spanish warrant	June 10, 1795	111	Allowed	B	12			
44	Richard Lee	Jordan Morgan	640	Waters of Sunflower cr'k	Occupancy	1797	115	Allowed	D	14			
45	Francis Stringer	Francis Stringer	640	Tombigbee	Pre-emption	1797	117	Rejected	D	14	Pre-emption	D	14
46	William Williams	William Williams	101	Same	Occupancy	Mar. 3, 1803	119	Allowed	D	14	Pre-emption	E	5
47	Peter Malone	John Woods	278	Same	Occupancy	—	120	Allowed	A	1			
48	Heirs of T. Bassett	Thomas Bassett	1,050	Same	British patent	—	122	Allowed	A	1			
49	Same	Same	750	Same	Same	—	124	Allowed	B	11			
50	John Chestang	John Chestang	480	Same	Spanish warrant	Jan. 30, 1795	146	Allowed	B	11			
51	Same	John Tally	480	Same	Same	Nov. 27, 1787	149	Allowed	B	11			
52	Same	Cornelius McCurtin	2,080	Mobile river	Same	Dec. 23, 1784	158	Rejected	D	13			
53	Cornelius McCurtin	Wyche Whatley	480	Tombigbee	Same	Jan. 6, 1794	163	Rejected	B	9			
54	Wyche Whatley	Patrick Brewer	134	Sunflower creek	Pre-emption	Mar. 3, 1803	165	Allowed	B	12			
55	Richard Brashear	Daniel Barker	640	Tombigbee	Occupancy	1797	167	Rejected	B	12			
56	Wiley Barker	Charles Brewer	583	Muddy Branch	Same	1797	168	Allowed	B	12			
57	Heirs of C. Brewer	Adam Hollinger	800	Tombigbee	Spanish warrant	June 10, 1795	169	Allowed	B	12			
58	Francis Boykin	Julian de Castro	335	Same	Occupancy	—	173	Rejected	B	12	Pre-emption		
59	J. F. and Ct. M'Grew	Same	640	Same	Same	1797	178	Allowed	B	12	Pre-emption	D	4
60	Julian de Castro	Anna Munger	504	Same	Same	1797	179	Allowed	B	10			
61	Anna Munger	James Watkins	680	Mill creek	Same	1797	181	Allowed	B	10			
62	James Watkins	William Powell	400	Tombigbee	Spanish warrant	June 10, 1795	182	Rejected	B	10			
63	Heirs of Wm. Powell	James Powell	594	Same	Occupancy	1797	186	Allowed	B	10			
64	James Powell	Joseph House	640	House's Mill creek	Same	1797	187	Rejected	B	10			
65	Joseph House	James Copelin	640	Three River lake	Same	1797	189	Allowed	B	10			
66	Heirs of Jas. Copelin	Josiah Skinner	185	Tombigbee	Pre-emption	Mar. 3, 1803	191	Rejected					
67	Josiah Skinner	Figures Lewis	129	Three River lake	Same	Mar. 3, 1803	192	Allowed					
68	Figures Lewis	Anthony Hoggatt	732	Tombigbee	Spanish warrant	Feb. 9, 1788	194	Allowed					
69	James Callier	Daniel Johnson	800	Same	Same	June 10, 1795	199	Allowed					
70	Daniel Johnson	Constant M'Grew	604	Same	Occupancy	1797	201	Allowed	C	3			
71	Constant M'Grew	Alexander M'Grew	640	Waters of Smith's creek	Same	1797	204	Rejected	C	3			
72	John M'Grew	James M'Grew	400	Tombigbee	Spanish warrant	Feb. 9, 1788	206	Allowed	B	2			
73	Heirs of J. M'Grew	John Turnbull	1,600	Same	Same	July 31, 1787	210	Rejected					
74	Samuel Mims												

No.	By whom claimed	In whose favor	Quantity	Watercourse		Nature of claim	Date	No.	Cl.		Decision
75	Geo. Brewer, Jr.	Valentine de Broca	800	Same	Same	Oct. 22, 1787	214	B	10		Allowed
76	John Johnston	John Johnston	400	Same	Same	June 10, 1795	221	C	3		Allowed
77	John Cannada	John Cannada	533	Same	Pre-emption	Mar. 3, 1803	225	D	14		Allowed
78	Sanders Rea	Sanders Rea	158	Johnston's creek	Same	Mar. 3, 1803	226	D	14		Allowed
79	J. Baptiste Trennier	J. Baptiste Trennier	397	Mobile river	Spanish warrant	Sept. 1, 1787	228	B	11		Rejected
80	James Frazier	James Frazier	1,600	Tombigbee	Same	July 31, 1787	233	B	12		Allowed
81	Daniel Johnston	Daniel Spillards	640	Waters of Tombigbee	Occupancy	1797	237				Allowed
82	Daniel Johnston	William Burk	640	Tombigbee	Same	1797	239				Rejected
83	Heirs of Wm. Burk	Thomas Jones	640	Bilbo's creek	Same	1797	241				Allowed
84	Young Gains	Young Gains	780	Tombigbee	Spanish warrant	Oct. 22, 1787	242	B	2		Allowed
85	Same	Dominique de Olive	800	Waters of Laura's creek	Same	Mar. 15, 1788	246	B	2		Rejected
86	Zachariah Landrum	Zachariah Landrum	114	Tolla creek	Pre-emption	Mar. 3, 1803	252	D	14		Allowed
87	Ranson Harwell	Ranson Harwell	197	Tolla creek	Same	Mar. 3, 1803	253	D	4		Allowed
88	James Denley	James Denley	400	Tombigbee	Spanish warrant	Oct. 2, 1787	255	B	2		Allowed
89	Nathaniel Ross	Henry Slaughter	164	Basset's creek	Pre-emption	Mar. 3, 1803	258	D			Rejected
90	William Murrell	William Murrell	175	Tolla creek	Same	Mar. 3, 1803	260	D	10		Allowed
91	Edward Creighton	Benjamin King	32	Tombigbee	Same	Mar. 3, 1803	261	B			Allowed
92	Nicholas Perkins	Thomas Wheat	306	Same	Spanish warrant	Oct. 22, 1787	266				Allowed
93	Same	Daniel Johnston	200	Same	Same	-	272		10		Allowed
94	Anthony Espaho	John Turnbull	500	Same	Same	July 31, 1787	281		10		Rejected
95	John Callier	Wilford Hoggatt	781	Same	Same	Feb. 9, 1788	289	C	3		Allowed
96	Rawleigh Green	Rawleigh Green	201	Same	Pre emption	Mar. 3, 1803	295	D	14		Allowed
97	Thomas Goodwin	Daniel Kennada	286	Ryan's lake	Same	Mar. 3, 1803	296	D	13		Allowed
98	John Gordon	John Gordon	113	Laura's creek	Same	Mar. 3, 1803	298	B	2		Allowed
99	James Denley	Daniel Ward	1,000	Tombigbee	Spanish warrant	Oct. 22, 1787	300	C	3		Allowed
100	Cornelius Rain	Cornelius Rain	400	Same	Same	June 10, 1795	305	C	3		Allowed
101	Ann Lawrence	Moses Moore	800	Same	Same	Oct. 22, 1787	308				Allowed
102	Francis Fontinella	F. Fontinella	800	Same	Same	June 10, 1795	314				Rejected
103	Heirs of P. Trouillet	Peter Trouillet	800	Same	Same	Feb. 9, 1798	317		12		Rejected
104	John Brewer	Ch. Arban de Muy	800	Same	Same	Oct. 22, 1787	320	B	9		Allowed
105	James Denley	Solomon Johnston	280	Sunflower creek	Same	June 10, 1795	327	B	11		Allowed
106	Simon Andrey	Simon Andrey	479	Tombigbee	Same	May 10, 1787	331				Rejected
107	John Baker	John Baker	1,600	Same	Spanish permit	Jan. 9, 1787	335	C	3		Allowed
108	Same	Same	400	Same	Spanish warrant	July 2, 1787	338	C	3		Allowed
109	Edwin Lewis	Edwin Lewis	696	Same	Pre-emption	Mar. 3, 1803	342	D	13		Allowed
110	James Huccaby	Matthew Robinson	467	Tolla creek	Same	Mar. 3, 1803	344	D	14		Allowed
111	Joseph Westmorland	Lewis Crane	190	Same	Same	Mar. 3, 1803	345	E	5		Allowed
112	Adam Scott	Adam Scott	160	Barrow's lake	Same	Mar. 3, 1803	347	D	13		Allowed
113	James Bilbo	James Bilbo	479	Tombigbee	Same	Mar. 3, 1803	348				Rejected
114	Eliu Hall Bay	William Fradgley	173	Same	British patent	Mar. 13, 1776	350				Rejected
115	Same	Same	27	Same	Same	Mar. 13, 1776	357		1		Rejected
116	John Sutherland	John Sutherland	500	Same	Same	Oct. 22, 1779	374	A	1		Rejected
117	Heirs of A. Rochon	Augustine Rochon	925	Same	Same	Dec. 4, 1779	393	A			Allowed
118	Same	Same	550	Same	Same	June 16, 1777	400				Allowed
119	Francis Coleman	Charles Walker	500	Same	Same	Jan. 27, 1777	407				Rejected
120	Same	Abraham Little	100	Same	Same	Feb. 16, 1778	416				Rejected
121	James Hoggatt	William Wall	250	Same	Same	Mar. 20, 1778	424				Rejected
122	Joshua Howard	Arthur Moore	324	Same	Same	-	435				Rejected
123	Robert Abrahams	Robert Abrahams	500	Same	British warrant of survey	Dec. 15, 1778	441				Rejected
124	Isaac Standley	Isaac Standley	100	Waters of Laura's creek	Pre-emption	Mar. 3, 1803	444	D	13		Allowed
125	T. and J. Walker	T. and J. Walker	480	Same	Same	-	445	D	4		Allowed
126	William Hunt	Dennis M'Clendon	189	Same	Same	-	446	D	13		Allowed

N—Continued.

When presented	No.	By whom claimed	Name of original grantee or claimant	Quantity claim'd in acres or arpents	Situation	Whence derived	Date of patent, order of survey, or settlement	Recorded, Vol I. Page	What	Entered in register. Letter	Page	Under what title allowed	Entered in register. Letter	Page
1804. March 26	127	William Gilliam	John Clark	102	Sunflower creek	Pre-emption	Mar. 3, 1803	447	Allowed	D	14			
26	128	Jordan Morgan	Jordan Morgan	638	Tombigbee	Occupancy	1797	449	Rejected	—	—	Pre-emption	D	4
15	129	John Brewer	John Brewer	640	Johnston's creek	Same	1797	450	Allowed	B	12			
26	130	Thomas Goodwin	Hiram Munger	374	Ryan's lake	Same	1797	451	Rejected	—	12	Pre-emption	D	14
29	131	Heirs of M. Bilbo	Matthew Bilbo	401	Tombigbee	Same	1797	453	Allowed	B	12			
26	132	William Coleman	Simon Favre	498	Same	Same	—	454	Rejected	—	—			
26	133	Ann Lawrence	Ann Lawrence	640	Same	Same	1797	456	Allowed	B	12			
28	134	George Brewer, jr.	George Brewer, jr.	629	Same	Same	1797	458	Allowed	B	10			
27	135	Joseph Chestang	Joseph Chestang	640	Same	Same	1797	459	Allowed	B	11			
28	136	Noah K. Hutson	Henry Nail	297	Same	Same	1797	460	Allowed	C	3			
16	137	John Pickering	John Pickering	280	Waters of Tolla creek	Pre-emption	Mar. 3, 1803	461	Allowed	—	—	Pre-emption		14
26	138	Hezekiah Carter	Robert Jones	358	Ryan's lake	Occupancy	1797	462	Rejected	—	—			
26	139	Edmund Smith	Edmund Smith	432	Waters of Mobile	Pre-emption	Mar. 3, 1803	464	Allowed	D	13			
23	140	Robert Sorrel, sen.	Robert Sorrel, sen.	320	Waters of Bassett's creek	Same	—	466	Allowed	D	13			
26	141	P. Donnerly	P. Donnerly	448	Same	Same	—	467	Allowed	D	13			
26	142	Joseph Wilson	Joseph Dunbar	561	Tombigbee	Same	—	468	Allowed	D	14			
28	143	John Denley	John Denley	640	Same	Same	—	470	Allowed	D	4			
29	144	Heirs of E. Chaney	Levin Hainsworth	253	Waters of Tolla	Same	—	471	Allowed	D	14			
24	145	Sandford M'Clendon	Sandford M'Clendon	99	Same	Same	—	472	Allowed	D	4			
26	146	Thomas Malone	Thomas Malone	330	Tombigbee	Same	—	473	Allowed	D	13			
27	147	John Warmack	John Warmack	240	Waters of Tolla	Same	—	475	Allowed	D	13			
28	148	Wm. H. Hargrave	Stephen Williams	262	Sunflower creek	Same	—	476	Allowed	D	13			
28	149	Thos. Sullivant, jr.	Thos. Sullivant, jr.	190	Three River lake	Same	—	478	Allowed	D	13			
28	150	Thomas Sullivant	Thomas Sullivant	240	Waters of Johnston's creek	Same	—	479	Allowed	D	13			
28	151	George Dickey	George Dickey	640	Tombigbee	Same	—	480	Allowed	D	14			
28	152	John Dunn	John Dunn	391	Same	Same	—	481	Allowed	D	14			
28	153	Solomon Boykin	Elizabeth Reed	502	Bassett's creek	Same	—	482	Allowed	D	14			
29	154	Priscilla Miles	Priscilla Miles	456	Waters of House's Mill do.	Same	—	483	Allowed	E	5			
28	155	Charles Cassiter	Charles Cassiter	100	Waters of Tolla	Same	—	485	Allowed	E	5			
28	156	Wm. H. Hargrave	Wm. H. Hargrave	318	Sunflower creek	Same	—	486	Rejected	—	—			
30	157	P. Cartwright	P. Cartwright	159	Waters of Tolla	Same	—	487	Allowed	D	13			
30	158	George Farrar	George Farrar	160	Bilbo's creek	Same	—	488	Allowed	D	13			
15	159	Edward Creighton	Isham Beard	640	Waters of Tombigbee	Occupancy	1797	489	Rejected	—	—	Pre-emption	D	13
27	160	James Callier	Isabella Trouillet	640	Mobile river	Same	1797	490	Rejected	—	—			
29	161	Cornelius Rain	James Farr	344	Tombigbee	Same	1797	492	Rejected	—	—			
26	162	Joseph Bates, jr.	Joseph Bates, jr.	640	Same	Same	1797	493	Rejected	—	—			
19	163	Simon Andry	Simon Favre	10	Mobile river	Pre-emption	Mar. 3, 1803	495	Allowed	D	4	Pre-emption	D	13
29	164	J. M'Grew, sen.	J. M'Grew, sen.	637	Waters of Tombigbee	Occupancy	1797	497	Allowed	C	3			
30	165	John F. M'Grew	J. Flood M'Grew	630	Tolla creek	Same	1797	498	Rejected	—	—	Pre-emption	D	13

Day	No.	Claimed by	In favor of	Situation	Quantity	Nature of claim	Date of claim	No.	Decision	Class	No.
29	166	Clark M'Grew	Clark M'Grew	Tolla creek	640	Occupancy	1797	499	Allowed	C	3
28	167	John Hines	Fred. Smith	Tombigbee	640	Same	1797	500	Rejected	B	2
27	168	Benjamin Harrison	Jacob Miller	Ryan's lake	378	Same	1797	502	Allowed	D	13
30	169	Simpson Whaley	Simpson Whaley	Barrow's lake	100	Pre-emption	Mar. 3, 1803	506	Allowed	D	14
30	170	Benjamn Few	Turnbull and Joice	Tombigbee	500	Same	-	507	Allowed	B	2
31	171	Richard Hawkins	Richard Hawkins	Barrow's lake	640	Occupancy	1797	509	Allowed		
31	172	John Hawkins	John Hawkins	Same	151	Pre-emption	Mar. 3, 1803	510	Allowed	D	4
31	173	Wilson Carman	Wilson Carman	Mobile river	691	Same	-	511	Allowed	D	4
31	174	Adam Hollinger	A. Hollinger	Poll bayou	612	Same	-	512	Allowed	D	4
31	175	Nath. Christmas	Nath. Christmas	Tombigbee	85	Occupancy	1797	513	Allowed		
31	176	Seth Dean	John J. Abner	Poll bayou	640	Pre-emption	Mar. 3, 1803	514	Rejected		
31	177	Same	Jesse Thomas	Waters of Tombigbee	640	Same	-	515	Allowed		
31	178	Same	Seth Dean	Tombigbee	640	Same	-	516	Allowed		
31	180	Same	Jas. Low	Bilbo and Bates's creek	640	Same	-	517	Allowed		
31	181	Same	John Wallis	Tombigbee	639	Same	-	519	Allowed		
31	182	Same	Ch. Walker	Same	2,000	British patent	April 3, 1770	591	Rejected	B	10
30	183	Same	Francis Juzan	Mobile river	1,000	British patent	-	530	Rejected	B	12
31	184	Edmund Smith	John Dawson	Waters of Tombigbee	150	Occupancy	-	531	Withd'n		
31	185	Jacob Miller	Jacob Miller	Ryan's lake	640	Spanish warrant	1797	535	Withd'n		
30	186	Devisees of Mrs. Nar-bonne.	Maria J. Narbonne	Mobile river	3,200	Spanish warrant	July 2, 1787	547	Allowed	B	11
31	187	Thomas Bates	Thomas Bates	Same	628	Occupancy	1797	551	Allowed	E	5
26	188	Hardy Wootton	William Hunt	Sunflower creek	615	Spanish warrant	May 14, 1787	553	Allowed	B	11
23	189	Palagn J. Juzant,	Peter Juzant	Mobile river	1,134	Pre-emption	Mar. 3, 1803	v 2, p.1	With'n	B	11
26	190	William and J. Pierce	William and J. Pierce	Tombigbee	57	Same	Mar. 3, 1803	5	Not in time		
30	191	Edward Lloyd Wailes	John Baker	Waters of Tombigbee	480	Same	-	6	Allowed		
19	192	John B. Trenier	John B. Trenier	Mobile river	1,000	Spanish warrant	Oct. 14, 1793	15	Allowed		
19	193	Simon Andrey	Simon Andrey	Same	48	Same	Feb. 3, 1793	15	Rejected		
19	194	Benjamin King	William Jackson	Tombigbee	350	Same	-	15	Allowed		
26	186	Thomas Malone	John Arnot	Same	480	Same	July 2, 1787	{547 v1}			

CLAIMS PRESENTED EAST OF TOMBIGBEE.

Day	No.	Claimed by	In favor of	Situation	Quantity	Nature of claim	Date of claim	No.	Decision	Class	No.
February 4	1	James Carpenter, heir at law, &c.	Richard, Caleb, and Joseph Carpenter	Alabama river	1,000	British patent	July 22, 1769	1	Allowed	A	1
March 10	2	Nicholas Weeks	Dominique D'Olive	Mobile river	1,199 6/10	Spanish warrant	Dec. 26, 1794	6	Allowed	A	
19	3	Same	Same	Same	1,199	Same	Jan. 27, 1787	10	With'n by claimant		
19	4	Otto V. T. Barberie	Peter De Forge	Tensaw river	520	Lease & release	Nov. 1, 1768	13	Rejected		
19	5	Same	Francis Daran	Same	542	Mesne convey'e	Jan. 11, 1764	24	Rejected		
19	6	Joseph Thompson	Adam Hollinger	Alabama	730	Spanish warrant	Oct. 12, 1787	30	Allowed	B	
19	7	Samuel Mims	Samuel Mims	Same	982	Same	Feb. 21, 1787	34	With'n by claimant		
19	8	Heirs of W. Powell	William Powell	Tombigbee	800	Same	June 10, 1795	36	Not rec'd as being on Ind. land		
19	9	Geral Byrne	Peter Beverest	Tensaw river	-	Bill of sale	June 13, 1792	39	Do. as being within southern boundary	B	10

N—Continued.

Notice		**Claim**				**Title**			**Commissioners' decision**					
When presented.	No.	Name of original grantee or claimant.	By whom claimed.	Quantity claim'd in acres or arpents.	Situation.	Whence derived.	Date of patent, order of survey, or settlement.	Recorded, vol 1. Page.	What.	Entered in register. Letter	Page	When allowed under different titles. Under what title allowed.	Entered in register. Letter	Page
1804. March 19	10	John B. Trenier	John B. Trenier	1,000	Tombigbee	Spanish warrant	Oct. 14, 1793	Page vol. 2, p. 15	Allowed—see Reg'r, p. 23, No. 192					4
" 19	11	Simeon Andry	Simeon Andry	48	Same	Same	Feb. 2, 1793	vol. 2, p. 15	Allowed—see Reg'r, p. 23, No. 193.					
" 19	12	John Linder, jr.	Heirs of J. Linder, jr.	800	Alabama	Same	May 2, 1788	50	Allowed	B	11			
" 20	13	John Morris	John Morris	400	Tombigbee	Same	Oct. 22, 1787	53	Not rec'd, on Indian land	B	11			
" 20	14	Hardy Perry	Hardy Perry	800	Same	Same	Feb. 9, 1788	55	Same					
" 21	15	John Turnbull	Anthony Espaho	800	Same	Same	Jan. 14, 1790	58	Rejected					
" 21	15	Adam Hollinger	Adam Hollinger	1,000	Same	Same	Jan. 30, 1795	62	Allowed	B	9			
" 20	16	Narc. Broutin	Narc. Broutin	800	Alabama	Same	Jan. 10, 1794	66	Allowed	B	12			
" 20	18	Same	Same	400	Tombigbee	Same	Sep. 14, 1787	71	Withdrawn					
" 23	19	Thomas Bates, jr.	Thomas Bates, jr.	640	Same	Occupancy	1797	73	Rejected					
" 26	20	Richard Turvin	Richard Turvin	640	Same	Same	1797	74	Rejected					
" 26	21	Mich. Melton	Heirs of Mich. Melton	611	Tensaw lake	Same	1797	76	Allowed	B	12			
" 19	22	John Johnson	John Johnson	800	Tombigbee	Spanish warrant	June 10, 1795	83	Not received; Indian land					
" 26	23	James Mills	James Mills	299	Alabama	Same	June 3, 1788	85	Allowed	B	12			
" 26	24	Same	Lemuel Henry	491	Same	Same	June 3, 1788	85	Allowed	B	11			
" 19	25	Conrad Selhoof	William Buford	800	Same	Same	Feb. 9, 1788	91	Allowed	B	12			
" 23	26	Joseph Bates, sen.	Joseph Bates, sen.	1,000	Tombigbee	Same	Aug. 16, 1795	95	Allowed	B	9			
" 23	27	Peter Juzan	Petiaga L. Juzan	558	Mobile river	Same	-	98	Withdrawn					
" 23	28	Mich. Skipper	George Weekly	161	Alabama	Same	Feb. 9, 1788	99	Allowed	B	9			
" 23	29	John Trouillet	John Trouillet	639	Mobile river	Occupancy	1797	102	Rejected					
" 26	30	John Mills	John Mills	355	Alabama	Same	1797	106	Allowed	B	10		I	-
" 26	31	Benj. Stedham	Benj. Stedham	133	Same	Same	1797	106	Rejected					
" 26	32	Jeremiah Philips	Jeremiah Philips	322	Same	Same	1797	107	Withdrawn			Pre-emption	D	
" 26	33	Benj. Hovan	Benj. Hovan	566	Same	Same	1797	107	Allowed	B	9			
" 26	34	Moses Stedham	Moses Stedham	640	Pine-log creek	Same	1797	108	Allowed	B	12			
" 26	35	Thomas Malone	Thomas Malone	-	Tombigbee	Spanish warrant	-	109	Not received, as being on Indian land					
" 27	36	Abram Walker	Jesse Ross	630	Hollow creek	Occupancy	1797	110	Allowed	B	10			
" 27	37	John Randon	John Randon	301	Alabama	Same	1797	111	Allowed	B	11			
" 27	38	William Mills	Frs. Killingworth	640	Pine-log creek	Same	1797	112	Allowed	B	11			
" 27	39	George Philips	William M'Daniel	632	Major's creek	Same	1797	113	Allowed	B	11			
" 27	40	Corn. Dunn	Corn. Dunn	251	Hollow creek	Pre-emption	March 3, 1803	114	Allowed	D	4			

Date	No.	Claimant	Original claimant	Acres	Location	Nature of claim	Date	No.	Decision	Book	No.
" 27	41	Josiah Fletcher	J. Fletcher	601	Alabama	Occupancy	1797	115	Allowed	B	11
" 97	42	James Randon	J. Randon	630	Hollow creek	Same	1797	115	Rejected	B	10
" 98	43	Jos. Stiggins	Jos. Stiggins	635	Tensaw lake	Same	1797	116	Allowed	B	11
" 98	44	Jordon Proctor	Jordon Proctor	634	Same	Same	1797	116	Rejected	B	10
" 28	45	Richard Coleman	Richard Coleman	634	Same	Same	1797	117	Allowed	B	12
" 28	46	Reuben Dyer	Reuben Dyer	640	Tensaw river	Same	1797	117	Allowed	B	12
" 28	47	Jas. Cochran	Samuel Lyons	640	Tensaw lake	Same	1797	118	Allowed		
" 28	48	Simeon Wells	Jas. Proctor	636	Lawrence creek	Same	1797	119	Allowed		
" 31	49	Heirs of Val. DuBroca	Valentine DuBroca	640	Mobile river	Same	1797	120	Allowed	B	9
" 31	50	John Weekly	James Farr	636	Tensaw lake	Same	1797	120	Rejected		
" 31	51	William Collins	Charles Conway	638	Red Hill creek	Same	1797	121	Allowed	B	2
" 31	52	George Weekly	George Weekly	640	Stedham's lake	Same	1797	122	Rejected		
" 31	53	William Buford	Same	640	Major's creek	Same	1797	122	Rejected		
" 31	54	Francis Steele	Francis Steele	640	Tensaw lake	Same	1797	123	Allowed	B	11
" 31	55	William Webber	William Webber	640	Red Hill creek	Same	1797	124	Allowed	B	12
" 31	56	Young Gains	Young Gains	800	Tombigbee	Same	1797	124	Not received, as being on Indian land		
" 31	57	Samuel Frend	Samuel Frend	640	Pine-log creek	Occupancy	1797	125	Allowed	B	10
" 31	58	William Shields	William Shields	633	Alabama river	Same	1797	125	Rejected		
" 31	59	William H. Buford	Glode Rasby	640	Major's creek	Same	1797	126	Withdrawn by the claimant		
" 31	60	John Baker	John Baker	—	Tombigbee	Spanish warrant	June 10, 1795	126	Not received, as being on Indian land	D	4
" 31	61	John Trouillet	John Trouillet	640 9/16	Mobile	Occupancy	1797	127	Rejected		
" 31	62	William Weekly	William Weekly	139 6/16	Waters of Alabama	Pre-emption	March 3, 1803	127	Allowed		
" 31	63	Jos. Lawrence	Jos. Lawrence	800	Tombigbee	Occupancy	1797	128	Not received, as being on Indian land	B	11
April 14	64	James Callier	James Callier	320	Mobile river	Pre-emption	March 3, 1803	128	Withdrawn by the claimant		
March 31	65	Jos. Campbell	Aug. & Louisa Rochon	2,337	Same	2 Span. warrants	March 9, 1794	129	Allowed		
" 31	66	Samuel Mims	William Clark	174	Alabama	British patent	Aug. 6, 1778	130	Rejected		
" 31	67	Same	Same	350	Same	Same	1778	136	Rejected		
" 31	68	Heirs of P. De Forge	Peter De Forge	108	Wat's of Tensaw river	Same	1778	136	Rejected		
April 4	69	Same	Same	250	Tensaw creek	Same	Ap'l 16, 1779	141	Rejected		
" 4	70	Theodore Gilliard	Allen Grant	100	Briar creek	Same	Oct. 13, 1779	146	Not rec'd, as being within the southern boundary		
" 4	71	George Burdon	George Burden	269	Escambia river	Same	Jan. 29, 1780	166	Same		
" 4	72	Theodore Gilliard	Jos. Lamb	200	Same	Same	May 2, 1779	172	Same		
" 4	73	George Burdon	George Burdon	800	Briar creek	Same	Aug. 17, 1779	183	Rejected		
" 4	74	Same	Same	200	Same	Same	1779	189	Rejected		
" 4	75	Theodore Gilliard	Francis Lewis	300	Escambia	Same	June 16, 1777	194	Not rec'd, as being within south'n boun'ry	B	2
" 4	76	Same	Charles Ward	500	Same	Same	March 2, 1779	206			
" 4	77	Same	Same	500	Same	Same	March, 1779	212			
1805. April 30	78	Jos. Thompson	Jos. Thompson	640	Hollow creek	Occupancy	1797	223	Allowed	B	2
" 30	79	William J. Pierce	Francis Ballard	640	Alabama	Same	1797	224	Rejected		
" 30	80	Nath. Christmas	Mich'l Hartley	640	Tombigbee	Same	1797	227	Allowed	B	12
" 30	81	James Callier	Joseph Campbell	640	Mobile river	Same	1797	228	Allowed	B	

N—Continued.

When presented.	No.	By whom claimed.	Name of the original grantee or claimant.	Quantity claim'd in acres or arpents.	Situation.	Whence derived.	Date of patent, order of survey, or settlement.	Recorded, vol. 1.	What.	Entered in register. Letter	Page	Under what title allowed.	Entered in register. Let'r.	Page.
1805, April 30	82	William John Pierce	Jeremiah Phillips	640	Alabama river	Occupancy	March, 1797	Page 229	Allowed	B	11			
1804, June 11	83	Joseph Stiggins	John Johnson	800	Tensaw lake	Spanish warrant	Feb. 9, 1788	232	Allowed	B	2			
" 11	84	Benjamin Few	Benjamin Few	640	Mobile river	Pre-emption	Mar. 3, 1803	236	Rejected					
1805, April 30	85	Samuel Mims	Samuel Mims	640	Alabama	Occupancy	1797	237	Allowed	D	4			
" 27	86	Lemuel Henry	M. Hardy	640	Tombigbee	Same	1797	239	Rejected					
" 30	87	Nath. Christmas	Nath. Christmas	160	Same	Pre-emption	Mar. 3, 1803	242	Rejected					
1804, June 11	88	John Milliken	William Cannon	-	Alabama	Same	-	243	Withdrawn by the claimant					
" 1	89	Abijah Hunt	Aug. Rochon	1,000	Mobile	Deed of conv'ce	Dec. 16, 1801	243	Rejected					
1805, April 30	90	Heirs of Alexander McCullagh	Thomas Underwood	500	Alabama	Same	Jan. 1, 1779	246	Rejected					

MISSISSIPPI TERRITORY, *Washington county:*

FORT STODDERT, *Thursday, February* 2, 1804.

Be it remembered that, in pursuance of an act of the seventh Congress of the United States, passed on the third of March, one thousand eight hundred and three, entitled, "An act regulating the grants of land, and providing for the disposal of the lands of the United States south of the State of Tennessee," and in virtue of commissions, by Thomas Jefferson, President of the United States, to Ephraim Kirby, and Robert Carter Nicholas, to wit:

THOMAS JEFFERSON, *President of the United States of America: To all who shall see these presents, greeting:*

Know ye, that, reposing special trust and confidence in the integrity. diligence, and discretion of Ephraim Kirby, of Connecticut, and Robert Carter Nicholas, of Kentucky, I do appoint them commissioners of the United States in Washington county, in the Mississippi territory, for the purpose of ascertaining the rights of persons claiming lands in the said territory east of Pearl river, in pursuance of the articles of agreement and cession between the United States and Georgia, of the three first sections of the act of Congress, entitled, "An act regulating the grants of land, and providing for the disposal of the lands of the United States south of the State of Tennessee;" and do authorize and empower them to execute and fulfil the duties of their respective offices, according to law: and to have and to hold the same, with all the rights and emoluments thereunto legally appertaining unto them, the said Ephraim Kirby, and Robert Carter Nicholas, during the pleasure of the President of the United States for the time being, as to both or either of them.

In testimony whereof, I have caused these letters to be made patent, and the seal of the United States to be hereunto affixed.

Given under my hand, at the city of Washington, the twelfth day of July, in the year of our Lord one thousand eight hundred and three, and of the Independence of the United States of America the twenty-eighth.

[L. s.]

THOMAS JEFFERSON.

By the President:
JAMES MADISON, *Secretary of State.*

Who, in conformity thereto, severally took and subscribed the following oath, to wit:

I, Ephraim Kirby, do solemnly swear that I will impartially exercise and discharge the duties imposed upon me, by an act of Congress, entitled, "An act regulating the grants of land, and providing for the disposal of the lands of the United States south of the State of Tennessee," to the best of my skill and judgment.

EPHRAIM KIRBY.

Sworn and subscribed before me, Andrew Richardson, a Justice of the Peace for the county Alleghany, in the commonwealth of Pennsylvania, in due form, at Pittsburg, this seventeenth day of October, in the year of our Lord one thousand eight hundred and three.

ANDREW RICHARDSON.

PENNSYLVANIA, *Alleghany county, to wit:*

I, Tarlton Bates, Prothonotary of the Court of Common Pleas for the said county, do hereby certify that the above is the proper signature of Andrew Richardson; that the said Andrew Richardson is one of the commonwealth's Justices of the Peace in and for the said county, duly appointed, commissioned, and acting; and that full and entire faith and credit are and ought to be given to all his acts as such.

In testimony of which I have hereto set my hand, and the seal of the said court, at Pittsburg, this seventeenth day of October, in the twenty-eighth year of Independence, in the year of our Lord one thousand eight hundred and three.

[L. s.]

T. BATES.

I, Robert Carter Nicholas, do solemnly swear that I will impartially exercise and discharge the duties imposed upon me by an act of Congress, entitled, "An act regulating the grants of land, and providing for the disposal of the lands of the United States south of the State of Tennessee," to the best of my skill and judgment.

ROBERT C. NICHOLAS.

Subscribed, and sworn before me, James Caller, a Justice of the Peace for the county of Washington, in the Mississippi territory, in due form, at Fort Stoddert, in said county, this first day of February, in the year of our Lord one thousand eight hundred and four.

JAMES CALLER, *J. P.*

And also, in pursuance of a commission to Joseph Chambers, by the President of the United States, as follows, to wit:

THOMAS JEFFERSON, *President of the United States of America: To all who shall see these presents, greeting:*

Know ye, that, reposing special trust and confidence in the integrity, diligence, and discretion of Joseph Chambers, of the Mississippi territory, I do appoint him register of the land office of the United States in the county of Washington, in the Mississippi territory, for the lands lying east of Pearl river; and do authorize him to execute and fulfil the duties of that office according to law: and to have and to hold the said office. with all the rights and emoluments thereunto legally appertaining unto him, the said Joseph Chambers, during the pleasure of the President of the United States for the time being, and until the end of the next session of the Senate of the United States, and no longer.

In testimony whereof, I have caused these letters to be made patent, and the seal of the United States to be hereunto affixed.

Given under my hand, at the city of Washington, the twelfth day of July, in the year of our Lord one thousand eight hundred and three; and of the Independence of the United States of America the twenty-eighth.

[L. s.]

THOMAS JEFFERSON.

By the President:
JAMES MADISON, *Secretary of State.*

Who also took and subscribed the following oath, to wit: I, Joseph Chambers, do solemnly swear that I will impartially exercise and discharge the duties imposed upon me, by an act of Congress, entitled, "An act regulating the grants of land, and providing for the disposal of the lands of the United States south of the State of Tennessee," to the best of my skill and judgment.

JOSEPH CHAMBERS.

Subscribed and sworn before me, James Caller, a Justice of the Peace for the county of Washington, Mississippi territory, in due form, at Fort Stoddert, this second day of February, in the year of our Lord one thousand eight hundred and four.

JAMES CALLER, *J. P.*

The said Ephraim Kirby, Robert Carter Nicholas, and Joseph Chambers, met and formed the board, and the board then proceeded to the choice of a clerk: whereupon, David Parmelee 2d was unanimously appointed, who, being notified of his appointment, accepted the same, and appeared, took and subscribed the oath required by law, to wit:

I, David Parmelee 2d, do solemnly swear, that I will truly and faithfully enter and record all minutes, proceedings, and decisions of the board of commissioners for the county of Washington, appointed under, and by virtue of an act of the United States, entitled "An act regulating the grants, and providing for the disposal of the lands of the United States south of the State of Tennessee, and will and faithfully do and perform all other acts and things in said act pointed out as the duty of a clerk of the said board.

DAVID PARMELEE, 2d.

Sworn, and subscribed in presence of the board of commissioners, February 2, 1804.

Test: EPHRAIM KIRBY,
One of the Commissioners.

The board then adjourned until Friday, the 4th instant.

FRIDAY, *February* 3, 1804.

The board met according to adjournment. Present: Ephraim Kirby, Robert C. Nicholas, Joseph Chambers.

Proceeded to the adoption of certain rules and regulations, for conducting the business which might come before them; which rules were ordered to be published and posted up in some conspicuous places by the clerk, for the information of all concerned.

The board then adjourned until Saturday, the 4th instant.

75

SATURDAY, *February* 4, 1804.
The board met according to adjournment. Present: Ephraim Kirby, Robert C. Nicholas, Joseph Chambers. Adjourned until Monday, the 6th instant.

MONDAY, *February* 6, 1804.
The board met according to adjournment. Present: Ephraim Kirby, Robert C. Nicholas, Joseph Chambers. Adjourned until Tuesday, the 7th instant.

TUESDAY, *February* 7, 1804.
The board met according to adjournment. Present: Ephraim Kirby, Robert C. Nicholas, Joseph Chambers. Adjourned until Wednesday, the 8th instant.

WEDNESDAY, *February* 8, 1804.
The board met according to adjournment. Present: Ephraim Kirby, Robert C. Nicholas, Joseph Chambers. Adjourned until Thursday, the 9th instant.

THURSDAY, *February* 9, 1804.
The board met according to adjournment. Present: Ephraim Kirby, Robert C. Nicholas, Joseph Chambers. Adjourned until Friday, the 10th instant.

FRIDAY, *February* 10, 1804.
The board met according to adjournment. Present: Ephraim Kirby, Robert C. Nicholas, Joseph Chambers. Adjourned until Saturday, the 11th instant.

SATURDAY, *February* 11, 1804.
The board met according to adjournment. Present: Ephraim Kirby, Robert C. Nicholas. Adjourned until Monday, the 13th instant.

MONDAY, *February* 13, 1804.
The board met according to adjournment. Present: Ephraim Kirby, Robert C. Nicholas.

ISAAC RYAN's case, No. 1 on the docket of the board, and No. 4 on the books of the Register.

Claim.—A donation of six hundred and thirty-five acres, under the second section of the act.

The claimant presented his claim, together with a surveyor's plot of the land claimed, in the following words and figures, to wit:

To the Commissioners appointed in pursuance of the act of Congress, passed the third day of March, 1803, for receiving and adjusting the claim to lands south of Tennessee, and east of Pearl river.

Please to take notice, that the following tract of land, situated on the waters of Bassett's creek, bounded as follows: beginning at a black gum, south, eighty-six degrees west, thirty-three chains; south, twenty-two degrees west, thirty-two chains; south, fifty-eight degrees east, eighty chains; north fifty-three degrees east, fifty chains, to a gum; north seven degrees west, seventy chains; to a beach on the side of Bassett's creek; thence to the beginning; containing six hundred thirty-five acres, having such forms and marks, natural and artificial, as are fully represented in the plot annexed; which said tract of land is claimed under and in virtue of the second section of the aforesaid act of Congress as a donation, and is now exhibited unto the register of the land office established east of Pearl river, to be recorded as directed by said act. To all which he begs leave to refer, as also to the copy of the plot* hereunto annexed.

ISAAC RYAN.
[Plot omitted.]
FEBRUARY 13, 1804.

Entered in record of claims, vol. 1, page 20, by EDWARD LLOYD WAILES, for

JOSEPH CHAMBERS, *Register.*

Francis Boykin, of the county of Washington, in the Mississippi territory, of lawful age, was produced aa a witness in support of this claim, and, being duly sworn before the board, did depose, that he had lived within the county of Washington aforesaid thirteen years, and had been acquainted with Isaac Ryan, the present claimant, since the year 1795, and knew that, in the spring of

*This plot, and all those following on in this subject, have been omitted in printing, the tracts being already sufficiently described in the notices filed by the claimants.

the year 1797, and ever since, the said Ryan had lived on the lands by him claimed, lying on Bassett's creek, and that he had, from that time to the present, continued to occupy and cultivate the same; and that the said Ryan was in the year 1797, the head of a family; and this witness further deposed, that, to the best of his knowledge and belief, the lands described in the claimant's plot or survey now exhibited, are not claimed by virtue of any British or Spanish grant, or order, or warrant of survey.

The board ordered that the case be postponed for consideration, and then adjourned until Tuesday the 14th instant.

TUESDAY, *February* 14, 1804.
The board met according to adjournment. Present: Ephraim Kirby, Robert C. Nicholas. Adjourned until Wednesday, the 15th instant.

WEDNESDAY, *February* 15, 1804.
The board met according to adjournment. Present: Ephraim Kirby, Robert C. Nicholas. Adjourned until Thursday, the 16th instant.

THURSDAY, *February* 16, 1804.
The board met according to adjournment, Present: Ephraim Kirby, Robert C. Nicholas. Adjourned until Friday, the 17th instant.

FRIDAY, *February* 17, 1804.
The board met according to adjournment. Present: Ephraim Kirby, Robert C. Nicholas. Adjourned until Saturday, the 18th instant.

SATURDAY, *February* 18, 1804.
The board met according to adjournment. Present: Ephraim Kirby, Robert C. Nicholas. Adjourned until Monday, the 20th instant.

MONDAY, *February* 20, 1804.
The board met according to adjournment. Present: Ephraim Kirby, Robert C. Nicholas. Adjourned until Tuesday, the 21st instant.

TUESDAY, *February* 21, 1804.
The board met according to adjournment. Present: Ephraim Kirby, Robert C. Nicholas. Adjourned until Wednesday, the 22d instant.

WEDNESDAY, *February* 22, 1804.
The board met according to adjournment. Present: Ephraim Kirby, Robert C. Nicholas. Adjourned until Thursday, the 23d instant.

THURSDAY, *February* 23, 1804.
The board met according to adjournment. Present: Ephraim Kirby, Robert C. Nicholas. Adjourned until Friday, the 24th instant.

FRIDAY, *February* 24, 1804.
The board met according to adjournment. Present: Ephraim Kirby, Robert C. Nicholas. Adjourned until Saturday, the 25th instant.

SATURDAY, *February* 25, 1804.
The board met according to adjournment. Present: Ephraim Kirby, Robert C. Nicholas. Adjourned until Monday, the 27th instant.

MONDAY, *February* 27, 1804.
The board met according to adjournment. Present: Ephraim Kirby, Robert C. Nicholas. Adjourned until Tuesday, the 28th instant.

TUESDAY, *February* 28, 1804.
The board met according to adjournment. Present: Ephraim Kirby, Robert C. Nicholas.

JAMES MORGAN's case, No 2 on the docket of the board, and No. 5 on the books of the register.

Claim.—A right of pre-emption of three hundred and twenty acres and five-eighths of an acre, under the third section of the act.

The claimant presented his claim, together with a surveyor's plot of the land claimed, in the following words and figures, to wit:

To the Commissioners appointed in pursuance of the act of Congress passed the 3d day of March, 1803, for receiving and adjusting the claims to lands south of Tennessee and east of Pearl river.

Please to take notice, that the following tract of land, situated on the waters of House's mill creek, beginning at a lightwood stake, and running north, sixteen and a half degrees, east, one hundred and ninety poles, to a stake and pine; thence, north, seventy-three and a half degrees west, two hundred and seventy poles, to a small post oak; thence, south, sixteen and a half degrees west, one hundred and ninety poles, to a pine; thence, in a direct line to the beginning; containing three hundred and twenty acres and five-eighths of an acre, having such marks, natural and artificial, as are fully represented in the plot annexed: which is claimed under and by virtue of the third section of the said act of Congress as a pre-emption, and is now exhibited to the register of the land office east of Pearl river, to be recorded as directed by said act. To all which he begs leave to refer, as also to the copy of the plot hereunto annexed.

JAMES MORGAN,
Legal representative of John Burney.

[Plot omitted.]

Surveyed for James Morgan a tract of land containing three hundred and twenty and five-eighths acres, lying in Washington county, on one of the head branches of House's mill creek, beginning at a lightwood stake near the branch, and runs north, sixteen and a half degrees east, one hundred and ninety poles, to a stake and pine corner; thence, north, seventy-three and a half degrees west, two hundred and seventy poles, to a small post oak corner; thence, south, sixteen and a half degrees west, one hundred and ninety poles, across the branch, to a pine corner; from thence, a direct line to the place of beginning. Surveyed 1st February, 1804, by J. Malone.

Entered in record of claims, vol. 1, page 21, by EDWARD LLOYD WAILES, for

JOSEPH CHAMBERS, *Register.*

In support of the right of representation, the said James Morgan produced a deed of conveyance from John Burney, bearing date the 4th day of December, 1803, duly executed, assigning, relinquishing, and conveying to the said James Morgan all the said Burney's right and claim to the land described.

Edward Lloyd Wailes, of the county of Washington, in the Mississippi territory, was produced as a witness, and, being duly sworn before the board, did depose, that John Burney, the person on whose right the present claimant appears, did, on the 3d day of March last, inhabit and cultivate the land now claimed by the said Morgan, as his legal representative; and that the said Burney was at that time the head of a family, and that he had heard and believed that the said James Morgan, since he purchased the said right or improvement of the said Burney, had resided, and still did reside, on the premises; and that he had no knowledge that the same land was claimed by virtue of any British or Spanish grant, warrant, or order of survey.

The board ordered that the case be postponed for consideration.

WILLIAM MORGAN's case, No. 3 on the docket of the board, and No. 8 on the books of the register.

Claim.—A right of pre-emption of three hundred and nineteen acres, and nine-fortieths of an acre, under the third section of the act.

The claimant presented his claim, together with a surveyor's plot of the land claimed, in the following words and figures, to wit:

To the Commissioners appointed in pursuance of the act of Congress passed the 3d day of March, 1803, for receiving and adjusting the claims of lands south of Tennessee and east of Pearl river.

WASHINGTON COUNTY, *February* 26, 1804.

Please to take notice, that the following tract of land, situated on the waters of Bassett's creek, in Washington county, beginning at a small pine, and running south, sixty and a half degrees west, two hundred and twenty-six poles, to a small black jack corner; thence, south, twenty-seven and a half degrees east, two hundred and twenty-six poles, to a lightwood stake corner; thence, north, sixty and a half degrees east, two hundred and twenty-six poles, to a post oak corner; thence, in a direct line to the place of beginning; containing three hundred and nineteen acres and nine-fortieths of an acre: having such marks, natural and artificial, as are

represented in the plot annexed, which is claimed under and by virtue of the third section of the said act of Congress as a pre-emption, and now exhibited to the register of the land office east of Pearl river, to be recorded as directed by said act. To all which he begs leave to refer, as also to the copy of the plot herewith annexed.

WILLIAM MORGAN.

[Plot omitted.]

Surveyed for William Morgan a tract of land, containing three hundred and nineteen and nine-fortieths acres, lying in the county of Washington, on a branch of Bassett's creek. Beginning at a small pine, running south sixty and a half degrees, west two hundred and twenty-six poles, to a small black jack corner; thence, south twenty-seven and a half degrees, east two hundred and twenty-six poles, to a light wood stake corner; thence, north sixty and a half degrees, east two hundred and twenty-six poles, to a post-oak and two pines, marked as corner trees; thence, a direct line to the beginning. Surveyed 30th January, 1804, by J. Malone.

Entered in the record of claims, vol. 1, page 38, by EDWARD LLOYD WAILES, for

JOSEPH CHAMBERS, *Register.*

James Morgan, of the county of Washington, in the Mississippi territory, was produced as a witness, and being duly sworn before the board, did depose, that William Morgan, the present claimant, did, on the 3d day of March last, inhabit and cultivate the lands now by him claimed, and still continues to inhabit and cultivate the same: and that the said William was at that time the head of a family, and that, to the best of his knowledge and belief, the said land was not claimed by virtue of any British or Spanish grant, orders, or warrants of survey, or elder possession than that of the said William.

The board ordered that the case be postponed for consideration, and adjourned until Wednesday, the 29th instant.

WEDNESDAY, *February* 29, 1804.

The board met according to adjournment. Present: Ephraim Kirby, Robert C. Nicholas.

Adjourned until Thursday, the 1st day of March next.

THURSDAY, *March* 1, 1804.

The board met according to adjournment. Present: Ephraim Kirby, Robert C. Nicholas.

Adjourned until Friday, the 2d instant.

FRIDAY, *March* 2, 1804.

The board met according to adjournment. Present: Ephraim Kirby, Robert C. Nicholas.

Adjourned until Saturday, the 3d instant.

SATURDAY, *March* 3, 1804.

The board met according to adjournment. Present: Ephraim Kirby, Robert C. Nicholas, Joseph Chambers.

NATHAN BLACKWELL's case, No. 4 on the docket of the board, and No. 14 on the books of the register.

Claim.—A donation of six hundred and forty acres, under the second section of the act.

The claimant presented his claim, together with a surveyor's plot of the land claimed, in the following words and figures, to wit:

To the Commissioners appointed in pursuance of the act of Congress, passed the 3d day of March, 1803, for receiving and adjusting the claims to lands south of Tennessee and east of Pearl river.

Please to take notice, that the following tract of land, situated on the waters of Tombigbee, in the county of Washington, beginning at a yellow leaf sapling, running north, sixty-seven degrees west, ninety chains, to a red oak corner; thence, north, twenty-three degrees east, seventy-one chains, to a stake; thence, south, sixty-seven degrees east twenty-five chains, to the first lake; thence, thirty-five chains, to the corner and sweet gum; thence, south, twenty degrees east, sixty chains, to a stake; thence, south, forty-two degrees west, twenty-seven chains, to the beginning; containing six hundred and forty acres, having such forms and marks, both natural and artificial, as are fully represented in the plot annexed; which said tract of land is claimed by Nathan Blackwell, in and by virtue of the second section of the said act, as a donation, and is now exhibited to the register of the land office east of Pearl river, to be recorded as directed by said act. To all which he begs leave to refer, as also to a copy of the plot herewith filed.

NATHAN BLACKWELL.

MARCH 3, 1804.

[Plot omitted.]

Surveyed six hundred and forty acres of land, for Nathan Blackwell, of Washington county, Mississippi territory, under a donation claim, beginning at a yellow leaf sapling, running north, sixty-seven degrees west, ninety chains, to red oak corner; thence, north, twenty-three degrees east, seventy-one chains, to a stake; thence, south, sixty-seven degrees east, twenty-five chains, to the first lake; thence, thirty-five chains to the corner and sweet gum; thence, south, twenty degrees east, sixty chains, to a stake; south, thence, forty-two degrees west, twenty-seven chains, to the beginning.

WILLIAM GILLIAM.

FEBRUARY 18, 1804.

Entered in record of claims vol. 1, page 44, by EDWARD LLOYD WAILES, for

JOSEPH CHAMBERS, *Register.*

Adam Hollinger, of the county Washington, in the Mississippi territory, was produced as a witness, and, being duly sworn before the board, did depose, that Nathan Blackwell, the present claimant, was in possession of the land now claimed in the year 1795, and has continued to inhabit and cultivate the same ever since; and that he was also at that time the head of a family, and of full age.

Young Gains, of the county of Washington, in the Mississippi territory, was also produced as a witness, and, being duly sworn before the board, deposed, that Nathan Blackwell did inhabit and cultivate the tract of land, represented by the plot annexed to his notice now presented to the board of commissioners, previous to the 27th of October, 1797, and had continued to inhabit and cultivate the same ever since; and that he was at that time the head of a family, and of full age. He also said that he did not know that the land claimed by said Blackwell is claimed by any British or Spanish grant, warrant, or order of survey, except a small part by Francis Boykin, under a Spanish warrant of survey, as he believed.

The board ordered that the case be postponed for consideration; then adjourned until Monday, the 5th instant.

MONDAY, *March* 5, 1804.

The board met according to adjournment. Present: Ephraim Kirby, Robert C. Nicholas.

Adjourned until Tuesday, the 6th instant.

TUESDAY, *March* 6, 1804.

The board met according to adjournment. Present: Ephraim Kirby, Robert C. Nicholas.

Adjourned until Wednesday, the 7th instant.

WEDNESDAY, *March* 7, 1804.

The board met according to adjournment. Present: Ephraim Kirby, Robert C. Nicholas.

STERLING DUPREE's case, No. 5 on the docket of the board, and No. 13 on the books of the register.

Claim.—The right of representation to four hundred and ninety-five acres, under the second section of the act, as assignee and legal representative of Emanuel Cheney. The claimant presented his claim, together with a surveyor's plot of the land claimed, in the following words and figures, to wit:

To the Commissioners appointed in pursuance of the act of Congress passed the 3d day of March, 1803, for receiving and adjusting the claims to lands south of Tennessee and east of Pearl river.

Please to take notice, that the following tract of land, situated on the waters of Tombigbee river, in the county of Washington, beginning at a white oak, running south, sixty-four degrees west, twenty chains; thence, south, forty-five degrees west, fifteen chains, to a post oak corner; thence, south seventy-five degrees west, forty-six chains, to a post oak corner; thence, south, four degrees east, seventy-three chains, to a maple corner, thence, north, fifty-six degrees east, eighty chains, to a

stake on the bank of Tombigbee river; thence, up the river to the beginning containing four hundred and ninety-five acres, having such forms and marks, natural and artificial, as are fully represented in the plot annexed: which said land is claimed by Sterling Dupree, in and by virtue of a donation right derived from Emanuel Cheney, and is now exhibited to the register of the land office, east of Pearl river, to be recorded as directed by said act. To all which he begs leave to refer, as also to a copy of the plot herewith filed.

STERLING DUPREE.

FEBRUARY 29, 1804.

[Plot omitted.]

The above plot represents a tract of land surveyed for Sterling Dupree, on Nanna Hubba.

NATT. CHRISTMAS.

Chain bearers, David Dupree and Edmund Smith, sworn.

This day, David Dupree and Edmund Smith came before me, and made oath, that they have given a just account of the admeasurement of the above plot to the best of their knowledge.

Given under my hand, this 29th February, 1804.

JAMES CALLER, *J. P.*

Entered in record of claims, vol. 1, page 42, by ED-WARD LLOYD WAILES, for

JOSEPH CHAMBERS, *Register.*

In support of the right of representation, the said Sterling Dupree produced a deed of conveyance from Emanuel Cheney, bearing date the 19th day of July, 1801, duly executed, assigning, relinquishing, and conveying to the said Sterling Dupree all the said Emanuel Cheney's right and claim to the said land, and to the improvements made thereon.

Thomas Bates, of the county of Washington, in the Mississippi territory, was produced as a witness, and, being duly sworn before the board, deposed, that Emanuel Cheney, in the month of September, 1798, built a house upon the lands now claimed; and in the month of December following, he removed into the house; and in the year following, he commenced the cultivation of the land; that the said Cheney was at that time the head of a family, and had three children; that, about two years after, the said Cheney gave up the possession to Sterling Dupree, who entered into the occupancy of the said house and lands, and has continued in the occupancy of the same until this time; that, to the best of his knowledge, the said lands are not claimed by any English or Spanish grant, order or warrant of survey.

The board then ordered that the case be postponed for consideration; and adjourned until Thursday, the 8th instant.

THURSDAY, *March* 8, 1804.

The board met according to adjournment. Present: Ephraim Kirby, Robert C. Nicholas.

The board adjourned until Friday, the 9th instant.

FRIDAY, *March* 9, 1804.

The board met according to adjournment. Present: Ephraim Kirby, Robert C. Nicholas.

Adjourned until Saturday, the 10th instant.

SATURDAY, *March* 10, 1804.

The board met according to adjournment. Present: Ephraim Kirby, Robert C. Nicholas, Joseph Chambers.

Adjourned until Monday, the 12th instant.

MONDAY, *March* 12, 1804.

The board met according to adjournment. Present: Ephraim Kirby, Robert C. Nicholas, Joseph Chambers.

Adjourned until Tuesday, the 13th instant.

TUESDAY, *March* 13, 1804.

The board met according to adjournment. Present: Ephraim Kirby, Robert C. Nicholas, Joseph Chambers.

Adjourned until Wednesday, the 14th instant.

WEDNESDAY, *March* 14, 1804.

The board met according to adjournment. Present: Ephraim Kirby, Robert C. Nicholas, Joseph Chambers.

JAMES GRIFFIN's case, No. 6 on the docket of the board, and No. 9 on the books of the Register.

Claim.—A donation of six hundred and eighteen acres, under the second section of the act.

The claimant presented his claim, together with a surveyor's plot of the land claimed, in the following words and figures, to wit:

To the Commissioners appointed in pursuance of the act of Congress passed the 3d day of March, 1803, for receiving and adjusting the claims to lands south of Tennessee and east of Pearl river.

Please to take notice, that the following tract of land, situated on the waters of Smith's creek, in the county of Washington, beginning at a pine stake, and running thence south, fifty degrees east, sixty-eight chains fifty links, to a black oak; thence, south, forty degrees west, ninety chains, to a pine; thence north, fifty degrees west, sixty-eight chains fifty links, to a stake; thence, north, forty degrees east, ninety chains, to the beginning; containing six hundred and eighteen acres, having such forms and marks, natural and artificial, as are fully represented in the plot annexed: which said tract of land is claimed by James Griffin, in and by virtue of the second section of the said act of Congress as a donation; and is now exhibited to the register of the land office east of Pearl river, to be recorded as directed by said act. To all which he begs leave to refer, as also to a copy of the plot herewith filed.

JAMES GRIFFIN, his x mark.
FEBRUARY 28, 1804.
[Plot omitted.]

The above plot is truly surveyed and made out by me, Robert Ligon, this 14th day of February, Anno Domini 1804. Beginning at or near the house that Thomas Baker evacuated some days since; beginning on a stake and running south, fifty degrees east; thence, south, forty degrees west; thence, north, fifty degrees west; thence, north, forty degrees east, to the beginning; including in the above lines six hundred and eighteen acres.
Entered in record of claims, vol. 1, page 39, by EDWARD LLOYD WAILES, for

JOSEPH CHAMBERS, *Register.*

John McGrew, senior, of the county of Washington, in the Mississippi territory, was produced as a witness, and, being duly sworn before the board, deposed, that James Griffin moved, settled upon, and cultivated the land now claimed, and represented by the plot presented to the board of commissioners, before the year 1797, and has continued to inhabit and cultivate the same ever since; that he then was, has continued to be, and now is, the head of a family, and of full age.

Question. Do you know whether this land is claimed by any British or Spanish claim?

Answer. I have understood that there is both a British and Spanish claim for this land, but I have never seen either.

Question. Do you know whether James Griffin, the claimant, claims any other lands in this territory in virtue of any British or Spanish title?

Answer. I do not know that he does, but believe that he does not.

Robert Ligon, of the county of Washington, in said territory, surveyor, was produced as a witness, and, being duly sworn before the board, did depose, that the plot of James Griffin's donation claim is a true and correct representation, natural and artificial, of the land claimed; and that the claimant resides within the limits of this claim.

Question. Do you know and believe the chain carriers to be men of credibility?

Answer. I believe they are, but am not well acquainted with them, and cannot therefore answer positively that they are.

The board ordered that the case be adjourned for consideration.

ELISHA SIMMONS's case, No. 7 on the docket of the board, and No. 19 on the books of the Register.

Claim.—A right of pre-emption of four hundred and fifty-four acres, under the third section of the act.

The claimant presented his plot of the land claimed, in the words and figures following, to wit:

To the Commissioners appointed in pursuance of the act of Congress passed the 3d day of March, 1803, for receiving and adjusting claims to lands south of Tennessee and east of Pearl river.

Please to take notice, that the following tract of land, lying on the west side of Tombigbee river, consisting of four hundred and fifty-four acres, is claimed by Elisha

Simmons, of Washington county, and Mississippi territory, under and in virtue of an improvement and actual cultivation made previous to, and had and continued on, the third day of March, 1803, to the date hereof; which claim to the aforesaid four hundred and fifty-four acres is now delivered unto the register of the land office to be established east of Pearl river, to be recorded as directed by said act. To all which he begs leave to refer, as also to the plot thereof, herewith filed.

ELISHA SIMMONS.
FEBRUARY 24th, 1804.
[Plot omitted.]

Made out the 9th day of February, 1804, by me, Robert Ligon. Chain carriers, Rolly Green, Reuben Westmolan.

Entered in record of claims, vol. 1, page 52, by EDWARD LLOYD WAILES, for

JOSEPH CHAMBERS, *Register.*

William Rogers, of the county of Washington, in the Mississippi territory, was produced as a witness, and, being duly sworn before the board, deposed, that Elisha Simmons moved, lived, built a house on the place represented by the plot now presented to the commissioners, in the month of February, 1801, and has lived on the same ever since; and that he had then, and now has, a wife and two children.

Question. Do you know whether this land is claimed by any British or Spanish grants?

Answer. I do not know.

Question. Do you know of any other claims for this land than pre-emptions?

Answer. I do not.

Robert Ligon of said county, surveyor, was produced as a witness, and, being duly sworn before the board, deposed:

Question. Is the plot now presented by Elisha Simmons, for a claim of pre-emption of four hundred and fifty-four acres of land, a true and correct one of the land thereby represented?

Answer. It is.

Question. Are the chain carriers men of credibility?

Answer. I believe they are.

John McGrew, senior, of the county aforesaid, was also produced as a witness, and, being duly sworn before the board, deposed, that he believes that the claimant settled and lived on the land claimed about the time mentioned by William Rogers, and has continued on the same ever since, that he is the head of a family, and was so at that time.

Question. Is there any British or Spanish grants for this land?

Answer. There is a Spanish grant in the name of James Frazier, which I believe will be presented.

The board ordered that the case be postponed for consideration.

WILLIAM ROGERS's case, No. 8 on the docket of the board, and No. 25 on the books of the Register.

Claim.—A right of pre-emption of three hundred and eighty-eight acres, under the third section of the act.

The claimant presented his claim, together with a surveyor's plot of the land claimed, in the following words and figures, to wit:

To the Commissioners appointed in pursuance of the act of Congress passed 3d day of March, 1803, for receiving and adjusting the claims to lands south of the Tennessee and east of Pearl river.

Please to take notice, that the following tract of land, situated on the west side of Tombigbee river, Washington county, butted on said river, and bounded on the southwest by Kirkland's old line beginning at a sassafras, his old corner, and runs with the old line south, seventy degrees west, fifty-five chains, to a small pine corner; on the northwest, by lands within Kirkland's survey, running north, twenty degrees west, fifty-five chains, to a small yellow leaf and *whortleberry* corner; on the northeast by said survey, and runs north, seventy degrees east, ninety two chains fifty links, to a stooping maple on the river bank; and from thence, the meanders of the river to the place of the beginning: having such marks, natural and artificial, as are represented in the plot annexed, containing three hundred and eighty-eight acres; is claimed by William Rogers, under and by virtue of a settlement, bearing date the 7th day of February, 1800, and now exhibited to the register of the land office established east of Pearl river, to be recorded as directed by said act. To all which he begs leave to refer, as also to the copy of the plot herewith filed.

[Plot omitted]

Surveyed 17th February, 1804, by J. Malone. Chain carriers, John Cozby, Peter Cartwright. Test: R. Green.

WILLIAM ROGERS, his + mark.

Entered in record of claims, vol. 1, page 72, by Edward Lloyd Wailes, for

JOSEPH CHAMBERS, Register.

Mississippi Territory, *Washington County:*
　　　　　　　　　　　　　　　March 12th, 1804.

I do hereby certify that Peter Cartwright and William Shaw were sworn before me; that they impartially carried the chain for measuring a tract of land for William Rogers, claimed by virtue of settlement and cultivation, on the 3d of March, 1803.

R. HARWELL, J. P.

Elijah Simmons, of the county of Washington, in the Mississippi territory, was produced as a witness, and, being duly sworn before the board, deposed, that William Rogers moved, settled, built, and cultivated the land claimed by the plot now presented to the board, in February, 1800, and has continued to inhabit and cultivate the same ever since; that he was the head of a family and of full age, in the said month of February, 1800, and is at this time the head of a family.

Question. Do you know whether there is any British, Spanish, or donation claim for this land?

Answer. I do not know of any.

John McGrew, senior, of said county, was also produced as a witness, and, being duly sworn before the board, deposed, that William Rogers moved, settled, built, and cultivated the land claimed and represented by the plot now presented to the board, in February, 1800, and has continued to inhabit and cultivate the same ever since; and that he was the head of a family and of full age in the said month of February, 1800, and is at this time the head of a family.

Question. Do you know of any British or Spanish grant, or warrant, order of survey, or claim of donation for this land?

Answer. I have understood, and believe, that there are both a British and Spanish claim for this land, but I have never seen either.

The board ordered that the case be postponed for consideration.

Matthew Shaw's case, No. 9 on the docket of the board, and No. 32 on the books of the Register.

Claim.—A right of pre-emption of three hundred and thirty-three acres, two roods, and twenty-two poles, under the third section of the act.

The claimant presented his claim, together with a surveyor's plot of the land claimed, in the words following and figures, to wit:

To the Commissioners appointed in pursuance of the act of Congress, passed the third day of March, 1803, for receiving and adjusting the claims to lands south of the Tennessee and east of Pearl river.

Please to take notice, that the following tract of land, situated on the west side of Tombigbee, butted on said river, bounded on the southwest by George Robbins and vacant land, on the southeast by vacant land, and on the northeast by vacant land and William Rogers; beginning on a hackberry on the river bank, and runs with Robbins's line south, sixty degrees west, fifty-nine chains fifty links, to a sweet gum corner; thence, south, eighty-one degrees west, fifty chains fifty links, to a hickory corner; thence, south, forty-two degrees west, eight chains, to a pine corner; thence, south, thirty degrees east, thirty-two chains, to a small pine corner; thence, north, seventy degrees east, thirteen chains fifty links, to William Rogers's corner, the same course continued; in all, one hundred and six chains, to Rogers's corner maple on the river bank; and from thence, the meanders of the river to the place of beginning; having such marks, natural and artificial, as are represented in the plot annexed, containing three hundred and thirty-three acres, two roods; twenty-two poles is claimed by Matthew Shaw, under and by virtue of a settlement, in the year one thousand eight hundred and two, and now exhibited unto the Register of the Land Office established east of Pearl river, to be recorded as directed by said act. To all which he begs leave to refer, as also to the copy of the plot herewith filed.

[Plot omitted.]

Surveyed 2d March, 1804, by J. Malone. Chain carriers, William Rogers, Peter Cartwright.

Entered in record of claims, vol. 1, page 86, by Edward Lloyd Wailes, for

JOSEPH CHAMBERS, Register.

Mississippi Territory, *Washington county.*
　　　　　　　　　　　　　　　March 12th, 1804.

I do hereby certify that William Rogers and Peter Cartwright were sworn before me, that they impartially carried the chain for the measuring of a tract of land for Matthew Shaw, claimed by settlement and cultivation, on the 3d of March, 1803.

R. HARWELL, J. P.

William Rogers, of the county of Washington, in the Mississippi territory, was produced as a witness, and, being duly sworn before the Board, deposed: that Matthew Shaw moved, settled, built upon, and cultivated the land claimed and represented by the plot now presented to the Board of Commissioners, in the summer or fall of the year 1802, and has continued to inhabit and cultivate the same ever since; that he then was, has continued to be, and now is, the head of a family, and of full age.

Question. Do you know whether this land is claimed by any British, Spanish, or donation claim?

Answer. I do not know of any.

Elijah Simmons, of said county, was produced as a witness, and, being duly sworn before the Board, deposed, that Matthew Shaw moved, settled, built upon, and cultivated the land claimed and represented by the plot now presented to the Board of Commissioners, in the year 1802, and has continued to inhabit and cultivate the same ever since; that he was then, has continued to be, and now is, the head of a family, and of full age.

Question. Do you know whether this land is claimed by any British, Spanish, or donation claim?

Answer. I do not know of any.

The Board ordered that the case be postponed for consideration; then adjourned until Thursday, the 15th inst.

　　　　　　Thursday, *March* 15, 1804.

The Board met according to adjournment. Present: Ephraim Kirby, Robert C. Nicholas, Joseph Chambers.

James Caller's case, No. 10 on the docket of the Board, and No. 31 on the books of the Register.

Claim.—A right of representation to five hundred and seventy-three acres, two roods, and fifteen poles, under the second section of the act, as assignee and legal representative of Jesse Briant and Henry Snelgrove.

The claimant presented his claim, together with a surveyor's plot of the land claimed, in the following words and figures, to wit:

To the Commissioners appointed in pursuance of the act of Congress passed 3d day of March, 1803, for receiving and adjusting the claims to lands south of the Tennessee, and east of Pearl river.

Please to take notice, that the following tract of land, situated on the west side of Tombigbee river, on the waters of Smith's creek, butted on said river, and bounded by Chestang's claim above, and the heirs of James McGrew below, beginning on a small maple on the river bank, and running with Stewart's old line, south, twenty-five degrees west, crossing the river road at forty-nine chains thirty-five links, to a small pine station; at seventy-one chains, to a small branch; at one hundred and one chains, another; at one hundred and two chains, another; in all, one hundred and three chains, to a white oak corner; thence, north, sixty-five degrees west, crossing the main road at forty-seven chains to a small pine station, in all fifty-five chains fifty links, to a small pine corner on Stewart's old line, on the upper side; thence, with the old line north, twenty-five degrees east, crossing the main or public road at nine chains sixty links, the river road at sixty-five chains fifty links, to a small bay station, crossing the branch at sixty-nine chains below the confluence of the above; in all, ninety-nine chains fifty links, to the old corner and elm on the river bank; thence, the meanders of the river, to the place of beginning; having such marks, natural, as are represented in the plot annexed, containing five hundred and seventy-three acres, two roods and fifteen poles, is claimed by James Caller, legal representative of Henry Snelgrove, under and by virtue of a settlement bearing date in the year 1797, and now exhibited to the Register of the Land Office, established east of Pearl river, to be recorded as directed by said act. To all which he begs leave to refer, as also to the copy of the plot herewith filed.

JAMES CALLER,
Representative of Jesse Bryant and Henry Snelgrove.

[Plot omitted.]

Surveyed 9th March, 1804, by J. Malone. Chain carriers, Richard S. Bryan and Hartwell Hardaway.

Entered in record of claims, vol.1, page 83, by Edward Lloyd Wailes, for

JOSEPH CHAMBERS, Register.

MISSISSIPPI TERRITORY, *Washington County:*
MARCH 10, 1804.

Hartwell Hardaway and Richard S. Bryan came personally before me, John Murrell, and made oath that they carried the chain in surveying a tract of land, by Thomas Malone, for James Caller, on Smith creek, on one side, and Tombigbee river on the other, to the best of their skill and judgment.

Sworn to before me,   JOHN MURRELL, *J. P.*
HARTWELL HARDAWAY,
RICH. SMITH BRYAN.

In support of the right of representation, the said James Caller produced a deed of conveyance from Jesse Bryant, dated the 19th day of September, 1800, duly executed, assigning, relinquishing, and conveying, to Henry Snelgrove, all the said Bryant's right and claim to said land and the improvements made thereon; also, a deed of conveyance from said Henry Snelgrove, bearing date the 14th day of June, 1803, duly executed, assigning, relinquishing, and conveying, to the said James Caller, all the said Henry Snelgrove's right and claim to the said land, and the improvements made thereon.

Francis Boykin, of the county aforesaid, was produced as a witness, and, being duly sworn before the Board, deposed, that the land now claimed by James Caller was inhabited and cultivated by me, in the year 1795; that I removed from and abandoned the same, in the month of December of the same year; that Jesse Bryant occupied the same in the said month of December, 1795, and continued to inhabit and cultivate the same in the year 1798; and further, that the said land has been inhabited and cultivated by the said Bryant, or Henry Snelgrove, ever since the month of December, 1795; and that Jesse Bryant was, at that time, head of a family; that the plot, now exhibited by the said Caller to the Board, represents a correct view of the land claimed.

George Brewer was also produced as a witness, and being duly sworn before the Board, deposed, that Jesse Bryant inhabited and cultivated the land, now claimed by James Caller, in the year 1797; and that the same land has continued to be inhabited and cultivated by the said Bryant or Henry Snelgrove ever since; and that Bryant and Snelgrove are the heads of families, and were at that time.

The Board ordered that the case be postponed for consideration.

ISAAC RYAN's case.—The following certificate was exhibited, to wit:

MARCH 10, 1804.

This day came before me, Thomas Basset and James Finn, and, being duly sworn, say that they carried the chain for Isaac Ryan's land, to the best of their skill and ability, so help them God.
WILLIAM H. HARGROVE, *J. P.*
ROBERT LIGON, *Surveyor.*

JAMES MORGAN's case.—Sampson Mounger, George Brewer, and Micajah Wall, were produced as witnesses, and, being duly sworn, deposed, that John Burney, as the legal representative of whom James Morgan claims the right of preference to purchase the tract of land represented by a plot exhibited by the said Morgan to the Board, inhabited and cultivated on the same, before and on the 3d day of March, 1803, by his representative; and that the said Burney was the head of a family.

Question. Do you know of any British, Spanish, or donation claim for this land?

Sampson Mounger.—I do not know of any, but have heard that John McGrew claims the same in virtue of a donation.

George Brewer.—John McGrew has told me that he claims this land in virtue of a donation.

Micajah Wall.—John McGrew has told me that he claims this land in virtue of a donation, and have heard, and believe, that he has surveyed the same.

EPHRAIM BARKER's case, No. 11 on the docket of the Board, and No. 34 on the books of the Register.

Claim.—A donation of six hundred and forty acres, under the second section of the act. The claimant presented his claim, together with a surveyor's plot of the land claimed, in the words and figures following, to wit:

To the Commissioners appointed in pursuance of the act of Congress, passed the 3d day of March, 1803, for receiving and adjusting the claims to lands south of Tennessee, and east of Pearl river.

Please to take notice, that the following tract of land, situate on Tombigbee river, in the county of Washing-

ton, beginning at a willow corner, and running thence, north, seventy-nine degrees west, fifty-five chains thirty-four links, to a small gum; thence, north, forty-five degrees east, one hundred and forty-four chains, to a tupelo gum; thence, south, seventy-seven degrees east, fifty-five chains, to a gum; thence, south, forty-five degrees west, seventy-nine chains, to the river; thence, with the river, to the beginning; containing six hundred and forty acres; is claimed by Ephraim Barker in and by virtue of the second section of the said act, as a donation; having such shape, form, and marks, both natural and artificial, as are fully represented in the plot annexed, and is now exhibited to the Register of the Land Office established east of Pearl river, to be recorded as directed by said act. To all which he begs leave to refer, as also to a copy of the plot herewith filed.

EPHRAIM BARKER, his + mark.
MARCH 15, 1804.

[Plot omitted.]

Entered in record of claims, vol. 1, page 90, by ED-WARD LLOYD WAILES, for
JOSEPH CHAMBERS, *Register.*

The following certificate was exhibited, to wit:

MISSISSIPPI TERRITORY, *Washington county,* ss:

This day personally came before me John Clark and William Barker, and made oath that they performed their duty faithfully and impartially in carrying the chain around a tract of land, surveyed by William Gilliam, surveyor, for Ephraim Barker, on the 18th of February, 1804, lying on the west side of Tombigbee river, and bounded partly on the bank of said river.

Given under my hand and seal this 12th of March, 1804.
FIGURES LEWIS, *J. P.*

John Brewer, Esquire, and Wiley Barber were produced as witnesses, and, being duly sworn, deposed, that Ephraim Barker commenced to cultivate the land now claimed by him in the fall of the year 1797, and has continued to cultivate the same ever since; and that he was, at that time, the head of a family.

The board ordered that the case be postponed for consideration.

HIRAM MOUNGER's case, No. 12 on the docket of the board, and No. 33 on the books of the register.

Claim.—A donation of six hundred and forty acres under the second section of the act.

The claimant presented his claim, together with a surveyor's plot of the land claimed, in the following words and figures, to wit:

To the Commissioners appointed in pursuance of the act of Congress, passed the 3d day of March, 1803, for receiving and adjusting the claims to lands south of Tennessee, and east of Pearl river.

Please to take notice, that the following tract of land, beginning on a pine, and running south, forty-four degrees east, one hundred and forty-four chains, down the Sunflower creek, to a tupelo gum; and thence, south, forty-seven degrees west, twenty-three chains, to stake in fifteen feet from black gum; and thence, north, thirty five degrees west, fifty-four chains, to tupelo gum; and thence, north, sixty-five degrees west, twenty-five chains fifty links, to water oak, and thence, south, seventy degrees west, thirty-five chains, to swamp bush; and thence, north, forty degrees west, thirty-five chains, to willow oak; and thence, north, forty-six degrees east, seventy-two chains, to the beginning pine; including six hundred and forty acres, being vacant land, now delivered to the register of the land office to be established east of Pearl river, to be recorded as directed by said act. To all which he begs leave to refer, as also to the copy of the plot hereunto filed.

HIRAM MOUNGER.
MARCH 14, 1804.

[Plot omitted.]

The above survey was surveyed on the last day of February, beginning as follows, viz: on a pine; and thence, south, forty-four degrees east, one hundred and forty-four chains, directly down the said creek, to tupelo gum; thence, south, forty-seven degrees west, twenty-three chains; thence, north, thirty-five degrees west, fifty-four chains; thence, north, sixty-five degrees west, twenty-five chains fifty links; thence, south, seventy degrees west, thirty-five chains to branch; and up the said branch, amounting to fifty-seven chains; and thence, north, forty-six degrees east, to the beginning; bounded on the opposite of the said creek by vacant land, and on the opposite side by Charles Brewer, deceased.

Surveyed by me, Robert Ligon.—Chain carriers, James Danly, George Dieke.

Robert Ligon, surveyor, was produced as a witness, and, being duly sworn, deposed, that the plot now exhibited by Hiram Mounger, for the land claimed by him, presents a correct description, natural and artificial, of the same.

MARCH 10, 1804.

This day came before me, James Danley, and George Dieke, and swore that they carried the chain, in surveying a tract of land for Hiram Mounger, without favor or affection, to the best of their skill and ability, so help them God.

WILLIAM H. HARGRAVE, J. P.
ROBERT LIGON, Surveyor.

John Brewer was produced as a witness, and, being duly sworn, deposed, that Hezekiah Wheat inhabited and cultivated the land now claimed by Hiram Mounger, in the year 1796; and that the same has been cultivated ever since; and that he has heard Hezekiah Wheat say that he had exchanged this land with Hiram Mounger for other lands claimed and improved by said Mounger; and that said Hezekiah Wheat was, in the year 1796, above twenty-one years of age; and that the plot now exhibited by said Mounger presents a correct view of the land claimed by him; and that he lives within the limits of his claim and survey.

Question. Do you know of any British or Spanish claim?

Answer. Do not know of any.

Solomon Wheat was produced as a witness, and, being duly sworn, deposed, that his brother, Hezekiah Wheat, and himself, inhabited and cultivated the land now claimed by Hiram Mounger, in the year 1795 or 1796, and that the same has been cultivated and inhabited ever since; that, in the year 1798, his brother, Hezekiah Wheat, exchanged this land with said Mounger for other lands claimed and improved by him, and that the plot, now presented by Hiram Mounger to the board, exhibits correct view of the land claimed by him, and that he lives within the limits of his claim and survey.

The board ordered that the case be postponed for consideration.

SAMPSON MOUNGER's case, No. 13 on the docket of the Board, and No. 35 on the books of the Register.

Claim.—A donation of six hundred and thirty-four acres under the second section of the act.

The claimant presented his claim, together with a surveyor's plot of the land claimed, in the words and figures following, to wit:

To the Commissioners appointed in pursuance of the act of Congress, passed the 3d day of March, 1803, for receiving and adjusting the claims to lands south of the Tennessee and east of Pearl river.

Please to take notice, that the following tract of land, situated on Mill creek, bounded as follows, viz.: beginning at a red oak corner; thence, south, fifty-four degrees east, seventy chains; thence, south, thirty degrees west, eighty chains, to a pine corner; thence, north, fifty-four degrees west, eighty-three chains, to an oak corner; thence, north, thirty-six degrees east, fifty-three chains, to a pine corner; thence, south, sixty-four degrees east, thirteen chains; thence, north, thirty-two degrees east, twenty-five chains, to the beginning: having such marks, natural and artificial, as are represented in the plot annexed, containing six hundred and thirty-four acres; is claimed by Sampson Mounger, under and by virtue of the second section of the act, bearing date 3d March, 1803: the said Mounger claims no other lands in the territory, and now exhibited unto the register of the land office established east of Pearl river, to be recorded as directed by said act. To all which he begs leave to refer, as also to the copy of the plot herewith filed.

SAMPSON MOUNGER.
[Plot omitted.]

Surveyed by Thomas Bilbo for Sampson Mounger, 9th February, 1804. Chain carriers, George Brewer and Osburn Brewer.

THOMAS BILBO.

Entered in record of claims, vol. 1, page 91, by EDWARD LLOYD WAILES, for

JOSEPH CHAMBERS, Register.

John Brewer, George Brewer, Jun., and, Hiram Mounger, were produced as witnesses, and, being duly sworn, the said John and Hiram deposed, that Sampson Mounger built upon the tract of land claimed and represented by the plot exhibited to the board, in the year 1797; and that he was at that time the head of a family.

Question. Do you know that this land is claimed by a British or Spanish claim?

Answer. We do not.

The said George deposed, that Sampson Mounger built upon the tract of land claimed in the fall of the year 1797, and that he planted and cultivated within the limits of the same in the year 1798.

GEORGE BREWER, Jun. attorney for the heirs or legal representatives of William Brewer, deceased; case No. 14 on the docket of the board, and No. 37 on the books of the register.

Claim.—A donation of five hundred and ninety-four acres under the second section of the act.

The claimant, as attorney aforesaid, presented his claim, together with a surveyor's plot of the land claimed, in the following words and figures, to wit:

To the Commissioners appointed in pursuance of the act of Congress, passed the 3d day of March, 1803, for receiving and adjusting the claims to lands south of the Tennessee, and east of Pearl river.

Please to take notice, that the following tract of land, situated on the Tombigbee, beginning at a cypress corner, made conditional between Sullivant and the party, on a lake, known by Sullivant's landing, on the island by the name of the Three Rivers, and running south, eighty degrees east, seventy-nine chains fifty links; thence, north, ten degrees east, to Tombigbee, and up the said river to a cut-off; thence, with the cut-off to said lake, across on the west side of said lake; and thence, south, seventy degrees west, to an old line; and thence, south, fifty-one degrees west, with the said line to a black oak; thence, north, fifty-five degrees east, to the beginning cypress: having such marks, natural and artificial, as are represented in the plot annexed, containing five hundred and ninety-four acres, and is claimed by the heirs of William Brewer, Sen. deceased, under and by virtue of the second section, to wit, a donation title; and now exhibited unto the register of the land office established east of Pearl river, to be recorded as directed by said act. To all which they beg leave to refer, as also to the copy of the plot herewith filed.

GEORGE BREWER, Jun.,
Attorney in fact for the heirs.
MARCH, 15, 1804.
[Plot omitted.]

The above survey was surveyed the 23d of February, in the year 1804, per me, Robert Ligon, for the heirs of William Brewer, deceased, beginning on a cypress, at a landing on the east side of said lake, known by the name of Sullivant's landing, in the island known by the name of the Three River island, and running south, eighty degrees east, seventy-nine chains and fifty links; thence, north, ten degrees east, to Tombigbee, and up the said river to a cut-off; thence with the cut-off to said lake, across on the west side of said lake; and thence, south, seventy degrees west, to an old line; and thence, south, fifty-one degrees west, with the said line, to black oak; thence. south, thirty-five degrees east, to white oak, on one of the small creeks; and thence, north, fifty-five degrees east, to the beginning cypress.

You, Wiley Barker and William Barker, do solemnly swear that you have faithfully executed the employment of chain-carriers, without favor or affection, to the best of your skill and ability: so help you God.

WILLIAM H. HARGRAVE, J. P.

For the Three River tract, for the heirs of William Brewer, deceased. ROBERT LIGON, Surveyor.

FEBRUARY 1st, 1793.

Articles of agreement made and agreed upon, by and between George Brewer and Owen Sulliven, respecting his lands and possessions in the island.

The said Brewer agrees, if the said Sulliven will go and take possession of his houses and cleared land, and keep possession until the said Brewer call for the same again for himself, to give the said Sulliven half the land in the island; Sulliven to begin at the lower end of Mr. Brewer's old clearing; the island to be divided in the middle; Brewer to keep the upper end, and Sullivan the lower end of the said island of lands, lying at the mouth of the Three Rivers, over the lake. The above conditions are agreed upon by us.

GEO. BREWER,
OWEN SULLIVEN, his × mark.

N. B. And further agrees that, let Sulliven build a house on any part of the land, he would not dispossess him.

Entered in record of claims, vol. 1, page 94, by EDWARD LLOYD WAILES, for

JOSEPH CHAMBERS, *Register.*

Wiley Barker, Richard Brashears, and Robert Ligon, surveyor, were produced as witnesses; and, being duly sworn, the said Barker deposed, that William Brewer inhabited and cultivated the land now claimed in the year 1793 or 1794, and that he died previous to the year 1797, and that this land was not cultivated by any of his family in the year 1797, or since; and that he heard Owen Sulliven and George Brewer, Jun. for the representatives of William Brewer, deceased, agree upon a conditional line, mentioned in the notice, and upon a cypress for the corner tree to this line; and that said Sullivan and Brewer agreed that Brewer's heirs should have the land lying above, or on the north side of the conditional line; and that Owen Sulliven should have the land lying below, or on the south side of this line.

The said Brashears deposed, that William Brewer, deceased, inhabited and cultivated the land now claimed in the year 1792; that he died in the year 1793, or 1794; that Owen Sulliven inhabited and cultivated the same land for the representatives of William Brewer, deceased, as by an agreement between George Brewer and said Sulliven may more fully appear; and that Owen Sullivan continued to inhabit and cultivate this land until within one or two years last past, when he died; that he saw the articles of agreement, now presented to the board, between George Brewer and Owen Sullivan, signed and delivered for the purposes therein mentioned; and that he also saw James Bilbo subscribe the same as a witness.

Robert Ligon, surveyor, deposed, that the plot now exhibited by George Brewer for donation to the heirs of William Brewer, deceased, represents a correct view, natural and artificial, of the land so claimed.

The board ordered that the case be postponed for consideration.

SOLOMON WHEAT'S case, No. 15 on the docket of the board, and No. 36 on the books of the register.

Claim.—A donation of two hundred and fifty-seven acres and one hundred and thirty-eight poles, under the second section of the act.

The claimant presented his claim, together with a surveyor's plot of the land claimed, in the words and figures following, to wit:

To the Commissioners appointed in pursuance of the act of Congress, passed the 3d day of March, 1803, for receiving and adjusting the claims to lands south of Tennessee and east of Pearl river.

Please to take notice, that the following tract of land, situated on the waters of Bassett's creek, in Washington county, beginning on a pine, and running north, sixty degrees east, twenty-five chains; thence, south, thirty degrees east, sixty chains, to a lake; thence, five chains, to a hackberry station, twenty-six chains and fifty links to a large sycamore, fifteen chains to the corner white oak; thence, south, sixty degrees west; twenty-three chains, to the beginning; containing two hundred and fifty-seven acres and one hundred and thirty-eight poles, having such shape, form, and marks, both natural and artificial, as are represented in the plot herewith filed; is claimed by Solomon Wheat, in and by virtue of the second section of said act, as a donation. To all which he begs leave to refer, as also to a copy of the plot herewith filed.

SOLOMON WHEAT, his × mark.

MARCH 15, 1804.

[Plot omitted.]

FEBRUARY 22d, 1804.

Then surveyed for Solomon Wheat, of Washington county, Mississippi territory, under a donation claim of land, two hundred and fifty-seven acres and one hundred and thirty-eight poles: beginning at a pine running north, sixty degrees east, twenty-five chains, to a pine; thence, south, thirty degrees east, sixty-five chains, to a lake; thence, to a fore-and-aft hackberry, five chains;

thence to a cypress, twenty-six chains and fifty links, to a cypress pond; thence, to a white oak corner, fifteen chains and fifty links; thence, south, sixty degrees west, ninety-seven chains to Scot's beginning corner; thence, north, forty-one degrees west, fifteen chains, to the beginning.

WILLIAM GILLIAM.

Chain carriers, Benjamin Harrison and Thomas Goodwin.

Entered in record of claims, vol. 1, page 93, by EDWARD LLOYD WAILES, for

JOSEPH CHAMBERS, *Register.*

This may certify that Benjamin Harrison and Thomas Goodwin came before me, and made oath that they were chain bearers to William Gilliam, on a survey of a tract of land surveyed for Solomon Wheat, and that they gave a true account of the admeasurement as such. Given under my hand, this 15th day of March, 1804.

JAMES CALLER, *J. P.*

Sampson Mounger, Hiram Mounger, Ephraim Barker, and Richard Brashear, were produced as witnesses, and, being duly sworn, the said Hiram deposed, that, in the year 1796, or 1797, he commenced to clear, and did clear, about two acres of land; and, on the 10th day of September, he went to the State of Georgia, for the purpose of assisting his father to remove to the settlement on the Tombigbee river; and, in October, 1797, he returned to this country; in the year 1798, he exchanged the land by him claimed, with Solomon and Hezekiah Wheat, for another tract of land claimed by them; and that the plot now exhibited by Solomon Wheat is a true representation of the land by him now claimed, also of a part of the land transferred by him to Solomon and Hezekiah Wheat; and that Solomon and Hezekiah Wheat have divided the improvement, by a conditional line made between them, as they have both told him; further, that they both intend claiming a donation under and in virtue of the labor and improvement made by him in 1796, or 1797; that he was at that time twenty-one years of age.

Question. Do you know of any British or Spanish claim for this land?

Answer. I do not.

The said Barker deposed, that Hiram Mounger did clear some land on the tract now claimed by Solomon Wheat, in the year 1797, and that he was at that time, and has continued to be, an inhabitant of this country, and was twenty-one years of age; and further, that he has heard said Mounger say that he exchanged said improvement and claim with Solomon and Hezekiah Wheat, for other lands claimed and improved by them.

The said Brashear deposed, that he saw Hiram Mounger clearing land, in the year 1797, on the tract now claimed by Solomon Wheat, and that said Mounger told him that he had exchanged this improvement and claim to this land with Solomon and Hezekiah Wheat, for other lands claimed and improved by them; and that Solomon Wheat now inhabits and cultivates within the limits of this claim and survey; further, that he believes that Hiram Mounger was, at the time of his settlement, twenty-one years of age.

The said Sampson Mounger deposed, that his son Hiram Mounger was born in the year 1772.

The board ordered that the case be postponed for consideration.

RICHARD BRASHEAR'S case, No. 16 on the docket of the Board, and No. 55 on the books of the Register.

Claim.—A donation of six hundred and forty acres, under the second section of act.

The claimant, as assignee and legal representative of Patrick Brewer, presented his claim, together with a surveyor's plot, of the land claimed, in the words and figures following to wit:

To the Commissioners appointed, pursuant to the act of Congress, the 3d March, 1803, for receiving and adjusting claims to lands south of Tennessee and east of Pearl river.

Please to take notice, that the following tract of land is claimed by Richard Brashear, of Washington county, Mississippi territory, under and in virtue of a settlement made by Patrick Brewer, in June, 1797, transferred by said Brewer to Sampson Mounger, 1798, and by said Mounger to James Denley in the same year, and by said Denley to George Dickey, in 1799, and by said Dickey to this claimant in May, 1800, bounded as follows, to wit: beginning on a white oak, and running north, thirty degrees west, eighty chains, to a tupelo gum; thence,

76

south, sixty degrees west, eighty chains to a pine; thence, south, thirty degrees east, eighty chains, to a pine; thence, north, sixty degrees east, eighty chains, to the beginning; including in said lines six hundred and forty acres, now delivered to the register of the land office to be established east of Pearl river, to be recorded as directed by said act. To all which he begs leave to refer, as also to the copy of the plot herewith filed.

RICHARD BRASHEAR.

MARCH 15th, 1804.

[Plot omitted.]

The above is justly and truly laid off by me, ROBERT LIGON.

Laid off the 14th July, 1803, for Richard Brashear, beginning on a white oak, and running north, thirty degrees west, eighty chains, to a tupelo gum; and from thence, south, sixty degrees west, eighty chains, to a pine; and thence, south, thirty degrees east, eighty chains, to a pine; thence, north, sixty degrees east, eighty chains; to beginning: including in said lines six hundred and forty acres; at the time of the survey, it was bounded by adjacent and undefined claims, including part of a claim held by Watley, and also the public ground, as the place appointed for the seat of justice in Wahington county.

Entered in record of claims, vol. 1, page 165, by EDWARD LLOYD WAILES, for

JOSEPH CHAMBERS, Register.

MISSISSIPPI TERRITORY, Washington County:

This day came before me John Denley, and, being duly sworn, says that he carried the chain for Richard Brashear's land, without favor or affection, to the best of his skill and ability, so help him God. March 12th, 1804.

WILLIAM H. HARGRAVE, J. P.

MISSISSIPPI TERRITORY, Washington County, ss.

I, David Gains, do swear that I have faithfully executed the office of chain carrier, to a survey of land made by Robert Ligon, and claimed by Richard Brashear. Sworn before me, this 10th of March, 1804.

JOHN MURRELL, J. P.

ROBERT LIGON, Surveyor.

Sampson Mounger and Hiram Mounger were produced as witnesses, and, being duly sworn, the said Hiram deposed, that, in the year 1797, Patrick Brewer built upon the tract of land claimed and represented by the plot exhibited to the board, and cultivated upon the same. Knows that he was the head of a family previous to this time; and believes that he continued to be so in the year 1797, and that he was twenty-one years of age; that he has heard Patrick Brewer acknowledge that he transferred his right of claim to this land to Sampson Mounger, and Sampson Mounger that he transferred his right of claim to James Denley, and James Denley that he transferred his right to George Dickey, and George Dickey that he transferred his right of claim to Richard Brashear, at the several dates as specified in the notice of claim, now exhibited by the said Brashear for the said tract; and that the said Brashear has remained in the possession of the same ever since.

The said Sampson deposed, that he purchased from Patrick Brewer, in the year 1798, and, in the same year, transferred the same to James Denley; further, that I know the said Brewer to have been the head of a family, and twenty-one years of age.

Question. Do you know whether there is any British or Spanish claim for this land?

Answer. We do not know of any.

The Board ordered that the case be postponed for consideration.

MICAJAH WALL's case, No. 17 on the docket of the Board, and No. 39 on the books of the Register.

Claim.—A right of pre-emption to three hundred and twenty acres and five-eighths of an acre, under the third section of the act.

The claimant presented his claim, together with a surveyor's plot of the land claimed in the following words and figures, to wit:

To the Commissioners appointed in pursuance of the act of Congress passed the 3d day of March, 1803, for receiving and adjusting claims to lands south of Tennessee and east of Pearl river.

Please to take notice, that the following tract of land, situated on Smith's creek, in the county of Washington, beginning at James Morgan's northeast corner stake and

pine, and runs north, seventy-three and a half degrees west, two hundred and seventy poles, to a small post oak, James Morgan's northwest corner; thence, north, sixteen and a half degrees east, one hundred and ninety poles, crossing the spring branch to a small black-jack corner; thence, south, seventy-three and a half degrees east, crossing spring branch, two hundred and seventy poles, to a light wood stake corner; from thence, a direct line to the beginning, containing three hundred and twenty acres and five-eighths of an acre; is claimed by Micajah Wall, in and by virtue of the third section of the said act, as a pre-emption: having such shape, form, and marks, both natural and artificial, as are fully represented in the plot annexed, and is now exhibited to the register of the land office, established east of Pearl river, to be recorded as directed by said act. To all which he begs leave to refer, as also to a copy of the plot herewith filed.

MICAJAH WALL.

MARCH 15, 1804.

[Plot omitted.]

Surveyed for Micajah Wall a tract of land, containing three hundred and twenty and five-eighths acres, lying in Washington county, on the waters of Smith's creek; beginning at James Morgan's northeast corner stake and pine corner; and runs north, seventy-three and a half degrees west, two hundred and seventy poles, to a small post oak, James Morgan's northwest corner: thence, north, sixteen and a half degrees east, one hundred and ninety poles, crossing his spring branch, to a small black-jack corner; thence, south, seventy-three and a half degrees east, crossing another spring branch, two hundred and seventy poles, to a light wood stake corner; and from thence a direct line to the beginning. Surveyed 1st February, 1804, by

J. MALONE.

Entered in record of claims, vol. 1, page 100, by EDWARD LLOYD WAILES, for

JOSEPH CHAMBERS, Register.

Sampson Mounger and George Brewer were produced as witnesses, and being duly sworn, deposed, that Micajah Wall, the present claimant, has inhabited and cultivated the land represented by the plot now exhibited to the Board, more than two years last past; and, during this whole time, hath been at the head of a family.

Question. Do you know of any British, Spanish, or donation claim for this land?

Sampson Mounger.—I do not know of any, but have heard that John McGrew claims the same, in virtue of a donation.

George Brewer.—John McGrew has told me, that he claims this land by virtue of a donation.

The board ordered that the case be postponed for consideration; then adjourned until Friday, the 16th instant.

FRIDAY, March 16, 1804.

The board met according to adjournment. Present: Ephraim Kirby, Robert C. Nicholas, Joseph Chambers.

RICHARD LEE's case, No. 18 on the docket of the Board and No. 44 on the books of the Register.

Claim.—A donation of six hundred and forty acres, as assignee and legal representative of Jordan Morgan, under the second section of the act.

The claimant presented his claim, together with a surveyor's plot of the land claimed, in the following words and figures, to wit:

To the Commissioners appointed in pursuance of the act of Congress, passed the 3d day of March, 1803, for receiving and adjusting claims south of the Tennessee and east of Pearl river.

Please to take notice, that the following tract of land, beginning at a small hickory, upon a line run by Thomas Bilbo for James Denley, on his tract, lying above or north of Thomas Wheat's land; and running thence, south, eighty-five degrees west, seven chains, to a pine; thence, north, fifty-five degrees west, seventy-five chains, to a hickory; thence, north, twelve degrees west, sixty-four chains, to a water oak; thence, east, eighty chains, to a white oak; and thence, south, to the beginning, one hundred and four chains; including in said lines six hundred and forty acres of land; bounded on the east by lands of James Denley and John Brewer, on the south by lands of John Brewer, on all other sides by adjacent undefined claims. This land is claimed by Richard Lee, of Washington county, Mississippi territory, under and in virtue of a settlement made by Jordan Morgan, in the month of August, or early in September, 1797, and sold by said Morgan to William Vardeman in the year 1799, and by John Caller, Esq., in behalf of said Vardeman, to this reporter, in the year 1801, April 16th; now delivered to the register of the land office to be established east of Pearl river, to be recorded as directed by said act. To all which he begs leave to refer, as also to the copy of the plot herewith filed.

R. LEE.

MARCH 14, 1804.

[Plot omitted.]

The annexed survey was made the 10th of March, 1804, by the undersigned, for Richard Lee, having such marks, natural and artificial, as the above plot represents, beginning at a small hickory, upon a line run by Thomas Bilbo for James Denley, on his tract lying above or north of Thomas Wheat's land; and running thence, south, eighty-five degrees west, seven chains, to a pine; thence, north, fifty-five degrees west, seventy-five chains, to a hickory; thence, north, twelve degrees west, sixty-four chains, to a water oak; thence, east, eighty chains to a white oak; and thence, south, to the beginning; one hundred and four chains, bounded on the east by lands of James Denley and John Brewer, on the south by lands of John Brewer, on all other sides by adjacent undefined claims. This land surveyed for a donation claim.

ROBERT LIGON, Surveyor.

Entered in record of claims, vol. 1, page 115, by EDWARD LLOYD WAILES, for

JOSEPH CHAMBERS, Register.

MISSISSIPPI TERRITORY, Washington County, ss:

Personally appeared before me, one of the Justices of the Peace, for said county, George Dickney and James Donnelly, who, after being duly sworn, say that they have this day truly and honestly performed the duty of chain carriers, in a survey of land claimed by Richard Lee, in the Sunflower neck.

Sworn before me, this 10th day of March, 1804.

WILLIAM H. HARGRAVE, J. P.

ROBERT LIGON, Surveyor.

Richard Brashear, Ephraim Barker, and Solomon Wheat, were produced as witnesses, and, being duly sworn, the said Brashear deposed, that, in 1797, Jordan Morgan inhabited and cleared upon the land now claimed by Richard Lee, under and by virtue of a habitation and improvement made by the said Morgan; also, that said Morgan has told me that he had, for a valuable consideration, transferred the land to William Vardeman; and that, immediately upon Morgan's quitting the habitation and improvement of this land, William Vardeman entered upon the same; and that Morgan was at that time twenty-one years of age.

The said Barker deposed, that, he believed that, in the year 1797, Jordan Morgan inhabited and improved the land now claimed by Richard Lee, in virtue of a purchase under Morgan; and that said Morgan has told me he transferred his right to the land now claimed to William Vardeman for a valuable consideration; and that, immediately upon Morgan's quitting the said habitation and improvement, William Vardeman entered thereon; and that Jordan Morgan was at that time twenty-one years of age.

The said Wheat deposed, that, in the year 1797, Jordan Morgan inhabited and improved the land now claimed by Richard Lee, in virtue of a purchase under said Morgan.

The Board ordered that the case be postponed for consideration.

WILEY BARKER's case, No. 19 on the docket of the Board, and No. 56 on the books of the Register.

Claim.—A donation of six hundred and forty acres, as legal representative to Daniel Barker, deceased, under the second section of the act.

The claimant presented his claim, together with a surveyor's plot of the land claimed, in the words and figures following, to wit:

To the Commissioners appointed pursuant to the act of Congress, passed the 3d of March, 1803, for receiving and adjusting claims to lands south of the Tennessee and east of Pearl river.

Please to take notice, that the following tract of land is claimed by Wiley Barker, of Washington county, Mississippi territory, by virtue of a legacy of Daniel Barker, deceased, to which the settlement was made by the said Daniel Barker, and held until 1803, and held in occupation until this period, to wit: beginning on a tupelo gum and conditional line made between James

Coplen, deceased, and Daniel Barker, deceased, and running south, sixty degrees west, eighty chains and fifty links, to a sweet gum; and from thence, north, thirty degrees west, seventy-nine chains fifty links, to a post oak; and from thence, north, sixty degrees east, eighty chains fifty links, to an ash; and thence, south, thirty degrees east, seventy-nine chains fifty links, to the beginning tupelo gum; including in said lines six hundred and forty acres, now delivered to the Register of the Land Office established east of Pearl river, to be recorded as directed by said act. To all which he begs leave to refer, as also to the copy of the plot hereunto filed.

WILEY BARKER,
Legatee of Daniel Barker.

MARCH 15, 1804.

[Plot omitted.]

The above survey was surveyed the 24th February, 1804, per me, Robert Ligon, for the legatees of Daniel Barker, deceased, beginning on a tupelo gum, and running south, sixty degrees west, eighty chains fifty links, to black gum; and thence, north, thirty degrees west, seventy-nine chains fifty links, to post oak; thence, north, sixty degrees east, eighty chains fifty links, ash; thence, to the beginning tupelo gum; lying on the northeast by lands called Caller's, and on the northwest, and northeast, and southeast, on vacant land. Surveyed by me,

ROBERT LIGON.

N. B. The said land lies opposite the upper end of what is called the Three River Island.

Chain carriers, John Brewer, William Barker.

Entered in record of claims, vol. 1, page 167, by EDWARD LLOYD WAILES, for

JOSEPH CHAMBERS, Register.

You, John Brewer and William Barker, do solemnly swear that you have executed the employment of chain carriers, without favor or affection, to the best of your skill and ability: so help you God.

WILLIAM H. HARGRAVE, J. P.

ROBERT LIGON, Surveyor.

John Brewer, Esq. Ephraim Barker, and Richard Brashear, were produced as witnesses, and, being duly sworn, the said Brewer and Brashear deposed, that Daniel Barker, in the year 1797, commenced to cultivate and improve the land now claimed by Wiley Barker, in virtue of a legacy, and that he continued to inhabit the same until the year 1803, when he died; also, that he cultivated the same from the year 1798, until his death; and that he was twenty-one years of age at the date of his settlement.

The said Ephraim Barker deposed, that he was present at the death of his son, Daniel Barker, and that he heard him give to Wiley Barker the land now claimed a short time previous to his decease; and that Daniel Barker then requested him particularly to take notice that it was his will and desire that all his right and interest in this land should be vested in Wiley Barker, and that he was twenty-one years of age at the time of his settlement, which was in the year 1797; and that Daniel Barker departed this life in the year 1803, and that the present claimant immediately entered into the possession and cultivation of this land, and has continued in the possession and cultivation thereof ever since.

The board ordered that the case be postponed for consideration.

WYCHE WATLEY's case, No. 20 on the docket of the Board, and No. 54 on the books of the Register.

Claim.—A right of pre-emption of one hundred and thirty-four acres, as assignee and legal representative of Rebecca Kimbre, under the third section of the act.

The claimant presented his claim, together with a surveyor's plot of the land claimed, in the following words and figures, to wit:

To the Commissioners appointed in pursuance of the act of Congress passed the 3d day of March, 1803, for receiving and adjusting claims south of the Tennessee and east of Pearl river.

Please to take notice that the following tract of land, situated on the east side of the Sunflower creek, near the seat of justice for Washington county, beginning on a black oak, and running south, twenty-three degrees west, fifty-four chains to a pine on the above creek; and thence, down the said creek, south, sixty-three-degrees east, eight chains, to a pine, one-eighth of a mile from said seat of justice; and thence, north, fifty-two degrees east, thirty-six chains, to a pine; and thence, south, fifty-five degrees east, seven chains, to pine; thence, north, fifty-two degrees east, one chain, to a post oak, to a line of Richard Lee's, and ¦with the said line four chains to the said Lee's corner; thence, north, twelve degrees west, thirty chains, to swamp on stake; thence, south, eighty-six degrees west, twenty-five chains, to the beginning black oak; including in said lines one hundred and thirty-four acres, and also the two improvements made by Mrs. Kimbre. This land is claimed by Wyche Watley, of Washington county, Mississippi territory, now delivered to the Register of the Land Office to be established east of Pearl river, to be recorded as directed by said act. To all which he begs leave to refer, as also to the copy of the plot hereunto filed.

WYCHE WATLEY.

MARCH 15, 1804.

[Plot omitted.]

The above survey was completed the 9th day of March by me, Lobert Ligon, for Wyche Watley, claimed by pre-emption, having such forms and marks, natural and artificial, as the above plot represents; beginning on the lake on a black oak, and running south, twenty-three degrees west, fifty-four chains, near the Sunflower creek; and from thence, south, sixty-three degrees east, eight chains; and thence, north, fifty-two degrees east, thirty-six chains; south, fifty-five degrees east, seven chains; thence, north, fifty two degrees east, nine chains; thence, north, sixty degrees west, four chains, with Lee's line; thence running north, twelve degrees west, thirty chains, with said Lee's line, to Cypress swamp; thence, south, eighty-six degrees west, twenty-five chains, to the beginning, running into Brashear's line.

Entered in record of claims, vol. 1, page 163, by EDWARD LLOYD WAILES, for

JOSEPH CHAMBERS, Register.

MARCH 10, 1803.

This day came before me James Donley and James Danley, and swore that they faithfully and truly carried the chain for to survey a tract of land for Wyche Watley, without favor or affection, to the best of their skill and ability: so help them God.

WILLIAM H. HARGRAVE, J. P.

ROBERT LIGON, Surveyor.

The said Watley produced a deed of conveyance from Rebecca Kimbre, bearing date the 9th day of October, 1802, duly executed, assigning, relinquishing, and conveying to the said Watley all the said Kimbre's right, title, and claim to said tract of land and the improvements made thereon.

Hiram Mounger, Ephraim Barker, Wiley Barker, and Richard Brashears, were produced as witnesses, and being duly sworn, the said Mounger deposed, that Rebecca Kimbre, in the year 1802, inhabited and cultivated on the land now claimed by Wyche Watley, as her representative; that, in the fall or winter of the same year, Mrs. Kimbre removed from and ceased to cultivate this land; and that the said land and improvement remained uncultivated and unoccupied from the time that Mrs. Kimbre left the same, until the month of December or January, 1803, when the said Wyche Watley occupied and commenced the further cultivation thereof; and that Mrs. Kimbre was the head of a family.

Question. At what time did Mr. Watley set out for the purpose of removing his family to the settlements on the Tombigbee, and at what time did he return with them?

Answer. He set out in the spring of the year 1803, and returned to this settlement with them in the fall or winter of the same year.

The said Ephraim Barker deposed that he knew nothing about the settlement made by Mrs. Kimbre.

The said Wiley Barker deposed, that he knew nothing, of his own knowledge, of the settlement made by Mrs. Kimbre.

The said Brashear deposed, that Rebecca Kimbre inhabited and cultivated the land now claimed in the year 1802, and that she was at that time the head of a family.

Question. Did you see Rebecca Kimbre sign and deliver, for the purpose therein mentioned, the instrument now presented to the Board, purporting to be a transfer from Rebecca Kimbre to Wyche Watley of the land now claimed, and did you see John Denley subscribe to the same as a witness?

Answer. I did.

Question put to Hiram Mounger. Was the land delivered to Mr. Watley or his agent by Mrs. Kimbre, and at what time?

Answer. Rebecca Kimbre, in the month of October, 1802, delivered the land now claimed to me, as the agent of Wyche Watley, and for his use and benefit.

The Board ordered that the case be postponed for consideration.

JOHN BREWER's case, No. 21 on the docket of the Board, and No.——on the books of the Register.

Claim.—A donation of six hundred and forty acres, under the second section of the act.

The claimant presented his claim, together with a surveyor's plot of the land claimed, in the following words and figures, to wit:

To the Commissioners appointed pursuant to the act of Congress passed on the 3d of March, 1803, for receiving and adjusting of claims to lands south of the Tennessee and east of Pearl river.

Please to take notice, that the following tract of land, to wit: beginning on an ironwood, upon a line of the heirs of Charles Brewer, and running south, seventy degrees east, forty chains; thence squaring the course each way, lying on the south side of the land claimed by said heirs, and the same distance on the north side of Johnson's creek; this land is claimed by John Brewer, of Washington county, Mississippi territory, under and by virtue of a settlement made by this claimant in June, 1797, now delivered to the Register of the Land Office to be established east of Pearl river, to be recorded as directed by said act. To all which he begs leave to refer; as also to the plot herewith filed.

JNO. BREWER.

MARCH 15, 1804.

[Plot omitted.]

The above admeasurement is truly taken and laid down per me, Robert Ligon, this 15th day of February, 1804, beginning on the corner of the orphans of Charles Brewer, and running eighty chains each way, lying on the south side of said tract, and on the north side of Johnson's creek.

Chain carriers, Wiley Roberts, James Danley.

Entered in record of claims, vol. 1, page——, by EDWARD LLOYD WAILES, for

JOSEPH CHAMBERS, Register.

You, James Danley and Wiley Roberts, do solemnly swear that you have faithfully and truly executed the employment of chain carriers, without favor or affection: so help you God.

WILEY ROBERTS.
JAMES DANLEY.

WILLIAM H. HARGRAVE, J. P.

ROBERT LIGON, Surveyor.

Richard Brashear and Hiram Mounger were produced as witnesses, and being duly sworn, did depose, that, in the year 1797, John Brewer inhabited and cultivated the land now claimed, and has continued to inhabit and cultivate the same ever since; also, that he was at the time of his settlement the head of a family.

The board ordered that the case be postponed for consideration.

FIGURES LEWIS's case, No. 22 on the docket of the Board, and No. —— on the books of the Register.

Claim.—A right of pre-emption of one hundred and twenty-nine acres, and thirty-six poles, under the third section of the act.

The claimant presented his claim, together with a surveyor's plot of the land claimed, in the following words and figures, to wit:

To the Commissioners appointed in pursuance of the act of Congress passed the 3d day of March, 1803, for receiving and adjusting the claims to lands south of the Tennessee and east of Pearl river.

Please to take notice, that the following tract of land, situate on the west side of Tombigbee river, and on the west side of the most westerly prong of the Three Rivers, butted and bounded as follows, viz: beginning at a tupelo gum, and over cup oak, standing on the west bank of the western prong of the Three Rivers, a little above Barker's landing, in an old line, running on the old line south, fifty degrees west, forty-three chains and seventy-five links, to a turkey oak corner; thence, south, thirty-three degrees east, forty-six chains and thirty links, to a water oak station; thence, course continued, fifteen chains and forty-five links, to a sweet gum corner; thence, south, ten degrees east, eleven chains, to a sweet gum station; thence, course continued, five chains and fifty links, to a water oak corner, standing on the north bank of Sullivan's creek; thence, down the meanders of said creek, south, seventy-five degrees east, nine chains, to the mouth, where it makes into the before mentioned Three Rivers; thence, up the meanders of the said west prong of Three Rivers, to the beginning; having such marks, natural and artificial, as are represented in the plot annexed, containing one hundred and twenty-nine acres and thirty-six poles, is claimed by Figures Lewis, of Washington county, as a pre-emption, under and by virtue of a settlement made by him, the said F. Lewis, on or about the 1st of December, 1803, and now exhibited unto the Register of the Land Office established east of Pearl river, to be recorded as directed by said act. To all which he begs leave to refer, as also to the copy of the plot herewith filed.

FIGURES LEWIS.

[Plot omitted.]

Surveyed for Figures Lewis, of Washington county, one hundred and twenty-nine acres and thirty-six poles of land, which represents the above plot, lying and being in the county of Washington, and on the west side of Tombigbee river, and on the west side of the most westerly prong of the Three Rivers, butted and bounded as followeth, viz: beginning at tupelo gum, and over cup oak, standing on the west bank of the western prong of the Three Rivers, a little above Barker's landing, in an old line, running on the old line, south, fifty degrees west, forty-three chains and seventy-five links, to a turkey oak corner; thence, south, thirty-three degrees east, forty-six chains and thirty links to a water oak station; thence, course continued, fifteen chains and forty-five links, to a sweet gum corner; thence, south, ten degrees east, eleven chains. to a sweet gum station; thence, course continued, five chains and fifty links, to a wateroak corner, standing on the north bank of Sullivan's creek; thence, down the meanders of said creek, south, seventy-four degrees east, nine chains, to the mouth, where it makes in to the before mentioned Three Rivers; thence, up the meanders of said west prong of Three Rivers, to the beginning.

Surveyed the 1st day of March, 1804, by me,

WILLIAM GILLIAM.

Chain carriers, Wiley Barker, and William Barker.
Entered in record of claims, vol. 1, page ——, by
EDWARD LLOYD WAILES, for
JOSEPH CHAMBERS, Register.

MISSISSIPPI TERRITORY, Washington County, ss:

This day came before me, Figures Lewis, one of the Justices of the Peace for said county, Wiley Barker, and William Barker, chain carriers, and made oath, that they would do justice, and render a true account of the outs in measuring round a tract of land surveyed by Mr. Gilliam for me. Given under my hand, this 2d of March, 1804.

FIGURES LEWIS, J P.

Wiley Barker and Ephraim Barker were produced as witnesses, and, being duly sworn, they deposed, that, in the month of December, 1803, Figures Lewis commenced to build and improve the land now claimed, and has inhabited and cultivated the same ever since; and that he was at that time the head of a family.

Question. Do you know whether this land is claimed by any British, Spanish, or donation claim?

Answer. We do not know of any British or Spanish claim, but do know that all, or the greater part thereof, is claimed by the representatives of William Brewer, deceased, in virtue of a donation claim.

The Board ordered that the case be postponed for consideration.

GEORGE BREWER, Jun., case, No. 23 on the docket of the Board, and No. 62 on the books of the Register.

Claim.—A donation of six hundred and twenty acres, as assignee and legal representative of James Watkins under the second section of the act.

The claimant presented his claim, together with a surveyor's plot of the land claimed, in the words and figures following, to wit:

To the Commissioners appointed in pursuance of the act of Congress passed the 3d of March, 1803, to receive and adjust the claims to lands south of Tennessee and east of Pearl river.

MISSISSIPPI TERRITORY, Washington County:
March 6, 1804.

Please to take notice, that the following tract of land, situated on Bassett's creek, butting and bounded as fol

lows: beginning on a red oak corner, on the lower line of George Brewer's Spanish claim, south, fifty-four degrees east, seventy chains, to a corner pine, along Mr. Sampson Mounger's line; thence, south, thirty-six degrees west, forty-five chains, to a corner white oak, on said Mounger's line; thence, south, sixty degrees east, forty chains, to a corner pine; thence, north, thirty degrees east, ninety chains, to corner stake; thence, north, sixty degrees west, one hundred and ten chains, to a corner red oak; thence, to the beginning first mentioned, having such marks, natural and artificial, as are represented in the plot annexed, containing six hundred and twenty acres, is claimed by George Brewer, Jun. as the legal representative of James Watkins and George Johnston, under and by virtue of occupancy; the said tract herein specified being inhabited and cultivated, the said claimants legally represented by George Brewer, Jun. on the day of the evacuation of the Spanish troops from this territory, agreeable to the second section of an act of Congress entitled an act, &c. and for a long time previous to that time; and the same does not appear to be claimed by virtue of any of the preceding provisions of the act, and the said claimant, legally represented by George Brewer, claims no other lands in the territory, and now exhibited to the Register of the Land Office established east of Pearl river, to be recorded as directed by said act. All of which he begs leave to refer, as also to the plot hereto fixed.

GEORGE BREWER, JUN.

Surveyed by Thomas Bilbo, February, 1804. Chain carriers, Sampson Mounger, John Hall.

Entered on record of claims, vol. 1, page 181, by
EDWARD LLOYD WAILES, for
JOSEPH CHAMBERS, Register.

[Plot omitted.]

MISSISSIPPI TERRITORY, Washington County:

Appeared before me, Wm. Pierce, one of the Justices for said county, John Hall and Sampson Mounger, and made oath that they rendered a true adjustment of the outs in a survey made by Thomas Bilbo, for Mr. Watkins, as donation right, to George Brewer, Jun., his resentative: as witness my hand and seal.

Sworn before me, the 26th day of March, 1804.

WILLIAM PIERCE, J. P.

Sampson Mounger, and John Caller, Esq. were produced as witnesses, and, being duly sworn, the said Caller deposed, that James Watkins inhabited and improved upon the land now claimed, in the year 1797, and also in the months of March and April, 1798; and that James Watkins was, in the year 1797, twenty-one years of age.

The said Mounger deposed, that James Watkins inhabited and improved upon the land now claimed, in the year 1797, and also in the months of March and April, 1798; and that James Watkins was, in the year 1797, twenty-one years of age. That James Watkins told me that he had transferred his right to the land now claimed unto George Johnston for a valuable consideration, and that immediately after James Watkins quit the possession of the land, and George Johnston entered the possession thereof, that George Johnston has told me, that he had, for a valuable consideration, transferred his right to the land now in question to Alexander McGrew, and I know that said McGrew possessed himself of the same; I have heard Alexander McGrew say that he had, for a valuable consideration, transferred his claim to this land to Julian Castro, and do know that Julian Castro possessed himself thereof. Julian Castro has told me that he had transferred, for a valuable consideration, his right to the same land to George Brewer, Jun., and I do know that said Brewer took possession thereof, in the year 1800 or 1801, and has continued in the possession and improvement thereof ever since.

The Board ordered that the case be postponed for consideration.

JOSIAH SKINNER's case, No. 24 on the docket of the Board, and No. 67 on the books of the Register.

Claim.—A right of pre-emption of one hundred and eighty-five acres, under the second section of the act.

The claimant presented his claim, together with a surveyor's plot of the land claimed, in the following words and figures, to wit:

To the Commissioners appointed in pursuance of the act of Congress passed the 3d day of March, 1803, for receiving and adjusting the claims to lands south of Tennessee and east of Pearl river.

Please to take notice, that the following tract of land, situated on the waters of Tombigbee river, in the county of Washington, beginning on a red oak, being Thomas's corner, and runs thence, south, eighty-six degrees west, forty chains, to a stake; thence, north, forty-five degrees west, fifty chains, to a lightwood stump; thence, south, forty degrees west, one chain and fifty links, to a pine corner; thence, south, thirty-eight degrees east, one hundred and five chains, to a gum corner; thence, south, eighty degrees east, forty chains, to the river; thence, with the river to the beginning; containing one hundred and eighty-five acres, having such shape, form, and marks, both natural and artificial as are represented in the plot annexed, and is now exhibited to the Register of the Land Office established east of Pearl river, to be recorded as directed by said act. To all which he begs leave to refer, as also to a copy of the plot herewith filed, March 16, 1804: the above land is claimed under and by virtue of the third section of said act, as a pre-emption.

JOSIAH SKINNER.
[Plot omitted.]

This plot represents a tract of land surveyed for Josiah Skinner, beginning on a red oak corner, of Thomas Carson's, standing on the bank of Tombigbee river; running thence, south, eighty-six degrees west, forty chains, to a stake on Carson's line; thence north, forty-five degrees west, fifty chains, to a lightwood stump; thence, south, forty degrees west, one chain and fifty links, to a pine; thence, south, thirty-eight degrees east, one hundred and five chains, to a sweet gum; thence, south, eighty degrees east, forty chains, to an ash on the bank of the river; thence, up the various courses of the river, to the beginning; containing one hundred and eighty-five acres.

Surveyed 10th day of March, 1804.

NATT. CHRISTMAS.

Entered in the record of claims, vol. 1, page —, by EDWARD LLOYD WAILES, for
JOSEPH CHAMBERS, Register.

Adam Hollinger and Natt. Christmas were produced as witnesses, and, being duly sworn, they deposed: that Josiah Skinner commenced to inhabit and cultivate the land now claimed in the fall of the year 1802; and do believe that he continued to inhabit and cultivate the same until after the third day of March, 1803; and that he was on said third day of March the head of a family.

The Board ordered that the case be postponed for consideration.

ANNA MOUNGER's case, No. 25 on the docket of the Board, and No. 61 on the books of the Register.

Claim.—A donation of five hundred and four acres, under the second section of the act.

The claimant presented her claim, together with a surveyor's plot of the land claimed, in the following words and figures, to wit:

To the Commissioners appointed in pursuance of the act of Congress, passed the 3d day of March, 1803, for receiving and adjusting the claims to lands south of the Tennessee, and east of Pearl river.

Please to take notice, that the following tract of land, situated on the Tombigbee river, butting and bounding as follows, viz: beginning on a large sycamore, running south, forty-eight degrees west, one hundred and twenty-six chains, forty-nine links, to a pine; thence, north, forty-two degrees west, forty chains, to a pine; thence, north, forty-eight degrees east, one hundred and twenty-six chains, forty-nine links, to a hackberry corner on the river; thence, down the river Tombigbee, to the beginning; having such marks, natural and artificial, as are represented in the plot annexed, containing five hundred and four acres of land; is claimed by Anna Mounger, under and by virtue of occupancy, the said tract therein specified being inhabited and cultivated by the claimant since the year 1797, and she claims no other lands in the territory; and now exhibited to the Register of the Land Office established east of Pearl river, to be recorded, as directed by said act. To all which she begs leave to refer, as also to the copy of the plot herewith filed.

ANNA MOUNGER.
[Plot omitted.]

Surveyed by Thomas Bilbo, for Anna Mounger. Chain carriers, George Brewer, Jun. and John Hall. Entered in record of claims, vol. 1, page 179, by EDWARD LLOYD WAILES, for
JOSEPH CHAMBERS, Register.

MISSISSIPPI TERRITORY, Washington County:

Appeared before me, William Pierce, one of the Justices for the said county, John Hall, and made oath that he rendered a true adjustment of the outs as chain carrier in a survey made by Thomas Bilbo for Anna Mounger as donation right: as witness my hand and seal. Sworn before me, this twenty-sixth day of March, 1804.
WILLIAM PIERCE, J. P.

MISSISSIPPI TERRITORY, Washington County:

Personally appeared before me George Brewer, and made oath, that he carried the chain for a tract of land, surveyed for Anna Mounger, to the best of his knowledge. Given under my hand, March 30th, 1804. Sworn to before
JON. CALLIER, J. P.

George Brewer, Jun., Francis Boykin, and James Caller, Esq. were produced as witnesses, and, being duly sworn, the said Brewer and Boykin testified, that Elijah Thompson, the late husband of Anna Mounger, inhabited and cultivated the land now claimed by Anna Mounger, in the year 1796, and part of the year 1797; some time in the first part of this year, Elijah Thompson died, without lawful issue; that Anna Mounger, his wife, continued to inhabit and cultivate the same land, until sometime in the month of December, 1798, when she intermarried with Sampson Mounger; and that Sampson Mounger continued, after his intermarriage, to cultivate the year following.

The said Caller testified, that in the year 1802, he came into the possession of the land now claimed by Anna Mounger, by authority of Joshua Howard, who claimed the same, under an English title, but finding that the present claimant asserted her right to the land, and not finding any satisfactory title in Howard, he gave up the possession.

Question to each of the witnesses. Do you know whether this land is claimed by any Spanish or English title?
Answer. We do not.
Question to each of the witnesses. Do you know whether the present claimant makes claim to any other lands in this territory, by force of any British or Spanish grant, warrant, or order of survey?
Answer. We do not.

The board ordered that the case be postponed for consideration.

THOMAS CARSON's case, No. 26 on the docket of the Board, and No. 38 on the books of the register.

Claim.—A donation of six hundred and forty acres, as assignee and legal representative of John Jacob Abner, under the second section of the act.

The claimant presented his claim, together with a surveyor's plot of the land claimed, in the following words and figures, to wit:

To the Commissioners appointed in pursuance of the act of Congress passed the 3d day of March, 1803, for receiving and adjusting the claims to lands south of Tennessee, and east of Pearl river.

Please to take notice, that the following tract of land, situated on the waters of the Tombigbee river, in the county of Washington, beginning at a stake at the mouth of the lake, called the Polbyu, and running south, eighty-six degrees west, eighty chains, to a pine corner; thence, south, eleven degrees east, eighty chains, to a pine corner; thence, north, eighty-six degrees east, eighty chains to a red oak standing on the river; thence, up the river to the beginning; containing six hundred and forty acres; having such shape, form, and marks, both natural and artificial, as are represented in the plot annexed; which said tract of land is claimed by Thomas Carson, legal representative of John Jacob Abner, in and by virtue of the second section of the said act, as a donation, and is now exhibited to the register of the land office established east of Pearl river, to be recorded as directed by said act. To all which he begs leave to refer, as also to a copy of the plot herewith filed.

THOMAS CARSON,
Legal representative of John Jacob Abner.
MARCH 16, 1804.
[Plot omitted.]

This plot represents a tract of land, surveyed for Thomas Carson, beginning at red oak corner, on the bank of Tombigbee, running up the bank of the river, as the plot directs, eighty chains, to a stake at the mouth of Polbyu; thence south, eighty-six degrees west, eighty chains, to a pine; thence, south, eleven degrees east, eighty chains to a pine; thence, to the beginning; containing six hundred and forty acres. Surveyed the 12th of March, 1804.

NATT. CHRISTMAS.

Chain bearers, John Barnett, Godwin Mirack.
Entered in record of claims, volume 1, pages 97 and 98, by EDWARD LLOYD WAILES, for
JOSEPH CHAMBERS, *Register*.

This day came John Barnett and Goodwin Mirack before me, and made oath that, in all cases where they have borne the chain, they have done it to the best of their knowledge, and rendered a true account of the measurement; and that they would, in all cases hereafter, do the same in like manner.
Sworn before me this 5th of March, 1804.
JOSEPH THOMPSON, *J. P.*

The said Thomas Carson, in support of the right of representation, produced a deed of conveyance from John Jacob Abner, bearing date the 31st day of July, 1802, duly executed, assigning, relinquishing, and conveying to the said Carson, his heirs and assigns, all the said Abner's right, title, interest, and claim to the said land, and the improvements made thereon.
Adam Hollinger, Francis Boykin, and Richard Barrow, were produced as witnesses, and being duly sworn, the said Hollinger deposed, that John Jacob Abner did, in the year 1797, and for many years before, inhabit and cultivate the land now claimed, and continued to inhabit and cultivate the same, until after he sold his right to Thomas Carson; that the said Abner was, in the year 1797, the head of a family: in the spring of the year 1803, Thomas Carson entered into possession of the premises, and has so continued ever since.
The said Boykin testified, that Abner was in possession of the land in the year 1792 or 1793, but does not know that he lived there in 1797.
The said Barrow testified, that John Jacob Abner did inhabit and cultivate the land in question in the year 1797, and has continued to cultivate the same until the last year; and that he was of full age, and the head of a family in year 1797.
The board ordered that the case be postponed for consideration.

The Heirs of CHARLES BREWER, case No. 27 on the docket of the Board, and No. 57 on the books of the Register.
Claim.—A donation of five hundred and eighty-two acres, under the second section of the act.
The claimants presented their claim, together with a surveyor's plot of the land claimed, in the following words and figures, to wit:
To the Commissioners appointed in pursuance of the act of Congress, passed the 3d of March, 1803, for receiving and adjusting claims to lands south of the river Tennessee, and east of Pearl river.
MARCH 14, 1804.
Please to take notice, that the following tract of land, beginning on a tupelo gum near the bank of Sunflower creek, or on a stake in and about fifteen feet from said gum, and bounding on five lines of Hiram Mounger's survey, and cornering on a stake in the branch, and running south, twenty degrees west, forty-four chains; thence, south, seventy degrees east, one hundred and twenty-seven chains, to the beginning. This land is claimed by the heirs of Charles Brewer, late of Washington county, Mississippi territory, deceased, under, and by virtue of, a settlement made by the said Charles Brewer, in September, 1797, and now delivered to the register of the land office, to be recorded as directed by said act. To which they beg leave to refer, as also to the copy of the plot herewith filed.
EPHRAIM BARKER, his × mark,
For the heirs of Charles Brewer.

[Plot omitted.]

Test, RICHARD LEE.
The within plot is surveyed for the remains of Charles Brewer, deceased, beginning on a tupelo gum, near the bank of the Sunflower creek, or on a stake in and about fifteen feet from said gum, and binding on five lines of Hiram Mounger's survey, and corners on a stake in the branch, and running south, twenty degrees west, forty-four chains; thence, south, seventy degrees east, one hundred and twenty-seven chains, to the beginning.

Surveyed by me, Robert Ligon. Chain carriers, Stephen Williams, George Dickey.
Entered in record of claims, vol. 1, page 168, by EDWARD LLOYD WAILES, for
JOSEPH CHAMBERS, *Register*.
MARCH 10, 1804.
This day came before me George Dickey and Stephen Williams, and swore that they had faithfully and truly carried the chain in surveying a tract of land for the heirs of Charles Brewer, deceased, without favor or affection, to the best of their skill and ability: so help them God.
WILLIAM H. HARGRAVE, *J. P.*
ROBERT LIGON, *Surveyor*.

John Brewer, Esq. and Hiram Mounger, were produced as witnesses, and being duly sworn, they deposed, that the deceased Charles Brewer commenced the improvement of the land in question, in the fall of the year 1797, by clearing a little land, &c.: his family being sickly, he did not make a crop on the land in the year 1798, but came on to the land with his family in the fall of the year 1798, and continued to inhabit and cultivate the same until his decease, which was in the year 1802; his family have since continued to inhabit and cultivate the same land until the present time. The said Charles Brewer was the head of a family in the year 1797.
The board ordered that the case be postponed for consideration.

JAMES CALLER, Esq., case No. 28 on the docket of the Board, and No. 40 on the books of the Register.
Claim.—A donation of five hundred and sixty-seven acres and six-tenths of an acre, as assignee and legal representative of Joseph Anderson, under the second section of the act.
The claimant presented his claim, together with a surveyor's plot of the land claimed, in the words and figures following, to wit:

To the Commissioners appointed in pursuance of an act of Congress passed the 3d of March, 1803, for receiving and adjusting claims to lands south of the Tennessee river, and east of the Pearl river.
FORT STODDERT, *March* 15, 1804.
Please to take notice, that the following tract of land lying west of the Tombigbee river, butting and bounding northwardly, beginning at a sycamore on the bank of said river, being the conditional corner between Joseph Anderson and Jacob Abner, running south, seventy-six degrees west, to another black jack corner, agreed upon by the said Anderson and Abner; thence, to a stake on the same course, distance seventy chains; thence, south, three degrees east, seventy-five chains, to a black gum on the side of a small branch; thence, north, eighty-seven degrees east, seventy chains, to a stake on the river bank at Rochon's corner; then up the meanders of said river to the beginning corner; bounded northwardly by Jacob Abner's land, and southeastwardly by Rochon's land, west by vacant land, and on the east by the Tombigbee river, lying in the county of Washington, Mississippi territory, about two miles above Nanna Hubba bluff; is claimed by James Caller, the legal representative of Joseph Anderson, the said Joseph Anderson having settled thereon on the ——— day of ——— 1798; and conveyed by said Anderson to Seth Dean, on the 3d of December, 1803, and from said Dean conveyed to James Caller, on the 16th day of January, 1804, under and by virtue of the donation, agreeably to the second section of an act of Congress, passed the 3d of March, 1803, as may appear by that act, to all which he begs leave to refer, as also to the copy of the plot now handed or delivered to the register of the land office to be established east of Pearl river, and to be recorded agreeably to that act.
JAMES CALLER.
JOSEPH ANDERSON.
[Plot omitted.]
MARCH 14, 1804.
Surveyed for James Caller, the legal representative of Joseph Anderson, a tract of land on the west side of the river Tombigbee, containing five hundred and sixty-seven and six-tenths acres; beginning at a sycamore on the bank of said river, being the conditional corner between the said Anderson and Jacob Abner, running south, seventy-six degrees west, to another black jack corner agreed on by the said Anderson and Abner; then to a stake on the same course, distance seventy chains; thence, south, three degrees east, seventy-five chains, to

a black gum on the side of a small branch; thence, north, eighty-seven degrees east, seventy chains, to a stake on the river bank, at Rochon's corner; then up the meanders of said river to the beginning corner; bounded northwardly by Jacob Abner's land, and south-eastwardly by Rochon's land, west by vacant land, and on the east by the Tombigbee river, lying in the county of Washington, Mississippi territory.

Surveyed by James Gordon. Chain bearers, Joseph Bates, Sen., William Weathers.

Entered in record of claims, volume I, page 101, by EDWARD LLOYD WAILES, for

JOSEPH CHAMBERS, *Register.*

[Plot omitted.]

Joseph Bates, Sen. and William Weathers, made oath, as chain bearers to James Gordon, surveyor, they have given a true account of the lands they admeasured for him as such, to the best of their knowledge.

JAMES CALLER, *J. P.*

In support of the right of representation, the claimant exhibited a deed of conveyance from Joseph Anderson, bearing date the 3d day of December, 1803, assigning and conveying to Seth Dean all the said Anderson's right, claim, and interest in the said tract of land, and the improvements made thereon; also produced a deed of conveyance from said Dean, bearing date the 18th day of January, 1804, conveying and assigning to the said James Caller all the said Dean's right and claim to the said tract of land, and to the improvements made thereon.

Adam Hollinger was produced as a witness, and being duly sworn, deposed, That the said Joseph Anderson entered into the land in question early in the year 1798, (believes in the month of February,) and cultivated a small crop that season, and lived on the land in a school-house; that the year following he built a house on the land, and continued there to inhabit and cultivate until about this time last year; he then sold his improvement, and moved off. At the time when he first went on to said land, he had a wife and family of children.

Question by James Caller. Did you ever hear John Jacob Abner say that he and Anderson had agreed upon a conditional line between their respective possessions?

Answer. I did hear Abner say so, but do not know where the line was.

The Board ordered that the case be postponed for consideration."

HOWEL DUPREE's case, No. 29 on the docket of the Board, and No. 42 on the books of the Register.

Claim.—A donation of six hundred and thirteen acres, as assignee and legal representative of William Hillis, under the second section of the act.

The claimant presented his claim, together with a surveyor's plot of the land claimed, in the words and figures following, to wit:

To the Commissioners appointed in pursuance of the act of Congress passed the 3d day of March, 1803, for receiving and adjusting of the claims of land south of Tennessee and east of Pearl river.

Please to take notice. that the following tract of land is claimed by Howel Dupree, of Washington county, Mississippi territory, under, and in virtue of, a settlement made by William Hillis in the year 1795, now delivered to the register of the land office to be established east of Pearl river, to be recorded as directed by said act. To which he begs leave to refer, as also to the copy of the plot herewith filed.

HOWEL DUPREE.

MARCH 15, 1804.

[Plot omitted.]

The above survey is just and true as it stands stated, surveyed the 14th day of March, 1804, by me, Robert Ligon, and having such marks, natural and artificial, as the plot represents; beginning on a line run for Creighton's survey, and running north, thirty-four degrees west, seventeen chains, to a sassafras; and from thence north, thirty-seven degrees east, thirty-five chains to pine; and from thence south, eighty-five degrees east, to water oak; and from thence north, twenty degrees east, thirty-four chains, to swamp bush; and from thence, meandering the river, and on its west side, to where the rivers Tombigbee and Alabama intersect each other, and corner on a sweet gum on the bank of said river, and running south, eighty degrees west, one hundred and fifty-two chains, to the beginning stake, including, in said lines, the improvement made by Hillis and transferred to Dupree, to which the same implies the surveying.

Entered in record of claims, vol. 1, page 108, by EDWARD LLOYD WAILES, for

JOSEPH CHAMBERS, *Register.*

MISSISSIPPI TERRITORY, *Washington County:*

MARCH 30, 1804.

Personally appeared before me John Hines and Edmund Smith, and made oath on the Holy Evangelists of Almighty God, deposed, and said, that they carried the chain for a tract of land surveyed for Howel Dupree, and that they effected the duty to the best of their skill and judgment, as directed by the surveyor.

Given under my hand. Sworn to before me,

JON. CALLIER, *J. P.*

The claimant exhibited a deed of conveyance from William Hillis, bearing date the 9th day of November, 1801, assigning and conveying to the said Howel Dupree all the said Hillis's right, interest, and claim to the said tract of land, and to the improvements made thereon.

Richard Barrow was produced as a witness, and, being duly sworn, deposed, that, in the year 1795, William Hillis commenced the improvement and cultivation of the land now claimed, and continued to inhabit and improve the same until he sold his right to Howel Dupree in the year 1801; the last part of the time the said Hillis rented the land. When Dupree purchased the right of Hillis, he took the possession, and has continued to inhabit and cultivate the same until this time; that the said Hillis, at the time of his inhabiting, as aforesaid, the said land, in the year 1797, was the head of a family.

Question. Were you present when the said Hillis assigned his right to the land in question to the said Dupree?

Answer. I was; it was done at my house.

Question. Did you see it executed and delivered by Hillis?

Answer. I did, and signed it myself as a witness.

The board ordered that the case be postponed for consideration.

JAMES SCOTT's case, No. 30 on the docket of the Board, and No. 41 on the books of the Register.

Claim.—A donation of three hundred and seventy-five acres and twenty poles, as assignee and legal representative of Gabriel Burrows, under the second section of the act.

The claimant presented his claim, together with a surveyor's plot of the land claimed, in the words and figures following, to wit:

To the Commissioners appointed in pursuance of the act of Congress passed the 3d day of March, 1803, for receiving and adjusting the claims of lands south of Tennessee and east of Pearl river.

Please to take notice, that the following tract of land, situated on the waters of Bassett's creek, in the county of Washington, beginning at a pine and running south, thirty degrees east, one hundred and twenty-two chains, to a gum corner; thence south, sixty degrees west, twenty-five chains, to a gum corner; thence north, thirty degrees west, seventy-nine chains, to a cypress corner; thence north, sixty degrees west, twenty-five chains, to a red oak; thence north, forty-five degrees west, thirty chains fifty links, to red oak; thence north, sixty-seven degrees east, fifty chains thirty links, to the beginning; containing three hundred and seventy-five acres and twenty poles, having such shape, form, and marks, both natural and artificial, as are represented in the plot herewith annexed: is claimed by James Scott, legal representative of Gabriel Burrows, and is now exhibited to the register of the land office established east of Pearl river; to be recorded as directed by said act. To all which he begs leave to refer, as also to a copy of the plot herewith filed.

JAMES SCOTT,

Legal representative of Gabriel Burrows.

MARCH 15, 1804.

[Plot omitted.]

FEBRUARY 18, 1804.

I have surveyed, for James Scott, three hundred and seventy-five acres and twenty poles of land, on the west side of Tombigbee river; its buttings and boundaries are as hereafter set down: beginning at a pine, running south, thirty degrees east, to a sweet gum, seventy-five chains, to an open pond; thence, to a tupelo gum corner, forty-seven chains; thence south, sixty degrees west, twenty-five chains; thence north, thirty degrees west, to a black gum station on Lee's line, forty-seven chains; thence to a cypress corner, thirty-three chains; thence north, sixty-five degrees west, to a forked red oak corner, twenty-five chains; thence north, forty-five degrees west, to a mulberry station, twelve chains, thence, to a red oak sapling corner, eighteen chains twenty- five links,, to the beginning, north, sixty-seven degrees east, fifty chains thirty links.

WILLIAM GILLIAM.

Chain carriers, Solomon Wheat and Benjamin Harrison.

Entered in record of claims, vol. 1, page 106, by EDWARD LLOYD WAILES, for

JOSEPH CHAMBERS, *Register.*

MISSISSIPPI TERRITORY, *Washington County:*
MARCH 13, 1804.

This day came before me, one of the justices assigned to keep the peace in said county, Solomon Wheat and Benjamin Harrison, and did swear that they carried the chain round the land that was run for James Scott, to the best of their knowledge: so help them God.

WILLIAM H. HARGRAVE, *J. P.*

The claimant exhibited a deed of conveyance from Gabriel Burrows, bearing date the 19th day of September, 1799, relinquishing and conveying to the said Scott all the said Burrows's right, title, and claim, to the said tract of land, and the improvements made thereon.

Hiram Mounger was produced as a witness, and, being duly sworn, deposed, that about Christmas, in the year 1797, Gabriel Burrows removed on to the land in question, with his family, erected a house, and commenced the clearing of the land, and raised a crop upon the same the following season; that he continued to inhabit and cultivate the same until he sold his possessions to James Scott; the said James Scott then came into the possession of the premises, and has continued to inhabit and cultivate the same until this time; that the said Burrows was, at the time of commencing his settlement, as aforesaid, the head of a family.

The board ordered that the case be postponed for consideration, and adjourned until Saturday, the 17th instant.

SATURDAY, *March* 17, 1804.
The board met, according to adjournment. Present: Ephraim Kirby, Robert C. Nicholas, Joseph Chambers.
Adjourned until Monday, the 19th instant.

MONDAY, *March* 19, 1804.
The board met, according to adjournment. Present: Ephraim Kirby, Robert C. Nicholas, Joseph Chambers.
Adjourned until Tuesday, the 20th instant.

TUESDAY, *March* 20, 1804.
The board met, according to adjournment. Present: Ephraim Kirby, Robert C. Nicholas, Joseph Chambers.

THOMAS BASSETT's case, No. 31 on the docket of the Board, and No. 49 on the books of the Register.

Claim—Of seven hundred and fifty acres, as administrator of Nathaniel Bassett, deceased, who was son and heir of Thomas Bassett, deceased, under a British grant, confirmed by a Spanish warrant of survey, under the first section of the act.

The claimant exhibited his claim, together with a surveyor's plot of the land claimed, in the following words and figures, to wit:

To the Commissioners appointed in pursuance of the act of Congress, passed the 3d day of March, 1803, for receiving and adjusting the claims to lands south of the Tennessee and east of Pearl river.

Please to take notice that the following tract of land, situated on the river Tombigbee, in the county of Washington, beginning at a sassafras, running thence, north, eighty-two degrees west, one hundred and twenty-five chains and seventy-five links, to a pine corner; thence, south, eighty degrees west, fifty-nine chains and twenty-eight links, to a black jack; thence, south, eighty- two degrees east, ninety-two chains, to a white ash on the river; thence, with the river, to the beginning; containing seven hundred and fifty acres, is claimed by Thomas Bassett, administrator of Nathaniel Bassett, in and by virtue of a British and Spanish grant, having such shape, form, and marks, both natural and artificial, as are fully represented in the plot annexed, and is now exhibited to the register of the land office, to be recorded as directed by said act. To all which he begs leave to refer, as also to a copy of the plot herewith filed.

THOMAS BASSETT,
Administrator of Nathaniel Bassett.
MARCH 19, 1804.
[Plot omitted.]

The above survey was surveyed the 27th day of February, 1804, for Thomas Bassett, the representative of Thomas Bassett his brother, lying and situated on the upper end of Mackintosh bluff, partly surround the basin, beginning on a sassafras, on the west side of the above river, and running north, eighty-two degrees west, one hundred and twenty-five chains, seventy-five links; thence, south, eight degrees west, fifty-nine chains, twenty-eight links; thence, south, eighty-two degrees east, ninety-two chains, to the above river or basin, including Hinston and Powel within the survey, amounting, by estimation, to seven hundred and fifty acres.

N. B. The within survey was surveyed by me, Robert Ligon.

Chain carriers. Francis Stringer, William Barker.

You, Francis Stringer and William Barker, do swear and affirm, that you have justly and truly carried the chain, as directed by the surveyor, to the best of your skill and ability, for Thomas Bassett; land situated on M'Intosh bluff.

JOHN BREWER, *J. P.*

ROBERT LIGON, *Surveyor.*

In support of this claim, the following written documents were introduced, to wit:

I, Nathaniel Bassett, inhabitant of this city, in the best form of law, before your excellency, appear and say, that from my late father, and my brother Thomas and myself inherited a certain quantity of land, situated on the river Tombigbee, formerly in the district of Mobile, but now included in the American territory, according to the limits lately fixed, which land consists of a plantation of one thousand and fifty acres, possessed by my brother, and another of seven hundred and fifty, whereupon lives, with our consent, Mr. Powel; which possessions were the property of our father, who had the titles thereof, from the time they were under the English government, having since, and while they belonged to the Spanish dominions, presented the said original documents to his excellency Stephen Miro, formerly Governor General of these provinces, who was pleased to confirm us, by the title we obtained from him, in the legal possession which we enjoyed. But several accidents happened to my mother, Lucy Bassett, having caused the seizure of her property, and among other things of the said titles, which were put in the public deposit; they were destroyed there in the fire of the year 1794. It being now necessary to ascertain the loss, in order to prove, in the American territory, that I am the legal owner of the aforesaid lands, I beg your excellency to be pleased to order an information to be taken, without delay, and deposition to be received, as well of the persons who saw us in peaceable possession of them, when the said river and its lands were delivered to this Government, as of those who have seen, not only the English titles which we had got, but also the confirmation granted to us in virtue of them, by the aforesaid Governor Miro. And to that end I beg your excellency to admit the justification I offer, issuing order for the witnesses whom I will present to be examined according to the tenor of what I have heretofore exposed, and to deliver me the whole after its execution, to the use, and with reserve of my rights; which favor I solicit with justice; and swear, &c.

NATHANIEL BASSETT.

It being presented, the information solicited by the petitioner will be received. Mr. Peter Derbigny, interpreter public, being called, if necessary, with the usual formalities, the execution of the present order is committed to the Notary, who, after it is duly complied with, will deliver it as is solicited.

[Here follows the Civil Governor's half signature.]

It is so ordered by his honor Don Nicholas Vidal, Lieutenant Governor, Auditor of War for the provinces of Louisiana and West Florida, and Civil Governor temporary of the same, since the death of the Governor General, vice Patron Royal, and sub-delegate of the posts revenues, for His Majesty, who signed it in the city of New Orleans, the seventh day of July, one thousand eight hundred.

NARC. BROUTIN, *Notary Public.*
The same day I informed Mr. Nathaniel Bassett of the above.

BROUTIN, *Notary Public.*

The same day I communicated the above to Mr. Peter Derbigny, who said he accepted of the commission of interpreting therein given to him, and swore in the name of Almighty God to fulfil it faithfully. In witness whereof he has set his signature to the present.

PETER DERBIGNY.
Before me: NARC. BROUTIN, *Notary Public.*

In the city of New Orleans, the seventh day of July, one thousand eight hundred, Mr. Nathaniel Bassett presented as a witness, in the information by him solicited, according to the order given for its execution, Mr. Augustin Rochon, inhabitant of the town of Mobile, actually in this city, and in virtue of the commission to me conferred by the foregoing decree, and through the interpretation of Mr. Peter Derbigny, I received the oath which he made by the Almighty God, and the Holy Cross, according to law, to declare the truth in what will be under his knowledge, and being interrogated agreeably to the tenor of the foregoing petition, he said, that it is certain, to him known and notorious, that Nathaniel Bassett and his parents possessed some lands on the river Tombigbee, in the district of Mobile; and that he, the deponent, saw the said Nathaniel and his parents in quiet and peaceable possession of the said lands, at the time that the said river, and lands belonging to it, were given up to this crown; and further, he affirms that his present deposition contains the truth, agreeably to his oath; and after it was read to him, he ratified and confirmed it; he is said to be twenty-seven years of age, and signed with the above named interpreter; which I do attest.

AUGUSTIN ROCHON,
PETER DERBIGNY.

Before me: NARC. BROUTIN, *Notary Public.*

In the city of New Orleans, the eighth day of July, one thousand eight hundred, Mr. Nathaniel Bassett, in the information by him solicited, according to the order given for its execution, presented as a witness Mr. Anthony Mendez, of whom, in virtue of a commission to me conferred by the foregoing decree, I received the oath which he made by the Almighty God, and the Holy Cross, according to law, to declare the truth in what will be under his knowledge; and being interrogated after the tenor of the foregoing petition, he said, that the contents of the said petition are the exact truth, for the deponent held in his own hands, the titles of property of the said lands, written in the English language; and he further affirms, that his present deposition is faithful and true, agreeably to his oath, and after it was read to him, he ratified and confirmed it; he is said to be above the age of majority, and signed it; which I do certify.

ANTHONY MENDEZ.

Before me: NARC. BROUTIN, *Notary Public.*

In the city of New Orleans, the ninth day of July, one thousand eight hundred, Mr. Nathaniel Bassett, in the information by him solicited, and ordered to be taken, presented as a witness Mr. Simon Favre, of whom, in virtue of the commission to me conferred by the foregoing decree, and through the interpretation of Mr. Peter Derbigny, I received the oath which he made, by the Almighty God, and the Holy Cross, according to law, to answer the truth in what will be under his knowledge; and being interrogated after the tenor of the foregoing petition, he said, that it is certain, and to him well known, that Mr. Thomas Bassett, father of the petitioner, since the time that the English Government was owning and had the effectual possession of the plantations situated on the river Tombigbee, one of them at a place called Thomas's Bluff, and the other at the place called Thichapataw, which now bears the name of Bayou Bassett, or Bassett's creek; that when the district of Mobile, wherein were included the said plantations, was given up to the crown, the sons of the said Thomas Bassett became Spanish subjects, and, as such, continued to possess the said lands; that the deponent also knows that one Stgoe Powel lives on one of the said plantations, although he is not informed for what motive. And he further says, that this is all that is known to him concerning this matter, and that it is the truth agreeably to the oath he has taken; and after it was read to him, he ratified and confirmed it. He is said to be forty years of age, and signed with the above named interpreter; which I do certify.

SIMON FAVRE.

Before me: NARC. BROUTIN, *Notary Public.*

In the city of New Orleans, the same day, month, and year, Mr. Nathaniel Bassett, in the information by him solicited, and ordered accordingly to be taken, presented as a witness, Mr. Charles Parent, of whom, in virtue of the commission to me conferred by the foregoing decree, and through the interpretation of Mr. Peter Derbigny, I received the oath that he made by the Almighty God, and the Holy Cross, according to law, to declare the truth; and being interrogated after the tenor of the foregoing petition, he said, that he knows and heard that the father of the petitioner possessed two plantations on the river Tombigbee, in the district of Mobile, in the time of the English dominion; and that, when the district of Mobile was given up to this crown, the said Bassett, father and son, became Spanish subjects, and remained in possession of the said lands; he further says, that his present deposition contains the truth, agreeably to the oath he has taken; and after it was read to him, he ratified and confirmed it. He is said to be sixty-three years of age, and signed with the above named interpreter; which I do certify.

CHARLES PARENT.
PETER DERBIGNY.

Before me: NARC. BROUTIN, *Notary Public.*

In the city of New Orleans, the twelfth day of July, one thousand eight hundred, Mr. Nathaniel Bassett, in the information by him solicited, and ordered accordingly, presented as a witness Mrs. Mary Fitzgerald, of whom, in virtue of the commission conferred to me, and through the public interpreter, I received the oath which she made, by the Almighty God, and the Holy Cross, according to law, to declare the truth; and being interrogated after the tenor of the foregoing petition, she said that the only thing she can declare is, that, before the last fire, she saw the titles of grant of the lands mentioned in said petition, written in the English language, in possession of the petitioner, and confirmed by his excellency Stephen Miro, formerly Governor of this province; and she further says that her present deposition contains the truth, agreeably to the oath she has made. Is said to be more than thirty years of age, and signed with the above named interpreter; which I do certify.

MARY FITZGERALD.
PETER DERBIGNY.

Before me: NARC. BROUTIN, *Notary Public.*

In the city of New Orleans, the fifteenth day of July, one thousand eight hundred, before me, the Notary, appeared James Lemaire, witness presented by Mr. Nathaniel Bassett, in the information by him solicited, of whom, in virtue of the commission to me conferred by the preceding decree, I received the oath which he made by Almighty God, and the Holy Cross, according to law, to declare the truth; and being interrogated after the tenor of the foregoing petition, he said, that about two years before the fire of 1794, the petitioner showed him two titles of grant of some lands, which his father possessed on the river Mobile, at the place called Tombigbee; the first in the English language, which his aforesaid father had since the time of the English dominion, and the others in Spanish, being given by his excellency Governor Stephen Miro, whereby he left the petitioner in peaceable possession of the said lands, because, when said territory was given up to Spain, he, the said petitioner, became a Spanish subject; that he cannot ascertain, with any degree of precision, what was the exact quantity of said lands, but believes that one tract contained above a thousand acres, and the other more than seven hundred of superficies; and he further says, that his present deposition contains the truth, agreeably to the oath he has taken, and after it was read to him, he ratified and confirmed it. Is said to be thirty years of age, and signed it; which I do certify.

JAMES LEMAIRE.

Before me: NARC. BROUTIN, *Notary Public.*

I, Nathaniel Bassett, inhabitant of this city, in pursuance of the instance by me moved, with a view of justifying that my brother Thomas and myself are truly the owners of two plantations, situated on the river Tombigbee, the one at a place called Thomas's bluff, and the other at Thichapataw, now known by the name of Bayou Bassett, or Bassett's creek; the first containing one thousand and fifty acres, and the other seven hundred and fifty, on one of which is now living, Mr. Powel, before your excellency appear and say, that I have sufficiently proved, by the depositions of Augustin Rochon, Anthony Mendez, Simon Favre, Charles Parent, James Lemaire, and Mary Fitzgerald, that we legally possess and own the said tracts of land, according to the titles of them, which the said witnesses have seen, as well as those granted by the English Government, as those granted by the Spanish, which titles perished in the fire of the year '94; in consequence of which, and to the end of justifying my right, and legal possession of the aforesaid lands, and that the said justification may be equivalent to the original titles destroyed by the fire, so that I may be acknowledged as legal owner of the said tracts, in the United States, in which territory they are now included, according to the late limits, I beg of your excellency to give your approbation to the said justification, as far as is by law required, giving it the necessary sanction by your decree, and the intervention of your royal authority; ordering, at the same time, that the original writings be delivered to me with such authenticated copies as I may want, to present myself where, and in the manner that will be convenient to my interest. And to that end, I entreat of your excellency to issue the orders I am soliciting with justice. swearing, &c.

NATHANIEL BASSETT.

Let the writings be brought before the tribunal: follows the Civil Governor's half signature.
It has been so ordered by his excellency Don Nicholas Maria Vidal, &c. the 24th of July, 1800.

NARC. BROUTIN, Not. Pub.

The same day, I, the notary, went to Mr. Nathaniel Bassett's lodgings, and notified him the foregoing decree.
BROUTIN, Not.

Having seen the information, made at the request of Mr. Nathaniel Bassett, we approve it, inasmuch as is by law required, ordering to deliver the original of it to said Bassett, agreeably to his petition, with such copies as he may want for the purposes to him convenient, he paying their amount, together with that of the costs of the present writings, according to their just tax.

NICHOLAS M. VIDAL.

It was so ordered by his excellency Don Nicholas Maria Vidal, &c. in New Orleans, the 4th day of August, 1800.

NARC. BROUTIN, Not. Pub.

The same day I communicated the contents of the foregoing decree to Mr. Nathaniel Bassett.
BROUTIN, Not.

[Here follows the taxation of the costs.]
I, Peter Derbigny, interpreter to His Catholic Majesty in and for the province of Louisiana, do certify that the above is a true and faithful translation from the original, written in Spanish. In testimony whereof, I have hereunto set my hand, the thirteenth day of May, one thousand eight hundred and one. (The 24th of July, 1800, interlined before signed.)

PETER DERBIGNY.

I, Nathaniel Bassett, inhabitant of this city, in the information which I have been permitted to give, to the end of justifying that my brother Thomas and myself are the only legal owners of the two plantations, one of which contains one thousand and fifty acres, and the other seven hundred and fifty, both granted to our father, with the usual titles, since the time of the English dominion in the river Tombigbee, formerly in the jurisdiction of Mobile, and now included within the American territory by the late limits; the said property having been confirmed to us by new titles under the Spanish Government, before your excellency appear and say: that, to the end of proving more fully the date of the Spanish titles which were destroyed in the fire that happened in this city in the year 1794, he wishes your excellency may be pleased to order that Mr. Bernard Molina, Mr. Anthony Mendez, and Mr. Augustin Camano, shall declare, upon oath, if they know and are assured that, before the said fire, they saw in my hands and possession the two above said titles, dated in June, 1787, by which his excellency Don Stephen Miro, then Governor of this province, confirmed to me the property and privilege which I had upon the said plantations or tracts of land; and, it being so done, in order to give more force and validity to these proofs, and hold them as a part and as the end of the present information. I beg of your excellency to approve them, so far as is by law required, and confirm them by your judicial decree, and the interposition of the authority which you represent, ordering the whole of the proceedings to be delivered to me original, with the copies which I will ask for the purposes that will tend to establish my rights; the costs of which I am ready to pay. I, therefore, beg of your excellency to be good enough to issue the order, which I solicit with justice; to which end I do swear, &c.

NATHANIEL BASSETT.

The persons named in the above shall swear and declare as is solicited before the notary to whom it is committed; and, after it shall be done, the papers will be brought before the tribunal.

[Here follow the signatures or flourishes of the Governor and Auditor.]
It is so ordered by his excellency Don Manuel de Salcedo, colonel of the royal armies, Civil and Military Governor of the provinces of Louisiana and West Florida, inspector of the troops and militia of the same, vice patron royal, and judge sub-delegate of the superintendency of the posts for His Majesty, who signed it with Don Nicholas Maria Vidal, lieutenant governor, high judge of the war in and for these provinces, and counsellor general of the government of the same, in the city of New Orleans, the 21st day of October, 1801.

NARCISSE BROUTIN, Not. Pub.

In the city of New Orleans, the 22d day of October, 1801, before me, the notary, appeared Don Augustin Camano, of whom, in virtue of the commission which is given to me by the foregoing decree, I received the oath which he made by the Almighty, and a sign of the Holy Cross, according to law, to answer the truth that will be laid before him, and being interrogated agreeably to the tenor of the preceding petition, he said it is true and certain that, before the fire which broke out in this city in the year 1794, he saw in the hands and possession of the petitioner the titles of two tracts of land situated on the river Tombigbee, formerly in the jurisdiction of Mobile; one of one thousand and fifty acres, the other of seven hundred and fifty; which titles were signed by his excellency Don Esteban Miro, Governor General of this province, under date of the month of June, 1787, and by them the aforesaid Governor confirmed the property and rights which the petitioner had upon the said tracts ever since the English dominion; and he further affirms that his present deposition contains the truth, agreeably to his oath, and, after it was read to him, he ratified and confirmed it: said to be of fifty-three years of age, and signed it, which I do attest.

AUGUSTIN CAMANO.

Before me: NARCISSE BROUTIN, Not. Pub.

In the same day, month, and year, I, the notary, in virtue of the commission which is conferred unto me by the foregoing decree, received the oath of Don Bernard Molina, sub-lieutenant of the armies, who took it by the Almighty God, the right hand laid on the hilt of his sword, swearing to answer the truth to the questions that will be asked of him; and, being interrogated after the tenor of the foregoing petition presented by Mr. Nathaniel Bassett, he said, that, before the fire which happened in this city in the year 1794, he saw in the hands and possession of said Bassett, two titles of two tracts of land or plantations, situated on the river Tombigbee, formerly in the jurisdiction of Mobile, one of one thousand and fifty acres, and the other of seven hundred and fifty; said titles bearing date of the month of June, 1787; signed by the then Governor General of this province, confirming thereby the property and rights which the said Bassett had to said lands, in the time of the English dominion; and he further affirms that his present deposition contains the truth, agreeably to his oath; and, after it was read to him, he ratified and confirmed it: said to be above the age of majority, and signed, which I do attest.

BERNARD MOLINA.

Before me: NARCISSE BROUTIN, Not. Pub.

In the city of New Orleans, the 30th day of October, 1801, before me, the notary, appeared Don Anthony Mendez, of whom, in virtue of the commission which is conferred unto me by the foregoing decree, I received the oath, which he made by the Almighty God and the Holy Cross, according to law, swearing to answer the truth to the questions that shall be asked of him, and, being interrogated after the tenor of the foregoing decree, he said, that he is certain and knows positively that, before the fire of the year 1794, Mr. Athanasius Bassett had in his possession the titles of property of the lands expressed in his foregoing petition, and that the deponent himself kept in his hands the primitive titles in English in the year 1780, being at Mobile, which titles were destroyed, by the same fire, with those granted by his excellency Don Stephen Miro, former Governor of this province; and he said that what he has declared is the truth, agreeably to the oath which he has taken; that he is forty-nine years of age; and he signed it; which I do attest.

ANTHONY MENDEZ.

Before me: NARCISSE BROUTIN, Not. Pub.

The whole being seen, we approve, as far as the law admits it, the information received at the request of Mr. Nathaniel Bassett, and order it to be delivered to him original, with such copies as he will ask for the purposes which may be convenient to him, he paying the amount and the costs, according to a just tax.

MANUEL DE SALCEDO.
NICHOLAS MARIA VIDAL.

It has been so ordered by his excellency Don Manuel de Salcedo, &c. who signed it, with Don Nicholas Maria Vidal, &c. in the city of New Orleans, the 1st day of December, 1801.

NARCISSE BROUTIN, Not. Pub.

[Here follow the ratification of the decree and taxation of the costs.]

I, Peter Derbigny, interpreter to His Catholic Majesty, in and for the province of Louisiana, do certify that the above is a true and faithful translation from the original written in Spanish. In testimony whereof I have hereunto set my hand the 19th day of May, 1802. [The words *then* and *with* scratched out before signing.]

PETER DERBIGNY.

Don Manuel de Salcedo, coronel de lo reales exercito, gobernador solitico y militar de las provincias de la Luisiana y Florida Occidental, inspector de la tropa veterana y milicia de ellas, vice patron real y suez subdelagado de la superintendencia general de correo, &c.

Certifico que Don Pedro Derbigny, dequien parece firmad el documento antecedente, es interprete publico por Su Magested de etto provincia, y que es surerdadera firma a la que se debe dar entera fé y credita; y para que conste doy la presente firmada de mi mano, sellada con el sello de mi arma refrendada, por el infrascrito comisario honorario de guerra, secretario por Su Magestad de este Gobernador, en la Nueva Orleans, a dos de Junis, 1802.

[L. S.]   MANUEL DE SALCEDO.
ANDREZ LOPEZ ARMETTO.

Certified that the signature within this document is the same that his excellency the Governor General puts in all public and private papers signed by him.

[L. S.]   JOAQUIN DE OSORNO.

MOBILE, March 6, 1804.

Entered in the Register's Office, vol. 1, page 127 to 145, by Edward Lloyd Wailes, for

JOSEPH CHAMBERS, Register.

I, Thomas Price, of the post of Mobile, English interpreter for his Majesty the King of Spain, do solemnly swear by the Almighty God, and by the Holy Cross, that this is a true and faithful translation of the Spanish writings hereto annexed.   THOMAS PRICE.

Subscribed and sworn before the Board, March 20, 1804.
Attest: DAVID PARMELEE 2d, Clerk.

The following depositions were exhibited, to wit:
The deposition of Wilford Hocket, who deposeth and says, that, at the time the British exercised jurisdiction on and about the river Tombigbee, he lived there, and that he knew Thomas Bassett to live and be in possession of a tract of land, said to contain five hundred acres, on the Tombigbee river, at the upper end of what was called Macintosh's bluff; and that, when the Spanish came to exercise jurisdiction there, the family of Bassetts went to New Orleans; some time after, say in the year 1788, the deponent being in company with Nathaniel Bassett, a Mr. Powel applied to said Bassett to purchase said land, but said Bassett refused selling it, saying he intended to return to and live on it as soon as he could arrange his business at New Orleans. After this, Mr. Powel requested liberty to live on said land: Bassett observed he might, on condition that he would leave it when thereunto requested.

WILFORD HOGGATT.

NATCHEZ, November 12, 1801.
Sworn to and subscribed before me,
SAMUEL BROOKS, Justice Peace.

The deposition of Anthony Hocket, Esquire, who deposeth and says, that, some time in the year 1788, the deponent being in company with Nathaniel Bassett, a Mr. Powel applied to said Bassett, and requested liberty to go on to a tract of land, belonging to said Bassett, at M'Intosh's bluff, until he could supply himself elsewhere: said Bassett replied that he might, if he would, leave or deliver it to him whenever he, the said Bassett, should request it.

ANTHONY HOGGATT.
NATCHEZ, November 12, 1801.
Sworn to and subscribed before me,
SAMUEL BROOKS, Justice Peace.

Young Gains and James Dean were produced as witnesses, and being duly sworn, the said Gains deposed:
Question. Do you believe that the land now claimed by Thomas Bassett, as the legal representative of Nathaniel Bassett, lying on Thomas's bluff, was inhabited and cultivated on the 27th day of October, 1795?
Answer. I do believe that this land or some part thereof, was cultivated by William Powel, his sons, or widow, on the 27th day of October, 1795.

The said Dean deposed:
In the latter part of the year 1788, I heard William Powel ask of Nathaniel Bassett, the brother of the present claimant, leave to settle upon and cultivate the land now in question; and that Nathaniel Bassett told William Powel that he might settle upon and cultivate the same, provided he, Powel, would deliver to him, Nathaniel Bassett, possession when he should require him, Powel, so to do; to which Powel assented, but said that he expected that Basset would not want the possession within a short time. Basset then told Powel he could not certainly say: for he might want it shortly, or perhaps not within two or three years; and this was previous to Powel's taking possession of the land.
Question. Do you know whether this land was inhabitated and cultivated by William Powel, his widow, or sons, on the 27th day of October, 1795?
Answer. It was cultivated by them, or some of them, on the 27th day of October, 1795.

The Board ordered that the case be postponed for consideration.

THOMAS BASSETT's case, No 32 on the docket of the Board, and No. 48 on the books of the Register.

Claim—Of one thousand and fifty acres, as son and heir of Thomas Bassett, deceased, under a British grant, confirmed by a Spanish warrant of survey, under the second section of the act.

The claimant presented his claim, together with a surveyor's plot of the land claimed, in the following words and figures to wit:

To the Commissioners appointed in pursuance of he ac, of Congress passed the 3d day of March, 1803, for receiving and adjusting the claims to lands south of Tennessee, and east of Pearl river.

Please to take notice, that the following tract of land, situated on the waters of Bassett's creek, in the county of Washington, beginning at a cotton tree, running thence, north, sixty-seven degrees west, ninety-seven chains and fifty links, to a pine; thence, south, twenty-three degrees west, eighty-three chains and sixteen links to a pine; thence, south, sixty-seven degrees east, two hundred and twenty-three chains, to Tombigbee river, a maple corner; thence, with the river, as the same meanders, to the beginning; containing one thousand and fifty acres, having such shape, form, and marks, both natural and artificial, as are fully represented in the plot annexed: is claimed by Thomas Bassett, and in by virtue of a British grant and a Spanish grant; and is now exhibited to the Register of the Land Office established east of Pearl river, to be recorded. To all which he begs leave to refer, as also to a copy of the plot herewith filed.

THOMAS BASSETT.

MARCH 19, 1804.
[Plot omitted.]

The above survey was surveyed the 2d day of March, 1804, by me, Robert Ligon, for Thomas Bassett, an inhabitant of this county, having such marks, forms, and boundaries, natural and artificial, as will hereafter be described, as follows, viz: beginning on the west side of the above river, and crossing the same, for compliment, on the front line, and extends north, sixty-seven degrees west, one hundred and fifty-seven chains, to a large lake or swamp, impassable; thence, striking a square, north, twenty-three degrees east, eighty-three chains sixteen links to old British survey, said to be done for the father of Thomas Bassett, and following the said line, ninety-seven chains fifty links, to a pine; south, twenty-three degrees west, eighty-three chains sixteen links, to a pine; thence, aiming to butt said line, to the aforesaid swamp; including, in said lines, by estimation, one thousand and fifty acres.

Entered in record of claims, vol. 1, page 122, by EDWARD LLOYD WAILES, for

JOSEPH CHAMBERS, Register.

MARCH 10, 1804.
This day came before me Isaac Rains and Joel Walker, and swore that they faithfully and truly carried the chain, to the best of their skill and ability, without favor or affection: so help them God.

WILLIAM H. HARGRAVE, J. P.
ROBERT LIGON, Surveyor.

In support of this claim, the same written documents recorded in the preceding case, excepting the two depositions, were applied; also, Young Gains, Francis Stringer, and James Dean, were introduced as witnesses, and, being duly sworn, the said Gains deposed, that I saw Thomas Bassett, the father of the present claimant, in the occupancy and cultivation of the tract of land now claimed, before the year 1781, and during the dominion of the British Government over this country, having large improvements thereon, it being the same tract whereon the present claimant has lived, lying above the mouth of Bassett's creek; and I always understood and believed that Thomas Bassett's father had obtained a grant from the British Government of West Florida for the same tract of land; and that the said Thomas Bassett, the father of the present claimant, as I was informed and do believe, was murdered by the Indians, in or before the year 1781.

Question. Do you know that Thomas Bassett, the present claimant, inhabited and cultivated the land now in question on the 27th day of October, 1795?

Answer. He did inhabit and cultivate the same on the 27th day of October, 1795.

Question. Of what age was Thomas Bassett at the time he was murdered?

Answer. He was about thirty-seven years of age, or upwards.

Question. Which is the true Bassett's creek, the one that runs into the Tombigbee river on its eastern or left bank, or that which empties itself into the same river on the western or right bank?

Answer. I believe they are both properly called by the name of Bassett's creek; the one on the right bank of the Tombigbee, from his having lived on or near the same, and the one on the left from Thomas Bassett's having been murdered thereon; and that the tract of land now in question lies on the west bank of the Tombigbee.

Question put to the said Dean. Do you know that Thomas Bassett, the present claimant, inhabited and cultivated the land now in question on the 27th day of October, 1795, and has continued to inhabit and cultivate the same ever since?

Answer. I do know that he did cultivate and inhabit the same on the 27th day of October, 1795, and has continued to do so until this time.

Question 2d. Do you know whether or not Thomas Bassett, the present claimant, was twenty-one years of age in the month of June, 1787?

Answer. I do not certainly know, but believe that he was twenty-one years of age at that time.

The said Stringer deposed:

I do believe that Thomas Bassett, the present claimant, inhabited and cultivated the land now claimed on the 27th day of October, 1795, and do know that he has continued to have the same land inhabited and cultivated ever since.

The Board ordered that the case be postponed for consideration.

CORNELIUS McCURTIN's case, No. 33 on the docket of the Board, and No. 53 on the books of the Register.

Claim—Of four hundred and eighty acres, by virtue of a Spanish grant or order of survey, under the first section of the act.

The claimant presented his claim, together with a surveyor's plot of the land claimed, in the following words and figures, to wit:

To the Commissioners appointed in pursuance of an act of Congress passed the 3d of March, 1803, for receiving and adjusting claims to land south of the Tennessee river and east of the Pearl river.

Please to take notice, that the following tract of land, lying west of the river Tombigbee, beginning on the bank of the river, at a sycamore corner, standing at the mouth of a gut on George Brewer's line, running up the river north eighty-six degrees west, thirty-eight chains, to a swamp oak bush on the bank of the river, thence, south, thirty degrees west, one hundred and twenty-six chains and forty-nine links, to a pine; thence, south, eighty-six degrees east, thirty-eight chains, to a pine; thence, north, thirty degrees west, one hundred and twenty-six chains and forty-nine links, to the beginning; bounded on the north by land of John Arnot, and on the south by John Stelly's land, near to Fort St. Stephen's: is claimed by Cornelius McCurtin, under and by virtue of a Spanish grant or order of survey, granted to Cornelius McCurtin, as may appear by the original grant now delivered to the Register of the Land Office (to be established east of Pearl river,) to be recorded as direct-

ed by that act. To all which he begs leave to refer, as also to the copy of the plot herewith filed.

CORNELIUS M'CURTIN.

[Plot omitted.]

Surveyed 23d February, 1804. Chain bearers, John Dease and John Dean.

The above plot represents a tract of land surveyed for Cornelius McCurtin, beginning on the west bank of Tombigbee river, on a sycamore corner, standing at the mouth of a gut, on George Brewer's line, running up the river north, eighty-six degrees west, thirty-eight chains, to a swamp oak bush on the bank of the river; thence, south, thirty degrees west, one hundred and twenty-six chains and forty-nine links, to a pine; thence, south, eighty-six degrees east, thirty-eight chains, to a pine; thence, north, thirty degrees west, one hundred and twenty-six chains and forty-nine links, to the beginning; containing four hundred and eighty acres.

NATT. CHRISTMAS.

Entered in record of claims, vol. 1, page 158, by EDWARD LLOYD WAILES, for

JOSEPH CHAMBERS, Register.

MISSISSIPPI TERRITORY, Washington County:

I do certify that John Dease made oath before me that he carried the chain for the measuring a tract of land for Cornelius McCurtin, as particularly as the nature of the case would admit of.

R. HARWELL, J. P.

MARCH 24, 1804.

In support of this claim, the following deed of conveyance and order of survey were exhibited, to wit:

TOMBIGBEE RIVER, July 19, 1790.

Know all men, by these presents: That I, Edward Lucas, have bargained and sold, unto Cornelius McCurtin, all my right and title of a tract of land, my property, bounding on the north side by John Arnot, and on the south by John Stilley, for the sum of fifty silver dollars, to me paid in hand, the receipt whereof I do hereby acknowledge.

Given under my hand, before witnesses, this day and date above mentioned.

EDWARD LUCAS.

BENJAMIN RAWLINS, } Witnesses.
JOHN ARNOT, }

Ante mi en et fueste, St. Estevan 19 de Julio, de 1790,

JOSEF DEVILLE DEGOUTIN.

His Excellency the GOVERNOR GENERAL of W. Florida:

Mr. Cornelius McCurtin, lieutenant of militia at Pensacola, and at present resident in Mobile, with the greatest respect, presents, and says, that, in the year of '90, he bought of Edward Lucas, in district of St. Stephen, twelve acres front of land, and forty back, bounded on the north by land of John Arnot's, and on the south by land of John Steely, (this is in that time,) which I bought for fifty Spanish milled dollars, and part at bill of sale, in consequence, that was authorized by Captain Josef Deville Degoutin, commandant at that time; and, not finding any document of grant in this office, in favor of Lucas, as at that time the Government was favorable to inhabitants, and did not exact the usual custom established; and, desiring the deponent to claim the same land as his property, he prays your excellency, in consideration of what he has said, that, by the Secretary of State, they may deliver him the titles of grant that correspond in good terms what he expects to receive from your excellency's goodness.

CORNELIUS McCURTIN.

MOBILE, 18th December, 1793.

His Excellency the GOVERNOR GENERAL of this province:

It is very true what the deponent declares in his petition; and, being informed by the inhabitants that, before the said McCurtin went to Pensacola, he always made his crops on said land, without molestation: in consequence of which, I think he can obtain the grant that he petitions for, detaining the originals in this office, and deliver in a copy of the same, in order that I should make known that said land is his property. Your excellency may use your pleasure.

MANUEL DE LANZOS.

MOBILE, December 20, 1793.

NEW ORLEANS, January 26, 1794.

The Surveyor General of this province, or his deputy, shall establish this individual upon the twelve acres front, and forty back, that he bought, situated on the place that he mentions in his petition, and not causing prejudices to his neighbors, remitting the original diligence, in order that I may furnish him with the titles of grant.

BARON CARONDELET.

This is a true copy of the original grant by which it was drawn, and that remains in this office of my command, which I do certify.

JOAQUIN DE OSORNO. [L. S.]
Mobile, *March* 6, 1804.

The above is a copy of the Spanish grant.

THOMAS PRICE.

I, Thomas Price, of the post of Mobile, English interpreter for His Majesty the King of Spain, do solemnly swear by the Almighty God, and by the Holy Cross, that this is a true and faithful translation of the Spanish grant or writing hereto annexed.

THOS. PRICE.

Subscribed and sworn before the Board, March 20, 1804.—Attest: DAVID PARMELEE 2d, *Clerk.*

Entered in record of claims, vol. 1, page 168, by EDWARD LLOYD WAILES, for

JOSEPH CHAMBERS, *Register.*

James Dean was produced as a witness, and, being duly sworn, deposed, that Cornelius M'Curtin cultivated the land now claimed in the year 1790, and that he, M'Curtin, was, in the year 1793, above thirty years old, and the head of a family.

The Board ordered that the case be postponed for consideration.

JOHN CHASTANG's case, No. 34 on the docket of the Board, and No. 50 on the books of the Register.

Claim—Of four hundred and eighty acres, by virtue of a Spanish warrant of survey, under the first section of the act.

The claimant presented his claim, together with a surveyor's plot of the land claimed, in the words and figures following, to wit:

To the Commissioners appointed, in pursuance of an act of Congress, passed the 3d of March, 1803, for receiving and adjusting claims to land south of the Tennessee river and east of the Pearl river.

Please to take notice, that the following tract of land, lying west of the Tombigbee river, butting and bounding on the north by the church at Fort St. Stephen's, and on the south by land granted to John Talley, is claimed by John Chastang, under and by virtue of a Spanish grant or order of survey, granted to John Chastang, as may appear by the original grant, now delivered to the register of the land office, (to be established east of Pearl river,) to be recorded as directed by that act. To all which he begs leave to refer as also to the copy of the plot herewith filed.

CHASTANG JEUNE.
[Plot omitted.]

Surveyed for John Chastang, by Thomas Bilbo, February 21, 1804. Chain carriers, John Stearman and David Gains.

Entered in record of claims, vol. 1, page 146, by EDWARD LLOYD WAILES, for

JOSEPH CHAMBERS, *Register.*

David Gains and William Stearman came before me, the subscriber, one of the Justices of the Peace for Washington county, and made oath, that they carried the chain faithfully and impartially, on a survey made by Thomas Bilbo for Doctor John Chastang. Sworn before me, this 2d day of April, 1804.

R. HARWELL, *J. P.*

In support of this claim, a Spanish grant or warrant of survey was exhibited, in the words and figures following, to wit:

Mobile, *December* 28, 1794.

His Excellency the GOVERNOR GENERAL:

Don John Chastang, inhabitant established on Tombigbee river, with the greatest respects due to his excellency, represents, these five years past he has been established on a tract of land, which contains twelve acres front, with its corresponding profounder, limited on the north by land appertaining to the parish of this post, and on the south by land of John Talley; the same never had any proprietor, unless the petitioner, who is established thereon; and, being established thereon without the corresponding titles of concession, he humbly begs your excellency to order the Secretary of General Government to despatch the corresponding title of concession, in form, to the end that he may prove, at all times that he is the real proprietor of said land; which favor

he expects from the great justification of your excellency.

JOHN CHASTANG.
Mobile, *December* 28, 1794.

His Excellency the GOVERNOR GENERAL of these provinces:

With the greatest confidence I can assure it to be the truth what the petitioner solicits above, having myself seen the place whereon he was established, which was granted to him when he was a resident on the same place, whereon Fort St. Stephens now stands; and, by informations taken by me from the eldest inhabitants of this river, the land he solicits doth not appertain to any person; in consequence of which, it appears that it may be granted. The concession the above petitioner solicits, he having a sufficient number of negroes to cultivate the same, your excellency may dispose as it may seem best.

MANUEL DE LANZOS.
New Orleans, *January* 30, 1795.

The Surveyor General of this province, or some individual named by him, shall establish the petitioner on the twelve acres front of land, with its profounder of forty, as customary, as it is vacant, not causing prejudice to any neighbors, at the same place mentioned in the above petition, with the precise conditions of making the road, and clearing regularly, in the peremptory space of one year; and if, at the precise space of three years, the land is not settled, after which period it cannot be established, this grant to remain null: under which supposition, the business of settling the limits will be carried on in the tract and remitted me, to provide the interested party with titles in form.

THE BARON OF CARONDELET, *Register.*

This is a copy of the original within these archives of this place, which I certify.

MANUEL DE LANZOS.
Mobile, *February* 16. 1795.

The above was compared exact with the original in this office under my charge, by me,

JOAQUIN DE OSORNO.

The above is a true copy of the Spanish grant.

THOMAS PRICE.

The words "that part of" have been erased, not corresponding with the Spanish copy, and "the" added.

THOMAS PRICE.

I, Thomas Price, of the post of Mobile, English interpreter for his Majesty the King of Spain, do solemnly swear by the Almighty God, and by the Holy Cross, that this is a true and faithful translation of the Spanish grant or writing hereto annexed.

THOMAS PRICE.

Subscribed and sworn before the Board, March 20, 1804.—Attest: DAVID PARMELEE 2d, *Clerk.*

Entered in record of claims, vol. 1, page ——, by EDWARD LLOYD WAILES, for

JOSEPH CHAMBERS, *Register.*

John Baker and Robert Welch were produced as witnesses, and, being duly sworn, the said Baker deposed, that Doctor John Chastang inhabited and cultivated the land now in question on the 27th day of October, 1795, and that the said Chastang was, at that time, between forty and fifty years of age.

The said Welch deposed, that Doctor Chastang inhabited and cultivated the land now in question in the fall of the year 1795, but did not know whether or not he did so inhabit and cultivate on the 27th day of October, 1795; and that he was, in the year 1795, above forty years of age.

The Board ordered that the case be postponed for consideration.

JOHN CHASTANG's case, No. 35 on the docket of the Board, and No. 51 on the books of the Register.

Claim—Of four hundred and eighty acres, as assignee and legal representative of John Talley, by virtue of a Spanish warrant, under the second section of the act.

The claimant presented his claim, together with a surveyor's plot of the land claimed, in the following words and figures, viz.:

To the Commissioners appointed in pursuance of the act of Congress passed the 3d day of March, 1803, for receiving and adjusting the claims to lands south of the Tennessee and east of Pearl river.

Please to take notice, that the following tract of land, lying west of the Tombigbee river, butting and bounding on the north by Don John Chastang's land, on the south by lands belonging to the heirs of Charles Stewart, is claimed by John Chastang, as the legal representative of John Talley, having now in his possession said Talley's bill of sale for said land, bearing date 29th December, 1794, under and by virtue of a Spanish grant or order of survey, granted to the said John Talley, as may appear by the original grant, now delivered to the Register of the Land Office, (to be established east of Pearl river,) to be recorded as directed by that act. To all which he begs leave to refer, as also to a copy of the plot herewith filed.

CHASTANG, Jeune.

February 21, 1804.

[Plot omitted.]

Surveyed by Thomas Bilbo, for John Chastang. Chain carriers, John Stearman and David Gains, Jun.

THOMAS BILBO.

Entered in record of claims, volume 1, page 149, by Edward Lloyd Wailes, for

JOSEPH CHAMBERS, Register.

In support of this claim. a warrant of survey and a bill of sale were exhibited, in the words and figures following, viz.:

His excellency Don Estevan Miro, colonel of the royal army, governor civil and military of the city and province of the Louisiana, &c. &c.

Mobile, November 12, 1787.

John Talley, inhabitant of Mobile jurisdiction, with great respects to your excellency, petitions and says, that there are found on Tombigbee river, twelve acres of land, formerly of James Smith, limited north and south by lands the property of Charles Stewart, deceased; said land was abandoned in the year '80, and until this present has not been claimed by him nor any other empowered; he begs your excellency's generosity in granting him to be the proprietor of said land, with its profounder, as customary; with papers of titles from the Secretary of Government, which may correspond with the concession; for which favor he will be forever thankful.

JOHN TALLEY.

At Mobile, November 17, 1787.

Don Vicent Folch, captain in the fixed Louisiana regiment, commandant civil and military of said place and its jurisdiction, certifies, that the land the petitioner solicits is vacant, by informations taken from different inhabitants who know said place, for which I sign these presents.

VICENT FOLCH.

New Orleans, November 27, 1787.

The surveyor of this province, Don Carlos Laveau Trudeau, shall establish the individual on that part of land of twelve acres front, with its profounder of forty, as customary, as it is vacant, not causing any prejudice to neighbors, at the same place mentioned in the above petition, with the precise conditions of making the road and clearing regularly, in peremptory space of one year; and if, at the precise space of three years, the land is not settled, after which period it cannot be established, this grant to remain null; under which supposition, the business of settling the limits will be carried on in the with titles in form.

ESTEVAN MIRO.

t act and remitted me to provide the interetd party Certifies that the above is a copy of the original in the office of this place, Mobile, December, 28, 1787.

SANTIAGO DE LA SAUSSAYE,
 Notary Public.

The above was compared exact with the original in this office under my charge, by me,

JOAQN. DE OSORNO.
 THOMAS PRICE.

The above is a copy of the Spanish grant.

I, Thomas Price, of the post of Mobile, English interpreter for His Majesty the King of Spain, do solemnly swear by the Almighty God, and by the Holy Cross, that this is a true and faithful translation of the Spanish grant, or writing hereto annexed.

THOMAS PRICE.

Subscribed and sworn before the Board, March 20, 1804.—Attest: David Parmelee 2d, Clerk.

A bill of sale.—To all to whom these may come: I, John Talley, inhabitant on Tombigbee river, in St. Stephen's jurisdiction, have really and effectually sold to Don John Chastang, doctor. and inhabitant on the same river, a plantation situate one quarter of a league distance from the fort St. Stephen's, and half-quarter of a league from the same river, limited, on the north side by the said Don John Chastang, and on the south by the heirs of Charles Stewart, containing twelve acres front, with its profounder as customary, of forty; the same that was granted to me by his excellency the Governor General of this province, which the copy of concession will prove, dated the 27th of November, in the year 1787, signed by his excellency Estevan Miro, the copy of which is signed by Santiago de la Saussaye, Public Notary of Mobile: said copy I deliver to the purchaser, together with the above plantation, including a house thereon, and every thing else thereunto belonging, and eleven head of cattle, for and in consideration of eighty-five silver dollars to me in hand paid, in the presence of the commandant and the witnesses undersigned; renouncing all rights and claims to said land and cattle above mentioned, by giving up full possession to the purchaser, or any other person for him: which sale I warrant and defend from any claimers, by all the laws of justice, established by His Catholic Majesty: and being present, Don John Chastang accepted this bill of sale in his favor, for the above sum mentioned, for him to use as real proprietor of the same land, which I proved to be my own by the above titles mentioned; which titles may serve for him and his heirs. I, Don Pedro Rola, lieutenant in Louisiana regiment, commandant civil and military of said fort and its jurisdictions, accompanied with the evidence of assistance, knowing both parties contracting, and sign these presents with the two evidences, at Fort St. Stephen's the 23d of December, 1794.

JOHN TALLEY, his + mark.
 JOHN CHASTANG.

Gines Fernandez,
 Bartholome Villacicentio, } Witnesses.

Before me,

PEDRO ROLA.

This is a copy of the original, in the archives under my charge, Mobile, February 7, 1804.

JOAQ. DE OSORNO.

The above was compared exact with the original in this office under my charge, by me,

JOAQ. DE OSORNO.

The above is a bill of the Spanish original.

THOMAS PRICE.

I, Thomas Price, of the post of Mobile, English interpeter for His Majesty the King of Spain, do solemnly swear by the Almighty God, and by the Holy Cross, that this is a true and faithful translation of the Spanish conveyance or writing hereto annexed.

THOMAS PRICE.

Subscribed and sworn before the Board, March 20, 1804.—Attest: David Parmelee 2d, Clerk.

Entered in record of claims, vol. 1, page 149, by Edward Lloyd Wailes, for

JOSEPH CHAMBERS, Register.

The claimant exhibited a writing, by him subscribed, in the following words and figures, to wit:

To the Board of Commissioners,

Fort Stoddert, March 20, 1804.

Whereas I. John Chastang, have laid in claims before the commissioners, for lands at Fort Stephen's, the survey of which includes that garrison: Be it known to the said commissioners now in session at Fort Stoddert, that I, the said John Chastang, am not disposed to claim any land that my titles do not fully represent; should I have claimed or had surveyed any land at the above mentioned place, that the said commissioners may think proper to hold for public use or benefit, they are perfectly at liberty to deduct it, and it is my sincere wish that they should do so; was the said land at this time entirely at my disposal, as a good citizen of the United States, it would give me great pleasure to accommodate that Government with so much as might be thought necessary for public use.

CHASTANG.

John Baker and Robert Welch were produced as witnesses, and, being duly sworn, they deposed:

Question put to said Baker. Do the lands now in question join the land belonging to Doctor Chastang?

Answer. It does.

Question to both of said witnesses. Did Doctor John Chastang inhabit and cultivate the land now claimed on the 27th day of October, 1795?

Answer. He had improvements on the tract now claimed, as we believe, in October, 1795.

Question to the same witness. Was John Talley twenty-one years of age in the year 1787?

Answer. He was above forty years of age.

The Board ordered that the case be postponed for consideration.

JOHN CHASTANG's case, No. 36 on the docket of the Board, and No. 52 on the books of the Register.

Claim—Of nineteen hundred and thirty-eight and four-tenths acres, by virtue of a Spanish grant, or order of survey, under the first section of the act.

The claimant presented his claim, together with a surveyor's plot of the land claimed, in the words and figures following, to wit:

To the Commissioners appointed in pursuance of an act of Congress passed the 3d of March, 1803, receiving and adjusting the claims to lands south of the Tennessee and east of Pearl river.

FORT STODDERT.

Please to take notice, that the following tract of land, lying west of the Mobile river, butting and bounding on the south by Grog Hall creek, on the north by Cedar creek, on the east by said river, and on the other side by vacant land, is claimed by John Chastang, under and by virtue of a Spanish grant or order of survey, granted to the said John Chastang, as may appear by the original grant now delivered to the Register of the Land Office, (to be established east of Pearl river,) to be recorded as directed by that act. To all which he begs leave to refer, as also to the copy of the plot herewith filed.   CHASTANG JEUNE.

[Plot omitted.]

Surveyed for John Chastang a tract of land on the west side of the Mobile river, containing one thousand nine hundred and thirty-eight and four-tenths acres, beginning at the mouth of Grog Hall creek, on the north side thereof, at a water oak, running due west seventy-nine chains to a black jack; thence, due north, one hundred and ninety-five chains, to a laurel on the bank of Cedar creek, the course to the river being impassable; but beginning a second time at the mouth of Grog Hall creek, and taking the meanders of said river Mobile by course and distance, as nearly as the nature of the way would admit, to a sycamore tree, I find the laurel on Cedar creek bank to be one hundred and forty-seven chains, bearing north, sixty-one degrees east, to the said sycamore, bounded eastwardly by the said Mobile river, on all other sides by vacant land; lying in the county of Washington, Mississippi territory.

Surveyed by James Gordon, February, 28, 1804. Chain bearers, Gabriel Tissrah, James Callier.

Entered in record of claims, vol. 1, page—, by EDWARD LLOYD WAILES, for

JOSEPH CHAMBERS, *Register.*

MISSISSIPPI TERRITORY, *Washington County:*
MARCH 17, 1804.

This day came James Callier, and made oath, before the Holy Evangelists of Almighty God, deposeth and saith, that he carried the chain for a tract of land surveyed for Doctor John Chastang, the premises that he now resides on, and that he effected the duty to the best of his skill and judgment, as directed by the surveyor. Given under my hand. Sworn to before

JOHN CALLIER, J. P.

In support of this claim a Spanish grant, or order of survey, was exhibited, in the following words and figures, to wit:

His Excellency Don HENRIQUE GRIMAREST, Lieutenant Colonel of the royal army, Governor civil and military of Mobile, and its jurisdiction, &c., with the humblest supplication, Mr. Chastang, (youngest.)

Should your excellency please to grant him a tract of land, situate on Mobile river, about twelve leagues distance from this place, bounded, on the one side, by a creek that separates said land from Grog Hall, and, on the other side, by another called Cedar creek, which separates it from that of Cambey; with the profounder, as customary; with the old fields belonging to said tract, which is situate on the other side the river; for which favor I shall be forever thankful.

With the profoundest respects,

I am your most obedient and most humble servant,

CHASTANG, (youngest.)

MOBILE, *December* 23, 1784.

Shall be examined the above land the petitioner demands; and should there be found in the last treaty between the Spanish and the King of Great Britain no opposition, or nothing found contrary to said treaty, and

not causing prejudice to any person, he may be provided with titles, in form, to take possession of said land.

GRIMAREST.

MOBILE, *January* 18, 1785.

Don PEDRO FAVROT, Commandant of Mobile, and its district.

We give to Mr. Chastang, (youngest,) the contents of his request to enjoy and cultivate said land, as though it had been granted him, until the ratification. The same will be forwarded to him by his excellency Don Estevan Miro, Governor of this province.

PEDRO FAVROT.

MOBILE, *June* 20, 1798.

Don Manuel De Lanzos, captain in the royal army, retired commandant civil and military of Mobile and its jurisdiction, certifies that Don John Chastang, neighbor of this jurisdiction, and as inhabitant of said jurisdiction, solicits me for the concession original, from his excellency the Governor General of these provinces, given in favor, the above land mentioned in the petition, and the decisions of the commandants of this place. Said concession was certainly granted, but they do not exist in these archives; no doubt they have been mislaid and cannot be found: notwithstanding, by the informations I have taken, I am convinced that it is legally his, in consequence of the original document which he presents; which is returned to him for his security.

MANUEL DE LANZOS.

MOBILE, *March* 8, 1804.

This is a copy of the above document original, presented for the interested party.

JOAQUIN DE OSORNO.

THOMAS PRICE.

This is translated from the above document.

I, Thomas Price, of the post of Mobile, English interpreter for His Majesty the King of Spain, do solemnly swear by the Almighty God, and by the Holy Cross, that this is a true and faithful translation of the Spanish grant, or writing hereto annexed.

THOMAS PRICE.

Subscribed and sworn before the Board, March 20, 1804.—Attest: DAVID PARMELEE 2d, *Clerk.*

Entered in record of claims, vol. 1, page 155, by EDWARD LLOYD WAILES, for

JOSEPH CHAMBERS, *Register.*

The Board ordered that the case be postponed for consideration.

GEORGE ROBBINS's case, No. 37 on the docket of the Board, and No. 26 on the books of the Register.

Claim—A donation of six hundred and forty acres, as assignee and legal representative of Zadock Brashear, under the second section of the act.

The claimant presented his claim, together with a surveyor's plot of the land claimed, in the words and figures following, to wit:

To the Commissioners appointed in pursuance of the act of Congress passed the 3d day of March, 1803, for receiving and adjusting the claims to lands south of the Tennessee and east of Pearl river.

Please to take notice, that the following tract of land, situated on the west side of Tombigbee river, bounded on the southwest by lands claimed by Young Gains, on the southeast by vacant land, and on the northeast by the claim of John Cozby: beginning on a large sycamore, on the river bank, and runs south, sixty degrees west, fifty chains, to a red oak; thence, south, thirty degrees east, one hundred and fifteen chains, to a black gum; thence, north, sixty degrees east, sixty chains, to an elm on the river bank; and from thence, the meanders of the river, to the place of beginning; having such marks, natural and artificial, as are represented in the plot annexed, containing six hundred and forty acres; is claimed by George Robbins, legal representative of Zadock Brashear, under and by virtue of a settlement, bearing date in the year one thousand seven hundred and eighty-four, and now exhibited unto the Register of the Land Office established east of Pearl river, to be recorded as directed by said act. To all which he begs leave to refer, as also to the copy of the plot herewith filed.

GEORGE ROBBINS.

[Plot omitted.]

Entered in record of claims, vol. 1, page 73, by EDWARD LLOYD WAILES, for

JOSEPH CHAMBERS, *Register.*

MISSISSIPPI TERRITORY, *Washington County:*

Joseph Lawrence and William Shaw came forward and made oath, that they carried the chain for Thomas

Bilbo, while he was surveying a tract of land for George Robbins, to their best skill and judgment, this tenth day of March, 1804.

JOSEPH LAWRENCE,
WILLIAM SHAW.

Sworn to before me, JOHN MURRELL, *J. P.*

The claimant exhibited a deed of conveyance from Zadock Brashear, bearing date the 14th day of April, 1799, assigning and conveying to the said Robbins, all the said Brashear's right and title to the improvements which he had made on said tract of land.

Young Gains, Sen. and Robert Welch were produced as witnesses, and being duly sworn, the said Gains deposed, that Zadock Brashear did inhabit and cultivate the land now in question about the years 1791, 1792, and 1793, and then moved out of this territory into the Spanish country, and had lived there ever since; that Brashear's cultivation and improvement was considerably large, and after he went off the place was possessed by the Indians; but how long he could not say.

The said Welch deposed, that he agrees with the testimony given by Young Gains, Senior; and further, that Indians, who were the relations of Zadock Brashear's wife, inhabited and cultivated on the land now claimed, in the years 1797 and 1798; and that Zadock Brashear was in the year 1797 twenty-one years of age.

The Board ordered that the case be postponed for consideration.

JOHN BAPTIST TRENIER's case, No. 38 on the docket of the Board, and No. 79 on the books of the Register.

Claim—Of three hundred and twenty-seven acres, one rood, and fifteen poles, by virtue of a Spanish warrant of survey, under the first section of the act.

The claimant exhibited his claim, together with a surveyor's plot of the land claimed, in the following words and figures, viz.:

To the Commissioners appointed in pursuance of the act of Congress passed the 3d day of March, 1803, for receiving and adjusting the claims to lands south of Tennessee and east of Pearl river.

Please to take notice, that the following tract of land, situated on the Mobile river, in the county of Washington, beginning at the mouth of Grog Hall creek, on a water oak; running thence, due west, one hundred and twenty-six chains, fifty-three links, to a stake corner; thence, south, forty-five degrees east, forty-seven chains fifty links, to a stake; thence, due east, one hundred and twenty-six chains fifty-three links, to a stake on the river bank; thence, the meanders of the river, to the mouth of the creek to the beginning; containing three hundred and twenty-seven acres, one rood, and fifteen poles, having such shape, form, and marks, both natural and artificial, as are represented in the plot hereunto annexed: is claimed by Nicholas Weeks, attorney for John Baptist Trenier, in and by virtue of a Spanish warrant of survey, and is now exhibited to the Register of the Land Office established east of Pearl river, to be recorded as directed by said act. To all which he begs leave to refer, as also to a copy of the plot annexed.

NICHOLAS WEEKS,
Attorney for Baptist Trenier.

[Plot omitted.]

Surveyed for Baptist Trenier a tract of land on the west side of the Mobile river, containing three hundred and twenty-seven acres, one rood, and fifteen poles; beginning at the mouth of Grog Hall creek, on a water oak, running due west one hundred and twenty-six chains fifty-three links, on John Chastang's line, to a stake corner; thence south, forty-five degrees east, forty-seven chains fifty links, to a stake; thence, due east, one hundred and twenty-six chains fifty-three links, to a stake on the river bank; thence, the meanders of the river, to the mouth of Grog Hall creek, the beginning corner; bounded northwardly by John Chastang's land, and eastwardly by said river, lying in Washington county, Mississippi territory. Surveyed March 26, 1804, by JAMES GORDON.

Chain carriers, Hartwell Hardaway and Daniel Murphey.

Entered in record of claims, vol. 1, page 228, by EDWARD LLOYD WAILES, for

JOSEPH CHAMBERS, *Register.*

This day came Hartwell Hardaway and Daniel Murphey, and made oath, as chain bearers to James Gordon, surveyor, they have given a true account of the admeasurement of a tract of land surveyed for Baptist Trenier.

JAMES CALLIER.

MARCH 29, 1804.

In support of this claim, a Spanish warrant of survey was exhibited, in the words and figures following, viz.:

His Excellency Don ESTEVAN MIRO, Colonel of the royal army, Governor General of the city and province of Louisiana, &c.

John Baptist Trenier, inhabitant of Mobile jurisdiction, with the greatest respect lays before your excellency, and says, that, having a small stock, and no range for them of his own, he prays your excellency's goodness in granting him a concession of land of twenty acres front, situate on Tombigbee river, called Grog Hall, bounded on the north by land the property of Don John Chastang, and on the south by land the property of Simon Andry; the above land, evacuated by Mr. Magilivrey these seven years past, and until now never has been claimed by the proprietor, nor any other person empowered for him: he begs your excellency to grant him the above petition, with papers of titles necessary from the Secretary of Government which may correspond with the concession; for which favor from your excellency he will be forever thankful.

JOHN BAPTIST TRENIER.

MOBILE, *July* 27, 1787.

Don Vicente Folch, captain in the Louisiana regiment of fixed infantry, and commandant civil and military of Mobile and its district, certifieth, that, having taken information of the inhabitants of this district, the land the above petitioner solicits is vacant.

VICENTE FOLCH.

NEW ORLEANS, *September* 1, 1787.

The surveyor of this province, Don Charles Trudeau, shall establish that part of twenty acres front which the above petitioner solicits, with its profounder of forty acres back, as customary, at the same place as above mentioned in the petition, it being vacant, not causing any prejudice to the neighbors, with the precise conditions of making the road, and clearing regularly, in the peremptory space of one year; and if, at the precise space of three years, the land is not settled, during which period it cannot be alienated, this grant to remain null: under which supposition, the business of settling the limits will be carried on in the tract, and remitted me to provide the interested party with titles in form.

ESTEVAN MIRO.

MOBILE, *July* 20, 1802.

This is a copy of the original that exists in the office under my charge.

JOAQUIN DE OSORNO.

The above compared exact with the original, by me,
JOAQUIN DE OSORNO.

The above was translated from the Spanish grant.

THOMAS PRICE.

I, Thomas Price, of the post of Mobile, English interpreter for his Majesty the King of Spain, do solemnly swear by the Almighty God, and by the Holy Cross, that this is a true and faithful translation of the Spanish grant or writing hereto annexed.

THOMAS PRICE.

Subscribed and sworn before the Board, March 20, 1804.—Attest: DAVID PARMELEE 2d, *Clerk.*

Entered in record of claims, vol. 1, page 228, by EDWARD LLOYD WAILES, for

JOSEPH CHAMBERS, *Register.*

The Board ordered that the case be postponed for consideration.

JAMES CALLIER's case, No. 39 on the docket of the Board, and No. 69 on the books of the Register.

Claim—Of seven hundred and thirty-two acres, as assignee and legal representative of Anthony Hoggatt, by virtue of a Spanish warrant of survey, under the first section of the act.

The claimant exhibited his claim, together with a surveyor's plot of the land claimed, in the following words and figures, to wit:

To the Commissioners appointed in pursuance of an act of Congress passed the 3d day of March, 1803, for receiving and adjusting claims south of the Tennessee river and east of the Pearl river.

Please to take notice, that the following tract of land, lying west of the Tombigbee river, butting and bounding as follows, viz.: beginning on the river bank at a small hackberry, marked with an X and three chops, as a corner, and runs south, forty-eight degrees west, crossing the back swamp at thirty-seven chains, to a large cypress fore and aft tree, and seventy-seven chains, crossing a small branch to a large chesnut fore and aft tree; continuing the same course, one hundred and twenty-six chains forty-nine links, to a lightwood stake corner marked with an X and three chops; thence north, forty-two degrees west, sixty-three chains twenty-four links and a half, to a lightwood stake corner marked with an X and three chops; thence north, forty-eight degrees east, crossing a small branch at twelve chains fifty links, another at twenty-six chains, another at fifty chains, another at sixty-seven chains, the back swamp at eighty-two chains twenty-five links, ninety-seven chains, to a small sycamore on the bank of the river marked with an X and three chops, a corner; and from thence to the beginning: is claimed by James Callier, under and by virtue of a Spanish grant, or order of survey, to Anthony Hoggatt, and is now exhibited unto the Register of the Land Office established east of Pearl river, to be recorded as directed by said act. To all which he begs leave to refer, as also to a copy of the plot herewith filed.

JAMES CALLIER,
Legal representative of Anthony Hoggatt.
MARCH 19, 1804.

[Plot omitted.]

WASHINGTON COUNTY, *Mississippi Territory.*

Surveyed for James Callier a tract of land, lying on the west side of the river Tombigbee, beginning on the river bank at a small hackberry, marked with an X and three chops, as a corner, and runs south, forty-eight degrees west, crossing the back swamp at thirty-seven chains, to a large cypress fore and aft tree, and seventy-seven chains, crossing a small branch, to a large chesnut fore and aft tree, continuing the same course one hundred and twenty-six chains forty-nine links, to a lightwood stake corner, marked with an X and three chops; thence, north, forty-two degrees west, sixty-three chains twenty-four links and a half, to a lightwood stake corner, marked with an X and three chops; thence, north, forty-eight degrees east, crossing a small branch at twelve chains fifty links, another at twenty-six chains, another at fifty chains, another at sixty-seven chains, the back swamp at eighty-two chains twenty-five links; ninety-seven chains, to a small sycamore on the bank of the river, marked with an X and three chops, a corner; and from thence to the beginning. Surveyed 13th February, 1804, by J. MALONE.

Chain carriers, George Brewer and Robert Callier.

His Excellency ESTEVAN MIRO, Colonel of the royal armies, civil and military Governor of the city and province of Louisiana, &c.

Anthony Hoggatt, inhabitant of the jurisdiction of Mobile, with the most profound respect declares to your excellency, that there is found on this river of Tombigbee twenty acres of vacant land, the which, until the present, has not had a proprietor, in attention to this, and with the view of cultivating tobacco, he hopes from the generosity of your excellency, to grant him the proprietary in them, with those of the ordinary depth, and that your excellency may order the corresponding titles of concession to be delivered by the Secretary's office of Government for so much: he solicits your excellency that it may be ordered as asked for; in the which he will receive favor. ANTONIO HOGGATT.

MOBILE, *January* 21, 1788.

Don Vicente Folch, captain of the fixed regiment of Louisiana, commandant civil and military of the aforementioned place and district, certifies, that the land that the petitioner solicits for is found vacant, according to information taken (to this effect) from several inhabitants who have knowledge of it; and that it may be plain and evident, these presents are given in the said place. Fecit ut supra. VICENTE FOLCH.

NEW ORLEANS, *February* 9, 1788.
The Surveyor General of this province, Don Carlos Laveau Trudeau, will establish this petitioner upon the twenty acres of land in front that he solicits for, with the ordinary depth of forty, in the place indicated in the preceding memorial, being vacant, and not causing prejudice to any, with the precise conditions of making the road and clearing in the term of one year; and to remain null this concession if, at the expiration of three, the land will not be found established, this grant to remain null; under which supposition, the business of settling the limits will be carried on in the tract, and remitted me, to provide the interested party with titles in form. ESTEVAN MIRO.

MOBILE, *March* 10, 1788.
Certifies that the foregoing copy is like the original that remains in the archives of this place.

SANTIAGO DE LA SAUSSAYE.

The above was compared exact with the original in this office under my charge, by me,
JOAQUIN DE OSORNO.

The above is a copy of the Spanish grant.
THOMAS PRICE.

I, Thomas Price, of the post of Mobile, English interpreter for His Majesty the King of Spain, do solemnly swear by the Almighty God, and by the Holy Cross, that this is a true and faithful translation of the Spanish grant, or writing hereto annexed.
THOMAS PRICE.

Subscribed and sworn before the Board, March 20, 1804.—Attest: DAVID PARMELEE 2d, *Clerk.*

On the back of the original Spanish grant, or warrant of survey, are two endorsements, in the following words and figures, to wit:

I do hereby relinquish my right and title of the within grant, to Robert Welch.
ANTHONY HOGGATT.
Witness present, JACOB PHILLIS.

I do hereby assign over to James Callier all my right and title to the within tract of eight hundred acres of land, for and in consideration of six hundred dollars, this 11th of August, 1802.
ROBERT WELCH. [L. S.]
JOSEPH CAMPBELL.

Entered in record of claims, vol. 1, page 194, by EDWARD LLOYD WAILES, for
JOSEPH CHAMBERS, *Register.*

The Board ordered that the case be postponed for consideration.

Adjourned until Wednesday, the 21st instant.

WEDNESDAY, *March* 21, 1804.

The board met according to adjournment. Present: Ephraim Kirby, Robert C. Nicholas, Joseph Chambers.

JAMES CALLIER's case, representative of Anthony Hoggatt. Thomas Price, Robert Welch, and Young Gains, were produced as witnesses, and, being duly sworn, the said Price deposed, that Robert Welch settled upon and cultivated the land now in question in the year 1791 or 1792, and that the same land was previously inhabited and cultivated by Anthony Hoggatt; that Robert Welch inhabited and cultivated this land on the 27th day of October, 1795, and continued in the habitation and cultivation of the same, from the said year 1791 or 1792, until the latter part of the year 1798, or the commencement of the year 1799; and that, on the 9th of February, 1788, Anthony Hoggatt was upwards of twenty-five years of age.

Question. Do you know the time that Anthony Hoggatt first settled upon the land now in question, and whether he inhabited, cultivated, or claimed any land other than this on the Tombigbee river?

Answer. He settled upon this land in the year 1786 or 1787, and continued to inhabit the same until the year 1791 or 1792, when, as I understood, he transferred the same to Robert Welch; and I never understood that he claimed any other land on the river Tombigbee than that now claimed by James Callier.

The said Gains deposed, I saw Anthony Hoggatt in the habitation and cultivation of the land now claimed in the year 1788 or 1789, and do know that he continued there until the year 1792 or 1793, when, as I was informed, and did believe, he transferred the same to Robert Welch; and that Robert Welch settled upon the land immediately after Anthony Hoggatt quitted the same, and continued to inhabit and cultivate thereon, until after the year 1795; and that he, Welch, did actually inhabit and cultivate the same on the 27th day of October, 1795; and that Anthony Hoggatt was, as I believe, on the 7th day of February, 1788, upwards of twenty-five years of age.

Question. Do you know whether Anthony Hoggatt claimed or inhabited any other land on the Tombigbee river, than this now claimed by James Callier?

Answer. I do believe he did not.

The said Welch deposed: I settled upon the land now in question, in virtue of a purchase from Anthony Hoggatt, in the year 1792 or 1793, and continued to inhabit and cultivate the same until the year 1799; and that I did actually inhabit and cultivate the same on the 27th of October, 1795; that, in the year 1799, I was engaged as an interpreter of the Choctaw language for American garrison of Fort Stoddert, to which post I removed in this year, and left my wife and family on the land now in question; that, in the winter of the year 1799, my wife and family quitted the possession of this land; but, previous to her doing so, she did rent the same to William Vardeman, upon his agreeing to pay her annually, for the use of same, thirty barrels of corn, Spanish measure, and to keep the house and fences in good repair; that, in pursuance of said agreement between my wife and said Vardeman, I received from him thirty barrels of corn, for the first year's rent; and that he afterwards refused to pay me rent, or to go off, alleging, as the reason, that he had a British grant for the same, and I do acknowledge I did transfer my right to this land, agreeably to the true intent and meaning of the endorsement on the original warrant of survey.

The Board ordered that the case be postponed for consideration.

CORNELIUS MCCURTIN's case. Doctor John Chastang and Wilson Carman, Esq. were produced as witnesses, and, being duly sworn, Chastang deposed, that, by recurring to a correspondence between Cornelius McCurtin and himself, he finds that, in September, 1791, Mr. McCurtin requested him to take care of the plantation, being the land now in question, and that he did do the same until the year 1796; that, in November, 1791, a man by the name of Stewart was in possession of the house and improvements which were on the land, of which he advised Mr. McCurtin by letter, and he, Stewart, continued there some time, but does not know when he left it, nor how far he considered himself the tenant of McCurtin; that, in the year 1792, Barton Hanna applied to me, as the agent of McCurtin, to rent the plantation, but we did not agree upon the rent, and I referred him to Mr. McCurtin, but do not know what agreement was eventually made between them, but believe he lived on the land a short time.

Question. Did Cornelius McCurtin, or any person in his behalf, inhabit and cultivate the lands now claimed in the year 1795, or on the 27th of October, in that year?

Answer. Not to my knowledge.

The said Carman deposed, that, in the month of November, 1800, Cornelius McCurtin constituted me his agent or attorney, and committed to me the charge of this land, with power to rent or sell it; and, subsequent to this time, an application was made to me to purchase the same, but we did not agree on the price.

The Board ordered that the case be postponed for consideration.

JOSEPH HOUSE's case, No. 40 on the docket of the Board, and No. 65 on the books of the Register.

Claim.—A donation of six hundred and forty acres, under the second section of the act.

The claimant exhibited his claim, together with a surveyor's plot of the land claimed, in the words and figures following, viz.:

To the Commissioners appointed in pursuance of the act of Congress, passed the 3d day of March, 1803, for receiving and adjusting the claims to lands south of Tennessee and east of Pearl river.

MARCH 16, 1804.

Please to take notice, that the following tract of land, situate on the west side of Tombigbee river, beginning at a branch of Bassett's creek, on a pine, running south, fifty degrees east, eighty chains, to a corner pine; thence, south, thirty-two degrees west, to a corner stake, eighty chains; thence, north, fifty-eight degrees west, eighty chains, to a corner pine; thence, north, thirty-two degrees east, eighty chains, to the beginning: containing six hundred and forty acres: is claimed by Joseph House, of Washington county, having such forms and marks, both natural and artificial, as are represented in the plot annexed; the said land is claimed in and by virtue of the second section of the said act of Congress, by a donation, bearing date in the year 1797, and now exhibited to the Register of the Land Office, to be recorded as directed by said act. To all which he begs leave to refer, as also to a copy of the plot hereunto annexed.

YOUNG GAINS,
Legal representative of Joseph House.

[Plot omitted.]

Surveyed for Joseph House, six hundred and forty acres of land lying in the pine woods.

THOMAS BILBO.

Chain carriers, David Gains, Jun. and Joseph Lawrence. March 16, 1804.

Entered in record of claims, vol. 1, page 187, by EDWARD LLOYD WAILES, for

JOSEPH CHAMBERS, *Register.*

Francis Stringer and Thomas Bassett were produced as witnesses, and being duly sworn, they deposed:

Question. Have you or do you expect any interest, either directly or indirectly, by the establishment of Joseph House in this donation?

Both answered. We have no interest, nor do we expect any.

Question. Do you know whether Joseph House, the claimant, has any British or Spanish grant, warrant, or order of survey, in his own name for land in this territory?

Answer. We believe he has not.

Said witnesses also deposed, that, in the winter of the year 1799, Robert House, the father of Joseph House, the claimant, entered upon the land now claimed in virtue of an agreement between him and Thomas Bassett, for the purpose of taking care of and attending a mill; and that Joseph House entered upon the same in the year 1800, and continued thereon until the year 1801, when he purchased Thomas Bassett's right to this mill.

The said Stringer further testified, that he believed that Solomon Boykin had or intended to present a claim for a right of preference to purchase a tract of land, in virtue of a settlement made by Joseph House, the present claimant.

The Board ordered that the case be postponed for consideration.

FRANCIS STRINGER's case, No. 41 on the docket of the Board, and No. 45 on the books of the Register.

Claim.—A donation of six hundred and forty acres, under the second section of the act.

The claimant presented his claim, together with a surveyor's plot of the land claimed, in the words and figures following, to wit:

To the Commissioners appointed in pursuance of the act of Congress passed the 3d day of March, 1803, for receiving and adjusting the claims to lands south of Tennessee, and east of Pearl river.

MARCH 19, 1804.

Please to take notice, that the following tract of land, situated on Stringer's mill branch, on Tombigbee, in the county of Washington, beginning at a stake, running north, forty-seven degrees east, one hundred and twenty-seven chains and fifty links to a water oak; thence, south, forty-three degrees east, thirty chains, to a stake; thence, north, sixty-two degrees east, forty-one chains fifty links, to an ash; thence, with the meanders of the river, thirty-five chains fifty links, to a maple; thence, south, sixty-two degrees west, thirty chains fifty links, to a bay; thence, north, forty-three degrees west, twenty-four chains, to a stake; thence, south, forty-seven degrees west, one hundred and fourteen chains fifty links, to a stake; thence, with a straight line to the beginning: containing six hundred and forty acres, having such shape, form, and marks, both natural and artificial, as are fully represented in the plot annexed: is claimed by Francis Stringer, in and by virtue of the second section of the said act as a donation, and is now exhibited to the Register of the Land Office, to be recorded as directed. To all which he begs leave to refer, as also to the copy of the plot herewith filed.

FRANCIS STRINGER.

[Plot omitted.]

Surveyed 12th March, 1804, by J. Malone.—Chain carriers, John Holleway and John Dunn.

Entered in record of claims, vol. 1, page 117, by EDWARD LLOYD WAILES, for

JOSEPH CHAMBERS, *Register.*

Thomas Bassett was produced as a witness, and, being duly sworn, did depose:

Question. Have you or do you expect any interest, either directly or indirectly, by the establishment of this claim?

Answer. I have not any interest, nor do I expect any.

He further deposed, that Francis Stringer settled and built upon the land now claimed in the month of February, of the year 1798: I do not recollect that he made a crop on the premises in that year; but that he cleared some land; that, from the year 1798 until the present time, he continued to cultivate and inhabit the land now in question.

Question. Do you know whether Francis Stringer was, in the year 1798, the head of a family?

Answer. I believe at that time he was more than twenty-one years of age, and he was the head of a family.

Question. Do you know whether Francis Stringer has either a British or Spanish claim for land in this territory?

Answer. I do not certainly know, but believe he has not.

The Board ordered that the case be postponed for consideration.

JOHN HINSON, administrator of the estate of Owen Sullivant, deceased, case No. 42 on the docket of the Board, and No. 43 on the books of the Register.

Claim—Of four hundred acres, by virtue of a Spanish warrant of survey, under the first section of the act.

The claimant presented his claim, together with a surveyor's plot of the land claimed, in the words and figures following, to wit:

To the Commissioners appointed in pursuance of the act of Congress, passed the 3d day of March, 1803, for receiving and adjusting the claims to lands south of Tennessee, and east of Pearl river.

Please to take notice, that the following tract of land, situated on an island, opposite the Three Rivers, beginning at a hickory on the banks of Tombigbee, and running thence, up the river, the various courses as plotted, to a gum, at Baker's cut off; thence, with Baker's cut off, the courses as plotted, to a willow, at the mouth of the Three River lake; thence, with the east bank of the Three River lake; thence, down the Three River lake, the courses plotted, sixty-six chains and fifty links, to a hickory; thence, north, thirty-eight degrees east, thirty-seven chains, to a stake; thence, south, sixty-four degrees east, seventy-six chains, to a stake; thence, as plotted, to the beginning; containing four hundred acres, and has such marks, both natural and artificial, as are represented in the plot annexed: is claimed by John Hinson, administrator of Owen Sullivant; and is now exhibited to the Register of the Land Office established east of Pearl river, to be recorded as directed by said act. To all which he begs leave to refer, as also to a copy of the plot within.

JOHN HINSON,
Administrator of the estate of Owen Sullivant.
MARCH 15, 1804.

{Plot omitted.}

Surveyed 9th of March 1804, by Natt. Christmas. Chain bearers, John Wheat, James Bilbo.

MISSISSIPPI TERRITORY, *Washington County,*
May Term, 1803.

To John Hinson: You are the administrator of the will [L .S.] of Owen Sullivant, deceased, with the will annexed; proceed as the law in such cases directs, and of your proceedings thereon make due return.

Test: R. LEE, *Clerk W. C. C.*

In support of this claim, a Spanish warrant was exhibited in the following words and figures, to wit:

FORT ST. STEPHEN'S, *April* 12, 1795.
His Excellency the GOVERNOR GENERAL:

Owen Sullivant, inhabitant in the jurisdiction of St. Stephen's, with the greatest respect due to your excellency, represents and lays before your excellency, and says, that, about sixteen leagues from St. Stephen's, there is a tract of land vacant, containing about ten acres front, with corresponding profounder, of forty back; situate at the Three Rivers; beginning at the mouth, running upwards until bounded by vacant land; he is desirous of peaceable possession, without causing prejudice to any person whatever: he begs your excellency to grant him the above petition, with papers necessary from the Secretary of Government, which may correspond with the cession: for which favor he will be forever thankful.

OWEN SULLIVANT.

FORT ST. STEPHEN'S, *May* 12, 1795.
His Excellency the GOVERNOR GENERAL:

By the best information from the inhabitants of this post, that the land the above demands is King's commons, therefore, cannot cause any prejudice to any neighbors, your excellency may dispose as it may seem best.

ANTONIO PALAO.

NEW ORLEANS, *June* 10, 1795.
The Surveyor General of this province, or some other individual named by him for that business, shall establish that part of land of ten acres front, with its profounder

of forty acres back, as customary, at the same place mentioned in the above petition; with the precise conditions of making the road and clearing regularly in the peremptory space of one year; and if at the precise space of three years the land is not settled, during which period it cannot be alienated, this grant to remain null; under which supposition, the business of settling the limits will be carried on in the tract, and remitted me to provide the interested party with titles in form.

THE BARON OF CARONDELET.

ST. STEPHEN'S, *January* 7, 1796.
Registered. The above is a copy of the original in this office, under my charge.

FERNANDO LESORE.

The above was compared exact with the original in this office by me,

JOAQUIN DE OSORNO.

[L. S.]   The above is a copy of the Spanish grant.

I, Thomas Price, of the post of Mobile, English interpreter for His Majesty the King of Spain, do solemnly swear, by the Almighty God, and by the Holy Cross, that this is a true and faithful translation of the Spanish grant or writing hereto annexed.

THOS. PRICE.

Subscribed and sworn before the Board, March 21st, 1804.—Attest: DAVID PARMELEE 2d, *Clerk.*

Entered in record of claims, vol. 1, page 111, by EDWARD LLOYD WAILES, for

JOSEPH CHAMBERS, *Register.*

MISSISSIPPI TERRITORY, *Washington County:*

I do hereby certify, that John Wheat and James Bilbo qualified before me to perform their duty faithfully and impartially, as chain bearers to a tract of land, now about to be surveyed by Natt. Christmas, surveyor, which is claimed by John Hinson, administrator, with the will annexed of Owen Sullivant, deceased, as part of said deceased's estate, by virtue of a warrant of survey, obtained from the Spanish Government in favor of said deceased; beginning at the mouth of the Three Rivers. Given under my hand and seal, this 9th day of March, 1804.

FIGURES LEWIS, *J. P.* [L. S.]
The Board ordered that the case be postponed for consideration.

DANIEL JOHNSON'S case, No. 43 on the docket of the Board, and No. 70 on the books of the Register.

Claim—Of eight hundred acres, by virtue of a Spanish warrant of survey, under the first section of the act.

The claimant presented his claim, together with a surveyor's plot of the land claimed, in the following words and figures, to wit:

To the Commissioners appointed in pursuance of the act of Congress passed the 3d day of March, 1803, for receiving and adjusting claims to lands south of Tennessee, and east of Pearl river.

Please to take notice, that the following tract of land, situated on the west side of Tombigbee river, in the county of Washington, beginning at the water oak on the river Tombigbee, and running west, one hundred and twenty chains seventy links to a post oak; thence, south, sixty-three chains twenty-five links, to an ironwood; thence, east, one hundred and forty chains and twenty links, to a sycamore on the river bank; thence, up the various courses of the river, to the beginning; containing eight hundred acres, and hath such forms and marks, both natural and artificial, as are fully represented in the plot annexed: is claimed by Daniel Johnson, in and by virtue of a Spanish warrant of survey; and is now exhibited to the Register of the Land Office established east of Pearl river, to be recorded as directed by said act. To all which he begs leave to refer, as also to a copy of the plot herewith filed.

DANIEL JOHNSON.

MARCH 20, 1804.

[Plot omitted.]

Surveyed 20th March, 1804, by John Dease. Chain bearers, James Dean and Amos Reed.

In support of this claim, a Spanish warrant of survey was exhibited in words and figures following, to wit:

FORT ST. STEPHEN'S, *May* 11, 1795.
His Excellency the GOVERNOR GENERAL:

Daniel Johnson, with the profoundest respect, represents and lays before your excellency, and says, that he being desirous of settling himself on Tombigbee river, there is a tract of land about sixteen leagues distance below Fort St. Stephen's, containing twenty acres front, with its customary profounder back, bounded on the north by a bayou or creek, called the Three Mouth creek, and on the south by vacant land; he desires to cultivate the same, not causing prejudice to any person whatever: he begs your excellency to grant him the above petition, with papers of titles necessary, which may correspond with the grant; for which favor from your excellency he will be forever thankful.

DANIEL JOHNSON.

FORT ST STEPHEN'S, *May* 11, 1795.
His Excellency the GOVERNOR GENERAL:
By the best information taken from the inhabitants of this post, that the land the above petitioner solicits is vacant lands, and King's commons, your excellency may dispose as is best, as it cannot cause any prejudice to any person.

ANTONIO PALAO.

NEW ORLEANS, *June* 10, 1795.
The Surveyor General of this province shall establish that part of twenty acres front, with the profounder back, as customary, of forty acres, which the petitioner solicits in the above petition, as the land is vacant, and at the same place as abovementioned in the petition, without causing any prejudice to any neighbors, with the precise conditions of making the road and clearing regularly, in peremptory space of one year; and if at the precise space of three years the land is not settled, during which period it cannot be alienated, this grant remains null; under which supposition, the business of settling the limits will be carried on in the tract, and remitted me to provide the interested party with titles in form.

THE BARON OF CARONDELET.

FORT ST. STEPHEN'S, *September* 15, 1795.
Certifieth that the above is copy of the original in these archives, under my charge.

FERNANDO LISORE.

The above was compared exact with the original in this office, by me.

JOAQN. DE OSORNO. [L. S.]

The above is a copy of the Spanish grant.

THOS. PRICE.

I, Thomas Price, of the post of Mobile, English interpreter for His Majesty the King of Spain, do solemnly swear by the Almighty God, and by the Holy Cross, that this is a true and faithful translation of the Spanish grant or writing hereto annexed.

THOS. PRICE.

Subscribed and sworn before the Board, March 21, 1804.—Attest: DAVID PARMELEE 2d, *Clerk.*
Entered in record of claims, vol. 1, page 199, by EDWARD LLOYD WAILES, for

JOSEPH CHAMBERS, *Register.*

The Board ordered the case postponed for consideration.

JOHN JOHNSON's case, No. 44 on the docket of the Board, and No. 76 on the books of the Register.
Claim—Of four hundred acres, by virtue of a Spanish warrant of survey, under the second section of the act.
The claimant presented his claim, together with a surveyor's plot of the land claimed, in the words and figures following, to wit:

To the Commissioners appointed in pursuance of the act of Congress passed the 3d day of March, 1803, for receiving and adjusting the claims to lands south of the Tennessee, and east of Pearl river.

MARCH 20, 1804.
Please to take notice, that the following tract of land, situated on the west side of Tombigbee river, in the county of Washington, beginning on said river at a pine; thence, south, forty-seven degrees west, one hundred and twenty-six chains forty-nine links, to a corner pine; thence, north, forty-three degrees west, thirty-one chains, to a corner stake; thence, north, forty-seven degrees east, one hundred and twenty-six chains forty-nine links, to a corner red oak; thence, down the meanders of the river, to the beginning; containing four hundred acres, and hath such forms and marks, both natural and artificial, as are fully represented in the plot annexed: is claimed by John Johnson, in and by virtue of a Spanish warrant of survey; and is now exhibited to the Register of the Land Office established east of Pearl river, to be recorded as directed by said act. To all which

he begs leave to refer, as also to a copy of the plot herewith filed.

JOHN HINSON, for
JOHN JOHNSON.
[Plot omitted.]
Surveyed for John Johnson four hundred acres of land. Chain carriers, James Bilbo and Joseph Lawrence.

THOMAS BILBO.

MARCH 21, 1803.
The claimant exhibited a Spanish warrant of survey in the following words and figures, to wit:

ST. STEPHEN'S, *May* 11, 1795.
His Excellency the GOVERNOR GENERAL:
John Johnson, inhabitant in the jurisdiction of St. Stephen's, with the greatest respect due to your excellency, represents and lays before your excellency, and says, that he is established on a tract of land, about eighteen leagues distance from this fort, containing ten acres front, with its customary profounder, or back, bounded the south by Moses Moor, and on the north by William Powell, and, until this present, has no other proprietor but the one who has possession; but, not being legal, begs your excellency to grant him the above petition, with papers necessary from the secretary of Government, which may correspond with the grant: for which favor from your excellency he will be forever thankful.

JOHN JOHNSON.

ST. STEPHEN'S, *May* 11, 1795.
His Excellency the GOVERNOR GENERAL:
By the best information from the inhabitants of this post, that the land the above petitioner solicits is King's commons, therefore cannot cause any prejudice to neighbors, your excellency may dispose as it may seem best.

ANTONIO PALAO.

NEW ORLEANS, *June* 10, 1795.
The Surveyor General of this province, or some other individual named by him for that business, shall establish that part of land of ten acres front, with its forty acres back, as customary, in the profounder, without causing prejudice to neighbors, as the land proves vacant, at the same place mentioned in the above petition, with the precise conditions of making the road and clearing regularly, in the peremptory space of one year; and if at the precise space of three years the land is not settled, during which period it cannot be alienated, this grant to remain null; under which supposition, the business of settling the limits will be carried on in the tract, and remitted me, to provide the interested party with titles in form.

THE BARON OF CARONDELET.

ST. STEPHEN'S, *September* 15, 1795.
Certifieth the above is a true copy of the original that remains in this office under my charge.

FERNANDO LISORE.

The above is a true copy of the Spanish grant.
THOS. PRICE.

The above was compared exact with the original in this office under my charge,

JOAQN. DE OSORNO. [L. S.]

I, Thomas Price, of the post of Mobile, English interpreter for His Majesty the King of Spain, do solemnly swear by the Almighty God, and by the Holy Cross, that this is a true and faithful translation of the Spanish grant or writing hereto annexed.

THOS. PRICE.

Subscribed and sworn before the Board, March 21, 1804.—Attest: DAVID PARMELEE 2d, *Clerk.*
Entered in record of claims, vol. 1, page 221. by EDW. LLOYD WAILES, for,

JOSEPH CHAMBERS, *Register.*

James Bilbo and Joseph Lawrence came before me, and made oath that, as chain bearers for Thomas Bilbo, surveyor, in surveying a tract of land for John Johnson, they gave a true account of the admeasurement, to the best of their knowledge.

JAMES CALLER, J. P.

MARCH 21, 1804.
The Board ordered that the case be postponed for consideration.

YOUNG GAINS's case, No. 45 on the docket of the Board, and No. 84 on the books of the Register.
Claim—Of seven hundred and eighty acres, by virtue of a Spanish warrant of survey, under the first section of the act.
The claimant presented his claim, together with a surveyor's plot of the land claimed, in the words and figures following, to wit:

To the Commissioners appointed in pursuance of the act of Congress, passed the 3d day of March, 1803, for receiving and adjusting the claims to lands south of Tennessee, and east of Pearl river.

Please to take notice, that the following tract of land, situated on the Tombigbee river, beginning at a sycamore on the bank of the river, and running thence, south, thirty-nine degrees west, one hundred and twenty-six chains and forty-nine links, to a corner red oak; thence, south, sixty-six degrees east, sixty-three chains twenty-two links, to a corner post oak; thence, north, thirty-nine degrees east, one hundred and twenty-six chains forty-nine links, to the river; thence, with the meanders of the river, to the beginning; containing seven hundred and eighty acres, having such shape, forms, and marks, natural and artificial, as are represented in the plot annexed: is claimed by Young Gains, in and by virtue of a Spanish warrant of survey, bearing date the 22d day of October, 1787, and is now exhibited to the Register of the Land Office east of Pearl river, to be recorded as directed by said act. To all which he begs leave to refer, as also to a copy of the plot herewith filed.

YOUNG GAINS.

MARCH 20, 1804.

[Plot omitted.]

Surveyed 25th March, 1804, by Thomas Bilbo. Chain carriers, George Gullett and Joseph Lawrence.

In support of this claim, a Spanish warrant of survey was exhibited, in the following words and figures, viz:

His Excellency Don ESTEVAN MIRO, Colonel of the royal army, Governor civil and military of the city and province of the Louisiana, &c.

MOBILE, October 10, 1787.

Young Gains, inhabitant of Mobile jurisdiction, with the greatest respects to your excellency, represents and says, that there is a tract of land on Tombigbee river, containing twenty acres, formerly the property of Mr. Dallas, limited on the north by John Arnot, and on the south by vacant land; said tract, since the year 1780, never has been claimed by the proprietor, nor any other person empowered by him; the above petitioner begs your excellency to grant him the above tract of land, with the profounder, as customary, with papers of titles from the Secretary of Government, which may correspond with the concession; for which favor he will be forever thankful.

YOUNG GAINS.

MOBILE, October 10, 1787.

Don Vicent Folch, captain in the Louisiana regiment, and commandant civil and military of Mobile and its jurisdiction, certifieth that the land the above petitioner solicits is vacant, and by information from different inhabitants of this district, who have knowledge of said land.

VICENT FOLCH.

NEW ORLEANS, October 22, 1787.

The surveyor of this province, Don Carlos Laveau Trudeau, shall establish that part of land of twenty acres front, by its profounder of forty, as customary, as it is vacant, not causing prejudice to any person, at the same place mentioned in the above petition, with the precise conditions of making the road and clearing regularly in the peremptory space of one year; and if at the precise space of three years the land is not settled, during which period it cannot be alienated, this grant to remain null; under which supposition, the business of settling limits will be carried on in the tract, and remitted me to provide the interested party with titles in form.

ESTEVAN MIRO.

MOBILE, December 4, 1798.

This is a copy of the original in this office, under my charge, which I certify.

MANUEL DE LANZOS.

The above is a copy of the Spanish grant.

THOMAS PRICE.

The above was compared exact with the original in this office, under my charge, by me,

JOAQUIN DE OSORNO.

I, Thomas Price, of the post of Mobile, English interpreter for His Majesty the King of Spain, do solemnly swear by the Almighty God, and by the Holy Cross, that this is a true and faithful translation of the Spanish grant or writing hereto annexed.

THOMAS PRICE.

Subscribed and sworn before the Board, March 21st, 1804.—Attest: DAVID PARMELEE 2d, Clerk.

Entered in record of claims, vol. 1, page 242, by EDWARD LLOYD WAILES, for

JOSEPH CHAMBERS, Register.

Joseph Lawrence and George Gullett, chain carriers for the survey in this case, were sworn before John Callier, Esq., Justice of Peace.

The Board ordered that the case be postponed for consideration.

YOUNG GAINS's case, No. 46 on the docket of the Board, and No. 85 on the books of the Register.

Claim—Of eight hundred acres, as assignee and legal representative of Dominique de Olive, by virtue of a Spanish warrant of survey, under the first section of the act.

The claimant presented his claim, together with a surveyor's plot of the land claimed, in the following words and figures, to wit:

To the Commissioners appointed in pursuance of the act of Congress, passed the 3d day of March, 1803, for receiving and adjusting the claims to lands south of Tennessee, and east of Pearl river.

Please to take notice, that the following tract of land, situated on the west side of Tombigbee river, beginning at a cotton, running north, seventy degrees west, thirty-seven chains, to a stake; thence, west, eighty-four chains, to a corner oak; thence north, twenty-eight degrees west, forty-three chains, to a corner gum; thence, north, twenty-four chains, to a stake on the bank of Bassett's creek: thence, east, one hundred and forty-four chains, to a branch; thence, south, forty-five degrees east, twenty chains, to a corner maple on the bank of the river; thence, with the river to the beginning, containing eight hundred acres; is claimed by Young Gains, legal representative of Dominique de Olive, having such forms and marks, both natural and artificial, as are represented in the plot annexed: the said land is claimed in and by virtue of the first section of the said act of Congress, by a Spanish grant bearing date the 15th March, 1788, and now exhibited to the register of the land office, to be recorded as directed by said act. To all which he begs leave to refer, as also to a copy of the plot hereunto annexed.

YOUNG GAINS.

Legal representative of Dominique de Olive.

[Plot omitted.]

Surveyed 24th February, 1804, by Thomas Bilbo. Chain carriers, George Gullett and David Gains, Jun.

A Spanish warrant of survey and a bill of sale were exhibited in support of this claim, in the words and figures following, to wit:

MOBILE, January 29, 1788.

His Excellency the GOVERNOR GENERAL:

Dominique de Olive, inhabitant of Mobile jurisdiction, with the greatest respect to your excellency, represents and says, that there is a tract of vacant land on Tombigbee river, containing twenty acres, limited on the north by vacant land, and on the north by Monsieur Dubroca, which until now has never had any proprietor; begs your excellency to grant him the above tract of land, with the profounder as customary, with papers of titles necessary from the Secretary of Government, which may correspond with the concession; for which favor he will be forever thankful.

DOMINIQUE DE OLIVE.

MOBILE, May 4, 1788.

Don Vicent Folch, captain in the Louisiana regiment of fixo, and commandant of civil and military of Mobile and its jurisdiction, certify, that by information from the different inhabitants, that part of land the above petitioner solicits remains vacant.

VICENT FOLCH.

NEW ORLEANS, March 15, 1788.

The commandant of Mobile shall establish that part of twenty acres front, with the profounder of forty as customary, as it is vacant, and not causing prejudice to any neighbors, at the same place mentioned in the above petition, with the precise conditions of making the road and clearing regularly, in the peremptory space of one year; and if at the precise space of three years the land is not settled, during which period it cannot be alienated, this grant to remain null; under which supposition the business of settling the limits will be carried on in the tract, and remitted me, to provide the interested party with titles in form.

ESTEVAN MIRO.

MOBILE, March 5, 1804.

This is a copy of the original in this office under my charge.

JOAQUIN DE OSORNO.

The above is a copy of the Spanish grant.

THOMAS PRICE.

The above is compared exact with the original in this office, under my charge, by me,

JOAQUIN DE OSORNO.

I, Thomas Price, of the post of Mobile, English interpreter for his Majesty the King of Spain, do solemnly swear by the Almighty God, and by the Holy Cross, that this is a true and faithful translation of the Spanish grant or writing hereto annexed.

THOMAS PRICE.

Subscribed and sworn before the Board, March 21st, 1804.—Attest: DAVID PARMELEE 2d, *Clerk.*

Know all men by these presents: I, Dominique de Olive, inhabitant of this place, really and effectually sold and delivered unto Young Gains, inhabitant of Tombigbee river, one tract of land of twenty acres front, by forty in the profounder; limited on the south by land of Valentine Dubroca, and on the north by vacant land, above place called the Sunflower: said land obtained first by concession from his excellency the Governor General of these provinces, the original of which exists in the office of this place, dated the 12th day of March, 1788; said land I have sold and delivered unto said Gains for the sum of eighty silver dollars, which I have received, which said sum I am fully satisfied with, for which I pass this bill of sale with form and regularity, renouncing all rights to said land, and give full possession to Young Gains, with all rights and titles for the same; therefore give up all rights, titles and claims to said land sold and delivered to Young Gains, as above mentioned; in test of which, I sign these presents, in the presence of the commandant of Mobile, the 3d day of December, 1798, I, Don Manuel Lanzos, commandant civil and military of said place, accompanied with two evidences of assistance, who have knowledge of both contracting parties, shall sign these presents with the two evidences of assistance; Dominique de Olive shall sign with a cross, as customary.

YOUNG GAINS,
DOMINIQUE, his x mark.

JOSE LOPEZ, FRANCISCO CANTERO.
Before me,　　MANUEL DE LANZOS.
This is a copy of the original in the office under my charge, which I certify the day and date as abovementioned.

MANUEL DE LANZOS.

The above is a copy of the Spanish bill of sale.

THOS. PRICE.

This was compared exact with original by me.

JOAQ. DE OSORNO. [L. S.]

I, Thomas Price, of the post of Mobile, English interpreter for His Majesty the King of Spain, do solemnly swear by the Almighty God, and by the Holy Cross, that this is a true and faithful translation of the Spanish grant, or writing hereto annexed.

THOS. PRICE.

Subscribed and sworn before the Board, March 21, 1804. Attest: DAVID PARMELEE 2d, *Clerk.*

Entered in record of claims, vol. 1, page 246, by EDWARD LLOYD WAILES, for

JOSEPH CHAMBERS, *Register.*

David Gains, Jun. and George Gullett, chain carriers for the survey in this case, were sworn before

JOHN CALLIER, J. P.

The board ordered that the case be postponed for consideration.

JAMES FRAZIER's case, No. 47 on the docket of the Board, and No. 80 on the books of the Register.

Claim—Of sixteen hundred acres, by virtue of a Spanish warrant of survey, under the first section of the act.

The claimant presented his claim, together with a surveyor's plot of the land claimed, in the words and figures following, to wit:

To the Commissioners appointed in pursuance of the act of Congress, passed the 3d day of March, 1803, for receiving and adjusting the claims to lands south of Tennessee and east of Pearl river.

Please to take notice, that the following tract of land, situated on the west side of Tombigbee river, including part of Toller creek, in the county of Washington; beginning at a cotton tree, running thence, south, forty-four degrees west, one hundred and thirty-three chains and ninety links, to a red haw; thence, north, forty-six degrees west, ninety-five chains, to Toller creek; thence, with the creek north, forty-four degrees east, eighteen chains fifty links, to a persimmon tree; thence, north, for-

ty-six degrees west, thirty-one chains fifty links, to a stake on the north fork of Toller creek: thence, north, forty-four degrees east, one hundred and three chains, to the river, a sweet gum corner; thence, with the meanders of the river, to the beginning; and hath such forms and marks, both natural and artificial, as are fully represented in the plot annexed, containing sixteen hundred acres: is claimed by James Frazier, in and by virtue of a Spanish warrant of survey, bearing date the 31st day of July, 1787, and is now exhibited to the Register of the Land Office to be established east of Pearl river, to be recorded as directed by said act. To all which he begs leave to refer, as also to a copy of the plot herewith filed.

J. F. McGREW, for
JAMES FRAZIER.

MARCH 30, 1804.
[Plot omitted.]

Surveyed March 20, 1804, by Robert Ligon.

A Spanish warrant of survey was exhibited in this case, in the following words and figures, to wit:

Don ESTEVAN MIRO, colonel of His Majesty's royal troops, Governor of the city and province of Louisiana, &c. &c.

MOBILE, *June* 6, 1787.

James Frazier, inhabitant in the jurisdiction of Mobile, with profoundest respect to your excellency, petitions and says, that existeth and is on Tombigbee river forty acres of land, formerly the property of Mr. Farmer, limited on the east side by a tract of land the property of John Turnbull, and on the west side by another of the same, which was forsaken by the widow Farmer, in the year 1780, and until this present has never been claimed by the proprietor, nor any other person for him empowered; and as the attention of the above petitioner is to cultivate tobacco and Indian corn, he begs your excellency to grant him the above petition, with papers necessary from the Secretary of Government, which may correspond with the same.

JAMES FRAZIER.

Don Pedro Favrot, captain in Louisiana regiment, commandant civil and military at this place, certifieth, by information from four of the inhabitants of character of this place, the land above mentioned was forsaken by the same individuals as above mentioned, and at the same time as specified above; and as it may be credited at any time, I give these presents at Mobile, this 7th June, 1787.

PEDRO FAVROT.

NEW ORLEANS, *July* 31, 1787.

The Surveyor General of this province, Don Carlos Laveau Trudeau, shall establish the petitioner on that part of land of forty acres front by its profounder of forty back, as customary, at the same place mentioned in the above petition, not causing prejudice to any person whatsoever, with the precise conditions of making the road and clearing regularly in the peremptory space of one year; and if at the precise space of three years the land is not settled, during which period it cannot be alienated, this grant to remain null; under which supposition, the business of settling the limits will be carried on in the tract, and remitted me, to provide the interested party with titles in form.

ESTEVAN MIRO.

MOBILE, *February* 29, 1804.

The above was compared with the original in this exact by me.

JOAQ. DE OSORNO. [L. S.]

The above copy is exact from the Spanish grant.

THOS. PRICE.

I, Thomas Price, of the post of Mobile, English interpreter for His Majesty the King of Spain, do solemnly swear by the Almighty God, and by the Holy Cross, that this is a true and faithful translation of the Spanish grant, or writing hereto annexed.

THOS. PRICE.

Subscribed and sworn before the Board, March 21, 1804.—Attest: DAVID PARMELEE 2d, *Clerk.*

Entered in record of claims, vol. 1, page 232, by EDWARD LLOYD WAILES, for

JOSEPH CHAMBERS, *Register.*

The Board ordered that the case be postponed for consideration.

JAMES POWELL, executor of William Powell, deceased, case No. 48 on the docket of the Board, and No. 63 on the books of the Register.

Claim—Of four hundred acres, by virtue of a Spanish warrant of survey, under the first section of the act.

The claimant exhibited his claim, together with a surveyor's plot of the land claimed, in the words and figures following, to wit:

To the Commissioners appointed in pursuance of the act of Congress passed the 3d day of March, 1803, for receiving and adjusting the claims to lands south of Tennessee and east of Pearl river.

Please to take notice, that the following tract of land, situated on the west side of Tombigbee river, butting and bounding on the east by said river, to the south by John Johnson's land, beginning on a red oak, west by vacant land, and north by James Powell's land, containing four hundred acres; and hath such forms and marks, both natural and artificial, as are fully represented in the plot annexed: is claimed by James Powell, executor for the estate of William Powell, in and by virtue of a Spanish warrant of survey, and is now exhibited to the Register of the Land Office established east of Pearl river, to be recorded as directed by said act. To all which he begs leaves to refer, as also to a copy of the plot herewith filed.

JAMES POWELL.
Executor of William Powell.

MARCH 20, 1804.

[Plot omitted.]

Surveyed 22d ———, 1804, by John Dease. Chain carriers, James Dean and Amos Read.

In support of this claim, a Spanish warrant of survey was exhibited, in the following words and figures, viz.

FORT ST. STEPHEN'S, 11*th May*, 1795.
To his Excellency the GOVERNOR GENERAL:

William Powell, inhabitant in the jurisdiction of St. Stephen's, with the greatest respect, represents and lays before your excellency, that having been settled on a tract of land these ten years past, situate in distance about eighteen leagues from this Fort St. Stephen's, on up-land, the same leads down to Mobile, which contains about ten acres front, bounded on the south by John Johnson, and on the north by Owen Sullivant; the land being vacant, begs your excellency to grant him the titles of cession: for which favor from your excellency he will be forever thankful:

WILLIAM POWELL.

FORT ST. STEPHEN'S, 11*th May*, 1795.
To His Excellency the GOVERNOR GENERAL:

By information from the different inhabitants of this post, it appears that the land is vacant, and within the King's dominion; therefore, cannot cause any prejudice to any.

ANTONIO PALAO.

NEW ORLEANS, 10*th June*, 1795.

The Surveyor of the province shall establish that part of ten acres of land front, the same that solicits the petitioner, with forty back, as customary, as it appears to be vacant land, and not causing any prejudice to the neighbors, with the precise conditions of making the road, and clearing regularly, in the peremptory space of one year; and if at the precise space of three years the land is not settled, during which period it cannot be alienated, this grant to lay null, under which supposition, the business of settling the limits will be carried on in the tract, and remitted me, to provide the interested party with titles in form.

THE BARON OF CARONDELET.

Certifieth that the above is a copy of the original in the office under my charge, at Fort St. Stephen's, October 6th, 1795.

FERNANDO LESORE.

Translated from the Spanish grant—copied.

THOMAS PRICE.

The above was compared to this original in the office, by me,

JOAQ. DE OSORNO. [L. S.]

I, Thomas Price, of the post of Mobile, English interpreter for His Majesty the King of Spain, do solemnly swear by the Almighty God, and by the Holy Cross, that this is a true and faithful translation of the Spanish grant or writing hereto annexed

THOMAS PRICE.

Subscribed and sworn before the Board, March 21st, 1804.—Attest: DAVID PARMELEE 2d, *Clerk.*

Entered in record of claims, volume 1, page 182, by EDW. LLOYD WAILES, for

JOSEPH CHAMBERS, *Register.*

The Board ordered that the case be postponed for consideration.

SIMON ANDRY's case, No. 49 on the docket of the Board, and No. 106 on the books of the Register.

Claim—Of four hundred and seventy-nine acres, by virtue of a Spanish warrant of survey, under the first section of the act.

The claimant presented his claim, together with a surveyor's plot of the land claimed, in the words and figures following, to wit:

To the Commissioners appointed in pursuance of the act of Congress passed the 3d day of March, 1803, for receiving and adjusting claims to land south of the Tennessee river and east of the Pearl river.

FORT STODDERT, *March* 21, 1804.

Please to take notice, that the following tract of land, lying west of the Mobile river, butting and bounding on the north by Grog Hall creek, and on the south by Joseph Chastang, on the east by the said river, and west by vacant land, is claimed by Simon Andrey, under and by virtue of a Spanish grant, or order of survey, granted to the said Simon Andrey, as may appear by the original grant now delivered to the Register of the Land Office, (to be established east of Pearl river) to be recorded as directed by that act. To all which he begs leave to refer, as also to the copy of the plot herewith filed.

CHASTANG, Jeune, acting for

SIMON ANDREY.

[Plot omitted.]

Surveyed, 20 h March, 1804, by James Gordon. Chain bearers. Gabriel Tissrah and William Weathers.

In support of this claim, a Spanish warrant of survey was exhibited in the words and figures following, viz.:

MOBILE, *April* 13, 1787.

Senor Don ESTEVAN MIRO, colonel of the royal troops, and Governor of civil and military in the province of the Louisiana, &c.:

Simon Andrey, inhabitant of Mobile jurisdiction, with the greatest submission and respect, says, that on the river Tombigbee, there is forty acres of land that has been evacuated by Mr. Magillivrey these eight years past, lying and situate between the property of Mr. Chastang on the southeast side, and on the northeast side by a place called Grog Hall, so named by said Mr. Magillivrey, above mentioned, comprehending both sides of the river; and that the petitioner having slaves in number sufficient to cultivate the above mentioned lands, humbly begs your excellency to favor him with a grant for the same, having paid due attention that no person whatever hath laid any claims since the evacuation of the above mentioned lands; he therefore begs your excellency to favor him of being proprietor of the above mentioned forty acres of land front, with its profounder, that corresponds, as customary, and begs your excellency would give directions to the secretary of despatches for the same.

God preserve you many years.

Signed for   SIMON ANDREY.

Don Pedro Favrot, captain in the Louisiana regiment of fixo, and commandant of civil and military of Mobile, &c. certifieth, that having taken a second information from four credible inhabitants, who declare, that the above mentioned forty acres of land, front on the river, at the place above named, have been abandoned or evacuated by the same person above named, as long as the same term of time of eight years past, as above mentioned; and being convinced of the fact of the above information, I have signed these presents, the 13th of April, 1787.

PEDRO FAVROT.

NEW ORLEANS, *May* 14, 1787.

The commandant of Mobile post shall establish the petitioner on twelve acres of land only, front on the river, and forty acres back in the profounder, as customary, without causing any detriment; the petitioner may have choice of the above twelve acres front on the river within the boundary of the above mentioned forty acres front on the river, by him petitioned for, with these express obligations: that, within the term of one year, he shall make roads and lawful improvements; and if neglected for the term of three years, the same land shall become vacant; observing these express conditions, that, during the above mentioned term of three years, he, the petitioner, shall not convey, bargain for, or sell, or cause it to be done, any part of the above mentioned twelve acres of lands front on the river, until intelligence shall be given of the above obligation being completed, which may correspond with the titles in due form.

ESTEVAN MIRO.

The above is a true copy of the original in the office of this place.

SANTIAGO DE LA SAUSSAYE,
Public Writer in Mobile.

MOBILE, *July* 8, 1787.
Translated from a copy of the original in this office.

THOMAS PRICE.

I, Thomas Price, of the post of Mobile, English Interpreter for His Majesty the King of Spain, do solemnly swear by the Almighty God, and by the Holy Cross, that this is a true and faithful translation of the Spanish grant or writing hereto annexed.

THOMAS PRICE.

Subscribed and sworn before the Board, March 21, 1804.—Attest: DAVID PARMELEE 2d, *Clerk.*

Entered in record of claims, vol. 1, page 331, by EDWARD LLOYD WAILES, for

JOSEPH CHAMBERS, *Register.*

Gabriel Tissrah and William Weathers, chain carriers for the survey in this case, were sworn before

JAMES CALLIER, Esq., *Justice of Peace.*

The Board ordered that the case be postponed for consideration.

SIMON ANDREY's case, No. 50 on the docket of the Board, and No. 163 on the books of the Register.

Claim.—A right of pre-emption of forty-one acres, as legal representative of Charlotte Haurale, under the third section of the act.

The claimant presented his claim, together with a surveyor's plot of the land claimed, in the following words and figures, to wit:

To the Commissioners appointed in pursuance of an act of Congress passed the 3d of March, 1803, for receiving and adjusting claims to lands south of the Tennessee river and east of Pearl river.

FORT STODDERT, *March* 21, 1804.

Please to take notice, that the following tracts of land, one lying on the west, and the other on the east side of Mobile river, beginning at a persimon tree, and adjoining to lands claimed by Joseph Chastang, for the lands on the west side of the river; the land on the east side of said river beginning at the green oak landing, and running until it also joins to lands of the said Joseph Chastang, is claimed by Simon Andrey, as the legal representative of Charlotte Maurale, under and by virtue of the third section of an act of Congress passed the 3d March, 1803, for pre-emption, to be recorded agreeably to that act. To all which he begs leave to refer, as also to the copy of the plots herewith filed.

CHASTANG, Jeune, acting for
SIMON ANDREY.
[Plot omitted.]

Surveyed February 20, 1804, by James Gordon. Chain carriers, Joseph Campbell and Gabriel Tissrah.

In support of claim, a writing was exhibited in the following words and figures, to wit:

I, the subscriber, Simon Favre, do give, and, by these presents, have given, unto Charlotte Haurale, in consideration of her good services done me, a tract of land on the bluff, beginning at my persimon tree, until it joins Mr. Chastang's boundary, which contains about one and a half acres on the river; and, on the opposite side of the said river another tract of land, beginning at my landing, called the Green Oak, until it joins also Mr. Chastang's boundary, forming about two acres front on the river, with the same profounder as customary; and that it may be well understood that the said Charlotte Haraule shall enjoy the same fully and peaceably, she being the only heir to the said lands, in promising her to warrant the same from all troubles or impeachments whatever.

Given, in the presence of evidences at my plantation, the twenty-third of June, one thousand seven hundred and seventy-three.

SIMON FAVRE.

DUVAL, } Test.
P. SUZAN, }

The above is a true copy of the original.

THOMAS PRICE.

I, Thomas Price, of the post of Mobile, English interpreter for His Majesty the King of Spain, do solemnly swear by the Almighty God, and by the Holy Cross, that this is a true and faithful translation of the writing hereto annexed.

THOS. PRICE.

Subscribed and sworn before the Board, March 21, 1804.—Attest: DAVID PARMELEE 2d, *Clerk.*

79

Entered in record of claims, vol. 1, page 495, by EDWARD LLOYD WAILES, for

JOSEPH CHAMBERS, *Register.*

The Board ordered that the case be postponed for consideration.

GEORGE BREWER, Junior's, case, No 51 on the docket of the Board, and No. 75 on the books of the Register.

Claim—Of eight hundred acres, as assignee and legal representative of Valentine Dubroca, by virtue of a Spanish warrant of survey, under the first section of the act.

The claimant presented his claim, together with a surveyor's plot of the land claimed, in the following words and figures, to wit:

To the Commissioners appointed in pursuance of the act of Congress passed the 3d day of March, 1803, for receiving and adjusting the claims to lands south of Tennessee and east of Pearl river.

Please to take notice, that the following tract of land, situated on the waters of Tombigbee, in the county of Washington, beginning at sweet gum, and running west, one hundred and five chains, to a sweet gum corner; thence, south, sixty-three chains twenty-five links, to a laurel corner; thence, east, one hundred and seventy-seven chains, to a stake corner on the river; thence, with the meanders of the river, to the beginning; containing eight hundred acres, having such shape, form, and marks, both natural and artificial, as are fully represented in the plot annexed: is claimed by George Brewer, Jr., as legal representative of Valentine Dubroca, in and by virtue of a Spanish warrant of survey, and is now exhibited to the Register of the Land Office established east of Pearl river, to be recorded as directed by said act. To all which he begs leave to refer, as also to a copy of the plot herewith filed.

GEORGE BREWER, Jun.

MARCH 16, 1804.
[Plot omitted.]

Surveyed February 21, 1804, by Robert Ligon.

A Spanish warrant of survey and bill of sale were exhibited in this case, in the following words and figures, viz:

MOBILE, *October* 2, 1787.

His Excellency the GOVERNOR GENERAL:

Valentine Dubroca, inhabitant of Mobile jurisdiction, with the greatest respects to your excellency, petitions and says, there is found on Tombigbee river twenty acres of land, limited on the north by land of Dominique de Olive, and on the south by vacant land, which never had any proprietor; in attention of which, he expects from your excellency the favor of granting him the above petition, with the corresponding papers of titles, from the Secretary of Government, which may correspond with the concession: for which favor from your excellency he will be forever thankful.

VALENTINE DUBROCA.

MOBILE, *October* 2, 1787.

Don Vicent Folch, captain in the fixed Louisiana regiment, commandant civil and military of Mobile, and its jurisdiction, certifies, that the land the petitioner solicits is found vacant, by information taken to that purpose from several inhabitants knowing the same.

VICENT FOLCH.

NEW ORLEANS, *October* 22, 1787.

The surveyor of this province, Don Carlos Laveau Trudeau, shall establish this individual on that part of land of twenty acres front, which he solicits, with the profounder as customary, of forty, at the same place mentioned in the above petition, as it is vacant, not causing any prejudice to any neighbors, with the precise conditions of making the road and clearing regularly in the peremptory space of one year; and if, at the precise space of three years, the land is not settled, after which period it cannot be established, this grant to remain null; under which supposition, the business of settling the limits will be carried on in the tract, and remitted me, to provide the interested party with titles in form.

This is a copy, compared to the original existing in the archives under my charge, which I certify.

JOAQUIN DE OSORNO. [L. S.]

MOBILE, *February* 24, 1804.

The above is a copy of the Spanish grant.

THOMAS PRICE.

I, Thomas Price, of the post of Mobile, English interpreter for His Majesty the King of Spain, do solemnly swear by the Almighty God, and by the Holy Cross, that this is a true and faithful translation of the Spanish grant or writing hereto annexed.

THOMAS PRICE.

Subscribed and sworn before the Board, March 21, 1804.—Attest: DAVID PARMELEE 2d, *Clerk.*

To all to whom these may come:

I, Valentine Dubroca, neighbor of Mobile jurisdiction, hath really and effectually sold to George Brewer, inhabitant of Tombigbee river, one tract of land, containing twenty acres, situate at a place called Sunflower on said river, limited on the north side by one of Dominique de Olive, and on the south by another of Arban Durny; said land is my own property, by concession from his excellency the Governor General, in the year one thousand seven hundred and eighty-seven, the original of which exists in the archives of this place, the copy of which I sold to the purchaser, safe, without mortgage or claims on the same, for the sum of sixty silver dollars, which I have received, and am satisfied; renouncing all rights, titles, and claims, me and my heirs, to said land and possessions thereunto belonging, and give full possession to the purchaser, his heirs, and assigns, forever, to dispose or make use of for him, his heirs, and assigns: and, being present said George Brewer, he accepts this bill of sale and titles to said land above mentioned, for the same sum we bargained for, in which he is well satisfied. In testimony of which, this is dated at Mobile, the twenty-sixth day of June, one thousand seven hundred and ninety-eight.

I, Don Manuel de Lanzos, commandant civil and military of said province, accompanied with two evidences of assistance, knowing both parties contracting, and sign, with the two evidences. And I, the said commandant, &c.

VALENTINE DUBROCA.

FRANCISCO CONTERO, } *Witnesses.*
GARONEMO YAUANAS, }

Before me,

MANUEL DE LANZOS.

MOBILE, *June* 26, 1798.

This is a copy of the original that passed before me, for which I certify.

MANUEL DE LANZOS.

The above is a bill of sale of the Spanish original.

THOMAS PRICE.

The above was compared exact with the original in this office under my charge, by me,

JOAQUIN DE OSORNO. [L. S.]

Entered in record of claims, vol. 1, page 214, by EDWARD LLOYD WAILES, for

JOSEPH CHAMBERS, *Register.*

I, Thomas Price, of the post of Mobile, English interpreter for His Majesty the King of Spain, do solemnly swear by the Almighty God, and by the Holy Cross, that this is a true and faithful translation of the Spanish grant or writing hereto annexed.

THOMAS PRICE.

Subscribed and sworn before the Board, March 21st, 1804.—Attest: DAVID PARMELEE 2d, *Clerk.*

The Board ordered that the case be postponed for consideration.

JOHN BREWER's case, No. 52 on the docket of the Board, and No. 104 on the books of the Register.

Claim—Of eight hundred acres, as assignee and legal representative of Charles Arbon Demoy, by virtue of a Spanish warrant of survey, under the first section of the act.

The claimant presented his claim, together with a surveyor's plot of the land claimed, in the following words and figures, to wit:

To the Commissioners appointed in pursuance of the act of Congress passed the 3d day of March, 1803, *for receiving and adjusting the claims to lands south of Tennessee, and east of Pearl river.*

Please to take notice, that the following tract of land, situated on the Tombigbee river, in the county of Washington, beginning at a cotton tree, being James Denley's corner, running thence, due west, eighty-one chains and fifty links, to a white oak; thence, north, sixty-three chains twenty-five links, to an ironwood; thence, east, one hundred and seventy chains, to a stake corner on the river; thence, with the river, to the place of beginning; containing eight hundred acres, having such shape, form, and marks, both natural and artificial, as are fully represented in the plot annexed: is claimed by John

Brewer, as legal representative of Charles Abon Demoy, in and by virtue of a Spanish warrant of survey, and now exhibited to the Register of the Land Office established east of Pearl river, to be recorded as directed by said act. To all which he begs leave to refer, as also to a copy of the plot herewith filed.

JOHN BREWER,
Legal representative of Charles Arbon Demoy.
MARCH 16, 1804.

[Plot omitted.]

Surveyed 20th February, 1804, by Robert Ligon. Chain carriers, James Danley, George Dickey.

A Spanish warrant of survey and a bill of sale were exhibited in this case in the words and figures following, viz:

His Excellency Don ESTEVAN MIRO, Colonel of the royal army, Governor civil and military of the city and province of the Louisiana, &c. &c.

MOBILE, *October* 10*th*, 1787.

Charles Abon Demoy, inhabitant in Mobile jurisdiction, with the greatest respect to your excellency, represents and says there is on Tombigbee river forty acres of vacant land, which land never has had any proprietor, limited on the north side by land, the property of Valentine Dubroca, and on the south by a tract of land of Daniel Ward's; and with intention to cultivate tobacco and corn on said land, begs your excellency's goodness in granting me the above forty acres as real proprietor of the same, with the profounder, as customary; for which favor he will be ever thankful.

CHARLES ABON DEMOY.

MOBILE, *October* 10*th*, 1787.

Don Vincent Folch, captain in the fixed Louisiana regiment, commandant civil and military of Mobile and its district, certifies, that what the petitioner solicits is found vacant by the information taken for that purpose from several inhabitants knowing the same.

VINCENT FOLCH.

NEW ORLEANS, *October* 22*d*, 1787.

The surveyor of this province, Don Charles Laveau Trudeau, shall establish this individual on that part of land of twenty acres front, which he solicits, with its profounder, as customary, of forty, at the same place mentioned in the above petition, as it is vacant, not causing prejudice to any neighbors, with the precise conditions of making the road, and clearing regularly, in the peremptory space of one year; and if, at the precise space of three years, the land is not settled, after which period it cannot be established, this grant to remain null; under which supposition, the business of settling the limits will be carried on the tract, and remitted me, to provide the interested party with titles in form.

ESTEVAN MIRO.

This is exact with the original, from which is written this copy, and existing in the archives of this place, under my charge; the same I certify at Mobile, the 23d of October, 1800. MANUEL DE LANZOS.

This was compared with the original existing in the office under my charge.

JOAQUIN DE OSORNO. [L. S.]

The above is a copy of the Spanish grant.

THOS. PRICE.

I, Thomas Price, of the post of Mobile, English interpreter for his Majesty the King of Spain, do solemnly swear by the Almighty God, and by the Holy Cross, that this is a true and faithful translation of the Spanish grant or writings hereto annexed.

THOS. PRICE.

Subscribed and sworn before the Board, March 21st, 1804.—Attest: DAVID PARMELEE 2d, *Clerk.*

To all to whom these may come:

Charles Arbon Demoy, inhabitant of Mobile jurisdiction, hath really and effectually sold unto John Brewer, inhabitant established on Tombigbee river, United States territory, since the limitation, a tract of land my own property, containing twenty acres front, with the profounder as customary of forty; said land limited on one side by land of Valentine Dubroca, deceased, and on the other side by land, the purchaser's property; the above land proves to be my own property by titles of concession from his excellency the Governor General of these provinces, warranted to me in the year one thousand seven hundred and eighty-seven, the original of which exists in the archives of this place, of which I took a copy of certification from the commandant; the same I sold to said purchaser, safe from all mortgages or claims, with all the improvements, for the sum of two hundred silver dollars, which I received and am satisfied, and by these renounce all rights, titles, and claims to said lands and possessions thereunto belonging, and by these give full possession to said purchaser, his heirs and assigns, forever, to dispose of for him his heirs and assigns; and, as the purchaser is not present to accept in his favor the bill of sale with titles for said said land, accept for him, and in his favor, John Baptist Dubroca and Thomas Price, who hold themselves satisfied, according to the above contract, passing receipts on both sides, both being satisfied. In testimony of which, these are dated at Mobile, the twenty-third day of October, one thousand eight hundred.

I, Don Manuel De Lanzos, captain retired from the regiment fixed of the Louisiana, commandant civil and military of Mobile place and its jurisdiction, accompanied with two evidences of assistance, who is knowing the vender and the two persons who accepted in favor of the purchaser, having no Notary Public, they all sign these with me, at Mobile, the same day and year above dated.

CHARLES ARBON DEMOY.

For the purchaser: John Baptist Dubroca, Thomas Price. Evidences of assistance: Salvador Gormez, Augustin Blanco.

Before me,　　MANUEL DE LANZOS.

This is a copy of the original passed before me, and existing in the archives of this place under my charge, which I certify, the day above dated.

MANUEL DE LANZOS.

The above is a bill of sale of the Spanish grant.

THOS. PRICE.

The above was compared exact with the original in this office under my charge, by me.

JOAQUIN DE OSORNO. [L. S.]

I, Thomas Price, of the post of Mobile, English interpreter for His Majesty the King of Spain, do solemnly swear by the Almighty God, and by the Holy Cross, that this is a true and faithful translation of the Spanish grant or writings hereto annexed.

THOS. PRICE.

Subscribed and sworn before the Board, March 21st, 1804.—Attest: DAVID PARMELEE 2d, Clerk.

Entered in record of claims, vol. 1, page 320, by EDWARD LLOYD WAILES, for

JOSEPH CHAMBERS, Register.

The Board ordered that the case be postponed for consideration.

The heirs of JAMES McGREW, case No. 53 on the docket of the Board, and No. 73 on the books of the Register.

Claim—Of four hundred acres, by virtue of a Spanish warrant of survey, under the first section of the act.

The claimants presented their claim, together with a surveyor's plot of the land claimed, in the following words and figures, to wit:

To the Commissioners appointed, in pursuance of the act of Congress passed the 3d day of March, 1803, to receive and adjust claims to lands east of Pearl river.

Please to take notice, that the following tract of land, situated on the west side of the river Tombigbee, butting and bounded as follows: beginning on a corner cotton tree above Reams's line and lands claimed by Young Gains, &c. about two miles below Fort St. Stephen's, (supposed;) thence, running south, eighteen degrees west, one hundred and twenty-six chains fifty links, to a corner red oak; thence, north, seventy-two degrees west, thirty-one chains and fifty links, to a corner stake; thence, north, eighteen degrees east, one hundred and twenty-six chains fifty links, to a corner cotton tree on the bank of the river; thence, down the meanders of the river to the first mentioned station; having such marks, natural and artificial, as are represented in the plot annexed, containing four hundred acres; is claimed by James McGrew; or by his heirs, to wit: Peggy McGrew, Eliza McGrew, or Eliza De Castro, Alexander McGrew, Giles McGrew, James McGrew, Jane McGrew, Nancy McGrew, Keziah McGrew, John McGrew, and Wm. Mc Grew, children of said James McGrew, under and by virtue of a Spanish warrant or order of survey, granted unto him, the said James McGrew- on the day of; and the said claimant did, on the 27th day of October, 1795, inhabit and cultivate the tract herein specified, agreeably to the requisitions of the first section of an act of Congress, entitled an act, and the

same does not appear to be claimed by any preceding provision of the act, and now exhibited to the Register of the Land Office, established east of Pearl river, to be recorded as is directed by said act. To all which they beg leave to refer, as also to the plot hereto fixed, &c. &c.

Presented February 29th, 1804, by
ELIZABETH DE CASTRO, her × mark.
Witness, EDWIN LEWIS.
[Plot omitted.]

Surveyed in February, 1804, by Robert Ligon. Chain carriers, Young Gains, Dawson Grimes.

In support of this claim, a Spanish warrant of survey was exhibited in the following words and figures, to wit:

Don ESTEVAN MIRO, Colonel of the royal army, Governor civil and military of the city and province of Louisiana, &c. &c.

MOBILE, 12th January, 1788.

James McGrew, inhabitant of this jurisdiction of Mobile, with the greatest respect to your excellency, represents and says, that there is on the Tombigbee river ten acres of vacant land, which, until now, has never been claimed by any proprietor; he begs your excellency to grant him, with the profounder customary, with papers of titles necessary from the Secretary of Government, that may correspond with the concession; for which favor he will be forever thankful.

JAMES McGREW.

Don Vicent Folch, captain in regiment of fixed of the Louisiana, commandant civil and military of Mobile and its district, certifieth, that the land the petitioner solicits is vacant, by information from the different inhabitants who are knowing to the same place, for which I sign these presents the day and date above mentioned.

VICENT FOLCH.

NEW ORLEANS, 9th February, 1788.

The surveyor of this province, Don Carlos Laveau Trudeau, shall establish that part of land of ten acres front, with its profounder of forty acres as customary, as it is vacant, and not cause prejudice to any neighbors, at the place mentioned in the above petition, with the precise conditions of making the road, and clearing regularly in the peremptory space of one year; and if at the precise space of three years the land is not settled, during which period it cannot be alienated, this grant to remain null; under which supposition, the business of settling the limits will be carried on in the tract, and remitted me to provide the interested party with titles in form.

ESTEVAN MIRO.

MOBILE, March 6th, 1788.

Certifieth the above is a copy of the original existing in the office of this place.

SANTIAGO DE LA SAUSSAYE,
Public Notary.

The above is a copy of the Spanish grant.

THOS. PRICE.

The above is compared exact with the original in this office, under my charge, by me.

JOAQ. DE OSORNO. [L. S.]

I, Thomas Price, of the post of Mobile, English interpreter for His Majesty the King of Spain, do solemnly swear, by the Almighty God, and by the Holy Cross, that this is a true and faithful translation of the Spanish grant, or writing hereto annexed.

THOS. PRICE.

Subscribed and sworn before the Board, March 21st, 1804.—Attest: DAVID PARMELEE 2d, Clerk.

Entered in record of claims, vol. 1, page 206, by EDWARD LLOYD WAILES, for

JOSEPH CHAMBERS, Register.

The Board ordered that the case be postponed for consideration.

FRANCIS BOYKIN's case, No. 54 on the docket of the Board, and No. 58 on the books of the Register.

Claim—Of eight hundred acres, as representative of Adam Hollinger, by virtue of a Spanish warrant of survey, under the first section of the act.

The claimant exhibited his claim, together with a surveyor's plot of the land claimed, in the following words and figures, to wit:

To the Commissioners appointed, in pursuance of an act of Congress, passed the 3d day of March, 1803, for receiving and adjusting the claims to lands south of Tennessee and east of Pearl river,

Please to take notice, that the following tract of land situated on the river Tombigbee, in the county of Washington, beginning at an elm, and running north, sixty-seven degrees west, one hundred and thirty-eight chains, to a stake; thence, south, twenty-three degrees west, sixty-three chains twenty-four links, to a black gum; thence, south, sixty-seven degrees east, one hundred and fifteen chains, to a cotton tree standing on the river; thence, with the river, to the beginning, containing eight hundred acres, having such shape, form, and marks, both natural and artificial, as are represented in the plot annexed: is claimed by Francis Boykin under and by virtue of a Spanish warrant of survey, dated the 10th day of June, 1795, and now exhibited to the Register of the Land Office east of Pearl river, to be recorded as directed by said act. To all which he begs leave to refer, as also to a copy of the plot herewith filed.

FRANCIS BOYKIN.

MARCH 15th, 1804.

[Plot omitted.]

Surveyed 5th of March, 1804, by Robert Ligon. Chain carriers, Rice Wells, William McGee.

In support of this claim, a Spanish warrant of survey was exhibited, in the words and figures following, viz:

St. Stephen's, May 1st, 1795.

His Excellency the Governor General:

Adam Hollinger, with the greatest respect to your excellency, represents and says, that, these five years past he has been settled on a tract of land, about ten miles distance from the fort, on Mobile side; the said land contains twenty acres, limited next to the fort by Nathaniel Blackwell, and on the other side by land of Mr. Bassett's; the same was vacant when the petitioner took possession; he begs your excellency to grant him the above petition, with papers of titles necessary which may correspond with the concession; for which favor he will be forever thankful.

ADAM HOLLINGER.

St. Stephen's, 6th May, 1795.

His Excellency the Governor General:

By information from the inhabitants of this post, that the land above mentioned is King's commons, and not causing any prejudice to any neighbors, your excellency may dispose as it may seem best.

ANTONIO PALAO.

New Orleans, 10th June, 1795.

The Surveyor General of this province, or some individual named by him for that business, shall establish that part of land of twenty acres front, with its profounder of forty acres, as customary, as it is vacant, not causing any prejudice to any neighbors, at the same place mentioned in the above petition, with the precise conditions of making the road, and clearing regularly in the peremptory space of one year; and, if at the precise space of three years the land is not settled, during which period it cannot be alienated, this grant to remain null; under which supposition, the business of settling the limits will be carried on in the tract, and remitted me, to provide the interested party with titles in form.

THE BARON OF CARONDELET.

Registered: FERNANDO LISORE.

The above is a copy of the Spanish grant.

THOS. PRICE.

The above was compared exact with the original in this office under my charge, by me,

JOAQ. DE OSORNO. [L. S.]

I, Thomas Price, of the post of Mobile, English interpreter for His Majesty the King of Spain, do solemnly swear by the Almighty God, and by the Holy Cross, that this is a true and faithful translation of the Spanish grant or writing hereto annexed.

THOS. PRICE.

Subscribed and sworn before the Board, March 21st, 1804. Attest: David Parmelee 2d, Clerk.

On the back of the original Spanish warrant there is an endorsement in the following words and figures, viz:

For value received of Francis Boykin, of the county of Washington, I do assign, transfer, release, and forever quit claim to the said Francis Boykin, all my interest, right, and title to all the lands which can or ought to be claimed or holden by virtue of the foregoing order or warrant of survey from the Spanish Government.

Witness my hand the 21st of March, 1804.

ADAM A. HOLLINGER, his x mark.

Test: Edward Lloyd Wailes.

Entered in record of claims, vol. 1, page 169, by Edward Lloyd Wailes, for

JOSEPH CHAMBERS, Register.

Rice Wells and William McGeehe, chain carriers for the survey in this case, were sworn before John Callier, Esq. Justice of Peace.

The Board ordered that the case be postponed for consideration.

Ann Lawrence's case, No. 55 on the docket of the Board, and No. 101 on the books of the Register.

Claim—Of eight hundred acres, as legal representative of Moses Moore, by virtue of a Spanish warrant of survey, under the first section of the act.

The claimant presented her claim, together with a surveyor's plot of the land claimed, in the following words and figures, to wit:

To the Commissioners appointed in pursuance of the act of Congress, passed the 3d day of March, 1803, for receiving and adjusting claims to land south of Tennessee, and east of Pearl river.

Please to take notice, that the following tract of land, situated on the west side of the river Tombigbee, in the county of Washington, beginning on said river at an oak; thence, south, twenty-five degrees east, fourteen chains; thence, south, thirty-six degrees east, one hundred and ten chains; thence, south, seventeen degrees east, seventeen chains; thence, south, seventy degrees east, seventy-seven chains, to a corner stake; thence, north, seventeen degrees east, ninety-three chains, to a sassafras; thence, west, twenty-five chains; thence, north, sixty-eight degrees west, twenty-five chains; thence up the meanders of said river to the beginning; containing eight hundred acres, and hath such forms and marks, both natural and artificial, as are fully represented in the plot annexed: is claimed by the widow Ann Lawrence, legal representative of Moses Moore, in and by virtue of a Spanish warrant of survey, and is now exhibited to the Register of the Land Office established east of Pearl river, to be recorded as directed by said act. To all which she begs leave to refer, as also to a copy of the plot herewith filed.

JOSEPH LAWRENCE,

For Ann Lawrence,

Legal representative of Moses Moore.

MARCH 20, 1804.

[Plot omitted.]

Chain carriers, James Bilbo and William Phelps. Surveyed 19th March, 1804, by Thomas Bilbo.

In this case, a Spanish warrant of survey was exhibited, in the words and figures following, viz.:

Mobile, October 1, 1787.

His Excellency the Governor General of the province of Louisiana:

Moses Moore, inhabitant in the jurisdiction of Mobile, with the greatest respect to your excellency, represents and says, that there is found on Tombigbee river a tract of land of twenty acres, formerly the property of Mr. McIntosh, interpreter and commissary of the Chickasaw Indians, in the English times; limited on the north by the same land, and on the south by Sunflower; which was evacuated by said McIntosh in the year eighty, and, until this present, never has been claimed by him, nor no other for him empowered. The petitioner being necessitated for such a tract to cultivate tobacco and Indian corn, he begs your excellency to grant him the above petition, with the profounder as customary, with papers of titles necessary, from the secretary of Government, which may correspond with the concession; for which favor he will be forever thankful.

MOSES MOORE.

Don Vicent Folch, captain in Louisiana regiment of infantry, and commandant civil and military of Mobile and its jurisdiction, certifies that the land the above petitioner solicits is vacant, by information from the different inhabitants of this district.

VICENT FOLCH.

New Orleans, October 22, 1787.

The surveyor of this province, Don Carlos Laveau Trudeau, shall establish that part of land of twenty acres front, with its profounder of forty acres, as customary, as it is vacant, not causing any prejudice to any neighbors, at the same place mentioned in the above petition, with the precise conditions of making the road, and clearing regularly, in the peremptory space of one year; and if, at the precise space of three years, the land is not settled, during which period it cannot be alienated, this grant to remain null; under which supposition, the business of setting the limits will be carried on in the tract, and remitted me to provide the interested party with titles in form.

ESTEVAN MIRO.

This is a copy compared with the original in this office, Mobile, March 5, 1804.

JOAQ. DE OSORNO.

The above is a copy of the Spanish grant.

THOMAS PRICE.

The above compared with the original exact in this office under my charge.

JOAQ. DE OSORNO. [L. s.]

I, Thomas Price, of the post of Mobile, English interpreter for His Majesty the King of Spain, do solemnly swear by the Almighty God and the Holy Cross, that this is a true and faithful translation of the Spanish grant or writing hereto annexed.

THOMAS PRICE.

Subscribed and sworn before the Board, March 21, 1804.—Attest: DAVID PARMELEE 2d, *Clerk.*

Entered in record of claims, volume 1, page 308, by EDWARD LLOYD WAILES, for

JOSEPH CHAMBERS, *Register.*

In support of the right of representation, the claimant exhibited the last will and testament of the said Moses Moore, bearing date the 25th of July, 1791, in which he willed and devised to the said Ann Lawrence all his right and title to the land now claimed, which she was to have and possess after the decease of Margaret, the widow of said Moore; which said will was duly executed, proved, and approved.

The Board ordered that the case be postponed for consideration.

JOHN CALLIER's case, No. 56 on the docket of the Board, and No. 95 on the books of the Register.

Claim—Of seven hundred and eighty-one acres, one rood, and eleven poles, as assignee and legal representative of Adam Hollinger, by virtue of a Spanish warrant of survey, under the first section of the act.

The claimant presented his claim, together with a surveyor's plot of the land claimed, in the words and figures following viz.:

To the Commissioners appointed in pursuance of the act of Congress passed the 3d day of March, 1803, for receiving and adjusting the claims to lands south of Tennessee, and east of Pearl river.

Please to take notice, that the following tract of land, situated on the west side of Tombigbee river, Washington county, butted on said river, and bounded on the north by Carny's old improvement; on the west by vacant land, and on the south by the claims of Francis Stringer and Thomas Malone; beginning on a hackberry on the river bank, and runs south, forty-seven degrees west, at thirty-two chains, the back swamp at one hundred and thirty chains, crossing Stringer's mill branch; in all, one hundred and thirty chains, to a small pine corner; thence, south, forty-three degrees east, at thirty chains, crossing a small branch; in all, sixty-three chains twenty-four links, to a pine corner; thence, north, forty-seven degrees east at seventeen chains, crossing the mill branch at eighty chains, crossing the back swamp; in all, one hundred and twenty-three chains, to an elm corner on the river bank; thence, the meanders of the river, to the beginning; having such marks, natural and artificial, as are represented in the annexed plot, containing seven hundred and eighty-one acres, one rood, and eleven poles: is claimed by John Callier, legal representative of Adam Hollinger, under and by virtue of a Spanish grant bearing date the 9th day of February, 1788, and now exhibited unto the Register of the Land Office established east of Pearl river, to be recorded as directed by said act. To all which he begs leave to refer, as also to the copy of the plot herewith filed.

JOHN CALLIER.

[Plot omitted.]

Chain carriers, Noah Pelcher, and Francis Stringer. Surveyed March 20, 1804, by Thomas Malone.

In support of this claim, a Spanish warrant of survey was exhibited, in the following words and figures, to wit:

MOBILE, *January* 21, 1788.

His Excellency Don ESTEVAN MIRO, colonel of the royal army, Governor civil and military of the city and province of Louisiana, &c.

Wilford Hoggatt, inhabitant in Mobile jurisdiction, with the greatest respect to your excellency, says, there are found on this river Tombigbee twenty acres of vacant land: said land until now never had any proprietor; in attention of this, begs your excellency's generosity in granting him the proprietary of said land, with

the profounder, as customary, with papers of titles from the secretary of Government, which may correspond with the concession: for which favor he will be forever thankful.

WILFORD HOGGATT.

Don Vicent Folch, captain in the fixed Louisiana regiment, commandant civil and military of the above-mentioned place and district, certifies that the land the petitioner solicits is found vacant, as by information taken to that effect of several inhabitants who are well acquainted with the same; for which I sign these presents, at the place abovementioned, the day and date above.

VICENT FOLCH.

NEW ORLEANS, *February* 9, 1788.

The Surveyor General of this province, Don Carlos Laveau Trudeau, shall establish that part of land of twenty acres front, with the profounder, as customary, of forty, at the same place mentioned in the above petition, as it is vacant, not causing prejudice to any neighbors, with the precise conditions of making the road, and clearing regularly, in the peremptory space of one year: and if, at the precise space of three years, the land is not settled, after which period it cannot be established, this grant to remain null; under which supposition, the business of settling the limits will be carried on in the tract, and remitted me to provide the interested party with titles in form.

ESTEVAN MIRO.

This is a copy of the original existing in the archives under my charge.

JOAQ. OSORNO.

MOBILE, *March* 16, 1804.

The above is a copy of the Spanish grant.

THOMAS PRICE.

I, Thomas Price, of the post of Mobile, English interpreter for His Majesty the King of Spain, do solemnly swear by the Almighty God and by the Holy Cross, that this is a true and faithful translation of the Spanish grant or writing hereto annexed.

THOMAS PRICE.

Subscribed and sworn before the Board, March 21, 1804.—Attest: DAVID PARMELEE 2d, *Clerk.*

Entered in record of claims, volume 1, page 289, by EDWARD LLOYD WAILES, for

JOSEPH CHAMBERS, *Register.*

The claimant exhibited a bill of sale from the said Adam Hollinger, bearing date the 20th day of February, 1800, duly executed, assigning and conveying to the said John Callier all his, the said Hollinger's right, title, and claim to the said tract of land, and the improvements and buildings made thereon.

The Board ordered that the case be postponed for consideration.

JAMES DENLEY's case, No. 57 on the docket of the Board, and No. 88 on the books of the Register.

Claim—Of four hundred acres, by virtue of a Spanish warrant of survey, under the first section of the act.

The claimant presented his claim, together with a surveyor's plot of the land claimed, in the following words and figures, to wit:

To the Commissioners appointed in pursuance of the act of Congress passed the 3d day of March, 1803, for recording and adjusting claims to lands south of the Tennessee, and east of Pearl river.

MARCH 16, 1804.

Please to take notice, that the following tract of land, situated on the west side of Tombigbee river, in the county of Washington, beginning at Perkins's line, and extending thirty-one chains and sixty-two links for a front; thence, north, twenty degrees, east to the river, and then return back to the beginning, and reverse the course ninety-eight chains fifty links to a sweet gum, in high water, where it was impassable; and hath such forms and marks, both natural and artificial, as are fully represented in the plot annexed, containing four hundred acres: is claimed by James Denley in and by virtue of a Spanish warrant of survey, and is now exhibited to the Register of the Land Office east of Pearl river, to be recorded as directed by said act. To all which he begs leave to refer, as also to a copy of the plot herewith filed.

JAMES DENLEY.

[Plot omitted.]

Surveyed by Robert Ligon. Chain carriers, James Denley and George Dickey.

The claimant produced a Spanish warrant of survey in the following words and figures, to wit:

MOBILE, *October* 9, 1787.

His Excellency the GOVERNOR GENERAL:

James Denley, inhabitant of Mobile jurisdiction, with the greatest respect to your excellency, says, there is found on Tombigbee river ten acres of land, formerly the property of Mr. Magillivrey, by the name of Sunflower, situate on the east side by land of Daniel Johnson, and on the west side by vacant land; the above land was abandoned in the year '80, and until this present has not been claimed by the proprietor nor any other person empowered for him; in attention of which, begs your excellency's generosity, in granting him as proprietor of said land with the profounder, as customary, with the papers of titles necessary from the Secretary of Government, which may correspond with the concession; for which favor he will be forever thankful.

JAMES DENLEY.

Don Vicent Folch, captain in the fixed Louisiana regiment, commandant civil and military of Mobile and its jurisdiction, certifies, the land the petitioner solicits is existing vacant, by information from the inhabitants who are well knowing the said land.

VICENT FOLCH.

MOBILE, *October* 9, 1787.

NEW ORLEANS, *October* 22, 1787.

The surveyor of this province, Don Carlos Laveau Trudeau, shall establish this individual on that part of ten acres front of land, with the profounder, as customary, of forty, at the same place the above petitioner solicits, as it is vacant, and not causing prejudice to any neighbor, with the precise conditions of making the road and clearing regularly in peremptory space of one year; and if at the precise space of three years the land is not settled, after which period it cannot be established, this grant to remain null; under which supposition, the business of settling the limits will be carried on in the tract, and remitted me, to provide the interested party with titles in form.

ESTEVAN MIRO.

This is a copy compared with the original existing in the archives of this place under my charge.

JOAQUIN DE OSORNO. [L. S.]

MOBILE, *February* 24, 1804.

The above is a copy of the Spanish grant.

THOMAS PRICE.

I, Thomas Price, of the post of Mobile, English interpreter for His Majesty the King of Spain, do solemnly swear by the Almighty God, and by the Holy Cross, that this is a true and faithful translation of the Spanish grant or writing hereto annexed.

THOMAS PRICE.

Subscribed and sworn before the Board, March 21, 1804.—Attest: DAVID PARMELEE 2d, *Clerk.*

The Board ordered that the case be postponed for consideration.

JAMES DENLEY's case, No. 58 on the docket of the Board, and No. 105 on the books of the Register.

Claim—Of two hundred and eighty acres, as assignee and legal representative of Solomon Johnson, by virtue of a Spanish warrant of survey, under the first section of the act.

The claimant exhibited his claim, together with a surveyor's plot of the land claimed, in the following words and figures, to wit:

To the Commissioners appointed in pursuance of the act of Congress passed the 3d day of March, 1803, for receiving and adjusting claims to lands south of Tennessee, and east of Pearl river.

MARCH 21, 1804.

Please to take notice, that the following tract of land, situated in the county of Washington, butting and bounding on the east side by the Sunflower creek and lands surveyed for Hiram Mounger, and on the south side by Hargrave's claim, and on the west by Morgan's claim, and hath such forms and marks, both natural and artificial, as are fully represented in the plot annexed, containing two hundred and eighty acres: is claimed by James Denley, legal representative of Solomon Johnson, in and by virtue of a Spanish warrant of survey, bearing date the 10th day of June, 1795; is now exhibited to the Register of the Land Office established east of Pearl river, to be recorded as directed by said act. To all which he begs leave to refer, as also to a copy of the plot herewith filed.   JAMES DENLEY.

[Plot omitted.]

Surveyed the 24th of February, 1804, by Robert Ligon.

In support of this claim a Spanish warrant was produced, in the following words and figures, viz.:

His Excellency the GOVERNOR GENERAL:

ST. STEPHEN's *May* 11, 1795.

Solomon Johnson, inhabitant of the district of St. Stephen's, with the greatest respect to your excellency, represents and says, that he has been established these four years on a tract of land, in distance about six leagues below Fort St. Stephen's on Mobile side, containing seven acres front, with the profounder, as customary, limited on one side by James Donnelly, and on the north side by John Brewer; and, as it has no proprietor, prays your excellency to grant him the said land, with papers of titles from the Secretary of the Government, which may correspond with the concession in form; for which favor he will be forever thankful.

SOLOMON JOHNSON.

His Excellency the GOVERNOR GENERAL:

By information from the inhabitants of this post, the petitioner solicits is vacant, and King's commons; and not causing prejudice to any neighbors, your excellency may dispose of it as may seem best.

ANTONIO PALAO.

NEW ORLEANS, *June* 10, 1795.

The Surveyor General of this province, or any individual named by him, shall establish this individual on that part of seven acres of land front, with the profounder back as customary, of forty, at the same place the above petitioner solicits, as it is vacant, not causing prejudice to any neighbor, with the precise conditions of making the road and clearing regularly in peremptory space of one year; and if at the precise space of three years the land is not settled, after which period it cannot be established, this grant to remain null; under which supposition, the business of settling the limits will be carried on in the tract, and remitted me to provide the interested party with titles in form.

THE BARON OF CARONDELET.

Certifies the above to be a copy of the original existing in the archives under my charge.

FERNANDO LESORE.

ST. STEPHEN's, *Sept.* 21, 1792.

The above is a copy of the Spanish grant.

THOMAS PRICE.

The above was compared exact with the original in this office under my charge, by me,

JOAQN. DE OSORNO. [L. S.]

I, Thomas Price, of the post of Mobile, English interpreter for His Majesty the King of Spain, do solemnly swear by the Almighty God, and by the Holy Cross, that this is a true and faithful translation of the Spanish grant hereto annexed.

THOMAS PRICE.

Subscribed and sworn before the Board, March 21, 1804.—Attest: DAVID PARMELEE 2d, *Clerk.*

On the back of the said Spanish warrant of survey is an endorsement in the following words and figures, to wit:

FORT STODDERT, *March* 20, 1804.

I hereby assign all my right, title, and interest, of the within Spanish warrant of survey to James Denley, for value received.

Test: EDWARD LLOYD WAILES,

JOHN BREWER.

Entered in record of claims, vol. 1, page 327, by EDWARD LLOYD WAILES, for

JOSEPH CHAMBERS, *Register.*

The Board ordered that the case be postponed for consideration.

NICHOLAS PERKIN's case, No. 59 on the docket of the Board, and No. 92 on the books of the Register.

Claim—Of three hundred and six acres, as assignee and legal representative of Thomas Wheat, by virtue of a Spanish warrant of survey, under the first section of the act.

The claimant presented his claim, together with a surveyor's plot of the land claimed, in the following words and figures, to wit:

To the Commissioners appointed in pursuance to the act of Congress passed the 3d day of March, 1803, for receiving and adjusting claims to lands south of Tennessee and east of Pearl river.

Please to take notice, that the following tract of land, situated on the west side of Tombigbee river, in the county of Washington, beginning at a sassafras, being Ward's corner, running south, twenty degrees west, one hundred and fifteen chains, to a sweet gum corner; thence south, twenty degrees east, twenty-six chains, to a stake corner; thence north, twenty degrees east, one hundred and twenty-two chains, to a stake on the river; thence, with the river to the beginning; and hath such forms and marks, both natural and artificial, as are fully represented in the plot annexed, containing three hundred and six acres: is claimed by Nicholas Perkins, legal representative of Thomas Wheat, in and by virtue of a Spanish warrant of survey, and is now exhibited to the Register of the Land Office established east of Pearl river, to be recorded as directed by said act. To all which he begs leave to refer, as also to a copy of the plot herewith filed.

NICHOLAS PERKINS,
Representative of Thomas Wheat.

MARCH 21, 1804.

[Plot omitted.]

The claimant produced a Spanish warrant of survey in the words and figures following, to wit:

His Excellency Don ESTEVAN MIRO, Colonel of the royal army, Governor civil and military of the city and province of the Louisiana, &c.

Thomas Wheat, inhabitant of Mobile jurisdiction, with the greatest respect to your excellency, says, there are found on Tombigbee river eight acres of land, formerly the property of Mr. Magillevrey, in the year eighty, situated on the east of land of Mr. Daniel Wards, and on the west of John Johnson; since which, said land has not been claimed by the owner, nor any other person empowered by him; he begs your excellency to grant him the above petition, with the profounder, as customary, with papers of titles necessary from the Secretary of Government, which may correspond with the concession; for which favor he will be forever thankful.

THOMAS WHEAT.

MOBILE, October 9, 1787.

Don Vicent Folch, Captain in the Louisiana fixed regiment, commandant civil and military of Mobile and its district, certifies, the land the above petitioner solicits is vacant, by the best information from the different inhabitants of this place, for which I sign these presents at said place, day and date above mentioned.

VICENT FOLCH.

NEW ORLEANS, October 22, 1787.

The surveyor of this province, Don Carlos Laveau Trudeau, shall establish that part of land of eight acres front, with its profounder of forty acres, as customary, at the same place mentioned in the above petition, as it is vacant, not causing any prejudice to any person, with the precise conditions of making the road, and clearing regularly in the peremptory space of one year; and if at the precise space of three years the land is not settled, during which period it cannot be alienated, this grant to remain null; under which supposition, the business of settling the limits will be carried on in the tract, and remitted me to provide the interested party with titles in form.

ESTEVAN MIRO.

Certify the above copy was compared with the original in the office of this place. Mobile, December 16, 1787.

SANTIAGO DE LA SAUSSAYE.

The above is a copy of the Spanish grant.

THOMAS PRICE.

The above was compared exact with the original in this office under my charge, by me,

JOAQN. DE OSORNO. [L. S.]

I, Thomas Price, of the post of Mobile, English interpreter for his Majesty the King of Spain, do solemnly swear by the Almighty God, and by the Holy Cross, that this is a true and faithful translation of the Spanish grant or writing hereto annexed.

THOMAS PRICE.

Subscribed and sworn before the Board, March 21, 1804.—Attest: DAVID PARMELEE 2d, Clerk.

Entered in record of claims, vol. 1, page 266, by EDWARD LLOYD WAILES, for

JOSEPH CHAMBERS, Register.

The claimant produced a deed of conveyance from Thomas Wheat, bearing date the 19th day of August, 1803, duly executed, assigning and conveying to the said Nicholas Perkins, his heirs, &c., all the said Wheat's right, title, and interest to the said tract of land, and the improvements made thereon; also a letter of attorney, of the same date, from said Wheat, authorizing the said

Perkins to prosecute said claim before the Board of Commissioners, for his own use and benefit.

The Board ordered that the case be postponed for consideration.

NICHOLAS PERKINS's case, No. 60 on the docket of the Board, and No. 93 on the books of the Register.

Claim—Of two hundred acres, as assignee and legal representative of Daniel Johnson, by virtue of a Spanish warrant of survey, under the first section of the act.

The claimant presented his claim, together with a surveyor's plot of the land claimed, in the following words and figures, to wit:

To the Commissioners appointed in pursuance of the act of Congress passed the 3d day of March, 1803, for receiving and adjusting the claims to lands south of Tennessee, and east of Pearl river.

Please to take notice, that the following tract of land, situated on the west side of Tombigbee, in the county of Washington, beginning at a stake on the river, and runs south, twenty degrees west, one hundred and twenty-two chains, on Wheat's line, to his stake corner; thence, south, seventy degrees east, fifteen chains and seventy-five links, to a sweet gum corner; thence, north, twenty degrees east, one hundred and forty-one chains, to Tombigbee; thence, with the river to the beginning; containing two hundred acres, having such shape, forms, and marks, natural and artificial, as are represented in the plot annexed: is claimed by Nicholas Perkins, legal representative of Daniel Johnson, in and by virtue of a Spanish warrant of survey, and is now exhibited to the Register of the Land Office east of Pearl river, to be recorded as directed by said act. To all which he begs leave to refer, as also to a copy of the plot herewith filed.

NICHOLAS PERKINS,
Legal Representative of Daniel Johnson.

MARCH 21, 1804.

[Plot omitted.]

Surveyed by William Gilliam.

A Spanish warrant of survey was exhibited in the following words and figures, to wit:

To His Excellency ESTEVAN MIRO, Colonel of the royal armies, civil and military, Governor of the city and province of Louisiana, &c.

Daniel Johnson, inhabitant in the jurisdiction of Mobile, with the most profound respect, says to your excellency, that there is five acres of land on the river of Tombigbee, formerly belonging to Mr. McGillivray, named Sunflower, situated on the east side of a tract of land belonging to Thomas Wheat, and on the west side of James Denley's tract of land; the which land was abandoned in the year eighty, and since has not been reclaimed by the proprietor, nor by his agent: in consideration whereof, your excellency will be pleased to grant him said acres, running back as usual, ordering that the necessary titles may be delivered through the Government's Secretary's Office. He humbly petitions you may grant his request, in which he will receive a favor.

DANIEL JOHNSON.

MOBILE, October 9, 1787.

Don Vicent Folch, captain of the fixed regiment of Louisiana, civil and military commandant of the place of Mobile and its district, certifies that the land petitioned for as above, is found vacant, according to information taken from inhabitants who could have knowledge of this circumstance.

VICENT FOLCH.

MOBILE, October 9, 1787.

NEW ORLEANS, October 22, 1787.

The surveyor of this province, Don Carlos Laveau Trudeau, will settle the petitioner on the five acres of land for which he petitioned, running back as usual forty acres, in the place mentioned in the preceding memorial, it being vacant, and not causing any injury, with the precise conditions of making the road and proper clearing, in the precise space of one year; this concession to be null, if, at the precise expiration of three, the land may not be found settled; under which position the survey shall be made, remitting it to me, to provide to the interested titles in form.

ESTEVAN MIRO.

MOBILE, March 17, 1804.

I do hereby certify that the above is a faithful and true translation rendered from the original copy in the Spanish language that remains in these archives.

JOAQUIN DE OSORNO. [L. S.]
THOMAS PRICE.

I, Thomas Price, of the post of Mobile, English interpreter for His Majesty the King of Spain, do solemnly swear by the Almighty God, and by the Holy Cross, that this is a true and faithful translation of the Spanish grant or writing hereto annexed.

THOMAS PRICE.

Subscribed and sworn before the Board, March 21st, 1804.—Attest: DAVID PARMELEE 2d, *Clerk*.

Entered in record of claims, vol. 1, page 272, by ED-WARD LLOYD WAILES, for

JOSEPH CHAMBERS, *Register*.

The claimant exhibited a deed of conveyance from Daniel Johnson, bearing date 17th August, 1801, duly executed, assigning and conveying to Solomon Johnson, his heirs, &c. all the said Daniel's right and title to said tract of land, and the improvements made thereon; also, a deed of conveyance from the said Solomon, bearing date 21st May, 1803, duly executed, releasing and conveying to William H. Hargrave all the said Solomon's right and title to said premises; also, a deed of conveyance from the said Hargrave, dated the 1st day of September, 1803, duly executed, releasing and conveying to the said Perkins all the said Hargrave's right and title to the said tract of land and the improvements thereon made.

The Board ordered that the case be postponed for consideration.

CORNELIUS RAIN's case, No. 61, on the docket of the Board, and No. 100 on the books of the Register.

Claim—Of four hundred acres, by virtue of Spanish warrant of survey, under the first section of the act.

The claimant presented his claim, together with a surveyor's plot of the land claimed, in the following words and figures, to wit:

To the Commissioners appointed in pursuance of the act of Congress passed the 3d day of March, 1803, *for receiving and adjusting claims to lands south of Tennessee and east of Pearl river.*

Please to take notice, that the following tract of land, situated on the west side of Tombigbee river, in the county of Washington, beginning at a gum on said river, and running north, eighty-five degrees west, one hundred and ten chains, to a water oak; thence north, five degrees east, to cotton wood, forty-six chains sixty-two and a half links, to said river; thence, down the meanders of the river, to the beginning; containing four hundred acres, and hath such forms and marks, both natural and artificial, as are fully represented in the plot annexed; is claimed by Cornelius Rain, in and by virtue of a Spanish grant, and is now exhibited to the Register of the Land Office established east of Pearl river, to be recorded as directed by the said act. To all which he begs leave to refer, as also to a copy of the plot herewith filed.

CORNELIUS RAIN.

MARCH 19, 1804.

[Plot omitted.]

Surveyed March 20, 1804, by John Dease. Chain carriers, James Powel and James Dean.

The claimant produced a Spanish warrant of survey, in the words and figures following, to wit:

FORT ST. STEPHEN'S, *May* 11, 1795.

His Excellency the GOVERNOR GENERAL:

Cornelius Rain, inhabitant of Tombigbee river, with the greatest respect, represents and lays before your excellency, that there is a tract of land, distance about eighteen leagues and two miles below Fort St. Stephen's, and about half a league from where he is now a resident, containing ten acres front with its corresponding profounder, bounded on the north by land the property of Moses Moore, and on the south by a creek called Lawrence's creek: he begs your excellency to grant him the above petition, with papers necessary from Secretary of the Government, which may correspond with the cession: for which favor from your excellency he will be forever thankful.

CORNELIUS RAIN.

FORT ST. STEPHEN'S, *May* 11, 1795.

His Excellency the GOVERNOR GENERAL:

By the best information from the different inhabitants of this post, the land the above petitioner solicits is vacant and within the King's dominion, King's commons.

ANTONIO PALAO.

NEW ORLEANS, *June* 10, 1795.

The Surveyor General of this province shall establish that part of ten acres of land front on the river, the same that the above petitioner solicits in the above petition, with forty acres back, as customary, without

causing prejudice to any neighbors, with the precise conditions of making the road and clearing regularly in the peremptory space of one year; and if, at the precise space of three years, the land is not settled, during which period it cannot be alienated, this grant to remain null; under which supposition, the business of settling the limits will be carried on in the tract, and remitted me to provide the interested party with titles in form.

THE BARON OF CARONDELET.

The above is a copy of the Spanish grant, copied.

THOMAS PRICE.

The above compared exact with the original in this office, by me,

JOAQUIN DE OSORNO.

I, Thomas Price, of the post of Mobile, English interpreter for his Majesty the King of Spain, do solemnly swear by the Almighty God, and by the Holy Cross, that this is a true and faithful translation of the Spanish grant or writing hereto annexed.

THOMAS PRICE.

Subscribed and sworn before the Board, March 21, 1804.—Attest: DAVID PARMELEE 2d, *Clerk*.

Entered in record of claims, vol. 1, page 305, by ED-WARD LLOYD WAILES, for

JOSEPH CHAMBERS, *Register*.

The Board ordered that the case be postponed for consideration.

JOHN F. M'GREW AND CLARK M'GREW's case, No. 62 on the docket of the Board, and No. 59 on the books of the Register.

Claim—Of three hundred and thirty-five acres and thirty-one poles, as assignees and legal representatives of Julian de Castro, by virtue of a Spanish warrant of survey, under the first section of the act.

The claimants presented their claim, together with a surveyor's plot of the land claimed, in the following words and figures, to wit:

To the Commissioners appointed in pursuance of the act of Congress, passed the 3d day of March, 1803, *for receiving and adjusting the claims to lands south of the Tennessee, and east of Pearl river.*

Please to take notice, that the following tract of land, situated on the west side of Tombigbee river, Washington county, butted on said river, and bounded on the south by the claim of Thomas Malone, on the west by vacant land, and the north by the claim of Mrs. Conner M'Grew, or the heirs of James M'Grew; beginning on a small sweet gum on the river bank, and runs a conditional line between the claimants and Thomas Malone, south, twenty-four degrees west, one hundred and twenty-six chains and forty-nine links, to a corner stake, with a post oak, red oak, and two pines, pointers, (having crossed two branches, one at thirty chains fifty links, the other at thirty-two chains eighty links;) thence, north, sixty-six degrees west, twenty-six chains fifty links, to a red oak corner; thence, north, twenty-four degrees east, one hundred and twenty-six chains forty-nine links, to a cherry corner on the river bank; thence, the meanders of the river, to the beginning; having such marks, natural and artificial, as are represented in the plot annexed, containing three hundred and thirty-five acres and thirty-one poles: is claimed by John F. M'Grew, legal representative of Julian de Castro, under and by virtue of a Spanish grant, bearing date the 10th day of June, 1795, and now exhibited unto the Register of the Land Office established east of Pearl river, to be recorded as directed by said act. To all which he begs leave to refer, as also to the copy of the plot herewith filed.

J. F. M'GREW AND CLARK M'GREW,

Legal representatives of Julian de Castro.

[Plot omitted.]

Surveyed 21st March, 1804, by J. Malone. Chain carriers, Richard Burney and George Brewer.

The claimants exhibited a Spanish warrant of survey, in the words and figures following, to wit:

ST. STEPHEN'S, *May* 1, 1795.

His Excellency the GOVERNOR GENERAL:

Julian de Castro, with the profoundest respect, represents to your excellency, and says, that he has been a residenter for these eight years on Tombigbee river, without obtaining any concession for land; and, being desirous of remaining a residenter, and there being a tract of land of ten acres on the upland, the same that runs down to Mobile, bounded on the north side by James M'Grew, and on the south side by Tobias Reams and not causing prejudice to any person, begs your excellency to grant him the above petition, with the corresponding titles, in form; for which favor he will be forever thankful.

JULIAN DE CASTRO.

St. Stephen's, *May* 5, 1795.

His Excellency the Governor General:

By the best information from the inhabitants of this post, that the land the above petitioner solicits is King's commons, and cannot cause any prejudice to any neighbors, your excellency may dispose as it may seem best.

ANTONIO PALAO.

New Orleans, *June* 10, 1795.

The Surveyor General of this province, or a person appointed by him for that business, shall establish that part of land of ten acres front, with the profounder, as customary, of forty back, at the same place as is mentioned in the above petition, with the precise conditions of making the road, and clearing regularly, in the peremptory space of one year; and if at the precise space of three years the land is not settled, during which period it cannot be alienated, this grant to remain null; under which supposition, the business of settling the limits will be carried on the tract, and remitted me, to provide the interested party with titles in form.

THE BARON OF CARONDELET.

Registered. The above is a true copy of the Spanish original.

THOMAS PRICE.

The above was compared exact with the original in this office, by me,

JOAQ. DE OSORNO.

I, Thomas Price, of the post of Mobile, English interpreter for His Majesty the King of Spain, do solemnly swear by the Almighty God, and by the Holy Cross, that this is a true and faithful translation of the Spanish grant, or writing hereto annexed.

THOMAS PRICE.

Subscribed and sworn before the Board, March 21, 1804.—Attest: David Parmelee 2d, *Clerk.*

The claimants also exhibited a writing, which is attached to said Spanish warrant of survey, in the following words and figures, to wit:

I transfer the within grants of land to J. F. McGrew and Clark McGrew, it being for value received. Witness my hand and seal, this 22d of July, 1802.

JULIAN DE CASTRO.

Entered in record of claims, vol. 1, page 173, by Edward Lloyd Wailes, for

JOSEPH CHAMBERS, *Register.*

The Board ordered that the case be postponed for consideration.

James Denley's case, No. 63 on the docket of the Board, and No. 99 on the books of the Register.

Claim—Of one thousand acres, as assignee and legal representative of Daniel Ward, by virtue of a Spanish warrant of survey, under the first section of the act.

The claimant presented his claim, together with a surveyor's plot of the land claimed, in the following words and figures, to wit:

To the Commissioners appointed in pursuance of the act of Congress passed the 3d day of March, 1803, for receiving and adjusting the claims to lands south of the Tennessee, and east of Pearl river.

Please to take notice, that the following tract of land, situated on the river Tombigbee, butting and bounding as follows: beginning at a red bud, running west, one hundred and twenty-six chains and forty-nine links; to an oak corner; north, seventy-nine chains and fifty-five links, from an oak corner to a magnolia; east, one hundred and thirty chains and forty-nine links, from a magnolia to a cotton wood; and from thence, to the beginning; having such marks, natural and artificial, as are represented in the plot annexed, containing one thousand acres: is claimed by James Denley, under and by virtue of a Spanish grant, bearing date the 22d day of October, 1787, and now exhibited unto the Register of the Land Office established east of Pearl river, to be recorded as directed by said act. To all which he begs leave to refer, as also to the copy of the plot herewith filed.

JAMES DENLEY.

[Plot omitted.]

Chain bearers, Hiram Mounger, George Dickey. Surveyed by Thomas Bilbo, for James Denley, 15th October, 1801.

In this case a Spanish warrant of survey was produced in support of this claim, in the words and figures following, viz.:

Mobile, *October* 12, 1787.

His Excellency the Governor General:

Daniel Ward, inhabitant of Mobile jurisdiction, with the greatest respects to your excellency, petitions and says, there are found on Tombigbee river fifty acres of land, formerly of James Mackintosh, deceased, which was abandoned in the year 1781, and until this present has not been claimed by the proprietor, nor any other person empowered for him; situate on the north side by land called the Sunflower; in attention of which, he expects from the generosity of your excellency, in granting him the proprietary of said land, with the profounder, as customary, with papers of titles from the Secretary of Government, which may correspond with the concession; for which favor he will be forever thankful.

DANIEL WARD.

Don Vicent Folch, captain in the fixed Louisiana regiment, commandant civil and military of Mobile and its jurisdiction, certifies that the land the above petitioner solicits is found vacant by information, taken to the above purpose, from several inhabitants, who are knowing to the same.

VICENT FOLCH.

New Orleans, *October* 22, 1787.

The Surveyor General of this province shall establish this individual on that part of land of twenty-five acres front, in the place of fifty he solicits in the above petition, with its profounder, as customary, of forty, at the same place mentioned in the above petition, as it is vacant, not causing any prejudice to any neighbors, with the precise conditions of making the road and clearing regularly in the peremptory space of one year; and, if at the precise space of three years, the land is not settled, after which period it cannot be established, this grant to remain null; under which supposition, the business of settling the limits will be carried on in the tract, and remitted me to provide the interested party with titles in form.

ESTEVAN MIRO.

Mobile, *February* 24, 1804.

This is compared with the original existing in the archives under my charge, by me.

JOAQUIN DE OSORNO.

The above is a copy of the Spanish grant.

THOMAS PRICE.

I, Thomas Price, of the post of Mobile, English interpreter for His Majesty the King of Spain, do solemnly swear by the Almighty God, and by the Holy Cross, that this is a true and faithful translation of the Spanish grant or writing hereto annexed.

THOMAS PRICE.

Subscribed and sworn before the Board, March 21, 1804.—Attest: David Parmelee 2d, *Clerk.*

Entered in record of claims, vol. 1, page 300, by Edward Lloyd Wailes, for

JOSEPH CHAMBERS, *Register.*

The claimant exhibited a bill of sale from John Joyce, as executor of Daniel Ward, deceased, bearing date the 12th of August, 1795, duly executed, relinquishing and conveying to the said James Denley all his, the said Joyce's, right, title, and claim, as executor aforesaid, to the said tract of land now claimed.

The board ordered that the case be postponed for consideration.

Lemuel Henry, attorney for Antonio Espaho, case No. 64 on the docket of the Board, and No. 94 on the books of the Register.

Claim—Of five hundred acres, as assignee and legal representative of John Turnbull, by virtue of a Spanish warrant of survey, under the first section of the act.

The claimant presented his claim, together with a surveyor's plot of land claimed, in the following words and figures, viz.:

To the Commissioners appointed in pursuance of the act of Congress passed the 3d day of March, 1803, for receiving and adjusting claims to lands south of Tennessee, and east of Pearl river.

March 20, 1804.

Please to take notice, that the following tract of land, situate on the west side of the Tombigbee river, on the lower end of Nanna Hubba, (a bluff so called,) in the county of Washington; beginning at a stake on said bluff, near Creighton's old houses; thence, south, fifty-nine degrees west, seventy-four chains, to a large chesnut corner; thence, south, sixty-two degrees east, fifty-one chains fifty links, to Howel Dupree's line;

thence, north, forty degrees east, twenty one chains, to Dupree's corner pine; thence, south, sixty-two degrees east, fifty-nine chains, to a stake; thence, north, thirty-nine degrees east, fifty-seven chains fifty links, to the river; thence, up the river, as plotted, to the beginning; and has such form and marks, both natural and artificial, as are fully represented in the plot annexed, containing five hundred acres, is claimed by Lemuel Henry, attorney in fact: for Antonio Espaho, legal representative of John Turnbull, in and by virtue of a Spanish warrant or order of survey, and is now exhibited to Register of the Land Office established east of Pearl river, to be recorded as directed by said act. To all which he begs leave to refer, as also to a copy of the plot herewith filed, this 20th of March, 1804.

LEMUEL HENRY,
Attorney in fact for Antonio Espaho.

Surveyed 21st March, 1804, by John Milliken.

[Plot omitted.]

The claimant exhibited a Spanish warrant of survey, in the words and figures following, viz:

MOBILE, *June* 6, 1787.

His Excellency ESTEVAN MIRO, Governor General of of this province, &c. &c.

John Turnbull, inhabitant in the district of Mobile, declares to your excellency, that there are situated on the Tombigbee river five hundred acres of land, at the distance of sixteen leagues from Mobile, in the place called La Naniaba, on the side of the firm land; and, for the greater security of the petitioner, he prays your excellency to grant him the proprietary, and that you may give to the Secretary of Government orders to render him the necessary titles and rights, to the end that he may be put in actual possession; and which favor he will ever bear in mind.

JOHN TURNBULL.

Don Pedro Favrot, captain of the Louisiana regiment, civil and military commandant of Mobile and its jurisdiction, certifies that, according to information taken from four of the most respectable inhabitants, this land, that the above named demands, belongs to him, per verbal testimony; and that he may make appear, whenever it is requisite, I here deliver him these presents, in Mobile, the 7th day of June, 1787.

NEW ORLEANS, *July* 31, 1787.

The Surveyor General of this province, Don Carlos Trudeau, will establish this petitioner on the five hundred acres in the place above mentioned in the foregoing memorial, not being prejudicial; on which supposition, the measurement will be extended in continuation, and remitted to me, that the requisite titles may be forwarded in form.

ESTEVAN MIRO.

MOBILE, *March* 6, 1804.

Don Joaquin de Osorno, captain of regiment of infantry of Louisiana, civil and military commandant of Mobile and its jurisdiction, &c., certifies that the above writing is copy of the original that exists in the archives at his charge.

JOAQUIN DE OSORNO.

The above is a copy of the Spanish grant.

THOMAS PRICE.

This was compared exact with the original in this office under my charge, by me.

JOAQUIN DE OSORNO. [L. S.]

I, Thomas Price, of the post of Mobile, English interpreter for His Majesty the King of Spain, do solemnly swear by the Almighty God, and by the Holy Cross, that this is a true and faithful translation of the Spanish grant or writing hereto annexed.

THOMAS PRICE.

Subscribed and sworn before the Board, March 21, 1804.—Attest: DAVID PARMELEE 2d, *Clerk.*

Entered in record of claims, vol. 1, page 281, by EDWARD LLOYD WAILES, for

JOSEPH CHAMBERS, *Register.*

The said Henry produced a deed of conveyance from Manuel Cheney, bearing date 20th of January, 1801, duly executed, relinquishing and conveying to Don Benjamin Dubroca all the said Cheney's right, title, and claim to said tract of land; also, produced a bill of sale from the said Dubroca, dated the 20th of February, 1801, duly executed, conveying to the said Antonio Espaho, all his, the said Dubroca's, right and title to said land; also, produced a certificate, in the words and figures following, to wit:

Don Joaquin de Osorno, captain of the royal troops, and commandant civil and military of Mobile and its jurisdiction, and sub-delegate to the royal intendency, &c. This certifieth that, in the Office of Records, under my charge, is a grant of a tract of land of John Turnbull, lying and situate on Nanna Hubba's bluff, Tombigbee river, containing five hundred acres; also, a tract of land lying and situate opposite Nanna Hubba's bluff aforesaid, containing twenty acres front on the river Tombigbee, and forty acres back, field or swamp land.

Given under my hand and seal, at Mobile, this fifth day of December, 1801.

JOAQUIN DE OSORNO. [L. S.]

There was also produced a power of attorney from said Espaho, bearing date 14th of May, 1803, duly executed, authorizing the said Lemuel Henry to transact all the said Espaho's business respecting the two tracts of land mentioned in the preceding certificate, and to bring suit or suits, if necessary, to recover said land, &c.

FRANCISCO FONTANILLA's case, No. 65 on the docket of the Board, and No. 102 on the books of the Register.

Claim—Of eight hundred acres, by virtue of a Spanish warrant of survey, under the first section of the act.

The claimant presented his claim, together with a surveyor's plot of the land claimed, in the following words and figures, to wit:

To the Commissioners appointed in pursuance of the act of Congress, passed the 3d of March, 1803, for receiving and adjusting claims to lands south of Tennessee and east of Pearl river.

Please to take notice, that the following tract of land, situated on the west side of Tombigbee river, near Fort St. Stephen's, beginning on a sycamore, running south, thirty-two degrees west, one hundred and twenty-six chains forty-nine links, to a black-jack; thence, north, fifty-eight degrees west, sixty-three chains twenty-four links, to a hickory; thence, north, thirty-two degrees east, one hundred and twenty-six chains forty-nine links, to an oak on the river; thence, with the meanders of the river, to the beginning; containing eight hundred acres, having such shape, form, and marks, as are represented in the plot annexed; is claimed by Francisco Fontanilla, and now exhibited to the Register of the Land Office east of Pearl river, to be recorded as directed by said act. To all which he begs leave to refer.

[Plot omitted.]

Chain carriers, Young Gains and David Gains. Surveyed 17th March, 1804, by Thomas Bilbo.

The claimant exhibited a Spanish warrant of survey, in the following words and figures, to wit:

ST. STEPHEN'S, *May* 4, 1795.

His Excellency the GOVERNOR GENERAL:

Francisco Fontanilla, with the greatest respect to your excellency, represents and says, that, having purchased from Julian de Castro the possessions he had on a tract of vacant land, near Fort St. Stephen's, formerly the property of an inhabitant by the name of Smith, the same is deceased, and left no heir; which land contains twenty acres front, with its corresponding profounder of forty acres, limited on the north by land the property of Stewart, and on the south by land the property of John Chastang, and causing no prejudice to any of the neighbors, begs your excellency to grant him the above petition, with papers of titles necessary from the Secretary of the Government, which may correspond with the concession; for which favor he will be forever thankful.

FRANCISCO FONTANILLA.

ST. STEPHEN'S, *May* 5, 1795.

His Excellency the GOVERNOR GENERAL:

By information from the inhabitants of this post, that the land above mentioned is King's commons, and not causing any prejudice to any neighbors, your excellency may dispose as it may seem best.

NEW ORLEANS, *June* 10, 1795.

The Surveyor General of this province, or some individual named by him for that business, shall establish that part of land of twenty acres front, with its profounder of forty acres, as customary, as it is vacant, not causing prejudice to any neighbors, at the same place mentioned in the above petition, with the precise conditions of making the road and clearing regularly, in the peremptory space of one year; and if, at the precise space of three years, the land is not settled, during which period it cannot be alienated, this grant to remain null; under which supposition, the business of settling the limits will be carried on in the tract, and remitted me, to provide the interested party with titles in form.

THE BARON OF CARONDELET.

The above is a copy of the Spanish grant.

THOMAS PRICE.

The above was compared exact with the original in this office under my charge, by me,

JOAQUIN DE OSORNO. [L. s.]

I, Thomas Price, of the post of Mobile, English interpreter for His Majesty the King of Spain, do solemnly swear, by the Almighty God, and by the Holy Cross, that this is a true and faithful translation of the Spanish grant or writing hereto annexed.

THOMAS PRICE.

Subscribed and sworn before the Board, March 21, 1804.—Attest: DAVID PARMELEE 2d, *Clerk.*

Entered in record of claims, vol. 1, page 314, by EDWARD LLOYD WAILES, for

JOSEPH CHAMBERS, *Register.*

The Board ordered the case to be postponed for consideration.

SAMUEL MIMS's case, No. 66 on the docket of the Board, and No. 74 on the books of the Register.

Claim—Of sixteen hundred acres, as assignee and legal representative of John Turnbull, by virtue of a Spanish warrant of survey, under the first section of the act.

The claimant presented his claim, together with a surveyor's plot of the land claimed, in the words and figures following, to wit:

To the Commissioners appointed in pursuance of the act of Congress passed the 3d day of March, 1803, for receiving and adjusting the claims to lands south of the Tennessee and east of Pearl river.

MARCH 20, 1804.

Please to take notice, that the following tract of land, situated on the west side of Tombigbee, on Toller creek, in the county of Washington, beginning at a gum on the river, and runs south, fifty-six degrees west, one hundred and twenty-six chains fifty links, to a stake in a prairie; thence, north, thirty-four degrees west, one hundred and twenty-six chains fifty links to a post and red oak; thence, north, fifty-six degrees east, one hundred and twenty-six chains fifty links to two red oaks on the bank of said river; thence, down the meanders of the river, to the beginning; and hath such forms and marks, both natural and artificial, as are fully represented in the plot annexed, containing sixteen hundred acres; is claimed by Samuel Mims, legal representative of John Turnbull, in and by virtue of a Spanish warrant of survey, and is now exhibited to the Register of the Land Office established east of Pearl river, to be recorded as directed by said act. To all which he begs leave to refer, as also to a copy of the plot herewith filed.

SAMUEL MIMS.

[Plot omitted.]

Surveyed 29th October, 1801, by Natt. Christmas. Sworn chain carriers, John Baker, Evin Boles.

In this case, the claimant produced a Spanish warrant of survey, in the following words and figures, viz:

His Excellency DON ESTEVAN MIRO, Colonel of the royal army, Governor civil and military of the city and province of Louisiana, &c.

MOBILE, *June* 6, 1787.

John Turnbull, neighbor in Mobile jurisdiction, by the great respect due to your excellency, represents and says, that there is a certain tract of land on Tombigbee river of forty acres, formerly of Mr. Farmer's; said land was abandoned by the widow Farmer in the year eighty; said land never has been claimed by the owner, nor any other person: limited on the east side by a large creek, and on the west side by land abandoned by the widow Farmer; in consequence of which, as the petitioner is necessitated for a tract of land to employ his negroes in raising tobacco and Indian corn, he begs your generosity to grant him the proprietary of said land with the profounder as usual, and begs your excellency to give orders to the Secretary of State to deliver him the titles of concession.

JOHN TURNBULL.

Don Pedro Favrot, captain of the fixed Louisiana regiment, commandant civil and military of the place of Mobile, certified, by informations taken from four inhabitants of note, who are knowing the land above petitioned for, that it has been abandoned by said Farmer; in consequence of which, I give this information at the request of the petitioner.

PEDRO FAVROT.

MOBILE, *June* 7, 1787.

NEW ORLEANS, *July* 31, 1787.

The Surveyor General of this province, Don Carlos Laveau Trudeau, shall establish that part of land of forty acres front, which the above solicits, by its profounder of forty acres, as customary, as it is vacant, not causing prejudice to any neighbors, at the same place mentioned in ths above petition, with the precise conditions of making the road and clearing regularly in the peremptory space of one year; and if at the precise space of three years, the land is not settled, during which period it cannot be established, this grant to remain null; under which supposition, the business of settling the limits will be carried on in the tract, and remitted me, to provide the interested with titles in form.

ESTEVAN MIRO.

Certified that the above is a copy of the original in the office of this place.

SANTIAGO DE LA SAUSSAYE, *P. Writer.*

MOBILE, *September* 3, 1787.

The above is a copy of the Spanish grant.

THOMAS PRICE.

The above was compared exact with the original in this office under my charge, by me,

JOAQN. DE OSORNO. [L. s.]

I, Thomas Price, of the post of Mobile, English interpeter for His Majesty the King of Spain, do solemnly swear by the Almighty God, and by the Holy Cross, that this is a true and faithful translation of the Spanish grant or writing hereto annexed.

THOMAS PRICE.

Subscribed and sworn before the Board, March 21, 1804.—Attest: DAVID PARMELEE 2d, *Clerk.*

Entered in record of claims, vol. I, page 210, by EDWARD LLOYD WAILES, for

JOSEPH CHAMBERS, *Register.*

The claimant produced a deed of conveyance from Anthony Espaho, bearing date the 10th day of March, 1801, duly executed, conveying to the said Samuel Mims all the said Espaho's right and title to the tract of land now claimed.

The Board ordered that the case be postponed for consideration.

Adjourned until Thursday, the 22d instant.

THURSDAY, *March* 22, 1804.

The Board met according to adjournment. Present: Ephraim Kirby, Robert C. Nicholas, Joseph Chambers.

JAMES CALLIER and JOSEPH CAMPBELL, executors of Maria Josephia Narbone, case No. 67 on the docket of the Board, and No. — on the books of the Register.

Claim—Of fifteen hundred and ninety-nine acres and three-tenths of an acre, by virtue of a sale at public auction, under authority of the French Government, in the year 1756, of lands previously owned and cultivated, and which have since continued to be inhabited and cultivated, by virtue of the title derived from said sale, under the respective Governments of England, Spain, and the United States, under the first section of the act.

The claimants presented their claim, together with a surveyor's plot of the land claimed, in the words and figures following, to wit:

To the Commissioners appointed in pursuance of an act of Congress, passed the 3d day of March, 1803, for receiving and adjusting claims to lands south of the Tennessee river and east of Pearl river.

Please to take notice, that the following tract of land, lying west of the Mobile river, bounded eastwardly by the said river, and on all other sides by vacant land, is claimed by the executors of the estate of Maria Josephia Narbone, wife of Anthony Narbone, deceased, for the use and benefit of the legatees of said estate, under and by virtue of the last will and testament of the late Maria Josephia Narbone, deceased, claimed under the first section of the above mentioned act of Congress; to all which the said executors beg leave to refer, as also to the copy of the plot now delivered, (to the Register of the Land Office to be established east of Pearl river) which plot is herewith filed.

FORT STODDERT, *March* 22, 1804.

JAMES CALLIER,　}
JOSEPH CAMPBELL, } *Executors.*

[Plot omitted.]

Surveyed 12th March, 1804, by James Gordon. Chain bearers, Gabriel Tissrah, William Weathers.

In support of this claim, the following written documents were produced, viz.:

[Contract of adjudication of the plantation in partnership of the late Montclain with Flandrin, No. 1.]

To Monsieur BOBE DESCLAUSEAUX, *King's Counsellor, Commissary of the Marine, and Judge of the royal jurisdiction of Mobile.*

Humbly prays Guilleaume Marcellin, substitute procurator for the vacant estates of this town, acting for and in the name of the succession of the late Barthelemy Montclain whilst living, merchant of this town, setting forth his desire to arrive before you at the sale of the estate, moveables, and immoveables of the said succession contained in the inventory taken after his decease, as well as the plantation of the said succession, in partnership with the named Louis Flandrin, inhabitant of this town, that the whole should be judicially sold to the highest and last bidder; the purchasers paying the costs of the said adjudication.

The petitioner further begs, as it is time to transmit to the hands of the procurator, for vacant estates at New Orleans, the amount of the said succession, that a dividend thereof may be made to the creditors of the same by the superior council, and that there may be in this town some that would be adjudicators at the sale, and who would purpose to retain for their debts the amount of the articles that might be adjudged to them, which cannot be done but for ready money:

May it please you to order that, notwithstanding there may be among the adjudicators at the said sale creditors of that succession; that, notwithstanding their debts, they may be obliged to pay into my hands, at the expiration of the term, you will please to limit the amount of their adjudication; and of which ordinance a mention shall be made in the publications and advertisements, that they may not plead ignorance thereof; and you will do justice.

MARCELLIN.

At MOBILE, *July* 22, 1756.

ADVERTISEMENT BY THE KING.

Judicial sale of Plantation.

It is made known to all it may concern : That, on the petition of the substitute procurator for vacant estates, in virtue of our ordinance at the foot of the said petition, that it shall be proceeded to the sale and adjudication of a plantation, situate on the river of Mobile, eleven leagues from Mobile, the half of which belongs to the succession of late Barthelemy Montclain, on account of his partnership with the named Louis Flandrin, in the said plantation, which consists as follows:

First, the place formerly called the plantation of Madame le Sueur, whereon is built a new house, thirty feet long, on twenty wide posts in the ground, covered with bark, clayed between said posts, with six windows and two doors, with a clayed chimney in the said house, and a piazza on one side, to the gable end whereof is an appentis, with a chimney, serving as a kitchen; beside said house is another small building, with posts in the ground, enclosed with stakes, serving as a fowl-house. To the right, in the entrance of the said plantation, is a great building sixty feet long, on thirteen wide, closed in with stakes, posts in the ground, and bark covered, serving for a negro house; to the left is a barn of twenty-five feet long, on eighteen wide posts in the ground, and enclosed with pallisadoes, to the gable end whereof is an appentis, with a chimney; all which buildings are enclosed with stakes set upright, which form a yard of twenty-five toises square. Aside of said plantation, on the river, to the left going up, is a desert of fifteen arpents in front on the river, on two in depth; on the other side, to the right, is another desert of ten arpents, on two of depth. The which sale of plantation, with its circumstances and dependencies above mentioned, shall be made by public sale, for three Sundays running, at the door of this parish church, at the going out of the mass, to be definitively adjudged at the said fifteenth day to the highest and last bidder, in paying the costs of his adjudication ; the purchaser whereof may enter in possession. But, in the course of the month of January of the next year, on account of the crop and other effects of which it cannot be cleared before that time, the purchaser is likewise to observe that, in case he should be a creditor of the said succession, he will be obliged, notwithstanding his credit, to pay the price of the said plantation into the hands of the said substitute.

BOBE DESCLOSEAUX.

MARCELLIN, *Notary or Register.*

At MOBILE, *July* 23, 1756.

Adjudication of the plantation of the partnership of late Montclain with the named Flandrin.

In the year 1756, Sunday, the 24th of July of the said year, at the request of Mr. Guilleaume Marcellin, substitute to the procurator for vacant estates in this town, acting for and in the name of the succession of the late Barthelemy Montclain, whilst living, merchant of this town, tending to his grant that sale should be made before us in a judicial manner, of the effects of the said deceased, and that proclamations should be made, and advertisements set up, to arrive at the sale of the immoveables thereof in the usual and accustomed house; in consequence whereof, and according to our ordinance, the plantation that the said deceased had on the river of Mobile, in partnership with the named Louis Flandrin, inhabitant of this place, the half of which is belonging to his succession, had been published and advertised to be entirely sold, with its buildings and its deserts, such as they are specified by the publications and advertisements set up by the adjudication, to the highest and last bidder, subject to the charges, clauses, and conditions mentioned in the advertisements.

Whereon, we, Jean Baptiste Claude Bobé Desclauseaux, King's Counsellor, Commissary of the Marine, and Judge of the royal jurisdiction of Mobile, accompanied with Mr. Francis Cæsar Bernoudy, deputy King's Attorney General, and of our Register, at the door of this parish church, at the going out of the great mass, after having caused the said advertisement to be publicly read and proclaimed aloud by Cerinque, the crier, the judiciary sale of said plantation warranted against all trouble, debts, hypothecations, and other hindrances that might be thereon, advertising that he may not enter in possession but in the course of the month of January of the ensuing year 1757, on account of the crop and other effects of which the plantation cannot be cleared but at the time; and a sufficient number of people being assembled, and none opposing, we have proceeded, in presence of the said Flandrin, to the first adjudication as follows:

First, after many publications, the said plantation has been set up by Mr. Oliver to the sum of eight hundred livres; and, after many outcries on the said price of eight hundred livres, and that none bid higher, we have adjourned to Sunday next, the second adjudication, and have for that purpose ordered new proclamations and fixings as where it may be needful. Done the day, month, and year as above.

FLANDRIN,

BOBE DESCLOSEAUX,

MARCELLIN, *Notary or Register.*

MARCELLIN, *Notary or Register.*

And Sunday, the 1st of August, of the said year, after the proclamations and setting up of advertisements, w' have order to the proceeding to the second adjudication of the sale of the said plantation; and after having caused *de nouveau* the reading of the said advertisement to be made aloud by the said crier, the judicial sale thereof at the door of this parish church, at the going out of the great mass, with a sufficient number of persons present, and the calling out of the price of eight hundred livres of the first and present adjudication; and Monsieur Aubert has appeared, who bid up to the sum of nine hundred livres; and after many callings out of the bidding of nine hundred livres by Mr. Aubert, and that none offered that bid higher, we have referred to next Sunday to proceed to the third and last adjudication of the said plantation, and have ordered for that purpose new publications and setting up of advertisements, where may be needful. Done the day, month, and year as above.

BOBE DESCLOSEAUX,

MARCELLIN, *Register.*

MARCELLIN, *Register.*

And Sunday, the 8th of August, of the said year 1756, after the proclamations and setting up of advertisements, ordered to proceed to the adjudication, simple and definitive, of the sale of said plantation; at the church door of this parish, at the going out of high mass, where we again ordered new proclamations by Cerinque, the crier; and, a sufficient number of people having assembled, we proceeded as follows, subject to the charges, clauses, and conditions mentioned in the advertisement; and after many publications of the price of nine hundred livres of Sunday last, appeared Mr. Bobé, who bid up to the sum of one thousand livres.

By Mr. Chastang, to that of twelve hundred livres;
By Mr. Bonnille, to that of twelve hundred and twenty livres;
By Flandrin, to that of fifteen hundred livres;

By Mr. Aubert, to that of seventeen hundred livres;
By Mr. Chastang, to that of eighteen hundred livres;
By Mr. Flandrin, to that of two thousand livres;
By Mr. Bobé, to that of two thousand two hundred livres;
By Mr. Bonnille, to that of two thousand four hundred livres.
By Flandrin, to that of two thousand four hundred and fifty livres;
By Monsieur Bonnille, to that of two thousand five hundred livres;
By Flandrin, to that of two thousand five hundred and twenty livres;
And as none offered to bid higher on the price of two thousand five hundred and twenty livres, after having got the said highest offer, and that the said Flandrin required of us to adjudge him the said plantation, purely and simply:

Whereon, we, King's Counsellor and Judge as above said, have, to Flandrin, as highest and last bidder, adjudged, and do adjudge, purely and simply, the said plantation above mentioned in the advertisement, with its circumstances and dependencies, to be enjoyed by him, his heirs, &c. in all property, in consideration of the sum of twelve hundred and sixty livres, which he shall pay to the succession of said deceased Barthelemy Montclain, for the half of the price of his bidding, on account of the partnership with him therein, at the end of the present year; for which purpose, the said Flandrin has affected and hypothecated all his goods and has signed.
Done the day, month, and year as above signed.
　　　　　FLANDRIN,
　　　　　BOBE DESCLOSEAUX,
　　　　　MARCELLIN, *Register.*

MARCELLIN, *Register.*
For copy conformable to the original remaining in the registry of the jurisdiction of Mobile, compared by us, Notary and Register of the said jurisdiction, at Mobile, 28th December, 1756.
　　　　　MARCELLIN, *Register.*

I, the subscribing Notary and Register of the jurisdiction of Mobile, and deputy procurator for vacant estates in said place, acknowledge to have received of Louis Flandrin, inhabitant, the sum of twelve hundred and sixty livres for the one half of the sale, by adjudication of the plantation of the partnership of the late Montclain with him, and of which, in my said capacity as procurator for vacant estates, I acquit and discharge him of the sum of twelve hundred and sixty livres, to be accounted for to the profit of the succession of the said deceased, in the account which I shall render of the said succession. Done at Mobile, 28th December, 1756.
　　　　　MARCELLIN.

A just translation of the annexed No. 1.
　　　　　E. LAGARDERE, *P. T. & J.*
[REGISTERED No. 2.]
We, Pierre Annibal Deville, Knight of the royal and military order of St. Louis, ancient King's Lieutenant of Mobile, do certify that Mr. Francois and Bernard Bernoudy, brothers, and Flandrin, hold and possess, since about seven years and a half, a plantation of twenty arpents in front on the usual depth, seated on the river of Mobile, eleven leagues above and of the same side as the town, at the bluff formerly called the Plantation of Mr. Lesueur, as well as a desert; also of twenty arpents front on the usual depths, where they make provisions for their negroes of the other side of the river facing the said plantation; the which plantations and deserts, partly proceeding from the succession of late Montclain, have been adjudged the 8th of August, 1756, to the said Flandrin, who has ceded the one half of both to the said Messrs. Francois and Bernard Bernoudy.
In testimony whereof, we have delivered to the said Messrs. Francois and Bernard Bernoudy, and Flandrin, the present certificate, to serve and avail to confirm their titles of property to the said plantations and deserts, as well as their dependencies.
At MOBILE, Dec. 24, 1763.
　　　　　DEVILLE.

We, the Director General commanding for the King at New Orleans, do certify that the plantation and desert, and their dependencies, mentioned at the other side, are to belong in full property to the said Francois and Bernard Bernoudy, and Flandrin, conformable to the intentions of His M. C. M., and to the power by him given to his governors and ordonators, to permit his subjects to settle in this department of Mobile, where they thought fit.
In testimony whereof, we have signed the present certificate, and caused our seal at arms to be set thereto,

and countersigned by our Secretary, at Mobile, 24th December, 1763.
　　　　　DABBADIE.

By my Lord DUVERGE.
A just translation of the annexed No. 2.
　　　　　E. LAGARDERE, *P. T. & J.*
No. 3.
I, the underwritten Francis Bernoudy, acknowledge to have this day sold, yielded, quitted, transferred, and made over, from henceforth and forever, with promise to warrant from all trouble and hindrance generally, whatsoever, Mr. Anthony Narbon, inhabitant of this city, the half of a plantation to me belonging, and that I had in partnership with the deceased Mr. Flandrin, spouse of the wife of said Narbon; the said plantation situated upon the river of Mobile, about eleven leagues above, upon the same side of this city.
[torn*] bluff called formerly the plantation of Mrs. [torn*] as well as the half of a desert, also of twenty arpents of front, with the accustomed depth this sale made paying the price and sum of four hundred dollars, money of Spain, that the said Mr. Narbon has paid me in his obligation one half payable on the tenth of January next, and the other half in the course of the month of August of the year one thousand seven hundred and sixty-five; for which payment, the said plantation shall continue made over and mortgaged even until the perfect payment thereof; after which I consent that the said Mr. Narbon enjoys the said plantation as of a property belonging to him, having delivered to him, for that effect, the titles concerning the said plantation.
Done and passed at the seventh of September, one thousand seven hundred and sixty-four, in presence of the witnesses under written; thus signs:
　　　　　BERNOUDY,
　　　　　NARBON, his + mark.
Witnesses, Vidal, Vincent, Robert Farmer.
A just translation of the annexed No. 3.
　　　　　E. LAGARDERE, *P. T. & J.*

BOARD OF COMMISSIONERS, *March* 22, 1804.
Doctor John Chastang, being under oath, did solemnly swear that this is a true translation from the papers in the French language hereto attached.—Attest: DAVID PARMELEE 2d, *Clerk.*
Entered in record of claims, vol 1. page —, by EDWARD LLOYD WAILES, for
　　　　　JOSEPH CHAMBERS, *Register.*

BOARD OF COMMISSIONERS, WASHINGTON COUNTY, *Thursday, March* 22, 1804.
James Callier, Esquire, one of the executors of the last will and testament of Maria Josephia Narbon, having appeared before the Board, and on solemn oath declared that there is a claim now depending before said Board by said executors, for and in behalf of the legatees of said deceased, for fifteen hundred and ninety-nine acres and three-tenths of an acre, on the west side of Mobile or Tombigbee river, founded upon a title derived under the French Government of Louisiana, in the year 1756; and that Simon Andrey, of the county of Washington, is deemed to be an important witness in support of said claim, and that he is now confined by severe sickness, and in such a state of health that it is impracticable to have him before said Board, to give his testimony in the premises:
Whereupon, it is ordered by the Board that the said Simon Andrey be duly qualified before some lawful magistrate of said county to give true and correct answers to the interrogatories hereto subjoined, and to such other interrogatories as shall be proposed to him; and that his answers shall be certified to this Board by the magistrate taking the same, in due form of law.
Attest:　　DAVID PARMELEE 2d, *Clerk.*
The Board ordered that the case be postponed for consideration.

JOSIAH SKINNER'S case: Edward Gatlan was produced as a witness, and, being duly sworn, deposed:
Question. Have you, or do you expect any interest from this claim?
Answer. I have no interest, nor do I expect any in virtue thereof.
Josiah Skinner did inhabit and cultivate the land now in question on the third day of March, 1803, and before and since that time; and that, on the third day of March, 1803, Josiah Skinner was the head of a family.

*The original MS. is here defective.

Question. Do you know whether this land is claimed in virtue of any British, Spanish, or donation claim?

Answer. I do not certainly know by what species of claim; but both James Callier and Thomas Carson have surveyed a part of this land.

Question. Has Skinner removed from the land now claimed, and if so, about what time?

Answer. He did remove from the same, and his removal took place after the 11th day of March, 1803; for I well recollect, from writings and other circumstances, that he was living on this land on the said 11th day of March; his removal, therefore, took place soon after this day, but do not recollect the particular day.

Question. To what place did Skinner remove, and for what purpose?

Answer. He removed from the land now in question to the pine woods, for the benefit of range for his own stock, and to take care of the cattle of Adam Hollinger; but, by an advertisement which I saw posted on the side of the house at the place now claimed, signed by Josiah Skinner, he forbade any person entering into the houses or premises he had quitted, for that he meant to continue his claim to this land.

Question. Did Josiah Skinner cultivate any land on that part of the tract now claimed, which lies next adjoining the Tombigbee river, on the 3d day of March, 1803?

Answer. He did not cultivate on that part of the tract now claimed on the 3d day of March, 1803, but had cleared land, and made preparations to cultivate.

The Board ordered that the case be postponed for consideration.

EDWARD CREIGHTON's case, No. 68 on the docket of the Board, and No. 91 on the books of the Register.

Claim.—A right of pre-emption of thirty-two acres and six-tenths, as assignee and legal representative of Benjamin King, under the third section of the act.

The claimant presented his claim, together with a surveyor's plot of the land claimed, in the following words and figures, to wit:

To the Commissioners appointed in pursuance of the act passed the 3d of March, 1803, for receiving and adjusting claims south of Tennessee and east of the Pearl river.

Please to take notice, that the following tract of land, beginning on a water oak, and running south, twenty-seven degrees west, five chains seventy-two links, to a stake; and from thence, south, eighty degrees west, fifteen chains, to an unknown bush; thence, north, seventeen degrees west, five chains, to a pine; and from thence, north, two degrees west, twelve chains, to a stake on the creek; and from thence, meandering the creek, to the beginning: this small tract of land is claimed by Edward Creighton in virtue of Benjamin King's improvement, and erecting thereon a cotton ginn, as described in the plot annexed, about the year 1800, transferred by the said Benjamin King to this reporter, who claims by right of pre-emption; John Callier, Esq. being a witness to the declaration of Joseph Bates, Senior, of the said tract of land, as plotted, being unclaimed or vacant land, now delivered to the Register of the Land Office to be established east of Pearl river, to be recorded as directed by said act. To all which he begs leave to refer, as also to the copy of the plot herewith filed.

EDWARD CREIGHTON,
Representative of Benjamin King.
MARCH 14, 1804.

[Plot omitted.]

Surveyed by Robert Ligon.

The claimant produced a deed of conveyance from Benjamin King bearing date the 11th day of March, 1803, duly executed and duly proven before James Farr, Justice of the Peace, relinquishing and conveying to the said Edward Creighton, in consideration of five hundred dollars, all his, the said King's, right, title, and interest to the said tract of land, and the buildings and improvements made thereon.

Entered in record of claims, vol. 1, page 261, by EDWARD LLOYD WAILES, for

JOSEPH CHAMBERS, Register.

John Hinds, chain carrier for the preceding survey, was sworn before John Brewer, Esquire, Justice of Peace.

Wilson Carman, and Andrew Barnard, were produced as witnesses, and, being duly sworn, the said Carman deposed, in answer to a question put to him by the Board, that he had no interest in, nor did he expect any, by the establishment of this claim.

That Benjamin King inhabited and improved upon the land now claimed in the month of June, 1801; but how long after he continued to inhabit the same, he did not know.

Question. Do you know whether this land was inhabited or cultivated on the 3d day of March, 1803, either by Benjamin King or Edward Creighton?

Answer. I do not know that either of them did inhabit the land in question on that day.

Question. Do you know whether this land is claimed by any British, Spanish, or donation claim?

Answer. I do not know that it is.

The said Barnard deposed:

Question. Have you or do you expect any interest in and by virtue of this claim?

Answer. I have not, nor do I expect any interest.

That Benjamin King built upon the land now in question, two years and half before he conveyed the same to Edward Creighton, and part of the said time cultivated a garden; and that said King did inhabit and cultivate the same on the 3d of March, 1803; that he put Creighton in possession of the premises in the month of April, 1803; and that Creighton has continued to inhabit and cultivate the same ever since; and that Benjamin King was on the 3d day of March, 1803, above twenty-one years of age.

The Board ordered that the case be postponed for consideration.

Adjourned until Friday the 23d instant.

FRIDAY, March 23, 1804.

The Board met according to adjournment. Present: Ephraim Kirby, Robert C. Nicholas.

EDWIN LEWIS's case, No. 69 on the docket of the Board, and No. 109 on the books of the Register.

Claim.—A right of pre-emption of six hundred and ninety-six acres, under the third section of the act.

The claimant presented his claim, together with a surveyor's plot of the land claimed, in the following words and figures, to wit:

To the Commissioners appointed in pursuance of the act of Congress, passed the 3d day of March, 1803, to receive and adjust the claims to lands south of Tennessee, and east of Pearl river.

WASHINGTON COUNTY, MISSISSIPPI TERRITORY,
March 16, 1804.

Please to take notice, that the following tract of land, situate on the west side of the river Tombigbee, butting and bounded as follows: beginning above Dr. Chastang's upper corner, and below Edwin Lewis's cotton house, above the first bayou above the Fort St. Stephen's, on the river bank, on an old line run by John Baker and Peter Malone; thence, runs the course of said line along the same, supposed to be forty-two degrees west, forty chains, to a corner stake; thence, north, forty-eight degrees west, one hundred and twenty chains, to a corner stake; thence, north, forty-two degrees east, one hundred and twelve chains, to a corner stake, on the river bank; thence, down the meanders of the river to the first station; having such marks, natural and artificial, as are represented in the plot annexed, containing six hundred and ninety-six acres; is claimed by Edwin Lewis, under and in virtue of a settlement or occupancy, he, the said claimant, having inhabited and cultivated the tract herein specified, agreeable to the third section of the act of Congress, entitled "An act regulating the grants of lands, and providing for the disposal of the lands of the United States south of the State of Tennessee," and the same does not appear to be claimed by any of the preceding provisions of the act; and the same was not inhabited nor cultivated, agreeable to the requisitions of said act, by any other person, &c.

This claimant further setteth forth, that he settled the same by consent of John Baker, in December, 1802, and he does not set forth this claim to injure or to impede said John Baker's right; but in case the same proves insufficient, then this claimant claims the first right to purchase the same, or any part thereof, to which there are no legal and superior claims, all of which are now exhibited to the Register of the Land Office established east of Pearl river, to be recorded as is directed by said act. All of which he begs leave to refer, as also to the plot herewith filed, &c. &c.

EDWIN LEWIS.
[Plot omitted.]

Entered in record of claims, volume 1, page 342, by EDWARD LLOYD WAILES, for

JOSEPH CHAMBERS, Register.

Thomas Price was produced as a witness, and, being duly sworn, did depose:

Question. Have you any interest, direct or indirect, in the establishment of this claim?

Answer. I have none.

Question. Did Edwin Lewis, the present claimant, inhabit and cultivate the land in question on the 3d of March last?

Answer. I do not know.

Question. Was he twenty-one years of age at that time?

Answer. I do not know.

Question. Is the land now in question claimed by virtue of any British or Spanish title?

Answer. I understand that it is claimed by the heirs of one Stewart, under an English title, but have no particular knowledge of the fact.

Question. Who inhabited this land at the evacuation of Fort St. Stephen's?

Answer. On part of the tract, there lived a man by the name of John Woods, and on another part a man by the name of John Berry; these were the only men living on the land at that time to my knowledge.

The Board ordered that the case be postponed for consideration.

RICHARD BARROW's case, No. 70 on the docket of the Board, and No. 28 on the books of the Register.

Claim.—A donation of six hundred and forty acres, under the second section of the act.

The claimant presented his claim, together with a surveyor's plot of the land claimed, in the words and figures following, to wit:

To the Commissioners appointed, in pursuance of the act of Congress passed the 3d day of March, 1803, for receiving and adjusting the claims to lands south of Tennessee and east of Pearl river.

MARCH 7, 1804.

Please to take notice, that the following tract of land, situated on the Mobile river, in the county of Washington, beginning at a gum corner, on the edge of Barrow's swamp, on the lake, running thence, south, seventy-seven degrees east, one hundred and fifty-five chains, to a willow corner, standing near two hickories on the bank of Mobile river, at the point of a sand bar, seven chains from the southern point of Joncy's island, thence, north, forty degrees east, seven chains, to a cotton tree on the lower part of said island; thence, up the west side of said island, north, ten degrees east, thirty-two chains and fifty links, to a willow corner; thence, west, five chains, to a birch corner; thence, north, ten degrees east, three chains, to a stake corner on Helverston's line, to the bank of the river: thence, north, seventy-seven degrees west, one hundred and fifty-five chains with Helverston's line, to a pine corner; thence, south, ten degrees west, forty chains, to the beginning, containing six hundred and forty acres; is claimed by Richard Barrow, in and by virtue of the second section of the said act, as a donation, and is now exhibited to the Register of the Land Office east of Pearl river, to be recorded as directed by said act. To all which he begs leave to refer, as also to a copy of the plot herewith.

RICHARD BARROW.
[Plot omitted.]

Chain bearers, Zachariah Worsly and Edmund Smith. Surveyed 2d March, 1804, by Natt. Christmas. Entered in record of claims, vol. 1, page 78, by ED-WARD LLOYD WAILES, for

JOSEPH CHAMBERS, *Register.*

The said chain bearers were sworn before James Callier, *J. P.*

Joseph Bates and Thomas Bates were produced as witnesses, and, being duly sworn, they did depose:

Question to said witnesses. Are you directly or indirectly interested in the establishment of this claim?

Answer. We are not.

Both testified, that Richard Barrow, the present claimant, did, antecedent to the year 1797, during that year, and subsequent thereto, inhabit and cultivate the land now by him claimed, and that he was at that time an aged man, and the head of a family.

Question to both witnesses. Is this land claimed by any British or Spanish grant, warrant, or order of survey?

Answer. Not to our knowledge.

The Board ordered that the case be postponed for consideration.

RACHEL HELVERSTON, in behalf of the heirs of Godfrey Helverston, deceased, case No. 71 on the docket of the Board, and No. 27 on the books of the Register.

Claim.—A donation of six hundred and forty acres, under the second section of the act.

The claimants presented their claim, together with a surveyor's plot of the claimed, in the following words and figures, to wit:

To the Commissioners appointed in pursuance of the act of Congress passed the 3d day of March, 1803, for receiving and adjusting the claims to lands south of Tennessee, and east of Pearl river.

MARCH 7, 1804.

Please to take notice, that the following tract of land, situated on the waters of Alabama river, on the west side, in the county of Washington, beginning at a cypress, and running thence, north, seventy-seven degrees west, one hundred and sixty chains, to a pine; thence, south, ten degrees west, forty chains, to a pine, it being Richard Barrow's corner; thence, south, seventy-seven degrees east, one hundred and sixty chains, along Richard Barrow's line, to a stake on the bank of Mobile river; thence, up the said river, north, ten degrees east, forty chains, to the beginning, containing six hundred and forty acres, having such shape, forms, and marks, both natural and artificial, as are fully represented in the plot annexed; which said tract of land is claimed by Rachel Helverston, for the heirs of Godfrey Helverston, deceased, in and by virtue of a donation, and is now exhibited to the Register of the Land Office east of Pearl river, to be recorded as directed by said act. To all which they beg leave to refer, as also to a copy of the plot herewith filed.

RICHARD BARROW, for
RACHEL HELVERSTON,
Acting for the heirs of Godfrey Helverston.
[Plot omitted.]

Chain bearers, Edmund Smith, Zachariah Worsly. Surveyed 2d March, 1804, by Natt. Christmas. Entered in record of claims, vol. 1, page 76, by ED-WARD LLOYD WAILES, for

JOSEPH CHAMBERS, *Register.*

The said chain bearers were sworn before James Callier, Esq., *J. P.*

Richard Barrow and Joseph Bates were produced as witnesses, and, being duly sworn, deposed:

Question. Are you directly or indirectly interested in the establishment of this claim?

Answer by each witness. I am not.

Both testified, that Godfrey Helverston, now deceased, commenced his improvements, on the land in question, in the year 1795, by building a house, and the following year by raising of crops, and that he continued to inhabit and cultivate the same from that time until the time of his death, which was in June last; and that, during said whole period, he was the head of a family, and twenty-one years of age; and that his widow and orphan children have lived on and cultivated the same land since the death of the said Godfrey.

Question to both witnesses. Is this land claimed by virtue of any British or Spanish grant, order, or warrant of survey?

Answer. Not to our knowledge.

Question. Do you know whether the deceased claimed or held any lands in this territory, by virtue of any English or Spanish grant, order, or warrant of survey?

Answer by both. He did not.

The Board ordered that the case be postponed for consideration.

PETER MALONE's case, No. 72 on the docket of the Board, and No. 47 on the books of the Register.

Claim.—A donation of two hundred and seventy-eight acres, two roods, and eight poles, as assignee and legal representative of John Woods, under the second section of the act.

The claimant presented his claim, together with a surveyor's plot of the land claimed, in the following words and figures, to wit:

To the Commissioners appointed in pursuance of the act of Congress passed the 3d day of March, 1803, for receiving and adjusting the claims to lands south of the Tennessee and east of Pearl river.

WASHINGTON COUNTY, MISSISSIPPI TERRITORY,
February 21, 1804.

Please to take notice, that the following tract of land, situated on the southwest side of Tombigbee river, butting and bounded as follows: by a line commencing on a cedar bush on the river bank, about five chains above the Fort St. Stephen's; thence, south, forty-seven degrees west, thirty-one chains seventy links, to a corner pine; thence, south, sixty-four degrees west, fifteen chains fifty links, to a red oak corner; thence, north, twenty-two degrees west, twenty-five chains, to a red bush; thence, north, fifty-four degrees west, eleven chains fifty links, to a small sassafras corner; thence, north, twenty-one degrees west, twenty-six chains fifty links, to a hickory corner; thence, north, fifty degrees east, thirty-eight chains, to a maple on the bank of the river; thence, the meanders of the river, to the beginning; having such marks, natural and artificial, as are represented in the plot annexed; containing two hundred and seventy-eight acres, two roods, and eight poles; is claimed by Peter Malone, the legal representative of John Woods, under and by virtue of the second section of the act, he, the said claimant, Peter Malone, having (as representative of said Wood,) no other claim to land in the territory; and that the same was cultivated and inhabited agreeable to the act of Congress entitled "An act, &c.;" and likewise, the said land does not appear to be claimed by virtue of the preceding provisions of the act, &c.

PETER MALONE.

[Plot omitted.]

Surveyed 13th February, 1804, by J. Malone. Chain carriers, Peter Malone and Colonel Josiah Bullock.

Entered in record of claims, vol. 1, page 120, by EDWARD LLOYD WAILES, for

JOSEPH CHAMBERS, Register.

The claimant exhibited a writing in the words and figures following, to wit:

ST. ESTEVAN, March 25, 1800.

This is to certify, that I have delivered my house and rails to Mr. Andres, according to Mr. Callier's letter to me. Given from under my hand, the day and date above written.

JOHN WOODS.

On the back of which writing is an endorsement in the words and figures following, viz.:

I endorse this instrument of writing over to Peter Malone, this 11th day of March, 1804.

ANDRAIS BARNAUD.

Josiah Bullock, one of the chain carriers for the preceding survey, was sworn, as such, before William Pierce, Justice of Peace.

Thomas Price was produced as a witness, and being duly sworn, deposed:

Question. Are you directly or indirectly interested in the establishment of this claim?

Answer. I am not.

He then testified, that he did not know the land represented by the plot before the Board, but knew that John Woods did, in the year 1798, live on a tract of land called Stewart's Reserve; that, in the fall of that year, he built his house, and commenced his cultivation in the year following; that John Woods was at this time a married man; that the place where Woods lived he always understood to be the property of one Stewart, who claimed the same by virtue of a British grant; and that he always understood that the Spanish Government refused to grant this land on the same account.

The Board ordered that the case be postponed for consideration.

JOHN TROUILLET, Executor of Peter Trouillet, case No. 73 on the docket of the Board, and No. 103 on the books of the Register.

Claim—Of eight hundred acres, by virtue of a Spanish warrant, under the first section of the act.

The claimant presented his claim, together with a surveyor's plot of the land claimed, in the words and figures following, to wit:

To the Commissioners appointed in pursuance of an act of Congress, passed the 3d day of March, 1803, for receiving and adjusting claims to land south of the Tennessee river and east of the Pearl river.

FORT STODDERT.

Please to take notice, that the following tract of land, lying west of the Tombigbee river, beginning on a maple, Thomas Bassett's corner, on the river aforesaid, and runs with his line, north, sixty-seven degrees west, one hundred and twenty-nine chains forty-nine links, to a stake corner; thence, south, twenty-three degrees west, sixty-three chains twenty-five links, to a stake; thence, south, sixty-seven degrees east, one hundred and twenty-three chains forty-nine links, to a stake on the river bank; thence, the meanders of the river, to the beginning: is claimed by John Trouillet, executor to the estate of Peter Trouillet, deceased, for the use and benefit of the heirs of the said Peter Trouillet, under and by virtue of a Spanish grant, or order of survey, granted to

the before named Peter Trouillet, as may appear by the original grant now delivered to the Register of the Land Office to be established east of Pearl river. To all which he begs leave to refer, as also to the copy of the plot herewith filed.

JOSEPH CAMPBELL.

[Plot omitted.]

Surveyed by J. Malone.

The claimant exhibited a Spanish warrant of survey in the following words and figures, to wit:

MOBILE, January 16, 1788.

His Excellency the GOVERNOR GENERAL:

Peter Trouillet, native and inhabitant of Mobile, with great respect to your excellency, represents and says, that, with intention to cultivate tobacco, and being informed that it was good land for that effect, begs your excellency to grant him a concession of twenty acres of land on said river, limited on the north by land the property of Madam Bassett, and on the south by land that is vacant; he begs your excellency to grant him the land above mentioned; for which favor he will be forever thankful.

PETER TROUILLET.

Don Vicent Folch, captain in the Louisiana regiment of fixo, commandant of civil and military of the said place and district, certifieth, that the land the above petitioner solicits is vacant, by information from the inhabitants who have knowledge of the same. In justification of which, I sign these presents at the said place and date as above mentioned.

VICENT FOLCH.

NEW ORLEANS, February 9, 1788.

The surveyor of this province, Don Carlos Laveau Trudeau, shall establish the above petitioner on that part of land of twenty acres front, with its profounder back as customary, of forty acres, at the same place mentioned in the above petition; as it is vacant, it cannot cause prejudice to any person; with the precise conditions of making the road and clearing regularly in peremptory space of one year; and if, at the precise space of three years, the land is not settled, during which period it cannot be alienated, this grant to remain null; under which supposition, the business of settling the limits will be carried on in the tract, and remitted me, to provide the interested party with titles in form.

ESTEVAN MIRO.

Don Joaquin Osorno, captain in the Louisiana regiment of infantry, and commandant of civil and military of Mobile and its jurisdiction, &c., certifieth, that the above is a copy taken from the original, in this office under my charge. Given from under my hand, in Mobile, the 18th of October, 1802.

JOAQN. DE OSORNO.

The above is a copy of the Spanish grant.

THOS. PRICE.

The above was compared with the original exact in this office.

JOAQN. DE OSORNO. [L. S.]

I, Thomas Price, of the post of Mobile, English interpreter for His Majesty the King of Spain, do solemnly swear, by the Almighty God, and by the Holy Cross, that this is a true and faithful translation of the Spanish grant or writing hereto annexed.

THOS. PRICE.

Subscribed and sworn before the Board, March 23d, 1804.—Attest: DAVID PARMELEE 2d, Clerk.

Entered in record of claims, vol. 1, page 317, by EDWARD LLOYD WAILES, for

JOSEPH CHAMBERS, Register.

The Board ordered that the case be postponed for consideration.

Adjourned until Saturday, the 24th instant.

SATURDAY, March 24, 1804.

The Board met according to adjournment. Present: Ephraim Kirby, Robert C. Nicholas.

JOHN BAKER's case, No. 74 on the docket of the Board, and No. 107 on the books of the Register.

Claim—Of fifteen hundred and ninety-nine acres, three roods, and twelve poles, by virtue of a Spanish warrant of survey, under the first section of the act.

The claimant presented his claim, together with a surveyor's plot of the land claimed, in the words and figures following, to wit:

To the Commissioners appointed in pursuance of the act of Congress passed the 3d day of March, 1803, for receiving and adjusting claims to lands south of Tennessee, and east of Pearl river.

Please to take notice, that the following tract of land, situated on the west side of Tombigbee, in the county of Washington, beginning at a stake near about the middle of a field on the river below my house; thence, south, twenty-nine degrees west, ninety-one chains; thence, south, forty-seven degrees east, one hundred and twenty-six chains forty-nine links; thence, north, twenty-nine degrees east, seventy-three chains seventy-five links, to the river; thence, with the river, to the beginning; fifteen hundred and ninety-nine acres, three roods, and twelve poles; and hath such forms and marks, both natural and artificial, as are fully represented in the plot annexed: is claimed by John Baker, in and by virtue of a Spanish warrant of survey, bearing date the 9th day of January, 1787, and is now exhibited to the Register of the Land Office established east of Pearl river, to be recorded as directed by said act. To all which he begs leave to refer, as also to a copy of the plot herewith filed.

JOHN BAKER.

MARCH 24, 1804.
[Plot omitted.]
The claimant produced a Spanish warrant of survey, in the following words and figures, viz.:

His Excellency DON PEDRO FAVROT, Commandant of this place:
John Baker, with the greatest respect due to your excellency, has the honor to represent his intention to quit the navigation, and endeavor to cultivate the land by two negroes; he expects to buy at the return of the schooner; in consequence of which, I beg your honor to grant me permission to establish one tract of land, containing forty acres front, and forty deep, as customary, formerly the property of Charles Walker, deceased, in the city of this place, situated on Tombigbee, and desire the petitioner to live peaceably and subject to His Catholic Majesty, by the conditions, to be a good settler and real Spaniard: the land above mentioned has no proprietor, and is right good to cultivate tobacco; I beg your excellency to grant the above land: for which favor from your excellency he will be forever thankful.

JOHN BAKER.
MOBILE, *January* 9, 1787.
It is granted to the above petitioner, and laid off agreeably to the Governor's royal orders; and the petitioner to give his oath to be true to the King and country, according to the orders from the General Government.

FAVROT.
MOBILE, *November* 12, 1803.
Don Joaquin de Osorno, captain of the regiment of infantry of Louisiana, commandant civil and military of Mobile and its jurisdiction, certifieth, existing in one bundle of concessions of land, in this office, is found the original in French writing, which I translate by the petitioner's demand, which I sign.

JOAQUIN DE OSORNO.

The above was compared exact by the original existing in this office under my charge.

JOAQUIN DE OSORNO.

I, Thomas Price, of the post of Mobile, English interpreter for His Majesty the King of Spain, do solemnly swear, by the Almighty God, and the Holy Cross, that, having examined the foregoing translation of the Spanish grant or writing thereto annexed, I find no material or essential errors contained in the same; but that all the substantial parts of said writing, viz., the dates, names of persons, the description of the lands, and number of acres, &c., are truly and correctly translated.

THOS. PRICE.
Subscribed and sworn before the Board, March 24, 1804.—Attest: DAVID PARMELEE 2d, *Clerk.*
Entered in record of claims, vol. 1, page 335, by EDWARD LLOYD WAILES, for
JOSEPH CHAMBERS, *Register.*

Doctor Chastang was produced as a witness, and, being duly sworn and questioned by the Board, testified, that he was not directly or indirectly interested in the establishment of this claim; that, in the year 1790, he removed on to his lands near Fort St. Stephen's, and at that time found John Baker, the present claimant, settled on his plantation near the same place, where he continued to live and cultivate until the year 1796, when

he, Chastang, removed from that neighborhood; that he understood that Baker had been at the same place some years previous to this time, and that he believed he continued there still, and was, as the deponent fully believed, more than twenty-one years of age in the year 1787.

Rolley Green and Joseph Westmoreland, chain carriers for the preceding survey, were sworn before Ransom Harwell, Esq. Justice of Peace.
The Board ordered that the case be postponed for consideration.

JOHN BAKER'S case, No. 76 on the docket of the Board, and No. 108 on the books of the Register.
Claim—Of four hundred acres, by virtue of a Spanish warrant of survey, under the first section of the act.
The claimant presented his claim, together with a surveyor's plot of the land claimed, in the following words and figures, to wit:

To the Commissioners appointed, in pursuance of the act of Congress passed the 3d day of March, 1803, for receiving and adjusting claims to lands south of Tennessee and east of Pearl river.

Please to take notice, that the following tract of land, situated on the west side of Tombigbee river, in the county of Washington, beginning at a stake about the middle of my bottom field, on the river below my dwelling house; running thence, south, twenty-nine degrees west, one hundred and thirty-four chains twenty-five links, to a stake; thence, north, sixty-one degrees west, thirty-one chains sixty links, to a stake; thence, north, twenty-nine degrees east, one hundred and fifteen chains, to the river; thence, with the river, to the beginning; containing four hundred acres, and hath such forms and marks, both natural and artificial, as are fully represented in the plot annexed: is claimed by John Baker, in and by virtue of a Spanish grant, bearing date 2d day of July, 1787, and is now exhibited to the Register of the Land Office established east of Pearl river, to be recorded as directed by said act. To all which he begs leave to refer, as also to a copy of the plot herewith filed.

JOHN BAKER.
MARCH 24, 1804.
[Plot omitted.]
The claimant produced a Spanish warrant of survey, in the words and figures following, viz.:

His Excellency Don ESTEVAN MIRO, Colonel of the royal army, Governor General of this city and province of Louisiana, &c. &c.
MOBILE, *June* 21, 1787.
John Baker, inhabitant of the jurisdiction of Mobile, with the great respect due to your excellency, represents and says, as having a small stock of cattle, and no pasture for them, he begs your excellency's goodness to grant him ten acres of land, situate on Tombigbee river, limited to the north side land, property of John Joyce, and on the south by land the King's commons; the above land was evacuated by Charles Walker, seven years past, and never been claimed by the proprietor nor any other person empowered by him: he begs your excellency to grant him the above petition, with the papers necessary from the Secretary of Government, which may correspond with the concession; for which favor from your excellency he will be ever thankful.

JOHN BAKER.
MOBILE, *June* 22, 1787.
Don Vicente Folch, captain of the Louisiana regiment, Commandant civil and military of Mobile and its district, certifieth, that the land the petitioner solicits is vacant, by information of the inhabitants of this district.

VICENTE FOLCH.
NEW ORLEANS, *July* 2, 1787.
The Commandant of Mobile shall establish this individual on that part of the ten acres of land front, by the profounder of forty back as customary, at the same place he solicits in the above petition, as it appears vacant, and not causing any prejudice to the neighbors, by the precise conditions of making the road and clearing regularly in the peremptory space of one year; and if, at the precise space of three years the land is not settled, after which period it cannot be established, and this grant to remain null; under which supposition, the business of settling the limits will be carried on in the tract, and remitted me, to provide the interested party with titles in form.

ESTEVAN MIRO.

Mobile, 3d September, 1787.

Certifieth that the above is a copy from the original existing in archives of this place.

SANTIAGO DE LA SAUSSAYE.

The above is compared exact by the original existing in this office under my charge.

JOAQN. DE OSORNO.

I, Thomas Price, of the post of Mobile, English interpreter for His Majesty the King of Spain, do solemnly swear, by the Almighty God, and the Holy Cross, that, having examined the foregoing translation of the Spanish grant or writing hereto annexed, I find no material or essential errors contained in the same; but that all the substantial parts of said writing, viz., the dates, names of persons, the description of lands, number of acres, &c. are truly and correctly translated.

THOMAS PRICE.

Subscribed and sworn before the Board, March 24, 1804. Attest, DAVID PARMELEE 2d, Clerk.

Entered in record of claims, volume 1, page 338, by EDWARD LLOYD WAILES, for

JOSEPH CHAMBERS, Register.

The testimony of Dr. John Chastang, recorded in the preceding case, was given and applied in support of this claim also.

The chain carriers for the survey in this case were the same persons, and sworn, as mentioned in the preceding case.

The Board ordered that the case be postponed for consideration.

JOHN DEASE's case, No. 76 on the docket of the Board, and No. 29 on the books of the Register.

Claim.—A right of pre-emption of fifty acres, under the third section of the act.

The claimant presented his claim, together with a surveyor's plot of the land claimed, in the following words and figures, to wit:

To the Commissioners appointed in pursuance of the act of Congress passed the 3d day of March, 1803, for receiving and adjusting claims to lands south of Tennessee, and east of Pearl river.

MARCH 9, 1804.

Please to take notice, that the following tract of land, situated on the waters of Tombigbee river, in the county of Washington, beginning at a pine, and running thence, north, twenty-two chains thirty-five links, to a corner pine; thence, west, twenty-two chains thirty-five links, to a pine; thence, south, twenty-two chains thirty-five links, to a pine; thence, east, twenty-two chains thirty-five links, to the beginning; containing fifty acres, having such shape, forms, and marks, natural and artificial, as are fully represented in the plot annexed; which said land is claimed by John Dease, in and by virtue of the third section of the said act, as a pre-emption; and is now exhibited to the Register of the Land Office east of Pearl river, to be recorded as directed by said act. To all which he begs leave to refer, as also to a copy of the plot herewith filed.

JOHN DEASE.

[Plot omitted.]

Chain bearers, James Powell, John Hinson. Surveyed 23d day of February, 1804, by Natt Christmas.

Entered in record of claims, volume 1, page 80, by EDWARD LLOYD WAILES, for

JOSEPH CHAMBERS, Register.

Daniel Johnson and James Powel, chain carriers for the preceding survey, were sworn before Ransom Harwell, Esq., Justice of the Peace.

James Powel and Daniel Johnson were produced as witnesses, and were duly sworn, and, being interrogated by the Board, both testified, that they were not directly or indirectly interested in the establishment of this claim; that, some time in the fall of the year 1802, John Dease, the present claimant, entered upon the land now claimed, and commenced the building of a mill; that he had, from that time to the present, continued the prosecution of said work; that he had built a house upon said land, for the accommodation of himself and workmen, and the last year cultivated a small garden; that he was twenty-one years of age on the 3d of March, 1803.

The Board ordered that the case be postponed for consideration.

RANSOM HARWELL's case, No. 77 on the docket of the Board, and No. 87 on the books of the Register.

Claim—A right of pre-emption of one hundred and ninety-seven acres, one rood, and twenty-seven poles, under the third section of the act.

The claimant presented his claim, together with a surveyor's plot of the land claimed, in the following words and figures, to wit:

To the Commissioners appointed in pursuance of the act of Congress passed the 3d day of March, 1803, for receiving and adjusting the claims to lands south of the Tennessee and east of Pearl river.

Please to take notice, that the following tract of land, situated on Tawler creek, Washington county, bounded on the southwest by the claim of Elisha Simmons, on the southeast by the claim of James Huckeby, and on the northeast by the claim of William Murrel, Senior, beginning at a willow oak, and runs north, thirteen degrees west, thirty-one chains sixty-two links, to a bay corner, near the creek Tawler; thence, south, seventy-five degrees west, at ten chains fifteen links, crossing his spring branch, in all twenty-six chains fifteen links, to a cherry corner, on Simmons's line; thence, with his line, south, forty-seven degrees west, at twelve chains fifty links, crossing the creek; at thirteen chains fifty links, crossing again; at seventeen chains thirty links, again; at twenty-four chains eighty-three links, crossing again; in all, forty-three chains fifty links, to a willow oak corner; thence, with Simmons's or Huckeby's southeast line, south, forty-five degrees east, forty-two chains fifty links, to a chinquepine corner; thence, north, twenty degrees east, twenty-three chains fifty links, to a large chesnut corner; thence, north, three degrees east, three chains thirty-eight links, to a hickory corner; thence, north, sixty degrees east, thirteen chains, to a hickory corner; thence, north, seventy-five degrees east, fourteen chains, to the beginning; having such marks, natural and artificial, as are represented in the plot annexed; containing one hundred and ninety-seven acres, one rood, and twenty-seven poles: is claimed by Ransom Harwell, of Washington county, under and by virtue of the third section of the above recited act, and now exhibited unto the Register of the Land Office established east of Pearl river, to be recorded as directed by said act. To all which he begs leave to refer, as also to the copy of the plot herewith filed.

[Plot omitted.]

Chain carriers, William Murrel, Senior, and William Murrel, Junior. Surveyed, 7th day of March, 1804, by J. Malone.

Entered in record of claims, vol. 1, page 253, by EDWARD LLOYD WAILES, for

JOSEPH CHAMBERS, Register.

The said chain carriers for the survey, in this case, were sworn before John M'Grew, Esq., Justice of the Peace.

John Baker and Edwin Lewis were produced as witnesses, and duly sworn; and, being interrogated by the Board, they both testified, that they were not, directly or indirectly, interested in the establishment of this claim; that Ransom Harwell, the present claimant, antecedent to, and on the 3d of March, 1803, did inhabit and cultivate the land now by him claimed; that he had a number of buildings, such as a dwelling house and necessary out-houses erected thereon, at the time above mentioned; that he has since continued to inhabit and cultivate the same; and that, on said 3d day of March, he was more than twenty-one years of age, and the head of a family.

The Board ordered that the case be postponed for consideration.

WILLIAM MURRELL's case, No. 78 on the docket of the Board, and No. 90 on the books of the Register.

Claim.—A right of pre-emption of one hundred and seventy-five acres, one rood, and twenty-one poles, under the third section of the act.

The claimant presented his claim, together with a surveyor's plot of the land claimed, in the following words and figures, viz.:

To the Commissioners appointed in pursuance of the act of Congress, passed the 3d day of March, 1803, for receiving and adjusting the claims of lands south of the Tennessee and east of Pearl river.

Please to take notice, that the following tract of land, situated on the waters of Tawler creek, bounded on the southwest by the claim of Ransom Harwell, and on the northeast by vacant land, beginning on a chinquepine, and runs south, forty-eight degrees west, thirteen chains fifty links, to a post oak; thence, south, ten degrees east, sixteen chains fifty links, to a red oak corner; thence, north, sixty-five degrees east, thirty-five chains fifty links, to a hickory corner; thence, north, twenty-one degrees east, thirty-three chains fifty links, to a lightwood stake corner, with a hickory, dogwood, white oak, and chesnut pointers; thence, north, thirteen degrees west, fifteen chains, to Ransom Harwell's beginning corner, water oak; thence, their dividing lines, south, seventy degrees west, fifteen chains, to a hickory corner; thence, south, sixty degrees west, thirteen chains, to a hickory corner; thence, south, three degrees west, three chains thirty-eight links, to a large chesnut corner; thence, south, twenty degrees west, twenty-three chains fifty links, to the beginning; having such marks, natural and artificial, as are represented in the plot annexed, containing one hundred and seventy-five acres, one rood, and twenty-one poles: is claimed by William Murrell, Senior, under and by virtue of the third section of the above recited act, and now exhibited to the Register of the Land Office established east of Pearl river, to be recorded as directed by said act. To all which he begs leave to refer, as also to the copy of the plot herewith filed.

WILLIAM MURRELL.

Witness, EDWIN LEWIS.
[Plot omitted.]

Surveyed 7th March, 1804, by J. Malone. Chain carriers, William Murrell, Jun. and Ransom Harwell.

Entered in record of claims, vol. 1, page 260, by EDWARD LLOYD WAILES, for
JOSEPH CHAMBERS, *Register.*

The chain carriers above named were sworn before James Callier, Esq. Justice of the Peace.

John Baker and Ransom Harwell were produced as witnesses, and, being duly sworn and interrogated by the Board, they both testified, that they were not directly or indirectly interested in the establishment of this claim; that William Murrell, the present claimant, settled on the land by him now claimed, previous to the 3d of March, 1803; that on that day, and ever since, he has there lived and cultivated largely; and that, on the 3d of March, 1803, he was advanced in life and the head of a family.

The Board ordered that the case be postponed for consideration.

JOHN JOHNSON's case: commenced in page 678.

James Powel and Daniel Johnson were produced as witnesses, and, being duly sworn and interrogated by the Board, they both testified that they had no interest in the establishment of this claim; that, in the year 1794, John Johnson, the present claimant, lived on and cultivated the land by him now claimed; that he had continued to live on and cultivate the same until the present time; and that he was at that time of full age and the head of a family.

The Board ordered that the case be postponed for consideration.

JOHN HIXSON, administrator of Owen Sullivan: case commenced in page 677.

Daniel Johnson and James Powel were produced as witnesses, and, being duly sworn and interrogated by the Board, they both testified that they had no interest in the establishment of this claim: that, in the year 1793, Owen Sullivan, lately deceased, did cultivate the lands now claimed by his administrator; that he continued to cultivate the same annually until the time of his death, which happened about one year ago; that the same lands have since been cultivated by the administrator of the deceased; that said Sullivan's place of dwelling was near said lands, on the other side of the lake, the said lands being low ground and not suitable for the erection of dwelling houses; that the said Sullivan had a cabin on said land for the purpose of protecting his workmen from the weather; and that the said Sullivan was, in the year 1795, a man in years and the head of a family.

The Board ordered that the case be postponed for consideration.

DANIEL JOHNSON's case: commenced in page 678.

James Powel was produced as a witness, and, being duly sworn and interrogated by the Board, he deposed, that he had no interest in the establishment of this claim; that, in the spring of the year 1795, Daniel Johnson, the present claimant, began to cultivate the land now by him claimed, and raised a crop the ensuing season; that he hath continued to cultivate the same land ever since; but, being an unmarried man, he lived in the family of his father, near by.

Question. Did this claimant cultivate this land for his own use solely, or for the benefit of his father?

Answer. I do not know positively, but always understood that he cultivated for himself solely.

Question. Was this claimant twenty-one years of age on the 11th day of June, 1795, or the head of a family?

Answer. He was not the head of a family, and I do not know positively that he was twenty-one years of age.

The Board ordered that the case be postponed for consideration.

JAMES POWEL, executor of William Powel: case commenced in page 682.

John Baker and Daniel Johnson were produced as witnesses, and being duly sworn and interrogated by the Board, they both testified, that they were not interested in the establishment of this claim; that, in the year 1793, the said William Powel, since deceased, lived upon and cultivated the land now claimed by James Powel, his executor; that he continued to cultivate and annually to raise crops on the said land until the time of his death, which happened in the year 1796; that his widow and family continued in the same cultivation and possession until the death of said widow, which took place about three months since; that, since that time, the family have continued in possession as before; and that the said William Powel was an aged man and the head of a family in the year 1793.

The Board ordered that the case be postponed for consideration.

JAMES POWEL's case, No. 79 on the docket of the Board, and No. 64 on the books of the Register.

Claim—Of five hundred and ninety-four acres, under the second section of the act, as a donation.

The claimant presented his claim, together with a surveyor's plot of the land claimed, in the following words and figures, to wit:

To the Commissioners appointed in pursuance of the act passed the 3d of March, 1803, for receiving and adjusting claims to lands south of Tennessee and east of the Pearl river.

Please to take notice, that the following tract of land, situated on the west side of the river Tombigbee, in the county of Washington, beginning at a water oak on William Powel's corner, and runs west forty-five chains, to a pine; thence, north, sixty-three chains, to a red oak; thence, east, forty-five chains, to a pine; thence, south, sixteen chains ninety-three links, to a pine; thence, east, one hundred and forty-one chains, to a sycamore on the river bank; thence, down the various courses of the river, to the beginning: containing five hundred and ninety-four acres, and hath such forms and marks, both natural and artificial, as are fully represented in the plot annexed: is claimed by James Powel, in and by virtue of the second section of the said act as a donation, and is now exhibited to the Register of the Land Office established east of Pearl river, to be recorded as directed by said act. To all which he begs leave to refer, as also to a copy of the plot herewith filed.

JAMES POWEL.

MARCH 24, 1804.
[Plot omitted.]

Surveyed 22d March, 1804, by John Dease. Chain bearers, James Dean and Amos Reed.

Entered in record of claims, vol. 1, page 186, by EDWARD LLOYD WAILES, for
JOSEPH CHAMBERS, *Register.*

Daniel Johnson was produced as a witness, and, being duly sworn and interrogated by the Board, deposed, that he had no interest in the establishment of this claim; that James Powel, the present claimant, commenced the cultivation of the land now by him claimed in the year 1795 or 1796; that he has continued annually to cultivate and raise crops on the same until the present time, and had a small cabin thereon, but resided near by the land in his mother's family, who was a widow; that he cultivated and improved this land for his own use and benefit; and that he was twenty-one years of age, and, as the witness believed, the head of a family in the year 1797.

The Board ordered that the case be postponed for consideration.

Adjourned until Monday, the 26th instant.

MONDAY, *March* 26, 1804.

The Board met according to adjournment. Present: Ephraim Kirby, Robert C. Nicholas.

ROBERT SORREL, Senior's, case, No. 80 on the docket of the Board, and No. 140 on the books of the Register.

Claim.—A right of pre-emption of three hundred and twenty acres, under the third section of the act.

The claimant presented his claim, together with a surveyor's plot of the land claimed, in the words and figures following, to wit:

To the Commissioners appointed in pursuance of the act of Congress passed the 3d day of March, 1803, to receive and adjust the claims to lands south of the Tennessee and east of Pearl river.

WASHINGTON COUNTY, MISSISSIPPI TERRITORY, *March* 23, 1804.

Please to take notice, that the following tract of land, lying and situated on Little creek, south branch of Bassett's creek, butting and bounded as follows: beginning on a station pine on the hill a little below Robert Sorrell's house; thence, running south, forty degrees west, fifty chains, to a corner pine, thence, south, sixty-six degrees west, one hundred and six chains, to a corner pine, near the bank of said creek; thence, north, thirty-three degrees west, twenty chains, to a corner stake; thence, north, fifty-two degrees east, eighty-eight chains, to a corner stake; thence, to the beginning; having such marks, natural and artificial, as are represented in the plot annexed; containing three hundred and twenty acres; is claimed by Robert Sorrel, Senior, under and by virtue of occupancy, the said claimant having inhabited and cultivated the tract herein specified on the 3d day of March, 1803, agreeable to the third section of the recited act, &c., and now exhibited to the Register of the Land Office established east of Pearl river, to be recorded as directed by said act. All of which he begs leave to refer, as also to the plot hereto fixed.

For ROBERT SORREL, Senior,
EDWIN LEWIS.
[Plot omitted.]

Entered in record of claims, vol. 1, page 466, by EDWARD LLOYD WAILES, for
JOSEPH CHAMBERS, *Register*.

Thomas Goodwin was produced as a witness, and, being duly sworn and interrogated by the Board, he testified, that he had no interest whatever in this claim; that, before the 3d of March, 1803, on that day, and since, Robert Sorrel, Sen. the present claimant, did inhabit and cultivate the land now by him claimed; and that he was at that time near seventy years of age and the head of a family.

EDWIN LEWIS's case: commenced in page 700.

John Pickering was produced as a witness, and being duly sworn and interrogated by the Board, he deposed, that he had no interest whatever in this claim; that, in the last of the year 1802, Edwin Lewis, the present claimant, employed him to erect certain buildings for said Lewis, on the land now in question; that he built a store, a kitchen, a dwelling house, and a warehouse, for the storage of cotton; that the said Lewis had, from that time to the present, continued to inhabit the same; that he had cultivated a small piece of land connected with said buildings; that he was thus inhabiting and cultivating on the 3d of March, 1803; and that the said Lewis was at that time more than twenty-one years of age.

The Board ordered that the case be postponed for consideration.

PATRICK DONNELLY's case, No. 81 on the docket of the Board, and No. 141 on the books of the Register.

Claim.—A right of pre-emption of four hundred and forty-eight acres and sixteen poles, under the third section of the act.

The claimant presented his claim, together with a surveyor's plot of the land claimed, in the words and figures following, to wit:

To the Commissioners appointed in pursuance of the act of Congress passed the 3d day of March, 1803, for receiving and adjusting the claims to lands south of Tennessee, and east of Pearl river.

Please to take notice, that the following tract of land, situated on the waters of Bassett's creek, on the west side of Tombigbee river, in the county of Washington, beginning at a pine corner, and runs south, thirty-two degrees east, forty chains, to a stake; thence, north, thirty-seven degrees east, one hundred and twenty-five chains fifty links, to a pine; thence, north, forty degrees west, forty chains, to a stake corner; thence, south, forty degrees west, one hundred and eleven chains, to the beginning; and hath such forms and marks, both natural and artificial, as are fully represented in the plot annexed, containing four hundred and forty-eight acres and sixteen poles: is claimed by Patrick Donnelly, in and by virtue of the third section of the said act, as a pre-emption, and is now exhibited to the Register of

the Land Office established east of Pearl river, to be recorded as directed by said act. To all which he begs leave to refer, as also to a copy of the plot herewith filed.

Exhibited by HARDY WOTTON, his x mark, for
PATRICK DONNELLY.
[Plot omitted.]

MARCH 26, 1804.

Surveyed 28th February, 1804, by William Gilliam. Chain carriers, Jordon Morgan and Henry Hill.

Entered in record of claims, vol. 1, page 467, by EDWARD LLOYD WAILES, for
JOSEPH CHAMBERS, *Register*.

The said Jordon Morgan and Henry Hill, chain carriers for the preceding survey, were sworn before William H. Hargrave, Esq., Justice of the Peace.

Jordon Morgan and John Kennedy were produced as witnesses, and being duly sworn and interrogated by the Board, they both testified that they had no interest whatever in this claim: that Patrick Donnelly, the present claimant, had lived upon the land now claimed ever since the year 1802; that the land is a pine barren, not fit for profitable cultivation; that the claimant has thereon a dwelling house, negro houses, cow-pens, &c. for the convenience of managing his stock of cattle, which subsist in the range, but no other cultivation than garden vegetables for the use of his household; and that the said Donnelly was, on the 3d day of March, 1803, more than twenty-one years of age.

William Gilliam, surveyor, was produced as a witness, and, being duly sworn, deposed, that the plot now exhibited to the Board is a true representation of the land now claimed, according to the best of his knowledge and belief; that it includes the buildings and improvements of the claimant; that he, the deponent, knew of no interfering claims except the claim of Robert Sorrel, Sen. which runs nearly half a mile into the northeast end of this tract.

The Board ordered that the case be postponed for consideration.

JOSEPH WILSON's case, No. 82 on the docket of the Board, and No. 142 on the books of the Register.

Claim.—A right of pre-emption of five hundred and sixty-one acres and sixteen poles, as assignee and legal representative of Joseph Dunbar, under the third section of the act.

The claimant presented his claim, together with a surveyor's plot of the land claimed, in the following words and figures, to wit:

To the Commissioners appointed in pursuance of the act of Congress passed the 3d day of March, 1803, for receiving and adjusting claims to land south of Tennessee, and east of Pearl river.

Please to take notice, that the following tract of land, situated on Tombigbee river, on the west side, in the county of Washington, beginning at a cedar post on the river bank, and runs north, eighty-five degrees east, sixty-five chains, to Cannady's hickory corner; thence with Cannady's line, south, five degrees east, thirty chains, to a stake; thence, south, seventy-eight degrees east, eighty-five chains, to the river, a maple corner; thence, with the meanders of the river, to the place of beginning; and hath such forms and marks, both natural and artificial, as are represented in the plot annexed, containing five hundred and sixty-one acres and sixteen poles; is claimed by Joseph Wilson, legal representative of Joseph Dunbar, in and by virtue of the third section of the said act, as a pre-emption, and is now exhibited to the Register of the Land Office established east of Pearl river, to be recorded as directed by said act. To all which he begs leave to refer, as also to a copy of the plot herewith filed.

JOSEPH WILSON,
Legal representative of Joseph Dunbar.
MARCH 26, 1804.
[Plot omitted.]

Chain carriers, John Cannady and Henry Hill. Surveyed by William Gilliam.

Entered in record of claims, vol. 1, page 468, by EDWARD LLOYD WAILES, for
JOSEPH CHAMBERS, *Register*.

The said chain carriers were sworn before William H. Hargrave, Esq., Justice of the Peace.

The claimant exhibited a deed of conveyance from Joseph Dunbar, bearing date the 12th day of March, 1804, duly acknowledged, relinquishing and assigning to the said Wilson all the said Dunbar's right, title, and interest to improvements made upon said tract of land.

Jordon Morgan and John Kennedy were produced as witnesses, and, being duly sworn and interrogated by the Board, they both testified that they had no interest whatever in this claim; that, in December, 1802, Joseph Dunbar did live upon and cultivate the land.now claimed by Joseph Wilson, as his legal representative; that he, Dunbar, continued there to live and cultivate until December, 1803, and raised a considerable crop on said land in the summer of 1803; that he sold his improvements to Joseph Wilson, the present claimant, who thereupon took possession of the premises, and has since continued to occupy and improve the same; that the said Joseph Dunbar was, on the 3d of March, 1803, apparently more than twenty-one years of age, and the head of a family.

William Gilliam, surveyor, was produced as a witness, and, being duly sworn, he deposed that the plot now before the Board is a true and correct representation of the land claimed, according to his best knowledge and belief; that it includes the buildings and improvements of the claimant; that he did not know of any interfering claim of any kind; that the figure of the plot was occasioned by other lines confining it to its present shape.

The Board ordered that the case be postponed for consideration.

EDMUND SMITH's case, No. 83 on the docket of the Board, and No. 139 on the books of the Register.

Claim.—A right of pre-emption of four hundred and twenty-two acres, under the third section of the act.

The claimant presented his claim, together with a surveyor's plot of the land claimed, in the following words and figures, to wit:

To the Commissioners appointed in pursuance of the act of Congress passed the 3d day of March, 1803, for receiving and adjusting claims to lands south of Tennessee, and east of Pearl river.

Please to take notice, that the following tract of land, situated on the west side of Tombigbee, in the county of Washington, beginning at a live oak, and runs north, seventy degrees west, one hundred and twenty-five chains, to a pine; thence, north, fifteen chains, to a pine on Howell Dupree's line; thence, with the said line, north, eighty degrees east, twenty chains, to a gum; thence, north, eighty-eight degrees east, ninety-four chains, to an elm on Gatlin's line; thence, with the said line, south, four degrees east, fifty-eight chains, to the beginning; and hath such forms and marks, both natural and artificial, as are fully represented in the plot annexed, containing four hundred and twenty-two acres: is claimed by Edmund Smith, in and by virtue of the third section of the said act as a pre-emption, and is now exhibited to the Register of the Land Office established east of Pearl river, to be recorded as directed by said act. To all which he begs leave to refer, as also to a copy of the plot herewith filed.

EDMUND SMITH.

MARCH 26, 1804.

[Plot omitted.]

Chain bearers, Sterling Dupree and Howell Dupree. Surveyed the 17th day of March, 1804, by Natt. Christmas.

Entered in record of claims, vol. 1, page 464, by EDWARD LLOYD WAILES, for

JOSEPH CHAMBERS, *Register.*

The above named chain bearers were sworn before James Callier, Esq., Justice of the Peace.

Howell Dupree was presented as a witness, and, being duly sworn and interrogated by the Board, he deposed that he had no interest, direct or indirect, in the establishment of this claim; that Edmund Smith, the present claimant, entered upon the land in question in the year 1801, built a house, and raised a crop on the land the next season; that he has continued to inhabit and cultivate the same until the present time; and that, on the 3d of March, 1803, he had a wife and family of children.

The Board ordered that the case be postponed for consideration.

JAMES SCOTT, representative of Gabriel Burrows: case commenced in page 663.

William Gilliam, surveyor, was presented as a witness, and, being duly sworn, he deposed that the plot presented is truly made, according to his knowledge and belief; that the irregularity of the figure of this land was occasioned by an accommodation with the adjoining claimants, to avoid litigation; that he did not know of any interfering claims of any kind with the land now claimed.

The Board ordered that the case be postponed for consideration.

EDWIN LEWIS's case, No. 84 on the docket of the Board, and No. 20 on the books of the Register.

Claim.—A right of pre-emption of one hundred and seventy-five acres, as assignee and legal representative of Dennis McClendon, and John McCole, under the third section of the act.

The claimant presented his claim, together with a surveyor's plot of the land claimed, in the following words and figures, to wit:

To the Commissioners appointed in pursuance of the act of Congress, passed on the 3d day of March, 1803, for receiving and adjusting the claims to lands south of the Tennessee, and east of Pearl river.

Please to take notice, that the following tract of land, situated on Fulsom's and Tawler creeks, butting and bounded as follows: beginning on a water oak on Tawler, at the mouth of Fulsom's creek; thence, running down the said Tawler creek, twelve chains, to a corner stake; thence, an east course, sixty-four chains, to a corner stake; thence, south, seven degrees west, forty-six chains, to a corner maple on the bank of Fulsom's creek; thence, west, fourteen chains, to a line run by Edwin Lewis; thence, north, seven degrees east, to a white pine corner; thence, down the meanders of the said Fulsom's creek, to the first mentioned station; having such marks, natural and artificial, as are represented in the plot hereunto annexed, containing one hundred and seventy-five acres: is claimed by Edwin Lewis, as the legal representative of John McCole and Dennis McClendon, under and by virtue of occupancy, the aforesaid persons legally represented said Edwin Lewis, having inhabited and cultivated the tract herein specified, on the third day of March, 1803, agreable to the third section of the act of Congress, entitled "An act," &c. and for a considerable time before that time: and the same does not appear to be claimed by any of the preceding provisions of the act, and now exhibited to the Register of the Land Office established east of Pearl river, to be recorded as directed by said act. To all which he begs leave to refer, as also to the plot hereunto fixed, &c.,

EDWIN LEWIS.

MISSISSIPPI TERRITORY, WASHINGTON COUNTY, *February 22, 1804.*

[Plot omitted.]

Entered in record of claims, vol. 1, page 53, by EDWARD LLOYD WAILES, for

JOSEPH CHAMBERS, *Register.*

The claimant exhibited a deed of conveyance from Dennis McClendon, bearing date the 14th day of February, 1803, duly executed, relinquishing and conveying to John McCole all the said McClendon's claim, title, and interest to the said tract of land, and the improvements made thereon.

The claimant also produced a deed of conveyance from the said John McCole, bearing date the 25th of February, 1804, duly executed, assigning and conveying to the said Edwin Lewis all the said John McCole's title, claim, and interest to the said land, and the improvements thereon made.

John Pickering and John McCole were presented as witnesses, and, being duly sworn and interrogated by the Board, they both deposed, that they had no interest in the establishment of this claim.

The said Pickering testified, that, in the year 1802, Dennis McClendon entered upon the land now claimed by Edwin Lewis, as the legal representative of McCole and McClendon; that said McClendon erected a house, and raised some corn on the same land in that year, and continued to inhabit and cultivate the same until the 15th of April, 1803, and that the said McClendon had, on the 3d day of March, 1803, a wife and family of children.

The said McCole testified, that, on the 3d of March, 1803, Dennis McClendon lived upon the land now claimed by Edwin Lewis, and continued there until the 15th of April, 1803, when he removed off; and that he, the deponent, took possession thereof, having, previous to the 3d of March, 1803, purchased the improvements of said Dennis McClendon; that, in the course of the summer 1803, he, the said McCole, agreed to sell said improvements to Edwin Lewis, the present claimant; that, in pursuance of said agreement, did, on the 25th of February, 1804, execute a written conveyance for that purpose.

The Board ordered that the case be postponed for consideration.

JOSEPH BATES, Junior's, case, No. 85 on the docket of the Board, and No. 162 on the books of the Register.

Claim.—A donation of six hundred and forty acres, under the second section of the act.

The claimant presented his claim, together with a surveyor's plot of the land claimed, in the words and figures following, viz.:

To the Commissioners appointed in pursuance of the act of Congress passed the 3d day of March, 1803, for receiving and adjusting the claims to lands south of Tennessee, and east of Pearl river.

Please to take notice, that the following tract of land, situated on the west side of the Tombigbee, in the county of Washington, beginning on a gum corner on the west bank of the Tombigbee: running thence, north, forty-five degrees west, one hundred and nine chains, to a pine; thence, south, forty-five degrees west, one hundred and three chains, to a post oak; thence, south, forty-five degrees east, thirty-two chains, to a post oak corner; thence, south, sixty-two degrees east, fifteen chains, to a dogwood, near a spring on the bank of a branch; thence, down the meanders of the branch, as laid down in the plot, to the river; thence, up the river the various courses, as laid down in the plot, to the beginning; containing six hundred and forty acres: is claimed by Joseph Bates, Jun. by virtue of the second section of the said act, as a donation, having such forms and marks, both natural and artificial, as are fully represented in the plot annexed, and is now exhibited to the register of the land office established east of Pearl river, to be recorded as directed by said act. To all which he begs leave to refer, as also to a copy of the plot herewith filed. JOSEPH BATES, Jun.

[Plot omitted.]

Surveyed February 18, 1804, by Natt. Christmas. Chain bearers, Sterling Dupree, Thomas Bates.

Entered in record of claims, vol. 1, page 493, by EDWARD LLOYD WAILES, for

JOSEPH CHAMBERS, *Register.*

Richard Turvin and Thomas Bates, Jun. were presented as witnesses, and, being duly sworn and interrogated by the Board, they both deposed, that they had no interest whatever in this claim.

The said Thomas testified, that Joseph Bates, Jun. the present claimant, was twenty-two years of age in the year 1797: that, being unmarried, he lived in the family of his father, Joseph Bates, Sen., upon the land now in question; that he acted for himself, independent of his said father, and did, during the years 1797 and 1798, cultivate the land now by him claimed, for his own use and benefit; that his father lived upon the land, and did also cultivate some part of it at the same time, but claims no part of it.

The said Turvin testified, that Joseph Bates, Jun., the present claimant, lived on the land now by him claimed in the year 1797, in the family with his father.

The Board ordered that the case be postponed for consideration.

HARDY WOOTTON's case, No. 86 on the docket of the Board, and No. 188 on the books of the Register.

Claim.—A donation of six hundred and fifteen acres and fifty-six poles, as assignee and legal representative of William Hunt, under the second section of the act.

The claimant presented his claim, together with a surveyor's plot of the land claimed, in the words and figures following, to wit:

To the Commissioners appointed in pursuance of the act of Congress passed the 3d day of March, 1803, for receiving and adjusting the claims to lands south of Tennessee, and east of Pearl river.

Please to take notice, that the following tract of land, situated on the Sunflower creek, in the county of Washington, on the west side of Tombigbee, beginning at Carter's line, south, twenty-one degrees east, sixty chains, to a pine station; thence, forty chains, to a corner on Sunflower creek, standing in the prison bounds; thence, south, eighty-seven degrees east, through Richard Brashear's field, to a pine station, forty-one chains twenty-five links, to a hazel corner, twenty-three chains seventy-five links; thence, north, twenty-one degrees west, seventeen chains, to a red oak station; thence, continuing the same course, seven chains and fifty links, to a new line; thence, on the same course to a gum station, continuing the same course to Carter's line, sixty-four chains on Carter's line, south, seventy-five degrees east, forty-one chains fifty links, to a tupelo gum corner; thence, north, eighty degrees east, twenty-six chains, to the beginning stake corner; containing six hundred

and fifteen acres and fifty-six poles. As a donation, this land is claimed by Hardy Wootton, legal representative of William Hunt, having such shape, forms, and marks, both natural and artificial, as are represented in the plot annexed, and is now exhibited to the Register of the Land Office established east of Pearl river, to be recorded as by said act directed. To all which he begs leave to refer, as also to a copy of the plot herewith filed.
HARDY L. WOOTTON, his x mark.
Legal representative of William Hunt.

MARCH 26, 1804.

[Plot omitted.]

Surveyed March 14, 1804, by William Gilliam. Chain carriers, Solomon Wheat and Joseph Wheat.

Entered in record of claims, vol. 1, page 553, by EDWARD LLOYD WAILES, for

JOSEPH CHAMBERS, *Register.*

The claimant exhibited a deed of conveyance from William Hunt, bearing date the 8th day of November, 1800, duly executed and acknowledged, relinquishing and conveying to the said Hardy Wootton all the said Hunt's right, title, and claim to the improvements made upon said tract of land.

On the back of said deed are two endorsements, in the following words and figures, to wit:

I do hereby assign over all my right, title, and claim to the within, for the use mentioned, from myself and my heirs forever, to Thomas Ware and his heirs; likewise the said Ware is to have possession the 1st day of February, 1802: as witness my hand, this 26th day of January, 1802.
HARDY WOOTTON.

JOSEPH SHARP, } *Test.*
CHARLES REED, }

I do hereby sign over all my right, title, and claim to the above privileges: as witness my hand, this 6th November, 1802.

THOMAS WARE.

A deed of conveyance was also produced from Daniel Johnson, as attorney for John Linder, bearing date the 29th day of February, 1804, duly executed, relinquishing and assigning to the said Hardy Wootton all the said Linder's right, title, and claim, to the abovementioned improvements.

Jordan Morgan and Solomon Wheat were produced as witnesses, and, being duly sworn and interrogated, they both testified, that they had no interest in the establishment of this claim; that, in the summer season of the year 1797, William Hunt entered upon the lands now claimed, erected a house, sowed some turnips, &c. the same year; that he raised a crop the year following, and continued to live on and cultivate the said land until he sold his improvements to Hardy Wootton in the year 1800, when he removed off, and Wootton entered into possession; that, in the year 1797, William Hunt had a wife and two children.

The said Wheat further testified, that he was not confident that Hunt sowed turnips on the land in the year 1797, but knew that he lived there, because he, the deponent, helped him to raise his house.

William Gilliam, surveyor, was presented as a witness, and, being duly sworn, deposed, that the plot, by him returned, of the land now claimed is a true representation thereof, according to the best of his knowledge and belief; that he knew of no interfering claim to that part of this tract which lies northerly of Watley's upper line; that there were several claims, houses, and possessions on the other part.

The Board ordered that the case be postponed for consideration.

HEZEKIAH CARTER's case, No. 87 on the docket of the Board, and No. 138 on the books of the Register.

Claim.—A donation of three hundred and fifty-eight acres and thirty-six poles, as assignee and legal representative of Robert Jones, under the second section of the act.

The claimant presented his claim, together with a surveyor's plot of the land claimed, in the following words and figures to wit:

To the Commissioners appointed in pursuance of the act of Congress passed the 3d day of March, 1803, for receiving and adjusting claims to land south of Tennessee, and east of Pearl river

Please to take notice that the following tract of land, situated on Sunflower creek, on the west side of Tombigbee river, in the county of Washington, beginning at a white pine, running, south, forty-five degrees west, fifty-two chains, to a red oak; thence, south, twenty-five degrees east, thirty-one chains, to a pine; thence, north, eighty degrees east, thirty-three chains, to a gum corner; thence, south, seventy-five degrees east. forty-two chains, to a hornbean corner; thence, south, seventy degrees east, twenty chains, to a mulberry corner; thence, north, sixty degrees east, three chains, to a yellow leaf sapling; thence, north, thirty degrees west, forty-six chains, to a cypress; thence, north, sixty-five-degrees west, twenty-five chains, to a red oak; thence, north, forty-five degrees west, thirty-five chains twenty-five links, to the beginning;and hath such forms and marks, both natural and artificial, as are fully represented in the plot annexed, containing three hundred and fifty-eight acres and thirty six poles: is claimed by Hezekiah Carter, legal representative of Robert Jones, in and by virtue of the second section of the said act, as a donation,and is now exhibited to the Register of the Land Office established east of Pearl river, to be recorded as directed by said act. To all which he begs leave to refer, as also to a copy of the plot herewith filed.

HEZEKIAH CARTER, his + mark.

MARCH 26, 1804.

[Plot omitted.]

Chain carriers, Jeremiah Morgan and Benjamin Harrison.

Entered in record of claims, vol. 1, page 462, by EDWARD LLOYD WAILES, for
JOSEPH CHAMBERS, *Register.*

The claimant exhibited a deed of conveyance from Robert Jones, bearing date the 10th day of November, 1800, duly executed, relinquishing and assigning to Hardy Wootton all the said Jones's right and interest to the improvements made on said tract of land. On the back of which deed is an endorsement in the words and figures following, viz.:

I do hereby assign over all my right, title, and claim to the within mentioned, to Hezekiah Carter, his heirs, from me and my heirs forever. In witness whereof, I have set my hand this 25th day of January, 1802.

HARDY WOOTTON.

Witnessed: JOHN CLOOP,
JOSEPH SHARP.

Solomon Wheat and Jordan Morgan were produced as witnesses, and being duly sworn and interrogated by the Board, they both testified, that they were in no way interested in this claim; that, in the latter part of January, or the beginning of February, in the year 1798, Robert Jones entered upon the land now claimed, built a house, cleared about six or seven acres, and raised a crop that season; that he continued to inhabit and cultivate the same until the year 1800, when he sold his improvements to Hardy Wootton, who entered into the possession and cultivation, and so continued until he sold to Hezekiah Carter, the present claimant, who then entered into the possession and cultivation of the same, and had so continued until the present time; and that the said Robert Jones was, in the year 1798, an aged man, and the head of a family.

William Gilliam, surveyor, was presented as a witness; and, being duly sworn, deposed, that the plot by him returned is truly and correctly made, according to the best of his knowledge and belief; that this land is bounded on all sides by other claims, except the line on the northwest end, which is the reason of the irregularity of its shape; that Mr. Lee has since varied the figure of his survey; and that he, the deponent, knew of no interfering claim of any kind.

The Board ordered that the case be postponed for consideration.

JOHN CANNEDA'S case, No. 88 on the docket of the Board, and No. 77 on the books of the Register.

Claim.—A right of pre-emption of five hundred and thirty-three acres, under the third section of the act.

The claimant presented his claim, together with a surveyor's plot of the land claimed, in the following words and figures, to wit:

To the Commissioners appointed in pursuance of the act of Congress passed the 3d day of March, 1803, for receiving and adjusting the claims to lands south of Tennessee, and east of Pearl River.

Please to take notice, that the following tract of land, situated on the river Tombigbee, in the county of Washington, beginning at a cedar post, and runs north, eighty-five degrees east, sixty-five chains, to a hickory corner; thence, south, five degrees east, sixty-five chains, to an elm; thence south, eighty-five degrees west, one hundred chains, to a stake on Denley's line; thence,

north, twenty degrees east, fifty-one chains, fifty links, to the river; thence, with the river to the beginning; and hath such shape, form, and marks, both natural and artificial, as are represented in the plot annexed, containing five hundred and thirty-three acres: is claimed by John Canneda, in and by virtue of the third section of the said act, as a pre-emption, and is now exhibited to the Register of the Land Office established east of Pearl river, to be recorded as directed by said act. To all which he begs leave to refer, as also to a copy of the plot herewith filed.

JOHN CANNEDA.

[Plot omitted.]

MARCH 26, 1804.

Surveyed 9th March, 1804, by William Gilliam. Chain carriers, Joseph Wilson and Henry Hill.

Entered in record of claims, vol. 1, page 225, by EDWARD LLOYD WAILES, for
JOSEPH CHAMBERS, *Register.*

The said Henry Hill and Joseph Wilson, chain carriers for the preceding survey, were sworn before William H. Hargrave, Justice of the Peace.

Jordan Morgan and Thomas Wheat were presented as witnesses; and, being duly sworn and interrogated by the Board, they both testified, that they were not interested in the establishment of this claim; that John Canneda, the present claimant, inhabited and cultivated the land now in question, in the year 1802, and ever since; that he was, on the 3d of March, 1803, more than twenty-one years of age.

William Gilliam, surveyor, was produced as a witness; and, being duly sworn, deposed, that the plot now presented to the Board contains a true and correct representation of the land claimed, according to the best of his knowledge and belief; that it includes the buildings and improvements of the claimant; and that he knew of no interfering claims of any kind.

The Board ordered that the case be postponed for consideration.

SOLOMON WHEAT'S case : commenced in page 58.

William Gilliam, surveyor, was produced as a witness; and, being duly sworn, deposed, that the plot now presented is truly and correctly made, according to the best of his knowledge and belief; that this claim is bounded by other claims, and, therefore, necessarily surveyed in its present form; that he knew of no interfering claims.

The Board ordered that the case be postponed for consideration.

JOHN PICKERING'S case, No. 89 on the docket of the Board, and No. 137 on the books of the Register.

Claim.—A right of pre-emption of two hundred and eighty acres under the 3d section of the act.

The claimant presented his claim, together with a surveyor's plot of the land claimed, in the words and figures following, to wit:

To the Commissioners appointed in pursuance of the act of Congress, passed the 3d day of March, 1803, for receiving and adjusting claims to lands south of Tennessee and east of Pearl river.

WASHINGTON COUNTY, M. TERRITORY, *March* 5, 1804.

Please to take notice, that the following tract of land, situated on Pickering's branch, north of Tawler creek, butting and bounded as follows: beginning on a wild plum tree, in a prairie called the Cow Stump prairie, on the east side of Pickering's branch; thence, west, sixty chains, to a corner stake; thence, north, twenty degrees, east, fifty chains, to a corner stake; thence, east, sixty chains, to a corner stake; thence, south, twenty degrees west, fifty chains, to the beginning; having such marks, natural and artificial, as are represented in the plot annexed; containing two hundred and eighty acres: is claimed by John Pickering, under and by virtue of occupancy, he, the said claimant, having inhabited and cultivated the tract herein specified, on the 3d day of March, 1803, agreeable to an act of Congress, entitled An act, &c. and the same does not appear to be claimed by any of the preceding provisions of said act, and now exhibited to the Register of the Land Office established east of Pearl river, to be recorded as directed by said act. All of which he begs leave to refer, as also to the plot hereto fixed, &c.

For JOHN PICKERING,
EDWIN LEWIS.

[Plot omitted.]

Entered in record of claims, vol. 1, page 461, by EDWARD LLOYD WAILES, for
JOSEPH CHAMBERS, *Register.*

William Coleman was presented as a witness; and, being duly sworn, deposed, that he was in nowise interested in this claim; that he was in the State of Georgia on the 3d of March, 1803, and could not say that the present claimant inhabited and cultivated the land in question at that time; that, when he returned from Georgia, in the month of May, 1803, he found John Pickering, the present claimant, working upon this land; that he had a house partly raised, about ten acres under fence, and five or six acres cleared, which appeared to have been cleared the preceding winter; that he raised on said land a crop of corn that season; that the said John Pickering had at that time a wife and a number of children.

The Board ordered that the case be postponed for consideration.

RICHARD S. BRYAN and GEORGE BREWER, Senior's case, No. 90 on the docket of the Board, and No. 6 on the books of the Register.

Claim.—A right of pre-emption of three hundred and nineteen acres, under the third section of the act.

The claimants presented their claim, together with a surveyor's plot of the land claimed, in the following words and figures, viz. :

To the Commissioners appointed in pursuance of the act of Congress, passed the 3d day of March, 1803, for receiving and adjusting the claims to lands south of Tennessee and east of Pearl river.

Please to take notice, that the following tract of land, situated on the waters of Tawler creek, in the county of Washington, beginning at a corner cherry tree, and running thence, south, seventy degrees west, sixty-five chains; thence, south, twenty degrees east, forty-nine chains; thence, north, twenty degrees east, sixty-five chains; thence, north, twenty degrees. west forty-nine chains, to the beginning; containing three hundred and nineteen acres, having such forms and marks, both natural and artificial, as are represented in the plot annexed; which said tract of land is claimed by Richard Smith Bryan and George Brewer, senior, under the firm of Bryan and Brewer, in and by virtue of right of pre-emption, and is now exhibited to the Register of the Land Office established east of Pearl river, to be recorded as by said act directed. To all which they beg leave to refer, as also to a copy of the plot herewith filed.

RICHARD SMITH BRYAN.
GEORGE BREWER, Senior.
FEBRUARY 22, 1804.
[Plot omitted.]

Surveyed 13th February, 1804, by Thomas Bilbo. Chain carriers, James Huckaby and John McCole.

John McCole was produced as a witness, and, being duly sworn, testified, that he had no interest in the establishment of this claim; that John Sluder entered upon the lands now claimed in the fall of the year 1802, built a small house, cut over about four acres of land, and commenced the cultivation of a garden on the same; that he continued to inhabit and cultivate the same until the month of April, 1803, when he moved off, having previously sold his improvement; that the said John Sluder was, on the 3d of March, 1803, the head of a family.

That, some time in the month of February, 1803, Richard S. Bryan, one of the firm of Bryan and Brewer, and one of the present claimants, began to make improvements on another part of the land now claimed, to wit, on Tawler's creek, near where they have since erected a mill; that the improvement then commenced was, as the deponent understood, the building of a dwelling house; that the present claimants had purchased the improvements which had been made by John Sluder on the other part of said land; took possession of the same in the month of June, 1803.

The Board ordered that the case be postponed for consideration.

EDWIN LEWIS's case, No. 91 on the docket of the Board, and No. 21 on the books of the Register.

Claim.—A right of pre-emption of four hundred acres, as assignee and legal representative of William Green, under the third section of the act.

The claimant presented his claim, together with a surveyor's plot of the land claimed in the following words and figures, to wit:

To the Commissioners appointed in pursuance of the act of Congress passed the 3d day of March, 1803, for receiving and adjusting the claims to lands south of Tennessee, and east of Pearl river.

WASHINGTON COUNTY, M. TERRITORY, *Feb.* 22, 1804.
Please to take notice that the following tract of land,

situated on Tawler's bayou or creek, above Fulsom's creek, butting and bounded as follows: By a line commencing at a water oak, at the mouth of Fulsom's creek, on the bank of Tawler; thence, up the said Fulsom's creek, about south, sixty degrees east, fifty-eight chains, to a corner white pine, on the south side of said creek; thence, south, seven degrees west, seventy chains, to a corner hickory; thence, north, eighty-three degrees west, fifty chains, to a corner stake; thence, north, seven degrees east, to the first mentioned water oak or beginning; having such marks, natural and artificial, as are represented in the plot annexed, containing four hundred acres; is claimed by Edwin Lewis, as the legal representative of William Green, under and by virtue of occupancy, he, the said William Green, having settled the same in January, 1802, and did likewise inhabit and cultivate the tract herein specified on the 3d day of March, 1803, agreeable to an act of Congress, entitled an Act, &c.; and the said William Green did, on the 7th day of June, 1803, assign a deed of conveyance of his right unto the said Edwin Lewis, and likewise two depositions on the sixth day of August, (of the same date,) and the said Edwin had, a long time previous to those assignments, agreed with the said William Green, for a part of the said premises; and the same does not appear to be claimed by any of the preceding provisions of the act, and no part thereof was inhabited and cultivated, at that time required by the said act, by any other person, and now exhibited unto the Register of the Land Office east of Pearl river, to be recorded as directed by said act. To all which he begs leave to refer, as also to the plot hereto fixed, &c.

EDWARD LEWIS.
[Plot omitted.]

Surveyed, 15th of February, 1804, by Robert Ligon. Entered in record of claims, vol. 1, page 55, by EDWARD LLOYD WAILES, for

JOSEPH CHAMBERS, *Register.*

The claimant exhibited a deed from William Green, dated the 7th day of June, 1803, conveying to Edwin Lewis all the said Green's right, title, and claim to the said tract of land and the improvements thereon.

John Pickering was presented as a witness, and, being duly sworn and interrogated by the Board, deposed, that he had no interest in the establishment of this claim; that William Green entered upon the land, now claimed by Edwin Lewis, as his legal representative, in the month of January, 1802, erected a house, cleared and fenced a few acres, and raised a crop that year; that he continued to live on and cultivate the same land until the fall of the year 1803, and raised a crop thereon in the summer of the same year; that the said Green was, on the 3d of March, 1803, more than twenty-one years of age, and the head of a family.

The Board ordered that the case be postponed for consideration.

JAMES CALLIER, representative of Bryant and Snellgrove: case commenced in page 651.

Richard Smith Bryant was produced as a witness, and being duly sworn and interrogated by the Board, he deposed, that he had no interest in this claim; that, on the 4th of June, 1803, he was present when Henry Snellgrove agreed to convey to James Callier, Esquire, his improvement and all his right to the land now in question, and when he did actually convey the same by an instrument under his hand, to which he, the deponent, subscribed as a witness; that, according to his understanding, the transaction was fair and *bona fide.*

The Board ordered that the case be postponed for consideration.

NATHAN BLACKWELL's case: commenced in page 643.

William Gilliam, surveyor, was presented as a witness, and being duly sworn, deposed, that this plot is truly and correctly made, to the best of his knowledge and belief; that Francis Boykin's line, as it is now surveyed, takes nine poles and twenty links upon the lower or southwardly side of the present claim; that he, the witness, had surveyed and measured the lands claimed by said Boykin, and found that the survey of said Boykin includes more than his quantity of acres, to the amount of this interference; that he knew of no other claim that interfered with this plot.

The Board ordered that the case be postponed for consideration.

Adjourned until Tuesday the 27th instant.

TUESDAY, *March* 27, 1804.
The Board met according to adjournment. Present: Ephraim Kirby, Robert C. Nicholas.

Benjamin Harrison's case, No. 92 on the docket of the Board, and No. 168 on the books of the Register.

Claim.—A donation of three hundred and seventy-eight acres, as assignee and legal representative of Jacob Miller, under the second section of the act.

The claimant presented his claim, together with a surveyor's plot of the land claimed, in the following words and figures, to wit:

To the Commissioners appointed in pursuance of the act of Congress passed the 3d of March, 1803, for receiving and adjusting of claims to lands south of Tennessee, and east of Pearl river.

Please to take notice, that the following tract of land, situated on the west side of Tombigbee, in the county of Washington, beginning at Thomas Goodwin's stake corner, and runs, north, sixty-five degrees east, eighty chains thirty links, to Ryan's upper corner; thence, south, sixty degrees east, eighty-three chains, to a sweet bay corner; thence, north, forty-two degrees east, three chains, to a sweet gum corner on Ryan's lake; thence, down Ryan's lake to Thomas Goodwin's elm corner, nineteen chains; thence, south, forty degrees west eleven chains, to a hornbeam; thence, north, thirty degrees west, one hundred and eight chains, to the beginning; containing three hundred and seventy-eight acres,having such shape, form, and marks, both natural and artificial, as are represented in the plot annexed: is claimed by Benjamin Harrison, legal representative of John Acworth, attorney in fact for Jacob Miller, in and by virtue of the second section of the said act, as a donation, as is now exhibited to the Register of the Land Office, to be recorded as directed by said act. To all which he begs leave to refer, as also to a copy of the plot herewith filed.

BENJAMIN HARRISON,
Representative of John Acworth, Attorney for Jacob Miller.

March 27, 1804.

[Plot omitted.]

Surveyed, 20th February, 1804, by William Gilliam. Chain carriers, Thomas Goodwin and Hezekiah Carter. Entered in record of claims, vol. 1, page 502, by Edward Lloyd Wailes, for

JOSEPH CHAMBERS, *Register.*

The claimant exhibited sundry legal deeds of conveyance, duly executed and on file, by virtue of which all the right and title which the said Jacob Miller had to the said tract of land and the improvements made thereon, became vested in the said Benjamin Harrison; in consequence of which, he obtained and now holds the possession of the premises.

Jordan Morgan was presented as a witness, and, being duly sworn and interrogated by the Board, deposed, that in the month of October, 1797, Jacob Miller, the person under whom Benjamin Harrison claims the land now in question, did inhabit and cultivate the same; that he had a cabin and some small improvements; that he continued until some time in the year following, when he sold his improvements and possession to John James, who entered into the possession of the same, and continued some time; then sold his improvement to the deponent; that he entered into possession, and raised one crop on the land, then sold his right to Shered Hatley, who also entered into the possession, and there continued until he sold to Joseph Jackson, who took possession and continued there until he sold to Benjamin Harrison, the present claimant; that he entered into the possession, and had continued therein ever since; that, at the time when he, the deponent, saw Jacob Miller in possession of the premises, in the year 1797, he was a married man, as was John James to whom he sold.

William Gilliam, surveyor, was produced as a witness, and, being duly sworn, deposed, that the plot now before the Board was truly and correctly made, according to the best of his knowledge and belief; that the house and improvements of the claimant were within the plot, and that he knew of no interfering claim or claims.

The Board ordered that the case be postponed for consideration.

William Gilliam's case, No. 93 on the docket of the Board, and No. 127 on the books of the Register.

Claim.—A right of pre-emption of one hundred and two acres, as assignee and legal representative of John Clark, under the third section of the act.

The claimant presented his claim, together with a surveyor's plot of the land claimed, in the following words and figures, viz.:

To the Commissioners appointed in pursuance of the act of Congress passed the 3d of March, 1803, for receiving and adjusting claims to lands south of Tennessee and east of Pearl river.

Please to take notice, that the following tract of land, situated on Sunflower creek, on the west side of Tombigbee river, in the county of Washington, beginning at a pine corner, running south, seven degrees east, forty chains, to a lightwood stake; thence, south, sixty-five degrees west, thirty-four chains, to a pine corner; thence, north, seven degrees west, twenty chains, to a pine corner on the creek; thence, north, forty degrees east, forty-five chains, to the beginning; containing one hundred and two acres, and hath such forms and marks, both natural and artificial, as are fully represented in the plot annexed: is claimed by William Gilliam, legal representative of John Clark, in and by virtue of the third section of the said act, as a pre-emption; and is now exhibited to the Register of the Land Office established east of Pearl river, to be recorded as directed by said act. To all which he begs leave to refer, as also to a copy of the plot herewith filed.

WILLIAM GILLIAM.

March 26, 1801.

[Plot omitted.]

Surveyed, March 13, 1804, by William Gilliam. Chain carriers, James Leonard and Hardy Wootton. Entered in record of claims, vol. 1, page 447, by Edward Lloyd Wailes, for

JOSEPH CHAMBERS, *Register.*

The claimant exhibited a deed of conveyance from John Clark, dated 18th February, 1803, assigning to the said Gilliam all the said Clark's right and claim to said tract of land and the improvements made thereon.

The said Leonard and Wootton, chain carriers for the survey in this case, were sworn before William H. Hargrave, Esq., Justice of Peace.

Solomon Wheat and Hardy Wootton were presented as witnesses, and, being duly sworn and interrogated by the Board, they both testified, that they were not interested in this claim; that the land now claimed by William Gilliam was settled and cultivated by John Clark, in the year 1802; that Clark sold his possession to the present claimant; that he moved his family on to the land, and raised a crop there in the summer of 1803; that they could not positively say whether he resided there on the 3d March, 1803; that he was, at that time, the head of a family.

The Board ordered that the case be postponed for consideration.

Jordan Morgan's case, No. 94 on the docket of the Board, and No. 128 on the books of the Register.

Claim.—A donation of six hundred and thirty-eight acres, under the second section of the act.

The claimant presented his claim, together with a surveyor's plot of the land claimed, in the following words and figures, to wit:

To the Commissioners appointed in pursuance of the act of Congress passed the 3d day of March, 1803, for receiving and adjusting claims to lands south of the Tennessee, and east of Pearl river.

Please to take notice, that the following tract of land, situated on the Sunflower lake, on the west side of Tombigbee, in the county of Washington, beginning at a sassafras corner, on Perkins's line, thence, south, twenty degrees west, sixty-two chains, to a white oak corner; then, due west, ninety-four chains, to a stake on James Denley's line; thence, south, ten degrees east, fifty-eight chains, to a black oak corner on James Denley's line; thence, west, one hundred and twenty-six chains, to the beginning; and hath such forms and marks, both natural and artificial, as are fully represented in the plot annexed, containing six hundred and thirty-eight acres: is claimed by Jordan Morgan, in and by virtue of the second section of the said act, as a donation; and is now exhibited to the Register of the Land Office established east of Pearl river, to be recorded as directed by said act. To all which he begs leave to refer, as also to a copy of the plot herewith filed.

JORDAN MORGAN, his × mark.

March 26, 1804.

[Plot omitted.]

Chain carriers, Wiley Roberts and Hardy Wootton. Entered in record of claims, vol. 1, page 449, by Edward Lloyd Wailes, for

JOSEPH CHAMBERS, *Register.*

The above named chain carriers were sworn before William H. Hargrave, Esquire, Justice of the Peace.

Solomon Wheat and Thomas Wheat were presented as witnesses, and, being duly sworn and interrogated by the Board, they both deposed, that they were not interested in this claim.

The said Thomas testified, that, in the year 1798, the present claimant, Jordan Morgan, having married his daughter, he agreed to give him half of his improvements where he then lived, which was upon the land now claimed by said Morgan; that he entered upon the same land that year, and cultivated from twelve to fifteen acres in corn; that he afterwards relinquished to Morgan the whole improvements; that he lived there about three years from the time when he first came; and that he was, when he first entered upon said land, above twenty-one years of age, and a married man.

Question by the claimant. Do you remember that you assisted me to haul my house and to haul rails, when I first came on to the land, and at what time of the year was it?

Answer. I do remember it, and it was in the spring season; but I cannot name the exact time.

The said Solomon testified, that, in the spring, or the first part of the summer, of 1798, Jordan Morgan, the present claimant, entered, with his family upon the land by him now claimed, and raised a crop that year; that he has been off and on several times since, and had raised crops; that he, the deponent, was not able to ascertain, with precision, the years when he was off or on; that, at the time when he first went into the possession of said land, he was above twenty-one years of age, and a married man.

William Gilliam, surveyor, was presented as a witness, and, being duly sworn, he deposed, that the plot of the land claimed, which is now before the Board, was truly and correctly made, according to the best of his knowledge and belief; that it included the buildings and cultivation of the claimant; that he knew of no interfering lines or claims of any kind; that this tract was bounded on three sides by the lines of other claimants.

The Board ordered that the case be postponed for consideration.

JAMES CALLIER's case, No. 95 on the docket of the Board, and No. 160 on the books of the Register.

Claim.—A donation of six hundred and forty acres, as assignee and legal representative of Isabella Trouillet, the wife of Joseph Campbell, under the second section of the act.

The claimant presented his claim, together with a surveyor's plot of the land claimed, in the following words and figures, to wit:

To the Commissioners appointed in pursuance of an act of Congress passed the 3d day of March, 1803, for receiving and adjusting claims to land south of the Tennessee river, and east of the Pearl river.

Please to take notice, that the following tract of land, lying west of the Mobile river, bounded eastwardly by the said river, and on all other sides by vacant lands, is claimed by James Callier, legal representative of Isabella Trouillet, at present the wife of Joseph Campbell; the said land having been settled in the year 1795, by the said Isabella Trouillet, who has occupied the same down to the present day, under and by virtue of the second section of the above mentioned act of Congress, for granting donation lands. To all which he begs leave to refer, as also to a copy of the plot now delivered to the Register of the Land Office, to be established east of Pearl river, which said plot is herewith filed.

JAMES CALLIER.

FORT STODDERT, March 27, 1804.
[Plot omitted.]

Surveyed 23d March, 1804, by James Gordon. Chain bearers, William Weathers, Joseph Edmonson.

Entered in record of claims, vol. —, page —, by EDWARD LLOYD WAILES, for
JOSEPH CHAMBERS, Register.

The claimant produced a deed of conveyance from Joseph Campbell, bearing date 20th of October, 1802, duly executed, conveying to the said Callier all the said Campbell's right and title to said tract of land.

Doctor John Chastang was presented as a witness, and, being duly sworn and interrogated by the Board, he deposed, that he had no interest in this claim, that, in the years 1796, 1797, and 1798, and, as he believed, in the year 1799, Isabella Trouillet, then the widow of Peter Trouillet, had a number of negroes living upon and cultivating the land now in question; that Madame Trouillet resided, at that time, in Mobile.

The Board ordered that the case be postponed for consideration.

JOSEPH CHASTANG's case, No. 96 on the docket of the Board, and No. 135 on the books of the Register.

Claim.—A donation of six hundred and thirty-nine acres and eight-tenths of an acre, under the second section of the act.

The claimant presented his claim, together with a surveyor's plot of the land claimed, in the following words and figures, to wit:

To the Commissioners appointed in pursuance of an act of Congress passed the 3d day of March, 1803, for receiving and adjusting claims to land south of the Tennessee, and east of the Pearl river.

Please to take notice, that the following tract of land lying on the west side of the Mobile river, butting and bounding as follows, viz.: beginning at a stake at Simon Andry's fence on the bank of the said river, running north, sixty-two degrees west, ninety-nine chains, to a pine; thence, south, four degrees west, ninety-seven chains, to a stake; thence, due east, ninety-one chains and sixty-links, to a red oak on the bank of the river; thence, up the meanders, to the beginning, on a straight line, fifty-one chains; bounded westwardly on vacant land, northwardly by Charlotte Herau's land, and eastwardly by the Mobile river; is claimed by Joseph Chastang, under and by virtue of the second section of the above mentioned act of Congress, for granting donation land. To all which he begs leave to refer; also, to the copy of the plot now delivered to the Register of the Land Office to be established east of Pearl river, which plot is herewith filed.

JOSEPH CHASTANG.

FORT STODDERT, March 26, 1804.
[Plot omitted.]

Surveyed March 24, 1804, by James Gordon. Chain bearers, Gabriel Tissrah, William Weathers.

Entered in record of claims, vol. I, page 459, by EDWARD LLOYD WAILES, for
JOSEPH CHAMBERS, Register.

Joseph Chastang appeared before the Board, and, on solemn oath, declared, that Simon Andry, of the county of Washington, is (as he believes) a material witness in his case, now pending before the Board, wherein he claims a donation of six hundred and thirty-nine acres and eight-tenths of an acre; and that the said Simon Andry is now confined to his bed by severe sickness, and in such state of health that it is not practicable to have him personally before said Board to give his testimony in the premises.

Whereupon, it is ordered by the Board, that the testimony of the above named witness may be taken in said case, before any lawful magistrate of said county (who is disinterested in said case,) being certified to the Board in due form of law.

Attest: DAVID PARMELEE 2d, Clerk.

John Chastang, Esquire, was presented as a witness, and, being duly sworn and interrogated, by the Board, he deposed, that in the year 1766 or 1767, Joseph Chastang, the present claimant, purchased the lands now in question, and went immediately into the possession and cultivation of the same, and continued there until the country was taken from the English by the Spaniards, when the Indians became so troublesome and dangerous that he was obliged to move down to Mobile: that when he, the deponent, came on to his plantation (which was near by the claimant's) in October, 1796, he found one of the sons of the present claimant, on his plantation, with his negroes, conducting his business as overseer; that he believed that one of the claimant's sons was there, with the negroes, as overseer, until the year 1798, when the said Joseph Chastang returned to his plantation now claimed, and had lived there ever since; that the present claimant was near sixty years of age in the year 1797.

Question. You say that this claimant purchased the lands now claimed in the years 1766 or 1767, and has ever since possessed the same; why does he not claim the lands by virtue of that title?

Answer. I have understood that the Indians burnt several of his houses, in one of which were his title papers, and thereby it has become impossible for him to produce this written evidence of his title.

The Board ordered that the case be postponed for consideration.

THOMAS GOODWIN's case, No. 97 on the docket of the Board, and No. 130 on the books of the Register.

Claim.—A donation of three hundred and seventy-four acres, as assignee and legal representative of Hiram Mounger, under the second section of the act.

The claimant presented his claim, together with a surveyor's plot of the land claimed, in the words and figures following, to wit:

To the Commissioners appointed in pursuance of the act of Congress passed the 3d day of March, 1803, for receiving and adjusting claims to lands south of Tennessee, and east of Pearl river.

Please to take notice, that the following tract of land, situated on Ryan's lake, on the west side of Tombigbee river, in the county of Washington, beginning at Wheat's pine corner, and running thence, north, sixty degrees east, eighteen chains, to a lightwood stake; thence, south, thirty degrees east, one hundred and eight chains, to a hornbeam; thence, north, sixty degrees east, forty chains and fifty links, to a hornbeam on Ryan's lake; thence, south, twenty-seven degrees east, forty chains, to a red oak; thence, south, sixty degrees west, twenty-eight chains, to a sweet gum; thence, north, fifty-six degrees west, forty chains, to Wheat's white oak corner; thence, with a straight line, to the beginning; and hath such forms and marks, both natural and artificial, as are fully 'represented in the plot annexed, containing three hundred and seventy-four acres: is claimed by Thomas Goodwin, as legal representative of Hiram Mounger, in and by virtue of a donation claim, and is now exhibited to the Register of the Land Office, east of Pearl river, to be recorded as directed by said act. To all which he begs leave to refer, as also to the copy of the plot herewith filed.

THOMAS GOODWIN.

MARCH 24, 1804.

[Plot omitted.]

Chain carriers, Hezekiah Carter and Ambrose Miles. Entered in record of claims, vol. 1, page 451, by ED-WARD LLOYD WAILES, for

JOSEPH CHAMBERS, *Register.*

The said chain carriers for the preceding survey were sworn before William H. Hargrave, Esquire, Justice of the Peace.

The claimant produced a deed of conveyance from John Wheat, dated the 13th day of July, 1803; conveying to the said Thomas Goodwin, all the said Wheat's right and claim to the said tract of land, and the improvements made thereon.

Jordan Morgan was presented as a witness, and, being duly sworn and interrogated by the Board, deposed, that he was not interested in this claim; that, in the year 1797, he passed across this land, and found an improvement there, which he understood was made by Hiram Mounger; that, in the year 1798, Hiram Mounger exchanged his possession and improvement on this land, for the possession and improvement of Hezekiah and Solomon Wheat, on another tract; that two or three improvements were made in different parts of the tract, given up by Mounger to the Wheats; that the Wheats being brothers, made a partition of the land among themselves; that the land now in question is a part of the original tract, which was claimed by virtue of the settlement and improvement of Hiram Mounger; that Thomas Goodwin, the present claimant, then lived on one of those improvements; that Frederick Smith performed labor at the same place in the year 1798, and raised a crop there in the year 1799; and the same year sold his labor and improvement to John Wheat, a brother of Solomon and Hezekiah; that, whether Smith improved there by the consent of the Wheats or not, he, the deponent, could not be positive; though he presumed, it was by consent, as Smith was a connexion of the family by marriage, and lived in the house with them during that time; that Hiram Mounger was upwards of twenty-one years of age in the year 1797.

William Gilliam, surveyor, and Solomon Wheat, were produced as witnesses, and being duly sworn, the said Wheat deposed, that Hiram Mounger had made some improvements on the land, now claimed by Thomas Goodwin, before the exchange took place, as mentioned by the last witness; that Smith had also begun to labor there in the year 1798, before Solomon and Hezekiah Wheat entered into possession; that, after they came into possession, they agreed with Smith upon a partition line, between the improvements where Smith was at work and the improvements where Mounger lived, which line was truly represented by the plot then before the Board; that Smith afterwards sold his improvements and possession to John Wheat, as he, the deponent, had heard them say; that John Wheat sold to Thomas Goodwin, as he had heard them both say; that he knew that Goodwin took possession, and had since continued to live at the same place.

The said Gilliam testified, that the plot of the land claimed by Thomas Goodwin, then before the Board, was truly and correctly made, according to the best of his knowledge and belief; that he knew of no interfering claims of any kind; that the irregular shape of this survey was occasioned by the lines of adjoining claimants.

The Board ordered that the case be postponed for consideration.

WILLIAM WILLIAMS's case, No. 98 on the docket of the Board, and No. 46 on the books of the Register.

Claim.—A right of pre-emption of one hundred and one acres, three roods, and twenty-seven poles, under the third section of the act.

The claimant presented his claim, together with a surveyor's plot of the land claimed, in the following words and figures, to wit:

To the Commissioners appointed, in pursuance of the act of Congress passed the 3d day of March, 1803, for receiving and adjusting the claims to lands south of the Tennessee and east of Pearl river.

Please to take notice, that the following tract of land, situated on the west side of Tombigbee, butted on the same, bounded on the southwest and southeast by vacant land, and on the northeast by George Robbins; beginning on a cotton tree, and runs south, fifty-six degrees west, thirty-one chains, to a white oak; thence, south, twenty-five degrees east, at twenty-five chains crossing a small branch; in all, sixty chains twenty-seven links, to a stake with two wahoos, a hickory, and dogwood pointers; thence, north, sixty degrees east, twenty chains and fifty links, with Robbins's line to his corner, a large sycamore on the river bank; thence, the meanders of the river, to the beginning; having such marks, natural and artificial, as are represented in the plot annexed; containing one hundred and one acres, three roods, and twenty-seven poles: is claimed by William Williams, under and by virtue of a settlement bearing date the 20th day of February, 1803, and now exhibited unto the Register of the Land Office east of Pearl river, to be recorded as directed by said act. To all which he begs leave to refer, as also to the copy of the plot herewith filed.

WILLIAM WILLIAMS.

[Plot omitted.]

Chain carriers, Henry Nail, Edward Williams. Surveyed 28th February, 1804, by J. Malone. Entered in record of claims, vol. page 119, by ED-WARD LLOYD WAILES, for

JOSEPH CHAMBERS, *Register.*

Richard Hawkins and Edward Williams were produced as witnesses, and, being duly sworn and interrogated by the Board, they both deposed, that they had no interest in the establishment of this claim; that William Williams, the present claimant, did inhabit and cultivate the land by him claimed before and on the 3d of March, 1803, and raised a crop thereon in the summer following; and that he was, on the third of March, 1803, an aged man, and the head of a family.

The Board ordered that the case be postponed for consideration.

JAMES HUCKABY's case, No. 99 on the docket of the Board, and No. 110 on the books of the Register.

Claim.—A right of pre-emption of four hundred and sixty-seven acres, as assignee and legal representative of Matthew Robinson, under the third section of the act.

The claimant presented his claim, together with a surveyor's plot of the land claimed, in the following words and figures, to wit:

To the Commissioners appointed in pursuance of the act of Congress passed the 3d day of March, 1803, for receiving and adjusting claims to land south of Tennessee, and east of Pearl river.

Please to take notice, that the following tract of land, situated on the south side of Tawler creek, in the county of Washington, beginning at a stake on said creek, running east eighty chains, to a poplar corner; thence, north, fifty-three chains, to a chestnut; thence, north, forty-five degrees west, thirty-five chains, to a hackberry on said creek; thence, up said creek, to the beginning; and hath such forms and marks, both natural and artificial, as are fully represented in the plot annexed; containing four hundred and sixty-seven acres: is claimed by James Huckaby, legal representative of Matthew Robinson, in and by virtue of the third section of the above recited act, as a pre-emption; and is now exhibited to the Register of the Land Office, established east of Pearl river, to be recorded as directed by said act. To all which he begs leave to refer, as also to a copy of the plot herewith filed.

WILLIAM COLEMAN, for

JAMES HUCKABY,

Representative of Matthew Robinson.

MARCH 27, 1804.

[Plot omitted.]

Surveyed 4th March, 1804, by Thomas Bilbo. Chain carriers, Reuben Westmoreland, Richard Smith Bryan. Entered in record of claims, vol. 1, page 344, by ED-WARD LLOYD WAILES, for

JOSEPH CHAMBERS, *Register.*

The said chain carriers were sworn before William Pierce and Joseph Thompson, Justices of the Peace.

The claimant exhibited a deed from Matthew Robinson, dated 22d January, 1803, conveying to the said James Huckaby all the said Robinson's right to said tract of land and the improvements made thereon.

Richard Smith Bryan and William Coleman were presented as witnesses, and, being duly sworn and interrogated by the Board, they both deposed, that they were not interested in this claim; that, in the latter part of the year 1801, Matthew Robinson commenced to improve upon the land claimed by James Huckaby, and live there with his family through the year 1802, and raised a crop that year; that he afterwards sold his improvements to James Huckaby; that he continued to live on the land, by the consent of Huckaby, some time after, but whether the said Robinson or the said Huckaby lived there on the 3d of March, 1803, they, the witnesses, could not be positively certain; but were certain that, when Robinson moved off, Huckaby moved on to the land, and did cultivate and raise a crop thereon, in the summer of the year 1803; and that both Robinson and Huckaby were heads of families on the 3d of March, 1803.

The Board ordered that the case be postponed for consideration.

NICHOLAS PERKINS, representative of Thomas Wheat: case commenced in page 690.

John Baker was produced as a witness, and, being duly sworn and interrogated by the Board, deposed, that he had no interest in this claim; that Thomas Wheat, the person under whom the present claim is made, was an old inhabitant of this county; that, on the 27th day of October, 1795, and before and since, until lately, the said Thomas Wheat did inhabit and cultivate the land then question; that, on the 22d of October, 1787, the said Thomas Wheat was more than twenty-one years of age, and the head of a family.

Thomas Wheat and William Gilliam, surveyor, were produced as witnesses, and, being duly sworn, the said Gilliam deposed, that the plot before the Board was made by him; that it was true and correct, according to his best knowledge and belief; that he knew of no interfering claims.

The said Wheat testified, that he did sell and convey his title to the land now claimed to Nicholas Perkins, the present claimant; that the instrument of conveyance, now produced to the Board, was his free act and deed for that purpose.

Jordan Morgan and Hezekiah Carter, chain carriers for the survey in this case, and also for the survey in the said Perkins's case, commenced in page 691, were sworn before William H. Hargrave, Esq., Justice of the Peace.

The Board ordered that the case be postponed for consideration.

JOHN WAMACK's case, No. 100 on the docket of the Board, and No. 147 on the books of the Register.

Claim.—A right of pre-emption of two hundred and forty acres, under the third section of the act.

The claimant presented his claim, together with a surveyor's plot of the land claimed, in the following words and figures, to wit:

To the Commissioners appointed in pursuance of an act of Congress passed the 3d day of March, 1803, for receiving and adjusting claims to lands south of the Tennessee, and east of Pearl river.

Please to take notice, that the following tract of land, situated on the west side of the river Tombigbee, beginning at a large pine, and runs south, sixty-two degrees west, crossing a small branch at six chains and fifty links, forty chains, to a stake; thence, north, twenty-eight degrees west, sixty chains, to a black jack corner; thence, north, sixty-two degrees east, forty chains, to a stake, and from thence to the beginning: containing two hundred and forty acres: is claimed by John Wamack, un-

der and by virtue of the third section of the above recited act of Congress; is now exhibited to the Register of the Land Office, established east of Pearl river, for the purpose of being recorded as directed by the above recited act. To all which he begs leave to refer, as also to the plot herewith filed.

JOHN WAMACK.

MARCH 26, 1804.

[Plot omitted.]

Surveyed 18th February, 1804, by J. Malone. Chain carriers, Peter Cartwright and John Walker.

Entered in record of claims, vol. 1, page 475, by ED-WARD LLOYD WAILES, for

JOSEPH CHAMBERS, *Register.*

The said chain carriers for the preceding survey were sworn before William Pierce, Justice of Peace.

Richard S. Bryan and William Coleman were produced as witnesses, and, being duly sworn and interrogated by the Board, they deposed, that they were in no way interested in the establishment of this claim.

The said Coleman further testified, that, in July, 1802, he was at the house of John Wamack, the present claimant, on the lands which are now by him claimed; that he then had considerable land in cultivation; that he, said Coleman, then went into Georgia, and returned in the month of May, 1803, and found the said Wamack still there inhabiting and cultivating; that he continues there still; and that he verily believed that Wamack was there on the 3d of March, 1803; that he was, at that time, more than twenty-one years of age, and the head of a family.

Question by the claimant's attorney. What is the state of John Wamack's improvements on the land by him now claimed?

Answer. I suppose that he has between thirty and forty acres under cultivation.

The said Bryan testified, that he was at the house of John Wamack, the present claimant, on the land now by him claimed, the last of February, or the 1st of March, 1803; that he then lived there with his family; had considerable land in cultivation; that he has ever since continued to live there; and that he was, at that time, more than twenty-one years of age, and the head of a family.

Thomas Malone, surveyor, was presented as a witness, and, being duly sworn, deposed, that the plot then before the Board was truly and correctly made, according to the best of his knowledge and belief; that it includes the house and improvements of the claimant; that he knew of no interfering lines or claims of any kind.

The Board ordered that the case be postponed for consideration.

Adjourned until Wednesday, the 28th instant.

WEDNESDAY, *March* 28, 1804.

The Board met according to adjournment. Present: Ephraim Kirby, Robert C. Nicholas.

NICHOLAS PERKINS, representative of Daniel Johnson: case commenced in page 691.

James Denley, John Denley, and William H. Hargrave, were presented as witnesses, and, being duly sworn and interrogated by the Board, they all deposed, that they had no interest in this claim.

The said James testified, that Daniel Johnson, in whose right the present claimant appears, deceased about two years before; that he would then have been (if living) upwards of seventy years of age; that he resided in this county in the year 1795, and until the time of his death; that the land in question was, some part of it, under cultivation in the year 1795; but could not say that it was by Daniel Johnson.

The said John testified, that he could not say, with positive certainty, as to the precise time, but knew that, about year 1795, the land in question was cultivated by the son of Daniel Johnson, deceased; that, before the year 1795, and in that year, and until his death, the said Daniel Johnson did reside in this county, not far from this land, and that he was an aged man at the time of his death.

The said Hargrave testified, that the deed of conveyance, dated the 21st day of September, 1803, under his signature, then before the Board, by which he conveyed all his right and interest in the land now claimed by Nicholas Perkins, Esq., the present claimant, was his free act and deed, and was by him executed and delivered for the purposes therein mentioned.

William Gilliam, surveyor, Hiram Mounger, and John Brewer, were produced as witnesses, and, being duly sworn, the said Gilliam deposed, that, on the 21st of May, 1800, he saw Solomon Johnson execute and deliver a deed to William H. Hargrave, conveying the lands now in question; that he was called and subscribed as a witness; and that he saw Samuel Long also subscribe as a witness to the same instrument; that, upon inspection of the deed of Solomon Johnson, then exhibited in evidence before the Board, he was satisfied that it was the same original instrument to which he subscribed as a witness; that he surveyed, and made the plot then before the Board; that it was correctly made, according to the best of his knowledge and belief; that a small portion of one line could not be measured, by reason of high water, and was laid down by conjecture.

The said Brewer and Mounger both testified, that, from the year 1791, until within three years past, the land in question has been cultivated by Daniel Johnson, deceased, or for his use.

The Board ordered that the case be postponed for consideration.

NICHOLAS PERKINS, representative of Thomas Wheat: case commenced in page 690.

John Brewer, Esq. and Hiram Mounger were produced as witnesses, and, being duly sworn and interrogated by the Board, they deposed, that they were not interested in this claim; that, before the year 1795, in that year, and until within a short time past, Thomas Wheat, the person in whose right the present claimant appears, did inhabit and cultivate the land in question, and that they believed that said Thomas Wheat was more than twenty-one years of age, and the head of a family on the 22d day of October, 1787.

The Board ordered that the case be postponed for consideration.

JOHN BAKER's two cases: one commenced in page 703, the other in page 704.

George Brewer was produced as a witness in said cases; and, being duly sworn and interrogated by the Board, he testified, that, in the year 1794, he became acquainted with John Baker, the present claimant, at his place of residence, on the lands now in question; that the said Baker had continued to reside and cultivate there ever since.

The Board ordered that these cases be postponed for consideration.

WILLIAM GILLIAM's case: commenced in page 713.

William Hargrave and John Denley were presented as witnesses; and, being sworn and interrogated by the Board, they deposed, that they were not in any way interested in this claim; and that Hargrave testified, that he was present when John Clark sold his possession and improvement on the land in question, on the 18th of February, 1803; that, by their request, he drew and witnessed a writing which said Clark executed: that, within a few days after, he was present when Clark gave to Gilliam the possession of the place; that Gilliam went there himself, and raised a crop that season, but did not move his family into the house immediately; that Gilliam was, on the 3d of March, 1803, the head of a family.

The said Denley testified, that he was present when John Clark sold his possessions to William Gilliam, and witnessed the writing; that he knew that the possession was peaceably surrendered up by Clark to Gilliam; that Gilliam went to work on the land that spring, and raised a crop thereon the ensuing season; that, in the course of the same spring, he moved into the house, and had there lived ever since.

The Board ordered that the case be postponed for consideration.

EPHRAIM BARKER's case: commenced in page 652.

William Gilliam, surveyor, was presented as witness, and, being duly sworn, deposed, that the plot of the land claimed, then presented to the Board, was correctly made according to the best of his knowledge and belief; that said plot did not include any dwelling house, as it usually overflowed annually, and was unfit for a dwelling place; that it included the cultivated field of the claimant; that he, Gilliam, knew of no interfering lines or claims.

Question. Is this position such that a family could not reside upon it?

Answer. It is very much surrounded by ponds and lakes: I cannot say how far the health of inhabitants might be affected by that: the annual overflowings, I think, would probably sweep a house off if one should be placed there.

The Board ordered that the case be postponed for consideration.

BENJAMIN HARRISON's case: commenced in page 712.

Hiram Mounger was produced as a witness, and, being duly sworn, deposed, that he was not interested in the establishment of this claim; that, in the latter part of the year 1797, Jacob Miller settled upon the land in question, and as he, Mounger, understood, sold it afterwards to one James, who cultivated it in the year 1798; that from James the possession and improvement passed through several persons to Benjamin Harrison, the present claimant, who then lived upon the same; that both Jacob Miller and James were each the head of a family in the year 1797.

The Board ordered that the case be postponed for consideration.

FRANCIS STRINGER's case: commenced in page 676.

John Dunn and Reuben Holleway, chain carriers for the survey in this case, were sworn before John Callier, Esq., Justice of the Peace.

John Callier, Esq. was produced as a witness, and, being duly sworn and interrogated by the Board, deposed, that he had no interest in the establishment of this claim; that, in the month of January, or February, 1798, he assisted Francis Stringer to erect a house on the land which he now claims; that he believed that Stringer got into it with his family in the month of February, and had continued to live and cultivate there ever since, and believed that he made a crop on the same land in the year 1798; that the said Stringer was, at that time, more than twenty-one years of age; and that, according to the best of his recollection, said Stringer did cut his timber or logs for his house in the year 1797.

The Board ordered that the case be postponed for consideration.

NOAH KINNER HUTSON's case, No. 101 on the docket of the Board, and No. 136 on the books of the Register.

Claim.—A donation of two hundred and ninety-seven acres three roods and five poles, as assignee and legal representative of Henry Nail, under the second section of the act.

The claimant presented his claim, together with a surveyor's plot of the land claimed, in the following words and figures, to wit:

To the Commissioners appointed in pursuance of the act of Congress passed the 3d day of March, 1803, for receiving and adjusting the claims to lands south of the Tennessee, and east of Pearl river.

Please to take notice, that the following tract of land, situated in Washington county, on the west side Tombigbee, butted on said river, and bounded on the north by land claimed by Mrs. Ann Lawrence, on the west, by vacant land, and on the south, by the claim of James Callier: beginning at a small sweet gum on the river bank, said Callier's corner, and runs with the river, south, eighty-seven degrees west, fifteen chains; thence, south, eighty-two degrees west, twenty-two chains fifty links; thence, north, eighty-two degrees west, twelve chains fifty links; thence, south, eighty-seven degrees west, nineteen chains; thence, north, eighty-five degrees west, five chains fifty links; thence, north, eighty-seven degrees west, four chains forty links to a sassafras corner, on the river bank; thence, south, thirteen degrees west, forty-four chains fifty links, to a small pine corner; thence, south, fifty-nine degrees east, twenty-six chains, to a stake on James Callier's line; thence, with his line north, forty-eight degrees east, eighty-seven chains, to the beginning: having such marks, natural and artificial, as are represented in the plot annexed, containing two hundred and ninety-seven acres, three roods and five poles; is claimed by Noah Kinner Hutson, legal representative of Henry Nail, under and by virtue of the section of the above recited act, and now exhibited unto the Register of the Land Office, established east of Pearl river, to be recorded as directed by said act: to all which he begs leave to refer, as also to the copy of the plot herewith filed.

        NOAH KINNER HUTSON, his x mark,
          Legal representative of Henry Nail.

March 8, 1804.

[Plot omitted.]

Surveyed 23d March, 1804, by J. Malone. Chain carriers, George Hutson and James Whitington.

Entered in record of claims, vol. 1, page 460, by EDWARD LLOYD WAILES, for

        JOSEPH CHAMBERS, *Register.*

The said chain carriers for the preceding survey were sworn before John Callier, Esq., Justice of the Peace.

John Callier, Esq. and George Brewer were produced as witnesses, and, being duly sworn and interrogated by the Board, they deposed, that they were in no way interested in this claim; and the said Brewer testified, that, in the year 1794, Henry Nail, the person in whose right the present claimant appears, built upon and cultivated the land in question, and continued to live there until the year 1797 or 1798, when he removed off, but kept up the cultivation by means of other people until the year 1801 or 1802; when he sold his possessions and improvements to Noah Kinner Hutson, the present claimant; that he, Brewer, drew the writings for the parties, which, he understood, had since been lost by accident; that, in the year 1797, Henry Nail was the head of a family; that the present claimant had been in possession ever since the purchase which he made of Nail, as aforesaid.

The said Callier testified, that when he came into this country, in the year 1797, he found Henry Nail living on the land in question; that it appeared to be an old possession; that he knew that Nail continued there until the year 1799; that, in the year 1797, Henry Nail had a wife and family of children.

Thomas Malone, surveyor, was presented as a witness, and, being duly sworn, deposed, that he made the plot then before the Board; that, according to his knowledge and belief, it was correct; that it included the dwelling house and improvements of the claimant; that there was an interfering claim; that the line of Mrs. Lawrence run across this plot, near to the house, on the westerly side thereof; that he knew of no other interference.

The Board ordered that the case be postponed for consideration.

SIMON ANDREY's two cases: one commenced in page 682, the other case commences in page 683.

Joseph Chastang was produced as a witness in these two cases, and being duly sworn and interrogated by the Board, deposed, that Simon Andry, the present claimant, was more than fifty years of age; that, between and in the year 1795, the plantation of the said Simon Andry, on the land now claimed, was inhabited and cultivated by his slaves; that the said Andry being an interpreter of the Choctaw language, resided principally in Mobile, but occasionally visited this plantation to inspect the business, &c.; that the cultivation was continued in that manner until the year 1797, when he moved on to the land himself, and had ever since resided there the principal part of the time; that the said two tracts of land, claimed by said Andry, are adjoined and form the said plantation.

The Board ordered that the cases be postponed for consideration.

WILLIAM COLEMAN's case, No. 102 on the docket of the Board, and No. 132 on the books of the Register.

Claim.—A donation of four hundred and ninety-seven acres, two roods, and six poles, as assignee and legal representative of Simon Favre, under the second section of the act.

The claimant presented his claim, together with a surveyor's plot of the land claimed, in the following words and figures, to wit:

To the Commissioners appointed in pursuance of the act of Congress passed the 3d day of March, 1803, for receiving and adjusting the claims to lands south of the Tennessee, and east of Pearl river.

Please to take notice, that the following tract of land, situated on the west side Tombigbee, butted on said river, and bounded on the southwest by Stewart's old survey, beginning on the river bank, just above a bayou or branch, at the upper end of the bluff, on which stands Fort St. Stephen's, at a small ironwood, and runs with the old line south, twenty-five degrees west, crossing the bayou at one chain, in all forty-two chains ninety links, to a stake corner, with two red oak pointers on James Griffin's line; thence, on agreed line between the claimant and said Griffin, north, fifty degrees west, eighteen chains eighty-seven links, to a stake corner; thence, an agreed line south, forty degrees west, fifty-five chains, to a pine corner; thence, north, sixty-five degrees west, thirty-four chains, fifty links, to a stake with a hickory and red oak pointers; thence north, twenty-five degrees east, at fifty-eight chains, a small branch, in all, one hundred and sixteen chains, to a small locust tree on the river bank; thence, the meanders of the river to the beginning, having such marks, natural and artificial, as are represented in the plot annexed, containing four hundred and ninety-seven acres, two roods, and six poles: is claimed by William Coleman, of Washington county, legal representative of Simon Favre, under and by virtue of the second section of the above recited act, and now exhibited unto the Register of the

Land Office, established east of Pearl river, to be recorded as directed by said act. To all which he begs leave to refer, as also to the copy of the plot herewith filed.

WILLIAM COLEMAN,
Legal representative of Simon Favre.
[Plot omitted.]

Surveyed 17th March, 1804, by J. Malone. Chain carriers, Nace Russel, James Griffin, and Dawson Grimes.

The claimant exhibited a deed of conveyance in the words and figures following, to wit:

Sepan quantos esta carta vieren que yo Simon Favre, interpreto de Indios en este Puesto, vendo legalmente, a Juan Berry, una cara, y una cerca de penchas, con todas las caranas que existen dentro de la mencionada cerca, sovre la Tierra, de Mon. Esturd en el Preiri de Doscientos Banni les de mahir en Espiga, que derena Vivnanme en el Emban ladeno de este Juente á la findel mes de Octubre de este presente ano; vasa cuyas condiciones me sepano de todo el derecho de propiedad que tengo en dichos edificios, y cedo todo mi derecho en el mencionado Juan Berry, livnandele los citados en el tiempo de la evaquarios de este piesto; y para que conste lo simmo en el suerte de En. Estevan de Tombeibe, en presencia de los dos testigos, por Francisco Fontanillas y Thomas Price, a los quatro dias del mes de Enero de mil setecientos noventa y nueve anos.

SIMON FAVRE.

FRAN. FONTANILLAS, THOMAS PRICE.
Ante mi,   **FERNANDO LESORO.**

On the back of which said deed is an assignment in the words and figures following, viz.:

I do hereby assign all the within contents to William Coleman, for value received of him, the said Coleman, this 21st September, 1800.

JOHN BERRY.

Attest: LEVIN AINSWORTH, his x mark.
      THOMAS WILLIAMS.

Entered in record of claims, vol. 1, page 454, by EDWARD LLOYD WAILES, for

JOSEPH CHAMBERS, *Register.*

The said Russel, Griffin, and Grimes, chain carriers for the preceding survey, were sworn before William Pierce, Justice of the Peace.

Francis Stringer, John Callier, and John F. McGrew, were produced as witnesses, and, being duly sworn and interrogated by the Board, they all deposed, that they were not in any way interested in this claim; and the said Stringer and McGrew testified, that, in the latter part of the year 1796, or the first part of the year 1797, Simon Favre entered into the possession and improvement of the land now claimed by William Coleman, as his legal representative; that said Favre continued to reside on and cultivate the same land, raised crops annually until after the Spaniards had evacuated that part of the Mississippi territory, in the spring of the year 1799; and that, in the year 1797, the said Favre was the head of a family.

The said Callier testified, that he saw Simon Favre living on the land in question, in the year 1797; that he then had a good crop of corn which had grown thereon that year; that he, Callier, went into Georgia and returned in June 1799, and that said Simon Favre had removed with his family out of the country; and he understood that Favre sold his possession and improvement to John Berry, who raised a crop on that land in the year 1800; that Berry afterwards sold to William Coleman, the present claimant, as he had heard both the parties declare.

The Board ordered that the case be postponed for consideration.

FIGURES LEWIS's case: commenced in page 659.

William Gilliam, surveyor, was presented as a witness, and, being duly sworn, deposed, that the plot then presented was correctly and truly made, according to the best of his knowledge and belief; that it included the dwelling house and improvements of the claimant; that, from information, he understood that George Brewer had surveyed Sullivan's island, and crossed and included the whole of that survey, except a small corner.

Thomas Sullivan was produced as a witness, and, being duly sworn and interrogated by the Board, testified, that he was in no way interested in this claim; that near about the 15th of February, 1803, Figures Lewis entered upon the land then claimed, and set two negroes to work on the same; that said Lewis lived at another place, but was there every two or three days superintending his business; that his work was continued until he moved there with his family in the spring season following: that, on the 3d of March, 1803, his work was progressing, one small house was then finished, and two others partly done; that said Lewis had continued to live there ever since he moved on in the spring, 1803.

The Board ordered that the case be postponed for consideration.

DANIEL JOHNSON's case: commenced in page 678.

Bridget Burk was produced as a witness, and, being duly sworn and interrogated by the Board, deposed, that she was frequently in the family of the present claimant's father in the year 1795; that she then understood from the family, that Daniel Johnson, the present claimant, was more than twenty-one years of age; that she lived in the family in the year 1796, and always understood the same thing; that, in the year 1796, Daniel Johnson lived with his father, but carried on business by himself: that he used to go out to work with his men, which she understood to be upon the land now claimed, but could not say positively that it was upon the land.

The Board ordered that the case be postponed for consideration.

DANIEL JOHNSON's case, No. 103 on the docket of the Board, and No. 83 on the books of the Register.

Claim.—A donation of six hundred and forty acres, as legal representative of William Burk, under the second section of the act.

The claimant presented his claim, together with a surveyor's plot of the land claimed, in the following words and figures, to wit:

To the Commissioners appointed in pursuance of the act of Congress passed the 3d day of March, 1803, for receiving and adjusting claims to lands south of Tennessee and east of Pearl river.

MARCH 26, 1804.

Please to take notice, that the following tract of land, situated on the west side of Tombigbee river, in the county of Washington, beginning at a water oak, running thence, north, one hundred and forty-three chains forty-six links, to a red oak corner; thence, north, eighty-one chains twenty-five links, to a corner stake; thence, east, forty-two chains and forty-six links, to a water oak on the Three River lake; thence, down the meanders of said lake, to the beginning; containing six hundred and forty acres, and hath such forms and marks, both natural and artificial, as are fully represented in the plot annexed: is claimed by Daniel Johnson, legal representative of William Burk, in and by virtue of a deed of conveyance from William Burk to the widow Elizabeth McKim, and from the widow E. McKim to said D. Johnson, and is now exhibited to the Register of the Land Office established east of Pearl river, to be recorded as directed by said act. To all which he begs leave to refer, as also to a copy of the plot herewith filed.

[Plot omitted.]

Surveyed 22d March, 1804, by John Dease. Chain bearers, James Dean, Amos Reed.

Entered in record of claims, vol. 1, page 239, by EDWARD LLOYD WAILES, for JOSEPH CHAMBERS, *Register.*

The claimant exhibited a deed from Elizabeth McKim, bearing date the 3d of September, 1803, duly executed, conveying to the said Daniel Johnson all the said Elizabeth's right and claim to the said tract of land, and the improvements made thereon.

Ephraim Barker and Bridget Burk were produced as witnesses, and, being duly sworn and interrogated by the Board, they deposed, that they were not interested in the establishment of this claim.

The said Burk testified, that, in the year 1797, William Burk, now deceased, then the husband of the witness, commenced the improvement of the land in question, by clearing a little land, preparing for a garden, planting some fruit trees. &c. and moved on with the family in the month of January or February, 1798, and raised a crop on the land that year; that in the last part of the same year, he sold his possession and improvement to the widow Elizabeth McKim, who took possession, and continued to inhabit and cultivate the same until last year, except one year that she rented it.

The said Barker testified, that, in the year 1797, William Burk began his improvements on the land now in question, by building a smoke house, and beginning his dwelling house, &c.; that he moved his family on in the year 1798; that he, Barker, saw that year a crop of corn growing there; that Burk was a married man in the year 1797.

The Board ordered that the case be postponed for consideration.

SOLOMON BOYKIN's case, No. 104 on the docket of the Board, and No. 153 on the books of the Register.

Claim.—A right of pre-emption of five hundred and two acres, as assignee and legal representative of Elizabeth Reed, under the third section of the act.

The claimant presented his claim, together with a surveyor's plot of the land claimed, in the following words and figures, to wit:

To the Commissioners appointed in pursuance of the act of Congress, passed the 3d day of March, 1803, for receiving and adjusting claims to lands south of the Tennessee, and east of Pearl river.

MARCH 20, 1804.

Please to take notice, that the following tract of land, situated on the waters of Bassett's creek, on the west side of Tombigbee, in the county of Washington, beginning at sweet gum, on a lake; thence, with the lake, to a sweet gum; thence, north, sixty-seven degrees west, eighty-three chains, to a post oak corner; thence, south, twenty-three degrees west, eighty-two chains, to a black gum, on Bassett's creek; thence, with the said creek, to the beginning, and hath such marks and forms, both natural and artificial, as are fully represented in the plot annexed, containing five hundred and two acres: is claimed by Solomon Boykin, legal representative of Elizabeth Reed, in and by virtue of the third section of the said act, as a pre-emption; and is now exhibited to the Register of the Land Office established east of Pearl river, to be recorded as directed by said act. To all which he begs leave to refer, as also to a copy of the plot herewith filed.

SOLOMON BOYKIN,
Legal representative of Elizabeth Reed.
[Plot omitted.]

Surveyed 7th of March, 1804, by Robert Ligon.

Entered in record of claims, vol. 1, page 482, by EDWARD LLOYD WAILES, for JOSEPH CHAMBERS, *Register.*

Kinchen Boykin and John Smith, chain carriers for the preceding survey, were sworn before John Callier, Esq. Justice of Peace.

Robert Ligon and Francis Boykin were presented as witnesses, and, being duly sworn and interrogated by the Board, they deposed, that they were not interested in this claim; that, in the year 1802, Robert House inhabited and improved the land in question, and that he sold his possession and improvement to the widow Elizabeth Reed, who went into possession, and continued there, from the spring of the year 1803, until about the month of December, 1803, when she relinquished her claim to House, not being able to pay him the purchase money; that, during the time that she lived there, in the spring and summer of 1803, she cultivated a small garden for family purposes, which was the only cultivation she had on the land; that, when she relinquished and left the place, House sold it to the present claimant, who immediately went into possession, and has continued in possession ever since; that Elizabeth Reed was more than twenty-one years of age on the 3d of March, 1803.

The said Ligon further testified, that he knew that Elizabeth Reed was in possession of the premises before and on the 3d of March, 1803; that the plot of the land claimed was made by him; that it was accurately laid down according to the best of his knowledge and belief; that he knew of no interfering lines or claims.

The Board ordered that the case be postponed for consideration.

Adjourned until Thursday, the 29th instant.

THURSDAY, *March* 29, 1804.

The Board met according to adjournment. Present: Ephraim Kirby, Robert C. Nicholas, Joseph Chambers.

EDNA BILBO, administratrix of Matthew Bilbo, deceased, case No. 105 on the docket of the Board, and No. 131 on the books of the Register.

Claim.—A donation of four hundred and one acres, under the —— section of the act.

The claimant presented her claim, together with a surveyor's plot of the land claimed, in the following words and figures, to wit:

To the Commissioners appointed in pursuance of the act of Congress passed the 3d day of March, 1803, for receiving and adjusting the claims to lands south of Tennessee and east of Pearl river.

MARCH 29, 1804.

lease to take notice, that the following tract of land, lying on an island called Bilbo's island, in the county of Washington, beginning at the most northernmost part of the island, and running down the eastward river to the confluence of the same; thence, up the southwest river, to the confluence of the creek known by the name of Bilbo's creek; thence, northwardly, to the beginning; containing four hundred and one acres, having such shape, form, and marks, natural and artificial, as are represented in the plot annexed, is claimed by Edna Bilbo, for the heirs of Matthew Bilbo, and now exhibited to the Register of the Land Office east of Pearl river, to be recorded as directed by said act. To all which she begs leave to refer.

EDNA BILBO,
For the heirs of Matthew Bilbo.

[Plot omitted.]

Surveyed 16th March, 1804, by Robert Ligon. Chain carriers, George Farrar and Cornelius Rain.
Entered in record of claims, vol. 1, page 452, by ED-WARD LLOYD WAILES, for

JOSEPH CHAMBERS, Register.

The chain carriers above named were sworn before Figures Lewis, Esq., Justice of Peace.
The claimant produced letters of administration granted to her, and duly authenticated, bearing date 8th April, 1804.
John Callier and Cornelius Rain were presented as witnesses, and, being duly sworn and interrogated, they deposed, that they had no interest, nor did they expect any, in this claim.
The said Callier testified, that Matthew Bilbo came to this county with him, in the winter of the year 1797, and, as he, Callier, believed, cultivated the land in question, in the year 1798, and continued to cultivate the same until his death; that his wife had cultivated the same ever since; that the land, being low ground, was subject to be inundated, and therefore not suitable to build and live upon; that Matthew Bilbo built his dwelling house on the high land near the same, and that he was, in the year 1797, the head of a family.
The said Rain testified the same, as did said Callier, excepting the words " with him," which words Rain omitted.
Robert Ligon, surveyor, was presented as a witness, and, being duly sworn, deposed, that he surveyed the land then in question, and made the plot exhibited to the Board, which gave a true representation of said land; that it had such marks natural as are therein represented, and that he knew of no interfering lines.
The Board ordered that the case be postponed for consideration.

BRIDGET BURKE, administratrix of William Burke, deceased, case No. 106 on the docket of the Board, and No. 83 on the books of the Register.
Claim.—A donation of six hundred and forty acres, as assignee and legal representative of Thomas Jones, under the —— section of the act.
The claimant presented her claim, together with a surveyor's plot of land claimed, in the following words and figures, viz.:

To the Commissioners appointed in pursuance of the act of Congress passed the 3d day of March, 1803, for receiving and adjusting claims to land south of Tennessee and east of Pearl river.

Please to take notice, that the following tract of land, situated on the west side of Tombigbee, in the county of Washington, beginning at a sassafras on the river bank, and running north, seventy-three degrees west, one hundred and one chains and twenty links, to a water oak; thence, north, seventeen degrees east, forty chains, to a cypress; thence, south, eighty degrees west, fifty-seven chains, to a pine; thence, south, ten degrees east, fifty chains, to a pine on Bilbo's creek; thence, down said creek to the river, and up the various courses of the river to the beginning; and hath such forms and marks, both natural and artificial, as are fully represented in the plot annexed, containing six hundred and forty acres: is claimed by the widow Bridget Burke, in and by virtue of a deed of conveyance from Thomas Jones to the deceased William Burke; and is now exhibited to the Register of the Land Office established east of Pearl river, to be recorded as directed by said act. To all which she begs leave to refer, as also to a copy of the plot herewith filed.

BRIDGET BURKE, her x mark,
Administratrix of her deceased husband, Wm. Burke.
MARCH 26, 1804.

[Plot omitted.]

Surveyed March 22, 1804, by John Dease. Chain bearers, James Dean and James Powel.

Entered in record of claims, vol. 1, page 241, by ED-WARD LLOYD WAILES, for

JOSEPH CHAMBERS, Register.

The claimant produced letters of administration to her, duly granted and authenticated, bearing date the 16th day of September, 1803.
Ephraim Barker and Francis Stringer were presented as witnesses, and being duly sworn and interrogated by the Board, they deposed, that they were not interested in this claim; that Thomas Jones, the person in whose right the present claimant appears, moved his family on to the land in question in the year 1796; made a crop thereon in 1797; that his family continued to reside there until the last part of the year 1798, when William Burke, now deceased, purchased the possession and improvements which Jones had made, and removed there with his family, and there continued until the time of his death, which happened in the course of last year; that the said Thomas Jones was the head of a family in the year 1797.
The Board ordered that the case be postponed for consideration.

ANN LAWRENCE's case, No. 107 on the docket of the Board, and No. 133 on the books of the Register.
Claim.—A donation of six hundred and forty acres, under the second section of the act.
The claimant presented her claim, together with a surveyor's plot of the land claimed, in the following words and figures, to wit:

To the Commissioners appointed in pursuance of the act of Congress passed the 3d day of March, 1803, for receiving and adjusting the claims to lands south of Tennessee, and east of Pearl river.

Please to take notice, that the following tract of land, situated on the west side of Tombigbee river, in the county of Washington, beginning at a stake on the river bank, and runs south seventeen degrees west, crossing a small branch at forty chains ninety links, another at sixty-six chains, in all, eighty-eight chains, to a large pine corner; thence, north, seventy-three degrees west, crossing Brewer's mill creek at sixty chains, about two chains below the mill, in all, eighty chains, to a stake corner; thence, north, seventeen degrees east, seventy-two chains, to a water oak, George Brewer's corner, on the river bank; thence, the meanders of the river, to the beginning, containing six hundred and forty acres; having such forms and marks, both natural and artificial, as are fully represented in the plot annexed; is claimed by Ann Lawrence, in and by virtue of the second section of the act, as a donation, and is now exhibited to the Register of the Land Office, established east of Pearl river, to be recorded as directed by said act. To all which she begs leave to refer, as also to a copy of the plot herewith filed.

JOSEPH LAWRENCE, for
ANN LAWRENCE.

MARCH 28th, 1804.
[Plot omitted.]

Surveyed 13th February, 1804, by J. Malone. Chain carriers, Kenith Hutson and David Gains, Junior.
Entered in record of claims, vol. 1, page 456, by EDWARD LLOYD WAILES, for

JOSEPH CHAMBERS, Register.

Young Gains and George Brewer, Junior, were presented as witnesses, and, being duly sworn and interrogated by the Board, they testified, that they had no interest whatever in this claim; that Ann Lawrence had inhabited and cultivated upon the land then in question ever since the year 1795; that she was, on the 27th of October, 1797, above twenty-five years of age.
The Board ordered that the case be postponed for consideration.

JOHN DUNN's case, No. 108 on the docket of the Board and No. 152 on the books of the Register.
Claim.—A right of pre-emption of three hundred and ninety-one acres, one rood, and thirty-nine poles, under the third section of the act.
The claimant presented his claim, together with a surveyor's plot of the land claimed, in the following words and figures, to wit:

To the Commissioners appointed in pursuance of the act of Congress passed the 3d day of March, 1803, for receiving and adjusting claims to lands south of the Tennessee, and east of Pearl river.

Please to take notice, that the following tract of land, situated on Tombigbee river, butted on said river, and bounded north by the claim of Francis Stringer, and on the west by vacant land, and on the south by the claim of Nathan Blackwell, beginning on Stringer's maple corner, on the river bank, and runs with his line south, sixty-two degrees west, thirty chains fifty links, to a bay corner; thence, north, forty-three degrees west, twenty-four chains, to a stake, with two sassafras and a mulberry pointer; thence, south, forty-seven degrees west, seventy-three chains, to a small pine corner; thence, south, forty-three degrees east, seventeen chains to a small red oak corner; thence north, thirty-eight degrees east, twelve chains fifteen links to a stake, Nathan Blackwell's corner; thence with his line south, sixty-eight degrees east, sixty-three chains, (passing Blackwell's sweet gum corner one chain fifty links) to a stake corner on the river bank; thence, the meanders of the river, to the beginning; having such marks, natural and artificial, as are represented in the plot annexed; containing three hundred and ninety-one acres, one rood, and thirty-nine poles: is claimed by John Dunn, under and by virtue of a settlement in the year 1802, and now exhibited unto the Register of the Land Office, established east of Pearl river, to be recorded as directed by said act. To all which he begs leave to refer, as also to the copy of the plot herewith filed.

JOHN DUNN.

March 24, 1804.

[Plot omitted.]

Surveyed 24th March, 1804, by J. Malone. Chain carriers, Kinchen Boyken and Rice Wells. Entered in record of claims, vol. 1, page 481, by Edward-Lloyd Wailes, for

JOSEPH CHAMBERS, Register.

The said chain carriers, Boykin and Wells, were sworn before John Callier, Esq., Justice of the Peace.

Francis Boykin and Francis Stringer were produced as witnesses, and, being duly sworn and interrogated by the Board, they deposed, that they were not interested in the establishment of this claim; that John Dunn, the present claimant, built a house and moved his family on to the land, then in question, in the year 1802; that he had continued to live there ever since, and made a crop on the land in 1803; that, on the 3d of March of that year he was the head of a family.

The Board ordered that the case be postponed for consideration.

Thomas Malone's case, No. 109 on the docket of the Board, and No. 146 on the books of the Register.

Claim.—A right of pre-emption of three hundred and thirty acres, under the third section of the act.

To the Commissioners appointed in pursuance of the act passed the 3d day of March, 1803, for receiving and adjusting the claims to lands south of the Tennessee, and east of Pearl river.

Please to take notice, that the following tract of land, situated on the west side of Tombigbee river, Washington county, butted on said river, and bounded on the north by the claim of Colonel John Callier, on the west by vacant land, and on the south by the claim of Francis Stringer, beginning on an elm, on the river bank, Colonel Callier's lower corner; and runs with his line south, forty-seven degrees west, twenty-four chains eighty-six links, to an ironwood corner; thence, south, thirty-seven degrees east, forty-four chains seventy-five links, to a white oak corner; thence, north, forty-seven degrees east, thirty-two chains, to a white oak corner, an agreed line between the claimant and F. Stringer; thence, south, forty-three degrees east, thirty chains, to a stake corner; thence, north, sixty-three degrees east, forty-one chains fifty links, to a large ash, on the river bank; thence, the meanders of the river, to the beginning; having such marks, natural and artificial, as are represented in the plot annexed; containing three hundred and thirty acres: is claimed by Thomas Malone, under and by virtue of the third section of the above recited act, and now exhibited unto the Register of the Land Office established east of Pearl river, to be recorded as directed by said act. To all which he begs leave to refer, as also to the copy of the plot herewith filed.

T. MALONE.

March 23, 1804.

[Plot omitted.]

Surveyed 23d March, 1804, by J. Malone. Chain carriers, Noah Pelcher and Francis Stringer. Entered in record of claims, volume 1, page 473, by Edward Lloyd Wailes, for

JOSEPH CHAMBERS, Register.

The above named chain carriers were sworn before Figures Lewis, Esquire, Justice of the Peace.

John Callier and James Callier, Esquires, were presented as witnesses, and, being duly sworn and interrogated by the Board, they deposed, that they were not interested in this case; that Thomas Malone, the present claimant, went to reside on the land in question in the year 1802, and had cultivated it ever since, and resided there on the 3d of March, 1803; that he was, at that time, more than twenty-one years of age.

The Board ordered that the case be postponed for consideration.

James Callier, representative of Bryant and Snelgrove: case commenced in page 651.

James Griffin was produced as a witness, and, being duly sworn, testified, that the parties Jesse Briant and Henry Snelgrove executed and delivered the writing presented to the Board, on the 19th day of September, 1800, for purposes therein mentioned, and agreeably to the tenor thereof, as it had been read to him; that he made his mark as a witness to the same, as did also Samuel Griffin witness the same in his presence.

The Board ordered that the case be postponed for consideration.

Edward Creighton, representative of Benjamin King: case commenced in page 699.

John Callier, Esquire, was presented as a witness, and being duly sworn, testified, that in the year 1801, he went in company with Benjamin King to look out a piece of vacant land on which to erect a cotton gin; that he pitched upon the land now in question, and according to his, the witness's, best recollection, erected his cotton gin there in the same year, or in the beginning of the year 1802, and continued to reside there until after the 3d of March, 1803; that, on that day, King was more than twenty-one years of age.

The Board ordered that the case be postponed for consideration.

Heirs of James Copelen, case No. 110 on the docket of the Board, and No. 66 on the books of the Register.

Claim.—A donation of six hundred and forty acres, under the second section of the act.

The claimants presented their claim, together with a surveyor's plot of the land claimed, in the following words and figures, to wit:

To the Commissioners appointed in pursuance of the act of Congress passed the 3d day of March, 1803, for receiving and adjusting claims to lands south of Tennessee, and east of Pearl river.

Please to take notice, that the following tract of land, situated on the Three River lake, on the west side of Tombigbee river, in the county of Washington, beginning on the bank of the Three River lake, on a water oak; running, thence, up the branch of the lake north, nine degrees west, forty chains, to a stake; thence, south, sixty degrees west, twelve chains, to Barker's corner, on a sweet gum; thence, the same course, continued with his line eighty chains, to the other corner, on a sweet gum; course still continued twenty-four chains, to a sweet gum, on the Boggy swamp; course continued fifty-seven chains further, to a stake; thence, south, thirty degrees west thirty-eight chains, to a stake; thence, to the beginning; and hath such forms and marks, both natural and artificial, as are fully represented in the plot annexed, containing six hundred and forty acres: is claimed by the heirs of James Copelen, deceased, in and by virtue of the second section of the said act of Congress, as a donation, and is now exhibited to the Register of the Land Office established east of Pearl river, to be recorded as directed by said act. To all which they beg leave to refer, as also to a copy of the plot herewith filed.

The Heirs of JAMES COPELEN.

March 24, 1804.

[Plot omitted.]

Surveyed the 20th of March, 1804, by Natt. Christmas. Chain bearers, Edward Smith and William Rain. Entered in record of claims, vol. 1, page 189, by Edward Lloyd Wailes, for

JOSEPH CHAMBERS, Register.

Ephraim Barker and Elizabeth Bates were presented as witnesses, and, being duly sworn and interrogated by the Board, they deposed, that they had no interest in this case : and the said Barker testified that James Copelen, deceased, built, settled, and improved on the tract of land then in question, in the latter part of the year 1797; that he made a crop on the same in the year 1798, and continued to inhabit and cultivate the same from the year 1797 until his death, which happened about one year since; that said Copelen was the head of a family in the year 1797.

The said Elizabeth testified, that James Copelen, deceased, inhabited the land then in question between seven and eight years last past, and did continue to inhabit and cultivate the same until his decease, which happened about one year since; and that said Copelen was the head of a family when he settled upon this land.

The Board ordered that the case be postponed for consideration.

THOMAS SULLIVANT's case, No. 111 on the docket of the Board, and No. 150 on the books of the Register.

Claim.—A right of pre-emption of two hundred and forty acres, under the third section of the act.

The claimant presented his claim, together with a surveyor's plot of the land claimed, in the following words and figures, viz.:

To the Commissioners appointed in pursuance of the act of Congress, passed the 3d day of March, 1803, *for receiving and adjusting the claims to land south of Tennessee, and east of Pearl river.*

Please to take notice, that the following tract of land, situated on the west side of Tombigbee river, in the county of Washington, beginning at a black gum, thence, running south seventy-five degrees west, sixty chains, to a pine; thence, north, fifteen degrees west, forty chains, to a stake: thence, north, seventy-five degrees east, sixty chains, to a stake; thence, south, fifteen degrees east, forty chains, to the beginning; containing two hundred and forty acres, having such shape, form, and marks, both natural and artificial, as are represented in the plot annexed: is claimed by Thomas Sullivant, in and by virtue of the third section of the said act, as a pre-emption, and is now exhibited to the Register of the Land Office east of Pearl river, to be recorded as directed by said act. To all which he begs leave to refer, as also to the plot annexed.

THOMAS SULLIVANT, his x mark.

MARCH 28, 1804.

[Plot omitted.]

Surveyed by William Gilliam. Chain carriers, Owen Sullivant and Thomas Sullivant.

Entered in record of claims, vol. 1, page 479, by EDWARD LLOYD WAILES, for

JOSEPH CHAMBERS, *Register.*

Ephraim Barker and John Denley were produced as witnesses, and being duly sworn and interrogated by the Board, they deposed, that they had no interest in this claim; that the claimant inhabited and cultivated the land then in question on the 3d of March, 1803; and that he was on that day the head of a family.

The Board ordered that the case be postponed for consideration.

THOMAS SULLIVANT, Junior's case, No. 112 on the docket of the Board, and No. 149 on the books of the Register.

Claim.—A right of pre-emption of one hundred and ninety acres, under the third section of the act.

The claimant presented his claim, together with a surveyor's plot of the land claimed, in the following words and figures, to wit:

To the Commissioners appointed, in pursuance of the act of Congress passed the 3d day of March, 1803, *for receiving and adjusting claims to lands south of Tennessee, and east of Pearl river.*

Please to take notice, that the following tract of land, situate on three River lake, in the county of Washington, beginning at a hickory; thence, north, thirty-eight degrees east, thirty-seven chains, to a stake; thence, south, sixty-four degrees east, seventy-six chains, to a stake; thence, south four degrees east, twenty-six chains, to a hickory corner; thence, up the Three River lake, as is plotted, to the beginning; and hath such forms and marks, both natural and artificial, as are fully represented in the plot annexed; containing one hundred and ninety acres: is claimed by Thomas Sullivant, Junior, in and by virtue of a pre-emption; and is now exhibited to the Register of the Land Office established east of Pearl river, to be recorded as directed by said act. To all which he begs leave to refer, as also to a copy of the plot herewith filed.

THOMAS SULLIVANT, his x mark, for

THOMAS SULLIVANT, JUN.

MARCH, 1804.   [Plot omitted.]

Surveyed, 9th of March, 1804, by Natt. Christmas. Chain bearers, John Wheat, James Bilbo.

Entered in record of claims, vol. 1, page 478, by EDWARD LLOYD WAILES, for

JOSEPH CHAMBERS, *Register.*

Thomas Sullivant, Senior, and Ephraim Barker were produced as witnesses, and being duly sworn and interrogated by the Board, they deposed, that they were not in any way interested in this claim: that the land in question being low land, and subject to annual inundation, could not be built upon, but Thomas Sullivant, Jun. the claimant, cultivated on the same from the year 1802, by himself or representative, until the then present time; and that said Thomas Sullivant was, on the 3d of March, 1803, the head of a family.

The Board ordered that the case be postponed for consideration.

SANDERS REA's case, No. 113 on the docket of the Board, and No. 78 on the books of the Register.

Claim.—A right of pre-emption of one hundred and fifty-eight acres, under the third section of the act.

The claimant presented his claim, together with a surveyor's plot of the land claimed, in the following words and figures, to wit:

To the Commissioners appointed in pursuance of the act of Congress passed the 3d day of March, 1803, *for receiving and adjusting claims to lands south of Tennessee, and east of Pearl river.*

Please to take notice, that the following tract of land, situated on the west side of Tombigbee river, on the waters of Johnson's creek, in the county of Washington, beginning at a water oak, and running thence, north, twenty-two degrees east, thirty-one chains seventy-five links, to a water oak corner; thence, north, sixty-eight degrees west, fifty chains; thence, south, twenty-two degrees west, thirty-one chains seventy-five links, to a pine corner; thence, south, sixty-eight degrees east, fifty chains, to the beginning; and hath such forms and marks, both natural and artificial, as are fully represented in the plot annexed; containing one hundred and fifty acres: is claimed by Sanders Rea, in and by virtue of the third section of the act, as a pre-emption; and is now exhibited to the Register of the Land Office east of Pearl river, to be recorded as directed by said act. To all which he begs leave to refer, as also to a copy of the plot herewith filed.

SANDERS REA, his x mark.

MARCH 28, 1804.

[Plot omitted.]

Surveyed by Robert Ligon.

Entered in record of claims, vol. 1, page 226, by EDWARD LLOYD WAILES, for

JOSEPH CHAMBERS, *Register.*

Solomon Boykin and Jonas Rea, chain carriers for the preceding survey, were sworn before John Callier and Figures Lewis, Esquires, Justices of the Peace.

Robert Ligon and Edward Lloyd Wailes were produced as witnesses, and, being duly sworn and interrogated by the Board, they testified, that they were not interested in this claim; that they believed that Sanders Rea had inhabited upon the land then claimed from the year 1802 until the then present time; that he was, on the 3d of March, 1803, the head of a family.

The said Ligon further testified, that this land was surveyed by him; that the plot then presented to the Board gave a true representation of the land then claimed; that John Brewer, Esquire, claims about fifty acres thereof, from the north side, under and by virtue of a donation.

The Board ordered that the case be postponed for consideration.

RICHARD S. BRYAN and GEORGE BREWER, Senior: case commenced in page 711.

James Huckaby, one of the chain carriers for the survey in this case, was sworn before William Pierce, Justice of Peace.

John Gordon was presented as a witness, and, being duly sworn and interrogated by the Board, testified, that he was not interested in this claim; that he saw laborers in the employment and for the use of Richard S. Bryan, improving upon the land then in question, in the month of February, 1803; that he believed that said land had been in a continual state of improvement from the said month of February, 1803, until the then present time; and that he believed the said Bryan was, on the 3d day of March, twenty-one years of age.

Question. Do you know whether Sluder inhabited and cultivated within the limits of the tract now claimed, and about what time, and for whose use?

Answer. I saw John Sluder living within the limits of the tract of land now in question in the month of February, 1803; but whether for his own account, or for the benefit of said Bryant, I do not know.

The Board ordered that the case be postponed for consideration.

JOHN CALLIER, representative of Adam Hollinger: case commenced in page 688.

Noah Pelcher and Francis Stringer, chain carriers for the survey in this case, were sworn before Figures Lewis, Esquire, Justice of Peace.

John Baker, George Brewer, and Francis Boykin, were produced as witnesses, and, being duly sworn and interrogated by the Board, they deposed, that they had no interest whatever in this case.

The said Baker testified, that Wilford Hoggatt, the person in whose favor the Spanish warrant of survey for the land in question issued, was a resident on said land at and before the date of said warrant, in the year 1798, and did perform the conditions on which said warrant was to become valid; that he was, at the date of said warrant, more than twenty-one years of age, and the head of a family; that said land had been annually cultivated ever since, by some person holding under said Hoggatt; and that, in the year 1795, it was cultivated by Adam Hollinger, a resident in this county, then claiming said land by a title derived from said Hoggatt.

The said Brewer testified, that he came to this country in the year 1791, and that Wilford Hoggatt then lived upon and cultivated the land in question; and, from that period, agreed with the testimony of John Baker, as above; and further, that he, Brewer, heard Wilford Hoggatt say, that he had sold said land to Leonard Marbury; and also understood, from the information of others, that Marbury, by his attorney, John Joyce, sold the same to Adam Hollinger.

The said Boykin testified, that, when he came to this country, in the year 1791, Hoggatt was in the possession of the said land; that, about the year 1783, Hoggatt sold to Marbury, who afterwards sold, by his attorney, Joyce, to Adam Hollinger, who cultivated the same in 1795; that said land had been peaceably possessed and cultivated by the several persons holding title under said Hoggatt, to the then present time.

FRANCIS BOYKIN, representative of Adam Hollinger: case commenced in page 687.

Francis Stringer, George Brewer, Junior, John Baker, and Nathan Blackwell, were presented as witnesses, and, being duly sworn and interrogated by the Board, they deposed, that they were not interested in this claim.

The said Brewer and Stringer testified, that, in the year 1795, Adam Hollinger inhabited and cultivated the land in question; that they believed that said Boykin entered into the possession thereof in the year 1796; that he had ever since continued to inhabit and cultivate the same; that Adam Hollinger, on the 10th of June, 1795, was the head of a family.

The said Stringer further testified, that he heard the said Hollinger say that he had sold and transferred said land to Francis Boykin for a valuable consideration.

The said Baker testified, that Adam Hollinger did inhabit and cultivate on the land then in question in May, 1795; that he, Baker, knew that the same had been inhabited and cultivated ever since, either by said Hollinger, or Francis Boykin, the present claimant; that Adam Hollinger, on the 10th of June, 1795, was the head of a family.

The said Blackwell testified, that, on the 27th of October, 1795, Adam Hollinger inhabited and cultivated the land in question; that he had heard said Hollinger say that he had sold the same to Francis Boykin; and that Boykin entered into the possession thereof on the day that Hollinger quitted the same, which he, Blackwell, believed was in the month of December, 1795; that said Boykin had continued to inhabit and cultivate on said land ever since.

The Board ordered that the case be postponed for consideration.

JOHN BREWER, representative of Charles Arbon Demoy: case commenced in page 685.

Hiram Mounger and Ephraim Barker were produced as witnesses, and, being duly sworn and interrogated by the Board, they deposed, that they had no interest in this case; that, from the year 1791, until the 27th day of October, 1795, and afterwards, Charles Arbon Demoy, by his slaves, inhabited and cultivated the land in question; that they believed that said Charles Arbon Demoy was, on the 27th of October, 1787, more than twenty-one years of age.

Robert Ligon, surveyor, was presented as a witness, and, being duly sworn, deposed, that the plot then presented to the Board exhibited a true representation of the land then claimed; that he surveyed the same; that he knew of no other claim which interfered with said land, and believed there was none.

The Board ordered that the case be postponed for consideration.

JAMES DENLEY, representative of Daniel Ward: case commenced in page 693.

Hiram Mounger and George Dickey, chain carriers for the survey in this case, were sworn before William H. Hargrave, Esq., Justice of the Peace.

Hiram Mounger and Ephraim Barker were presented as witnesses, and, being duly sworn and interrogated by the Board, they deposed, that they were not in any way interested in this case; that, in the year 1791, the land in question had the appearance, and they believed was cultivated many years previous thereto; that it had been cultivated every year since that time; and that James Denley inhabited and cultivated the same, by his slaves, on the 27th day of October, 1795.

John Baker and Thomas Bilbo, surveyor, were produced as witnesses, and, being duly sworn, the said Baker testified, that, on the 22d of October, 1787, Daniel Ward was more than twenty-one years of age; that Ward cultivated the same land in question, agreeable to the tenor of his Spanish grant for the same; and that James Denley cultivated the same, by his slaves, on the 27th of October, 1795; that said land being subject to inundations prevents it from being a proper site for a dwelling house or houses to be built upon.

The said Bilbo testified, that he surveyed the land then in question; that the plot exhibits a true representation of the land claimed, with such marks, natural and artificial, as were therein laid down; that there were no lines of other claims that interfered with that; that its lines did not interfere with those of any other claim that he knew of.

The Board ordered that the case be postponed for consideration.

JAMES DENLEY, representative of Solomon Johnson: case commenced in page 690.

Hiram Mounger and Ephraim Barker were produced as witnesses, and being duly sworn and interrogated by the Board, they deposed, that they had no interest whatever in this claim; that, in the year 1795, the land in question was cultivated by Solomon Johnson, or for his use; that he was then a resident in this county; and that they fully believe, from his appearance, that he was at that time more than twenty-one years of age.

Robert Ligon, surveyor, was produced as a witness, and, being duly sworn, deposed, that he surveyed the land then in question, and made the plot then exhibited to the Board, which gave a correct view of the land in question, and had marks, natural and artificial, as were in that plot represented, and that he did not know of any interfering lines.

The Board ordered that the case be postponed for consideration.

JAMES DENLEY'S case: commenced in page 689.

George Dickey and James Donally, chain carriers for the survey in this case, and also for the survey in the said Denley's preceding case, were sworn before William H. Hargrave, Justice of the Peace.

John Brewer, Esquire, and Hiram Mounger, were presented as witnesses, and being duly sworn and interrogated by the Board, they deposed, that they had no interest in this case; that from and previous to the year 1791, James Denley cultivated the land then in question by his slaves or tenants, and that he did actually so cultivate the same on 27th day of October, 1795; and that, on the 22d day of October, 1787, James Denley, as they believed, was more than twenty-one years of age.

Robert Ligon, surveyor, was produced as a witness, and, being duly sworn, deposed, that he surveyed the land then in question, and made the plot then exhibited to the Board, which gave a correct representation of said land, as circumstances would enable him to make, a part thereof being so deeply covered with water as to prevent an actual measurement thereof to be taken; that he knew of no interfering lines.

The Board ordered that the case be postponed for consideration.

Adjourned until Friday, the 30th instant.

FRIDAY, *March* 30, 1804.

The Board met according to adjournment. Present: Ephraim Kirby, Robert C. Nicholas, Joseph Chambers.

EDWIN LEWIS, representative of William Green: case commenced in page 711.

Robert Ligon, surveyor, was presented as a witness, and being duly sworn, deposed, that he surveyed the land then in question; that the plot exhibits a true representation of the land claimed; that there is an improvement claimed by Richard S. Bryan, which improvement was made by said Bryan within the limits of said survey.

ANN LAWRENCE, representative of Moses Moore: case commenced in page 688.

John Baker, James Denley, Ephraim Barker, Daniel Johnson, and Young Gains, were produced as witnesses, and, being duly sworn and interrogated by the Board, they deposed, that they were not interested in this case.

The said Baker and Denley testified, that they knew that Moses Moore inhabited and cultivated the land then in question, from the year 1786 until his death, which happened in the year 1791, and that he was the head of a family on the 22d day of October, 1787.

The said Barker testified, that he believed that Margaret Moore, the widow of the deceased, left her son, Cornelius Rain, on the land then in question, who did cultivate and inhabit the same on the 27th day of October, 1795, and as he, Barker, believed, for account of the said Margaret Moore.

The said Johnson testified, that he believed that the land in question was cultivated in the year 1795 by Cornelius Rain; that said Rain told him that said cultivation was for his own use and account; that he, Johnson, and his father commenced cultivation on said land in the year 1800, as well as he recollected, by the consent of Mrs. Lawrence; that one of them had continued to cultivate thereon ever since; that he had heard his father, John Johnson, say that he was to pay Mrs. Lawrence rent for the cultivation of the land the last year.

Question. Is Mrs. Moore, the widow of Moses Moore, dead, and at or about what time did she die?

Answer. She is dead, and her death happened in the year 1800, according to my best understanding and belief.

The said Gains testified, that in or about the year 1800 or 1801, Daniel Johnson applied to him to rent the land in question; that he told him that Cornelius Rain was the proper person to apply to for that purpose, as Mrs. Moore, then Mrs. Linder, had the use of it, by will, during her life time, and that he believed that Cornelius Rain, her son, acted as her agent; he, Johnson, replied and said, that Mrs. Linder, late Mrs. Moore, was deceased; he, Gains, then told him he would speak to Mrs. Lawrence, and accordingly did so; that she agreed that it should be rented to Mr. Daniel Johnson, or his father, John Johnson, for the consideration that he would put and keep up a good and sufficient fence round the field, which he or they agreed to do, and, as he believed, did do.

The Board ordered that the case be postponed for consideration.

The HEIRS OF JAMES MCGREW: case commenced in page 686.

Young Gains, Jun. and Dawson Grimes, chain carriers for the survey in this case, were sworn before William Pierce, Esquire, Justice of the Peace.

George Brewer, Jun. and Francis Boykin were produced as witnesses, and, being duly sworn and interrogated by the Board, they deposed, that they were not in any way interested in this claim; that they knew that James McGrew, deceased, did, on the 27th of October, 1795, inhabit and cultivate, before and since, upon a tract of land lying below Fort St. Stephen's on the Tombigbee river, but they could not say whether the land so inhabited and cultivated lay within the lines represented by the plot then exhibited to the Board; that they believed that the said James McGrew was more than twenty-one years of age on the 9th day of February, 1788.

John Baker was presented as a witness, and, being duly sworn, deposed, that he knew that James McGrew did cultivate and inhabit on the land in question in the year 1788, and that James McGrew, or his family, cultivated on the same land on the 27th day of October, 1795; that said James McGrew was, on the 9th day of February, 1788, the head of a family, and more than twenty-one years of age.

The Board ordered that the case be postponed for consideration.

GEORGE BREWER, Jun., representative of Valentine Dubroca: case commenced in page 684.

John Baker, James Denley, and Hiram Mounger, were presented as witnesses, and, being duly sworn and interrogated by the Board, they deposed, that they had no interest in this case.

The said Baker and Denley testified, that from the year 1787 until 1796, Valentine Dubroca, by his son and slaves, inhabited and cultivated the land in question, and that he did actually inhabit and cultivate the same on the 27th of October, 1795; and that the said Dubroca was, on the 22d of October, 1787, more than twenty-one years of age.

The said Mounger testified, that, from the year 1791, until 1796, the land in question was cultivated by the overseer and slaves of Valentine Dubroca and Dominique de Olive.

Robert Ligon, surveyor, was produced as a witness, and being duly sworn, deposed, that he surveyed the land in question; that the plot exhibits a true and correct representation of the same, agreeably to the tenor of the Spanish warrant of survey under which it was claimed, and had such marks, natural and artificial, as were therein represented.

The Board ordered that the case be postponed for consideration.

The HEIRS OF EMANUEL CHENEY, case No. 114 on the docket of the Board, and No. 144 on the books of the Register.

Claim.—A right of pre-emption of two hundred and fifty-three acres, two roods, and twenty-six poles, as representatives of Levin Hainsworth, under the third section of the act.

The claimants presented their claim, together with a surveyor's plot of the land claimed, in the following words and figures, to wit:

To the Commissioners appointed in pursuance of the act of Congress passed the 3d day of March, 1803, for receiving and adjusting the claims to lands south of the Tennessee, and east of Pearl river.

Please to take notice, that the following tract of land, situated in Washington county, on the waters of McGrew's creek, and bounded on all sides by vacant land, beginning at a post oak, and runs north, seventy-three degrees east, fifty-five chains, to a red oak corner; thence, north, fourteen degrees east, sixteen chains ten links, to a large red oak; thence, north, sixty-one degrees west, sixty chains sixteen links, to a post oak corner; thence, south, thirty-five degrees west, twenty-seven chains fifty links, to a post oak; thence, to the beginning; having such marks, natural and artificial, as are represented in the plot annexed; containing two hundred and fifty-three acres, two roods, and twenty-six poles; is claimed by the heirs of Emanuel Cheney, legal representatives of Levin Hainsworth, under and by virtue of the third section of the above recited act, and now exhibited unto the Register of the Land Office, established east of Pearl river, to be recorded as directed by said act. To all which they beg leave to refer, as also to the copy of the plot herewith filed.

SALLY CHENEY, *Administratrix*,
J. J. M'GREW, *Admin. of the estate of Emanuel Cheney deceased*,
Legal representatives of Levin Hainsworth.

MARCH 29, 1804.

[Plot omitted.]

Surveyed March 29th, 1804, by T. Malone. Chain carriers, William McGrew and William Kerr.

Entered in record of claims, vol. 1, page 471, by EDWARD LLOYD WAILES, for

JOSEPH CHAMBERS, *Register.*

William Hunt and John Gordon were produced as witnesses, and, being duly sworn and interrogated by the Board, they deposed, that they had no interest, directly or indirectly, in this claim; that Levin Hainsworth inhabited and cultivated the land in question on the 3d day of March, 1803, and before that time; that he, Hainsworth, was, on the said 3d day of March, 1803, the head of a family; that Levin Hainsworth had told them that he sold and delivered his possession and improvements to the said Emanuel Cheney, deceased, for a valuable consideration; that they believed that said bargain took place in the summer of the year 1803; that, in the latter part of that year, said Hainsworth removed therefrom, and said Emanuel Cheney entered into the possession of the same, and did inhabit and cultivate the same until his death, which happened in the latter part of the year 1803.

Thomas Malone, surveyor, was presented as a witness, and, being duly sworn, deposed, that he surveyed the land then in question, and made the plot exhibited to the Board, which gave a true representation of the land claimed; that there were no lines that interfered with that claim, and that its lines did not interfere with any other claim; that he believed all the adjoining land to be vacant.

The Board ordered that the case be postponed for consideration.

GEORGE BREWER, Junior's, case, No. 115 on the docket of the Board, and No. 134 on the books of the Register.

Claim.—A donation of six hundred and twenty-nine acres, two roods, and thirty-six poles, under the second section of the act.

The claimant presented his plot of the land claimed, together with a surveyor's plot of the land claimed, in the following words and figures, to wit:

To the Commissioners appointed in pursuance of the act of Congress passed the 3d day of March, 1803, for receiving and adjusting claims to lands south of Tennessee, and east of Pearl river.

Please to take notice, that the following tract of land, situated on the west side of Tombigbee, in the county of Washington, beginning at a water oak, on Mrs. Lawrence's line, running south, thirty degrees west, one hundred and twenty chains, to a stake; thence, north, sixty degrees west, fifty-three chains twenty-two links, to a stake; thence, with Thomas Malone's line, north, thirty degrees east, one hundred and twenty chains, to a sycamore on the river; thence, with the river to the beginning; and hath such forms and marks, both natural and artificial, as are fully represented in the plot annexed, containing six hundred and twenty-nine acres, two roods, and thirty-six poles: is claimed by George Brewer, Jun. in and by virtue of the second section of the said act, as a donation; and is now exhibited to the Register of the Land Office established east of Pearl river, to be recorded as directed by said act. To all which he begs leave to refer, as also to a copy of the plot herewith filed.

                                        GEORGE BREWER, JUN.
MARCH 28, 1804.
          [Plot omitted.]

Surveyed for George Brewer by T. Malone.

Entered in record of claims, vol. 1, page 458, by EDWARD LLOYD WAILES, for
                    JOSEPH CHAMBERS, *Register.*

Hiram Mounger, James Denley, and John Baker were presented as witnesses, and, being duly sworn, they deposed, that they had no interest in this claim; that George Brewer, Jun. had been in the uninterrupted cultivation and habitation of the land in question, from the year 1794, until the 30th of March, 1804; and that said Brewer was the head of a family in the year 1797.

The Board ordered that the case be postponed for consideration.

WILLIAM H. HARGRAVE's case, No. 116 on the docket of the Board, and No. 148 on the books of the Register.

Claim.—A right of pre-emption of two hundred and sixty-two acres, as assignee and legal representative of Stephen Williams, under the third section of the act.

The claimant presented his claim, together with a surveyor's plot of the land claimed, in the words and figures following, to wit:

To the Commissioners appointed in pursuance of the act of Congress passed the 3d day of March, 1803, for receiving and adjusting claims to land south of Tennessee, and east of Pearl river.

Please to take notice, that the following tract of land, situated on the west side of Tombigbee, on the Sunflower creek, in the county of Washington, beginning at the commencement of Lee's and Denley's line; running thence, north, fifty-five degrees west, seventy chains, to a post oak corner, on Watley's survey; and thence, with said survey, to Brashear's line, and with the said line to a white oak, and thence, a square, with the said line, to a creek called the Sunflower, and down the said creek to Denley's line, and with the said line to the beginning; and hath such forms and marks, both natural and artificial, as are fully represented in the plot annexed, containing two hundred and sixty-two acres: is claimed by William H. Hargrave, representative of Stephen Williams, in and by virtue of the third section of the said act, as a pre-emption, and is now

exhibited to the Register of the Land Office established east of Pearl river, to be recorded as directed by said act. To all which he begs leave to refer, as also to a copy of the plot herewith filed.
                              WILLIAM H. HARGRAVE,
                              Representative of Stephen Williams.
MARCH 28th, 1804.
          [Plot omitted.]

Surveyed by Robert Ligon.

Entered in record of claims, vol. 1, page 476, by EDWARD LLOYD WAILES, for
                    JOSEPH CHAMBERS, *Register.*

The claimant exhibited a deed of conveyance from Stephen Williams, duly executed, conveying to the said William H. Hargrave all the said Williams's right and interest to the said tract of land, and the improvements thereon made.

Hiram Mounger and James Denley were presented as witnesses, and, being duly sworn and interrogated by the Board, they deposed, that they were not interested in this case; that Stephen Williams built a house upon the land then in question in the year 1801; that said Williams was a blacksmith, and continued to inhabit the land on the 3d day of March, 1803; and that Williams was on said 3d day of March, more than twenty-one years of age; that William H. Hargrave, by the consent, and under Williams, made a crop on said land, in the summer of said year 1803, and that said Hargrave continued in the possession when Williams removed therefrom, and was still in possession of the same; that he had heard Stephen Williams, the person under whom said Hargrave claims, say that he sold said land to said Hargrave.

John Denley and Robert Ligon, surveyor, were presented as witnesses, and, being duly sworn, the said Denley testified, that he saw Stephen Williams sign and deliver the instrument of writing then presented to the Board, purporting to be a conveyance of the land in question from said Williams to said Hargrave; and that since James Denley subscribed his name as a witness thereto, that said instrument of writing was made, executed, and delivered for the purposes therein mentioned, in and about six months ago.

The said Ligon deposed, that he surveyed the land in question; that the plot represents a true and correct view of the land claimed, with such marks, natural and artificial, as were therein represented.

Question. Why was said land located in such unshapely form?

Answer. I had no chain carriers, and it is bounded on all sides by other lands actually surveyed by me, and was put in the present form to prevent an interference with other claims.

The Board ordered that the case be postponed for consideration.

WILLIAM H. HARGRAVE's case, No. 117 on the docket of the Board, and No. 156 on the books of the Register.

Claim.—A right of pre-emption of three hundred and eighteen acres, under the third section of the act.

The claimant presented his claim, together with a surveyor's plot of the land claimed, in the following words and figures, viz.:

To the Commissioners appointed in pursuance of the act of Congress passed 3d day of March, 1803, for receiving and adjusting claims to lands south of Tennessee and east of Pearl river.

Please to take notice, that the following tract of land, situated on the waters of Sunflower creek, in the county of Washington, beginning at Jordan Morgan's white oak corner, on Nicholas Perkins's line, running thence, west, sixty chains, to a stake; thence, south, twenty degrees west, fifty-three chains, to a stake; thence, parallel with the first line, to Perkins's sweet gum corner, sixty chains; thence, along Perkins's line, fifty-three chains, to the beginning; having such shape, form, and marks, both natural and artificial, as are represented in the plot annexed: is claimed by William H. Hargrave, in and by virtue of the third section of the said act, as a pre-emption, and is now exhibited to the Register of the Land Office east of Pearl river, to be recorded as directed by said act. To all which he begs leave to refer, as also to the plot annexed.
                              WILLIAM H. HARGRAVE.
MARCH 29, 1804.
          [Plot omitted.]

Surveyed March 29, 1804, by William Gilliam.

Entered in record of claims, vol. 1, page 486, by EDWARD LLOYD WAILES, for
                    JOSEPH CHAMBERS, *Register.*

Hiram Mounger and John Denley were presented as witnesses, and, being duly sworn and interrogated by the Board, they deposed, that they were not interested in this case; that William H. Hargrave commenced to improve upon the land then in question in the year 1802, and had ever since continued occasionally to labor thereon; that he had rails split, and a small piece of ground fenced, on the 3d of March, 1803, but that the land being subject to inundation, and it being difficult to procure water in the summer season, was, therefore, not a suitable place for a habitation either for whites or blacks; that the said Hargrave had continued to claim the said land from the year 1802 until the then present time; and that Hargrave was the head of a family on the 3d of March, 1803.

The Board ordered that the case be postponed for consideration.

RICHARD S. BRYAN and GEORGE BREWER, Sen.: case commenced in page 711.

James Bilbo, surveyor, was presented as a witness, and, being duly sworn, deposed, that he surveyed the land then in question, and that the plot exhibits a true representation of the land claimed, with such marks, natural and artificial, as were therein laid down; that he did not know that the lines of said claim interfered with those of any other claim, except, on the northwest corner, it interfered with land surveyed under a settlement made by Ebenezer Fulsom, which interference, he, Bilbo, thought did not contain more than ten or twelve acres.

Question. Do you know about what time Richard S. Bryan commenced to improve upon the land now claimed ?

Answer. He commenced building a house thereon in the month of February, 1803, and has continued to improve thereon ever since.

The Board ordered that the case be postponed for consideration.

YOUNG GAINS, representative of Dominique de Olive: case commenced in page 680.

John Baker and James Denley were presented as witnesses, and being duly sworn and interrogated by the Board, they deposed, that they had no interest in this case; that, previous to and from the year 1791, until the year 1796, Dominique de Olive, by his overseer and slaves, did actually inhabit and cultivate the land in question on the 27th day of October, 1795; and that Dominique de Olive was, on the 15th of March, 1788, more than twenty-one years of age.

Thomas Bilbo, surveyor, and Hiram Mounger, were presented as witnesses, and, being duly sworn, the said Mounger testified, that, from the year 1791, until the year 1796, the land in question was cultivated by the overseer and slaves of Dominique de Olive and Valentine Dubroca.

The said Bilbo deposed, that he surveyed the land in question; that the plot exhibits a true and correct representation of the same, agreeably to the tenor of the Spanish warrant of survey under which it was claimed, and had such marks, natural and artificial, as were therein laid down; that said survey includes a small part of the old improvement; and that the lines of George Brewer's survey includes all the old improvement and nearly one-third of the land then in question.

The Board ordered that the case be postponed for consideration.

HOWELL DUPREE, representative of William Hillis: case commenced in page 663.

Adam Hollinger, and Robert Ligon, surveyor, were presented as witnesses, and, being duly sworn, the said Hollinger testified, that he knew that William Hillis inhabited and cultivated the land in question in the year 1797, and did believe that he continued to inhabit and cultivate thereon until near the end of that year, and that said William Hillis was, in the year 1797, above twenty-one years of age.

The said Ligon deposed, that he surveyed the land then in question; that the plot exhibited a true and correct representation of the land claimed, and had such marks, natural and artificial, as were therein laid down.

Question. Why did you make said survey of such an unusual and uncomely form?

Answer. I did it to avoid the lines of other claimants.

The Board ordered that the case be postponed for consideration.

JAMES CALLIER, representative of Isabella Trouillet: case commenced in page 714.

Isabella Campbell was presented as a witness, and, being duly sworn, the instrument or writing of conveyance from Joseph Campbell to James Callier, dated 20th

October, 1802, being read to her, she was interrogated, and answered as follows, viz.:

Question. Did you before know of such instrument or writing of conveyance?

Answer. I did.

Question. Why did you not sign it?

Answer. I was not asked to sign it.

Question. Do you know that, by agreeing to this instrument, you convey the birth-right of your children?

Answer. I do know it.

Question. Has this transaction taken place with your full approbation and consent?

Answer. It has.

Question. Has your husband made use of no undue influence, persuasion, or coercive means, to induce you to agree to this instrument?

Answer. He has not.

Question. Who made the first proposal to you to sell such right as you may have in or on the land now in question?

Answer. My husband, Joseph Campbell.

Question. What reason did your husband give you to induce you to part with this property?

Answer. He gave none.

Question. What reason had you to part with your right to this land?

Answer. I parted with it from necessity.

Question. What was the consideration, or do you know of any consideration being paid to your husband, for your right in and to this land?

Answer. It was a bargain and sale made by my husband, and I do not know what consideration was given.

Question. How came you to part with the property of your children, without knowing there was some consideration paid therefor?

Answer. I gave my consent.

Doctor John Chastang and Wilson Carman, being under oath, deposed, that they had well and truly, according to the best of their skill and ability, interpreted the oath administered to the witness, and the interrogatories put by the Board to the witness, and her answers to those interrogatories.

The Board ordered that the case be postponed for consideration.

EDMUND SMITH's case: commenced in page 708.

Sterling Dupree was presented as a witness, and, being duly sworn and interrogated by the Board, he deposed, that he was not interested in this case; and further testified, in the same words as Howell Dupree had done, whose testimony is recorded in page 370.

WILLIAM HUNT, representative of Dennis McClendon, case No. 118 on the docket of the Board, and No. 126 on the books of the Register.

Claim.—A right of pre-emption of one hundred and eighty-nine acres and two poles, under the third section of the act.

The claimant presented his claim, together with a surveyor's plot of the land claimed, in the following words and figures, viz.:

To the Commissioners appointed in pursuance of the act of Congress passed the 3d of March, 1803, for receiving and adjusting the claims to lands south of Tennessee and east of Pearl river.

Please to take notice, that the following tract of land, situated in Washington county, on the waters of Laura's creek, butted and bounded on all sides by vacant land, beginning on a pine, and runs north, fifty degrees west, thirty-eight chains fifty links, to a small pine corner; thence, north, forty-five degrees east, crossing a branch at twenty chains, in all fifty-six chains, to a large red oak corner; thence, south, thirty-five degrees east, nineteen chains sixty-five links, to a black-jack corner; on John F. M'Grew's line; thence south, eighteen degrees east, crossing a branch at nine chains forty links, again at fifty, and again at seventy links, in all twenty-two chains seventy links, to a white oak corner; thence, to the beginning; having such marks, natural and artificial, as are represented in the plot annexed, containing one hundred and eighty-nine acres and two poles: is claimed by William Hunt, legal representative of Dennis McClendon, who was the legal representative of John Sluder, who was the legal representative of Levin Hainsworth, under and by virtue of the third section of the above recited act, and now exhibited unto the Register of the Land office established east of Pearl river, to be recorded as directed by said act. To all which he begs leave to refer, as also to the copy of the plot herewith filed.

MARCH 19, 1804.   WILLIAM HUNT.

[Plot omitted.]

Surveyed 19th March, 1804, by T. Malone. Chain carriers, Shields Marsh, John Hopkins.

Entered in record of claims, vol. 1, page 446, by ED-WARD LLOYD WAILES, for

JOSEPH CHAMBERS, *Register.*

The said Marsh and Hopkins, chain carriers for the preceding survey, were sworn before John McGrew, Justice of Peace.

Samford McClendon and John Gordon were presented as witnesses, and, being duly sworn and interrogated by the Board, they deposed, that they had no interest in this case.

The said McClendon testified, that he moved to this country about three years since; that Henry Sluder came with him; that, soon after their arrival, he was present when said Henry Sluder purchased the land and improvement now in question, from Levin Hainsworth; that he heard Henry Sluder tell John Sluder to settle upon the land and improve it, and that he might have it if he did not return; that he, McClendon, was also present when John Sluder sold the same to Dennis McClendon, and when said McClendon sold to William Hunt, the present claimant; that he knew that William Hunt inhabited and cultivated thereon on the 3d of March, 1803, and had continued to inhabit and cultivate the same ever since.

The said Gordon testified, that William Hunt did inhabit and cultivate on the land in question on the 3d of March, 1803, and before and since that time.

Question. Was William Hunt the head of a family on the 3d of March, 1803?

Answer by both of said witnesses. He was.

Thomas Malone, surveyor, was produced as a witness, and being duly sworn, deposed, that he surveyed the land then in question; that the plot represents a true exhibition of the same; that there were no lines of other claims that interfered with that claim, and that its lines did not interfere with any other, except on the northwest corner of said tract Hunt's line crossed the old Indian boundary; that, by this interference, he did not include more than one or two acres of land on the Indian or north side of said boundary.

The Board ordered that the case be postponed for consideration.

JOHN MCGREW, Sen.; Esq, case No. 119 on the docket of the Board, and No. 164 on the books of the Register.

Claim.—A donation of six hundred and twenty-seven acres, under the second section of act.

The claimant presented his claim, together with a surveyor's plot of the land claimed, in the following words and figures, to wit:

To the Commissioners appointed in pursuance of an act of Congress passed the 3d day of March, 1803, for receiving and adjusting claims south of Tennessee, and east of Pearl river.

MARCH 29, 1804.

Please to take notice, that the following tract of land, situate, lying, and being in the county of Washington, on the west side of the Tombigbee, beginning on a stake near the house of John McGrew, Esq. and running north, eight degrees west, forty-three chains, to a holly; thence, north, sixty degrees east, eighty-six chains seventy-five links, to a white oak; thence, south, thirty-four degrees east, fifty-six chains twenty-eight links, to a poplar; and thence, south, twenty-five degrees west, forty chains, to a white oak; from thence, south, eighty-five degrees west, fifty-three chains and fifty links, to a hickory; and from thence to the beginning; bounded on the north by lands claimed by John Baker, and on the east by Stewart's old line, or William Coleman's lands: is claimed by John McGrew, Sen., Esq., under and by virtue of the second section of the above recited act, and is now exhibited to the Register of the Land Office established east of Pearl river, for the purpose of being recorded as directed by said act. To all which he begs leave to refer, as well as the plot herewith filed.

JOHN McGREW, Sen.

[Plot omitted.]

Surveyed 21st March, 1804, by Robert Ligon.

Entered in record of claims, vol. 1, page 497, by ED-WARD LLOYD WAILES, for

JOSEPH CHAMBERS, *Register.*

John Rail and John McGrew, Jun., chain carriers for the preceding survey, were sworn before R. Harwell, Justice of Peace.

Lemuel Henry, George Brewer, Jun. and James Denley, were presented as witnesses, and, being duly sworn and interrogated by the Board, they deposed, that they had no interest in this case.

The said Brewer and Denley testified, that John McGrew from the year 1791, and previous thereto, until the then present time, had inhabited and cultivated upon the tract of land in question; and that said McGrew was the head of a family in the year 1797.

Question to Mr. Denley. Do you know whether or not John McGrew, the present claimant, was among the first settlers above Bassett's creek, after the conquest of this country by the Spaniards?

Answer. He was.

The said Henry testified, that he believed that John Linder subscribed with his own hand his name to the writing, certifying that a permit was given to John McGrew to settle upon certain lands.

Robert Ligon, surveyor, was produced as a witness, and being duly sworn, testified, that he surveyed the land then in question; that the plot exhibited a true representation of the same, with the marks, natural and artificial, as were therein laid down; that he knew of no other lines interfering with those of this claim, nor of its lines interfering with those of any other claim, except on the northwest corner where it crossed a line, which was supposed to be the line of a British survey; that the interference included upwards of fifty acres of land.

JOSHUA HOWARD's case, No. 120 on the docket of the Board, and No. 121 on the books of the Register.

Claim—Of two hundred and fifty acres, as assignee and legal representative of Arthur Moor, and Mary Moor, his wife, by virtue of a deed from them, under the first section of the act.

The claimant presented his claim, together with a surveyor's plot of the land claimed, in the words and figures following, to wit:

Joshua Howard, a citizen of the Mississippi territory, claims two hundred and fifty acres of land, lying on the west side of Tombigbee river, in the county of Washington; which tract of land was originally granted to Arthur Moor, by the British Government of West Florida, by order of survey, bearing date in the year 1777, which order of survey, together with the necessary documents accompanying the same, was deposited in the proper office in Pensacola, and by the said officer carried away from there at the evacuation thereof, when captured by the Spaniards; and the aforesaid Arthur Moor, and Mary, his wife, by their deed, legally and fully executed, bearing date the 5th day of July, in the year 1780, did convey unto the aforesaid Joshua Howard the aforesaid two hundred and fifty acres of land; and the said Joshua Howard was an actual settler in the Mississippi territory on the 27th October, 1795.

JOSHUA HOWARD.

[Plot omitted.]

The claimant produced a deed of conveyance in the following words and figures, to wit:

This indenture, made the fifth day of July, in the year of our Lord one thousand seven hundred and eighty, between Arthur Moor, and Mary, his wife, of the district of Mobile, in the province of West Florida, of the one part, and Joshua Howard, of the district aforesaid, of the other part, witnesseth, that the said Arthur Moor, and Mary, his wife, for and in consideration of the sum of two hundred dollars to them in hand paid by the said Joshua Howard, the receipt whereof the said Arthur Moor, and Mary, his wife, do hereby acknowledge, and themselves therewith fully satisfied, contented, and paid, have bargained and sold, aliened, enfeoffed, released, and confirmed, and by these presents do bargain, sell, alien, enfeoff, release, convey, and confirm, unto the said Joshua Howard, all that tract or parcel of land lying and being in the district and province aforesaid, situate on the west side of the river Tombigbee, by distance above the town of Mobile about one hundred and five miles; bounded on the northeast by said river, northwest by land surveyed for John Lott, and on the other sides by vacant land, having such shape, form, and marks, both natural and artificial, as are represented in the plot annexed to His Majesty's letters patent to the said Arthur Moor, bearing date the —— of ——, and contains two hundred and fifty acres: to have and to hold the above described two hundred and fifty acres of land, and premises above mentioned, with the appurtenances, unto the said Joshua Howard, his heirs and assigns, forever, in as full and ample a manner as the same was granted to the said Arthur Moor by the aforesaid letters patent: and the said Arthur Moor, and Mary, his wife, for themselves and their heirs, do covenant and agree to and with the said Joshua Howard, his heirs, and assigns, that he, the said Arthur Moor, and Mary his wife, are seised of a good, lawful and indefeasible state of inheritance, in fee simple, of and in all and singular the premises above mentioned, and of every part thereof, with the appurtenances, without any manner of condition, mortgage, limitation of use or uses, or other matter, cause, or thing, to alter, change, or determine the same: and also, that he, the said Arthur Moor, and Mary his wife, now have good rightful power and lawful authority, in their own right, to bargain, sell, and convey the above described tract of land and premises with the appurtenances, unto the said Johua Howard, his heirs and assigns, to the only proper use and behoof of the said Joshua Howard, his heirs and assigns, according to the true intent and meaning of these presents; and that also he, the said Joshua Howard, his heirs and assigns, shall and may, from time to time, and at all times hereafter, peaceably and quietly have, hold, occupy, possess, and enjoy all and singular the premises above mentioned, to be hereby granted, with the appurtenances, without the let, trouble, hindrance, molestation, interruption, and denial of him, the said Arthur Moor, and Mary, his wife, their heirs, and assigns, and of all and every other person and persons whatever claiming, or to claim, by, from, or under them, or any of them: and further, that he, the said Arthur Moor, and Mary, his wife, and their heirs, and all and every other person and persons, and their heirs, any thing having or claiming in the premises above mentioned, or any part thereof, by, from, or under him or them, shall and will, at all times hereafter, at the request and cost of the said Joshua Howard, his heirs, and assigns, make, do, and execute all and every further and other lawful and reasonable acts and assurances in the law whatsoever, for the further, better, and more perfect conveying and assuring of the premises hereby granted, with the appurtenances, according to the true intent and meaning of these presents. In witness whereof, the said Arthur Moor, and Mary, his wife, have hereunto set their hands and seals, the day and year first above written.

ARTHUR A. MOOR, his x mark.
MARY MOOR, her x mark.

Sealed and delivered, [the words "and Mary, his wife," interlined before sealing,] in the presence of
ABEDNEGO LLEWELLYNN,
WILLIAM JOYNER.

On the back of said deed are endorsements and certificates in the words and figures following, to wit:
Received on the day of the date of the within written indenture, of and from the within named Joshua Howard, the sum of two hundred dollars, being in full for the consideration money within mentioned.

ARTHUR A. MOOR, his × mark.
MARY MOOR, her × mark.

Witnesses, ABEDNEGO LLEWELLYNN,
WILLIAM JOYNER.

Be it remembered, that, on the 27th day of December, in the year of our Lord one thousand seven hundred and ninety-eight, appeared before William Dunbar, thereunto authorized, William Joyner, one of the subscribing witnesses to the within instrument of writing, who, being duly sworn, did depose and say, that he saw the within named Arthur and Mary Moor sign, seal, and deliver the within instrument, as their voluntary act and deed, and also sign the receipt hereon endorsed ; and that the names of Abednego Llewellynn and William Joyner are of the proper hand-writing of the said Abednego Llewellynn, and of him, this deponent; and I, having inspected the same, and finding therein no material erasures, interlineations, or obliterations, do hereby certify the same.   WILLIAM DUNBAR,
Judge of Probate, pro tem.

Entered on record in the county of Adams, Mississippi territory, liber A, pages 12, 13, 14 and 15.
JOHN HENDERSON, Recorder.
NATCHEZ, June 10, 1799.

The claimant exhibited the following papers in support of his claim, to wit:

MR. ARTHUR MORE,
                          To JOHN McGILLIVRAY, Dr.
1777, July 15. To ½ gallon rum, at 6rs., 1 lb. sugar, 2 rs. - - - - - 8
    "   "   1 barrel potato seed, 2 dls. of Mr. L. in March - - 2
    " Nov. 29. 2 horse bells, at 5rs. - - 1
                                          ———
                                          3 8
Cr. By cash paid Mr. Little,   2 8
                                          ———
                          Owes, $1 0

Owes, $1 0
To paid for surveying 250 acres land for your acct. - - 20 1
To interest on do. from the 17th February, 1778, to the 4th of March, 1780, is 24 months, 17 days, at 8 per ct. per annum,   3 3½
                                          ————
                                          24 4½
Cr. By cash had of you - - 8 5
                                          ————
                                          $15 9½

MOBILE, 4th March, 1780. Received the contents in full.   For JOHN McGILLIVRAY,
LACHR. McGILLIVRAY.

Two hundred and fifty acres, situated on the west side of the river Tombigbee, distant above the town of Mobile, about one hundred and five miles, bounded on the northeast by said river, northwest by land surveyed for John Lott, on the other sides by vacant land.

Entered in record of claims, vol. 1, page 435, by EDWARD LLOYD WAILES, for

JOSEPH CHAMBERS, Register.

Thomas Malone, John Callier, and James Denley were presented as witnesses, and, being duly sworn and interrogated by the Board, said witnesses deposed, that they were not interested in this claim.

The said Callier testified, that, in the year 1799, he wrote to Joshua Howard offering to purchase the land in question, which he had been informed belonged to Howard ; and that he agreed to take four hundred dollars therefor; that he, Callier, accordingly agreed with Howard for the land in the year 1799; that, in consequence of said agreement, the same was cultivated in the year 1801; that, after that time, the agreement for said land entered into between said Howard and himself was cancelled, and he surrendered to Howard all the right, title, or claim which he had acquired under and by the purchase or agreement with said Howard.

The said Denley testified, that he had heard that Joshua Howard claimed, and continued to claim, said land, under a British title previous to and since the year 1795; and did believe that, on the 27th day of October, 1795, Howard did reside within said territory, near to the town of Natchez, and did actually know that said land was not cultivated in the year 1795 by Howard or his representatives ; that it was in that year cultivated by Mr. Elijah Thompson, or his widow, and for their own use and account.

Question by Mr. Gilmore, attorney for the claimant. Do you know from any circumstance, and from what circumstances, that Elijah Thompson, or his widow, cultivated this land for his own use and account?

Answer. They, or one of them, have told me that they did cultivate for their own use and account, and intended claiming the land in virtue of their settlement.

The said Malone testified, that, in the year 1802, Joshua Howard, the claimant, came to this country to receive the payment for the land in question, in pursuance of a sale or agreement entered into, concerning the premises, between said Howard and Colonel John Callier; that, upon the investigation of James Callier, who wished to become the purchaser, under John Callier, questioned the ability of Howard to make him a good and sufficient legal title to said land; and, therefore, Howard and said Colonel John Callier agreed to cancel the agreement to bargain which was made between them in relation thereto; that he, Malone, afterwards rented the land and plantation then in question, the terms of which lease will fully appear by an instrument of writing signed by Joshua Howard and the said Malone, and dated the fifth day of October, 1802, which was then before the Board.

Robert Ligon, surveyor, was produced as a witness, and, being duly sworn, deposed, that he surveyed the land then in question, and made said plot, which exhibits a true representation of the land claimed, with such marks, natural and artificial, as were therein laid down; that, in making said survey, he found marked trees which appeared to be evidences of an ancient line.

The Board ordered that the case be postponed for consideration.

CHARLES CASSETER's case, No. 121 on the docket of the Board, and No. 155 on the books of the Register.

Claim.—A right of pre-emption of one hundred acres, under the third section of the act.

The claimant presented his claim, together with a surveyor's plot of the land claimed, in the following words and figures, to wit:

To the Commissioners appointed, in pursuance of the act of Congress passed the 3d day of March, 1803, for receiving and adjusting the claims to lands south of the Tennessee and east of Pearl river.

Please to take notice, that the following tract of land, situated on the west side of Tombigbee, Washington-county, on the waters of Santibogue and Laura's creek, bounded on all sides by vacant land, beginning on a hickory, and runs north, forty-three degrees east, thirty-one chains sixty links, (crossing a fork of his spring branch at two chains from the beginning,) to a stake, with a black-jack pointer; thence, south, forty-seven degrees east, thirty-one chains sixty links, to a black-jack with two black-jack pointers; thence, south, forty-three degrees west, thirty-one chains sixty links, to a pine corner; thence, north, forty-seven degrees west, crossing the other prong of the spring branch at twenty-one chains, another small branch at twenty-five chains, in all thirty-one chains sixty links, to the beginning; having such marks, natural and artificial, as are represented in the plot annexed, containing one hundred acres: is claimed by Charles Casseter, under and by virtue of a settlement bearing date December, 1802, and now exhibited unto the Register of the Land Office, established east of Pearl river, to be recorded as directed by said act. To all which he begs leave to refer, as also to the copy of the plot herewith filed.

                     CHARLES CASSETER.

FEBRUARY 29, 1804.

               [Plot omitted.]

Surveyed 29th February, 1804, by T. Malone. Chain carriers, John Walker and Isaac Stanley. Entered in record of claims, vol. 1, page 485, by EDWARD LLOYD WAILES, for

        JOSEPH CHAMBERS, *Register.*

The said Walker, chain carrier for the above survey, was sworn before William Pierce, Esq., Justice of Peace.

Raleigh Green and Samford McClendon were presented as witnesses, and, being duly sworn and interrogated by the Board, they deposed, that they had no interest in this case; that Charles Casseter inhabited and cultivated the land in question on the 3d day of March, 1803, and before that time, and ever since; that he was, on said 3d day of March, 1803, more than twenty-one years of age.

Thomas Malone, surveyor, was produced as a witness, and, being duly sworn, deposed, that he surveyed the land in question; and made the plot then exhibited to the Board; that it gave a true and correct view of the land claimed, with such marks, natural and artificial, as were therein laid down; and that the land lay on the west side of the Tombigbee river, and below the old Indian boundary; that there were no interfering lines that he knew of, but as he believed, it was bounded on all sides by vacant land.

The Board ordered that the case be postponed for consideration.

Adjourned until Saturday, the 31st instant.

          SATURDAY, *March 31st,* 1804.

The Board met according to adjournment. Present: Ephraim Kirby, Robert C. Nicholas, Joseph Chambers.

PETER CARTWRIGHT's case, No. 122 on the docket of the Board, and No. 157 on the books of the Register.

Claim.—A right of pre-emption of one hundred and fifty-nine acres one rood, and thirty poles, under the first section of the act.

The claimant presented his claim, together with a surveyor's plot of the land claimed, in the following words and figures, to wit:

To the Commissioners appointed in pursuance of the act of Congress passed the 3d day of March, 1803, for receiving and adjusting the claims to lands south of the Tennessee and east of Pearl river.

Please to take notice, that the following tract of land, situated on the West side of Tombigbee, Washington county, bounded on the southeast by Mimms's claim and vacant land, on the northeast, northwest, and south-west by vacant land; beginning on a hickory on Mimms's line, and runs south, eighty-four degrees east, fifteen chains, to a stake corner, with a large red oak pointer; thence, north, nine degrees east, thirty-three chains fifty links, (crossing a branch of Tawler at twenty chains,) to a white oak corner; thence, north, thirty degrees west, thirty-three chains, to a poplar corner; thence, south, fifty-seven degrees west, thirty-three

           84

chains fifty links, to a stooping bay corner; thence, Mimms's old line to the beginning; having such marks, natural and artificial, as are represented in the plot annexed, containing one hundred and fifty-nine acres, one rood, thirty poles: is claimed by Peter Cartwright, under and by virtue of a settlement in the year 1801, and now exhibited unto the Register of the Land Office established east of Pearl river, to be recorded as directed by said act. To all which he begs leave to refer, as also to the copy of the plot herewith filed.

                PETER CARTWRIGHT.

              [Plot omitted.]

Chain carriers, John Wannack and John Walker. Entered in record of claims, vol. 1, page 487, by EDWARD LLOYD WAILES, for

        JOSEPH CHAMBERS, *Register.*

The said chain carriers for the above survey were sworn before William Pierce, Justice of Peace.

Raleigh Green was presented as a witness, and, being duly sworn and interrogated by the Board, deposed, that he was not interested in this claim; that Peter Cartwright inhabited and cultivated the land in question on the 3d day of March, 1803, and before that time, and ever since; that said Cartwright was, on the 3d day of March, 1803, the head of a family.

Thomas Malone, surveyor, was produced as a witness, and, being duly sworn, deposed, that he surveyed the land in question, and made said plot, which exhibited a true representation of the land then claimed, with such marks, natural and artificial, as were therein laid down; that there were no other lines that interfere with the lines of said claim that he knew of; that it lies on the west side of Tombigbee river, and below the old Indian boundary line.

The Board ordered that the case be postponed for consideration.

ISAAC STANLEY's case, No. 123 on the docket of the Board, and No. 124 on the books of the Register.

Claim.—A right of pre-emption of one hundred acres, under the third section of the act.

The claimant presented his claim, together with a surveyor's plot of the land claimed, in the following words and figures, to wit:

To the Commissioners appointed in pursuance of the act of Congress passed the 3d day of March, 1803, for receiving and adjusting claims to lands south of the Tennessee, and east of Pearl river.

Please to take notice, that the following tract of land, situated in Washington county, on the waters of Laura's creek, butted and bounded on all sides by vacant land, beginning on a hickory, and runs north, ten degrees east, crossing a branch of Laura's creek at fifteen chains, another at eighteen chains, in all twenty-five chains to a stake with a sweet gum and two red oak pointers; thence, north, eighty degrees west, crossing a branch at three chains, again at three chains fifty links, again at four chains, again at twenty-two chains, in all forty chains, to a stake with two hickories and a red oak, pointers; thence, south, ten degrees west, twenty-five chains, to a red oak; thence to the beginning; having such marks, natural and artificial, as are represented in the plot annexed, containing one hundred acres: is claimed by Isaac Stanley, under and by virtue of the third section of the above recited act, and now exhibited unto the Register of the Land Office established east of Pearl river, to be recorded as directed by said act. To all which he begs leave to refer, as also to the copy of the plot herewith field.

              ISAAC STANLEY, his + mark.

MARCH 3, 1804.

             [Plot omitted.]

Surveyed 3d of March, 1804, by T. Malone. Chain carriers, John Walker and John Gordon. Entered in record of claims, vol. 1, page 444, by EDWARD LLOYD WAILES, for

        JOSEPH CHAMBERS, *Register.*

The said Walker and Gordon, chain carriers for the preceding survey, were sworn before William H. Hargrave, Esq., Justice of Peace.

Raleigh Green and Samford McClendon were presented as witnesses, and, being duly sworn and interrogated by the Board, they deposed, that they were not interested in this case; that Isaac Stanley did inhabit and cultivate the land in question on the 3d day of March, 1803, and before that time, and ever since; that said Isaac Stanley was, on the 3d day of March, 1803, the head of a family.

Thomas Malone, surveyor, was presented as a witness, and, being duly sworn, deposed, that he surveyed the land in question, and made said plot, that it exhibited a true and correct representation of the land claimed, with such marks, natural and artificial, as were therein laid down: that there were no lines that he knew of, in other claims, interfering with the lines of this claim, excepting one of the lines of Tandy and John Walker's survey; that said land lay on the west side of Tombigbee river, and below the old Choctaw boundary line.

The Board ordered that the case be postponed for consideration.

TANDY WALKER and JOHN WALKER's case, No. 124 on the docket of the Board, and No. 125 on the books of the Register.

Claim.—A right of pre-emption of four hundred and nineteen acres, two roods, and thirty-eight poles, under the third section of the act.

The claimants presented their claim, together with a surveyor's plot of the land claimed, in the words and figures following, to wit:

To the Commissioners appointed in pursuance of the act of Congress passed the 3d day of March, 1803, for receiving and adjusting claims to lands south of the Tennessee, and east of Pearl river.

Please to take notice, that the following tract of land, situated on the west side of Tombigbee river, in the county of Washington, beginning at a hickory, running south, fifty degrees west, thirty chains fifty links, to a sweet gum; thence, south, twelve degrees west, thirty chains, to a black oak; thence, south, sixty-three degrees east, sixty-one chains, to a pine; thence, east, twenty-five chains fifty links, to a sweet gum corner; thence, north, fifty degrees east, forty chains, to a pine corner; thence, north, fifty-seven degrees west, ninety-five chains, to the beginning corner; and hath such forms and marks, both natural and artificial, as are represented in the plot annexed, containing four hundred and nineteen acres, two roods, thirty-eight poles: is claimed by Tandy Walker and John Walker, in and by virtue of the third section of the said act, as a pre-emption, and is now exhibited to the Register of the Land Office established east of Pearl river, to be recorded as directed by said act. To all which they beg leave to refer, as also to the copy of the plot herewith filed.

JOHN WALKER, his × mark,
For self and brother Tandy.
MARCH 31, 1804.
[Plot omitted.]

Surveyed 19th February, 1804, by T. Malone. Chain carriers, Charles Casserty and John Walker.
Entered in record of claims, vol. 1, page 445, by EDWARD LLOYD WAILES, for
JOSEPH CHAMBERS, *Register.*

The said Casserty, chain carrier for the above survey, was sworn before William Pierce, Justice of Peace.

Samford McClendon and Raleigh Green were presented as witnesses, and, being duly sworn and interrogated by the Board, they deposed, that they had no interest in this claim; that Tandy Walker inhabited and cultivated on the land in question on the 3d day of March, 1803; that both Tandy and John Walker cultivated on the same land before and since that time; that Tandy Walker was, on the 3d day of March, 1803, the head of a family: and that John Walker was at that time, as they, the witnesses, believed, twenty-one or more years of age.

Thomas Malone, surveyor, was produced as a witness, and, being duly sworn, deposed, that he surveyed the land in question, and made said plot, which exhibited a true and correct view of the land in question, with such marks, natural and artificial, as were therein laid down; that said land lay on the west side of the Tombigbee, and below the old Indian boundary; that there were interfering lines with said claim, viz.: William McGrew on the southwest and southeast corners, and Isaac Stanley's on the west corner; that McGrew's interference, he, Malone, supposed might include twenty-five or thirty acres of land; that Stanley's interference did not include more than six or seven acres of land.

The Board ordered that the case be postponed for consideration.

JAMES HUCKABY, representative of Matthew Robinson: case commenced in page 651.
John Gordon was presented as a witness, and, being duly sworn and interrogated by the Board, he deposed,

that he was not interested in this case; that Matthew Robinson inhabited and cultivated on the land in question on the 3d day of March, 1803, and before that time, and continued so to do until he sold the same unto James Huckaby; and that said Robinson was, on the 3d day of March, 1803, the head of a family.

The Board ordered that the case be postponed for consideration.

RAWLEY GREEN's case, No. 125 on the docket of the Board, and No. 96 on the books of the Register.
Claim.—A right of pre-emption of two hundred and one acres and thirty-one poles, under the third section of the act.

The claimant presented his claim, together with a surveyor's plot of the land claimed, in the following words and figures, to wit:

To the Commissioners appointed in pursuance of the act of Congress passed 3d day of March, 1803, for receiving and adjusting claims to lands south of the Tennessee and east of Pearl river.

Please to take notice, that the following tract of land, situated on the west side of Tombigbee river, butted on said river, bounded on the northeast by the line dividing Robert Farmer's and Kirkland's surveys, and lying altogether within the lines of Farmer's survey, beginning at a sassafras, and runs the dividing line between the claimant and John Westmoreland, south, seventy degrees west, seventy chains, to a sweet gum; thence, north, forty degrees west, twenty-nine chains, to a red oak on Farmer's old line; thence, with the old line, north, seventy degrees east, seventy-four chains fifty links, to a sassafras on Farmer's corner; thence, the meanders of the river, to the beginning, having such marks, natural and artificial, as are represented in the plot annexed; containing two hundred and one acres and thirty-one poles: is claimed by Rawley Green, under and by virtue of a settlement bearing date the 3d day of March, 1803, and now exhibited unto the Register of the Land Office, established east of Pearl river, to be recorded as directed by said act. To all which he begs leave to refer, as also to the copy of the plot herewith filed.

RAWLEY GREEN.
FEBRUARY 27, 1804.
[Plot omitted.]

Surveyed February 27, 1804, by T. Malone. Chain carriers, Joseph Westmoreland, Elisha Simmons.
Entered in record of claims, vol. 1, page 295, by EDWARD LLOYD WAILES, for
JOSEPH CHAMBERS, *Register.*

John Baker and William Shaw were produced as witnesses, and, being duly sworn, the said Shaw deposed, that Rawley Green inhabited and cultivated the land then in question on the 3d day of March, 1803, and before and since that time; that said Green was the head of a family on the 3d day of March, 1803.

The said Baker deposed, that he had seen a Spanish grant for said land, in the names of John Turnbull and James Frazier.

The Board ordered that the case be postponed for consideration.

SAMFORD McCLENDON's case. No. 126 on the docket of the Board, and No. 145 on the books of the Register.
Claim.—A right of pre-emption of ninety-nine acres, under the third section of the act.

The claimant presented his claim, together with a surveyor's plot of the land claimed, in the words and figures following, to wit:

To the Commissioners appointed in pursuance of the act of Congress passed the 3d day of March, 1803, for receiving and adjusting claims to lands south of the Tennessee, and east of Pearl river.

Please to take notice, that the following tract of land, situated in Washington county, on the waters of Laura's creek, butted and bounded on all sides by vacant land; beginning on a post oak, and runs south, seventy-one degrees west, thirty-seven chains eighty-six links, to a small post oak; thence, south, twenty-two degrees west, twenty chains, to a stake with a pine and Spanish oak, pointers; thence, north, seventy-one degrees east, forty-seven chains fifty links, to a white oak; thence, to the beginning; having such marks, natural and artificial, as are represented in the plot annexed, containing ninety-nine acres: is claimed by Samford McClendon, under and by virtue of the third section of the above recited act, and now exhibited unto the Register of the Land Office established east of Pearl river, to be recorded as directed by said act. To all which he begs leave to refer, as also to the copy of the plot herewith filed.

SAMFORD McCLENDON.

MARCH 22, 1804.

[Plot omitted.]

Surveyed March 22, 1804, by T. Malone. Chain carriers, Zachariah Landrum and John Gordon.

Entered in record of claims, vol. 1, page 472, by EDWARD LLOYD WAILES, for

JOSEPH CHAMBERS, *Register.*

The above named chain carriers were sworn before Ransom Harwell, Justice of the Peace.

William Hunt and John Gordon were produced as witnesses, and, being duly sworn and interrogated by the Board, they deposed, that they had no interest in this claim; that Sandford McClendon did inhabit and cultivate the land in question on the 3d day of March, 1803, and before that time, and ever since; that said McClendon was on said 3d day of March the head of a family.

Thomas Malone, surveyor, was presented as a witness, and, being duly sworn, deposed, that he surveyed the land in question, and made said plot, which exhibited a true and correct representation of the land claimed, with such marks, natural and artificial, as were therein laid down; that the lines of this claim did not, that he knew of, interfere with the lines of any other claim, nor were there lines of other claims interfering with this; that said land lay on the west side of Tombigbee river, and below the old Choctaw boundary line.

The Board ordered that the case be postponed for consideration.

ZACHARIAH LANDRUM's case, No. 127 on the docket of the Board, and No. 86 on the books of the Register.

Claim.—A right of pre-emption of one hundred and fourteen acres, under the third section of the act.

The claimant presented his claim, together with a surveyor's plot of the land claimed, in the following words and figures, viz.:

To the Commissioners appointed, in pursuance of the act of Congress passed the 3d day of March, 1803, for receiving and adjusting claims to lands south of the Tennessee, and east of Pearl river.

Please to take notice, that the following tract of land, situated on the west side of Tombigbee, Washington county, on the waters of Laura's creek, butted and bounded on all sides by vacant land, beginning on a red oak, and runs, north, seventeen degrees west, crossing a small branch at eight chains fifty links, another at nine chains fifty links, in all twenty-eight chains fifty links, to a stake with two post oaks and a sweet gum, pointers; thence; north, seventy-three east, forty chains, to a stake with a Spanish oak and two hickory pointers; thence, south, seventeen degrees east, twenty-eight chains fifty links, with a post oak and maple pointers; thence to the beginning; having such marks, natural and artificial, as are represented in the plot annexed, containing one hundred and fourteen acres: is claimed by Zachariah Landrum, under and by virtue of the third section of the above recited act; and now exhibited unto the Register of the Land Office established east of Pearl river, to be recorded as directed by said act. To all which he begs leave to refer, as also to the copy of the plot herewith filed.

ZACHARIAH LANDRUM.

MARCH 22, 1804.

[Plot omitted.]

Surveyed 22d March, 1804, by T. Malone. Chain carriers, John Gordon and Isaac Stanley.

Entered in record of claims, vol. 1, page 252, by EDWARD LLOYD WAILES, for

JOSEPH CHAMBERS, *Register.*

John Walker and Samford McClendon were presented as witnesses, and being duly sworn and interrogated by the Board, they deposed, that they were not interested in this claim.

The said McClendon testified, that he knew that Zachariah Landrum inhabited and cultivated the land in question on the 3d of March, 1803, and before that time, and ever since; and that he was at that time the head of a family.

The said Walker testified, that he left this country in February, 1803, at which time Zachariah Landrum was in the habitation and cultivation of the land in question; that when he, Walker, returned in the winter of the same year, he found Landrum in the possession of the same land, which had the appearance of having

been cultivated during the time that he, Walker, was absent; that said Landrum was, before and after the month of February, 1803, the head of a family.

Thomas Malone, surveyor, was presented as a witness, and, being duly sworn, deposed, that he surveyed the land in question, and made said plot, which exhibited a true and correct view of the land claimed, with such marks, natural and artificial, as were therein laid down; that he knew of no interfering lines; and that said land lay on the west side of the Tombigbee river, and below the old Choctaw boundary line.

The Board ordered that the case be postponed for consideration.

JOHN GORDON's case, No. 128 on the docket-of the Board, and No. 98 on the books of the Register.

Claim.—A right of pre-emption of one hundred and thirteen acres and twenty-five poles, under the third section of the act.

The claimant presented his claim, together with a surveyor's plot of the land claimed, in the following words and figures, to wit:

To the Commissioners appointed in pursuance of the act of Congress passed the 3d day of March, 1803, for receiving claims to lands south of the Tennessee, and east of Pearl river.

Please to take notice, that the following tract of land, situated on the waters of Laura's creek, on the west side of Tombigbee river, Washington county, butted and bounded on all sides by vacant land, beginning at a post oak, and runs south, five degrees east, at twenty-two chains fifty links, crossing a branch of Laura's creek at twenty-six chains fifty links, in all, thirty-three chains fifty links, to a stake, with two hickory and two red oak pointers; thence, south, fifty-seven degrees east, eleven chains fifty-seven links, to a red oak corner; thence, north, eighty-five degrees east, twenty chains to a stake, with a chesnut, hickory, and red oak pointers; thence, north, five degrees west, crossing Laura's creek, at twenty-nine chains; in all, forty chains, to a red bay, and from thence to the beginning; having such marks, natural and artificial, as are represented in the plot annexed, containing one hundred and thirteen acres and twenty-five poles; is claimed by John Gordon, under and by virtue of the third section of the above recited act, and now exhibited unto the Register of the Land Office, east of Pearl river, to be recorded as directed by said act. To all which he begs leave to refer, as also to the copy of the plot herewith filed.

JOHN GORDON.

MARCH 22, 1804.

[Plot omitted.]

Surveyed 3d of March, 1804, by T. Malone. Chain carriers, Isaac Stanley and Zachariah Landrum.

Entered in record of claims, volume 1, page 298, by EDWARD LLOYD WAILES, for

JOSEPH CHAMBERS, *Register.*

The above named chain carriers were sworn before R. Harwell, Justice of the Peace.

Rawley Green and Samford McClendon were presented as witnesses, and, being duly sworn and interrogated by the Board, they deposed, that they were not interested in this claim; that John Gordon, the present claimant, before the 3d of March, 1803, on that day, and ever since, had resided upon and cultivated the land in question; and that, on said 3d of March, he was above twenty-one years of age, and the head of a family.

Thomas Malone, surveyor, was presented as a witness, and, being duly sworn, he deposed, that he surveyed and plotted the land in question, and that the plot exhibited was a correct representation thereof, according to the best of his knowledge and belief; that he knew of no interfering lines or claims.

The Board ordered that the case be postponed for consideration.

JOHN F. McGREW and CLARK McGREW, representatives of Julian de Castro: case commenced in page 639.

Nathan Blackwell and Francis Boykin were presented as witnesses, and being duly sworn, they deposed, that Julian de Castro inhabited and cultivated the land then in question on the 27th day of October, 1795, and that said de Castro was, on the 10th of June, 1795, the head of a family, and more than twenty-one years of age.

The Board ordered that the case be postponed for consideration.

JOHN McGREW, Junior's, case, No. 129 on the docket of the Board, and No. 72 on the books of the Register.

Claim.—A donation of six hundred and forty acres, under the second section of the act.

The claimant presented his claim, together with a surveyor's plot of the land claimed, in the following words and figures, to wit:

To the Commissioners appointed in pursuance of the act of Congress passed the 3d day of March, 1803, for receiving and adjusting the claims to lands south of the Tennessee, and east of Pearl river.

Please to take notice, that a-tract of land, lying on the west side of Tombigbee, in Washington county, in the hickory flat, bounded as follows: beginning at a small black-jack, and running south, seventy-three degrees east, eighty chains, to a hickory; thence, south, seventeen degrees west, eighty chains, to a large pine; thence, north, seventy-three degrees east, eighty chains, to a large pine; thence, south, seventeen degrees east, eighty chains, to the beginning: is claimed by John McGrew, Jun., of Washington county, Mississippi territory, by virtue of a settlement made by Alexander McGrew, who actually inhabited and cultivated the aforesaid land in 1797, when the evacuation took place, and conveyed by him to the said claimant, and now delivered to the Register of the Land Office, established east of Pearl river, for the purpose of being recorded. To all which he begs leave to refer, as also to the plot herewith filed.

JOHN McGREW, JUN.

[Plot omitted.]

Surveyed 22d February, 1804, by T. Malone. Chain carriers, John F. McGrew and Benjamin King.

Entered in record of claims, vol. 1, page 204, by EDWARD LLOYD WAILES, for

JOSEPH CHAMBERS, *Register.*

George Brewer and Joseph Lawrence were produced as witnesses, and, being duly sworn and interrogated by the Board, they deposed, that they were not interested in this case.

The said Brewer testified, that some time in the spring of the year 1798, he was on said land, and saw some signs of a little labor having been done, such as a few trees cut down; that a small patch appeared as if something had been planted there, but did not know who performed said labour, nor that any person lived on the land that year, nor that any crop was raised there, nor that Alexander McGrew was twenty-one years of age at that time, or a married man.

The said Lawrence testified, that in the summer of the year 1798, he saw a small pen on said land, with corn growing in it, which appeared to have been planted, but did not know who performed said work, nor that any person resided on the land that year, nor that any other improvement or cultivation was made there that year; that he did not know that Alexander McGrew was twenty-one years of age in the year 1798, but believed he was.

The said witnesses further deposed, that they understood that Alexander McGrew did the work above mentioned, or caused it to be done; and also that they never knew or heard that he did afterwards either inhabit or cultivate the said land, but that it had since been cultivated by others not claiming under him.

Thomas Malone, surveyor, was presented as a witness, and, being duly sworn, deposed, that he surveyed and plotted the land in question, and believed the plot exhibited to be correct; that the plot included the greater part of James Morgan's and Micajah Wall's surveys.

The Board ordered that the case be postponed for consideration.

JAMES CALLIER, [representative] of Isabella Trouillet, the wife of Joseph Campbell: case commenced in page 714.

Adam Hollinger, Richard Barrow, George Brewer, Junior, Richard Hawkins, and Augustine Rochon, were produced as witnesses, and, being duly sworn and interrogated by the Board, they deposed, that they had no interest in this case.

The said Brewer testified, that, in the fall of the year 1796, or 1797, as he was passing by the place in question, some negroes came out of the houses, and he asked those negroes to whom they belonged; that they told him to Peter Trouillett, or Mrs. Trouillet; that he did not certainly recollect which.

The said Hollinger testified, that he knew that negroes belonging to Peter Trouillet, from the year 1794 until 1799, inhabited on the land in question, but cultivated on the east side of the river Tombigbee; that he did not know that they cultivated on the west side of said river.

Question. Do you know whether Peter Trouillet or Isabella Trouillet resided within the territory at any time, and, if so, about what time?

Answer. I do not know that Peter Trouillet did reside within the territory, but am certain that Isabella Trouillet did reside on the land in question at the time the American troops arrived at the garrison of Fort Stoddert, and commenced to build, I believe the year preceding.

Question. Where did Isabella Trouillet reside before the time you have mentioned?

Answer. She resided within the town of Mobile.

Question. Was not Alexander Trouillet acting as the overseer of Isabella Trouillet in the year 1797, at the place in question?

Answer. I have always understood that he was. at that time, acting as the overseer of Isabella Trouillet.

The said Hawkins testified, that, in the year 1797, he saw negroes, said to belong to Madam Trouillet, inhabiting and cultivating upon the land in question; and that Madam Trouillet at that time resided in the town of Mobile, and continued to reside there until the fall of the year 1799, when she moved and made her residence on the place in question, and continued to reside thereon until the spring of the year 1803.

Question. Did you, or did you not, understand that Isabella Trouillet was a widow in the year 1797?

Answer. I did understand that she was a widow at that time.

The said Barrow testified, that he knew that negroes, said to belong to Peter Trouillet, or the widow Trouillet, inhabited and cultivated the land in question from the year 1794 until the American troops arrived here and commenced to build the garrison Fort Stoddert; that Isabella Trouillet removed from Mobile, and did certainly inhabit on the land in question at the time the American troops came to this place, and that he believed she did remove and so inhabit the year preceding.

The said Rochon testified, that Isabella Campbell, late Isabella Trouillet, was a widow in the years 1796 and 1797, before which time, her late husband, Peter Trouillet, died.

The Board ordered that the case be postponed for consideration.

LEMUEL HENRY, attorney in fact for Antonio Espaho' representative of John Turnbull: case commenced in page 694.

Adam Hollinger, Thomas Bates, and Richard Barrow, were presented as witnesses, and, being duly sworn and interrogated by the Board, they deposed, that they had no interest in this case.

Question to said Hollinger. Do you know that the land now in question was inhabited and cultivated on the 27th of October, 1795, or not?

Answer. I do not know that it was.

Question. Do you know whether or not John Turnbull lived in the Mississippi territory on the 27th of October, 1795?

Answer. I have been informed that John Turnbull did, on the 27th of October, 1795, live at or near Baton Ronge, on the Mississippi river.

Question. Has John Turnbull, since the 27th of October, 1795, resided within this territory?

Answer. I believe he has not.

Question. Was John Turnbull, on the 1st of July, 1787, twenty-one years of age?

Answer. I think he was near forty years of age at that time.

Question. Do you know whether Michael Hartley at the time he purchased the land in question, agreed with John Turnbull, or John Joyce, his agent, that if he did not pay him three hundred dollars at the expiration of three years from the date of said purchase, the land so purchased by Hartley should again become the property of John Turnbull?

Answer. I do not know that he did, but that he did agree to give three hundred dollars for the land; and, having failed in making the payment of the three hundred dollars at the expiration of the three years, he again gave up the possession of the land to John Turnbull or his agent.

The said Barrow testified, that one Alexander inhabited and cultivated the land in question in the years 1794 and 1795; that, in the fall of the year 1795, he quitted the possession, and Michael Hartley moved on to the same soon after Alexander quitted it; Michael Hartley cultivated it in the years 1796, 1797, and 1798; and further, that Hartley purchased said land from John Turnbull, or John Joyce, his agent, for the consideration of three hundred dollars, to have been paid within three years from the date of the purchase, which payment he failed to make, and again gave up the land to John Turnbull or his agent, and Turnbull released him from his obligation to pay the three hundred dollars; that Emanuel Cheney afterwards purchased said land from John Turnbull, for the consideration of three hundred dollars; and that he, Barrow, saw the bill of sale which Turnbull gave Cheney for said land, in which he covenanted to warrant and defend the same against all persons.

Question. Did John Turnbull live in the territory on the 27th of October, 1795?

Answer. I do not know that he did, but believe he did not.

The said Bates testified, that said land had been cultivated and inhabited for the last fifteen years; but for whom, or for whose use or account it was cultivated on the 27th day of October, 1795, he did not know.

Question. Was John Turnbull a resident within the Mississippi territory on the 27th of October, 1795, or since?

Answer. I believe he was not, nor has he been since.

John Milliken, surveyor, was presented as a witness, and, being duly sworn, deposed, that he surveyed the land in question; that said plot exhibited a true and correct representation of the same, with such marks, natural and artificial, as were therein laid down; that the lines of this tract interfered with the lines of Howel Dupree's claim; that Colonel Benjamin Few set up a claim for the whole of said land that lay within the dotted lines.

The Board ordered that the case be postponed for consideration.

EDWIN LEWIS's case, No. 130 on the docket of the Board, and No. 23 on the books of the Register.

Claim.—A donation of six hundred and forty acres, as assignee and legal representative of Henry Nail, under the second section of the act.

The claimant presented his claim, together with a surveyor's plot of the land claimed, in the following words and figures, to wit:

To the Commissioners appointed in pursuance of the act of Congress passed the 3d day of March, 1803, for receiving and adjusting claims to lands south of the Tennessee, and east of Pearl river.

WASHINGTON COUNTY, MISSISSIPPI TERRITORY, *February 22, 1804.*

Please to take notice, that the following tract of land, situate on the southwest side of the river Tombigbee, butting and bounded as follows: by a line beginning on the mouth of the first bayou, or small creek or branch below the Hatchatigiby bluff or lake; thence, running due west, forty-four chains, to a corner stake; thence, running north, thirty chains, to a corner stake; thence, running north, forty-five degrees east, sixty chains, to a corner stake; thence, running due north, to a corner stake on the lower side or bank of Sintabogue; thence, down the meanders of said Sintabogue creek to the river Tombigbee; thence, down the meanders of the bank of the river to the beginning or first mentioned station; having such marks, natural and artificial, as are represented in the plot annexed, containing six hundred and forty acres: is claimed by Henry Nail, and by his legal representative, Edwin Lewis, under and by virtue of occupancy; he, the said Henry Nail, having occupied the same for some time previous to the final evacuation of the Spanish troops from this territory, and did, on the day of the evacuation of the Spanish troops, inhabit and cultivate the tract herein specified, and ever since unto this day, agreeable to the second and third sections of the act of Congress, entitled "An act regulating the grants of lands, and providing for the sale of the lands of the United States south of the State of Tennessee;" and that he, the said claimant, claims no other land in the territory, and the same does not appear to be claimed by any of the preceding provisions of the act; and now exhibited to the Register of the Land Office established east of Pearl river, to be recorded as directed by said act. To all which he begs leave to refer, as also to the plot hereunto fixed, &c.

For HENRY NAIL,
EDWIN LEWIS.
[Plot omitted.]

Entered in record of claims, vol. 1, page 62, by ED-WARD LLOYD WAILES, for

JOSEPH CHAMBERS, *Register.*

The claimant produced a deed of conveyance from Henry Nail, bearing date the 29th day of October, 1803, relinquishing and conveying to the said Edwin Lewis all the said Nail's right, interest and claim to the said tract of land, and to the improvements made thereon.

Young Gains and Henry Nail were presented as witnesses, and, being duly sworn and interrogated by the Board, they deposed, that they had no interest in this claim.

The said Gains testified, that he believed Henry Nail settled and built on the land then in question in the latter part of the year 1797, or the beginning of the year 1798; that he was certain that Nail did inhabit and cultivate on the same previous to the final evacuation of said territory by the Spanish troops; that the old Choctaw line and that marked by General Wilkinson as such, in the month of August, 1803, ran across said tract, and struck the river just below the Hatchatigiby lake, as appeared by the dotted line on the plot; and that Henry Nail was, in the year 1797, the head of a family.

The said Nail testified, that he did improve and make some small cultivation on the land some short time before the Spanish troops evacuated said territory, which was in the fall of the year preceding that event.

Question. Have you or do you expect that there will be any other claim for land in this territory, in your name?

Answer. I sold my right to Mr. Hudson of an improvement or labor which I had made on a tract of land, but sold no land previous to my settlement and cultivation of the land now in question.

Question to said Gains. Do you think it would not be difficult to prove the settlement and cultivation of this land, on account of its remote situation from other white inhabitants?

Answer. It would, for, as well as I can recollect, there are no white families nearer than John Baker and John M'Grew, Esquires; a distance of seven or eight miles from this land.

The Board ordered that the case be postponed for consideration.

Adjourned until Monday, the 2d day of April next.

MONDAY, *April* 2, 1804.

The Board met according to adjournment. Present: Ephraim Kirby, Robert C. Nicholas, Joseph Chambers.

Adjourned until Tuesday, the 3d instant.

TUESDAY, *April* 3, 1804.

The Board met according to adjournment. Present: Ephraim Kirby, Robert C. Nicholas, Joseph Chambers.

Adjourned until Wednesday, the 4th instant.

WEDNESDAY, *April* 4, 1804.

The Board met according to adjournment. Present: Ephraim Kirby, Robert C. Nicholas.

Adjourned until Thursday, the 5th instant.

THURSDAY, *April* 5, 1804.

The Board met according to adjournment. Present: Ephraim Kirby, Robert C. Nicholas.

Adjourned until Friday, the 6th instant.

FRIDAY, *April* 6, 1804.

The Board met according to adjournment. Present: Ephraim Kirby, Robert C. Nicholas.

WILSON CARMAN's case, No. 131 on the docket of the Board, and No. 173 on the books of the Register.

Claim.—A right of pre-emption of six hundred and ninety-one acres and five poles, under the third section of the act.

The claimant presented his claim, together with a surveyor's plot of the land claimed, in the words and figures following, to wit:

To the Commissioners appointed in pursuance of an act of Congress, passed the 3d day of March, 1803, for receiving and adjusting claims to land south of the Tennessee, and east of the Pearl river.

Please to take notice, that the following tract of land, lying west of the Tombigbee river, butting and bounding as follows, viz.: beginning in and about fifteen chains below Fort Stoddert, on the said river, and running due west, forty chains, to a stake; thence, south, nine degrees east, one hundred and seven chains, to a stake; thence, east, eighteen chains, to a tupelo gum, a station in water; thence, calling for the mouth of the bayou Chouheala, from calculation, nineteen chains; thence, according to Lieutenant Gain's measurement, to the beginning: is claimed by Wilson Carman, under and by virtue of the third section of the above mentioned act of Congress for granting pre-emption lands. To all which he begs leave to refer, as also the copy of the plot now delivered to the Register of the Land Office to be established east of Pearl river, which plot is herewith filed.

W. CARMAN.

Fort Stoddert, *March* 31, 1804.

[Plot omitted.]

Chain carriers, Augustin Rochon and Nathan Blackwell. Surveyed March 31, 1804, by Robert Ligon.

Entered in record of claims, vol. 1, page 511, by Edward Lloyd Wailes, for

JOSEPH CHAMBERS, *Register.*

The said Rochon and Blackwell, chain carriers for the preceding survey, were sworn before James Callier, Justice of the Peace.

Captain James Sterret and Godfrey Bartles were presented as witnesses, and, being duly sworn and interrogated by the Board, they deposed, that they were not interested in this case.

The said Sterret testified, that in November, 1802, he came to Fort Stoddert to pay the troops, when the present claimant lived upon the land now claimed; that he was at that time the head of a family, and more than twenty-one years of age; and that having lately come to Fort Stoddert, he found the claimant living at the same place; and that he had, as Sterret believed, lived there ever since he first saw him.

The said Bartles testified, that Wilson Carman, the present claimant, had, for several years last past, cultivated and resided upon the land in question, and in particular on the 3d day of March, 1803, and was at that time the head of a family.

The Board ordered that the case be postponed for consideration.

Simpson Whaley's case, No 132 on the docket of the Board, and No. 169 on the books of the Register.

Claim.—A right of pre-emption of one hundred acres, under the third section of the act.

The claimant presented his claim, together with a surveyor's plot of the land claimed, in the following words and figures, to wit:

To the Commissioners appointed in pursuance of the act of Congress passed the 3d of March, 1803, for receiving and adjusting claims to lands south of Tennessee, and east of Pearl river.

March 30, 1804.

Please to take notice, that the following tract of land, situate on the west side of the Mobile river, in the county of Washington, beginning at a pine on the side of a lake a little above Fort Stoddert, running west, eighty chains to a pine; thence, south, twelve chains fifty links to a lightwood stake; thence, east, eighty chains to a water oak, on the side of said lake; thence, up the said lake to the beginning; and has such form and marks, both natural and artificial, as are fully represented in the plot annexed; containing one hundred acres: is claimed by Simpson Whaley, in and by virtue of the said act of Congress; giving the right of pre-emption, and is now exhibited to the Register of the Land Office, established east of Pearl river, to be recorded as directed by said act. To all which he begs leave to refer, as also to the copy of the plot herewith filed.

SIMPSON WHALEY.

[Plot omitted.]

Surveyed 23d of March, 1804, by James Gordon. Chain bearers, Gabriel Tissrah and William Weathers.

Entered on record of claims, vol. 1, page 506, by Edward Lloyd Wailes, for

JOSEPH CHAMBERS, *Register.*

The above named chain carriers were sworn before James Callier, Esq., Justice of the Peace.

Wilson Carman and Godfrey Bartles were presented as witnesses, and, being duly sworn and interrogated by the Board, they deposed, that they had no interest in this case; that Simpson Whaley, the present claimant, began to improve upon the land by him claimed before the 3d of March, 1803: that he removed on to it in the spring of 1803, but could not positively say when; that he had resided and cultivated there to the present time; and that he was more than twenty-one years of age, and the head of a family.

James Gordon, surveyor, was produced as a witness, and, being duly sworn, deposed, that he surveyed and made the plot then exhibited to the Board, and believed it to be correctly made; that it included the house and improvement of the said claimant, and that he, Gordon, knew of no interfering lines or claims.

The Board ordered that the case be postponed for consideration.

Adjourned until Saturday the 7th instant.

Saturday, *April* 7, 1804.

The Board met according to adjournment. Present: Ephraim Kirby, Robert C. Nicholas.

Robert Ligon, surveyor, was presented as a witness, and, being duly sworn, deposed, that he made the surveys and plots returned to the Board of Commissioners by the following claimants, to wit: John Denley's pre-emption, six hundred and forty acres; Edward Creighton, representative of Benjamin King, pre-emption, thirty-two and six-tenths acres; George Dickey's pre-emption, six hundred and forty acres; Edward Creighton, representative of Isram Miller, donation, six hundred and forty acres; William McGrew's donation, six hundred and thirty-eight acres: Levin Haynsworth's pre-emption, three hundred and ninety-six acres; Solomon Johnson's donation, six hundred and forty acres; Clark McGrew's donation, six hundred and forty acres; Isaac Ryan's donation, six hundred and forty acres; Francis Boykin's Spanish warrant, eight hundred acres; Thomas Bassett's British grant, confirmed by Spanish warrant, one thousand and fifty acres. And that said plots respectively contained true representations of the land therein described, according to the best of his knowledge and belief, and did include the plantation and improvements of the several claimants; and that he knew of no interfering lines or claims.

The Board ordered that the said cases be postponed for consideration.

Wiley Barker, representative of Daniel Barker: case commenced in page 603.

Robert Ligon, surveyor, was presented as a witness, and, being duly sworn, deposed, that he made the survey and plot of the land in question, and believed it to be correct; that it included the buildings and cultivated fields of the claimant; that he, Ligon, had understood that this claim was interfered with on the lower or south line by a British grant, but did not know to what extent.

The Board ordered that the case be postponed for consideration.

Wilson Carman's case: commenced in page 669.

Robert Ligon, surveyor, was presented as a witness, and being duly sworn, deposed, that he made the survey and plot of the land in question, and that it was a correct representation thereof, according to the best of his knowledge and belief; that he believed that the whole of said survey was claimed by James Callier, Esq., as the representative of Joseph Campbell's wife.

The Board ordered that the case be postponed for consideration.

The Heirs of Charles Brewer: case commenced in page 607.

Robert Ligon, surveyor, was produced as a witness, and being duly sworn, deposed, that he surveyed and plotted the land in question, and that he believed the plot then exhibited to be correct, and that it included the improvements of the claimant: that he knew of no interfering claims or lines.

The Board ordered that the case be postponed for consideration.

Thomas Bassett, administrator of Nathaniel Bassett: case commenced in page 609.

Robert Ligon, surveyor, was presented as a witness, and, being duly sworn, deposed, that he made the survey and plot of the land in question, and that it was correct, according to his best knowledge and belief, and included the buildings noted on said plot; that he understood that the claim of Daniel Johnson interfered with this upon the upper or north line, and that the claim of Powel covered the southern part of said tract.

The Board ordered that the case be postponed for consideration.

Richard Lee, representative of Jordan Morgan: case commenced in page 602.

Robert Ligon, surveyor, was produced as a witness, and, being duly sworn, deposed, that he surveyed and plotted the land in question, and that he believed it was correct, and included the improvements of the claimant; that he understood that Hardy Wotton's claim interfered with this in part, but that he, Ligon, did not know to what extent, and knew of no other interference.

The Board ordered that the case be postponed for consideration.

WYCHE WATLEY, representative of Rebecca Kimbre: case commenced in page 603.

Robert Ligon, surveyor, was produced as a witness, and, being duly sworn, deposed, that he made the survey and plot of the land in question, and that it was correct, according to his knowledge and belief, and included the improvements of the claimant; that the said plot was at first interfered with by the claim of Richard Brashear; that the parties had since accommodated the business by mutual consent, and called him to witness the amicable adjustment which was made, by which Brashear withdrew his claim to that part which was first included in said survey; that Hardy Wotton had, as the deponent understood, exhibited a claim which covered the whole of said plot, and a part of three adjoining ones, viz.: Brashear's, Lee's and Hargrave's.

The Board ordered that the case be postponed for consideration.

RICHARD BRASHEAR's case: commenced in page 601.

Robert Ligon, surveyor, was presented as a witness, and, being duly sworn, deposed, that he made the survey and plot of the land in question; that it was true and correct, as he believed, and that it included the improvements of the claimant; that it also included a part of the claim of Wyche Watley; but that said Brashear, in the presence of said Ligon, agreed to waive his claim to all the land which said interference covered; that he knew of no other interference with his claim, except that he had heard that Hardy Wotton had run into a part of it.

The Board ordered that the case be postponed for consideration.

JAMES FRAZIER's case: commenced in page 623.

Robert Ligon, surveyor, was produced as a witness, and, being duly sworn, deposed, that he made the survey and a plot of the land in question, and believed it to be correct; that it included the principal part of the old improvement of the claimant, and five others, and part of the sixth; that the claims of Elisha Simmons, William Murrell, Ransom Harwell, and Joseph Westmoreland, and part of the claim of Raleigh Green, were included within said plot; and that, on the lower or south side, it also interfered with the claim of John Baker.

The Board ordered that the case be postponed for consideration.

JOHN BREWER's case: commenced in page 604.

Robert Ligon, surveyor, was presented as a witness, and, being duly sworn, deposed, that he made the survey and plot of the land in question, and believed it to be correct, and that it included the house and improvements of the claimant; that on the southeast side it interfered with the claim of Sanders Rea, about fifty acres; that he knew of no other interference.

The Board ordered that the case be postponed for consideration.

CONSTANT McGREW's case, No. 133 on the docket of the Board, and No. 71 on the books of the Register.

Claim.—A donation of six hundred and four acres, under the second section of the act.

The claimant presented her claim, together with a surveyor's plot of the land claimed, in the following words and figures, to wit:

To the Commissioners appointed in pursuance of the act of Congress passed the 3d day of March, 1803, for receiving and adjusting claims to lands south of Tennessee, and east of Pearl river.

MISSISSIPPI TERRITORY, Washington County: MARCH 2, 1804.

Please to take notice, that the following tract of land, situate on the west side of river Tombigbee, butting and bounded as follows: beginning on a corner of Doctor Chastang's lower line, on the bank of the river; thence, running south, twenty-five degrees west, along the said line, eighty chains, to a corner stake; thence, running south, sixty-five degrees east, eighty chains, to a corner pine on James McGrew's upper line; thence, north, eighteen degrees east, along the said James McGrew's line, eighty-one chains, to a corner cotton tree on the bank of the river, being James McGrew's upper corner; thence, the meanders of the river, to the beginning or station first mentioned; having such marks, natural and artificial, as are represented in the plot annexed, containing six hundred and four acres: is claimed by Constant McGrew, under and by virtue of occupancy; the said claimant having inhabited and cultivated the tract

herein specified agreeable to the second section of the act of Congress, entitled "An act regulating grants of land, and providing for the sale of lands of the United States," &c. and a long time previous to and after that time; and the same does not appear to be claimed by any of the preceding provisions of the act, and the said claimant was qualified agreeable to the requisitions of the law, and claims no other land in the territory, and now exhibited to the Register of the Land Office, established east of Pearl river, to be recorded as directed by the said act. All of which this claimant begs leave to refer, as also to the plot hereto fixed, &c. &c.

CONSTANT McGREW, her x mark.
[Plot omitted.]

Entered in record of claims, vol. 1, page 201, by EDWARD LLOYD WAILES, for

JOSEPH CHAMBERS, Register.

Robert Ligon, surveyor, was presented as a witness, and, being duly sworn, deposed, that he surveyed the land in question, but did not make the plot, and could not say as to its correctness; but knew, from the natural marks, that it included the improvements of the claimant; that the greatest part of this claim was also claimed by James Callier, as the assignee of Bryant and Snelgrove; that he knew of no other interference..

The Board ordered that the case be postponed for consideration.

JOHN FLOOD McGREW's case, No. 134 on the docket of the Board, and No. 165 on the books of the Register.

Claim.—A donation of six hundred and forty acres, under the second section of the act.

The claimant presented his claim, together with a surveyor's plot of the land claimed, in the following words and figures, to wit:

To the Commissioners appointed in pursuance of the act of Congress passed the 3d day of March, 1803, for receiving and adjusting the claims to lands east of Pearl river, and south of Tennessee.

Please to take notice, that the following tract of land, situated on the north fork of Tawler creek, in the county of Washington, on the west side of Tombigbee; beginning at a hickory, running thence, south, sixty-four degrees west, ninety chains, to a corner post oak; thence, north, twenty-six degrees west, seventy chains to a corner black jack; thence, north, sixty-four degrees east, ninety chains, to a stake corner; thence, south, twenty-six degrees east, seventy chains, to the beginning; containing six hundred and thirty acres, having such shape, form, and marks, natural and artificial, as are represented in the plot annexed: is claimed by John Flood McGrew, in and by virtue of the second section of the said act of Congress, and is now exhibited to the Register of the Land Office east of Pearl river, to be recorded as directed by said act. To all which he begs leave to refer, as also to a copy of the plot annexed.

J. F. McGREW.

MARCH 29, 1804.
[Plot omitted.]

Surveyed by me, Robert Ligon.

Entered in record of claims, vol. 1, page 498, by EDWARD LLOYD WAILES, for

JOSEPH CHAMBERS, Register.

Robert Ligon, surveyor, was produced as a witness, and, being duly sworn, deposed, that he made the survey and plot of the land in question, and believed it to be correct, and that it included a small improvement; that he understood that the claim of John Gordon interfered with this in a small degree, on the northeast side; that he knew of no other interference.

The Board ordered that the case be postponed for consideration.

JOHN HINES's case, No. 135 on the docket of the Board, and No. 167 on the books of the Register.

Claim.—A donation of six hundred and forty acres, as representative of Frederick Smith, under the second section of the act.

The claimant presented his claim, together with a surveyor's plot of the land claimed, in the following words and figures, to wit:

To the Commissioners appointed in pursuance of the act of Congress passed the 3d of March 1803, for receiving and adjusting claims to lands south of the river Tennessee, and east of Pearl river.

Please to take notice, that the following tract of land, situated on the west side of Tombigbee, in the county of Washington, beginning at James Denley's, and running south, twenty degrees west, one hundred and fifteen chains; thence, north, seventy degrees west, twenty-five chains fifty links; thence, north, twenty degrees east, one hundred and thirty chains, to a sweet gum; thence, with a straight line, twenty-five chains fifty links, to a sweet gum on the river; thence, with the river, to the beginning: containing six hundred and forty acres; having such shape, form, and marks, both natural and artificial, as are represented in the plot annexed: is claimed by John Hines, representative of Frederick Smith, in and by virtue of the second section of the act, as a donation, and is now exhibited to the Register of the Land Office established east of Pearl river, to be recorded as directed by said act. To all which he begs leave to refer, as also to a copy of the plot herewith filed.

JOHN DENLEY, for
JOHN HINES,
Representative of Frederick Smith.
MARCH 28, 1804.

[Plot omitted.]
Surveyed the 26th March, 1804, by Robert Ligon. Chain carriers, James Denley and James Donley.
Entered in record of claims, vol. 1, page 500, by EDWARD LLOYD WAILES, for
JOSEPH CHAMBERS, *Register.*
The claimant exhibited two writings, in the following words and figures, to wit:
Know all men by these presents, that I, Thomas Ware, have bargained and sold to Daniel Kannady an improvement made by John Wheat on the river joining Captain Hargrave's: likewise, he doth warrant and defend it from James Lovel and his heirs, this 12th day of November, 1802.

THOMAS WARE.
Test: HEZEKIAH CARTER, his x mark.
Know all men by these presents, that I, Daniel Kannady, do bargain and sell unto George Farrar a certain tract of land, that I, Daniel Kannady, did buy of Thomas Ware, formerly called Smith's improvement, below the Sunflower. I, Daniel Kannady, warrant and defend it from James Lovel, or his heirs or assigns, this 17th day of December, 1804.

DANIEL KANNADY.
Witness: BEN. BALDWIN.
Upon the back of the last recited writing is an endorsement in the words and figures following, to wit:
For and in consideration of the sum of fifty dollars, to me in hand paid, I do sell unto John Hines the within bill of sale, and all and every thing claimed thereby, as given under my hand this 14th of March, 1804.

GEORGE FARRAR.
Robert Ligon, surveyor, was presented as a witness, and, being duly sworn, deposed, that he made the survey and plot of the land in question; that it was true and correct, as he believed; that it included the improvements of the claimant; that he understood that that part of said land which adjoins the river was claimed by John Kennedy; that he had not heard of any other interfering claim.
Benjamin Baldwin and Richard Brashears were presented as witnesses, and, being duly sworn, they deposed, that they were not interested in the establishment of this claim. The said Baldwin testified, that the first knowledge he had of said land was about the month of July, 1802; that he believed that there was no person then living upon it, and, not having a general knowledge of the plot, could not say that he knew that any person lived upon the land in question at any time since he first saw it, until lately a Mr. Hills, he thought, had moved on to it. The said Brashears testified, that, according to the best of his knowledge, Frederick Smith settled upon the land in question, in the year 1797, at the place called the Old Field; that the next year his wife was wounded and scalped by the Indians at that place, after which he removed off; and that he, Brashears, did not know any thing of the succession of occupants since that time.
James Denley was produced as a witness, and, being duly sworn, deposed, that, to the best of his knowledge, Frederick Smith settled upon the land in question in the year 1797; that he never saw Smith's house or improvement; but he believed that he had made some improvement; that said Smith sold his claim to this improvement to John Wheat for one gallon of *taffia.*
The Board ordered that the case be postponed for consideration.
Adjourned until Monday the 9th instant.

MONDAY, *April* 9, 1804.
The Board met according to adjournment. Present: Ephraim Kirby, Robert C. Nicholas.

ALEXANDER McCULLAGH's case, No. 136 on the docket of the Board, and No. 1 on the books of the Register.
Claim—Of two hundred acres of land, by virtue of a British grant, under the first section of the act.
The claimant presented his claim, together with a surveyor's plot of the land, in the following words and figures, to wit:
To the Commissioners appointed for receiving and adjusting claims to lands in the Mississippi territory by virtue of an act of Congress passed the 3d day of March, 1803.
GENTLEMEN:
Be pleased to take notice, that the following tract of land, situate, lying, and being within the Mississippi territory is claimed by Alexander McCullagh, nephew and heir at law of Alexander McCullagh, formerly of Pensacola, in the province of West Florida, deceased, who died intestate, and that the grant mentioned in the following list or schedule, and now delivered to the Register of the Land Office, opened under and by virtue of the said act for lands lying east of Pearl river, together with a copy of the plot for the same, now also delivered in said office, will evince his right and title to said tract of land. To all which, for greater certainty, reference is hereby made.

ALEXR. McCULLAGH.
List or schedule of the tract of land referred to in the following notification, viz.: Lot No. 1, two hundred acres. This is a tract of two hundred acres of land, situate on the west side of the river Tombigbee, about three-quarters of a mile above McIntosh's bluff; bounded to the north by land of Adam Tate, on the south by land surveyed for Thomas Bassett, east by the river Tombigbee, and on the west by vacant land. The title to this land will appear by the original grant to Alexander McCullagh, bearing date the 6th of April, 1778, for two hundred acres of land, situated as above stated. A copy of the plot taken from the original grant of the above mentioned land is hereto annexed, and also herewith delivered into the Land Office.
[Plot omitted.]
GEORGE THE THIRD, *by the grace of God, of Great Britain, France, and Ireland, King, defender of the faith, and so forth. To all to whom these presents shall come, greeting:*
Whereas, our loving subject, Alexander McCullagh, in his humble petition, presented to our trusty and well beloved Peter Chester, Esquire, our Captain General and Governor-in-chief in and over our province of West Florida aforesaid, bearing date the 10th day of February, now last past, did set forth in substance, that, by virtue of our royal proclamation of the 17th day of October, in the third year of our reign, a certain Thomas Wigglesworth did, on the 13th day of February, which was in the year of our Lord 1776, obtain a warrant for surveying two hundred acres of land, in consideration of his services in America, last war, as a non-commissioned officer, and some time after departed this life: that, before his death, the said Thomas Wigglesworth did, for a valuable consideration, grant, bargain, sell, assign, transfer, and set over unto the petitioner, all his estate, right, title, and interest of, in, and unto the same tract of land of two hundred acres of land; and, on account of the death of the said Thomas Wigglesworth, as aforesaid, before the passing of a patent for the said lands, the said petitioner could not obtain proper titles thereto, unless the same was granted to himself, therefore prayed that our letters patent for the said tract might be made out and passed for the same unto, and in the name of, the said petitioner, his heirs, and assigns; which tract of land, so purchased by the said Alexander McCullagh from the said Thomas Wigglesworth before his decease, as aforesaid, we being willing to grant unto the said Alexander McCullagh, according to the prayer of this petition: *now know ye,* That we, of our special grace, certain knowledge, and mere motion, have given and granted, and by these presents, for us, our heirs and successors, do give and grant unto the said Alexander McCullagh, his heirs and assigns, all that tract of land herein before mentioned, situate on the west side of the river Tombigbee, about three quarters of a mile above McIntosh's bluff, bounded on the north by land surveyed for Adam Tate, on the south by land surveyed for Thomas Bassett, east by the river Tombigbee, and on the west by vacant land, in our province of West Florida, and having such shape, form, and marks, both natural and artificial, as are represented in the plot thereof hereunto annexed, as drawn by the Surveyor General of lands, which said tract of land contains two hundred acres, and is bounded as by the further certi-

ficate hereunto likewise annexed, under the hand of our said Surveyor General of lands in our said province, may more fully and at large appear; together with all woods, underwoods, timber, and timber-trees, lakes, ponds, fishing waters, water-courses, profits, commodities, hereditaments, and appurtenances whatsoever thereunto belonging or in any wise appertaining; together, also, with the privilege of hunting, hawking, and fowling in and upon the same, and all mines and minerals; reserving to us, our heirs and successors, all mines of gold and silver: to have and to hold the said tract of land, and all and singular the premises hereby granted, with the appurtenances, unto the said Alexander McCullagh, his heirs and assigns, in free and common soccage; yielding and paying unto us, our heirs and successors, or to the Receiver General of our customs, for the time being, or to such other officer as shall be appointed to receive the same, a quit-rent of one half-penny sterling, per acre, at the feast of St. Michael every year; the first payment to commence on the said feast of St. Michael which shall first happen after the expiration of ten years from the date hereof, or within fourteen days after annually: *Provided, always,* (and this present grant is upon condition,) *nevertheless,* That the said Alexander McCullagh, his heirs and assigns, shall and do, within three years after the date hereof, for every fifty acres of plantable land hereby granted, clear and cultivate three acres, at least, in that part thereof which he or they shall judge most convenient and advantageous, or else do clear and drain three acres of swampy or sunken ground, or do drain three acres of marsh, if any such shall be contained therein; and shall further, within the time aforesaid, put and keep upon every fifty acres thereof, accounted barren, three neat cattle, and continue the same thereon until three acres for every fifty acres be fully cleared and improved; and if it shall so happen that there be no part of the said tract of land fit for present cultivation, without manuring and improving the same, that if the said Alexander McCullagh, his heirs and assigns, shall, within three years from the date hereof, erect on some part of the said tract of land one good dwelling house, to contain at least twenty feet in length and sixteen in breadth, and put on his said land the like number of three neat cattle, as aforesaid, on every fifty acres therein contained; or, otherwise, if any part of the said tract of land shall be stony or rocky ground, not fit for pasture culture, shall and do, within three years, as aforesaid, besides erecting the said house, begin to employ thereon, and continue to work for three years then next ensuing, in digging in any stone quarry or mine, one good and able hand for every hundred acres thereof, it shall be accounted a sufficient cultivation and improvement: *Provided, also,* That every three acres which shall be cleared and worked, or cleared and drained, as aforesaid, shall further be accounted a sufficient seating, cultivation, and improvement, to save forever from forfeiture fifty acres of land, in any part of the tract hereby granted; and the said Alexander McCullagh, his heirs and assigns, shall be at liberty to withdraw his or their stock, or to forbear working in any quarry or mine, in proportion to such cultivation and improvements aforesaid, as shall be made upon the plantable lands, swamps, sunken grounds, or marshes therein contained: *Provided, also,* That this grant shall be duly registered in the Register's office in this province, within six months from the date hereof; and, also, that a docket thereof shall be entered in the Auditor's office, within the same time, if such establishment shall take place in this province. *Provided, always,* That the said Alexander McCullagh, his heirs and assigns, at any time hereafter, having seated, planted, cultivated, and improved the said land, or any part thereof, according to the directions and conditions above mentioned, and make proof of such seating, planting, cultivation, and improvement, in the general court, or the court of the county district or precinct where the land lieth, and have such proof certified to the Register's office, and there entered with the record of this grant, a copy of which, duly attested, shall be admitted on trial to prove the seating and planting the said land: *Provided always, nevertheless,* That if the said Alexander McCullagh, his heirs and assigns, do not in all things fully comply with and fulfil the respective directions and conditions herein above set forth, for the proper cultivation of the said land, within the time herein above limited for completion thereof; or if the said Alexander McCullagh, his heirs, or assigns, shall not pay to us, our heirs, or successors, or to the Receiver General of our quit-rents, or to the proper officer appointed to receive the same, the said quit-rent of one half-penny sterling per acre, on the said feast of St. Michael, or within fourteen days

after, annually, for every acre contained in this grant, that then, and in either of these cases respectively, this grant be void, any thing contained therein to the contrary notwithstanding; and the said lands, tenements, hereditaments, and premises hereby specified, and every part thereof, shall revert to us, our heirs and successors, fully and absolutely as if the same had not been granted.

Given under the great seal of our province of West Florida: Witness our trusty and well beloved Peter Chester, Esquire, our Captain General and Governor-in-chief in and over our said province, at Pensacola, this sixth day of April, in the year of our Lord one thousand seven hundred and seventy-eight, and the eighteenth year of our reign.

　　　　　　　　　　　　　PETER CHESTER.

Passed the Secretary's Office.
　　PH. LIVINGSTON, Jun., *Deputy Secretary.*

WEST FLORIDA, *ss.*
　Pursuant to a fiat from his excellency Peter Chester, Esquire, Captain General, Governor, and Commander-in-chief in and over His Majesty's province of West Florida, &c. to me directed, bearing date the 6th day of April, 1778, I have perused and inspected the within letters patent, and do hereby certify there is no error therein apparent to me.
　　　　　　　R. WEGG, *Attorney General.*

　　　　　　AUDITOR'S OFFICE, *April* 6, 1778.
　A docket of the within grant is entered in book B, folio 34.
　　　　　J. LORIMER, *Deputy Auditor.*

　　　　SECRETARY'S OFFICE, *April* 6, 1778.
WEST FLORIDA, *ss.*
　I do hereby certify, that the within letters patent, Surveyor General's certificate, and the certificate of the Attorney General, are recorded in the Secretary and Register's Office of the province of West Florida in liber A, No. 2, page 506, and examined and compared with the said record, by
　　PH. LIVINGSTON, Jun., *Deputy Secretary.*

　Entered in record of claims, vol. 1, page 1, by EDWARD LLOYD WAILES, for
　　　　　JOSEPH CHAMBERS, *Register.*

　The Board ordered that the case be postponed for further consideration.

　OTTO V. T. BARBERIE, attorney in fact for the heirs of Robert Farmar, case No. 137 on the docket of the Board, and No. 2 on the books of the Register.
　Claim—Of one thousand acres, by virtue of a British grant, under the first section of the act.
　The claimant presented his claim, together with a surveyor's plot of the land claimed, in the following words and figures, to wit:
To the Commissioners appointed in pursuance of the act of Congress passed the 3d day of March, 1803, *for receiving and adjusting the claims to lands south of Tennessee, and east of Pearl river.*
　Please to take notice, that the following tract of land, situated on the west side of the river Tombigbee, distant from the town of Mobile one hundred and thirty miles, bounded eastwardly by the river Tombigbee, northwardly by lands surveyed for Moses Kirkland and vacant land, and on all other sides by vacant land, and hath such forms and marks, both natural and artificial, as are represented in the plot annexed; containing one thousand acres, more or less: is claimed by Otto V. T. Barberie, of New York, attorney in fact for the heirs of Major Robert Farmar, under and by virtue of a British grant, dated the 6th August, 1778, now delivered to the Register of the Land Office established east of Pearl river, to be recorded as directed by said act. To all which he begs leave to refer, as also to a copy of the plot herewith filed.
　　　　　　　OTTO V. T. BARBERIE.
　　　　　　　[Plot omitted.]

WEST FLORIDA, *ss.*
GEORGE THE THIRD, *by the grace of God, of Great Britain, France, and Ireland, King, defender of the faith, &c. To all to whom these presents shall come, greeting:*
　Know ye, that we, of our special grace, certain knowledge, and mere motion, have given and granted, and, by these presents, for us, our heirs and successors, do give and grant unto Robert Farmar, his heirs and assigns, all that tract of land situated on the west side of the river Tombigbee, distant from the town of Mobile about one hundred and thirty miles, bounded eastwardly

by the river Tombigbee, northwardly by land surveyed for Moses Kirkland, and vacant land, and on all other sides by vacant land, in our province of West Florida, and having such shape, form, and marks, both natural and artificial, as are represented in the plot thereof hereunto annexed, as drawn by our Surveyor General of lands, which said tract of land contains one thousand acres, and is bounded as by the further certificate hereunto likewise annexed, under the hand of our Surveyor General of lands in our said province, may more fully and at large appear; together with all woods, underwoods, timber and timber trees, lakes, ponds, fishings, waters, water courses, profits, commodities, hereditaments, and appurtenances whatsoever thereunto belonging, or in anywise appertaining; together, also, with privilege of hunting, hawking, and fowling in and upon the same, and all mines and minerals; reserving unto us, our heirs and successors, all mines of gold and silver: to have and to hold the said tract of land, and all and singular the premises hereby granted, with the appurtenances, unto the said Robert Farmar, his heirs and assigns, forever, in free and common soccage; yielding and paying to us, our heirs, and successors, to the Receiver General of our quit-rents for the time being, or to such other officer as shall be appointed to receive the same, a quit-rent of one halfpenny sterling per acre, at the feast of St. Michael every year; the first payment to commence on the said feast of St. Michael which shall first happen after the expiration of two years from the date hereof, or within fourteen days after the said feast, annually: *Provided always*, (and this present grant is upon condition,) *nevertheless*, That the said Robert Farmar, his heirs and assigns, shall and do, within three years after the date thereof, for every fifty acres of plantable land hereby granted, clear and cultivate three acres, at least, in that part thereof which he or they shall judge most convenient and advantageous; or else do clear and drain three acres of swampy or sunken ground; or do drain three acres of marsh, if any such shall be contained therein; and shall further, within the time aforesaid, put and keep upon every fifty acres thereof accounted barren three neat cattle, and continue the same thereon, until three acres for every fifty acres be fully cleared and improved; and if it shall so happen that there be no part of the said land fit for present cultivation without manuring and improving the same, if the said Robert Farmar, his heirs and assigns, shall, within three years from the date hereof, erect on some part of the said tract of land one good dwelling house, to contain at least twenty feet in length and sixteen feet in breadth, and put on his said land the like number of three neat cattle, as aforesaid, on every fifty acres therein contained; or, otherwise, if any part of the said tract of land should be stony or rocky ground, not fit for culture or pasture, shall and do, within three years as aforesaid, besides erecting the said house, begin to employ thereon, and continue to work for three years then next ensuing, in digging in any stone quarry or mine, one good and able hand for every hundred acres thereof, it shall be accounted a sufficient cultivation and improvement: *Provided, also*, That every three acres which shall be cleared and worked or cleared and drained, as aforesaid, shall be accounted a sufficient seating, planting, cultivation, and improvement, to save forever from forfeiture fifty acres of land in any part of the tract hereby granted: and the said Robert Farmar, his heirs or assigns, shall be at liberty to withdraw his or their stock, or to forbear working in any quarry or mine, in proportion to such cultivation and improvements as shall be made upon the plantable lands, swamp, sunken grounds, or marshes therein contained: *Provided, also*, That this grant shall be duly registered in the Register's Office of this province, within six months from the date hereof; and also, that a docket thereof shall be entered in the Auditor's Office within the same time, if such establishment shall take place in this province: *Provided, always*, That the said Robert Farmar, his heirs and assigns, at any time hereafter, having seated, planted, cultivated, and improved the said land, or any part thereof, according to the directions and conditions above mentioned, may make proof of such seating, planting, cultivation, and improvement in the general court, or in the court of the county, district, or precinct where the land lieth, and have such proof certified in the Register's Office, and there entered with the record of this grant, a copy of which, duly attested, shall be admitted on trial, to prove the seating and planting of the said land: *Provided always, nevertheless*, That if the said Robert Farmar, his heirs or assigns, do not in all things fully comply with and fulfil the respective directions and conditions herein above set forth, for the proper cultivation of the said

land, within the time herein above limited for the completion thereof; or, if the said Robert Farmar, his heirs or assigns, shall not pay to us, our heirs and successors, or to the Receiver General of our quit-rents, or to the proper officer appointed to receive the same, the said quit-rent of one halfpenny sterling per acre, on the said feast of St. Michael, or within fourteen days after, annually, for every acre contained in this grant; that then, and in either of these cases, respectively, this grant shall be void, any thing contained herein to the contrary notwithstanding; and the said lands, tenements, hereditaments, and premises hereby specified, and every part or parcel thereof, shall revert to us, our heirs and successors, fully and absolutely, as if the same had never been granted.

Given under the great seal of our province of West Florida: Witness our trusty and well beloved Peter Chester, Esquire, our Captain General, Governor, and Commander-in-chief in and over our said province, at Pensacola, this sixth day of August, in the year of our Lord one thousand seven hundred and seventy-eight, and in the eighteenth year of our reign.

[G. S.] PETER CHESTER.

Passed the Secretary's Office.
PH. LIVINGSTON, Jun., *Deputy Secretary*.

WEST FLORIDA, *ss.*

Pursuant to a fiat from his excellency Peter Chester, Esquire, Captain General, Governor, and Commander in-chief in and over His Majesty's province of West Florida, and to me directed, bearing date the sixth day of August, 1778, I have perused and inspected the within letters patent, and do hereby certify that there is no error therein apparent to me.
E. H. BAY, for
E. R. WEGG, *Attorney General*.

AUDITOR'S OFFICE, *August* 6, 1778
A docket of the within grant is entered in book B, folio 44, by
J. LORIMER, *Deputy Auditor*.

WEST FLORIDA, SECRETARY'S OFFICE,
August 6, 1778.
I do hereby certify that the within letters patent, Surveyor General's certificate, and the certificate of the Attorney General, are recorded in the Secretary and Register's Office of the province of West Florida, in liber A, No. 3, page 434. Examined and compared with the said record by
PH. LIVINGSTON, Jun., *Deputy Secretary*.

Entered in record of claims, volume 1, page 6, by
EDW. LLOYD WAILES, for
JOSEPH CHAMBERS, *Register*.

The Board ordered that the case be postponed for consideration.

OTTO V. T. BARBERIE, attorney in fact for the heirs of Robert Farmar, case No. 138 on the docket of the Board, and No. 3 on the books of the Register.
Claim—Of eight hundred acres, by virtue of a British grant, under the first section of the act.
The claimant presented his claim, with a surveyor's plot of the land claimed, in the following words and figures to wit:

To the Commissioners appointed in pursuance of the act of Congress passed the 3d *day of March*, 1803, *for receiving and adjusting the claims to lands south of Tennessee, and east of Pearl river.*

Please to take notice, that the following tract of land, situated on the west side of the river Tombigbee, at the high bluff, known by the name of Architcpy, adjoining the Choctaw boundary grant of land, bounded southwardly by the river Tombigbee, and on all other sides by vacant land; and hath such forms and marks, both natural and artificial, as are represented in the plot annexed, containing eight hundred acres, more or less: is claimed by Otto V. T. Barberie, of New York, attorney in fact for the heirs of Major Robert Farmar, under and in virtue of a British grant, dated the 6th day of August, 1778, now delivered to the Register of the Land Office established east of Pearl river, to be recorded as directed by said act. To all which he begs leave to refer, as also to a copy of the plot herewith filed.

OTTO V. T. BARBERIE.
FEBRUARY 8, 1804.
[Plot omitted.]

WEST FLORIDA, *ss.*

GEORGE THE THIRD, *by the grace of God, of Great Britain, France, and Ireland, King, defender of the faith, &c. To all to whom these presents shall come, greeting:*

Know ye, that we, of our special grace, certain knowledge, and mere motion, have given and granted, and by these presents, for us, our heirs and successors, do give and grant, unto Robert Farmar, his heirs and assigns, all that tract of land situated on the west side of the river Tombigbee, at the high bluff, known by the name of Architicpy, adjoining the Choctaw boundary grant of lands, [bounded] southwardly by the river Tombigbee, and on all other sides by vacant land, in our province of West Florida, and having such shape, form, and marks, both natural and artificial, as are represented in the plot thereof hereunto annexed, as drawn by our Surveyor General of lands; which said tract of land contains eight hundred acres, and is bounded as by the further certificate hereunto likewise annexed, under the hand of our said Surveyor General of lands in our said province, may more fully and at large appear, together with all woods, underwoods, timber, and timber trees, lakes, ponds, fishings, waters, watercourses, profits, commodities, hereditaments, and appurtenances whatsoever thereunto belonging, or in anywise appertaining; together also, with privileges of hunting, hawking, and fowling in and upon the same, and all mines and minerals, reserving to us, our heirs and successors, all mines of gold and silver: to have and to hold the said tract of land, and all and singular the premises hereby granted, with the appurtenances, unto the said Robert Farmar, his heirs and assigns, forever, in free and common soccage, yielding and paying unto us, our heirs and successors, or to the Receiver General of our quit-rents for the time being, or to such other officer as shall be appointed to receive the same, a quit-rent of one halfpenny sterling per acre, at the feast of St. Michael every year; the first payment to commence on the said feast of St. Michael which shall first happen after the expiration of two years from the date hereof, or within fourteen days after the said feast, annually: *Provided always,* (and this present grant is upon condition,) *nevertheless,* That the said Robert Farmar, his heirs or assigns, shall and do, within three years after the date hereof, for every fifty acres of plantable lands hereby granted, clear and cultivate three acres, at least, in that part thereof which he or they may judge most convenient and advantageous; or else do clear and drain three acres of swampy or sunken ground, or do drain three acres of marsh, if any such shall be contained therein; and shall further, within the time aforesaid, put and keep upon every fifty acres thereof accounted barren three neat cattle, and continue the same thereon, until three acres for every fifty acres be fully cleared and improved; and if it shall so happen that there be no part of the said tract of land fit for present cultivation, without manuring and improving the same, if the said Robert Farmar, his heirs or assigns, shall, within three years from the date hereof, erect on some part of the said tract of land one good dwelling house, to contain at least twenty feet in length and sixteen feet in breadth, and put on the said tract of land the like number of three neat cattle, as aforesaid, on every fifty acres herein contained; or, otherwise, if any part of the said land shall be stony or rocky ground, not fit for culture or pasture, shall and do, within three years, as aforesaid, besides erecting the said house, begin to employ thereon, and continue to work for three years then next ensuing, in digging in any stone quarry or mine, one good and able hand for every hundred acres thereof, it shall be accounted a sufficient seating, cultivation, and improvement, to save forever from forfeiture fifty acres of said land, in any part of the tract hereby granted.

And the said Robert Farmar, his heirs and assigns, shall be at liberty to withdraw his or their stock, or to forbear working in any quarry or mine, in proportion to such cultivation and improvement aforesaid, as shall be made upon the plantable lands, swamps, sunken grounds, or marshes therein contained: *Provided, also,* That this grant shall be duly registered in the Register's Office of this province within six months from the date hereof, and also that a docket thereof shall be entered in the Auditor's Office, within the same time, if such establishment shall take place in this province: *Provided always,* That the said Robert Farmar, his heirs and assigns, at any time hereafter, having seated, planted, cultivated, and improved the said land, or any part thereof, according to the directions and conditions above mentioned, may make proof of such seating, planting, cultivation, and improvement, in the general court, or in the court of the county, district, or precinct where the said land lieth, and have such proof certified to the Register's Office, and there entered with the record of this grant, a copy of which, duly attested, shall be admitted, on trial, to prove the seating and planting the said land : *Provided always, nevertheless,* That if the said Robert Farmar, his heirs and assigns, do not in all things fully comply with and fulfil the respective directions and conditions herein above set forth for the proper cultivation of the said land, within the time herein above limited for the completion thereof; or, if the said Robert Farmar, his heirs or assigns, shall not pay to us, our heirs and successors, or to the Receiver General of our quit-rents, or to the proper officer appointed to receive the same, the said quit-rent of one halfpenny sterling per acre on the said feast of St. Michael, or within fourteen days after, annually, for every acre contained in this grant; that then, and in either of these cases, respectively, this grant shall be void, any thing contained therein to the contrary notwithstanding; and the said lands, tenements, hereditaments, and premises, hereby specified, and every part and parcel thereof, shall revert to us, our heirs and successors, fully and absolutely, as if the same never had been granted.

Given under the great seal of our province of West Florida: Witness our trusty and well beloved Peter Chester, Esq., our Captain General, Governor, and Commander-in-chief in and over our said province, at Pensacola, this sixth day of August, in the year of our Lord one thousand seven hundred and seventy-eight, and in the eighteenth year of our reign.

[G. S.]   PETER CHESTER.

Passed the Secretary's office.

PH. LIVINGSTON, JR., *Dep. Secretary.*

WEST FLORIDA, *ss.*

Pursuant to a fiat from his excellency, Peter Chester, Esquire, Captain General, Governor, and Commander-in-chief in and over His Majesty's province of West Florida, &c., to me directed, bearing date the 6th day of August, 1778, I have perused and inspected the within letters patent, and do hereby certify that there is no error therein apparent to me.

E. R. WEGG, *Attorney General.*

AUDITOR'S OFFICE, *August* 6, 1788.

A docket of the within grant is entered in book B, folio 44.

J. LORIMER, *Deputy Auditor.*

WEST FLORIDA, SECRETARY'S OFFICE, *August* 6, 1778.

I do hereby certify that the within letters patent, Surveyor General's certificate, and the certificate of the Attorney General, are recorded in the Secretary and Register's Office of the province of West Florida, in liber A, page 433. Examined and compared with the said record, by

PH. LIVINGSTON, JR., *Dep. Secretary.*

Entered in record of claims, volume 1, page 13, by EDWARD LLOYD WAILES, for

JOSEPH CHAMBERS, *Register.*

The Board ordered that the case be postponed for consideration.

WILLIAM VARDEMAN's case, No. 139 on the docket of the Board, and No. 7 on the books of the Register.

Claim—Of three hundred acres, as assignee and legal representative of John Lott, Junior, by virtue of a British grant, under the first section of the act.

The claimant presented his claim, together with a plot of the land claimed, in the words and figures following, to wit:

To the Commissioners appointed in pursuance of the act of Congress passed the 3d day of March, 1803, for receiving and adjusting the claims to lands south of Tennessee, and east of Pearl river.

Please to take notice, that the following tract of land, situated on the waters of Tombigbee river, in the county of Washington, bounded on the west side by land surveyed for Jesse Wall, on the north by the river Tombigbee, and on the south by lands surveyed for Arthur Moor, and southwestwardly by vacant land, containing three hundred acres, having such shape, form and marks, both natural and artificial, as are fully represented in the plot annexed: is claimed by William Vardeman, legal representative of John Lott, by virtue of a British patent, and is now exhibited to the Register of the Land

Office east of Pearl river, to be recorded as directed by said act. To all which he begs leave to refer, as also to a copy of the plot herewith filed.

WM. VARDEMAN.

GEORGE THE THIRD, *by the grace of God, of Great Britain, France, and Ireland, King, defender of the faith, &c. To all to whom these presents shall come, greeting:*

Know ye, that we, of our special grace, certain knowledge, and mere motion, have given and granted, and, by these presents, for us, our heirs and successors, do give and grant, unto John Lott, Junior, his heirs and assigns, all that tract of land situated on the west side of the river Tombigbee, distant above the town of Mobile about one hundred and five miles, bounded on the west by land surveyed for Jesse Wall, north by the river Tombigbee, southeastwardly by land surveyed for Arthur Moore, and southwestwardly by vacant land, in our said province of West Florida, and having such shape, form and marks, both natural and artificial, as are represented in plot thereof hereunto annexed, as drawn by our Surveyor General of lands; which said tract of land contains three hundred acres, and is bounded as by the further certificate hereunto likewise annexed, under the hand of our said Surveyor General of lands in our said province, may more fully and at large appear; together with all woods, underwoods, timber, and timber trees, lakes, ponds, fishings, waters, watercourses, profits, commodities, hereditaments, and appurtenances whatsoever thereunto belonging, or in any wise appertaining; together, also, with privilege of hunting, hawking, and fowling in and upon the same, and all mines and minerals, reserving to us, our heirs and successors, all mines of gold and silver: to have and to hold the said tract of land, and all and singular the premises hereby granted, with the appurtenances, unto the said John Lott, Junior, his heirs and assigns, forever, in free and common soccage; yielding and paying unto us, our heirs and successors, or to the Receiver General of our quitrents for the time being, or to such other officer as shall be appointed to receive the same, a quit-rent of one halfpenny sterling per acre, at the feast of St. Michael every year; the first payment to commence on the said feast of St. Michael, which shall first happen after the expiration of ten years from the date hereof, or within fourteen days after the said feast, annually: *Provided always,* (and this present grant is upon condition,) *nevertheless,* That this grant shall be duly registered in the Register's Office in this province, within six months from the date hereof, and also that a docket thereof shall be entered in the Auditor's Office within the same time, if such establishment shall take place in this province: *Provided, also,* That if the said John Lott, Junior, his heirs and assigns, do not in all things fully comply with and fulfil the conditions herein above set forth for the registering this grant, within the time herein above limited for the completion thereof; or, if the said John Lott, Junior, his heirs or assigns, shall not pay to us, our heirs and successors, or to the Receiver General of our quit-rents, or to the proper officer as shall be appointed to receive the same, the said quit-rent of one half penny sterling per acre, on the said feast of St. Michael, or within fourteen days thereafter, annually, for every acre contained in this grant; that then, and in either of these cases, respectively, this grant shall be void, any thing therein contained to the contrary notwithstanding; and the said lands, tenements, and hereditaments, hereby specified, and every part and parcel thereof, shall revert to us, our heirs, and successors, fully and absolutely, as if the same had never been granted.

Given under the great seal of our province of West Florida: Witness our trusty and well beloved Peter Chester, Esquire, our Captain General, Governor, and Commander-in-chief in and over our said province, at Pensacola, the sixteenth day of February, in the year of our Lord one thousand seven hundred and seventy-eight, and the eighteenth year of our reign.

[G. S.] PETER CHESTER.

Passed the Secretary's office.

PH. LIVINGSTON, JUN. Dep. Sec.

WEST FLORIDA, ss.

Pursuant to a fiat from his excellency Peter Chester, Esquire, Captain-General and Governor-in-chief in and over His Majesty's province of West Florida, &c. to me directed, bearing the date 16th day of February, 1778, I have perused and inspected the within letters patent, and do certify that there is no error therein apparent to me.

E. R. WEGG, *Attorney General.*

AUDITOR'S OFFICE, *February* 16, 1778.
A docket of the within grant is entered in book B, folio 29.

J. LORIMER, *Deputy Auditor.*

PENSACOLA, SECRETARY'S OFFICE, *February* 16, 1778.
I do hereby certify that the within letters patent, Surveyor General's certificate, together with the certificate of the Attorney General, are recorded in the Secretary and Register's Office of the province of West Florida, in liber A, No. 2, page 468, &c.
Examined and compared with the said record, by
PH. LIVINGSTON, JUN., *Deputy Secretary.*
[Plot omitted.]

Entered in record of claims, vol. 1, page 23, by EDWARD LLOYD WAILES, for

JOSEPH CHAMBERS, *Register.*

The claimant exhibited deeds of lease and release from John Lott, Jun., bearing date the 24th and 25th of September, 1780, duly executed, conveying to Hubard Rees and John Whitehead all the said John Lott's right, title, and interest in and to said tract of land.

Also, exhibited a deed of conveyance from John Whitehead, bearing date the 27th day of October, 1800, duly executed, conveying to William Vardeman all the said Whitehead's right, title, and interest in and to the said tract of land.

The Board ordered that the case be postponed for consideration.

The HEIRS OF JOHN McINTOSH, case No. 140 on the docket of the Board, and No. 24 on the books of the Register.

Claim—Of five hundred acres, by virtue of a British grant, under the first section of the act.

The claimants presented their claim, together with a surveyor's plot of the land claimed, in the following words and figures, to wit:

To the Commissioners appointed in pursuance of the act of Congress passed the 3d day of March, 1803, *for receiving and adjusting the claims to lands south of Tennessee, and east of Pearl river.*

Please to take notice, that the following tract of land, situated as follows: beginning on or below the east end of bluff of the Tomies, or Turkey bluff, on a willow corner, on the river bank; thence, a line of marked trees, south, seventeen degrees east, one hundred and twenty-two Gunter's chains forty-six links, to a corner gum; thence, south, seventy-three degrees west, forty chains twenty-eight links, to an oak corner; thence, north, seventeen degrees west, one hundred and twenty-two chains forty-six links, to a corner oak on the river bank; thence, the meanders of the river Tombigbee, to the first mentioned station, having such marks, natural and artificial, as are represented in the plot annexed, containing five hundred acres: is claimed by the legal representatives of John McIntosh, deceased, under and by virtue of a British patent, legally and fully executed, bearing date the twelfth day of September, 1775, and now exhibited to the Register of the Land Office, established east of Pearl river, to be recorded as directed by said act. To all which they beg leave to refer, as also to a copy of the plot herewith filed.

Exhibited by
EDWIN LEWIS,
For the heirs.
[Plot omitted.]

WEST FLORIDA, ss.

GEORGE THE THIRD, *by the grace of God, of Great Britain, France, and Ireland, King, defender of the faith, &c. To all whom these presents shall come, greeting:*

Know ye, that we, of our special grace, certain knowledge, and mere motion, have given and granted, and, by these presents, do give and grant, unto John McIntosh, his heirs and assigns, all that tract of land situated on the west side of the river Tombigbee, about sixty-three miles northwardly from the town of Mobile, on the east end of the bluff of the Tomies, or Turkey bluff, butting and bounding northwestwardly by the said river, and on all other sides by vacant land, in our province of West Florida, and having such shape, form, and marks, both natural and artificial, as are represented in the plot annexed, as drawn by our Surveyor General of lands in our said province of West Florida; which said tract of land contains five hundred acres, and is bounded, as by the further certificate hereunto likewise annexed, under the hand of our said Surveyor General of lands in our said province of West Florida, may more fully and at large appear; together with all woods, underwoods, timber, and timber trees, lakes, ponds, fishings, waters, water courses, profits, commodities, hereditaments, and appurtenances whatsoever thereunto belonging, or in anywise appertaining; together, also, with the privilege of hunting, hawking, and fowling in and upon the same, and all mines and minerals; reserving unto us, our heirs and successors, all mines of gold and silver: to have and to hold the said tract of land, and all and singular the premises hereby granted, with the appurtenances, unto the said John McIntosh, his heirs and assigns, forever, in free and common soccage, yielding and paying unto us, our heirs and successors, or to the Receiver General of our quit-rents for the time being, or to such other officer as shall be appointed to receive the same, a quit-rent of one halfpenny sterling per acre, at the feast of St. Michael every year; the first payment to commence on the said feast of St. Michael which shall first happen after the expiration of two years from the date hereof, or within fourteen days after the said feast, annually: *Provided always*, (and this present grant is upon condition,) *nevertheless*, That the said John McIntosh, his heirs and assigns, shall and do, within three years after the date hereof, for every fifty acres of plantable land hereby granted, clear and cultivate three acres, at least, in that part thereof which he or they shall judge most convenient and advantageous; or else do clear and drain three acres of swampy or sunken ground, or do drain three acres of marsh, if any such shall be contained therein; and shall further, within the time aforesaid, put and keep upon every fifty acres thereof accounted barren three neat cattle, and continue the same thereon, until three acres for every fifty acres be fully cleared and improved; and if it shall so happen that there be no part of the said tract of land fit for present cultivation, without manuring and improving the same, if the said John McIntosh, his heirs or assigns, shall, within three years from the date hereof, erect on some part of the said tract of land one good dwelling house, to contain at least twenty feet in length and sixteen feet in breadth, and put on his said land the like number of three neat cattle, as aforesaid, on every fifty acres therein contained: or otherwise, if any part of the said tract of land shall be stony or rocky ground, not fit for culture or pasture, shall and do, within three years, as aforesaid, besides erecting the said house, begin to employ thereon, and continue to work for three years then next ensuing, in digging any stone quarry or mine, one good and able hand for every fifty acres thereof, it shall be accounted a sufficient cultivation and improvement; to save forever from forfeiture fifty acres of land in any part of the tract hereby granted; and the said John McIntosh, his heirs and assigns, shall be at liberty to withdraw his or their stock, or to forbear working in any quarry or mine, in proportion to such cultivation and improvements aforesaid, as shall be made upon the plantable lands, swamps, sunken grounds, or marshes therein contained : *Provided, also*, That this grant shall be duly registered in the Register's Office of this province, within six months from the date hereof, and also that a docket thereof shall be entered in the Auditor's within the same time, if such establishment shall take place in this province: *Provided always*, That the said John McIntosh, his heirs and assigns, at any time hereafter, having seated, planted, cultivated, and improved the said land, or any part thereof, agreeable to the directions and conditions above mentioned, and make proof of such seating, planting, cultivation, and improvement, in the general court, or in the court of the county, district, or precinct where the said land lieth, and have such proof certified to the Register's Office, and there entered with the record of this grant, a copy of which, duly attested, shall be admitted on trial, to prove the seating and planting the said land : *Provided always, nevertheless*, That if the said John McIntosh, his heirs and assigns, do not in all things fully comply with and fulfil the respective directions and conditions herein above set forth for the proper cultivation of the said land, within the time limited for the completion thereof ; or, if the said John McIntosh, his heirs or assigns, shall not pay to us, our heirs and successors, or to the Receiver General of our quit-rents, or to the proper officer appointed to receive the same, the said quit-rent of one halfpenny sterling per acre on the said feast of St. Michael, or within fourteen days after, annually, for every acre contained in this grant; that then, and in either of these cases, respectively, this grant shall be void, any thing therein contained to the contrary notwithstanding; and the said lands, tenements, and premises, hereby specified, and every part or parcel thereof, shall revert to us, our heirs and successors, fully and absolutely, as if the same never had been granted.

Given under the great seal of our province of West Florida: Witness our trusty and well beloved Peter Chester, Esq. our Captain General, Governor, and Commander-in-chief in and over our said province, at Pensacola, this twelfth day of September, in the year of our Lord 1775, and in the fifteenth year of our reign.

[G. S.] PETER CHESTER.

Pursuant to a fiat from his excellency Peter Chester, Esquire, Captain General, Governor, and Commander-in-Chief in and over His Majesty's province of West Florida, &c. to me directed, bearing date the 12th day of September, 1775, I have perused and inspected the within letters patent, and do certify that there is no error therein apparent to me.

E. R. WEGG, *Attorney General.*

WEST FLORIDA, SECRETARY'S OFFICE, *September* 12, 1775.

I do hereby certify that the within letters patent, Surveyor General's certificate, and the certificate of the Attorney General, are recorded in the Secretary and Register's Office of the province of West Florida, in liber A, No. 3, page 111.

Examined and compared with the said record by

ALEXANDER McCULLAGH, *Dep. Sec.*

Entered in record of claims, vol. 1, page 24, by EDWARD LLOYD WAILES, for

JOSEPH CHAMBERS, *Register.*

The Board ordered that the case be postponed for consideration.

ELIHU HALL BAY's case, No. 141 on the docket of the Board, and No. 113 on the books of the Register.

Claim—Of one hundred and seventy-three acres, as assignee and legal representative of William Fradgley, by virtue of a British grant, under the first section of the act.

The claimant presented his claim, together with a surveyor's plot of the land claimed, in the following words and figures, to wit:

To the honorable the Commissioners appointed in pursuance of the act of Congress passed the 3d day of March, 1803, *for receiving and adjusting claims to lands south of Tennessee, and east of Pearl river.*

DECEMBER 20, 1803.

GENTLEMEN:

Please to take notice, that the following tract of land, on the west side of Tombigbee river, for one hundred and seventy-three acres, about sixty-two miles above the town of Mobile, butting and bounding (at the time of survey,) westwardly on lands granted to John McIntosh, northwardly on said river, and on all other sides by vacant lands: is claimed by Elihu Hall Bay, of Charleston, South Carolina, under and by virtue of a grant to one William Fradgley under the great seal of West Florida, signed by Governor Chester, dated the 15th March, 1776; also a lease and release from the grantee to Elihu Hall Bay, the claimant for the same, as may appear by the original grant and conveyance now delivered unto the Register of the Land Office, now established east of Pearl river, to be recorded as directed by the said act. To all which he begs leave to refer, as also to a copy of the plot annexed to the original grant, herewith filed.

ELIHU H. BAY.

[Plot omitted.]

WEST FLORIDA, *ss.*

GEORGE THE THIRD, *by the grace of God, of Great Britain, France, and Ireland, King, defender of the faith, &c. To all to whom these presents shall come, greeting:*

Know ye, that we, of our special grace, certain knowledge, and mere motion, have given and granted, and, by these presents, for us, our heirs and successors, do give and grant, unto William Fradgley, a reduced non-commissioned officer, his heirs and assigns, all that tract of land situated on the west of the river Tombigbee, about sixty-two miles above Mobile, butting and bounding westwardly on land granted unto John McIntosh, northerly on said river, and on all other sides by vacant land, in our province of West Florida, and having such shape, form, and marks, both natural and artificial, as are represented in the plot thereof hereunto annexed, as drawn by our Surveyor General of lands; which said tract of land contains one hundred and seventy-three acres, and is bounded as by the further certificate hereunto likewise annexed, under the hand of our Surveyor General of lands in our said province, may more fully and at large appear; together with all woods, underwoods, timber, and timber trees, lakes, ponds, fishings, waters, water courses, profits, commodities, hereditaments, and appurtenances whatsoever thereunto belonging, or in anywise appertaining; together, also, with privilege of hunting, hawking, and fowling in and upon the same, and all mines and minerals; reserving to us, our heirs and successors, all mines of gold and silver: to have and to hold the said tract of land, and all and singular the premises hereby granted, with the appurtenances, unto the said William Fradgley, his heirs and assigns, forever, in free and common soccage; yielding and paying unto us, our heirs and successors, or to the Receiver General of our quit-rents for the time being, or to such other officer as shall be appointed to receive the same, a quit-rent of one halfpenny sterling per acre, at the feast of St. Michael every year; the first payment to commence on the said feast of St. Michael which shall first happen after the expiration of ten years from the date hereof, or within fourteen days after, annually: *Provided always*, (and this present grant is upon condition) *nevertheless*, That the said William Fradgley, his heirs or assigns, shall and do, within three years after the date hereof, for every fifty acres of plantable land hereby granted, clear and cultivate three acres, at least, in that part thereof which he or they shall judge most convenient and advantageous, or else do clear and drain three acres of swampy or sunken ground, or do drain three acres of marsh, if any such shall be contained therein: and shall farther, within the time aforesaid, put and keep upon every fifty acres thereof accounted barren three neat cattle, and continue the same thereon, until three acres for every fifty acres be fully cleared and improved; and if it shall so happen that there be no part of the said tract of land fit for present cultivation, without manuring and improving the same, if the said William Fradgley, his heirs and assigns, shall, within three years from the date hereof, erect on some part of the said tract of land one good dwelling house, to contain at least twenty feet in length and sixteen feet in breadth, and put on his said land the like number of three neat cattle, as aforesaid, on every fifty acres therein contained, or, otherwise, if any part of the said tract of land shall be stony and rocky ground, not fit for culture or pasture, shall and do, within three years, as aforesaid, besides erecting the said house, begin to employ thereon, and continue to work for three years then next ensuing, in digging any stone quarry or mine, one good and able hand for every hundred acres thereof, it shall be accounted a sufficient seating, cultivation, and improvement: *Provided also*, That every three acres which shall be cleared and worked, or cleared and drained, as aforesaid, shall further be accounted a sufficient seating, planting, cultivation, and improvement, to save forever from forfeiture fifty acres of land in any part of the tract hereby granted. And the said William Fradgley, his heirs and assigns, shall be at liberty to withdraw his or their stock, or to forbear working in any stone quarry or mine, in proportion to such cultivation and improvements aforesaid, as shall be made upon the plantable lands, swamps, sunken grounds, or marshes therein contained: *Provided, also*, that this grant shall be duly registered in the Register's Office within this province, in six months from the date hereof, and also a docket thereof shall be entered in the Auditor's office within the same time, if such establishment shall take place in this province: *Provided always*, That the said William Fradgley, his heirs and assigns, at any time hereafter, having seated, planted, cultivated, and improved the said land, or any part thereof, according to the directions and conditions above mentioned, may make proof of such seating, planting, cultivation, and improvement, in the general court, or in the court of the county, district, or precinct where the land lieth, and have such proof certified to the Register's Office, and there entered with the record of this grant, a copy of which, duly attested, shall be admitted on trial, to prove the seating and planting the said land: *Provided always*, *nevertheless*, That if the said William Fradgley, his heirs and assigns, do not in all things fully comply with and fulfil the respective directions and conditions herein above set forth for the proper cultivation of the said land, within the time herein above limited for the completion thereof; or, if the said William Fradgley, his heirs or assigns, shall not pay to us, our heirs and successors, or to the Receiver General of our quit-rents, or to the proper officer appointed to receive the same, the said quit-rent of one halfpenny sterling per acre, on the said feast of St. Michael, or within fourteen days after, annually, for every acre contained in this grant; that then, and in either of these cases, respectively, this grant shall be void, any thing therein contained to the contrary notwithstanding; and the said lands, tenements, hereditaments, and premises, hereby specified, and every part and parcel thereof, shall revert to us, our heirs and successors, fully and absolutely, as if the same never had been granted. This grant being in pursuance of our royal proclamation of the 7th day of October, in the third year of our reign.

Given under the great seal of our province of West Florida: Witness our trusty and beloved Peter Chester, Esquire, our Captain General, Governor, and Commander-in-chief in and over our said province, at Pensacola, this thirteenth day of March, in the year of our Lord one thousand seven hundred and seventy-six, and in the sixteenth year of our reign.

[G. S.] PETER CHESTER.

Passed the Secretary's Office.

PH. LIVINGSTON, JUN., *Deputy Secretary.*

WEST FLORIDA, *ss.*

Pursuant to a fiat from his excellency Peter Chester, Esquire, Captain General, Governor and Commander-in-chief in and over His Majesty's province of West Florida, &c., to me directed, bearing date the 13th day of March, 1776, I have perused and inspected the within letters patent, and hereby certify that there is no error therein apparent to me.

E. R. WEGG, *Attorney General, by*
E. H. BAY, *his Attorney.*

WEST FLORIDA, SECRETARY'S OFFICE, *March* 16, 1776.

I do hereby certify that the within letters patent, Surveyor General's certificate, and the certificate of the Attorney General, are recorded in the Secretary's and Register's Office of the province of West Florida, in liber A, No. 3. page 141.

Examined and compared with the said record by

PH. LIVINGSTON, JUN., *Deputy Secretary.*

The claimant exhibited deeds of lease and release from William Fradgley, bearing date the 14th and 15th of March, 1776, duly executed, conveying to the said Elihu Hall Bay all the said Fradgley's right, title, and interest in and to the said tract of land.

Entered in record of claims, vol. 1, page 350, by EDWAD LLOYD WAILES, for

JOSEPH CHAMBERS, *Register.*

The Board ordered that the case be postponed for consideration.

ELIHU HALL BAY's case, No. 142 on the docket of the Board, and No. 114 on the books of the Register.

Claim—Of twenty-seven acres of land, as assignee and legal representative of William Fradgley, by virtue of a British grant, under the first section of the act.

The claimant presented his claim, together with a surveyor's plot of the land claimed, in the following words and figures, to wit:

To the honorable Commissioners appointed in pursuance of the act of Congress passed the 3d day of March,1803, for receiving and adjusting claims to lands south of the Tennessee and east of Pearl river.

GENTLEMEN:

Please to take notice, that the following tract of land of twenty-seven acres, on the west side of Tombigbee river, about sixty-two miles above the town of Mobile, at a place known by the name of Tomies bluff; butting and bounding northerly on said river, northeastwardly on John McIntosh's land, and on all other sides by vacant land: is claimed by Elihu Hall Bay, of Charleston, South Carolina, under and by virtue of a grant to William Fradgley, dated the 15th March, 1776, for the same, and indentures of lease and release from Fradgley to E. H. Bay for this tract; which grant and indentures of lease and release are all now delivered unto the Register of the Land Office established east of Pearl river, as directed by said act, with a copy of the plot annexed to the original grant. To all which he begs leave to refer.

E. H. BAY.

DECEMBER 20, 1803.

[Plot omitted.]

A plot of twenty-seven acres of land on Tombigbee river, claimed by Elihu Hall Bay, of Charleston, South Carolina.

E. H. BAY.

DECEMBER 20, 1803.

WEST FLORIDA, ss.

GEORGE THE THIRD, *by the grace of God, of Great Britain, France, and Ireland, King, defender of the faith, &c. To all to whom these presents shall come, greeting:*

Know ye, that we, of our special grace, certain knowledge, and mere motion, have given and granted, and, by these presents, for us, our heirs and successors, do give and grant, unto William Fradgley, a reduced non-commissioned officer, his heirs and assigns, all that tract of land, situated northerly, about sixty-three miles above the town of Mobile, on the west side of Tombigbee river, at a place known by the name of Tomies bluff; butting and bounding northerly on the said river Tombigbee, and on all other sides by vacant land, in our province of West Florida; and having such shape, form, and marks, both natural and artificial, as are represented in the plot thereof hereunto annexed, as drawn by our Surveyor General of lands; which said tract of land contains twenty-seven acres, and is bounded as by the further certificate hereunto likewise annexed, under the hand of our said Surveyor General of lands in our said province, may more fully and at large appear: together with all woods, underwoods, timber, and timber-trees, lakes, ponds, fishings, waters, watercourses, profits, commodities, hereditaments, and appurtenances whatsoever thereunto belonging, or in anywise appertaining: together, also, with privilege of hunting, hawking, and fowling in and upon the same, and all mines and minerals, reserving to us, our heirs and successors, all mines of gold and silver: to have and to hold the said tract of land, and all and singular the premises hereby granted, with the appurtenances, unto the said William Fradgley, his heirs and assigns, forever, in free and common soccage; yielding and paying unto us, our heirs and successors, or to the Receiver General of our quit-rents for the time being, or to such other officer as shall be appointed to receive the same, a quit-rent of one halfpenny sterling per acre, at the feast of St. Michael every year; the first payment to commence on the said feast of St. Michael which shall first happen after the expiration of ten years from the date hereof, or within fourteen days after the said feast, annually : *Provided always,* (and this present grant is upon condition) *nevertheless,* That the said William Fradgley, his heirs and assigns, shall and do, within three years after the date hereof, for every fifty acres of plantable land hereby granted, clear and cultivate three acres, at least, in that part thereof which he or they may judge most convenient and advantageous, or else do clear and drain three acres of swampy or sunken ground, or do drain three acres of marsh, if any such shall be contained therein; and shall further, within the time aforesaid, put and keep upon every fifty acres thereof accounted barren three neat cattle, and continue the same thereon, until three acres for every fifty acres be fully cleared and improved; and if it shall so happen that there be no part of the said tract of land fit for present cultivation, without manuring and improving the same, if the said William Fradgley, his heirs or assigns, shall within three years from the date hereof, erect on some part of the said tract of land one good dwelling house, to contain at least twenty feet in length and sixteen feet in breadth, and put on his said land the like number of three neat cattle, as aforesaid, on every fifty acres therein contained ; or, otherwise, if any part of the said land shall be stony and rocky ground, not fit for culture or pasture, shall and do, within three years as aforesaid, besides erecting the said house, begin to employ thereon and continue to work for three years then next ensuing, in digging any stone quarry or mine, one good and able hand for every hundred acres thereof, it shall be accounted a sufficient cultivation and improvement : *Provided, also,* That every three acres which shall be cleared and drained, as aforesaid, shall further be accounted a sufficient seating, planting, cultivation and improvement, to save forever from forfeiture fifty acres of land in any part of the tract hereby granted; and the said William Fradgley, his heirs and assigns, shall be at liberty to withdraw his or their stock, or to forbear working in any quarry or mine, in proportion to such cultivation and improvements aforesaid as shall be made upon the plantable lands, swamps, sunken grounds, or marshes therein contained : *Provided, also,* That this grant shall be duly registered in the Register's Office within six months from the date hereof, and also a docket thereof shall be entered in the Auditor's Office within the same time, if such establishment shall take place in this province : *Provided, always,* That the said William Fradgley, his heirs and assigns, at any time hereafter, having seated, planted, cultivated, and improved the said land, or any part thereof, according to the directions and conditions above mentioned, may make proof of such seating, planting, cultivation, and improvement, in the general court, or the court of the county, district, or precinct where the said land lieth, and have such proof certified to the Register's Office, and there entered with the record of this grant, a copy of which, duly attested, shall be admitted on trial, to prove the seating and planting of the said land: *Provided always, nevertheless,* That if the said William Fradgley, his heirs and assigns, do not in all things fully comply with and fulfil the respective directions and conditions above set forth, for the proper cultivation of the said land, within the time hereunto above limited for the completion thereof; or, if the said William Fradgley, his heirs or assigns, shall not pay to us, our heirs and successors, or to the Receiver General of our quit-rents, or to the proper officer appointed to receive the same, the said quit-rent of one halfpenny sterling per acre, on the said feast of St. Michael, or within fourteen days after, annually, for every acre contained in this grant; that then, and in either of these cases respectively, this grant shall be void, any thing herein contained to the contrary notwithstanding ; and the said lands, tenements, hereditaments, and premises hereby specified, and every part and parcel thereof, shall revert to us, our heirs and successors, fully and absolutely, as if the same never had been granted. This grant being in pursuance of our royal proclamation of the seventh day of October, in the third year of our reign.

Given under the great seal of our province of West Florida: Witness our trusty and well beloved Peter Chester, Esquire, our Captain General, Governor, and Commander-in-chief in and over our said province, at Pensacola, this thirteenth day of March, in the year of our Lord one thousand seven hundred and seventy-six, and the sixteenth year of our reign.
[G. S.]   PETER CHESTER.

Passed the Secretary's Office.

PH. LIVINGSTON, JUN., *Dep. Sec.*

WEST FLORIDA, ss.

Pursuant to a fiat from his excellency Peter Chester, Esquire, Captain General, Governor, and Commander-in-chief in and over our Majesty's province of West Florida, &c. &c., to me directed, bearing date the thirteenth day of March, 1776, I have perused and inspected the within letters patent, and do hereby certify that there is no error therein apparent to me.

E. R. WEGG, *Atty. General, by*
ELIHU HALL BAY, *his Attorney.*

WEST FLORIDA, SECRETARY'S OFFICE, *March* —, 1776.

I do hereby certify, that the within letters patent, Surveyor General's certificate, and the certificate of the Attorney General, are recorded in the Secretary's and Register's Office of the province of West Florida, in liber A, No. 3, page 142.

Examined and compared with the said record by

PH. LIVINGSTON, JUN., *Dep. Sec.*

The claimant exhibited deeds of lease and release from William Fradgley, bearing date the 14th and 15th days of March, 1776, duly executed, conveying to the said Elihu Hall Bay all the said Fradgley's right, title, and interest, to the said tract of land.

Entered in record of claims, vol. 1, page 357, by EDWARD LLOYD WAILES, for

JOSEPH CHAMBERS, *Register.*

The Board ordered that the case be postponed for consideration.

ELIHU HALL BAY's case, No. 143 on the docket of the Board, and No. 115 on the books of the Register.

Claim—Of five hundred acres, as assignee and legal representative of John Sutherland, by virtue of a British grant, under the first section of the act.

The claimant presented his claim, together with a surveyor's plot of the land claimed, in the following words and figures, to wit:

To the Honorable the Commissioners appointed in pursuance of the act of Congress passed the 3d day of March, 1803, for receiving and adjusting claims to lands south of the river Tennessee, and east of Pearl river.

GENTLEMEN:

Please to take notice, that the following tract of land, situated on the west side of Tombigbee river, about one hundred and twelve miles above the town of Mobile, joining the Tombigbee river to the northeast, bounded on the northwest by lands surveyed to Charles Walker, and on the other two sides by vacant land; containing five hundred acres: is claimed by Elihu Hall Bay, of Charleston, South Carolina, under and by virtue of a grant, under the great seal of West Florida, dated the 22d October, 1779, to John Sutherland, signed by Governor Chester, a bargain and sale from John Sutherland, by Elihu Hall Bay, his attorney, to Henry Beaumont, dated the 13th day of November, 1779. Also, a bargain and sale from Henry Beaumont back to Elihu Hall Bay, for said tract of land, dated 15th of November, 1779; which grant and intermediate conveyances are all now delivered unto the Register of the Land Office established east of Pearl river, as directed by said act, with a copy of the plot of the said land to the original grant annexed. To all which he begs leave to refer.

E. H. BAY.

DECEMBER 20, 1803.

[Plot omitted.]

A plot of five hundred acres of land claimed by Elihu Hall Bay, of Charleston, South Carolina.

E. H. BAY.

DECEMBER 20, 1803.

WEST FLORIDA, ss.

GEORGE THE THIRD, *by the grace of God, of Great Britain, France, and Ireland, King, defender of the faith, &c.   To all to whom these presents shall come, greeting:*

Know ye, that we, of our special grace, certain knowledge, and mere motion, have given and granted, and, by these presents, for us, our heirs and successors, do give and grant, unto John Sutherland, a reduced master's mate in our navy, his heirs and assigns, all that tract of land, situated on the west side of the river Tombigbee, distant from the town of Mobile about one hundred and twelve miles, joining the river Tombigbee at the northeast, bounded on the northwest side by land surveyed for Chas. Walker, and on the other two sides by vacant land, in our province of West Florida, and having such shape, form, and marks, both natural and artificial, as are represented in the plot thereof hereunto annexed, as drawn by our Surveyor General of lands; which said tract of land contains five hundred acres, and is bounded as by the further certificate hereunto likewise annexed, under the hand of our said Surveyor General of lands, in our said province, may more fully and at large appear; together with all woods, underwoods, timber, and timber trees, lakes, ponds, fishings, waters, watercourses, profits, commodities, hereditaments, and appurtenances whatsoever thereunto belonging, or in any wise appertaining, together, also, with privilege of hunting, hawking, and fowling in and upon the same, and all mines and minerals; reserving to us, our heirs and successors, all mines of gold and silver: to have and to hold the said tract of land, and all and singular the premises hereby granted, with the appurtenances, unto the said John Sutherland, his heirs and assigns, forever, in free and common soccage, yielding and paying unto us, our heirs and successors, or to the Receiver General of our quit-rents for the time being, or to such other officer, as shall be appointed to receive the same, a quit-rent of one halfpenny sterling per acre, at the feast of St. Michael every year; the first payment to commence on the said feast of St. Michael, which shall first happen after the expiration of ten years from the date hereof, or within fourteen days after the said feast annually: *Provided always,* (and this present grant is upon condition,) *nevertheless:* That the said John Sutherland, his heirs or assigns, shall and do within three years after the date hereof, for every fifty acres of plantable land hereby granted, clear and cultivate three acres, at least, in that part thereof which he or they shall judge most convenient and advantageous; or else do clear and drain three acres of swampy or sunken ground, or do drain three acres of marsh, if any such shall be contained therein; and shall further, within the time aforesaid, put and keep upon every fifty acres thereof accounted barren three neat cattle, and continue the same thereon; until three acres for every fifty acres be fully cleared and improved; and if it shall so happen that there be no part of the said land fit for present cultivation, without manuring and improving the same, if the said John Sutherland, his heirs or assigns, shall, within three years from the date hereof, erect on some part of the said tract of land one good dwelling house, to contain at least twenty feet in length and sixteen feet in breadth, and put on his said land the like number of three neat cattle, as aforesaid, on every fifty acres therein contained; or, otherwise, if any part of the said tract of land shall be stony and rocky ground, not fit for culture or pasture, shall and do, within three years, as aforesaid, besides

erecting the said house, begin to employ thereon, and continue to work for three years then next ensuing, in digging any stone quarry or mine, one good and able hand for every hundred acres thereof, it shall be accounted a sufficient cultivation and improvement: *Provided also,* That every three acres which shall be cleared and worked, or cleared and drained, as aforesaid, shall further be accounted a sufficient seating, planting, cultivation, and improvement, to save forever from forfeiture fifty acres of land, in any part of the tract hereby granted; and the said John Sutherland, his heirs and assigns, shall be at liberty to withdraw his or their stock, or to forbear working in any stone quarry or mine in proportion to such cultivation and improvements as shall be made upon the plantable lands, swamps, sunken grounds, or marshes therein contained: *Provided also,* That this grant shall be duly registered in the Register's Office of this province within six months from the date hereof, and also, that a docket thereof shall be entered in the Auditor's Office within the same time, if such establishment shall take place in this province: *Provided, always,* That the said John Sutherland, his heirs and assigns, at any time hereafter, having seated, planted, cultivated, and improved the said land, or any part thereof, according to the directions and conditions above mentioned, may make proof of such seating, planting, cultivation, and improvement, in the general court, or in the court of the county, district, or precinct where the said land lieth, and have such proof certified to the Register's Office, and there entered with the record of this grant, a copy of which, duly attested, shall be admitted on trial to prove the seating, planting, cultivation, and improvement of the said land: *Provided, always, nevertheless,* That if the said John Sutherland, his heirs and assigns, do not in all things fully comply with and fulfil the respective directions and conditions herein above set forth for the proper cultivation of the said land, within the time herein above limited for the completion thereof; or, if the said John Sutherland, his heirs or assigns, shall not pay to us, our heirs and successors, or to the Receiver General of our quit-rents, or to the proper officer appointed to receive the same, the said quit-rent of one halfpenny sterling per acre, on the feast of St. Michael, or within fourteen days after, annually, for every acre contained in this grant; that then, and in either of these cases, respectively, this grant shall be void, any thing therein contained to the contrary notwithstanding; and the said lands, tenements, hereditaments, and premises, hereby specified, and every part and parcel thereof, shall revert to us, our heirs and successors, fully and absolutely, as if the same had never been granted. This grant being in pursuance of our royal proclamation of the seventh day of October, in the third year of our reign.

Given under the great seal of our province of West Florida: Witness our trusty and well beloved Peter Chester, Esquire, our Captain General, Governor, and Commander-in-chief in and over our said province, at Pensacola, this twenty-second day of October, in the year of our Lord one thousand seven hundred and seventy-nine, and in the nineteenth year of our reign.

[G. S.]　　　PETER CHESTER.

Passed the Secretary's Office.

ELIHU HALL BAY, *Deputy Secretary.*

WEST FLORIDA, ss.

Pursuant to a fiat from his excellency Peter Chester, Esquire, Captain General Governor, and Commander-in-chief in and over His Majesty's province of West Florida, &c., to me directed, bearing date the 22d day of October, 1779, I have perused and inspected the within letters patent, and do hereby certify that there is no error therein apparent to me.

E. G. WEGG, *Attorney General.*

WEST FLORIDA, SECRETARY'S OFFICE,
Pensacola, 22d *October,* 1779.

I do hereby certify, that the within letters patent, Surveyor General's certificate, and the certificate of the Attorney General, are recorded in the Secretary and Register's Office of the Province of West Florida, in liber A, No. 3, page 532.

Examined and compared with the said record, by

ELIHU HALL BAY,
Dep. Secretary and Register.

AUDITOR'S OFFICE, PENSACOLA, 22d *October,* 1779.

A docket of the within grant is entered in this office, in book B, page—by J. LORIMER, *Dep. Auditor.*

Entered in record of claims, vol. 1, page 374, by ED-WARD LLOYD WAILES, for

JOSEPH CHAMBERS, *Register.*

The claimant produced a deed of conveyance from John Sutherland, executed by Elihu Hall Bay, as attorney for said Sutherland, dated 13th day of November, 1779, conveying to Henry Beaumont all the said Sutherland's right, title, and claim to the said tract of land.

The claimant also produced a deed of conveyance from Henry Beaumont, bearing date the 15th day of November, 1779, conveying to Elihu Hall Bay all the said Beaumont's right, title, and claim to the said tract of land.

The Board ordered that the case be postponed for consideration.

AUGUSTIN ROCHON's heirs, case No. 144 on the docket of the Board, and No. 116 on the books of the Register.

Claim—Of two hundred and twenty-five acres of land, as the legal representatives of Augustin Rochon, deceased, by virtue of a British grant, under the first section of the act.

The claimants presented their claim, together with a surveyor's plot of the land claimed, in the following words and figures, to wit:

To the Commissioners appointed in pursuance of the act of Congress passed the 3d day of March, 1803, for receiving and adjusting claims to land south of Tennessee and east of Pearl river.

FORT STODDERT, *March* 12, 1804.

Please to take notice, that the following tract of land, lying west of Tombigbee river, butting and bounding northwardly by Lewis Forneret's land, southerly by Daniel Mortimer's land, eastwardly by said river, and on the other side by vacant land; about two miles above Nanna Hubba bluff, and about sixty-two miles from the town of Mobile: is claimed by Louise Rochon, widow, for and in behalf of the heirs of Augustin Rochon, deceased, under and by virtue of a British patent granted to Augustin Rochon, deceased, late husband of the said Louise, as may appear by the original patent now delivered to the Register of the Land Office to be established east of Pearl river, to be recorded as directed by said act. To all which he begs leave to refer, as also to a copy of the plot herewith filed.

AUGUSTIN ROCHON,
Attorney for Louise Rochon.
[Plot omitted.]

WEST FLORIDA, ss.

GEORGE THE THIRD, *by the grace of God, of Great Britain, France, and Ireland, King, defender of the faith, &c. To all to whom these presents shall come, greeting:*

Know ye, that we, of our special grace, certain knowledge, and mere motion, have given and granted, and, by these presents, for us, our heirs and successors, do give and grant, unto Augustin Rochon, his heirs and assigns, all that tract of land situated on the west side of the river Tombigbee, about two miles above the bluff of the Nanna Hubba, and about sixty-two miles above the town of Mobile, bounded northwardly by Lewis Forneret's land, southwardly by Daniel Mortimer's land, eastwardly by said river, and on the other side by vacant land, in our said province of West Florida, and having such shape, form, and marks, both natural and artificial, as are represented in the plot thereof hereunto annexed, as drawn by our Surveyor General of lands, in our said province of West Florida; which said tract of land contains two hundred and twenty-five acres, and is bounded as by the further certificate hereunto likewise annexed, under the hand of our said Surveyor General of lands in our said province, may more fully and at large appear: together with all woods, underwoods, timber, and timber trees, lakes, ponds, fishings, waters, water courses, profits, commodities, hereditaments, and appurtenances whatsoever thereunto belonging, or in anywise appertaining: together, also, with privilege of hunting, hawking, and fowling in and upon the same, and all mines and minerals, reserving to us, our heirs and successors, all mines of gold and silver: to have and to hold the said tract of land, and all and singular the premises hereby granted, with the appurtenances, unto the said Augustin Rochon, his heirs and assigns, forever, in free and common soccage, yielding and paying unto us, our heirs and successors, or to the Receiver General of our quit-rents for the time being, or to such other officer as shall be appointed to receive the same, a quit-rent of one halfpenny sterling per acre ,

at the feast of St. Michael every year; the first payment to commence on the said feast of St. Michael which shall first happen after the expiration of two years from the date hereof, or within fourteen days after the said feast, annually: *Provided always,* (and this present grant is upon condition,) *nevertheless,* That the said Augustin Rochon, his heirs or assigns, shall and do, within three years after the date hereof, for every fifty acres of plantable land hereby granted, clear and cultivate three acres, at least, in that part thereof which he or they shall judge most convenient and advantageous; or else do clear and drain three acres of swampy or sunken ground, or do drain three acres of marsh, if any such shall be contained therein; and shall further, within the time aforesaid, put and keep upon every fifty acres thereof accounted barren three neat cattle, and continue the same thereon, until three acres for every fifty be fully cleared and improved; and if it shall so happen that there be no part of the said land fit for present cultivation, without manuring and improving the same, if the said Augustin Rochon, his heirs and assigns, shall, within three years from the date hereof, erect on some part of the said tract of land one good dwelling house, to contain at least twenty feet in length and sixteen feet in breadth, and put on his said land the like number of three neat cattle, as aforesaid, on every fifty acres therein contained; or otherwise, if part of the said tract of land shall be stony or rocky ground, not fit for culture or pasture, shall and do, within three years, as aforesaid, besides erecting the said house, begin to employ thereon, and continue to work for three years then next ensuing, in digging any stone quarry or mine, one good and able hand for every hundred acres thereof, it shall be accounted a sufficient cultivation and improvement: *Provided also,* That every three acres which shall be cleared and worked, or cleared and drained, as aforesaid, shall further be accounted a sufficient seating, planting, cultivation, and improvement, to save forever from forfeiture fifty acres of land in any part of the said tract hereby granted. And the said Augustin Rochon, his heirs and assigns, shall be at liberty to withdraw his or their stock, or to forbear working in any quarry or mine, in proportion to such cultivation and improvements aforesaid as shall be made upon plantable lands, swamps, sunken grounds or marshes therein contained: *Provided always,* That this grant shall be duly registered in the Register's Office of this province, within six months from the date hereof, and also a docket thereof shall be entered in the Auditor's Office within the same time, if such establishment shall take place in this province: *Provided always,* That the said Augustin Rochon, his heirs and assigns, shall at any time hereafter, having seated, planted, cultivated, and improved the said land, or any part thereof, according to the directions and conditions above mentioned, may make proof of such seating, planting, cultivation, and improvement, in the general court, or in the court of the county, district, or precinct where the said land lieth; and have such proof certified to the Register's Office, and there entered with the record of this grant, a copy of which, duly attested, shall be admitted on trial, to prove the seating and planting of the said land: *Provided always, nevertheless,* That if the said Augustin Rochon, his heirs and assigns, do not in all things fully comply with and fulfil the respective directions and conditions herein above set forth, for the proper cultivation of the said land, within the time herein above limited for the completion thereof, or if the said Augustin Rochon, his heirs and assigns, shall not pay to us, our heirs and successors, or to the Receiver General of our quit-rents, or to the proper officer appointed to receive the same, the said quit-rent of one halfpenny sterling per acre, on the said feast of said St. Michael, or within fourteen days after the said feast, annually, for every acre contained in this grant; that then, and in either of these cases, respectively, this grant shall be void, any thing contained therein to the contrary notwithstanding; and the said lands, tenements, hereditaments, and premises, hereby specified, and every part and parcel thereof, shall revert to us, our heirs and successors, fully and absolutely, as if the same never had been granted:

Given under the great seal of our said province of West Florida: Witness our trusty and well beloved Peter Chester, Esq. our Captain General, Governor, and Commander-in-chief in and over our said province, at Pensacola, this fourth day of December, in the year of our Lord one thousand seven hundred and seventy-nine, and in the twentieth year of our reign.

[G. S.] PETER CHESTER.

Passed the Secretary's office.

ELIHU HALL BAY, *Dep. Sec'y.*

West Florida, ss.

Pursuant to a fiat from his excellency Peter Chester, Esquire, Captain General, Governor, and Commander-in-chief in and over His Majesty's province of West Florida, &c. &c. to me directed, bearing date the fourth day of December, 1779, I have perused and inspected the within letters patent, and do hereby certify that there is no error therein apparent to me.

E. R. WEGG, *Attorney General.*

West Florida, Secretary's Office,
Pensacola, 4th December, 1779.

I do hereby certify, that the within letters patent, Surveyor General's certificate, and the certificate of the Attorney General, are recorded in the Secretary and Register's Office of the province of West Florida, in liber A, No. 3, page 534.

Examined and compared with the said record, by

ELIHU HALL BAY, *Dep. Sec. and Reg*

Pensacola, Auditor's Office, *4th December,* 1779.

A docket of the within grant is entered in book B, page —, by

J. LORIMER, *Deputy Auditor.*

Entered in record of claims, vol. 1, page 393, by
Edward Lloyd Wailes, for
JOSEPH CHAMBERS, *Register.*

The Board ordered that the case be postponed for consideration.

The heirs of Augustin Rochon, case No. 145 on the docket of the Board, and No. 117 on the books of the Register.

Claim—Of five hundred and fifty acres of land, by virtue of a British patent, under the first section of the act.

The claimants presented their claim, together with a surveyor's plot of the land claimed, in the following words and figures, to wit:

To the Commissioners appointed in pursuance of the act of Congress passed the 3d day of March, 1803, *for receiving and adjusting the claims to lands south of Tennessee, and east of Pearl river.*

Fort Stoddert, *12th March,* 1804.

Please to take notice, that the following tract of land, lying west of the river Tensaw, butting and bounding on the north by land surveyed to Charles Parent; northwestward by land possessed by Lewis Duret; south by land possessed by John Trouillet, and southwestward by the river Tensaw, about thirty-six miles above the town of Mobile: is claimed by Louise Rochon, widow, for and in behalf of the heirs of Augustin Rochon, deceased, under and by virtue of a British patent granted to Augustin Rochon, deceased, late husband of the said Louise, as may appear by the original patent now delivered to the Register of the Land Office established east of Pearl river, to be recorded as directed by said act. To all which she begs leave to refer, as also to a copy of the plot herewith filed.

AUGUSTIN ROCHON, Attorney for
LOUISE ROCHON.
[Plot omitted.]

West Florida, ss.

GEORGE the Third, *by the grace of God, of Great Britain, France, and Ireland, King, Defender of the Faith, &c. To all to whom these presents shall come, greeting:*

Know ye, that we, of our special grace, certain knowledge, and mere motion, have given and granted; and, by these presents, for us, our heirs and successors, do give and grant, unto Augustin Rochon, his heirs and assigns, all that tract of land situated on the west side of the river Tensaw, about thirty-six miles above the town of Mobile, bounded on north by land surveyed to Charles Parent, northward by land surveyed to Lewis Duret, south by land possessed by John Trouillet, and southwestward by the river Tensaw, in our province of West Florida, and having such shape, form, and marks, both natural and artificial, as are represented in the plot thereof hereunto annexed, as drawn by our Surveyor of lands; which said tract of land contains five hundred and fifty acres, and is bounded as by the further certificate, hereunto likewise annexed, under the hand of our said Surveyor General of lands in our said province will more fully and at large appear; together with all woods, underwoods, timber, and timber trees, lakes, ponds, fishings, waters, water courses, profits, commodities, hereditaments, and appurtenances whatsoever, thereunto belonging, or in any wise appertaining; toge-

ther, also, with privilege of hunting, hawking, and fowling in and upon the same, and all mines and minerals, reserving unto us, our heirs and successors, all mines of gold and silver: to have and to hold the said tract of land, and all and singular the said premises hereby granted, with the appurtenances, unto the said Augustin Rochon, his heirs and assigns, forever, in free and common soccage, yielding and paying unto us, our heirs and successors, or to the Receiver General of our quit-rents for the time being, or to such other officer as shall be appointed to receive the same, a quit-rent of one halfpenny sterling per acre, at the feast of St Michael every year; the first payment to commence on the said feast of St. Michael which shall first happen after the expiration of two years, or within fourteen days after the said feast, annually: *Provided always,* (and this present grant is upon condition,) *nevertheless,* That the said Augustin Rochon, his heirs and assigns, shall and do, within three years after the date hereof, for every fifty acres of plantable lands hereby granted, clear and cultivate three acres, at least, in that part thereof which he or they shall judge most convenient and advantageous; or else, do clear and drain three acres of swampy or sunken ground, or do drain three acres of marsh, if any such shall be contained therein; and shall further, within the time aforesaid put and keep upon every fifty acres thereof accounted barren three neat cattle, and continue the same thereon, until three acres for every fifty acres be fully cleared and improved; and if it shall so happen that there be no part of the said tract of land fit for present cultivation, without manuring and improving the same, if the said Augustin Rochon, his heirs or assigns, shall, within three years from the date hereof, erect on some part of the said tract of land one good dwelling house, to contain at least twenty feet in length and sixteen in breadth, and put on his said land the like number of three neat cattle, as aforesaid, on every fifty acres therein contained: or, otherwise, if any part of the said tract of land shall be stony and rocky ground, not fit for culture or pasture, shall and do within three years, as aforesaid, besides erecting the said house, begin to employ thereon, and continue to work, for three years then next ensuing, in digging any stone quarry or mine, one good and able hand for every hundred acres thereof, it shall be accounted a sufficient cultivation and improvement: *Provided, also,* That every three acres which shall be cleared and worked, or cleared and drained, as aforesaid, shall further be accounted a sufficient cultivation and improvement, to save forever from forfeiture fifty acres of land in any part of the said tract hereby granted. And the said Augustin Rochon, his heirs or assigns, shall be at liberty to withdraw his or their stock, or to forbear working in any quarry or mine, in proportion to such cultivation and improvement: *Provided always,* That the said Augustin Rochon, his heirs and assigns, at any time hereafter, having seated, planted, cultivated, and improved the said land, or any part thereof, according to the directions and conditions above mentioned, may make proof of such seating, planting, cultivation, and improvement, in the general court, or, in the court of the county, district, or precinct where the said land lieth, and have such proof certified to the Register's Office, and there entered with the record of this grant, a copy of which, duly attested, shall be admitted on trial, to prove the seating and planting the said land: *Provided always, nevertheless,* That, if the said Augustin Rochon, his heirs and assigns, do not in all things fully comply with and fulfil the respective directions and conditions herein above set forth, for the proper cultivation of the said land, within the time herein above limited for the completion thereof; or, if the said Augustin Rochon, his heirs and assigns, shall not pay to us, our heirs and successors, or to the Receiver General of our quit-rents, or to the proper officer appointed to receive the same, the said quit-rent of one halfpenny sterling per acre, on the said feast of St. Michael, or within fourteen days after annually, for every acre contained in this grant; that then, and in either of these cases, respectively, this grant shall be void, any thing herein contained to the contrary notwithstanding; and the said lands, tenements, hereditaments, and premises, hereby specified, and every part and parcel thereof, shall revert to us, our heirs and successors, fully and absolutely as if the same never had been granted.

Given under the great seal of our province of West Florida: Witness our trusty and well beloved Peter Chester, Esquire, our Captain General, Governor, and Commander-in-chief in and over our said province, at Pensacola, this sixteenth day of June, in the year of our Lord one thousand seven hundred and seventy-seven, and the seventeenth year of our reign.

[G. S.]   PETER CHESTER.

Passed the Secretary's Office.

PH. LIVINGSTON, Jun., *Deputy Sec.*

WEST FLORIDA, *ss.*

Pursuant to a fiat from his excellency Peter Chester, Esquire, Captain General, Governor, and Commander-in-chief in and over His Majesty's province of West Florida, &c. to me directed, bearing date the 16th day of June, 1777, I have perused and inspected the within letters patent, and do hereby certify that there is no error therein apparent to me.

ELIHU HALL BAY, for
E. R. WEGG, *Attorney General.*

WEST FLORIDA, SECRETARY'S OFFICE, *June* 16, 1777.

I do hereby certify that the within letters patent, Surveyor General's certificate, and the certificate of the Attorney General, are recorded in the Secretary's and Register's Office of the province of West Florida, in liber A, No. 3, page 284. Examined and compared with the said record by

PH. LIVINGSTON, Jun., *Deputy Secretary.*

AUDITOR'S OFFICE, *June* 16, 1777.

A docket of the within grant is entered in book B, folio 4, by

J. LORIMER, *Deputy Auditor.*

Entered in record of claims, vol. 1, page 400, by ED-WARD LLOYD WAILES, for

JOSEPH CHAMBERS, *Register.*

The Board ordered that the case be postponed for consideration.

FRANCIS COLEMAN'S case, No. 146 on the docket of the Board, and No. 118 on the books of the Register.

Claim—Of five hundred acres of land, as assignee and legal representative of Charles Walker, by virtue of a British grant, under the first section of the act.

The claimant presented his claim, together with a surveyor's plot of the land claimed, in the words and figures following, to wit:

To the Honorable the Board of Commissioners appointed in pursuance of the act of Congress, passed the 3d day of March, 1803, *for receiving and adjusting the claims to lands south of Tennessee, and east of Pearl river.*

Please to take notice, that the following tract of land, situated on the west side of Tombigbee, beginning on a point immediately above the Black Rock, on the river Tombigbee, and running west, twenty-one degrees thirty minutes south, fifty-six chains fifty links, to the corner; thence, north, twenty-one degrees thirty minutes west, fifty-eight chains and fifty links, to the river; thence, along said river, to the beginning; containing five hundred acres, more or less: is claimed by Francis Coleman, of Jefferson county, State of Georgia, under and by virtue of a British patent, granted to Charles Walker, conveyed by Charles Walker to Joel Walker, and by Joel Walker to the claimant, and now delivered to the Register of the Land Office established, in pursuance of the aforesaid act of Congress, east of Pearl river, to be recorded as directed by said act of Congress. To all which he begs leave to refer, as also to a copy of the plot herewith filed.

WILLIAM COLEMAN,
Attorney in fact for Francis Coleman.
[Plot omitted.]

GEORGE THE THIRD, *by the grace of God, of Great Britain, France, and Ireland, King, defender of the faith, &c. To all to whom these presents shall come, greeting:*

Know ye, that we, of our special grace, certain knowledge, and mere motion, have given and granted, and, by these presents, for us, our heirs and successors, do give and grant, unto Charles Walker, his heirs and assigns, all that tract of land situated on a point immediately above the Black Rock, on the river Tombigbee, about one hundred and twelve miles above the town of Mobile, which tract of land is bounded by the river Tombigbee on the northeast, south, and southwest, and part by vacant land, and on the west by vacant land in our province of West Florida; and having such shape, form, and marks, both natural and artificial, as are represented in the plot thereof hereunto annexed, as drawn by our Surveyor General of lands; which said

tract contains five hundred acres, and is bounded as by the further certificate, hereunto likewise annexed, under the hand of our said Surveyor General of lands in our said province may more fully and at large appear; together with all woods, underwoods, timber, and timber trees, lakes, ponds, fishings, waters, water courses, profits, commodities, hereditaments, and appurtenances, whatsoever, thereunto belonging, or in any wise appertaining; together, also, with privilege of hunting, hawking, and fowling in and upon the same, and all mines and minerals, reserving unto us, our heirs and successors, all mines of gold and silver: to have and to hold the said tract of land, and all and singular the premises hereby granted, with the appurtenances, unto the said Charles Walker, his heirs and assigns, forever, in free and common soccage; yielding and paying unto us, our heirs and successors, to the Receiver General of our quit-rents for the time being, or to such other officer as shall be appointed to receive the same, a quit-rent of one halfpenny sterling per acre, at the feast of St. Michael every year; the first payment to commence on the said feast of St. Michael which shall first happen after the expiration of ten years from the date hereof, or within fourteen days after the said feast, annually: *Provided always,* (and this present grant is upon condition,) *nevertheless,* That this grant shall be duly registered in the Register's Office of this province within six months from the date hereof, and also that a docket thereof shall be entered in the Auditor's Office within the same time, if such establishment shall take place in this province: *and provided, also,* That if the said Charles Walker, his heirs and assigns, do not in all things fully comply with and fulfil the respective directions and conditions herein above set forth for registering this grant, within the time herein above limited for the completion thereof; or if the said Charles Walker, his heirs or assigns, shall not pay to us, our heirs and successors, or to the Receiver General of our quit-rents, or to the proper officer appointed to receive the same, the said quit-rent of one halfpenny sterling per acre, on the said feast of St. Michael, or within fourteen days after, annually, for every acre contained in this grant; that then, and in either of these cases, respectively, this grant shall be void, any thing therein contained to the contrary notwithstanding; and the said lands, tenements, hereditaments, and premises, hereby specified, and every part and parcel thereof, shall revert to us, our heirs and successors, fully and absolutely, as if the same never had been granted.

Given under the great seal of our province of West Florida: Witness our trusty and well beloved Peter Chester, Esquire, our Captain General, Governor, and Commander-in-chief in and over our said province, at Pensacola, the twenty-seventh day of January, in the year of our Lord one thousand seven hundred and seventy-seven, and in the seventeenth year of our reign.

[G. S.]   PETER CHESTER.

Passed the Secretary's Office.

PH. LIVINGSTON, Jr., *Dep. Sec.*

Pursuant to a fiat from his excellency Peter Chester, Esq. our Captain General, Governor, and Commander-in-chief in and over His Majesty's province of West Florida, &c. &c. to me directed, bearing date the 27th day of January, 1777, I have perused and inspected the within letters patent, and do hereby certify that there is no error therein apparent to me.

E. R. WEGG, *Attorney General.*

PENSACOLA, *January* 27, 1777.

I do hereby certify that the within letters patent, Sur-veyor General's certificate, and the certificate of the Attorney General, are recorded in the Secretary and Register's Office of the province of West Florida, in liber A, No. 2, page 286, &c. Examined and compared with the said record by

PH. LIVINGSTON, Jr., *Dep. Sec.*

Entered in record of claims, volume 1, page 406, by EDWARD LLOYD WAILES, for

JOSEPH CHAMBERS, *Register.*

The claimant exhibited a deed of conveyance from Joel Walker, bearing date the 21st day of December, 1798; also, a deed from Mary Walker, the wife of said Joel, bearing date the 28th day of December, 1798, duly executed and proven, conveying and relinquishing to Francis Coleman, in and by the first mentioned deed, all the said Joel's right, title, interest, and claim in and to the said tract of land, and in and by the other said deed, conveying and relinquishing to the said Coleman all the said Mary's right, title, interest, and estate, in or to said tract of land.

The Board ordered that the case be postponed for consideration.

FRANCIS COLEMAN's case, No. 147 on the docket of the Board, and No. 119 on the books of the Register.

Claim—Of one hundred acres, as legal representative of Abraham Little, by virtue of a British grant, under the first section of the act.

The claimant presented his claim, together with a surveyor's plot of the land claimed, in the following words and figures, to wit:

To the Commissioners appointed in pursuance of the act of Congress, passed the 3d of March, 1803, for receiving and adjusting claims to lands south of Tennessee, and east of Pearl river.

Please to take notice, that the following tract of land, situated on the west side of Tombigbee, bounded to the north by land surveyed for Frederick George Mulcaster, to the northwestward by the river Tombigbee, and on all other sides by vacant land, and hath such marks, both natural and artificial, as are fully represented in the plot annexed: is claimed by Francis Coleman, of Jefferson county, and State of Georgia, under and by virtue of a British patent, granted to Abraham Little, and by Abraham Little to Frances Walker, and from Frances Walker to Joel Walker, and from Joel Walker to said claimant; and is now exhibited to the Register of the Land Office established east of Pearl river, to be recorded as directed by said act. To all which he begs leave to refer, as also to the plot herewith filed.

WM. COLEMAN,
Attorney in fact for Francis Coleman.
[Plot omitted.]

GEORGE THE THIRD, *by the grace of God, of Great Britain, France, and Ireland, King, defender of the faith, &c. To all to whom these presents shall come, greeting:*

Know ye, that we, of our special grace, certain knowledge, and mere motion, have given and granted, and, by these presents, for us, our heirs and successors, do give and grant, unto Abraham Little, his heirs and assigns, all that tract of land situated on the west side of the river Tombigbee, about one hundred and thirteen miles from the town of Mobile, bounded to the northward by land surveyed for Frederick George Mulcaster, to the northeast by the river Tombigbee, and on the other sides by vacant land, in our said province of West Florida; and having such shape, form, and marks, both natural and artificial, as are represented in the plot thereof, hereunto annexed, as drawn by our Surveyor General of lands in our said province of West Florida; which said tract of land contains one hundred acres, and is bounded, as by the further certificate hereunto likewise annexed, under the hand of our said Surveyor General of lands in our province, may more fully and at large appear; together with all woods, underwoods, timber, and timber trees, lakes, ponds, fishings, waters, watercourses, profits, commodities, hereditaments, and appurtenances whatsoever hereunto belonging, or in any wise appertaining; together, also, with privilege of hunting, hawking, and fowling in and upon the same, and all mines and minerals; reserving to us, our heirs and successors, all mines of gold and silver: to have and to hold the said tract of land, and all and singular the premises hereby granted, with the appurtenances, unto the said Abraham Little, his heirs and assigns, forever, in free and common soccage; yielding and paying unto us, our heirs and successors, or to the Receiver General of our quit-rents for the time being, or to such other officer as shall be appointed to receive the same, a quit-rent of one halfpenny sterling per acre, at the feast of St. Michael every year; the first payment to commence on the said feast of St. Michael, which shall first happen after the expiration of two years from the date hereof, or within fourteen days after the said feast, annually: *Provided always,* (and this present grant is upon condition,) *nevertheless,* That the said Abraham Little, his heirs and assigns, shall and do, within three years after the date hereof, for every fifty acres of plantable land hereby granted, clear and cultivate three acres, at least, in that part thereof which he or they shall judge most convenient and advantageous; or else, do clear and drain three acres of swampy or sunken ground, or do drain three acres of marsh, if any such shall be contained therein; and shall further, within the time aforesaid, put and

keep upon every fifty acres thereof accounted barren, three neat cattle, and continue the same thereon, until three acres for every fifty acres be fully cleared and improved; and if it shall so happen that there be no part of the said tract of land fit for present cultivation, without manuring and improving the same, if the said Abraham Little, his heirs and assigns, shall, within three years from the date hereof, erect on some part of the said tract of land one good dwelling-house, to contain at least twenty feet in length and sixteen feet in breadth, and put on his said land the like number of three neat cattle, as aforesaid, on every fifty acres therein contained; or otherwise, if any part of the said land shall be stony or rocky ground, not fit for culture or pasture, shall and do, within three years, as aforesaid, besides erecting the said house, begin to employ thereon, and continue to work for three years then next ensuing, in digging any stone quarry or mine, one good and able hand for every hundred acres thereof, it shall be accounted a sufficient seating, planting, cultivation, and improvement; *Provided also,* That every three acres which shall be cleared and worked, or cleared and drained, as aforesaid, shall further be accounted a sufficient seating, cultivation, and improvement, to save forever from forfeiture fifty acres of land in any part of the tract hereby granted; and the said Abraham Little, his heirs and assigns, shall be at liberty to withdraw his or their stock, or to forbear working in any quarry or mine, in proportion to such cultivation and improvement, as aforesaid, as shall be made upon the plantable lands, swamps, sunken grounds, or marshes therein contained: *Provided, also,* That this grant shall be duly registered in the Register's Office of this province within six months from the date hereof, and also that a docket thereof shall be entered in the Auditor's Office within the same time, if such establishment shall take place in this province: *Provided always,* That the said Abraham Little, his heirs and assigns, at any time hereafter, having seated, planted, cultivated, and improved the said land, or any part thereof, according to the directions and conditions above mentioned, may make proof of such seating, planting, cultivation, and improvement, in the general court, or in the court of the county, district, or precinct where the said land lieth; and have such proof certified to the Register's Office, and there entered with the record of this grant, a copy of which, duly attested, shall be admitted on trial, to prove the seating and planting of the said land: *Provided always, nevertheless,* That if the said Abraham Little, his heirs and assigns, do not in all things fully comply with and fulfil the respective directions and conditions herein above set forth, for the proper cultivation of the said land within the time limited for the completion thereof; or, if the said Abraham Little, his heirs or assigns, shall not pay to us, our heirs and successors, or to the Receiver General of our quit-rents, or to the proper officer appointed to receive the same, the said quit-rent of one halfpenny sterling per acre at the said feast of Saint Michael, or within fourteen days after the said feast, annually, for every acre contained in this grant; then, and in either of these cases, respectively, this grant shall be void, any thing contained therein to the contrary notwithstanding; and the said lands, tenements, hereditaments, and premises, hereby specified, and every part and parcel thereof, shall revert to us, our heirs and successors, fully and absolutely, as if the same never had been granted.

Given under the great seal of our province of West Florida: Witness our trusty and well beloved Peter Chester, Esq. Captain General, Governor, and Commander-in-chief in and over our said province, at Pensacola, this 16th day of February, 1778, and in the eighteenth year of our reign.

[G. S.] PETER CHESTER.

Passed the Secretary's Office.

PH. LIVINGSTON, Jun., *Deputy Secretary.*

WEST FLORIDA, *ss.*

Pursuant to a fiat from his excellency Peter Chester, Esq., Captain General, Governor, and Commander-in-chief in and over His Majesty's province of West Florida, &c. to me directed, bearing date the 16th day of February, 1778, I have perused and inspected the within letters patent, and do hereby certify that there is no error therein apparent to me.

E. R. WEGG, *Attorney General.*

WEST FLORIDA, SECRETARY'S OFFICE,
February 16, 1778.

I do hereby certify that the within letters patent, Surveyor General's certificate, and the certificate of the

Attorney General, are recorded in the Secretary and Register's office of the province of West Florida, in liber A, No. 3, page 385, &c. Examined and compared with the said record by

PH. LIVINGSTON, Jun., *Deputy Secretary.*

AUDITOR'S OFFICE, *Feb.* 16, 1778.

A docket of the within grant is entered in book B, folio 28, per

J. LORIMER, *Deputy Auditor.*

Entered in record of claims, vol. 1, page 416, by EDWARD LLOYD WAILES, for

JOSEPH CHAMBERS, *Register.*

The claimant produced a deed from Joel Walker, bearing date the 21st day of December, 1798, conveying all the said Joel's right, title, interest, and claim in and to the said tract of land.

The Board ordered that the case be postponed for consideration.

JAMES HOGGATT'S case, No. 148 on the docket of the Board, and No. 120 on the books of the Register.

Claim—Of two hundred and fifty acres, as legal representative of William Wall, and Eleanor, his wife, by virtue of a British grant, under the first section of the act.

The claimant presented his claim, together with a surveyor's plot of the land claimed, in the following words and figures, to wit:

MISSISSIPPI TERRITORY, WASHINGTON COUNTY,
February 4, 1804.

James Hoggatt, a citizen of the territory aforesaid, claims two hundred and fifty acres of land, lying on the west side of the river Tombigbee, formerly granted by His British Majesty to William Wall, by letters patent, bearing date the 20th day of March, 1778; which original patent is in the possession of the present claimant, and a plot hereof is thereunto annexed; and by the said William Wall, and Eleanor, his wife, by their deed, legally and fully executed, bearing date the 3d day of November, 1778, did convey unto the said James Hoggatt the said two hundred and fifty acres of land.

JAMES HOGGATT.

[Plot omitted.]

WEST FLORIDA, *ss.*

GEORGE THE THIRD, *by the grace of God, of Great Britain, France, and Ireland, King, defender of the faith, &c. To all to whom these presents shall come, greeting:*

Know ye, that we, of our special grace, certain knowledge, and mere motion, have given and granted, and, by these presents, for us, our heirs, and successors, do give and grant, unto William Wall, his heirs and assigns, all that tract of land, situated on the west side of the river Tombigbee, bounded on the northwest by lands surveyed for William Tucker, on the northeast side by the river Tombigbee, and on all other sides by vacant land, in our province of West Florida; and having such shape, form, and marks, both natural and artificial, as are represented in the plot thereof hereunto annexed, as drawn by our Surveyor General of lands; which said tract of land contains two hundred and fifty acres, and is bounded as by the further certificate hereunto likewise annexed, under the hand of our said Surveyor General of lands in our said province, will more fully and at large appear; together with all woods, underwoods, timber, and timber trees, lakes, ponds, fishings, waters, watercourses, profits, commodities, hereditaments and appurtenances whatsoever thereunto belonging, or in anywise appertaining; together, also, with privilege of hunting, hawking, and fowling in and upon the same, and all mines and minerals, reserving unto us, our heirs and successors, all mines of gold and silver: to have and to hold the said tract of land, and all and singular the premises hereby granted, with the appurtenances, unto the said William Wall, his heirs and assigns, forever, in free and common soccage, yielding and paying unto us, our heirs and successors, or to the Receiver General of our quit-rents for the time being, or to such other officer as shall be appointed to receive the same, a quit-rent of one halfpenny sterling per acre, at the feast of St. Michael every year; the first payment to commence on the said feast of St. Michael which shall first happen after the expiration of ten years from the date hereof, or within fourteen days after the said feast, annually; *Provided always*, (that this present grant is upon condition,) *nevertheless*, That this grant shall be duly registered in the Register's office of this province, within six months from the date hereof, and also that a docket shall be entered in the Auditor's office within the same time, if

such establishment shall take place in this province: *And provided, also*, That if the said William Wall, his heirs and assigns, do not in all things fully comply with and fulfil the conditions herein above set forth, for the registering this grant within the time limited for the completion thereof; or, if the said William Wall, his heirs and assigns, shall not pay to us, our heirs and successors, or to the Receiver General of our quit-rents, or to the proper officer appointed to receive the same, the said quit-rent of one halfpenny sterling per acre, on the said feast of St. Michael, or within fourteen days after the said feast, annually, for every acre contained in this grant; that then, and in either of these cases, respectively, this grant shall be void, any thing therein contained to the contrary notwithstanding; and the said lands, tenements, hereditaments, and premises, hereby specified, and every part and parcel thereof, shall revert to us, our heirs and successors, as fully and absolutely as if the same never had been granted.

Given under the great seal of our province of West Florida: Witness our trusty and well beloved Peter Chester, Esq. our Captain General, Governor, and Commander-in-chief in and over our said province, at Pensacola, this 20th of March, 1778, and in the eighteenth year of our reign.

[o. s.]   PETER CHESTER.

Passed the Secretary's Office.

PH. LIVINGSTON, Jun., *Deputy Secretary.*

WEST FLORIDA, *ss.*

Pursuant to a fiat from his excellency Peter Chester, Esq., Captain General, Governor, and Commander-in-chief in and over His Majesty's province of West Florida, &c. &c. to me directed, bearing date the 20th day of March, 1778, I have perused and inspected the within letters patent, and do hereby certify that there is no error therein apparent to me.

E. R. WEGG, *Attorney General.*

PENSACOLA, SECRETARY'S OFFICE, *March* 20, 1778.

I do hereby certify that the within letters patent, Surveyor General's certificate, and the certificate of the Attorney General, are recorded in the Secretary and Register's Office of this province, in lib. A, No. 2, page 500.

Examined and compared with the said record, by

PH. LIVINGSTON, Jun., *Deputy Secretary.*

AUDITOR'S OFFICE, *March* 20, 1778.

A docket of the within grant is entered in book B, folio 33, per

J. LORIMER, *Deputy Auditor.*

Entered in record of claims, vol. 1, page 424, by EDWARD LLOYD WAILES, for

JOSEPH CHAMBERS, *Register.*

The claimant exhibited a deed of conveyance from William Wall, and Eleanor his wife, bearing date the 3d day of November, 1778, conveying to the said claimant all the said William and Eleanor's right, title, interest, claim, and demand in and to the said two hundred and fifty acres of land.

The Board ordered that the case be postponed for consideration.

ROBERT ABRAHAM'S case, No. 149 on the docket of the Board, and No. 122 on the books of the Register.

Claim—Of five hundred acres, by virtue of a British patent, under the first section of the act.

The claimant presented his claim, together with a surveyor's plot of the land claimed, in the following words and figures, to wit:

To the Commissioners appointed in pursuance of the act of Congress passed the 3d day of March, 1803, for receiving and adjusting claims to lands south of Tennessee, and east of Pearl river.

Please to take notice, that the following tract of land, situated on the west side of the river Tombigbee, in the county of Washington, butting and bounding northeast by said river, west by John Matthew's land, and on all sides by vacant land, containing five hundred acres, having such shape, form, and marks, both natural and artificial, as are represented in the plot annexed: is claimed by Richard Burney, attorney in fact for Robert Abrahams, in and by virtue of a British patent, and is now exhibited to the Register of the Land Office established east of Pearl river, to be recorded as directed by said act. To all which he begs leave to refer, as also to a copy of the plot herewith filed.

RICHARD BURNEY,
Attorney in fact for Robert Abrahams.

MARCH 26, 1804.

[Plot omitted.]

By His Excellency PETER CHESTER, Esquire, Captain General, Governor, and Commander-in-chief in and over His Majesty's province of West Florida, &c. &c.

To ELIAS DURNFORD, Esquire, *Surveyor General.*

You are hereby directed and required to measure, or cause to be admeasured and laid out, to Robert Abrahams, a plantation or tract of land containing five hundred acres, situated on the west side of the river Tombigbee, about one hundred and fifteen miles from the town of Mobile, in West Florida, observing His Majesty's instructions in laying out the same, taking the utmost care you can that the same has not been heretofore run out on any warrant or patent, but be vacant land, and return a plot thereof hereunto annexed, certified by you in the Secretary's Office within six months from this date.

Given under my hand and seal at arms, at Pensacola, this 15th day of December, A. D. 1778.

PETER CHESTER.

Secretary's Office, certified by
ELIHU HALL BAY, *Deputy Secretary.*

WEST FLORIDA, *ss.*

Pursuant to a warrant from his excellency Peter Chester, Esq., Captain General, Governor, and Commander-in-chief in and over His Majesty's province of West Florida, to me directed, bearing date the 28th day of January, 1779, I have caused to be surveyed and laid out unto Robert Abrahams, a plantation or tract of land containing five hundred acres, situated on the west side of the river Tombigbee, bounded on the northeast by said river, distance from the town of Mobile about one hundred and fifteen miles, joining, west, a tract of land surveyed for John Matthews, and on the other sides by vacant land, and hath forms and marks, both natural and artificial, as are fully represented in the plot annexed. Certified this 28th day of January, A. D. 1779, by

ELIAS DURNFORD, *Surveyor General.*

PENSACOLA, *January* 28, 1779.
Received from Robert Abrahams the Surveyor General's fees for his five hundred acres on the river Tombigbee.

THOMAS DURNFORD.

Received of Mr. Robert Abrahams 19 3½, for his fees on his grant of five hundred acres, including Attorney General and Auditor's fees for the Secretary's Office.

R. W. CARR.

Entered in record of claims, vol. 1, page 441, by EDWARD LLOYD WAILES, for

JOSEPH CHAMBERS, *Register.*

The Board ordered that the case be postponed for consideration.

SETH DEAN's case, No. 150 on the docket of the Board, and No. 180 on the books of the Register.

Claim—Of two thousand acres, as assignee and legal representative of Charles Walker, under the first section of the act.

To the Commissioners appointed in pursuance of the act of Congress passed the 3d day of March, 1803, for receiving and adjusting the claims to lands south of Tennessee, and east of Pearl river.

Please to take notice, that the following land, situated on the west side of Tombigbee river, about fifty-eight miles above the town of Mobile, and about eight miles above the fork of the Alabama, in the county of Washington, beginning at a pine, thence, south, eighty degrees west, eighty-one chains seventy-nine links, to a pine; thence, south, eighty degrees east, two hundred and thirty-six chains, to a willow; thence, the meanders of the river, to an oak; thence, north, eighty degrees west, two hundred and forty-five chains, to the beginning; and hath such shape, forms, and marks, both natural and artificial, as are represented in the plot annexed, containing two thousand acres: is claimed by Seth Dean, legal representative of Charles Walker, in and by virtue of a British patent, and is now exhibited to the Register of the Land Office established east of Pearl river, to be recorded as directed by said act. To

all which he begs leave to refer, as also to a copy of the plot herewith filed.

SETH DEAN,
Legal representative of Charles Walker.

[Plot omitted.]

WEST FLORIDA, *ss.*

GEORGE THE THIRD, *by the grace of God, of Great Britain, France, and Ireland, King, defender of the faith, &c. To all to whom these presents shall come, greeting:*

Know ye, that we, of our special grace, certain knowledge, and mere motion, have given and granted, and, by these presents, for us, our heirs and successors, do give and grant, unto Charles Walker, his heirs and assigns, all that tract of land situated about fifty-eight miles above the town of Mobile, and about eight miles above the mouth of the Alabama, butting southwardly by lands laid out unto Alexander McIntosh, eastwardly by Tombigbee river, and on all other sides by vacant land; in our province of West Florida, and having such shape, form, and marks, both natural and artificial, as are represented in the plot thereof hereunto annexed, as drawn by our Surveyor General of lands; which said tract of land contains two thousand acres, and is bounded as by the further certificate, hereunto likewise annexed, under the hand of our said Surveyor General of lands, in our said province, may more fully and at large appear; together with all woods, underwoods, timber, and timber trees, lakes, ponds, fishings, waters, water courses, profits, commodities, hereditaments, and appurtenances whatsoever thereunto belonging, or in anywise appertaining; together, also, with privilege of hunting, hawking, and fowling in and upon the same, and all mines and minerals, reserving unto us, our heirs and successors, all mines of gold and silver: to have and to hold the said tract of land, and all and singular the premises hereby granted, with the appurtenances, unto the said Charles Walker, his heirs and assigns, forever, in free and common soccage; yielding and paying unto us, our heirs and successors, or to the Receiver General of our quit-rents for the time being, or to such other officer as shall be appointed to receive the same, a quit-rent of one halfpenny sterling per acre at the feast of St. Michael every year; the first payment to commence on the said feast of St. Michael which shall first happen after the expiration of two years from the date hereof, or within fourteen days after the said feast, annually: *Provided always,* (and this present grant is upon condition,) *nevertheless,* That the said Charles Walker, his heirs and assigns, shall and do, within three years after the date hereof, for every fifty acres of plantable lands hereby granted, clear and cultivate three acres, at least, in that part thereof which he or they may judge most convenient and advantageous, or else do clear and drain three acres of swampy or sunken ground, or do drain three acres of marsh, if any such shall be contained therein; and shall further, within the time aforesaid, put and keep upon every fifty acres thereof accounted barren three neat cattle, and continue the same thereon, until three acres for every fifty acres be fully cleared and improved; and if it shall so happen that there be no part of the said tract of land fit for present cultivation, without manuring and improving the same, if the said Charles Walker, his heirs and assigns, shall, within three years from the date hereof, erect on some part of the said tract of land one good dwelling house, to contain at least twenty feet in length and sixteen feet in breadth, and put upon his said land the like number of three neat cattle, as aforesaid, on every fifty acres therein contained; or, otherwise, if any part of the said land shall be stony or rocky ground, not fit for culture or pasture, shall and do, within three years, as aforesaid, besides erecting the said house, begin to employ thereon, and continue to work for three years then next ensuing, in digging any stone quarry or mine, one good and able hand for every hundred acres thereof, it shall be accounted a sufficient cultivation and improvement: *Provided, also,* That every three acres which shall be cleared and worked, or cleared and drained, shall further be accounted a sufficient seating, planting, cultivation, and improvement, to save forever from forfeiture fifty acres of land, in any part of the tract hereby granted; and the said Charles Walker, his heirs and assigns, shall be at liberty to withdraw his or their stock, or to forbear working in any quarry or mine, in proportion to such cultivation and improvements, as shall be made upon the plantable lands, swamps, sunken grounds, or marshes therein contained: *Provided, also,* That this grant shall be duly registered in the Register's Office of this province, within six months from the date hereof, and also that a docket thereof shall be entered in the Auditor's Office within the same time, if such establishment shall take place in this province: *Provided, always,* That the said Charles Walker, his heirs and assigns, at any time hereafter, having seated, planted, cultivated, and improved the said land, or any part thereof, according to the directions and conditions above mentioned, may make proof of such seating, planting, cultivation, and improvement, in the general court, or in the court of the county, district, or precinct, where the said land lieth, and have such proof certified to the Register's Office, and there entered with the record of this grant; a copy of which, duly attested, shall be admitted on trial, to prove the seating and planting of the said land: *Provided always, nevertheless,* That if the said Charles Walker, his heirs and assigns, do not in all things fully comply with and fulfil the respective directions and conditions herein above set forth for the proper cultivation of the said land, within the time herein above limited for the completion thereof; or, if the said Charles Walker, his heirs or assigns, shall not pay to us, our heirs and successors, or to the Receiver General of our quit-rents, or to the proper officer appointed to receive the same, the said quit-rent of one halfpenny sterling per acre, on the said feast of St. Michael, or within fourteen days after, annually, for every acre contained; that then, and in either of these cases, respectively, this grant shall be void, any thing herein contained to the contrary notwithstanding; and the said lands, tenements, hereditaments, and premises, hereby granted, and every part and parcel thereof, shall revert to us, our heirs and successors, fully and absolutely, as if the same never had been granted.

Given under the great seal of our province of West Florida: Witness our trusty and well beloved Elias Durnford, Esq. Lieutenant Governor and Commander-in-chief in and over our said province, at Pensacola, this third day of April, in the year of our Lord 1770, and in the ninth year of our reign.

[G. S.]   ELIAS DURNFORD.
Signed in council, this 3d April, 1770.
FRANCIS POUSSETT, *Dep. Cl'k Council.*
Entered in record of claims, vol. 1, page 521, by Edward Lloyd Wailes, for
JOSEPH CHAMBERS, *Register.*

The claimant exhibited a deed of conveyance from Mary Walker, as relict and sole executrix of Joel Walker, deceased, bearing date the 25th day of November, 1799, conveying and relinquishing all her right, title, interest, claim, and demand of, in and unto the said tract of two thousand acres of land, unto David Walker; also, one other deed from David Walker and Charlotte Walker, bearing date the 3d day of September, 1801, conveying and relinquishing all their right, title, interest, and claim of the aforesaid tract of land, unto the said Seth Dean.

The Board ordered that the case be postponed for consideration.

SETH DEAN's case, No. 151 on the docket of the Board, and No. 182 on the books of the Register.

Claim—Of one hundred and fifty acres, as legal representative of John Dawson, by virtue of a British grant under the first section of the act.

The claimant presented his claim, together with a surveyor's plot of the land claimed, in the following words and figures, to wit:

To the Honorable Board of Commissioners appointed to settle claims to lands south of Tennessee and east of Pearl river:

GENTLEMEN:

The annexed plot represents a tract of land originally granted to John Dawson, and by the said Dawson willed to his wife Elizabeth, who intermarried with Thomas Davis, and by said Davis conveyed to me, as by a deed bearing date 27th day of January, 1801, will more fully appear; which plot, will, and deed, is now delivered to the Register of the Land Office east of Pearl river, to be recorded as directed by an "Act of Congress passed the 3d day of March, 1803." To all which he begs leave to refer.

SETH DEAN,
Legal representative of John Dawson.
MARCH 31, 1804.
[Plot omitted.]
Surveyed the 3d day of October, 1776, by Elias Durnford, Surveyor General of West Florida.

The claimant exhibited part of a seal, and a small piece of paper, which appear to be remnants of a British grant, the writing being illegible, and no entire sentence remaining.

Entered in record of claims, vol. 1, page 531, by Edward Lloyd Wailes, for
JOSEPH CHAMBERS, *Register.*

The claimant produced a will and testament of John Dawson, bearing date the 6th day of December, 1790, duly executed and proven, in and by which will he devised to his wife Elizabeth Dawson all his right and title to the said tract of land; also, a deed from Thomas Davis, bearing date the 27th day of January, 1801, conveying all his right, title, interest, and claim in the said tract of land unto the said Seth Dean.

The Board ordered that the case be postponed for consideration.

SETH DEAN's case, No. 152 on the docket of the Board, and No. 181 on the books of the Register.

Claim—Of one thousand acres, by virtue of a deed of conveyance from Francis Juzant.

The claimant presented his claim in the following words and figures, to wit:

To the Honorable Board of Commissioners appointed to settle the claims to lands south of Tennessee and east of Pearl river.

GENTLEMEN:

The annexed deed for a tract or two tracts of land, lying on the west side of the river Tombigbee, situated on both sides of Cedar creek, below Fort Stoddert, I purchased of Francis Juzant, heir-at-law of Peter Juzant, deceased, which land the said Peter Juzant obtained from the Spanish Government; which deed is now exhibited to the Register of the Land Office established east of Pearl river, to be recorded as directed by the "Act of Congress passed the 3d day of March, 1803." To which deed I beg leave to refer.

SETH DEAN,
Representative of Francis Juzant.
MARCH 31, 1804.

MISSISSIPPI TERRITORY:

This indenture, made this 25th day of December, in the year of our Lord 1802, and in the twenty-sixth year of American independence, between Francis Juzant of the one part, citizen of the Creek nation, and Seth Dean, of the territory aforesaid, of the other part, witnesseth: That the said Francis Juzant, for and in consideration of the sum of one hundred dollars to him in hand paid by the said Seth Dean, at and before the sealing and delivery of these presents, the receipt whereof is hereby acknowledged, hath granted, bargained, sold, and confirmed to the said Seth Dean, his heirs and assigns, all that tract or tracts of land that was formerly the property of Peter Juzant, deceased, adjoining the west bank of the river Tombigbee, near or on both sides of the mouth of Cedar creek, supposed to contain one thousand acres of land, more or less: to have and to hold the above tract of land, with all and singular the improvements thereunto belonging, or in anywise appertaining, unto the said Seth Dean, his heirs and assigns, forever; and the said Francis Juzant, for himself, and his heirs and assigns, warrant and defend the right and titles of the beforementioned premises, against all persons lawfully claiming the same, unto the said Seth Dean, his heirs or assigns.

In witness whereof, he hath set his hand and seal, the day and year above written.

FRANCIS JUZANT.

Signed, sealed, and delivered in the presence of
ROBERT WALTON,
WILLIAM WALTON.

Entered in record of claims, vol. 1, page 530, by Edward Lloyd Wailes, for
JOSEPH CHAMBERS, *Register.*

The Board ordered that the case be postponed for consideration.

THOMAS BATES's case, No. 153 on the docket of the Board, and No. 187 on the books of the Register.

Claim.—A donation of six hundred and twenty-eight acres, under the second section of the act.

The claimant presented his claim, together with a surveyor's plot of the land claimed, in the following words and figures, to wit:

To the Commissioners appointed in pursuance of the act of Congress passed the 3d day of March, 1803, for receiving and adjusting claims to lands south of Tennessee, and east of Pearl river.

Please to take notice, that the following tract of land, situated on Tombigbee river, in the county of Washington, beginning at a sassafras ; thence, south, forty-four degrees west, eighty chains, to a pine; south, forty-seven chains, to a pine; thence, south, fourty-four degrees east, eighty-chains, to a gum ; thence, north, fifty degrees east, twelve chains, to the river; thence, with the river, to the beginning; and hath such forms and marks, both natural and artificial, as are fully represented in the plot annexed; containing six hundred and twenty-eight acres: is claimed by Thomas Bates, in and by virtue of the second section of the act, as a donation; and is now exhibited to the Register of the Land Office established east of Pearl river, to be recorded as directed by said act. To all which he begs leave to refer, as also to a copy of the plot herewith filed.

                    THOMAS T. BATES, his x mark.
MARCH 31, 1804.
            [Plot omitted.]
Surveyed the 15th of March, 1804, by Natt Christmas. Sworn chain bearers, Wm. Vaughn and Rob't Sharp.
Entered in record of claims, vol. 1, page 551, by EDWARD LLOYD WAILES, for
            JOSEPH CHAMBERS, Register.

The said Vaughn and Sharp. chain carriers for the preceding survey, were sworn before James Farr, Justice of Peace.
Richard Hawkins and James Powell were presented as witnesses, and being duly sworn and interrogated by the Board, they deposed, that they had no interest in this claim; that Thomas Bates, the present claimant, did, before the year 1797, during that year, and ever since, inhabit and cultivate the land in question; and that he was at said time the head of a family, and twenty-one years of age.
The Board ordered that the case be postponed for consideration.

ANN LAWRENCE, representative of Moses Moore: case commenced in page 628.
James Bilbo and William Phelps, chain carriers for the survey in this case, were sworn before John Callicr and R. Harwell, Esquires, Justices of the Peace.
James Powel and Thomas Bilbo, surveyors, were presented as witnesses, and, being duly sworn, the said Powel deposed, that Moses Moore, deceased, did live upon and cultivate the land in question at the time of his death; that, after his death, Cornelius Rain, who was the son of the widow, did inhabit and cultivate the said land, and was in possession thereof on the 27th of October, 1795, (as the witness understood) under the authority and by the permission of the widow of said Moses Moore.
The said Bilbo testified, that he made the survey and plot of the land in question; that it was correct, according to his knowledge and belief ; that he believed that the upper end of this claim was covered by a British grant in the name of John McIntosh, and that the lower end was embraced by a Spanish permission, in favor of Cornelius Rain; that the improvements, which were originally made by Moses Moore, deceased, were included within this survey.
The Board ordered that the case be postponed for consideration.

JAMES POWEL'S case: commenced in page 643.
James Dean, one of the chain carriers for the survey in this case, was sworn before Figures Lewis, Esq., Justice of Peace.
Cornelius Rain was presented as a witness, and, being duly sworn and interrogated by the Board, deposed, that, before the year 1797, throughout that year, and ever since, James Powel, the present claimant, had lived upon the land in question, and cultivated the same; and that, in the year 1797, he was the head of a family, and more than twenty-one years of age.
The Board ordered that the case be postponed for consideration.

CORNELIUS RAIN'S case : commenced in page 632.
James Dean and James Powel, chain carriers for the survey in this case, were sworn before R. Harwell, Justice of Peace.
Thomas Bates and James Powel were presented as witnesses, and, being duly sworn and interrogated by

the Board, they deposed, that they were not interested in this claim; that Cornelius Rain, the present claimant, as they believed, was a married man, and twenty-one years of age on the 10th day of June, 1795; and that he had inhabited and cultivated the land in question from that time to the then present time.
John Dease, surveyor, was presented as a witness, and, being duly sworn, deposed, that he surveyed and plotted the land in question, and believed it to be correct; that it included the improvements of the claimant; that he understood that this survey interfered with the claim of Mrs. Lawrence, but that it could not be run in any other form without excluding this claimant's improvements.
The Board ordered that the case be postponed for consideration.

JAMES FARR's case, No. 154 on the docket of the Board, and No. 161 on the books of the Register.
Claim.—A donation of three hundred and forty-four acres, under the second section of the act.
The claimant presented his claim, together with a surveyor's plot of the land claimed, in the words and figures following, to wit:

To the Commissioners appointed in pursuance of the act of Congress passed the 3d day of March, 1803, for receiving and adjusting claims to lands south of Tennessee, and east of Pearl river.
                                        MARCH 29, 1804.
Please to take notice, that the following tract of land, situated on the west side of the Tombigbee river, in the county of Washington, beginning on said river at a white oak, running thence, south, forty-seven degrees west, twenty chains, to a pine; thence, south, seventeen degrees west, sixty-nine chains, to a corner stake; thence, north, sixty-six degrees east, fifty-nine chains, to a corner stake; thence, north, thirty-six degrees west, fifty-four chains; thence, south, twenty-five degrees west, fourteen chains, to the river; thence, along the meanders of said river, to the beginning; and hath such forms and marks, both natural and artificial, as are fully represented in the plot annexed, containing three hundred and forty-four acres: is claimed by Cornelius Rain, attorney in fact for James Farr, in and by virtue of the second section of this act, as a donation, and is now exhibited to the Register of the Land Office established east of Pearl river, to be recorded as directed by said act. To all which he begs leave to refer, as also to a copy of the plot herewith filed.
                    CORNELIUS RAIN,
                        Attorney in fact for James Farr.
            [Plot omitted.]
Surveyed 23d March, 1804, by Thomas Bilbo. Chain carriers, John Johnston and Jacob Nealy.
Entered in record of claims, vol. 1, page 492, by EDWARD LLOYD WAILES, for
            JOSEPH CHAMBERS, Register.

The said chain carriers for the above survey were sworn before Figures Lewis and R. Harwell, Esquires, Justices of Peace.
James Powel was presented as a witness, and, being duly sworn and interrogated by the Board, deposed, that, in the spring of the year 1797, James Farr cultivated the land in question, and raised a crop upon it that year, and left it in the winter of the year following ; that, at that time, he appeared to be twenty-one years of age, or upwards.
Thomas Bilbo, surveyor, was produced as a witness, and, being duly sworn, deposed, that he made the survey and plot of the land in question, and believed it to be correct, and that it included the house and improvement of the claimant; that he, the witness, believed that the claim of John McIntosh, under a British grant, interfered on the lower side of this survey.
The Board ordered that the case be postponed for consideration.
Adjourned until Tuesday the 10th instant.

                    TUESDAY, April 10th, 1804.
The Board met according to adjournment. Present: Ephraim Kirby, Robert C. Nicholas.

JAMES BILBO's case, No. 155 on the docket of the Board, and No. 113 on the books of the Register.
Claim.—A right of pre-emption of four hundred and seventy-nine acres, under the third section of the act.
The claimant presented his claim, together with a surveyor's plot of the land claimed, in the following words and figures, to wit:

To the Commissioners appointed in pursuance of the act of Congress passed the 3d day of March, 1803, for receiving and adjusting claims to lands south of Tennessee, and east of Pearl river.

MARCH 24, 1804.

Please to take notice, that the following tract of land, situated on the west side of Tombigbee river, in the county of Washington, beginning at a beech, running thence, west, one hundred and four chains, to a corner swamp oak; thence, south, twenty-six degrees east, fifty-seven chains, to a post oak; thence, north, forty-eight degrees east, seven chains; thence, east, ninety-seven chains, to a corner water oak, on Sullivan's lake; thence, with the lake, to the beginning; containing four hundred and seventy-nine acres, having such forms and marks, natural and artificial, as are represented in the plot annexed: is claimed by James Bilbo, in and by virtue of the third section of the said act, as a pre-emption, and is now exhibited to the Register of the Land Office, established east of Pearl river, to be recorded as by said act directed. To all which he begs leave to refer, as also to a copy of the plot herewith filed.

JAMES BILBO.

[Plot omitted.]

Surveyed 22d March, 1804, by Thomas Bilbo. Chain carriers, James Dean and Amos Reed.

Entered in record of claims, vol. 1, page 348, by EDWARD LLOYD WAILES, for

JOSEPH CHAMBERS, *Register.*

Thomas Bilbo, surveyor, was presented as a witness, and, being duly sworn, deposed, that he made the surveys and plots returned to the Board of Commissioners by the following claimants, to wit:

George Robbins, representative of Zadock Brashear, donation, six hundred and forty acres; George Brewer, representative of James Watkins and George Johnson, donation, six hundred and twenty acres; Young Gains, attorney for Joseph House, donation, six hundred and forty acres; Sampson Mounger, donation, six hundred and thirty-four acres; Anna Mounger, donation, five hundred and four acres; George Farrar, pre-emption, one hundred and sixty acres; James Bilbo, pre-emption, four hundred and seventy-nine acres; and John Johnson, Spanish warrant, four hundred acres; and that the said plots respectively contain true representations of the land therein described, according to the best of his knowledge and belief; that they included the plantations and improvements of the several claimants; and that he knew of no interfering lines or claims.

The Board ordered that the case be postponed for consideration.

GEORGE FARRAR's case, No. 156 on the docket of the Board, and No. 158 on the books of the Register.

Claim.—A right of pre-emption of one hundred and sixty acres, under the third section of the act.

The claimant presented his claim, together with a surveyor's plot of the land claimed, in the following words and figures, to wit:

To the Commissioners appointed in pursuance of the act of Congress passed the 3d day of March, 1803, for receiving and adjusting claims to lands south of Tennessee, and east of Pearl river.

MARCH 30, 1804.

Please to take notice, that the following tract of land, situated on the west side of Tombigbee river, about two miles from the river, on a large creek called Bilbo's creek, in the county of Washington, beginning at a corner pine on the north side of said creek, running thence, south, six degrees west, forty chains, across said creek, to a corner pine; thence north, eighty-four degrees west forty chains to a corner pine; thence, north, six degrees east, forty chains, across said creek, to a corner stake; thence, south, eighty-four degrees east, forty chains, to the beginning, and hath such forms and marks, both natural and artificial, as are fully represented in the plot annexed; containing one hundred and sixty acres: is claimed by George Farrar, in and by virtue of the third section of this act, as a pre-emption, and is now exhibited to the Register of the Land Office established east of Pearl river, to be recorded as directed by said act. To all which he begs leave to refer, as also to a copy of the plot herewith filed.

GEO. FARRAR.

[Plot omitted.]

Surveyed the 28th March, 1804, by Thomas Bilbo. Chain carriers, Cornelius Rain and Jacob Neal.

Entered in record of claims, vol. 1, page 488, by EDWARD LLOYD WAILES, for

JOSEPH CHAMBERS, *Register.*

The Board ordered that the case be postponed for consideration.

EDWARD YOUNG's case, No. 157 on the docket of the Board, and No. 15 on the books of the Register.

Claim.—A donation of four hundred and eighty-eight acres, under the second section of the act.

The claimant presented his claim, together with a surveyor's plot of the land claimed, in the following words and figures, viz.:

To the Commissioners appointed in pursuance of the act of Congress passed the 3d day of March, 1803, for receiving and adjusting the claims to lands south of Tennessee, and east of Pearl river.

MARCH 3, 1804.

Please to take notice, that the following tract of land, situated on the waters of Tombigbee, in the county of Washington, beginning at a corner sycamore, and running thence, south, sixty degrees west, forty chains; thence, north, thirty degrees west, eighty-five chains; north, sixty degrees east, seventy-five chains; thence, with the river, to the beginning; containing four hundred and eighty-eight acres, having such shape, form, and marks, both natural and artificial, as are represented in the plot annexed; which said tract of land is claimed by Edward Young, under and by virtue of the second section of the said act, as a donation, and is now exhibited to the Register of the Land Office east of Pearl river, to be recorded as by the said act directed. To all which he begs leave to refer, as also to a copy of the plot herewith filed. Presented by me,

For EDWARD YOUNG,
YOUNG GAINS.

[Plot omitted.]

Surveyed 16th February, 1804, by Thomas Bilbo. Chain carriers, John Young and Joseph Lawrence.

Entered in record of claims, vol. 1, page 46, by EDWARD LLOYD WAILES, for

JOSEPH CHAMBERS, *Register.*

Thomas Bilbo, surveyor, was presented as a witness, and, being duly sworn, deposed, that he made the survey and plot of the land in question, and believed it to be correct, and that it contained the improvements of the claimant; and that he, the witness, understood that the claim of William Williams covered the house and the lower part of this claim, but had no particular knowledge of the fact.

The Board ordered that the case be postponed for consideration.

DANIEL YOUNG's case, No. 158 on the docket of the Board, and No. 16 on the books of the Register.

Claim.—A donation of six hundred and forty acres, under the second section of the act.

The claimant presented his claim, together with a surveyor's plot of the land claimed, in the following words and figures, to wit:

To the Commissioners appointed in pursuance of the act of Congress passed the 3d day of March, 1803, for receiving and adjusting the claims to lands south of Tennessee, and east of Pearl river.

MARCH 3, 1804.

Please to take notice, that the following tract of land, situated on the waters of Fulsom's creek, in the county of Washington, beginning on a red oak, and running north, forty-six degrees east, eighty chains; thence, south, forty-four degrees east, eighty chains; south, forty-six degrees east, eighty chains; thence, to the beginning; containing six hundred and forty acres, having such forms and marks, both natural and artificial, as are represented in the plot annexed; which said tract of land is claimed in and by virtue of the second section of the said act, by Daniel Young, and is now exhibited to the Register of the Land Office east of Pearl river, to be recorded as by said act directed. To all which he begs leave to refer, as also to a copy of the plot herewith filed. Presented by me, YOUNG GAINS, for

DANIEL YOUNG.

[Plot omitted.]

Surveyed 15th February, 1804, by Thomas Bilbo. Chain carriers, John Young and Joseph Lawrence.

Entered in record of claims, vol. 1, page 48, by EDWARD LLOYD WAILES, for

JOSEPH CHAMBERS, *Register.*

Thomas Bilbo, surveyor, was presented as a witness, and, being duly sworn, deposed, that he made the survey and plot of the land in question, and believed it to be correct, and that it included the plantation and improvements of the claimant; that the claim of James Huckaby covered near one-half of this survey, on the northwesterly side; that the claim of Byant and Brewer, perhaps, interfered in a small degree upon the southwesterly line.

The Board ordered that the case be postponed for consideration.

JAMES HUCKABY, representative of Matthew Robinson: case commenced in page 651.

Thomas Bilbo, surveyor, was presented as a witness, and, being duly sworn, deposed, that he made the survey and plot of the land in question; and believed it to be correct, and that it included the plantation and improvements of the claimant; that about one-half of this claim, on the east corner, was covered by the claim of Daniel Young, and knew of no other interfering claim.

The Board ordered that the case be postponed for consideration.

FRANCISCO FONTANILLA's case: commenced in page 634.

Young Gains, Jun. and David Gains, chain carriers for the survey in this case, were sworn before John Mc-Grew, Esq., Justice of the Peace.

Thomas Bilbo, surveyor, was presented as a witness, and, being duly sworn, deposed, that he made the survey and plot of the land in question, and believed it to be correct; and that it contained the plantation and improvements of the claimant; that about one-third part of this survey, on the lower side, was covered by the claim of Doctor John Chastang; that he, Bilbo, understood that the donation claims of Julian De Castro, Peter Malone, William Coleman, and James Griffin, were also laid upon the upper part of this claim.

The Board ordered that the case be postponed for consideration.

DANIEL JOHNSON, representative of Daniel Spillard: case No. 159 on the docket of the Board, and No. 81 on the books of the Register.

Claim.—A donation of six hundred and forty acres, under the second section of the act.

The claimant presented his claim, together with a surveyor's plot of the land claimed, in the following words and figures, to wit:

To the Commissioners appointed in pursuance of the act of Congress passed the 3d day of March, 1803, for receiving and adjusting claims to land south of Tennessee, and east of Pearl river.

MARCH 30, 1804.

Please to take notice, that the following tract of land, situated on the west side of Tombigbee river, in the county of Washington, beginning at a post oak, running south, seventy degrees west, fifty chains, to a stake; thence, south, twenty degrees east, one hundred and twenty eight chains, to a stake; thence, north, seventy degrees east, fifty chains, to a stake; thence, north, twenty degrees west, one hundred and twenty-eight chains, to the beginning; and hath such forms and marks, both natural and artificial, as are fully represented in the plot annexed; containing six hundred and forty acres: is claimed by Daniel Johnston, legal representative of Daniel Spillard, in and by virtue of the second section of this act, as a donation, and is now exhibited to the Register of the Land Office established east of Pearl river, to be recorded as directed by said act. To all which he begs leave to refer, as also to a copy of the plot herewith filed.

DANIEL JOHNSTON.
[Plot omitted.]

Surveyed 29th March, 1804, by Daniel Johnston. Chain bearers, Amos Reed and William D. C. Phelps.

The claimant exhibited two writings, in the following words and figures, to wit:

Know all men by these presents, That I, Archibald Reed, have bargained, sold, and delivered unto James Bilbo all my right, title, and claim of my improvement near Solomon Johnson. first improved by Daniel Shiler, for value received of him. Given under my hand, this 11th day of February, 1804.

ARCHIBALD REED.

Witness, WILLIAM D. PHELPS.

I endorse all my right and title of the above bill of sale to Daniel Johnston, for value received, of him: Witness my hand, this 25th March, 1804.

JAMES BILBO.

Witness, JOHN DEASE.

Entered in record of claims, vol. 1, page 237, by EDWARD LLOYD WAILES, for

JOSEPH CHAMBERS, Register.

John Dease, surveyor, was presented as a witness, and, being duly sworn, deposed, that he surveyed the land in question, but did not make the plot; that it was made by another person from his field notes, and that he believed it to be correct, and that it included the plantation and improvements of the claimant; that he knew of no interfering lines or claims, unless the northeast corner might interfere in a small degree with the claim of Wiley Barker; that it might also interfere in a small degree with Copeland's claim on the southeast corner.

The Board ordered that the case be postponed for consideration.

DANIEL JOHNSTON, representative of William Burke: case commenced in page 655.

John Dease, surveyor, was presented as a witness, and, being duly sworn, deposed, that he made the survey and plot of the land in question, and believed it to be correct, and that it included the improvements of the claimant; that he believed that it covered nearly the whole of James Bilbo's pre-emption claim; that he believed that the claim of the representatives of James Copeland, deceased, also interfered on the north corner, and probably covered the improvement.

The Board ordered that the case be postponed for consideration.

BRIDGET BURKE, administratrix of William Burke, deceased: case commenced in page 656.

James Powel and James Dean, chain carriers for the survey in this case, were sworn before R. Harwell, Esquire, Justice of Peace.

John Dease, surveyor, was presented as a witness, and, being duly sworn, deposed, that he made the survey and plot of the land in question, and believed it to be correct; and that it contained the improvement of the claimant; that he knew of no interfering lines or claims; and that its present shape was in consequence of other claims which bound it on all sides but one.

The Board ordered that the case be postponed for consideration.

YOUNG GAINS's case : commenced in page 621.

Thomas Bilbo, surveyor, was presented as a witness, and, being duly sworn, deposed, that he made the survey and plot of the land in question, and that he believed it to be correct; that it included the improvements of the claimant; that he understood that the claim of George Brewer, Jr. interfered with this on the lower side, and Thomas Malone on the upper side, but in what manner did not know.

The Board ordered that the case be postponed for consideration.

JOHN CHASTANG, representative of John Talley: case commenced in page 616.

Thomas Bilbo, surveyor, was presented as a witness, and, being duly sworn, deposed, that he made the survey and plot of the land in question, and believed it to be correct; and that it contained the improvements of the claimant; that it adjoins the other claim of Doctor Chastang for four hundred and eighty acres, under a Spanish warrant, on the lower side thereof; that he knew of no interference.

The Board ordered that the case be postponed for consideration.

JOHN CHASTANG's case: commenced in page 614.

Thomas Bilbo, surveyor, was presented as a witness, and, being duly sworn, deposed, that he made the survey and plot of the land in question, and believed it to be correct ; and that it contained the plantation and improvements of the claimant; that about two thirds of this survey, on the upper side, was covered by the claim of Francisco Fontanilla; and that the claim of James Griffin interfered upon the back end.

The Board ordered that the case be postponed for consideration.

DANIEL JOHNSON's case: commenced in page 620.

Amos Reed and James Dean, chain carriers for the survey in this case, were sworn before Figures Lewis and John Callier, Esquires, Justices of the Peace.

John Dease, surveyor, was presented as a witness, and, being duly sworn, deposed, that he made the survey and plot of the land in question, and believed it to be correct; and that it included the improvements of the claimant; that the British claim of Alexander McCullagh covered about one-quarter part of this claim, on the south side; and had heard of a British grant, in favor of Adam Tate, which must also cover a part of this claim, on the north side.

The Board ordered that the case be postponed for consideration.

JAMES POWEL, executor of William Powel, deceased: case commenced in page 623.

John Dease, surveyor, was presented as a witness, and, being duly sworn, deposed, that he made the survey and plot of the land in question, and believed it to be correct; and that it contained the improvements of the claimant; that about one-third of this claim, on the north side, was included in the claim of the representative of Nathaniel Bassett, deceased; that he knew of no other interference.

The Board ordered that the case be postponed for consideration.

JAMES POWEL's case: commenced in page 643.

John Dease, surveyor, was presented as a witness, and, being duly sworn, deposed, that he made the survey and plot of the land in question, and believed it to be correct; and that it included the improvements of the present claimant; that nearly the whole of this claim was covered by the claim of the representative of Nathaniel Bassett, deceased, except a small point on the river, at the upper corner, and also on the north end; that he knew of no other interference.

The Board ordered that the case be postponed for consideration.

Adjourned until Wednesday, the 11th instant.

WEDNESDAY, April 11, 1804.
The Board met according to adjournment. Present: Ephraim Kirby, Robert C. Nicholas.
Adjourned until Thursday, the 12th instant.

THURSDAY, April 12, 1804.
The Board met according to adjournment. Present: Ephraim Kirby, Robert C. Nicholas.

JOSEPH CHASTANG's case: commenced in page 650.

James Gordon, surveyor, was presented as a witness, and, being duly sworn, deposed, that he made the survey and plot of the land in question, and believed it to be correct; and that it included the dwelling-house and improvements of the claimant; that he knew of no interfering line or claim.

The claimant produced a deposition, taken in pursuance of an order of the Board, recorded in page 714; which deposition is in the following words and figures, to wit:

TUESDAY, April 3, 1804.
Personally appeared before me Simon Andry, and, being qualified agreeable to law, testifies as follows: that, some time in the year 1795, Ushan Chastang entered on the land in question with negroes, the property of Joseph Chastang, as he understood, and cultivated the said land until the American line was run, on both sides of the river; all of which time the said Joseph Chastang resided in Mobile; and, after the line was run, the said Joseph moved up, and has continued to cultivate and inhabit to the present day.

Sworn to before me,
JAMES CALLIER, J. P.
The Board ordered that the case be postponed for consideration.

SIMON ANDRY's case: commenced in page 624.

William Mitchel was produced as a witness, and, being duly sworn and interrogated by the Board, deposed, that he was not interested in this claim; that, before the year 1795, and ever since, Simon Andry had been settled upon and cultivated the land in question, by his slaves; but having an overseer there, and being there occasionally himself, he resided principally in Mobile, until about six or seven years ago; that he made this place his steady residence; and that he then was upwards of fifty years of age.

James Gordon, surveyor, was presented as a witness, and, being duly sworn, deposed, that he made the survey and plot of the land in question, and believed it to be correct; that this survey, together with another small one adjoining, which was claimed under a different title, included the buildings and improvements of the claimant, (part of the buildings coming within this plot, and part within the other;) that, on the north or upper side of this survey, the claim of John Baptist Trenier interfered to a very considerable extent.

The Board ordered that the case be postponed for consideration.

SIMON ANDRY, representative of Charlotte Haurale: case commenced in page 625.

The testimony of William Mitchel, recorded in the preceding case in this page, was applied in this case; his knowledge being the same in both cases.

James Gordon, surveyor, was presented as a witness, and, being duly sworn, deposed, that he made the survey and plot of the land in question, and believed it to be correct: that the piece on the west side of the river, containing forty-one acres, included part of the buildings and improvements of the claimant; that he, Gordon, knew of no interfering lines or claims.

The Board ordered that the case be postponed for consideration.

JOHN BAPTISTE TRENIER's case: commenced in page 617.

James Gordon, surveyor, was presented as a witness, and, being duly sworn, deposed, that he made the survey and plot of the land in question, and believed it to be correct; and that it included the dwelling-house and improvement of the claimant; but that the claim of Simon Andry included the said buildings and improvements, and the whole of this claim, except about thirty-five acres.

The Board ordered that the case be postponed for consideration.

JOHN CHASTANG's case: commenced in page 614.

James Gordon, surveyor, was presented as a witness, and, being duly sworn, deposed, that he made the survey and plot of the land in question, and believed it to be correct; and that it included the dwelling and improvements of the claimant; that he, Gordon, knew of no interfering lines or claims.

The Board ordered that the case be postponed for consideration.

JAMES CALLIER, representative of Isabella Trouillet, the wife of Joseph Campbell: case commenced in page 650.

James Gordon, surveyor, was presented as a witness, and, being duly sworn, deposed, that he made the survey and plot of the land in question, and believes that three of the lines which he run out, to wit, on the north end, west side, and south end, to be correctly delineated; but the line which pursues the meanders of the waters, and bounds thereon, he did not run, but laid the same down by conjecture.

Question by the claimant. Whether you did or did not make a correct plot of the land in question, according to the best of your knowledge at the time?

Answer. I did, as I was not able to take the meanders of the river.

Question by the claimant. Were you not instructed to run out this land so as not to include more than six hundred and forty acres?

Answer. I was instructed to run half a mile out, from the place of beginning, two miles down, and half a mile east, to the river.

The Board ordered that the case be postponed for consideration.

JAMES CALLIER's case, representative of Joseph Anderson: commenced in page 607.

James Gordon, surveyor, was produced as a witness, and being duly sworn, deposed, that he made the survey and plot of the land in question, and believed it to be correct; and that it included the improvements of the claimant: that it interfered with the claim of Thomas Carson, about one-half, on the north side.

The Board ordered that the case be postponed for consideration.

JAMES CALLIER and JOSEPH CAMPBELL, executors of Maria Josephia Narbone: case commenced in page 635.

James Gordon, surveyor, was presented as a witness, and, being duly sworn, deposed, that he made the survey and plot of the land in question, and believed it to be correct; and that it included the dwelling and improvements of the claimant; and that there were no interfering lines or claims.

The Board ordered that the case be postponed for consideration.

Adjourned until Friday, the 13th instant.

FRIDAY, *April* 13, 1804.
The Board met according to adjournment. Present: Ephraim Kirby, Robert C. Nicholas.
Adjourned until Saturday, the 14th instant.

SATURDAY, *April* 14, 1804.
The Board met according to adjournment. Present: Ephraim Kirby, Robert C. Nicholas.

YOUNG GAINS's case: commenced in page 621.
Adam Hollinger and Nathan Blackwell were presented as witnesses, and, being duly sworn and interrogated by the Board, they deposed, that they had no interest in this claim; that according to their knowledge and belief, the land in question was inhabited and improved by a person of the name of Lucas, as early as the year 1790, and that it continued to be inhabited and cultivated by a person of the name of Burrows through the year 1795; but whether these persons were tenants to the present claimant or not, they did not know; that the present claimant was an inhabitant of the Mississippi territory on the 27th of October, 1795, before that time, and ever since; and that, on the 22d of October, 1787, he was more than twenty-one years of age.
Question by the claimant. Did you ever know or hear that Burrows ever offered to sell the land in question, or exercise any act of exclusive ownership?
Answer by both. We never did.
The Board ordered that the case be postponed for consideration.
Adjourned until Monday, the 16th instant.

MONDAY, *April* 16, 1804.
The Board met according to adjournment. Present: Ephraim Kirby, Robert C. Nicholas, Joseph Chambers.

BENJAMIN FEW's case, No. 160 on the docket of the Board, and No. 170 on the books of the Register.
Claim.—A right of pre-emption of five hundred acres, as representative of Turnbull and Joyce, under the third section of the act.
The claimant presented his claim, together with a surveyor's plot of the land claimed, in the following words and figures, to wit:

To the Commissioners appointed in pursuance of the act of Congress passed the 3d day of March, 1803, for receiving and adjusting claims to land south of Tennessee, and east of Pearl river.

Please to take notice, that the following tract of land, situated on Nanna Hubb bluff, on the west side of Tombigbee river, in the county of Washington, beginning at a stake at the old corner, said to be Turnbull's; running thence, with the river, south, fifty-two degrees east, thirty-two chains; thence, south, seventy-three degrees east, thirty-one chains, to a sassafras; thence, south, twenty-eight degrees west, eighty-one chains fifty links, to a stake; thence, north, sixty-two degrees west, sixty-three chains, to a stake; thence, north, twenty-eight degrees east, eighty-one chains fifty links, to the beginning; and hath such forms and marks, both natural and artificial, as are fully represented in the plot annexed; containing five hundred acres: is claimed by Benjamin Few, under the third section of the act, &c.; the said Turnbull claimed this land under a Spanish warrant, [which] is now exhibited to the Register of the Land Office established east of Pearl river, to be recorded as directed by said act. To all which he begs leave to refer, as also to a copy of the plot herewith filed.
                    BENJAMIN FEW.
MARCH 30, 1804.
[Plot omitted.]
Surveyed March 28, 1804, by John Milliken. Chain bearers, James McConnell and Edmund Smith.
Entered in record of claims, vol. 1, page 507, by EDWARD LLOYD WAILES, for
    JOSEPH CHAMBERS, *Register.*

Natt Christmas, Richard Barrow, and John Milliken, surveyor, were presented as witnesses, and, being duly sworn, the said Christmas deposed, that, some time in the year 1802, he as sheriff, was directed by Lemuel Henry, Esquire, attorney at law, to advertise and sell one hundred acres of land, lying, as he believed, within the lines of the plot or survey then exhibited to the Board, in virtue of an execution issued from the court of Washington county, Mississippi territory, in favor of Michael Milton, against the property of Turnbull and Joyce; that he did accordingly advertise and put said land to sale; at which sale, Colonel Benjamin Few was the highest

bidder, and became the purchaser; that he, Christmas, gave him a sheriff's deed for the said one hundred acres of land; that, in two or three days after the sale, he put said Few in possession of said land; and that he had continued to inhabit and cultivate the same ever since.
The said Barrow deposed, that Colonel Benjamin Few had, according to his best belief, cultivated and inhabited on the land in question from the year 1802, and that Few was more than twenty-one years of age.
The said Milliken deposed, that he surveyed the land in question, and made the plot, but only measured the river, with its meanders, and plotted the other lines for complement of land; that said plot interfered with the claim of Howel Dupree, in or about the red dots; that Lemuel Henry's claim, as representative of John Turnbull, covered all of said land, except that part interfering with Dupree; that said Few inhabited and cultivated within the limits of this survey.
The Board ordered that the case be postponed for consideration.
Adjourned until Tuesday, the 17th instant.

TUESDAY, *April* 17, 1804.
The Board met according to adjournment. Present: Ephraim Kirby, Robert C. Nicholas, Joseph Chambers.
Adjourned until Wednesday, the 18th instant.

WEDNESDAY, *April* 18, 1804.
The Board met according to adjournment. Present: Ephraim Kirby, Robert C. Nicholas, Joseph Chambers.

RICHARD HAWKINS's case, No. 161 on the docket of the Board, and No. 171 on the books of the Register.
Claim.—A donation of six hundred and forty acres, under the second section of the act.
The claimant presented his claim, together with a surveyor's plot of the land claimed, in the following words and figures, to wit:

To the Commissioners appointed in pursuance of the act of Congress passed the 3d day of March, 1803, for receiving and adjusting claims to land south of Tennessee, and east of Pearl river.

Please to take notice, that the following tract of land, situate on the west side of Tombigbee, on Barrow's lake, in the county of Washington, beginning at a cypress on the point where Barrow's creek empties into Barrow's lake, running thence, down the lake, south, thirty-four degrees west, fifty-two chains, to a cypress on the bank; thence, north, sixty-two degrees west, one hundred and twenty-five chains, to a stake; thence, north, forty-five degrees east, fifty-two chains, to a stake; thence to the beginning; and hath such forms and marks, both natural and artificial, as are fully represented in the plot annexed, containing six hundred and forty acres: is claimed by Richard Hawkins, in and by virtue of the second section of the act, as a donation, and is now exhibited to the Register of the Land Office established east of Pearl river, to be recorded as directed by said act. To all which he begs leave to refer, as also to a copy of the plot herewith filed.
                    RICHARD HAWKINS.
    [Plot omitted.]
MARCH 31, 1804.
Surveyed March, — 1804, by Natt Christmas. Chain bearers, William Gibson and David Matthias.
Entered in record of claims, vol. 1, page 509, by EDWARD LLOYD WAILES, for
    JOSEPH CHAMBERS, *Register.*

Natt Christmas, surveyor, was presented as a witness, and being duly sworn, deposed, that he surveyed the land in question; that the plot then exhibited gave a true and correct representation of the land claimed, with such marks, natural and artificial, as were therein laid down; that said Hawkins resided within the limits of this survey; that there was an interference between this claim and the claim of Simpson Whaley, on the line north, forty-two degrees east, somewhere near to the lake, as he had been informed.
The said Gibson and Matthias, chain carriers for the above survey, were sworn before William H. Hargrave, Justice of Peace.
The Board ordered that the case be postponed for consideration.

JOSEPH BATES, Junior's case: commenced in page 646.
Natt Christmas, surveyor, was presented as a witness, and, being duly sworn, deposed, that he surveyed the land in question, and that the plot exhibited gave a true

and correct representation of the land claimed, with such marks, natural and artificial, as were therein laid down; that the claimant lived within the limits of said survey; that there was an interference of a few acres on the line north, sixty-three degrees east, on the branch which makes a part of said line, between this claim and the claim of Edward Creighton, representative of Benjamin King; that he only knew of said interference upon information.

The Board ordered that the case be postponed for consideration.

ADAM HOLLINGER's case, No. 162 on the docket of the Board, and No. 174 on the books of the Register.

Claim.—A right of pre-emption of six hundred and twelve acres, under the third section of the act.

The claimant presented his claim, together with a surveyor's plot of the land claimed, in the following words and figures, to wit:

To the Commissioners appointed in pursuance of an act of Congress passed the 3d day of March, 1803, for receiving and adjusting claims to land south of the Tennessee river, and east of the Pearl river.

Please to take notice, that the following tract of land, lying west of the Tombigbee river, beginning on a stake, on the west bank of the said river, at the mouth of the Poll bayou, on the south side of the said creek, on Eason's corner; thence, running with his line, south, eighty-six degrees west. eighty chains, to a pine; thence, south, eleven degrees east,twenty-five chains, to a pine; thence, south, seventy-seven degrees west, twenty-eight chains, to a gum ; thence, north, eleven degrees east, one hundred and five chains, to a pine; thence, north, eighty degrees east, seventy-one chains, to a stake, on the bank of the Tombigbee river; thence, down the river, to the beginning: is claimed by Adam Hollinger, under and by virtue of the third section of the above mentioned act of Congress. To all which he begs leave to refer, as also to the copy of the plot now delivered to the Register of the Land Office to be established east of Pearl river; which plot is herewith filed.

W. CARMAN,
Attorney in fact for Adam Hollinger.

FORT STODDERT, *March* 31, 1804.

[Plot omitted.]

Surveyed the 15th day of March, 1804, by Natt Christmas. Chain bearers, John Barnet and Goodwin Mirick.

Entered in record of claims, vol. 1, page 512, by ED-WARD LLOYD WAILES, for

JOSEPH CHAMBERS, *Register.*

Natt Christmas, surveyor, Joseph Bates, senior, and Lemuel Henry, were presented as witnesses, and being duly sworn, the said Christmas deposed, that there were two interferences with the lines of this survey, viz.: Thomas Bates, senior, and Seth Dean, both run over the line north, eleven degrees east, a considerable distance; Dean near three hundred acres, and Bates above two hundred acres.

The said Bates and Henry deposed that Adam Hollinger inhabited and cultivated the land in question on the third day of March, 1803, and before, and ever since that time; and that said Hollinger was, on the third day of March, 1803, the head of a family.

The Board ordered that the case be postponed for consideration.

SETH DEAN's case, No. 163 on the docket of the Board and No. 176 on the books of the Register.

Claim.—A donation of six hundred and forty acres, as representative of John Jacob Abner, under the second section of the act.

The claimant presented his claim, together with a surveyor's plot of the land claimed, in the following words and figures, viz.:

To the Commissioners appointed in pursuance of the act of Congress passed the 3d day of March, 1803, for receiving and adjusting claims to lands south of Tennessee, and east of Pearl river.

Please to take notice, that the following tract of land, situated on the west side of Tombigbee river, in the county of Washington, beginning at a corner stake, running north, seventy-two degrees west, eighty chains, to a lightwood stake; thence, south, eighty degrees west fifteen chains, to a pine ; thence, north, fifteen degrees east, eighty chains, to a corner stake; thence, south, seventy-two degrees east, seventy-five chains, to the river; thence with the river to the beginning ; having such shape, form and marks, natural and artificial, as are represented in the plot annexed, containing six hundred and forty acres: is claimed by Seth Dean, representative of John Jacob Abner, in and by virtue of the second section of the said act, and is now exhibited to the Register of the Land Office east of Pearl river, to be recorded as directed by said act. To all which he begs leave to refer, as also to a copy of the plot herewith filed.

SETH DEAN,
Representative of John Jacob Abner.

MARCH 31, 1804.

[Plot omitted.]

Surveyed 31st March, 1804, by Seth Dean. Chain carriers, Jesse Thomas and David Dupree.

Entered in record of claims, vol. 1, page 514, by ED-WARD LLOYD WAILES, for

JOSEPH CHAMBERS, *Register.*

The Board ordered that the case be postponed for consideration.

SETH DEAN's case, No. 164 on the docket of the Board, and No. 178 on the books of the Register.

Claim.—A right of pre-emption of six hundred and forty acres, under the third section of the act.

The claimant presented his claim, together with a surveyor's plot of the land claimed, in the following words and figures, to wit:

To the Commissioners appointed in pursuance of the act of Congress passed the 3d day of March, 1803, for receiving and adjusting claims to lands south of Tennessee, and east of Pearl river.

Please to take notice, that the following tract of land, situated on the west side of the river Tombigbee in the county of Washington, beginning on the said river, running thence, north, eighty degrees west, ninety chains, to a corner stake; thence, north, sixty-six chains, to a stake; thence east, ninety chains, to a stake on said river; thence, to the beginning; and hath such forms and marks, both natural and artificial, as are fully represented in the plot annexed; containing six hundred and forty acres, is claimed by Seth Dean, in and by virtue of the third section of this act, as a pre-emption, and is now exhibited to the Register of the Land Office established east of Pearl river, to be recorded as directed by said act. To all which he begs leave to refer, as also to a copy of the plot herewith filed.

SETH DEAN.

MARCH 24, 1804.

[Plot omitted.]

Entered in record of claims, vol. 1, page 516, by ED-WARD LLOYD WAILES, for

JOSEPH CHAMBERS, *Register.*

Natt Christmas, surveyor, was presented as a witness, and, being duly sworn, deposed, that he made the plot of the land in question, from his field notes of adjoining lines, and believed it to be correct; that it included an improvement originally made by the claimant, then in the occupancy of Mrs. Copeland; that this tract was claimed by Thomas Bates and Adam Hollinger, representatives of William Cheney, except a few acres on the west side ; that the interference of Hollinger was on the south side about one half, and Bates' interference on the north more than one half, and extended on to the claim of Hollinger.

The Board ordered that the case be postponed for consideration.

GEORGE DICKEY's case, No. 165 on the docket of the Board, and No. 151 on the books of the Register.

Claim.—A right of pre-emption of six hundred and forty acres, under the third section of the act.

The claimant presented his claim, together with a surveyor's plot of the land claimed, in the following words, to wit:

To the Commissioners appointed for adjusting claims and rights of lands south of Tennessee, and east of the Pearl river.

Please to take notice, that the above survey is claimed by George Dickey, as a pre-emption lying and situated about three miles below the Sunflower, beginning on a sassafras, running west with Danley's line, until hindered by water; thence, returning back to the beginning; thence, meandering the river down, one hundred and fourteen chains fifty links, to a sassafras; thence, west, until hindered by water; claiming, by the said pre-emption, six hundred and forty acres; bounding on the north by Denley, and on other sides by vacant land or undefined claims.

JOHN DENLEY, for

GEORGE DICKEY.

[Plot omitted.]

MARCH 3, 1804.

Chain carriers, James Donley and Hiram Mounger Partly surveyed on the 23d March, 1804, by Robert Ligon.

Entered in record of claims, vol. 1, page 460, by EDWARD LLOYD WAILES, for

JOSEPH CHAMBERS, Register.

John Denley was presented as a witness, and, being duly sworn and interrogated by the Board, deposed, that the claimant began to work on the land in question in the year 1801, and worked upon it at times ever since, but did not know that he had ever made a crop upon it, but believed that he had about six acres well cleared; that the land was low, and subject to inundation, and was unfit for a place of residence; that the claimant had not resided upon it; that George Dickey, the claimant, was the head of a family on the 3d of March, 1803.

The Board ordered that the case be postponed for consideration.

THOMAS SULLIVANT, Junior's case: commenced in page 658.

Natt Christmas, surveyor, was presented as a witness, and, being duly sworn, deposed, that he made the surveys and plots returned to the Board by the following claimants, to wit: Thomas Sullivant, junior, pre-emption, one hundred and ninety acres; Edmund Smith, pre-emption, four hundred and twenty-two acres; John Dease, pre-emption, fifty acres; heirs of Godfrey Helverston, donation, six hundred and forty acres; and Seth Dean, representative of John Wallace, pre-emption, six hundred and thirty-nine acres; and that the said plots respectively contained true representations of the land therein described, according to his best knowledge and belief; that they included the plantations and improvements of the several claimants; and that he knew of no interfering lines or claims.

The Board ordered that the case be postponed for consideration.

THOMAS BATES's case: commenced in page 687.

Natt Christmas, surveyor, was presented as a witness, and, being duly sworn, deposed, that he made the survey of the land in question, that the plot then exhibited gave a true and correct representation of the land claimed, with such marks, natural and artificial, as were therein laid down; that there were two interferences with the lines of this claim, viz.: the lines of Seth Dean's claim, and the lines of Adam Hollinger's claim, as representative of William Cheney; that Adam Hollinger's claim interfered with this claim, running from the line south forty-four degrees east, nearly with the crooked line, intended to represent a fence, to the river Tombigbee; that Dean's claim interfered with this claim, running with a line to the north-east of the fence, from the south line, forty-four degrees east, to the same river Tombigbee, as by the scratched line on the plot may better appear.

The Board ordered that the case be postponed for consideration.

JOSIAH SKINNER's case: commenced in page 605.

Natt Christmas, surveyor, was presented as a witness, and, being duly sworn, deposed, that he surveyed the land now in question; that the plot exhibited gives a true and correct representation of the land claimed, with such marks, natural and artificial, as were therein laid down; that the improvements of the claimant were within the lines of this survey; that he had been informed that James Callier, Esquire's, claim, as representative of Joseph Anderson, interfered with the whole of this land, except the narrow niche of land, which he knew run within the limits of Thomas Carson's claim, and which Skinner run by the consent of Carson, given in his, Christmas's, presence.

The Board ordered that the case be postponed for consideration.

EDWARD GATLAND's case, No. 166 on the docket of the Board, and No. 11 on the books of the Register.

Claim.—A right of pre-emption of three hundred and six acres, under the third section of the act.

The claimant presented his claim, together with a surveyor's plot of the land claimed, in the following words and figures, to wit:

To the Commissioners appointed in pursuance of the act of Congress passed the 3d day of March, 1803, for receiving and adjusting the claims to lands south of Tennessee, and east of Pearl river.

Please to take notice, that the following tract of land, situated on the waters of Mobile river, in the county of Washington, beginning at a gum, and running thence, south, ten degrees east, sixty chains, to a gum; thence, south, two degrees east, ten chains, to a gum; thence, south, seventeen degrees west, thirty-four chains fifty links, to a cypress corner; thence, north, seventy-eight degrees west, eighteen chains, to a live oak corner; thence, north, nine degrees west, ninety-three chains, to a gum corner; thence, to the beginning; containing three hundred and six acres, having such forms and marks, both natural and artificial, as are fully represented in the plot annexed: which said tract of land is claimed by Edward Gatland, in and by virtue of the third section of the said act as a pre-emption, and is now exhibited to the Register of the Land Office east of Pearl river, to be recorded as directed by said act. To all which he begs leave to refer, as also to copy of the plot herewith filed.

EDWARD GATLAND.

FEBRUARY 29, 1804.

[Plot omitted.]

Surveyed 27th February, 1804, by Natt Christmas. Chain bearers, Sterling Dupree and David Dupree, who were sworn before James Callier, Justice of the Peace.

Entered in record of claims, vol. 1, page 41, by EDWARD LLOYD WAILES, for

JOSEPH CHAMBERS, Register.

Natt Christmas, surveyor, James Callier, and Joseph Bates, Sen. were presented as witnesses, and, being duly sworn, the said Christmas deposed, that he surveyed the land now in question; that the plot exhibited gave a true and correct representation of the land claimed, with such marks, natural and artificial, as were therein laid down; that a negro house and field of the claimant were within the limits of this survey; that there was an interference between the lines of this claim and the claim of Howel Dupree, to the extent of a straight line drawn from the two small crosses on the lines north, nine degrees west, and south, ten degrees east, and on the north end of this survey; that he only knew of this interference from information, but the fact, he believed, would more at large appear, reference being had to the survey of Howel Dupree's claim.

The said Callier and the said Bates deposed, that the claimant commenced to improve upon the land in question in the winter of the year 1802, and made a crop of corn thereon in the following year, and had continued to cultivate the same ever since; that this being swamp or low land, it was not a suitable place for a dwelling house; that they believed that the waters covered nearly the whole of this land, at some seasons of the year; that, on the 3d of March, 1803, and before, and ever since that time, the claimant was the head of a family.

The Board ordered that the case be postponed for consideration.

HEIRS OF JAMES COPELEN: case commenced in page 657.

Natt Christmas, surveyor, was presented as a witness, and, being duly sworn, deposed, that he made the plot of the land then exhibited to the Board, and did actually survey and measure the same from the Three River lake, to the Boggy branch, but was prevented from the further survey and measurement by high waters; that he plotted the residue for complement, and also took the course of the lake from actual observation; that there were two interferences with the lines of this survey, viz.: George Brewer and Figures Lewis; that both those interferences were on the south side of this survey; that he only knew of those interferences from information that the fact will more at large appear, by referring to the plots of George Brewer, attorney for the heirs of Charles Brewer, and Figures Lewis's survey.

The Board ordered that the case be postponed for consideration.

Adjourned until Thursday, the 19th instant.

THURSDAY, *April* 19, 1804.

The Board met according to adjournment. Present: Ephraim Kirby, Robert C. Nicholas, Joseph Chambers.

LEMUEL HENRY, attorney in fact for Anthony Espaho: case commenced in page 633.

Joseph Bates, sen. and Natt Christmas were produced as witnesses, and, being duly sworn and interrogated by the Board, they deposed, that they had no interest in this claim; and the said witnesses further deposed, that a man of the name of Alexander inhabited and cultivated the land in question in the year 1793; that his, Alexander's negroes, continued to cultivate on this land in the years 1794 and 1795; that, in those last years, the negroes were under his, Bates's, direction; that said cultivation and habitation were under the permission of John Turnbull, as he, Bates, was informed by Alexander, Joyce, and Turnbull; that after Alexander quitted the possession, a man by the name of Hartly contracted with John Turnbull for the purchase of said land; and, in full consideration therefor was to pay him three hundred dollars; that, in pursuance of said contract to purchase, said Hartly entered into possession of the premises in the winter of the year 1795, or spring of the year 1796, and continued to inhabit and cultivate thereon, until the fall or winter of 1799, when, having failed to make the payment of three hundred dollars, he told him, Bates, that he had given up the land to Turnbull again, and had cancelled his obligation to pay the said three hundred dollars; that he had also heard Joyce say that he had released Hartly from the payment of the three hundred dollars, in consequence of said Hartly's having given up the land, or rather the right he had acquired by said contract to purchase; that neither Turnbull nor Joyce were inhabitants within the Mississippi territory on the 27th of October, 1795, or since that time.

Question. Has the right to this land always been admitted to be in John Turnbull?

Answer. I have understood that the right was always admitted to be in John Turnbull, or persons claiming under him.

Question to said Christmas by the claimant's attorney. Did you or did you not see in the possession of Mr. Norwood an English grant for the land in question, in favor of John Turnbull?

Answer. I did never see any such grant.

The Board ordered that the case be postponed for consideration.

NATT CHRISTMAS's case, No. 167 on the docket of the Board, and No. 175 on the books of the Register.

Claim.—A right of pre-emption of eighty-five acres, under the third section of the act.

The claimant presented his claim, together with a surveyor's plot of the land claimed, in the following words and figures, to wit:

To the Commissioners appointed in pursuance of the act of Congress passed the 3d day of March, 1803, for receiving and adjusting claims to lands south of Tennessee and east of Pearl river.

Please to take notice, that the following tract of land, situated on the west side of the river Tombigbee, on the bluff known by the name of Nanna Hubba, in the county of Washington; beginning on said river, running thence, north, three degrees west, twenty-one chains; thence, north, sixteen degrees east, twenty-three chains twenty-five links; thence, north, fifty-three degrees west, six chains; thence, north, five degrees west, twelve chains; thence, south, sixty degrees west, seventeen chains; thence, south, twenty-five chains; thence, north, eighty degrees east, thirty-two chains, to the beginning; containing eighty-five acres, and hath such forms and marks, both natural and artificial, as are fully represented in the plot annexed: is claimed by Natt Christmas, in and by virtue of the third section of this act, and is now exhibited to the Register of the Land Office established east of Pearl river, to be recorded as directed by said act. To all which he begs leave to refer, as also to a copy of the plot herewith filed.

MARCH 31, 1804.   NATT CHRISTMAS.

[Plot omitted.]

Surveyed 28th March, 1804, by J. Milliken. Chain carriers, John Ackworth and Josiah Kirk.

Entered in record of claims, vol. 1, page 513, by EDWARD LLOYD WAILES, for

JOSEPH CHAMBERS, Register.

Joseph Bates, Sen. and Edward Gatland were produced as witnesses, and, being duly sworn and interrogated by the Board, they deposed, that they had no interest in this claim: that the claimant has inhabited and cultivated on the land in question from the year 1801 until the then present time; that he did actually inhabit and cultivate on the same on the 3d day of March, 1803;

and that Natt Christmas, the claimant, was, on the said 3d day of March, 1803, the head of a family.

The Board ordered that the case be postponed for consideration.

Adjourned until Friday, the 20th instant.

FRIDAY, April 20, 1804.

The Board met according to adjournment. Present: Ephraim Kirby, Robert C. Nicholas, Joseph Chambers.

Adjourned to Saturday, the 21st instant.

SATURDAY, April 21, 1804.

The Board met according to adjournment. Present: Ephraim Kirby, Robert C. Nicholas, Joseph Chambers.

SETH DEAN's case: commenced in page 693.

Jesse Thomas and William Wallace were presented as witnesses, and, being duly sworn and interrogated by the Board, they deposed, that they had no interest in this claim: that Seth Dean commenced to improve upon the land then in question in the year 1802, and that he did actually inhabit and cultivate the same on the 3d day of March, 1803; and that said Dean was, on said 3d day of March, the head of a family; and that Mrs. Copeland then lived on said land.

The Board ordered that the case be postponed for consideration.

SETH DEAN's case, No. 168 on the docket of the Board, and No. 180 on the books of the Register.

Claim.—A right of pre-emption of six hundred and thirty-nine acres, as assignee and legal representative of John Wallace, under the third section of the act.

The claimant presented his claim, together with a surveyor's plot of the land claimed, in the following words and figures, to wit:

To the Commissioners appointed in pursuance of the act of Congress passed on the 3d day of March, 1803, for receiving and adjusting the claims to lands south of Tennessee and east of Pearl river.

Please to take notice, that the following tract of land, situated on the west side of the river Tombigbee, in the county of Washington, beginning at a sassafras on said river, running thence south, forty-four degrees west, ninety chains, to a pine; thence, north, forty-six degrees west, eighty chains, to a stake on Bilbo's creek; thence, on said creek, north sixty-four degrees east, seventy-one chains, to a stake; thence north, fourteen degrees east, forty chains, to a gum: thence along the said river, to the beginning: having such shape, form, and marks, natural and artificial, as are represented in the plot annexed: is claimed by Seth Dean, legal representative of John Wallace, in and by virtue of the third section of this act, as a pre-emption, and now exhibited to the Register of the Land Office, to be recorded as directed by said act. To all which he begs leave to refer, as also to a copy of the plot herewith filed.

SETH DEAN,
Representative of John Wallace.

MARCH 31, 1804.

[Plot omitted.]

Chain bearers, William Vaughn and Robert Sharp. Entered in record of claims, vol. 1, page 519, by EDWARD LLOYD WAILES, for

JOSEPH CHAMBERS, Register.

The claimant produced a deed of conveyance from John Wallace, bearing date the 31st of October, 1803, duly executed, relinquishing and conveying to the said Seth Dean all the said Wallace's right and interest in or to the said tract of land, together with the improvements made thereon.

William Walton was presented as a witness, and being duly sworn and interrogated by the Board, deposed that he was not interested in this claim; that he saw John Wallace sign, seal, and deliver to Seth Dean the deed then presented to the Board, on the day and for the purposes therein mentioned, and that he subscribed thereto as a witness.

Edna Bilbo and Richard Hawkins were presented as witnesses, and being duly sworn, the said Bilbo deposed that John Wallace built and settled upon the land then in question before the 3d of March, 1803, and cultivated a garden only on said land the ensuing season; and that John Wallace was, on said 3d day of March, the head of a family.

The said Hawkins deposed, that John Wallace built and settled upon the land then in question before the 3d day of March, 1803, and that said Wallace was, on the said 3d day of March, the head of a family.

The Board ordered that the case be postponed for consideration.

SETH DEAN's case, No. 169 on the docket of the Board, and No. 179 on the books of the Register.

Claim.—A right of pre-emption of six hundred and forty acres, as assignee and legal representative of James Lowe, under the third section of the act.

The claimant presented his claim, together with a surveyor's plot of the land claimed, in the following words and figures, viz.:

To the Commissioners appointed in pursuance of the act of Congress passed the 3d day of March, 1803, for receiving and adjusting the claims to lands south of Tennessee and east of Pearl river.

Please to take notice, that the following tract of land, situated on the west side of Tombigbee river, in the county of Washington, beginning on a corner stake, running thence, north, eighty degrees west, sixty-four chains, to Bates's creek; thence, along said creek, to Bilbo's creek, to a corner stake on said creek; thence, south, fifty-eight degrees west, thirty-eight chains, to a pine; thence, south, eighty-four degrees west, forty chains, to a corner pine; thence, south, six degrees east, one hundred chains, to a corner stake; thence, north, eighty degrees east, eighty-four chains, to the beginning, having such shape, form and marks, natural and artificial, as are represented in the plot annexed: is claimed by Seth Dean, representative of James Lowe, in virtue of the third section of the said act, and is now exhibited to the Register of the Land Office established east of Pearl river, to be recorded as directed by said act. To all which he begs leave to refer, as also to a copy of the plot annexed.

SETH DEAN,
Representative of James Lowe.

MARCH 31, 1804.

[Plot omitted.]

Surveyed 31st March, 1804 by Seth Dean. Chain carriers, David Dupree and George Farrar.

Entered in record of claims, vol. 1, page 517, by EDWARD LLOYD WAILES, for

JOSEPH CHAMBERS, Register.

The claimant exhibited a deed of conveyance from James Lowe, duly executed, bearing date the 9th day of February, 1804, conveying to the said Dean all the said Lowe's right, claim, and interest to the said tract of land.

Sherwood B. Bonner, Edna Bilbo, and Richard Hawkins, were presented as witnesses, and, being duly sworn and interrogated by the Board, they deposed, that they had no interest in this case; and said Bonner further testified, that he saw James Lowe with his own hand sign, seal, and deliver unto Seth Dean the instrument of writing then presented to the Board; and that he, Bonner, subscribed to said writing, when made, as a witness, as did also Aaron Grinage.

The said Bilbo and Hawkins further deposed, that James Lowe built a house, and lived upon the land in question, before the 3d of March, 1803, and did inhabit on said land on the said 3d day of March, and cultivated cotton and potatoes thereon the ensuing season; that James Lowe was, on the 3d day of March, 1803, the head of a family, and more than twenty-one years of age.

The Board ordered that the case be postponed for consideration.

SETH DEAN's case, No. 170 on the docket of the Board, and No. 177 on the books of the Register.

Claim.—A right of pre-emption of six hundred and forty acres, as legal representative of Jesse Thomas, under the third section of the act.

The claimant presented his claim, together with a surveyor's plot of the land claimed, in the following words and figures, to wit:

To the Commissioners appointed in pursuance of the act of Congress passed the 3d day of March, 1803, for receiving and adjusting the claims to lands south of Tennessee and east of Pearl river.

Please to take notice, that the following tract of land, situated on the west side of Tombigbee, in the county of Washington, beginning at a corner pine, about a mile from the river; running thence, south, twenty degrees east one hundred and sixteen chains, to a corner; thence, north, forty degrees west, seventy chains, to a corner stake and pine; thence, south, fifty degrees west, sixty chains, to a corner stake; thence, north, twenty degrees

west eighty-four chains, to a corner stake; thence, north, eighty degrees east, eighty-six chains to the beginning; and hath such forms and marks, both natural and artificial, as are fully represented in the plot annexed, containing six hundred and forty acres: is claimed by Seth Dean, legal representative of Jesse Thomas, in and by virtue of the third section of this act, as a pre-emption, and is now exhibited to the Register of the Land Office established east of Pearl River, to be recorded as directed by said act. To all which he begs leave to refer, as also to the copy of the plot herewith filed.

SETH DEAN,
Representative of Jesse Thomas.

MARCH 31, 1804.

[Plot omitted.]

Surveyed March 31, 1804, by Thomas Bilbo. Chain carriers, Jesse Thomas and David Dupree.

Entered in record of claims, vol. 1, page 515, by EDWARD LLOYD WAILES, for

JOSEPH CHAMBERS, Register.

Jesse Thomas and William Walton were presented as witnesses, and, being duly sworn and interrogated by the Board, they deposed, that they were not interested in this case; and said Thomas further testified, that he sold his claim to the land then in question to Seth Dean, for the consideration of forty-eight dollars; that he commenced his improvement in the year 1802, and had inhabited and cultivated on said land ever since, and did actually inhabit and cultivate the same on the 3d day of March, 1803; and was, on the said 3d day of March, the head of a family.

The said Walton deposed, that he knew that, on the 3d day of March, 1803, Jesse Thomas did actually cultivate and inhabit the said land; and that said Thomas was, on said 3d day of March, the head of a family.

The Board ordered that the case be postponed for consideration.

SETH DEAN, representative of John Dawson: case commenced in page 687.

Jesse Thomas was produced as a witness, and, being duly sworn and interrogated by the Board, deposed, that he saw Thomas Davis sign, seal, and deliver, with his own hand, unto Seth Dean, the deed or instrument of writing then presented to the Board; and that he did, at the same time, subscribe his name thereto as a witness, as did also C. Helber in his presence.

Thomas Bassett was presented as a witness, and, being duly sworn, deposed, that John Dawson, during the possession of this country by the British Government, inhabited and cultivated on a tract of land, some distance above the mouth of the Three Rivers, and which land he supposed was represented by the plot then exhibited; that he did confidently believe that neither John Dawson, nor his legal representative or representatives, resided within the Mississippi territory on the 27th day of October, 1795.

The Board ordered that the case be postponed for consideration.

SETH DEAN, representative of Francis Juzant: case commenced in page 687.

William Walton was presented as a witness, and, being duly sworn and interrogated by the Board, deposed, that he was not interested in this claim; that he saw Francis Juzant sign, seal, and deliver to Seth Dean the deed then presented to the Board, on the day and date therein mentioned, purporting to be a conveyance of one thousand acres of land, on the west side of the Tombigbee river, and on both sides of the mouth of Cedar creek; that he saw Robert Walton subscribe the same as a witness.

The Board ordered that the case be postponed for consideration.

Adjourned until Monday, the 23d instant.

MONDAY, April 23, 1804.

The Board met according to adjournment. Present: Ephraim Kirby, Robert C. Nicholas, Joseph Chambers.

Adjourned until Tuesday, the 24th instant.

TUESDAY, April 24, 1804.

The Board met according to adjournment. Present: Ephraim Kirby, Robert C. Nicholas, Joseph Chambers.

Adjourned until Wednesday, the 25th instant.

WEDNESDAY, April 25, 1804.

The Board met according to adjournment. Present: Ephraim Kirby, Robert C. Nicholas, Joseph Chambers.

RICHARD BARROW's case: commenced in page 639.

Natt Christmas, surveyor, was presented as a witness, and, being duly sworn, deposed, that he run three lines of the survey of the land then claimed, and plotted the fourth line for complement; that the plot then exhibited, presents a true and correct view of the land claimed, with such marks, natural and artificial, as are therein noted; that there were no lines that interfered with this claim, nor did the lines of this claim interfere with that of any other, except with that of Hawkins's, as had been stated.

The Board ordered that the case be postponed for consideration.

NATT CHRISTMAS's case: commenced in page 695.

John Milliken, surveyor, was presented as a witness, and, being duly sworn, deposed, that he surveyed the land then in question, and made the plot exhibited to the Board, which gave a true and correct view of said land, with such marks, natural and artificial, as were therein noted; that the houses and improvements of the claimant were within the limits of said survey; that there was a claim of Edward Creighton's, as representative of Benjamin King, that interfered with this claim, beginning at a corner stake, and running to the south of the spring branch, or the north line of said survey, in or about twenty acres ; that the interference is represented by the dotted line; that Sterling Dupree's claim covered the whole of said land.

The Board ordered that the case be postponed for consideration.

THOMAS CARSON's case, as representative of John Jacob Abner: commenced in page 606.

Natt Christmas, surveyor, was presented as a witness, and, being duly sworn, deposed, that he surveyed the land in question, and made the plot then exhibited to the Board, which gave a true and correct view of the land claimed, with such marks, natural and artificial, as are therein noted; that he had been informed by Mr. James Gordon that he run a line of the survey or claim of the representative of Joseph Anderson, over the south line of Carson's survey, to the extent of upwards of two hundred acres; that Josiah Skinner had also run over the south line of said survey, but, by the consent of Mr. Thomas Carson, given in his, Christmas's presence, that the original improvements of John Jacob Abner were within the limits of said survey.

The Board ordered that the case be postponed for consideration.

JAMES CALLIER's case, as representative of Joseph Anderson: commenced in page 607.

Thomas Bates, Senior, was presented as a witness, and, being duly sworn and interrogated by the Board, deposed, that Joseph Anderson inhabited and cultivated the land claimed in the year 1798, and continued to inhabit and cultivate on the same until about two years last past; that said land had been inhabited and cultivated since Anderson left it, by William Walton, as a tenant of Seth Dean, who purchased, as he Bates, understood and believed, Anderson's right to this claim; that Joseph Anderson was the head of a family in the month of February, 1798.

The Board ordered that the case be postponed for consideration.

SAMUEL MIMS, representative of John Turnbull: case commenced in page 635.

Natt Christmas, surveyor, was presented as a witness, and being duly sworn, deposed, that upwards of one year ago he surveyed the land in question, and made the plot exhibited to the Board, in pursuance of an order to me issued from the court of Washington county; that the plot exhibited a true and correct view of the land then claimed, with such marks, natural and artificial, as were on the plot noted; that there were two men, one of the name of Causby, and the other of the name of Rogers, who were then living within the limits of this survey.

The Board ordered that the case be postponed for consideration.

STERLING DUPREE, representative of Emanuel Cheney: case commenced in page 596.

Natt Christmas, surveyor, was presented as a witness, and, being duly sworn, deposed, that he surveyed the land in question, and made plot exhibited to the Board, which gave a true and correct view of the land claimed, with such marks, natural and artificial, as were therein noted; that there was a claim in his own name that interfered with the line of the said survey, cornering on the margin of the Tombigbee river, represented

by the cross on Dupree's plot, the extent of which interference would more fully appear by reference to the plot of his survey; that there was a claim of Edward Creighton's, as representative of Benjamin King, that interfered with the lines of this survey; that the extent of said interference will more fully appear by a reference to the plot of his survey, and the plot of the survey of said Creighton, representative of said King.

Edna Bilbo and Richard Hawkins were presented as witnesses, and, being duly sworn and interrogated by the Board, they deposed, that they were not interested in this claim; that Emanuel Cheney settled upon the land in question late in the year 1798, but did not make any cultivation; that he inhabited and cultivated on said land in the year 1799, but the cultivation of this was a garden only.

The said Hawkins further deposed, that Earles built the house on said land in which Cheney lived, some time in the summer or fall of the year 1798; that said Earles told him he had sold the same to Emanuel Cheney.

The said Bilbo further testified, that Emanuel Cheney, in the year 1797, was the head of a family, and more, than twenty-one years of age; the said Hawkins also deposed, that said Cheney was, in the year 1798, the head of a family, and more than twenty-one years of age.

The Board ordered that the case be postponed for consideration.

ADAM SCOTT's case, No. 171 on the docket of the Board, and No. 112 on the books of the Register.

Claim.—A right of pre-emption of one hundred and sixty acres, under the third section of the act.

The claimant presented his claim, together with a surveyor's plot of the land claimed, in the following words and figures, to wit:

To the Commissioners appointed in pursuance of the act of Congress passed the 3d day of March, 1803, for receiving and adjusting claims to land south of Tennessee, and east of Pearl river:

Please to take notice, that the following tract of land, situated on the west side of Tombigbee river, in the county of Washington, beginning at Barrow's lake, and runs down the river thirteen chains fifty links, to a holly; thence, west, twelve chains, to a pine; thence, south, thirty-seven chains twenty-five links, to a stake; thence, west, twenty-eight chains, to a stake; thence, north, fifty-one chains, to a stake; thence, east, forty-three chains, to the beginning; containing one hundred and sixty acres, and hath such marks, both natural and artificial, as are fully represented in the plot annexed: is claimed by Adam Scott, in and by virtue of the third section of the act, as a pre-emption, and is now exhibited to the Register of the Land Office established east of Pearl river, to be recorded as directed by said act. To all which he begs leave to refer, as also to a copy of the plot herewith filed.

ADAM SCOTT,

MARCH 29, 1804.

[Plot omitted.]

Surveyed by John Milliken. Chain bearers, Cordeal N. Daniels and William Patten.

Entered in record of claims, vol. —, page 347, by EDWARD LLOYD WAILES, for

JOSEPH CHAMBERS, *Register.*

John Milliken, surveyor, was presented as a witness, and, being duly sworn, deposed, that he began at a corner tree on Barrow's lake, and meandered the lake to a holly, a station tree, in or about a hundred yards to the north of the garrison burying ground, and continued the measurement of the line, west, twelve chains, and south, thirty-seven chains twenty-five links, to a stake; and plotted the other lines for complement; that there were no other lines that interfered with the lines of this survey that he knew of, except the lines of James Callier's survey, made by James Gordon; that the houses and improvements of the claimant were within the limits of this survey.

Godfrey Bartles and Richard Hawkins were presented as witnesses, and, being duly sworn and interrogated by the Board, they deposed, that Adam Scott, the claimant, inhabited and cultivated the land in question on the 3d day of March, 1803, and before and since that time; and that said Adam Scott was, on said 3d day of March, the head of a family, and more than twenty-one years of age.

The Board ordered that the case be postponed for consideration.

JOHN HAWKINS's case, No. 172 on the docket of the Board, and No. 172 on the books of the Register.

Claim.—A right of pre-emption of one hundred and fifty-one acres, under the third section of the act.

The claimant presented his claim, together with a surveyor's plot of the land claimed, in the following words and figures, to wit:

To the Commissioners appointed in pursuance of the act of Congress passed the third day of March, 1803, for receiving and adjusting the claims to lands south of Tennessee and east of Pearl river.

Please to take notice, that the following tract of land, situated on the west side of Tombigbee, in the county of Washington, beginning on a gum, on a point of land between Barrow's lake and Mobile river, running thence, up the courses and distances, as laid down in the plot, to a willow on Richard Barrow's corner; thence wes forty chains to a stake in Barrow's lake swamp; thence down the lake, as laid down in the plot, to the beginning; and hath such forms and marks, both natural and artificial, as are represented in the plot annexed, containing one hundred and fifty-one acres: is claimed by John Hawkins, in and by virtue of the third section of said act, as a pre-emption, and is now exhibited to the Register of the Land Office established east of Pearl river, to be recorded as directed by said act. To all which he begs leave to refer, as also to the copy of the plot herewith filed.

                                        JOHN HAWKINS.
MARCH 31, 1804.
            [Plot omitted.]

Surveyed March, 1804, by Natt Christmas. Chain bearers; Robert Lucas and Matthew Murry.

Entered in record of claims, vol. 1, page 510, by EDWARD LLOYD WAILES, for

            JOSEPH CHAMBERS, *Register.*

Natt Christmas, surveyor, Joseph Bates, and Richard Hawkins, were presented as witnesses, and, being duly sworn, the said Christmas deposed, that he surveyed the land in question, and made the plot then exhibited, which gave a true and correct view of the land claimed, with such marks, natural and artificial, as were therein noted; that there were no lines that interfered with said survey that he knew of.

The said Bates and Hawkins deposed, that, before the 3d of March, 1803, and ever since, the land in question had been cultivated by the claimant, and for his use, but, being low land, subject to inundation, could not be made a place of residence; that John Hawkins, the claimant, was, on said 3d day of March, the head of a family.

The Board ordered that the case be postponed for consideration.

Adjourned until Thursday, the 26th instant.

                            THURSDAY, *April* 26, 1804.
The Board met according to adjournment. Present: Ephraim Kirby, Robert C. Nicholas, Joseph Chambers.

GEORGE FARRAR's case: commenced in page 689.

Richard Hawkins and Seth Dean were presented as witnesses, and, being duly sworn, they deposed, that George Farrar inhabited and cultivated on said land before and ever since the 3d of March, 1803, and was, on said 3d of March, more than twenty-one years of age.

Question to said witnesses. Do you, or either of you, know that the present claimant was the owner, or did ever claim said land, or the improvements, on or before the 3d day of March, 1803?

Answer by both witnesses. He did not.

Question. Do you know under what pretensions the present claimant occupied and possessed the land and improvements now in question on the 3d day of March, 1803?

Answer. We know only that he lived there and made a crop on this land in that year, as a cropper.

The said Dean further deposed, that, on the day that this land was surveyed, he heard Mrs. Bilbo say, that, as she could not take in said land in her claim, George Farrar, the present claimant, might purchase it himself from the United States.

The Board ordered that the case be postponed for consideration.

Adjourned until Friday, the 27th instant.

                            FRIDAY, *April* 27, 1804.
The Board met according to adjournment. Present: Ephraim Kirby, Robert C. Nicholas.

HEIRS OF JAMES McGREW: case commenced in page 627.

Adam Hollinger was produced as a witness, and, being duly sworn and interrogated by the Board, deposed that

he had no interest in this case; that James McGrew deceased, did inhabit and improve the land in question many years ago, he believed as much as fourteen years, and continued there until the time of his death, which was after the year 1795; that his widow and family continued at the same place until after the Americans took possession of this country, in the year 1799; and that said James McGrew was the head of a family, and more than twenty-one years of age, on the 9th of February, 1788.

The Board ordered that the case be postponed for consideration.

CONSTANT McGREW's case: commenced in page 671.

John Baker and Young Gains were presented as witnesses, and, being duly sworn and interrogated by the Board, they deposed that they had no interest in this claim; and the said Baker further testified, that the widow Constant McGrew, the present claimant, had been in the occupancy of the land in question many years; that she lived upon it with her husband before the year 1794, about which time she became a widow, and had continued to inhabit and improve the same ever since.

The said Gains deposed, that he did not certainly know that Mrs. Constant McGrew inhabited and cultivated within the limits of the survey then exhibited in the year 1797, but his belief was that she did inhabit and cultivate on the said land in that year; that James McGrew died in or about the year 1797, as well as the witness recollected; that James McGrew, at the time of his leaving this country, and for some short time before his death, inhabited and cultivated on the place represented by Mr. Ligon to have been divided by the lower line of said survey, some distance from the river; that, in or about the year 1788, James McGrew lived at the improvement where Mr. Gahey lived, and near to the river; that Mrs. M'Grew was, in the year 1797, more than twenty-one years of age.

Adam Hollinger and Robert Ligon were presented as witnesses, and, being duly sworn, the said Ligon deposed, that he did not make the plot exhibited, but had retraced the lines from the lower line on the river, until he was prevented from pursuing the upper line to its junction with the river by high water; that Mrs. McGrew told him, at that time, that a stump, a line tree, was a corner to the piazza of the house in which she lived, and that the principal part of the house, or all, except a corner of the piazza, was in the limits of the Spanish grant, and that she intended to support the Spanish grant, in virtue of her habitation in that house; that the upper line of this tract run five chains within the limits of Doctor Chastang's claim; that Mrs. McGrew told him, Ligon, that she was glad that the line had left a sufficiency of the improvement within the limits of the donation, to support it, or to support her rights; that he did not exactly remember the words, but that they were to that effect.

The said Hollinger deposed, that Mrs. McGrew was, in the year 1797, more than twenty-one years of age.—Vide his deposition, in the case of the heirs of James McGrew, recorded in preceding case.

The Board ordered that the case be postponed for consideration.

Adjourned until Saturday, the 28th instant.

                            SATURDAY, *April* 28, 1804.
The Board met according to adjournment. Present: Ephraim Kirby, Robert C. Nicholas.

CLARK McGREW's case, No. 173 on the docket of the Board, and No. 166 on the books of the Register.

Claim.—A donation of six hundred and forty acres, under the second section of the act.

The claimant presented his claim, together with a surveyor's plot of the land claimed, in the words and figures following, to wit:

To the Commissioners appointed in pursuance of an act of Congress passed the 3d of March, 1803, for receiving and adjusting claims to lands south of the State of Tennessee, and east of Pearl river.

Please to take notice, that the following tract of land, situated on the west side of the Tombigbee river, lying and being in Washington county, beginning near Tawler creek, on a black gum, and running north, thirteen degrees west, seventy chains, to a hickory; thence, north, nine degrees east, thirty-two chains, to a hickory; thence, north fifty-five degrees east, ninety-four chains, to a water oak; thence, south, forty-six degrees east, twenty-nine chains, to a persimmon; thence, to the beginning:

is claimed by Clark McGrew, under and by virtue of the second section of the above recited act, and is now exhibited to the Register of the Land Office established east of Pearl river, for the purpose of being recorded as directed by said act. To all which he begs leave to refer, as well as to the plot herewith filed.

CLARK McGREW.

March 29, 1804.

[Plot omitted.]

Surveyed 20th March, 1804, by Robert Ligon.
Entered in record of claims, vol. 1, page 499, by Edward Lloyd Wailes, for

JOSEPH CHAMBERS, *Register.*

The claimant exhibited a deposition, as follows, to wit:

Washington County, Mississippi Territory,
April 26, 1804.

This day came Thomas Ettridge before me, one of the Justices assigned to keep the peace for said county, and made oath that, previous to 1797, and of the date of 1797, he saw Clark McGrew's tract of land in a state of improvement, about six acres of land in cultivation; and that Clark McGrew's negro resided on the tract of land in the year 1797, and has always continued the possession until the present year. And further this deponent saith not.

THOMAS ETTRIDGE.

Given under my hand and seal. Sworn to before JOHN CALLIER, *Justice of Peace.*

John McGrew, Esquire, was presented as a witness, and, being duly sworn, deposed, that, in the year 1796, there was a small piece of land claimed within the limits of this survey, and that Clark McGrew has continued to make a small crop every year since that time on the same; that he never had himself resided on said land more than two or three nights at a time, having made his, the said John's, house his home: that Clark McGrew was, in the year 1797, more than twenty-one years of age.

The Board ordered that the case be postponed for consideration.

Joseph Westmoreland's case, No. 174 on the docket of the Board, and No. 111 on the books of the Register.
☞ *Claim.*—A right of pre-emption of one hundred and ninety-three acres and thirty-six poles, as legal representative of Lewis Crane, under the third section of the act.

The claimant presented his claim, together with a surveyor's plot of the land claimed, in the following words and figures, to wit:

To the Commissioners appointed in pursuance of the act of Congress, passed the 3d day of March, 1803, for receiving and adjusting the claims to lands south of Tennessee, and east of Pearl river.

Please to take notice, that the following tract of land, situated on the Tombigbee river, butted on the west side said river, bounded on the southwest by a line dividing him, the claimant, and Raleigh Green, lying altogether within the lines of Robert Farmar's survey, beginning on a sassafras, Raleigh Green's southwest corner, and runs with their dividing line south, seventy degrees west, sixty chains fifty links, to a poplar corner; thence, south, twenty degrees east, thirty chains, to a pine with two wahoos, pointers; thence, north, seventy degrees east, sixty-eight chains, to a stake on the river bank; thence, the meanders of the river, to the beginning; having such marks, natural and artificial, as are represented in the plot annexed, containing one hundred and ninety-three acres thirty-six poles: is claimed by Joseph Westmoreland, legal representative of Lewis Crane, under and by virtue of a settlement bearing date the 3d day of March, 1803, and now exhibited unto the Register of the Land Office established east of Pearl river, to be recorded as directed by said act. To all which he begs leave to refer, as also to the copy of the plot herewith filed.

JOSEPH WESTMORELAND.

February 27, 1804.

[Plot omitted.]

Surveyed 27th February, 1804, by T. Malone. Chain carriers, Raleigh Green and Elisha Simmons.
Entered in record of claims, vol. 1, page 345, by Edward Lloyd Wailes, for

JOSEPH CHAMBERS, *Register.*

The claimant exhibited a deed of conveyance from Lewis Crane, bearing date the 28th of March, 1803, relinquishing and conveying to the said Westmoreland all the said Crane's right and claim to said tract of land.

John Baker and James Davis were presented as witnesses, and, being duly sworn and interrogated by the Board, they deposed, that, in the year 1802, Lewis Crane lived upon the land in question, and raised a crop, and had a small house; that, in the spring of the year 1803, he sold his possession and improvement to Joseph Westmoreland, who moved on, and Crane moved off, but could not say the precise time when the exchange took place; that Westmoreland raised a crop on the land the last year; that Lewis Crane was the head of a family, and twenty-one years of age, on the 3d of March, 1803.

Thomas Malone, surveyor, was presented as a witness, and, being duly sworn, deposed, that he made the survey and plot of the land in question, and believed it to be correct, and that it included the dwelling-house and improvements of the claimant; that this claim was wholly included within the claim of Robert Farmar, under a British grant; that he knew of no other.

The Board ordered that the case be postponed for consideration.

Simon Andrey's case: commenced in page 624.
James Callier and Wilson Carman were presented as witnesses, and, being duly sworn and interrogated by the Board, they deposed, that they had no interest in this case; that part of the dwelling-houses and other buildings of the claimant stand on the land in question, and also his garden; that he resided there on the 3d of March, 1803, and ever since, and on said day was more than twenty-one years of age.

The Board ordered that the case be postponed for consideration.

John Flood McGrew's case: commenced page 671.
Levin Hainsworth and William McGrew were presented as witnesses, and, being duly sworn and interrogated by the Board, they deposed, that they were not interested in this case; the said Hainsworth further deposed, that, when he came to this country, in the last part of the year 1799, and was looking out for a farm or plantation, John Flood McGrew showed him the land in question as belonging to himself; that there had at that time some labor been done upon it, but no house erected, nor the appearance of any crop in that year; that, about the year 1801, he put a family on said land, and some stock; that he, the witness, believed that, at the time first mentioned, the claimant was more than twenty-one years of age.

The said William further deposed, that, in the year 1798, the claimant began to work on the land by him then claimed, and did some work on the same every year, until the year 1801, when he put a family on, which had remained there ever since, and had raised crops.

John McGrew, Esq. was produced as a witness, and, being duly sworn, deposed, that John Flood McGrew was, in the year 1797, more than twenty-one years of age.

The Board ordered that the case be postponed for consideration.

Levin Hainsworth's case, No. 175 on the docket of the Board, and No. 18 on the books of the Register.
Claim.—A right of pre-emption of three hundred and ninety-six acres, under the third section of the act.

The claimant presented his claim, together with a surveyor's plot of the land claimed, in the following words and figures, to wit:

To the Commissioners appointed in pursuance of the act of Congress, passed the 3d day of March, 1803, for receiving and adjusting claims to land south of the Tennessee and east of Pearl river.

Please to take notice, that the following tract of land, situated below Sintabogue, on Pine Barren creek, butting and bounded as follows, to wit: beginning on a corner hickory; thence, running south, eighty-two degrees west, eighty-two chains fifty links, to a corner sassafras; thence north, twelve degrees west, forty-eight chains, to a corner sweet gum; thence, north, eighty-two degrees east, eighty-two chains and fifty links, to a corner stake; thence, south, twelve degrees east, forty-eight chains, to the beginning; having such marks, natural and artificial, as are represented in the plot annexed, containing three hundred and ninety-six acres: is claimed by Levin Hainsworth, under and by virtue of occupancy; he, the said Hainsworth, having inhabited and cultivated the tract herein specified on the 3d day of March, 1803, agreeable to an act of Congress, entitled "An act," &c. and likewise the said claimant occupied the said tract from the year 1801, until this day.

LEVIN HAINSWORTH, his + mark.

Witness : JOSEPH CHAMBERS.

[Plot omitted.]

FEBRUARY, 21st, 1804.

Surveyed by me, Robert Ligon. Chain carriers, William McGrew and John McGrew.

Entered in record of claims, volume 1, page 50, by EDWARD LLOYD WAILES, for

JOSEPH CHAMBERS, *Register.*

William McGrew was presented as a witness, and, being duly sworn and interrogated by the Board, deposed, that the claimant built two small cabins on the land in question in the year 1801, and made other improvements; that the Indians being troublesome, as this land was above the former Indian line, he did not reside there steadily; that, on the 3d of March, 1803, his people were there at work, and he was, at that time, more than twenty-one years of age.—Vide surveyor's testimony in this case, in page 670.

The Board ordered that the case be postponed for consideration.

PRISCILLA MILES's case, No. 176 on the docket of the Board, and No. 154 on the books of the Register.

Claim.—A right of pre-emption of four hundred and fifty-six acres, under the third section of the act.

The claimant presented his claim, together with a surveyor's plot of the land claimed, in the following words and figures, to wit:

To the Commissioners appointed in pursuance of the act of Congress passed the 3d day of March, 1803, for receiving and adjusting claims to lands south of the Tennessee, and east of Pearl river.

Please to take notice, that the following tract of land, situated on the waters of House's Mill creek, Washington county, butted and bounded on all sides by vacant land, beginning on a hickory, and runs south seventy-two degrees east, twenty-five chains fifty links, to a large pine corner; thence, south, eighty-six degrees east, ninety chains, to a stake with three pines, pointers; thence, north, four degrees east, forty chains, to a pine corner; thence, south, eighty-six degrees west one hundred and fifteen chains, to a stake corner, with two pines, pointers; thence, to the beginning; having such marks, natural and artificial, as are represented in the plot annexed, containing four hundred and fifty-six acres and twelve poles: is claimed by Priscilla Miles, of Washington county, Mississippi territory, under and by virtue of the third section of the above recited act, and now exhibited unto the Register of the Land Office established east of Pearl river, to be recorded as directed by said act. To all which she begs leave to refer, as also to the copy of the plot herewith filed.

PRISCILLA MILES.

MARCH 26, 1804.

[Plot omitted.]

Surveyed 26th March, 1804, by T. Malone. Chain carriers, George McGee and William Morgan.

Entered in record of claims, vol. 1, page 483, by EDWARD LLOYD WAILES, for

JOSEPH CHAMBERS, *Register.*

The above named chain carriers were sworn before John Callier, Esquire, Justice of Peace.

Thomas Malone, surveyor, was presented as a witness, and, being duly sworn, deposed, that he made the survey and plot of the land in question, and believed it to be correct; that it included the dwelling and the greater part of the claimant's improvements, and that he, Malone, knew of no interfering line or claim, and believed there was none; that, in September, 1802, he was at said place, and the present claimant then lived there, had a dwelling house, some cleared land, and appearance of cultivation, and had continued there ever since; that she was at that time a widowed lady, considerably advanced in years.

James Callier was presented as a witness, and, being duly sworn and interrogated by the Board, deposed, that he was not interested in this case; that Priscilla Miles, the present claimant, lived upon and cultivated the land in question on the 3d of March, 1803, before that time, and ever since, and at that time was more than twenty-one years of age.

The Board ordered that the case be postponed for consideration.

JOHN PICKERING's case: commenced in page 647.

William McGrew was presented as a witness, and, being duly sworn and interrogated by the Board, de-

posed, that he had no interest in this claim; that, before the 3d of March, 1803, John Pickering had two houses partly built upon the land in question, and some ground cleared; that he raised a crop of eight or ten acres the ensuing season, and moved his family on at the beginning of the fall.

The Board ordered that the case be postponed for consideration.

EDWARD CREIGHTON's case, No. 177 on the docket of the Board, and No. 159 on the books of the Register.

Claim.—A donation of six hundred and forty acres, as legal representative of Isram Beard, under the second section of the act.

The claimant presented his claim, together with a surveyor's plot of the land claimed, in the following words and figures, to wit:

To the Commissioners appointed in pursuance of the act of Congress passed on the 3d day of March, 1803, for receiving and adjusting claims south of the Tennessee, and east of Pearl river.

Please to take notice, that the following tract of land, situated about one mile from Nanna Hubba bluff, beginning on a line of Howel Dupree's, running north, thirty-four degrees east, to a tupelo gum; thence, north fifty-six degrees east, five chains, to a tupelo gum ; from thence, south, fifty-six degrees west ninety-one chains, to a whortleberry; from thence, south, thirty-four degrees east, seventy-two chains and fifty links; and from thence, north fifty-six degrees east, ninety-one chains, to the beginning, including within the said lines six hundred and forty acres of land; bounded on the east by Howel Dupree's donation claim, and on all the rest by vacant land or undefined claims: this land is claimed by Edward Creighton, of Washington county, Mississippi territory, under and in virtue of a settlement made by Isram Beard, on or before the month of August, 1797, by him transferred to Jacob Miller, and by said Miller to this reporter, in July 21st, 1802, now delivered to the Register of the Land Office, to be established east of Pearl river, to be recorded as directed by said act. To all which he begs leave to refer, as also to a copy of the plot herewith filed.

EDWARD CREIGHTON.

MARCH 14, 1804.

[Plot omitted.]

Surveyed 14th March, 1804, by Robert Ligon. Chain carriers, John Hines and Howel Dupree.

Entered in record of claims, vol. 1, page 489, by EDWARD LLOYD WAILES, for

JOSEPH CHAMBERS, *Register.*

The claimant exhibited a deed of conveyance from Jacob Miller, bearing date 21st July, 1802, assigning and conveying to the said Creighton all the said Miller's right and claim to said land, and the improvements thereon.

Rachel Helverson was presented as a witness, and, being duly sworn and interrogated by the Board, deposed, that she had not any interest in this claim; that Isram Beard settled upon the land in question in the year 1798, by building a house, and raised a small crop the year following, that he did not live there more than two years before he parted with his possession to Jacob Miller, who took peaceable possession of the same; that, at the time of the settlement above mentioned, Isram Beard was the head of a family.—Vide surveyor's testimony in page 670.

Richard Barrow was produced as a witness, and, being duly sworn, deposed, that, in the latter part of the year 1798, Isram Beard settled upon the land in question, and, in the year 1799, cultivated thereon; that Isram Beard was the head of a family.

The Board ordered that the case be postponed for consideration.

WILLIAM McGREW's case, No. 178 on the docket of the Board, and No. 17 on the books of the Register.

Claim.—A donation of six hundred and thirty-eight acres, under the second section of the act.

The claimant presented his claim, together with a surveyor's plot of the land claimed, in the following words and figures, to wit:

To the Commissioners appointed in pursuance of the act of Congress passed the 3d day of March, 1803, for receiving and adjusting claims to land south of Tennessee, and east of Pearl river.

Please to take notice, that the following tract of land, situated on the south side of Tombigbee river, on the branch of Toller creek, called Coffee-house creek, or William McGrew's creek, butting and bounding as follows, to wit: beginning at a corner pine on the south side of said creek, thence running north, sixty degrees east, seventy chains and fifty links, to a corner chesnut; thence, north, thirty degrees west, ninety chains fifty links, to a corner chinque-pine; thence, south, sixty degrees west, seventy chains fifty links, to a corner stake; thence, south, thirty degrees east, to the beginning; and such forms and marks, natural and artificial, as are represented in the plot annexed, containing six hundred and thirty-eight acres: is claimed by William McGrew, under and by virtue of occupancy, the said William McGrew having inhabited and cultivated the tract herein specified on the day of the evacuation of the Spanish troops, agreeable to an act of Congress, entitled, "An act regulating the grants of land, and providing for the disposal of the lands of the United States south of the State of Tennessee." The said land was likewise occupied previous, and ever since, unto this day, by the said claimant, who was above twenty-one years of age at the time required by the act, and claims no other land in the territory; and it does not appear to be claimed by any other person, &c. &c.

WILLIAM McGREW.

FEBRUARY 21, 1804.

[Plot omitted.]

Surveyed 13th February, 1804, by Robert Ligon. Chain carriers, Levin Hainsworth and John McGrew. Entered in record of claims, vol. 1, page 49, by ED-WARD LLOYD WAILES, for

JOSEPH CHAMBERS, *Register.*

John McGrew, Senior, and Levin Hainsworth were presented as witnesses, and, being duly sworn and interrogated by the Board, they deposed, that they had no interest in this case.

The said Hainsworth also testified, that when he came to this country, in the latter part of the year 1799, William McGrew, the present claimant, showed him the land in question as his plantation; that it had the appearance of having been cultivated several years; that there were the remains of an old house and a temporary shed, and four or five acres under cultivation, part of which appeared to have had a crop on it the preceding summer.

The said John McGrew, Senior, further deposed, that he did not see the improvements of his son, the present claimant, upon the land in question, until several years after it commenced; that his own house was the frontier house, the said claimant a single man, and lived in the family with him; that, in the year 1797, the claimant commenced said improvement, as he believed; that he used to go regularly off to work, with working people and tools; and he, the witness, always understood from the claimant; that it was at said place, and fully believed that it was: that he continued to improve in this manner annually, until he was married, about two years ago, when he moved there to live; that the claimant was born in the year 1776.—Vide surveyor's testimony, in page 670.

The Board ordered that the case be postponed for consideration.

RICHARD HAWKINS's case: commenced in page 692.

Joseph Bates and John Hawkins were presented as witnesses, and, being duly sworn and interrogated by the Board, they deposed, that they were not interested in this case; and the said Joseph also deposed, that, in the fall of the year 1797, the present claimant entered upon the land in question, erected a house, and began to clear the lands; that, by himself or his son, he had continued to inhabit and cultivate the same until the then present time, and raised crops regularly; and that he was, in the year 1797, more than twenty-one years of age.

The said John further deposed, that, in January, 1798, he came into this country, and found his father Richard Hawkins, living upon the land in question, and that he had there lived and cultivated ever since, except about two years, when the claimant resided at Tensaw; and his improvements on the land in question were occupied by another person in his behalf.

The Board ordered that the case be postponed for consideration.

JOHN McGREW, Junior, representative of Alexander McGrew: case commenced in page 668.

James McGrew and John McGrew, Esquires, were presented as witnesses, and, being duly sworn and interrogated by the Board, they deposed, that they were not interested in this case; and the said James also deposed, that he helped Alexander McGrew to build a

house, and to plant a little corn on the land in question, as he, witness, believed, in the year 1798; that Alexander McGrew had done some labor on the land before that time, but that he did not inhabit the land, nor did any person live there in his behalf.

The said John deposed, that he knew that Alexander McGrew was, in the year 1797, more than twenty-one years of age.

The Board ordered that the case be postponed for consideration.

JULIAN DE CASTRO's case, No. 179 on the docket of the Board, and No. 60 on the books of the Register.

Claim.—A donation of six hundred and forty acres, under the second section of the act.

The claimant presented his claim, together with a surveyor's plot of the land claimed, in the following words and figures, to wit:

To the Commissioners appointed in pursuance of the act of Congress for receiving and adjusting the claims to lands south of Tennessee, and east of Pearl river.

Please to take notice, that a certain tract of land, lying on the Tombigbee river, and containing six hundred and forty acres, bounded as follows: beginning at a whortleberry on said river, and running south, twenty-seven degrees west, to a stake corner; thence, south, sixty-four degrees east, to a hickory corner; thence, north, twenty-seven degrees east, to a stake on said river; thence, along the meanders of said river, to the place of beginning: is claimed by Julian de Castro, by virtue of a certificate setting forth the same, and which tract will more particularly appear from a plot and survey thereof herewith filed; he therefore prays that this claim may be recorded.

JULIAN DE CASTRO.

[Plot omitted.]

Surveyed, 16th of February, 1804, by T. Malone. Chain carriers, Thomas Barker, and —— Pie. Entered in record of claims, vol. 1, page 178, by ED-WARD LLOYD WAILES, for

JOSEPH CHAMBERS, *Register.*

William McGrew was presented as a witness, and, being duly sworn and interrogated by the Board, deposed, that according to the best of his recollection, Julian de Castro, the present claimant, lived on the land in question in the year 1789; and about that time moved off to another place about three miles distant, where he resided about three years; and he then moved with his family out of the territory, and did not return until the year 1801.

Thomas Malone, surveyor, was presented as a witness, and, being duly sworn, deposed, that he made the survey and plot of the land in question, and believed it to be correct; and that it included the dwelling house and improvements of the claimant; that this claim included the claim of Peter Malone altogether; also, some part of the claim of James Griffin; also, a part of John Baker's one thousand six hundred acres claim; that it also covered about half a mile front of the claim of Edward Lloyd Wailes, and of William Coleman; that it probably included about half the front of the claim of Doctor Chastang.

The Board ordered that the case be postponed for consideration.

EDWARD LLOYD WAILES's case, No. 180 on the docket of the Board, and No. 191 on the books of the Register.

Claim.—A right of pre-emption of four hundred and eighty acres, as assignee and legal representative of John Baker, under the third section of the act.

The claimant presented his claim, together with a surveyor's plot of the land claimed, in the words and figures following, to wit:

To the Commissioners appointed in pursuance of the act of Congress passed 3d day of March, 1803, for receiving and adjusting the claims to lands south of Tennessee, and east of Pearl river.

Please to take notice, that the following tract of land, situated on the west side of Tombigbee river, near Fort St. Stephen's, in the county of Washington, beginning at Doctor John Chastang's upper line, on a small ironwood, standing on the river bank, and runs with his line south, twenty-five degrees west, eighty chains, to a stake; thence, north, sixty-five degrees west, sixty chains, to a stake; thence north, twenty-five degrees east, eighty chains, to a stake; thence, with the meanders of the river to the beginning; containing four hundred and eighty acres, and hath such shape, form, and marks, both natural and artificial, as are fully represented in the plot annexed: is claimed by Edward Lloyd Wailes, assignee of John Baker, legal representative of John Berry, who purchased the said land at sheriff's sale, and has had the same in possession from the 5th of October, 1801, until the present time; and claims the right of purchasing the said land, under the third section of the said act, and is now exhibited to the Register of the Land Office established east of Pearl river, to be recorded as directed by said act. To all which he begs leave to refer, as also to a copy of the plot herewith filed.

EDWARD LLOYD WAILES,
Representative of John Baker.
MARCH 30, 1804.
[Plot omitted.]

Surveyed by T. Malone.
Entered in record of claims, vol. 2, page 6, by EDWARD LLOYD WAILES, for
JOSEPH CHAMBERS, *Register.*

The claimant exhibited a deed from Elijah Powel, as deputy sheriff for said county, duly executed, acknowledged, and recorded, bearing date the 5th of October, 1801, conveying to the said John Baker the said tract of land; which deed was given in consequence of a writ of attachment against the lands and tenements of John Berry, in virtue of which writ, directed to the said Powel, by the county court in said county, to execute and return according to law, he sold at public auction, and deeded said land as above stated.

On the back of said deed is written as follows, to wit: I hereby assign all my right, title, interest, claim, and demand of the within deed, and all the right, title, interest, and claim of the land therein mentioned, to Edward Lloyd Wailes, his heirs and assigns, and I do warrant and defend the said land unto the said Edward Lloyd Wailes, against myself and my heirs only.
JOHN BAKER.

Witness, OTTO T. V. BARBERIE.

The claimant also produced three other instruments of writing, as follows, to wit:

I, Pleasant Rose, have received in possession, for John Baker, or his heirs, eight hundred acres of land, including a certain improvement made by John Berry, and adjoining Fort St. Stephen's, and sold by virtue of a writ of attachment, by the sheriff of Washington county, to the said Baker; the said eight hundred acres to be returned upon demand to the said Baker, except one lot, to include the house that the said Rose now lives in, which said house and lot the said Rose is to continue in for and during the term of two years, and pay unto the said Baker one dollar per annum; and for the true performance, the said Rose doth oblige himself to forfeit and pay to the said Baker, or his heirs, in case of refusal, the sum of fifty thousand dollars.

Given under my hand and seal, this 16th day of September, 1802.
PLEASANT ROSE.

Witness, WILLIAM BREWER.

I, John Baker, do hereby oblige myself and heirs to pay unto Pleasant Rose for all the improvements he shall make upon a lot rented him, where he now lives, for two years, after the expiration of the said term, the said improvements to be valued and paid in cotton, or country produce.

Given under my hand, this 16th day of September, 1802.
JOHN BAKER.

Witness, WILLIAM BREWER.

JUNE 20, 1803. Received of John Baker one hundred dollars in full satisfaction for improving and cultivating the aforesaid land.
PLEASANT ROSE.

EMANUEL CHENEY, his ✕ mark.

Joseph Westmoreland and James Davis were presented as witnesses, and, being duly sworn, and interrogated by the Board, they deposed, that they had not any interest in this case; that Pleasant Rose did live on the land in question some short time before the 3d of March, 1803, and, as they understood, as a tenant to John Baker; but, whether he, or any other person, was there on said 3d of March they could not certainly say; that the improvements were two small cabins; that a small garden was made since the 3d of March, 1803.

Question by the claimant. Do you not know that John Murrel did live on another part of this land on the 3d of March, 1803?

Answer by both. John Murrel did live on a part of the land now claimed on the 3d of March, 1803, and raised a crop there the last year; that the place where Murrel lived was two or three hundred yards from the place first spoken of, where Rose lived.

Question to J. Westmoreland. Did you ever hear Pleasant Rose say that John Baker had settled with him, and paid him for the labor which he did on said land?

Answer. I heard Rose say that Baker had settled with him, and paid him for work which he had done for Baker, part of which I understood to be on this land.

Question. Was John Baker twenty-one years of age on the 3d of March, 1803?

Answer by both. He was.

Thomas Malone, surveyor, was presented as a witness, and, being duly sworn, deposed, that he made the plot of the land in question from his minutes of an adjoining line which he had surveyed, and believed it to be correct; that it included the house and improvements where Pleasant Rose lived, and also the house and improvements where John Murrel lived; that, on the southeast corner, there was a small interference with the claim of James Griffin; that he, Malone, believed that the greater part of this survey was included in the lines of John Baker's one thousand six hundred acres claim; that the greater part, if not the whole, of Peter Malone's claim, was included in the lines of this, and also the greater part of the claim of William Coleman; that the east side of this also included about half a mile of the front of Julian de Castro's donation claim.

George Robbins and Thomas Ettridge were presented as witnesses, and, being duly sworn, the said Robbins deposed, that Pleasant Rose inhabited and built a house on the land in question in the year 1802; that John Baker told him that he had settled Pleasant Rose at said place, to sell spirits for account of Baker; that he believed that Rose continued on said land until the month of March, 1803, but could not say certainly that he did do so.

The said Ettridge deposed, that he knew that Pleasant Rose inhabited upon the land in question on the 3d of March, 1803; that he had a small garden of about thirty feet square, on which he, Ettridge, saw six or seven stalks of corn growing; that Rose told him that he had never received any thing for building the house.

The Board ordered that the case be postponed for consideration.

Adjourned until Monday the 30th instant.

MONDAY, *April* 30, 1804.
The Board met according to adjournment. Present: Ephraim Kirby, Robert C. Nicholas.

JOHN CALLIER, representative of Adam Hollinger: case commenced in page 629.

Thomas Malone, surveyor, James Dean, and Nathan Blackwell, were presented as witnesses, and, being duly sworn, the said Malone deposed, that he made the survey and plot of the land in question, and believed it to be correct, and that it included the dwelling house and improvements of the claimant; that he understood that a British claim, in the name of Hoggatt, was within this survey on the east or lower side.

The said Dean deposed, that he always understood and heard Wilford Hoggatt say that the place he lived on, and which John Callier now claims as his representative, was his own, and had heard said Wilford Hoggatt also say, that he had obtained a Spanish grant, in favor of his brother James Hoggatt, for eight hundred acres of land, next adjoining below the place he then lived on.

The said Blackwell deposed, that he was present when Leonard Marbury tendered the last payment for the consideration money of the purchase of the tract of land in question, at which time said Marbury presented a bond to him, Hoggatt, purporting as he, the witness, understood, to require that Wilford Hoggatt would indemnify him, Marbury, against all other claims; that Hoggatt flew into a passion, and refused to sign it; but he, witness, understood that, some short time afterwards, he did consent, received the payment, and did actually sign said bond; that Marbury, on quitting this country, made and authorized John Joyce to be his agent, and that he, Joyce, acted as such, without any person questioning his authority so to do, as well in conveying the land in question to Adam Hollinger, as in transferring other property belonging to the said Marbury; that Hollinger gave to Callier, in his, Blackwell's, presence, at Mobile, the bill of sale of the same land, as he understood, from John Joyce, as agent to Leonard Marbury, to him, Hollinger, and that Callier appeared to be well satisfied therewith.

The Board ordered that the case be postponed for consideration.

FRANCIS STRINGER's case: commenced in page 619.

Thomas Malone, surveyor, was presented as a witness, and, being duly sworn, deposed, that he made surveys and plots returned to the Board of Commissioners by the following claimants, to wit: Francis Stringer's donation, six hundred and forty acres; Thomas Malone's pre-emption, three hundred and thirty acres; John Dunn's pre-emption, three hundred and ninety-one acres; William Morgan's pre-emption, three hundred and nineteen acres; Peter Cartwright's pre-emption, one hundred and fifty-nine acres; and Priscilla Miles's pre-emption, four hundred and fifty-six acres; and that the said plots respectively contain true representations of the land therein described, according to the best of his knowledge and belief, and did include the plantations and improvements of the several claimants; that he knew of no interfering lines or claims.

The Board ordered that the case be postponed for consideration.

WILLIAM MURRELL's case: commenced in page 643.

Thomas Malone, surveyor, was presented as a witness, and, being duly sworn, deposed, that he made the survey and plot of the land in question, and believed it to be correct, and that it included the dwelling house and improvements of the claimant; that the principal part of said survey on the north was included in the claim of Elisha Simmons; that a small corner on the south was included in the claim of James Huckaby.

The Board ordered that the case be postponed for consideration.

THOMAS MALONE's case, No. 181 on the docket of the Board, and No. 186 on the books of the Register.

Claim—Of four hundred and eighty acres, as assignee and legal representative of John Arnot, by virtue of a Spanish warrant, or order of survey, under the second section of the act.

The claimant presented her claim, together with a surveyor's plot of the land claimed, in the following words and figures, to wit:

To the Commissioners appointed in pursuance of the act of Congress passed the 3d day of March, 1803, for receiving and adjusting the claims to lands south of the Tennessee, and east of Pearl river.

Please to take notice, that the following tract of land, situate on the west side of Tombigbee, beginning on a sweet gum corner of Flood McGrew's claim, and runs with his line south, twenty-four degrees west, one hundred and twenty-four chains forty-nine links, to a stake corner; thence, north, sixty-six degrees east thirty-seven chains, and twenty links, to a corner stake; thence, north, twenty-four degrees east, one hundred and twenty-eight chains, forty-nine links, to a corner sweet gum on the bank of the river; thence, the meanders of the river, to the beginning first mentioned; having such marks, natural and artificial, as are represented in the plot annexed, containing four hundred and eighty acres of land: is claimed by Thomas Malone, representative of John Arnot, under and by virtue of a Spanish warrant of survey, bearing date the —— day of —— and now exhibited to the Register of the Land Office established east of Pearl river, to be recorded as is directed by said act. All of which he begs leave to refer to, as also to the copy of the plot annexed, &c.

For THOS. MALONE,
EDWIN LEWIS.

MARCH 31, 1804.

[Plot omitted.]

Surveyed March, 1804, by T. Malone. Chain carriers, John Dean and George Brewer.

Entered in record of claims, vol. 1, page 547, by EDWARD LLOYD WAILES, for

JOSEPH CHAMBERS, *Register.*

The claimant exhibited a Spanish warrant of survey, in the following words and figures, to wit:

His Excellency Don ESTEVAN MIRO, Colonel of the Royal Army, Governor General of the city and province of Louisiana.

John Arnot, inhabitant in the jurisdiction of Mobile, with the greatest respect for your excellency, represents and says, that there is in the river Tombigbee a tract of forty acres of land, of which ten or twelve acres was formerly owned by a Doctor Dallas, situated on the east side by Benjamin James's land, and on the west side by the said land of the above mentioned Doctor Dallas, which was abandoned by him in the year 1779, and until this present has not been reclaimed by the proprietor, nor by any person by him empowered, (with an intention of what has been expressed, as also to the petitioner,) he, with a few head of cattle and hogs for his support, expects from your excellency's generosity the favor of granting him the above petition, with titles from the Secretary of Government, which correspond with the concession; for which favor from your excellency, he will be forever thankful.

JOHN ARNOT.

MOBILE, 26th June, 1787.

MOBILE, June 27, 1787.

Don Vincent Folch, captain in the fixed regiment of Louisiana, commandant civil and military of this district, certifies that the land which the petitioner solicits is vacant, from information taken for that purpose.

VINCENT FOLCH.

NEW ORLEANS, July 2, 1787.

The Commandant of the post of Mobile, shall establish the petitioner upon the twelve acres of land, with the profounder, as customary, of forty, at the place he solicits, being vacant, not causing prejudice, upon the precise condition of making the road and clearing regularly, in the space of one year; and if at the end of three years, the land is not settled, during which period it cannot be alienated, this grant to remain null; under which supposition, the business of settling the same is to be carried on in the tract, and remitted me to provide the interested party with titles in form.

ESTEVAN MIRO.

This is a copy of the original, which exists in the archives under my charge, remitted to me.

JOAQN. DE OSORNO. [L. S.]

John Baker and Doctor John Chastang were presented as witnesses, and, being duly sworn, the said Baker deposed, that he had compared this translation with the Spanish original or grant hereto attached; and that, to the best of his understanding, it was truly and correctly translated, as to names, dates, and quantity of acres.

The said Chastang deposed, that the foregoing is a true translation of the Spanish warrant or order of survey hereto annexed, according to the best of his knowledge and belief.

The claimant produced a deed of conveyance from John Arnot, bearing date the 18th day of December, 1794, duly executed, conveying to Tobias Reams all the said Arnot's right, claim, and title to the said tract of land, and the improvements thereon.

Thomas Malone, surveyor, was presented as a witness, and, being duly sworn, deposed, that he made the survey and plot of the said land, and believed it to be correct, and that it included the house and other improvements made under the original claimant, except about lengths of fence. That the claim of Cornelius McCurtin interfered with this, on the east side, about half way in front; thence, towards the southwest corner, so as to include something more than half of this tract; that he also understood that a claim of Young Gains ran diagonally across this, a little south of the house, so as to include the greater part of said survey on the south; and knew of no other interfering lines or claims with this.

John McGrew and John Baker were presented as witnesses, and, being duly sworn and interrogated by the Board, they deposed, that they were not interested in this case; that John Arnot settled upon the land in question, in the year 1787, and continued to inhabit and cultivate thereon for some time; that John Arnot was, on the 2d July, in the year 1787, more than twenty-one years of age; and that they believed that said land had been inhabited and cultivated by him, or some person under him, ever since that time; that Arnot had told them that he had sold his right to one Tobias Reams, and that they knew that Reams entered into and enjoyed the peaceable possession thereof, under his purchase from Arnot.

John Callier and James Callier were presented as witnesses, and, being duly sworn, the said John deposed, that he was authorized, by a letter from his brother Thomas Callier, to cancel the bargain or purchase of land, which he had made with Tobias Reams, for his, Thomas's use, and account, and which he, witness, accordingly did; and in pursuance of that power re-conveyed the land to Reams, in the manner endorsed on the Spanish writing.

The said James deposed, that he saw a letter; and had understood that Thomas Callier authorized John Callier to cancel the bargain or purchase of land, which he had made for his account with Tobias Reams, and that said John Callier did accordingly do so, by reconveying said land to said Tobias Reams, in the manner endorsed on said Spanish writing.

The Board ordered that the case be postponed for consideration.

THOMAS GOODWIN's case, No. 182 on the docket of the Board, and No. 97 on the books of the Register.

Claim.—A right of pre-emption of two hundred and eighty-six acres, as legal representative of Daniel Kannada, under the third section of the act.

The claimant presented his claim, together with a surveyor's plot of the land claimed, in the words and figures following, to wit:

To the Commissioners appointed in pursuance of the act of Congress passed the 3d day of March, 1803, for receiving and adjusting claims to lands south of the Tennessee, and east of Pearl river.

Please to take notice that the following tract of land, situated on the waters of Bassett's creek, in the county of Washington, beginning at a hornbeam, and running north, forty degrees east, eleven chains, to a lake; forty chains, to a beech corner; thence, north, fifty degrees east, twenty chains, to a hickory; thence, south, forty degrees east, fifty-five chains to an elm corner; thence, south, forty chains, on Brewer's line, to a stake corner; south, sixty-seven degrees west, twenty-nine chains, to a red oak; thence, north, twenty-seven degrees west, forty chains, to the beginning; and hath such forms and marks, both natural and artificial, as are fully represented in the plot annexed, containing two hundred and eighty-six acres; is claimed by Thomas Goodwin, legal representative of Daniel Kannada, in and by virtue of the third section of the said act, as a pre-emption, and is now exhibited to the Register of the Land Office established east of Pearl river, to be recorded as directed by said act. To all which he begs leave to refer, as also to a copy of the plot herewith filed.

THOMAS GOODWIN,
Legal representative of Daniel Kannada.
MARCH 26, 1804.

[Plot omitted.]

Chain carriers, Ambrose Miles and Hezekiah Carter. Entered in record of claims, vol. 1, page 296, by EDWARD LLOYD WAILES, for

JOSEPH CHAMBERS, *Register.*

The claimant exhibited a deed from John Kannada, bearing date the 14th day of August, 1803, duly executed, conveying to Nathaniel Ross all the said Kannada's right, title, and claim to said tract of land, and the improvements thereon made. On the back of which deed is an assignment as follows, to wit:

MARCH 6, 1804.

I endorse all my right and title to Thomas Goodwin, of the within mentioned: as witness my hand and seal.

NATHANIEL ROSS.

Test, STEPHEN CLAY.

Benjamin Baldwin was presented as a witness, and, being duly sworn and interrogated by the Board, he deposed that he had no interest in this case; that Daniel Kannada purchased the improvements upon the land in question, about the last of December, 1802, or beginning of January, 1803; and was in possession on the 3d of March, 1803; and raised a crop of about one hundred bushels of corn the following season, by the cultivation of a tenant, having about twelve acres under improvement; that there was no dwelling house upon the land, it being low land and generally subject to inundation every year. That Daniel Kannada was more than twenty-one years of age on the 3d of March, 1803.

William Gilliam, surveyor, was presented as a witness, and, being duly sworn, deposed, that he made the survey in question, and believed it to be correct; and that it included the cultivated field of the claimant: that he, Gilliam, knew of no interfering lines or claims.

The Board ordered that the case be postponed for consideration.

JOHN BAKER's case: commenced in page 640.

Thomas Malone, surveyor, was presented as a witness, and being duly sworn, deposed, that he made the survey and plot of the land in question, and believed it to be correct; and that it included part of the improvements of the claimant; that his dwelling house and other improvements were on adjoining land, claimed by him under another warrant; that the southwestwardly side of

this tract interfered with the donation claim of John McGrew, Sen.; that it also interfered with the claims of Peter Malone, Julian de Castro, James Griffin, William Coleman, Doctor Chastang, and Edward Lloyd Wailes.

The Board ordered that the case be postponed for consideration.

JOHN BAKER's case: commenced in page 641.

Thomas Malone, surveyor, was produced as a witness, and, being duly sworn, deposed, that he made the plot of the land in question, and believed it to be correct ; and that it included the dwelling house, and part of the improvements of the claimant; that, on the east side, it interfered with the claim of John McGrew, senior, but in what manner he could not say.

The Board ordered that the case be postponed for consideration.

JAMES MORGAN, representative of John Burney: case commenced in page 594.

Thomas Malone, surveyor, was presented as a witness, and being duly sworn, deposed, that he made the survey and plot of the land in question, and believed it to be correct, and that it included the dwelling house and improvements of the claimant; that this was principally included in the donation claim of John McGrew, junior, representative of Alexander McGrew, on the northeast side, which was distinguished by a dotted line on the plot; that there might be a strip of something more than two hundred yards wide, which was not included.

The Board ordered that the case be postponed for consideration.

RANSOM HARWELL's case: commenced in page 642.

Thomas Malone, surveyor, was presented as a witness, and, being duly sworn, deposed, that he made the survey and plot of the land in question, and believed it to be correct, and that it included the dwelling house and improvements of the claimant; and that he believed that this survey was wholly included in the survey and claim of Elisha Simmons.

The Board ordered that the case be postponed for consideration.

WILLIAM ROGERS's case: commenced in page 597.

Thomas Malone, surveyor, was produced as a witness, and, being duly sworn, deposed, that he made the survey and plot of the land in question, and believed it to be correct, and that it included the dwelling house and improvements of the claimant: that, from the best of his information and belief, there was no interference with this claim.

The Board ordered that the case be postponed for consideration.

JAMES CALLIER, representative of Bryant and Snelgrove: case commenced in page 598.

Thomas Malone, surveyor, was produced as a witness, and being duly sworn, deposed, that he made the survey and plot of the land in question, and believed it to be correct, and that it included the dwelling house and improvements made by Henry Snelgrove; that the claim in the name of the heirs of Jas. McGrew, under a Spanish warrant, intersects a small corner of this on the northeast; that the claim of Constant McGrew, for a donation, comprehends the whole front of this survey, and extends back within nineteen chains of the rear.

The Board ordered that the case be postponed for consideration.

RICHARD LEE, representative of Jordan Morgan: case commenced in page 602.

George Dickey, John Callier, and William Vardeman, were presented as witnesses, and being duly sworn and interrogated by the Board, they deposed, that they had no interest in this case. And the said Dickey testified, that he came to this country from South Carolina in the year 1799, and one of the first houses which he went to was Jordan Morgan's on the land in question; that it appeared to have been erected in the winter preceding; that he had, at the same time, a smith's shop erected, and the tools of his trade, and but small cultivation; that, some time after, Morgan went out of possession, and William Vardeman came in; that, at a subsequent period, Vardeman went out, and the place was afterwards improved by the tenants of Esquire Lee, the present claimant, and had been so continued to that time.

Question by the claimant. When you came to the house of Jordan Morgan, as you have mentioned, was he not married to Mr. Wheat's daughter, and had a child ?

Answer. He was married, and had a child at that time.

The said Callier deposed, that he sold William Vardeman's claim to the land in question to Richard Lee, and paid to him, Vardeman, the consideration money, which he received, and confirmed his Callier's bargain and sale to Lee; that he, Callier, had always understood, and did believe, that Lee entered into the peaceable and quiet possession of said land, in virtue of said sale, and continued quietly to possess the same without opposition, until lately, as he understood, some person or persons had set up claim or claims to all or a part of said land.

The said Vardeman deposed, that, in May, 1799, he purchased and settled upon the land in question, and continued thereon until some time in the latter part of that year, or beginning of the year 1800, when he removed therefrom, and rented another place; that, some time afterwards, Colonel Callier, in his, Vardeman's, behalf, and for his account, sold his right or claim to the improvements and land to Richard Lee; which bargain and sale he, Vardeman, confirmed; that neither Jordan Morgan, nor any other person, set up claim to said land at that time, that he knew of, nor had they since, until very lately; that Jordan Morgan inhabited on said land at the time that he, Vardeman, purchased his claim and improvements.

The Board ordered that the case be postponed for consideration.

WILLIAM WILLIAMS's case : commenced in page 651.

Thomas Malone, surveyor, was presented as a witness, and, being duly sworn, deposed, that he made the survey and plot of the land in question, and believed it to be correct; that it included the dwelling house and improvements of the claimant; that from his knowledge of the natural marks referred to in the survey of Edward Young for a donation, and from an inspection of his plot returned to the Board, the whole of this claim was included within that survey.

The Board ordered that the case be postponed for consideration.

PETER MALONE, representative of John Woods: case commenced in page 639.

Thomas Malone. surveyor, was produced as a witness, and, being duly sworn, deposed, that he made the survey and plot of the land in question, and believed it to be correct; that it included the dwelling house and improvements of the claimant.

George Harris and Siddie Harris were produced as witnesses, and, being duly sworn and interrogated by the Board, they deposed, that they had no interest in this case; that they knew that Peter Malone inhabited and cultivated on the land in question, before and since the 3d day of March, 1803, and that they believed that he actually did inhabit thereon on the said 3d day of March; and that Peter Malone was at that time the head of a family.

The Board ordered that the case be postponed for consideration.

MICAJAH WALL's case: commenced in page 602.

Thomas Malone, surveyor, was presented as a witness, and, being duly sworn, deposed, that he made the survey and plot of the land in question, and believed it to be correct; that it included the dwelling house and improvements of the claimant ; that this survey was wholly included in the claim of John McGrew, junior, as the representative of Alexander McGrew, and that he knew of no other interference.

The Board ordered that the case be postponed for consideration.

MATTHEW SHAW's case: commenced in page 598.

Thomas Malone, surveyor, was presented as a witness, and being duly sworn, deposed, that he made the survey and plot of the land in question, and believed it to be correct ; that it included the dwelling house and improvements of the claimant; and that he knew of no interference.

The Board ordered that the case be postponed for consideration.

WILLIAM COLEMAN, representative of Simon Favre : case commenced in page 654.

Thomas Malone, surveyor, was presented as a witness, and, being duly sworn, deposed, that he made the survey and plot of the land in question; and believed it to be correct; that it included the improvements of the claimant, but not his dwelling house, which was se-

veral miles off from the land claimed; that this survey included the whole of Peter Malone's claim; that the east side of this comprehends the greater part of the claim of Edward Lloyd Wailes, and that John Baker's. one thousand six hundred acres' survey runs from south to north diagonally across this, and included a great part of it; that the claim of Julian de Castro for a donation interfered nearly in the same manner as did said Wailes's claim.

Augustin Rochon was presented as a witness, and, being duly sworn, deposed, that, Simon Favre was an interpreter of the Choctaw language for the Spanish garrison at Fort Confederation, on the Tombigbee river, until that garrison was evacuated by the Spanish troops in the year 1796 or 1797; that said Favre was then attached to the garrison of Fort St. Stephen's, on the same river, as an interpreter, and continued in this service at said post until it was evacuated by the Spanish troops; that he then removed to New Orleans, and there acted as interpreter for the Spanish Government, in which service and capacity he still continued.

The Board ordered that the case be postponed for consideration.

ANN LAWRENCE's case: commenced in page 656.

Thomas Malone, surveyor, was presented as a witness, and, being duly sworn, deposed, that he made the survey and plot of the land in question, and believed it to be correct; that it included the dwelling house and improvements of the claimant; that this claim embraced almost the whole of the claim of Noah Kenner Hutson, except a little on the river at the northeast corner; that the south corner interfered with the claim of James Callier, under Anthony Hoggatt: and knew of no other interference.

The Board ordered that the case be postponed for consideration.

JAMES CALLIER, representative of Anthony Hoggatt: case commenced in page 617.

Thomas Malone, surveyor, was presented as a witness, and, being duly sworn, deposed, that he carried the compass part of the way in making a survey of the land in question, and that Mr. Bilbo carried the compass the remaining part; and that, from his own minutes, and those of Mr. Bilbo, he made this plot, and believed it to be correct; that it included the dwelling and improvements of the claimant; that, from the best of his knowledge and information, the claim of William Vardeman, under a British grant to John Lott, covered the whole width of this claim on the front, but how far back he was not able to say.

The Board ordered that the case be postponed for consideration.

GEORGE BREWER, Junior's, case: commenced in page 661.

Thomas Malone, surveyor, was produced as a witness, and, being duly sworn, deposed, that he made the survey and plot of the land in question, and believed it to be correct; that it included the dwelling house and improvements of the claimant; that the claim of Young Gains, under a Spanish warrant, included more than half the front of this, and running diagonally, intersected the west line of this survey, about half way back from the river, so that it embraced the northwest corner; that he had understood that a British grant, in the name of Abrahams, interfered with some part of this, but in what manner he did not know.

The Board ordered that the case be postponed for consideration.

BENJAMIN KING's case, No. 183 on the docket of the Board, and No. 194 on the books of the Register.

Claim—Of three hundred and fifty acres, by virtue of a deed of conveyance from William Jackson to Israel Foalsome, pre-supposing a British grant to said Jackson, under the first section of the act.

The claimant presented his claim, together with a surveyor's plot of the land claimed, in the words and figures following, to wit:

To the Commissioners appointed in pursuance of the act of Congress passed the 3d day of March, 1803, for receiving and adjusting claims to lands south of the Tennessee, and east of Pearl river.

Please to take notice, that the following tract of land, situated on the waters of the Tombigbee, in the county of Washington, beginning at Stewart's old line; south, twenty-five degrees west, one hundred and ten chains, to a red oak corner; thence, south, sixty-five degrees

89

east, thirty-one chains, sixty links, to a stake; thence, north, twenty-five degrees east, one hundred and fifteen chains fifty links, to the river; and thence, with the river, to the beginning; containing three hundred and fifty acres: is claimed by Benjamin King, legal representative of Israel Foalsome, and now exhibited to the Register of the Land Office to be established east of Pearl river, to be recorded as directed by said act. To all which he begs leave to refer, as also to a copy of the plot herewith filed.

BENJAMIN KING,
Representative of Israel Foalsome.
[Plot omitted.]

Surveyed 24th February, 1804. Chain carriers, Peter Nelms and Benjamin King.
Entered in record of claims, vol. 2, page 15, by Edward Lloyd Wailes, for
JOSEPH CHAMBERS, *Register.*

The claimant produced deeds of lease and release from William Jackson, bearing date the 3d and 4th days of March, 1780, duly executed, conveying to Israel Foalsome all the said Jackson's right, title, and interest in or to said tract of land.
The Board ordered that the case be postponed for consideration.

JOHN DENLEY's case, No. 184 on the docket of the Board, and No. 143 on the books of the Register.
Claim.—A right of pre-emption of six hundred and forty acres, under the third section of the act.
The claimant presented his claim, together with a surveyor's plot of the land claimed, in the following words and figures, viz.:

To the Commissioners appointed for adjusting claims and rights of land south of the Tennessee, and east of Pearl river.

Please to take notice, that the above survey is claimed by John Denley, as a pre-emption, lying and situated about two miles below the Sunflower, beginning on a red elm on the west side of Tombigbee, running west, until hindered by water; thence, returning to the beginning; thence, meandering the river down, until it intersects with George Dickey; thence, west, till hindered by water; claiming the said pre-emption six hundred and forty acres, binding on the south by George Dickey, and on all other sides by vacant land or undefined claims.

JOHN DENLEY.
MARCH 28, 1804.
[Plot omitted.]

Surveyed 23d March, 1804, by Robert Ligon. Chain carriers, Hiram Mounger and James Dunley.
Entered in record of claims, vol. 1, page 470, by Edward Lloyd Wailes, for
JOSEPH CHAMBERS, *Register.*

George Dickey was presented as a witness, and, being duly sworn and interrogated by the Board, deposed, that he had no interest in this claim; that the present claimant began to work on said land in the year 1801; that, in the year 1803, he raised a crop of about five acres of corn and pumpkins on it; that he was, on the 3d of March, 1803, twenty-one years of age; but being an unmarried man, lived in the family with his father, and had no dwelling house or other houses on said land.—Vide surveyor's testimony, in page 670.
The Board ordered that the case be postponed for consideration.

NATHANIEL Ross's case, No. 185 on the docket of the Board, and No. 89 on the books of the Register.
Claim.—A right of pre-emption of one hundred and sixty-four acres and thirty-six poles, as representative of Henry Slaughter, under the third section of the act.
The claimant presented his claim, together with a surveyor's plot of the land claimed, in the following words and figures, to wit:

To the Commissioners appointed in pursuance of the act of Congress passed the 3d day of March, 1803, for receiving and adjusting claims to land south of the Tennessee, and east of Pearl river.

Please to take notice, that the following tract of land, situated on the waters of Bassett's creek, in the county of Washington, beginning at a red oak on Isaac Ryan's line; running, thence, north, twenty degrees east, fifteen chains, to a water oak; thence, north, sixty-five degrees east, thirty-three chains, to a gum; thence, north, thirty degrees west, thirty-five chains, to a red oak; thence,

south, fifty-two degrees west, thirty-five chains, to a red oak; thence, south, sixteen degrees west, thirty chains, to a red oak sapling; thence, south, sixty-three degrees east, twenty-one chains fifty links, to the beginning; and hath such forms and marks, both natural and artificial, as are fully represented in the plot annexed, containing one hundred and sixty-four acres and thirty-six poles, is claimed by Nathaniel Ross, representative of Henry Slaughter, in and by virtue of the said act, as a pre-emption, and is now exhibited to the Register of the Land Office established east of Pearl river, to be recorded as directed by said act. To all which he begs leave to refer, as also to a copy of the plot herewith filed.

BENJAMIN BALDWIN, for
NATHANIEL ROSS.
[Plot omitted.]

Chain carriers, Benjamin Harrison and Hezekiah Carter.
Entered in record of claims, vol. 1, page 258, by Edward Lloyd Wailes, for
JOSEPH CHAMBERS, *Register.*

The above named chain carriers were sworn before William H. Hargrave, Esq., Justice of the Peace.
Benjamin Baldwin was presented as a witness, and, being duly sworn and interrogated by the Board, deposed, that he had no interest in this claim; that Daniel Kannada purchased the improvements on said land, together with the improvement in the swamp, now claimed by Thomas Goodwin of Henry Slaughter; and he understood that Daniel Kannada sold the whole to his brother, John Kannada, who sold the same to Nathaniel Ross; that said Ross sold the swamp part to Thomas Goodwin, as he, witness, had heard, and retained the upland, which is now in question; that on this part there was a cabin, but there was no cultivation in the year 1803, nor was it inhabited by any body on the 3d of March in that year, nor until the close of the year; Thomas Goodwin resided there a short time; that Nathaniel Ross, Daniel Kannada, and John Kannada, were each of them twenty one years of age on the 3d of March, 1803.
William Gilliam, surveyor, was presented as a witness, and, being duly sworn, deposed, that he made the survey and plot of the land in question, and believed it to be correct; that it included the dwelling house and improvements of the claimant; that he had not heard of any interfering lines or claims.
The Board ordered that the case be postponed for consideration.
Adjourned until Tuesday, the 1st of May next.

TUESDAY, May 1, 1804.
The Board met according to adjournment. Present: Ephraim Kirby, Robert C. Nicholas.
Adjourned until Wednesday, the 2d instant.

WEDNESDAY, May 2, 1804.
The Board met according to adjournment. Present: Ephraim Kirby, Robert C. Nicholas.

WILLIAM H. HARGRAVE's case: commenced in page 661.
William Gilliam, surveyor, was produced as a witness, and, being duly sworn, deposed, that he made the survey and plot in question, and believed it to be correct; that it included a small improvement of the claimant; that he knew of no interfering lines or claims.
The Board ordered that the case be postponed for consideration.

THOMAS SULLIVANT's case: commenced in page 658.
William Gilliam, surveyor, was presented as a witness, and, being duly sworn, deposed, that he made the plot of the land in question, from a survey which he had previously made, and believed it to be correct; that it included the dwelling-house and improvements of the claimant; that he knew of no interfering lines.
The Board ordered that the case be postponed for consideration.

WILLIAM GILLIAM, representative of John Clark: case commenced in page 649.
William Gilliam, surveyor, was presented as a witness, and, being duly sworn, deposed, that he made the survey and plot of the land in question, and believed it to be correct; that it contained the dwelling-house and improvements of the claimant; that he knew of no interfering claim.
The Board ordered that the case be postponed for consideration.
Adjourned until Thursday, the 3d instant.

THURSDAY, *May* 3, 1804.

The Board met according to adjournment. Present: Ephraim Kirby, Robert C. Nicholas, Joseph Chambers.

Adjourned until Friday, the 4th instant.

FRIDAY, *May* 4, 1804.

The Board met according to adjournment. Present: Ephraim Kirby, Robert C. Nicholas, Joseph Chambers.

Adjourned until Saturday, the 5th instant.

SATURDAY, *May* 5, 1804.

The Board met according to adjournment. Present: Ephraim Kirby, Robert C. Nicholas, Joseph Chambers.

SETH DEAN, representative of Charles Walker: case commenced in page 686.

Thomas Bassett was presented as a witness, and, being duly sworn, deposed, that more than twenty years ago, he saw negroes belonging to Charles Walker clearing ground on the west side of Tombigbee river, opposite the cut-off, just below the mouth of the creek, as well as he recollected; that he believed neither Charles Walker nor his legal representative or representatives, resided within the Mississippi territory on the 27th day of October, 1795; that he had understood that Joel Walker, nephew to Charles Walker, inherited the whole of the estate of his uncle, Charles Walker, deceased.

William Coleman was presented as a witness, and being duly sworn and interrogated by the Board, deposed, that he had no interest in this claim.

Question. Do you know the widow of Joel Walker, nephew of Charles Walker?

Answer. I did know her, and her name was Mary, to the best of my recollection; she had a child, and I have heard that it was dead. I have heard from the brothers of Joel Walker, William and David Walker, that this child was dead; and I believe that this child died between the years 1798 and 1801.

The Board ordered that the case be postponed for consideration.

FRANCIS COLEMAN, representative of Charles Walker: case commenced in page 683.

John McGrew, Sen., was presented as a witness, and, being duly sworn and interrogated by the Board, deposed, that he had no interest in this case; that he knew that Charles Walker settled upon the land in question in or about the year 1778, built a house and made two or three crops on said land; that he believed that Walker died in the year 1780; that neither Charles Walker, nor his representative or representatives, resided within the Mississippi territory on the 27th day of October, 1795; that he thought Walker had cleared, and under cultivation, within the limits of said land, about forty acres.

The Board ordered that the case be postponed for consideration.

Adjourned until Monday, the 7th instant.

MONDAY, *May* 7, 1804.

The Board met according to adjournment. Present: Ephraim Kirby, Robert C. Nicholas, Joseph Chambers.

JAMES CALLIER and JOSEPH CAMPBELL, executors of Maria Josephia Narbone, deceased: case commenced in page 635.

The following deposition, taken pursuant to an order of the Board, recorded in page 699, was exhibited, to wit:

Question. Have you any interest, direct or indirect, in the establishment of this claim?

Answer. I have no interest, direct or indirect.

Question. How long have the lands now claimed been in the occupancy and possession of the present claimants, and those under whom they hold?

Answer. About forty-five years.

Question. Have these persons held an uninterrupted possession, holding out all others therefrom, and no other person claiming any right thereto?

Answer. They have held an uninterrupted possession of the lands now claimed, holding out all others therefrom, and no person or persons have made any claim thereto.

Question. When did Anthony Narbone, the husband of Maria Josephia Narbone, die?

Answer. About ten years since.

Question. Did he die in possession of the premises?

Answer. He died in possession of the premises, and on the lands now claimed.

Question. Did Maria Josephia Narbone, his widow, continue to inhabit and possess the same until her death, and at what time did she die?

Answer. Maria Josephia Narbone, the widow of Anthony Narbone, deceased, did continue to inhabit and possess the said land until her death; and that she died about eighteen months ago, on the said premises.

Question. Have the premises been inhabited and cultivated by the heirs of Maria Josephia Narbone since her death, and, if so, by which of them?

Answer. The premises have been inhabited and cultivated by one of the heirs of said deceased, viz.: Isabella Campbell.

Question. What kind of cultivation has been made on the land in question, from your first knowledge of the place, until the present time?

Answer. Corn, pease, potatoes, rice, and sometimes tar.

SIMON ANDRY.

Personally appeared before me, James Farr, Esquire, one of the Justices of the Peace for the county of Washington, in the Mississippi territory, Simon Andry, and, being duly sworn to make true and correct answers to such questions as should be proposed to him, did, on oath, make the answers to the abovementioned questions, as above stated.

Sworn before me, this 27th day of April, 1804.

JAMES FARR, *J. P.*

John Chastang and Augustin Rochon were presented as witnesses, and being duly sworn and interrogated by the Board, they deposed, that they had no interest in this case.

The said Chastang further deposed, that, when he first came into this country, which was in the year 1765, Mr. Anthony Narbone, now deceased, was settled upon the land in question, and, from appearance, and as he then understood, had been settled there many years before; that he continued to live there until the time of his death, which happened about the year 1794; and that Maria Josephia Narbone, his widow, lived there until she died, about eighteen months since; and that one of her heirs, to wit, Isabella Campbell, had resided there ever since.

The said Rochon also deposed, that, as long ago as he could remember, to wit, about the year 1781, Anthony Narbone lived on the land in question; that, for a time, the Indians became so troublesome, that Mr. Narbone was compelled to quit his plantation, and remove into Mobile; but as soon as the danger was over, [he returned to it,] and lived there until he died; that his widow lived there until she died, and, since her death, her daughter Isabella, the present wife of Joseph Campbell, had resided at the same place.

The Board ordered that the case be postponed for consideration.

JOHN CHASTANG's case: commenced in page 614

The following notice, plot, and testimony, were produced by the claimant, as a part of said case, to wit:

To the Commissioners appointed in pursuance of an act of Congress passed the 3d day of March, 1803, for receiving and adjusting claims to land south of the Tennessee river and east of Pearl river.

Please to take notice, that the following tract of land lying east of Mobile river, butting and bounding on the north by lands claimed by Peter Juzant, on the south by lands claimed by Baptist Trennier, on the west by said river and on the other side by vacant land: is claimed by John Chastang, under and by virtue of a Spanish grant or order of survey, granted to the said John Chastang, as may appear by the original grant now delivered to the Register of the Land Office to be established east of Pearl river, to be recorded as directed by said act. To all which he begs leave to refer, as also to the copy of the plot herewith filed.

CHASTANG, JEUNE.

[Plot omitted.]

FORT STODDERT.

Surveyed 29th February, 1804, by James Gordon. Chain bearers, Joseph Campbell and Gabriel Tissrah.

The deposition of Simon Andry, taken pursuant to an order of the Board, was exhibited, as follows, to wit:

Question. Are you, directly or indirectly, interested in the establishment of the claim in question?

Answer. I am not interested, directly or indirectly, in the claim.

Question. Did Doctor John Chastang, the present claimant, inhabit and cultivate the land now by him claimed on the 22d of October, in the year 1795; and, if so, what kind of cultivation?

Answer. Doctor John Chastang did inhabit and cultivate the land in question on the 22d of October, 1795, on both sides of the river, and that he has so continued to inhabit and cultivate the said lands to the present time, and that he made corn, pease, rice, and potatoes thereon.

Question. Was Doctor Chastang the head of a family, or twenty-one years of age, on the 18th of January, 1785?

Answer. He was the head of a family, and twenty-one years of age, at that time.

SIMON ANDRY.

Personally appeared before me, James Callier, Esquire, one of the Justices of the Peace for the county of Washington, in the Mississippi territory, Simon Andry, and, being duly sworn to make true and correct answers to such questions as should be proposed to him, did, on oath, make the answers to the above mentioned questions, as above stated. Sworn before me, the 27th day of April, 1804.

JAMES CALLIER, J. P.

Augustin Rochon was presented as a witness, and, being duly sworn, deposed, that Doctor Chastang established himself on the land in question in the year 1795, by building upon the same, and putting a number of his negroes there; that, some time after, probably in the year following, he removed from his upper plantations, near Fort St. Stephen's, to this place, where he had resided ever since.

Simon Andry was presented as a witness, and, being duly sworn, deposed, that, at the time Doctor Chastang petitioned for the land whereon he now lives, the old fields on the opposite side of the river extended the whole length of his concession on the west side, commencing on the east, or opposite side of that channel of the river from that whereon said Chastang resides, and running up the bank of the said channel of the river, until nearly opposite the mouth of Cedar or Cambey creek, and, in extent from the river, in and about three acres.

The Board ordered that the case be postponed for consideration.

HEIRS OF AUGUSTIN ROCHON, deceased, two cases: one commenced in page 681, and the other in page 682.

The deposition of Simon Andry, taken pursuant to an order of the Board, was exhibited, as follows, to wit:

Question. Are you, directly or indirectly, interested in the claim in question?

Answer. I am not interested directly or indirectly.

Question. Did you know Augustin Rochon, deceased, and at what time did he die?

Answer. I did know Augustin Rochon, deceased, before his death, and he died about the year 1780.

Question. Did he, at any time before his death, reside within this territory, and cultivate any of the lands which are now claimed by his heirs or executors?

Answer. Augustin Rochon, deceased, did reside in this territory before his death, and cultivate the lands now claimed by his executors or heirs.

Question. Do you know whether his widow or either of his heirs resided within the Mississippi territory throughout the year 1795, and whether either of them cultivated any of the lands of said deceased within said territory?

Answer. The son of Augustin Rochon, deceased, did live on and cultivate the lands of the said deceased throughout the year 1795.

Question. What kind of cultivation did he make?

Answer. Corn, pease, potatoes, and rice in the summer; in the winter he made tar.

SIMON ANDRY.

Personally appeared before me, James Callier, Esquire, one of the Justices of the Peace for the county of Washington, in the Mississippi territory, Simon Andry, and, being duly sworn to make true and correct answers to such questions as should be proposed to him, did, on oath, make the answers to the above mentioned questions, as above stated. Sworn before me, this 27th day of April, 1804.

JAMES CALLIER, J. P.

Doctor John Chastang was presented as a witness, and, being duly sworn, deposed, that, before the death of Augustin Rochon, deceased, he saw his laboring people working upon and cultivating the lands now claimed by his heirs; that he could not say from positive knowledge that Augustin, the son of the deceased, continued to do the same after the death of his father, but that he knew that his people were here in the year 1795; and believed that he resided here also during a part of said year.

The Board ordered that the case be postponed for consideration.

Adjourned until Thursday, the 10th instant.

THURSDAY, May 10, 1804.

The Board met according to adjournment. Present: Ephraim Kirby, Robert C. Nicholas.

Adjourned until Saturday, the 12th instant.

SATURDAY, May 12, 1804.

The Board met according to adjournment. Present: Ephraim Kirby, Robert C. Nicholas, Joseph Chambers.

Adjourned until Monday, the 14th instant.

MONDAY, May 14, 1804.

The Board met according to adjournment. Present: Ephraim Kirby, Robert C. Nicholas, Joseph Chambers.

ROBERT SORREL, Senior's case: commenced in page 643.

Thomas Bassett was presented as a witness, and, being duly sworn and interrogated by the Board, deposed, that he had no interest in this claim; that Robert Sorrel, Sen., was living on the land in question, had land cleared and corn growing last spring was a year since; and, from the quantity of labor that appeared to have been done, he must have lived there previous to the 3d day of March, 1803; and was, at that time, more than forty years of age.

The Board ordered that the case be postponed for consideration.

JAMES FRAZIER's case: commenced in page 623.

John McGrew was produced as a witness, and, being duly sworn, deposed, that James Frazier settled and commenced to improve upon the land in question, in the fall of the year 1788 or 1789, and made four or five crops thereon, and then removed to Natchez, and from thence to Chickasaw nation, where he had resided ever since; that when Frazier quitted said land he told him to take care of the same for him; that he, McGrew, put on a man by the name of Stilly, who made a crop thereon in the year 1795; and that James Frazier was, on the 31st of July, 1787, more than twenty-one years of age.

The Board ordered that the case be postponed for consideration.

JAMES FARR's case: commenced in page 688.

Daniel Johnson was presented as a witness, and, being duly sworn and interrogated by the Board, deposed, that he was not interested in this claim; that, in the year 1795, the land in question was settled upon and cultivated by Cornelius Rain, as well as he, Johnson recollected; that he had understood that James Farr cultivated and inhabited said land, in the year 1797, in the employment of Cornelius Rain.

The Board ordered that the case be postponed for consideration.

EDWIN LEWIS's case, as representative of William Green: commenced in page 648.

John McGrew, Esquire, was presented as a witness, and, being duly sworn and interrogated by the Board, deposed, that he had no interest in this case; that William Green settled, built houses, and improved upon the land in question, about two years last past, and continued thereon until last fall; and was, on the 3d of March, 1803, more than twenty-one years of age.

The Board ordered that the case be postponed for consideration.

EDWIN LEWIS's case: commenced in page 648.

John McGrew, Esquire. was presented as a witness, and, being duly sworn, deposed, that Edwin Lewis settled upon the land in question before the 3d of March, 1803, built houses, and cultivated last summer one or two acres of land; that he had resided thereon before and ever since the 3d of March last; and was, he, McGrew, thought, more than twenty-one years of age.

The Board ordered that the case be postponed for consideration.

HEIRS OF JOHN McINTOSH: case commenced in page 676.

John McGrew, Esquire, and Thomas Bassett were presented as witnesses, and, being duly sworn and interrogated by the Board, they deposed, that they had no interest in this claim. And the said McGrew deposed, that John McIntosh had land cleared, and negroes working on said land, in the year 1780 or 1781; and that it was said that the land was cultivated, at that time, for the account of John McIntosh.

The said Bassett deposed, that he knew that said land was inhabited and cultivated, at the time that the British held this country, by his, McIntosh's, negroes and overseer.

The Board ordered that the case be postponed for consideration.

Joshua Howard, representative of Arthur Moore and wife: case commenced in page 663.

John McGrew, Esquire, and Thomas Bassett were presented as witnesses, and, being duly sworn, deposed, that they knew that Arthur Moore inhabited and cultivated on the land in question, when the British held possession of this country. And the said McGrew also deposed, that said Moore conveyed said land to Joshua Howard; that he had understood, and did believe, that said Howard did reside within the Mississippi territory on the 27th day of October, 1795.

The Board ordered that the case be postponed for consideration.

James Hoggatt's case, as representative of William Wall and wife: commenced in page 685.

John McGrew, Esquire, and Thomas Bassett were presented as witnesses, and, being duly sworn, the said McGrew deposed, that James Hoggatt lived at or near the land, near to where Colonel Callier now lives, in the year 1780; that Hoggatt had a plantation and barn on the said place; that he, McGrew, understood from William Wall and James Hoggatt, that the land thus inhabited and cultivated by James Hoggatt, in the year 1780, was the same which Hoggatt purchased from said Wall; that he did not know whether or not James Hoggatt, or his legal representative, resided within the Mississippi territory on the 27th day of October, 1795; that he knew that Wilford Hoggatt resided one year at or near the same place, in the low grounds where James Hoggatt lived, and afterwards removed from the low grounds, or swamp, to the pure lands, some distance from the river; that Marbury entered upon this land after Wilford Hoggatt quitted it; that, after Marbury quitted the possession Adam Hollinger entered thereon; that Wilford Hoggatt first came to this country after the conquest of it by the Spaniards, which was before the year 1795, at which time, he said he had come to get his and his brother's land; that Wilford Hoggatt removed from this country to the Mississippi river, near to the town of Natchez, where he had resided ever since, as the witness believed.

The said Bassett deposed, that he knew that James Hoggatt lived, in the year 1789, or before that time, in or about the same place, on the river Tombigbee, where Colonel Callier now lives; that he asked Wilford Hoggatt, as well as he, Bassett, recollected, some time in the year 1791, why he settled upon the land claimed by his brother, James Hoggatt, and whereon he had formerly lived; he said that his own place, or land, was entirely wood land, and as the place of his brother had considerable quantity of land that had been formerly cleared, it was much easier to clear up again; and that when his brother James Hoggatt came to this country, if he came at all, he might clear him, Wilford Hoggatt, as much land, and he would give him up his land again; that he, Bassett, believed that Wilford Hoggatt resided within the Mississippi territory on the 27th of October, 1795.

The Board ordered that the case be postponed for consideration.

Heirs of Robert Farmer, deceased, two cases: commenced in pages 673 and 674.

John McGrew, Esq. was presented as a witness, and, being duly sworn, deposed, that, soon after the Americans took possession of this country, Colonel John McKee came to his house, and requested him to get some persons to settle upon Major Robert Farmer's land, and said that he would pay for whatever labor they might do; that he, McGrew, accordingly agreed with Elijah Simmons and William Rogers to settle upon the lower tract, for account of the representatives of Farmer; that he had since understood that their settlements were made without the limits of Farmer's claim, which happened from his, McGrew's not being well acquainted with the lines of Farmer's land; that McKee gave him, McGrew, the plot of the said lower tract only.

The Board ordered that the case be postponed for consideration.

Adjourned until Thursday, the 17th instant.

Thursday, May 17, 1804.
The Board met according to adjournment. Present: Ephraim Kirby, Robert C. Nicholas, Joseph Chambers.

James Scott's case, representative of Gabriel Burrows: commenced in page 608.

John Smith was presented as a witness, and, being duly sworn and interrogated by the Board, deposed, that he had no interest in this claim; that Gabriel Burrows

moved, built, and cleared ground, on the place in question, in the year 1797, and in that year cultivated about one acre in corn, and planted peach trees; that Burrows resided and cultivated on said land; one or two years after that, sold it to James Scott, the present claimant, who had resided on the same ever since Burrows quitted it; and that he, Smith, always understood that Burrows had sold his claim to Scott; that, in the year 1797, Gabriel Burrows had a wife and family of three children.

The Board ordered that the case be postponed for consideration.

Adjourned until Friday, the 18th instant.

Friday, May 18, 1804.
The Board met according to adjournment. Present: Ephraim Kirby, Robert C. Nicholas, Joseph Chambers.
Adjourned until Monday, the 21st instant.

Monday, May 21, 1804.
The Board met according to adjournment. Present: Ephraim Kirby, Robert C. Nicholas, Joseph Chambers.
Adjourned until Wednesday, the 23d instant.

Wednesday, May 23, 1804.
The Board met according to adjournment. Present: Ephraim Kirby, Robert C. Nicholas, Joseph Chambers.

Elihu Hall Bay's three cases, in two of which he claims, as representative of William Fradgley; the other, as representative of John Sutherland, the two first cases commenced in pages 677–678, the other case in page 679. In each of these cases the Board adjudged as follows, to wit:

On due consideration, the Board is of opinion that this claim is not supported agreeably to the articles of agreement and cession between the United States and the State of Georgia, and the said claimant is not confirmed in his title to said land.

Heirs of John McIntosh, deceased: case commenced in page 676.

On due consideration, the Board is of opinion that this claim is not supported agreeably to the articles of agreement and cession between the United States and the State of Georgia, and the said claimants are not confirmed in their title to said land.

James Hoggatt, representative of William Wall and and wife: case commenced in page 685.

On due consideration, the Board is of opinion that this claim is not supported agreeably to the articles of agreement and cession between the United States and the State of Georgia, and the said claimant is not confirmed in his title to said land.

Heirs of Robert Farmer, deceased; two cases, commenced, one in page 673, the other in page 674; in each of which cases the Board adjudged as follows, to wit:

On due consideration, the Board is of opinion that this claim is not supported agreeably to the articles of agreement and cession between the United States and the State of Georgia, and the said claimants are not confirmed in their title to said land.

Benjamin King, representative of Israel Foalsome: case commenced in page 705.

Claim.—Three hundred and fifty acres, founded on a deed of conveyance from William Jackson to Israel Foalsome, presupposing a British grant to said Jackson; but no such grant being produced, or proved ever to have existed, the Board, on due consideration, is of opinion that this claim is not supported, and the claimant is not confirmed in his claim to said land.

Heirs of Augustin Rochon, deceased; two cases, commenced, one in page 681, the other in page 682; in each of which cases the Board adjudged as follows, to wit:

On due consideration, the Board is of opinion that this claim is supported agreeably to the articles of agreement and cession between the United States and the State of Georgia, and the said claimants are confirmed in their title to said land.

Seth Dean, representative of Francis Juzant: case commenced in page 687.

Claim.—One thousand acres, by virtue of a deed of conveyance from Francis Juzant, pretending to be the son and heir of Peter Juzant, deceased: this claim is founded on a supposed British grant to the said Peter Juzant; but no such grant being produced, nor any evidence that it ever existed, the Board, on due consideration, is of opinion that this claim is not supported, and the claimant is not confirmed in his claim to said land.

SETH DEAN, representative of John Dawson: case commenced in page 687.

On careful inspection of the paper produced, as the original patent or grant, in support of this claim, the same being mutilated, illegible, and altogether unintelligible; on due consideration, the Board is of opinion that the said paper, claimed to be the original patent, or grant, is destitute of the parts essential to its validity, and, therefore, the said claimant is not confirmed in his claim to said land.

SETH DEAN, representative of Charles Walker: case commenced in page 686.

On due consideration, and careful inspection of the original patent or grant produced in support of this claim, the Board is of opinion that the said patent or grant is not legally and fully executed, and, therefore, the said claimant is not confirmed in his title to said land.

FRANCIS COLEMAN's two cases, commenced, one in page 683, as representative of Charles Walker, the other case in page 684, as representative of Abraham Little; in each of which cases the Board adjudged as follows, to wit:

On due consideration, the Board is of opinion that this claim is not supported agreeably to the articles of agreement and cession between the United States and the State of Georgia, and the said claimant is not confirmed in his title to said land.

ALEXANDER McCULLAGH, representative of Alexander McCullagh, deceased: case commenced in page 672.

On due consideration, the Board is of opinion that this claim is not supported agreeably to the articles of agreement and cession between the United States and the State of Georgia, and the said claimant is not confirmed in his title to said land.

WILLIAM VARDEMAN, representative of John Lott, Jun.: case commenced in page 675.

On due consideration, the Board is of opinion that this claim is not supported agreeably to the articles of agreement and cession between the United States and the State of Georgia, and the said claimant is not confirmed in his title to said land.

ROBERT ABRAHAM's case: commenced in page 685.

On due consideration, the Board is of opinion that this claim is not supported agreeably to the requirements of law, and the said claimant is not confirmed in his claim to said land.

JOSHUA HOWARD, representative of Arthur Moore and wife: case commenced in page 663.

Claim.—Two hundred and fifty acres, founded on deeds of conveyance from Arthur Moore, and Mary Moore his wife, pre-supposing a British grant to said Arthur Moore, of the lands claimed; but no such grant being produced, nor any evidence that it ever existed, the Board, on due consideration, is of opinion that this claim is not supported, and the claimant is not confirmed in his title or claim to said land.

THOMAS BASSETT, son and heir of Thomas Bassett, deceased: case commenced in page 612.

On due consideration, the Board is of opinion that the existence and subsequent loss of the said grant from the British Government of West Florida to said Thomas Bassett, deceased, is proved, and that this claim is supported agreeably to the requirements of law; and the Board doth confirm to the lawful heirs of the said Thomas Bassett, deceased, their title to the said land, to be located as follows, to wit:

Beginning on the west side of the Tombigbee river, on the margin thereof, at a cotton tree; thence, north, sixty-seven degrees west, with the line of the old British survey, seventy-nine chains fifty links; thence, south, twenty-three degrees west, eighty-three chains sixteen links; thence, south, sixty-seven degrees east, two hundred and twenty-three chains, to the margin of Tombigbee river; thence, up the same, with the meanders thereof, to the place of beginning.

THOMAS BASSETT, administrator of Nathaniel Bassett, deceased: case commenced in page 609.

On due consideration, the Board is of opinion that the existence and subsequent loss of the said grant from

the British Government of West Florida to said Thomas Bassett, deceased, is proved, and that this claim is supported agreeably to the requirements of law; and the Board doth confirm to the lawful heirs of the said Thomas Bassett, deceased, their title to said land, to be located as follows, viz.:

Beginning on the west margin of the Tombigbee river, about three quarters of a mile above McIntosh's bluff, at a sassafras, being the corner of the old British survey, and also the corner of lands granted by the British Government to Alexander McCullagh; thence, north, eighty-seven degrees west, one hundred and twenty-five chains seventy-five links, in the said old line; thence, south, three degrees west, fifty-nine chains, twenty-eight links, in said old line; thence, south, eighty-seven degrees east, ninety-two chains, in said old line, to the river; and thence up the margin of the same to the place of beginning.

JAMES CALLIER and JOSEPH CAMPBELL, executors of Maria Josephia Narbone, deceased: case commenced in page 635.

On full investigation of the circumstances attending this case, and on due consideration thereof, the Board is of opinion that the long uninterrupted possession of such part of the lands now claimed as is hereafter described, under several successive Governments, affords as high evidence of a complete and perfect title as a grant from either of said Governments fully executed. Although this claim is not brought within the literal provisions of the act of Congress of the 3d of March, 1803, the Board is of opinion that it is well supported within the spirit and intent of said act; and doth, thereupon, confirm to the lawful heirs or legatees of the said Maria Josephia Narbone, deceased, title to the following tracts of land, to wit:

Beginning on the west margin of the west branch of the Tombigbee, or Mobile river, ten chains above the present dwelling house of Joseph Campbell; thence, down the margin of said river sixty-three chains twenty-five links; thence, due south, seven chains fifty links; thence, up the course of said river, sixty-three chains, twenty-five links, keeping, in all places, seven chains and fifty links therefrom; thence, due north, to the place of beginning: also, beginning on the east side of the west channel of said river, opposite the place of beginning before mentioned; and thence, running from the east margin of said west channel due north, seven chains fifty links; thence, down the course of the said margin, sixty-three chains twenty-five links, keeping, in all places, seven chains fifty links therefrom; thence, due south, to the margin of said channel, and up the same to the place of beginning; containing forty acres of land on each side of said west channel of said river. And the Board doth order, that a certificate be granted to them accordingly.

Adjourned until Friday the 25th instant.

FRIDAY, *May* 25, 1804.

The Board met according to adjournment. Present: Ephraim Kirby, Robert C. Nicholas, Joseph Chambers.

JAMES CALLIER, representative of Anthony Hoggatt: case commenced in page 617.

On due consideration, the Board is of opinion that this claim is supported agreeably to the requirements of law, and that the claimant is entitled to a patent for seven hundred and thirty-two acres of land, to be located as follows, to wit:

Beginning on the west margin of the Tombigbee river, at the upper corner of Anna Mounger's five hundred and four acre donation tract; thence, up the margin of said river, so far as to make sixty-three chains twenty-five links, in a straight line; thence, south, thirty-three degrees west, so far, that a due west line therefrom, to said Anna Mounger's northwest corner, and from thence, with her line north, fifty degrees east, to the place of beginning, shall include seven hundred and thirty-two acres: *Provided, nevertheless,* That the said claimant first obtain, before a court of competent jurisdiction, a judicial decision in his favor against the adverse claim, by virtue of a grant from the British Government of West Florida to John Lott, Jun., of three hundred acres, bearing date February 16, 1778. And the Board doth order that a certificate be issued to him accordingly.

LEMUEL HENRY, attorney for Antonio Espaho: case commenced in page 633.

On due consideration, the Board is of opinion that this claim is not supported agreeably to the requirements of law, and the claimant is not entitled to a patent for said land by him claimed, in manner and form aforesaid.

JOHN FLOOD McGREW and CLARK McGREW, representatives of Julian de Castro: case commenced in page 632.

On due consideration, the Board is of opinion that this claim is supported agreeably to the requirements of law, and that the claimants are entitled to a patent for three hundred and thirty-five acres of land, to be located as follows, to wit:

Beginning on the west margin of the Tombigbee river, at the upper corner of Thomas Malone's four hundred and eighty acre tract, in the right of John Arnot; thence, with the line of said tract, due south, one hundred and twenty-six chains forty-nine links, to his southwest corner; thence, due west, twenty-six chains fifty links; thence, due north, to the river; and down the margin of the same, to the place of beginning. And the Board doth order that a certificate be granted to them accordingly.

CORNELIUS RAIN'S case: commenced in page 632.

On due consideration, the Board is of opinion that this claim is supported agreeably to the requirements of law, and that the claimant is entitled to a patent for four hundred acres of land, to be located as follows, to wit:

Beginning on the west margin of the Tombigbee river, at the lower corner of Moses Moore's Spanish warrant, confirmed to Ann Lawrence, his legal representative; thence, down the margin of said river so far, as in a straight line, due east and west, shall make thirty-six chains and twenty links; thence, south, seventeen degrees east, so far, that a due west line therefrom shall strike the southeast corner of the lands confirmed to said Ann Lawrence upon the Spanish warrant of said Moses Moore; and thence with said Ann Lawrence's line north, seventeen degrees west, to the place of beginning : *Provided, nevertheless,* That the said claimant first obtain, before a court of competent jurisdiction, a judicial decision in his favor, against the adverse claim under a grant from the British Government of West Florida to William Fradgley, bearing date March 13th, 1776. And the Board doth order that a certificate be granted to him accordingly.

JAMES FRAZIER'S case: commenced in page 623.

On due consideration, the Board is of opinion that this claim is not supported agreeably to the requirements of law, and the claimant is not entitled to a patent for the land by him claimed, in manner and form aforesaid.

JAMES POWEL, executor of William Powel, deceased: case commenced in page 623.

On due consideration, the Board is of opinion that this claim is supported agreeably to the requirements of law, and that the lawful heirs of the said William Powel, deceased, are entitled to a patent for four hundred acres of land, to be located in the following manner, to wit :

Beginning on the west margin of the Tombigbee river, near the cotton gin of Major Hinson, being the lower corner of lands confirmed to the heirs of Thomas Bassett, deceased; thence, down the margin of said river to the upper corner of John Johnson's Spanish warrant; thence, with said Johnson's line, south, seventeen degrees east, forty-six chains; thence, west, so far, that a due north line therefrom to the line of said Bassett's land, and thence with said line to the place of beginning, shall include four hundred acres. And the Board doth order that a certificate be granted to them accordingly.
Adjourned until Saturday, the 26th instant.

SATURDAY, *May 26th*, 1804.
The Board met according to adjournment. Present : Ephraim Kirby, Robert C. Nicholas, Joseph Chambers.

NICHOLAS PERKINS, representative of Daniel Johnson: case commenced in page 631.

On due consideration, the Board is of opinion that this claim is supported agreeably to the requirements of law, and that the claimant is entitled to a patent for two hundred acres of land, to be located as follows, to wit:

Beginning on the margin of the Tombigbee river, at the lower corner of said Perkins's three hundred and six acre tract, claimed under Thomas Wheat's Spanish warrant; thence, with the line of said tract to the southeast corner thereof ; thence, south, seventy degrees east so far, that a line therefrom, north, twenty degrees east, to the margin of said river, and thence, up the same to the place of beginning, shall include two hundred acres.

NICHOLAS PERKINS, representative of Thomas Wheat: case commenced in page 630.

On due consideration, the Board is of opinion that this claim is supported agreeably to the requirements of law, and that the claimant is entitled to a patent for three hundred and six acres of land, to be located as follows, to wit:

Beginning on the west margin of the Tombigbee river, at a sassafras, at the mouth of Steep Gut, being the place called Ward's old corner, and is also a northeast corner of Jordan Morgan's pre-emption, and the southeast corner of James Denley's one thousand acre tract, claimed under Daniel Ward's Spanish warrant; thence, south, twenty degrees west, one hundred and fifteen chains ; thence, south, seventy degrees east, twenty-six chains ; thence, north, twenty degrees east, to the margin of Tombigbee river; and thence, up the margin of said river, to the place of beginning. And the Board doth order that a certificate be granted to him accordingly.

ANN LAWRENCE, representative of Moses Moore: case commenced page 628.

On due consideration, the Board is of opinion that this claim is supported agreeably to the requirements of law, and that the claimant is entitled to a patent for eight hundred acres of land, to be located as follows, to wit :

Beginning on the west margin of the Tombigbee river, at an oak corner, being the upper corner of lands formerly granted by the British Government of West Florida to John McIntosh; thence, down the margin of said river, so far as to make sixty-three chains and twenty-one links, in a straight line; thence, south, seventeen degrees east, so far that a due west line therefrom, sixty-three chains twenty-one links, and from thence, north seventeen degrees west, to the place of beginning, shall include eight hundred acres. *Provided, nevertheless,* That the said claimant first obtain, before a court of competent jurisdiction, a judicial decision in her favor against the adverse claim by virtue of a grant from the British Government of West Florida to John McIntosh, bearing date September 12th, 1775; also, against the claim by virtue of a British grant to William Fradgley, bearing date March 13th, 1776. And the Board doth order that a certificate be granted to her accordingly.

JOHN HINSON, administrator of Owen Sullivant: case commenced in page 620.

On due consideration, the Board is of opinion, that this claim is supported agreeably to the requirements of law, and that the lawful heirs of the said Owen Sullivant, deceased, are entitled to a patent for four hundred acres of land, to be located as follows, to wit:

Beginning on the west margin of the Tombigbee river, at the upper side of the mouth of Three River lake ; thence, up the margin of said river, to a sweet gum, at the mouth of Barker's cut off, or bayou, which unites the upper part of said lake to the river; thence, with said cut-off, or bayou, to a willow on the east margin of said lake; thence, down the margin of shid lake, sixty-six chains fifty links, to a hickory; thence, north, thirty-eight degrees east, thirty-seven chains, to a stake; thence, south, sixty-four degrees east, seventy-six chains, to a stake; thence, with the waters of a branch of said lake, to the place of beginning. And the Board doth order that a certificate be granted to them accordingly.
Adjourned until Monday, the 28th instant.

MONDAY, *May 28th*, 1804.
The Board met according to adjournment. Present : Ephraim Kirby, Robert C. Nicholas, Joseph Chambers.

JOHN CHASTANG'S case: commenced in page 614.

On due consideration, the Board is of opinion that this claim is supported agreeably to the requirements of law, and that the claimant is entitled to a patent for four hundred and eighty acres of land, to be located as follows, to wit :

Beginning at the southwest corner of John Chastang's four hundred and eighty acre tract, in the right of John Tally; thence, with the line of said tract, due north, to the west margin of Tombigbee river; thence, up the margin of said river to the mouth of a bayou or gut, a few chains below the former priest's house of the parish of fort St. Stephen's; thence, due south, twenty chains; thence, due west, so far that a line therefrom, due south, and thence, due east, to the place of beginning, shall include four hundred and eighty acres. And the Board doth order that a certificate be granted to him accordingly.

JOHN CHASTANG, representative of John Talley: case commenced in page 614.

On due consideration, the Board is of opinion, that this claim is supported agreeably to the requirements of law, and that the claimant is entitled to a patent for four hundred and eighty acres of land, to be located as follows, to wit:

Beginning at an elm on the west margin of the Tombigbee river, being Stewart's old corner, a few chains below the mouth of Smith's creek, and being also the upper corner of James Callier's five hundred and seventy-three acre tract, in the right of Bryant and Snelgrove; thence, up the margin of said river so far as to make thirty-seven chains and twenty links, in a due west line; thence, due south, so far that a line therefrom due east, thirty-seven chains and twenty links, to the line of said Callier's tract; and thence, with said line due north, to the place of beginning, shall include four hundred and eighty acres. And the Board doth order that a certificate be granted to him accordingly.

HEIRS OF JAMES McGREW, deceased: case commenced in page 627.

On due consideration, the Board is of opinion, that this claim is supported agreeably to the requirements of law, and that the lawful heirs of the said James McGrew, deceased, are entitled to a patent for four hundred acres of land, to be located as follows, viz.:

Beginning on the west margin of the Tombigbee river, at the upper corner of John Flood and Clark McGrew's three hundred and thirty-five acre tract, in the right of Julian De Castro; thence, with the line of said tract due south, to the southwest corner thereof; thence, due west, thirty-one chains fifty links; thence, due north, to the river, and down the same to the place of beginning. And the Board doth order that a certificate be granted to them accordingly.

JOHN BAKER's case: commenced in page 640.

On due consideration, the Board is of opinion, that this claim is not supported, and that the claimant is not entitled to a patent for the land by him claimed, in manner and form aforesaid.

JOHN TROUILLET, executor of Peter Trouillet, deceased: case commenced in page 640.

On due consideration, the Board is of opinion that this claim is not supported agreeably to the requirements of law, and that the claimants are not entitled to a patent for the land by them claimed, in manner and form aforesaid.

JOHN BAKER's case: commenced in page 641.

On due consideration, the Board is of opinion, that this claim is supported agreeably to the requirements of law, and that the claimant is entitled to a patent for four hundred acres of land, to be located as follows, to wit:

Beginning on the west margin of the Tombigbee river, at twenty-five chains below his present dwelling house; thence, due south, so far that a line therefrom due west, thirty-one chains sixty-three links; and thence, due north, to the river, and down the same to the place of beginning, shall include four hundred acres. Provided, nevertheless, That the said claimant first obtain, before a court of competent jurisdiction, a judicial decision in his favor, against the adverse claim, by virtue of a grant from the British Government of West Florida, to John Southerland, bearing date the 22d day of October, 1779; also against the adverse claim by virtue of a grant from said Government of West Florida to Charles Walker, bearing date the 27th day of January, 1777. And the Board doth order that a certificate be granted to him accordingly.

SIMON ANDRY's case: commenced in page 624.

On due consideration, the Board is of opinion, that this claim is supported agreeably to the requirements of law, and that the claimant is entitled to a patent for four hundred and eighty acres of land, to be located as follows, to wit:

Beginning at a stake at said Andry's Bluff; thence, north, sixty-two degrees west, forty-two chains ninety-eight links; thence, north, fifty-one degrees east, thirty-seven chains ninety-two links; thence, south, sixty-two degrees east, forty-two chains ninety-eight links, to the river bank; thence, down the margin of said river to the place of beginning; provided that said western lines shall not be so extended as to include more than four hundred and eighty acres. And the Board doth order that a certificate be granted to him accordingly.

JOHN BAPTIST TRENNIER's case: commenced in page 617.

On due consideration, the Board is of opinion, that this claim is supported agreeably to the requirements of law, and that the claimant is entitled to a patent for three hundred and twenty-seven acres of land, to be located as follows, to wit:

Beginning at the corner of land allowed to John Chastang, at the mouth of Grog Hall creek; and thence, pursuing down the margin of the Mobile river to the upper corner of land allowed to Simon Andry; thence, westwardly, pursuing the course of the lines of the said Simon Andry and John Chastang so far, as to include the number of acres above mentioned.

DANIEL JOHNSON's case: commenced in page 620.

On due consideration, the Board is of opinion that this claim is supported agreeably to the requirements of law, and that the claimant is entitled to a patent for eight hundred acres of land, to be located as follows, to wit:

Beginning on the west margin of the Tombigbee river, on the lower side of the mouth of a bayou or creek, called the Three Mouthed creek, or Three River lake; thence, down the margin of said river so far as to make sixty-three chains and twenty-five links, in a straight line; thence, north, eighty-seven degrees west, so far, that a line therefrom due north, sixty-three chains twenty-five links; and thence, south, eighty-seven degrees east, to the place of beginning; shall include eight hundred acres: Provided, nevertheless, That the said claimant first obtain, before a court of competent jurisdiction, a judicial decision in his favor, against the adverse claim by virtue of a grant from the British Government of West Florida to Alexander McCullagh, bearing date the 6th day of A. D. 1778. And the Board doth order that a certificate be granted to him accordingly.

Adjourned until Tuesday, the twenty-ninth instant.

TUESDAY, May 29, 1804.

The Board met according to adjournment. Present: Ephraim Kirby, Robert C. Nicholas, Joseph Chambers.

SAMUEL MIMS, representative of John Turnbull: case commenced in page 635.

On due consideration, the Board is of opinion that this claim is not supported agreeably to the requirements of law, and the claimant is not entitled to a patent for the land by him claimed, in manner and form aforesaid.

FRANCISCO FONTANILLA's case: commenced in page 634.

On due consideration, the Board is of opinion that this claim is not supported agreeably to the requirements of the law, and the claimant is not entitled to a patent for the land by him claimed, in manner and form aforesaid.

JAMES DENLEY, representative of Daniel Ward: case commenced in page 633.

On due consideration, the Board is of opinion, that this claim is supported agreeably to the requirements of law, and the claimant is entitled to a patent for one thousand acres of land, to be located as follows, to wit:

Beginning on the west margin of the Tombigbee river, at a sassafras, at the mouth of Steep Gut, so called, being the place called Ward's old corner, and is also a north-east corner of Jordan Morgan's pre-emption, and the northwest corner of Nicholas Perkins's three hundred and six acre tract, claimed under Thomas Wheat's Spanish warrant; thence, due west, one hundred and twenty-six chains forty-nine links; thence, due north, so far that a due east line therefrom to the margin of said river, and thence, down the margin of the same to the place of beginning, shall include one thousand acres. And the Board doth order, that a certificate be granted to him accordingly.

JOHN JOHNSON's case: commenced in page 621.

On due consideration, the Board is of opinion that this claim is supported agreeably to the requirements of law, and the claimant is entitled to a patent for four hundred acres of land, to be located as follows, to wit:

Beginning on the west margin of the Tombigbee river, at an oak, being the upper corner of Moses Moore's Spanish warrant, claimed by his representative, Ann Lawrence; thence, up the margin of said river thirty-one chains seventy-five links; thence, south, seventeen degrees east, so far that a line therefrom to the southwest corner of said Ann Lawrence's land, and from thence, with her line north, seventeen degrees west, to the place of beginning, shall include four hundred acres: Provided, nevertheless, That the said claimant first obtain, before a court of competent jurisdiction, a judicial decision in his favor against the adverse claim, by virtue of a grant from the British Government of West Florida, to William Fradgley, bearing date the 13th day of March, 1776. And the Board doth order that a certificate be granted to him accordingly.

FRANCIS BOYKIN, representative of Adam Hollinger: case commenced in page 627.

On due consideration, the Board is of opinion that this claim is supported agreeably to the requirements of law, and that the claimant is entitled to a patent for eight hundred acres of land, to be located as follows, to wit:

Beginning on the west margin of the Tombigbee river, near Bassett's old field, at the upper corner of a grant from the British Government of one thousand and fifty acres to Thomas Bassett, deceased; thence, in the course of said Bassett's line north, sixty-seven degrees west, so far that a line therefrom, due north, seventy chains, and thence, south, sixty-seven degrees east, to the margin of said river; and thence down the same to the place of beginning, shall include eight hundred acres. And the Board doth order that a certificate be granted to him accordingly.

JAMES DENLEY's case: commenced in page 629.

On due consideration, the Board is of opinion that this claim is supported agreeably to the requirements of law, and that the claimant is entitled to a patent for four hundred acres of land, to be located as follows, to wit:

Beginning on the margin of the Tombigbee river, at the lower corner of Nicholas Perkins's two hundred acre tract, claimed under Daniel Johnson's Spanish warrant; thence, with the line of said Perkins, south, twenty degrees west, to the said Perkins's southeast corner; thence, south, seventy degrees east, so far that a line therefrom, north, twenty degrees east, to the margin of said river, and thence up the same to the place of beginning, shall include four hundred acres. And the Board doth order that a certificate be granted to him accordingly.

JAMES DENLEY, representative of Solomon Johnson: case commenced in page 630.

On due consideration, the Board is of opinion that this claim is supported agreeably to the requirements of law, and the claimant is entitled to a patent for two hundred and eighty acres of land, to be located as follows, to wit:

Beginning at the southwest corner of James Denley's one thousand acre tract, claimed under Daniel Ward's Spanish warrant, and the northwest corner of Jordan Morgan's six hundred and forty acre pre-emption; thence, due south, with the line of said Morgan, fifty-five chains; thence, due west, fifty-two chains; and thence, due north, fifty-five chains; thence, due east, fifty-two chains, to the beginning. And the Board doth order that a certificate be granted to him accordingly.

CORNELIUS McCURTIN's case: commenced in page 613.

On due consideration, the Board is of opinion that this claim is not supported agreeably to the requirements of law, and the claimant is not entitled to a patent for the land by him claimed, in manner and form aforesaid.

JOHN CALLIER, representative of Wilford Hoggatt: case commenced in page 629.

On due consideration, the Board is of opinion that this claim is supported agreeably to the requirements of law, and that the claimant is entitled to a patent for eight hundred acres of land, to be located as follows, to wit:

Beginning at the northwest corner of Thomas Malone's six hundred and forty acre pre-emption right; thence, north, fifty degrees east, to the west margin of the Tombigbee river; thence, up the margin of the same so far, as to make sixty-three chains twenty-five links in a straight line; thence, south, fifty degrees west, so far that a line therefrom, south, forty degrees east, sixty-three chains twenty-five links, and thence, north, fifty degrees east, to the place of beginning, shall include eight hundred acres: Provided, nevertheless, That said claimant first obtain, before a court of competent jurisdiction, a judicial decision in his favor against the adverse claim, by virtue of a grant from the British Government of West Florida to William Wall, bearing date the 20th day of March, 1778. And the Board doth order that a certificate be granted to him accordingly.

Adjourned until Wednesday, the 30th instant.

WEDNESDAY, May 30, 1804.

The Board met according to adjournment. Present: Ephraim Kirby, Robert C. Nicholas, Joseph Chambers.

JOHN McGREW, senior's case: commenced in page 663.

On due consideration, the Board is of opinion that the present claim is supported agreeably to the requirements of law, and the claimant is entitled to a patent for six hundred and twenty-seven acres of land, to be located as follows, to wit:

Beginning at the southwest corner of Edward Lloyd Wailes's six hundred and forty acre pre-emption tract, in the right of John Baker; thence, with the line of said tract, due north, eighty chains, to the line of Edwin Lewis's one hundred and sixty acre pre-emption tract; thence, with said line, to the southwest corner thereof; thence, due north, with said Lewis's line, and the line of Peter Malone, twenty-eight chains in all; thence, west, thirty-four chains; thence, south, one hundred and eight chains; thence, east, direct to the place of beginning: Provided, nevertheless, That the said claimant first obtain, before a court of competent jurisdiction, a judicial decision in his favor against the adverse claim, by virtue of a grant from the British Government of West Florida to John Sutherland, bearing date the 22d day of October, 1779. And the Board doth order that a certificate be granted to him accordingly.

JOHN FLOOD McGREW's case: commenced in page 671.

On due consideration, the Board is of opinion that the present claim is not supported, but that the claimant may be entitled, under the 3d section of the act, to a right of pre-emption to five hundred and six acres of land, to be located as follows, to wit:

Beginning at a hickory, being the same place mentioned in his plot returned to the Register's Office, as his beginning corner; thence, south, sixty-four degrees west, ninety chains; thence, due north, seventy-eight chains; thence, north, sixty-four degrees east, fifty-four chains; thence, to the beginning. And the Board doth order, that a certificate be granted to him accordingly, if requested.

JOHN McGREW, Junior's, case, as representative of Alexander McGrew: commenced in page 668.

On due consideration, the Board is of opinion that the present claim is not supported agreeably to the requirements of law, and the claimant is not entitled to a patent for the land by him claimed, in manner and form aforesaid.

CONSTANT McGREW's case: commenced in page 671.

On due consideration, the Board is of opinion that the present claim is not supported agreeably to the requirements of law, and the claimant is not entitled to a patent for the land by her claimed, in manner and form aforesaid.

DANIEL YOUNG's case: commenced in page 689.

On due consideration, the Board is of opinion that the present claim is not supported agreeably to the requirements of law, and the claimant is not entitled to a patent for the land by him claimed, in manner and form aforesaid.

EDWARD YOUNG's case: commenced in page 689.

On due consideration, the Board is of opinion that the present claim is not supported agreeably to the requirements of law, and the claimant is not entitled to a patent for the land by him claimed, in manner and form aforesaid.

JOHN HINES, representative of Frederick Smith: case commenced in page 671.

On due consideration, the Board is of opinion that the present claim is not supported agreeably to the requirements of law, and the claimant is not entitled to a patent for the land by him claimed in manner and form aforesaid.

CLARK McGREW's case: commenced in page 698.

On due consideration, the Board is of opinion that the present claim is supported according to the requirements of law, and that the claimant is entitled to a patent for six hundred and forty acres of land, to be located as follows, to wit:

Beginning at a black gum, near Tawler creek, being the same place mentioned in his plot returned to the Register's Office as his beginning corner; thence, north, thirteen degrees west, seventy chains; thence, north, nine degrees east, thirty-two chains; thence, north, fifty-five degrees east, ninety-four chains; thence, south, forty-six degrees east, to Tawler creek; thence, with the meanders of the said creek, so far that a line therefrom to the place of beginning, shall include six hundred and forty acres. And the Board doth order that a certificate be granted to him accordingly.

WILLIAM McGREW's case: commenced in page 700.
On due consideration, the Board is of opinion that the present claim is not supported, but that the claimant may be entitled, under the third section of the act, to a right of pre-emption to six hundred and thirty-eight acres of land, to be located as follows, to wit:
Beginning at a corner pine, on the south side of a branch of Tawler creek; thence, north, sixty degrees east, seventy chains fifty links; thence, north, thirty degrees west, ninety chains fifty links; thence, south, sixty degrees west, seventy chains fifty links; and thence, south, thirty degrees east, to the place of beginning. And the Board doth order that a certificate be granted to him accordingly.

HEIRS OF WILLIAM BREWER, deceased: case commenced in page 600.
On due consideration, the Board is of opinion that the present claim is not supported agreeably to the requirements of law; and the claimants are not entitled to a patent for the land by them claimed, in manner and form aforesaid.

THOMAS BATES's case: commenced page 687.
On due consideration, the Board is of opinion that the present claim is supported agreeably to the requirements of law, and that the claimant is entitled to a patent for six hundred and twenty-eight acres of land, to be located as follows, to wit:
Beginning on the west margin of the Tombigbee river, at the northeast corner of Seth Dean's pre-emption; and thence, with the said Dean's line south, eighty-six degrees west, seventy chains; thence, due north, so far that a line due east therefrom to the west margin of the Tombigbee river, and thence, down the margin of the said river to the place of beginning, shall include six hundred and twenty-eight acres. And the Board doth order that a certificate be granted to him accordingly.

HARDY WOOTTON, representative of William Hunt: case commenced in page 646.
On due consideration, the Board is of opinion that the present claim is supported agreeably to requirements of law; and that the claimant is entitled to a patent for six hundred and fifteen acres of land, to be located as follows, to wit:
Beginning at the northwest corner of Richard Lee's six hundred and forty acre donation, in the right of Jordan Morgan; and thence, with said Lee's line due south, to the northeast corner of William H. Hargrave's three hundred and twenty acre tract; and thence, with the line of said Hargrave and Wyche Watley's line, due west, to the northwest corner of said Watley's one hundred and forty-two acre tract; thence, due north, so far that a line therefrom due east, and thence, due south to the place of beginning, shall contain six hundred and fifteen acres. And the Board doth order that a certificate be granted to him accordingly.

HEIRS OF JAMES COPELEN: case commenced in page 657.
On due consideration, the Board is of opinion that the present claim is supported agreeably to the requirements of law, and that the claimants are entitled to a patent for six hundred and forty acres of land, to be located as follows, to wit:
Beginning on the west margin of the Three River lake, half way between the present dwelling house of Mrs. Copelen and Wiley Barker, on a due east line; thence, down the margin of said lake, to the upper or northeast corner of Figures Lewis's three hundred and twenty acre pre-emption; and thence, with said Lewis's line, due west, so far that a line therefrom due north, and thence, due east, to the place of beginning, shall include six hundred and forty acres. And the Board doth order that a certificate be granted to them accordingly.

JAMES GRIFFIN's case: commenced in page 596.
On due consideration, the Board is of opinion that the present claim is supported agreeably to the requirements of law, and that the claimant is entitled to a patent for six hundred and eighteen acres of land, to be located as follows, to wit:

Beginning at the southwest corner of James Callier's donation, in the right of Jesse Bryant: thence, in the line of the said tract, due north, to the southeast corner of John Chastang's four hundred and eighty acre tract, in the right of John Talley; thence, due west, with Chastang's lines, to the southwest corner of his four hundred and eighty acre tract in his own right; thence, with the line of the said Chastang, due north, thirty-four chains; thence, due west, thirty-three chains; thence, south, eighty chains; thence, east, to the place of beginning. And the Board doth order that a certificate be granted to him accordingly.

NOAH K. HUTSON, representative of Henry Nail: case commenced in page 653.
On due consideration, the Board is of opinion that this claim is supported agreeably to the requirements of law, and that the claimant is entitled to a patent for two hundred and ninety-seven acres of land, to be located as follows, to wit:
Beginning on the west margin of the Tombigbee river, at the upper corner of James Callier's seven hundred and thirty-two acre tract, in the right of Wilford Hoggatt's Spanish warrant; thence, up the margin of said river, so far that a due south line therefrom to said Callier's line, and thence, with said Callier's line, north, thirty-three degrees east, to the place of beginning, shall include two hundred and ninety-seven acres. And the Board ordered that a certificate be granted to him accordingly.

EDWIN LEWIS, representative of Henry Nail: case commenced in page 669.
On due consideration, the Board is of opinion that this claim is not supported agreeably to the requirements of law, and the claimant is not entitled to a patent for the land by him claimed in manner and form aforesaid.

JAMES POWEL's case: commenced in page 643.
It appears to the Board that the land now claimed by the claimant is covered by a grant from the British Government of West Florida to Thomas Bassett, late of this territory, deceased. Therefore, on due consideration, the Board is of opinion that this claim is not supported, and the claimant is not entitled to a patent for the land by him claimed, in manner and form aforesaid.

JOSEPH BATES, Junior's, case: commenced in page 646.
On due consideration, the Board is of opinion that this claim is not supported agreeably to the requirements of law, and the claimant is not entitled to a patent for the land by him claimed in manner and form aforesaid.
Adjourned until Thursday the 31st instant.

THURSDAY, May 31, 1804.
The Board met according to adjournment. Present: Ephraim Kirby, Robert C. Nicholas, Joseph Chambers.

DANIEL JOHNSON, representative of William Burk: case commenced in page 655.
On due consideration, the Board is of opinion that this claim is supported agreeably to the requirements of law, and that the claimant is entitled to a patent for three hundred and twenty acres of land, to be located as follows, to wit:
Beginning on the west bank of the Tombigbee, at the mouth of the Three River lake, being the upper or northeast corner of his Spanish warrant for eight hundred acres; thence, in the line of said Spanish warrant, north, eighty-seven degrees west, so far that a line therefrom, due north, twenty-five chains, and thence, due east, to the margin of said lake, and thence, with the margin of the said lake to the place of beginning, shall include three hundred and twenty acres. And the Board doth order that a certificate be granted to him accordingly.

HIRAM MOUNGER's case: commenced in page 599.
On due consideration, the Board is of opinion that this claim is supported agreeably to the requirements of law, and that the claimant is entitled to a patent for six hundred and forty acres of land, to be located as follows, to wit:
Beginning on the north line of John Brewer's six hundred and forty acre donation, at the southeast corner of the heirs of Charles Brewer's pre-emption; thence, with the line of said heirs, due north, thirty-three chains seventy-five links, to their northeast corner; thence, still with the line of said heirs, due west, sixty chains, to their northwest corner; thence, due north, so far that a line therefrom, due east, shall strike the southwest cor-

ner of James Denley's two hundred and eighty acre tract, claimed under a Spanish warrant to Solomon Johnson; and thence, still due east with said Denley's line, so far that a line therefrom, due south, to John Brewer's six hundred and forty acre donation, and with the line thereof, due west, to the place of beginning, shall include six hundred and forty acres. And the Board doth order that a certificate be granted to him accordingly.

THOMAS CARSON, representative of John J. Abner: case commenced in page 606.

On due consideration, the Board is of opinion that this claim is supported agreeably to the requirements of law, and that the claimant is entitled to a patent for six hundred and forty acres of land, to be located as follows, to wit:

Beginning at a stake at the lower side of the mouth of Poll bayou; thence, south, eighty-six degrees west, ninety-one chains; thence, south, eleven degrees east, seventy chains; thence, north, eighty-six degrees east, to the margin of the river Tombigbee; and thence, up the margin of said river, to the place of beginning. And the Board doth order that a certificate be granted to him accordingly.

JAMES CALLIER, representative of Bryant and Snelgrove: case commenced in page 598.

On due consideration, the Board is of opinion that this claim is supported according to the requirements of law, and that the claimant is entitled to a patent for five hundred and seventy-three acres of land, to be located as follows, to wit:

Beginning at an elm, on the west margin of the Tombigbee river, being Stewart's old corner, a few chains below the mouth of Smith's creek; thence due south, one hundred and five chains; thence, due east, so far that a due north line therefrom to the river, and up the same to the place of beginning, shall include five hundred and seventy-three acres. And the Board doth order that a certificate be granted to him accordingly.

DANIEL JOHNSTON, representative of Daniel Spillard: case commenced in page 690.

On due consideration, the Board is of opinion, that this claim is not supported agreeably to the requirements of law, and the claimant is not entitled to a patent for the land by him claimed, in manner and form aforesaid.

HOWELL DUPREE, representative of William Hillis: case commenced in page 608.

On due consideration, the Board is of opinion that this claim is supported agreeably to the requirements of law, and that the claimant is entitled to a patent for six hundred and thirteen acres of land, to be located as follows, to wit:

Beginning at the northwest corner of Edward Gatland's pre-emption, and thence, with said Gatland's line, south, seventy-seven degrees east, to said Gatland's northeast corner, on the margin of Mobile river; thence, up the margin of said river, twenty chains; thence, north, sixty-five degrees west, so far that a line therefrom to the place of beginning will include six hundred and thirteen acres; bounded eastwardly by the Mobile river, and southwardly by Edward Gatland's pre-emption. And the Board doth order, that a certificate be granted to him accordingly.

JOSEPH HOUSE's case: commenced in page 619.

On due consideration, the Board is of opinion that this claim is not supported agreeably to the requirements of law, and the claimant is not entitled to a patent for the land by him claimed, in manner and form as aforesaid.

STERLING DUPREE, representative of Emanuel Cheney: case commenced in page 596.

On due consideration, the Board is of opinion that the present claim is not supported, but that the claimant may be entitled, under the third section of the act, to the right of pre-emption to three hundred and twenty acres of land, to be located as follows, to wit:

Beginning at the northwest corner of Col. Benjamin Few's pre-emption, thence with the said Few's line; north, fifty-six degrees east, to said Few's beginning corner, on the margin of Tombigbee river; thence up the margin of said river, thirty chains; thence due west, so far that a line therefrom to the place of beginning shall contain three hundred and twenty acres, bounded southwardly by Col. Benjamin Few's pre-emption, eastward-

ly on the Tombigbee river, and northwardly on Major Natt Christmas's pre-emption. And the Board doth order that a certificate be granted to him accordingly, if required.

ANN LAWRENCE's case: commenced in page 656.

On due consideration, the Board is of opinion that the present claim is supported agreeably to the requirements of law, and the claimant is entitled to a patent for five hundred and twenty acres of land, to be located as follows, to wit:

Beginning on the northwest corner of James Callier's seven hundred and thirty-two acre tract, in the right of Wilford Hoggatt's Spanish warrant; thence, in the course of said Callier's line north, thirty-three degrees east, to the southwest corner of Noah Kenner Hutson's two hundred and ninety-seven acre donation; thence, with said Hutson's line, due north, to the west margin of the Tombigbee river; thence, up the same so far as to make sixty chains, upon a due west line; thence, due south, seventy chains; thence, due east, so far, that a line therefrom, due south, will strike the place of beginning. And the Board doth order that a certificate be granted to her accordingly.

GEORGE BREWER, Jun., representative of James Watkins: case commenced in page 605.

On due consideration, the Board is of opinion that this claim is supported agreeably to the requirements of law, and the claimant is entitled to a patent for four hundred and ten acres of land, to be located as follows, to wit:

Beginning at George Brewer, Jun's. six hundred and twenty-nine acre donation, on his own right, at the southwest corner thereof; thence, with the line of the said tract, due east, fifty chains to the corner thereof; thence, due north, to the corner of Mrs. Lawrence's five hundred and twenty acre tract; thence, with the line of said tract, due east, to a corner thereof; thence, still with the line of said tract, due south, to the corner thereof; which is also the southwest corner of James Callier's tract, in the right of Hoggatt; thence, due west, so far, that a line therefrom, due north, will strike the place of beginning. And the Board doth order that a certificate be granted to him accordingly.

JOHN BREWER's case: commenced in page 604.

On due consideration, the Board is of opinion that this claim is supported agreeably to the requirements of law, and the claimant is entitled to a patent for six hundred and forty acres of land, to be located as follows, to wit:

Beginning at the northeast corner of Sanders Rhea's pre-emption right of one hundred and sixty acres; thence, with said Rhea's line, due west, eighty chains; thence, due north, eighty chains; thence, due east, eighty chains; thence, due south, to the place of beginning. And the Board doth order that a certificate be granted to him accordingly.

WILEY BARKER, representative of Daniel Barker: case commenced in page 603.

On due consideration, the Board is of opinion that this claim is supported agreeably to the requirements of law, and the claimant is entitled to a patent for six hundred and forty acres of land, to be located as follows, to wit:

Beginning, half way between the present dwelling house of said Barker and the present dwelling house of Mrs. Copelen, on the west margin of the Three River lake, on a due east line, and thence, with the line of the heirs of James Copelen, due west, to the northwest corner of said Copelen's land; thence, due north, fifty-two chains; thence, due east, to the margin of the Three River lake, or in case the lake doth not so far extend, then to a point parrallel therewith; thence, to and with the margin of said lake to the place of beginning, and to include six hundred and forty acres within these lines, or less, as the case may be. And the Board doth order that a certificate be granted to him accordingly.

JAMES FARR's case: commenced in page 688.

On due consideration, the Board is of opinion that this claim is not supported agreeably to the requirements of law, and the claimant is not entitled to a patent for the land by him claimed, in manner and form as aforesaid.

PETER MALONE, representative of John Woods: case commenced in page 639.

On due consideration, the Board is of opinion that this claim is not supported, but that the claimant may be entitled, under the third section of the act, to a right of pre-emption to one hundred and sixty acres of land, to be located as follows, to wit:

Beginning at the northwest corner of Edwin Lewis's one hundred and sixty acre pre-emption tract; thence, with the line of the said tract, due east, one hundred and fifteen chains, to John Chastang's line; thence, due north, fourteen chains; thence, due west, one hundred and fifteen chains; thence, due south, fourteen chains, to the place of beginning: *Provided, nevertheless,* That the said claimant first obtain before a court of competent jurisdiction, a judicial decision in his favor, against the adverse claim by virtue of a grant from the British Government of West Florida, to John Sutherland, bearing date the 22d day of October, 1779. And the Board doth order that a certificate be granted to him accordingly, if requested.

Adjourned until Friday, the 1st of June next.

FRIDAY, *June* 1, 1804.
The Board met according to adjournment. Present: Ephraim Kirby, Robert C. Nicholas, Joseph Chambers.

RICHARD LEE, representative of Jordan Morgan : case commenced in page 602.

On due consideration, the Board is of opinion that this claim is supported agreeably to the requirements of law, and the claimant is entitled to a patent for six hundred and forty acres of land, to be located as follows, to wit:

Beginning at the southwest corner of James Denley's one thousand acre tract, claimed under Daniel Ward's Spanish warrant, which is also the northwest corner of Jordan Morgan's six hundred and forty acre pre-emption, and the northeast corner of James Denley's two hundred and eighty acre tract; and thence, with the line of the said last mentioned tract, due west, to the northwest corner thereof, and in the same course sixty chains; thence, due north, one hundred and six chains seventy-five links; thence, due east, sixty chains; thence, due south, to the northwest corner of James Denley's one thousand acre tract, and in the same course with the line of said tract, to the place of beginning. And the Board doth order that a certificate be granted to him accordingly.

ANNA MOUNGER's case : commenced in page 606.

On due consideration, the Board is of opinion that this claim is supported agreeably to the requirements of law, and the claimant is entitled to a patent for five hundred and four acres of land, to be located as follows, to wit:

Beginning on the west margin of the Tombigbee river, at the upper corner of John Callier's eight hundred acre tract, in the right of Wilford Hoggatt; thence, with the said Callier's line, south, fifty degrees west, to his northwest corner; thence, due west, so far that a line there from north, fifty degrees east, to the margin of the river; and thence, down the same to the place of beginning, shall include five hundred and four acres. And the Board doth order that a certificate be granted to her accordingly.

HEIRS OF CHARLES BREWER, deceased: case commenced in page 607.

On due consideration, the Board is of opinion that this claim is not supported agreeably to the requirements of law, but that upon the evidence exhibited, the claimants are entitled, under the third section of the act, to a right of pre-emption to two hundred acres of land, to be located as follows, to wit:

Beginning on the north line of John Brewer's six hundred and forty acre donation, thirty chains, east, of the northwest corner thereof; thence, along said line, due west, to said corner, and in same course sixty chains; thence, due north, thirty-three chains and seventy-five links; thence, due east, sixty chains; thence, due south, thirty-three chains seventy-five links, to the place of beginning. And the Board doth order that a certificate be granted to them accordingly.

JULIAN DE CASTRO's case: commenced in page 701.

On due consideration, the Board is of opinion that this claim is not supported agreeably to the requirements of law, and the claimant is not entitled to a patent for the land by him claimed, in manner and form aforesaid.

ISAAC RYAN's case: commenced in page 594.

On due consideration, the Board is of opinion that this claim is supported agreeably to the requirements of law, and the claimant is entitled to a patent for six hundred and forty acres of land, to be located as follows, to wit:

Beginning at the northwest corner of Benjamin Harrison's six hundred and forty acre tract, claimed in the right of Jacob Miller; thence, with said Harrison's line,

due east, one hundred and sixty chains, to his northeast corner; thence, due north, forty chains; thence, due west, one hundred and sixty chains; thence, due south, to the place of beginning. And the Board doth order that a certificate be granted to him accordingly.

EDNA BILBO, administratrix of Matthew Bilbo, deceased: case commenced in page 655.

On due consideration, the Board is of opinion that this claim is supported agreeably to the requirements of law, and the claimants are entitled to a patent for four hundred and one acres of land, to be located as follows, to wit:

Bounded on all sides by the waters of the Tombigbee river, being an island in said river, about two miles above the bayou called the Cut-off. And the Board doth order that a certificate be granted to her accordingly.

JAMES SCOTT, representative of Gabriel Burrows: case commenced in page 608.

On due consideration, the Board is of opinion, that this claim is supported agreeably to the requirements of law, and the claimant is entitled to a patent for three hundred and twenty acres of land, to be located as follows, to wit:

Beginning on the northeast corner of Hezekiah Carter's three hundred and twenty acre tract, and thence, with the line of said Carter, due west, eighty chains; thence, due north, forty chains; thence, due east, eighty chains; thence, due south, to the place of beginning. And the Board doth order that a certificate be granted to him accordingly.

BENJAMIN HARRISON, representative of Jacob Miller: case commenced in page 649.

On due consideration, the Board is of opinion that this claim is supported agreeably to the requirements of law, and the claimant is entitled to a patent for six hundred and forty acres of land, to be located as follows, to wit:

Beginning at the northwest corner of Thomas Goodwin's three hundred and twenty acre tract, claimed in the right of Hiram Mounger; thence, due east, in the line of said Goodwin to his northeast corner, and continuing in the same course one hundred and sixty chains in all; thence, due north, forty chains; thence, due west, one hundred and sixty chains; thence, due south, to the place of beginning. And the Board doth order that a certificate be granted to him accordingly.

NATHAN BLACKWELL's case: commenced in page 595.

On due consideration, the Board is of opinion that this claim is supported agreeably to the requirements of law, and that the claimant is entitled to a patent for six hundred and forty acres of land, to be located as follows, to wit:

Beginning on the margin of Tombigbee river, on the west side thereof, at the upper corner of Francis Boykin's Spanish warrant in the right of Adam Hollinger, for eight hundred acres; thence, in the course of said Boykin's line north, sixty-seven degrees west, one hundred and sixty-five chains; thence, due north, sixteen chains; thence, due east, to the margin of said river; and with the same to the place of beginning. And the Board doth order that a certificate be granted to him accordingly.

RICHARD BARROW's case: commenced in page 639.

On due consideration, the Board is of opinion that this claim is supported agreeably to the requirements of law, and the claimant is entitled to a patent for six hundred and forty acres of land, to be located as follows, to wit:

Beginning at a willow, standing near to two hickories, on the west bank of Mobile river, being the northeast corner of John Hawkins's pre-emption; thence, pursuing up the margin of said river so far as to make forty chains, in a straight line; thence, north, seventy-seven degrees west, so far that a line from thence, south, ten degrees west, to Barrow's creek, and a line from the place of beginning north, seventy-seven degrees west, till it strikes Barrow's creek; and thence, with the meanders of said creek, shall include six hundred and forty acres, exclusive of a small island in the Mobile river called Tony's island. And the Board doth order that a certificate be granted to him accordingly.

EPHRAIM BARKER's case: commenced in page 599.

On due consideration, the Board is of opinion, that this claim is supported, and the claimant is entitled to a patent for six hundred and forty acres of land, to be located as follows, to wit:

Beginning on the west margin of the Tombigbee river, on the upper side of Barker's cut-off, or the bayou which leads from the upper end of Three River lake into the river; thence, with the upper margin of said bayou, to the eastern margin of said lake; thence, along margin of said lake, and to the northeast corner of Wiley Barker's donation; thence, with the line of said Wiley, due west, to the southeast corner of Sanders Rhea's pre-emption, thence, with said Rhea's line due north, to his northeast corner; thence, due east, so far that a line due south, therefrom, to the margin of the Tombigbee river, and down the same to the place of beginning, shall include six hundred and forty acres. And the Board doth order that a certificate be granted to him accordingly.

HEIRS OF GODFREY HELVERSTON: case commenced in page 639.

On due consideration, the Board is of opinion that this claim is supported agreeably to the requirements of law, and the claimants are entitled to a patent for six hundred and forty acres of land, to be located as follows, to wit:

Beginning on the west bank of the Mobile river, at the northeast corner of Richard Barrow's donation claim; thence, north, seventy-seven degrees west, with the line of said Barrow to his northwest corner; thence, north, ten degrees east, so far that a line south, seventy-seven degrees east, to the west shore of the Mobile river, shall include six hundred and forty acres; bounded east, on the west margin of Mobile river; and south, upon the land of Richard Barrow. And the Board doth order that a certificate be granted to them accordingly.

Adjourned until Saturday, the 2d day of June.

SATURDAY, June 2, 1804.

The Board met according to adjournment. Present: Ephraim Kirby, Robert C. Nicholas, Joseph Chambers.

EDWARD CREIGHTON, representative of Isram Beard: case commenced in page 700.

On due consideration, the Board is of opinion that this claim is not supported agreeably to the requirements of law; and the claimant is not entitled to a patent for the land by him claimed, in manner and form aforesaid.

SETH DEAN, representative of John Jacob Abner; case commenced in page 693.

On due consideration, the Board is of opinion that this claim is not supported agreeably to the requirements of law, and the claimant is not entitled to a patent for the land by him claimed, in manner and form aforesaid.

FRANCIS STRINGER's case: commenced in page 619.

On due consideration, the Board is of opinion that this claim is not supported agreeably to the requirements of law, but that the claimant may be entitled, under the third section of the act, to a right of pre-emption to six hundred acres of land, to be located as follows, to wit:

Beginning on the west margin of the Tombigbee river, at the upper corner of John Dunn's six hundred and forty acre pre-emption; thence, with said Dunn's line, due west, to his northwest corner; thence, due north, forty-three chains eighty links; thence, due east, to the said river; and thence, down the margin of the same to the place of beginning. And the Board doth order that a certificate be granted to him accordingly, if requested.

GEORGE ROBBINS, representative of Zadock Brashear: case commenced in page 616.

Thomas Eldridge was presented as a witness, and, being duly sworn, deposed, that, in the year 1797, an Indian inhabited and cultivated the land in question, for the use and account of Zadock Brashear; that said Brashear sent him clothing by him, the deponent, which he delivered him for his services in taking care of the houses and plantation of Brashear; that, in the year 1799, said Brashear sent me a letter requesting I would inform the Indian that he might quit the land, as he had sold his right to a man by the name of Robbins; that this Indian lived with Brashear while he resided on said place, and continued to live thereon, from the time Brashear removed therefrom, for account of said Brashear, until the year 1799; that, some time after, he informed the Indian that Brashear had sold it; that said

Brashear was, in the year 1799, the head of a family, and more than twenty-one years of age.

On due consideration, the Board is of opinion that this claim is not supported agreeably to the requirements of law, but that the claimant may be entitled, under the third section of the act, to a right of pre-emption to six hundred and forty acres of land, to be located as follows, to wit:

Beginning at the northwest corner of Matthew Shaw's three hundred and twenty acre tract; thence, with the line of said tract, due east, to the west margin of Tombigbee river; thence, up the same so far as to make ninety-five chains on a due north line; thence, due west, so far that a line therefrom, due south, shall strike the place of beginning. And the Board doth order that a certificate be granted to him accordingly, if requested.

GEORGE BREWER, Junior's case: commenced in page 661.

On due consideration, the Board is of opinion that this claim is supported agreeably to the requirements of law, and that the claimant is entitled to a patent for six hundred and twenty-nine acres of land, to be located as follows, to wit:

Beginning on the west margin of the Tombigbee river, at the upper end of Ann Lawrence's five hundred and twenty acre tract; thence, up the margin of said river so far as to make fifty chains on a due west line; thence, due south, so far that a line therefrom, due east, fifty chains, and thence, due north, to the place of beginning, shall include six hundred and twenty-nine acres. And the Board doth order that a certificate be granted to him accordingly.

SAMPSON MOUNGER's case: commenced in page 600.

On due consideration, the Board is of opinion that this claim is supported agreeably to the requirements of law, and that the claimant is entitled to a patent for six hundred and thirty-four acres of land, to be located as follows, to wit:

Beginning at the southwest corner of George Brewer, Jun.'s four hundred and ten acre tract, in the right of James Watkins, thence with the line of said tract, due east, eighty five chains, to his southeast corner; which is also the southwest corner of James Callier's seven hundred and thirty-two acre tract; thence, due south, seventy-six chains; thence, west, eighty-five chains; thence, due north, to the place of beginning. And the Board doth order that a certificate be granted to him accordingly.

BRIDGET BURKE, administratrix of William Burke, deceased: case commenced in page 656.

On due consideration, the Board is of opinion that this claim is supported, and that the heirs of the said William Burke, deceased, are entitled to a patent for six hundred and forty acres of land, provided the same shall be contained within the following lines, viz.:

Beginning at the northeast corner of James Lowe's pre-emption, claimed by his representative Seth Dean; thence, with said Lowe's line, due east, to the northwest corner of John Wallace's pre-emption, claimed by his representative Seth Dean; and thence, with the said Wallace's line, due east to the west margin of the Tombigbee river, near the mouth of Bilbo's creek; thence, up the margin of said river, to the mouth or outlet of Rain's lake; thence, along the lower margin of said lake, to the lower line of Cornelius Rain's land; thence, with the said Rain's line, south, seventeen degrees east, to his southeast corner; thence, with his line, due west, to the southeast corner of Ann Lawrence's land; thence, with said Lawrence's line to her south-west corner; and thence, to the place of beginning. And the Board doth order that a certificate be granted to them accordingly.

RICHARD HAWKINS's case: commenced in page 692.

On due consideration, the Board is of opinion, that this claim is supported, and that the claimant is entitled to a patent for six hundred and forty acres of land, to be located as follows, to wit:

Beginning on the margin of Barrow's lake, opposite to a large pine tree on the bluff, being the north east corner of Simpson Whaley's land; thence, pursuing up the margin of said lake, northwardly, to the mouth of Barrow's creek, thence, up said creek, westwardly, so far that a line due south therefrom, to intersect a line from the place of beginning, due west, in the course of said Whaley's line, shall include six hundred and forty acres. And the Board doth order that a certificate be granted to him accordingly.

THOMAS GOODWIN, representative of Hiram Mounger: case commenced in page 650.

Jordan Morgan and Solomon Wheat were presented as witnesses, and, being duly sworn and interrogated by the Board, they deposed, that they were not interested in this claim; that they knew that John Wheat inhabited and cultivated on the land in question, before and on the 3d day of March, 1803; that the said John Wheat or Thomas Goodwin had inhabited and cultivated on the same land ever since; and that John Wheat was, on the 3d day of March, 1803, more than twenty-one years of age.

On due consideration, the Board is of opinion that this claim is not supported, but that the claimant may be entitled, under the third section of the act, to a right of pre-emption to three hundred and twenty acres of land, to be located as follows, to wit:

Beginning on the northeast corner of Solomon Wheat's two hundred acre tract; thence, with said Wheat's line, due west, fifty chains, to his northwest corner; thence, with said Wheat's line, due south, forty chains, to his southwest corner, on the line of James Scott's three hundred and twenty acre tract; thence with said Scott's line, due west, to his northwest corner, and continuing the same course, in all forty-five chains; thence, due north, fifty-five chains; thence, due east, ninety-five chains; thence, due south, to the place of beginning. And the Board doth order that a certificate be granted to him accordingly, if requested.

JAMES CALLIER, legal representative of Joseph Anderson: case commenced in page 607.

Adam Hollinger and Jesse Thomas were produced as witnesses, and, being duly sworn, the said Hollinger deposed, that he understood and did believe, that William Walton inhabited and cultivated the land whereon Joseph Anderson formerly lived on the 3d day of March, 1803; and also understood and believed, that this cultivation was made by said Walton under a purchase from said Anderson.

The said Thomas deposed, that William Walton inhabited on the land in question, on the 3d of March, 1803; and made a crop thereon the ensuing season; that, in the month of January, 1803, as well as he, Thomas, recollected, the said Anderson removed with his family to Mobile, and resided, as the witness understood, at or near Mobile, until the month of December, 1803, when he returned with his family to this country; and after a few weeks he removed with his family to the Mississippi country; that he sold his improvement, with all its advantages, to Seth Dean, and that James Callier became bound to him, Thomas, for the payment of the consideration which Dean was to make to him for his said improvements; and, from this circumstance, I considered my improvements vested in Callier.

Adjourned until Monday, the 4th instant.

MONDAY, June 4, 1804.

The Board met according to adjournment. Present: Ephraim Kirby, Robert C. Nicholas, Joseph Chambers.

EDWARD CREIGHTON, representative of Benjamin King: case commenced in page 638.

On due consideration, the Board is of opinion that the present claimant is entitled to a right of pre-emption to one hundred acres of land, to be located as follows, to wit:

Beginning on the west margin of the Tombigbee river, at the upper corner of Natt Christmas's pre-emption; thence, up the margin of the river ten chains; thence, north, fifty degrees east, so far, that a straight line to the northwest corner of said Christmas's pre-emption, and thence, with said Christmas's line, to the place of beginning, shall include one hundred acres, bounded southwardly on said Christmas, and eastwardly on the river Tombigbee: and the Board doth order that a certificate be granted to him accordingly.

JAMES BILBO's case: commenced in page 688.

On due consideration, the Board is of opinion that this claim is not supported, and the same is accordingly disallowed.

SANDERS REA's case: commenced in page 659.

On due consideration, the Board is of opinion that the present claimant is entitled to a right of pre-emption to one hundred and sixty acres of land, to be located as follows, to wit:

Beginning at the northwest corner of Wiley Barker's six hundred and forty acre donation; thence, due north, thirty-one chains and seventy-five links; thence, due east, fifty-five chains; thence, due south, to said Barker's line; thence, with the said line, due west, to the place of beginning, including one hundred and sixty acres. And the Board doth order that a certificate be granted to him accordingly.

ADAM SCOTT's case: commenced in page 697.

On due consideration, the Board is of opinion that the present claimant is entitled to a right of pre-emption to one hundred acres of land, to be located as follows, to wit:

Beginning on the margin of Barrow's lake, a little north of the burying ground of Fort Stoddert, at a holly, being one of the corners referred to in the plot which the claimant returned to the Register; thence, along the margin of the said lake, northwardly, thirteen chains and fifty links, to a water oak near Welch's landing, being the first corner referred to in the claimant's plot; thence, due west, so far that a due south line from the extreme point of this line to the extreme point of a line due west from the place of beginning, shall include one hundred acres. And the Board doth order that a certificate be granted to him accordingly.

RICHARD S. BRYAN and GEORGE BREWER, Senior's, case: commenced in page 648.

On due consideration, the Board is of opinion that the present claimants are entitled to right of pre-emption to three hundred and twenty acres of land, to be located as follows:

Beginning at a corner cherry tree on Fulsom's creek, being the place of beginning described in the plot of the claimants entered in the Register's Office; thence, south, seventy degrees west, sixty-five chains; thence, south, twenty degrees east, forty-nine chains; thence, north, seventy degrees east, sixty-five chains; thence, north, twenty degrees west, forty-nine chains, to the place of beginning. And the Board doth order that a certificate be granted to them accordingly.

EDWARD GATLAND's case: commenced in page 694.

On due consideration, The Board is of opinion that the present claimant is entitled to a right of pre-emption; to three hundred and twenty acres of land, to be located as follows, viz.:

Beginning at the northwest corner of Edmund Smith's pre-emption; thence, along said Smith's line, south, seventy-seven degrees east, to his northeast corner; thence, along the line of said Smith, south, nine degrees east, to a live oak, being said Smith's southeast corner; thence, along the line of Godfrey Helverston's heirs, south, seventy-seven degrees east, to the margin of Mobile river: thence, up the west margin of said river, forty-nine chains; thence, north, seventy-seven degrees west, so far that a line therefrom south, ten degrees west, will strike the place of beginning: bounded eastwardly, by the Mobile river, southwardly, by Godfrey Helverston's heirs and Edmund Smith's pre-emption, and, northwardly, by Howell Dupree's donation. And the Board doth order that a certificate be granted to him accordingly.

FIGURES LEWIS's case: commenced in page 604.

On due consideration, the Board is of opinion that this claimant is entitled to a right of pre-emption to three hundred and twenty acres of land, to be located as follows:

Beginning on the west margin of Three River lake, three chains above the present dwelling-house of said Lewis; thence, down the margin of said lake, to the northeast corner of Daniel Johnson's three hundred and twenty acre donation, in the right of William Burke; thence, with the line of said Johnson, due west, so far that a line therefrom, due north, and thence, due east, to the place of beginning, shall include three hundred and twenty acres. And the Board doth order that a certificate be granted to him accordingly.

ADAM HOLLINGER's case: commenced in page 693.

On due consideration, the Board is of opinion that this claimant is entitled to a right of pre-emption to six hundred and forty acres of land, to be located as follows;

Beginning at the mouth of the Poll bayou, on the lower side thereof, which is also the beginning corner of Thomas Carson's donation; thence, up the margin of Tombigbee river, sixty chains; thence, south, eighty-six degrees west, one hundred and six chains; thence, due south, so far that a straight line therefrom to the northwest corner of Thomas Carson's donation, and thence, with said Carson's line, north, eighty-six degrees east, to the place of beginning, shall include six hundred and forty acres. And the Board doth order that a certificate be granted to him accordingly.

JOSEPH WESTMORELAND, representative of Lewis Crane: case commenced in page 699.

On due consideration, the Board is of opinion that this claimant is entitled to a right of pre-emption to one hundred and ninety-seven acres of land, to be located as follows, viz.:

Beginning at the northwest corner of Ransom Harwell's three hundred and twenty acre pre-emption tract; thence, with the line of said tract, due east, thirty-four chains, to the line of William Murrell's tract; thence, with the said Murrell's line, due north, to the west margin of the Tombigbee river; thence, up the margin of the same, twenty-three chains; thence, due west, twenty chains; thence, due south, to the place of beginning: *Provided, nevertheless,* That the said claimant first obtain, before a court of competent jurisdiction, a judicial decision in his favor against the adverse claim, by virtue of a grant from the British Government of West Florida to Robert Farmar, of one thousand acres, bearing date the 6th day of August, 1778. And the Board doth order that a certificate be granted to him accordingly.

JOSIAH SKINNER's case: commenced in page 605.

On due consideration, the Board is of opinion that this claim is not supported, and the same is accordingly rejected.

EDWIN LEWIS's case: commenced in page 638.

On due consideration, the Board is of opinion that this claimant is entitled to a right of pre-emption to one hundred and sixty acres of land, to be located as follows, to wit:

Beginning at the northwest corner of Edward Lloyd Wailes's six hundred and forty acre pre-emption tract, in the right of John Baker; thence, due east, eighty chains, in the line of said tract, to John Chastang's line; thence, with said line, fourteen chains; thence, due west, one hundred and fifteen chains; thence, due south, fourteen chains; thence, due east to the beginning: *Provided, nevertheless,* That the said claimant first obtain, before a court of competent jurisdiction, a judicial decision in his favor against the adverse claim, by virtue of a grant from the British Government of West Florida to John Sutherland, bearing date the 22d day of October, 1779. And the Board doth order that a certificate be granted to him accordingly.

JAMES HUGKABY's case: commenced in page 651.

On due consideration, the Board is of opinion that this claimant is entitled to a pre-emption right for four hundred and fifteen acres of land, to be located as follows:

Beginning at the southeast corner of Elisha Simmon's six hundred and forty acre pre-emption tract; thence, in the line of said tract, due north, to a corner of Ransom Harwell's three hundred and twenty acre tract; thence, due west, to the southwest corner of said tract; thence, due south, so far that a line therefrom due east shall strike the place of beginning. And the Board doth order that a certificate be granted to him accordingly.

WILLIAM WILLIAMS's case: commenced in page 651.

On due consideration, the Board is of opinion that this claimant is entitled to a right of pre-emption to three hundred and twenty acres of land, to be located as follows, viz.:

Beginning on the west margin of the Tombigbee river, at the upper corner of George Robbins's six hundred and forty acre tract; thence, up the margin of the said river, so far as to make thirty-three chains on a due north line; thence, due west, so far that a due south line therefrom, thirty-three chains, and thence, due east, to the place of beginning, shall include three hundred and twenty acres. And the Board doth order that a certificate be granted to him accordingly.

WYCHE WATLEY's case: commenced in page 603.

On due consideration, the Board is of opinion that this claimant is entitled to a right of pre-emption to one hundred and forty-two acres of land, to be located as follows:

Beginning at the northeast corner of Richard Brashear's six hundred and forty acre pre-emption in the right of Patrick Brewer, on the line of William H. Hargrave's three hundred and twenty acre tract; thence, with said Brashear's line, due west, seventy-one chains, to his northwest corner; thence, due north, twenty chains; thence, due east, seventy-one chains; and thence, due south, to the place of beginning. And the Board doth order that a certificate be granted to him accordingly.

RANSOM HARWELL's case: commenced in page 642.

On due consideration, the Board is of opinion that this claimant is entitled to a right of pre-emption to three hundred and twenty acres of land, to be located as follows:

Beginning at the southeast corner of William Murrell's one hundred and sixty acre pre-emption tract; thence, with the line of said tract, due north, fifty chains; thence, due west, thirty-four chains; thence, due south, seventy-nine chains; thence, due east, fifty-four chains, to the line of Elisha Simmons; thence, with said line, due north, to William Murrell's southeast corner; thence, with the said Murrell's line, to the place of beginning: *Provided, nevertheless,* That the said claimant first obtain, before a court of competent jurisdiction, in his favor, against the adverse claim, by virtue of a grant from the British Government of West Florida to Robert Farmar, bearing date the 6th day of August, 1778. And the Board doth order that a certificate be granted to him accordingly.

JAMES MORGAN, representative of John Burney: case commenced in page 594.

On due consideration, the Board is of opinion that this claimant is entitled to a right of pre-emption to three hundred and twenty acres of land, to be located as follows:

Beginning at a lightwood stake, being the beginning corner described in the claimant's plot returned in the office of the Register; thence, north, sixteen and a half degrees east, forty-seven chains fifty links; thence, north, seventy-three and a half degrees west, sixty-seven chains fifty links; thence, south, sixteen and a half degrees west, forty-seven chains fifty links; thence, direct to the place of beginning. And the Board doth order that a certificate be granted to him accordingly.

EDWIN LEWIS, representative of McCole and McClendon: case commenced in page 645.

On due consideration, the Board is of opinion that this claimant is entitled to a right of pre-emption to one hundred and sixty acres of land, to be located as follows:

Beginning at the northwest corner of Edwin Lewis's three hundred and twenty acre tract, in the right of William Green; thence, due north, thirty-two chains; thence, due east, fifty chains; thence, due south, thirty-two chains; thence, direct to the place of beginning. And the Board doth order that a certificate be granted to him accordingly.

EDWIN LEWIS, representative of William Green: case commenced in page 648.

On due consideration, the Board is of opinion that this claimant is entitled to a right of pre-emption to three hundred and twenty acres of land, to be located as follows:

Beginning at the southeast corner of Bryan and Brewer's three hundred and twenty acre tract; thence, in the line of said tract, north, twenty degrees west, forty-nine chains, to the northeast corner thereof; thence due north, twenty-five chains; thence, due east, fifty chains; thence, due south, seventy-one chains; thence, direct to the place of beginning. And the Board doth order that a certificate be granted to them accordingly.

MICAJAH WALL's case: commenced in page 602.

On due consideration, the Board is of opinion that this claimant is entitled to a right of pre-emption to three hundred and twenty acres of land, to be located as follows:

Beginning at the northeast corner of James Morgan's three hundred and twenty acre pre-emption tract, in the right of John Burney; thence, north, seventy-three and a half degrees west, sixty-seven chains fifty links; thence north, sixteen and a half degrees east, forty-seven chains fifty links; thence, south, seventy-three and a half degrees east, sixty-seven chains fifty links; thence, direct to the place of beginning. And the Board doth order that a certificate be granted to him accordingly.

RAWLEY GREEN's case: commenced in page 666.

On due consideration, the Board is of opinion that the claimant is entitled to a right of pre-emption to three hundred and twenty acres of land, to be located as follows:

Beginning at the northwest corner of Joseph Westmoreland's one hundred and ninety-seven acre tract; thence, with the line of said tract, due east, to the west margin of the said river Tombigbee; thence up the margin of the river, twenty-two chains; thence, due west, eighty chains; thence, due south, fifty-three chains; thence, due east, to Westmoreland's line; and thence, with said line, to the place of beginning: *Provided, nevertheless,* That the said claimant first obtain, before a court of competent jurisdiction, a judicial decision in his favor against the adverse claim by virtue of a grant from the British Government of West Florida to Robert Farmar of one thousand acres, bearing date the 6th day of August, 1778. And the Board doth order that a certificate be granted to him accordingly.

BENJAMIN FEW's case: commenced in page 692.

On due consideration, the Board is of opinion that this claimant is entitled to a right of pre-emption to six hundred and forty acres of land, to be located as follows:

Beginning on the west bank of the Tombigbee river, at a place a few paces north of a deep gully or ravine near to a house now occupied by Lemuel Henry, and being a stake corner, formerly agreed upon by Sterling Dupree and Colonel Benjamin Few; thence, south, fifty-six degrees west, so far that a line therefrom, south, sixty-five degrees east, will strike the northwest corner of Howell Dupree's donation; thence, in the course of said Dupree's line, south, sixty-five degrees east, so far that a line therefrom due north, to the west margin of the Tombigbee, and up the margin of said river, to the place of beginning, shall include six hundred and forty acres. And the Board doth order that a certificate be granted to him accordingly.

YOUNG GAINS, representative of Dominique de Olive: case commenced in page 622.

Augustin Rochon was presented as a witness, and, being duly sworn, deposed, that he had frequently seen Dominique de Olive laboring and attending to his crop and negroes, on the land now claimed by Young Gains, as his representative.

Question. About what time did you see him on this plantation last?

Answer. About nine or ten years past.

That on this plantation there was a good store house and negro houses; that said Olive lived in the store house at such times as he resided on the plantation; that there was a large field, containing in or about thirty or forty acres cleared and cultivated.

The Board ordered that the case be postponed for consideration.

GEORGE BREWER, Jun., representative of Valentine Dubroca: case commenced in page 625.

Augustine Rochon was presented as a witness, and, being duly sworn, deposed, that he saw the son of Dubroca resided on the land in question, and overlooked the negroes of his father then working on this land; that this cultivation took place in the year 1795; that young Dubroca resided in the territory at that time, being an interpreter of the Indian language at Fort St. Stephen's.

The Board ordered that the case be postponed for consideration.

JAMES CALLIER, representative of Isabella Trouillet: case commenced in page 650.

Alphaces Sayre was produced as a witness, and, being duly sworn and interrogated by the Board, deposed, that he was not interested in this claim; that from the year 1800 to the year 1804, Joseph Campbell and Isabella Trouillet, his wife, inhabited and cultivated on the land now in question; that the extent of the cultivation was a garden, turnip field, and such like domestic cultivation; that on the 3d day of March, 1803, said Campbell was from home, and on business at or near New Orleans, but his family was then resident on said land; that Mr. Campbell and himself found them there on their return from New Orleans; that he had always understood, that Campbell left some property in his hands on this land, and in the care of Alexis Trouillet, in order that he might have a home whenever he came there on business.

The Board ordered that the case be postponed for consideration.

JOHN B. TRENNIER's case, No. 186 on the docket of the Board, and No. 192 on the books of the Register.

Claim—Of nine hundred and ninety-nine acres and nine-tenths of an acre, by virtue of a Spanish warrant of survey, under the first section of the act.

The claimant presented his claim, together with a surveyor's plot of the land claimed, in the following words and figures, to wit:

To the Commissioners appointed in pursuance of the act of Congress passed the 3d day of March, 1803, for receiving and adjusting the claims to lands south of Tennessee, and east of Pearl river.

Please to take notice, that the following tract of land, situated on the east side of the west channel of the Mobile river, in the county of Washington, beginning at John Chastang's corner, running thence, east, one hundred and fifteen chains fifty-six links, to a stake; thence, south, nine degrees west, seventy-nine chains; thence, west, one hundred and fifteen chains fifty-six links to a red oak, on the bank of the said river; thence up the meanders of the river to the beginning: containing nine hundred and ninety-nine acres and nine-tenths of an acre, having such shape, form, and marks as are represented in the plot annexed: is claimed by Nicholas Weeks, attorney, for said John Baptist Trennier, in and by virtue of a Spanish warrant of survey; and is now exhibited to the Register of the Land Office established east of Pearl river, to be recorded as directed by said act. To all which he begs leave to refer, as also to a copy of the plot herewith filed.

NICHOLAS WEEKS,
Attorney for John B. Trennier.

March, 1804.

[Plot omitted.]

Surveyed 3d March, 1804, by James Gordon. Chain bearers, James Callier, Hartwell Hardaway.

MOBILE, *September* 20, 1793.

His Excellency the Governor and Intendant General:

John Baptist Trennier, for him, and in his name, as lawful attorney for him, Simon Andrey, both inhabitants of this place, with the greatest respect represents, and lays before your excellency, and says, that there is a tract of land vacant, situate on the east side of Tombigbee river, containing twenty-five acres front, bounded on the north side by a creek called Hardrick, and on the south side by land the property of the petitioner; and as there never appeared any proprietor until now, he begs your excellency to grant him the above tract of land, it being vacant; and he being necessitated for such a tract of land, after his retire from the service as interpreter at Natchez, and that he may have some place of his own to retire to, and having slaves in number sufficient to cultivate the same, he begs your excellency to grant him the above petition, with papers of titles necessary which may correspond with the grant, for which favor he will be forever thankful.

SIMON ANDRY.

MOBILE, *October* 11, 1793.

His Excellency the Governor and Intendant General:

The person who petitions, in the name of John Baptist Trennier, is duly authorized and empowered as his lawful attorney, who has charge of all his property ever since he was named interpreter for the Walnut Hills. I next was informed, by some of the oldest inhabitants, that the land the above petitioner solicits is vacant, and that he has slaves sufficient to cultivate the same. Your excellency may dispose as it may seem best.

MANUEL DE LANZOS.

NEW ORLEANS, *October* 14, 1793.

The surveyor general, or any individual named by him for that business, shall establish that part of twenty-five acres front which the petitioner solicits, with forty in the profounder back as customary, not causing prejudice to neighbors, with the precise conditions of making the road, and clearing regularly in the peremptory space of one year; and if at the precise space of three years the land is not settled, during which period it cannot be alienated, this grant to remain null, under which supposition the business of settling the limits will be carried on in the tract, and remitted me, to provide the interested party with titles in form.

THE BARON DE CARONDELET.

Don Pedro Olivier, Captain in the Louisiana regiment of infantry, and commandant, civil and military, of Mobile and its jurisdiction, certifieth, that the above concession of land is copied here exact from the original in these archives under my charge, for which I sign these presents, at Mobile, this thirty-first day of October, one thousand seven hundred and ninety-five.

PEDRO OLIVIER.

The above was compared exact with the original, by me.

JOAQN. DE OSORNO.

Translated from the Spanish grant,

THOS. PRICE.

I, Thomas Price, of the post of Mobile, English interpreter for his Majesty the King of Spain, do solemnly swear, by the Almighty God, and by the Holy Cross, that this is a true and faithful translation of the Spanish grant, or writing hereunto annexed.

THOMAS PRICE.

Subscribed and sworn before the Board, March the 20th, 1804.—Attest: DAVID PARMELEE 2d, *Clerk.*

Entered in record of claims, vol. 2, page 15, by EDWARD LLOYD WAILES, for

JOSEPH CHAMBERS, *Register.*

Simon Andrey was presented as a witness, and, being sworn, deposed, that he was agent for John Baptist Trennier, and did, with his negroes, cultivate the land in question, on the 27th day of October, 1795; that said Trennier did at that time reside at, or near, the town of Natchez, and within the Mississippi territory, and that he was, in the month of October, 1793, more than twenty-five years of age.

The Board ordered that the case be postponed for consideration.

SIMON ANDREY's case, No. 187 on the docket of the Board, and No. 193 on the books of the Register.

Claim—Of forty-nine acres and nine-tenths of an acre, by virtue of a Spanish warrant of survey, under the first section of the act.

The claimant presented his claim, together with a surveyor's plot of the land claimed, in the following words and figures, to wit:

To the Commissioners appointed in pursuance of an act of Congress passed the 3d day of March, 1803, for receiving and adjusting claims to lands south of the Tennessee river, and east of Pearl river.

Please to take notice, that the following tract of land, lying east of the Mobile river, butting and bounding as follows, viz.: beginning at a stake on the bank of the river, running south fifty-five degrees, east, four chains seventy-four links, to a stake on Charlotte Heraul's line; thence, south, fifty degrees east, seven chains fifty links; thence, south, fifty-two degrees east, six chains; thence, south, fifty-four degrees east, seven chains fifty links; thence, south, forty-four degrees east, nine chains; thence, south, eighty degrees east, thirteen chains fifty links; thence, south, eighty-nine degrees east, twenty chains fifty links; thence, north, sixty-eight degrees east, three chains fifty links; thence, north, sixty-three degrees east, seven chains twenty links; thence, north, forty-two degrees east, ten chains fifty links; thence, north, twenty degrees east, five chains; thence, north, fifteen degrees east, five chains; thence, north, one degree west, five chains; thence, north,eight degrees west, one chain; thence south, eight degrees east, four chains seventy-four links, to a stake on the river; thence, down the meanders, to the beginning corner, bounded southwardly by Charlotte Heraul's land: is claimed by Simon Andrey, under and by virtue of a Spanish warrant, or order of survey, granted to the said Simon Andrey, as may appear by the original grant now delivered to the Register of the Land Office, to be established east of Pearl river, to be recorded as directed by said act. To all which he begs leave to refer, as also to a copy of the plot herewith filed.

CHASTANG, JUN.,
Acting for Simon Andrey.

FORT STODDERT, *March* 21, 1804.
[Plot omitted.]

Surveyed by James Gordon. Chain bearers, Joseph Campbell and Gabriel Tissrah.

MOBILE, *January* 18, 1793.

Seignior Governor and Intendant General:

Simon Andrey, inhabitant of this district, with the greatest respect, represents to your excellency and says, that the land whereon he now lives, and for which he has a grant, is of no further use to him than for building his houses and keeping his stock or cow-pen; the land being very poor, and not fit for cultivation, he begs your excellency to grant him on the east side of the

river Tombigbee, opposite the place whereon his house now stands, which land is suitable for cultivation; but there not being more than one and a half acres back from the river that is tillable land, after which it is a low, boggy, over-flowing land not to be inhabited, and in consequence of the narrow limits on the bank of the river not fit for cultivation, he begs your excellency to grant him thirty-two acres front on the river, as above mentioned in this petition, for which favor he will be forever thankful.

SIMON ANDREY.

Seignior Governor General of this Province, &c.

I have been informed by several inhabitants of this river, who confirm the above lands petitioned for to be vacant lands, and that the back part being inhabitable, is, as it is represented ; but the front on the river being good tillable land, he having slaves in number sufficient to maintain and cultivate the same, he begs your excellency in favoring his petition, for which he will forever pray.

MANUEL DE LANZOS.

MOBILE, *January* 19, 1793.

NEW ORLEANS, *February* 2, 1793.

The commandant of Mobile shall establish that part of thirty-two acres of land front, on the river, as mentioned in the petition, with its back or profounder of one and a half acres, as is mentioned in the above memorial, as it proves to be vacant land, without causing any detriment whatever, with these conditions precisely, of clearing roads and making lawful improvements within the term of one year: but should it be neglected for the term of three years, the same land shall again become vacant; and, during the above term of three years, the petitioner shall not convey, bargain, or sell any part of the above lands, or cause it to be done, but shall give information of his fulfilling the above obligation within said term of time, that it may correspond with the titles given in regular form.

THE BARON DE CARONDELET.

The above is a true copy of the original in this office under my charge, which I certify in Mobile.

MANUEL DE LANZOS.

Translated from a copy of the original in Mobile.

THOMAS PRICE.

I, Thomas Price, of the post of Mobile, English interpreter for His Majesty the King of Spain, do solemnly swear, by the Almighty God, and by the Holy Cross, that this is a true and faithful translation of the Spanish grant or writing hereto annexed.

THOS. PRICE.

Subscribed and sworn before the Board, March 21st, 1804.—Attest: DAVID PARMELEE 2d, *Clerk.*

Entered in record of claims, vol. 2, page 15, by EDWARD LLOYD WAILES, for

JOSEPH CHAMBERS, *Register.*

Augustin Rochon was presented as a witness, and, being duly sworn, deposed, that Simon Andrey did cultivate the land in question on the 27th of October, 1795, and that said Andrey was, in the month of February, 1793, more than twenty-five years of age.

The Board ordered that the case be postponed for consideration.

Adjourned until Tuesday the 5th instant.

TUESDAY, *June* 5, 1804.

The Board met according to adjournment. Present: Ephraim Kirby, Robert C. Nicholas, Joseph Chambers.

NATT CHRISTMAS's case: commenced in page 695.

On due consideration, the Board is of opinion, that this claimant is entitled to a right of pre-emption to two hundred and seventy acres of land, to be located as follows: beginning at the northeast corner of Sterling Dupree's pre-emption on the west margin of the Tombigbee river ; thence, up the margin of said river twenty-five chains ; thence, north, sixty degrees west, so far that a straight line therefrom to the northwest corner of Sterling Dupree's pre-emption ; and thence, with said Dupree's line to the place of beginning, shall include two hundred and seventy acres, bounded southwardly by said Dupree, and eastwardly on the river Tombigbee. And the Board doth order that a certificate be granted to him accordingly.

SIMPSON WHALEY's case: commenced in page 670.

On due consideration, the Board is of opinion, that this claimant is entitled to a right of pre-emption to one hundred acres of land, to be located as follows: beginning on the west margin of Barrow's lake, at a water-oak, near Welch's landing, being the northeast corner of Adam Scott's claim; thence, northwardly, along the margin of said lake, opposite to a large pine tree on the bluff, which was the corner designated in the plot of the claimant, as returned to the Register; and thence, due west, to and from said tree, so far that a line due south to the extreme point of this line, to the extreme point of a line due west from to the place of beginning, shall include one hundred acres, bounded south on Adam Scott's line. And the Board doth order that a certificate be granted to him accordingly.

ELISHA SIMMONS's case: commenced in page 597.
On due consideration, the Board is of opinion, that this claimant is entitled to a right of pre-emption to six hundred and forty acres of land, to be located as follows: beginning on the west margin of the Tombigbee river, on the upper side of the mouth of Salt creek; thence, up the margin of said river, so far as to make thirty-eight chains on a due west line; thence, due south, so far that due east therefrom thirty-eight chains; and thence due north to the place of beginning, shall include six hundred and forty acres: *Provided, nevertheless,* That the said claimant first obtain, before a court of competent jurisdiction, a judicial decision in his favor against the adverse claim, by virtue of a grant from the British Government of West Florida to Robert Farmar, bearing date the 6th day of August, 1778. Also against the adverse claim by virtue of a like grant to Abraham Little, bearing date the 16th day of February, 1778. And the Board doth order that a certificate be granted to him accordingly.

SETH DEAN, representative of Jesse Thomas: case commenced in page 696.
On due consideration, the Board is of opinion, that this claimant is entitled to a right of pre-emption to one hundred and ninety acres of land, to be located as follows: beginning at the southwest corner of Augustin Rochon's British grant; thence, with the said Rochon's line, north, twenty-one degrees east, to the south line of James Callier's pre-emption; thence, with said Callier's line, south, eighty-six degrees west, to said Callier's southwest corner; thence, south, eleven degrees east, twenty-seven chains; thence, north, eighty-six degrees east, to the place of beginning. And the Board doth order that a certificate be granted to him accordingly.

SETH DEAN's case: commenced in page 693.
On due consideration, the Board is of opinion that this claimant is entitled to a right of pre-emption to three hundred and twenty acres of land, to be located as follows: beginning on the west margin of the Tombigbee river, at the northeast corner of Adam Hollinger's pre-emption, and thence up the margin of said river, twenty-five chains; thence, south, eighty-six degrees west, one hundred and thirty-one chains; thence, due south, so far, that a straight line therefrom to the northwest corner of Adam Hollinger's pre-emption, and thence, with said Hollinger's line, north, eighty-six degrees east, to the place of beginning, shall include three hundred and twenty acres. And the Board doth order that a certificate be granted to him accordingly.

SETH DEAN, representative of James Lowe: case commenced in page 696.
On due consideration, the Board is of opinion, that this claimant is entitled to a right of pre-emption to six hundred and forty acres of land, to be located as follows: beginning at the northeast corner of the pre-emption right allowed to the representative of John Wallis; thence, with the line of said Wallis's pre-emption, due south, to the southwest corner thereof; and thence, with the same line, due east, to the northwest corner of Thomas Bates's donation; and thence, with said Bates's line, due south fifty chains; and thence, due west, so far that a line therefrom due north, and thence due east to the place of beginning, shall include six hundred and forty acres. And the Board doth order that a certificate be granted to him accordingly.

SETH DEAN, representative of John Wallace: case commenced in page 695.
On due consideration, the Board is of opinion that this claimant is entitled to a right of pre-emption to three hundred and twenty acres of land, to be located as follows: beginning on the margin of the Tombigbee river, three chains above the mouth of Bilbo's creek; thence, down the margin of said river to the northeast corner of Thomas Bates's donation; thence, with the line of said Bates due west, so far that a line therefrom due north, and thence due east to the place of beginning, shall include three hundred and twenty acres. And the Board doth order that a certificate be granted to him accordingly.

JOHN PICKERING's case: commenced in page 647.
On due consideration, the Board is of opinion that this claimant is entitled to a right of pre-emption of two hundred and eighty acres of land, to be located as follows:
Beginning at a wild plum tree in a prairie, being the place described in his plot returned to the Register's Office, as his beginning corner; thence, west, sixty chains; thence, south, twenty degrees, west; fifty chains; thence, east, sixty chains; thence, north, twenty degrees east, fifty chains, to the place of beginning. And the Board doth order that a certificate be granted to him accordingly.

TANDY WALKER AND JOHN WALKER's case: commenced in page 666.
On due consideration, the Board is of opinion that the claimants are entitled to a right of pre-emption to three hundred and twenty acres of land, to be located as follows:
Beginning at a pine corner, described in the plot returned by the claimants to the Register's Office; thence, east, twenty-five chains, fifty links, crossing Laura's creek at thirteen chains; thence, north, fifty degrees east, forty chains; thence, north, fifty-seven degrees west, eighty chains; thence, south, thirty degrees west, sixty-nine chains; thence, south, sixty-three degrees east, forty-six chains, to the place of beginning. *Provided, nevertheless,* That the said claimants first obtain, before a court of competent jurisdiction, a judicial decision in their favor against the adverse claim, by virtue of a grant from the British Government of West Florida to Robert Farmar, bearing date the 6th of August, 1778. And the Board doth order that a certificate be granted to them accordingly.

PATRICK DONNELLY's case: commenced in page 644.
On due consideration, the Board is of opinion that this claimant is entitled to a right of pre-emption to three hundred and twenty acres of land, to be located as follows:
Beginning on the north side of Little Bassett's creek, at the northwest corner of the tract, so far from the present dwelling house of the claimant, as to leave the same in the centre of said tract; thence, due east, fifty-six chains seventy links; thence, due south, fifty-six chains, seventy links; thence, due west, fifty-six chains, seventy links; thence, due north, to the place of beginning. And the Board doth order that a certificate be granted to him accordingly.

WILLIAM MURRELL's case: commenced in page 643.
On due consideration, the Board is of opinion, that this claimant is entitled to a right of pre-emption to one hundred and sixty acres of land, to be located as follows:
Beginning on the west side of the Tombigbee river, at the upper corner of Elisha Simmons's six hundred and forty acre pre-emption tract; thence, up the margin of said river so far as to make twenty chains on a due west line; thence, due south, so far, that a due east line therefrom to the line of said Simmons's tract, and thence, with said line due north, to the place of beginning, shall include one hundred and sixty acres: *Provided, nevertheless,* That the said claimant first obtain, before a court of competent jurisdiction, a judicial decision in his favor against the adverse claim, by virtue of a grant from the British Government of West Florida to Robert Farmar, bearing date the 6th day of August, 1778. Also against the adverse claim by virtue of a like grant to Abraham Little, bearing date the 16th day of February, 1778. And the Board doth order that a certificate be granted to him accordingly.

ISAAC STANLEY's case: commenced in page 665.
On due consideration, the Board is of opinion that this claimant is entitled to a right of pre-emption to one hundred acres of land, to be located as follows:
Beginning at a hickory corner, being the place described as the beginning in the plot of the claimant returned to the Register's Office; thence, north, ten degrees east, twenty-five chains; thence, north, eighty degrees west, forty chains; thence, south, ten degrees west, twenty-five chains; thence, direct to the place of beginning. And the Board doth order that a certificate be granted to him accordingly.

Bates due west, so far that a line therefrom due north, and thence due east to the place of beginning, shall include three hundred and twenty acres. And the Board doth order that a certificate be granted to him accordingly.

ZACHARIAH LANDRUM's case: commenced in page 667.

On due consideration, the Board is of opinion that this claimant is entitled to a right of pre-emption to one hundred and fourteen acres of land, to be located as follows, to wit:

Beginning at a red oak, being the same described in the plot returned to the Register's Office, as his beginning corner; thence, north, seventeen degrees west, twenty-eight chains fifty links; thence, north, seventy-three degrees east, forty chains; thence, south, seventeen degrees east, twenty-eight chains fifty links; thence, direct to the place of beginning. And the Board doth order that a certificate be granted to him accordingly.

JOSEPH WILSON, representative of Joseph Dunbar: case commenced in page 644.

On due consideration, the Board is of opinion that this claimant is entitled to a right of pre-emption to six hundred and forty acres of land, to be located as follows:

Beginning on the margin of the Tombigbee river, on the west side thereof, half way between the claimant's house and the house of John Kennedy, which is also said Kennedy's beginning corner; thence, east, fifteen chains, with said Kennedy's line; thence, with said Kennedy's, due south, to the southeast corner of said Kennedy's pre-emption; thence, due east, so far that a line therefrom due north, to the margin of said river, and thence, with the same, pursuing the meanders thereof, to the place of beginning, shall include six hundred and forty acres. And the Board doth order that a certificate be granted to him accordingly.

MATTHEW SHAW's case: commenced in page 598.

On due consideration, the Board is of opinion that this claimant is entitled to a right of pre-emption to three hundred and twenty acres of land, to be located as follows:

Beginning on the west margin of the Tombigbee river, at the upper corner of William Rogers's three hundred and twenty acre tract; thence, up the margin of said river, so far as to make thirty-three chains on a due north line; thence, due west, so far that a line therefrom, due south, shall strike the northwest corner of said Rogers's tract; and thence, with the line of said tract, due east, to the place of beginning. And the Board doth order that a certificate be granted to him accordingly.

SOLOMON BOYKIN, representative of Elizabeth Reed: case commenced in page 655.

On due consideration, the Board is of opinion that this claimant is entitled to a right of pre-emption to six hundred and forty acres of land, to be located as follows:

Beginning at the northeast corner of Isaac Ryan's six hundred and forty acre donation tract; and thence, with said Ryan's line, due west, to his northwest corner; and thence, due north, forty chains; thence, due east, one hundred and sixty chains; and thence, due south, to the place of beginning. And the Board doth order that a certificate be granted to him accordingly.

ROBERT SORREL, Senior's case: commenced in page 643.

On due consideration, the Board is of opinion that this claimant is entitled to a right of pre-emption to three hundred and twenty acres of land, to be located as follows:

Beginning on the north side of Little Bassett's creek, at the northwest corner of the tract, so far from the present dwelling house of the claimant, as to leave the same in the centre of said tract; thence, due east, fifty-six chains seventy links; thence, due south, fifty-six chains seventy links; thence, due west, fifty-six chains seventy links; thence, due north, to the place of beginning. And the Board doth order that a certificate be granted to him accordingly.

PRISCILLA MILES's case: commenced in page 700.

On due consideration, the Board is of opinion that this claimant is entitled to a right of pre-emption to one hundred and sixty acres of land; to be located as follows:

Beginning at the northwest corner of the tract, so far from the present dwelling house of the claimant, as to leave the same in the centre of said tract; thence, due east, forty chains; thence, due south, forty chains; thence, due west, forty chains; thence, due north, forty chains, to the place of beginning. And the Board doth order that a certificate be granted to her accordingly.

THOMAS MALONE's case: commenced in page 657.

On due consideration, the Board is of opinion that this claimant is entitled to a right of pre-emption to six hundred and forty acres of land, to be located as follows:

Beginning on the west margin of the Tombigbee river, on the upper corner of Francis Stringer's six hundred and forty acre pre-emption right; thence, with said Stringer's line, due west, to his northwest corner; thence, due north, forty chains; thence, due east, to the river; and thence, down the margin of the same, to the place of beginning. And the Board doth order that a certificate be granted to him accordingly.

Adjourned until Wednesday, June the 6th.

WEDNESDAY, June 6, 1804.

The Board met according to adjournment. Present: Ephraim Kirby, Robert C. Nicholas, Joseph Chambers.

WILLIAM ROGERS's case: commenced in page 597.

On due consideration, the Board is of opinion that this claimant is entitled to a right of pre-emption to three hundred and twenty acres of land, to be located as follows:

Beginning on the west margin of the Tombigbee river, at the upper corner of Raleigh Green's three hundred and twenty acre tract; thence, up the margin of said river, so far, as to make thirty-six chains on a due north line; thence, due west, so far that a line therefrom, due south, shall strike the northwest corner of said Green's tract; and thence, with said Green's line due east, to the place of beginning. And the Board doth order that a certificate be granted to him accordingly.

JOHN CANNEDA's case: commenced in page 647.

On due consideration, the Board is of opinion that this claimant is entitled to a right of pre-emption to six hundred and forty acres of land, to be located as follows:

Beginning on the margin of the Tombigbee river, on the west side thereof, at a place half way between the said claimant's dwelling house, and the house of Joseph Wilson; thence, due east, fifteen chains; thence, due south, so far that a line due west therefrom, to the lower line of James Denley's'four hundred acre tract, and thence, with said line north, twenty degrees east, to the margin of the river, and thence, down the margin of the same, with the meanders thereof, to the place of beginning, shall include six hundred and forty acres. And the Board doth order that a certificate be granted to him accordingly.

WILSON CARMAN's case: commenced in page 669.

On due consideration, the Board is of opinion that this claimant is entitled to a right of pre-emption to one hundred and sixty acres of land, to be located as follows;

Beginning on the west bank of the Mobile river, near the house where Alexis Trouillett now lives, at the place established for the upper corner of land allowed to James Callier; thence, up the margin of said river, to a place below Fort Stoddert, near said Carman's landing, and also near where the present fence of said Carman strikes the river, and due east from a large oak tree near the river bank; thence, due west, so far that a due south line from the extreme point of this line to the extreme point of a due west line, from the place of beginning, shall include one hundred and sixty acres; which shall be bounded south on the north line of James Callier's land. And the Board doth order that a certificate be granted to him accordingly.

JOHN DENLEY's case: commenced in page 706.

On due consideration, the Board is of opinion that this claimant is entitled to a right of pre-emption to one hundred and sixty acres of land, to be located as follows:

Beginning on the margin of the Tombigbee river, on the west side thereof, at the upper corner of George Dickey's one hundred and sixty acre pre-emption; thence, with the line of said Dickey, due north, to his northeast corner; thence, due east, thirteen chains seventy-five links; thence, due south, to the margin of said river, and thence, down the same, to the place of beginning; to include the number of acres above mentioned. And the Board doth order that a certificate be granted to him accordingly.

THOMAS SULLIVANT, Junior's, case: commenced in page 658.

On due consideration, the Board is of opinion that this claimant is entitled to a right of pre-emption to one hundred and ninety acres of land, to be located as follows:

Beginning on the west margin of the Tombigbee river, on the upper side of the mouth of Three River lake, at a hickory, being the lower corner of a Spanish warrant; confirmed to the heirs of Owen Sullivant, deceased; thence, with the waters of the upper branch of said lake, to the northeast corner of said Sullivant's land; thence, north, sixty-four degrees west, seventy-six chains, in the line of said Sullivant's land, to a corner stake; thence, in said line, south, thirty-eight degreees west, thirty-seven chains, to the bank of the Three River lake; thence, down the margin of said lake to the place of beginning. And the Board doth order that a certificate be granted to him accordingly.

LEVIN HAINSWORTH's case: commenced in page 699.

On due consideration, the Board is of opinion that this claim is not supported, and the same is accordingly disallowed.

NATHANIEL ROSS, representative of Henry Slaughter: case commenced in page 706.

On due consideration, the Board is of opinion that this claim is not supported, and the same is accordingly disallowed.

WILLIAM H. HARGRAVE's case: commenced in page 661.

On due consideration, the Board is of opinion that this claim is not supported, and the same is accordingly rejected.

THOMAS SULLIVANT's case: commenced in page 658.

On due consideration, the Board is of opinion that this claimant is entitled to a right of pre-emption to two hundred and forty acres of land, to be located as follows:

Beginning at a black gum, on the southeast corner, being the beginning corner in the plot returned by this claimant to the Register's Office; and thence, due west, sixty chains; thence, due north, forty chains; thence, due east, sixty chains; thence, due south, forty chains, to the place of beginning. And the Board doth order that a certificate be granted to him accordingly.

JOHN DUNN's case: commenced in page 656.

On due consideration, the Board is of opinion that this claimant is entitled to a right of pre-emption to six hundred and forty acres of land, to be located as follows:

Beginning on the west margin of the Tombigbee river, at the upper corner of Nathan Blackwell's six hundred and forty acre donation, and thence with said Blackwell's line, due west, to his northwest corner; thence, due north, fifty-five chains eighty links; thence, due east, to said river; and down the same, to the place of beginning. And the Board doth order that a certificate be granted to him accordingly.

WILLIAM HUNT's case: commenced in page 662.

On due consideration, the Board is of opinion that this claimant is entitled to a right of pre-emption to one hundred and sixty acres of land, to be located as follows:

Beginning at the southeast corner of the tract, thence, north, fifty degrees west, thirty-eight chains fifty links; thence, north, fifty-six degrees east, fifty-seven chains; thence, south, thirty-five degrees east, nine chains sixty-five links; thence, south, eighteen degrees east, twenty-two chains seventy links; thence, direct to the place of beginning. And the Board doth order that a certificate be granted to him accordingly.

WILLIAM H. HARGRAVE, representative of Stephen Williams: case commenced in page 661.

On due consideration, the Board is of opinion that this claimant is entitled to a right of pre-emption to three hundred and twenty acres of land, to be located as follows:

Beginning at the southwest corner of Richard Lee's six hundred and forty acre donation, in the right of Jordan Morgan; thence, with said Lee's line, due east, to the northwest corner of James Denley's two hundred and eighty acre tract; thence, with said Denley's line, due south, to his southwest corner, on the line of Hiram Mounger's six hundred and forty acre donation; thence, with said Mounger's line, due west, thirty-two chains

fifty links, and thence, due north, so far that a due east line therefrom to Richard Lee's line, and thence, with said line, due south, to the place of beginning, shall include three hundred and twenty acres. And the Board doth order that a certificate be granted to him accordingly.

PETER CARTWRIGHT's case: commenced in page 665.

On due consideration, the Board is of opinion that this claimant is entitled to a right of pre-emption to one hundred and sixty acres of land, to be located as follows:

Beginning at a hickory, being the same described in his plot returned to the Register's Office as his beginning corner; thence, south, eighty-four degrees east, fifteen chains; thence, north, nine degrees east, thirty-three chains fifty links; thence, north, thirty degrees west, thirty-three chains; thence, south, fifty-seven degrees west, thirty-three chains fifty links; thence to the beginning. And the Board doth order that a certificate be granted to him accordingly.

WILLIAM MORGAN's case: commenced in page 595.

On due consideration, the Board is of opinion that this claimant is entitled to a right of pre-emption to three hundred and twenty acres of land, to be located as follows:

Beginning at the northwest corner of said tract, so far from the present dwelling of the claimant as to leave the same in the centre thereof; thence, due east, fifty-six chains fifty links; thence, due south, fifty-six chains fifty links; thence, due west, fifty-six chains fifty links; thence, due north, to the beginning. And the Board doth order that a certificate be granted to him accordingly.

EDMUND SMITH's case: commenced in page 645.

On due consideration, the Board is of opinion that this claimant is entitled to a right of pre-emption to four hundred and twenty-two acres of land, to be located as follows:

Beginning at a live oak, on the north line of the lands of Godfrey Helverston's heirs, eighteen chains from the west bank of Mobile river; thence, north, nine degrees west, along the line of Edward Gatland, thirty chains, to a corner; thence, north, seventy-seven degrees west, so far that a line from the extreme point of this line south, ten degrees west, to intersect a line from the place of beginning; north, seventy-seven degrees west, shall include four hundred and twenty-two acres; bounded south on the lands of Godfrey Helverston's heirs, east and north by Edward Gatland's pre-emption. And the Board doth order that a certificate be granted to him accordingly.

JOHN WAMACK's case: commenced in page 652.

On due consideration, the Board is of opinion that this claimant is entitled to a right of pre-emption to two hundred and forty acres of land, to be located as follows:

Beginning at a pine, being the same described in his plot returned to the Register's Office as his beginning corner; thence, south, sixty-two degrees west, forty chains; thence, north, twenty-eight degrees west, sixty chains; thence, north, sixty-two degrees east, forty chains; thence, direct to the beginning. And the Board doth order that a certificate be granted to him accordingly.

GEORGE FARRAR's case: commenced in page 689.

On due consideration, the Board is of opinion that this claimant is entitled to a right of pre-emption to three hundred and twenty acres of land, to be located as follows:

Beginning at the place where John Johnson's Spanish warrant, Moses Moore's Spanish warrant, claimed by Ann Lawrence, his representative, and Bridget Burk's donation corner together; thence, with said Bridget Burk's line, to the northwest corner of James Lowe's pre-emption; thence, with the line of said Lowe's land, due south, twenty-five chains; thence, due west, seventy chains; thence, due north, so far that a line therefrom, due east, to John Johnson's line, and thence with said Johnson's line, due east, to the place of beginning, shall include three hundred and twenty acres. And the Board doth order that a certificate be granted to him accordingly.

GEORGE DICKEY's case: commenced in page 693.

On due consideration, the Board is of opinion that this claimant is entitled to a right of pre-emption to one hundred and sixty acres of land, to be located as follows:

Beginning on the margin of the Tombigbee river, on the west side thereof, at the upper corner of Ephraim Barker's donation; thence, with said Barker's line, due north, to his corner; and continuing the same course so far that a line therefrom, due east, thirteen chains and twenty-five links, and thence, due south, to the margin of said river, and thence down the same to the place of beginning, shall include one hundred and sixty acres. And the Board doth order that a certificate be granted to him accordingly.

JOHN DEASE's case: commenced in page 642.
On due consideration, the Board is of opinion that this claimant is entitled to a right of pre-emption to three hundred and twenty acres of land, to be located as follows:
Beginning on the southeast corner, on the east side of Bilbo's creek, and so far therefrom as to leave the mill dam and saw mill of the said Dease, which are now erected, in the centre of said tract; and thence, due west, fifty-six chains seventy links; thence, due north, fifty-six chains seventy links; thence, due east, fifty-six chains seventy links; thence, due south, fifty six chains seventy links, to the place of beginning. And the Board doth order that a certificate be granted to him accordingly.

HEIRS of EMANUEL CHENEY's case: commenced in page 660.
On due consideration, the Board is of opinion that the lawful heirs of the said Emanuel Cheney, deceased, are entitled to the right of pre-emption to two hundred and fifty-three acres of land, to be located as follows:
Beginning at a post oak, being the same described in their plot returned to the Register's Office as their beginning corner; thence, north, seventy-three degrees east, fifty-five chains; thence, north, fourteen degrees east, sixteen chains ten links; thence, north sixty-one degrees west, sixty chains sixteen links; thence, south, thirty-five degrees west, twenty-seven chains fifty links; thence, direct to the beginning. And the board doth order that a certificate be granted to them accordingly.

CHARLES CASSETER's case: commenced in page 664.
On due consideration, the Board is of opinion that this claimant is entitled to one hundred acres of land, to be located as follows:
Beginning at a hickory, being the same described in his plot returned to the Register's Office as his beginning corner; thence, north, forty-three degrees, east, thirty-one chains sixty links; thence south, forty-seven degrees east, thirty-one chains'sixty links; thence, south, forty-three degrees west, thirty-one chains sixty links; thence, north, forty-seven degrees west, thirty-one chains sixty links, to the beginning: Provided nevertheless, That the said claimant first obtain, before a court of competent jurisdiction, a judicial decision in his favor against the adverse claim, by virtue of a grant from the British Government of West Florida to Robert Farmar, bearing date the 6th of August, A. D. 1778. And the Board doth order that a certificate be granted to him accordingly.

JOHN HAWKINS's case: commenced in page 698.
On due consideration, the Board is of opinion that this claimant is entitled to a right of pre-emption to one hundred and fifty acres of land, to be located as follows:
Beginning at a willow, standing near two hickories, on the bank of Mobile river, being the southeast corner of Richard Barrow's donation claim; thence, westwardly, with said Barrow's line, till it strikes Barrow's creek; thence, down the margin of said creek and lake, so far that a due east line from thence, to the Mobile river shall include one hundred and fifty acres; to be bounded eastwardly by the west shore of the Mobile river, northwardly by Richard Barrow's south line, westwardly by the eastern shore of Barrow's creek and lake, and southwardly by a due east line drawn from said lake to the river Mobile. And the Board doth order that a certificate be granted to him accordingly.

SAMFORD McCLENDON's case: commenced in page 666.
On due consideration, the Board is of opinion that this claimant is entitled to a right of pre-emption to one hundred acres of land, to be located as follows:
Beginning at a post oak, being the same described in his plot returned to the Register's Office as his beginning corner; thence, south, seventy-one degrees west, thirty-seven chains eighty-six links; thence, south, twenty-two degrees west, twenty chains; thence, north,

seventeen degrees east, forty-seven chains fifty links; thence, direct to the beginning. And the Board doth order that a certificate be granted to him accordingly.

SIMON ANDREY's case: commenced in page 624.
On due consideration, the Board is of opinion that this claimant is entitled to a right of pre-emption to twenty four acres of land, to be located as follows:
Beginning at a stake, the corner of lands confirmed to Joseph Chastang, on the west bank of Mobile river; thence, running up the margin thereof, to the corner of lands confirmed to said Andrey, under the first section of the act; and thence, back with the courses of said Andrey and Chastang, so far as to include twenty-four acres. And the Board doth order that a certificate be granted to him accordingly.

JOHN GORDON's case: commenced in page 667.
On due consideration, the Board is of opinion that this claimant is entitled to a right of pre-emption to one hundred and thirteen acres of land, to be located as follows:
Beginning at a post oak, being the same described in his plot returned to the Register's Office as his beginning corner ; thence, south, five degrees east, thirty-three chains fifty links; thence, south, fifty-seven degrees east, eleven chains fifty-seven links; thence, north, eighty-five degrees east, twenty chains; thence, north, five degrees west, forty chains; and from thence to the beginning. And the Board doth order that a certificate be granted to him accordingly.

THOMAS GOODWIN, representative of Daniel Kennedy case commenced in page 704.
On due consideration, the Board is of opinion that this claimant is entitled to a right of pre-emption to three hundred and twenty acres of land, to be located as follows:
Beginning at the northeast corner of Thomas Goodwin's three hundred and twenty acre tract, claimed in the right of Hiram Mounger; thence, with the line of said tract, due south, to the northeast corner of Solomon Wheat's two hundred acre tract, and continuing the same course, forty-nine chains and fifty links in all; thence, due east, sixty-five chains; thence, due north, to Benjamin Harrison's southeast corner; thence, with said Harrison's line, due west, to the place of beginning. And the Board doth order that a certificate be granted to him accordingly.

WILLIAM GILLIAM, representative of John Clark: case commenced in page 649.
On due consideration, the Board is of opinion that this claimant is entitled to a right of pre-emption to one hundred and sixty acres of land, to be located as follows:
Beginning on the north side of a branch, which runs near to the present dwelling house of the claimant, at a pine, being his beginning corner mentioned in his plot entered in the Register's Office; thence, due south, forty chains; thence, due west, forty chains; thence, due north, forty chains; thence, due east, to the place of beginning. And the Board doth order that a certificate be granted to him accordingly.
Adjourned until Saturday the 9th instant.

SATURDAY, June 9, 1804.
The Board met according to adjournment. Present: Ephraim Kirby, Robert C. Nicholas, Joseph Chambers.
Adjourned until Tuesday, the 12th instant.

TUESDAY, June 12, 1804.
The Board met according to adjournment. Present: Ephraim Kirby, Robert C. Nicholas, Joseph Chambers.

RICHARD BRASHEAR, representative of Patrick Brewer: case commenced in page 601.
John Brewer, Esquire, and Solomon Wheat, were presented as witnesses, and, being duly sworn and interro} gated, they deposed, that they had no interest in this claim; that the said Brashear inhabited and cultivated on the land in question before the 3d day of March, 1803, on that day, and that he had continued to reside and cultivate thereon ever since.

SOLOMON WHEAT's case: commenced in page 601.
Jordan Morgan and Richard Brashear were presented as witnesses, and, being duly sworn and interrogated, they deposed, that they were not interested in this case; that Solomon Wheat inhabited and cultivated on the land in question on the 3d day of March, 1803, and had continued to inhabit and cultivate the same ever since.

The Board ordered that the case be postponed for consideration.

SOLOMON JOHNSON'S case: commenced in page 728.

John Brewer, Esquire, and Jordan Morgan, were presented as witnesses, and, being duly sworn and interrogated, they deposed, that they knew that Solomon Johnson inhabited and cultivated the land in question before and on the 3d day of March, 1803, and had continued to inhabit and cultivate thereon ever since; and that said Johnson; was, on said 3d day of March, more than twenty-one years of age, and a married man.

The Board ordered that the case be postponed for consideration.

JORDAN MORGAN'S case: commenced in page 649.

Richard Brashear and Solomon Wheat were presented as witnesses, and, being duly sworn and interrogated, they deposed, that they were not interested in this case.

The said Brashear further testified, that Jordan Morgan inhabited and cultivated on said land before and on the 3d day of March, 1803, and that the same land had been cultivated ever since by William H. Hargrave, Esquire, for account of said Morgan.

The said Wheat also testified, that he believed that Jordan Morgan inhabited and cultivated on said land before and on the 3d day of March, 1803; that he saw William H. Hargrave, Esquire, cultivating thereon in the summer of 1803.

The Board ordered that the case be postponed for consideration.

HEZEKIAH CARTER, representative of Robert Jones: case commenced in page 646.

Jordan Morgan and Thomas Wheat were presented as witnesses, and, being duly sworn and interrogated, they deposed, that they had no interest in this case; that said Carter inhabited and cultivated on the land in question before and on the 3d day of March, 1803, and had continued to inhabit and cultivate the same ever since; that said Carter was, on said 3d day of March, more than twenty one years of age.

The Board ordered that the case be postponed for consideration.

Adjourned until Friday, the 15th instant.

FRIDAY, June 15, 1804.
The Board met according to adjournment. Present: Ephraim Kirby, Robert C. Nicholas.
Adjourned until Monday, the 18th instant.

MONDAY, June 18, 1804.
The Board met according to adjournment. Present: Robert C. Nicholas.
Adjourned until Thursday, the 21st instant.

THURSDAY, June 21, 1804.
The Board met according to adjournment. Present: Ephraim Kirby, Robert C. Nicholas.
Adjourned until Saturday the 23d instant.

SATURDAY, June 23, 1804.
The Board met according to adjournment. Present: Ephraim Kirby, Robert C. Nicholas.

JOHN BREWER, representative of Charles Arbon Demoy: case commenced in page 626.

Richard Brashear and John Denley were presented as witnesses, and, being duly sworn and interrogated, they deposed, that they had no interest in this claim; that Charles Arbon Demoy resided on the land in question, superintending his business and laborers, in the year 1795, and fully believed that he continued there until after the 25th of October, 1795; that his principal residence was at Mobile, and on a plantation which he had below; but that he spent a part of his time every year at this place, where he had a black family; and, from particular circumstances, knew that he was here as above mentioned.

The Board ordered that the case be postponed for consideration.

Adjourned until Tuesday, the 26th instant.

TUESDAY, June 26, 1804.
The Board met according to adjournment. Present: Ephraim Kirby, Robert C. Nicholas.
Adjourned until Friday, the 29th instant.

FRIDAY, June 29, 1804.
The Board met according to adjournment. Present: Ephraim Kirby, Robert C. Nicholas, Joseph Chambers.

YOUNG GAINS, representative of Dominique de Olive: case commenced in page 622.

On due consideration, the Board is of opinion that this claim is supported agreeably to the requirements of law, and that the claimant is entitled to a patent for eight hundred acres of land, to be located as follows, to wit:

Beginning on the margin of the Tombigbee river, on the west side thereof, at the upper corner of George Brewer, Junior's eight hundred acre tract, claimed under Valentine Dubroca's Spanish warrant; thence, with said Brewer's line, due west, so far that a line therefrom, due north, sixty-three chains and twenty-five links, and thence, due west, to the margin of said river, and thence, down the same, with the meanders thereof, to the place of beginning, shall include eight hundred acres. And the Board doth order that a certificate be granted to him accordingly.

THOMAS MALONE, representative of John Arnot: case commenced in page 703.

On due consideration, the Board is of opinion that this claim is supported agreeably to the requirements of law, and that the claimant is entitled to a patent for four hundred and eighty acres, to be located as follows, to wit:

Beginning on the west bank of the Tombigbee river, at the upper corner of George Brewer, Junior's, six hundred and twenty-nine acre donation tract, in his own right; thence, up the margin of said river, so far as to make thirty-seven chains and twenty links, on a due west line; thence, due south, so far that a due east line therefrom, thirty-seven chains and twenty links, to George Brewer, Junior's, line, and thence, with the same, due north, to the place of beginning, shall include four hundred and eighty acres. And the Board doth order that a certificate be granted to him accordingly.

JOHN CHASTANG'S case: commenced in page 614.

On due consideration, the Board is of opinion that this claim is supported agreeably to the requirements of law, and that the claimant is entitled to one thousand nine hundred and thirty-eight acres of land, to be located on the west side of the west channel of the Mobile river, as follows, to wit:

Beginning at the mouth of Groghall creek, on the north side thereof, and thence, running up the west margin of the Mobile river, to the mouth of Cedar creek; and thence, extending westwardly, upon the south margin of said creek, and due west from the mouth of Groghall creek, so far that a due north and south line, drawn between the extreme western points of said lines, shall include one thousand nine hundred and thirty-eight acres. And, also, on the east side of said west channel of Mobile river, beginning opposite to the mouth of Groghall creek; thence, due east, eleven chains; thence, northwardly, up said river, pursuing the meanders thereof, at the distance of eleven chains from the east margin thereof, to a point, directly opposite to the mouth of Cedar creek, and due east therefrom; and thence, due west, eleven chains, to the river. And the Board doth order that a certificate be granted to him accordingly.

GEORGE BREWER, representative of Valentine Dubroca: case commenced in page 625.

On due consideration, the Board is of opinion that this claim is supported agreeably to the requirements of law, and that the claimant is entitled to a patent for eight hundred acres of land, to be located as follows, to wit:

Beginning on the margin of the Tombigbee river, on the west side thereof, at the upper corner of John Brewer's eight hundred acre tract, claimed under Charles Arbon Demoy; thence, with said Brewer's line, due west, so far that a line therefrom, due north, sixty-three chains twenty-five links, and thence, due east, to the margin of said river, and thence, down the same, with the meanders thereof, to the place of beginning, shall include eight hundred acres. And the Board doth order that a certificate be granted to him accordingly.

JOHN BREWER, representative of Charles Arbon Demoy: case commenced in page 626.

On due consideration, the Board is of opinion that this claim is supported agreeably to the requirements of law, and that the claimant is entitled to a patent for eight hundred acres of land, to be located as follows, to wit:

Beginning on the west margin of the Tombigbee river, at the upper corner of James Denley's one thousand acre tract, claimed under Daniel Ward's Spanish warrant; thence, with the line of said James Denley, due west, one hundred and four chains; thence, due north, so far that a line therefrom due east, to the margin of said river, and down the same to the place of beginning, shall include eight hundred acres. And the Board doth order that a certificate be granted to him accordingly.

JOSEPH CHASTANG'S case: commenced in page 650.

On due consideration, the Board is of opinion that this claim is supported agreeably to the requirements of law, and that the claimant is entitled to a patent for six hundred and forty acres of land, to be located as follows, to wit:

Beginning at a stake at Simon Andry's fence, on the bank of the river Mobile; thence, down the west margin of said river, so far as to make fifty-one chains in a due south line; thence, south, sixty-four degrees west, so far that a line therefrom, due north shall strike the southwest corner of John Baptist Trennier's three hundred and twenty-seven acre tract; thence, with the line of tract, north, fifty-one degrees east, to the southwest corner of Simon Andry's twenty-four acre pre-emption tract; thence, with the line of said tract, to the place of beginning. And the Board doth order that a certificate be granted to him accordingly.

RICHARD BRASHEAR, representative of Patrick Brewer: case commenced in page 601.

On due consideration, the Board is of opinion that this claim is not supported; but that, upon the evidence exhibited, the said Richard Brashear is entitled, under the third section of said act, to a right of pre-emption to six hundred and forty acres of land, to be located as follows, to wit:

Beginning on Hiram Mounger's line, at the southwest corner of William H. Hargrave's three hundred and twenty acre pre-emption, in the right of Stephen Williams; thence, with said Mounger's line, due west, to his northwest corner and in the same course, seventy-one chains; thence, due north, ninety chains; thence, due east, seventy-one chains, to said Hargrave's line; and thence, with the line of said Hargrave, due south, to the place of beginning. And the Board doth order that a certificate be granted accordingly.

JAMES CALLIER, representative of Joseph Anderson: case commenced in page 607.

On due consideration, the Board is of opinion that this claim is not supported; but that, upon the evidence exhibited, the said James Callier is entitled, under the third section of said act, to a right of pre-emption to six hundred and forty acres of land, to be located as follows, to wit:

Beginning on the west bank of the Tombigbee river, at the southeast corner of Thomas Carson's donation; and thence, with said Carson's lower line, south, eighty-six degrees west, one hundred and sixty chains; thence, south, eleven degrees east, forty chains; thence, north, eighty-six degrees east, to the west margin of the river Tombigbee; thence, up the margin of said river, to the place of beginning. And the Board doth order that a certificate be granted to him accordingly.

JAMES CALLIER, representative of Isabella Trouillet: case commenced in page 650.

On due consideration, the Board is of opinion that this claim is not supported; but that, upon the evidence exhibited, the said James Callier is entitled, under the third section of said act, to a right of pre-emption to six hundred and forty acres of land, to be located as follows, to wit:

Beginning on the west bank of the river Mobile, on the bluff near where Alexis Trouillet now lives, so that a due west line therefrom will leave said house twenty-five links on the south side of said line; thence, running due west eighty chains, or one mile, and thence, due south, so far that a due east line therefrom to the west bank of the sluice, or bayou, which puts out from the Mobile below Fort Stoddert, and thence, up the margin of said bayou and river, to the place of beginning, shall include six hundred and forty acres, exclusive of one half of an acre fronting on the river bank, where the cotton house now stands, and extending back so as to leave said house as nearly central as may be, which said half acre is reserved for the future use and disposition of the United States. And the Board doth order that a certificate be granted to him accordingly.

JORDAN MORGAN'S case: commenced in page 649.

On due consideration, the Board is of opinion that this claim is not supported; but that, upon the evidence exhibited, the claimant is entitled, under the third section of said act, to a right of pre-emption, to six hundred and forty acres of land, to be located as follows, to wit:

Beginning on the west margin of the Tombigbee river, at a sassafras, at the mouth of Steep Gut, being the place called Ward's old corner, and is also the northeast corner of Nicholas Perkins's three hundred and six acre tract, claimed under Thomas Wheat's Spanish warrant, and the southeast corner of James Denley's one thousand acre tract, claimed under Daniel Ward's Spanish warrant; thence with said Denley's line, due west, one hundred and twenty-six chains forty-nine links; thence, due south, so far that a due east line therefrom to the line of said Perkins above mentioned, and thence, with said Perkins's line, to the place of beginning, shall include six hundred and forty acres. And the Board doth order that a certificate be granted accordingly.

SOLOMON WHEAT'S case: commenced in page 601.

On due consideration, the Board is of opinion that this claim is not supported; but that, upon the evidence exhibited, the claimant is entitled, under the third section of said act, to a right of pre-emption to two hundred acres of land, to be located as follows, to wit:

Beginning at the northeast corner of James Scott's three hundred and twenty acre tract; thence, with the line thereof, due west, fifty chains; thence, due north, forty chains; thence, due east, fifty chains; thence, due south, to the place of beginning. And the Board doth order that a certificate be granted to him accordingly.

SOLOMON JOHNSON'S case: commenced in page 726.

On due consideration, the Board is of opinion that this claim is not supported, but that, upon the evidence exhibited, the claimant is entitled, under the third section of the act, to a right of pre-emption to one hundred acres of land, to be located as follows, to wit:

Beginning at the northeast corner on the north side of a branch of Johnson's creek, so far from the present dwelling house of the said Johnson, as to leave his said dwelling house in the centre of said tract; thence, due south, thirty-one chains seventy-five links; thence, due west, thirty-one chains, seventy-five links; thence, due north, thirty-one chains seventy-five links, thence, due east to the place of beginning, containing one hundred acres. And the Board doth order that a certificate be granted to him accordingly.

HEZEKIAH CARTER, representative of Robert Jones: case commenced in page 646.

On due consideration, the Board is of opinion that this claim is not supported; but that, upon the evidence exhibited, the claimant is entitled, under the third section of the act, to a right of pre-emption to three hundred and twenty acres of land, to be located as follows, to wit:

Beginning at the northeast corner of Hardy Wootton's six hundred and fifteen acre donation, in the right of William Hunt; thence, with said Wootton's line, due west, eighty chains; thence, due north, forty chains; thence, due east, eighty chains; thence, due south, to the place of beginning. And the Board doth order that a certificate be granted to him accordingly.

Adjourned until Tuesday, the 3d instant.

TUESDAY, *July* 3, 1804.

The Board met according to adjournment. Present: Ephraim Kirby, Robert C. Nicholas, Joseph Chambers.

JOHN BAPTIST TRENNIER'S case: commenced in page 720.

On due consideration, the Board is of opinion that this claim is supported agreeably to the requirements of law, and that the claimant is entitled to a patent for one thousand acres, to be located in the following manner, to wit:

Beginning on the east bank of the west channel of the Mobile river, opposite to the mouth of Groghall creek, at the lower corner of land confirmed to Doctor John Chastang, then running down the margin of said river, so far as to make seventy-nine chains in a straight line; thence, due east, so far that a line drawn from the extreme point of this line to the east point of a line due east, from the place of beginning, shall include one thousand acres. *Provided, nevertheless,* That this tract shall not extend down the river so far as to interfere with the lines of the land confirmed to Simon Andrey. And the Board doth order that a certificate be issued to him, the said claimant, accordingly.

SIMON ANDREY'S case: commenced in page 721.

On due consideration, the Board is of opinion that this claim is supported agreeably to the requirements of law, and that the claimant is entitled to a patent for forty-eight acres of land, to be located in the following manner, to wit:

Beginning at a stake on the east bank of the west channel of the Mobile river, at the place where the plot returned by this claimant to the Register commences; and thence, following down the east margin of said river, one hundred and one chains and twenty links; thence, east, so far that a corresponding line with the margin of said river, to a point due east from the place of beginning, shall include forty-eight acres. And the Board doth order that a certificate be granted to him accordingly.

WILLIAM COLEMAN, representative of Simon Favre: case commenced in page 654.

On due consideration, the Board is of opinion that this claim is not supported agreeably to the requirements of law, and the claimant is not entitled to a patent for the land by him claimed, in the manner and form aforesaid.

YOUNG GAINS's case: commenced in page 621.

On due consideration, the Board is of opinion that this claim is not supported agreeably to the requirements of law, and the claimant is not entitled to a patent for the land by him claimed, in the manner and form aforesaid.

Adjourned until Friday, the 6th instant.

FRIDAY, July 6, 1804.
The Board met according to adjournment. Present: Ephraim Kirby, Robert C. Nicholas, Joseph Chambers.
Adjourned until Monday, the 9th instant.

MONDAY, July 9, 1804.
The Board met according to adjournment. Present: Ephraim Kirby, Robert C. Nicholas.
Adjourned until Thursday, the 12th instant.

THURSDAY, July 12, 1804.
The Board met according to adjournment. Present: Robert C. Nicholas.
Adjourned until Saturday, the 14th instant.

SATURDAY, July 14, 1804.
The Board met according to adjournment. Present: Ephraim Kirby, Robert C. Nicholas.
Adjourned until Monday, the 16th instant.

MONDAY, July 16, 1804.
The Board met according to adjournment. Present: Ephraim Kirby, Robert C. Nicholas.

EDWARD LLOYD WAILES, representative of John Baker: case commenced in page 701.

Joseph Westmoreland and Elijah Simmons were presented as witnesses, and, being duly sworn, they deposed, that they were acquainted with the hand writing of Pleasant Rose, and having inspected two papers then before the Board of Commissioners, the one purporting to be an agreement made by said Rose with John Baker, respecting the possession and occupancy of the land in question, dated the 16th day of September, 1802, and the other a receipt to said Baker for one hundred dollars, in satisfaction for improvements made on said land, dated June 20, 1803, that they verily believed that the name of Pleasant Rose, subscribed to said papers, was written by said Rose, and that the same was his genuine signature; that Emanuel Cheney, one of the subscribing witnesses to said writings, was dead, and that William Brewer, the other subscribing witness, did not reside within this territory. The said Westmoreland further testified, that since he gave his former testimony in this case, he had recollected several circumstances, from which he was fully convinced that the said Pleasant Rose was in the occupancy and possession of the land in question after the 3d of March, 1803, as well as before that time; that he verily believed that said Rose resided there on said 3d of March.

On due consideration, the Board is of opinion that this claimant is entitled to a right of pre-emption to six hundred and forty acres of land, to be located as follows, to wit:

Beginning at the northeast corner of James Griffin's six hundred and eighteen acre donation tract, on the line of John Chastang: thence, with said line, due north, eighty chains; thence, due west, eighty chains; thence, due south, eighty chains; thence, due east, eighty chains, to the place of beginning; and the board doth order that a certificate be granted to him accordingly.

SOLOMON JOHNSON's case, No. 188 on the docket of the Board, and No. 30 on the books of the Register.

Claim.—A donation of six hundred and forty acres, under the second section of the act.

The claimant presented his claim, together with a surveyor's plot of the land claimed, in the words and figures, following, viz.:

To the Commissioners appointed in pursuance of the act of Congress passed the 3d day of March, 1803, for receiving and adjusting the claims to lands south of Tennessee and east of Pearl river.

Please to take notice, that the following tract of land, situated on the waters of Johnson's creek, in the county of Washington, beginning at a white oak, and running south, fifty degrees west, fifty-five chains, to a red oak; thence, south, thirty-three degrees west, forty-five chains, to a pine; thence north eighty-three degrees west, sixty-five chains, to a dogwood; thence, north, seventy degrees west, eighty-two chains, to a pine; thence, with Johnson's creek, to the beginning; containing six hundred and forty acres, having such shape, form and marks, both natural and artificial, as are fully represented in the plot annexed: is claimed by Solomon Johnson, in and by virtue of the second section of said act, as a donation, and is now exhibited to the Register of the Land Office east of Pearl river, to be recorded as directed by said act. To all which he begs leave to refer, as also to the copy of the plot herewith filed.

SOLOMON JOHNSON, his ⋈ mark.
MARCH 13, 1804.
[Plot omitted.]

Entered in record of claims, vol. 1, page 81, by EDWARD LLOYD WAILES, for
JOSEPH CHAMBERS, Register.

The foregoing notice and plot ought to have been entered in vol. 2, page 518.

HOBUCKINTOOPA, WEDNESDAY, May 1, 1805.
The Board of Commissioners convened at this place. Present: Robert C. Nicholas, Joseph Chambers.

NICHOLAS WEEKS, executor of Dominique de Olive; case No. 189 on the docket of the Board, and No. 2 on the books of the Register.

Claim.—Of eleven hundred and ninety-nine acres and six tenths of an acre, by virtue of a Spanish warrant of survey, under the first section of the act.

The claimant presented his claim, together with a surveyor's plot of the land claimed, in the words and figures following, to wit:

To the Commissioners appointed in pursuance of the act of Congress passed the 3d day of March, 1803, for receiving and adjusting claims to lands south of the river Tennessee, and east of Pearl river.

Please to take notice, that the following tract of land, situated on the east side of the Mobile river, in Washington county, beginning at a gum, and running thence, south, sixty-two degrees east, one hundred and thirty-six chains and thirty-nine links, to a stake; thence, north, eight degrees east, ninety-four chains eighty links, to a stake; thence, south, sixty-two degrees east, one hundred and thirty-six chains thirty-nine links, to a beech; thence, with the river, to the beginning; containing one thousand one hundred and ninety-nine acres and six-tenths of an acre, having such shape, forms, and marks, both natural and artificial, as are represented in the plot annexed: which said tract of land is claimed by Nicholas Weeks, executor of Dominique de Olive, in and by virtue of a Spanish warrant of survey, and is now exhibited to the Register of the Land Office east of Pearl river, to be recorded as directed by said act. To all which he begs leave to refer, as also to a copy of a plot herewith filed.

NICHOLAS WEEKS,
One of the Executors of Dominique de Olive.
MARCH 10, 1804.
[Plot omitted.]

Surveyed March 8, 1804, by James Gordon. Chain bearers, William Weathers, John Burgess.

In support of this claim a Spanish warrant was exhibited in the words and figures following, to wit:

MOBILE, December 6, 1793.
To his Excellency the Governor General of these provinces:

Dominique de Olive, an old inhabitant of this place, with the most profound respect due to your excellency, lays before you, that, at the end of the year 1791, or a[t] the commencement of 1792, he solicited, through the means of the commandant of Mobile, at that epoch, a cession of land of thirty acres front, with the ordinary depth of forty, bounded on the north with a tract belonging to M. Narcis Broutan, and on the south by another belonging to M. Augustin Rochon, the same that was then found vacant, having no proprietor; the aforesaid commandant knowing this, permitted him to clear, labor, and cultivate the land, it being so that it is more than five years ago since he possessed it, gathering therefrom his victuals, without any one appearing to reclaim it; and having solicited the copy of the original cession, it was not to be found in the archives of this place, therefore he humbly begs of your excellency to grant him another cession of the same tract for security at all times, for which he will be forever thankful.

DOMINIQUE DE OLIVE.

MOBILE, *December* 6, 1794.
To his Excellency the Governor General of these provinces:
There is no doubt remains with me in what the petitioner relates to your excellency; but, in order to be more certain, I listened to other old inhabitants of probity, who have assured me of the same, and the original document could have been very easily mislaid in these archives, and it seems to me that no prejudice will occur by granting another cession; but your excellency's benevolence will dispose of it for the best.

MANUEL DE LANZOS.

NEW ORLEANS, *December* 26, 1794.
The Surveyor General of this province, or the person named for this purpose, will settle the above named petitioner upon the thirty acres of land in front that he solicits, with the ordinary depth of forty acres, in the place that the preceding memorial describes, being vacant, and not causing any prejudice to the neighbors, with the precise conditions of making the road, and clearing regularly, in the peremptory space of one year; and if, at the precise space of three years, the land is not settled, (during which period it cannot be alienated,) this grant to remain null; under which supposition, the business of settling the limits will be carried on in the tract, and remitted me, to provide the interested party with titles in form.

BARON DE CARONDELET.

MOBILE, *January* 10, 1804.
Copy of the original grant that remains in the archives of this place commanded by me, the which I certify.

JOAQUIN DE OSORNO. [L. S.]

I, Thomas Price, of the post of Mobile, English interpreter for his Majesty the King of Spain, do solemnly swear by the Almighty God, and by the Holy Cross, that this is a true and faithful translation of the Spanish grant or writing hereto annexed.

THOMAS PRICE.

Subscribed and sworn before the Board, March 20, 1804.—Attest: DAVID PARMELEE 2d, *Clerk.*
Entered in record of claims, (east side of Tombigbee,) vol. 1, page 6, by EDWARD LLOYD WAILES, for
JOSEPH CHAMBERS, *Register.*
The Board ordered that the case be postponed for consideration.
Adjourned until Saturday, the 4th instant.

SATURDAY, *May* 4, 1805.
The Board met according to adjournment. Present: Robert C. Nicholas, Joseph Chambers.
Adjourned until Monday, the 6th instant.

MONDAY, *May* 6, 1805.
The Board met according to adjournment. Present: Robert C. Nicholas, Joseph Chambers.

BENJAMIN FEW's case, No. 190 on the docket of the Board, and No. 84 on the books of the Register.
Claim.—A right of pre-emption of six hundred and forty acres, under the third section of the act.
The claimant presented his claim, together with a surveyor's plot of the land claimed, in the words and figures following, to wit:
To the Commissioners appointed to settle and adjust claims to lands south of Tennessee, and east of the Pearl river.
GENTLEMEN:
The annexed plot represents a tract of land situated on the east of the Mobile river, about one mile below the forks of the Alabama and Tombigbee rivers, contain-

ing six hundred and four acres; is claimed by the subscriber in virtue of the third section of the act of Congress, passed the 3d day of March, 1803, which plot is now delivered to the Register of the Land Office, to be recorded agreeably to the aforesaid act of Congress. To all which he begs leave to refer.

BENJAMIN FEW.

Surveyed March 23, 1804, by John Milliken. Chain bearers, John Airs and David Williams.
Entered in record of claims, (east side,) vol. 1, page —, by EDWARD LLOYD WAILES, for
JOSEPH CHAMBERS, *Register.*
The above named chain bearers were sworn before James Callier, Justice of the Peace.
Natt Christmas was presented as a witness, and, being duly sworn, deposed, that some time in January, 1802, Benjamin Few came to his house with his negroes from Georgia; that he (Christmas) was confident that Few built, inhabited and cultivated on the land claimed, in the said month of January, and that he had inhabited and cultivated on said land ever since, by his negroes and overseers, until January or February last, when his negroes and overseers removed therefrom for a short time; that they soon afterwards returned to the improvement and cultivation thereof, that he believed Few was in the actual habitation and cultivation thereof on the 3d day of March, 1803; and that said Benjamin Few was, on the said 3d day of March, more than twenty-one years of age; that he had heard that said land was claimed in virtue of a Spanish warrant of survey, granted to Dominique de Olive, but that he had never seen said warrant.
The Board ordered that the case be postponed for consideration.
Adjourned until Thursday, the 9th instant.

THURSDAY, *May* 9, 1805.
The Board met pursuant to adjournment. Present: Robert C. Nicholas, Joseph Chambers.
Adjourned until Saturday, the 11th instant.

SATURDAY, *May* 11, 1805.
The Board met according to adjournment. Present: Robert C. Nicholas, Joseph Chambers.

NICHOLAS WEEKS, executor of Dominique de Olive: case commenced on page 728.
John Baker and Gabriel Tisrah were presented as witnesses, and, being duly sworn, the said Baker deposed, that in the year 1795, and for several years before and after, Dominique de Olive cultivated on the land in question; that he resided on said land in the summer season, and at Mobile, with his family in the winter; that he left a negro or two, on the plantation in the seasons of winter, and took therefrom his other negroes, as was customary among French planters, during the winter months; that on the 26th day of December, 1794, Dominique de Olive was more than twenty-one years of age.
The said Tisrah deposed, that Dominique de Olive cultivated and lived, in the summer season, on the land in question, in the year 1795, and continued thereon, with about ten negroes, until after Fort Stoddert was built; that he was an old man on the 26th of December, 1794, and the head of a family.
The Board ordered, that the case be postponed for consideration.
Adjourned until Monday, the 13th instant.

MONDAY, *May* 13, 1805.
The Board met according to adjournment. Present: Robert C. Nicholas, Joseph Chambers.

JOSEPH THOMPSON, representative of Adam Hollinger; case, No. 191 on the docket of the Board, and No. 6 on the books of the Register.
Claim.—A right to seven hundred and thirty acres, by virtue of a Spanish warrant of survey, under the first section of the act.
The claimant presented his claim, together with a surveyor's plot of the land claimed, in the words and figures following, viz.:
To the Commissioners appointed in pursuance of the act of Congress passed the 3d day of March, 1803, for receiving and adjusting claims to land south of the Tennessee, and east of Pearl river.
Please to take notice, that the following tract of land, situated on the east of the Tombigbee, fronting on the Alabama river, in the county of Washington, beginning on the Alabama river, on John Randon's line, running south, twenty-three degrees east, seventeen chains,

to a cypress; thence, south, fifty-six degrees west, eleven chains, George Weekley's corner, which is a cotton tree; thence, south, thirty-seven degrees west, five chains, to a stake, on Weekley's line; south, fifty-six degrees west, thirty-six chains to a gum corner; thence due west, with Phillips's line, ninety chains, to a stake; thence, north, five degrees west, seventy-seven chains, to Mimms's line, to a stake; thence, south, seventy degrees east, seventy chains fifty links to a sassafras corner; thence, with the river to the beginning; and bath such forms and marks, both natural and artificial, as are fully represented in the plot annexed, containing seven hundred and thirty acres: is claimed by Joseph Thompson, legal representative of Adam Hollinger, in and by virtue of a Spanish warrant and survey, and is now exhibited to the Register of the Land Office, established east of Pearl river, to be recorded as directed by said act. To all which he begs leave to refer, as also to a copy of the plot herewith filed.

JOSEPH THOMPSON,
Legal representative of Adam Hollinger.
MARCH 26, 1804.
[Plot omitted.]

Surveyed March 24, 1804, by John Milliken. Sworn chain bearers, James McConnell and William Thomas. In support of this claim, a Spanish warrant of survey was exhibited in the words and figures following, to wit:

His Excellency Don ESTEVAN MIRO, Colonel of the Royal Army, Governor civil and military of the city and province of Louisiana, &c.

Adam Hollinger, inhabitant of Mobile jurisdiction, with the greatest respect to your excellency, represents and says, there is found on Tensaw river, twenty acres of land, on an island by the name of Nanna Hubba; the said land until now never had any proprietor: he begs your excellency to grant him the above petition, with papers of titles necessary, from the Secretary of Government, which may correspond with the concession, for which favor he will be forever thankful.

ADAM HOLLINGER.
MOBILE, *October* 10, 1787.

Don Vicent Folch, captain of the Louisiana regiment of infantry, commandant civil and military of the place of Mobile, and its district, certifies, that the land the petitioner solicits is vacant, by information from the different inhabitants, who are knowing to the said place of land, above mentioned. Mobile, the day and date above mentioned.

VICENT FOLCH.

NEW ORLEANS, *October* 22, 1787.
The Surveyor General of this province, Don Carlos Laveau Tredeau, shall establish that part of land of twenty acres front, with its profounder of forty acres, as customary, as it is vacant, not causing any prejudice to any neighbors, at the same place mentioned in the above petition, with the precise conditions of making the road and clearing regularly, in the peremptory space of one year; and if, at the precise space of three years, the land is not settled, during which period it cannot be alienated, this grant to remain null; under which supposition the business of settling the limits will be carried on in the tract, and remitted to me to provide the interested party with titles in form.

ESTEVAN MIRO.

MOBILE, *November* 29, 1787.
Certified that the above is a true copy of the original in the office of this place.
SANTIAGO DE LA SAUSSAYE,
Notary Public.
The above is a copy of the Spanish grant.
THOMAS PRICE.
The above was compared exact with the original in this office under my charge, by me,
JOAQN. DE OSORNO. [L. S.]

I, Thomas Price, of the post of Mobile, English interpreter to His Majesty the King of Spain, do solemnly swear by the Almighty God, and by the Holy Cross, that this is a true translation of the Spanish grant or writing hereto annexed.

THOMAS PRICE.
Subscribed and sworn, before the Board, March 21, 1804.—Attest: DAVID PARMELEE 2d, *Clerk.*
Entered in record of claims, (east of Tombigbee,) vol. 1, page 30, by EDWARD LLOYD WAILES, for
JOSEPH CHAMBERS, *Register.*

William Pierce and John Mills were presented as witnesses, and, being duly sworn, they deposed, that the land now claimed was cultivated by Joseph Thompson, the present claimant, on the 27th day of October, 1795, who had continued to cultivate the same ever since; that, in consequence of the said land being situated in an island, and being occasionally covered by the water, it was an improper and unhealthy situation for a dwelling-house; that the principal cultivation made by said Thompson, for the support of himself and family, had been on the land in question.

Question. Was Adam Hollinger on the 22d of October, 1787, twenty-one years of age?
Answer. Adam Hollinger was, on the 22d of October, 1787, as they believed, more than twenty-one years of age.
Question. Are you, or either of you, interested, or to be interested, in the establishment of this claim?
Answer. We are not.

On the back of the said Spanish warrant of survey is an endorsement in the words and figures following, to wit:

FORT STODDERT, *March* 26, 1804.
For a valuable consideration, I hereby assign and make over to Joseph Thompson, Esquire, all my right, title, interest, and claim, of and unto the within Spanish warrant of survey, to him, his heirs and assigns, forever In witness whereof I hereunto set my hand and seal, the day and year above written.
ADAM HOLLINGER, his × mark.
Witness, EDWARD LLOYD WAILES.

The Board ordered that the case be postponed for consideration.

JOSEPH THOMPSON's case, No. 192 on the docket of the Board, and No. 78 on the books of the Register.

Claim.—A donation of six hundred and forty acres, under the second section of the act.

The claimant presented his claim, together with a surveyor's plot of the land claimed, in the words and figures following, viz.:

To the Commissioners appointed in pursuance of the act of Congress passed the 3d day of March, 1803, for receiving and adjusting claims to land south of Tennessee, and east of Pearl river.

Please to take notice, that the following tract of land, situated on the east side of the Alabama river on Hollow creek, adjoining Samuel Mimms on the south, and James Randon on the north, containing six hundred and forty acres: is claimed by Joseph Thompson, in and by virtue of the second section of said act, as a donation, and is now exhibited to the Register of the Land Office established east of Pearl river, to be recorded as directed by said act. To all which he begs leave to refer, as also to a copy of the plot herewith filed.

WILLIAM PIERCE, for
JOSEPH THOMPSON.
APRIL 30, 1805.
[Plot omitted.]

Surveyed 29th April, 1804, by J. Milliken.
Entered in record of claims, (east side,) vol. 1, page—
JOSEPH CHAMBERS, *Register.*

John Mills and William Pierce were presented as witnesses, and, being duly sworn and interrogated by the Board, they deposed, that they were not interested in this claim; that Joseph Thompson, the claimant, did inhabit and cultivate the land in question, in the year 1797, long before, and ever since that time, viz.: that he had been in the continual occupation and cultivation thereof, in and about fourteen years last past, and that the said Joseph Thompson was, in the year 1797, more than twenty-one years of age, and the head of a family. The Board ordered that the case be postponed for consideration.

WILLIAM PIERCE and JOHN PIERCE; case No. 193 on the docket of the Board, and No. 82 on the books of the Register.

Claim.—A donation of six hundred and forty acres, as representatives of Jeremiah Phillips, under the second section of the act.

The claimants presented their claim, together with a surveyor's plot of the land claimed, in the words and figures following, to wit:

To the Commissioners appointed in pursuance of the act of Congress, passed the 3d day of March, 1803, for receiving and adjusting claims to land south of Tennessee and east of Pearl river.

Please to take notice, that the following tract of land, situate on the east side of the river Tombigbee, in the county of Washington, beginning at the Alabama river, running north, thirty degrees west, sixty chains, to a gun; west, twenty-eight chains; south, twelve degrees east, one hundred and twenty-five chains; and hath such forms and marks, both natural and artificial, as are represented in the plot annexed, containing six hundred and forty acres: is claimed by William and John Pierce, in and by virtue of a donation, and is now exhibited to the Register of the Land Office established east of Pearl river, to be recorded as directed by said act. To all which they beg leave to refer, as also to a copy of the plot herewith filed.

April 29, 1805.   W. & JOHN PIERCE.

[Plot omitted.]

Surveyed by J. Milliken.

Entered in record of claims, (east side,) vol. 1, page —.

JOSEPH CHAMBERS, *Register.*

The claimants exhibited a deed of conveyance from Jeremiah Phillips, bearing date the 27th of April, 1805, duly executed and duly proven, conveying to William and John Pierce, all his the said Philips's right, title, and claim to said tract of land, and the improvements thereon made.

John Mills and George Weekley were presented as witnesses, and being duly sworn and interrogated by the Board, they deposed that they were not interested in this claim; that the land in question was situated in Nanna Hubba island; that it could not be inhabited, by reason of its being frequently covered with water, and that the said land was actually cultivated, by the said Jeremiah Phillips, in the year 1797; that he was at that time twenty-one years of age, and the head of a family.

The Board ordered that the case be postponed for consideration.

John Mills's case, No. 194 on the docket of the Board, and No. 30 on the books of the Register.

Claim.—A donation of three hundred and fifty-five acres, under the second section of the act.

The claimant presented his claim, together with a surveyor's plot of the land claimed, in the words and figures following, to wit:

To the Commissioners appointed in pursuance of a n *act of Congress, passed the 3d day of March, 1803, for receiving and adjusting claims to lands south of the Tennessee river, and east of Pearl river.*

Please to take notice, that the following tract of land, situated on the east side of Tombigbee in Nanna Hubba island, in the county of Washington, beginning at two willows, thence, up the Alabama river, north, twenty-one degrees west, to three cotton trees; thence, across said island, south, thirty degrees to a corner maple, on said river; thence, down said river, to the beginning, south, fifty-five degrees east; containing three hundred and fifty five acres, having such shape, form, and marks, both natural and artificial, as are represented in the plot annexed: is claimed by John Mills, in and by virtue of the second section of this act, as a donation, and is now exhibited to the Register of the Land Office, to be recorded as directed by said act. To all which he begs leave to refer, as also to a copy of the plot herewith filed.

JOHN MILLS.

March 26, 1804.

[Plot omitted.]

Surveyed February 13, 1804, by John Milliken. Chain bearers, James Mills and Francis Killingworth.

Entered in record of claims, (east side,) vol. 1, page 106, by Edward Lloyd Wailes, for

JOSEPH CHAMBERS, *Register.*

Joseph Thompson and Moses Stedham were presented as witnesses, and, being duly sworn and interrogated by the Board, they deposed, that they were not interested in this claim; that John Mills, the present claimant, cultivated the land in question in the year 1797, and had continued in the occupancy and cultivation thereof ever since; that they believed that the said Mills was, in the year 1797, more than twenty-one years of age, and that he was the head of a family.

The Board ordered that the case be postponed for consideration.

Francis Killingworth, representative of William Mills: case No. 195 on the docket of the Board, and No. 38 on the books of the Register.

Claim.—A donation of six hundred and forty acres, under the second section of the act.

The claimant presented his claim, together with a surveyor's plot of the land claimed, in the words and figures following, to wit:

To the Commissioners appointed in pursuance of the act of Congress passed the 3d day of March, 1803, for receiving and adjusting claims to lands south of Tennessee, and east of Pearl river.

Please to take notice, that the following tract of land, situated on the east side of Tombigbee and Alabama rivers, in the county of Washington, beginning on a pine corner; running thence, south, seventy-five degrees east, nine chains; thence, north, twenty degrees east, twenty-four chains, to a pine corner; thence, north, seventy-five degrees east, eighty-two chains, to a pine corner; thence, south fifteen degrees, east, sixty-four chains, to a stake corner; thence, south, seventy-five degrees west, one hundred and five chains, to a stake corner; thence, to the beginning; and hath such shape, forms and marks, both natural and artificial, as are fully represented in the plot annexed, containing six hundred and forty acres: is claimed by Francis Killingworth, legal representative of William Mills, in and by virtue of the second section of this act, as a donation, purchased of said William Mills, and is now exhibited to the Register of the Land Office established east of Pearl river, to be recorded as directed by said act. To all which he begs leave to refer, as also to a copy of the plot herewith filed.

FRANCIS KILLINGWORTH.

March 26, 1804,

[Plot omitted.]

Surveyed February 15, 1804, by John Milliken. Chain bearers, James Mills and William McDaniel.

Entered in record of claims, (east of Tombigbee,) vol. 1, page 111, by Edward Lloyd Wailes, for

JOSEPH CHAMBERS, *Register.*

In support of this claim, the last will and testament of Thomas Hudson, deceased, was exhibited, bearing date the 25th day of February, 1800, duly executed and proven; in and by which the said Hudson devised and bequeathed to Sarah Hall, (the daughter of Charles Hall,) all his estate, both real and personal, "by her freely to be possessed and enjoyed."

A certificate was also exhibited, in the following words, to wit:

I do hereby certify that I joined in matrimony William Mills and Sarah Hall, agreeable to the laws of this territory. Given under my hand, 17th March, 1800.

JAMES THOMPSON, *J. P.*

A writing in the words following was also exhibited, viz.:

This obligation witnesseth, that I have this day bargained and sold a certain tract of land formerly the property of Thomas Hudson, deceased, and now the property of William and Sarah Mills, to Francis Killingworth, for the sum of two hundred dollars; and I do further obligate myself to quit claim of the said land for the two hundred dollars. As witness my hand, this 4th day of February, 1804.

WILLIAM MILLS.

Witness, John Mills.

Joseph Thompson and John Mills were presented as witnesses, and, being duly sworn and interrogated by the Board, they deposed, that they were not interested in this claim; that the land now claimed by Francis Killingworth was inhabited and cultivated in the year 1797, by Thomas Hudson; and that said Hudson was, in the year 1797, more than twenty-one years of age; that the same Francis Killingworth, in whose name this claim is filed, was dead.

The Board ordered that the case be postponed for consideration.

George Weekley, representative of Michael Skipper; case No. 196 on the docket of the Board, and No. 28 on the books of the Register.

Claim.—A right to one hundred and sixty-one acres, by virtue of a Spanish warrant of survey, under the first section of the act.

The claimant presented his claim, together with a surveyor's plot of the land claimed, in the words and figures following, to wit:

To the Honorable Commissioners appointed to settle claims to lands south of Tennessee and east of Pearl river.

MARCH 23, 1804.

GENTLEMEN:

Please to take notice, that I claim one hundred and sixty-one acres of land, on the east side of the river Tombigbee, and on the west side of the river Alabama, by virtue of a Spanish warrant, in the name of Michael Skipper, dated the 9th February, 1788, which is now delivered to the Register of the Land Office to be recorded, to which I beg leave to refer, as also to the within plot.

GEORGE WEEKLEY.

[Plot omitted.]

Surveyed 16th February, 1804, by John Milliken. Chain bearers, Robert Dunn, James McConnell.

The claimant exhibited a Spanish warrant of survey, in the words and figures following, to wit:

His Excellency Don ESTEVAN MIRO, Colonel of the Royal army, Governor civil and military of the city and province of the Louisiana, &c. &c. &c.

MOBILE, *January* 18, 1788.

Michael Skipper, inhabitant of Mobile jurisdiction, with the greatest respects, represents to your excellency, and says, that there is, on Tenshaw river, twelve acres of land that never had any proprietor until this present time; he begs your excellency to grant him the said land, with the profounder as customary; with papers of titles from the Secretary of Government, which may correspond with the concession; for which favor he will be forever thankful.

MICHAEL SKIPPER.

Don Vicent Folch, captain of the fixed Louisiana regiment, commandant, civil and military, of Mobile and its district, certify, that the land the petitioner solicits is vacant, by information from the different inhabitants of note, who are knowing said land; to which I sign these presents, the above day and date.

VICENT FOLCH.

NEW ORLEANS, *February* 9, 1788.

The surveyor of this province, Don Carlos Laveau Tredeau, shall establish that part of land of twelve acres front, with the profounder of forty acres, as customary, as it is vacant, not causing any prejudice to any neighbors, at the same place mentioned in the above petition, with the precise conditions of making the road, and clearing regularly, in the peremptory space of one year; and if, at the precise space of three years, the land is not settled, during which period it cannot be established, this grant to remain null, under which supposition, the business of settling the limits will be carried on in the tract, and remitted me, to provide the interested party with titles in form.

ESTEVAN MIRO.

MOBILE, *March* 11, 1788.

Certified that the above is compared with the original in the office at this place.

SANTIAGO DE LA SAUSSAYE, *Pub. Not'y.*

The above is a copy of the Spanish grant.

THOMAS PRICE.

The above was compared exact with the original in this office, under my charge, by me,

JOAQUIN DE OSORNO. [L. S.]

I, Thomas Price, of the post of Mobile, English interpreter for His Majesty the King of Spain, do solemnly swear, by the Almighty God, and the Holy Cross, that this is a true and faithful translation of the Spanish grant or writing hereto annexed.

THOMAS PRICE.

Subscribed and sworn before the Board, March 23, 1804.—Attest: DAVID PARMELEE 2d, *Clerk.*

Entered in record of claims, (east of Tombigbee,) vol. 1, page 99, by EDWARD LLOYD WAILES, for

JOSEPH CHAMBERS, *Register.*

The claimant exhibited a deed of conveyance, in Spanish, from Michael Skipper, purporting to convey to John Joyce all the said Skipper's right, title, and claim to said tract of land; on the back of which deed of conveyance there are two endorsements or assignments, in the following words and figures, to wit:

MOBILE, *March* 2, 1792.

I do hereby assign unto Cornelius Dunn, his heirs and assigns, all my right and title to the tract of land, houses, &c. mentioned on the other side, having received the full consideration money agreed upon between Mr. Cornelius Dunn and me.

JOHN JOYCE.

TENSAW, *November* 1, 1796.

I do hereby assign unto George Weekley, his heirs and assigns, all my right and title to the tract of land, houses, &c. mentioned, on west side of Alabama river, having received the full consideration agreed upon between Mr. George Weekley and me.

CORNELIUS DUNN.

John Randon and Cornelius Dunn were brought forward as witnesses, and, being duly sworn and interrogated by the Board, they deposed, that they were not interested in this claim; that the land in question was cultivated and inhabited by Cornelius Dunn, on the 27th day of February, 1795; and that Michael Skipper was at that time twenty-one years of age.

The Board ordered that the case be postponed for consideration.

NARCISO BOUTIN's case, No. 197 on the docket of the Board, and No. 17 on the books of the Register.

Claim.—A right to eight hundred acres, by virtue of a Spanish warrant of survey, under the first section of the act,

The claimant presented his claim, together with a surveyor's plot of the land claimed, in the words and figures following, to wit:

To the Commissioners appointed in pursuance of the act of Congress passed the 3d day of March, 1803, for receiving and adjusting the claims to lands south of Tennessee, and east of Pearl river.

WASHINGTON COUNTY, MISSISSIPPI TERRITORY, *March* 20, 1804.

Please to take notice, that the following tract of land, situated on the east side of the Alabama river, beginning at a stake corner, running north, thirty-four degrees east, seventy-two chains, to a stake corner; thence, south, fifty-six degrees east, sixty-three chains and twenty-four links, to a corner stake; thence, south, twenty-seven degrees west, one hundred and twenty-seven chains, to a corner stake on Olive Domie's line; thence, north, sixty-three degrees west, forty-seven chains, on the aforesaid line, to the river; thence, with the river, to the beginning; containing eight hundred acres: is claimed by Narciso Broutin, having such forms and marks, both natural and artificial, as are represented in the plot annexed. The said land is claimed in and by virtue of the first section of the said act of Congress, by a Spanish grant, bearing date the 10th January, 1794, and now exhibited to the Register of the Land Office, to be recorded, as directed by said act. To all which he begs leave to refer, as also to a copy of the plot hereunto annexed.

YOUNG GAINS,

Attorney in fact for Narciso Broutin.

Surveyed 19th March, 1804, by Thomas Bilbo. Chain carriers, John Johnson, Esquire, and Joseph Lawrence.

The claimant exhibited a Spanish warrant of survey, in the following words and figures, to wit:

MOBILE, *December* 22, 1793.

His Excellency the Governor and Intendant General:

Don Narciso Broutin, lieutenant of militia, of this place, with the greatest respects to your excellency, represents and says, that, between the two rivers Tombigbee and Alabama, there is a tract of twenty acres of land front, limited on the north by vacant land, and on the south the same, which land is vacant and King's commons, and, being desirous of cultivating the same, begs your excellency to grant him the above petition, with papers of titles necessary, which may correspond with the cession, for which favor he will be forever thankful.

NARCISO BROUTIN.

MOBILE, *December* 23, 1793.

His Excellency the Governor and Intendant General:

By information from the inhabitants of this jurisdiction, the land abovementioned is vacant, having no claimant, and his intention is to cultivate the same. Your excellency may dispose as it may seem best.

MANUEL DE LANZOS.

NEW ORLEANS, *January* 10, 1794.

The Surveyor General, or some individual named by him for that business, shall establish that part of twenty acres front, with the profounder of forty acres, as customary, as it is vacant, not causing prejudice to any person, at the same place mentioned in the above petition, with the precise conditions of making the road, and clearing regularly, in the peremptory space of one year; and if, at the precise space of three years, the land is not settled, during which period it cannot be alienated, this grant to remain null; under which supposition, the business of settling the limits will be carried on in the tract, and remitted me, to provide the interested party with titles in form.

THE BARON OF CARONDELET.

MOBILE, *February* 2, 1794.

Certifieth this is a copy of the original in this office under my charge.

MANUEL DE LANZOS.

The above is a copy of the Spanish grant.

THOMAS PRICE.

The above was compared exact with the original in this office, under my charge, by me.

JOAQUIN DE OSORNO.

I, Thomas Price, of the post of Mobile, English interpreter for His Majesty the King of Spain, do solemnly swear, by the Almighty God, and by the Holy Cross, that this is a true and faithful translation of the Spanish grant or writing hereto annexed.

THOMAS PRICE.

Subscribed and sworn before the Board, March 21st, 1804.—Attest: David Parmelee 2d, *Clerk.*
Entered in record of claims, (east side) vol. 1, page 66, by Edward Lloyd Wailes, for

JOSEPH CHAMBERS, *Register.*

Cornelius Dunn was presented as a witness, and, being duly sworn and interrogated by the Board, he deposed, that he had no interest in this claim; that, to the best of his recollection, the land in question was cultivated by Narciso Broutin, or to his use, on the 27th day of October, 1795; that the said Broutin was, on the 10th day of January, 1794, more than twenty-one years of age, and the head of a family; that the said Broutin was, on the 27th day of October, 1795, an inhabitant of the town of Mobile, and that his principal place of cultivation was on the land in question; that he, Dunn, knew of no interfering claim.

The Board ordered that the case be postponed for consideration.

Heirs of John Linder, Junior; case, No. 198 on the docket of the Board, and No. 12 on the books of the Register.
Claim.—A right to eight hundred acres, by virtue of a Spanish warrant of survey, under the first section of the act.

The claimants presented their claim, together with a surveyor's plot of the land claimed, in the words and figures following, viz :

To the Commissioners appointed in pursuance of the act of Congress passed the 3d of March, 1803, for receiving and adjusting claims to lands south of the Tennessee, and east of Pearl river.

Please to take notice, that the following tract of land, situated on the east of Tombigbee and Alabama rivers, and west side of Tensaw lake, in the county of Washington, beginning on the Alabama river, and west side of Tensaw lake, at an ash and maple; thence, north, seventy-five degrees east, one hundred and twenty-seven chains, to a hickory corner; thence, north, fifteen degrees west, sixty-three chains, to a cypress corner; thence, south, seventy-five degrees west, one hundred and twenty-seven chains, partly on Pine-log creek, to a boggy gut and stake; thence, down the Alabama river to the beginning; and hath such marks, natural and artificial, as are fully represented in the plot annexed, containing eight hundred acres: is claimed by John Mills, attorney in fact for the heirs of John Linder, Junior, in and by virtue of a Spanish warrant of survey, and is now exhibited to the Register of the Land Office established east of Pearl river, to be recorded as directed by said act. To all which he begs leave to refer, as also to a copy of the plot herewith filed.

JOHN MILLS.
For the heirs of John Linder, Junior.
March 26, 1804.
[Plot omitted.]

Surveyed 10th February, 1804, by John Milliken. Chain bearers, James Mills and Francis Killingworth. The claimants exhibited a Spanish warrant of survey, in the following words and figures, to wit:

His Excellency Estevan Miro, Colonel of the Royal army, Governor civil and military of the city and province of the Louisiana, &c. &c.
John Linder, Jun. inhabitant of Mobile jurisdiction, with the greatest respect to your excellency, petitions and says, there is found on the Tensaw river, twenty acres of vacant land, situate on the west side of said river, which said land, until this present, never had any proprietor: he prays your excellency to grant him, as proprietor of said land, with the profounder as customary, and deliver him, through the Secretary of Government, the corresponding titles of concession, for which favor from your excellency the petitioner will be forever thankful.

JOHN LINDER, Jun.

Don Vicent Folch, captain in fixed Louisiana regiment, commandant civil and military of Mobile place

and its jurisdiction, certifies, that the land the petitioner solicits is found vacant by information taken to that effect, from several inhabitants who are well knowing to the said land, for which I sign these presents the day and date above.

VICENT FOLCH.

New Orleans, *May* 2, 1788.
The commandant will inform me the reasons of the above petitioner's soliciting that tract of land, and whether he is in great necessity for it or not.

MIRO.

New Orleans, *June* 3, 1788.
The commandant of Mobile shall establish this individual on the twenty acres of land front he solicits, with the profounder, as customary, of forty, at the same place mentioned in the above petition, as it is vacent, not causing prejudice to neighbors, with the precise conditions of making the road and clearing regularly, in the peremptory space of one year; and if, at the precise space of three years, the land is not settled, after which period it cannot be established, this grant to remain null, under which supposition the business of settling the limits will be carried on in the tract, and remitted me to provide the interested party with titles in form.

ESTEVAN MIRO.

Mobile, *May* 14, 1798.
Compared with the original existing in the archives of this place, from which this copy was drawn, the same I certify.

MANUEL DE LANZOS.

The above is a copy of the Spanish grant.
THOS. PRICE.

The above was compared exact with the original in this office, under my charge, by me,

JOAQUIN DE OSORNO.

I, Thomas Price, of the post of Mobile, English interpreter for His Majesty the King of Spain, do solemnly swear, by the Almighty God, and by the Holy Cross, that this is a true and faithful translation of the Spanish grant or writing hereunto annexed.

THOS. PRICE.

Subscribed and sworn the Board, March 21st, 1804.—Attest: David Parmelee 2d, *Clerk.*
Entered in record of claims, (east side,) vol. 1, page 50, by Edward Lloyd Wailes, for

JOSEPH CHAMBERS, *Register.*

Joseph Thompson and Moses Sedham were presented as witnesses, and, being duly sworn and interrogated by the Board, they deposed, that they were not interested in this claim; that the land claimed by the heirs of John Linder, Junior, was inhabited and cultivated by them on the 27th day of October, 1795, and that it had been inhabited and cultivated ever since; that they, the deponents, believed that John Linder, Junior, in whose name the land in question is claimed, was, on the 3d day of June, 1788, the head of a family, and twenty-one years of age.

Question. Does or does not the improvement, made by John Linder, Jun. in his life-time, and by his heirs since his death, extend from the dwelling houses to a point on the Alabama river, next adjoining the head of the Tensaw lake, where it makes out of the Alabama.
Answer by both. It does.
The Board ordered that the case be postponed for consideration.

Benjamin Hooven's case, No. 199 on the docket of the Board, and No. 33 on the books of the Register.
Claim.—A donation of five hundred and sixty-six acres, under the second section of the act.
The claimant presented his claim, together with a surveyor's plot of the land claimed, in the following words and figures, to wit.

To the Commissioners appointed in pursuance of the act of Congress passed the 3d day of March, 1803, for receiving and adjusting the claims to lands south of Tennessee, and east of Pearl river.

Please to take notice that the following tract of land, situated on the east side of Tombigbee river, on the Alabama river, beginning on a peach tree, runs south, seventy-eight degrees west, forty-two chains, to a cypress corner; thence, with Pine log creek, to the river; thence, south, eighty-six degrees west, twenty-four chains; thence, north, thirty-nine degrees west, fifty-four chains; thence, north, seventy-five degrees west, eight chains; thence, south, fifty-eight degrees, west eight chains fifty links; south, twenty-six degrees west eight chains; thence south, fourteen .chains; thence south, twenty-six degrees east, twenty-six chains; thence, south, fifty-four degrees east, to boggy-gut; thence, with the gut to Mills's corner; thence, north, eighty-six degrees east, and one hundred and fourteen chains, to a wild plum; thence, north, fifteen degrees west, twenty chains, to the beginning; containing five hundred and sixty-six acres; having such forms and marks, both natural and artificial, as are represented in the plot annexed: is claimed by Benjamin Hooven, in and by virtue of a donation right; and is now exhibited to the Register of the Land Office established east of Pearl river, to be recorded as directed by said act. To all which he begs leave to refer, as also to a copy of the plot herewith filed.

BENJAMIN HOOVEN.

March 26, 1804.

[Plot omitted.]

Surveyed 22d March, 1804, by John Milliken. Chain bearers, James McConnell and Levi Qualls.

Entered in record of claims, vol. 1, (on the east side) page 107, by Edward Lloyd Wailes, for

JOSEPH CHAMBERS, *Register.*

John Mills and John Dunn were presented as witnesses, and, being duly sworn and interrogated by the Board, deposed, that they were not interested in this claim ; that Benjamin Hooven, the claimant, settled upon the land in question, in the spring of the year 1797; and had continued to inhabit and cultivate the same ever since ; that the said Hooven was, in the year 1797, twenty-one years of age, and the head of a family.

The Board ordered that the case be postponed for consideration.

Josiah Fletcher's case, No. 200 on the docket of the Board, and No. 41 on the books of the Register.

Claim.—A donation of six hundred and one acres, under the second section of the act.

The claimant presented his claim, together with a surveyor's plot of the land claimed, in the words and figures following, to wit:

To the Commissioners appointed in pursuance of the act of Congress passed the 3d day of March, 1803, for receiving and adjusting claims to lands south of Tennessee, and east of Pearl river.

Please to take notice, that the following tract of land, situated on the east side of Tombigbee, in the cut-off island, commonly called Nanna Hubba island, in the county of Washington, beginning at a cotton tree; thence, south, five degrees east, one hundred and twenty chains, to a gum; thence, south, eighty-eight degrees west, forty-eight chains, to a stake ; thence, north, thirty degrees east, twenty-six chains, to a sassafras; thence, with the Alabama and the cut-off to the beginning cotton tree; and hath such forms and marks, both natural and artificial, as are fully represented in the plot annexed, containing six hundred and one acres: is claimed by Josiah Fletcher, in and by virtue of the second section of the said act as a donation; and is now exhibited to the Register of the Land Office east of Pearl river, to be recorded as directed by said act. To all which he begs leave to refer, as also to a copy of the plot herewith filed.

JOSIAH FLETCHER, his mark.

March 27, 1804.

[Plot omitted.]

Surveyed 20th February, 1804, by John Milliken. Chain bearers, James McConnell and Robert Dunn.

Entered in record of claims, (east side) vol. 1, page 115, by Edw. Lloyd Wailes, for

JOSEPH CHAMBERS, *Register.*

Cornelius Dunn and George Weekley, Junior, were presented as witnesses, and, being duly sworn and interrogated by the Board, they deposed, that they were not interested in this claim; that Josiah Fletcher, the claimant, did, on the 27th day of October, 1797, cultivate and inhabit the land in question; that he was at that time more than twenty-one years of age, and the head of a family.

The Board ordered that the case be postponed for consideration.

Moses Stedham's case, No. 201 on the docket of the Board, and No. 34 on the books of the Register.

Claim.—A donation of six hundred and forty acres, under the second section of the act.

The claimant presented his claim, together with a surveyor's plot of the land claimed, in the words and figures following, to wit:

To the Commissioners appointed in pursuance of the act of Congress passed the third of March, 1803, for receiving and adjusting the claims to lands south of Tennessee and east of Pearl river.

Please to take notice, that the following tract of land, situated on the east side of Tombigbee, on Curry's Lake, in the county of Washington, beginning at a white oak on the lake, and runs down the lake, south, forty degrees west; thence, south, six degrees west; thence, to Pine Log creek, to a cypress; thence, at the first beginning corner, and running with George Weekley's line; thence, north, sixty-eight degrees east, to a black oak on Mimms's line; thence, south, twenty-two degrees east, to a pine; thence, to and with the creek, to a cypress; and hath such shape, form, and marks, both natural and artificial, as are represented in the plot annexed; containing six hundred and twenty-eight acres: is c'aimed by Moses Stedham, in and by virtue of the second section of the said act, as a donation; and is now exhibited to the Register of the Land Office established east of Pearl river, to be recorded as directed by said act. To all which he begs leave to refer, as also to a copy of the plot herewith filed.

MOSES STEDHAM, his + mark.

March 26, 1804.

[Plot omitted.]

Surveyed 17th February, 1804, by John Milliken Chain bearers, James McConnell and Benjamin Hooven.

Entered in record of claims, (east side,) vol. 1, page 108, by Edward Lloyd Wailes, for

JOSEPH CHAMBERS, *Register.*

Cornelius Dunn and Josiah Fletcher were presented as witnesses, and, being duly sworn and interrogated by the Board, they deposed, that they were not interested in this claim; that Moses Stedham, the claimant, did, in the year 1797, cultivate and inhabit the land in question; and that he was at that time more than twenty-one years of age, and the head of a family.

The Board ordered that the case be postponed for consideration.

Cornelius Dunn's case, No. 202 on the docket of the Board, and No. 40 on the books of the Register.

Claim.—A right of pre-emption of two hundred and fifty-two acres, under the third section of the act.

The claimant presented his claim, together with a surveyor's plot of the land claimed, in the words and figures following, to wit:

To the Commissioners appointed in pursuance of the act of Congress, passed the 3d day of March, 1803, for receiving and adjusting claims to lands south of Tennessee, and east of Pearl river.

Please to take notice, that the following tract of land, situated on the east side of Tombigbee, on the waters of Holly creek, in the county of Washington, beginning at an elm corner, and runs south, twenty-four chains, to a persimmon; thence, east, one hundred and three chains and a half, to a pine; thence, north twenty-five degrees west, twenty-nine chains fifty links, to Holly creek; thence, with the meanders of said creek, to the beginning; and hath such forms and marks, both natural and artificial, as are fully represented in the plot annexed; containing two hundred and fifty-two acres: is claimed by Cornelius Dunn, in and by virtue of the third section of the said act, as a pre-emption; and is now exhibited to the Register of the Land Office established east of Pearl river, to be recorded as directed by said act. To all which he begs leave to refer, as also to a copy of the plot herewith filed.

CORNELIUS DUNN.

March 27, 1804.

[Plot omitted.]

Surveyed 18th February, 1804, by John Milliken. Entered in record of claims, (east side,) vol. 1, page 114, by Edward Lloyd Wailes, for

JOSEPH CHAMBERS, *Register.*

Josiah Fletcher and John Randon were presented as witnesses, and, being duly sworn and interrogated by the Board, they deposed, that they were not interested in this claim; that Cornelius Dunn, the claimant, did, on the 3d day of March, 1803, cultivate and inhabit the land in question, and that he was at that time more than twenty-one years of age, and the head of a family.

The Board ordered that the case be postponed for consideration.

JOHN RANDON's case, No. 203 on the docket of the Board, and No. 37 on the books of the Register.

Claim.—A donation of three hundred and one acres, under the second section of the act.

The claimant presented his claim, together with a surveyor's plot of the land claimed, in the words and figures following, to wit:

To the Commissioners appointed in pursuance of the act of Congress passed the 3d day of March, 1803, for receiving and adjusting claims to land south of the Tennessee, and east of Pearl river.

Please to take notice, that the following tract of land, situated on the east side of Tombigbee river, in the Nanna Hubba Island, butting on the river Alabama, beginning at two willows, and running south, twenty-three degrees east, seventeen chains, twenty-five links, to a cypress; thence, south, five degrees east, fifteen chains, to a cotton tree; thence, south, thirty-five degrees east, forty-four chains fifty links, to the Alabama river; thence, with the Alabama river, to the beginning, containing three hundred and one acres, having such shape, form, and marks, both natural and artificial, as are represented in the plot annexed, and is now exhibited to the Register of the Land Office east of Pearl river, to be recorded as directed by said act. To all which he begs leave to refer. The above tract of land is claimed by John Randon, in and by virtue of the second section of the said act of Congress, as a donation.

JOHN RANDON.

MARCH 27, 1804.

[Plot omitted.]

Surveyed 22d February, 1804, by John Milliken. Chain carriers, James McConnell and William Thomas.

Entered in record of claims, (east side of Tombigbee,) vol. 1, page 111, by EDWARD LLOYD WAILES, for

JOSEPH CHAMBERS, *Register.*

Cornelius Dunn and George Weekley were presented as witnesses, and, being duly sworn and interrogated by the Board, they deposed, that they had no interest in this claim; that John Randon, the claimant, did, in the year 1797, cultivate and inhabit the land in question; that he was at that time more than twenty-one years of age, and the head of a family.

The Board ordered that the case be postponed for consideration.

GEORGE WEEKLY's case, No. 204 on the docket of the Board, and No. 52 on the books of the Register.

Claim.—A donation of six hundred and forty acres, under the second section of the act.

The claimant presented his claim, together with a surveyor's plot of the land claimed, in the words and figures following, to wit:

To the Commissioners appointed in pursuance of the act of Congress passed the 3d day of March, 1803, for receiving and adjusting the claims to lands south of Tennessee, and east of Pearl river.

Please to take notice, that the following tract of land, situated on the east side of Tombigbee and Alabama rivers, beginning on Stedham's lake, and runs north, eighty-eight degrees east, forty-four chains, to a pine corner; thence, north, sixty-eight degrees east, thirty-two chains, to a black oak; thence, south, twenty-two degrees east, sixty-three chains fifty links, to a pine, on Killingworth's line; thence, north, seventy-five degrees east, seventy-four chains to a stake; thence, north, fifteen degrees west, fifty-eight chains, to a stake; thence, due west, one hundred and thirty-eight chains, to Mimms's corner, on Stedham's lake, thence, with the lake, to the beginning; containing six hundred and forty acres; and hath such forms and marks, both natural and artificial, as are fully represented in the plot annexed: is claimed by George Weekley, in and by virtue of the second section of the said act, as a donation; and is now exhibited to the Register of the Land Office established east of Pearl river, to be recorded as directed by said act. To all which he begs leave to refer, as also to a copy of the plot herewith filed.

GEORGE WEEKLEY.

MARCH 31, 1804.

[Plot omitted.]

Surveyed March 8, 1804, by John Milliken. Chain bearers, John Ackworth and James McConnell.

Entered in record of claims, (east of Tombigbee,) vol. 1, page 122, by EDWARD LLOYD WAILES, for

JOSEPH CHAMBERS, *Register.*

Cornelius Dunn and John Randon were presented as witnesses, and, being duly sworn and interrogated by the Board, they deposed, that they were not interested in this claim; that George Weekley, the claimant, did, in the year 1797, cultivate and inhabit the land in question; and that he was at that time twenty-one years of age, and the head of a family.

The Board ordered that the case be postponed for consideration.

JAMES RANDON's case, No. 205 on the docket of the Board, and No. 42 on the books of the Register.

Claim.—A donation of six hundred and thirty acres, under the second section of the act.

The claimant presented his claim, together with a surveyor's plot of the land claimed, in the words and figures following, viz.:

To the Commissioners appointed in pursuance of the act of Congress passed the 3d day of March, 1803, for receiving and adjusting claims to lands south of Tennessee, and east of Pearl river.

Please to take notice, that the following tract of land, situated on the east side of Tombigbee river, on the waters of Holly creek, in the county of Washington, beginning at Mimms's pine corner, and runs west, one hundred and fifty-six chains, to a white oak corner on Holly creek; thence, with the creek, as it meanders; thence, east one hundred and twenty-four chains, to a gum; thence, south, forty-five chains, to the beginning; containing six hundred and thirty acres, having such shape, form, and marks, both natural and artificial, as are represented in the plot annexed: is claimed by James Randon, in and by virtue of the second section of the said act, as a donation; and is now exhibited to the Register of the Land Office east of Pearl river, to be recorded as directed by said act. To all which he begs leave to refer, as also to a copy of the plot herewith filed.

Exhibited to the Register by John Randon, for his brother.

JAMES RANDON.

MARCH 27, 1804.

[Plot omitted.]

Surveyed 27th February, 1804, by John Milliken. Chain carriers, James McConnel and William Thomas. Entered in record of claims, (east side,) vol. 1, page 115, by EDWARD LLOYD WAILES, for

JOSEPH CHAMBERS, *Register.*

Cornelius Dunn and George Weekley were presented as witnesses, and being duly sworn and interrogated by the Board, they deposed, that they had no interest in this claim; that the land in question was cultivated in the year 1797; that the claimant, James Randon, lived with his brother, John Randon, and was owner of part of the slaves by whom the cultivation was made on said land; and that said James was at that time more than twenty-one years of age.

The Board ordered that the case be postponed for consideration.

WILLIAM WEEKLEY's case, No. 206 on the docket of the Board, and No. 62 on the books of the Register.

Claim.—A right of pre-emption of one hundred and thirty-nine acres, under the third section of the act.

The claimant presented his claim, together with a surveyor's plot of the land claimed, in the words and figures following, to wit:

To the Commissioners appointed in pursuance of the act of Congress passed the 3d day of March, 1803, for receiving and adjusting claims to lands south of the Tennessee, and east of the Pearl river.

Please to take notice, that the following tract of land, situated on the east side of Tombigbee river, in the county of Washington, beginning at a pine; running thence, north, sixty-six degrees west, fifty-two chains, to a stake; thence, south, twenty-four degrees west, twenty-two chains, to a pine; thence, south, fifty degrees east, twenty-seven chains; thence, east, forty chains fifty links, to a pine; thence, north, seventeen degrees west, seventeen chains, to the beginning; and hath such forms and marks, both natural and artificial, as are represented in the plot annexed, containing one hundred and thirty-nine acres: claimed by William Weekley, in and by virtue of a pre-emption, and is now established east of Pearl river, to be recorded as directed by said act. To all which he begs leave to refer, as also to a copy of the plot herewith filed.

WILLIAM WEEKLEY.

MARCH 31, 1804.

[Plot omitted.]

Surveyed 24th March, 1804, by John Milliken. Chain bearers, James McConnel and Levi Qualls.

Entered in record of claims, (east side) vol. 1, page 127, by EDWARD LLOYD WAILES, for

JOSEPH CHAMBERS, *Register.*

John Mills and William Pierce were presented as witnesses, and, being duly sworn and interrogated by the Board, they deposed, that they were not interested in this claim; that William Weekley, the claimant, did, on the 3d day of March, 1803, actually inhabit and cultivate the land in question, and that he was at that time the head of a family, and twenty-one years of age; that they knew of no interfering claim.

The Board ordered that the case be postponed for consideration.

BENJAMIN STEDHAM's case, No. 207 on the docket of the Board, and No. 31 on the books of the Register.

Claim.—A donation of one hundred and thirty-three acres, under the second section of the act.

The claimant presented his claim, together with a surveyor's plot of the land claimed, in the words and figures following, to wit:

To the Commissioners appointed in pursuance of the act of Congress passed on the 3d day of March, 1803, for receiving and adjusting claims to lands south of Tennessee, and east of Pearl river.

Please to take notice, that the following tract of land, situated on the east side of Tombigbee, and on the Alabama, in the county of Washington, beginning at a cotton tree, south, sixty degrees west, seventy chains fifty links, to a stake; thence, north, fifty-four degrees east, thirty-seven chains; thence, south, thirty-five degrees east, sixty-two chains, to the river; thence, with the river, to the beginning; and hath such forms and marks, both natural and artificial, as are fully represented in the plot annexed, containing one hundred and thirty-three acres: is claimed by Benjamin Stedham, in and by virtue of the second section of the said act, as a donation, and is now exhibited to the Register of the Land Office established east of Pearl river, to be recorded as directed by said act. To all which he begs leave to refer, as also to a copy of the plot herewith filed.

BENJAMIN STEDHAM, his + mark.

MARCH 26, 1804.

[Plot omitted.]

Surveyed 16th February, 1804, by John Milliken. Sworn chain carriers, Moses Stedham and James McConnel.

Entered in record of claims, (east side,) vol. 1, page 106, by EDWARD LLOYD WAILES, for

JOSEPH CHAMBERS, *Register.*

Josiah Fletcher and John Randon were presented as witnesses, and, being duly sworn and interrogated by the Board, they deposed, that they were not interested in this claim; that, about eighteen or nineteen years ago, Benjamin Stedham commenced the improvement of the land in question; that, in the year 1797, cultivation was made on said land by Moses Stedham, his son.

The Board ordered that the case be postponed for consideration.

JESSE ROSS's case, representative of Abraham Walker; No. 208 on the docket of the Board, and No. 36 on the books of the Register.

Claim.—A donation of six hundred and thirty acres, under the second section of the act.

The claimant presented his claim, together with a surveyor's plot of the land claimed, in the following words and figures, to wit:

To the Commissioners appointed in pursuance of the act of Congress passed the 3d day of March, 1803, for receiving and adjusting claims to land south of Tennessee, and east of Pearl river.

Please to take notice, that the following tract of land, situated on Hollow creek, east side of Tombigbee and Alabama rivers, in the county of Washington, beginning on Hollow creek, at an ash corner; thence, east, fifty-six chains fifty-seven links, to a gum; thence, south, ninety-six chains, to a corner stake; thence, west, seventy-six chains, to a corner stake on Hollow creek; thence, up the meanders of said creek, to the beginning; and hath such forms and marks, both natural and artificial, as are fully represented in the plot annexed, containing six hundred and thirty acres: is claimed by Jesse Ross, legal representative of Abraham Walker, in and by virtue of the second section of this act, as a donation,

and is now exhibited to the Register of the Land Office established east of Pearl river, to be recorded as directed by said act. To all which he begs leave to refer, as also to a copy of the plot herewith filed.

JESSE ROSS,

Legal representative of Abraham Walker.

MARCH 27, 1804.

[Plot omitted.]

Surveyed February 18th, 1804, by John Milliken. Chain bearers, Wiseman Walker and Ezekiel Reaves.

Entered in record of claims, (east side,) vol. 1, page 110, by EDWARD LLOYD WAILES, for

JOSEPH CHAMBERS, *Register.*

George Weekley and Cornelius Dunn were presented as witnesses, and, being duly sworn and interrogated by the Board, they deposed that they were not interested in this claim; that the land in question was cultivated and inhabited by Abraham Walker in the year 1797; the said Walker was at that time twenty-one years of age; and that they knew of no interfering claim.

The Board ordered that the case be postponed for consideration.

LEMUEL HENRY's case, representative of John Linder, Senior; No. 209 on the docket of the Board, and No. 24 on the books of the Register.

Claim.—A right of four hundred and ninety-one acres, by virtue of a Spanish warrant of survey, under the first section of the act.

The claimant presented his claim, together with a surveyor's plot of the land claimed, in the words and figures following, viz.:

To the Commissioners appointed in pursuance of the act of Congress passed the 3d day of March, 1803, for receiving and adjusting claims to land south of Tennessee, and east of Pearl river.

Please to take notice, that the following tract of land, situated on the east side of Tombigbee and Alabama rivers, in the county of Washington, beginning at the mouth of the Tensaw lake, on the Alabama river, on an ash and maple; thence, down said lake, north, seventy-five degrees east, seventy-eight chains, to a corner stake; thence, south, fifteen degrees east, sixty-three chains, to a corner stake; thence, south, seventy-five degrees west, and seventy-eight chains, across Linder's lake, to a water oak corner; thence, north, fifteen degrees west, sixty-three chains, to the beginning; and hath such forms and marks, both natural and artificial, as are fully represented in the plot annexed, containing four hundred and ninety-one acres: is claimed by Lemuel Henry, legal representative of John Linder, Senior, in and by virtue of a Spanish grant, and is now exhibited to the Register of the Land Office established east of Pearl river, to be recorded as directed by said act. To all which he begs leave to refer, as also to a copy of the plot herewith filed.

LEMUEL HENRY,

Legal representative of John Linder, Senior, deceased.

MARCH 26, 1804.

[Plot omitted.]

Surveyed February 11th, 1804, by John Milliken. Chain bearers, Francis Killingworth and James Mills.

The claimant exhibited a Spanish warrant in support of this claim, in the words and figures following, to wit:

His Excellency Estevan Miro, Colonel of the Royal army, Governor civil and military of the city and province of the Louisiana, &c. &c.

John Linder, father, inhabitant of Mobile jurisdiction, with the greatest respects to your excellency, petitions and says, there are found on Tensaw river twenty acres of vacant land, situate on the east side of said river; said land, until this present, never had any proprietor. He prays your excellency to grant him as proprietor of said land, with the profounder, as customary, and order the despatches from the Secretary of Government, the corresponding titles of concession; for which favor from your excellency the petitioner will be forever thankful.

JOHN LINDER.

MOBILE, *April* 23, 1788.

Don Vicent Folch, captain in the fixed Louisiana regiment, commandant civil and military of this place and its jurisdiction, certifies, that the land the petitioner solicits is found vacant, by information taken to that effect from several inhabitants, who are well knowing the said land; for which I sign these presents, the day and date above.

VICENT FOLCH.

NEW ORLEANS, *May 2d*, 1788.

The commandant will inform the reasons the above petitioner solicits the above tract of land, and whether he was in great necessity for it or not.

MIRO.

NEW ORLEANS, *June 3d*, 1788.

The commandant of Mobile shall establish this individual on the twenty acres of land front he solicits, with the profounder, as customary, of forty, at the same place mentioned in the above petition, as it is vacant, not causing prejudice to any neighbors, with the precise conditions of making the road, and clearing regularly, in the peremptory space of one year; and if at the precise space of three years the land is not settled, after which period it cannot be established, this grant to remain null; under which supposition, the business of settling the limits will be carried on in the tract, and remitted me, to provide the interested party with titles in form.

ESTEVAN MIRO.

The above compared with the original, from which this copy was drawn, existing in these archives under my charge, which I certify.

MANUEL DE LANZOS.

MOBILE, *May 14th*, 1798.

The above is a copy of the Spanish grant.

THOMAS PRICE.

The above compared exact with the original in this office, under my charge, by me,

JOAQUIN DE OSORNO.

I, Thomas Price, of the post of Mobile, English interpreter for His Majesty the King of Spain, do solemnly swear by the Almighty God, and by the Holy Cross, that this is a true translation of the Spanish grant or writing hereto annexed.

THOMAS PRICE.

Subscribed and sworn before the Board, March 21st, 1804.—Attest: DAVID PARMELEE 2d, *Clerk*.

Entered in record of claims, (east of Tombigbee,) vol. 1, page 85, by EDWARD LLOYD WAILES, for

JOSEPH CHAMBERS, *Register*.

The claimant exhibited a deed of conveyance from John Linder, Senior, bearing date the 6th day of November, 1800, conveying to John Mills and Mary, his wife, all the said Linder's right and title to the land described in said Spanish warrant. A deed was also exhibited, from John Mills, bearing date the 21st day of May, 1803, conveying to Lemuel Henry all the said John Mills's right and title to five hundred acres of the aforesaid tract of land, fronting on the Alabama river, with the improvements made thereon.

William Pierce and Moses Stedham were presented as witnesses, and, being duly sworn, and interrogated by the Board, they deposed, that they had no interest in this claim; that John Linden, Senior, in whose name the land in question is claimed, cultivated the same on the 27th day of October, 1795; that they believed that he inhabited the same on the same day and year; that they well recollected that he resided in the Mississippi territory on the 27th day of October, 1795; and that they did believe that John Linder, Senior, was, on the 3d day of June, 1788, more than twenty-one years of age, and the head of a family.

The Board ordered that the case be postponed for consideration.

JAMES MILLS, representative of John Linder, Senior; case, No. 210 on the docket of the Board, and No. 23 on the books of the Register.

Claim.—A right to two hundred and ninety-nine acres, by virtue of a Spanish warrant of survey, under the first section of the act.

The claimant presented his claim, together with a surveyor's plot of the land claimed, in the words and figures following, to wit:

To the Commissioners appointed in pursuance of the act of Congress passed the 3d day of March, 1803, for receiving and adjusting the claims to land south of Tennessee, and east of Pearl river.

Please to take notice, that the following tract of land, situate on the east side of Tombigbee and Alabama rivers, and on the west side of Tensaw lake, in the county of Washington, beginning at a black oak, north, seventy-five degrees east, forty-seven chains fifty links, to a hickory corner; thence, south, fifteen degrees east, sixty-three chains to a stake corner; thence south, seventy-five degrees west. forty-seven chains fifty links to a stake; thence, north, fifteen degrees west, sixty-three chains, to

the beginning; and hath such forms and marks, both natural and artificial, as are fully represented in the plot annexed, containing two hundred and ninety-nine acres: is claimed by James Mills, legal representative of John Linder, Senior, deceased, in and by virtue of a Spanish warrant, or order of survey, and is now exhibited to the Register of the Land Office east of Pearl river, to be recorded as directed by said act. To all which he begs leave to refer, as also to a copy of the plot herewith filed.

LEMUEL HENRY, for
JAMES MILLS,
Legal representative of John Linder, Sen.

MARCH 26, 1804.

[Plot omitted.]

Surveyed February 11, 1804, by John Milliken. Chain bearers, James Mills and Francis Killingworth.

Entered in record of claims, (east side,) vol. 1, page 85, by EDWARD LLOYD WAILES, for

JOSEPH CHAMBERS, *Register*.

The Spanish warrant, together with the deed of conveyance, from John Linder, Senior, to John Mills, and the testimony of William Pierce and Moses Stedham, recorded in the preceding case of Lemuel Henry, commenced in page 814, were exhibited and applied in support of this claim.

The claimant also exhibited a deed from John Mills, bearing date the 21st day of May, 1803, conveying to James Mills all the right, title, and interest of the said John Mills, in and to three hundred acres of land, on the east side of the Alabama river, and the east end of a tract of twenty acres front on said river, and forty back.

The Board ordered that the case be postponed for consideration.

Adjourned until Tuesday the 14th instant.

TUESDAY, *May* 14, 1805.

The Board met according to adjournment. Present: Robert C. Nicholas, Joseph Chambers.

WILLIAM PIERCE and JOHN PIERCE, representatives of Francis Ballard, case No. 211 on the docket of the Board, and No. 79 on the books of the Register.

Claim.—A right of donation of six hundred and forty acres, under the second section of the act.

The claimants presented their claim, together with a surveyor's plot of the land claimed, in the following words and figures, to wit:

To the Commissioners appointed in pursuance of the act of Congress passed the 3d day of March, 1803, for receiving and adjusting claims to land south of Tennessee, and east of Pearl river.

Please to take notice, that the following tract of land, situate on the east side of the river Tombigbee, in the county of Washington, beginning at the Alabama river, running north, thirty degrees west, sixty chains, to a gum; west, twenty-eight chains; south, twelve degrees east, one hundred and twenty-five chains; and hath such forms and marks, both natural and artificial, as are fully represented in the plot annexed, containing six hundred and forty acres: is claimed by William and John Pierce, in and by virtue of a donation, and is now exhibited to the Register of the Land Office established east of Pearl river, to be recorded as directed by said act. To all which he begs leave to refer, as also to a copy of the plot herewith filed.

WILLIAM & JOHN PIERCE.

APRIL 29, 1805.

[Plot omitted.]

The claimants presented a writing, as follows, to wit:

MISSISSIPPI TERRITORY, *May* 30, 1801.

This is to certify, that I have sold and conveyed to Seth Dean all my right, claim, or title to two improvements, that is to say, the place where I now live, and my swamp-field in the cut-off, and all claims near or adjoining; and for the above land and privileges I have received one hundred and twenty dollars. As witness my hand.

FRANCIS BALLARD. [L. S.]

In presence of
JOSEPH OGDON, his + mark,
ABRAHAM WALKER, his × mark,
ANDREW MCNEELY.

On the back of which writing is an endorsement, as follows, viz.:

I endorse the within claims, and mine, also, to Mr. David Allen, for the sum of one hundred and forty dollars. Witness my hand, this 7th day of October, 1801.

SETH DEAN. [L. S.]

Signed in presence of
 MOSES STEDHAM, his x mark.
 DONALD McCOY.

Entered in record of claims, (east side,) vol. 1, page —.
 JOSEPH CHAMBERS, *Register.*

The claimants also exhibited a deed from David Allen, bearing date the 25th day of April, 1805, conveying to William and John Pierce all the said Allen's right, title, and claim to the land claimed in this case.

George Weekley was presented as a witness, and, being duly sworn and interrogated by the Board, he deposed, that he had no interest in this claim; that, some time in the year 1796, he moved to this country, and, in the latter end of the same year, or the beginning of the year 1797, as well as he recollected, Francis Ballard moved to this country, and commenced the cultivation of the land in question by his son-in-law and a negro; that the cultivation was continued about three or four years, when the said Francis Ballard removed to the Mississippi; and that he was, in the year 1797, twenty-one years of age, and the head of a family.

The Board ordered that the case be postponed for consideration.

WILLIAM SHIELD's case, No. 212 on the docket of the Board, and No. 58 on the books of the Register.

Claim.—A donation of six hundred and thirty-two acres, under the second section of the act.

The claimant presented his claim, together with a surveyor's plot of the land claimed, in the words and figures following, to wit:

To the Commissioners appointed in pursuance of the act of Congress passed the 3d day of March, 1803, for receiving and adjusting claims to land south of Tennessee and east of Pearl river.

Please to take notice, that the following tract of land, situated on the east side of Tombigbee river, in the county of Washington, beginning at a cotton tree, running thence, north, forty degrees west, fifty-six chains, to a stake; thence, south, fifty degrees west, one hundred and thirteen chains, to a stake; thence, south, forty degrees east, fifty-six chains, to a stake on the river; thence, with the meanders of the river, to the beginning; and hath such forms and marks, both natural and artificial, as are fully represented in the plot annexed, containing six hundred and thirty-two acres: is claimed by Shields, in and by virtue of the second section of the act, as a donation, and is now exhibited to the Register of the Land Office established east of Pearl river, to be recorded as directed by said act. To all which he begs leave to refer, as also to a copy of the plot herewith filed.

WILLIAM SHIELDS, his x mark.

MARCH 31, 1804.

[Plot omitted.]

Surveyed February 14, 1804, by John Milliken. Chain carriers, John Phillips and Charles Woolf.

Entered in record of claims, (east side,) vol. 1, page 125, by EDWARD LLOYD WAILES, for
 JOSEPH CHAMBERS, *Register.*

George Weekley was presented as a witness, and, being duly sworn and interrogated by the Board, he deposed, that he was not interested in this claim; that, as well as he recollected, William Shields, early in the year 1797, moved from Pensacola to Tensaw, and commenced the cultivation of the land in question; that he continued to cultivate the same for about four or five years, and that he knew of no interfering claim; and that he was, at that time, twenty-one years of age, and the head of a family.

The Board ordered that the case be postponed for consideration.

Adjourned until Wednesday, the 15th instant.

WEDNESDAY, *May* 15, 1805.

The Board met according to adjournment. Present: Robert C. Nicholas, Joseph Chambers.

NATT CHRISTMAS, representative of Michael Hartly; case No. 213 on the docket of the Board, and No. 80 on the books of the Register.

Claim.—A donation of six hundred and forty acres, under the second section of the act.

The claimant presented his claim, together with a surveyor's plot of the land claimed, in the words and figures following, viz.:

To the Commissioners appointed in pursuance of the act of Congress passed the 3d day of March, 1803, for receiving and adjusting claims to lands south of Tennessee, and east of Pearl river.

Please to take notice, that the following tract of land, lying in the island known by the name of Nanna Hubba, formed by the cut-off of the rivers Tombigbee and Alabama, in the county of Washington, beginning on a stake, on the east bank of the Tombigbee river, (thirty chains northwardly, or above a corner already fixed, between Benjamin Few and Sterling Dupree, on the west bank of the river,) running thence, east, one hundred and eighty eight chains, to the Alabama river; thence, down the bank of the Alabama, to the mouth of the Fork lake; thence, with the margin of the lake, to the Tombigbee river; thence, up the margin of said river, to the beginning; containing six hundred and forty acres: is claimed by Natt Christmas, as representative of Michael Hartly, as a donation, by virtue of the second section of said act, and is now delivered to the Register of the Land Office, east of Pearl river, to be recorded agreeably to the directions of said act. To all which he begs leave to refer, as also to a copy of the plot herewith filed.

NATT CHRISTMAS.

APRIL 30, 1805.

[Plot omitted.]

Entered in record of claims, (east side,) vol. 1, page —.
 JOSEPH CHAMBERS, *Register.*

The claimant exhibited a deed from Michael Hartly, bearing date the 27th day of April, 1805, conveying to Natt Christmas all the said Hartly's right and title to said tract of land.

The Board ordered that the case be postponed for consideration.

JAMES CALLIER, representative of Joseph Campbell; case No. 214 on the docket of the Board, and No. 81 on the books of the Register.

Claim.—A donation of six hundred and forty acres, under the second section of the act.

The claimant presented his claim, together with a surveyor's plot of the land claimed, in the words and figures following, to wit:

To the Commissioners appointed in pursuance of the act of Congress passed the 3d day of March, 1803, for receiving and adjusting claims to lands south of the Tennessee, and east of Pearl river.

Please to take notice, that the following tract of land, situated on the east side of Tombigbee river, nearly opposite Fort Stoddert, beginning ten chains below the bend, running eighty chains down the river, thence, so as to contain six hundred and forty acres, in a square tract, is claimed by James Callier, legal representative of Joseph Campbell, under a conveyance from said Campbell, and acknowledged by Isabella Campbell, before the former Board of Commissioners, sitting at Fort Stoddert, by a settlement made by said Isabella Campbell, in 1797.

JAMES CALLIER.

APRIL 30, 1805.

Entered in record of claims, (east side,) vol. 1, page —.
 JOSEPH CHAMBERS, *Register.*

[Plot omitted.]

Michael Hartly was presented as a witness, and, being duly sworn and interrogated by the Board, he deposed, that he was not interested in this claim; that the land in question was cultivated in the year 1797, by Mrs. Trouillet, widow of Pierre or Peter Trouillet, and that she was at that time twenty-one years of age, and the head of a family.

The deed of conveyance from Joseph Campbell to James Callier, which was exhibited in said Callier's case, No. 95, and noted in vol. 1, page 407, was applied in support of this case.

The Board ordered that the case be postponed for consideration.

Adjourned until Thursday, the 16th instant.

THURSDAY, *May* 16th, 1805.

The Board met according to adjournment. Present: Robert C. Nicholas, Joseph Chambers.

SIMEON WILKS, representative of James Proctor; case No. 215 on the docket of the Board, and No. 48 on the books of the Register.

Claim.—A donation of six hundred and thirty-six acres, under the second section of the act.

The claimant presented his claim, together with a surveyor's plot of the land claimed, in the following words and figures, to wit:

To the Commissioners appointed in pursuance of the act of Congress passed the 3d day of March, 1803, for receiving and adjusting the claims to lands south of the Tennessee and east of Pearl river.

Please to take notice, that the following tract of land, situated on the Tensaw lake, on the east side of Tombigbee, in the county of Washington, beginning at a hickory, running north, eighty degrees east, eighty chains, to a stake; thence, south, ten degrees east, eighty chains, to a pine; thence, to a water oak on the lake; thence, north, ten degrees west, eighty chains, to the beginning; and hath such forms and marks, both natural and artificial, as are fully represented in the plot annexed, containing six hundred and thirty-six acres: is claimed by Simeon Wilks, legal representative of James Proctor, in and by virtue of the second section of the act, as a donation, and is now exhibited to the Register of the Land Office, established east of Pearl river, to be recorded as directed by said act. To all which he begs leave to refer, as also to a copy of the plot herewith filed.

SIMEON WILKS, legal representative of
JAMES PROCTOR.
MARCH 28, 1804.
[Plot omitted.]

Surveyed March 12th, 1804, J. Milliken. Sworn chain carriers, James M'Connell and Levi Qualls.

The claimant exhibited a writing in the words and figures following, to wit: Know all men by these presents, that I, James Proctor, have given up possession and all my claim of the improvement that Simeon Wilks now lives on, to him the said Wilks, for his proper use.

Given under my hand, this 15th day of January, 1803.
JAMES PROCTOR.

Witness, RICHARD COLEMAN, his x mark.

Entered on record of claims, (east side,) vol. 1, page 119, by EDWARD LLOYD WAILES, for
JOSEPH CHAMBERS, *Register.*

Richard Coleman and Joseph Stiggins were presented as witnesses, and being duly sworn and interrogated by the Board, they deposed, that they had no interest in this claim; that James Proctor did, in the year 1797, actually inhabit and cultivate the land in question; and that he was at that time twenty-one years of age, and the head of a family.

The Board ordered that the case be postponed for consideration.

WILLIAM COLLINS, representative of Charles Conway: case No. 216 on the docket of the Board, and No. 51 on the books of the Register.

Claim.—A donation of six hundred and thirty-eight acres, under the second section of the act.

The claimant presented his plot of the land claimed, in the words and figures following, to wit:

To the Commissioners appointed in pursuance of the act of Congress passed the 3d day of March, 1803, for receiving and adjusting claims to lands south of Tennessee, and east of Pearl river.

Please to take notice, that the following tract of land, situated on the east side of the river Tombigbee, bounded to the west by Tensaw lake, to the south by John Weekley's land, and on all other sides by vacant lands; and hath such marks, both natural and artificial, as are fully represented in the plot annexed, containing six hundred and thirty-eight acres, is claimed by William Collins, under and in virtue of a donation right, now delivered to the Register of the Land Office, established east of the Pearl river, to be recorded as directed by said act. To all which he begs leave to refer, as also to a copy of the plot herewith filed.

W. BUFORD, for
WILLIAM COLLINS.
MARCH 31, 1804.
[Plot omitted.]

Surveyed March 21, 1804. Sworn chain bearers, James M'Connell and Levi Qualls.

Entered in record of claims, (east side,) vol. 1, page 121, by EDWARD LLOYD WAILES, for
JOSEPH CHAMBERS, *Register.*

Richard Coleman and Joseph Stiggins were presented as witnesses, and, being duly sworn and interrogated by the Board, they deposed, that they were not inte-

rested in this claim; that Charles Conway did not inhabit or cultivate the land in question in the year 1797. The said Coleman further testified, that, as well as he recollected, the land was cultivated in the year 1797, but by whom, or for whose use, he did not know. The said Stiggins also testified, that, as well as he recollected, Richard Hawkins settled upon the land in question, in the year 1798.

The Board ordered that the case be postponed for consideration.

JOHN WEEKLEY, representative of James Farr; case No. 217 on the docket of the Board, and No. 50 on the books of the Register.

Claim.—A donation of six hundred and thirty-six acres, under the second section of the act.

The claimant presented his claim, together with a surveyor's plot of the land claimed, in the following words and figures, to wit:

To the Commissioners appointed in pursuance of the act of Congress passed the 3d day of March, 1803, for receiving and adjusting claims to lands south of the Tennessee, and east of Pearl river.

Please to take notice, that the following tract of land, situate on the east side of the river Tombigbee, bounded to the west by Tensaw lake, and to the south by Richard Coleman and Simeon Wilks, and hath such marks, both natural and artificial, as are fully represented in the plot annexed, containing six hundred and thirty-six acres: is claimed by John Weekley, under and by virtue of a donation, now delivered to the Register of the Land Office, established east of the Pearl river, to be recorded as directed by said act. To all which he begs leave to refer, as also to the copy of the plot herewith filed.

W. BUFORD, for
JOHN WEEKLEY.
MARCH 31, 1804.
[Plot omitted.]

Surveyed March 21, 1804, by J. Milliken. Sworn chain carriers, James McConnell and Levi Qualls.

Entered in record of claims, (east side,) vol. 1, page 120, by EDWARD LLOYD WAILES, for
JOSEPH CHAMBERS, *Register.*

The claimant exhibited a deed from James Farr, bearing date the 14th day of March, 1804, conveying to John Weekley all the said Farr's right and claim to the said tract of land.

Joseph Stiggins and Richard Coleman were presented as witnesses, and, being duly sworn and interrogated by the Board, deposed, that they were not interested in this claim; that James Farr did actually inhabit and cultivate the land in question, in the year 1797; that he was at that time twenty-one years of age, and the head of a family, and that he knew of no interfering claim.

The Board ordered that the case be postponed for consideration.

WILLIAM WEBBER's case, No. 218 on the docket of the Board, and No. 55 on the books of the Register.

Claim.—A donation of six hundred and forty acres, under the second section of the act.

The claimant presented his claim, together with a surveyor's plot of the land claimed, in the words and figures following, to wit:

To the Commissioners appointed in pursuance of the act of Congress passed the 3d day of March, 1803, for receiving and adjusting the claims to lands south of Tennessee, and east of Pearl river.

Please to take notice, that the following tract of land, situated on the east of Tombigbee, in the county of Washington, beginning at a stake, running east, eighty chains, to a stake; thence, north, eighty chains, to a hickory; thence, west, eighty chains, to a pine; thence, south, eighty chains, to the beginning; and hath such forms and marks, both natural and artificial, as are represented in the plot annexed, containing six hundred and forty acres: is claimed by William Webber, in and by virtue of the second section of the said act of Congress, and is now exhibited to the Register of the Land Office, established east of Pearl river. To all which he begs leave to refer, as also to a copy of the plot herewith filed.

W. BUFORD, for
WILLIAM WEBBER.
MARCH 31, 1804.
[Plot omitted.]

Entered in record of claims, (east side,) vol. 1, page 124, by EDWARD LLOYD WAILES, for
JOSEPH CHAMBERS, *Register.*

Joseph Stiggins and Richard Coleman were presented as witnesses, and, being duly sworn and interrogated by the Board, they deposed, that they were not interested in this claim; that William Webber cultivated and inhabited the land in question in the year 1797, and that he was at that time twenty-one years of age, and the head of a family; that they knew of no interfering claim.

The Board ordered that the case be postponed for consideration.

FANNY STEEL'S case, No. 219 on the docket of the Board, and No. 54 on the books of the Register.

Claim.—A donation of six hundred and forty acres, under the second section of the act.

The claimant presented her claim, together with a surveyor's plot of the land claimed, in the words and figures following, to wit:

To the Commissioners appointed in pursuance of the act of Congress passed the 3d day of March, 1803, for receiving and adjusting claims to lands south of Tennessee, and east of Pearl river.

Please to take notice, that the following tract of land, situate on the east side of the river Tombigbee, bounded on the north by Tensaw lake, and on all other sides by vacant land, and hath such marks, both natural and artificial, as are fully represented in the plot annexed, containing six hundred and forty acres: is claimed by Frances Steel, under and in virtue of a donation right, now delivered to the Register of the Land Office, established east of the Pearl river, to be recorded as directed by said act. To all which she begs leave to refer, as also to a copy of the plot herewith filed.

W. BUFORD, for
FRANCES STEEL.
[Plot omitted.]

Surveyed March 17th, 1804, by J. Milliken. Chain carriers, James M'Connell and Levi Qualls.

Entered in record of claims, (east side,) vol. 1, page 123, by EDWARD LLOYD WAILES, for
JOSEPH CHAMBERS, *Register.*

Joseph Stiggins and Reuben Dyer were presented as witnesses, and, being duly sworn and interrogated by the Board, they deposed, that they had no interest in this claim; that Fanny Steel did, in the year 1797, actually inhabit and cultivate the land in question; and that she was, at that time, twenty-one years of age, and the head of a family; and that they knew of no interfering claims.

The Board ordered that the case be postponed for consideration.

JORDAN PROCTOR'S case, No. 220 on the docket of the Board, and No. 44 on the books of the Register.

Claim.—A donation of six hundred and thirty-four acres, under the second section of the act.

The claimant presented his claim, together with a surveyor's plot of the land claimed, in the words and figures following, to wit:

To the Commissioners appointed in pursuance of the act of Congress passed the 3d day of March, 1803, for receiving and adjusting claims to lands south of Tennessee, and east of Pearl river.

Please to take notice, that the following tract of land, situated on the east side of Tombigbee, on lake Tensaw, in the county of Washington, beginning on a hickory on the lake, south, sixty-one degrees west, eighteen chains fifty links, to a stake; thence, north, twenty-eight degrees west, one hundred and fifty-one chains; thence, north, sixty-nine degrees east, eighteen chains fifty links, to the lake; thence, with the meanders of the lake, to the beginning; and hath such forms and marks, both natural and artificial, as are fully represented in the plot annexed, containing six hundred and thirty-four acres: is claimed by Jordan Proctor, in and by virtue of the second section of the said act of Congress, as a donation, and is now exhibited to the Register of the Land Office, established east of Pearl river, to be recorded as directed by said act. To all which he begs leave to refer, as also to a copy of the plot herewith filed.

JORDAN PROCTOR.
MARCH 28, 1804.
[Plot omitted.]

Surveyed March 13, 1804, by John Milliken. Chain bearers, James McConnell and Levi Qualls.

Entered in record of claims, (east side,) vol. 1, page 116, by EDWARD LLOYD WAILES, for
JOSEPH CHAMBERS, *Register.*

Joseph Stiggins and Richard Coleman were presented as witnesses, and being duly sworn and interrogated by the Board, they deposed, that they had no interest in this claim. And the said Coleman further testified, that, to the best of his recollection, in the year 1796, Jordan Proctor cultivated about five acres of the land in question, and that he was, at that time, twenty-one years of age. The said Stiggins also deposed, that, as well as he recollected, some time in the latter end of the year 1797, or the beginning of 1798, he passed by the plantation of Jordan Proctor, and saw the said Proctor at work in his field; that, from appearances, he, Stiggins, did suppose that there had been some land cleared and cultivated previous to that time; and that the said Proctor was, at that time, twenty-one years of age.

The Board ordered that the case be postponed for consideration.

HEIRS OF MICHAEL MILTON: case No. 221 on the docket of the Board, and No. 21 on the books of the Register.

Claim.—A donation of six hundred and eleven acres, under the second section of the act.

The claimants presented their claim, together with a surveyor's plot of the land claimed, in the following words and figures, to wit:

To the Commissioners appointed in pursuance of the act of Congress passed the 3d day of March, 1803, for receiving and adjusting the claims to lands south of Tennessee, and east of Pearl river.

Please to take notice, that the following tract of land, situated on the lake Tensaw, on the east side of Tombigbee, beginning on the lake, and running with it, north, eighty-five degrees west, one hundred and forty-eight chains fifty links, to a mulberry; thence, south, eighteen degrees east, thirty-eight chains fifty links, to a sweet gum; thence, south, seventy-eight degrees east, one hundred and sixty chains, to a dogwood; thence, north, thirteen degrees west, thirty-eight chains fifty links, to the lake, containing six hundred and eleven acres, having such shape, form, and marks, both natural and artificial, as are represented in the plot annexed: is claimed by the heirs of Michael Milton, in and by virtue of a donation, and now exhibited to the Register of the Land Office, established east of Pearl river, to be recorded as by said act directed. To all which they beg leave to refer, as also to a copy of the plot herewith filed.

BENJAMIN HOOVEN,
For the heirs of Michael Milton.
[Plot omitted.]

Surveyed March 8, 1804, by John Milliken. Chain bearers, James McConnell and Levi Qualls.

Entered in record of claims, (east side,) vol. 1, page 76, by EDWARD LLOYD WAILES, for
JOSEPH CHAMBERS, *Register.*

Reuben Dyer and Joseph Stiggins were presented as witnesses, and, being duly sworn and interrogated by the Board, they deposed, that they were not interested in this claim; that Michael Milton did, in the year 1797, actually inhabit and cultivate the land in question; and that he was, at that time, twenty-one years of age, and the head of a family; and that they knew of no interfering claim.

The Board ordered that the case be postponed for consideration.

REUBEN DYER'S case, No. 222 on the docket of the Board, and No. 46 on the books of the Register.

Claim.—A donation of six hundred and forty acres, under the second section of the act.

The claimant presented his claim, together with a surveyor's plot of the land claimed, in the following words and figures, viz.:

To the Commissioners appointed in pursuance of the act of Congress passed the 3d day of March, 1803, for receiving and adjusting the claims to lands south of Tennessee, and east of Pearl river.

Please to take notice, that the following tract of land, situate on the east side of Tombigbee river, being part of an island, in the county of Washington, beginning on the forks of Tensaw lake and river, at a water oak; running thence, north, ten degrees west, forty chains; thence, north, forty-four degrees west, thirty-three chains; thence, north, seventy-six degrees west, thirty-seven chains; thence, south, twenty-two degrees west, thirty-nine chains; thence, north, fifty-five degrees west, nineteen chains fifty links; thence, north, twenty-four degrees west, twenty-five chains fifty links; thence, north, forty-one degrees west, twenty-four chains; thence, north, sixty-six degrees west, ten chains; thence, south, thirty-four degrees east, twenty-three chains; thence, south, fourteen degrees east, thirty-three chains; thence, south, twenty-six degrees east, twenty-one chains; thence, south, twenty degrees west, sixteen chains; thence, south, fifty degrees west, seventeen chains, to a water oak; thence, south, eighty-nine degrees east, one hundred and twenty-eight chains fifty links, to the beginning; containing six hundred and forty acres, having such shape, forms, and marks, natural and artificial, as are represented in the plot annexed: is claimed by Reuben Dyer, in and by virtue of the second section of this act, as a donation, and is now exhibited to the Register of the Land Office, east of Pearl river, to be recorded as directed by said act. To all which he begs leave to refer, as also to a copy of the plot herewith filed.

REUBEN DYER.

March 28, 1804.

[Plot omitted.]

Surveyed March 20, 1804, by John Milliken. Chain bearers, James McConnell and Levi Qualls.

Entered in record of claims, (east side,) vol. 1, page 117, by EDWARD LLOYD WAILES, for
JOSEPH CHAMBERS, *Register.*

Joseph Stiggins and Reuben Dyer were presented as witnesses, and, being duly sworn and interrogated by the Board, they deposed, that they were not interested in this claim; that Reuben Dyer, the claimant, did, in the year 1797, cultivate the land in question, and had continued to cultivate the same ever since; that, from its being frequently covered with water, it was rendered unfit to reside on; that the said Dyer was, at that time, twenty-one years of age, and the head of a family; and that they knew of no interfering claim.

The Board ordered that the case be postponed for consideration.

RICHARD COLEMAN's case, No. 223 on the docket of the Board, and No. 45 on the books of the Register.

Claim.—A donation of six hundred and thirty-four acres, under the second section of the act.

The claimant presented his claim, together with a surveyor's plot of the land claimed, in the words and figures following, to wit:

To the Commissioners appointed in pursuance of the act of Congress passed the 3d day of March, 1803, for receiving and adjusting claims to lands south of Tennessee, and east of Pearl river.

Please to take notice, that the following tract of land, situated on the east side of Tombigbee river, on the Tensaw lake, in the county of Washington, beginning at a black oak, and running thence, north, sixty-four degrees east, fifty-six chains fifty-seven links, to a stake; thence, north, twenty-six degrees west, one hundred and thirteen chains fourteen links, to a maple and bay; thence, south, sixty-four degrees west, thirty-six chains, to the lake; thence, with the lake, south, thirty-one degrees east, eighty-nine chains, to the beginning, and hath such forms and marks, both natural and artificial, as are fully represented in the plot annexed, containing six hundred and thirty-four acres; is claimed by Richard Coleman, in and by virtue of the second section of the said act, as a donation, and is now exhibited to the Register of the Land Office, established east of Pearl river, to be recorded as directed by said act. To all which he begs leave to refer, as also to a copy of the plot herewith filed.

For RICHARD COLEMAN,
JOSEPH STIGGINS.

March 28, 1804.

[Plot omitted.]

Surveyed March 12, 1804, by John Milliken. Chain bearers, James McConnell and Levi Qualls.

Entered in record of claims, (east side,) vol. 1, page 117, by EDWARD LLOYD WAILES, for
JOSEPH CHAMBERS, *Register.*

Joseph Stiggins and Benjamin Pyburn were presented as witnesses, and, being duly sworn and interrogated by the Board, they deposed that they had no interest in this claim; that Richard Coleman, the claimant, did, in the year 1797, actually inhabit and cultivate the land in question; and that he was, at that time, twenty-one years of age, and the head of a family.

The Board ordered that the case be postponed for consideration.

JOSEPH STIGGINS's case, No. 224 on the docket of the Board, and No. 43 on the books of the Register.

Claim.—A donation of six hundred and thirty-five acres, under the second section of the act.

The claimant presented his claim, together with a surveyor's plot of the land claimed, in the following words and figures, to wit:

To the Commissioners appointed in pursuance of the act of Congress passed the 3d day of March, 1803, for receiving and adjusting the claims to lands south of Tennessee, and east of Pearl river.

Please to take notice, that the following tract of land, situated on the east side of Tombigbee river, in the county of Washington, beginning on a water oak on Coleman's or Tensaw lake, running thence, north, thirty-two degrees west, ten chains; thence, north, ten degrees west, eighteen chains, to a red bay tree; thence, up the meanders of said Tensaw or Stiggins's lake, to a bay, and on to a water oak corner; thence, south, fifty-five degrees east, twenty-four chains, to a corner stake; thence, south, sixty-one degrees east, one hundred and sixty-nine chains, to the beginning, being part of an island, and hath such forms and marks, both natural and artificial, as are fully represented in the plot annexed, containing six hundred and thirty-five acres: is claimed by Joseph Stiggins, in and by virtue of the second section of this act, as a donation, and is now exhibited to the Register of the Land Office established east of Pearl river, to be recorded as directed by said act. To all which he begs leave to refer, as also to a copy of the plot herewith filed.

JOSEPH STIGGINS.

MARCH 28, 1804.

[Plot omitted.]

Surveyed March 10, 1804, by John Milliken. Chain bearers, James McConnell and Levi Qualls.

Entered in record of claims, (east side,) vol. 1, page 116, by EDWARD LLOYD WAILES, for
JOSEPH CHAMBERS, *Register.*

Richard Coleman and Reuben Dyer were presented as witnesses, and, being duly sworn and interrogated by the Board, they deposed, that they were not interested in this claim; that Joseph Stiggins, the claimant, did, in the year 1797, cultivate the land in question; and that he was, at that time, twenty-one years of age, and the head of a family; that they knew of no interfering claim.

The Board ordered that the case be postponed for consideration.

JAMES COCKRAM, representative of Samuel Lyons; case, No. 225 on the docket of the Board, and No. 47 on the books of the Register.

Claim.—A donation of six hundred and forty acres, under the second section of the act.

The claimant presented his claim, together with a surveyor's plot of the land claimed, in the words and figures following, to wit:

To the Commissioners appointed in pursuance of the act of Congress passed the 3d day of March, 1803, for receiving and adjusting claims to lands south of Tennessee and east of Pearl river.

Please to take notice, that the following tract of land, situated on the east side of Tombigbee, on lake Tensaw, in the county of Washington, beginning at a cypress, and running north, seventy-three degrees east, eighty chains; thence, north, seventeen degrees west, eighty chains, to a pine; thence, south, seventy-three degrees west, eighty chains, to a tupelo gum; thence, south, seventeen degrees east, eighty chains, to the beginning; containing six hundred and forty acres, having such shape, forms, and marks, natural and artificial, as are represented in the plot annexed: is claimed by James Cockram, legal representative of Samuel Lyons, in and by virtue of a donation, and is now exhibited to the Register of the Land Office east of Pearl river, to be recorded as directed by said act. To all which he begs leave to refer, as also to a copy of the plot herewith filed.

JAMES COCKRAM, his + mark,
Legal representative of Samuel Lyons.

MARCH 28, 1804.

[Plot omitted.]

Surveyed March 26, 1804, by John Milliken. Chain bearers, Levi Qualls and John Milliken.

The claimant exhibited a writing as follows, to wit:

WASHINGTON COUNTY, *May* 29, 1802.

Received of James Cockram forty dollars, in full, for all my claim to the house and improvements on which I now live, together with all the crop now growing on said improvement, which I have this day sold, and am ready to deliver to him when called for.

SAMUEL LYONS, his × mark.

Witness : ELIJAH SMITH.

Entered in record of claims, (east side,) vol. 1, page 118, by EDWARD LLOYD WAILES, for

JOSEPH CHAMBERS, *Register.*

Reuben Dyer, Joseph Stiggins, and Benjamin Pyburn were presented as witnesses, and, being duly sworn and interrogated by the Board, they deposed, that they were not interested in this claim. The said Stiggins further testifies, that Samuel Lyons did, in the year 1797, actually inhabit and cultivate the land in question, and continued to cultivate the same until his death, which happened, as well as he recollected, in the fall of the year 1802; and that he was, in 1797, twenty-one years of age, and the head of a family.

The said Pyburn also deposed, that Samuel Lyons did inhabit and cultivate the land in question ; but in what year, he, Pyburn, did not recollect: that Lyons was twenty-one years of age, and the head of a family.

The said Dyer further testified, that Samuel Lyons did, in the year 1797, actually inhabit and cultivate the land in question; and that he was, at that time, twenty-one years of age, and the head of a family.

The Board ordered that the case be postponed for consideration.

SAMUEL TREND's case, No. 226 on the docket of the Board, and No. 57 on the books of the Register.

Claim.—A donation of six hundred and forty acres, under the second section of the act.

The claimant presented his claim, together with a surveyor's plot of the land claimed, in the words and figures following, to wit:

To the Commissioners appointed in pursuance of the act of Congress passed the 3d day of March, 1803, for receiving and adjusting claims to lands south of Tennessee and east of Pearl river.

Please to take notice that the following tract of land, situated on the east side of Tombigbee and Alabama rivers, in the county of Washington, beginning at a stake, running thence, north, fifteen degrees east, eighty chains, to a cypress, on Pine-log creek; thence, north, seventy-five degrees east, eighty chains, to a stake; thence, south, fifteen degrees west, eighty chains, to a stake; thence, south, seventy-five degrees west, eighty chains, across said creek, to the beginning; and hath such forms and marks, both natural and artificial, as are fully represented in the plot annexed; containing six hundred and forty acres: is claimed by Samuel Trend, in and by virtue of the second section of this act, as a donation; and is now exhibited to the Register of the Land office, established east of Pearl river, to be recorded as directed by said act. To all which he begs leave to refer, as also to a copy of the plot herewith filed.

WILLIAM SHIELDS, his ⋈ mark, for
SAMUEL TREND.

MARCH 31, 1804.

[Plot omitted.]

Surveyed February 15th, 1804, by John Milliken. Chain bearers, William McDaniel and James Mills.

Entered in record of claims, (east side,) vol. 1, page 125, by EDWARD LLOYD WAILES, for

JOSEPH CHAMBERS, *Register.*

William Pierce and Joseph Stiggins were presented as witnesses, and, being duly sworn and interrogated by the Board, they deposed, that they had no interest in this claim; that the land in question was actually inhabited and cultivated by Samuel Trend, in the year 1797; and that he was, at that time, twenty-one years of age, and the head of a family; and the lands claimed by the heirs of Francis Killingworth interfere with this claim.

The Board ordered that the case be postponed for consideration.

WILLIAM BUFORD, representative of Conrad Selhoof; case No. 227 on the docket of the Board, and No. 25 on the books of the Register.

Claim.—A right to eight hundred acres, by virtue of a Spanish warrant of survey, under the first section of the act.

The claimant presented his claim, together with a surveyor's plot of the land claimed, in the words and figures following, viz.:

To the Register appointed in pursuance of the act of Congress passed the 3d day of March, 1803, for recording claims to the south of Tennessee, and east of Pearl river.

Please to take notice, that the following tract of land, situated on the east side of the river Tombigbee, bounded to the south and southwest by Tensaw river, and hath such natural marks as are represented by a Spanish warrant of survey hereunto annexed ; containing eight hundred acres, or twenty acres front on said river, and forty back; granted to Conrad Selhoof, and transferred, by legal conveyances, to the present claimant William Buford. The Register will further please to take notice, that the said tract of land, including Piney island, is at this time so covered by water, that an accurate survey cannot be made on the same; and that, when a proper board shall be appointed for adjusting the claims to lands lying in that part of Washington county, the claimant will exhibit the necessary plot and other documents to establish the said claim.

W. BUFORD, *Claimant.*

MARCH 31, 1804.

[Plot omitted.]

The claimant exhibited a Spanish warrant in the words and figures following, viz.:

His excellency Don Estevan Miro, Colonel of the royal army, Governor civil and military of the city and province of Louisiana, &c.

Conrad Selhoof, inhabitant of Mobile jurisdiction, with great respect to your excellency, says, that there is found a tract of land on Tensaw river, containing twenty acres, by the name of Pine island; which land, until now, never had any proprietor; he begs your excellency to grant him the above petition, and deliver him the titles necessary from the Secretary of Government, which may correspond with the concession ; for which favor he will forever be thankful.

CONRAD SELHOOF.

MOBILE, *January* 15, 1788.

Don Vicent Folch, captain in the Louisiana regiment of fixed, commandant civil and military of said place and its jurisdiction, certified, that the land the petitioner solicits is vacant, by information taken from different inhabitants, who are well informed of said place, for which I sign at said place the day and date above mentioned.

VICENT FOLCH.

NEW ORLEANS, *February* 9, 1788.

The surveyor of this province, Don Laveau Trudeau, shall establish that part of land of twenty acres front, which the petitioner solicits, with its profounder of forty, as customary; as it is vacant, not causing prejudice to any neighbors, at the same place mentioned in the above petition; with the precise conditions of making the road and clearing regularly, in peremptory space of one year; and if, at the precise space of three years, the land is not settled, after which period it cannot be established, this grant to remain null; under which supposition, the business of settling the limits will be carried on in the tract, and remitted to me to provide the interested party with titles in form.

ESTEVAN MIRO.

MOBILE, *April* 4, 1788.

Certifies that the above is a true copy of the original, in the office at this place.

SANTIAGO DE LA SAUSSAYE, *Public Notary.*

The above is a copy of the Spanish grant.

THOMAS PRICE.

The above was compared exact with the original in this office under my charge, by me.

JOAQ. DE ORSONO. [L. s.]

I, Thomas Price, of the post of Mobile, English interpreter for His Majesty the King of Spain, do solemnly swear by the Almighty God, and by the Holy Cross, that this is a true and faithful translation of the Spanish grant, or writing hereto annexed.

THOS. PRICE.

Subscribed and sworn before the Board, March 21st, 1804.—Attest: DAVID PARMELEE 2d, *Clerk.*

Upon the back of said order of survey, there are two writings or conveyances in the words and figures following, to wit:

Know all men by these presents, that I, Cornelius McCurtin, by virtue of a power of attorney to me given by the widow Colate, of New Orleans, have made over unto John Linder, Esquire, his heirs or assigns, forever, the within grant, with all the rights and titles of said Madam Colate. Given under my hand this 10th day of March, 1794. As by power of attorney from the widow Colate.

CORNELIUS McCURTIN.

Know all men by these presents, that I, John Linder, Esquire, Senior, have hereby bargained and sold unto John Linder, Junior, the within premises, or his heirs, executors, administrators, and assigns, forever, for which I hereby warrant and defend against all persons whatsoever, or my heirs, executors, administrators, or assigns, for value received: as witness my hand and seal, this 11th day of June, 1798.

JNO. LINDER.

Witnesses, JAMES McALPINE,
JOHN MILLS.

Entered in record of claims, (east side,) vol. 1, page 91, by EDWARD LLOYD WAILES, for

JOSEPH CHAMBERS, Register.

The claimant exhibited a deed from John Linder, duly executed, and bearing date the 24th day of October, 1803, conveying to William H. Buford all the right, title, and interest, of the said Linder in said tract of land, and the improvements thereon made.

Reuben Dyer, Joseph Stiggins, and Richard Coleman, were presented as witnesses, and, being duly sworn and interrogated by the Board, they deposed, that they were not interested in this claim. The said Stiggins also deposed, that he knew nothing of this claim but from hearsay.

The said Dyer also deposed, that Mr. Collett, many years past, lived upon the land in question; that he, Dyer, knew of no person, either by the name of Collett or Selhoof, being on said land, in the year 1795; that the person called Collett was, when he knew him, an elderly man; and that the said Collett died on the land in question; and that an inventory of his estate was taken by Robert Lard.

The said Coleman also deposed, that, as well as he recollected, John Linder, Senior, in the year 1795, informed him that he had the land in question in cultivation, but that he, Coleman, did not know it of his own knowledge.

The Board ordered that the case be postponed for consideration.

Adjourned until Saturday, the 18th instant.

SATURDAY, May 18, 1805.
The Board met according to adjournment. Present: Robert C. Nicholas, Joseph Chambers.

ADAM HOLLINGER's case, No. 228 on the docket of the Board, and No. 16 on the books of the Register.

Claim.—A right to nine hundred and ninety-nine acres and five-tenths of an acre, under the first section of the act, by virtue of a Spanish warrant or order of survey.

The claimant presented his claim, together with a surveyor's plot of the land claimed, in the words and figures following, to wit:

To the Commissioners appointed in pursuance of an act of Congress passed the 3d of March, 1803, for receiving and adjusting claims to lands south of the Tennessee river, and east of Pearl river.

Please to take notice, that the following tract of land, lying east of the river Tombigbee, butting and bounding as follows, viz.: beginning at a tupelo gum, on the bank of the Cut-off, thence, down the meanders, to the mouth of said Cut-off, to a willow; thence, down the river Tombigbee, to a maple corner; thence, north, eighty-six degrees east, one hundred and twenty-six chains, fifty-three links; thence, a straight line, to the beginning; bounded by Tombigbee river on the west, and northwardly by the Cut-off, on the other sides by vacant land: is claimed by Adam Hollinger, under and by virtue of a Spanish grant or order of survey granted to Adam Hollinger, as may appear by the original grant now delivered to the Register of the Land Office, to be established east of Pearl river, to be recorded agreeably to that act. To all which he begs leave to refer, as also to the copy of the plot herewith filed.

W. CARMAN,
Attorney for Adam Hollinger.

FORT STODDERT, March 21, 1804.
[Plot omitted.]

Said warrant of survey was exhibited in the words following, viz.:

MOBILE, December 24, 1794.
His Excellency the GOVERNOR GENERAL:

Adam Hollinger, inhabitant of this jurisdiction, with the most profound respect, represents before your excellency and says, that, within the district of Tombigbee exists and is twenty-five acres of vacant land, on a creek called Boukanonga, and on the right hand of said creek, up the river. Said land has no proprietor; and having slaves in number sufficient to cultivate the same, he begs your excellency to grant him the above petition, with papers necessary from the Secretary of Government, which may correspond with the concession, for which favor he will be forever thankful.

ADAM HOLLINGER.

MOBILE, December 27, 1794.
His excellency the Governor General of these provinces, by information from the old settlers of said river, it appears that the land the above petitioner solicits is vacant, and has no proprietor, and the number of slaves in possession of the above petitioner, it suffers no difficulty in granting the above petition, as it may seem best.

MANUEL DE LANZOS.

NEW ORLEANS, January 30th, 1795.
The surveyor of this province, Don Carlos Laveau Trudeau, or some other named by him, shall establish the petitioner on the twenty-five acres of land front, with the profounder, as customary, of forty acres back, as it appears vacant, and not causing any prejudice to any neighbors, with the precise conditions of making the road and clearing regularly, in the peremptory space of one year; and if, at the precise space of three years, the land is not settled, during which period it cannot be alienated, this grant to remain null; under which supposition the business of settling the limits will be carried on in the tract, and remitted me to provide the interested party with titles in form.

THE BARON OF CARONDELET.

MOBILE, February 16, 1795.
Registered. Certifieth the above is a copy of the original concession, that remains in these archives, under my charge.

MANUEL DE LANZOS.

The above is a copy of the Spanish grant.
THOS. PRICE.

The above was compared exact with the original in this office, by me,
JOAQUIN DE OSORNO. [L. S.]

I, Thomas Price, of the post of Mobile, English interpreter for his Majesty the King of Spain, do solemnly swear by the Almighty God, and by the Holy Cross, that this is a true and faithful translation of the Spanish grant or writing hereto annexed.

THOS. PRICE.

Subscribed and sworn before the Board, March 21st, 1804.—Attest; DAVID PARMELEE 2d, Clerk.

Entered in record of claims, (east of Tombigbee,) vol. 1, page 62, by EDWARD LLOYD WAILES, for

JOSEPH CHAMBERS, Register.

John Jacob Abner and Joseph Bates, senior, were presented as witnesses, and, being duly sworn and interrogated by the Board, they deposed, that they were not interested in this claim; that, in the year 1795, a man by the name of Watkins cultivated the land in question, as a tenant at will of Adam Hollinger; that, in the same year, in the month of August, Adam Hollinger commenced a clearing on the land, by his overseer and hands, and in the latter end of the same year removed himself and family to the place where he now lives; that the said land had been cultivated by the said Hollinger ever since, and that Adam Hollinger was, at that time, twenty-one years of age, and the head of a family.

The Board ordered the case to be postponed for consideration.

JOSEPH BATES, Senior's, case, No. 229 on the docket of the Board, and No. 26 on the books of the Register.

Claim.—A right to one thousand acres, by virtue of a Spanish warrant of survey, under the first section of the act.

The claimant presented his claim, together with a surveyor's plot of the land claimed, in the words and figures following, viz.:

To the Commissioners appointed in pursuance of the act of Congress, passed the 3d of March, 1803, for receiving and adjusting the claims to lands south of Tennessee, and east of Pearl river.

Please to take notice, that the following tract of land, situated on the east bank of Tombigbee river, beginning on a cedar post on said east bank; running thence with Thomas Bates, Junior's, line, south, forty-five degrees east, eighty chains, to a stake; thence, north, forty-five degrees east, sixty-four chains, to a stake; thence, south, forty-five degrees east, eighty chains, to a stake; thence, south, forty-five degrees west, eighty chains, to a stake; thence, north, forty-five degrees west, eighty chains, to a stake; thence, north, fifteen degrees east, sixteen chains, to a stake; thence, north, seventy-five degrees west, eighty chains, to a cedar post on the bank of the river; thence up the river the courses and distances, as laid down in the plot, to the beginning; and hath such forms and marks, both natural and artificial, as are fully represented in the plot annexed, containing one thousand acres: is claimed by Joseph Bates, Senior, in and by virtue of a Spanish grant, and is now exhibited to the Register of the Land Office, established east of Pearl river, to be recorded as directed by said act. To all which he begs leave to refer, as also to a copy of the plot herewith filed.

JOSEPH BATES, Senior.

MARCH 23, 1804.

[Plot omitted.]

Surveyed March 19th, 1804. by Natt Christmas. Chain bearers, Sterling Dupree and Thomas Bates.

The claimant exhibited an order of survey as follows, to wit:

MOBILE, *July 20th,* 1795.

His Excellency the GOVERNOR GENERAL:

Joseph Bates, inhabitant of this district, with the greatest respect to your excellency, represents and says, there is a tract of vacant land, situate on Tombigbee river, in distance about eighteen leagues from this place, limited on the north by land of John Turnbulls, and on the south by vacant land facing my own plantation; and, being necessitated for land to cultivate, begs your excellency to grant him twenty-five acres front, with its profounder of forty, as customary; the said land never had any proprietor. He begs your excellency to grant the above petition, with orders to the Secretary to deliver him the corresponding concession; for which favor he will be forever thankful.

JOSEPH BATES.

MOBILE, *July 27th,* 1795.

His excellency the Governor General of this province, by information from the inhabitants of that settlement, the land is vacant, and of consequence King's commons: not causing any prejudice to any neighbors, you may dispose as it may seem best.

NEW ORLEANS, *August* 18, 1795.

The Surveyor General of this province, or some individual named by him for that business, shall establish that part of land, of twenty-five acres front, with its profounder of forty acres, as customary, as it is vacant, not causing prejudice to any neighbors, at the same place mentioned in the above petition, with the precise conditions of making the road and clearing regularly in the peremptory space of one year; and if, at the precise space of three years, the land is not settled, during which period it cannot be alienated, this grant to remain null: under which supposition, the business of settling the limits will be carried on in the tract, and remitted me to provide the interested party with titles in form.

THE BARON OF CARONDELET.

MOBILE, *March* 6, 1804.

This is a copy compared with the original in this office under my charge.

JOAQUIN DE OSORNO. [L. S.]

The above is a copy of the Spanish grant.

THOMAS PRICE.

I, Thomas Price, of the post of Mobile, English interpreter for His Majesty the King of Spain, do solemnly swear by the Almighty God, and by the Holy Cross, that this is a true and faithful translation of the Spanish grant or writing hereto annexed.

THOMAS PRICE.

Subscribed and sworn before the Board, March 21st, 1804.—Attest: DAVID PARMELEE 2d, *Clerk.*

Entered on record of claims, (east of Tombigbee) vol. 2, page 95, by EDWARD LLOYD WAILES, for

JOSEPH CHAMBERS, *Register.*

Natt Christmas, surveyor, was presented as a witness, and, being duly sworn, deposed, that he made the plot exhibited to the Board by Joseph Bates with his Spanish warrant of survey, which included the improvement and cleared lands of the claimant; that an actual survey of the river or front of this land was made, and a few chains on the upper and lower lines running out from the river; that, in consequence of high water, it was impossible to complete the survey, except by plotting the same.

Adam Hollinger and John Jacob Abner were presented as witnesses, and, being duly sworn and interrogated by the Board, they deposed, that they were not interested in this claim. The said Abner testified further, that, in the year 1791, he was at Joseph Bates, Senior's, and saw considerable improvements and cultivation on the land in question; that he, the said Bates, had continued to cultivate thereon ever since; that he was, on the 18th day of August, 1795, twenty-one years of age, and the head of a family.

The said Hollinger also deposed, that Joseph Bates, Senior, cultivated the land in question in the year 1795; and had continued to cultivate the same ever since; that, on the 18th day of August, 1795, he was twenty-one years of age, and the head of a family.

The Board ordered that the case be postponed for consideration.

RICHARD TURVIN's case, No. 230 on the docket of the Board, and No. 20 on the books of the Register.

Claim.—A donation of six hundred and forty acres, under the second section of the act.

The claimant presented his claim, together with a surveyor's plot of the land claimed, in the words and figures following, viz.:

To the Commissioners appointed in pursuance of the act of Congress passed the 3d day of March, 1803, for receiving and adjusting claims to land south of Tennessee, and east of Pearl river.

Please to take notice, that the following tract of land, situated on the east side of Tombigbee river, in the county of Washington, beginning on a maple standing on the bank of Tombigbee river, at Adam Hollinger's corner, running down the bank of said river, south, forty degrees east, thirty-eight chains, to a lake; continued two chains further to an oak corner; thence, along the banks of the river south, nine degrees east, twenty chains; thence, south, nine degrees west, fifteen chains; thence, south, forty-nine degrees west, five chains, south, forty-two degrees west, seven chains and fifty links, to a swamp oak corner; thence, to Thomas Bates, Junior's, line; thence, south, forty-five degrees east, thirteen chains, to an ash station at the edge of the swamp, continued in all eighty-four chains, to a stake; thence, north, forty-five degrees east, seventy-seven chains and fifty links, to a stake; thence, north, forty-five degrees west, eighty-nine chains, to the beginning; and hath such forms and marks, both natural and artificial, as are fully represented in the plot annexed, containing six hundred and forty acres; is claimed by Richard Turvin, in and by virtue of the second section of the said act, as a donation, and is now exhibited to the Register of the Land Office established east of Pearl river. To all which he begs leave to refer, and to be recorded as directed by said act; also to a copy of the plot herewith filed.

RICHARD TURVIN, his x mark.

MARCH 26, 1804.

[Plot omitted.]

Surveyed February 22d, 1804, by Natt Christmas. Chain bearers, Thomas Bates, John Barnet.

Entered in record of claims, (east side,) vol. 1, page 74, by EDWARD LLOYD WAILES, for

JOSEPH CHAMBERS, *Register.*

John Jacob Abner and Adam Hollinger were presented as witnesses, and, being duly sworn and interrogated by the Board, they deposed, that they were not interested in this claim; that the land in question was not cultivated until the year 1798.

The Board ordered the case to be postponed for consideration.

SAMUEL MIMS's claim, No. 231 on the docket of the Board, and No. 85 on the books of the Register.

Claim.—A donation of six hundred and forty acres, under the second section of the act.

The claimant presented his claim, together with a surveyor's plot of the land claimed, in the words and figures following, to wit:

To the Commissioners appointed in pursuance of the act of Congress passed the 3d day of March, 1803, for receiving and adjusting claims to land south of Tennessee, and east of Pearl river.

Please to take notice, that the following tract of land, situated on the east side of the Tombigbee river, in the county of Washington, beginning on the Alabama river, or Cut-off, at a sweet gum; south, five degrees east, one hundred and nine chains; south, eighty-five degrees west, seventy-one chains, at a stake; north, five degrees west, eighty chains, at a stake; and hath such forms and marks, both natural and artificial, as are fully represented in the plot annexed, containing six hundred and forty acres: is claimed by Samuel Mims, in and by virtue of a donation, and is now exhibited to the Register of the Land Office, established east of Pearl river, to be recorded as directed by said act. To all which he begs leave to refer, as also to a copy of the plot herewith filed.

W. PIERCE, for
SAMUEL MIMS.

APRIL 29, 1805.
[Plot omitted.]
Entered in record of claims, (east side,) vol. 1, page 237.

JOSEPH CHAMBERS, *Register.*

William Pierce and Adam Hollinger were presented as witnesses, and, being duly sworn and interrogated by the Board, they deposed, that they had no interest in this claim; that Samuel Mims did, in the year 1797, actually cultivate the land in question, lying in Nanna Hubba Island; that he was at that time twenty-one years of age, and the head of a family; and that they knew of no interfering claim.
The Board ordered that the case be postponed for consideration.

JAMES CALLIER, representative of Joseph Campbell: case commenced in page 738.

Joseph Bates, Sen. and John Jacob Abner, were presented as witnesses, and, being duly sworn and interrogated by the Board, they deposed, that they were not interested in this claim; and the said Bates testified, that the land in question was cultivated in the year 1797, by hands belonging to Isabella Trouillet, widow of Peter Trouillet; that he did not know whether Mrs. Trouillet resided on the bluff, opposite the land in question at that time, or whether she was then living in the town of Mobile; that Alexis Trouillet informed him that he was the overseer of Mrs. Trouillet, and was cultivating the land to her use, and that she was at that time, as he, Bates, believed, twenty-one years of age, and the head of a family. The said Abner also testified, that he did not see the land in question in the year 1797, but from seeing the hands of Mrs. Trouillet pass to and from the place in question, and from being told by Alexis Trouillet, that he was the overseer of Mrs. Trouillet, he had reason to believe that the land was cultivated to her use, and that she was, at that time, as he believed, twenty-one years of age, and the head of a family.
The Board ordered that the case be postponed for consideration.

NATT CHRISTMAS, representative of Michael Hartly: case commenced in page 738.

Joseph Bates, Sen., Adam Hollinger, and Richard Turvin, were presented as witnesses, and, being duly sworn and interrogated by the Board, they deposed, that they had no interest in this claim; the said Bates and Hollinger testified, that the land in question was cultivated by Michael Hartly in the year 1796, 1797, and 1798; that the situation of the land was such as would not admit of being inhabited, and that said Hartly was, in the year 1797, twenty-one years of age, and the head of a family. The said Turvin also testified, that Michael Hartly cultivated the land in question in the years 1797 and 1798; that, from the low situation of the land, it would not admit of being inhabited; that said Hartly was, in 1797, twenty-one years of age, and the head of a family.
The Board ordered that the case be postponed for consideration.

BENJAMIN FEW's case: commenced in page 729.

Adam Hollinger was presented as a witness, and, being duly sworn, he deposed, that Benjamin Few had raised three successive crops, independent of the one now growing on the land in question; and that he was,

on the 3d day of March, 1803, twenty-one years of age, and the head of a family.
The Board ordered that the case be postponed for consideration.

LEMUEL HENRY, representative of Michael Hartly; case, No. 232 on the docket of the Board, and No. 86 on the books of the Register.

Claim.—A donation of six hundred and forty acres, under the second section of the act.

The claimant presented his claim, together with a surveyor's plot of the land claimed, in the words and figures following, to wit:

To the Honorable the Board of Commissioners appointed in pursuance of the act of Congress passed the 3d of March, 1803, for the adjusting of claims to land south of Tennessee and east of Pearl river.

Please to take notice, that Lemuel Henry, legal representative of Michael Hartly, claims a tract of land of six hundred and forty acres, as a donation, situate on the lower end of the Nanna Hubba Island, beginning at a cedar post, on the east bank of the Tombigbee river, running north, fifty-seven degrees east, five hundred poles, to the Alabama river, and down both rivers for complement, as by the plot herewith filed will more fully appear.

LEMUEL HENRY.
[Plot omitted.]

Surveyed by Lemuel Henry.
Entered in record of claims, (east side,) vol. 1, page 239.

JOSEPH CHAMBERS, *Register.*

The claimant exhibited a deed, bearing date the 22d day of April, 1805, from Michael Hartly, conveying to Lemuel Henry all the said Hartly's right to said tract of land.
Adam Hollinger, Joseph Bates, Senior, and Richard Turvin, were presented as witnesses, and, being duly sworn and interrogated by the Board, they deposed, that they were not interested in this claim. The said Bates and Hollinger testified, that the land in question was cultivated by Michael Hartly in the years 1796, 1797, and 1798; that the situation of the land was such as would not admit of being inhabited; and that the said Hartly was, in the year 1797, twenty-one years of age, and the head of a family. The said Turvin testified, that Michael Hartly cultivated the land in question in the years 1797 and 1798; that, from the low situation of the land, it would not admit of being inhabited, and that said Hartly was, in 1797, twenty-one years of age and the head of a family.
The Board ordered that the case be postponed for consideration.

SAMUEL MIMS, representative of William Clark; case, No. 233 on the docket of the Board, and No. 66 on the books of the Register.

Claim.—A right to one hundred and seventy-four acres, by virtue of a British grant, under the first section of the act.

The claimant presented his claim, together with a surveyor's plot of the land claimed, in the words and figures following, to wit:

To the Commissioners appointed, in pursuance of the act of Congress passed the 3d day of March, 1803, for receiving and adjusting claims to lands south of Tennessee and east of Pearl river.

Please to take notice, that the following tract of land, situated about eighty miles from the town of Mobile, in the county of Washington, bounded on the west by the river Alabama, and on the other sides by a laggoon, and hath such forms and marks, both natural and artificial, as are fully represented in the plot annexed, containing one hundred and seventy-four acres: is claimed by Samuel Mims, legal representative to William Clark, in and by virtue of a British grant, and is now exhibited to the Register of the Land Office, established east of Pearl river, to be recorded as directed by said act. To all which he begs leave to refer, as also to a copy of the plot herewith filed.

SAMUEL MIMS.

MARCH 31, 1804.
[Plot omitted.]

Surveyed, 1778, by Elias Durnford, *S. G.*
A grant was exhibited in the words and figures following, to wit:

WEST FLORIDA, *ss:*

GEORGE THE THIRD, *by the grace of God, of Great Britain, France, and Ireland, King, defender of the faith, &c. To all to whom these presents shall come, greeting:*

Know ye, that we, of our special grace, certain knowledge, and mere motion, have given and granted, and, by these presents, for us, our heirs and successors, do give and grant, unto William Clark, his heirs and assigns, all that tract of land situated about eighty-five miles from the town of Pensacola, bounded on the west by the river Alabama, and on the other sides by a laggoon, in our province of West Florida, and having such shape, form, and marks, both natural and artificial, as are represented in the plot thereof hereunto annexed, as drawn by our Surveyor General of lands; which said tract of land contains one hundred and seventy-four acres, and is bounded as by the further certificate hereunto likewise annexed, under the hand of said Surveyor General of lands, in our said province, may more fully and at large appear; together with all woods, underwoods, timber, and timber trees, lakes, ponds, fishings, waters, watercourses, profits, commodities, hereditaments, and appurtenances whatsoever hereunto belonging, or in anywise appertaining; together, also, with privilege of hunting, hawking, and fowling in and upon the same, and all mines and minerals, reserving to us, our heirs and successors, all mines of gold and silver; to have and to hold the said tract of land, and all and singular the premises hereby granted, with the appurtenances, unto the said William Clark, his heirs and assigns, forever, in free and common soccage, yielding and paying unto us, our heirs and successors, or to the Receiver General of our quit-rents for the time being, or to such other officer as shall be appointed to receive the same, a quit-rent of one halfpenny sterling per acre, at the feast of St. Michael every year; the first payment to commence on the said feast of St. Michael, which shall first happen after the expiration of ten years from the date hereof, or within fourteen days after the said feast annually: *Provided, always,* (and this present grant is upon condition,) *nevertheless,* That this grant shall be duly registered in the Register's Office of this province, within six months from the date hereof, and also, that a docket thereof shall be entered in the Auditor's Office within the same time, if such establishment shall take place in this province: *And provided, also,* That if the said William Clark, his heirs and assigns, do not in all things fully comply with, and fulfil the condition herein above set forth, for the registering of this grant, within the time herein above limited for the completion thereof; or if the said William Clark, his heirs and assigns, shall not pay to us, our heirs and successors, or to the Receiver General of our quit-rents, or to the proper officer appointed to receive the same, the said quit-rent of one halfpenny sterling per acre, on the said feast of St. Michael, or within fourteen days after, annually, for every acre contained in this grant; that then, and in either of these cases, respectively, this grant shall be void, any thing herein contained to the contrary notwithstanding; and the said lands, tenements, hereditaments, and premises, hereby specified, and every part and parcel thereof, shall revert to us, our heirs and successors, as fully and absolutely, as if the same had never been granted.

Given under the great seal of our province of West Florida: Witness our trusty and well beloved Peter Chester, Esquire, our Captain General, and Governor-in-chief in and over our said province, at Pensacola, this sixth day of August, in the year of our Lord one thousand seven hundred and seventy-eight, and in the eighteenth year of our reign.

PETER CHESTER.

Passed the Secretary's Office.

PH. LIVINGSTON JUN., *Dep. Sec.*

WEST FLORIDA:

Pursuant to a fiat from his excellency Peter Chester, Esq., Captain General and Governor-in-chief in and over His Majesty's province of West Florida, &c. to me directed, bearing date the 4th day of August, 1778, I have perused and inspected the within letters patent, and do hereby certify that there is no error therein apparent to me.

ELIHU HALL BAY, for
E. R. WEGG, *Attorney General.*

AUDITOR'S OFFICE, *August* 6, 1778.

A docket of the within grant is entered in book B, folio 42, by

J. LORIMER, *Deputy Auditor.*

PENSACOLA, *Secretary's Office.*

I do hereby certify, that the within letters patent, Surveyor General's certificate, together with the certificate of the Attorney General, are recorded in the Secretary and Register's Office of the province of West Florida, in liber A, No. 4, page 42, &c. Examined and compared with the said record.

PHILIP LIVINGSTON, JUN., *Dep. Sec.*

Upon the back of which grant there is an endorsement, in the following words and figures, to wit: I deliver the within grant to Jesse McCall, Esq., as conveyed to him twenty-seventh May, 1801, by me,

A. GINDRAT.

Entered in record of claims, (east side,) vol. 1, by EDWARD LLOYD WAILES, for

JOSEPH CHAMBERS, *Register.*

The claimant exhibited a deed from A. Gindrat, bearing date the 27th day of May, 1801, conveying to Jesse McCall, Esq., all the said Gindrat's right and title to said land; also a deed from Jesse McCall, bearing date the 23d day of September, 1801, conveying to Samuel Mims all the said McCall's right, title, and interest in said tract of land.

Adam Hollinger and William Pierce were presented as witnesses, and, being duly sworn and interrogated by the Board, they deposed, that they were not interested in this claim. The said Hollinger also testified, that the land in question was cultivated by Samuel Mims in the year 1795; that said land adjoined the land on which he resided, and that his principal support was had from his cultivation on this land. The said Pierce also deposed, that the land in question was cultivated in the year 1795, by Samuel Mims, and that, from a conversation which he heard between the said Mims and William Clark, he was induced to believe that said land was then the property of said William Clark, and that Mims was tenant at will of him, said Clark; and that he, Clark, was an inhabitant and resident in the State of Georgia on the 27th day of October, 1795; that the land in question was adjoined to that on which the said Mims resided, and that his principal support was had from this land.

The Board ordered that the case be postponed for consideration.

SAMUEL MIMS, representative of William Clark; case No. 234 on the docket of the Board, and No. 67 on the books of the Register.

Claim.—A right to three hundred and fifty acres, by virtue of a British grant, under the first section of the act.

The claimant presented his claim, together with a surveyor's plot of the land claimed, in the words and figures following, to wit:

To the Commissioners appointed in pursuance of the act of Congress passed the 3d day of March, 1803, for receiving and adjusting the claims to lands south of Tennessee, and east of Pearl river.

Please to take notice, that the following tract of land, situated on the east side of Tombigbee and Alabama river, in the county of Washington, butting and bounded west, by the Alabama river and a laggoon, and all other sides by vacant land, and hath such forms and marks, natural and artificial, as are represented in the plot annexed, containing three hundred and fifty acres, is claimed by Samuel Mims, legal representative of William Clark, in and by virtue of a British patent, and is now exhibited to the Register of the Land Office established east of Pearl river, to be recorded as directed by said act. To all which he begs leave to refer, as also to a copy of the plot herewith filed.

SAMUEL MIMS.

MARCH 31, 1804.

[Plot omitted.]

Surveyed by Elias Durnford, Surveyor General.

The claimant exhibited a British grant as follows, to wit:

WEST FLORIDA, *ss.*

GEORGE THE THIRD, *by the grace of God, of Great Britain, France, and Ireland, King, defender of the faith, &c. To all to whom these presents shall come, greeting:*

Know ye, that we, of our special grace, certain knowledge, and mere motion, have given and granted, and by these presents, for us, our heirs and successors, do give and grant, unto William Clark, his heirs and assigns, all that tract of land situated on the east side of Alabama river, bounded west by said river and by a laggoon, and on all other sides by vacant land, in our province of West Florida, and having such shape, form, and marks, both natural and artificial, as are represented in the plot thereof hereunto annexed, as drawn by our Surveyor General of lands, which said tract of land contains three hundred and fifty acres, and is bounded as by the further certificate hereunto likewise annexed, under the hand of our said Surveyor General of lands, in our said province, may more fully and at large appear; together with all woods, underwoods, timber, and timber trees, lakes, ponds, fishings, waters, water courses, profits, commodities, hereditaments, and appurtenances whatsoever thereunto belonging, or in anywise appertaining; together, also, with privilege of hunting, hawking, and fowling in and upon the same, and all mines and minerals, reserving to us, our heirs and successors, all mines of gold and silver: to have and to hold the said tract of land, and all and singular the premises, hereby granted, with the appurtenances, unto the said William Clark, his heirs and assigns, forever, in free and common soccage, yielding and paying unto us, our heirs and successors, or to the Receiver General of our quit-rents for the time being, or to such other officer as shall be appointed to receive the same, a quit-rent of one halfpenny sterling per acre, at the feast of St. Michael every year, the first payment to commence on the said feast of St. Michael which shall first happen after the expiration of ten years from the date hereof, or within fourteen days after said feast annually. *Provided, always,* and this present grant is upon condition, *nevertheless,* That this grant shall be duly registered in the Register's Office of this Province, within six months from the date hereof, and also that a docket thereof shall be entered in the Auditor's Office within the same time, if such establishment shall take place in this province. *And provided, also,* That if the said William Clark, his heirs or assigns, do not in all things fully comply with, and fulfil the condition herein above set forth, for the registering of this grant, within the time herein above limited for the completion thereof; or, if the said William Clark, his heirs or assigns, shall not pay to us, our heirs and successors, or to the Receiver General of our quit-rents, or to the proper officer appointed to receive the same, the said quit-rent of one halfpenny sterling per acre, on the said feast of St. Michael, or within fourteen days after, annually, for every acre contained in this grant, that then, and either of these cases respectively, this grant shall be void, any thing therein contained to the contrary notwithstanding; and the said lands, tenements, hereditaments, and premises, hereby specified, and every part and parcel thereof, shall revert to us, our heirs and successors, fully and absolutely, as if the same had never been granted.

Given under the great seal of our province of West Florida : Witness our trusty and well beloved Peter Chester, Esq., our Captain General, and Governor-in-chief in and over our said province, at Pensacola, this sixth day of August, in the year of our Lord one thousand seven hundred and seventy-eight, and in the eighteenth year of our reign.
[c. s.]   PETER CHESTER.

Passed the Secretary's Office.
   PH. LIVINGSTON, Jun., *Dep. Sec.*

WEST FLORIDA :
 Pursuant to a fiat from his excellency Peter Chester, Esq., Captain General and Governor-in-chief in and over His Majesty's province of West Florida, &c. to me directed, bearing date the sixth day of August, 1778, I have perused and inspected the within letters patent, and do hereby certify that there is no error therein apparent to me.
   E. R. WEGG, *Attorney General.*

AUDITOR'S OFFICE, *August* 6, 1778.
 A docket of the within grant is entered in book B, folio 42.
   J. LORIMER, *Deputy Auditor.*

PENSACOLA, *Secretary's Office.*
 I do hereby certify that the within letters patent, Surveyor General's certificate, together with the certificate of the Attorney General, are recorded in the Secretary and Register's Office of the province of West Florida, in liber A, No. 4, page 44. Examined and compared with the said record by
   PH. LIVINGSTON, Jun.; *Deputy Secretary.*

Entered in record of claims, (east side,) vol. 1, page 136, by EDWARD LLOYD WAILES, for
   JOSEPH CHAMBERS, *Register.*

The claimant exhibited two deeds, one from A. Gindrat, bearing date the 16th day of June, 1801; conveying to Jesse McCall all the said Gindrat's right, title, and interest, in and to said tract of land; the other deed from Jesse McCall, bearing date the 23d of September, 1801, conveying to Samuel Mims all the said McCall's right, title, and claim, to said land, and the improvement thereon.

Adam Hollinger and William Pierce were presented as witnesses, and, being duly sworn and interrogated by the Board, they deposed, that they had no interest in this claim; Adam Hollinger further testified, that the land in question was cultivated and inhabited by Samuel Mims. The said Pierce also deposed, that in the year 1795, the land in question was cultivated by Samuel Mims; that, from a conversation which he heard between the said Mims and William Clark, he was induced to believe, that the land was then the property of the said Clark, and that he, the said Mims, was the tenant at will of him, the said Clark, and that said Clark was an inhabitant and resident in the State of Georgia, on the 27th day of October, 1795.
The Board ordered that the case be postponed for consideration.

JOSEPH STIGGINS, representative of John Johnson: case No. 235 on the docket of the Board, and No. 83 on the books of the Register.
 Claim.—A right to eight hundred acres, by virtue of a Spanish warrant of survey, under the first section of the act.
The claimant presented his claim, together with a surveyor's plot of the land claimed, in the words and figures following, to wit :

To the Commissioners appointed in pursuance of an act of Congress passed the 3d day of March, 1803, for receiving and adjusting claims to land south of Tennessee and east of Pearl river

Please to take notice, that the following tract of land, lying east of the Mobile river, bounded on the east by lands belonging to the United States, south, by Mrs. Steel's donation, west, by the Tensaw lake, and north, by a donation of Joseph Stiggins, representative of Coleman and others, is claimed by Joseph Stiggins, representative of John Johnson, Esq. by virtue of the first section of said act, under a Spanish warrant, bearing date the 9th February, 1788. To all which he begs leave to refer, as also to a copy of the plot herewith filed.
   JOSEPH STIGGINS,
   Representative of John Johnson, Esq.
May 11, 1804.
   [Plot omitted.]

It appearing from the files in this case, that there was no plot with the notice, which was filed with the Register on the 11th June, 1804, John Milliken, the surveyor, was duly sworn, and did depose, that, to the best of his recollection and belief, he filed a plot with said notice, on the 11th day of June, 1804; that the plot which he filed with the Register was afterwards brought to him by Stiggins; and that he, Milliken, made out a plot different from the one originally filed, and gave it to Stiggins; but whether he filed the altered plot or the original with the Register he could not say, but believed he did file the same, as amended, previous to the first of May, 1805, and that the plot now filed was conformable to the one amended by him for Stiggins.

The claimant exhibited a Spanish warrant of survey, in the words and figures following, to wit:
Don Estevan Miro, Colonel of the army, Governor of the province of Louisiana:
   MOBILE, *January* 14, 1788.
John Johnson, inhabitant within the jurisdiction of Mobile, with all due respect, represents to your excellency, that there is on the bank of the Tensaw river a vacant piece of land of twenty acres, which to this period never has had any proprietor, he therefore humbly expects that the generosity of your excellency will grant him the property of said land, with the ordinary depth, giving orders to the Secretary of Government, of your city, for the concession of the said titles; therefore he entreats your excellency to grant him this favor.
   JOHN JOHNSON

Don Vicent Folch, captain of the regiment of Louisiana and commandant of Mobile. I certify that the land which is solicited is vacant, according to the information that has been taken from several inhabitants, and in witness whereof I sign this, the date as above.

VICENT FOLCH.

NEW ORLEANS, *February 9*, 1788.
The surveyor of this province, Don Carlos Laveau Trudeau, will establish this petitioner on the twenty acres of land of front, which is solicited, with the common depth of forty acres, in the place indicated in the antecedent memorial, the same being vacant, and causing no prejudice to any one whatever, under the precise condition of making the road, and the regular clearing in the term of a year; and this concession to be null if, at the expiration of three years, the ground be not established, and until that time not to be alienated; after the fulfilment of which conditions the regular titles of propriety will be made out and granted.

ESTEVAN MIRO.

MOBILE, *March* 10, 1788.
I certify that the antecedent copy is equal to its original, which is in the archives of this place.

SANTIAGO DE LA SAUSSAYE.

PENSACOLA, *February* 22, 1804.
I do certify that the above is, to the best of my knowledge and judgment, a faithful translation of a Spanish document, transmitted to me by Mr. Joseph Stiggins, inhabitant of Tensaw.

JAMES INNERARITY.

Entered in record of claims, (east side,) vol. 1, page 232, by EDWARD LLOYD WAILES, for
JOSEPH CHAMBERS, *Register.*

The claimant exhibited three deeds or writings, that is to say, a deed from John Johnson, bearing date the 8th day of January, 1796, conveying to Arthur Rials, all right, title, and interest, which the said Johnson had to said tract of land, and the improvements thereon; a deed from Samuel Lyons, bearing date the 8th day of November, 1796, conveying to Joseph Stiggins all the said Lyons's right and title to said land and the improvements; also a deed from Arthur Rials, bearing date the 11th day of November, 1796, conveying to Joseph Stiggins all the said Rials's right, title, and claim to the aforesaid tract of land, and the improvements thereon made.

Reuben Dyer and Benjamin Pyburn were presented as witnesses, and being duly sworn and interrogated by the Board, they deposed, that they were not interested in this claim; that, as well as they recollected, the land in question was cultivated on the 27th day of October, 1795, by James Upton or William Hillis, and that the said land was cultivated for a considerable time before the year 1795, to the use of John Johnson, and continued in cultivation until it went into the possession of the said Upton or Hillis; that the said Johnson was, on the 9th day of February, 1788, twenty-one years of age, and the head of a family; that the cultivation of the said land, by the said Upton or Hillis, was to the use of Samuel Lyons.

The Board ordered that the case be postponed for consideration.

Adjourned until Tuesday, the 21st instant.

TUESDAY, *May* 21, 1805.
The Board met according to adjournment. Present: Robert C. Nicholas, Joseph Chambers.
Adjourned until Friday, the 24th instant.

FRIDAY, *May* 24, 1805.
The Board met according to adjournment. Present: Robert C. Nicholas, Joseph Chambers.
WILLIAM WEBBER's case: commenced in page 739.
William H. Buford was presented as a witness, and, being duly sworn, deposed, that he made the plot and survey of the land in question; that the land lay in the county of Washington, and that the Indian claims to the whole of the said land had been extinguished; that it included the improvements of the claimant; and that he, Buford, knew of no interfering claim.

The Board ordered that the case be postponed for consideration.

Adjourned until Saturday, the 25th instant.

SATURDAY, *May* 25, 1805.
The Board met according to adjournment. Present: Robert C. Nicholas, Joseph Chambers.

HEIRS OF VALENTINE DUBROCA's case, No. 236 on the docket of the Board, and No. 49 on the books of the Register.

Claim.—A donation of six hundred and thirty-nine acres and nine tenths of an acre, under the second section of the act.

The claimants presented their claim, together with a surveyor's plot of the land claimed, in the words and figures following, to wit:

To the Commissioners appointed in pursuance of an act of Congress passed the 3d day of March, 1803, *for receiving and adjusting claims to lands south of the Tennessee river, and east of the Pearl river.*

Please to take notice, that the following tract of land, lying east of the Mobile river, bounded northeastwardly by lands claimed by Joseph Campbell, as the legal representative of Augustin Rochon, westwardly by the Mobile river, and on the south, by vacant land, is claimed by Martin Dubroca, widow, for the use and benefit of the heirs to the estate of Valentine Dubroca, deceased, the said Marton Dubroca being his widow, and acting for said estate, under and by virtue of the second section of the above mentioned act of Congress, for granting donation lands. To all which she begs leave to refer, as also to the copy of the plot now delivered to the Register of the Land Office, to be established east of Pearl river, which plot is herewith filed.

FORT STODDERT, *March* 31, 1804.
MILAINE DUBROCA,
Acting for Marton Dubroca.
[Plot omitted.]

Surveyed March 26, 1804, by James Gordon.
Entered in record of claims, (east side,) vol. 1, page 120, by EDWARD LLOYD WAILES, for
JOSEPH CHAMBERS, *Register.*

Adam Hollinger and Richard Barrow were presented as witnesses, and, being duly sworn and interrogated by the Board, they deposed, that they had no interest in this claim. The said Barrow testified, that the land in question was cultivated by negroes, said to be the property of Dubroca, and superintended by a young man, son of said Dubroca, in the year 1797; but whether he cultivated to the use of the claimants, or to his own use, he did not know. The said Hollinger also testified, that Valentine Dubroca, by his negroes and one of his sons, cultivated a tract of land near the Sunflower.

Question. Do you know of more than one person by the name of Dubroca, who was the head of a family in the year 1795, 1796, or 1797?

Answer. I did not.

The Board ordered that the case be postponed for consideration.

JOSEPH CAMPBELL, representative of AUGUSTIN ROCHON AND LOUISA ROCHON; case No. 237 on the docket of the Board, and No. 65 on the books of the Register.

Claim.—A right to two thousand three hundred thirty-seven acres and five tenths of an acre, by virtue of two Spanish warrants of survey, under the first section of the act.

The claimant presented his claim, together with a surveyor's plot of the land claimed, in the words and figures following, viz.:

To the Commissioners appointed in pursuance of an act of Congress passed the 3d of March, 1803, *for receiving and adjusting claims to lands south of the Tennessee river, and east of the Pearl river.*

Please to take notice, that the following tract of land, lying east of the Mobile river, bounding northwardly by a bayou, which divides it from lands surveyed for the estate of Dominique, on the east by vacant land, southwardly, by lands known by the name of Daniel Ward's lands, and on the west, by the said river; is claimed by Joseph Campbell, legal representative of Augustin Rochon, said Rochon having sold said lands, or the titles thereof, to the said Joseph Campbell, under and by virtue of two Spanish grants or orders of survey, granted to Louisa Rochon and the said Augustin Rochon. To all which he begs leave to refer, as also to the copy of the plots, now delivered to the Register of the Land Office to be established east of Pearl river, which plots are herewith filed, and the grants entered.

JOSEPH CAMPBELL.
FORT STODDERT, *March* 31, 1804.
[Plot omitted.]

Surveyed 8th March, 1804, by James Gordon. Chain bearers, John Burgess, William Weathers.

Entered in record of claims, (east of Tombigbee,) vol. 1, page 129, by EDWARD LLOYD WAILES, for

JOSEPH CHAMBERS, *Register.*

Adam Hollinger and Richard Barrow were presented as witnesses, and being duly sworn and interrogated by the Board, they deposed, that they had no interest in this claim; that Augustin Rochon cultivated the land in question, from about the year 1793 until the evacuation of the Spanish troops in the year 1799; that they believed he was at that time, twenty-one years of age. That Augustin Rochon continued to cultivate the land in question, with the hands of Louisa Rochon, (his mother,) and his own, from the year 1793, until the evacuation of the Spanish troops, which took place in the year 1799.

The Board ordered that the case be postponed for consideration.

THOMAS BATES, Junior's, case, No. 238, on the docket of the Board, and No. 19 on the books of the Register.

Claim.—A donation of six hundred and forty acres, under the second section of the act.

The claimant presented his claim, together with a surveyor's plot of the land claimed, in the following words and figures, viz.:

To the Commissioners appointed in pursuance of the act of Congress passed the 3d day of March, 1803, for receiving and adjusting the claims to lands south of the Tennessee, and east of Pearl river.

Please to take notice, that the following tract of land, situated on the east side of Tombigbee, in the county of Washington, beginning on a cedar post in a field on the bank of Tombigbee river, running up the river bank, north, eighty-six degrees east, thirty chains; thence, north, sixty-eight degrees east, ten chains; thence, north, fifty-five degrees east, fifteen chains; thence, north, eighty-five degrees east, ten chains; thence, north, seventy-five degrees east, fifteen chains, to a swamp oak corner, to Richard Turvin on the bank of the river; thence, south, forty-five degrees east, seventy-five chains, crossing a cypress swamp to a stake; thence, south, sixty-two degrees west, eighty-six chains and fifty links, to a stake; thence, to the beginning; containing six hundred and forty acres, and hath such forms and marks, both natural and artificial, as are fully represented in the plot annexed: is claimed by Thomas Bates, Junior, in and by virtue of the second section of said act, as a donation, and is now exhibited to the Register of the Land Office established east of Pearl river, to be recorded as directed by said act. To all which he begs leave to refer, as also to the copy of the plot herewith filed.

THOMAS BATES, JUN.

MARCH 23, 1804.

[Plot omitted.]

Surveyed February 28, 1804, by Natt Christmas. Chain bearers, John Barnet, John Hawkins.

Entered in record of claims, (east side) vol. 1, page 73, by EDWARD LLOYD WAILES, for

JOSEPH CHAMBERS, *Register.*

Joseph Bates and Richard Barrow were presented as witnesses, and being duly sworn and interrogated by the Board, they deposed, that they were not interested in this claim. The said Bates testified, that before the year 1797, throughout that year and ever since, Thomas Bates, Jun., the present claimant, had inhabited and cultivated the land in question, and that in the month of April, 1797, he arrived at the age of twenty-one years.

Question. What kind of cultivation and improvement hath the claimant made on the land by him claimed?

Answer. Being an unmarried man, he lived near by the land, in my family, but carried on business by himself. The first year he cleared about seven acres, and in the year 1797 had a crop on the same; he has since regularly increased his improvements, to about forty acres now under cultivation; his buildings are a horse stable and corn house.

Question to the said Barrow. Who cultivated the land in question in the year 1797?

Answer. I do not know.

Question. Was Thomas Bates, Jun. twenty-one years of age in 1797?

Answer. I do not know, but I have reasons to believe he was.

Question. How many acres has the said Bates in cultivation?

Answer. I suppose about twenty acres at this time.

Natt Christmas, surveyor, was duly sworn, and did depose, that Thomas Bates, Junior's, donation claim exhibited to the board included the larger part of his improvements and cleared land; that an actual survey was made on the river or front of the land, and a few chains on the line above and below running out from the river; that in consequence of high water it was impracticable to complete the survey, except by plotting the same.

The Board ordered that the case be postponed for consideration.

JAMES CALLIER, representative of Joseph Campbell: case commenced in page 738.

Henry Weathers and Richard Barrow were presented as witnesses, and, being duly sworn and interrogated by the Board, they deposed, that they were not interested in this claim; that the land in question was cultivated to the use of the widow Trouillet in the year 1797, and that she was at that time the head of a family. The said Weathers also deposed that, in the year 1797, he was hired by the widow Trouillet to work on the land in question; that at that time she lived in the town of Mobile, as well as he recollected. The said Barrow further deposed, that he did believe that the widow Trouillet was living on the bluff, nearly opposite the land in question, in the year 1797.

The Board ordered that the case be postponed for consideration.

NATT CHRISTMAS and LEMUEL HENRY's case: the former commenced in page 738, the latter in page 745; each of whom claim as representative of Michael Hartly.

Rebecca Hartly and William Hartly were presented as witnesses, May 15th, 1805, and, being duly sworn and interrogated by the Board, the said Rebecca deposed, that she should be richer if Natt Christmas got the land than if Mr. Henry got it, but also said, that it made no difference with her, whether Natt Christmas obtained a right to the land or not, as he was to pay the same amount in either case; that, as well as she recollected, about three weeks ago, on Sunday, young Mr. Henry came to the dwelling house of Michael Hartly, and asked her if Mr. Hartly was at home; that she answered that he was not, and then asked him, Henry, if he was acquainted with Hartly; he said he was not, to which she replied, that Hartly had just taken his gun and walked out, and that he would return home in a short time; that Mr. Henry said he had come to qualify Mr. Hartly about a piece of land, opposite to Nanna Hubba Bluff, in the Nanna Hubba Island; that she told Henry that Mr. Hartly could swear nothing in his behalf; he said that made no difference, that he had come to qualify him, Hartly, to what he knew about the land, and nothing else; that Mr. Henry then accompanied her to the cow-pen, where she went to milk the cows; that they had no more conversation about the land until some time after dark, but, that, before this time, Mr. Henry and Mr. Hartly, her husband, had both returned to the house; that Mr. Henry then stated to her husband, that he, Henry, did not know what to do about the land, and wished that his brother had come himself, as he knew more about these things; but, that he would write down what he, Hartly, would swear to about the land, and take it and show it to his brother, and that he might then do as he pleased; that Mr. Henry then wrote down, as he read to them, that Michael Hartly had cultivated the land in Nanna Hubba Island, in the year 1797, for his own use, or words to that effect; that to that writing her husband made his mark. The conveyance made by Hartly to Henry being read to Mistress Hartly, she said, that she well recollected that Henry read from the beginning of the writing as far as the words in the year 1797, before and afterwards; but, that the words from thence to the end of the instrument, she did not recollect to have heard before, nor did she believe that it ever was read to her or to her husband; that she had heard read a copy of the instrument written by Henry. The said William deposed, that he was not interested in this claim; that he heard read a writing that John Henry wrote, and which his father, Mr. Hartly, made his mark to, but that it only stated, as well as he recollected, that his father cultivated the land in Nanna Hubba Island, in the year 1797, before and afterwards, that he had since heard read a copy of the writing made by John Henry, to which his father made his mark; that Henry said that he had come to qualify his father, that he would take the writing to his brother; that he did not think it would be of any account, but his brother might do with it as he pleased,

Joseph Bates, Senior, Thomas Bates, Junior, Henry Weathers, John Henry and Adam Hollinger were this day, 25th of May, presented as witnesses, and, being duly sworn and interrogated by the Board, they deposed, that they were not interested in this claim.

Question to John Henry. Did you subscribe your name to the instrument of writing from Michael Hartly to Lemuel Henry?

Answer. I did.

Question. Did you make this instrument of writing?

Answer. I did.

Question. Did you read the whole of this writing to the said Michael Hartly within his hearing?

Answer. I did, in the presence and hearing of him, his wife, and son.

Question. What consideration did you, or were you to give the said Hartly for the land conveyed by this instrument of writing?

Answer. I believe the principal consideration, or object of Mr. Hartly, was to prevent Antonio Espaho from obtaining the land in question, and twenty dollars, which I promised should be given to him by Lemuel Henry, in case he should obtain said land.

Question. Was you instructed by Lemuel Henry to get Michael Hartly, in case you should obtain any instrument of writing relative to the land in question, to certify in the body of the same, the time of cultivating the said land?

Answer. I was.

Question. When you found that Hartly refused to say or do any thing in support of Espaho's claim, did not Hartly anxiously embrace the opportunity of doing any thing in his power for the support of his own claim, whereby said Espaho might be defeated, and he, Hartly, obtain the sum of twenty dollars?

Answer. He said he would do any thing in his power.

Question. From the conversation which passed in Hartly's family, was it or not generally and well understood what was the contents and substance of the instrument of writing from said Hartly to said Henry?

Answer. It appeared to be well understood.

Question. From the instructions you received, were there any rational motives for you to commit a fraud?

Answer. None.

Question. Did you or not tell Mr. Hartly, that it was two years too late for him to get the land in question?

Answer. I told Mr. Hartly that it was two years too late for him to get a pre-emption.

Question. Did you not tell Mr. Hartly, after obtaining the instrument in writing, that it was of no account, but that you would take it to your brother, and he might do as he pleased with it?

Answer. I told him my brother would support Turnbull's claim if he could, and if he did, that this instrument in writing would die of course.

Question. Did you not tell Mr. Hartly that your brother had possession of the land in question; and that it was impossible for him, Hartly, to get the same?

Answer. I told him my brother had the land in possession, and would continue to hold it under Espaho's claim if he could; that my brother wished to avoid disputes, and had sent me to get his, Hartly's right if he had any.

Question. Why did you not get Mrs. Hartly, or her son William Hartly, to witness this instrument of writing?

Answer. Because they lived below the line, and I knew of no way of getting them above.

Question. Did you not get the paper on which this writing was made, from Mrs. Hartly?

Answer. I did not; the paper on which this writing was made I took with me in my pocket book. Mrs. Hartly did give a piece of paper, on which I began the instrument of writing, but found the ink spread on it in such a manner that it would not do, and I then took the paper from my pocket book on which the same is made.

Question. Did you not endeavor as much as in your power to keep Mr. Hartly ignorant of the value of his title?

Answer. I did not explain the law to him, and told him I did not think his claim very good, in consequence of Turnbull's claim to the same.

Question. Did you not tell Mr. Hartly that you would make Espaho pay you fifty dollars for riding down there to do his business?

Answer. I told him that Esapho ought to pay for my doing his business below the line, as I had understood by the contract between him and my brother, he was to do all that might be necessary below the line.

The said Weathers deposed, that he saw Michael Hartly sign the deed of conveyance from him to Natt Christmas, dated the 27th of April, by making his mark and acknowledging the same, and that he, Weathers, witnessed the same by making his mark thereon; that said deed was executed, as well as he recollected, on Sunday.

Question. Did any other person than yourself sign the instrument of writing from Hartly to Christmas, as a witness?

Answer. I do not recollect, I cannot read writing, and do not know whether there was any other witness or not, but the paper appears the same as when I made my mark thereto. Mr Milliken wrote my name, and was present when I made my mark.

Question. Was Major Christmas present at the making of this contract?

Answer. He was not.

Question. Did you hear the contract made?

Answer I did, and Mr Milliken gave his note for one hundred dollars, as a consideration therefor.

Question. Who went down for you as a witness?

Answer. Mr. Milliken.

Question. What was he to give you for coming up?

Answer. Nothing at all; I had business of my own at the Bluff.

Question. Did Mr. Milliken tell you it was absolutely necessary you should come up as a witness?

Answer. He told me that he wanted me to come and prove the deed which I had witnessed.

The said Thomas Bates, Jun., deposed, that he heard Mr. Milliken say that he was to give Mr. Hartly one hundred dollars, if he, Milliken, should hold the land in question.

Question. Did you hear Mr. Hartly say whether he was to have any thing for coming to the Board of Commissioners to testify to the instrument of writing from him to Natt Christmas?

Answer. I heard him say he was to have twenty-five dollars, and was to be paid on his return from the Board of Commissioners.

Question. Did you not hear Mr. Milliken say, that he told Mr. Hartly, if he had signed any other instrument of writing, conveying the land in question, not to sign the one to Natt Christmas?

Answer. He said he told him over and often, and that Hartly said that he had not signed any other writing.

The said Joseph Bates, Sen., deposed, that he heard Mr. Hartly say that he was to have one hundred dollars for the land in question, and twenty dollars for his coming up to the Board of Commissioners, as a witness in support of the claim of Natt Christmas.

The said Hollinger deposed, that he heard Mr. Milliken say that he had bought the land in question of Mr. Hartly, for Natt Christmas, and that said Christmas was to pay said Hartly one hundred dollars for the same, in case he, Christmas, should obtain it.

Question. Do you or not believe that, if a stranger was to apply to Mr. Hartly to purchase the land in question, that he would again sell it?

Answer. I do expect he would, although I know no harm of the man.

The Board ordered that the case be postponed for consideration.

ANTONIO ESPAHO, representative of John Turnbull: case No. 239 on the docket of the Board, and No. 15 on the books of the Register.

Claim.—A right to eight hundred acres, by virtue of a Spanish warrant of survey, under the first section of the act.

The claimant presented his claim, together with a surveyor's plot of the land claimed, in the words and figures following, viz.:

To the Commissioners appointed in pursuance of the act of Congress passed the 3d of March, 1803, for receiving and adjusting claims to land south of Tennessee, and east of Pearl river.

Please to take notice, that the following tract of land, situate on the east side of Tombigbee river in the county of Washington, beginning at a post on said river, being Bates's lower corner, and running north, twenty-seven degrees east, one hundred and twenty-three chains and fifty links, to a stake corner; thence, south, sixty-three degrees east, sixty-three chains, to a stake corner; thence, south, twenty-seven degrees west, one hundred and twenty-three chains fifty links, to the river; thence, up the said river, as plotted, to the beginning; and has such form and marks, both natural and artificial, as are fully represented in the plot annexed, containing eight hundred acres: is claimed by Lemuel Henry, attorney in fact for Antonio Espaho, legal representative of John Turnbull, in and by virtue of a Spanish warrant, or order of survey, and is now exhibited to the Register of the Land Office established east of Pearl river, to be recorded as directed by said act. To all which he begs leave to refer, as also to a copy of the plot herewith filed.

LEMUEL HENRY,
Attorney in fact for Antonio Espaho.

MARCH 30, 1804.
[Plot omitted.]

Chain bearers, James McConnell and Edmund Smith.
Surveyed March 28th, 1804, by J. Milliken.
A Spanish warrant of survey was exhibited as follows, to wit :

His Excellency Estevan Miro, Brigadier of the Royal army, Governor and Intendant General of the province of Louisiana and West Florida, &c. &c.

John Turnbull, inhabitant in the jurisdiction of Mobile, most respectfully solicits and declares, that there is on the Tombigbee river twenty acres of vacant land, situate opposite to land belonging to him, called la Nannahaba, the which, until now, has not had a possessor ; therefore, he hopes you may grant him the proprietary, and that your excellency may give orders unto the Secretary of Government to render him the necessary titles, to the end that he might be put in actual possession, and which favor he will ever bear in mind.

JOHN TURNBULL.

MOBILE, *January* 2, 1790.

MOBILE, *January* 4, 1790.

Don Vincente Folch, Captain of the Louisiana regiment, civil and military Commandant of Mobile and its district, certifies that the result of an inquiry made of several inhabitants, is that the land remains vacant, that the above named solicits, and as he has sufficient force to improve it, your excellency may make the cession if found suitable.

VINCENTE FOLCH.

NEW ORLEANS, *January* 14, 1790.

The Surveyor General of this province, Don Carlos Trudeau, will establish the above named petitioner in twenty acres of land in front, with the ordinary depth of forty, in the place above mentioned in the foregoing memorial, it not being prejudicial to any person, under which supposition the measurement will be extended in continuation and remitted to me, that I may forward to the party interested the corresponding titles in favor.

ESTEVAN MIRO.

MOBILE, *March* 6, 1804.

Don Joaquin de Osorno, Captain of regiment of infantry of Louisiana, Commandant civil and military of Mobile, certifies, that the above writing is a true copy of the original in the archives at my charge.

JOAQ. DE OSORNO.

The above is a copy of the Spanish grant.

THOMAS PRICE.

The above was compared exact with the original in this office, under my charge, by me,

JOAQ. DE OSORNO.

I, Thomas Price, of the post of Mobile, English interpreter for His Majesty the King of Spain, do solemnly swear by the Almighty God, and by the Holy Cross, that this is a true and faithful translation of the Spanish grant or writing hereto annexed.

THOMAS PRICE.

Subscribed and sworn before the Board, March 21, 1804.—Attest: DAVID PARMELEE 2d, *Clerk.*
Entered in record of claims, (east of Tombigbee,) vol. 1, page 58, by EDWARD LLOYD WAILES, for

JOSEPH CHAMBERS, *Register.*

Adam Hollinger, Richard Barrow, and Joseph Bates, Sen. were presented as witnesses, and being duly sworn and interrogated by the Board, they deposed, that they had no interest in this claim. The said Bates also deposed, that the land in question was cultivated in the years 1793, 1794, and 1795, by a man by the name of Alexander; that John Turnbull informed him, Bates, on Nanna Hubba bluff, that he, Turnbull, had permitted the said Alexander to cultivate the same, and that said Alexander informed him, Bates, that he was on the place by permission of said Turnbull, and that the said Turnbull was, on the 14th day of January, 1790, more than twenty-one years of age.

Question. Where did said Turnbull live in the year 1795?

Answer. I believe that he lived in the town of Mobile, but I am not confident.

Question to the said Barrow. Did John Turnbull cultivate the land in question, in the year 1795?

Answer. He did not; a man by the name of Alexander cultivated said land in the years 1794 and 1795.

Question. To whose use did Alexander cultivate this land?

Answer. To his own use, I believe.

Question. Did you ever hear Alexander say, that he cultivated this land for John Turnbull?

Answer. I did not, to my recollection.

Question. Did you ever know of Alexander's paying any rent to Turnbull?

Answer. I did not, but that John Turnbull was, on the 14th day of January, 1790, more than twenty-one years of age.

The said Hollinger deposed, that John Turnbull did not cultivate the land in question in the year 1795; that said land was, at that time, cultivated by a man of the name of Alexander, but whether to his own use or Turnbull's, he knew not; that on the 14th day of January, 1790, John Turnbull was more than twenty one years of age.

John Milliken, surveyor, being duly sworn, deposed, that he made the survey and plot returned to the Board of Commissioners, by Lemuel Henry, attorney in fact for Antonio Espaho, under a Spanish warrant of survey; that this claim interfered with the claim of Joseph Bates, Senior's, Spanish warrant, Natt Christmas's donation claim, as representative of Michael Hartly, Thomas Bates, Junior's, donation claim, and Lemuel Henry's donation claim, as representative of Michael Hartly, as represented in the general map of the Nanna Hubba Island, presented to the Board by said Milliken.

The Board ordered that the case be postponed for consideration.

Adjourned until Wednesday, the 29th instant.

WEDNESDAY, *May* 29, 1805.
The Board met according to adjournment. Present: Robert C. Nicholas, Joseph Chambers.

Adjourned until Saturday, the 1st day of June next.

SATURDAY, *June* 1, 1805.
The Board met according to adjournment. Present: Robert C. Nicholas, Joseph Chambers.

John Milliken, surveyor, being duly sworn, deposed, that he made the surveys and plots, returned to the Board of Commissioners, by the following claimants, to wit:

James Mills, representative of John Linder, Senior, Spanish warrant of survey; Lemuel Henry, representative of John Linder, Senior, Spanish warrant of survey; heirs of Michael Milton, donation claim; John Mills, donation claim; Moses Stedham, donation claim; Jesse Ross, representative of Abraham Walker, donation claim; John Randon, donation claim; William McDaniel, representative of George Phillips, donation claim; Joseph Stiggins, donation claim; Jordan Proctor, donation claim; Richard Coleman, donation claim; Reuben Dyer, donation claim; James Cockaram, representative of Samuel Lyons, donation claim; John Weekley, representative of James Farr, donation claim; William Collins, representative of Charles Conway, donation claim; George Weekley, donation claim; Francis Steel, donation claim; William Buford, representative of George Weekley, Senior, donation claim ; Cornelius Dunn, pre-emption claim; William Weekley, pre-emption claim; and Simeon Wilks, donation claim; that said plots respectively contained true representations of the land therein described, according to the best of his knowledge and belief, and did include the plantations and improvements of the several claimants; that he knew of no interfering lines or claims; that the plot exhibited to the Board, in the case of Joseph Stiggins, representative of John Johnson, was made and surveyed in part by him, Milliken; that he believed that it gave a correct view of the land claimed by said Stiggins, and included his houses and cleared land; and that it did not interfere with any other claim.

The Board ordered that these cases be postponed for consideration.

WILLIAM SHIELDS'S case: commenced in page 738.

John Milliken, surveyor, being duly sworn, deposed, that he made the survey and plot in this case; that he did not make an actual survey of this plot, further than twenty-five chains on the river bank, beginning on cotton tree, and plotted the balance of the survey; that this survey, as laid down in the general map of the Nanna Hubba Island, he believed to be a more correct representation of the land claimed; that it included the improvements of the claimant.

The Board ordered that the case be postponed for consideration.

JOSIAH FLETCHER's case: commenced in page 734.

John Milliken, surveyor, being duly sworn, deposed, that he made the survey and plot in this case; that this claim interferes with the claim of Joseph Thompson, under a Spanish warrant of survey, as described in the general map of the Nanna Hubba Island, which he made and presented to the Board.

The Board ordered that the case be postponed for consideration.

BENJAMIN FEW's case: commenced in page 729.

John Milliken, surveyor, being duly sworn, deposed, that he made the survey and plot in this case; that from information, he believed that this claim was entirely covered by the claim of Dominique de Olive, presented to the Board by Nicholas Weeks, executor of Dominique, under a Spanish warrant.

The Board ordered that the case be postponed for consideration.

SAMUEL TREND's case: commenced in page 742.

John Milliken, surveyor, being duly sworn, deposed, that he made the survey and plot in this case; that the larger part of this claim is included within the lines of the donation claim of Francis Killingworth, as described in the plot of this claimant.

The Board ordered that the case be postponed for consideration.

JOSEPH THOMPSON, representative of Adam Hollinger: case commenced in page 729.

John Milliken, surveyor, being duly sworn, deposed, that he made the survey and plot in this case; that this claim interfered with the donation claim of Samuel Mims, and the donation claim of Josiah Fletcher, as described in the general map of the Nanna Hubba Island which he presented to the Board.

The Board ordered that the case be postponed for consideration.

GEORGE WEEKLEY, representative of Michael Skipper: case commenced in page 731.

John Milliken, surveyor, being duly sworn, deposed, that he made the survey and plot in this case; that this claim interfered with the donation claim of Moses Stedham, as described in the general map of Nanna Hubba Island, which he presented to the Board.

The Board ordered that the case be postponed for consideration.

HEIRS OF JOHN LINDER, Jun.: case commenced in page 733.

John Milliken, surveyor, being duly sworn, deposed, that he made the survey and plot in this case; that this claim interfered with the donation claim of Benjamin Hooven, and included his buildings and nearly all of his cleared land, as described in the plot of this claim.

The Board ordered that the case be postponed for consideration.

FRANCIS KILLINGWORTH, representative of William Mills: case commenced in page 731.

John Milliken, surveyor, being duly sworn, deposed, that he made the survey and plot in this case; that this claim interfered with the donation claim of Samuel Trend, as described in the plot of the two surveys.

The Board ordered that the case be postponed for consideration.

BENJAMIN HOOVEN's case: commenced in page 733.

John Milliken, surveyor, being duly sworn, deposed, that he made the survey and plot in this case; that this claim interfered with the claim of Linder's heirs, under a Spanish warrant, as described in the plot of this claimant.

The Board ordered that the case be postponed for consideration.

JAMES RANDON's case: commenced in page 735.

John Milliken, surveyor, being duly sworn, deposed, that he made the survey and plot in this case; that this claim interfered with the donation claim of Joseph Thompson, as described in the plot of this claimant.

The Board ordered that the case be postponed for consideration.

SAMUEL MIM's case: commenced in page 744.

John Milliken, surveyor, being duly sworn, deposed, that he made the survey and plot in this case; that this claim interfered with the donation claim of Joseph Thompson, as described in the general map of the Nanna Hubba island, which said Milliken presented to the Board.

BENJAMIN STEDHAM's case: commenced in page 736.

John Milliken, surveyor, being duly sworn, deposed, that he made the survey and plot in this case; that this claim interfered with the donation claim of Francis Ballard, as described in the general map of the Nanna Hubba island, which said Milliken presented to the Board.

The Board ordered that the case be postponed for consideration.

JOSEPH THOMPSON's case: commenced in page 730.

John Milliken, surveyor, being duly sworn, deposed, that he made the survey and plot in this case; that this claim interfered with the donation claim of James Randon, as described in his plot.

The Board ordered that the case be postponed for consideration.

WILLIAM PIERCE and JOHN PIERCE, representatives of Jeremiah Phillips: case commenced in page 730.

John Milliken, surveyor, being duly sworn, deposed, that he made the survey, and Clinch Gray made the plot in this case; that the plot, laid in by the claimants, did not represent the land in question, as would more fully appear, by referring to said plot, and the general map of the Nanna Hubba island, presented to the Board by said Milliken; that the interferences would appear on the said general map, where the plot was altered, so as to give a true representation of the land claimed.

The Board ordered that the case be postponed for consideration.

WILLIAM PIERCE and JOHN PIERCE, representatives of Francis Ballard: case commenced in page 737.

John Milliken, surveyor, being duly sworn, deposed, that the plot exhibited to the Board in this case, was, as he believed, an exact copy of the one filed in the claim of William and John Pierce, as representatives of Jeremiah Phillips.

The Board ordered that the case be postponed for consideration.

Adjourned until Wednesday, the 5th instant.

WEDNESDAY, June 5, 1805.
The Board met according to adjournment. Present: Robert C. Nicholas, Joseph Chambers.
Adjourned until Saturday, the 8th instant.

SATURDAY, June 8, 1805.
The Board met according to adjournment. Present: Robert C. Nicholas, Joseph Chambers.

THOMAS BATES, Junior's case: commenced in page 749.

Michael Hartly was presented as a witness, and, being duly sworn and interrogated by the Board, deposed, that he had no interest in this claim; that, in the spring of the year 1797, he helped Thomas Bates, Jun., the present claimant, to roll his logs on the land in question, and that said Bates cultivated the same, in that year, to his own use; that he was at that time twenty-one years of age, as he, Hartly was informed by the family of the claimant.

The Board ordered that the case be postponed for consideration.

WILLIAM BUFORD, representative of Conrad Selhoof; case commenced in page 742.

Richard Coleman and Thomas Marshall were presented as witnesses, and, being duly sworn and interrogated by the Board, they deposed, that they were not interested in this claim; the said Coleman further deposed, that, as well as he recollected, in the year 1795, he saw Mr. John Linder, and a Mr. Lott, who was in the employment of said Linder, hauling corn to the house of said Linder, which corn, they both told him, they had brought out of Piney island, a plantation on the land in question; the said Marshall also deposed, that some time in the latter end of the year 1794, he came to Tensaw to live; that in the year 1795, he was on the land in question, at that time known as Collett's island; that he was on the island, and saw the hands of John Linder and his overseer, Mr. Lott, cultivating the land in question; that he got roasting ears out of the fields, and that he well recollected that these circumstances took place after the death of Townsen.

The Board ordered that the case be postponed for consideration.

NATT CHRISTMAS, representative of Michael Hartly: case commenced in page 738.

Michael Hartly appeared in person before the Board, and acknowledged the instrument of writing, or deed of conveyance, which is noted in page 738, to be his free and voluntary act, and for the uses and to the purposes mentioned in said deed.

The Board ordered that the case be postponed for consideration.

NATT CHRISTMAS's case, No. 210 on the docket of the Board, and No. 87 on the books of the Register.

Claim.—A right of pre-emption of one hundred and sixty acres, under the third section of the act.

The claimant presented his claim, together with a surveyor's plot of the land claimed, in the words and figures following, to wit:

To the Commissioners appointed in pursuance of an act of Congress passed the 3d day of March, 1803, for receiving and adjusting claims to land south of Tennessee, and east of Pearl river.

Please to take notice, that the following tract of land, lying in the island known by the name of Nanna Hubba, formed by the Cut-off of the rivers Tombigbee and Alabama, in the county of Washington, beginning on a cedar stake, being Joseph Bates's lower corner, near the bank of the river; running thence, north, seventy-five degrees east, eighty chains; thence, south, to the river Tombigbee; thence, up the margin of said river to the beginning; containing one hundred and sixty acres: is claimed by Natt Christmas, as a pre-emption, by virtue of the third section of said act, and is now exhibited to the Register of the Land Office east of Pearl river, to be recorded agreeably to the directions of said act. To all which he begs leave to refer, as also to a copy of the plot herewith filed.

NATT CHRISTMAS

[Plot omitted.]

APRIL 30, 1805.

Entered in record of claims, (east side,) vol. 1, page 242.

JOSEPH CHAMBERS, *Register.*

James Callier and William Buford were presented as witnesses, and, being duly sworn and interrogated by the Board, they deposed that they were not interested in this claim; that they believed that Natt Christmas, the claimant, cultivated the land in question, on the 3d of March, 1803, before and afterwards, and that he was at that time twenty-one years of age, and the head of a family.

The Board ordered that the case be postponed for consideration.

WILLIAM McDANIEL, representative of George Phillips; case No. 211 on the docket of the Board, and No. 39 on the books of the Register.

Claim.—A donation of six hundred and thirty-two acres, under the second section of the act.

The claimant presented his claim, together with a surveyor's plot of the land claimed, in the words and figures following, to wit:

To the Commissioners appointed in pursuance of the act of Congress passed the 3d day of March, 1803, for receiving and adjusting claims to lands south of Tennessee, and east of Pearl river.

Please to take notice, that the following tract of land, situated on the east side of Tombigbee, on Major's creek, in the county of Washington, beginning at an iron wood, and running north, seventy-five degrees east, seventy-seven chains, to a stake; thence, north, fifteen degrees west, forty-five chains, to a stake; thence, south, sixty-one degrees east, one hundred and forty-five chains, to a stake; thence, south, twenty chains, to a black gum; thence, north, eighty-four degrees east, seventy-two chains, to a pine; thence, north, sixty degrees west, thirty-five chains, to Major's creek; and thence, with the creek, to the beginning; containing six hundred and thirty-two acres, having such shape, form and marks, natural and artificial, as are represented in the plot annexed: is claimed by William McDaniel, legal representative of George Phillips, in and by virtue of the second section of said act, as a donation, and now exhibited to the Register of the Land Office, east of Pearl river, to be recorded as directed by said act. To all which he begs leave to refer, as also to the plot herewith filed.

WILLIAM McDANIEL,
Legal representative of George Phillips.

MARCH 27, 1804.

[Plot omitted.]

Surveyed March 23, 1804, by John Milliken. Chain bearers, James McConnell and Levi Qualls.

Entered in record of claims, (east side Tombigbee,) vol. 1, page 113, by EDWARD LLOYD WAILES, for

JOSEPH CHAMBERS, *Register.*

Richard Coleman and William Buford were presented as witnesses, and, being duly sworn and interrogated by the Board, they deposed, that they had no interest in this claim; the said Coleman testified, that, as well as he recollected, George Phillips inhabited and cultivated the land in question, in the year 1797, and continued thereon until his death; that he was, in the year 1797, twenty-one years of age, and the head of a family; that he, Coleman, believed that the land had been in cultivation ever since, to the use of the claimant; that he knew that the present claimant had derived his title to the land in question, from Wyseman Walker, the second husband of the wife of George Phillips; that said Phillips left, when he died, two children, a son and a daughter; the said Buford testified, that he had heard Wyseman Walker, the present husband of the late wife of George Phillips, deceased, say, that he, Walker, had sold said land to William McDaniel; that Mrs. Walker, late Mrs. Phillips, had two children by George Phillips, her first husband.

The Board ordered that the case be postponed for consideration.

WILLIAM BUFORD, representative of George Weekley, Sen.; case No. 242 on the docket of the Board, and No. 53 on the books of the Register.

Claim.—A donation of six hundred and forty acres, under the second section of the act.

The claimant presented his claim, together with a surveyor's plot of the land claimed, in the words and figures following, to wit:

To the Commissioners appointed in pursuance of the act of Congress, passed the 3d day of March, 1803, for receiving and adjusting claims to lands south of Tennessee, and east of Pearl river.

Please to take notice, that the following tract of land, situated on the east side of the river Tombigbee, bounded to the north, by the Major's creek and John Mills's lands, to the south by Conrad Selhoof, and to the west by Glade Rasley's claim, and hath such marks, both natural and artificial, as are fully represented in the plot annexed, containing six hundred and forty acres: is claimed by William Buford, under and in virtue of a donation right, now delivered to the Register of the Land Office, established east of Pearl river, to be recorded as directed by said act. To all which he begs leave to refer, as also to the copy of the plot herewith filed.

W. BUFORD.

[Plot omitted.]

Surveyed 22d March, 1804, by John Milliken. Chain bearers, James McConnell and Levi Qualls.

Entered in record of claims, (east side) vol. 1, page 123, by EDWARD LLOYD WAILES, for

JOSEPH CHAMBERS, *Register.*

Richard Coleman, Thomas Marshall, and John Milliken, were presented as witnesses, and, being duly sworn and interrogated by the Board, they deposed, that they were not interested in this claim; the said Coleman testified that, as well as he recollected, in the year 1797, the land in question was cultivated by Peter Rolly, a Spanish commandant, by permission of John Linder, Sen. who continued thereon until the evacuation of the Spaniards in 1799; that, as he, Coleman, believed, said Linder was, in the year 1797, twenty-one years of age, and the head of a family.

Question. Has said land been cultivated ever since the evacuation of the Spaniards or not?

Answer. I do not recollect to have seen the place evacuated.

Question. Has this land been constantly cultivated to the use of John Linder, Sen?

Answer. I know of no other claimant.

Question. By whom was this land cultivated on the 3d day of March, 1803?

Answer. I do not recollect.

The said Marshall deposed, that as well as he recollected, he came to live on the land in question, with Peter Rolly, a Spanish commandant, who was the tenant of John Linder, Senior; that said Rolly cultivated a considerable garden on said land, in that year; that, in the same year said Linder removed from the place in question, below the present boundary line, to a place called Honeycut's bluff.

The said Milliken deposed, that he had reason to believe that Arthur Patton resided on, and cultivated the land in question on the 3d of March, 1803; that he saw Mr. Patton on the place in the fall of the same year; and saw a crop on the land.

Lemuel Henry being duly sworn, deposed, that he always understood and did believe, that Arthur Patton inhabited and cultivated the land in question, on the third day of March, 1803, by and under the permission of John Mills, executor of John Linder.

The Board ordered that the case be postponed for consideration.

Adjourned until Tuesday, the 11th instant.

TUESDAY, *June* 11, 1805.
The Board met according to adjournment. Present: Robert C. Nicholas, Joseph Chambers.

Adjourned until Friday, the 14th instant.

FRIDAY, *June* 14, 1805.
The Board met according to adjournment. Present: Robert C. Nicholas, Joseph Chambers.

JOSEPH CAMPBELL, representative of Augustin Rochon and Louisa Rochon; case commenced in page 748. The claimant exhibited two Spanish warrants of survey, in the words and figures following, to wit:

MOBILE, *December* 31, 1793.
His Excellency the GOVERNOR GENERAL:
Mr. Augustin Rochon of this place, and Lieutenant of its militia, with respect, lays before you that there is on the river of Tombigbee twenty acres of vacant land, bounded on the south by a tract that the widow Rochon petitioned for, and on the north by a bayou without name, that divides it; and not having had until now any owner, and the petitioner having sufficient force for the cultivation, he respectfully prays that the proper titles may be passed through the Secretary's Office of Government; a favor he hopes to receive from your excellency

AUGUSTIN ROCHON.

MOBILE, *February* 20, 1794.
His Excellency the GOVERNOR GENERAL:
By the information I have taken from several planters in this jurisdiction, the twenty acres of land petitioned for as above is proved to be vacant, and belonging to the King; therefore, if your excellency thinks proper, the titles of concession may be passed the Secretary's Office of Government.

PEDRO OLIVIER.

NEW ORLEANS, *March* 9, 1794.
The Surveyor General of this province, or whoever may be so appointed, will settle the petitioner on ten acres of land in front, out of the twenty petitioned for, with the ordinary depth of forty acres; situated in the place expressed in the preceding memorial, and not to injure the neighbors; with the precise conditions of making a road and regular clearing, in the precise space of one year; and to remain null this concession, if, at the expiration of the precise space of three years, the land shall not be found settled, and not in a situation to be alienated: under which proposition the survey will be made and remitted to me, in order to furnish the interested the proper title in form.

BARON DE CARONDELET.

MOBILE, *February* 25, 1804.
Compared with the original that is in these archives.
JOAQUIN DE OSORNO.

I, Joseph Gordon, do solemnly swear by the name of the ever-living God, that this is a true translation of the Spanish order of survey hereunto annexed, according to my best knowledge and belief.

J. GORDON.
Subscribed and sworn before the Board, June 14, 1805.—Attest: DAVID PARMELEE 2d, *Clerk.*

MOBILE, *December* 31, 1793.
His Excellency the GOVERNOR GENERAL:
The widow Rochon of this place, with due respect, appears before you and says, that, on the Tombigbee river, there are thirty acres in front with the corresponding depth, of vacant land, having no proprietor: bounded on the north by a tract belonging to Mr. Augustin Rochon, and on the south by another that belonged formerly to Mr. Daniel Ward; and as it is desired that the petitioner has sufficient force for its cultivation, respectfully prays your excellency, that the corresponding titles

of right may be passed through the Secretary's Office of Government; a favor she hopes to receive from your excellency.

Widow ROCHON.

MOBILE, *January* 20, 1794.
His Excellency the GOVERNOR GENERAL:
By the information I have taken from several planters in this jurisdiction, the land petitioned for as above is proved to be vacant; and if your excellency thinks proper, the titles of concession may be passed.

PEDRO OLIVIER.

NEW ORLEANS, *March* 9, 1794.
The Surveyor General of this province, or whoever may be so appointed, will settle the petitioner on ten acres of land in front out of the thirty acres petitioned for, with the ordinary depth of forty acres; situated in the place pointed out in the preceding memorial, being vacant, and not to injure the neighbors; with the precise condition of making a road, and regular clearing in the precise space of one year; and to remain null this concession, if, at the end of the precise space of three years, the land shall not be found settled, and not in a situation to be alienated; under which proposition the survey will be made and remitted to me, in order to furnish the interested with titles in form.

THE BARON DE CARONDELET.

Confronted with the original that is in these archives.
JOAQUIN DE OSORNO.

I, Joseph Gordon, do solemnly swear in the name of the ever living God, that this is a true translation of the Spanish order of survey hereto annexed, according to my best knowledge and belief.

J. GORDON.
Subscribed and sworn before the Board, June 14, 1805.—Attest: DAVID PARMELEE 2d, *Clerk.*

On the back of the said Spanish orders of survey are two endorsements, in the words and figures following, to wit:
I do assign the within title papers or warrants to Joseph Campbell, for value received; as witness my hand and seal, this 27th day of February, 1804.

AUGUSTIN ROCHON. [L. s.]
Attest: R. H. GILMER, NICHOLAS WEEKS.

I do assign the within title papers or warrants to Joseph Campbell, for value received; as witness my hand and seal, this 27th day of February, 1804.

AUGUSTIN ROCHON.
Attest: R. H. GILMER, NICHOLAS WEEKS.

The claimant exhibited a power or letter of attorney from the widow Rochon, bearing date the 26th February, 1804, authorizing Augustin Rochon to do, in her behalf, as he might think fit in all things respecting her lands in the county of Washington, in the Mississippi territory.

Simon Andrey being duly sworn, deposed, that the lands now claimed under the Spanish warrants of survey, one in the name of Augustin Rochon, and the other in the name of the widow Rochon, were inhabited and cultivated on the 27th day of October, 1795, by said Augustin Rochon; that the cultivation was made by his slaves, and the slaves of the widow Rochon, his mother; and that she was twenty-one years of age, and the head of a family, on the 9th day of March, 1794.

The Board ordered that the case be postponed for consideration.

BENJAMIN STEDHAM's case: commenced in page 736.
Benjamin Hooven was presented as a witness, and, being duly sworn and interrogated by the Board, he deposed, that he was not interested in this claim; that the land in question was cultivated on the 3d of March, 1803, by Moses Stedham; but whether he cultivated to his own use or to the use of the claimant, he Hooven, did not know: that Moses Stedham was, on the 3d of March, 1803, twenty-one years of age, and the head of a family.

The Board ordered that the case be postponed for consideration.

Adjourned until Saturday, the 15th instant.

SATURDAY, *June* 15, 1805.
The Board met according to adjournment. Present: Robert C. Nicholas, Joseph Chambers.

NARCISO BROUTIN's case commenced in page 732.
The claimant exhibited a deposition in the words and figures following, viz.:

PENSACOLA, *February* 12, 1805.
His Excellency the GOVERNOR GENERAL:

Mr. James Innerarity of this place, agent for Mr. Young Gains, planter, in the district of Tombigbee, with the greatest respect appears before you and sets forth, that the said Gains, in order to assure to himself the possession of some lands which he has bought of Narcissus Broutin, in said district, when he was under the dominion of His Catholic Majesty, stands in need of the legal testimony of Geraud, of this place, in order to prove that the said lands were sowed and cultivated before the American Government took possession of the district; therefore, he prays your excellency to call before your tribunal the said Geraud, and make him deriver on oath what he knows of the following points: If he remembers having ascended the river Tombigbee in the month of October, in the year 1795? If afterwards, he observed a plantation situated at the conflux of the rivers Tombigbee and Alabama, on the east bank? If he knew to whom belonged that plantation before mentioned, and if the owner of it was a Spanish subject? If said plantation was cultivated and sowed at that time, and if there were houses built upon it? And after these declarations are made that the original may be returned for the purposes intended, which is a favor I hope to merit from the known justice of your excellency.　　JAMES INNERARITY.

PENSACOLA, *February* 13, 1805.
In order to legalize the declaration of Felix Geraud, for want of a notary, I named for the purpose Mr. Mathias Cervera and Francisco A. Navarro, the which they accepted, and offered to fulfil the charge preferred, in order to legalize the oath; and in due form presented themselves and signed with me.
　　　　VICENTE FOLCH,
　　　　FRANCISCO A. NAVARRO,
　　　　MATHIAS CERVERA.

On the same day, month, and year, Felix Geraud presented himself before me and the assisting witnesses: and it was demanded if he swore by God and the Cross to say the truth to the interrogatory set forth in this notice; he said, yes, he swore.

It was demanded by the tenor of it, the which was tated to him, and that he should make a true declaration of all. He said, that he remembered to have ascended the river Tombigbee in the year past of 1795; and that he saw there was a plantation between the rivers Tombigbee and Alabama, on the east bank, and that it belonged to Mr. Narcissus Broutin, a Spanish planter; that he had houses, &c.; that, in the time of which he spoke, his negroes were clearing the land of the plantation, and that he knew the said Broutin then sowed the said plantation; that is all he has to say on the business, the which he affirms and ratifies under the oath given; that he is in years, and signs this with me and the assisting witnesses.
　　　　FELIX GERAUD,
　　　　FOLCH,
　　　　FRANCISCO A. NAVARRO.
　　　　MATHIAS CERVERA.

I, Joseph Cordon, do solemnly swear by the ever-living God, that this is a true and faithful translation of the Spanish affidavit or writing hereto annexed, according to my best knowledge and belief.
　　　　　　J. GORDON.

Subscribed and sworn before the Board, June 15, 1805.—Attest: DAVID PARMELEE 2d, *Clerk.*

The Board ordered that the case be postponed for consideration.

Adjourned until Monday, the 17th instant.

MONDAY, *June* 17, 1805.
The Board met according to adjournment. Present: Robert C. Nicholas, Joseph Chambers.

Adjourned until Wednesday, the 19th instant.

WEDNESDAY, *June* 19, 1805.
The Board met according to adjournment. Present: Robert C. Nicholas, Joseph Chambers.

HEIRS OF VALENTINE DUBROCA: case commenced in page 748.

Simon Andrey was presented as a witness, and, being duly sworn, deposed, that he knew that Valentine Dubroca, under whom this claim is made, was the same person under whom George Brewer, as his representative, claims land in virtue of a Spanish warrant of survey, in the name of said Valentine Dubroca; and that said Dubroca died in the year 1799.

The Board ordered that the case be postponed for consideration..

Adjourned until Saturday, the 22d instant.

SATURDAY, *June* 22, 1805.
The Board met according to adjournment. Present: Robert C. Nicholas, Joseph Chambers.

Adjourned until Tuesday, the 25th instant.

TUESDAY, *June* 25, 1805.
The Board met according to adjournment. Present: Robert C. Nicholas, Joseph Chambers.

JAMES CARPENTER, heir at law to Richard, Caleb, and Joseph Carpenter: case, No. 243 on the docket of the Board, and No. 1 on the books of the Register.

Claim.—A right to one thousand acres, by virtue of a British grant, under the first section of the act.

The claimant presented his claim, together with a surveyor's plot of the land claimed, in the words and figures following, viz.:

To the Commissioners appointed in pursuance of an act of Congress passed the 3d day of March, 1803, for receiving and adjusting claims to lands south of Tennessee, and east of Pearl river.

Please to take notice, that the following tract of land, lying east of the Alabama river, butted and bounded to the south and southwest on the lands of Jacob Black well, on the north by the river, and on all other sides vacant, about forty-five miles from Mobile town, is claimed by James Carpenter, of Adams county, Mississippi territory, under and by virtue of a British patent granted to Richard, Caleb, and Joseph Carpenter, as may appear by the original patent, now delivered to the Register of the Land Office, to be established east of Pearl river, to be recorded as directed by that act. To all which he begs leave to refer, as also to the copy of the plot herewith filed.

　　　　JAMES CARPENTER,
Heir at law to Richard, Caleb, and Joseph Carpenter.
FEBRUARY 4, 1804.

[Plot omitted.]

WEST FLORIDA, *ss.*
GEORGE THE THIRD, *by the grace of God, of Great Britain, France, and Ireland, King, defender of the faith, &c. To all to whom these presents shall come, greeting:*

Know ye, that we, of our special grace, certain knowledge, and mere motion, have given and granted, and, by these presents, for us, our heirs and successors, do give and grant, unto Richard, Caleb, and Joseph Carpenter, their heirs and assigns, all that tract of land, situated on the east side of the Alabama river, butting and bounding to the south and southwest on the land of Jacob Blackwell, and on the northwest side on the river, and on all other parts by vacant land, about forty-five miles from Mobile town, in our province of West Florida, and having such shape, form, and marks, both natural and artificial, as are represented in the plot thereof hereunto annexed, as drawn by our Surveyor General of lands; which said tract of land contains one thousand acres, and is bounded as by the further certificate hereunto likewise annexed, under the hand of our said Surveyor General of lands, in our said province, may more fully and at large appear; together with all woods, underwoods, timber, and timber trees, lakes, ponds, fishings, waters, watercourses, profits, commodities, hereditaments, and appurtenances whatsoever thereunto belonging, or in anywise appertaining; together also with privilege of hunting, hawking, and fowling, in and upon the same, and all mines and minerals, reserving to us, our heirs and successors all mines of gold and siver: to have and to hold the said tract of land, and all and singular the premises hereby granted, with the appurtenances, unto the said Richard, Caleb, and Joseph Carpenter, their heirs and assigns forever, in free and common soccage, yielding and paying unto us, our heirs and successors, or to the Receiver General of our quit-rents for the time being, or to such other officer as shall be appointed to receive the same, a quit-rent of one half-penny sterling per acre, at the feast of St. Michael every year, the first payment to commence on the said feast of St. Michael, which shall first happen after the expiration of two years from the date hereof, or within fourteen days after the said feast annually: *Provided, always,* (and this present grant is upon condition,) *nevertheless,* That the said Richard, Caleb, and Joseph Carpenter, their heirs or assigns, shall and do, within three years after the date hereof, for every fifty acres of plantable land hereby granted, clear and cultivate three acres at least in that part thereof which he or they shall judge most convenient and advantageous, or else do clear and drain three acres of swampy or sunken ground, or do drain three acres of marsh, if any such shall be contained therein ; and shall further, within the time aforesaid, put and keep upon every fifty acres thereof, accounted barren, three neat cattle, and continue the same thereon until three acres for every fifty acres be fully cleared and improved : and if it shall so happen that there be no part of the said tract of land fit for present cultivation, without manuring and improving the same, if the said Richard, Caleb, and Joseph Carpenter, their heirs or assigns, shall, within three years from the date hereof, erect, on some part of the said tract of land, one good dwelling-house, to contain at least twenty feet in length, and sixteen feet in breadth ; and put on the said tract of land the like number of three neat cattle, as aforesaid, on every fifty acres therein contained ; or otherwise, if any part of the said tract of land shall be rocky or stony ground, not fit for culture or pasture, shall and do, within three years as aforesaid, besides erecting the said house, begin to employ thereon, and continue to work for three years then next ensuing, in digging any stone quarry or mine, one good and able hand for every hundred acres thereof, it shall be accounted a sufficient cultivation and improvement : *Provided, also,* That every three acres which shall be cleared and worked, or cleared and drained, as aforesaid, shall further be accounted a sufficient seating, planting, cultivation, and improvement, to save forever from forfeiture fifty acres of land in any part of the tract hereby granted: and the said Richard, Caleb, and Joseph Carpenter, their heirs and assigns, shall be at liberty to withdraw their stock, or to forbear working in any quarry or mine, in proportion to such cultivation and improvements aforesaid, as shall be made upon the plantable lands, swamps, sunken grounds, or marshes therein contained: *Provided, also,* That this grant shall be duly registered in the Register's Office of this province within six months from the date hereof ; and, also, that a docket thereof shall be entered in the Auditor's Office within the same time, if such establishment shall take place in this province: *Provided, always,* That the said Richard, Caleb, and Joseph Carpenter, their heirs and assigns, at any time hereafter, having seated, planted, cultivated and improved the said land, or any part thereof, according to the directions and conditions abovementioned, may make proof of such seating, planting, cultivation, and improvement, in the general court, or in the court of the county, district or precinct, where the said land lieth, and have such proof certified to the Register's Office, and there entered with the record of this grant, a copy of which, duly attested, shall be admitted on trial to prove the seating and planting of said land: *Provided, always, nevertheless,* That if the said Richard, Caleb, and Joseph Carpenter, their heirs and assigns, do not in all things fully comply with and fulfil the respective directions and conditions herein above set forth, for the proper cultivation of the said land, within the time herein above limited for the completion thereof: or, if the said Richard, Caleb, and Joseph Carpenter, their heirs or assigns, shall not pay to us, our heirs and successors, or to the Receiver General of our quit-rents, or to the proper officer appointed to receive the same, the said quit-rent of one halfpenny sterling per acre, on the said feast of St. Michael, or within fourteen days after, annually, for every acre contained in this grant, that then, and in either of these cases, respectively, this grant shall be void, any thing herein contained to the contrary notwithstanding; and the said lands, tenements, hereditaments, and premises hereby specified, and every part and parcel thereof, shall revert to us, our heirs and successors, fully and absolutely, as if the same had never been granted.

Given under the great seal of our province of West Florida: Witness our trusty and well beloved Monfort Brown, Esquire, our Lieutenant Governor, and Commander-in-chief in and over our said province, at Pensacola, this 22d day of July, in the year of our Lord 1769, and in the ninth year of our reign.

　　　　　　　　　　　　　　MONFORT BROWNE.

Signed in council, 22d July, 1769.
　　　FRANCIS POUSSETT, *Dep. Clk. Council.*
Recorded 24th July, 1769, book E, folio 19.
　　　FRANCIS POUSSETT, *Dep. Register.*

A deposition was also exhibited in the following words and figures, viz.:

Be it known to all men by these presents, that, on the 23d day of March, Anno Domini 1804, before me, Israel E. Trask, duly commissioned and qualified notary public in and for the city of New Orleans, personally came and appeared Mr. Stephen Watts of the city of New Orleans, who, being duly sworn, did depose and say, that he was personally knowing to the residence of the late Mr. Richard Carpenter, at Baton Rouge, in the province of West Florida, at the time that said province was surrendered to the arms of Spain; and also that the said Richard Carpenter afterwards moved to the district of Natchez, then under the sovereignty of Spain, where the said Richard continued, and died a Spanish subject.

In testimony whereof, I have hereunto subscribed my name, and affixed my seal, the day and year aforesaid.
　　　　　　I. E. TRASK, *Notary Public.* [L. s.]
Entered in record of claims, (east of Tombigbee,) vol. 1, page 1, by EDWARD LLOYD WAILES, for
　　　　　　JOSEPH CHAMBERS, *Register.*
The Board ordered that the case be postponed for consideration.

ALEXANDER MACULLAGH, representative of Thomas Underwood; case, No. 244 on the docket of the Board, and No. 90 on the books of the Register.

Claim.—A right to five hundred acres, by virtue of a British grant to Thomas Underwood, under the first section of the act.

The claimant presented his claim, without any plot, in the words and figures following, to wit:

To the Commissioners appointed for receiving and adjusting the claims to lands within the Mississippi territory south of Tennessee, and east of Pearl river, by virtue of an act of Congress passed the 3d of March, 1803.

GENTLEMEN:

Please to take notice, that the following tract of land, situate, lying, and being within the Mississippi territory, is claimed by Alexander Macullagh, nephew and heir at law of Alexander Macullagh, formerly of Pensacola, in the province of West Florida, deceased, who died intestate; and that the indenture, or deed of conveyance, mentioned in the following statement, and now delivered unto the Register of the Land Office, opened under and by virtue of said act, for lands lying east of Pearl river, will evince his right and title to the same. To all which for greater certainty, reference is hereby made.

　　　　　　ALEXANDER MACULLAGH.

This is a tract of five hundred acres of land, situate about sixty-five miles above the town of Mobile, on the east side of the Alabama river, butting and bounding west on said river, and all other sides by vacant land. The title to this tract will appear, first, by an indenture, or deed of conveyance, bearing date 1st January, 1779, from Thomas Underwood to Alexander Macullagh, for five hundred acres of land, the quantity now claimed. The original grant, or patent, to Thomas Underwood is lost or mislaid, but your claimant hopes that, reference being had to the British records of West Florida, it will appear to have existed; he therefore trusts, by such documents, the said claim will be satisfactorily established, should your honorable Board think the same sufficient.

Entered in record of claims, (on the east side,) vol. 1, page 246.

　　　　　　JOSEPH CHAMBERS, *Register.*

The claimant exhibited a deed of conveyance from Thomas Underwood, bearing date the 1st of January, 1779, legally and fully executed, and duly recorded, conveying to Alexander Macullagh all the said Underwood's right, title and claim in and to the said tract of land.

The Board ordered that the case be postponed for consideration.

ABIJAH HUNT, representative of Augustin Rochon; case, No. 215 on the docket of the Board, and No. 89 on the books of the Register.

Claim.—A right to one thousand acres, by virtue of a Spanish warrant of survey, under the first section of the act.

The claimant presented his claim, together with a surveyor's plot of the land claimed, in the words and figures following, viz.:

To the Commissioners appointed in pursuance of the act of Congress, passed the 3d day of March, 1803, for receiving and adjusting claims to lands south of Tennessee, and east of Pearl river.

Please to take notice, that the following tract of land, situated on the east side of the Tombigbee river, beginning at a live oak tree, nearly opposite to Fort Stoddert, running south, sixty-two degrees east, one hundred and twenty-six chains, fifty-three links, to a stake; thence, north, twenty-eight degrees east, seventy-eight chains seventy-five links to a stake; thence, north, sixty-two degrees west, one hundred and twenty-six chains fifty-three links, to a stake on the bank of the river; thence, down the said river, with its meanders, to the beginning: is claimed by Abijah Hunt, in and by virtue of a deed of conveyance from Joseph Campbell, who claims by virtue of a Spanish warrant, or order of survey, given by the Spanish Government to Augustin Rochon, and by him transferred to the said Joseph Campbell. To all which he begs leave to refer, as also to the plot annexed.

NICHOLAS PERKINS,
Agent for Abijah Hunt.
[Plot omitted.]

Entered in record of claims, (east side,) vol. 1, page 243, by EDWARD LLOYD WAILES, for
JOSEPH CHAMBERS, *Register.*

The claimant exhibited a deed from Joseph Campbell and Isabella Campbell, bearing date the 16th day of December, 1801, conveying to Abijah Hunt all the said Joseph's and Isabella's right, and title in and to the said tract of land.

The Board ordered that the case be postponed for consideration.

HEIRS OF ROBERT FARMER; case No. 246 on docket of the Board, and No. 5 on the books of the Register.

Claim.—A right to five hundred and forty-two acres, by virtue of a deed from Francis Daran, under the first section of the act.

The claimants presented their claim, together with a surveyor's plot of the land claimed, in the words and figures following, to wit:

To the Commissioners appointed in pursuance of the act of Congress, passed the 3d day of March, 1803, for receiving and adjusting claims to lands south of Tennessee and east of Pearl river.

Please to take notice, that the following tract of land or island, situated on the east side of Tombigbee river, eleven leagues from Mobile, on the Tensaw river and lake, first beginning on Tensaw lake, at three water oaks; thence, south, twenty degrees west, nine chains; thence, south, forty degrees west, thirty-six chains, to a white hickory, on the Tensaw river; thence, down said river, south, thirty-five degrees east, eighty chains; thence, south, fifteen degrees east, fifty-seven chains; thence, north, forty-five degrees east, nineteen chains; thence, north, eighty degrees east, forty-two chains, to a small water oak; thence, up Brier's creek, or Tensaw lake, north, thirty-five degrees west, thirty-eight chains; thence, north, sixty degrees west, thirty-one chains; thence, north, twenty-five degrees west, thirty-two chains; thence, north, forty-two degrees west, twenty-four chains; thence, north, thirty nine degrees east, twenty chains fifty links; thence, north, four degrees west, twenty chains, to a large cypress; thence, through Dyer's Cut-off, north, thirty-one degrees west, seven chains; thence, north, seventy degrees west, eight chains; thence south, seventy-five degrees west, ten chains, to the beginning; and hath such forms and marks, both natural and artificial, as are fully represented in the plot annexed; containing, in the whole island, five hundred and forty-two acres, more or less: is claimed by Otto V. G. Barberie, of New York, attorney in fact, for the heirs of Major Robert Farmer, under and in virtue of a deed of conveyance, from Francis Daran to Robert Farmer, dated Mobile, West Florida, on the eleventh day of June, 1764, now delivered to the Register of the Land Office established east of Pearl river, to be recorded as directed by said act. To all which he begs leave to refer, as also the copy of the plot herewith filed.

OTTO V. T. BARBERIE.
FORT STODDERT, *March* 19, 1804.
[Plot omitted.]

Surveyed March 15, 1804, by John Milliken. Chain bearers, James McConnell and Levi Qualls.
Entered in record of claims, (east side,) vol. 1, page 24, by EDWARD LLOYD WAILES, for
JOSEPH CHAMBERS, *Register.*

The claimants presented a writing in the following words and figures, to wit:

We, Peter Hannibal Develle, chevalier of the order royal and military of St. Louis, late lieutenant of the King at Mobile, certifies that the deceased, Mr. Boissy,

when living, an officer of the infantry, has laid out and established, fifteen years past, with the approbation of the governors and ordinators of the province of Louisiana, a plantation, situated at Tensaw, about eleven leagues from Mobile, containing seventy arpents of front; besides, there is comprised a low point of wood, bounded to the southeast by the river, and to the north by a bay, which land Madam Populus has held and possessed for some years past by inheritance of the said deceased Boissy, her husband. In faith of which, we have delivered the present certificate, for to serve him, and to validate the titles of property of the said land and its dependencies.

DEVELLE.

MOBILE, *December* 9, 1763.

Subjoined to the foregoing certificate is another writing in the French language, unaccompanied with any translation, purporting to be a certificate, bearing date the 9th day of December, 1763, from the then Governor of New Orleans, under his hand and seal, and countersigned by the Secretary of Government, certifying that the aforesaid land and its dependencies belonged to Madam Populus. Another writing in the French language, without any translation of the same, was exhibited; bearing date the 28th day of December, 1763, purporting to be a bill of sale from Madam Populus to Daran, conveying to him the land above mentioned.

The claimants also exhibited a deed from Francis Daran, bearing date the 11th day of June, 1764, conveying to Robert Farmer, Esquire, all the said Madam Populus's right and title to said land, and the buildings and improvements thereon.

The Board ordered that the case be postponed for consideration.

HEIRS OF ROBERT FARMER: case No. 247 on the docket of the Board, and No. 4 on the books of the Register.

Claim.—A right to five hundred and twenty acres, by virtue of a deed from Peter Deforge, under the first section of the act.

The claimants presented their claim, together with a surveyor's plot of the land claimed, in the words and figures following, to wit:

To the Commissioners appointed in pursuance of the act of Congress passed the 3d of March, 1803, for receiving and adjusting the claims to lands south of the Tennessee, and east of Pearl river.

Please to take notice, that the following tract of land, on the north end of an island, situate on the east side of Tombigbee river, on the Tensaw river, about eleven leagues from Mobile; first beginning on the Tensaw river at a small water oak; thence, up said river, north, thirty-five degrees west, sixty-five chains, to an elm and the forks of the lake and river; thence, up a creek, south, thirty-eight degrees west, twenty-eight chains; thence, south, seventy-seven degrees west, thirteen chains; thence, north, fifty-two degrees west, nineteen chains; thence, north, nineteen degrees west, seven chains; thence, south, seventy-five degrees west, thirteen chains fifty links, to a mulberry on the creek Sabordin; thence, down said creek, south, five degrees west, fourteen chains, to a gut; thence, south, thirty-four degrees west, forty chains; thence, south, twenty-four degrees east, eighty chains, to an ash; thence, across the island, north, seventy-nine degrees east, one hundred and ten chains, to the beginning; and hath such forms and marks, both natural and artificial, as are fully represented in the plot annexed; containing five hundred and twenty acres, more or less: is claimed by Otto V. T. Barberie, of New York, attorney in fact for the heirs of Major Robert Farmer, under and in virtue of a deed of conveyance from Peter Deforge to Robert Farmer, dated 1st of November, 1768, now delivered unto the Register of the Land Office established east of Pearl river, to be recorded as directed by said act. To all which he begs leave to refer, as also to the copy of the plot herewith filed.

OTTO V. T. BARBERIE.
FORT STODDERT, *March* 19, 1804.
[Plot omitted.]

Surveyed March 14, 1804, by J. Milliken. Sworn chain carriers, James M'Connell and Levi Qualls.
Entered in record of claims, (east side of Tombigbee,) vol. 1, page 13, by EDWARD LLOYD WAILES, for
JOSEPH CHAMBERS, *Register.*

The claimants exhibited a deed from James Lucian, bearing date the 25th day of March, 1767, conveying to Peter Deforge all the right and title of the said Lucian to his plantation, situated at Tensaw, bounding with the plantation of Lafrance.

Deeds of lease and release were also exhibited from Peter Deforge, bearing date the 1st day of November, 1768, conveying to Robert Farmer, Esquire, all the said Deforge's right, title, and interest in and to the said five hundred and twenty acres of land, and to the buildings and improvements thereon made.

The Board ordered that the case be postponed for consideration.

WILLIAM BUFORD, representative of Conrad Selhoof: case commenced in page 742.

The claimant returned the following order and affidavit, viz.:

BOARD OF COMMISSIONERS, WASHINGTON COUNTY,
Friday, May 24, 1805.

William Buford having appeared before the Board, and, on solemn oath, declared that he has a claim pending before the said Board, in his own behalf, as representative of Conrad Selhoof, for eight hundred acres of land, on the east side of the Alabama river, founded upon a title derived under a Spanish warrant of survey dated at New Orleans the 9th day of February, 1788 ; and that Mary Mills, wife of Major John Mills, and Mary Coleman, wife of Richard Coleman, are material and important witnesses in support of his said claim, and that they, he verily believes, and each of them are now in such a state of health, occasioned by severe sickness or personal inability, that it is impracticable for them, or either of them, personally to appear before the Board, to give their or either of their testimony in the premises.

W. H. BUFORD.

Whereupon, it is ordered by the Board that the said Mary Mills, wife of Major John Mills, and Mary Coleman, wife of Richard Coleman, be duly qualified before some lawful magistrate of the county, who is not interested in the case, to give true and correct answers to the interrogatories hereto subjoined, and to such other interrogatories as may be proposed to them or either of them; and their and each of their answers shall be certified to this Board, by the magistrate taking the same, in due form of law.

By order of the Board.
Attest: DAVID PARMELEE 2d, *Clerk.*

Question. Have you or either of you any interest in or by the establishment of the present claim ?

Answer. I have no interest in the establishment of the present claim.

Question. How long has the land now claimed been in the occupancy and possession of the present claimant, and those under whom he holds ?

Answer. It has been in the occupancy of Selhoof, or the man commonly called Collet, sixteen years, and in the possession of Buford, the representative of Selhoof, about eighteen months.

Question. Have these persons held an uninterrupted possession, holding out all others therefrom, and no other person claiming any right thereto ?

Answer. They have held an uninterrupted possession, and no person whatever, within my knowledge, has claimed any right thereto.

Question. Was the land now claimed by William Buford, as representative of Conrad Selhoof, inhabited and cultivated on the 27th day of October, 1795, and for whose use and benefit ?

Answer. In January, 1798, Selhoof, or commonly called Collet, departed this life; then, the heirs of Selhoof or Collet sold it to John Linder, senior, who cultivated it for one year, or perhaps more.

Question. Was Conrad Selhoof on the 9th day of February, 1788, the head of a family, or twenty-one years of age?

Answer. He was, on the 9th of February, 1788, the head of a family, and twenty-one years of age.

Question. What kind of cultivation and improvement was made on the land in question ?

Answer. Corn and rice were cultivated on the land in question.

Question. (by Mr. Buford.) Do you know Selhoof to be the man commonly called Collet ?

Answer. He was commonly called Collet, but he, at all times signed his name Selhoof.

Question. (by Mr. Buford.) Do you know of Cornelius McCurtin having power of attorney from the widow of Selhoof or the man called Collet ?

Answer. Cornelius McCurtin at all times acted as the attorney in fact for the widow of Selhoof or the man commonly called Collet.

MISSISSIPPI TERRITORY, *Washington County:*
Personally appeared before me, Mary Mills, wife of Major John Mills, and, being sworn, saith, that the answers to the within several questions are, true to the best of her knowledge. Sworn and subscribed to, before me, this 26th June, 1805.

MARY MILLS.

FIGURES LEWIS, *J. P.*

MISSISSIPPI TERRITORY, *Washington County.*
I do hereby certify, that Mary Mills, wife of Major John Mills, personally appeared before me, and subscribed the oath, above written, relative to the truth of the several within answers, and these interrogatories were sealed up by me this 26th June, 1805.

FIGURES LEWIS, *J. P.*

The Board ordered that the case be postponed for consideration.

Adjourned until Friday, the 28th instant.

FRIDAY, *June* 28, 1805.
The Board met according to adjournment. Present: Robert C. Nicholas, Joseph Chambers.

BENJAMIN STEDHAM's case: commenced in page 736.

Theodore Brightwell was presented as a witness, and, being duly sworn, deposed, that the land in question was cultivated by Moses Stedham, the son of the claimant, in the years 1801, 1802, and 1803; that the land being situated in an island, it was not usual for people to inhabit thereon; that he had seen corn growing on the cleared land, within the lines of this claim, in each of the years aforesaid; but could not say whether Moses Stedham cultivated by the permission, or for the use and account, of Benjamin Stedham, his father, or for his own use and account, and without his father's authority; that Benjamin Stedham, the claimant, was, on the 3d day of March, 1803, more than thirty years of age.

The Board ordered that the case be postponed for consideration.

HEIRS OF PETER DEFORGE; case No. 248 on the docket of the Board, and No. 68 on the books of the Register.

Claim.—A right to one hundred and eight acres, by virtue of a British grant, under the first section of the act.

The claimants presented their claim, together with a surveyor's plot of the land claimed, in the words and figures following, viz.:

To the Commissioners appointed in pursuance of the act of Congress passed the 3d *day of March,* 1803, *for receiving and adjusting claims to lands east of Pearl river.*

Please to take notice, that the following tract of land, situated on the west side of the river Tensaw, bounded on the southeast by land belonging to Robert Farmer, northeast by the river Tensaw, and on the other sides by vacant land, bearing date the 22d day of September, 1778, containing one hundred and eight acres, is claimed by the heirs of Peter Deforge, in and by virtue of a British grant, and is now exhibited to the Register of the Land Office established east of Pearl river, to be recorded as directed by said act. To all which he begs leave to refer, as also to a copy of the plot herewith filed.

FRANCISCO FONTANILLA,
Legal Representative of the heirs of Peter Deforge.

MARCH 31, 1804.

[Plot omitted.]

Surveyed 22d day of September, 1778, by Elias Durnford, Surveyor General.

A British grant was exhibited in the words and figures following, viz.:

WEST FLORIDA, *ss.*

GEORGE THE THIRD, *by the grace of God, of Great Britain, France, and Ireland, King, defender of the faith, &c. To all to whom these presents shall come, greeting:*

Know ye, that we, of our special grace, certain knowledge, and mere motion, have given and granted, and by these presents, for us, our heirs and successors, do give and grant, unto Peter Deforge, his heirs and assigns, all that tract of land, situated on the west side of the river Tensaw, bounded on the southeast by land belonging to Robert Farmer, Esq., northeast by the river Tensaw, and on the other sides by vacant land, distant from Pensacola about seventy miles, in our province of West Florida, and having such shape, form, and marks, both natural and artificial, as are represented in the plot thereof, hereunto annexed, as drawn by our Surveyor General of lands; which said tract of land contains one hundred and eight acres, and is bounded as by the further certificate hereunto likewise annexed, under the hand of our said Surveyor General of lands, in our said province, may more fully and at large appear; together with all woods, underwood, timber and timber trees, lakes, ponds, fishings, waters, watercourses, profits, commodities, hereditaments, and appurtenances whatsoever thereunto belonging, or in anywise appertaining; together, also, with privilege of hunting, hawking, and fowling in and upon the same, and all mines and minerals, reserving to us, our heirs and successors, all mines of gold and silver: to have and to hold the said tract of land, and all and singular the premises hereby granted, with the appurtenances, unto the said Peter Deforge, his heirs and assigns, forever, in free and common soccage; yielding and paying unto us, our heirs and successors, or to the Receiver General of our quit-rents for the time being, or to such other officer as shall be appointed to receive the same quit-rent of one halfpenny sterling per acre, at the feast of St. Michael every year; the first payment to commence on the said feast of St. Michael which shall first happen after the expiration of two years from the date hereof, or within fourteen days after the said feast annually: *Provided always*, (and this present grant is upon condition,) *nevertheless*, That the said Peter Deforge, his heirs or assigns, shall and do, within three years after the date hereof, for every fifty acres of plantable land hereby granted, clear and cultivate three acres; at least, in that part thereof which he or they shall judge most convenient and advantageous, or else do drain and clear three acres of swampy or sunken ground, or do drain three acres of marsh, if any such shall be contained therein; and shall further, within the time aforesaid, put and keep upon every fifty acres thereof, accounted barren, three neat cattle, and continue the same thereon until three acres for every fifty acres be fully cleared and improved: and if it shall so happen that there be no part of the said tract of land fit for present cultivation, without manuring and improving the same, if the said Peter Deforge, his heirs or assigns, shall, within three years from the date hereof, erect on some part of the said tract of land one good dwelling-house, to contain at least twenty feet in length, and sixteen in breadth, and put on his said land the like number of three neat cattle, as aforesaid, on every fifty acres therein contained; or, otherwise, if any part of the said tract of land shall be stony or rocky ground, not fit for culture or pasture, shall and do, within three years as aforesaid, besides erecting the said house, begin to employ thereon, and continue to work for three years then next ensuing, in digging any stone quarry or mine, one good and able hand for every hundred acres thereof, it shall be accounted a sufficient cultivation and improvement: *Provided, also*, that every three acres which shall be cleared and worked, or cleared and drained, as aforesaid, shall further be accounted a sufficient seating, planting, cultivation, and improvement, to save forever from forfeiture fifty acres of land in any part of the tract hereby granted; and the said Peter Deforge, his heirs and assigns, shall be at liberty to withdraw his or their stock, or to forbear working in any quarry or mine, in proportion to such cultivation and improvements aforesaid as shall be made upon the plantable lands, swamps, sunken grounds, or marshes therein contained: *Provided, also*, That this grant shall be duly registered in the Register's Office of this province, within six months from the date hereof; and, also, that a docket thereof shall be entered in the Auditor's Office, within the same time, if such establishment shall take place in this province: *Provided, always*, That the said Peter Deforge, his heirs and assigns, at any time hereafter, having seated, planted, cultivated, and improved the said land, or any part thereof, according to the conditions and directions, above mentioned, may make proof of such seating, planting, cultivation, and improvement, in the general court, or in the court of the county, district, or precinct where the said land lieth, and have such proof certified to the Register's Office, and there entered with the record of this grant, a copy of which, duly attested, shall be admitted on trial, to prove the seating and planting of the said land: *Provided always, nevertheless*, That, if the said Peter Deforge, his heirs and assigns, do not in all things fully comply with and fulfil the respective directions and conditions herein above set forth, for the proper cultivation of the said land, within the time herein above limited for the completion thereof; or, if the said Peter Deforge, his heirs or assigns, shall not pay to us, our heirs and successors, or to the Receiver General of our quit rents, or to the proper officer appointed to re-

ceive the same, the said quit-rent of one halfpenny sterling per acre, on the said feast of St. Michael, or within fourteen days after, annually, for every acre contained in this grant, that then, and in either of these cases, respectively, this grant shall be void, any thing contained therein to the contrary notwithstanding; and the said lands, tenements, hereditaments, and premises, hereby specified, and every part or parcel thereof, shall revert to us, our heirs, and successors, fully and absolutely as if the same had never been granted.

Given under the great seal of our province of West Florida. Witness our trusty and well beloved Peter Chester, Esquire, Captain General, Governor, and Commander-in-chief in and over our said province, at Pensacola, this 16th day of April, in the year of our Lord 1779, and in the nineteenth year of our reign.

PETER CHESTER.

Passed the Secretary's Office:
ELIHU HALL BAY,
Deputy Secretary. [L. S.]

WEST FLORIDA, *ss.*

Pursuant to a fiat from his excellency Peter Chester, Esquire, Captain General, Governor, and Commander-in-chief in and over his Majesty's province of West Florida, &c. to me directed, bearing date the 16th day of April, 1779, I have perused and inspected the within letters patent, and do hereby certify, that there is no error therein apparent to me.
E. R. WEGG, *Attorney General.*

PENSACOLA, AUDITOR'S OFFICE, *April* 16, 1779.

A docket of the within grant is entered in book B, page 59, per
J. LORIMER, *Deputy Auditor.*

PENSACOLA, WEST FLORIDA, SECRETARY'S OFFICE, *April* 16, 1779.

I do hereby certify that the within letters patent, Surveyor General's certificate, and the certificate of the Attorney General, are recorded in the Secretary and Register's Office of the province of West Florida, in liber A, No. 3, page 490.

Examined, and compared with the said record, by
ELIHU HALL BAY,
Deputy Secretary and Register.

Entered in record of claims, (east side,) vol. 1, page 141, by EDWARD LLOYD WAILES, for
JOSEPH CHAMBERS, *Register.*

The Board ordered that the case be postponed for consideration.

GEORGE BURDON's case, No. 249 on the docket of the Board, and No. 74 on the books of the Register.

Claim.—A right to two hundred acres, by virtue of a British grant, under the first section of the act.

The claimant presented this claim, together with a surveyor's plot of the land claimed, in the words and figures following, to wit:

This survey was made the 19th day of July, 1779, by virtue of a warrant from Peter Chester, Governor of West Florida, dated the 8th day of May, 1779, certified by Elias Durnford, Surveyor General.

Issac Gilliard and Benjamin Farrar claim this land, as attorneys in fact, for Mr. George Burdon.

WEST FLORIDA, *ss.*

GEORGE THE THIRD, *by the grace of God, of Great Britain, France, and Ireland, King, defender of the faith, &c. To all to whom these presents shall come; greeting:*

Know ye, that we, of our special grace, certain knowledge, and mere motion, have given and granted, and by these presents, for us, our heirs and successors, do give and grant, unto George Burdon, who served as a Lieutenant in America last war, his heirs and assigns, all that tract of land, situated on an island, enclosed by Tombigbee, Tensaw, and Brier creek; east by land surveyed for Joseph Jackson, and a small bayou, north, by a bayou, west by vacant land, in our province of West Florida; and having such shape, form, and marks, both natural and artificial, as are represented in the plot thereof hereunto annexed, as drawn by our Surveyor General of lands; which said tract of land contains two hundred acres, and is bounded as by the further certificate hereunto likewise annexed, under the hand of said Surveyor General of lands, in our said province, may more fully and at large appear; together with all woods, underwood, timber, and timber-trees, lakes, ponds, fishings, waters, water courses, profits, commodities, hereditaments, and appurtenances whatsoever thereunto belonging, or in anywise appertaining; together, also, with privilege of hunting, hawking, and fowling, in and upon the same, and all mines and minerals; reserving to us, our heirs and successors, all mines of gold and silver: to have and to hold the said tract of land, and all and singular the premises hereby granted, with the appurtenances, unto the said George Burdon, his heirs and assigns, forever, in free and common soccage; yielding and paying unto us, our heirs and successors, or to the Receiver General of our quit-rents, for the time being, or to such other officer as shall be appointed to receive the same quit-rent of one halfpenny sterling per acre, at the feast of St. Michael, every year, the first payment to commence on the said feast of St. Michael, which shall first happen after the expiration of ten years from the date hereof, or within fourteen days after the said feast annually. Provided, always, and this present grant is upon condition, nevertheless, that the said George Burdon, his heirs or assigns, shall and do, within three years after the date hereof, for every fifty acres of plantable land hereby granted, clear and cultivate three acres at least in that part thereof which he or they shall judge most convenient and advantageous; or else do clear and drain three acres of swampy or sunken ground; or do drain three acres of marsh, if any such shall be contained therein; and shall further, within the time aforesaid, put and keep upon every acre thereof, accounted barren, three neat cattle, and continue the same thereon until three acres, for every fifty acres, be fully cleared and improved: and if it shall so happen that there be no part of the said tract of land fit for present cultivation, without manuring and improving the same, if the said George Burdon, his heirs or assigns, shall, within three years from the date hereof. erect, on some part of the said tract of land, one good dwelling house, to contain at least twenty feet in length and sixteen feet in breadth, and put on his said land the like number of three neat cattle, as aforesaid, on every fifty acres therein contained; or, otherwise, if any part of the said tract of land shall be stony or rocky ground, not fit for culture or pasture, shall and do, within three years, as aforesaid, besides erecting the said house, begin to employ thereon, and continue to work for three years, then next ensuing, in digging any stone quarry or mine, one good and able hand for every hundred acres thereof, it shall be accounted a sufficient cultivation and improvement. Provided, also, That every three acres, which shall be cleared and worked, or cleared and drained, as aforesaid, shall further be accounted a sufficient seating, planting, cultivation, and improvement, to save forever from forfeiture fifty acres of land, in any part of the tract hereby granted. And the said George Burdon, his heirs and assigns, shall be at liberty to withdraw his or their stock, or to forbear working, in any quarry or mine, in proportion to such cultivation and improvements aforesaid, shall be made upon the plantable lands, swamps, sunken grounds, or marshes, therein contained: Provided, also, That this grant shall be duly registered in the Register's Office of this province, within six months from the date hereof, and also that a docket thereof shall be entered in the Auditor's Office within the same time, if such establishment shall take place in this province: Provided, always, That the said George Burdon, his heirs and assigns, at any time hereafter, having seated, planted, cultivated, and improved the said land, or any part thereof, according to the directions and conditions above mentioned, may make proof of such seating, planting, cultivation, and improvement in the general court, or in the court of the county, district, or precinct, where the said land lieth; and have such proof certified to the Register's Office, and there entered with the record of this grant, a copy of which, duly attested, shall be admitted on trial to prove the seating and planting of the said land: Provided, always, nevertheless, That if the said George Burdon, his heirs and assigns, do not in all things fully comply with, and fulfil the respective directions and conditions therein above set forth, for the proper cultivation of the said land within the time herein above limited for the completion thereof; or if the said George Burdon, his heirs or assigns, shall not pay to us, our heirs and successors, or to the Receiver General of our quit-rents, or to the proper officer appointed to receive the same, the said quit-rent of one halfpenny sterling, per acre, on the said feast of St. Michael, or within fourteen days after, annually, for every acre contained in this grant, that then, and in either of these cases, respectively, this grant shall be void; any thing contained herein to the contrary notwithstanding; and the said lands, tenements, hereditaments, and premises hereby specified, and every part or parcel thereof, shall revert to us, our heirs and successors, fully and absolutely, as if the same had never been granted. This grant being in pursuance of our royal proclamation, of the seventh day of October, in the third year of our reign.

Given under the great seal of our province of West Florida. Witness our trusty and well beloved Peter Chester, Esquire, Captain General Governor, and Commander-in-chief in and over said province, at Pensacola; this seventeenth day of August, in the year of our Lord one thousand seven hundred and seventy-nine, and in the nineteenth year of our reign.

PETER CHESTER.

Passed the Secretary's office.
ELIHU HALL BAY, Deputy Secretary.

WEST FLORIDA, ss.

Pursuant to a fiat from his excellency Peter Chester, Esquire, Captain General. Governor, and Commander-in-chief in and over His Majesty's province of West Florida, &c. &c., to me directed, bearing date the 17th day of August, 1779, I have perused and inspected the within letters patent, and do hereby certify that there is no error therein apparent to me.

PENSACOLA, AUDITOR'S OFFICE, August 17, 1779.
A docket of the within grant is entered in book B, page 65.

J. LORIMER, Deputy Auditor.

PENSACOLA, WEST FLORIDA, SECRETARY'S OFFICE, August 17, 1779.

I do hereby certify that the within letters patent, Surveyor General's certificate, and the certificate of the Attorney General are recorded in the Secretary and Register's Office of the province of West Florida, in liber N, No. 3, page 520.

Examined and compared with the said record, by——. Entered in record of claims (east side,) vol. 1, page 189.

JOSEPH CHAMBERS, Register.

The Board ordered that the case be postponed for consideration.

THEODORE GAILLARD, representative of Allen Grant; case, No. 250 on the docket of the Board, and No. 70 on the books of the Register.

Claim.—A right of one hundred acres of land, by virtue of a British grant of survey, under the first section of the act.

The claimant presented his claim, together with a surveyor's plot of the land claimed, in the words and figures following, viz.:

This survey was made the 22d day of September, 1779, by virtue of a warrant from Peter Chester, Governor of West Florida, dated the 9th day of July, 1779, certified by Elias Durnford, Surveyor General; this land is claimed by Isaac Gaillard and Benjamin Farrar, as attorneys in fact to Theodore Gaillard, who is the holder of Allen Grant's bond, to make titles to the said land, which bond and the patent is recorded with the Register of the district of Washington.
[Plot omitted.]

WEST FLORIDA, ss.

GEORGE THE THIRD, by the grace of God, of Great Britain, France, and Ireland, King, defender of the faith, &c. To all to whom these presents shall come, greeting.

Know ye, that we, of our special grace, certain knowledge, and mere motion, have given and granted, and, by these presents, for us, our heirs and successors, do give and grant. unto Allen Grant, his heirs and assigns, all that tract of land, situated on the east side of Brier creek, bounded west by lands surveyed for Samuel Fontanella, south by vacant land, and east by Joseph Jackson's land, in our province of West Florida, and having such shape, form and marks, both natural and artificial, as are represented in the plot thereof hereunto annexed, as drawn by our Surveyor General of land; which said tract of land contains one hundred acres, and is bounded as by the further certificate hereunto likewise annexed, under the hand of said Surveyor General of lands in our said province, may more fully and at large appear; together with all woods, underwood, timber and timber trees, lakes, ponds, fishings, waters, water courses, profits, commodities, hereditaments, and appurtenances, whatsoever thereunto belonging, or in any wise appertaining; together, also, with privilege of hunting, hawking, and fowling in andupon the same, and all mines and minerals, reserving to us, our heirs and successors, all mines of gold and silver: to have and to hold the said tract of land, and all and singular the premises hereby granted, with the appurtenances, unto the said Allen Grant, his heirs and assigns, forever, in free and common soccage, yielding and paying unto us, our heirs and successors, or to the Receiver General of our quit-rents for the time being, or to such other officer as shall be appointed to receive the same quit-rent of one half-penny sterling per acre, at the feast of St Michael every year; the first payment to commence on the said feast of St. Michael which shall first happen after the expiration of two years from the date hereof, or within fourteen days after the said feast, annually: *Provided, always,* (and this present grant is upon condition,) *nevertheless,* That the said Allen Grant, his heirs or assigns, shall and do, within three years, after the date thereof, for every fifty acres of plantable land hereby granted, clear and cultivate three acres at least in that part thereof which he or they shall judge most convenient and advantageous, or else do clear and drain three acres of swampy or sunken ground, or do drain three acres of marsh, if any such shall be contained therein; and shall further, within the time aforesaid, put and keep upon every fifty acres thereof, accounted barren, three neat cattle, and continue the same thereon until three acres for every fifty acres be fully cleared and improved: and if it shall so happen, that there be no part of the said tract of land fit for present cultivation without manuring and improving the same, if the said Allen Grant, his heirs or assigns, shall, within three years from the date hereof, erect on some part of the said tract of land one good dwelling-house, to contain at least twenty feet in length, and sixteen feet in breadth, and put on his said land the like number of three neat cattle as aforesaid, on every fifty acres therein contained; or, otherwise, if any part of the said tract of land shall be stony or rocky ground, not fit for culture or pasture, shall and do, within three years, as aforesaid, besides erecting the said house, begin to employ thereon, and continue to work for three years then next ensuing, in digging any stone quarry or mine, one good and able hand for every hundred acres thereof, it shall be accounted a sufficient cultivation and improvement: *Provided, also,* That every three acres which shall be cleared and worked, or cleared and drained, as aforesaid, shall further be accounted a sufficient seating, planting, cultivation, and improvement, to save forever from forfeiture fifty acres of land in any part of the tract hereby granted; and said Allen Grant, his heirs and assigns, shall be at liberty to withdraw his or their stock, or to forbear working in any quarry or mine, in proportion to such cultivation and improvements aforesaid, as shall be made upon the plantable lands, swamps, sunken grounds, or marshes therein contained: *Provided, also,* That this grant shall be duly registered in the Register's Office of this province within six months from the date thereof, and, also, that a docket thereof shall be entered in the Auditor's Office within the same time, if such establishment shall take place in this province : *Provided, always,* That the said Allen Grant, his heirs and assigns, at any time hereafter, having seated, planted, cultivated, and improved the said land, or any part thereof, according to the directions and conditions above mentioned, may make proof of such seating, planting, cultivation, and improvement in the general court, or in the court of the county, district, or precinct where the said land lieth, and have such proof certified to the Register's office, and there entered with the record of this grant, a copy of which, duly attested, shall be admitted on trial to prove the seating and planting of the said land: *Provided, always, nevertheless,* That if the said Allen Grant, his heirs and assigns, do not in all things fully comply with and fulfil the respective directions and conditions herein above set forth for the proper cultivation of the said land, within the time herein above limited for the completion thereof; or, if the said Allen Grant, his heirs and assigns, shall not pay to us, our heirs and successors, or to the Receiver General of quit-rents, or the proper officer appointed to receive the same, the said quit rent of one halfpenny sterling per acre, on the said feast of St. Michael, or within fourteen days after, annually, for every acre contained in this grant, that then, and in either of these cases, respectively, this grant shall be void, any thing contained herein to the contrary notwithstanding; and the said lands, tenements, hereditaments, and premises, hereby specified, and every part and parcel thereof, shall revert to us, our heirs and successors, fully and absolutely as if the same had never been granted.

Given under the great seal of our province of West Florida. Witness our trusty and well beloved Peter Chester, Esquire, our Captain General, Governor, and Commander-in-chief in and over our said province, at Pensacola, this fourth day of October, in the year of our Lord one thousand seven hundred and seventy-nine, and in the nineteenth year of our reign.

PETER CHESTER.

Passed the Secretary's office.
ELIHU HALL BAY, *Deputy Secretary.*

PENSACOLA, AUDITOR'S OFFICE, *October* 4, 1797. A docket of the within grant is entered in book B, page 67.

J. LORIMER, *Deputy Auditor.*

WEST FLORIDA, *ss.*
Pursuant to a fiat from his excellency Peter Chester, Esquire, Captain General, Governor, and Commander-in-chief in and over His Majesty's province of West Florida, &c. &c., to me directed, bearing date the 4th day of October, 1779, I have perused and inspected the within letters patent, and do hereby certify that there is no error therein apparent to me.

E. R. WEGG, *Attorney General.*

WEST FLORIDA, SECRETARY'S OFFICE, PENSACOLA, October 4, 1779.
I do hereby certify that the within letters patent, Surveyor General's certificate, and the certificate of the Attorney General, are recorded in the Secretary and Register's Office of the province of West Florida, in liber A, No. 3, page 530.
Examined and compared with the said record, by ——.
Entered in record of claims, (east side,) vol. 1, page 160.

JOSEPH CHAMBERS, *Register.*

The claimant exhibited a bond for three hundred dollars from Allen Grant to John Donaho, bearing date the 3d day of April, 1777, and conditioned that the said Grant should, when thereunto required, convey unto the said Donaho, by proper deeds of lease and release, one hundred acres of land.
The Board ordered that the case be postponed for consideration.

GEORGE BURDON's case, No. 251 on the docket of the Board, and No. 73 on the books of the Register.
Claim.—A right to eight hundred acres, by virtue of a British grant, under the first section of the act.
The claimant presented his claim, together with a surveyor's plot of the land claimed, in the words and figures following, to wit:
This survey was made the 19th day of July, 1779, by virtue of a warrant from Peter Chester, Esq., Governor of West Florida, dated the 8th day of May, 1779, certified by Elias Durnford, Surveyor General.
Isaac Gaillard and Benjamin Farrar claim these lands, as attorneys in fact for Mr. George Burdon.
[Plot omitted.]

WEST FLORIDA, *ss.*
GEORGE THE THIRD, *by the grace of God, of Great Britain, France, and Ireland, King, defender of the faith, &c. To all to whom these presents shall come, greeting:*
Know ye, that we, of our special grace, certain knowledge, and mere motion, have given and granted, and, by these presents, for us, our heirs and successors, do give and grant, unto George Burdon, who served as a Lieutenant in America last war, his heirs and assigns, all that tract of land, situated on an island between Brier creek and Tombigbee river, bounded on the south by Brier creek, east by land surveyed for George Burdon, north by a bayou and land surveyed for Thomas Scott, in our province of West Florida, and having such shape, form, and marks, both natural and artificial, as are represented in the plot thereof hereunto annexed, as drawn by our Surveyor General of lands; which said tract of land contains eight hundred acres, and is bounded as by the further certificate hereunto likewise annexed, under the hand of our said Surveyor General of lands in our said province, may more fully and at large appear; together with all woods, underwoods, timber, and timber trees, lakes, ponds, fishings, waters, water courses, profits, commodities, hereditaments, and appurtenances whatsoever thereunto belonging, or in any wise appertaining; together, also, with privilege of hunting, hawking, and fowling in and upon the same, and all mines and minerals, reserving to us, our heirs and successors, all mines of gold and silver: to have and to

hold the said tract of land, and all and singular the premises hereby granted, with the appurtenances, unto the said George Burdon, his heirs and assigns, forever, in free and common soccage; yielding and paying unto us, our heirs and successors, or to the Receiver General of our quit-rents for the time being, or to such other officer as shall be appointed to receive the same, a quit-rent of one halfpenny sterling per acre, at the feast of St. Michael every year, the first payment to commence on the said feast of St. Michael which shall first happen after the expiration of ten years from the date hereof, or within fourteen days after the said feast, annually: *Provided, always,* (and this present grant is upon condition,) *nevertheless,* That the said George Burdon, his heirs and assigns, shall and do, within three years after the date hereof, for every fifty acres of plantable land hereby granted, clear and cultivate three acres, at least, in that part thereof which he or they shall judge most convenient and advantageous, or else do clear and drain three acres of swampy or sunken ground, or do drain three acres of marsh, if any such shall be contained therein; and shall further, within the time aforesaid, put and keep upon every fifty acres thereof, accounted barren, three neat cattle, and continue the same thereon until three acres for every fifty acres be fully cleared and improved: and if it shall so happen that there be no part of the said tract of land fit for present cultivation, without manuring and improving the same, if the said George Burdon, his heirs and assigns, shall within three years from the date hereof, erect on some part of the said tract of land one good dwelling house, to contain at least twenty feet in length and sixteen feet in breadth, and put on his said land the like number of three neat cattle, as aforesaid, on every fifty acres therein contained; or, otherwise, if any part of the said tract of land shall be stony or rocky ground, not fit for culture or pasture, shall and do, within three years, as aforesaid, besides erecting the said house, begin to employ thereon, and continue to work for three years then next ensuing, in digging any stone quarry or mine, one good and able hand for every hundred acres thereof, it shall be accounted a sufficient cultivation and improvement: *Provided, also,* That every three acres which shall be cleared and worked, or cleared and drained as aforesaid, shall further be accounted a sufficient seating, planting, cultivation, and improvement, to save forever from forfeiture fifty acres of land in any part of the tract hereby granted; and the said George Burdon, his heirs and assigns, shall be at liberty to withdraw his or their stock, or to forbear working in any quarry or mine, in proportion to such cultivation and improvements aforesaid, as shall be made upon the plantable lands, swamps, sunken grounds, or marshes therein contained: *Provided, also,* That this grant shall be duly registered in the Register's Office of this province within six months from the date hereof; and, also, that a docket thereof shall be entered in the Auditor's Office within the same time, if such establishment shall take place in this province: *Provided, always,* That the said George Burdon, his heirs and assigns, at any time hereafter, having seated, planted, cultivated, and improved the said land, or any part thereof, according to the directions and conditions above mentioned, may make proof of such seating, planting, cultivation, and improvement, in the general court, or in the court of the county, district, or precinct where the said land lieth, and have such proof certified to the Register's Office, and there entered with the record of this grant, a copy of which, duly attested, shall be admitted on trial to prove the seating and the planting of the said land: *Provided always, nevertheless,* That if the said George Burdon, his heirs and assigns, do not in all things fully comply with and fulfil the respective directions and conditions herein above set forth for the proper cultivation of the said land, within the time herein above limited for the completion thereof; or if the said George Burdon, his heirs or assigns, shall not pay to us, our heirs, or successors, or to the Receiver General of our quit-rents, or to the proper officer appointed to receive the same, the said quit-rent of one halfpenny sterling per acre, on the said feast of St. Michael, or within fourteen days after, annually, for every acre contained in this grant, that then, and in either of these cases respectively, this grant shall be void, any thing contained therein to the contrary notwithstanding; and the said lands, tenements, hereditaments, and premises hereby specified, and every part or parcel thereof, shall revert to us, our heirs and successors, fully and absolutely as if the same had never been granted. This grant being in pursuance of our royal proclamation of the 7th day of October, in the third year of our reign.

Given under the great seal of our province of West Florida. Witness our trusty and well beloved Peter Chester, Esquire, Captain General, Governor and Commander in-chief in and over our said province, at Pensacola, this seventeenth day of August, in the year of our Lord one thousand seven hundred and seventy-nine, and in the nineteenth year of our reign.

                   PETER CHESTER,

Passed the Secretary's office.

West Florida, *ss.*

Pursuant to a fiat from his excellency, Peter Chester, Esquire, Captain General, Governor, and Commander-in-chief in and over his Majesty's province of West Florida, &c. &c., to me directed, bearing date the 17th day of August, 1779, I have perused and inspected the within letters patent, and do hereby certify that there is no error therein apparent to me.

Pensacola, Auditor's Office, *August* 17, 1779.

A docket of the within grant is entered in book B, page 65, per

           J. LORIMER, *Deputy Auditor.*

West Florida, Pensacola, Secretary's Office, *August* 17, 1779.

I do hereby certify that the within letters patent, Surveyor General's certificate, and the certificate of the Attorney General, are recorded in the Secretary and Register's Office of the province of West Florida, in liber A, page—, No. 3.

Examined and compared with the said record, by—. Entered in record of claims, (east side,) vol. 1, page 183.

           JOSEPH CHAMBERS, *Register.*

The Board ordered that the case be postponed for consideration.

John Trouillet's case, No. 252 on the docket of the Board, and No. 61 on the books of the Register.

Claim.—A donation of six hundred and thirty-nine acres and nine-tenths of an acre, under the second section of the act.

The claimant presented his claim, together with a surveyor's plot of the land claimed, in the words and figures following, to wit:

To the Commissioners appointed in pursuance of an act of Congress passed the 3d of March, 1803, for receiving and adjusting claims to lands south of the Tennessee river, and east of the Pearl river.

Please to take notice, that the following tract of land, lying east of the Mobile river, bounded southwardly by Jusant's land, eastwardly by vacant land, and westwardly by the said river, is claimed by John Trouillet, under and by virtue of the second section of the act of Congress above mentioned. To all which he begs leave to refer, as also to the copy of the plot now delivered to the Register of the Land Office to be established east of Pearl river, which plot is herewith filed.

           JOSEPH CAMPBELL,
              Acting for John Trouillet.

Fort Stoddert, *March* 23, 1804.

[Plot omitted.]

Surveyed March 19, 1804, by James Gordon. Chain bearers, Gabriel Tissrah, William Weathers.

Entered in record of claims, (east side,) vol. 1, page 127, by Edward Lloyd Wailes, for

           JOSEPH CHAMBERS, *Register.*

The Board ordered that the case be postponed for consideration.

John Trouillet's case, No. 253 on the docket of the Board, and No. 29 on the books of the Register.

Claim.—A donation of six hundred and thirty-nine acres and nine-tenths of an acre, as representative of Joseph Milon, under the second section of the act.

The claimant presented his claim, together with a surveyor's plot of the land claimed, in the words and figures following, to wit:

To the Commissioners appointed in pursuance of an act of Congress passed the 3d day of March, 1803, for receiving and adjusting claims to lands south of Tennessee, and east of Pearl river.

Please to take notice, that the following tract of land, lying east of the Mobile river, bounded eastwardly by a lake called the Cut-off to Tensaw, and on all other sides by vacant lands, is claimed by John Trouillet, under and by virtue of a bill of sale from Joseph Milon to John and Peter Trouillet. To all which he begs leave to refer, as also to the copy of the plot now delivered to the Register of the Land Office, to be established east of Pearl river, which plot is herewith filed.

JOSEPH CAMPBELL.

FORT STODDERT, *March* 31, 1804.
[Plot omitted.]

Surveyed March 24, 1804, by James Gordon. Chain bearers, William Weathers, Gabriel Tissrah.

Entered in record of claims, (east side,) vol. 1, page 102, by EDWARD LLOYD WAILES, for

JOSEPH CHAMBERS, *Register.*

The claimant exhibited a bill of sale from Joseph Milon, duly executed, and bearing date the 9th day of October, 1774, conveying all the said Milon's right and interest in and to the said tract of land to John and Peter Trouillet.

The Board ordered that the case be postponed for consideration.

Adjourned until Monday, the 1st day of July next.

MONDAY, *July* 1, 1805.

The Board met according to adjournment. Present: Robert C. Nicholas, Joseph Chambers.

Adjourned until Thursday, the 4th instant.

THURSDAY, *July* 4, 1805.

The Board met according to adjournment. Present: Robert C. Nicholas, Joseph Chambers.

Adjourned until Saturday, the 6th instant.

SATURDAY, *July* 6, 1805.

The Board met according to adjournment. Present: Robert C. Nicholas, Joseph Chambers.

Adjourned until Monday, the 8th instant.

MONDAY, *July* 8, 1805.

The Board met according to adjournment. Present: Robert C. Nicholas, Joseph Chambers.

SAMUEL MIMS, representative of William Clark: case commenced in page 745.

On due consideration, the Board is of opinion that this claim is not supported agreeably to the articles of agreement and cession, between the United States and the State of Georgia, and the said claimant is not confirmed in his title to said land.

SAMUEL MIMS, representative of William Clark: case commenced in page 746.

On due consideration, the Board is of opinion that this claim is not supported agreeably to the articles of agreement and cession, between the United States and the State of Georgia, and the said claimant is not confirmed in his title to said land.

HEIRS OF PETER DEFORGE: case commenced in page 758.

On due consideration, the Board is of opinion that this claim is not supported agreeably to the articles of cession and agreement between the United States and the State of Georgia, and the claimants are not confirmed in their title to said land.

GEORGE WEEKLEY, representative of Michael Skipper: case commenced in page 731.

On due consideration, the Board is of opinion that this claim is supported agreeably to the requirements of law, and the claimant is entitled to a patent for so many acres of land as may be included in the following limits, to wit: Beginning, at the mouth of a bayou or gut, on the west margin of the Alabama river, in the Nanna Hubba island, on two willows, it being the beginning corner as described in the claimant's plot, entered in the office of the Register, it being also the lower corner of John Randon's donation claim, in his own right, running from thence, north, thirty-five degrees west, until it intersects with the line of Joseph Thompson's claim, in virtue of a Spanish warrant of survey, in the name of Adam Hollinger; thence, with Thompson's said line, south, fifty-six degrees west, twenty-eight chains and fifty links; thence, south, thirty-five degrees east, to the margin of the Alabama river; and thence, up the west margin of said river, to the beginning.

JOSEPH THOMPSON, representative of Adam Hollinger: case commenced in page 729.

On due consideration, the Board is of opinion that this claim is supported agreeably to the requirements of law,

and the claimant is entitled to a patent for seven hundred and thirty acres of land, to be located as follows, to wit: Beginning, on the west margin of the Alabama river, in the Nanna Hubba island, at a willow, in a gut, being the beginning corner described in the claimant's plot, entered in the Office of the Register, and being also the upper corner of John Randon's donation claim, in his own right; running thence, south, twenty-three degrees east, seventeen chains; thence, south, fifty-six degrees west eleven chains; thence, south, thirty-seven degrees west, five chains; thence, south, fifty-six degrees west, thirty-six chains; thence, due west, ninety chains; thence, north, five degrees west, so far that a line drawn from the extreme point of the same, to the place of beginning, shall include seven hundred and thirty acres of land.

HEIRS OF JOHN LINDER, Junior: case commenced in page 733.

On due consideration, the Board is of opinion that this claim is supported agreeably to the requirements of law, and the claimant is entitled to a patent for eight hundred acres of land, provided so many acres be included within the following limits, to wit: Beginning at the mouth of the Tensaw lake, where it puts out of the Alabama river, at an ash and maple, being the beginning corner described in the claimant's plot, entered in the Office of the Register, and also the beginning corner of Lemuel Henry's four hundred and ninety-one acre tract, in virtue of a Spanish warrant of survey in the name of John Linder, Senior; running from thence, north, seventy-five degrees east, one hundred and twenty-seven chains; thence, return to the ash and maple, the place of beginning, before mentioned; and runs therefrom, up the margin of the Alabama river, to the mouth of Boggy gut, described in the aforesaid plot; and thence, up the margin of said gut, so far as to make sixty-three chains, in a straight line, from the ash and maple; thence, a line to be drawn from the termination of this line, to run northeastwardly, so as to leave the house and principal improvements of Benjamin Hooven on the north side thereof; this line to be continued so far that a line drawn from the extreme point thereof, running south fifteen degrees east, shall join the said line of one hundred and twenty-seven chains, at its termination.

JAMES CARPENTER, heir at law to Richard, Caleb, and Joseph Carpenter: case commenced in page 755.

An affidavit was exhibited in the words and figures following, viz.:

BOARD OF COMMISSIONERS, WASHINGTON,
Mississippi Territory, Monday, March 11, 1805.

Witness, Daniel Whitaker, sworn, says, that Richard Carpenter, the patentee, died previous to the 27th of October, 1795; and that his son, James Carpenter, the devisee and claimant, was a resident in the Mississippi territory on the 27th of October, 1795.

I do certify, that the above is a true extract from the journal of the Board of Commissioners, for lands west of Pearl river, in the claim of James Carpenter, under a Spanish patent to his father, legally and fully executed.

R. CLAIBORNE, *Clerk of the Board.*

On due consideration, the Board is of opinion that this claim is supported agreeably to the articles of agreement and cession between the United States and the State of Georgia, and that Richard, Caleb, and Joseph Carpenter, or their heirs or devisees, are confirmed in their title to said land.

Adjourned until Thursday, the 11th instant.

THURSDAY, *July* 11, 1805.

The Board met according to adjournment. Present: Robert C. Nicholas, Joseph Chambers.

HEIRS OF DOMINIQUE DE OLIVE: case commenced in page 728.

On due consideration, the Board is of opinion that this claim is supported agreeably to the requirements of law, and the claimants are entitled to a patent for one thousand two hundred acres of land, to be located as follows, viz.: Beginning at a gum, in the mouth of a creek or bayou, being the beginning corner described in the claimant's plot, entered in the Register's Office; running thence, south, sixty-two degrees east, one hundred and twenty-seven chains; thence, north, eight degrees east, ninety-four chains eighty links; thence, north, sixty-two degrees west, to the Mobile river; and down the river, with its meanders, to the beginning.

ADAM HOLLINGER's case: commenced in page 743.

On due consideration, the Board is of opinion, that this claim is supported agreeably to the requirements of law, and the claimant is entitled to a patent for one thousand acres of land, to be located as follows, viz.: Beginning on the margin of the bayou, called the Cut-off, at its mouth, where it puts out of the Tombigbee river, in the Nanna Hubba island: thence, down the Tombigbee river, with its meanders, so far as to make, in a straight line, seventy-nine chains; thence, north, eighty-six degrees east, one hundred and twenty-six chains forty-nine links; thence, in a straight line, to the lower margin of the Cut-off, and, with the said Cut-off, as it meanders, to the place of beginning, so as to include one thousand acres of land.

JOSEPH BATES, Senior's case: commenced in page 743.

On due consideration, the Board is of opinion that this claim is supported agreeably to the requirements of law, and the claimant is entitled to a patent for one thousand acres of land, provided so many acres be included within the following limits, to be located as follows, viz.: Beginning at a cedar post, near to the lower end of the claimant's cleared land, on the east bank of the Tombigbee river; being the same cedar post, acknowledged by the claimant, as the point at which the line should commence, which might separate or divide his claim from that of John Turnbull, or from the claim of the representatives of Michael Hartley; running, from said cedar post, north, seventy degrees east, one hundred and twenty-six chains forty-nine links; thence, at right angles, from the termination of the line last mentioned, seventy-nine chains; and from thence, south, seventy degrees west, to the river; and, with its meanders, to the place of beginning: Provided, That if the line, running at right angles from the termination of the line of one hundred and twenty-six chains forty-nine links, should strike the river Tombigbee, in running a less number than seventy-nine chains; thence, to run down the said river, from the point where it may intersect the same, with its meanders, to the place of beginning.

JOSEPH STIGGINS, representative of John Johnson: case commenced in page 747.

On due consideration, the Board is of opinion that this claim is supported agreeably to the requirements of law, and the claimant is entitled to a patent for eight hundred acres of land, to be located as follows, viz.: Beginning on the east margin of Tensaw lake, five chains and fifty links below the mouth of Pyburn's creek; running from thence, up the east margin of said lake, as it meanders, so far as to make, on a straight line, sixty-three chains twenty-five links; thence, from the extreme point of the line last mentioned, north, seventy-six degrees east, one hundred and twenty-four chains; thence, south, fourteen degrees east, sixty-three chains and twenty-five links; thence, a direct line, to the beginning.

LEMUEL HENRY, representative of John Linder, Senior: case commenced in page 736.

On due consideration, the Board is of opinion that this claim is supported agreeable to law, and the claimant is entitled to a patent for four hundred and ninety-one acres of land, to be located as follows, to wit: Beginning at the mouth of Tensaw lake, where it puts out of the Alabama river, at an ash and maple, being the beginning corner described in the claimant's plot, entered in the Register's Office; running thence, north, seventy-five degrees east, seventy-eight chains; thence, south, fifteen degrees east, sixty-three chains; thence, south, seventy-five degrees west, so far that a line from the extreme point of the same, to the place of beginning, shall include four hundred and ninety-one acres.

JAMES MILLS, representative of John Linder, Senior: case commenced in page 737.

On due consideration, the Board is of opinion that this claim is supported agreeably to the requirements of law, and the claimant is entitled to a patent for two hundred and ninety-nine acres of land, to be located as follows, to wit: Beginning at the northeast corner of Lemuel Henry's four hundred and ninety-one acre tract, in virtue of a Spanish warrant of survey, in the name of John Linder, Senior; running thence, north, seventy-five degrees east, forty-seven chains and fifty links; thence, south, fifteen degrees east, so far that a line from the extreme point of the same, south, seventy-five degrees west, to the line of Lemuel Henry's said tract, and, with said Henry's line, to the place of beginning, shall include two hundred and ninety-nine acres of land.

JOSEPH CAMPBELL, representative of Augustin Rochon and Louisa Rochon: case commenced in page 748.

On due consideration, the Board is of opinion that this claim is supported agreeably to the requirements of the act; but that the warrants or orders of survey, from the Spanish Government, in the name of Augustin Rochon, and the widow, alias Louisa Rochon, on which this claim is bottomed, granted, or ordered to be surveyed, for the said Augustin Rochon only four hundred acres, and for the widow Louisa Rochon only four hundred acres; and, therefore, that the claimant is entitled to a patent for four hundred acres of land, in and by virtue of the Spanish warrants or order of survey, in the name of Augustin Rochon, to be located as follows, viz.: Beginning on the east margin of the Mobile river, at a gum tree, in the mouth of a gut or bayou, being also the beginning corner of a tract of one thousand two hundred acres, confirmed to the heirs of Dominique de Olive, under a Spanish warrant or order of survey, bearing date New Orleans, 26th of December, 1794; and running with the line of said tract, south, sixty-two degrees east, one hundred and twenty-seven chains; thence, south, twenty-eight degrees west, so far that a line from the termination thereof, to run north, sixty-two degrees west, to the margin of the Mobile river; thence, up the same, as it meanders, to the beginning, shall include four hundred acres of land. Also, to a patent for four hundred acres of land, in virtue of a Spanish warrant or order of survey, in the name of the widow, alias Louisa Rochon, to be located as follows, viz.: Beginning on the east margin of the Mobile river, at the lower corner of the tract, confirmed to the claimant in virtue of a Spanish warrant or order of survey, in the name of Augustin Rochon, dated New Orleans, 9th of March, 1794; thence, with the line of said tract, south, sixty-two degrees east, one hundred and twenty-seven chains; thence, south, twenty-eight degrees west, so far that a line from the termination thereof, to run north, sixty-two degrees west, to the margin of the Mobile river; and, up the same, to the beginning, shall include four hundred acres of land.

ANTONIO ESPAHO, representative of John Turnbull: case commenced in page 750.

On due consideration, the Board is of opinion that this claim is not supported agreeably to the requirements of law, and the claimant is not entitled to a patent in manner and form aforesaid.

FRANCIS STEEL's case: commenced in page 740.

On due consideration, the Board is of opinion that this claim is supported agreeably to the requirements of law, and the claimant is entitled to a patent for six hundred and forty acres of land, to be located as follows, to wit: Beginning at a water oak, on the Tensaw lake, being the beginning corner described in the claimant's plot, entered in the Register's Office; running from thence, south, thirteen degrees east, forty-two chains; thence, south, eighty-five degrees east, fifty-four chains; thence, north, sixty-two chains; thence, northwestwardly, across Tensaw lake; thence, up the margin of said lake, so far that a line therefrom, south, twenty-two degrees west, to the margin of said lake; thence, up the margin thereof, to the place of beginning, shall include six hundred and forty acres of land.

WILLIAM WEBBER's case: commenced in page 735.

On due consideration, the Board is of opinion that this claim is supported agreeably to the requirements of law, and that the claimant is entitled to a patent for six hundred and forty acres of land, to be located as follows, to wit:

Beginning at a hickory, on the Indian line, as described in the claimant's plot, entered in the Register's Office; thence, with said Indian line, south, eighty chains; thence, west, eighty chains; thence, north, eighty chains; thence, east, eighty chains, to the beginning, to include six hundred and forty acres of land, and the improvements of the claimant.

Adjourned until Saturday, the 13th instant.

SATURDAY, July 13, 1805.

The Board met according to adjournment. Present: Robert C. Nicholas, Joseph Chambers.

GEORGE WEEKLEY's case: commenced in page 735.

On due consideration, the Board is of opinion that this claim is supported agreeably to the requirements of law, and the claimant is entitled to a patent for six hundred and forty acres of land, to be located as follows, viz.: Beginning on Stedham's lake, at the same place described in the claimant's plot entered in the Register's

Office; it being also the upper corner of Moses Stedham's donation tract of six hundred and twenty-eight acres; thence, north, eighty-eight degrees east, forty-four chains; thence, north, sixty-eight degrees east, thirty-two chains; thence, south, twenty-two degrees east, sixty-three chains and fifty links; thence, north, seventy-five degrees east, so far that a line drawn from the extreme point of the same, north, fifteen degrees west, fifty-eight chains; thence, due west, to the margin of the lake; thence, with its meanders, to the beginning.

WILLIAM COLLINS, representative of Charles Conway: case commenced in page 739.
On due consideration, the Board is of opinion that this claim is not supported agreeably to the requirements of law, and the claimant is not entitled to a patent in manner and form aforesaid.

JOHN WEEKLEY, representative of James Farr: case commenced in page 739.
On due consideration, the Board is of opinion that this claim is supported agreeably to the requirements of law, and the claimant is entitled to a patent for six hundred and thirty-six acres of land, to be located as follows, viz.:
Beginning at a water oak, on the east margin of the Tensaw lake, a small distance below the mouth of Farr's mill creek, being the beginning corner described in the claimant's plot entered in the Register's Office; running from thence, north, sixty-four degrees east, thirty-six chains; thence, south, twenty-six degrees east, thirty-eight chains; thence, north, eighty degrees east, sixty-three chains; thence, north, ten degrees west, so far, that a line drawn from the extreme point thereof, north, sixty-five degrees west, to the east margin of the Tensaw lake, and down the margin of said lake, as it meanders, to the beginning, shall include six hundred and thirty-six acres of land.

JAMES COCKRAM, representative of Samuel Lyons: case commenced in page 741.
On due consideration, the Board is of opinion that this claim is supported agreeably to the requirements of the law, and the claimant is entitled to a patent for six hundred and forty acres of land, to be located as follows, viz.:
Beginning at a cypress, on one of the branches of Rice creek, being the beginning corner described in the claimant's plot entered in the Register's Office; running from thence, north, seventy-three degrees east, eighty chains; thence, north, seventeen degrees west, eighty chains; thence, south, seventy-three degrees west eighty chains; thence, in a direct line to the beginning, to include six hundred and forty acres of land, and the improvements of the claimant.

JORDAN PROCTOR's case: commenced in page 740.
On due consideration, the Board is of opinion that this claim is not supported agreeably to the requirements of law, and the claimant is not entitled to a patent in manner and form aforesaid.

HEIRS OF MICHAEL MILTON: case commenced in page 740.
On due consideration, the Board is of opinion that this claim is supported agreeably to the requirements of law, and the claimants are entitled to a patent for six hundred and eleven acres of land, to be located as follows, viz.:
Beginning at a water oak, on the south side of Tensaw lake, being the beginning corner described in the claimant's plot entered in the Register's Office; running from thence, south, thirteen degrees east, thirty-eight chains fifty links; thence, north, seventy-eight degrees west, so far that a line from the termination of the same, north, thirteen degrees west, until it strikes the margin of said lake, and on the margin thereof, as it meanders, to the place of beginning, shall include six hundred and eleven acres of land.

RICHARD COLEMAN's case: commenced in page 741.
On due consideration, the Board is of opinion that this claim is supported agreeably to the requirements of law, and the claimant is entitled to a patent for six hundred and thirty-four acres of land, to be located as follows, viz.:
Beginning on the east margin of the Tensaw lake, at the upper corner of Joseph Stiggins's eight hundred acre tract, in virtue of a Spanish warrant of survey, in the name of John Johnson; running from thence, with Stiggins's line, north, seventy-six degrees east, fifty-seven chains; thence, north, twenty-six degrees west, so far that a line from the termination of the same, south, sixty-four degrees west, to Weekley's mill creek, and down the margin of the main branch of said creek, as it meanders, to Tensaw lake; thence, down the said margin of said lake, to the beginning, shall include six hundred and thirty-four acres of land.

JOHN RANDON's case: commenced in page 735.
On due consideration, the Board is of opinion that this claim is supported agreeably to the requirements of law, and the claimant is entitled to a patent for three hundred and one acres of land, to be located as follows, to wit:
Beginning at the mouth of a gut or bayou, on the west margin of the Alabama river, in the Nanna Hubba island, on two willows, it being also the beginning corner of George Weekley's one hundred and sixty-one acre tract, in virtue of a Spanish warrant of survey, in the name of Michael Skipper; thence, with the line of said Weekley's said tract, north, thirty-five degrees west, until it intersects the line of Joseph Thompson's claim, in virtue of a Spanish warrant of survey in the name of Adam Hollinger; thence, in the courses and with Thompson's lines, to the beginning corner of his said tract of land; thence, down the west margin of the Alabama river to the place of beginning.

JESSE ROSS, representative of Abraham Walker: case commenced in page 736.
No evidence being adduced to show that Jesse Ross, the claimant, is the legal representative of Abraham Walker, therefore—
On due consideration, the Board is of opinion that the claim of Abraham Walker is supported agreeably to the requirements of law, and that the said Abraham Walker is entitled to a patent for six hundred and thirty acres of land, to be located as follows, viz.:
Beginning at an ash, on the east margin of Hollow creek, it being the beginning corner described in the claimant's plot entered in the Register's Office; thence, east, fifty-six chains and fifty-seven links: thence, south, so far that a line from the termination of the same, to run west to the margin of said Hollow creek; and thence, up the margin of said creek, with its meanders, to the beginning, shall include six hundred and thirty acres of land, with the improvements of the claimant.

MOSES STEDHAM's case: commenced in page 734.
On due consideration, the Board is of opinion that this claim is supported agreeably to the requirements of law, and the claimant is entitled to a patent for six hundred and twenty-eight acres of land, to be located as follows, viz.:
Beginning at the beginning corner of George Weekley's donation tract of six hundred and forty acres, on Stedham's lake; running thence, with said Weekley's line, north, eighty-eight degrees east, forty-four chains; thence, north, sixty-eight degrees east, so far that a line drawn from the extreme point of the same, south, twenty-two degrees east, sixty-nine chains; thence, south, seventy-nine degrees east, until it strikes Pine Log creek; thence, on the margin of said creek, as it meanders, to Stedham's lake; thence, on the margin of said lake, with its meanders, to the beginning, shall include six hundred and twenty-eight acres of land.

JOHN MILLS's case: commenced in page 731.
On due consideration, the Board is of opinion that this claim is supported agreeably to the requirements of law, and the claimant is entitled to a patent for so many acres of land, as are included within the following limits, provided the same does not exceed six hundred and forty acres, viz.:
Beginning at three cotton trees, said to be in a gut, on the west margin of the Alabama river, in the Nanna Hubba island, being the same cotton trees described in the claimant's plot entered in the Register's Office; running from thence, down the said margin of said river, as it meanders, to a maple; being the same maple described in the aforesaid plot; thence, direct to the beginning.

HEIRS OF VALENTINE DUBROCA: case commenced in page 748.
On due consideration, the Board is of opinion that this claim is not supported agreeably to the requirements of law, and the claimants are not entitled to a patent in manner and form aforesaid.

JAMES CALLIER, representative of Joseph Campbell: case commenced in page 738.

On due consideration, the Board is of opinion that this claim is supported agreeably to the requirements of the act, and the claimant entitled to a patent for six hundred and forty acres of land, to be located as follows, viz.:

Beginning on the east margin of the Mobile river, ten chains below the first bend below Fort Stoddert; thence, down the river so far, as, when reduced to a straight line, to make eighty chains; thence, at right angles, (eastwardly) from the general course of the river, so as to include six hundred and forty acres of land.

RICHARD TURVIN's case: commenced in page 744.

On due consideration, the Board is of opinion that this claim is not supported agreeably to the requirements of law, and that the claimant is not entitled to a patent in manner and form aforesaid.

JOHN TROUILLET's case: commenced in page 762.

On due consideration, the Board is of opinion that this claim is not supported agreeably to the requirements of the act, and the claimant is not entitled to a patent for the land by him claimed.

JOHN TROUILLET, representative of Joseph Milon: case commenced in page 762.

On due consideration, the Board is of opinion that this claim is not supported agreeably to the requirements of law, and that the claimant is not entitled to a patent for the land by him claimed.

Adjourned until Tuesday the sixteenth instant.

TUESDAY, *July* 16, 1805.

The Board met according to adjournment. Present: Robert C. Nicholas, Joseph Chambers.

WILLIAM AND JOHN PIERCE, representatives of Francis Ballard: case commenced in page 737.

On due consideration, the Board is of opinion that this claim is not supported agreeably to the requirements of law, and the claimants are not entitled to a patent in manner and form aforesaid.

JOSIAH FLETCHER's case: commenced in page 734.

On due consideration the Board is of opinion that this claim is supported agreeably to the requirements of law, and the claimant is entitled to a patent for so many acres of land as may be included within the following limits, provided the quantity of land included therein does not exceed six hundred and forty acres, viz.:

Beginning at a sweet gum, on the margin of the Cut-off, in the Nanna Hubba island, being also the beginning corner of Samuel Mims's donation claim, in his own right; running from thence, south, five degrees east, until a line in this course intersects a line of Joseph Thompson's tract, in virtue of a Spanish warrant of survey, in the name of Adam Hollinger, and with the line of Thompson's said tract, to the margin of the Alabama river, and up the west margin thereof, as it meanders, to the mouth of the Cut-off; thence, on the south margin of the Cut-off as it meanders, to the beginning.

SAMUEL TREND's case: commenced in page 742.

On due consideration, the Board is of opinion that this claim is supported agreeably to the requirements of law, and the claimant is entitled to a patent for six hundred and forty acres of land, to be located as follows, viz.:

Beginning at a *point* on Pine Log creek, being also the beginning corner of Francis Killingworth's donation tract, as representative of William Mills; thence, with said Killingworth's line, south, forty-five degrees west, so far that a line drawn therefrom, north, ten degrees west, forty chains, shall leave the present dwelling-house of Samuel Trend, on the east side thereof; thence, from the termination of this line, east, one hundred and twenty chains; thence, south, ten degrees east, eighty chains; thence, west, so far, as to intersect said Killingworth's line; thence, with said Killingworth's lines to their intersection with Pine Log creek; thence, down the east margin of the said creek, as it meanders, to the point of beginning.

FRANCIS KILLINGWORTH, representative of William Mills: case commenced in page 731.

On due consideration, the Board is of opinion that this claim is supported agreeably to the requirements of law, and the claimant is entitled to a patent for six hundred and forty acres of land, to be located as follows, viz.:

Beginning at such a point on Pine Log creek, that a line drawn therefrom, south, forty-five degrees west, shall leave Francis Killingworth's plantation on the south side of the same, and the house of Samuel Trend on the north side thereof; the line in this course of south, forty-five degrees west, to be continued so far, that a line drawn from the termination thereof, south, ten degrees east, one hundred and seven chains, shall leave the plantation of the said Killingworth, on the east side thereof; thence, from the termination of the last mentioned line, east, sixty-six chains; thence, north, ten degrees west, one hundred and six chains; thence, west, to the east margin of Pine Log creek; thence, down the margin thereof, to the point of beginning: to include six hundred and forty acres.

BENJAMIN HOOVEN's case: commenced in page 733.

On due consideration, the Board is of opinion that this claim is supported agreeably to the requirements of law, and the claimant is entitled to a patent for five hundred and sixty-six acres of land, provided so many acres are included within the following limits, viz.: Beginning at the mouth of Pine Log creek, on the lower side of the same; thence, down the east margin of the Alabama river, to the mouth of a boggy gut, being the same gut described in the claimant's plot entered in the Register's Office, and also described in the location of the tract, in the name of the heirs of John Linder, Jun, in virtue of a Spanish warrant of survey; thence, up the margin of said gut, to the corner of the tract of the heirs of John Linder, Jun.: thence, in the course and with the line of said tract, northeastwardly, one hundred and fourteen chains; thence, north, fifteen degrees west, to the line of Moses Stedham's donation tract, and, with said Stedham's line and Pine Log creek, to the beginning.

JAMES RANDON's case: commenced in page 735.

On due consideration, the Board is of opinion that this claim is not supported agreeably to the requirements of law, and the claimant is not entitled to a patent in manner and form aforesaid.

SAMUEL MIMS's case: commenced in page 735.

On due consideration, the Board is of opinion that this claim is supported agreeably to the requirements of law, and the claimant is entitled to a patent for six hundred and forty acres of land, to be located as follows, to wit: Beginning at a sweet gum on the south margin of the Cut-off, in the Nanna Hubba island, being the beginning corner described in the claimant's plot entered in the Register Office, running from thence, south, five degrees east, until it intersects with a line of Joseph Thompson's claim, in virtue of a Spanish warrant of survey, in the name of Adam Hollinger; and thence, with said Thompson's lines, so far as to make eighty chains in a straight line from the place of beginning; thence, south, eighty-five degrees west, so far that a line drawn from the termination of the same, to run north, five degrees west, to the south margin of the Cut-off; thence, on the margin thereof, with its meanders, to the beginning, shall include six hundred and forty acres of land.

BENJAMIN STEDHAM's case: commenced in page 736.

On due consideration, the Board is of opinion that the present claim is not supported agreeably to the requirements of the second section of said act, but the same is supported agreeably to the requirements of the third section of said act, and the claimant is entitled to a right of pre-emption to one hundred and thirty-three acres of land, to be located as follows, viz.: Beginning at the lower corner of George Weekley's one hundred and sixty-one acre tract, in virtue of a Spanish warrant of survey, in the name of Michael Skipper, on the west margin of the Alabama river, in the Nanna Hubba islands; running from thence, with said Weekley's line, north, thirty-five degrees west, sixty-four chains; thence, in a direct line, to the Alabama river; and thence, up the said river, as it meanders, to the beginning: to include one hundred and thirty-three acres of land.

JOSEPH THOMPSON's case: commenced in page 730.

On due consideration, the Board is of opinion that this claim is supported agreeably to the requirements of law, and the claimant is entitled to a patent for six hundred and forty acres of land, to be located as follows, to wit: Beginning at a white oak, on the east margin of Hollow creek, being the beginning corner described in the claimant's plot entered in the Register's Office; running from thence, south, eighty-eight degrees east, eighty chains; thence, north, so far that a line from the termination of the same, to run north, eighty-eight degrees west, to the east margin of said creek; thence, down the east margin thereof, to the beginning, shall include six hundred and forty acres of land.

WILLIAM and JOHN PIERCE, representatives of Jeremiah Phillips; case commenced in page 730.

On due consideration, the Board is of opinion that this claim is supported agreeably to the requirements of law, and the claimants are entitled to a patent for six hundred and forty acres of land, to be located as follows, viz.: Beginning at the upper corner of John Mills's donation tract, in his own name, at three cotton trees, thence, up the west margin of the Alabama river, to the lower corner of Benjamin Stedham's pre-emption tract, thence, with the said Stedham's line, until it strikes the line of Joseph Thompson's tract, in virtue of a Spanish warrant of survey, in the name of Adam Hollinger; thence, westwardly, with said Thompson's line or lines, until it strikes the line of Samuel Mims's donation tract, in his own right; thence, with said Mim's line, so far that a direct line from the termination thereof to the margin of the Alabama river, and, up the margin of the same, to the lower corner of John Mills's donation tract; and thence, with said line, to the beginning, shall include six hundred and forty acres of land.

NATT CHRISTMAS, representative of Michael Hartley: case commenced in page 738.

On due consideration, the Board is of opinion that this claim is supported agreeably to the requirements of law, and the claimant is entitled to a patent for six hundred and forty acres of land, to be located as follows, viz.: Beginning at a cedar post on the east margin of the Tombigbee river, being the beginning corner of Joseph Bates's tract of one thousand acres, in virtue of a Spanish warrant of survey, in his own name; thence, with said Bates's line; north, seventy degrees east, one hundred and twenty-six chains forty-nine links; thence, return to the beginning cedar post; thence, down the east margin of the Tombigbee river, to its junction with the Alabama river; and, up the west margin thereof, so far that a direct line therefrom to the termination of the first mentioned line shall include six hundred and forty acres.

Adjourned until Friday, the 19th instant.

FRIDAY, *July* 19, 1805.

The Board met according to adjournment. Present: Robert C. Nicholas, Joseph Chambers.

THOMAS BATES, Junior's, case: commenced in page 749.

On due consideration, the Board is of opinion that this claim is not supported agreeably to the requirements of law, inasmuch as the land covered by this claim is within the limits of a Spanish warrant of survey in the name of Joseph Bates, the father of the claimant, allowed by the Board; and, therefore, the claimant is not entitled to a patent in manner and form aforesaid.

WILLIAM BUFORD, representative of George Weekly, senior: case commenced in page 753.

On due consideration, the Board is of opinion that this claim is not supported agreeably to the requirements of law, and the claimant is not entitled to a patent in manner and form aforesaid.

NATT CHRISTMAS's case: commenced in page 753.

On due consideration, the Board is of opinion that this claim is not supported agreeably to the requirements of law, and the claimant is not entitled to a right of pre-emption to the land by him claimed, inasmuch as a donation claim in the name of this claimant, as representative of Michael Hartley, was allowed by the Board, and includes within its limits all the improvements and land included within the lines of this claim.

BENJAMIN FEW's case: commenced in page 729.

On due consideration, the Board is of opinion that this claim is not supported agreeably to the requirements of law, inasmuch as there is a Spanish warrant of survey in the name of Dominique de Olive, supported agreeably to law, for the whole of the land included within the lines of this claim, and the same is therefore rejected.

WILLIAM WEEKLEY's case: commenced in page 735.

On due consideration, the Board is of opinion that this claim is supported agreeably to the requirements of law, and the claimant is entitled to a right of pre-emption to one hundred and thirty-nine acres of land, to be located as follows, to wit:

Beginning at a pine, being the beginning corner described in the claimant's plot entered in the Register's Office, running from thence, north, sixty-six degrees west, fifty-two chains; thence, south, twenty-four degrees west, twenty-two chains; thence, south, fifty degrees east, twenty-seven chains; thence, east, so far that a direct line from the termination of the same to the beginning shall include one hundred and thirty-nine acres of land, and the improvements of the claimant.

Adjourned until Monday, the 22d instant.

MONDAY, *July* 22, 1805.

The Board met according to adjournment. Present: Robert C. Nicholas, Joseph Chambers.

CORNELIUS DUNN's case: commenced in page 734.

On due consideration, the Board is of opinion that this claim is supported agreeably to the requirements of law, and the claimant is entitled to a right of pre-emption to two hundred and fifty-two acres of land, to be located as follows, to wit:

Beginning at an elm on the south margin of Hollow creek, being the beginning corner described in the claimant's plot, entered in the Register's Office; running from thence, south, twenty-four chains, thence, east, so far, that a line drawn from the termination of the same, due north, to the margin of Hollow creek, and thence, down the margin thereof to the place of beginning, shall include two hundred and fifty-two acres of land, and the improvements of the claimant.

SIMEON WILKS, representative of James Proctor: case commenced in page 738.

On due consideration, the Board is of opinion that this claim is supported agreeably to the requirements of law, and the claimant is entitled to a patent for six hundred and forty acres of land, to be located as follows, viz.: Beginning at a hickory, being the beginning corner described in the claimant's plot entered in the Register's Office; thence, north, eighty degrees east, eighty chains; thence, south, ten degrees east, eighty chains; thence, south, eighty degrees west, eighty chains; thence, in a direct line, to the beginning; to include six hundred and forty acres of land, and the improvements of the claimant.

REUBEN DYER's case: commenced in page 740.

On due consideration, the Board is of opinion that this claim is supported agreeably to the requirements of law, and the claimant is entitled to a patent for six hundred and forty acres of land, to be located as follows, viz.: Beginning at a water oak, nearly opposite to the confluence of Tensaw river and lake, being the beginning corner described in the claimant's plot entered in the Register's Office; running from thence up the margin of the Tensaw river, as it meanders, so far that a direct line therefrom to the place of beginning shall include six hundred and forty acres of land, and the improvements of the claimant.

JOSEPH STIGGINS's case: commenced in page 741.

On due consideration, the Board is of opinion that this claim is supported agreeably to the requirements of law, and the claimant is entitled to a patent for six hundred and forty-five acres of land, to be located as follows, viz.: Beginning at a white oak, on Coleman's or Tensaw lake, being the beginning corner described in the claimant's plot entered in the Register's Office; running from thence, north, thirty-two degrees west, ten chains; thence, north, ten degrees west, eighteen chains, to the margin of Tensaw lake; thence, up the margin of said lake, with its meanders, so far that a line from the termination thereof, south, fifty-five degrees east, twenty-four chains; thence, a direct line therefrom, to the beginning, shall include six hundred and thirty-five acres of land, and the improvements of the claimant.

LEMUEL HENRY, representative of Michael Hartly: case commenced in page 745.

On due consideration, the Board is of opinion that this claim is not supported agreeably to the requirements of law, and the claimant is not entitled to a patent in manner and form aforesaid.

Adjourned until Thursday, the 25th instant.

THURSDAY, *July* 25, 1805.

The Board met according to adjournment. Present: Robert C. Nicholas, Joseph Chambers.

THEODORE GAILLARD, representative of Allen Grant: case commenced in page 760.

On due consideration, the Board is of opinion that this claim is not supported agreeably to the articles of agreement and cession between the United States and the State of Georgia, and that the title to this land is not confirmed.

GEORGE BURDON's two cases; one commenced in page 759, the other in page 761, in each of which cases the Board adjudged as follows, viz.:

On due consideration, the Board is of opinion that this claim is not supported agreeably to the articles of agreement and cession between the United States and the State of Georgia, and the claimant is not confirmed in his title to said land.

HEIRS OF ROBERT FARMER's two cases; commenced in page 757, in each of which cases the Board adjudged as follows, viz.:

On due consideration, the Board is of opinion that this claim is not supported agreeably to the articles of agreement and cession between the United States and the State of Georgia, and the claimants are not confirmed in their claim to the said land.

Adjourned until Saturday, the 27th instant.

SATURDAY, July 27, 1805.

The Board met according to adjournment. Present: Robert C. Nicholas, Joseph Chambers.

ALEXANDER MACULLAGH, representative of Thomas Underwood: case commenced in page 756.

On due consideration, the Board is of opinion that this claim is not supported agreeably to the articles of agreement and cession between the United States and the State of Georgia, and the claimant is not confirmed in his claim to the said land.

Adjourned until Tuesday the 30th instant.

TUESDAY, July 30, 1805.

The Board met according to adjournment. Present: Robert C. Nicholas, Joseph Chambers.

Adjourned until Friday, the 2d day of August next.

FRIDAY, August 2, 1805.

The Board met according to adjournment. Present: Robert C. Nicholas, Joseph Chambers.

Adjourned until Monday, the 5th instant.

MONDAY, August 5, 1805.

The Board met according to adjournment. Present: Robert C. Nicholas, Joseph Chambers.

Adjourned until Thursday, 8th instant.

THURSDAY, August 8, 1805.

The Board met according to adjournment. Present: Robert C. Nicholas, Joseph Chambers.

Adjourned until Saturday, the 10th instant.

SATURDAY, August 10, 1805.

The Board met according to adjournment. Present: Robert C. Nicholas, Joseph Chambers.

WILLIAM McDANIEL, representative of George Phillips: case commenced in page 753.

Jeremiah Phillips was presented as a witness, and, being duly sworn, deposed, that George Phillips, his brother, moved upon, built a house, and cleared some ground upon the land in question, in the month of December, 1797; that said George Phillips died in the spring of the year 1798; that his widow, or William McDaniel, had inhabited and cultivated this land, as he, the deponent, believed, until this time, and that said McDaniel inhabited and cultivated said land on the third of March, 1803.

Question. Did George Phillips, deceased, leave a will?

Answer. He did.

Question. Did he make any disposition of this land in his will?

Answer. He did not, for in that day it was not considered he had any right to the land.

Question. Did your brother leave any children?

Answer. He did leave two, a boy and a girl, the girl is married, and the boy is an infant, under twenty-one years of age.

Question. Do you know whether they have transferred their right in this land to William McDaniel?

Answer. John Phillips, the son of George Phillips, eighteen or nineteen years of age, and James Farr, the husband of George Phillips's daughter, have transferred their right in said land to William McDaniel, as I have heard them both say.

On due consideration, the Board is of opinion that this claim is supported agreeably to the requirements of the act, and the claimant is entitled to a patent for six hundred and thirty-two acres of land, to be located as follows, viz.:

Beginning at an ironwood, being the beginning corner described in the claimant's plot, entered in the Register's Office; thence, north, seventy-five degrees east, seventy-seven chains; thence, north, fifteen degrees west, forty-five chains; thence, south, sixty-one degrees east, fourteen chains; thence, south, twenty chains; thence, north, eighty-four degrees west, seventy-two chains; thence, north, sixty degrees west, to Major's creek; thence, along the margin of said creek and its branches to the beginning, shall include six hundred and thirty-two acres.

WILLIAM BUFORD, representative of Conrad Selhoof: case commenced in page 742.

On due consideration, the Board is of opinion, that this claim is supported agreeably to the requirements of the act, and the claimant is entitled to a patent for eight hundred acres of land, to be located as follows, viz.:

Beginning on the east margin of the Tensaw river at a water oak; thence, down the margin of said river, so far as to make sixty-three chains, when reduced to a straight line; thence, south, seventy degrees east, one hundred and twenty-seven chains; thence, north, twenty degrees east, sixty-three chains; thence, direct to the beginning, shall include eight hundred acres; this land lying within the limits of Piney or Collet's island.

WILLIAM SHIELDS's case: commenced in page 738.

Jeremiah Phillips and William Buford were presented as witnesses, and, being duly sworn, the said Phillips deposed, that he did not know of his own knowledge that William Shields inhabited and cultivated this land in the year 1797; but, that it was in cultivation on the third day of March, 1803, or the year 1803, for the use of William Shields; the said Buford deposed, that he well remembered that the land in question was cultivated on the 3d of March, or in the summer of 1803, for the use of William Shields.

On due consideration, the Board is of opinion that this claim is not supported agreeably to the requirements of law, and the claimant is not entitled to a patent in manner and form aforesaid.

Adjourned until Tuesday, the 13th instant.

TUESDAY, August 13, 1805.

The Board met according to adjournment. Present: Robert C. Nicholas, Joseph Chambers.

ABIJAH HUNT, representative of Augustin Rochon: case commenced in page 756.

Elijah Smith was produced as a witness, and, being duly sworn, deposed, that he saw Joseph Campbell, and Isabell Campbell, sign, seal, execute and deliver their deed, for the purposes therein mentioned, bearing date 16th December, 1801; purporting to convey one thousand acres of land to Abijah Hunt, his heirs and assigns; also, that he subscribed his name thereto as a witness, and that Wilson Carman likewise subscribed his name thereto, as a witness, in the presence of him, the said Smith.

On due consideration, the Board is of opinion, that this claim is not supported agreeably to the requirements of law, and the claimant is not entitled to a patent in manner and form aforesaid.

JOHN PICKERING's case, PETER CARTWRIGHT's case: the former commenced in page 647, and the latter in page 665.

Thomas Malone, surveyor, being duly sworn, deposed that he made the survey of the claim of Peter Cartwright, and having followed the upper line of the heirs of Robert Farmer's claim, of one thousand acres, under a British grant, that he verily believed that a part of Cartwright's claim is within the lines of said Farmer's claim; also, that he believed that the greater part of the claim of John Pickering was also included within the limits of said Farmer's claim, and that the said Pickering told him that the greater part of his claim was actually within the limits of the said Farmer's said tract.

On further investigation and consideration, the Board is of opinion that a part of said Cartwright's claim, and a greater part of said Pickering's claim, is interfered with by the claim of Robert Farmer's heirs, in virtue of a grant, from the British Government of West Florida to Robert Farmer, for one thousand acres, bearing date the 6th day of August, 1778.

NOAH K. HUTSON, representative of Henry Nail: case commenced in page 653.

Thomas Bilbo, surveyor, being duly sworn, deposed, that the claim of John Lott, Jun., under a British grant, interfered with the southeast corner of Noah Kenner Hutson's donation claim.

On further investigation and consideration, the Board is of opinion that this claim be located as follows, viz.: Beginning on the west margin of the Tombigbee river, at the upper corner of James Callier's claim, as representative of Anthony Hoggatt; thence, south, thirty-three degrees west, ninety-one chains; thence, north, seventy-two degrees west, so far that a line to be drawn from the termination of the same, north, fifteen degrees east, to the margin of said river, and with the same to the place of beginning, shall include three hundred and twenty-nine acres of land: *Provided, nevertheless*, that the said claimant first obtain before a court of competent jurisdiction, a judicial decision in his favor, against the adverse claim, by virtue of a grant from the British Government of West Florida, to John Lott, Jun., of three hundred acres, bearing date the 16th February, 1778; and the Board doth order, that a certificate be issued to him accordingly.

Adjourned until Friday the 16th instant.

FRIDAY, *August* 16, 1805.

The Board met according to adjournment. Present: Robert C. Nicholas, Joseph Chambers.

JOHN MCGREW, Senior's case: commenced in page 663.

Stephen Hogg, surveyor, being duly sworn, deposed, that to his best belief and information, John McGrew, Senior's, donation tract, if located adjoining to the upper line of John Baker's tract of four hundred acres, in virtue of a Spanish warrant, will interfere with a grant of one hundred acres of land from the British Government of West Florida, to Abraham Little, also a grant of five hundred acres of land, from said Government, to Charles Walker.

On further investigation and consideration, the Board is of opinion, that this claim be located as follows, viz.: Beginning on the west margin of the Tombigbee river, at the upper corner of John Baker's tract of four hundred acres, in virtue of a Spanish warrant or order of survey, in his own right; thence, with Baker's said line, south, to the corner thereof; thence, west, so far that a line from the termination thereof, to run north to the west margin of the Tombigbee river, and down the same margin to the beginning, shall include six hundred and forty acres: *Provided nevertheless*, that the said claimant first obtain, before a court of competent jurisdiction, a judicial decision in his favor, against the adverse claim by virtue of a grant from the British Government of West Florida, of one hundred acres, to Abraham Little, bearing date the 16th day of February, 1778; also, against the adverse claim by virtue of a grant from said Government, to Charles Walker, of five hundred acres, bearing date the 27th day of January, 1777.

JOHN CALLIER, representative of Wilford Hoggatt: case commenced in page 629.

On further investigation and consideration, the Board is of opinion that this claim be located as follows, viz.: Beginning on a hackberry, on the bank of the Tombigbee river, being the beginning corner described in the claimant's plot, entered in the Register's Office; thence, to run south, fifty degrees west, so far that a line drawn from the termination thereof, south, forty-three degrees east, sixty-three chains and twenty-four links; thence, north, fifty degrees east, to the margin of the Tombigbee river; thence, up the river, as it meanders, to the beginning, shall include eight hundred acres of land.

ANN LAWRENCE's case: commenced in page 656.

On further investigation and consideration, the Board is of opinion that this claim be located as follows, viz.: Beginning on the west margin of the Tombigbee river, at the upper corner of Noah Kenner Hutson's donation tract, in right of Henry Nail; thence, south, fifteen degrees west, to the northwest corner of said Hutson's tract; thence, north, seventy-two degrees west, so far that a line drawn from the termination thereof, north, fifteen degrees east, to the margin of said river; and thence, down the river, with its meanders, to the beginning, shall include four hundred and forty-five acres of land.

GEORGE BREWER, Junior's, case: commenced in page 651.

On further investigation and consideration, the Board is of opinion that this claim be located as follows, viz.: Beginning on the west margin of the Tombigbee river, at the upper corner of Ann Lawrence's donation tract, in her own right; thence, south, fifteen degrees west, one hundred and twenty-two chains; thence, north, sixty-six degrees west, so far that a line drawn from the termination of the same, north, fifteen degrees east, to the west margin of said river; thence, down the same, with its meanders, to the beginning, shall include six hundred and twenty-nine acres of land.

THOMAS MALONE, representative of John Arnott: case commenced in page 703.

On further investigation and consideration, the Board is of opinion that this claim be located as follows, viz.: Beginning on the west margin of the Tombigbee river, at the upper corner of George Brewer, Junior's, donation tract, in his own right; thence, south, fifteen degrees west, one hundred and twenty-six chains forty-nine links; thence, north, seventy-eight degrees west, so far that a line therefrom, north, fifteen degrees east, to the margin of said river; thence, down the margin of the same, to the beginning, shall include four hundred and eighty acres of land.

JOHN F. MCGREW AND CLARK MCGREW, representatives of Julian de Castro: case commenced in page 632.

On further investigation and consideration, the Board is of opinion that this claim be located as follows, viz.: Beginning on the west margin of the Tombigbee river, at the upper corner of Thomas Malone's claim, in virtue of a Spanish warrant, in the name of John Arnott; thence, south, fifteen degrees west, one hundred and twenty-six chains and forty-nine links; thence, north, seventy-eight degrees west, so far that a line drawn from the termination thereof, north, fifteen degrees east, to the margin of the Tombigbee river, and thence, down the margin of the same, to the beginning, shall include four hundred acres of land.

HEIRS OF JAMES MCGREW: case commenced in page 627.

On further investigation and consideration, the Board is of opinion that this claim be located as follows, viz.: Beginning on the west margin of the Tombigbee river, at the upper corner of John Flood and Clark McGrew's claim, in virtue of a Spanish warrant, in the name of Julian de Castro; thence, south, fifteen degrees west, one hundred and twenty-six chains forty-nine links; thence, north, seventy-six degrees west, so far that a line drawn from the termination thereof, north, fifteen degrees east, to the margin of said river, and down the margin of the same, to the beginning, shall include four hundred acres of land.

GEORGE BREWER, Jun., representative of James Watkins: case commenced in page 605.

On further investigation and consideration, the Board is of opinion that this claim be located as follows, viz.: Beginning at the southwest corner of Noah Kenner Hutson's donation tract, in the right of Henry Nail, and on the line of James Callier's claim, in virtue of a Spanish warrant of survey, in the name of Anthony Hoggatt; thence, north, seventy-two degrees west, until it intersects the lower line of George Brewer's donation tract, in his own right; thence, south, fifteen degrees west, with said Brewer's said line, so far that a line drawn from the termination thereof, south, sixty-six degrees east, shall intersect the upper line of James Callier's claim, before mentioned, and with the same, to the beginning, shall include six hundred and twenty acres of land.

SAMPSON MOUNGER's case: commenced in page 609.

On further investigation and consideration, the Board is of opinion that this claim be located as follows, viz.: Beginning at the northwest corner of George Brewer, Junior's, donation tract, in his own right; thence, south, fifteen degrees west, eighty chains; thence, south, sixty-six degrees east, so far that a line from the termination thereof, north, fifteen degrees east, shall intersect the western boundary line of George Brewer, Junior's, donation tract, in the right of James Watkins; thence, with said line, north, sixty degrees west, until it intersects the line of said Brewer's claim, in his own right; thence, with said Brewer's line or lines, to the place of beginning, shall include six hundred and thirty-four acres of land.

THOMAS GOODWIN, representative of Hiram Mounger: case commenced in page 650.

On further investigation and consideration, the Board is of opinion that this claim be located as follows, viz.:

Beginning at a cedar post, set up by the claimant, and branded with the initials J. M. and B. H.; thence, north, thirty degrees west, thirty-five chains and thirty links; thence, south, sixty degrees west, eighteen chains; thence, south, thirty degrees east, so far that a line from the termination thereof, north, sixty degrees east, eighteen chains, and a line to be drawn from the termination of this line, to the beginning, shall include one hundred and twenty acres of land.

SOLOMON WHEAT's case: commenced in page 601.

On further investigation and consideration, the Board is of opinion that this claim be located as follows, viz.:

Beginning at a point on the south line of the tract of Thomas Goodwin, in the right of Hiram Mounger, twenty chains eighteen links from the southwest corner of said tract; thence in the course of and with said line, south, thirty degrees east, forty-one chains and eighty links; thence, south, sixty degrees west, twenty-four chains; thence, north, thirty degrees west, so far that a line from the termination of the same, direct to the beginning, shall include one hundred acres of land.

BENJAMIN HARRISON, representative of Jacob Miller: case commenced in page 649.

On further investigation and consideration, the Board is of opinion that this claim be located as follows, viz.:

Beginning at a cedar post, set up by the claimant, branded J. M. and B. H., being also the beginning corner of Thomas Goodwin's claim, in right of Hiram Mounger; from thence, north, thirty degrees west, so far that a line from the termination thereof, north, sixty-five degrees east, eight chains and thirty-one links; thence, south, fifty-eight degrees east, eighty three chains; thence, north, fifty degrees east, to a sweet gum corner on the margin of Ryan's lake, return to the beginning cedar post, and run therefrom south, thirty degrees east, so far that the whole length of the line, beginning at the cedar post, and running north, thirty degrees west, and south, thirty degrees east, shall be one hundred and seventy-three chains; thence, from the termination of this line, north, sixty degrees east, forty chains and fifty links; thence, north, twenty-seven degrees east, sixty-five chains; thence, north, forty degrees east, to the south margin of Ryan's lake; and thence, up the margin of the lake, to the sweet gum corner, shall include six hundred and forty acres of land.

PETER MALONE, representative of John Woods: case commenced in page 639.

On further investigation and consideration, the Board is of opinion that this claim be located as follows, viz.:

Beginning at the upper or northwest corner of John Chastang's tract of four hundred and eighty acres, in virtue of a Spanish warrant, or order of survey, in his own name; thence, with Chastang's line, fourteen chains; thence, west, one hundred and fifteen chains; thence, north, twenty-eight chains; thence, east, one hundred and fifteen chains; thence, direct to the beginning, to include three hundred and twenty acres, exclusive of one square acre adjoining his upper line, to include the store and dwelling-house of Edwin Lewis, in which Judge Toulmin now resides: *Provided, nevertheless,* That the said claimant first obtain, before a court of competent jurisdiction, a judicial decision in his favor against the adverse claim, by virtue of a grant from the British Government of West Florida to John Sutherland, bearing date the 22d day of October, 1779; and the Board doth order that a certificate be granted to him accordingly.

JAMES GRIFFIN's case: commenced in page 596.

On further investigation and consideration, the Board is of opinion that this claim be located as follows, viz.:

Beginning on the line of John Chastang's tract of four hundred and eighty acres, in virtue of a Spanish warrant, or order of survey, in his own right, at the southeast corner of Peter Malone's pre-emption tract of three hundred and twenty acres; thence, in the line of said Chastang, south, eighty chains; thence, west eighty chains; thence, north, eighty chains; thence, direct to the beginning, shall include six hundred and forty acres of land.

EDWIN LEWIS's case: commenced in page 638.

On further investigation and consideration, the Board is of opinion that this claim be located as follows, viz.: Beginning on the west margin of the Tombigbee river, at the mouth of a bayou or gut, near to the upper end of the bluff on which Fort St. Stephen's stands; thence, up the west margin of said bayou, so far as to make eight chains in a straight line; thence, in a direct line, to the northeast corner of Peter Malone's pre-emption of three hundred and twenty acres; thence, with said Malone's upper line, east, so far that one square acre on the south side thereof shall include the dwelling-house and store of the claimant, they being the same in which Judge Toulmin now resides; this east line to be continued so far on the line of said Malone, as to make twenty-eight chains; thence, north, forty degrees west, so far that a direct line therefrom to the west margin of the said river, and down the same, as it meanders, to the place of beginning, shall include one hundred and sixty acres, exclusive of five acres, to include, in the centre thereof, the cantonment at present occupied by the troops of the United States; the right of said five acres being reserved to the United States for their future use and disposition; and the Board doth order, that a certificate be issued accordingly.

EDWARD LLOYD WAILES, representative of John Baker: case commenced in page 701.

On further investigation and consideration, the Board is of opinion that this claim be located as follows, viz.: Beginning at the point where the line that runs north, forty degrees west, of Edwin Lewis's pre-emption tract of one hundred and sixty acres, leaves the upper line of Peter Malone's pre-emption tract of three hundred and twenty acres; thence, with said Lewis's line, north, forty degrees west, to the corner thereof; thence, north, twenty chains; thence, west, so far, that a line from the termination of this line, to run south, until it intersects the upper line of said Malone's said tract; and thence, with said line, to the beginning, shall include four hundred and eighty acres of land: *Provided, nevertheless,* That the claimant first obtain, before a court of competent jurisdiction, a judicial decision in his favor against the adverse claim, by virtue of a grant from the British Government of West Florida, to John Sutherland, bearing date the 22d day of October, 1779; and the Board doth order that a certificate be issued accordingly.

WILLIAM ROGERS's case: commenced in page 597.

On further investigation and consideration, the Board is of opinion that this claim be located as follows, viz.: Beginning at a sassafras, on the west margin of the Tombigbee river, being the beginning corner described in the claimant's plot, entered in the Register's Office, being also the upper corner of a tract granted by the British Government of West Florida to Robert Farmer, for one thousand acres; thence, south, seventy degrees west, fifty-five chains; thence, north, twenty degrees west, so far that a line from the termination of the same, north, seventy degrees east, to the margin of the Tombigbee river, and down the said margin to the place of beginning, shall include three hundred and eighty-eight acres of land.

MATTHEW SHAW's case: commenced in page 598.

On further investigation and consideration, the Board is of opinion that this claim be located as follows, viz.: Beginning on the west margin of the Tombigbee river, at the upper corner of William Rogers's pre-emption tract of three hundred and eighty-eight acres; thence, south, seventy degrees west, one hundred and six chains; thence, north, thirty degrees west, so far that a line from the termination of the same, north, seventy degrees east, to the west margin of the Tombigbee river, and down said margin to the place of beginning, shall include three hundred and thirty-three acres of land.

WILLIAM WILLIAMS's case: commenced in page 651.

On further investigation and consideration, the Board is of opinion that this claim be located as follows, viz.: Beginning at a sycamore, on the west margin of the Tombigbee river; thence, south, sixty degrees west, twenty chains and fifty links; thence, north, twenty-five degrees west, so far that a line from the termination of the same, north, fifty-six degrees east, to the west margin of the Tombigbee river, and down the said margin to the place of beginning, shall include one hundred and one acres of land.

GEORGE ROBBINS, representative of Zadock Brashear: case commenced in page 616.

On further investigation and consideration, the Board is of opinion that this claim be located as follows, viz.: Beginning at a sycamore on the west margin of the Tombigbee river, being also the beginning corner of William Williams's pre-emption tract of one hundred and one acres, and the same sycamore described in the claimant's plot, entered in the Register's Office; thence, south, sixty degrees west, fifty chains; thence, south, thirty degrees east, so far, that a line from the termination of the same, north, sixty degrees east, to the west margin of the Tombigbee river, and up the said margin to the place of beginning, shall include two hundred and twenty acres of land.

RAWLEY GREEN's case: commenced in page 666.

On further investigation and consideration, the Board is of opinion that this claim be located as follows, viz.: Beginning at a sassafras, being the beginning corner described in the claimant's plot, entered in the Register's Office; also, the beginning corner of William Rogers's pre-emption of three hundred and eighty-eight acres; thence, south, seventy degrees west, seventy-four chains; thence, south, forty degrees east, so far that a line from the termination of the same, north, seventy degrees east, to the west margin of the Tombigbee river, and up the said margin to the place of beginning, shall include two hundred and one acres.

JOSEPH WESTMORELAND's case: commenced in page 599.

On further consideration and investigation, the Board is of opinion that this claim be located as follows, viz.: Beginning on the west margin of the Tombigbee river, at the lower corner of Rawleigh Green's pre-emption of two hundred and one acres ; thence, south, seventy degrees west, sixty chains fifty links ; thence, south, twenty degrees east, so far that a line from the termination of the same, north, seventy degrees east, to the west margin of the Tombigbee river, and up the said margin to the beginning, shall include one hundred and ninety-seven acres.

RANSON HARWELL's case: commenced in page 642.

On further investigation and consideration, the Board is of opinion that this claim be located as follows, viz.: Beginning at a willow oak, being the same described in the claimant's plot, entered in the Register's Office, standing near to the branch that runs between the claimant's house and the house of William Murrell; thence, north, thirteen degrees west, thirty-one chains and sixty links ; thence, south, seventy-five degrees west, twenty-six chains and fifteen links; thence, south, forty-seven degrees west, forty-three chains and fifty links; thence, south, forty-five degrees east, so far that a line from the termination of the same to the place of beginning, shall include one hundred and ninety-seven acres.

WILLIAM MURRELL's case : commenced in page 643.

On further investigation and consideration, the Board is of opinion that this claim be located as follows, viz.: Beginning at a willow oak, being also the beginning corner of Ranson Harwell's pre-emption of one hundred and ninety-seven acres; thence, with the south line of said Harwell's tract, to his southwest corner; thence, south, forty-five degrees east, so far that a line from the termination of the same, to run parallel with the first mentioned line, and a line from the termination thereof to the place of beginning, shall include one hundred and sixty acres.

JAMES HUCKABY's case: commenced in page 651.

On further investigation and consideration, the Board is of opinion that this claim be located as follows, viz.: Beginning at a stake on the south margin of Tolla creek, a short distance below the confluence of Fulsom's and Tolla creeks, being the beginning corner described in the claimant's plot, entered in the Register's Office; thence, east, so far that a line from the termination of the same, to run north, until it intersects the upper line of Ransom Harwell's pre-emption tract; thence, in the course of said Harwell's line, north, forty-five degrees west, to the south margin of Tolla creek; and thence, up said margin to the place of beginning, shall include four hundred and sixty-seven acres.

EDWIN LEWIS, representative of McCole and Mc-Clendon: case commenced in page 645.

On further investigation and consideration, the Board is of opinion that this claim be located as follows, viz.: Beginning at a stake on the south margin of Tolla creek, a short distance below the confluence of Fulsom's and Tolla creeks, it being also the beginning corner of James Huckaby; thence, east, so far, that a direct line from the termination of the same, to the lower margin of Fulsom's creek; thence, with said margin of said creek, as it meanders, to its junction with Tolla creek; thence, down the south margin of Tolla creek to the beginning, shall include one hundred and sixty acres.

EDWIN LEWIS, representative of William Green: case commenced in page 648.

On further investigation and consideration, the Board is of opinion that this claim be located as follows, viz.: Beginning in the fork of Tolla and Fulsom's creeks, at their junction; thence, up the southern margin of Tolla creek, to the point where the line of Bryan and Brewer's pre-emption tract of three hundred and twenty acres crosses said Tolla creek; thence, in the course of said Bryan and Brewer's line, north, seventy degrees east, so far, that a direct line therefrom to Fulsom's creek, and with said creek, to the beginning, shall include one hundred and sixty acres.

ELISHA SIMMONS's case: commenced in page 597.

On further investigation and consideration, the Board is of opinion that this claim be located as follows, viz.: Beginning on the west margin of the Tombigbee river, at the lower corner of Joseph Westmoreland's pre-emption tract of one hundred and ninety-seven acres; thence, in a direct line to the northeast corner of Ransom Harwell's one hundred and ninety-seven acre pre-emption tract; thence, in the course of said line, south, thirteen degrees east, so far that a line from the termination of the same, to the west margin of the Tombigbee river, and up the said margin to the beginning, shall include one hundred and sixty acres of land.

JOHN FLOOD McGREW's case: commenced in page 671.

On further investigation and consideration, the Board is of opinion that this claim be located as follows, viz.: Beginning at a hickory, being the same described in the claimant's plot, entered in the Register's Office, as his beginning corner; thence, north, thirteen degrees west, forty chains; thence, south, seventy-seven degrees west, eighty chains; thence, south, thirteen degrees east, forty chains; thence, direct to the beginning, shall include three hundred and twenty acres of land.

ISAAC RYAN's case: commenced in page 594.

On further investigation and consideration, the Board is of opinion that this claim be located as follows, viz.: Beginning at the mouth of Ryan's lake, at its junction with Bassett's creek, at a black gum; thence, south, eighty-five degrees west, thirty chains; thence, south, twenty-one degrees west, thirty-three chains, to the corner of Benjamin Harrison's donation tract; thence, with said Harrison's line, south, fifty-eight degrees east, eighty-three chains; thence, north, fifty degrees east, four chains, to said Harrison's sweet gum corner: this line of north, fifty degrees east, to be continued so far that a line from the termination thereof, north, seven degrees west, to the southern margin of Bassett's creek, and up the same, to the place of beginning, shall include six hundred and forty acres of land.

SOLOMON BOYKIN, representative of Elizabeth Reed: case commenced in page 655.

On further investigation and consideration, the Board is of opinion that this claim be located as follows, viz.: Beginning at the mouth of the big lake, at a sweet gum, being the place of beginning described by the claimant's plot, entered in the Register's Office; thence, up the margin of said lake, to Bassett's line; thence, north, sixty-seven degrees west, so far that a line from the termination thereof, south, twenty-three degrees west, to the northern margin of Bassett's creek, and down the same to the place of beginning, shall include five hundred and two acres of land.

JAMES SCOTT, representative of Gabriel Burrows: case commenced in page 608.

On further investigation and consideration, the Board is of opinion that this claim be located as follows, viz.: Beginning at a pine, being the beginning corner described in the claimant's plot, entered in the Register's Office; thence in a direct line to the southwest corner of Solomon Wheat's pre-emption tract of one hundred acres; thence, in the course of said Wheat's line, south, thirty degrees east, so far as to make one hundred and twenty-two chains, from the beginning pine; thence, south, sixty degrees west, twenty-five chains; thence, north, thirty degrees west, seventy-nine chains; thence, north, forty-five degrees west, thirty chains and fifty links; thence, direct to the beginning; shall include three hundred and seventy-five acres of land.

HEZEKIAH CARTER, representative of Robert Jones: case commenced in page 646.
On further investigation and consideration, the Board is of opinion that this claim be located as follows, viz.:
Beginning at the point, where the line of James Scott's donation tract, running north, thirty degrees west, seventy-nine chains, terminates; thence, in the course of said Scott's line, north, sixty degrees west, twenty-five chains; thence, north, forty-five degrees west, twenty chains; thence, south, sixty-five degrees east, thirty chains; thence, direct to the beginning, shall include sixty acres of land.

THOMAS GOODWIN, representative of Daniel Kennedy: case commenced in page 704.
On further investigation and consideration, the Board is of opinion that this claim be located as follows, viz.:
Beginning on the margin of Ryan's lake at the point where the line of Benjamin Harrison's donation tract, running north, forty degrees east, strikes said lake; thence, up the south margin of said lake, forty chains; thence, north, fifty degrees east, twenty chains; thence, south, forty degrees east, fifty-five chains; thence, south, forty chains; thence, south, sixty-seven degrees west, to said Harrison's line; and from thence, with his line or lines, to the place of beginning, shall include two hundred and eighty-six acres of land.

NATHAN BLACKWELL's case: commenced in page 595.
On further investigation and consideration, the Board is of opinion that this claim be located as follows, viz.:
Beginning on the west margin of the Tombigbee river, at the upper corner of Francis Boykin's tract of eight hundred acres, in virtue of a Spanish warrant of survey, in the name of Adam Hollinger; thence, north, sixty-seven degrees west, to the said Boykin's line one hundred and twenty chains; thence, north, twenty-three degrees east, so far that a line from the termination thereof, south, sixty-seven degrees east, to the margin of the Tombigbee river, and down the margin of said river, as it meanders, to the beginning, shall include six hundred and forty acres of land.

JOHN DUNN's case: commenced in page 656.
On further investigation and consideration, the Board is of opinion that this claim be located as follows, viz.:
Beginning on the west margin of the Tombigbee river, at the upper corner of Nathan Blackwell's donation tract, of six hundred and forty acres; thence, north, sixty-seven degrees west, in the course of said Blackwell's line, eighty chains; thence, north, twenty-three degrees east, so far, that a line therefrom, south, sixty-seven degrees east, to the west margin of the Tombigbee river, and down the said margin to the beginning, shall include three hundred and twenty acres of land.

FRANCIS STRINGER's case: commenced in page 619.
On further investigation and consideration, the Board is of opinion that this claim be located as follows, viz.:
That a square tract of one hundred and sixty acres, running due north, due east, due south, and due west, shall include the present gin-house of the claimant in the centre thereof.
Adjourned until Monday, the 19th instant.

MONDAY August 19, 1805.
The Board met according to adjournment. Present: Robert C. Nicholas, Joseph Chambers,

THOMAS MALONE's case: commenced in page 657.
On further investigation and consideration, the Board is of opinion that this claim be located as follows, viz.:
Beginning on the west margin of the Tombigbee river, at the lower corner of John Callier's tract of eight hundred acres, in virtue of a Spanish warrant of survey, in the name of Wilford Hoggatt; thence, in the course of said Callier's line, south, fifty degrees west, eighty chains; thence, south, forty degrees east, so far that a line from the termination thereof, direct to the west margin of the Tombigbee river, and up the margin of the same, to the beginning, shall include three hundred and twenty acres of land.

WYCHE WATLEY's case: commenced in page 603.
On further investigation and consideration, the Board is of opinion that this claim be located as follows, viz.:
Beginning at the northwest corner of William H. Hargrave's pre-emption tract of three hundred and twenty acres; thence, west, seventy-one chains; thence, south, twenty-two chains; thence, east, to said Hargrave's line, and with said line, north, to the beginning, to include one hundred and fifty-six acres of land.

RICHARD BRASHEAR's case: commenced in page 601.
On further investigation and consideration, the Board is of opinion that this claim be located as follows, viz.:
Beginning at the southeast corner of Wyche Watley's one hundred and fifty-six acre pre-emption tract on the line of Hargrave; thence, west, with Watley's line, forty chains; thence, south, forty chains; thence, east, to Hargrave's line, and with said line to the beginning, shall include one hundred and sixty acres of land.

HIRAM MOUNGER's case: commenced in page 599.
On further investigation and consideration, the Board is of opinion that this claim be located as follows, viz.:
Beginning at the southwest corner of James Denley's tract of two hundred and eighty acres, in virtue of a Spanish warrant or order of survey, in the name of Solomon Johnston; thence, west, ninety chains; thence, south, fifty chains; thence, east, sixty chains; thence, south, thirty-three chains seventy-five links; thence, east, so far that a line from the termination thereof, north, to said Denley's line, and with said line west, to the place of beginning, shall include six hundred and forty acres of land.
Adjourned until Thursday, the 22d instant.

THURSDAY, August 22, 1805.
The Board met according to adjournment. Present: Robert C. Nicholas, Joseph Chambers.

WILLIAM GILLIAM, representative of John Clark: case commenced in page 649.
On further investigation and consideration, the Board is of opinion that this claim be located as follows, viz.:
Beginning at a pine on the north side of Sunflower creek, being the beginning corner described in the claimant's plot, entered in the Register's Office; thence, south, seven degrees east, forty chains; thence, south, sixty-five degrees west, thirty-four chains; thence, north, seven degrees west, so far, that a direct line therefrom to the place of beginning, shall include one hundred and two acres, and the improvements of the claimant.
Adjourned until Saturday, the 24th instant.

SATURDAY, August 24, 1805.
The Board met according to adjournment. Present: Robert C. Nicholas, Joseph Chambers.

JOHN and TANDY WALKER's case: commenced in page 666.
On further investigation and consideration, the Board is of opinion that the claim in virtue of a grant from the British Government of West Florida to Robert Farmer, bearing date the 6th day of August, 1778, does not interfere with this claim.

CLARK MCGREW's case: commenced in page 698.
On further consideration and investigation, the Board is of opinion that a part of this claim is interfered with by the claim of the heirs of Robert Farmer, in virtue of a grant from the British Government of West Florida to Robert Farmer, of one thousand acres, bearing date 6th of August, 1778.
Adjourned until Tuesday, the 27th instant.

TUESDAY, August 27, 1805.
The Board met according to adjournment. Present: Robert C. Nicholas, Joseph Chambers.
Adjourned until Friday, the 30th instant.

FRIDAY, August 30, 1805.
The Board met according to adjournment. Present: Robert C. Nicholas, Joseph Chambers.
Adjourned until Monday, the 2d day of September next.

MONDAY, September 2, 1805.
The Board met according to adjournment. Present: Robert C. Nicholas, Joseph Chambers.
Adjourned until Wednesday, the 4th instant.

WEDNESDAY, *September* 4, 1805.
The Board met according to adjournment. Present.
Robert C. Nicholas, Joseph Chambers.

NARCISO BROUTIN'S case: commenced in page 732.

Augustin Rochon was presented as a witness, and, being duly sworn, deposed, that in the year 1795, said Narciso Broutin, with some negroes, inhabited and cultivated a crop of corn on the land in question; that the family of Mr. Broutin resided in Mobile, but that he made the corn to provision his family.

Solomon Johnston (August 12) was presented as a witness, and, being duly sworn, deposed, that he knew the land claimed; that it lay just below the mouth of the Alabama river, nearly opposite to the upper end of a small island; that said land was inhabited and cultivated by Broutin's negroes, but at what time he could not say, but he knew that the negroes were Broutin's.

Question. Do you know whether Narciso Broutin, about the time you mention to have been on his place, cultivated any other land ?

Answer. I do not know.

On due consideration, the Board is of opinion that this claim is supported agreeably to the requirements of law, and that the claimant is entitled to a patent for eight hundred acres of land, to be located as follows, viz.:

Beginning on the east margin of the Mobile river, at the upper corner of a tract of one thousand two hundred acres, confirmed to the heirs of Dominique de Olive, in virtue of a Spanish warrant, or order of survey, in the name of said Dominique de Olive, dated New Orleans, 26th of December, 1794; thence, up the east margin of the Mobile and the Alabama rivers, so far as to make sixty-three chains twenty-four links, in a straight line; thence, south, sixty-two degrees east, so far that a direct line from the termination thereof shall strike the northeast corner of said Olive's tract; and thence, with his upper line, to the beginning, on the margin of the Mobile river, so as to include eight hundred acres.

Adjourned until Saturday, the 7th instant.

SATURDAY, *September* 7, 1805.
The Board met according to adjournment. Present:
Robert C. Nicholas, Joseph Chambers.
Adjourned until Tuesday, the 10th instant.

TUESDAY, *September* 10, 1805.
The Board met according to adjournment. Present:
Robert C. Nicholas, Joseph Chambers.
Adjourned until Thursday, the 12th instant.

THURSDAY, *September* 12, 1805.
The Board met according to adjournment. Present:
Robert C. Nicholas, Joseph Chambers.
Adjourned until Saturday, the 14th instant.

SATURDAY, *September* 14, 1805.
The Board met according to adjournment. Present:
Robert C. Nicholas, Joseph Chambers.

MISSISSIPPI TERRITORY, *Washington County,*
August 3, 1805.

SIR: In a private communication from a member of the Board of Commissioners, the Tensaw settlement was mentioned as being left in an unpleasant predicament. Upon further reflection, we have thought it our duty to advise you officially and more particularly on this subject.

As the ascertainment of the rights of persons to land on the east side of Tombigbee river, was not included in the provisions of the act of the 3d March, 1803, the inhabitants there conceived it optional with them, whether or not to enter their claims with the Register of the Land Office, by the 31st March, 1804. On the recommendation of the commissioners, the claims were perhaps generally, though not entirely, entered; but it is probable, and indeed certain, that many important documents necessary to correct adjudication on these claims, have not, in consequence of the abovementioned construction of the law, been entered. It is conceived that no Board which may be authorized to decide upon these claims, can do justice if the claimants are barred from completing their entries at the Register's Office. The act of the 27th March, 1804, supplementary to the act of the 3d of March, 1803, contains no provisions applicable to this object.

We looked a long time for official information that Congress had passed an act to enlarge the commissions which issued under the act of the 3d of March, 1803, declaring that the commissioners should, by virtue of those commissions, take cognizance of the claims east of Tombigbee river, but no communication of any kind, touching this subject, was received. Since the termination of the judicial business of the Board, namely, on the 26th July, the Register received a newspaper copy of the supplementary act referred to above. Had this act been announced in time, still it does not appear to contain any declaration investing the commissioners, heretofore appointed, with additional powers.

Both the acts abovementioned exclude from the jurisdiction of the commissioners all claims to land where the Indian title has not been extinguished. On inspection of the confirmation of the boundary line between the United States and the Choctaw nation, executed the 31st August, 1803, by General Wilkinson on the one part, and Mingo Poos-Coos and Alatala Hoomah on the other part, we find the limits thus described: beginning in the Hatcha Comisa or War river, where the limits between the United States and Spain cross the same; thence, up the channel of said river, to the confluence of Chickasaw Hay and Buckatannee rivers; thence, up the channel of the Buckatannee, to Bogue Hoomah, or Red creek; and thence, with the various courses in said instrument written, to the main branch of the Sintee Bogue or Snake creek; and thence, with said creek to the Tombigbee river; thence, down the main channel of the Tombigbee and Mobile rivers, to the abovementioned line of limits between the United States and Spain, and with the same to the point of beginning.

By report only we are informed that General Wilkinson, in behalf of the United States, run, marked, and confirmed a line of demarcation between the United States and the Creek Indians: beginning on the east side of the Tombigbee river, and on the north or upper side of the bayou, by the name of the Cut-off, (which flows between the Alabama and Tombigbee alternately as either of those rivers are the highest,) and thence, as specified in the said treaty. The island formed by these waters, called Nanna Hubba, containing about twenty thousand acres of the first quality of land, has been recently claimed by the Choctaw nation. These Indians refer to the beforementioned lines, settled on the 31st of August, 1803, as evidence of their never having relinquished their right to Nanna Hubba island. It is, however, certain, that, during the times when the British and Spanish Governments held the jurisdiction of this country, the island in question was in the occupancy and exclusive possession of their respective subjects; and has, in like manner, continued in the possession of the American citizens since the jurisdiction has been surrendered to the United States. It is believed that the Indian title was extinguished by the British, and that the same will appear by the *field notes* of Mr. Purcell, an English surveyor, and that these notes are, or were in the possession of General Wilkinson; and it is also said that General Wilkinson was fully of opinion that this island belonged to the United States. However satisfactory these circumstances may be, in the formation of private opinions, a judicial tribunal cannot proceed on such loose grounds; it must require official documents to justify its judgment. Any Board which may be appointed to adjust the claims on the east side of the Tombigbee, will find insuperable difficulties, unless the Government is pleased to furnish such official documents and other evidence as may lead to a correct decision.

On the 16th of July all the judicial business of the Board of Commissioners, which could come under its cognizance, by virtue of the law from which its appointment and authority were derived, was closed. Nothing remained to be done, but that the signature of a majority of the members be affixed to the certificates which have been adjudged to be issued; and, also, to report on the subject of British grants fully executed, required by the seventh section of the act. Under these circumstances, Mr. Nicholas, one of the commissioners, requested the consent of his colleagues to retire; the Board, considering that the object of its appointment was effected, and all the services to which it was particularly commissioned, draw near to the ultimate point, was of opinion that Mr. Nicholas might, with propriety, retire; and he has accordingly taken his departure for Kentucky.

We have the honor to be, with the greatest respect, your obedient servants,

EPHRAIM KIRBY,
JOSEPH CHAMERS,
Commissioners for adjusting claims to lands
east of Pearl river.

Hon. ALBERT GALLATIN. ESQ.

BOARD OF COMMISSIONERS, EAST OF PEARL RIVER,
Hobuckintoopa, Sept. 21, 1805.
SIR:
We have the satisfaction to communicate to you that on this day we finished the business of the Board, and adjourned *sine die.*

Uncontrollable circumstances have protracted the completion of this tedious and complex business much longer than had been anticipated by you.

Since the meeting of the Board at this place on the 1st day of May last. many complaints have been presented against the locations (previously made) of lands lying on the west side of the Tombigbee river; *and in all cases* where the party complaining convinced us more justice might be done by a revision of the case, we either made a new location, or so modified the old one as to us seemed right.

The locations, *in every instance,* have been effected, and the certificates issued, without any survey having been made under the authority of the United States. From this circumstance, we have experienced much perplexity, as we were compelled to act either from such doubtful information as we could obtain, from the witnesses and the private surveyors, presented by the claimants, or to postpone issuing the certificates until the respective claims might be surveyed under the authority of the United States. To the latter course, intrinsic objections presented themselves; and in adopting the former, difficulties in identifying the point or place at which certain tracts were to begin, unavoidably intervened. Hence it is our opinion, that it might more certainly establish the rights of individuals, as well as facilitate the progress of the business of the Surveyor of Public Lands, if he, or those acting under his authority, should be empowered by *law* to administer oaths, compel the attendance of witnesses, and take their testimony, in order to identify such points or places of beginning as could not, for want of the necessary information, be described with certainty in the certificates issued by the Board.

We have the honor to be, Sir, with perfect respect and esteem, your most obedient servants,
ROBERT C. NICHOLAS,
JOSEPH CHAMBERS.
The Honorable ALBERT GALLATIN, Esq.,
Secretary of the Treasury.

BOARD OF COMMISSIONERS, EAST OF PEARL RIVER,
September 14, 1805.
SIR:
Enveloped herewith you will receive the report (of British grants, legally and fully executed, and duly recorded) required from this Board by the 7th section of an act entitled "An act regulating the grants of land, and providing for the disposal of lands of the United States south of the State of Tennessee," passed on the 3d day of March, 1803.

We have the honor to be, Sir, with perfect respect and esteem, your most obedient servants,
ROBERT C. NICHOLAS,
JOSEPH CHAMBERS.
The Honorable ALBERT GALLATIN, Esq.,
Secretary of the Treasury.

Adjourned until Tuesday, the 17th instant.

TUESDAY, *September* 17, 1805.
The Board met according to adjournment. Present: Robert C. Nicholas, Joseph Chambers.

Adjourned until Thursday, the 19th instant.

THURSDAY, *September* 19, 1805.
The Board met according to adjournment. Present: Robert C. Nicholas, Joseph Chambers.

Adjourned until Saturday, the 21st instant.

SATURDAY, *September* 21, 1805.
The Board met according to adjournment. Present: Robert C. Nicholas, Joseph Chambers.

BOARD OF COMMISSIONERS, EAST OF PEARL RIVER,
Hobuckintoopa, Sept. 21, 1805.
SIR:
Enclosed you will receive a certificate, stating the day on which the clerk of this Board entered upon the duties of his office, and also the day on which the Board adjourned *sine die.*

The vouchers for all the incidental and contingent expenses to which this Board has been subjected, are certified by us, in duplicate, and will be presented for settlement by the clerk, Mr. Parmelee.

We have the honor to be, Sir, with perfect respect and esteem, your most obedient servants,
ROBERT C. NICHOLAS,
JOSEPH CHAMBERS.
The Honorable ALBERT GALLATIN, Esq.,
Secretary of the Treasury.

The Board ordered that the clerk take into his possession and safe keeping the books and papers, and cause them to be transmitted to, and lodged in the office of the Secretary of State, agreeably to a requisition in the sixth section of the act of Congress of the 3d of March, 1803, entitled "An act regulating the grants of land, and providing for the disposal of the lands of the United States south of the State of Tennessee."
Attest: DAVID PARMELEE 2d,
Clerk of the Board.

Adjourned *sine die.*

REGISTER A.

Abstract of Certificates entered with the Register of the Land Office west of Pearl river, during the month of April, 1805, grounded on British and Spanish patents.

Commissioners' certificates			Recorded.		Claim — To whom granted.	Claim — Name of original grantee.	Quantity allowed. (Acres.)	Situation.	Title — Whence derived.	Title — Date of patent.
When entered.	No.	Date.	Vol.	Page.						
1805. April 18,	1	Febr'y 26,	1	1	Thomas M. Green,	Margaret Stampley,	100	On the waters of Boyd's creek,	British,	Sept'r 1, 1777.
" 18,	2	Febr'y 26,	1	3	Thomas M. Green,	John Lum,	350	On the south side of Boyd's creek,	Do.	August 26, 1778.
" 18,	3	Febr'y 27,	1	5	Thomas M. Green,	John Smith,	200	On the waters of Cole's creek,	Do.	May 26, 1777.
" 18,	4	Febr'y 27,	1	7	Sarah Holmes	Sarah Holmes,	200	On Middle creek,	Do.	Sept'r 21, 1772.
" 18,	5	Febr'y 27,	1	9	Parker Canadine,	David Adam,	200	On the waters of Cole's creek,	Do.	Oct'r 23, 1777.
" 18,	6	Febr'y 27,	1	11	John Bolls	Andrew Cypress,	100		Do.	March 20, 1778.
" 18,	7	Febr'y 28,	1	13	Isaac and Joshua Alexander,	William Alexander,	600	On Second creek,	Do.	Sept'r 21, 1772.
" 18,	8	Febr'y 28,	1	15	Abner Green	Anthony Hutchins,	434	On Second creek,	Do.	August 2, 1773.
" 18,	9	Febr'y 28,	1	17	Abner Green	John Row,	250	On Second creek,	Do.	May 25, 1779.
" 18,	10	March 12,	1	19	John Talley	John Talley,	300		Do.	Oct'r 9, 1777.
" 18,	11	March 12,	1	21	John Collins	John Collins,	200	On the south fork of St. Catharine's,	Do.	March 20, 1778.
" 19,	12	April 17,	1	23	The legal representatives of William and Hanna Lum, deceased, and Jesse Lum,	Hanna, William, and Jesse Lum,	300	On the waters of Cole's creek,	Do.	Nov'r 14, 1776.
" 22,	17	April 17,	1	25	Margaret Gaillard, now the wife of Abraham Ellis,	Nathan Sweazy,	250	On the N. side of Homochitto river,	Do.	Oct'r 13, 1777.
" 22,	18	April 17,	1	27	Margaret Ellis, wife of Abraham Ellis,	John Lusk,	150	On Second creek,	Do.	Oct'r 11, 1777.
" 22,	19	April 17,	1	29	Abraham Ellis,	Richard Ellis,	1,850	On the waters of Cole's creek,	Do.	June 16, 1779.
" 22,	23	April 18,	1	31	Anne Hutchins, assignee of John Hutchins,	Anthony Hutchins,	1,000	On both sides of Second creek,	Do.	Sept'r 21, 1772.
" 25,	28	April 19,	1	33	Benjamin Bealk,	Benjamin Bealk,	800f.	On the waters of St. Catharine's,	Spanish,	Feb'y 10, 1789.
" 25,	41	April 23,	1	35	Celeste Hutchins,	Celeste Hutchins,	1,000f.	Near the White cliffs,	Do.	March 15, 1788.
" 26,	44	April 24,	1	52	Abraham Guice,	Abraham Guice,	240f.	On the waters of Homochitto river,	Do.	March 25, 1795.
" 26,	20	April 18,	1	37	The legal representatives of Charles Percy, deceased,	Charles Percy,	600	On the waters of Buffalo creek,	British,	Sept'r 23, 1779.
" 26,	21	April 18,	1	39	The legal representatives of Charles Percy, deceased,	James Smith Yarborough,	400	On the river Mississippi,	Do.	June 2, 1777.
" 26,	22	April 18,	1	42	The legal representatives of Charles Percy, deceased,	William Hiorn,	500	On the waters of Cole's creek,	Do.	Nov'r 19, 1777.
" 26,	26	April 19,	1	44	Jesse Carter	John Bolls,	100	On Second creek,	Do.	May 26, 1777.
" 26,	24	April 19,	1	46	John Ellis,	William Joiner,	500	On Second creek,	Do.	Sept'r 21, 1772.
" 26,	16	April 16,	1	48	John Ellis,	Zaccheus Routh,	400	On the waters of Cole's creek,	Do.	June 16, 1779.
" 27,	33	April 22,	1	50	Daniel Whitaker	Daniel Whitaker,	400f.	On the waters of St. Catharine's,	Spanish	March 6, 1788.

THOMAS H. WILLIAMS.

REGISTER A—Continued.

Abstract of Certificates entered with the Register of the Land Office west of Pearl river, during the month of May, 1805, grounded on British and Spanish patents.

When entered	No.	Date (1805)	Vol.	Page	To whom granted	Name of original grantee	Quantity allowed (Acres)	Situation	Whence derived	Date of patent
1805 May 6	34	April 22	1	54	Richard King	Richard King	500	On the river Big Black	Spanish	Sept'r 30, 1793
" " 6	138	May 3	1	56	Richard King	Richard King	600	On the river Big Black	Do.	Aug. 18, 1795
" " 8	56	April 26	1	58	Joseph Calvit	Joseph Calvit	386	On the waters of St. Catharine's creek	Do.	June 12, 1788
" " 8	57	April 26	1	60	Thomas Calvit	Thomas Calvit	200	On the waters of Cole's creek	Do.	Feb'y 27, 1789
" " 8	85	April 30	1	62	The legal representatives of Frederick Calvit, deceased	Frederick Calvit	500	On the waters of St. Catharine's creek	Do.	March 15, 1788
" " 10	133	May 3	1	64	Peter Nelson, and Margaret his wife	Margaret Leffiers	938	On the waters of Cole's creek	Do.	Sept'r 4, 1789
" " 10	25	April 19	1	65	Cato West	Cato West	800	On the waters of Cole's creek	Do.	Feb'y 27, 1789
" " 10	27	April 19	1	68	Cato West	Cato West	700	On Cole's creek	Do.	March 10, 1789
" " 13	53	April 25	1	70	John Bullen	Windsor Pipes	225	On the waters of St. Catharine's creek	Do.	April 21, 1789
" " 13	105	May 2	1	72	Prosper King	Prosper King	400	On the waters of the bayou Pierre	Do.	April 19, 1793
" " 13	106	May 2	1	74	Prosper King	Prosper King	200	On the river Big Black	Do.	Sept'r 1, 1793
" " 15	94	April 30	1	76	Jonathan Jones	John Courtney	400	On the waters of Fairchild's creek	Do.	March 6, 1793
" " 15	200	May 15	1	78	Richard Curtis	Richard Curtis	200	On the waters of Cole's creek	Do.	March 25, 1795
" " 15	37	April 20	1	80	William Foster	David Smith	400	On St. Catharine's creek	Do.	March 6, 1788
" " 16	29	April 23	1	82	Patsey Westly Moss	David Holt	250	On the waters of Cole's creek	Do.	March 10, 1789
" " 16	117	May 2	1	84	John Bolls	John Spyers	300	On St. Catharine's creek	Do.	Aug. 14, 1793
" " 16	109	May 2	1	86	John Bolls	John Bolls	350	On the waters of Second creek	Do.	Feb'y 10, 1789
" " 16	110	May 2	1	88	James Bolls	John Bolls	400	On St. Catharine's creek	Do.	Feb'y 10, 1789
" " 16	111	May 2	1	90	James Bolls	James Bolls	200	On Cole's creek	Do.	Jan'y 10, 1794
" " 16	112	April 20	1	92	Joseph Perkins	Christopher Butler	240	On Cole's creek	Do.	March 6, 1789
" " 17	31	April 20	1	94	Joseph Perkins	Joseph Perkins	177	On the river Big Black	Do.	Feb'y 25, 1788
" " 17	33	April 25	1	96	—	Robert Carter	300	On the waters of St. Catharine's creek	Do.	Feb'y 10, 1788
" " 17	54	April 30	1	98	Nathaniel Kennison	Nathaniel Kennison	500	On the waters of St. Catharine's creek	Do.	June 17, 1795
" " 18	82	April 29	1	100	John Griffing	John Griffing	600	On the waters of Cole's creek	Do.	Sept'r 30, 1793
" " 20	79	May 6	1	102	Gerard Brandon	David Monroe	1,000	On the waters of Cole's creek	Do.	March 20, 1789
" " 20	142	May 1	1	104	Tobias Brashear	Tobias Brashear	700	On the waters of the bayou Sara	Do.	March 20, 1795
" " 20	104	April 30	1	106	John Boothe	John Boothe	600	On the river Big Black	Do.	Jan'y 1, 1793
" " 20	83	May 13	1	108	Benjamin Beaulk, assignee of Jeptha Higdon	Jeptha Higdon	400	On the waters of the bayou Pierre	Do.	Nov'r 20, 1793
" " 20	182	May 16	1	110	William Bassett	Elizabeth Durbin	283	On the river Mississippi	Do.	Sept'r 1, 1793
" " 20	203	May 13	1	112	The legal representatives of Charles Boardman	Charles Boardman	1,000	On the waters of bayou Sara	Do.	March 6, 1788
" " 20	183	May 16	1	114	The legal representatives of C. Braxton, dec'd	Christian Braxton	240	On St. Catharine's creek	Do.	June 30, 1795
" " 20	114	May 2	1	116	Daniel Burnet	Daniel Burnet	1,000	On the waters of Cole's creek	Do.	Aug. 31, 1790
" " 20	204	May 16	1	118	The legal representatives of Charles Boardman, deceased	Charles Boardman	900	On the waters of the bayou Pierre	Do.	April 9, 1790
" " 20	123	May 2	1	120	John Bisland	John Bisland	850	On St. Catharine's creek	Do.	March 6, 1788
" " 20	124	May 2	1	122	John Bisland	John Bisland	850	On the waters of Fairchild's creek	Do.	April 9, 1790
" " 20	131	May 3	1	124	Alexander Bisland	Alexander Bisland	192	On the waters of St. Catharine's creek	Do.	Sept'r 1, 1795

ABSTRACT for MAY, 1805—Continued.

When entered	No.	Date	Vol.	Page	To whom granted	Name of original grantee	Quantity allowed	Situation	Whence derived	Date of patent
1805.		1805.					Acres.			
May 20,	91	April 30,	1	126	Abraham Ellis, in right of his wife Margaret,	William Case,	300	On Second creek,	British,	October 9, 1777.
" 20,	116	May 2,	1	128	Jeremiah Coleman,	John Jones,	600f.	On the waters of Fairchild's creek,	Spanish,	April 1, 1795.
" 20,	192	May 14,	1	130	Francis S. Girault,	Francis S. Girault,	395f.	On the river Mississippi,	Do.	June 20, 1795.
" 20,	172	May 13,	1	132	Abner Green,	Joseph Dyson,	400f.	On the waters of Fairchild's creek,	Do.	Feb'y 19, 1788.
" 20,	173	May 13,	1	134	Abner Green,	Abner Green,	665f.	On the waters of the bayou Pierre,	Do.	March 6, 1789.
" 20,	174	May 13,	1	136	Abner Green,	Abner Green,	600f.	On the river Mississippi,	Do.	Feb'y 12, 1788.
" 20,	175	May 13,	1	138	Abner Green,	Abner Green,	135f.	On St. Catharine's creek,	Do.	March 10, 1789.
" 20,	176	May 13,	1	140	Abner Green, in right of his wife Maria,	Maria Green,	500f.	On the waters of Second creek,	Do.	Feb'y 29, 1788.
" 20,	177	May 13,	1	142	Abner Green,	William Bassett,	400f.	On the waters of the bayou Pierre,	Do.	Oct'r 24, 1794.
" 20,	178	May 13,	1	144	Abner Green,	William Cunningham,	240f.	On Pine woods creek,	Do.	Sept'r 1, 1795.
" 20,	179	May 13,	1	146	Abner Green,	John Patterson,	350f.	On the waters of Second creek,	Do.	June 18, 1795.
" 20,	180	May 13,	1	148	Abner Green,	Daniel Burnet,	1,000f.	On the waters of the bayou Pierre,	Do.	June 20, 1795.
" 22,	73	April 29,	1	150	Gerard Brandon,	William Brocus,	600f.	On the waters of St. Catharine's creek,	Do.	Feb'y 29, 1788.
" 22,	74	April 29,	1	152	Gerard Brandon,	Gerard Brandon,	800f.	On the waters of the bayou Sara,	Do.	March 12, 1790.
" 22,	75	April 29,	1	154	James Bonnet,	James Romer,	400f.	On the waters of Fairchild's creek,	Do.	March 23, 1790.
" 22,	122	May 2,	1	156	John Bisland,	Jeremiah Bryan,	600f.	Between riv. Miss. & Fairchild's creek,	Do.	Feb'y 29, 1788.
" 22,	125	May 2,	1	158	John Bisland,	William Atchinson,	350f.		Do.	June 4, 1791.
" 22,	154	May 7,	1	160	The legal representatives of Adam Bickley,	Adam Bickley,	500f.	On the waters of Cole's creek,	Do.	August 14, 1794.
" 22,	121	May 2,	1	162	John Bisland,	James McIntyre,	500f.	On the waters of Fairchild's creek,	Do.	October 8, 1787.
" 22,	130	May 3,	1	164	John Bisland,	John Turnbull,	1,000f.	On the river Big Black,	Do.	June 22, 1791.
" 22,	161	May 9,	1	166	Richard Butler,	John Hardey,	200	On the waters of Second creek,	British,	Nov'r 12, 1778.
" 22,	220	May 21,	1	168	The legal representatives of Gabriel Benoist, deceased,	Gabriel Benoist,		On Fairchild's creek,	Spanish,	Jan'y 24, 1788.
" 22,	221	May 21,	1	170	The legal representatives of Gabriel Benoist, deceased,	Gabriel Benoist,	1,000f.	On the waters of Cole's creek,	Do.	August 14, 1794.
" 22,	222	May 21,	1	172	The legal representatives of Gabriel Benoist, deceased,	Gabriel Benoist,	1,000f.	On Fairchild's creek,	Do.	Jan'y 1, 1793.
" 22,	58	April 26,	1	174	Thomas M. Green,	Job Routh,	600f.	On Fairchild's creek,	Do.	May 30, 1793.
" 22,	59	April 26,	1	176	Thomas M. Green,	Jesse Smith,	400f.	On the waters of Cole's creek,	Do.	August 30, 1793.
" 22,	60	April 26,	1	178	Thomas M. Green,	David Odem,	240f.	On the waters of the bayou Pierre,	Do.	Dec'r 24, 1790.
" 22,	61	April 26,	1	180	Thomas M, Green,	Thomas M. Green,	375f.	On the waters of Cole's creek,	Do.	Feb'y 27, 1789.
" 22,	62	April 26,	1	182	Joseph Green,	Filmer and Abram Green,	700f.	On the waters of Fairchild's creek,	Do.	March 10, 1789.
" 22,	120	April 25,	1	184	Thomas Green,	Mary Foster,	500f.	Near the bayou Pierre,	Do.	Feb'y 12, 1788.
" 23,	52	April 25,	1	186	Thomas Foster and Levi Foster,	Thomas Green,	200f.	On Cole's creek,	Do.	March 6, 1788.
" 23,	76	April 2,	1	188	Peter Smith,	Peter Smith,	644f.	On St. Catharine's creek,	Do.	March 30, 1793.
" 23,	77	April 29,	1	190	Zachariah Smith, Jun.	Zachariah Smith,	400f.	On Percy's creek,	Do.	March 30, 1793.
" 23,	78	April 29,	1	192	James Smith,	James Smith,	500f.	On the waters of Buffalo creek,	Do.	March 28, 1791.
" 23,	171	April 29,	1	194	Robert Ford,	Robert Ford,	480f.	On the waters of Buffalo creek,	Do.	Feb'y 10, 1789.
" 23,	190	May 14,	1	196	Benajah Osmun,	Benajah Osmun,	500f.	On the waters of St. Catharine's creek,	Do.	March 10, 1795.
" 23,	199	May 25,	1	198	Peter Smith,	Zachariah Osmun,	600f.	On the waters of bayou Sara,	Do.	June 30, 1788.
" 23,	210	May 16,	1	200	Benajah Osmun,	Richard King,	115f.	On the waters of St. Catharine's creek,	Do.	August 30, 1794.

ABSTRACT for MAY, 1805—Continued.

When entered (1805)	Commissioners' certificates — No.	Date (1805)	Recorded — Vol.	Page	To whom granted	Name of original grantee	Situation	Quantity allowed (Acres)	Whence derived	Date of patent
May 23,	216	May 17,	1	202	John Lusk,	John Lusk,	On the river Homochitto,	300f.	Spanish,	May 29, 1795.
" 23,	217	May 17,	1	204	John Lusk,	John Lusk,	On the river Homochitto,	800f.	Do.	Feb'y 18, 1790.
" 23,	14	April 16,	1	206	Benjamin Farar, -	Evan Cameron,	On the west side of Second creek,	150	British,	July 22, 1776.
" 23,	90	April 30,	1	208	Benjamin Farar, in right of his wife Mary,	Richard Ellis,	Between Second creek & White cliffs,	1,000	Do.	June 16, 1779.
" 23,	92	April 30,	1	210	Benjamin Farar,	Michael Hooter,	On Second creek,	450	Do.	Sept'r 21, 1772.
" 23,	223	May 22,	1	212	Adam Bingaman,	Christian Bingaman,	On the waters of Cole's creek,	600	Do.	Oct'r 11, 1777.
" 23,	224	May 22,	1	214	Adam Bingaman,	Alexander McIntosh,	On the river Mississippi,	500	Do.	April 19, 1773.
" 23,	225	May 22,	1	216	Adam Bingaman,	Alexander McIntosh,	On Fairchild's creek,	400	Do.	May 5, 1777.
" 23,	226	May 22,	1	218	Adam Bingaman,	John Bentley,	On the waters of Fairchild's creek,	200	Do.	July 21, 1777.
" 23,	227	May 22,	1	220	Adam Bingaman,	William Brown, -	On the waters of Fairchild's creek,	150	Do.	July 21, 1777.
" 23,	228	May 22,	1	222	Adam Bingaman,	Philip Hannon, -	On the waters of Boyd's creek,	150	Do.	July 21, 1777.
" 23,	229	May 22,	1	224	Adam Bingaman,	Alexander McIntosh,	On the waters of Cole's creek,	200	Do.	Oct'r 9, 1777.
" 23,	230	May 22,	1	226	Adam Bingaman,	Samuel Gibson, -	On the waters of Cole's creek,	100	Do.	Oct'r 9, 1777.
" 23,	243	May 21,	1	228	Alexander Callender,	Alexander Callender,	On the waters of Cole's creek,	297f.	Spanish,	Jan'y 18, 1794.
" 24,	63	April 26,	1	230	Abraham Green,	Filmer and Abram Green,	On the waters of the bayou Pierre,	1,000f.	Do.	Feb'y 27, 1789.
" 24,	64	April 26,	1	232	Abraham Green,	Filmer and Abram Green,	On the waters of the bayou Pierre,	500f.	Do.	March 6, 1789.
" 24,	169	May 9,	1	234	Abraham Green and Everard Green,	Jacob Stampley, -	On Cole's creek,	350f.	Do.	April 8, 1791.
" 27,	30	May 30,	1	236	William Erwin,	William Erwin,	On Cole's creek,	500f.	Do.	Jan'y 30, 1787.
" 27,	95	April 30,	1	238	George Forman,	George Forman,	On the waters of Cole's creek,	150f.	Do.	March 4, 1795.
" 27,	96	April 30,	1	240	George Forman,	George Forman,	On the waters of Cole's creek,	200f.	Do.	March 4, 1795.
" 27,	38	April 23,	1	242	James Foster, -	James Foster, -	On St. Catharine's creek,	240f.	Do.	March 6, 1788.
" 28,	145	May 6,	1	244	Charles McKiernan,	Richard Harrison,	Near the Petit gulf,	555f.	Do.	March 24, 1790.
" 28,	244	May 1,	1	246	Charles McKiernan,	John Savage,	On the waters of Fairchild's creek,	337f.	Do.	Nov'r 20, 1793.
" 28,	101	May 24,	1	248	James Hoggatt,	John Armstreet, -	On the waters of Second creek,	506f.	Do.	March 22, 1795.
" 28,	102	May 24,	1	250	James Hoggatt,	Rebecca Dove, -	At the place called the Prairie,	229f.	Do.	June 20, 1795.
" 28,	184	May 14,	1	252	James Hoggatt,	John Bisland,	On the waters of Sandy creek,	750f.	Do.	March 6, 1788.
" 28,	185	May 14,	1	254	James Hoggatt,	Peter Nelson, -	On the river Big Black,	300f.	Do.	March 15, 1788.
" 29,	97	April 30,	1	256	Archibald Erwin,	Archibald Erwin,	On the waters of Cole's creek,	300f.	Do.	August 30, 1795.
" 29,	146	May 6,	1	258	John Martin, -	John Martin, -	On the waters of Cole's creek,	500f.	Do.	Feb'y 25, 1785.
" 29,	245	May 25,	1	260	The trustees of Bethel congregation,	Alexander Callender,		3f.	Do.	Jan'y 18, 1794.
" 30,	246	May 27,	1	262	The legal representatives of Joseph Bernard, deceased,	Joseph Bernard, -	On the river Mississippi,	800f.	Do.	April 10, 1795.
" 30,	247	May 27,	1	264	The legal representatives of Joseph Bernard, deceased,	Stephen Minor, -	On the river Mississippi,	500f.	Do.	May 6, 1786.

REGISTER'S OFFICE WEST OF PEARL RIVER, *June 1*, 1805.

THOMAS H. WILLIAMS.

REGISTER A—Continued.

Abstract of Certificates entered with the Register of the Land Office west of Pearl river, during the month of June, 1805, grounded on British and Spanish patents.

When entered	No.	Date	Vol.	Page	To whom granted	Name of original grantee	Quantity allowed	Situation	Whence derived	Date of patent
1805. June 3,	15	April 16,	1	266	Samuel Hutchins,	William Gorman,	Acres. 243	On Second creek,	British,	Sept'r 12, 1775.
" 3,	39	April 23,	1	268	Samuel Hutchins,	Samuel Hutchins,	200f.	Near Second creek,	Spanish,	Feb'y 29, 1788.
" 3,	40	April 23,	1	270	The legal representatives of Anthony Hutchins, deceased,	—	—	—		
" 3,	42	April 23,	1	272	The legal representatives of Anthony Hutchins, deceased,	Anthony Hutchins,	800f.	On the river Mississippi,	Do.	August 8, 1789.
" 3,	43	April 23,	1	274	The legal representatives of Anthony Hutchins, deceased,	Anthony Hutchins,	566f.	—	Do.	Feb'y 18, 1790.
" 3,	143	May 6,	1	276	Reuben Gibson,	Anthony Hutchins,	2,146f.	On the waters of Cole's creek,	Do.	Feb'y 18, 1790.
" 3,	98	April 30,	1	278	Richard Canadine,	Reuben Gibson,	220f.	On St. Catharine's creek,	Do.	March 4, 1789.
" 3,	99	April 30,	1	280	John J. Canadine,	Parker Canadine,	300f.	On the waters of Fairchild's creek,	Do.	March 15, 1789.
" 3,	100	April 30,	1	282	Parker Canadine, Jun. and George Rapalje Canadine,	Anthony Hutchins,	242f.	On the waters of Cole's creek,	Do.	March 31, 1790.
" 4,	119	May 2,	1	284	George Fitzgerald,	Parker Canadine,	508f.	On the waters of Cole's creek,	Do.	April 25, 1793.
" 4,	132	May 3,	1	286	George Fitzgerald,	John Farquhar,	360f.	—	Do.	Sept'r 3, 1784.
" 4,	163	May 9,	1	288	John Foster,	Charles Norwood,	400f.	On the river Homochitto,	Do.	May 9, 1786.
" 4,	164	May 9,	1	290	John Foster,	Elias Bonnell,	400f.	On the waters of St. Catharine's creek,	Do.	June 1, 1792.
" 4,	165	May 9,	1	292	John Foster,	John Foster,	214f.	On the river Homochitto,	Do.	March 15, 1789.
" 4,	144	May 6,	1	294	Joshua Howard,	John Foster,	800f.	On the waters of Second creek,	Do.	March 29, 1793.
" 4,	232	May 22,	1	296	John Henderson,	Henry Richardson,	400f.	On the waters of river Homochitto,	Do.	Feb'y 10, 1789.
" 4,	126	May 3,	1	298	John Bisland,	Alexander Henderson,	587f.	On the waters of St. Catharine's creek,	Do.	March 6, 1788.
" 4,	127	May 3,	1	300	John Bisland,	William West,	190f.	On the waters of St. Catharine's creek,	Do.	May 25, 1792.
" 4,	128	May 3,	1	302	John Bisland,	Hugh Coyle,	240f.	On the river Big Black,	Do.	Aug. 30, 1793.
" 4,	129	May 3,	1	304	John Bisland,	Maurice Joyce,	800f.	On the river Big Black,	Do.	June 22, 1791.
" 4,	260	May 3,	1	306	John Foster,	John Joyce,	1,000f.	On the river Homochitto,	Do.	June 22, 1791.
" 5,	139	May 3,	1	308	Richard Kidd,	Joshua Howard,	600f.	On the river Big Black,	Do.	April 9, 1794.
" 5,	140	May 27,	1	310	Richard King, in right of his wife,	Robert Kidd,	200f.	On St. Catharine's creek,	Do.	Nov'r 20, 1793.
" 5,	248	May 27,	1	312	Richard King,	Lewis Valleret,	335f.	On the waters of the river Big Black,	Do.	April 9, 1794.
" 5,	249	May 27,	1	314	John Girault,	Richard King,	1,180f.	On the waters of Cole's creek,	Do.	June 20, 1795.
" 6,	48	April 24,	1	316	The legal representatives of Henry Manadue, deceased,	William Gillespie,	265f.	On the waters of Cole's creek,	Do.	June 8, 1792.
" 6,	81	April 30,	1	318	James Jones,	Joseph Bonner,	600f.	On the waters of Cole's creek,	Do.	May 25, 1791.
" 6,	87	April 30,	1	320	William Lemon, and Sally his wife,	James Jones,	400f.	On the waters of Fairchild's creek,	Do.	June 20, 1795.
" 6,	103	May 1,	1	322	Frederick Kimble,	Isaac Tabor,	250f.	On the waters of the bayou Sara,	Do.	Aug. 14, 1793.
" 6,	113	May 2,	1	324	Stephen Miller,	Frederick Kimble,	acs. 57	On the waters of Cole's creek,	Do.	Sept'r 1, 1795.
" 6,	234	May 22,	1	326	The legal representatives of David Mitchell, deceased,	Patrick Sullivan,	400f.	On the waters of Second creek,	Do.	Feb'y 5, 1793.
" 6,	252	May 30,	1	328	Nathaniel Ivy,	David Mitchell,	400f.	On Second creek,	Do.	April 3, 1790.
" 6,	253	May 30,	1	330	William McIntosh,	Nathaniel Ivy,	317f.	On St. Catharine's creek,	Do.	March 22, 1795.

ABSTRACT FOR JUNE, 1805—Continued.

Commissioners' certificates.			Recorded.		Claim.				Title.	
When entered.	No.	Date.	Vol.	Page.	To whom granted.	Name of original grantee.	Quantity allowed.	Situation.	Whence derived.	Date of patent.
		1805.					Acres.			
1805. June 6,	254	May 30,	1	332	William McIntosh,	William McIntosh,	800f.	On the waters of the bayou Sara,	Spanish,	Sept'r 1, 1795.
" 6,	255	June 3,	1	334	Charles King, -	Charles King,	287f.	On the waters of St. Catharine's creek,	Do.	May 29, 1795.
" 6,	150	May 7,	1	336	Calvin Smith, -	David Mitchell,	400f.	On Second creek,	Do.	June 8, 1792.
" 6,	88	April 30,	1	338	John A. Davidson,	Stephen Scriber,	350f.	On the waters of Cole's creek,	Do.	Nov't 26, 1793.
" 6,	218	May 17,	1	340	Robert Dunbar,	Richard King,	600f.	On waters of St. C's & Fairchild's creek,	Do.	April 8, 1789.
" 6,	219	May 17,	1	342	Robert Dunbar,	Robert Dunbar,	800f.	On the waters of Cole's creek,	Do.	June 12, 1788.
" 8,	134	May 3,	1	344	The legal representatives of William Vousdan, deceased,	John Hoetler,	200	On the waters of the bayou Pierre,	British,	May 25, 1779.
" 8,	135	May 3,	1	346	The legal representatives of William Vousdan,	William Vousdan,	200	On the waters of the bayou Pierre,	Do.	Sept. 15, 1777.
" 8,	136	May 3,	1	348	The legal representatives of William Vousdan, deceased,	David Lejeune, -	400f.	At the place called Davion's rock,	Spanish,	March 20, 1789.
" 8,	137	May 3,	1	350	The legal representatives of William Vousdan,	David Ross,	600f.	On the river Mississippi,	Do.	April 14, 1790.
" 10,	278	June 5,	1	352	Thomas Calvit,	Thomas Calvit,	800f.	On the river Mississippi,	Do.	April 1, 1795.
" 10,	279	June 5,	1	354	Thomas Calvit,	Thomas Calvit,	200f.	On Cole's creek,	Do.	Feb'y 27, 1789.
" 10,	267	June 4,	1	356	William Brocus,	William Brocus,	1,000f.	On the waters of the bayou Pierre,	Do.	June 18, 1792.
" 10,	268	June 4,	1	358	William Brocus,	William Brocus,	1,000f.	On the waters of the bayou Pierre,	Do.	Jan'y 20, 1795.
" 10,	269	June 4,	1	360	William Brocus,	William Brocus,	400f.	On the waters of the bayou Pierre,	Do.	Feb'y 26, 1795.
" 10,	271	June 4,	1	362	The legal representatives of Charles Boardman, deceased,	John Baptiste Perret,	1,000f.	On the waters of Cole's creek,	Do.	June 19, 1788.
" 11,	36	April 23,	1	364	Christopher Guice,	Christopher Guice,	400f.	On the waters of the river Homochitto,	Do.	March 25, 1795.
" 11,	45	April 24,	1	366	Michael Guice,	Michael Guice,	500f.	On Cole's creek,	Do.	Feb'y 25, 1788.
" 11,	46	April 24,	1	368	The legal representatives of D. Grafton, dec'd,	Daniel Grafton, Sen.	300f.	Near Natchez,	Do.	Feb. 29, 1788.
" 11,	47	April 24,	1	370	The legal representatives of D. Grafton, dec'd,	Alexander Montgomery,	160f.	Adams county,	Do.	March 1, 1787.
" 11,	49	April 24,	1	372	Daniel Ogden,	Daniel Ogden,	500f.	On the waters of Thompson's creek,	Do.	Aug. 30, 1793.
" 11,	50	April 24,	1	374	Daniel Ogden,	Daniel Ogden,	500f.	On the waters of Thompson's creek,	Do.	May 25, 1792.
" 11,	51	April 24,	1	376	John Gibson,	John Gibson,	500f.	On the waters of the bayou Sara,	Do.	April 14, 1790.
" 11,	67	April 27,	1	378	Hezekiah Harman,	Hezekiah Harman,	700f.	On the waters of the bayou Pierre,	Do.	Jan'y 8, 1789.
" 11,	70	April 27,	1	380	The legal representative of N. Rob, deceased,	Nicholas Rob,	300f.	On the waters of the bayou Pierre,	Do.	Dec'r 1, 1794.
" 11,	84	April 30,	1	382	William Dunbar,	Isaac Johnson,	500f.	On the waters of Second creek,	Do.	Feb'y 29, 1788.
" 12,	13	April 16,	1	384	Isaac Fife,	Isaac Fife,	1,000	On the waters of Second creek,	British,	Sept'r 1, 1777.
" 12,	35	April 22,	1	386	Patrick Foley,	Patrick Foley,	1,500f.	On the bayou Pierre, -	Spanish,	Jan'y 1, 1793.
" 12,	55	April 25,	1	388	Elisha Flowers,	Elisha Flowers,	400f.	On the waters of the bayou Pierre,	Do.	June 25, 1791.
" 12,	71	April 27,	1	390	Thomas Cummins,	Thomas Cummins,	200f.	On the waters of the river Homochitto,	Do.	Aug. 30, 1793.
" 12,	80	April 29,	1	392	Palser Shilling,	Palser Shilling,	600f.	On river Mississippi,	Do.	March 15, 1789.
" 12,	86	April 30,	1	394	The legal representatives of Thomas Rule, dec'd,	Mark Oiler,	400f.	On the waters of St. Catharine's creek,	Do.	March 23, 1790.
" 12,	89	April 30,	1	396	Richard Dun, -	Richard Dun, -	250f.	On the waters of Fairchild's creek,	Do.	Feb'y 10, 1789.
" 12,	93	April 30,	1	398	-	-	-	-	Do.	April 8, 1789.
" 12,	290	June 7,	1	400	John Griffing, -	John Griffing, -	245f.	On the waters of Fairchild's creek,	Do.	Feb'y 16, 1789.
" 12,	291	June 7,	1	402	John Griffing, -	Gabriel Griffing, -	345f.	On the waters of Fairchild's creek,	Do.	Feb'y 16, 1789.

ABSTRACT for JUNE, 1805—Continued.

When entered.	No.	Date.	Vol.	Page.	To whom granted.	Name of original grantee.	Quantity allowed. (Acres.)	Situation.	Whence derived.	Date of patent.
1805. June 13,	118	May 2,	1	404	John Calliham,	James Stuart,	280f.	On the waters of Second creek,	Spanish,	March 25, 1795.
" 13,	147	May 6,	1	406	Jacob Cable,	Jacob Cable,	400f.	On the waters of Cole's creek,	Do.	March 10, 1789.
" 13,	154	May 7,	1	408	The legal representatives of Ephraim Coleman,	Ephraim Coleman,	300f.	On the waters of Cole's creek,	Do.	April 11, 1791.
" 13,	152	May 7,	1	410	Israel Coleman,	Israel Coleman,	300f.	On the waters of Cole's creek,	Do.	April 11, 1791.
" 13,	153	May 7,	1	412	John Ford,	John Ford,	800f.	On the waters of Cole's creek,	Do.	March 18, 1790.
" 13,	155	May 7,	1	414	Samuel Cobun,	Samuel Cobun,	300f.	On the waters of the bayou Pierre,	Do.	April 9, 1790.
" 13,	157	May 7,	1	416	Charles Cason,	Charles Cason,	300f.	On the waters of St. Catharine's creek,	Do.	March 15, 1789.
" 13,	166	May 9,	1	418	Patrick Cogan,	Patrick Cogan,	400f.	On the waters of the bayou Pierre,	Do.	Aug. 30, 1793.
" 14,	195	May 14,	1	420	Sarah Cleveland,	Elizabeth Durbin,	217f.	On the waters of the bayou Pierre,	Do.	Sept'r 1, 1793.
" 14,	205	May 16,	1	422	James Steel,	John Steel,	600f.	On the waters of the river Homochitto,	Do.	June 30, 1788.
" 14,	206	May 16,	1	424	Isaac Gaillard,	Isaac Gaillard,	800f.	On the river Homochitto,	Do.	Sept'r 1, 1795.
" 14,	207	May 16,	1	426	Isaac Gaillard,	Jesse Withers,	300f.	On the waters of the river Homochitto,	Do.	May 8, 1793.
" 14,	208	May 16,	1	428	Isaac Gaillard,	John Henderson,	1,152f.	On the waters of the river Homochitto,	Do.	Oct'r 4, 1787.
" 14,	209	May 16,	1	430	Isaac Gaillard,	Thomas Rule,	232f.	On the waters of the river Homochitto,	Do.	April 21, 1790.
" 14,	211	May 17,	1	432	Isaac Gaillard,	Isaac Gaillard,	1,000f.	On the river Homochitto,	Do.	March 15, 1789.
" 14,	149	May 7,	1	434	John Stowers and Windsor Pipes,	Moses Bonner,	400f.	On the waters of Fairchild's creek,	Do.	March 26, 1789.
" 17,	295	June 10,	1	436	Manuel Madden and James Bonner,	Manuel Madden,	788f.	On the waters of Fairchild's creek,	Do.	March 15, 1788.
" 17,	296	June 10,	1	438	Abraham Taylor,	Thomas Morgan,	250f.	On the waters of St. Catharine's creek,	Do.	March 10, 1789.
" 17,	65	April 26,	1	440	Everard Green,	Everard Green,	205f.	On Cole's creek,	Do.	Feb'y 12, 1788.
" 17,	66	April 27,	1	442	Everard Green,	Everard Green,	357f.	On Cole's creek,	Do.	Feb'y 12, 1788.
" 17,	283	June 6,	1	444	Benajah Osmun,	Joseph Ford,	370f.	On the waters of St. Catharine's creek,	Do.	April 28, 1790.
" 17,	284	June 6,	1	446	Benajah Osmun, assignee of the legal representatives of Andrew Bealle, deceased,	Andrew Bealle,	134f.	On the waters of St. Catharine's creek,	Do.	March 25, 1795.
" 17,	285	June 6,	1	448	Benajah Osmun, assignee of the legal representatives of Andrew Bealle, deceased,	John Hartley,	400f.	On the waters of St. Catharine's creek,	Do.	Feb'y 25, 1788.
" 17,	286	June 6,	1	450	Benajah Osmun, assignee of the legal representatives of Andrew Bealle, deceased,	Joseph Ford,	100f.	On the waters of St. Catharine's creek,	Do.	April 28, 1790.
" 17,	300	June 11,	1	452	Benajah Osmun, assignee of the legal representatives of Andrew Bealle, deceased,	Maria Girault,	100f.	On the waters of St. Catharine's creek,	Do.	July 17, 1790.
" 18,	156	May 7,	1	454	James Wade,	James Wade,	400f.	On the waters of Fairchild's creek,	Do.	March 15, 1788.
" 18,	148	May 7,	1	456	John Ellis,	Richard Ellis, Jun.	180f.	On the river Homochitto,	Do.	Jan'ry 31, 1788.
" 18,	170	May 13,	1	458	The legal representatives of G. Cochran dec'd.	George Cochran,	640f.	On the waters of Cole's creek,	Do.	Aug. 30, 1793.
" 18,	193	May 14,	1	460	John Ellis,	Benjamin Curtis,	400f.	On the waters of the river Homochitto,	Do.	Feb'y 28, 1795.
" 18,	194	May 14,	1	462	John Ellis,	John Ellis,	800f.	On the waters of the river Homochitto,	Do.	Jan'ry 31, 1788.
" 18,	235	May 23,	1	464	Robert Cochran,	Robert Cochran,	412f.	On the waters of the bayou Pierre,	Do.	April 10, 1795.
" 18,	236	May 23,	1	466	Robert Cochran,	Robert Cochran,	1,000f.	On the waters of Cole's creek,	Do.	April 9, 1790.
" 18,	237	May 23,	1	468	Robert Cochran,	Robert Cochran,	500f.	On the river Homochitto,	Do.	April 9, 1790.
" 18,	238	May 23,	1	470	The legal representatives of G. Cochran, dec'd.	Waterman Crane,	600f.	On the waters of the bayou Pierre,	Do.	Aug. 30, 1793.
" 18,	239	May 23,	1	472	The legal representatives of G. Cochran, dec'd.	George Cochran,	600f.	On the waters of the Petit Gulf creek,	Do.	Aug. 30, 1793.
" 18,	240	May 23,	1	474	The legal representatives of G. Cochran, dec'd.	Lewellen Price,	315f.	Claiborne county,	Do.	Aug. 30, 1793.
" 18,	241	May 23,	1	476	The legal representatives of G. Cochran, dec'd.	Waterman Crane,	600f.	On the waters of the bayou Pierre,	Do.	Aug. 14, 1794.
" 19,	107	May 2,	1	478	Anthony Hoggatt,	Rebecca Dove,	71f.	On the waters of St. Catharine's creek,	Do.	June 20, 1795.

ABSTRACT FOR JUNE, 1805—Continued.

Commissioners' certificates.			Recorded.		Claim.				Title.	
When entered.	No.	Date.	Vol.	Page.	To whom granted.	Name of original grantee.	Quantity allowed.	Situation.	Whence derived.	Date of patent.
1805. June 19,	115	May 2,	1	480	Wilford Hoggatt,	John Ratliffe,	*Acres.* 400f;	On the waters of Sandy creek,	Spanish,	Feb'y 10, 1789.
" 19,	159	May 8,	1	482	James Howard,	Anthony Hoggatt,	166f;	On the waters of Sandy creek,	Do.	Aug. 14, 1794.
" 19,	167	May 14,	1	484	Benjamin Holmes,	Benjamin Holmes,	400f;	On the waters of Sandy creek,	Do.	Feb'y 27, 1789.
" 19,	186	May 14,	1	486	Anthony Hoggatt,	James Oglesby,	500f;	On the waters of Second creek,	Do.	Jan'y 20, 1793.
" 19,	188	May 14,	1	488	Benjamin Holmes,	Benjamin Holmes,	100f;	On the waters of Sandy creek,	Do.	March 7, 1789.
" 19,	212	May 17,	1	490	John Ellis,	John Ellis,	426f;	On Buffalo creek,	Do.	June 20, 1793.
" 19,	213	May 17,	1	492	The legal representatives of C. Percy, deceased,	Andres Lopez Armesto,	800f;	On Buffalo creek,	Do.	May 4, 1787.
" 19,	214	May 17,	1	494	The legal representatives of C. Percy, deceased,	Charles Percy,	1,000f;	On the waters of the bayou Sara,	Do.	April 18, 1789.
" 19,	215	May 17,	1	496	The legal representatives of C. Percy, deceased,	Charles Percy,	2,400f;	Wilkinson county,	Do.	June 4, 1791.
" 19,	256	June 3,	1	498	The legal representatives of T. Reid, deceased	Susanna Percy,	800f;	On the waters of Buffalo creek,	Do.	June 20, 1795.
" 20,	108	May 6,	1	500		Thomas Reid,	500f;	On the waters of Cole's creek,	Do.	March 23, 1795.
" 20,	141	May 6,	1	502	John Stampley,	John Stampley,	200f;	On the waters of Cole's creek,	Do.	June 20, 1793.
" 20,	158	May 8,	1	504	Joseph Sessions,	Anthony Hoggatt,	acs. 125	On waters of Second & Sandy creeks,	Do.	Aug. 14, 1794.
" 20,	167	May 9,	1	506	Alexander Ross,	Alexander Ross,	1,000	Adams county,	Do.	Nov'r 19, 1777.
" 20,	168	May 9,	1	508	Alexander Ross,	Alexander Ross,	2,000	On the waters of Cole's creek,	British,	Nov'r 19, 1777.
" 20,	191	May 14,	1	510	David Swayze,	Nathan Swayze,	500f;	On the river Homochitto,	Spanish,	May 21, 1791.
" 20,	231	May 22,	1	512	Jacob Stampley,	Jacob Stampley,	250f;	On the waters of Cole's creek,	Do.	March 20, 1795.
" 20,	292	June 7,	1	514	George Selser,	Gabriel Griffin,	455f;	On the waters of Fairchild's creek,	Do.	Feb'y 16, 1789.
" 20,	293	June 7,	1	516	George Selser,	John Griffin,	145f;	On the waters of Fairchild's creek,	Do.	Feb'y 16, 1789.
" 20,	308	June 13,	1	518	Thomas Wilkins,	Thomas Wilkins,	1,000f;	On Buffalo creek,	Do.	Jan'y 23, 1788.
" 21,	309	June 13,	1	520	Thomas Wilkins,	Thomas Wilkins,	800f;	On the river Mississippi,	Do.	Sept'r 1, 1793.
" 21,	68	April 27,	1	522	Samuel Gibson,	Samuel Gibson,	850f;	On the waters of the bayou Pierre,	Do.	August 2, 1788.
" 21,	69	April 27,	1	524	Samuel Gibson,	James Kirk,	800f;	On the waters of the bayou Pierre,	Do.	April 8, 1788.
" 21,	72	April 27,	1	526	Randal Gibson,	Gibeon Gibson,	335f;	On the waters of St. Catharine's creek,	Do.	March 4, 1789.
" 21,	160	May 8,	1	528	Peter A. Vandorn,	Anthony Hoggatt,	400f;	On the waters of Sandy creek,	Do.	Aug. 14, 1794.
" 21,	162	May 9,	1	530	Randal Gibson,	Josiah Rondle,	240f;	On the waters of the bayou Pierre,	Do.	Aug. 30, 1795.
" 21,	181	May 13,	1	532	Thomas Vause,	Thomas Vause,	200f;	On the waters of the bayou Pierre,	Do.	June 20, 1795.
" 21,	196	May 14,	1	534	Jesse Greenfield,	Daniel Clark, Sen.	565f;	On Second creek,	Do.	Aug. 16, 1787.
" 21,	197	May 14,	1	536	Jesse Greenfield,	Ebenezer Rees,	700f;	On the waters of the bayou Pierre,	Do.	Aug. 16, 1794.
" 21,	198	May 14,	1	538	Jesse Greenfield,	Jesse Greenfield,	600f;	On the waters of the bayou Pierre,	Do.	Jan'y 28, 1789.
" 21,	294	June 7,	1	540	George Selser,	John Griffing,	10f;	On the waters of Fairchild's creek,	Do.	Feb'y 16, 1789.
" 24,	265	June 4,	1	542	John Hampton White,	John Hampton White,	1,000f;	Near the White cliffs,	Do.	April 20, 1791.
" 24,	265	June 4,	1	544	The legal representatives of M. White, dec'd,	Matthew White,	1,150f;	Near mouth of St. Catharine's creek,	Do.	March 6, 1788.
" 24,	272	June 4,	1	546	John Hampton White, legal representative of Charles White, deceased,	Charles White,	400f;	Near the White cliffs,	Do.	May 16, 1791.
" 24,	273	June 4,	1	548	John Hampton White, legal representative of Charles White, deceased,	Charles White,	400f;	Near the White cliffs,	Do.	April 20, 1791.
" 24,	281	June 5,	1	550	John Wall,	John Wall,	400f;	On the waters of the bayou Sara,	Do.	June 20, 1795.
" 24,	282	June 5,	1	552	John Wall,	John Wall,	500f;	On the Buffalo creek,	Do.	Sept'r 1, 1795.
" 24,	298	June 10,	1	554	Henry Turner,	Ebenezer Rees,	1,000f;	On the waters of Fairchild's creek,	Do.	Sept'r 27, 1788.
" 24,	316	June 17,	2	1	The legal representatives of Louisa Wylie, deceased,	Thomas M. Green,	100f;	On the waters of Fairchild's creek,	Do.	Feb'y 27, 1789.

ABSTRACT for JUNE, 1805—Continued.

Commissioners' certificates.					Claim.				Title.	
When entered.	No.	Date.	Vol.	Page.	To whom granted.	Name of original grantee.	Quantity allowed.	Situation.	Whence derived.	Date of patent.
1805.							Acres.			
June 24,	250	May 27,	2	3	William Ogden,	William Vousdan,	550f.	On the waters of Buffalo creek,	Spanish,	April 6, 1788.
" 24,	276	May 4,	2	5	Philetus Israel and Philander Smith,	Philetus Israel and Phil. Smith,	500f.	On Second creek,	Do.	March 6, 1788.
" 25,	259	June 3,	2	7	Catharine Surget,	Roger Doud,	500f.	Between Cole's creek and bayou Pierre,	Do.	August 8, 1789.
" 25,	269	June 4,	2	9	Catharine Surget,	Roger Doud,	540f.	On the waters of Cole's creek,	Do.	April 15, 1790.
" 25,	263	June 4,	2	11	The legal representatives of P. Surget, deceased,	Peter Surget,	1,000f.	On the waters of Second creek,	Do.	June 21, 1788.
" 25,	264	June 11,	2	13	The legal representatives of P. Surget, deceased,	Peter Surget,	3,000f.	On Second creek,	Do.	June 21, 1788.
" 25,	302	June 17,	2	15	The legal representatives of W. Gilbert, dec'd	William Gilbert,	1,000f.	On the waters of river Homochitto,	Do.	Jan'y 22, 1788.
" 25,	324	June 17,	2	17	Willis Bonner,	James McIntyre,	150f.	On the waters of Fairchild's creek,	Do.	Oct'r 8, 1787.
" 25,	325	June 18,	2	19	Thomas Foster,	Samuel Flowers,	80f.	On St. Catharine's creek,	Do.	April 8, 1789.
" 25,	337	June 18,	2	21	Thomas Foster,	Moses Bonner,	310f.	On St. Catharine's creek,	Do.	April 21, 1789.
" 25,	328	June 19,	2	23	Thomas Foster,	Susanna Spell,	105f.	On St. Catharine's creek,	Do.	Jan'y 28, 1789.
" 25,	341	June 20,	2	25	Thomas Foster,	Alexander Henderson,	100f.	On St. Catharine's creek,	Do.	March 6, 1788.
" 25,	345	June 20,	2	27	The legal representatives of W. Gilbert, dec'd	Richard Harrison,	398f.	On the waters of Sandy creek,	Do.	Feb'y 15, 1787.
" 26,	189	May 14,	2	29	The legal representatives of Wm. Calvit, dec'd	William Calvit,	80f.	On the waters of the bayou Sara,	Do.	March 15, 1788.
" 26,	201	May 15,	2	31	Abraham Horton,	Abraham Horton,	600f.	In the settlement of bayou Sara,	Do.	March 10, 1790.
" 26,	202	May 16,	2	33	Henry Hunter,	Henry Hunter,	2,000f.	On St. Catharine's creek,	Do.	Nov'r 20, 1793.
" 26,	349	June 20,	2	35	Joseph Harrison,	Gibson Gibson,	165f.	On Second creek,	Do.	March 10, 1789.
" 26,	351	June 21,	2	37	Alexander Ross,	Stephen Miner,	act. 855	On the waters of Cole's creek,	Do.	Aug. 15, 1787.
" 26,	361	June 21,	2	39	William Daniel,	William Daniel,	275f.	On the waters of river Homochitto,	Do.	March 4, 1795.
" 26,	251	May 30,	2	41	Gideon Hopkins,	Gideon Hopkins,	400f.	On the waters of Cole's creek,	Do.	May 21, 1791.
" 26,	277	June 7,	2	43	The legal representatives of Richard Harrison,	Richard Harrison,	661f.	On the waters of the bayou Sara,	Do.	Aug. 30, 1795.
" 26,	287	June 7,	2	45	Moses Lewis,	Moses Lewis,	500f.	On the waters of St. Catharine's creek,	Do.	March 22, 1795.
" 27,	257	June 5,	2	47	William Lewis,	Antonio Grass,	230f.	On the waters of Cole's creek,	Do.	Sept'r 1, 1793.
" 27,	288	June 5,	2	49	Joseph Ford,	Joseph Ford,	250f.	Between rivers Miss. & Homochitto,	Do.	April 28, 1790.
" 27,	261	June 4,	2	51	The legal rep's of Anthony Hutchins, deceased,	Richard Ellis,	320f.	On Second creek,	Do.	Jan'y 31, 1788.
" 27,	274	June 4,	2	53	Isaac Johnson,	Isaac Johnson,	800f.	On the River Mississippi,	Do.	March 26, 1789.
" 27,	275	June 4,	2	55	Benjamin Farar, in right of his wife Mary,	Richard Ellis,	150f.	On Cole's creek,	Do.	Jan'y 31, 1788.
" 28,	280	June 5,	2	57	William Fairbank,	William Fairbank,	200f.	On Buffalo creek,	Do.	Dec'r 20, 1794.
" 28,	289	June 7,	2	59	Benjamin Farar, in right of his wife,	Mary Ellis,	600f.	On the waters of Cole's creek,	Do.	Feb'y 16, 1789.
" 28,	233	May 22,	2	61	John Clark,	John Clark,	410f.	On the waters of the bayou Pierre,	Do.	April 10, 1795.
" 28,	242	May 23,	2	63	Waterman Crane,	Waterman Crane,	450f.	On the waters of the bayou Pierre,	Do.	Aug. 14, 1794.
" 28,	258	June 3,	2	65	Gibson Clark,	Gibson Clark,	600f.	On the waters of Cole's creek,	Do.	Feb'y 10, 1789.
" 28,	270	June 4,	2	67	The legal representatives of Narsworthy Hunter,	Narsworthy Hunter,	1,000f.	On the waters of St. Catharine's creek,	Do.	Sept'r 1, 1795.
" 28,	299	June 11,	2	69	Seth Lewis,	Maria Girault,	540f.	On the waters of St. Catharine's creek,	Do.	July 17, 1790.
" 28,	297	June 10,	2	71	George Killion,	George Killion,	400f.	On the waters of St. Catharine's creek,	Do.	March 15, 1789.
" 28,	301	June 11,	2	73	David Greenleaf,	David Greenleaf,	200f.	On the waters of river Big Black,	Do.	Feb'y 20, 1793.
" 28,	303	June 11,	2	75	John Collins,	Henry Phelps,	50f.	On the river Buffalo,	Do.	Aug. 30, 1793.
" 28,	305	June 12,	2	77	Richard Butler,	Francis Foussett,	1,000f.	Near Willing's bayou,	Do.	Nov'r 12, 1788.
" 28,	306	June 12,	2	79	Richard Butler,	John Hartley,	800f.	On the waters of Second creek,	Do.	Feb'y 25, 1788.

THOMAS H. WILLIAMS.

REGISTER A—Continued.

Abstract of Certificates entered with the Register of the Land Office west of Pearl river, during the month of July, 1805, grounded on British and Spanish patents.

Commissioners' certificates.			Recorded.		Claim.				Title.	
When entered.	No.	Date.	Vol.	Page.	To whom granted.	Name of original grantee.	Quantity allowed.	Situation.	Whence derived.	Date of patent.
1805. July 2,	364	June 24,	2	81	Ezra Ambrose and Earl Marbles,	Patrick Foley.	400 f.	On Buffalo creek,	Spanish,	Oct. 25, 1790.
" 3,	386	June 26,	2	83	Samuel Watson,	John Newman,	200 f.	On the waters of Sandy creek,	Do.	March 22, 1795.
" 3,	304	June 12,	2	85	John Ellis, -	Francis Poinsett,	1,000 f.	On the waters of bayou Sara,	Do.	August 20, 1795.
" 3,	372	June 25,	2	87	Richard King,	John Savage,	1,000 f.	On the waters of bayou Pierre,	Do.	August 14, 1794.
" 3,	310	June 13,	2	89	David Havard,	Beasley Pruct,	400 f.	On the waters of Sandy creek,	Do.	March 10, 1789.
" 3,	307	June 13,	2	91	Richard Butler,	Ezekiel Forman,	1,000 f.	On the waters of the bayou Sara,	Do.	June 10, 1795.
" 3,	311	June 13,	2	93	Lewis Moore,	William Tabor,	240 f.	On the waters of Cole's creek,	Do.	April 10, 1795.
" 3,	313	June 13,	2	95	Eunice McIntoah,	Eunice McIntosh,	565 f.	On St. Catharine's creek,	Do.	Jan'y 26, 1787.
" 5,	365	June 24,	2	97	Richard P. Smith,	Stephen Minor,	160 f.	On Second creek,	Do.	August 15, 1787.
" 5,	312	June 13,	2	99	Abram Ellis, assignee of John Ellis,	John Ellis,	1,040 f.	On the river Homochitto,	Do.	July 31, 1788.
" 5,	314	June 14,	2	101	James Carpenter,	Richard Carpenter,	800 f.	On waters of St. Catharine's creek,	Do.	June 12, 1788.
" 5,	315	June 14,	2	103	James McIntosh,	James McIntosh,	800 f.	About six miles S. E. from Natchez,	Do.	Feb'y 12, 1788.
" 5,	323	June 17,	2	105	Samuel Marshall,	James McIntyre,	350 f.	On the waters of Fairchild's creek,	Do.	Octob. 8, 1787.
" 5,	335	June 19,	2	107	Richard King,	James Morison,	400 f.	On waters of St. Catharine's creek,	Do.	April 19, 1793.
" 5,	339	June 19,	2	109	Isaac Gaillard,	Jacob Paul, Sen.	100 f.	On second creek,	British.	March 27, 1776.
" 5,	340	June 19,	2	111	Isaac Gaillard,	Jacob Paul, Jun.	100 f.	On second creek,	Do.	April 5, 1777.
" 8,	342	June 20,	2	113	John Henderson,	Alexander Henderson,	200 f.	On St. Catharine's creek,	Spanish.	March 6, 1788.
" 8,	317	June 17,	2	115	Adam Bingaman,	Adam Bingaman,	1,040 f.	On the waters of the bayou Sara,	Do.	Sept. 30, 1793.
" 8,	318	June 17,	2	117	Adam Bingaman,	Adam Bingaman,	500 f.	On waters of St. Catharine's creek,	Do.	May 15, 1789.
" 8,	319	June 17,	2	119	Adam Bingaman,	Adam Bingaman,	858 f.	On St. Catharine's creek,	Do.	May 15, 1789.
" 8,	320	June 17,	2	121	Lewis Bingaman,	Lewis Bingaman,	500 f.	On waters of St. Catharine's creek,	Do.	May 15, 1789.
" 8,	321	June 17,	2	123	Adam Bingaman,	Adam Bingaman,	9,600 feet,	Adjoining the city of Natchez,	Do.	May 15, 1789.
" 8,	322	June 17,	2	125	Adam Bingaman,	Adam Bingaman,	1,000 f.	Near St. Catharine's creek,	Do.	March 8, 1788.
" 8,	326	June 17,	2	127	Reuben Gibson,	Samuel Flowers,	acs. 31	On St. Catharine's creek,	Do.	April 21, 1789.
" 8,	329	June 18,	2	129	John Courtney,	Eustice Humphreys,	100 f.	On the water of Fairchild's creek,	Do.	Feb'y 27, 1789.
" 8,	331	June 18,	2	131	The legal representatives of Bernard Lintot, deceased,	-	-	-	-	-
" 8,	537	June 19,	2	133	John Ellis, -	Bernard Lintot,	30 f.	Below and near Natchez,	D.	March 6, 1789.
" 9,	538	June 18,	2	135	The legal representatives of Bernard Lintot, deceased,	William Cocke Ellis,	800 f.	On the waters of river Homochitto,	Do.	Feb'y 16, 1789.
" 9,	333	June 18,	2	137	William Kenner,	Bernard Lintot,	1,000 f.	On waters of St. Catharine's creek,	Do.	July 5, 1786.
" 9,	334	June 18,	2	139	John Stutlee,	John Stutlee,	764 f.	On the waters of the bayou Pierre,	Do.	Jan'y 20, 1793.
" 9,	338	June 19,	2	141	John Minor, -	John Minor,	400 f.	On the waters of Fairchild's creek,	Do.	June 8, 1792.
" 9,	344	June 20,	2	143	Peter Hill, -	Parker Canadine, Sen.	200 f.	On St. Catharine's creek,	Do.	March 15, 1789.
" 9,	346	June 20,	2	145	James Foster	Richard Harrison,	100 f.	On St. Catharine's creek,	Do.	Feb'y 15, 1787.
" 9,	348	June 20,	2	147	James Foster	Richard Harrison,	85 74/100	On St. Catharine's creek,	Do.	Feb'y 15, 1787.
" 9,	376	June 26,	2	149	Robert Moore,	Robert Moore,	345 f.	On St. Catharine's creek,	Do.	Feb'y 15, 1787.
" 9,	330	June 18,	2	151	Zachariah Smith,	Zachariah Smith,	30 f.	On the waters of Buffalo creek,	Do.	June 30, 1788.
" 9,	347	June 20,	2	153	States Trevilion,	Eustice Humphreys,	100 f.	On the waters of Fairchild's creek,	Do.	Feb'y 27, 1789.
" 9,			2	155	Asneath Willis,	Richard Harrison,	219 f.	On St. Catharine's creek,	Do.	Feb'y 15, 1687.

ABSTRACT FOR JULY, 1805—Continued.

When entered. (1805)	No.	Date. (1805)	Vol.	Page.	To whom granted.	Name of original grantee.	Quantity allowed. (Acres)	Situation.	Whence derived.	Date of patent.
July 10,	352	June 21,	2	155	Richard Curtis,	Richard Curtis,	400f	On the waters of Cole's creek,	Spanish,	Jan'y 25, 1795.
" 10,	354	June 21,	2	157	Sarah Carter, (late Kenner,)	Sarah Kenner,	250f	On Second creek,	Do.	May 21, 1791.
" 10,	355	June 21,	2	159	Jesse Carter,	Rachel Carter,	500f	On Second creek,	Do.	May 16, 1791.
" 10,	357	June 21,	2	161	William Barland,	John Bisland,	525f	On Second creek,	Do.	Sept'r 3, 1784.
" 10,	358	June 21,	2	163	Hugh Davis,	Landon Davis,	800f	On the waters of river Homochitto,	Do.	Feb'y 12, 1788.
" 10,	359	June 21,	2	165	The legal representatives of Martha Davis, deceased,		600f	On the waters of river Homochitto,	Do.	Feb'y 12, 1788.
" 10,	360	June 21,	2	167	Landon Davis,	Landon Davis,	800f	On the waters of river Homochitto,	Do.	March 15, 1789.
" 10,	374	June 25,	2	169	William Brocus,	William Brocus,	240f	On the waters of the bayou Pierre,	Do.	May 30, 1793.
" 10,	350	June 20,	2	171	Jonas Scoggin,	Jonas Scoggin,	695f	On the river Mississippi,	Do.	April 3, 1794.
" 11,	353	June 21,	2	173	Stephen Stephenson,	Stephen Stephenson,	300f	About nine miles east from Natchez,	Do.	March 15, 1789.
" 11,	343	June 20,	2	175	Ebenezer Rees,	Alexander Henderson,	423f	On St. Catharine's creek,	Do.	March 6, 1788.
" 11,	366	June 24,	2	177	John Smith,	John Smith,	450f	On the river Mississippi,	Do.	March 6, 1789.
" 11,	567	June 24,	2	179	John Smith,	Frederick Metzo,	300f	On the waters of Cole's creek,	Do.	Sept'r 30, 1793.
" 11,	368	June 24,	2	181	John Smith,	John Smith,	142f	On the river Mississippi,	Do.	March 6, 1789.
" 11,	369	June 24,	2	183		John Smith,	230f	On the waters of Fairchild's creek,	Do.	March 23, 1790.
" 11,	370	June 24,	2	185	Hugh Matthews,	John Stampley,	350f	On the waters of Cole's creek,	Do.	Jan'y 25, 1794.
" 11,	373	June 25,	2	187	Jesse Withers,	Thomas Jordan,	100f	On the waters of Fairchild's creek,	Do.	March 15, 1788.
" 11,	387	June 26,	2	189	Waterman Crane,	Waterman Crane,	400f	On the waters of the Bayou Pierre,	Do.	Jan'y 1, 1793.
" 11,	388	June 26,	2	191	Gasper Sinclair,	Gasper Sinclair,	400f	On the waters of Cole's creek,	Do.	Feb'y 27, 1789.
" 11,	362	June 24,	2	193	David Gibson,	John Ferguson,	500f	On the waters of St. Catharine's creek,	Do.	March 10, 1789.
" 12,	396	July 2,	2	195	Wm. Brooks, in right of his wife Elizabeth,	Eliz, Maria, Celeste Hutchins,	800f	On St. Catharine's creek,	Do.	May 25, 1791.
" 12,	397	July 2,	2	197	Wm. Brooks, in right of his wife Elizabeth,	William Wicks,	277f	On St. Catharine's creek,	Do.	April 3, 1790.
" 12,	398	July 2,	2	199	Wm. Brooks, in right of his wife Elizabeth,	Samuel Gibson,	150f	On waters of St. Catharine's creek,	Do.	April 8, 1789.
" 12,	399	July 2,	2	201	Wm. Brooks, in right of his wife Elizabeth,	William Vousdan,	140f	On waters of St. Catharine's creek,	Do.	June 8, 1792.
" 12,	400	July 5,	2	203	Wm. Brooks, in right of his wife Elizabeth,	William Vousdan,	71f	On waters of St. Catharine's creek,	Do.	May 29, 1795.
" 12,	401	July 11,	2	205	Wm. Brooks, in right of his wife Elizabeth,	Samuel Gibson,	380f	On St. Catharine's creek,	Do.	Jan'y 16, 1784.
" 12,	430	July 11,	2	207	The legal representatives of John Campbell, deceased,	John Campbell,	500	On the river Mississippi,	British,	Feb'y 11, 1772.
" 15,	415	July 9,	2	209	William B. Smith, Jun,	William B. Smith, Sen.	655f	On waters of St. Catharine's creek,	Spanish,	May 5, 1794.
" 15,	375	June 25,	2	211	John Girault, and James Spain,	Helena Spain,	186f	On the waters of Cole's creek,	Do.	Aug. 30, 1795.
" 15,	390	June 27,	2	213	Jonathan Guice,	Christopher Green,	706f	On the waters of Fairchild's creek,	British,	Nov'r 11, 1778.
" 15,	394	July 2,	2	215	Everard Green,	Everard Green,	38f	On the waters of Cole's creek,	Spanish,	Feb'y 12, 1788.
" 15,	404	July 5,	2	217	Matthew C. Tierney,	Matthew C. Tierney,	400f	On the waters of the bayou Pierre,	Do.	March 23, 1793.
" 15,	407	July 9,	2	219	Samuel Cooper, and Absalom Griffin,	William Cooper,	800f	On Sandy creek,	Do.	Jan'y 1, 1793.
" 15,	424	July 10,	2	221	Benjamin Brashears,	Benjamin Brashears,	400f	On the waters of the bayou Pierre,	Do.	March 20, 1795.
" 15,	425	July 11,	2	223	Jesse Hamilton,	Jesse Hamilton,	300f	On the waters of the bayou Pierre,	Do.	Feb'y 16, 1789.
" 15,	426	July 11,	2	225	Jesse Hamilton,	Jesse Hamilton,	800f	On waters of St. Catharine's creek,	Do.	Jan'y 31, 1788.
" 15,	439	July 11,	2	227	John Grafton,	William Atchinson,	200f	On the waters of Cole's creek,	Do.	June 4, 1791.
" 15,	432	July 11,	2	229	William Brooks,	David Ferguson,	87f	On waters of St. Catharine's creek,	Do.	Aug. 14, 1794.
" 15,	377	June 26,	2	231	James Bolls, and Wilson Bolls,	William Vousdan,	1,000f	On the waters of Cole's creek,	Do.	July 7, 1789.

ABSTRACT for JULY, 1805—Continued.

When entered	No.	Date.	Recorded. Vol.	Page.	To whom granted.	Name of original grantee.	Quantity allowed.	Situation.	Whence derived.	Date of patent.
1805.		1805.					Acres.			
July 15,	408	July 9,	2	233	Joseph Sessions,	James Perry,	100	On the waters of Second creek,	British,	Oct'r 9, 1777.
" 16,	336	June 19,	2	235	The legal representatives of John Lum, dec'd,	John Lum,	187f.	On St. Catharine's creek,	Spanish,	Dec'r 1, 1790.
" 16,	363	June 24,	2	237	Patrick Foley,	Patrick Foley,	1,300f.	On Buffalo creek,	Do.	Oct'r 25, 1794.
" 16,	371	June 24,	2	239	John Minor,	John Stumpley,	400f.	On the waters of Cole's creek,	Do.	Jan'y 25, 1794.
" 16,	378	June 26,	2	241	David Forman,	David Forman,	600f.	On the waters of the bayou Sara,	Do.	June 30, 1795.
" 16,	379	June 26,	2	243	The legal representatives of Ezekiel Forman, deceased,		600f.	On the waters of the bayou Sara,	Do.	June 30, 1795.
" 16,	380	June 26,	2	245	Augustina Forman,	Augustina Forman,	600f.	On the waters of the bayou Sara,	Do.	June 30, 1795.
" 16,	381	June 26,	2	247	Margaretta Forman,	Margaretta Forman,	600f.	On the waters of the bayou Sara,	Do.	June 30, 1795.
" 16,	382	June 26,	2	249	Frances Forman,	Frances Forman,	600f.	On the waters of the bayou Sara,	Do.	June 30, 1795.
" 15,	389	June 26,	2	251	The legal representatives of J. Fowler, dec'd,	John Fowler,	240f.	On St. Catharine's creek,	Do.	Feb'y 28, 1795.
" 16,	395	July 1,	2	253	Catharine Surget,	Richard Harrison,	750f.	On waters of the river Homochitto,	Do.	Feb'y 27, 1789.
" 17,	391	July 1,	2	255	William G. Forman,	Susanna Spell,	450f.	On waters of St. Catharine's creek,	Do.	April 20, 1784.
" 17,	392	July 1,	2	257	William G. Forman,	John Lum,	95f.	On St. Catharine's creek,	Do.	Jan'y 28, 1789.
" 17,	393	July 1,	2	259	William G. Forman,	John Hocombe,	135f.	On waters of St. Catharine's creek,	Do.	Dec'r 1, 1794.
" 17,	405	July 5,	2	261	Abram Ellis, assignee of John Ellis,	Abram Ellis,	667	On the waters of the river Homochitto,	British,	May 29, 1775.
" 17,	419	July 10,	2	263	Abram Ellis,	Thomas Murray,	1,000f.	On the waters of Second creek,	Spanish,	Feb'y 16, 1789.
" 17,	422	July 10,	2	265	Abram Ellis,	Sarah Mayes,	344f.	On the river Homochitto,	Do.	May 16, 1791.
" 17,	423	July 5,	2	267	Isaac Gaillard,	Ezekiel Forman,	100	On the river Homochito,	British,	July 23, 1791.
" 17,	406	July 9,	2	269	John Perkins,	Daniel McCoy,	225f.	On St. Catharine's creek,	Spanish,	Feb'y 28, 1795.
" 17,	416	July 9,	2	271	John Perkins,	Henry Green,	240f.	On the waters of Cole's creek,	Do.	Jan'y 1, 1793.
" 17,	417	July 9,	2	273	The legal representatives of D. McCoy, dec'd,	Henry Green,	300f.	On the river Homochitto,	Do.	May 10, 1789.
" 18,	383	June 26,	2	275	Henry Green,	Henry Green,	600f.	On the waters of Cole's creek,	Do.	April 8, 1791.
" 18,	384	June 26,	2	277	Henry Green,	Henry Green,	600f.	On the waters of Cole's creek,	Do.	Aug. 14, 1793.
" 18,	385	June 25,	2	279	Henry Green,	Henry Green,	600f.	On the waters of Cole's creek,	Do.	Sept'r 1, 1795.
" 18,	402	July 5,	2	281	The legal representatives of William Ferguson, deceased,	William Ferguson,	500f.	On the waters of Cole's creek,	Do.	March 15, 1789.
" 18,	403	July 5,	2	283	The legal representatives of William Ferguson, deceased,		150	On waters of St. Catharine's creek,	British,	August 6, 1778.
" 18,	409	July 9,	2	285	John Bolls,	John Bolls,	800f.	On the waters of Second creek,	Spanish,	May 26, 1787.
" 18,	410	July 9,	2	287	William Dunbar,	William Dunbar,	150f.	On the river Mississippi,	Do.	Jan'y 13, 1795.
" 18,	411	July 9,	2	289	William Dunbar,	William Dunbar,	800f.	On the waters of the bayou Sara,	Do.	May 16, 1791.
" 18,	412	July 9,	2	291	William Dunbar,	William Dunbar,	1,400f.	On the waters of the bayou Sara,	Do.	May 16, 1791.
" 18,	413	July 9,	2	293	William Dunbar,	William Dunbar,	800f.	On the waters of the bayou Sara,	Do.	May 5, 1794.
" 19,	414	July 9,	2	295	William Dunbar,	William Dunbar,	1,000f.	On the waters of the bayou Sara,	Do.	Nov't 20, 1793.
" 19,	418	July 9,	2	297	John Calvin,	John Calvin,	350f.	On the river Homochitto,	Do.	Feb'y 27, 1789.
" 19,	420	July 9,	2	299	Ann Dunbar,	Ann Dunbar,	1,000f.	On the waters of Feliciana creek,	Do.	Nov't 30, 1793.
" 19,	421	July 9,	2	301	William Dunbar, jun.,	William Dunbar, jun.,	525f.	On the waters of Feliciana creek,	Do.	Nov't 30, 1793.
" 19,	433	July 16,	2	303	John Wall,	John O'Reailey,	350f.	On the bayou Sara,	Do.	March 30, 1793.
" 19,	434	July 16,	2	305	Jeremiah Coleman,	Jeremiah Coleman,	200f.	On the waters of Fairchild's creek,	Do.	Jan'y 28, 1789.
" 19,	435	July 16,	2	307	The legal representatives of G. Griffing, dec'd,	Gabriel Griffing,		On the river Big Black,	Do.	Jan'y 10, 1794.

ABSTRACT FOR JULY, 1805—Continued.

| Commissioners' certificates | | | | | Claim | | | | Title | |
When entered.	No.	Date.	Vol.	Page.	To whom granted.	Name of original grantee.	Quantity allowed.	Situation.	Whence derived.	Date of patent.
1805. July 19,	436	1805. July 16,	2	309	The legal representatives of G. Griffing, dec'd,	Ezekiel Newman,	Acres. 200f.	On the river Big Black,	Spanish,	July 20, 1793.
" 19,	437	July 16,	2	311	The legal representatives of G. Griffing, dec'd,	Daniel Douglass,	200f.	On the river Big Black,	Do.	Jan'y 10, 1794.
" 22,	438	July 16,	2	313	Caleb Potter,	Moses Bonner,	600f.	On the river Mississippi,	Do.	April 8, 1789.
" 22,	439	July 16,	2	315	The legal rep's of Susanna Percy, deceased,	Caleb Potter,	540f.	On the waters of Buffalo creek,	Do.	Nov'r 20, 1793.
" 22,	427	July 11,	2	317	John Ellis,	Henry Hergenroeder,	800f.	On Buffalo creek,	Do.	Aug. 30, 1793.
" 22,	428	July 11,	2	319	John Ellis,	William Chabot,	1,500f.	On the river Homochitto,	Do.	July 7, 1789.
" 22,	431	July 11,	2	321	The legal representatives of J. Kirk, dec'd,	Jesse Carter,	800f.	On the river Homochitto,	Do.	May 21, 1791.
" 22,	440	July 18,	2	323	The legal representatives of J. Kirk, dec'd,	James Kirk,	1,930f.	Near the river Homochitto,	Do.	July 10, 1787.
" 22,	441	July 18,	2	325	Isaac Guion, in right of his wife Sarah,	Robert Casbol,	650f.	On the waters of Cole's creek,	Do.	March 15, 1789.
" 22,	442	July 18,	2	327	The legal representatives of A. Lewis, dec'd,	Sarah Lewis,	300f.	Adams county,	Do.	June 18, 1795.
" 22,	443	July 18,	2	329	The legal representatives of A. Lewis, dec'd,	Richard Goodwin,	600f.	On the river Mississippi,	Do.	July 10, 1787.
" 22,	444	July 18,	2	331	The legal representatives of A. Lewis, dec'd,	Asahel Lewis,	400f.	On the river Mississippi,	Do.	Feb'y 23, 1795.
" 23,	445	July 18,	2	333	The legal representatives of David Williams, deceased,	John Cadwallader, William, Mary, and Ann Williams,	1,000	Called the Grove Plantation,	' ' '	' ' '
" 23,	446	July 18,	2	335	Stephen Ambrose,	Stephen Ambrose,	400f.	On the river Homochitto,	British,	Feb'y 20, 1776.
" 23,	447	July 18,	2	337	The legal rep's of William Ferguson, dec'd,	Thomas Comstock,	1.50	Adams county,	Spanish,	March 6, 1789.
" 23,	448	July 19,	2	339	William Ellis,	John Foster,	186f.	On the waters of St. Catharine's creek,	British,	August 6, 1778.
" 24,	449	July 22,	2	341	The legal rep's of George Cochran, deceased,	Adam Snyder,	600f.	On the waters of the Petty Gulf creek,	Spanish,	March 15, 1789.
" 24,	450	July 22,	2	343	William Conner, in right of his wife Mary,	Ann Savage,	1,000f.	On Second creek,	Do.	Aug. 30, 1793.
" 24,	451	July 22,	2	345	Winthrop Sargent, in right of his wife Maria,		2,690f.	On the river Mississippi,	Do.	March 15, 1789.
" 24,	452	July 22,	2	347	The legal rep's of D. Williams, deceased,	David McIntosh Williams,	1,000f.	On the waters of St. Catharine's creek,	Do.	April 4, 1795.
" 25,	453	July 23,	2	349	The legal rep's of Dorothy Henderson, dec'd,	Dorothy Henderson,	300f.	On the river Mississippi,	Do.	May 23, 1787.
" 25,	454	July 23,	2	351	The legal rep's of James Nicholson, deceased,	William Webb,	600f.	On the waters of the river Homochitto,	Do.	Aug. 20, 1794.
" 25,	455	July 23,	2	353	The legal rep's of Wm. Murray, deceased,	Manuel Texada,	400f.	On the waters of Cole's creek,	Do.	Feb'y 12, 1788.
" 25,	456	July 23,	2	355	The legal rep's of Wm. Murray, deceased,	Stephen de Alba,	400f.	On the waters of Cole's creek,	Do.	Nov'r 27, 1788.
" 25,	457	July 23,	2	357	Lacey Rumsey,	Jane Rumsey,	2,000f.	On the waters of Second creek,	Do.	Oct'r 8, 1787.
" 25,	458	July 24,	2	359	Ferdinand L. Claiborne and Edward Wooldridge, assignees of James Wallace,	William O'Conner,	300f.	On the waters of Cole's creek,	Do.	May 3, 1795.
" 25,	459	July 24,	2	361	F. L. Claiborne, assignee of Patrick Connelly,	Abraham Horton,	179f.	On St. Catharine's creek,	Do.	March 3, 1789.
" 25,	460	July 24,	2	363	The legal representatives of A. Boyd, dec'd,	Alexander Boyd,	230	On the river Mississippi,	British,	Dec'r 15, 1768.
" 25,	461	July 24,	2	365	William Ratcliff,	William Ratcliff,	150	On Second creek,	Do.	Sept'r 21, 1772.
" 25,	462	July 24,	2	367	Ephraim Blackburn,	Jacob Adams,	263f.	On the waters of St. Catharine's creek,	Spanish,	June 4, 1791.
" 31,	463	July 25,	2	369	The legal rep's of Patrick Connelly, dec'd,	Dennis Collins,	248f.	On Cole's creek,	Do.	Sept'r 1, 1795.

THOMAS H. WILLIAMS.

REGISTER A—Continued.

Abstract of Certificates entered with the Register of the Land Office west of Pearl river, during the month of August, 1805, grounded on British and Spanish patents.

When entered	No.	Date	Recorded Vol.	Page	To whom granted	Name of original grantee	Quantity allowed (Acres)	Situation	Whence derived	Date of patent
1805. August 1,	464	July 30,	2	371	William McIntosh,	Christian Hortuck,	300f.	On the waters of the bayou Sara,	Spanish,	Sep'r 1, 1793.
" 1,	465	July 31,	2	373	The legal representatives of Gabriel Benoist, deceased,	Charles Fleurian,	600f.	On Fairchild's creek,	Do,	Aug. 8, 1789.
" 1,	466	July 31,	2	375	The legal representatives of Gabriel Benoist, deceased,					
" 5,	467	August 1,	2	377	Daniel Perry, Jun,	John Stephen Boree,	1,050f.	On Fairchild's creek,	Do,	May 12, 1789.
" 5,	468	August 1,	2	379	Jonathan Rucker, in right of his wife Ann,	Daniel Perry, Jun,	735f.	On the waters of Cole's creek,	Do,	March 15, 1789.
" 5,	469	August 1,	2	381	Barnabas Perry,	Daniel Perry, Sen,	250	On the waters of Cole's creek,	British,	May 6, 1776.
" 5,	470	August 1,	2	383	James McIntosh,	Daniel Perry, Sen,	325	On Second creek,	Do,	Sep'r 21, 1772.
" 5,	471	August 1,	2	385	John Noble Taylor, and the legal representatives of James Dallas, deceased,	Daniel Clark,	1,000	Near the city of Natchez,	Do,	Jan'y 15, 1768.
" 5,	472	August 1,	2	387	Daniel Clark,	Daniel Clark, Sen,	2,000	Near the city of Natchez,	Do,	Jan'y 15, 1768.
" 5,	473	August 1,	2	389	Daniel Clark,	Cæsar Archenard,	800f.	Wilkinson county,	Spanish,	March 29, 1794.
" 5,	474	August 1,	2	391	Daniel Clark,	Marcos Olivares,	1,000f.	On the waters of Cole's creek,	Do,	May 26, 1787.
" 6,	475	August 1,	2	393	Daniel Clark,	Bartholomew Le Breton,	800f.	On the river Mississippi,	Do,	June 14, 1787.
" 6,	476	August 1,	2	395	Daniel Clark,	Daniel Clark, Sen,	1,000f.	Wilkinson county,	Do,	Jan'y 28, 1789.
" 9,	477	August 7,	2	397	The legal representatives of Thomas Tyler, deceased,	Daniel Clark, Sen,	5,800f.	On the waters of the bayou Sara,	Do,	April 9, 1794.
" 9,	478	August 7,	2	399	The legal representatives of Thomas Tyler, deceased,	Peter Camus,	800f.	On the waters of Cole's creek,	Do,	Aug. 31, 1790.
" 9,	479	August 7,	2	401	George Overaker,	Richard Bacon,	131 14/100 acs.	On the river Mississippi,	Do,	April 20, 1784.
" 19,	480	August 8,	2	403	William Conner,	Richard Bacon,	200	On the river Mississippi,	Do,	April 20, 1784.
" 19,	481	August 8,	2	405	William Conner,	Samuel Lewis,	100	On Second creek,	British,	March 27, 1776.
" 19,	482	August 9,	2	407	John Bolls,	John R. Wiley,	400f.	On Second creek,	Do,	March 27, 1776.
" 22,	483	August 12,	2	409	John Jones,	David Greenleaf,	500f.	On the waters of the Bayou Pierre,	Spanish,	Aug. 30, 1793.
" 22,	484	August 15,	2	411	David Douglass,	David Douglass,	200f.	On the waters of Cole's creek,	Do,	June 18, 1795.
" 22,	485	August 15,	2	413	Thomas Burling,	Thomas Burling,	1,000f.	On the river Mississippi,	Do,	July 20, 1793.
" 22,	486	August 15,	2	415	The legal representatives of Joseph Bernard, deceased,	Joseph Bernard,	500f.	Adams county,	Do,	Dec'r 3, 1787.
" 22,	487	August 15,	2	417	Benjamin Faras,	Michael Fortier,	2,650f.	On the river Mississippi,	Do,	March 15, 1789.
" 22,	488	August 15,	2	419	William Dunbar,	William Brown,	450f.	On the waters of the bayou Pierre,	Do,	Jan'y 26, 1787.
" 22,	489	August 15,	2	421	David Greenleaf,	Daniel Perry,	400f.	On the waters of Cole's creek,	Do,	Aug. 8, 1789.
" 22,	490	August 15,	2	423	Adam Binguman,	Mark Oiler,	101f.	On St. Catharine's creek,	Do,	Feb'y 25, 1788.
" 22,	491	August 15,	2	425	Isaac Newman,	Charles King,	375f.	On the waters of Cole's creek,	Do,	Feb'y 10, 1789.
" 22,	492	August 15,	2	427	Ebenezer Rees,	Frances Cousset,	800f.	On the waters of Cole's creek,	Do,	April 8, 1791.
" 22,	493	August 15,	2	429	James Hoggatt and John Bell,	William Richey,	500f.	On the waters of Cole's creek,	Do,	July 7, 1789.
" 22,	494	August 15,	2	431	Ebenezer Rees,	William Thomas,	400f.	On the waters of Cole's creek,	Do,	Aug. 30, 1793.
" 22,	495	August 15,	2	433	Charles F. Todd,	James Spain,	200f.	On the waters of Cole's creek,	Do,	June 20, 1795.
" 23,	496	August 15,	2	435	Ebenezer Rees,	William Burch,	200f.	On the waters of Cole's creek,	Do,	Jan'y 10, 1794.

ABSTRACT FOR AUGUST, 1805—Continued.

When entered (1805)	No.	Date	Vol.	Page	To whom granted	Name of original grantee	Quantity allowed (Acres)	Situation	Whence derived	Date of patent
Aug. 23,	497	August 15,	2	437	Ebenezer Rees,	Ephraim Bates,	400f.	On Sandy creek,	Spanish,	March 24, 1790.
23,	498	August 15,	2	439	Ebenezer Rees,	William Lee,	400f.	On Sandy creek,	Do.	March 15, 1788.
23,	499	August 15,	2	441	William Collins and Elijah Cushing,	Thomas Jordan,	400f.	On the waters of Fairchild's creek,	Do.	March 15, 1788.
23,	500	August 15,	2	443	Robert Dunbar,	Robert Dunbar,	2,000f.	On the waters of Cole's creek,	Do.	Aug. 14, 1794.
26,	501	August 19,	2	445	The legal representatives of David Kennedy, deceased,		160f.		Do.	April 3, 1794.
26,	502	August 19,	2	447	Robert Turner,	Jonas Scoggin,	100f.	On the river Mississippi,	Do.	March 15, 1788.
26,	503	August 19,	2	449	Stephen Bullock,	Thomas Jordan,	400f.	On the waters of Fairchild's creek,	Do.	Jan'y 1, 1793.
26,	504	August 19,	2	451	James Allen Matthews, in right of his wife Elizabeth,	James Allen Matthews,		On the bayou Pierre, -	Do.	March 10, 1789.
26,	505	August 19,	2	453	James Allen Matthews,	John Ferguson,	act. 27	On the waters of St. Catharine's creek,	Do.	March 10, 1789.
26,	506	August 21,	2	455	Alexander Montgomery,	John Ferguson,	250f.	On the waters of St. Catharine's creek,	Do.	Feb'y 12, 1788.
26,	507	August 21,	2	457	Alexander Montgomery and Henry King,	Benjamin Curtis,	800f.	On the waters of St. Catharine's creek,	Do.	April 8, 1789.
26,	508	August 21,	2	459	The legal representatives of Narsworthy Hunter, deceased,	James Cole,	az. 150	On the waters of Cole's creek,	Do.	Nov'r 20, 1793.
26,	509	August 21,	2	461	Samuel P. Moore, James Moore, and Robert Moore,	Henry Hunter,	1,500	On the waters of the bayou Sara,	British,	Nov'r 28, 1768.
28,	510	August 26,	2	463	Joseph Sessions,	Wm., Walter, & Alex. Moore,	100f.	On the river Mississippi,	Spanish,	March 12, 1790.
28,	511	August 26,	2	465	William Nealans,	William Ratliff,	100f.	On the waters of Sandy creek,	Do.	Aug. 14, 1794.
28,	512	August 26,	2	467	William Nealans,	Anthony Hozgatt,	100f.	On the waters of Sandy creek,	Do.	March 12, 1790.
28,	513	August 26,	2	469	Leonard Pomet,	William Ratliff,		On the waters of Sandy creek,	Do.	Jan'y 7, 1795.
28,	514	August 26,	2	471	Abijah Hunt,	Andrew Gill,	Lot No.	2, of sq. No. 2, in city of Natchez,	Do.	Jan'y 23, 1793.
28,	515	August 26,	2	473	John Minor,	Benjamin Mousanto,	Lot No.	1 & 2, of sq. No. 3, in city of Natchez,	Do.	Jan'y 2, 1795.
28,	516	August 26,	2	475	Eunice McIntosh,	John Minor,	Lot No.	1, & of sq. No. 5, in city of Natchez,	Do.	Jan'y 15, 1795.
28,	517	August 26,	2	477	William Dunbar,	Eunice McIntosh,	Lot No.	3, of sq. No. 6, in city of Natchez,	Do.	Dec'r 15, 1794.
29,	518	August 27,	2	479	James Moore,	William Dunbar,	Lot No.	4, of sq. No. 6, in city of Natchez,	Do.	June 15, 1795.
29,	519	August 27,	2	481	Christopher Miller,	Jeremiah Routh,	Part of	2, of sq. No. 12, in city of Natchez,	Do.	Jan'y 15, 1795.
29,	520	August 27,	2	483	Thomas Hardesty,	James Moore,	Part of	lot No. 1, of sq. No. 12, in Natchez,	Do.	Jan'y 15, 1795.
29,	521	August 27,	2	485	Samuel Gibson,	Justus King,	509f.	lot No. 1, of sq. No. 12, in Natchez,	Do.	April 19, 1795.
29,	522	August 27,	2	487	John Perkins,	James Moore,	Part of	On the waters of the bayou Pierre,	Do.	Jan'y 15, 1795.
29,	523	August 27,	2	489	The legal representatives of William Vousdan, deceased,			lot No. 1, of sq. No. 12, in Natchez,	Do.	
29,	524	August 27,	2	491	The legal representatives of George Cochran, deceased,	William Vousdan,	10f.	In the city of Natchez,	Do.	Feb'y 17, 1795.
29,	525	August 27,	2	493	The legal representatives of George Cochran, deceased,	Stephen Minor,	12 44/100 f.	In the city of Natchez,	Do.	April 4, 1795.
29,	526	August 27,	2	495	John Girault,	George Cochran,	10f.	Near the city of Natchez,	Do.	June 20, 1795.
29,	527	August 27,	2	497	Paiser Shilling,	John Girault,	9 4/10 f.	Near the city of Natchez,	Do.	Feb'y 25, 1795.
29,	528	August 27,	2	499	Peter Walker, -	Phillippi Engel,	10f.	In the city of Natchez,	Do.	Feb'y 19, 1795.
30,	529	August 27,	2	501	Peter Walker, -	Peter Walker,	10f.	In the city of Natchez,	Do.	Feb'y 10, 1795.
30,	530	August 27,	2	503		Louis Valleret,	4f.	In the city of Natchez,	Do.	Feb'y 5, 1795.
30,					Daniel Douglass,	Daniel Douglass,	10f.	In the city of Natchez,	Do.	Feb'y 20, 1795.

ABSTRACT FOR AUGUST, 1805—Continued.

When entered.	Commissioners' certificates. No.	Date.	Recorded. Vol.	Page.	To whom granted.	Claim. Name of original grantee.	Quantity allowed.	Situation.	Title. Whence derived.	Date of patent.
1805.		1805.					Acres.			
Aug. 31,	531	August 28,	2	505	John Ellis,	Seth Doud,	113	On the waters of Second creek,	British,	Sept'r 8, 1777.
" 31,	532	August 28,	2	507	William Conner, and Mary his wife,	Robert Robertson,	100	On Second creek,	Do.	Dec'r 14, 1776.
" 31,	533	August 28,	2	509	Ann Martin,	Margaret Williams,	Lot No.	4, of sq. No. 25, in city of Natchez,	Spanish,	Sept. 30, 1795.
" 31,	534	August 28,	2	511	John Smith,	Jacob Phillippi,	600	On the waters of Cole's creek,	British,	July 22, 1769.
" 31,	535	August 28,	2	513	Adam Bingaman,	James Watkins,	500	On the waters of Cole's creek,	Do.	July 29, 1769.
" 31,	536	August 28,	2	515	Daniel McGillivray,	Daniel McGillivray,	300	On the waters of Cole's creek,	Do.	May 25, 1779.
" 31,	537	August 28,	2	517	David Lattimore and William Lattimore,	John Wilson,	Part of	lots No. 3 & 4, of sq. No. 11, Natchez,	Spanish,	Feb. 16, 1795.
" 31,	538	August 28,	2	519	John Rab,	John Wilson,	Part of	lots No. 3 & 4, of sq. No. 11, Natchez,	Do.	Feb. 16, 1795.
" 31,	539	August 28,	2	521	The legal representatives of Charles Watruns, deceased,	Francis Lennon,	5f.	Near the city of Natchez,	Do.	Feb. 6, 1795.
" 31,	540	August 28,	2	523	Ann Dunbar,	Ann Dunbar,	10 43/100 f.	Near the city of Natchez,	Do.	Sept'r 4, 1794.

REGISTER'S OFFICE WEST OF PEARL RIVER, *September* 1, 1805.

THOMAS H. WILLIAMS.

REGISTER A—Continued.

Abstract of Certificates entered with the Register of the Land Office west of Pearl river, during the month of September, 1805, grounded on British and Spanish patents.

| Commissioners' certificates | | | | | Claim | | | | Title | |
No.	When entered	Date	Vol.	Page	To whom granted	Name of original grantee	Quantity allowed (Acres)	Situation	Whence derived	Date of patent
	1805.	1805.								
541	Sept'r 3,	August 29	2	525	George Overaker,	George Overaker,	Lot No.	4, of sq. No. 14, in city of Natchez,	Spanish,	Jan'y 15, 1795.
542	" 3,	August 29	2	527	John Wall,	John Wall,	Lot No.	3, of sq. No. 14, in city of Natchez,	Do.	Jan'y 14, 1795.
543	" 3,	August 29	2	529	William Dunbar,	William Dunbar,	Lots No.	1 & 2, of sq. No. 14, in city Natchez,	Do.	Jan'y 15, 1795.
544	" 3,	August 29	2	531	Leonard Pomet,	William Barland,	Lot No.	1, of sq. No. 21, in city of Natchez,	Do.	May 8, 1786.
545	" 3,	August 29	2	533	Leonard Pomet,	William Barland,	Lot No.	2, of sq. No. 21, in city of Natchez,	Do.	May 8, 1786.
546	" 3,	August 29	2	535	James Moore,	Francis Ashton Watts,	Lot No.	3, in city of Natchez,	Do.	Jan'y 21, 1795.
547	" 3,	August 29	2	537	William Dunbar,	William Dunbar,	Lot No.	2, of sq. No. 3, in city of Natchez,	Do.	Oct'r 23, 1793.
548	" 3,	August 29	2	539	James Moore,	Edward McCabe,	Part of	lot No. 4, sq. No. 3, city Natchez,	Do.	July 15, 1794.
549	" 3,	August 29	2	541	Thomas Ewing,	Francis Lennon,	Part of	lot No. 4, sq. No. 10, city Natchez,	Do.	Dec'r 6, 1794.
550	" 3,	August 29	2	543	John Henderson,	Francis Lennon,	Part of	lot No. 4, sq. No. 10, city Natchez,	Do.	Dec'r 6, 1794.
551	" 3,	August 29	2	545	Robert Moore,	Francis Lennon,	Part of	lots No. 2 & 4, sq. No. 10, Natchez,	Do.	Dec'r 6, 1794.
356	" 3,	June 21	2	547	William Bailand,	William Barland,	Part of	In the city of Natchez,	Do.	May 8, 1786.
552	Sept'r 5,	Sept'r 3	2	549	The legal representatives of D. Mitchell, dec'd,	Amos Ogden,	366	On the waters of river Homochitto,	British,	Oct'r 27, 1772.
553	" 5,	Sept'r 3	2	551	William Gordon Forman,	Amos Ogden,	366	On the waters of river Homochitto,	Do.	Oct'r 27, 1772.
554	" 5,	Sept'r 3	2	553	James Moore,	Abraham Taylor,	250f.	On the waters of Well's creek,	Spanish,	Dec'r 20, 1794.
557	" 5,	Sept'r 3	2	555	James Moore,	William Fletcher,	300f.	On Sandy creek,	Do.	June 12, 1788.
558	" 5,	Sept'r 3	2	557	John Smith,	James Elliott,	200f.	On the waters of Cole's creek,	Do.	Oc'r 20, 1788.
559	" 5,	Sept'r 3	2	559	David Davis,	James Elliott,	245f.	On the waters of Cole's creek,	Do.	Oct'r 20, 1788.
560	Sept'r 10,	Sept'r 4	2	561	John Cammack,	William McIntosh,	100f.	On the waters of St. Catharine's creek,	Do.	Feb'y 12, 1788.
561	" 10,	Sept'r 4	2	563	John Ellis,	Theophilus Collins,	800f.	On the waters of the bayou Sara,	Do.	April 1, 1795.
562	" 10,	Sept'r 5	2	565	James Moore,	Edward McCabe,	500f.	On the waters of the bayou Pierre,	Do.	March 4, 1795.
563	" 10,	Sept'r 5	2	567	James Moore,	William Ryon,	160f.	On waters of St. C's & Second creeks,	Do.	March 10, 1789.
564	" 10,	Sept'r 5	3	1	James Moore,	Sarah Truly,	2,364f.	On St. Catharine's creek,	Do.	Jan'y 31, 1787.
565	" 10,	Sept'r 5	3	3	Abner Green,	Alexander Moore,	155f.	On the river Mississippi,	Do.	June 22, 1791.
566	" 10,	Sept'r 5	3	5	Job Routh,	John Stampley,	800f.	560 toises, near the city of Natchez,	Do.	June 4, 1785.
567	" 10,	Sept'r 5	3	7	The legal representatives of T. Tyler, dec'd,	Constantine McKenna,	24f.	On the bayou Pierre,	Do.	April 9, 1790.
568	" 10,	Sept'r 5	3	9	Job Routh,	Manuel Gayoso de Lemos,	1,000f.	Near the city of Natchez,	Do.	Sept'r 10, 1794.
569	" 10,	Sept'r 5	3	11	William Dunbar, Jun.	Manuel Gayoso de Lemos,	1,000f.	Near the city of Natchez,	Do.	Sept'r 14, 1794.
570	" 10,	Sept'r 5	3	13	Walter Burling,	William Dunbar, Jun.	300f.	On the waters of Cole's creek,	Do.	Aug. 14, 1794.
571	" 10,	Sept'r 5	3	15	William Dunbar, Jun.	Stephen Minor,	1,000f.	On the waters of Second creek,	Do.	May 25, 1792.
572	" 10,	Sept'r 5	3	17	Joseph Newman and George Newman,	Peter Camus,	300f.	On Second creek,	Do.	Aug. 20, 1795.
573	Sept'r 11,	Sept'r 9	9	19	Elijah Cushing,	Francis Lennon,	Part of 8f.	lot No. 2, sq. No. 10, city Natchez,	Do.	Dec'r 6, 1794.
574	" 11,	Sept'r 9	9	21	Isaac Locke,	John Scott,	7,31f.	In the city of Natchez,	Do.	Feb'y 16, 1795.
575	" 11,	Sept'r 9	9	23	William Lintot,	Philip Engel,	acs.150	In the city of Natchez,	Do.	June 15, 1795.
576	" 11,	Sept'r 9	9	25	John Stowers,	Philip Engel,	acs.150	In the city of Natchez,	Do.	June 15, 1795.
577	Sept'r 13,	Sept'r 11	11	27	Charles Mulholland,	Martin Owens,	37f.	On the waters of Fairchild's creek,	Do.	June 20, 1795.
578	" 13,	Sept'r 11	11	29	John Wraye,	Martin Owens,	acs.150	On the waters of Fairchild's creek,	Do.	June 20, 1795.
579	" 13,	Sept'r 11	11	31	Abner Pipes,	Martin Owens,	37f.	On the waters of Fairchild's creek,	Do.	June 20, 1795.
580	" 13,	Sept'r 11	11	33		David Odem,	acs.100	On the waters of Cole's creek,	Do.	Dec'r 24, 1790.

ABSTRACT for SEPTEMBER, 1805—Continued.

Commissioners' certificates					Claim			Situation	Title	
When entered.	No.	Date.	Vol.	Page.	To whom granted.	Name of original grantee.	Quantity allowed.		Whence derived.	Date of patent.
1805.		1805.					Acres.			
Sept'r 13,	581	Sept'r 11,	3	35	Abijah Hunt, -	David Odem,	195f.	On the waters of Cole's creek,	Spanish,	Dec'r 24, 1790.
" 13,	582	11,	3	37	John Girault, -	David Odem,	Lot No.	19, in the town of Greenville,	Do.	Dec'r 24, 1790.
" 13,	583	11,	3	39	Edward Turner, -	David Odem,	acs. 15	On the waters of Cole's creek,	Do.	Dec'r 24, 1790.
" 17,	584	16,	3	41	William Chaney, -	William Bell,	400f.	On the waters of Cole's creek,	Do.	October 1, 1794.
" 17,	585	16,	3	43	John Courtney, -	Clement Dyson,	160f.	On the waters of Fairchild's creek,	Do.	Nov'r 26, 1793.
" 17,	586	16,	3	45	Stephen Scriber, -	Joshua Collins,	200f.	On the waters of Fairchild's creek,	Do.	March 15, 1789.
" 17,	587	16,	3	47	Joseph Dove, -	Joseph Dove,	240f.	On the waters of Buffalo creek,	Do.	Sept'r 1, 1795.
" 17,	588	16,	3	49	Israel Leonard, -	Ishmer Andrews,	100f.	On the waters of St. Catharine's creek,	Do.	Jan'y 24, 1794.
" 17,	589	16,	3	51	Jacob Stampley, -	Alexander Boyd,	200f.	On the waters of river Big Black,	Do.	Oct'r 20, 1793.
" 17,	590	16,	3	53	Christian Harman, -	Charles Adams,	200f.	On the waters of St. Catharine's creek,	Do.	March 15, 1789.
" 17,	591	16,	3	55	Jacob Strupes, -	Charles Adams,	81 43	Acres, on waters St. Catharine's creek,	Do.	March 15, 1789.
" 17,	592	16,	3	57	John Lovelace, -	John Lovelace,	30f.	On the river Mississippi,	Do.	Jan'y 22, 1788.
" 17,	593	16,	3	59	John Wall, -	John Lovelace,	440f.	On the waters of Buffalo creek,	Do.	Jan'y 22, 1788.
" 17,	594	16,	3	61	John Wall, -	David Lejeunc,	200f.	On the waters of Buffalo creek,	Do.	April 8, 1789.
" 17,	595	16,	3	63	The legal representatives of Wm. Owens, dec'd,	William Henderson,	450f.	On the waters of Cole's creek,	Do.	Jan'y 22, 1793.
" 17,	596	16,	3	65	Thomas Wilkins and Stephen Minor, -	John Girault,	80f.	On the river Mississippi,	Do.	June 12, 1788.
" 17,	597	16,	3	67	Abijah Hunt, -	Alexander Moore,	716f.	On the bayou Pierre,	Do.	July 17, 1790.
" 17,	598	16,	3	69	Robert Moore, -	Samuel Gibson,	1,000f.	On the waters of the bayou Pierre,	Do.	March 15, 1789.
" 17,	599	16,	3	71	William Lindsey and Co.	Christian Harman,	Lot No.	1, sq. No. 2, in town of Gibson Port,	Do.	August 6, 1788.
" 17,	600	16,	3	73	Nicholas Robb, -	William Daniel,	600f.	On the waters of St Catharine's creek,	Do.	March 6, 1788.
" 18,	601	17,	3	75	Timothy O'Hara, -	Samuel Flowers,	105f.	Oo waters St. C's & Fairchild's creek,	Do.	Oct'r 20, 1795.
" 18,	602	17,	3	77	Samuel Flowers, -	William Butler,	900f.	On the waters of Cole's creek,	Do.	April 21, 1789.
" 18,	603	17,	3	79	Benjamin Faran, in right of his wife Mary,	Joseph Vidal,	600f.	On the river Mississippi,	Do.	Feb'y 16, 1789.
" 19,	604	18,	3	81	James Williams, -	Stephen Minor,	10f.	Near the city of Natchez,	Do.	Oct'r 25, 1793.
" 19,	605	18,	3	83	James Williams, -	Joseph Vidal,	30f.	Near the city of Natchez,	Do.	March 16, 1795.
" 19,	606	18,	3	85	Stephen Minor, -	Stephen Minor,	19 31	Near the city of Natchez,	Do.	Oct'r 25, 1793.
" 19,	607	18,	3	87	John Steele, -	Stephen Minor,	208 31	Near the city of Natchez,	Do.	March 6, 1795.
" 19,	608	18,	3	89	John Steele, -	Elizabeth Whipple,	31 9	On the waters of the bayou Pierre,	Do.	July 25, 1793.
" 19,	609	18,	3	91	St~phen Minor, -	Manuel Gayoso de Lemos,	800f.	Near the city of Natchez,	Do.	May 6, 1791.
" 19,	610	18,	3	93	Stephen Minor, -	Stephen Minor,	756f.	On the waters of Fairchild's creek,	Do.	Sept'r 12, 1794.
" 19,	611	18,	3	95	Stephen Minor, -	Lacey Rumsey,	12 65	Near the city of Natchez,	Do.	Sept'r 15, 1792.
" 19,	612	18,	3	97	David Ferguson, -	John Murdock,	500f.	On the waters of Cole's creek,	Do.	Oct'r 20, 1794.
" 19,	613	18,	3	99	Abijah Hunt and William G. Forman,	William Smith,	230f.	On the waters of the bayou Pierre,	Do.	March 25, 1795.
" 19,	614	18,	3	101	William Smith, -	Stephen Cole,	400f.	On the waters of Cole's creek,	Do.	March 15, 1789.
" 19,	615	18,	3	103	Patrick Gurnet, -	Patrick Gurnet,	240f.	On the waters of Cole's creek,	Do.	Feb'y 28, 1795.
" 19,	616	18,	3	105	William Thomas, -	Richard Miller,	300f.	On the waters of St. Catharine's creek,	Do.	March 8, 1792.
" 19,	617	18,	3	107	Richard Miller, -	John Newton,	200f.	On Second creek,	Do.	March 15, 1789.
" 19,	618	18,	3	109	Joshua Howard, -	John O'Conner,	200f.	On Buffalo creek,	Do.	March 22, 1795.
" 19,	619	18,	3	111	John O'Conner, -	Josiah Flowers,	330f.	On the waters of the bayou Pierre,	Do.	Aug. 30, 1793.
" 19,	620	18,	3	113	Josiah Flowers, -	David Mitchell,	100f.	350 toises, on waters St. Cath's creek,	Do.	April 10, 1795.
" 23,	621	20,	3	115	Samuel C. Young, -		195f.		Do.	April 20, 1784.

ABSTRACT for SEPTEMBER, 1805—Continued.

	Commissioners' certificates.				Claim.				Title.	
When entered.	No.	Date.	Recorded. Vol.	Page.	To whom granted.	Name of original grantee.	Quantity allowed.	Situation.	Whence derived.	Date of patent.
1805. Sept'r 23,	622	Sept'r 20,	3	117	Samuel C. Young,	Daniel Baker,	Acres. 200f.	On the waters of St. Catharine's creek,	Spanish,	April 20, 1784.
" 23,	623	Sept'r 20,	3	119	Joseph Killian and Abraham Galtney,	George Killian,	600f.	On the waters of St. Catharine's creek,	Do.	March 15, 1789.
" 23,	624	Sept'r 20,	3	121	The legal representatives of Martin Hestler, deceased,	Martin Hestler,	500f.	On the waters of Cole's creek,	Do.	Sept'r 1, 1795.
" 23,	625	Sept'r 20,	3	123	The legal representatives of Elias Bonnell, deceased,	John Girault,	361f.	On the waters of Second creek,	Do.	March 15, 1789.
" 23,	626	Sept'r 20,	3	125	Israel Smith,	David Mitchell,	14 19/100	Acres, on the waters of Second creek,	Do.	April 3, 1790.
" 24,	627	Sept'r 23,	3	127	David McFarlan,	David McFarlan,	400f.	On the waters of the bayou Pierre,	Do.	Aug. 30, 1795.
" 24,	628	Sept'r 23,	3	129	The legal representatives of George Cochran, deceased,	Lewis Evans,	Lot No. 2,	of sq. No. 19, in city of Natchez,	Do.	June 20, 1795.
" 25,	629	Sept'r 24,	3	131	James Moore,	James Moore,	Part of lot No. 1,	sq. No. 12, city Natchez,	Do.	Jan'y 15, 1795.
" 25,	630	Sept'r 24,	3	133	Israel Smith and Christian Gilbert,	Samuel Phipps,	400f.	On the waters of Second creek,	Do.	April 9, 1790.
" 25,	631	Sept'r 24,	3	135	Adam Bingaman,	Christian Bingaman,	450f.	On St. Catharine's creek,	Do.	March 8, 1788.
" 25,	632	Sept'r 24,	3	137	Daniel Clark,	Daniel Clark, Sen.	1,023f.	On the river Mississippi,	Do.	Feb'ry 6, 1787.
" 25,	633	Sept'r 24,	3	139	Elizabeth Whittle,	William Brocus,	196 62/100f.	On St. Catharine's creek,	Do.	July 20, 1786.
" 25,	634	Sept'r 24,	3	141	David Lattimore, assignee of Thomas Frazier,	William Brocus,	25	Acres, on waters St. Catharine's creek,	Do.	July 20, 1786.

THOMAS H. WILLIAMS.

REGISTER'S OFFICE WEST OF PEARL RIVER, *October* 1, 1805.

REGISTER A—Continued.

Abstract of Certificates entered with the Register of the Land Office west of Pearl river, during the month of October, 1805, grounded on British and Spanish patents.

Commissioners' certificates.					Claim.				Title.	
When entered.	No.	Date.	Recorded.		To whom granted.	Name of original grantee.	Quantity allowed.	Situation.	Whence derived.	Date of patent.
1805.		1805.	Vol.	Page.			Acres.			
October 1,	635	Sept'r 25,	3	143	Abijah Hunt and William G. Forman,	John Murdock,	500*f*	On the waters of Cole's creek,	Spanish,	Aug. 14, 1794.
" 1,	636	Sept'r 25,	3	145	Abijah Hunt and William G. Forman,	John Murdock,	400*f*.	On the waters of Cole's creek,	Do.	Aug. 14, 1794.
" 1,	637	Sept'r 25,	3	147	Abijah Hunt and William G. Forman,	John Murdock,	500*f*.	On the waters of Cole's creek,	Do.	Aug. 14, 1794.
" 1,	638	Sept'r 25,	3	149	Abijah Hunt and William G. Forman,	John Murdock,	500*f*.	On the waters of Cole's creek,	Do.	March 25, 1795.
" 2,	639	Sept'r 26,	3	151	Tobias Brashear,	Reuben Proctor,	200*f*.	On the waters of the bayou Pierre,	Do.	Oct'r 24, 1794.
" 2,	640	Sept'r 26,	3	153	Anthony Dougherty,	Benjamin Bealk,	134*f*.	Near the city of Natchez,	Do.	May 6, 1786.
" 3,	641	Sept'r 26,	3	155	Anthony Dougherty,	John Lusk,	137*f*.	Near the city of Natchez,	Do.	April 28, 1784.
" 3,	642	Sept'r 27,	3	157	Christopher Miller,	Daniel Douglass,	Part of	Lot No. 2, of sq. 11, in city Natchez,	Do.	March 3, 1795.
" 4,	643	Sept'r 27,	3	159	Daniel Douglass,	Daniel Douglass,	Lot No.	1, & part lot No. 2, sq. 11, in city Nat.	Do.	March 3, 1795.
" 4,	644	Sept'r 27,	3	161	David Lattimore, assignee of Abner Green,	William Barland,	Lots No.	2 & 4, of sq. No. 15, in city Natchez,	Do.	May 8, 1786.
" 5,	645	October 2,	3	163	Telfair Monson,	Telfair Monson,	400*f*.	On the waters of the bayou Sara,	Do.	April 10, 1795.
" 5,	646	October 2,	3	165	The legal representatives of Francis Poussett, deceased,	Francis Poussett,	1,000*f*.	On the waters of the bayou Sara,	Do.	March 22, 1795.
" 8,	647	October 2,	3	167	Daniel Clark,	Daniel Clark, senior,	600*f*.	On the river Mississippi,	Do.	Sept'r 30, 1793.
" 8,	648	October 2,	3	169	William Williams,	William Williams,	800*f*.	On the waters of the bayou Sara,	Do.	Aug. 30, 1795.
" 8,	649	October 2,	3	171	James Gibson,	Daniel Miller,	300*f*.	On the waters of the bayou Pierre,	Do.	Sept'r 30, 1793.
" 8,	650	October 2,	3	173	Anthony Dougherty,	John Row,	87*f*.	Near the city of Natchez,	Do.	May 15, 1795.
" 8,	651	October 2,	3	175	Job Routh and Jeremiah Routh,	John Row,	83*f*.	Near the city of Natchez,	Do.	May 15, 1795.
" 8,	652	October 3,	3	177	James Williams,	Toussaint Chabot,	1,600*f*.	On Buffalo creek,	Do.	July 7, 1789.
" 9,	653	October 3,	3	179	Robert Taylor and Isaac Taylor,	Jacob Cowperthwaite,	200*f*.	On the waters of Fairchild's creek,	Do.	October 8, 1787.
" 9,	654	October 3,	3	181	The legal representatives of Jacob Cowperthwaite, deceased,	Jacob Cowperthwaite,	800*f*.	On the waters of Fairchild's creek,	Do.	October 8, 1787.
" 10,	655	October 3,	3	183	Richard Graves,	Caleb Weeks,	*acs.* 28	On the waters of the bayou Sara,	Do.	May 25, 1791.
" 10,	656	October 3,	3	185	George Rapalje, in right of his wife Jane,	Jane Rapalje,	1,000*f*.	On the waters of the river Homochitto,	Do.	Feb'y 16, 1789.
" 14,	657	October 12,	3	187	Nathan Swayze, one of the legal representatives of Samuel Swayze, deceased,	Amos Ogden,	660	On the river Homochitto,	British,	Oct'r 27, 1772.
" 14,	658	October 12,	3	189	Samuel Swayze, one of the legal representatives of Samuel Swayze, deceased,	Amos Ogden,	786½	On the river Homochitto,	Do.	Oct'r 27, 1772.
" 14,	659	October 12,	3	191	Elijah Swayze, one of the legal representatives of Samuel Swayze, deceased,	Amos Ogden,	660	On the river Homochitto,	Do.	Oct'r 27, 1772.
" 14,	660	October 12,	3	193	The legal representatives of Obadiah Brown, deceased, in right of his wife Penelope, dec'd,	Amos Ogden,	1,276	On the river Homochitto,	Do.	Oct'r 27, 1772.
" 14,	661	October 12,	3	195	Hannah Curtis, one of the legal representatives of Samuel Swayze, deceased,	Amos Ogden,	1,026½	On the river Homochitto,	Do.	Oct'r 27, 1772.
" 14,	662	October 12,	3	197	Rhoda Lambert, one of the legal representatives of Samuel Swayze, deceased,	Amos Ogden,	1,026½	On the river Homochitto,	Do.	Oct'r 27, 1772.
" 14,	663	October 12,	3	199	The legal representatives of Stephen Swayze, deceased,	Amos Ogden,	1,026½	On the river Homochitto,	Do.	Oct'r 27, 1772.

ABSTRACT FOR OCTOBER, 1805—Continued.

Commissioners' certificates.					Claim.				Title.	
When entered.	No.	Date.	Recorded.		To whom granted	Name of original grantee.	Quantity allowed.	Situation.	Whence derived.	Date of patent.
			Vol.	Page.						
1805. Oct'r 14,	664	1805. October 12,	3	201	The legal representatives of Samuel Swayze, deceased,	Amos Ogden,	Acres. 464$\frac{1}{2}$	On the river Homochitto,	British,	Oct'r 27, 1772.
" 14,	665	October 12,	3	203	Gabriel Swayze, one of the legal representatives of Richard Swayze, deceased,	Amos Ogden,	3,057$\frac{1}{8}$	On the river Homochitto,	Do.	Oct'r 27, 1772.
" 14,	666	October 12,	3	205	Richard Swayze, one of the legal representatives of Richard Swayze, deceased,	Amos Ogden,	1,528$\frac{4}{7}$	On the river Homochitto,	Do.	Oct'r 27, 1772.
" 14,	667	October 12,	3	207	Caleb King, in right of his wife Mary,	Amos Ogden,	828$\frac{4}{7}$	On the river Homochitto,	Do.	Oct'r 27, 1772.
" 14,	668	October 12,	3	209	Sarah Swayze, wife of Richard Swayze, deceased,	Amos Ogden,	1,028$\frac{4}{7}$	On the river Homochitto,	Do.	Oct'r 27, 1772.
" 14,	669	October 12,	3	211	Job Cory, in right of his wife Lydia,	Amos Ogden,	728$\frac{4}{7}$	On the river Homochitto,	Do.	Oct'r 27, 1772.
" 15,	567	Sept'r 5,	3	213	James McIntosh,	Charles de Grand Pré,	2,847*f.*	On the river Homochitto,	Spanish,	Aug. 13, 1787.
" 15,	670	October 14,	3	215	Samuel Osborn,	James Cola,	412$\frac{1}{2}$	On the waters of Cole's creek,	British,	March 20, 1778.
" 15,	671	October 14,	3	217	States Trevilian,	James Cole,	137$\frac{1}{2}$	On the waters of Cole's creek,	Do.	March 20, 1778.
" 15,	672	October 14,	3	219	Henry Turner and Company,	Edward McCabe,	Part of	Lot No. 4, sq. No. 3, city Natchez,	Spanish,	July 15, 1794.
" 15,	673	October 14,	3	221	Maria Page,	Maria Page,	800*f.*	On the waters of Cole's creek,	Do.	July 7, 1789.
" 15,	674	October 14,	3	223	Stephen B. Minor and William Minor,	Stephen Minor,	1,180*f.*	On the waters of the river Big Black,	Do.	June 18, 1795.
" 15,	675	October 14,	3	225	James McIntosh,	James McIntosh,	800*f.*	On the waters of the bayou Sara,	Do.	March 22, 1795.
" 15,	676	October 14,	3	227	Eunice McIntosh,	Eunice McIntosh,	800*f.*	On the waters of the bayou Sara,	Do.	March 22, 1795.
" 20,	677	October 15,	3	229	The legal representatives of William Ferguson, deceased,	James Robertson,	250	On the waters of St. Catharine's creek,	British,	Nov'r 19, 1777.
" 20,	678	October 19,	3	231	James Williams,	Jason Lawrence,	1,000*f.*	On the river Homochitto,	Spanish,	March 15, 1789.
" 20,	679	October 19,	3	233	Robert K. Moore, William Wykoff, and William G. Garland,	Ebenezer Dayton,	400*f.*	On the river Homochitto.	Do.	March 29, 1793.
" 20,	680	October 19,	3	235	Robert Cochran,	Peter Piernas,	92*f.*	In the city of Natchez,	Do.	Feb'y 24, 1783.
" 21,	681	October 19,	3	237	David Ferguson,	David Ferguson,	1,000*f.*	On the waters of Cole's creek,	Do.	Aug. 14, 1793.
" 21,	682	October 19,	3	239	Manuel G. de Texada,	Michael Solabellas,	Lot No.	3, of sq. 2, in the city of Natchez,	Do.	May 7, 1793.
" 21,	683	October 19,	3	241	William Scott,	William Scott,	Lots No.	2 & 4, of sq. No. 27, in city Natchez,	Do.	Jan'y 15, 1795.
" 21,	684	October 19,	3	243	The legal representatives of George Cochran, deceased,	George Cochran,	Lot No.	1, of sq. No. 20, in city of Natchez,	Do.	June 20, 1795.
" 30,	685	October 26,	3	245	John Eldergill,	John Eldergill,	Lot No.	2, of sq. No. 18, in city of Natchez,	Do.	Jan'y 14, 1795.
" 30,	686	October 26,	3	247	The legal representatives of Patrick Connelly, deceased,	Richard King,	Lot No.	4, of sq. No. 32, in city of Natchez,	Do.	March 12, 1795.
" 30,	687	October 28,	3	249	George W. Humphreys,	William Vousdan,	500	On the waters of the bayou Pierre.	British,	March 19, 1779.

REGISTER'S OFFICE WEST OF PEARL RIVER, *November* 5, 1805.

THOMAS H. WILLIAMS.

REGISTER A—Continued.

Abstract of all the Certificates entered with the Register of the Land Office west of Pearl river, during the month of Feb., 1806, grounded on British and Spanish patents.

When entered.	No.	Date.	Vol.	Page.	To whom granted.	Name of original grantee.	Quantity allowed.	Situation.	Whence derived.	Date of patent.
1806. Feb'y 1,	688	January 6, 1806.	3	251	Legal representatives of David Mitchell,	Amos Ogden,	Acres. 240	On the Homochitto,	British,	Oct.r 27, 1772.
" 1,	689	January 6,	3	253	Richard, Prosper, Eliza, Catharine, and William Henry King,	Amos Ogden,	728¼	On the Homochitto,	Do.	Oct.r 27, 1772.
" 1,	690	January 6,	3	255	Thomas Calvit, assignee of Mary Oliver,	Mary Oliver,	150	On Cole's creek,	Do.	July 22, 1769.
" 1,	691	January 6,	3	257	James Moore, -	Joshua Stockstill,	500f.	On Sandy creek,	Spanish,	March 15, 1789.
" 1,	692	January 6,	3	259	James Moore, -	Louis Fore,	Lot No.	1, of sq. No. 4, Natchez,	Do.	Jan'y 7, 1795.
" 1,	693	January 6,	3	261	Legal representatives of Thomas Tyler,	William Barland,	16,500	Feet in Natchez,	Do.	May 8, 1786.
" 1,	694	January 6,	3	263	Legal representatives of William Moore,	William Moore,	Lots No.	1 & 3, of sq. No. 27, Natchez,	Do.	Jan'y 15, 1769.
" 1,	695	January 6,	3	265	Legal representatives of William Henderson,	William Tabor,	500f.	On the Homochitto,	Do.	Feb'y 10, 1769.
" 1,	696	January 6,	3	267	William Nyely,	William Tabor,	300f.	On the bayou Pierre,	Do.	April 10, 1795.
" 1,	697	January 7,	3	269	Martin and Ralph Price,	M. and R. Price,	Lot No.	1, of sq. No. 9, city of Natchez,	Do.	Aug. 30, 1793.
" 1,	698	January 7,	3	271	Daniel Douglass,	Maurice Stackpole,	400f.	On Cole's creek,	Do.	Feb'y 4, 1795.
" 1,	699	January 7,	3	273	Nicholas G. Ridgley,	William Curtis,	600f.	On Cole's creek,	Do.	Feb'y 28, 1795.
" 1,	700	January 7,	3	275	Nicholas G. Ridgley,	Abraham Thickston,	200f.	On Cole's creek,	Do.	Nov.r 20, 1793.
" 1,	701	January 7,	3	277	Abijah Hunt,	John Reed,	300f.	On Fairchild's creek,	Do.	June 12, 1788.
" 1,	702	January 7,	3	279	Abijah Hunt, -	Daniel Chambers,	800f.	On bayou Pierre,	Do.	Aug. 30, 1793.
" 1,	703	January 7,	3	281	William G. Forman,	James Fletcher,	1,000f.	On Fairchild's creek,	Do.	Sep.r 9, 1788.
" 1,	704	January 7,	3	283	David Greenleaf,	James Fletcher,	600f.	On Fairchild's creek,	Do.	Sep.r 9, 1788.
" 1,	705	January 7,	3	285	John Collins, -	Gilbert Leonard,	1,153f.	On Buffalo creek,	Do.	May 26, 1787.
" 1,	706	January 7,	3	287	Legal representatives of Daniel Clark, sen.	Gilbert Leonard,	1,600f.	On Buffalo creek,	Do.	May 26, 1787.
" 1,	707	January 7,	3	289	Daniel Clark, -	Rosalia de Grandpré,	500f.	On Second creek,	Do.	Aug. 13, 1787.
" 1,	708	January 7,	3	291	Daniel Clark, -	Peter Francis Rose,	100f.	On Buffalo creek,	Do.	May 26, 1787.
" 3,	709	January 8,	3	293	Peter B. Bruin, -	John Burnet,	200f.	On bayou Pierre,	Do.	Nov.r 4, 1784.
" 3,	710	January 8,	3	295	Legal representatives of William Henderson,	Squire Boon,	250f.	On bayou Pierre,	Do.	Oct.r 18, 1788.
" 3,	711	January 8,	3	297	Legal representatives of William Henderson,	Squire Boon,	200f.	On the Big Black,	Do.	Oct.r 18, 1788.
" 3,	712	January 8,	3	299	Legal representatives of William Henderson,	Squire Boon,	100	On the Big Black,	Do.	Oct.r 18, 1788.
" 3,	713	January 8,	3	301	Legal representatives of William Henderson,	William Ryan,	130f.	On the Big Black,	Do.	March 15, 1789.
" 3,	714	January 8,	3	303	Legal representatives of William Ryan,	Athanasius Martin,	800f.	On Second creek,	British,	Oct.r 9, 1777.
" 3,	715	January 13,	3	305	Everard Green,	Job Cory,	200f.	On Cole's creek,	Spanish,	June 8, 1792.
" 3,	716	January 13,	3	307	Richard King, -	Andrew Hare,	700f.	On St. Catharine's creek,	Do.	August 8, 1789.
" 3,	717	January 13,	3	309	Legal representatives of Andrew Hare,	Andrew Hare,	200f.	On the bayou Sara,	Do.	August 8, 1789.
" 3,	718	January 13,	3	311	Martha and Mary Rhea,	James Elliott,	100f.	On the bayou Sara,	Do.	Oct.r 20, 1788.
" 3,	719	January 13,	3	313	John Hopkins,	James Elliott,		On Cole's creek,	Do.	Oct.r 20, 1788.
" 3,	720	January 13,	3	315	John Griffing,	James Elliott,		On Cole's creek,	Do.	Oct.r 20, 1788.
" 3,	721	January 13,	3	317	John Hopkins, assignee of John Smith,	Stephen Minor,	875 62/100 f.	On the Mississippi,	Do.	March 6, 1795.
" 8,	722	January 15,	3	319	Stephen Minor,	William Barland,		Lot near the city of Natchez,	Do.	May 8, 1786.
" 8,	723	January 15,	3	321	Melling Woolley,	William Barland,		Lot near the city of Natchez,	Do.	May 8, 1786.
" 8,	724	January 15,	3	323	Robert and George Cochran,	William Barland,		Lot No. 1, of sq. No. 8, Natchez,	Do.	May 8, 1786.
" 8,	...	January 15,	3	325	George Furney,	William Barland,	Part of	Lot No. 1, of sq. No. 8, Natchez,	Do.	May 8, 1786.

ABSTRACT FOR FEBRUARY, 1806—Continued.

When entered	No.	Date.	Recorded. Vol.	Recorded. Page.	To whom granted.	Name of original grantee.	Quantity allowed.	Situation.	Whence derived.	Date of patent.
1805. Febr'y 8,	726	January 15,	3	327	John J. Walton,	William Barland,	Part of Lot No.	Lot No. 1, of sq. No. 8, Natchez,	Spanish,	May 8, 1786.
" 8,	727	January 15,	3	329	Ebenezer Ress,	William Barland,	Lot No.	3, of square No. 8, Natchez,	Do.	May 8, 1786.
" 8,	728	January 15,	3	331	John Girault,	William Barland,	-	Lot near the city of Natchez,	Do.	May 8, 1786.
" 8,	729	January 15,	3	333	Thomas Foster,	William Barland,	Lots No.	2 and 4, of sq. No. 17, Natchez,	Do.	May 8, 1786.
" 8,	730	January 15,	3	335	James Moore,	James Moore,	Lots No.	1 and 2, of sq. No. 13, Natchez,	Do.	Jan'y 18, 1795.
" 12,	731	January 15,	3	337	Robert Moore,	Robert Moore,	Lots No.	3 and 4, of sq. No. 13, Natchez,	Do.	Jan'y 18, 1795.
" 12,	732	January 16,	3	339	Robert Moore,	Geo. Rapalje, Lewis Charbona,	700f.	On the Mississippi,	Do.	March 31, 1786.
" 12,	733	January 16,	3	341	John J. Rodriques,	Geo. Rapalje, Lewis Charbona,	400f.	On the Mississippi,	Do.	March 31, 1786.
" 12,	734	January 16,	3	343	Isaac Guion,	Jacob Adams,	50f.	On St. Catharine's creek,	Do.	June 4, 1791.
" 12,	735	January 16,	3	345	John Minor,	Domingo Lorero,	Lot No.	4, of square No. 34, Natchez,	Do.	Jan'y 10, 1795.
" 12,	736	January 16,	3	347	Samuel S. Mahan,	Domingo Lorero,	Lot No.	3, of square No. 34, Natchez,	Do.	Jan'y 10, 1795.
" 12,	737	January 16,	3	449	David Ferguson, assignee of John Sullivan,	John Sullivan,	400f.	On Cole's creek,	Do.	June 20, 1795.
" 12,	738	January 16,	3	351	John Spiers,	Jacob Cobb,	350f.	On Sandy creek,	Do.	April 1, 1795.
" 12,	739	January 16,	3	353	Patrick Foley,	Patrick Foley,	500f.	On Buffalo creek,	Do.	April 12, 1790.

REGISTER'S OFFICE WEST OF PEARL RIVER, *March* 1, 1806.

THOMAS H. WILLIAMS.

REGISTER A—Continued.

Abstract of Certificates entered with the Register of the Land Office west of Pearl river, during the month of March, 1806, grounded on British and Spanish patents.

When entered.	No.	Date.	Recorded. Vol.	Recorded. Page.	To whom granted.	Name of original grantee.	Quantity allowed.	Situation.	Whence derived.	Date of patent.
1806. March 18,	740	1806. Feb'y 24,	3	355	The legal representatives of John Hartley, deceased,	Thaddeus Lyman,	Acres. 10,000	On the bayou Pierre, -	British,	Feb'y 2, 1775.
" 18,	741	Feb'y 24,	3	357	John Ellison, in right of his wife Salome,	Thaddeus Lyman,	10,000	On the bayou Pierre, -	Do.	Feb'y 2, 1775.
" 18,	742	Feb'y 24,	3	359	John Hutchins, -	Thomas Hutchins,	1,000	On the river Homochitto, -	Do.	July 15, 1775.
" 18,	743	Feb'y 24,	3	361	Joseph Calvit, -	Alexander McIntosh,	500	Near the little Gulf, -	Do.	March 6, 1770.
" 18,	744	Feb'y 24,	3	363	The legal representatives of Richard Harrison, deceased,					
" 18,	745	Feb'y 24,	3	365	Robert Moore, -	John J. Duforest,	600f.	On the waters of Cole's creek,	Spanish,	Jan'y 15, 1787.
" 19,	746	Feb'y 24,	3	367	Timothy O'Harra, -	John J. Duforest,	400f.	On the waters of Cole's creek,	Do.	Jan'y 15, 1787.
" 19,	747	Feb'y 27,	3	369	The legal representatives of David Forman, deceased,	Richard King, -	85f.	On the waters of St. Catharine's creek,	Do.	Aug. 20, 1794.
" 19,	748	Feb'y 27,	3	371	William Dunbar, -	Ezekiel Forman,	2,000f.	On Second creek,	Do.	June 1, 1792.
" 19,	749	March 5,	3	373	Henry Roach, -	William Dunbar,	Lot No. 100f.	l, of sq. No. 19, in city of Natchez,	Do.	March 12, 1793.
" 19,	750	March 5,	3	375	James Sterrett and Nathaniel Evans,	David Lejeune, -	100f.	Near Loftus's cliffs,	Do.	March 24, 1789.
" 19,	751	March 5,	3	377	James Sterrett and Nathaniel Evans,	David Lejeune, -	350f.	Near Loftus's cliffs,	Do.	March 24, 1789.
" 20,	752	March 5,	3	379	Daniel Ogden, -	Henry Roach, -	250f.	Near Loftus's cliffs,	Do.	June 23, 1788.
" 20,	753	March 10,	3	381	The legal representatives of David Odam, dec'd,	David Odam, -	225f.	Near Loftus's cliffs,	Do.	June 23, 1788.
" 20,	754	March 10,	3	383	Richard Canadine, -	Eustice Humphreys,	100f.	On the waters of Cole's creek,	Do.	Dec'r 24, 1790.
" 20,	755	March 10,	3	385	William Cole, -	William Cole, -	200f.	On the waters of Fairchild's creek,	Do.	Feb'y 27, 1789.
" 20,	756	March 10,	3	387	Solomon Cole, -	Solomon Cole, -	200f.	On waters of the river Homochitto,	Do.	Oct'r 20, 1793.
" 20,	757	March 10,	3	389	The legal representatives of George Cochran, deceased,			On the waters of Cole's creek,	Do.	Jan'y 10, 1794.
" 20,	758	March 10,	3	391	Robert Jones, -	James Todd,	240f.	On the waters of Cole's creek,	Do.	Jan'y 1, 1793.
" 20,	759	March 10,	3	393	Archibald Douglass, -	Robert Jones,	1,000f.	On Fairchild's creek,	Do.	Jan'y 18, 1788.
						Archibald Douglass,	200f.	On the river Big Black,	Do.	Oct'r 20, 1793.

REGISTER'S OFFICE WEST OF PEARL RIVER, *April* 1, 1806.

THOMAS H. WILLIAMS.

REGISTER A—Continued.

Abstract of Certificates entered with the Register of the Land Office west of Pearl river, grounded on British and Spanish patents, during the month of May, 1806.

| | Commissioners' certificates. | | | | Claim. | | | | | Title. |
| | | | Recorded. | | | | | | | |
When entered.	No.	Date.	Vol.	Page.	To whom granted.	Name of original grantee.	Quantity allowed.	Situation.	Whence derived.	Date of patent.
1806.		1806.					Acres.			
May 29,	760	March 27,	3	395	John Lovelace,	John Lovelace, -	200f.	On the Mississippi,	Spanish,	Jan'y 21, 1788.
" 29,	761	April 4,	3	397	George Overaker,	John Lusk,	157f.	On St. Catharine's creek,	Do.	April 28, 1784.
" 29,	762	April 4,	3	399	George Overaker,	Benjamin Beall,-	57f.	On St. Catharine's creek,	Do.	May 6, 1786.
" 29,	763	April 10,	3	401	George Mather,	James Mather,	2,000f.	On bayou Sara,	Do.	April 3, 1794.
" 29,	764	April 10,	3	403	James Andrews,	James Frazier,	800f.	On bayou Pierre,	Do.	Sept'r 1, 1795.
" 29,	765	April 10,	3	405	Leonard Pomet,	Joseph Vidal,	Lot No.	1, of sq. No. 2, Natchez,	Do.	
" 29,	766	April 10,	3	407	Christopher Miller, assignee of Thomas Bills,	Margaret Ury,	Lot No.	Lot No. 3, of sq. No. 12, Natchez,	Do.	
" 29,	767	April 10,	3	409	Margaret Ury, -	Margaret Ury,	Part of	Lot No. 3, of sq. No. 12, Natchez,	Do.	
" 30,	768	May 15,	3	411	David Ferguson,	Louis Fauré,	14f.	In the city of Natchez,	Do.	Feb'y 24, 1795.
" 30,	769	May 15,	3	413	David Ferguson,	Francis Lennan, -	5f.	In the city of Natchez,	Do.	Feb'y 6, 1795.
" 30,	770	May 15,	3	415	George D. Banks,	Daniel Clark,	500	On the Mississippi,	British,	Jan'y 2, 1768.
" 30,	771	May 15,	3	417	David Ferguson,	Emanuel Maddin,	100	On Second creek,	Do.	Feb'y 16, 1778.
" 30,	772	May 15,	3	419	David Ferguson,	William Hoyes,-	400	On Second creek,	Do.	Nov'r 14, 1776.
" 30,	773	May 16,	3	421	William Murray,	Cornelius McCann,	Half of	Lot No. 2, of sq. No. 32, Natchez,	Spanish,	April 6, 1795.
" 30,	774	May 16,	3	423	John J. Walton,	Richard Harrison,	Lot in	the city of Natchez,	Do.	March 1, 1783.
" 30,	775	May 16,	3	425	Stephen Minor,	Richard Harrison,	59f.	Near Natchez,	Do.	March 1, 1783.
" 30,	776	May 16,	3	427	Palser Shilling,	Richard Harrison,	2f.	Near Natchez,	Do.	March 1, 1783.
" 30,	777	May 16,	3	429	David Ferguson,	Richard Harrison,	2f.	Near Natchez,	Do.	March 1, 1783.
" 31,	778	May 27,	3	431	Nathaniel Tomlinson, -	Jacob Winfree, -	1,000	On Second creek,	British,	July 7, 1773.

THOMAS H. WILLIAMS.

REGISTER'S OFFICE WEST OF PEARL RIVER, *June 1, 1806.*

REGISTER A—Continued.

Abstract of Certificates entered with the Register of the Land Office west of Pearl river, during the month of September, 1806, grounded on British and Spanish patents.

When entered.	No.	Date.	Recorded. Vol.	Page.	To whom granted.	Name of original grantee.	Quantity allowed.	Situation.	Whence derived.	Date of patent.
1806.		1806.					Acres.			
Sept'r 8,	779	August 20,	3	433	Legal representatives of William Ferguson,	Thomas Harman,	325	Cole's creek, -	British,	April 22, 1777.
" 8,	780	August 20,	3	435	George Cochran and Patsey Harrison, -	Thomas Harman,	325	Cole's creek, -	Do.	April 22, 1777.
" 8,	781	August 20,	3	437	Ezekiel Dewit, in right of his wife,	William Kennison,	400f.	On the waters of Homochitto,	Spanish,	Aug. 20, 1794.
" 8,	782	August 20,	3	439	Phebe Dayton,	Phebe Calvit,	Lot No.	3, of sq. No. 13, Natchez,	Do.	Oct'r 24, 1795.
" 8,	783	August 20,	3	441	Robert Moore,	George Rapalje, -	231f.	Near city of Natchez,	Do.	March 1, 1788.
" 8,	784	August 20,	3	443	Robert Moore,	Ebenezer Rees, -	320f.	St. Catharine's creek,	Do.	June 20, 1795.
" 8,	785	August 20,	3	445	Legal representatives of Patrick Connelly,	Solomon Swayze,	Lot No.	1, of sq. No. 18, Natchez,	Do.	Oct'r 5, 1795.
" 8,	786	August 20,	3	447	Richard Sparks,	Benjamin Fooy, -	320f.	Bayou Pierre,	Do.	Aug. 29, 1791.

REGISTER'S OFFICE WEST OF PEARL RIVER, *October 1, 1806.*

THOMAS H. WILLIAMS.

REGISTER A —Continued.

Abstract of Certificates entered with the Register of the Land Office west of Pearl river, during the month of March, 1807, grounded on British and Spanish patents.

When entered.	Commissioners' certificates.		Recorded.		Claim.				Title.	
	No.	Date.	Vol.	Page.	To whom granted.	Name of original grantee.	Quantity allowed.	Situation.	Whence derived.	Date of patent.
1807.		1807.					Acres.			
March 7,	787	March 4,	3	449	Ferdinand L. Claiborne,	George Robbins,	400f.	Sandy creek,	Spanish,	Jan'y 20, 1793.
" 7,	788	March 4,	3	451	William Morrison,	Joseph Pagé,	720f.	Bayou Pierre,	Do.	April 13, 1790.
" 7,	789	March 4,	3	453	William Scott, in right of his wife Clara,	Henry Lafleur,	400f.	St. Catharine's creek,	Do.	March 1, 1787.
" 7,	790	March 4,	3	455	William Scott, in right of his wife Clara,	Charles Truffo,	100f.	St. Catharine's creek,	Do.	March 15, 1788.
" 7,	791	March 4,	3	457	George Cochran,	William Curtis,	200f.	Cole's creek,	Do.	Jan'y 20, 1793.
" 28,	792	March 18,	3	459	Peter A. Vandorn,	Richard Bell,	500f.	Cole's creek,	Do.	Feb'y 29, 1788.

LAND OFFICE, WEST OF PEARL RIVER, *May 1, 1807.*

THOMAS H. WILLIAMS, *Register.*

REGISTER A—Continued.

When entered.	Commissioners' certificates.		Recorded.		Claim.				Title.	
	No.	Date.	Vol.	Page.	To whom granted.	Name of original grantee.	Quantity allowed.	Situation.	Whence derived.	Date of patent.
1807.		1807.					Acres.			
April 7,	793	March 30,	3	461	Legal representatives of Robert Abrams,	Reuben Alexander	269f.	Second creek,	Spanish,	March 6, 1788.
" 9,	794	April 8,	3	463	Legal representatives of Anthony Hutchins,	Thomas Hutchins,	1,000f.	Second creek,	Do.	Feb'y 29, 1788.

LAND OFFICE, WEST OF PEARL RIVER, *May 1, 1807.*

THOS. H. WILLIAMS, *Register.*

REGISTER A—Continued.

Abstract of Certificates entered with the Register of the Land Office west of Pearl river, during the months of May and June, 1807, grounded on British and Spanish patents.

| Commissioners' certificates | | | | | To whom granted | Claim | | | Title | |
When entered	No.	Date	Recorded Vol.	Recorded Page		Name of original grantee	Quantity allowed	Situation	Whence derived	Date of patent
1807.		1807.					Acres.			
May 26,	795	May 19,	3	465	William Carney, assignee of Edward Murray,	Edward Murray,	1,000.	Bayou Pierre,	Spanish,	August 20, 1795.
" 26,	696	May 19,	3	467	Legal representatives of Robert Scott,	Robert Scott,	Lot No.	2, of square No. 4, Natchez,	Do.	Sept. 27, 1794.
June 22,	797	June 9,	3	469	Fergus A. Duplantier,	F. A. Duplantier,	1,740.	River Mississippi,	Do.	June 17, 1795.
" 22,	798	June 9,	3	471	Charles Trudeau,	Charles Trudeau,	1,180.	River Big Black,	British,	Octob. 20, 1794.
" 22,	799	June 9,	3	473	Zachariah Smith,	Joseph Vidal,	873	Buffalo creek,	Spanish,	April 11, 1795.
" 22,	800	June 9,	3	475	Legal representatives of Robert Scott,		Lot No.	4, of square No. 5, Natchez,	Do.	Nov. 16, 1792.
" 22,	801	June 9,	3	477	Francis Bazo and Anthony Grass,	F. Bazo and A. Grass,	800.	River Mississippi,	British,	May 4, 1775.
" 22,	802	June 9,	3	479	Hore Browse Trist,	Enoch Horton,	200	Second creek,	Spanish,	July 16, 1787.
" 22,	803	June 9,	3	481	James Mather,	Richard Deval,	800.	Cole's creek,	Do.	July 17, 1790.
" 22,	804	June 9,	3	483	Patrick Connelly,	John Girault,	90.	St. Catharine's creek,	Do.	Octob. 20, 1788.
" 22,	805	June 10,	3	485	Catharine Surget,	James Elliott,	800.	Cole's creek,	Do.	Sept. 21, 1772.
" 22,	806	June 11,	3	487	Legal representatives of Samuel Wells,	Innis Hooper,	257	Second creek,	British,	Sept. 21, 1772.
" 22,	807	June 11,	3	489	Legal representatives of Samuel Wells,	Samuel Wells,	1,000	Second creek,	Do.	May 8, 1786.
" 22,	808	June 12,	3	491	Andrew Marschalk,	William Barland,	Lot No.	4, of square No. 9, Natchez,	Spanish,	June 10, 1788.
" 22,	809	June 13,	3	493	Christopher Lea,	Joseph Dias,	12,800	feet, city of Natchez,	Do.	June 12, 1788.
" 22,	810	June 13,	3	495	Christopher Lea,	Alonzo Segovia,	9,600	feet, city of Natchez,	Do.	May 30, 1789.
" 22,	811	June 15,	3	497	James Moore,	Alexander de Bouille,	1,000.	Sandy creek,	Do.	
" 22,	812	June 15,	3	499	William Patterson,	Edward Patterson,	800.	Fairchild's creek,	Do.	March 20, 1789.
" 22,	813	June 15,	3	501	William Patterson,	Thomas Erwin,	800.	Fairchild's creek,	Do.	March 20, 1789.
" 22,	814	June 15,	3	503	William Patterson,	Thomas Patterson,	800.	Fairchild's creek,	Do.	March 20, 1789.
" 22,	815	June 11,	3	505	Legal representatives of William Moore,	John Tier,	Lot No.	5, of square No. 20, Natchez,	Do.	Jan'y 15, 1795.

WASHINGTON, MISSISSIPPI TERRITORY, July 1, 1807.

THOMAS H. WILLIAMS, Register.

REGISTER B.

Abstract of Certificates entered with the Register of the Land Office for the District west of Pearl river, during the month of September, 1806, on which patents may issue without the payment of purchase money.

When entered	No.	Date (1806)	Recorded Vol.	Recorded Page	To whom granted	Name of original grantee or claimant	Quantity allowed (Acres)	Situation	Whence derived	Date of order of survey or settlem't
Sept'r 1, 1806	1	June 2	4	1	John J. Walton, -	Rebecca McCabe,	Lot in	the city of Natchez,	Spanish,	May 6, 1795.
" 1	2	June 2	4	2	The legal representatives of Bernard Lintot,	Rebecca McCabe,	Lot in	the city of Natchez,	Do.	May 6, 1795.
" 1	3	June 2	4	4	John J. Walton, -	Charles M. Maltze,	Lot in	the city of Natchez,	Do.	
" 1	4	June 2	4	5	Leonard Pomet, -	Hugh Coyle,	Part of	lot No. 2, of sq. No. 8, Natchez,	Do.	March 2, 1793.
" 1	5	June 2	4	6	William Price, -	Hugh Coyle,	Part of	lot No. 2, of sq. No. 8, Natchez,	Do.	March 2, 1793.
" 1	6	June 2	4	7	Legal representatives of George Cochr—,	George Cochran,	Lot No.	2, of sq. No. 9, Natchez,	Do.	Aug. 25, 1794.
" 1	7	June 2	4	8	Juliana Stockpole,	Bridget Roberts,	Lot No.	3, of sq. No. 4, Natchez,	Do.	April 16, 1792.
" 1	8	June 2	4	9	Richard King, -	John Bolls,	Lot No.	4, of sq. No. 33, Natchez,	Do.	July 29, 1794.
" 1	9	June 2	4	10	Richard King, -	Prosper King,	Lot No.	5, of sq. No. 33, Natchez,	Do.	July 20, 1794.
" 1	10	June 2	4	11	Justus C. King,	Justus C. King,	Lot No.	2, of sq. No. 33, Natchez,	Do.	July 20, 1795.
" 1	11	June 2	4	12	John Eldergill,	Charles Jones,	Lot No.	1, of sq. No. 34, Natchez,	Do.	Aug. 29, 1795.
" 1	12	June 2	4	13	John Eldergill,	John Eldergill,	Lot No.	3, of sq. No. 25, Natchez,	Do.	Sept'r 19, 1795.
" 1	13	June 2	4	14	George Overaker,	Maria G. Sollivrellas,	Lot No.	4, of sq. No. 2, Natchez,	Do.	Feb'y 13, 1793.
" 1	14	June 4	4	15	Legal representatives of Moses Bonner,	Moses Bonner,	800f.	Fairchild's creek,	Do.	Feb'y 24, 1795.
" 1	15	June 4	4	16	Willis Bonner, -	Willis Bonner,	360f.	Fairchild's creek,	Do.	April 7, 1794.
" 1	16	June 4	4	17	Jonathan Guice,	Jonathan Guice,	400f.	Waters of Sandy creek,	Do.	March 28, 1794.
" 1	17	June 4	4	18	John Buller, -	John Buller,	355f.	Waters of St. Catharine's,	Do.	Feb'y 24, 1795.
" 1	18	June 4	4	19	Caleb Perkins, -	John Barton,	203f.	Waters of St. Catharine's,	Do.	April 7, 1791.
" 1	19	June 4	4	20	Legal representatives of Robert Watts,	Robert Watts,	400f.	Waters of Cole's creek,	Do.	Dec'r 18, 1789.
" 1	20	June 4	4	21	Wilford Hoggatt,	Hezekiah Williams,	244f.	Waters of Sandy creek,	Do.	Nov'r 1, 1788.
" 1	21	June 4	4	22	Nicholas Rabb,	David Lambert,	250f.	St. Catharine's creek,	Do.	March 19, 1789.
" 1	22	June 4	4	23	Barton Hannon,	Benjamin Bullock,	300f.	Second creek,	Do.	Jan'y 16, 1789.
" 1	23	June 4	4	24	Christian Harman,	Christian Harman,	132f.	St. Catharine's creek,	Do.	Jan'y 28, 1795.
" 1	24	June 4	4	25	William Scott, -	Peter Nelson,	200f.	Near the city of Natchez,	Do.	Aug. 20, 1782.
" 1	25	June 9	4	26	Thomas Ford, -	Thomas Ford,	640	Homochitto river,	Occupancy,	March 30, 1798.
" 1	26	June 9	4	27	Samuel Ratcliff,	Christopher Bingaman,	640	Homochitto river,	Do.	March 30, 1798.
" 1	27	June 9	4	28	Jacob Shilling, -	Jacob Shilling,	640	Well's creek,	Do.	March 30, 1798.
" 1	28	June 9	4	29	Jacob Guice, -	Jacob Guice,	640	Cole's creek,	Do.	March 30, 1798.
" 1	29	June 9	4	30	Alexander Farar,	Alexander Farar,	333¾	Cole's creek,	Do.	March 30, 1798.
" 1	30	June 9	4	31	Demsey White,	Demsey White,	640	St. Catharine's creek,	Do.	March 30, 1798.
" 1	31	June 10	4	32	Joseph Harrison,	Joseph Harrison,	328	Bayou Pierre,	Do.	March 30, 1798.
" 1	32	June 10	4	33	John B. Thery, assignee of Edmund Hall,	Henry Millburn,	640	Bayou Pierre,	Do.	March 30, 1798.
" 1	33	June 10	4	34	Austin Holbrook and David Berry,	John Cravens,	414	Sandy creek,	Do.	March 30, 1798.
" 1	34	June 10	4	35	Daniel Hawley, -	Daniel Hawley,	137½	Sandy creek,	Do.	March 30, 1798.
" 1	35	June 11	4	36	Ann Martin, -	Thomas Martin,	152	St. Catharine's creek,	Do.	March 30, 1798.
" 1	36	June 11	4	37	Leg'l representatives of Martin Hackler,	Martin Hackler,	640	Cole's creek,	Do.	March 30, 1798.
" 6	37	August 28	4	56	Benjamin Tyree, -	John Cammack,	Lot No.	3, of sq. No. 32, Natchez,	Spanish,	Nov'r 7, 1794.
" 6	38	August 28	4	57	Stephen Henderson and Arthur Andrews,	James Wylie,	Lot No.	1, of sq. No. 32, Natchez,	Occupancy,	March 30, 1798.

ABSTRACT for SEPTEMBER, 1806—Continued.

When entered.	No.	Date.	Recorded. Vol.	Page.	To whom granted.	Name of original grantee or claimant.	Quantity allowed.	Situation.	Whence derived.	Date of order of survey or settlem't.
1806. Septr 6,	39	August 28	4	42	James Gormley and Edward Pain,	John Read,	Acres. Half of	lot No. 2, of sq. No. 32, Natchez,	Spanish,	Oct'r 4, 1794.
" 6,	40	August 29	4	43	James Foster,	Zechariah Smith,	240f.	St. Catharine's creek,	Do.	May 5, 1786.
" 6,	41	August 29	4	44	Henry Stampley,	George Stampley,	400f.	Cole's creek,	Do.	Feb'y 26, 1788.
" 6,	42	August 29	4	45	John M. Alston,	Clement Dyson,	400f.	Cole's creek,	Do.	March 28, 1794.
" 6,	43	August 29	4	46	John Perkey,	Jacob Strupes,	127f.	St. Catharine's creek,	Do.	March 2, 1793.
" 6,	45	August 29	4	47		George Clare,	400f.	Cole's creek,	Do.	Nov'r 25, 1789.
" 6,	46	August 29	4	48	Legal representatives of Daniel Mygatt,	Daniel Mygatt,	155f.	Cole's creek,	Occupancy,	Nov'r 25, 1789.
" 6,	47	August 29	4	49	Abner Marble,	Abner Marble,	640	Cole's creek,	Do.	March 30, 1798.
" 6,	48	August 29	4	50	Abraham Mayes,	Abraham Mayes,	640	Cole's creek,	Do.	March 30, 1798.
" 6,	49	August 29	4	51	John M. Alston,	Thomas Dyson,	640	Cole's creek,	Do.	March 30, 1798.
" 6,	50	August 29	4	52	Frankey Dromgoole,	John Dyson,	640	Cole's creek,	Do.	March 30, 1798.
" 6,	51	August 29	4	53	Legal representatives of Barnabas Isinwood,	Barnabas Isinwood,	342	Cole's creek,	Do.	March 30, 1798.
" 6,	52	August 29	4	54	Wm. Brooks, assignee of Robert Throckmorton,	Simon Grimbear,	600	Cole's creek,	Do.	March 30, 1798.
" 6,	53	August 29	4	55	William Miller,	Samuel Mason,	402	Bayou Pierre,	Do.	March 30, 1798.
" 6,	54	August 29	4	56	Theophilus Marble,	Jonathan Curtis,	318	Cole's creek,	Do.	March 30, 1798.
" 6,	55	August 30	4	58	Edward King,	John Calvit,	310	Cole's and Sandy creeks,	Do.	March 30, 1798.
" 6,	56	Septr 4,	4	59	Samuel Bridges,	Nathan Green,	196	Cole's creek,	Do.	March 30, 1798.
" 6,	57	Septr 5,	4	60	Stephen Douglass,	John Ivers,	240f.	Bayou Pierre,	Spanish,	April 26, 1790.
Septr 9,	58	Septr 8,	4	61	Nathaniel Holly,	William Miller,	640	Bayou Pierre,	Occupancy,	March 30, 1798.
" 9,	59	Septr 8,	4	62	Thomas Ingles,	Nathaniel Holly,	640	Bayou Pierre,	Do.	March 30, 1798.
" 9,	60	Septr 8,	4	63	Thomas Crabb,	Enoch Bodwell,	640	Bayou Pierre,	Do.	March 30, 1798.
" 9,	61	Septr 8,	4	64	Lucius Smith,	Robert Ashley,	500	Bayou Pierre,	Do.	March 30, 1798.
Septr 11,	62	Septr 10,	4	65	Eliza and Ann Cobun,	Lucius Smith,	240f.	Bayou Pierre,	Spanish,	April 26, 1790.
" 11,	63	Septr 10,	4	66	Eliza and Ann Cobun,	Jacob Cobun,	324f.	Bayou Pierre,	Do.	Jan'y 11, 1787.
" 11,	64	Septr 10,	4	67	Abner Wilkinson,	Jacob Cobun,	476f.	Bayou Pierre,	Do.	Jan'y 11, 1787.
" 11,	65	Septr 10,	4	68	Legal representatives of Daniel Mygatt,	Josiah Smith,	240f.	Bayou Pierre,	Do.	July 22, 1789.
" 11,	66	Septr 10,	4	69	Simeon Hollayday,	Simeon Hollayday,	345f.	Bayou Pierre,	Do.	Nov'r 25, 1789.
" 11,	67	Septr 10,	4	70	Seth Rundell,	Thomas Ashley,	640	Bayou Pierre,	Occupancy,	March 30, 1798.
" 11,	68	Septr 10,	4	71	John Burns,	Charles Simmons,	640	Bayou Pierre,	Do.	March 30, 1798.
Septr 27,	69	Septr 22,	4	72	David Simmons,	Samuel Hackler,	640	Bayou Pierre,	Do.	March 30, 1798.
" 27,	44	August 29,	4	74	Willis McDonald,		400f.	Cole's creek,	Spanish,	March 2, 1793.
" 27,	70	Septr 26,	4	75			530	Cole's creek,	Occupancy,	March 30, 1798.
" 27,	71	Septr 26,	4	76	John Watts,	John Watts,	298	Cole's creek,	Do.	March 30, 1798.

REGISTER's OFFICE WEST OF PEARL RIVER, *October* 1, 1806.

THOMAS H. WILLIAMS.

REGISTER B—Continued.

Abstract of Certificates entered with the Register of the Land Office west of Pearl river, during the month of October, 1806, on which patents may issue without the payment of purchase money.

When entered.	No.	Date.	Recorded. Vol.	Page.	To whom granted:	Original grantee or claimant.	Quantity allowed.	Situation.	Whence derived.	Date of order of survey or settlement.
1806. Octob. 30,	72	August 28,	4	77	David Henderbrand,	David Henderbrand,	350f.	Cole's creek,	Spanish,	Feb'y 24, 1795.
" 30,	73	August 28,	4	78	Legal representatives of James Rapalje, dec'd.	James Rapalje,	890f.	Big Black,	Spanish,	April 26, 1790.
" 30,	74	August 28,	4	79	Isaac Rapalje,	Isaac Rapalje,	800f.	Big Black,	Spanish,	April 26, 1790.
" 30,	75	August 28,	4	80	Leonard Kipley,	Leonard Kipley,	350f.	Big Black,	Spanish,	Feb'y 24, 1795.
" 30,	76	August 28,	4	81	Abel Eastman,	Abel Eastman,	640	Big Black,	Occupancy,	March 30, 1798.
" 30,	77	August 28,	4	82	William Griffin,	William Griffing,	640	Big Black,	Occupancy,	March 30, 1798.
" 30,	78	August 28,	4	83	John Anderton,	John Anderton,	640	Big Black,	Occupancy,	March 30, 1798.
" 30,	79	August 28,	4	84	Anthony Glass,	Benjamin Steele,	640	Big Black,	Occupancy,	March 30, 1798.
" 31,	80	August 30,	4	85	Katura Proctor,	Katura Proctor,	640	Bayou Pierre,	Occupancy,	March 30, 1798.
" 31,	81	August 30,	4	86	Benjamin Newman,	Benjamin Newman,	670f.	St. Catharine's,	Spanish,	Dec. 29, 1791.
" 31,	82	August 30,	4	87	Samuel Holly,	Samuel Holly,	640	Bayou Pierre,	Occupancy,	March 30, 1799.
" 31,	83	August 30,	4	88	John Stowers,	John Stowers,	200	Big Black,	British,	Feb'y 11, 1779.

REGISTER'S OFFICE WEST OF PEARL RIVER, *November 1, 1806.*

THOMAS H. WILLIAMS.

REGISTER B—Continued.

Abstract of Certificates entered with the Register of the Land Office west of Pearl river, during the month of February, 1807, on which patents may issue without the payment of any purchase money.

When entered.	No.	Date.	Vol.	Page.	To whom granted.	Original grantee or claimant.	Quantity allowed.	Situation.	Whence derived.	Date of order of survey or settlem't.
1807. Feb. 9,	84	February 3,	4	89	Samuel Montgomery,	John Pollard,	640 Acres.	Bayou Pierre,	Occupancy,	March 30, 1798.
" 9,	85	February 3,	4	90	Darling Bradley,	Darling Bradley,	640	Wells's creek,	Do.	March 30, 1798.
" 9,	86	February 3,	4	91	David Carradine,	David Carradine,	640	Cole's creek,	Do.	March 30, 1798.
" 9,	87	February 3,	4	92	John James,	Robert Pendergrast,	448	River Homochitto,	Do.	March 30, 1798.
" 9,	88	February 3,	4	93	Joseph Ballin,	William Curtis,	640	Cole's creek,	Do.	March 30, 1798.
" 9,	89	February 3,	4	94	Ezra McCall,	Ezra McCall,	640	Bayou Pierre,	Do.	March 30, 1798.
" 9,	90	February 3,	4	95	William Howey,	William Howey,	640	Bayou Pierre,	Do.	March 30, 1798.
" 9,	91	February 3,	4	96	Legal representatives of Ephraim Coleman,	Ephraim Coleman,	173	Cole's creek,	Do.	March 30, 1798.
" 9,	92	February 3,	4	97	A. Gardner and J. Bedsil, assignees of Jesse Lum,	Jesse Lum,	640	Bayou Pierre,	Do.	March 30, 1798.
" 9,	93	February 3,	4	98	Legal representatives of Wm. Thompson,	William Thompson,	640	Bayou Pierre,	Do.	March 30, 1798.
" 9,	94	February 3,	4	99	Anthony Vauchere, assignee of Anthony Nicholas,	John Carroll,	204	Fairchild's creek,	Do.	March 30, 1798.
" 9,	95	February 3,	4	100	John Brooks,	John Brooks,	640	Cole's creek,	Do.	March 30, 1798.
" 9,	96	February 3,	4	101	Henry Mamadue,	Henry Mamadue,	640	Fairchild's creek,	Do.	March 30, 1798.
" 9,	97	February 3,	4	102	Henry Mamadue,	Anthony Delgan,	640	River Mississippi,	Do.	March 30, 1798.
" 9,	98	February 3,	4	103	William Ogtesley,	Benjamin Fletcher,	640	Wells's creek,	Do.	March 30, 1798.
" 9,	99	February 3,	4	104	James Clark,	James Clark,	105f.	Cole's creek,	Spanish,	Feb'y 24, 1795.
" 9,	100	February 3,	4	105	Philip Neville,	Philip Neville,	500f.	Cole's creek,	Do.	Jan'y 28, 1795.
" 9,	101	February 3,	4	106	George Fitzgerald,	George Fitzgerald,	1,000f.	Fairchild's creek,	Do.	March 19, 1795.
" 10,	102	February 4,	4	107	Legal representatives of James Magill,	James Magil,	500f.	Doud's creek,	Do.	April 25, 1790.
" 10,	103	February 4,	4	108	John Bishop, assignee of Wm. Kirkwood,	William Kirkwood,	479	River Mississippi,	Do.	March 28, 1794.
" 10,	104	February 4,	4	109	Ezekiel Perkins,	Joseph Perkins,	500f.	Wells's creek,	Do.	Feb'y 24, 1795.
" 10,	105	February 4,	4	110	Abraham Horton,	Samuel L. Wells,	400f.	Bayou Sara,	Do.	Aug. 1, 1789.
" 10,	106	February 4,	4	111	Samuel Davis,	Samuel Davis,	300f.	Cole's creek,	Do.	Jan'y 16, 1789.
" 10,	107	February 4,	4	112	Legal representatives of Henry Mamadue,	John Fenton,	400f.	Fairchild's creek,	Do.	June 3, 1795.
" 10,	108	February 4,	4	113	John Fenton,	Palser Shilling,	165f.	Second creek,	Do.	March 28, 1794.
" 10,	109	February 4,	4	114	Palser Shilling,	Hezekiah Williams,	400f.	River Mississippi,	Do.	Nov. 4, 1789.
" 10,	110	February 4,	4	115	Robert Miller,	Mary de Witt,	250f.	Wells's creek,	Do.	Feb'y 15, 1788.
" 10,	111	February 4,	4	116	Joseph Parnill,	William Silkrigs,	400f.	St. Catharine's creek,	Do.	Jan'y 3, 1787.
" 10,	112	February 4,	4	117	David Eldridge,	Lewellin Price,	300f.	St. Catharine's creek,	Do.	Sept. 1, 1795.
" 10,	113	February 4,	4	118	George Cochrun,	Thomas Daniel,	26f.	Bayou Pierre,	Do.	April 7, 1791.
" 10,	114	February 4,	4	119	Thomas Daniel,	William Bishop,	240f.	Cole's creek,	Do.	March 2, 1793.
" 10,	115	February 4,	4	120	William Montgomery,	Lewis Chachere,	345f.	St. Catharine's creek,	Do.	April 3, 1784.
" 10,	116	February 4,	4	121	Thomas Dawson,	Reuben Dunham,	500f.	River Mississippi,	Do.	May 12, 1787.
" 10,	117	February 4,	4	122	John Wall,	Reuben Dunham,	308f.	Bayou Sara,	Do.	May 12, 1787.
" 10,	118	February 4,	4	123	Daniel Clark,	Reuben Dunham,	2	Bayou Sara,	Do.	May 12, 1787.
" 10,	119	February 4,	4	124	Maurice Custard,	Thomas Martin,	100f.	Bayou Sara,	Do.	May 12, 1787.
" 10,	120	February 4,	4	125			600f.	Second creek,	Do.	March 2, 1793.

ABSTRACT FOR FEBRUARY, 1807—Continued.

When entered (1807.)	No.	Date (1807.)	Vol.	Page	To whom granted	Original grantee or claimant	Quantity allowed (Acres.)	Situation	Whence derived	Date of order of survey or settlem't
Feb'y 10,	121	February 4	4	126	John Holland and Abijah Hunt,	Charles Carter,	450f.	Wells's creek,	Spanish,	Jan'y 6, 1789.
" 11,	122	February 5	4	127		John Lusk,	800f.	River Homochitto,	Do.	Dec'r 27, 1794.
" 11,	123	February 5	4	128	Andrew Watkins,	Patrick Sullivan,	245f.	Cole's creek,	Do.	June 20, 1790.
" 11,	124	February 5	4	129	William McIntosh,	Andrew Thompson,	240f.	Wells's creek,	Do.	Nov'r 18, 1789.
" 11,	125	February 5	4	130	Charles King,	Joshua Flowers,	200f.	St. Catharine's creek,	Do.	Jan'y 20, 1788.
" 11,	126	February 5	4	131	Benjamin Farrar,	Isaac Johnson,	1,100f.	Second creek,	Do.	March 28, 1794.
" 11,	127	February 5	4	132	James Moore,	Cadder Rabby,	400f.	Sandy creek,	Do.	Feb'y 24, 1795.
" 11,	128	February 5	4	133	James Moore,	Thomas Hubbard,	400f.	Bayou Pierre,	Do.	April 26, 1790.
" 11,	129	February 5	4	134	James Moore,	Thomas Wells,	240f.	River Homochitto,	Do.	Feb'y 24, 1795.
" 11,	130	February 5	4	135	Philip Hoggatt, assignee of William Fletcher,	Benjamin Fletcher,	150f.	Sandy creek,	Do.	June 11, 1788.
" 11,	131	February 5	4	136	Samuel Heady,	Samuel Heady,	600f.	Second creek,	Do.	March 28, 1794.
" 11,	132	February 5	4	137	Henry Platner,	Henry Platner,	200f.	Cole's creek,	Do.	April 30, 1794.
" 11,	133	February 5	4	138	Henry Platner,	Henry Platner,	247f.	Second creek,	Do.	Sept'r 3, 1789.
" 11,	134	February 5	4	139	Charles Surget,	William Cobb,	100f.	Second creek,	Do.	July 28, 1787.
" 11,	135	February 5	4	140	Charles Surget,	Arthur Cobb,	400f.	St. Catharine's creek,	Do.	April 16, 1787.
" 16,	136	February 9	4	165	Samuel Timberlake,	William Cobb,	500f.	Sandy creek,	Do.	July 28, 1787.
" 16,	137	February 9	4	166	Joshua Howard,	Benjamin Lanier,	1,000f.	Buffalo creek,	Do.	March 18, 1795.
" 16,	138	February 9	4	167	Mordecai Throckmorton and James Spain,	Patrick Foley,	410f.	Cole's creek,	Do.	May 25, 1795.
" 16,	139	February 9	4	168	Legal representatives of Richard Harrison,	Richard Harrison,	240f.	Bayou Sara,	Do.	Oct'r 12, 1787.
" 16,	140	February 9	4	169	Patrick Foley,	Reuben Jelks,	240f.	Bayou Sara,	Do.	March 28, 1794.
" 16,	141	February 9	4	170	John F. Carmichael,	Thomas Viles,	300f.	Sandy creek,	Do.	March 2, 1793.
" 16,	142	February 9	4	171	Lyman Harding,	Daniel Harrigill,	lot	Under the bluff at Natchez,	Do.	March 10, 1789.
" 16,	143	February 9	4	172	William Lintot,	Rebecca McCabe,	600f.	River Homochitto,	Do.	June 29, 1795.
" 16,	144	February 9	4	173	Stephen Henderson,	Mordecai Richards,	480f.	Bayou Pierre,	Do.	Jan'y 14, 1792.
" 17,	145	February 10	4	174	Geo. W. Humphreys (in right of his wife Sara) and Maria Dillingham,	Sara and Maria Smith,	111f.	St. Catharine's creek,	Do.	Feb'y 25, 1795.
" 17,	146	February 10	4	175	Robert Moore,	William Ferguson,	52f.	Sandy creek,	Do.	Dec'r 11, 1782.
" 17,	147	February 10	4	176	Anthony Dougherty,	William Ferguson,	368f.	St. Catharine's creek,	Do.	Dec'r 11, 1782.
" 17,	148	February 10	4	177	Richard Miller,	Christian Harman,	600f.	Sandy creek,	Do.	Jan'y 28, 1795.
" 17,	149	February 10	4	178	Legal representatives of James Nicholson,	James Nicholson,	187f.	Buffalo creek,	Do.	Jan'y 11, 1788.
" 17,	150	February 10	4	179	John Smith,	Mark Cole,	240f.	Fairchild's creek,	Do.	Feb'y 14, 1789.
" 17,	151	February 10	4	180	Thomas Sullivan,	Thomas Sullivan,	600f.	Cole's creek,	Do.	April 7, 1791.
" 17,	152	February 10	4	181	David Ferguson, assignee of Jacob Crumpholt,	Jacob Crumpholt,	500f.	Cole's creek,	Do.	Octob. 30, 1790.
" 17,	153	February 10	4	182	Thomas White,	Sarah Armstrong,	500f.	Bayou Pierre,	Do.	Sept. 13, 1794.
" 17,	154	February 10	4	183	William Dunbar,	Alexander McCulloch,	400f.	Buffalo creek,	Do.	Nov'r 25, 1789.
" 17,	155	February 10	4	184	William Dunbar,	Henry Nicholson,	400f.	River Homochitto,	Do.	Jan'y 16, 1789.
" 17,	156	February 10	4	185	Walter Burling,	Samuel Cooper, -	400f.	Sandy creek,	Do.	Feb'y 24, 1795.
" 17,	157	February 10	4	186	Ebenezer Rees,	Elizabeth Douglass,	500f.	Cole's creek,	Do.	Jan'y 16, 1789.
" 17,	158	February 10	4	187	Lewis Evans,	Sylvester Staus,	500f.	Wells's creek,	Do.	May 5, 1795.
" 17,	159	February 10	4	188	Joshua Howard,	Thomas Berry,	500f.	Wells's creek,	Do.	May 5, 1795.

ABSTRACT FOR FEBRUARY, 1807—Continued.

When entered.	No.	Date.	Rec. Vol.	Rec. Page	To whom granted.	Name of original grantee.	Quantity allowed (Acres.)	Situation.	Whence derived.	Date of order of survey or settlem't.
1807. Feb'y 17,	160	February 10,	4	189	William Conner, in right of his wife Mary,	Mary Savage,	1,000f.	Buffalo creek,	Spanish,	March 28, 1794.
" 17,	161	February 10,	4	190	Edmund Johnson,	Edmund Johnson,	600f.	Cole's creek,	Do.	Oct'r 30, 1790.
" 18,	162	February 11,	4	191	Benjamin Hook, assignee of Simon Hook,	David Mulkey,	70	St. Catharine's creek,	Do.	March 30, 1798.
" 18,	163	February 11,	4	192	John Vanderal,	John Vanderal, Sen.	300	Cole's creek,	Occupancy,	March 30, 1798.
" 18,	164	February 11,	4	193	Legal representative of David Jones,	David Jones,	640	River Mississippi,	Do.	March 30, 1798.
" 18,	165	February 11,	4	194	Reuben Brassfield,	Reuben Brassfield,	640	Buffalo creek,	Do.	March 30, 1798.
" 18,	166	February 11,	4	195	Edward Lovelace,	Edward Lovelace,	331	River Mississippi,	Do.	March 30, 1798.
" 18,	167	February 11,	4	196	David Lambert, assignee of Wm. Everitt,	James McNeely,	450	Buffalo creek,	Do.	March 30, 1798.
" 18,	168	February 11,	4	197	Newel Vick, assignee of John Hamberlin,	John Hamberlin,	400	Cole's creek,	Do.	March 30, 1798.
" 18,	169	February 11,	4	198	John Chambers,	Isaac Erwin,	640	Wells' creek,	Do.	March 30, 1798.
" 18,	170	February 11,	4	199	James Simmons,	James Simmons,	640	Cole's creek,	Do.	March 30, 1798.
" 18,	171	February 11,	4	200	Mary Cole,	Mary Cole,	640	Cole's creek,	Do.	March 30, 1798.
" 18,	172	February 11,	4	201	Abraham Scriber,	William Bird,	120	Fairchild's creek,	Do.	March 30, 1798.
" 18,	173	February 11,	4	202	Alexander Montgomery,	Buckner Pitman,	225	Bayou Pierre,	Do.	March 30, 1798.
" 18,	174	February 11,	4	203	James McNeely,	William Bovard,	640	Buffalo creek,	Do.	March 30, 1798.
" 18,	175	February 11,	4	204	Samuel Lusk,	Samuel Lusk,	640	River Homochitto,	Do.	March 30, 1798.
" 18,	176	February 11,	4	205	Philip Sessions, assignee of Wm. Glasscock,	William Glasscock,	170	Second creek,	Do.	March 30, 1798.
" 18,	177	February 11,	4	206	Bailey E. Chancy,	Earle Marble,	400	Cole's creek,	Do.	March 30, 1798.
" 18,	178	February 11,	4	207	John Nugent,	Benjamin Carroll,	535	Buffalo creek,	Do.	March 30, 1798.
" 18,	179	February 11,	4	208	Ezekiel De Witt,	Ezekiel De Wit,	167	St. Catharine's creek,	Do.	March 30, 1798.
" 18,	180	February 11,	4	209	Israel Smith, assignee of Elijah Phipps,	Elijah Phipps,	640	Buffalo creek,	Do.	March 30, 1798.
" 18,	181	February 11,	4	210	William A. Lusk,	William A. Lusk,	640	Buffalo creek,	Do.	March 30, 1798.
" 18,	182	February 13,	4	211	James Davenport,	James Davenport,	600	Mississippi river,	Do.	March 30, 1798.
" 20,	183	February 13,	4	212	Abraham Clawson,	Thomas Splane,	637	Cole's creek,	Do.	March 30, 1798.
" 20,	184	February 13,	4	213	Abraham Martin,	John Odam and others,	640	Sandy creek,	Do.	March 30, 1798.
" 20,	185	February 13,	4	214	Abner Bickham,	Henry Jacobs,	640	River Homochitto,	Do.	March 30, 1798.
" 20,	186	February 13,	4	215	Joseph Sessions, assignee of John Mitchell,	John Mitchell,	640	Sandy creek,	Do.	March 30, 1798.
" 20,	187	February 13,	4	216	David Lattimore, assignee of Charles Marler,	Charles Marler,	640	Buffalo creek,	Do.	March 30, 1798.
" 20,	188	February 13,	4	217	William Ogden,	William Ogden,	605	Bayou Sara,	Do.	March 30, 1798.
" 20,	189	February 13,	4	218	William Fanner,	William Fanner,	500	Bayou Sara,	Do.	March 30, 1798.
" 20,	190	February 13,	4	219	Richard Sessions,	Robert Shuffield,	535	Sandy creek,	Do.	March 30, 1798.
" 20,	191	February 13,	4	220	John Erwin,	John Erwin,	635	Sandy creek,	Do.	March 30, 1798.
" 20,	192	February 13,	4	221	Phebe Goodwin,	Phebe Goodwin,	300	Bayou Pierre,	Do.	March 30, 1798.
" 20,	193	February 13,	4	222	John Searcy,	John Searcy,	640	Cole's creek,	Do.	March 30, 1798.
" 20,	194	February 13,	4	223	James Howard,	Sarah Kelly,	502	Sandy creek,	Do.	March 30, 1798.
" 20,	195	February 13,	4	224	Isma Foreman,	Isma Foreman,	320	Cole's creek,	Do.	March 30, 1798.
" 20,	196	February 13,	4	225	Legal representatives of Ruffin Gray,	Ruffin Gray,	270	River Homochitto,	Do.	March 30, 1798.
" 20,	197	February 13,	4	226	Ephraim Story,	Ephraim Story,	640	Bayou Pierre,	Do.	March 30, 1798.
" 20,	198	February 13,	4	227	Joseph White,	Joseph White,	640	Bayou Pierre,	Do.	March 30, 1798.
" 20,	199	February 13,	4	228	James Patton,	Eli Bunch,	640	Buffalo creek,	Do.	March 30, 1798.
" 20,	200	February 13,	4	229	Stephen Ambrose,	Augustus Roddy,	640	River Homochitto,	Do.	March 30, 1798.

ABSTRACT FOR FEBRUARY, 1807—Continued.

When entered.	Commissioners' certificates.				To whom granted.	Claim.			Title.	
	No.	Date.	Recorded.			Name of original grantee.	Quantity allowed.	Situation.	Whence derived.	Date of order of survey or settlem't.
			Vol.	Page.						
1807.		1807.					Acres.			
Feb'y 20,	201	February 13,	4	230	John Smith, -	John Smith, -	640	Bayou Pierre, -	Occupancy.	March 30, 1798.
" 20,	202	February 13,	4	231	Joseph Pannill, assignee of John Tally, Jun.	John Tally, Jun. -	640	River Homochitto, -	Do.	March 30, 1798.
" 24,	203	February 19,	4	232	Philip Sikes, -	Ebenezer Fulsome,	640	River Homochitto, -	Do.	March 30, 1798.
" 24,	204	February 19,	4	233	Elizabeth Swayze, -	Elizabeth Swayze, -	102	St. Catharine's creek,	Do.	March 30, 1798.
" 24,	205	February 19,	4	234	John Collins, assignee of Rebecca Graton,	Marian Sanders, -	640	Buffalo creek, -	Do.	March 30, 1798.
" 24,	206	February 19,	4	235	J. Holland and A. Hunt, -	James Hayes, -	640	River Homochitto, -	Do.	March 30, 1798.
" 24,	207	February 19,	4	236	Stephen Douglass, -	John Hamilton, -	500	Bayou Pierre, -	Do.	March 30, 1798.
" 24,	208	February 19,	4	237	Vincent Carter, -	Vincent Carter, -	640	Wells's creek, -	Do.	March 30, 1798.
" 24,	209	February 19,	4	238	Caleb Biggs, -	Caleb Biggs, -	640	Week's creek, -	Do.	March 30, 1798.
" 24,	210	February 19,	4	239	Henry Phipps, -	William Nicholson, -	640	Buffalo creek, -	Do.	March 30, 1798.
" 24,	211	February 19,	4	240	Thomas McCrorey, -	Thomas Lamphier, -	640	River Homochitto, -	Do.	March 30, 1798.
" 24,	212	February 19,	4	241	James Truly, -	James Truly, -	355	Cole's creek, -	Do.	March 30, 1798.

LAND OFFICE WEST OF PEARL RIVER, *March* 1, 1807.

THOMAS H. WILLIAMS.

102

REGISTER B—Continued.

Abstract of Certificates entered with the Register of the Land Office west of Pearl river, during the month of March, 1807, on which patents may issue without the payment of any purchase money.

When entered.	No.	Date.	Vol.	Page.	To whom granted.	Name of original grantee, or claimant.	Quantity allowed.	Situation.	Whence derived.	Date of order of survey or settlement.
1807. March 7,	213	March 4,	4	242	Adam Rum, -	Adam Rum, -	Acres. 500	Cole's creek, -	Occupancy,	March 30, 1798.
" 7,	214	March 4,	4	243	James Hyland, Sen., -	James Hyland, Sen., -	640	Big Black, -	Do.	March 30, 1798.
" 7,	215	March 4,	4	244	James Harman, -	James Harman, -	500	Bayou Pierre, -	Do.	March 30, 1798.
" 7,	216	March 4,	4	245	Jesse King, -	Elizabeth Reed, -	640	River Homochitto, -	Do.	March 30, 1798.
" 7,	217	March 4,	4	246	Thomas Lovelace, -	Thomas Lovelace, -	596	Buffalo creek, -	Do.	March 30, 1798.
" 7,	218	March 4,	4	247	John McCulloch, -	Lewis Davis, -	640	River Homochitto, -	Do.	March 30, 1798.
" 7,	219	March 4,	4	248	Richard King, assignee of Joseph Ford, -	Joseph Ford, -	640	River Homochitto, -	Do.	March 30, 1798.
" 7,	220	March 4,	4	249	Legal representatives of Joseph Miller, dec'd, -	Joseph Miller, -	350	Buffalo creek, -	Do.	March 30, 1798.
" 7,	221	March 4,	4	250	Justus Andrews, -	Justus Andrews, -	592	Buffalo creek, -	Do.	March 30, 1798.
" 7,	222	March 4,	4	251	James Howard, assignee of Zadock Barrow, -	Zadock Barrow, -	640	River Homochitto, -	Do.	March 30, 1798.
" 7,	223	March 4,	4	252	Littleberry West, -	Thomas Nicholls, -	290	Cole's creek, -	Do.	March 30, 1798.
" 7,	224	March 4,	4	253	Landon Davis, -	Landon Davis, -	640	River Homochitto, -	Do.	March 30, 1798.
" 9,	225	March 6,	4	254	William Adams, -	John Adams, -	201	St. Catharine's creek, -	Do.	Dec'r 3, 1794.
" 9,	226	March 6,	4	255	John H. White, -	John H. White, -	300f.	St. Catharine's creek, -	Spanish,	March 30, 1798.
" 9,	227	March 6,	4	256	Abijah Hunt, -	Harly Perry, -	600	Bayou Pierre, -	Occupancy,	April 26, 1790.
" 9,	228	March 6,	4	257	John Gaskins, -	John Gaskins, -	330f.	Cole's creek, -	Spanish,	March 30, 1798.
" 9,	229	March 6,	4	258	David Ferguson, assignee of Ebenezer Rees, -	Charles Howard, -	400	Fairchild's creek, -	Occupancy,	March 30, 1798.
" 9,	230	March 6,	4	259	Legal representatives of Charles Boardman, -	Abner Pipes, -	112f.	Fairchild's creek, -	Spanish,	Feb'y 2, 1793.
" 9,	231	March 6,	4	260	Legal representatives of Thomas L. White, -	Thomas L. White, -	500f.	Bayou Sara, -	Do.	May 20, 1794.
" 9,	232	March 6,	4	261	Simpson Holmes, -	Simpson Holmes, -	640	Beaver creek, -	Occupancy,	March 30, 1798.

LAND OFFICE WEST OF PEARL RIVER, *April* 1, 1807.

THOMAS H. WILLIAMS.

REGISTER B—Continued.

Abstract of Certificates entered with the Register of the Land Office west of Pearl river, during the month of April, 1807, on which patents may issue without the payment of any purchase money.

Commissioners' certificates.					Claim.				Title.	
When entered.	No.	Vol.	Page.	Date.	To whom granted.	Name of original grantee or claimant.	Quantity allowed.	Situation.	Whence derived.	Date of order of survey or settlem't.
1807. April 7,	233	4	262	March 30,	Richard King, -	Gibson Clark, -	600f.	River Mississippi,	Spanish,	May 12, 1787.
" 7,	234	4	263	March 30,	Richard King, -	John B. Lapoint, -	400f.	River Mississippi,	Do.	August 21, 1790.
" 7,	235	4	264	March 30,	Legal representatives of Abner Pipes, -	Abner Pipes, -	488f.	River Mississippi,	Do.	Feb'y 2, 1793.
" 7,	236	4	265	March 30,	William Kirkwood, -	William Kirkwood, -	71	River Mississippi,	Do.	March 28, 1794.
" 7,	237	4	266	March 30,	James Clark, assignee of Hugh Nelson,	James Clark, -	114	Wells's creek,	Do.	Feb'y 24, 1795.
" 7,	238	4	267	March 30,	John Girault, -	John Montgomery, -	597f.	Bayou Pierre,	Do.	Jan'y 13, 1793.
" 7,	239	4	268	March 30,	Legal representatives of David Kennedy,	Benjamin Monsanto,	500f.	River Mississippi,	Do.	Sept'r 22, 1788.
" 7,	240	4	269	March 30,	William Dunbar, -	Policarpo Ieguillo,	300f.	Buffalo creek,	Do.	March 28, 1794.
" 7,	241	4	270	March 30,	Legal representatives of Frederick Calvit,	Frederick Calvit,	300f.	River Mississippi,	Do.	July 26, 1792.
" 7,	242	4	271	March 30,	Samuel Phipps, -	Samuel Phipps,	370f.	Second creek,	Do.	Sept'r 24, 1793.
" 7,	243	4	272	March 30,	Legal representatives of John Vauchoré,	John St. Germain,	1,000f.	River Mississippi,	Do.	June 10, 1786.
" 7,	244	4	273	March 30,	Thomas Calvit, -	Richard Devall, -	500f.	Cole's creek,	Do.	Nov'r 12, 1788.
" 7,	245	4	274	March 30,	Robert Moore, -	Jacob Cable,	74f.	St. Catharine's creek,	Do.	Dec'r 10, 1782.
" 7,	246	4	275	March 30,	William Mackey, -	Philip Neville,	100f.	Bayou Pierre,	Do.	Jan'y 24, 1795.
" 7,	247	4	276	March 30,	Legal representatives of Ebenezer Dayton,	Russel Jones,	140f.	St. Catharine's creek,	Do.	Dec'r 23, 1784.
" 7,	248	4	277	March 30,	Legal representatives of Wm. Hamberlin,	William Hamberlin,	315	Cole's creek, -	Occupancy,	March 30, 1798.
" 7,	249	4	278	March 30,	Elias Barnes, assignee of Francis Nailer,	James Lobdill,	467f.	Bayou Pierre, -	Spanish,	July 16, 1792.
" 7,	250	4	279	March 30,	Francis Nailer, -	William Cooper, -	186f.	Second creek, -	Do.	Oct'r 1, 1787.
" 8,	251	4	280	April 8,	John Still Lee, -	Jesse Edwards, -	600	Big Black, -	Occupancy,	March 30, 1798.
" 13,	252	4	281	April 9,	Stephen Richards, -	Stephen Richards,	640	Bayou Pierre,	Do.	March 30, 1798.
" 13,	253	4	282	April 9,	William Stampley, -	William Stampley,	640	Cole's creek, -	Do.	March 30, 1798.
" 13,	254	4	283	April 9,	Simon Presler, -	Simon Presler, -	640	River Homochitto,	Do.	March 30, 1798.
" 13,	255	4	284	April 9,	Abijah Hunt, -	George Bailey,	640	Wells's creek,	Do.	March 30, 1798.
" 13,	256	4	285	April 9,	Abijah Hunt, -	James Erwin,	520	Sandy creek,	Do.	March 30, 1798.
" 13,	257	4	286	April 10,	Thos. Donaldson, in right of his wife Winifred,	Winifred Ryon,	500	Wells's creek,	Do.	March 30, 1798.
" 13,	258	4	287	April 10,	Adam Lanehart, -	Adam Lanehart,	500	Buffalo creek,	Do.	March 30, 1798.
" 13,	259	4	288	April 10,	Wilson Bolls, -	Wilson Bolls,	240	Big Black, -	Do.	March 30, 1798.
" 22,	260	4	289	April 13,	Thomas Foster, -	Stephen Douglass,	-	Lots No. 2 & 4, of sq. 80, Natchez,	Do.	March 30, 1798.
" 24,	261	4	290	April 22,	Francis Nailer, Jun.	John Burnet, Jun.	170	Bayou Pierre,	Do.	March 30, 1798.
" 24,	262	4	291	April 24,	Ebenezer Rees, -	John Odam, -	500f.	Bayou Pierre, -	Spanish,	Feb'y 24, 1795.

LAND OFFICE WEST OF PEARL RIVER, *May 1, 1807.*

THOS. H. WILLIAMS, *Register.*

REGISTER B—Continued.

Abstract of Certificates entered with the Register of the Land Office west of Pearl river, during the months of May and June, 1807, on which patents may issue without the payment of any purchase money.

	Commissioners' certificates.				Claim.				Title.	
When entered.	No.	Date.	Recorded. Vol.	Page.	To whom granted.	Name of original grantee or claimant.	Quantity allowed.	Situation.	Whence derived.	Date of order of survey or settlement.
1807.		1807.					Acres.			
May 1,	265	April 28,	4	292	William Spiller, assignee of Jeremiah Routh,	Jeremiah Routh, —	550	Cole's creek, —	Occupancy,	March 30, 1798.
" 1,	266	April 30,	4	293	Anthony Hoggatt, —	Anthony Hoggatt,	100f.	St. Catharine's creek, —	Spanish,	May 26, 1790.
" 2,	363	April 27,	4	294	William Smith, —	James Simmons,	550	Bayou Pierre, —	British,	Jan'y 8, 1777.
" 2,	364	April 27,	4	295	Eunice Humphreys, assignee of James Cole,	James Cole,	200	Cole's creek, —	Occupancy,	March 30, 1798.
" 14,	267	May 7,	4	296	John Clark, —	John Clark,	640	Bayou Pierre, —	Do.	March 30, 1798.
" 14,	258	May 12,	4	297	Hardiess Ellis, —	James Sanders,	234	Buffalo creek, —	Do.	March 30, 1798.
" 14,	269	May 12,	4	298	Abijah Hunt, —	Skipwith Durbin,	640	Wells's creek, —	Do.	March 30, 1790.
" 14,	270	May 12,	4	299	John Ritchie, —	David Waitman,	240f.	River Homochitto, —	Spanish,	April 26, 1790.
" 16,	271	May 15,	4	300	Richard King, —	William Cason,	640	River Homochitto, —	Occupancy,	March 30, 1798.
" 16,	272	May 16,	4	301	Levi Lusk, —	Levi Lusk,	320	River Homochitto, —	Do.	March 30, 1798.
" 16,	273	May 16,	4	302	Jacob Lusk, —	Jacob Lusk,	320	River Homochitto, —	Do.	March 30, 1798.
" 18,	274	May 16,	4	303	Thomas White, —	Thomas White,	640	Bayou Pierre, —	Do.	March 30, 1798.
" 18,	275	May 17,	4	304	William Lewis, —	Daniel Rayner,	260f.	St. Catharine's creek, —	Do.	March 28, 1794.
" 18,	276	May 17,	4	305	Thomas Freeman and John McKee, —	Louis Faure,	1,000f.	Cole's creek, —	Do.	Dec'r 29, 1791.
" 28,	277	May 17,	4	306	Simon Hook and Bartholomew James, —	James Stoddard,	203f.	St. Catharine's creek, —	Do.	Feb'ry 15, 1788.
June 3,	278	June 3,	4	307	Wm. Brooks, assignee of Jeptha Higdon,	Jeptha Higdon,	718f.	St. Catharine's creek, —	Do.	July 28, 1787.
" 3,	279	June 8,	4	308	Anthony Calvit, —	Anthony Calvit,	200f.	Mississippi river, —	Do.	Nov'r 2, 1794.
" 8,	280	June 8,	4	309	Anthony Glass, —	Anthony Glass,	640	Mississippi river, —	Occupancy,	March 30, 1798.
" 19,	281	June 9,	4	310	Samuel C. Young, —	Nathaniel Tomlinson,	128	St. Catharine's creek, —	Do.	March 30, 1798.
" 19,	282	June 9,	4	311	William Lintot, —	William Lintot,	Lots No.	1 and 2, of sq. No. 7, Natchez,	Do.	March 30, 1798.
" 19,	283	June 9,	4	312	John Williams, —	John Williams,	Lot No.	3, of sq. No. 26, Natchez,	Do.	March 30, 1798.
" 19,	284	June 10,	4	313	Thomas M. Green, —	Ebenezer Gosset,	200	Cole's creek, —	British,	
" 19,	285	June 10,	4	314	Thomas M. Green, —	Benjamin Roberts,	350	Cole's creek, —	Do.	
" 19,	287	June 10,	4	316	Thomas M. Green, —	Alexander Boyd,	123	Cole's creek, —	Do.	
" 19,	286	June 10,	4	315	Thomas M. Green, —	Henry Roach,	200	Cole's creek, —	Do.	
" 19,	288	June 11,	4	317	Legal representatives of Domingo Lorero,	Bertrand Febreau,	Lot No.	2, of sq. No. 25, Natchez,	Occupancy,	March 30, 1798.
" 19,	289	June 11,	4	318	James Moore, —	Andrew Scandlin,	Lot No.	1, of sq. No. 26, Natchez,	Do.	March 30, 1798.
" 19,	291	June 11,	4	320	Samuel P. Moore, —	James Rose,	Lot No.	4, of sq. No. 12, Natchez,	Do.	March 30, 1798.
" 19,	292	June 12,	4	321	John Stump, —	John Stump,	Lot No.	4, of sq. No. 26, Natchez,	Do.	March 30, 1798.
" 19,	293	June 12,	4	322	William Scott, —	John St. Germain, —	150f.	St. Catharine's creek, —	Spanish,	
" 19,	294	June 12,	4	323	Abijah Hunt, —	Ebenezer Smith, —	500f.	Bayou Pierre, —	Do.	Feb'ry 15, 1788.
" 19,	295	June 13,	4	324	Peter B. Bruin, —	Peter B. Bruin, —	640	Bayou Pierre, —	Occupancy,	March 30, 1798.
" 19,	296	June 13,	4	325	Jacob Airhard, —	Jacob Airhard,	Lot No.	1, of sq. No. 33, Natchez,	Spanish,	May 13, 1795.
" 19,	297	June 13,	4	326	Thomas M. Green, —	Joseph Dawes,	400	Cole's creek, —	British,	
" 19,	298	June 13,	4	327	Andrew A. Ellicott and John Walker, —	Peter Cabanne,	400f.	Homochitto river, —	Spanish,	Dec'r 1, 1788.
" 19,	299	June 13,	4	328	Ebenezer Rees, —	James White, —	400	Sandy creek, —	Occupancy,	March 30, 1798.
" 19,	300	June 13,	4	329	Benjah Osmun, assignee of A. Beall's heirs, —	John White, —	240f.	St. Catharine's creek, —	Spanish,	March 30, 1798.

LAND OFFICE WEST OF PEARL RIVER, *July* 1, 1807.

THOMAS H. WILLIAMS, *Register.*

REGISTER C.

Abstract of Certificates entered with the Register of the Land Office west of Pearl river, during the month of September, 1806, on which patents may issue without the payment of purchase money, but not until a judicial decision shall have been obtained against the conflicting British claims.

When entered.	No.	Date.	Recorded. Vol.	Recorded. Page.	To whom granted.	Name of original claimant.	Quantity allowed.	Situation.	Whence derived.	Date of order of survey or settlem't.	Name of claimant.	Name of original grantee or claimant.
1806.		1805.					Acres.					
Sept'r 1,	1	June 4,	4	38	Adam Tooley, -	Cadder Rabby, -	300f.	St. Catharine's creek,	Spanish,	May 26, 1790,	Heirs of D. Waugh, -	David Waugh.
" 1,	2	June 4,	4	39	Adam Tooley, -	James West, -	470f.	St. Catharine's creek,	Do.	March 28, 1794,	Heirs of D. Waugh, -	David Waugh.
" 1,	3	June 4,	4	40	Legal representatives of John Terry,	John Terry, -	700f.	Cole's creek, -	Do.	Dec'r 29, 1791,	Augustine Prevost, -	Augustine Prevost.
" 1,	4	June 4,	4	41	Anthony Hoggatt, -	John Tear, -	700f.	St. Catharine's creek,	Do.	Feb'ry 2, 1793,	Heirs of D. Waugh, -	David Waugh.

REGISTER'S OFFICE WEST OF PEARL RIVER, *October 1, 1806.*

THOMAS H. WILLIAMS.

REGISTER C—Continued.

Abstract of Certificates entered with the Register of the Land Office west of Pearl river, during the month of February, 1807, on which patents may issue without the payment of any purchase money, but not until a judicial decision shall have been obtained against the adverse British claims.

When entered.	No.	Date.	Recorded. Vol.	Recorded. Page.	To whom granted.	Name of original claimant.	Quantity allowed.	Situation.	Whence derived.	Date of order of survey or settlem't.	Name of claimant.	Name of original grantee or claimant.
1807.		1807.					Acres.					
Feb'ry 12,	5	Feb. 3,	4	141	Zachariah Kirkland, -	James Simmons, -	400f.	Mississippi river,	Spanish,	March 3, 1786,	Heirs of G. B. Rodney, -	Sir G. B. Rodney.
" 12,	6	Feb. 3,	4	143	Mordecai Throckmorton, -	John Holt, -	500f.	Cole's creek,	Do.	Feb'y 24, 1795,	Augustine Prevost, -	Augustine Prevost.
" 12,	7	Feb. 3,	4	145	Jesse Harper, -	Jesse Harper, -	500f.	Cole's creek,	Do.	Feb'y 24, 1795,	William Turpin, -	William Marshal.
" 12,	8	Feb. 3,	4	147	Jesse Harper, -	Jacob Shilling, -	500f.	Cole's creek,	Do.	March 28, 1794,	William Turpin, -	William Marshal.
" 12,	9	Feb. 3,	4	149	Cato West, -	Richard Trevilian, -	264f.	Cole's creek,	Do.	June 3, 1788,	Augustine Prevost, -	Augustine Prevost.
" 12,	10	Feb. 3,	4	151	John Burch, -	George Demoss, -	640	Cole's creek,	Occupancy,	March 30, 1798,	Augustine Prevost, -	Augustine Prevost.
" 12,	11	Feb. 3,	4	153	John Stabraker, -	John Stabraker, -	160	Mississippi river,	Do.	March 30, 1798,	Heirs of G. B. Rodney, -	Sir G. B. Rodney.
" 12,	12	Feb. 3,	4	155	Felix Hughes, -	Felix Hughes, -	640	Cole's creek,	Do.	March 30, 1798,	Ann Carr, Aug. Prevost,	John Firby, Aug. Prevost.
" 12,	13	Feb. 3,	4	157	John Cole, -	John Cole, -	600	Cole's creek,	Do.	March 30, 1798,	William Turpin, -	William Marshal.
" 12,	14	Feb. 3,	4	159	Prosper King, -	David Odan, -	640	Cole's creek,	Do.	March 30, 1798,	William Turpin, -	William Marshal.
" 12,	15	Feb. 3,	4	161	Hugh Slater, -	Hugh Slater, -	640	Cole's creek,	Do.	March 30, 1798,	Augustine Prevost, -	Augustine Prevost.
" 12,	16	Feb. 3,	4	163	George Jones, -	George Jones, -	640	Cole's creek,	Do.	March 30, 1798,	Augustine Prevost, -	Augustine Prevost.

LAND OFFICE WEST OF PEARL RIVER, *March 1, 1807.*

THOMAS H. WILLIAMS, *Register.*

REGISTER C—Continued.

Abstract of Certificates of pre-emption claims entered with the Register of the Land Office west of Pearl river, during the month of November, 1806.

When entered.	No.	Commissioners' certificates. Date.	Recorded. Vol.	Page.	To whom granted.	Name of original settler.	Quantity allowed.	Situation.
1806. Nov'r 15,	1	1806. September 4,			Reuben White,	Reuben White,	Acres. 100	Bayou Pierre.
" 15,	2	September 4,			Henry Ledbetter,	Henry Ledbetter,	200	Cole's creek.
" 15,	3	September 4,			James Hynum,	James Hynum,	226	Cole's creek.
" 15,	4	September 4,			Archibald Erwin,	Archibald Erwin,	450	Cole's creek.
" 15,	5	September 4,			John Martin,	John Pipes,	350	Cole's creek.
" 15,	6	September 4,			David Hunt,	David Hunt,	216	Cole's creek.
" 15,	7	September 4,			Thomas Fitzpatrick, assignee of James Milligan,	James Milligan,	438	Bayou Pierre.
" 15,	8	September 4,			Henry Kiper,	Joseph Green,	187	Cole's creek.
" 15,	9	September 4,			Arthur Brown Ross, assignee of Rachael Slone,	John Slone,	250	Bayou Pierre.
" 15,	10	September 4,			Charles Cissna,	Charles Cissna,	271	Cole's creek.
" 15,	11	September 4,			Aaron Neel,	Aaron Neel,	300	Bayou Pierre.
" 15,	12	September 4,			John Hill,	John Hill,	197	Bayou Pierre.
" 15,	13	September 4,			Samuel Boyd,	Samuel Boyd,	438	River Homochitto.
" 15,	14	September 4,			James Vincent,	James Vincent,	290	River Homochitto.
" 15,	15	September 4,			Thomas Morgan,	Thomas Morgan,	210	River Homochitto.
" 15,	16	September 4,			Francis Baldridge,	Benajah Spell,	640	Cole's creek.
" 15,	17	September 4,			Thomas Lacy,	Thomas Lacy,	320	Cole's creek.
" 15,	18	September 4,			William Lacy,	William Lacy,	320	Cole's creek.
" 15,	19	September 4,			Thomas Evans,	Thomas Evans,	500	Bayou Pierre.
" 15,	20	September 4,			Samuel Osborne,	Samuel Osborne,	67	River Mississippi.
" 15,	21	September 4,			Martin Cooper,	Martin Cooper,	200	Bayou Pierre.
" 15,	22	September 4,			Legal representatives of Christian Braxton,	Christian Braxton,	100	Bayou Pierre.
" 15,	23	September 4,			John Maylone,	Amos Hubbard,	100	River Mississippi.
" 15,	24	September 4,			Pliny Smith,	Phineas Smith,	640	River Mississippi.
" 15,	25	September 4,			John Woods,	John Woods,	250	Bayou Pierre.
" 15,	26	September 4,			Thomas Tompkins, assignee of James White,	James White,	100	River Mississippi.
" 15,	27	September 4,			Reuben Mayfield, assignee of John Delany,	John Delany,	243	River Mississippi.
" 15,	28	September 4,			William Kennison,	William Kennison,	372	River Homochitto.
" 15,	29	September 4,			Joseph Ford, Jun.,	Joseph Ford, Jun.,	304	River Homochitto.
" 15,	30	September 4,			Ebcaezer Clapp,	Ebenezer Clapp,	100	River Homochitto.
" 15,	31	September 4,			John Reed,	John Reed,	210	River Homochitto.
" 15,	32	September 4,			Joseph Slocomb,	Joseph Slocomb,	227	River Homochitto.
" 15,	33	September 4,			Moses Pipkin,	Moses Pipkin,	100	River Homochitto.
" 15,	34	September 4,			Henry Sloder,	Henry Sloder,	160	River Homochitto.
" 15,	35	September 4,			William Cissna,	William Cissna,	320	River Homochitto.
" 15,	36	September 5,			John Robinette,	John Robinette,	280	River Homochitto.
" 15,	37	September 5,			Joseph Galbreath,	Joseph Galbreath,	455	River Homochitto.
" 15,	38	September 5,			Asher Pipkin,	Asher Pipkin,	169	River Homochitto.
" 15,	39	September 8,			Samuel Lum, Sen.,	Samuel Lum, Sen.,	400	Bayou Pierre.

ABSTRACT for NOVEMBER, 1806—Continued.

When entered	No.	Date (1806)	Recorded Vol.	Recorded Page	To whom granted.	Name of original settler.	Quantity allowed. Acres.	Situation.
1805. Nov'r 15,	40	September 8,			James Bounds,	John Pollard,	200	Bayou Pierre.
" 15,	41	September 8,			Samuel Dearmond, assignee of David Lum,	Robert Thompson,	150	Bayou Pierre.
" 15,	42	September 8,			Ezekiel Evans,	Ezekiel Evans,	240	Bayou Pierre.
" 15,	43	September 9,			Joseph Quetgless, assignee of Jacob Drake,	Jacob Drake,	A lot below	the bluff in Natchez.
" 15,	44	September 9,			Hugh McD. Chisholm,	Hugh McD. Chisholm,	A lot below	the bluff in Natchez.
" 15,	45	September 9,			Robert Dunbar,	Robert Dunbar,	Lot No. 4,	of square No. 7, city of Natchez.
" 15,	46	September 9,			Robert Dunbar,	Robert Dunbar,	Lot. No. 3,	of square No. 7, Natchez.
" 15,	47	September 9,			Ferdinand L. Claiborne,	Ferdinand L. Claiborne,	Part of a lot	in the city of Natchez.
" 15,	48	September 9,			Legal representatives of John Scott,	John Scott,	Lot No. 4,	of square No. 1, Natchez.
" 15,	49	September 9,			Legal representatives of Andrew Beall,	Andrew Beall,	Lot No. 2,	of square No. 1, Natchez.
" 15,	50	September 9,			John Wilkins, Jun.,	-	Lot No. 3,	of square No. 3, Natchez.
" 15,	51	September 11,			Joshua Rundell,	Joshua Rundell,	100	Bayou Pierre.
" 15,	52	September 11,			Simeon Hollayday,	Simeon Hollayday,	170	Bayou Pierre.
" 15,	53	September 11,			Robert Hill, -	Robert Hill,	320	Bayou Pierre.
" 15,	54	September 11,			Gideon Lowry,	Robert Knox,	640	Bayou Pierre.
" 15,	55	September 11,			William Tabor,	William Tabor,	400	Bayou Pierre.
" 15,	56	September 11,			Andrew K. Boland,	Micajah Bennett	179	Bayou Pierre.
" 15,	57	September 11,			John Dennis, -	John Dennis, -	300	Bayou Pierre.
" 15,	58	September 22,			William M. Smith,	William M. Smith,	200	Cole's creek.
" 15,	59	September 22,			Jeremiah Watson,	Jeremiah Watson,	200	Cole's creek.
" 15,	60	September 22,			Marshall Stroud,	Marshall Stroud,	173	Cole's creek.
" 15,	61	September 22,			William Sharbut,	William Sharbut,	150	Bayou Pierre.
" 15,	62	September 26,			James King, -	Joseph Sanders,	225	River Homochitto.
" 15,	63	September 26,			Hezekiah Ford, assignee of Littleton Sanders,	Littleton Sanders,	414	River Homochitto.
" 15,	64	September 26,			John Calcote,	Darius Anderson,	320	River Homochitto.
" 15,	65	September 26,			James Owens,	James Owens,	294	River Homochitto.
" 15,	66	September 26,			Stephen Middleton,	Stephen Middleton,	155	River Homochitto.
" 15,	67	September 26,			Stephen Middleton,	Joseph Bradley,	112	River Homochitto.
" 15,	68	September 26,			James Scarlett, assignee of Reuben Mayfield,	Reuben Mayfield,	630	River Homochitto.
" 15,	69	September 26,			William Montgomery,	Benjamin Kitchens,	640	River Mississippi.
" 15,	70	September 26,			William Mackey,	William Mackey,	640	River Mississippi.
" 15,	71	October 29,			William Cooper,	William Cooper,	216	River Big Black.
" 15,	72	October 29,			Davenport Wiseman,	Davenport Wiseman,	297	River Big Black.
" 15,	73	October 29,			John Robinson, Jun.,	John Robinson, Jun.,	153	River Big Black.
" 15,	74	October 29,			Joseph Bullard,	Joseph Bullard,	200	River Big Black.
" 15,	75	October 29,			Legal representatives of Joseph Box, deceased,	Cyrus Marsh,	162	River Big Black.
" 15,	76	October 29,			George Sorrell,	George Sorrell,	204	River Big Black.
" 15,	77	October 29,			Raymond Robinson, -	William Dempsey,	350	River Big Black.
" 15,	78	October 29,			Duncan Cameron, -	Raymond Robinson,	365	River Big Black.
" 15,	79	October 29,			Hezekiah Wright, assignee of Duncan Cameron,	Duncan Cameron,	126	River Big Black.

ABSTRACT for NOVEMBER, 1806—Continued.

When entered.	Commissioners' certificates.				Claim.				
	No.	Date.	Recorded.		To whom granted.	Name of original settler.	Quantity allowed.	Situation.
			Vol.	Page.			Acres.	
1806,		1806,						
Nov'r 15,	80	October 29,	-	-	Duncan Cameron, -	William Knight,	211	River Big Black.
" 15,	81	October 29,	-	-	Legal representatives of Joseph Box, deceased,	Joseph Box, -	120	River Big Black.
" 15,	82	October 29,	-	-	Legal representatives of Samuel Lyon, deceased,	Samuel Lyon, -	200	River Big Black.
" 15,	83	October 29,	-	-	John Ragsdale,	John Ragsdale, -	405	River Big Black.
" 15,	84	October 29,	-	-	Harwood Jones,	Harwood Jones,	423	River Big Black.
" 15,	85	October 29,	-	-	Francis Jones,	Francis Jones,	300	River Big Black.
" 15,	86	October 29,	-	-	John L. Reynolds,	John Miller, -	120	River Big Black.
" 15,	87	October 29,	-	-	Vincent Fortner,	Vincent Fortner,	240	River Big Black.
" 15,	88	October 29,	-	-	William B. Elam,	Jesse Stephens,	200	River Big Black.
" 15,	89	October 29,	-	-	William Miller,	Thomas Beard,	320	River Big Black.
" 15,	90	October 29,	-	-	Jacob Phillips,	Jacob Phillips,	320	River Big Black.
" 15,	91	October 29,	-	-	Samuel Beard,	Samuel Beard,	211	River Big Black.
" 15,	92	October 29,	-	-	Larkin White, assignee of John Anthony,	Reuben Ray, -	500	River Big Black.
" 15,	93	October 30,	-	-	George Marshall,	Joseph Allen,	100	Bayou Pierre.
" 15,	94	October 30,	-	-	John McCaleb,	John McCaleb,	635	Bayou Pierre.
" 15,	95	October 30,	-	-	Henry Milburn,	Henry Millburn,	640	Bayou Pierre.
" 15,	96	October 30,	-	-	James McCaleb,	James McCaleb,	513	Bayou Pierre.
" 15,	97	October 30,	-	-	John Robinson, Sen.	Isaac Kemp, -	400	Bayou Pierre.
" 15,	98	October 30,	-	-	Edward Clark,	Edward Clark,	430	Bayou Pierre.
" 15,	99	October 30,	-	-	Joseph Moor, assignee of Jonathan Kemp,	Jonathan Kemp,	500	Bayou Pierre.
" 15,	100	October 30,	-	-	Reuben Ray, -	John Murphree,	100	Bayou Pierre.
" 15,	101	October 30,	-	-	John L. Reynolds, -	John L. Reynolds,	76	Bayou Pierre.
" 15,	102	October 30,	-	-	Samuel Dearmond, -	Samuel Dearmond,	640	Bayou Pierre.

REGISTER'S OFFICE WEST OF PEARL RIVER, *December* 1, 1806.

THOMAS H. WILLIAMS.

REGISTER D.

Abstract of Pre-emption Certificates entered with the Register of the Land Office west of Pearl river, during the month of December, 1806.

Commissioners' certificates.			Claim.			
When entered.	Number.	Date.	To whom granted.	Name of original settler.	Quantity allowed.	Situation.
1806. December		1806.			Acres.	
20,	103	December 15,	John Graves,	John Graves,	640	River Comite.
20,	104	December 15,	Richard Graves,	Richard Graves,	750	River Comite.
20,	105	December 15,	Robert Sims,	Robert Sims,	468	River Comite.
20,	106	December 15,	Leonard Hornsby,	Leonard Hornsby,	196	Beaver creek.
20,	107	December 15,	Micajah McCullen,	Micajah McCullen,	255	Beaver creek.
20,	108	December 15,	Jesse Lea, -	James Swain,	221	Beaver creek.
20,	109	December 15,	John Davis, assignee of Jesse Lea,	James Hazletop,	117	Beaver creek.
20,	110	December 15,	William Lawrence,	William Lawrence,	237	River Amite.
20,	111	December 15,	Jacob Currey,	Jacob Currey,	525	River Amite.
20,	112	December 15,	Moses Foster,	Moses Foster,	320	Beaver creek.
20,	113	December 15,	Edmund Andrews,	Edmund Andrews,	300	River Amite.
20,	114	December 15,	Robert Trentham,	Robert Trentham,	425	River Amite.
20,	115	December 15,	Mathew Tool, assignee of James Burney,	James Burney,	320	River Amite.
20,	117	December 15,	Henry Ratcliff,	Henry Ratcliff,	170	River Amite.
20,	118	December 15,	Abner Green,	Peter Ratcliff,	640	Beaver creek.
20,	119	December 15,	Francis Graves,	Francis Graves,	300	River Comite.
20,	120	December 15,	Christopher Nelson,	Christopher Nelson,	320	River Comite.
20,	121	December 15,	Samuel Lacey, assignee of Samuel Haper,	Samuel Harper,	274	River Comite.
20,	123	December 15,	Thomas Shropshire,	Thomas Shropshire,	100	Ueaver creek.
20,	124	December 15,	William Hickman	William Hickman,	150	Beaver creek.
20,	125	December 15,	Robert Montgomery, -	Robert Montgomery,	490	River Amite.
20,	126	December 15,	John Kneelan,	John Kneelan,	115	River Amite.
20,	127	December 15,	Matthew Tool, assignee of Robert Furlow,	Robert Furlow,	100	River Amite.
20,	128	December 15,	Isaac Jackson and W. Temple, assignees of John Berry,	John Berry,	534	Beaver creek.
20,	130	December 15,	William Curtis,	William Curtis,	383	Beaver creek.
20,	131	December 15,	William Burd,	William Burd,	320	Beaver creek.
20,	132	December 15,	John Courtney,	John Courtney,	590	River Amite.
20,	134	December 15,	David Drennon,	David Drennon,	174	River Amite.
20,	140	December 15,	David Callibam,	David Callibam,	217	Wells's creek.
20,	141	December 16,	William Hootsel,	William Hootsel,	390	Second creek.
20,	142	December 16,	Jane N. McCulloch,	Jane N. McCulloch,	234	River Homochitto.
20,	144	December 16,	Isaac Corey,	Isaac Corey,	200	River Homochitto.
20,	145	December 16,	Henry Moore,	James Erwin,	96	Wells's creek.
20,	146	December 16,	Joseph Montgomery,	Joseph Montgomery,	350	River Homochitto.
20,	151	December 16,	Joseph Erwin,	John House,	165	River Homochitto.
20,	154	December 16,	Francis Ballard,	Francis Ballard,	102	Sandy creek.
20,	156	December 16,	Nehemiah Carter,	Nehemiah Carter,	90	River Homochitto.
20,	162	December 16,	John Coale,	James McWaters,	183	River Homochitto.
20,	165	December 16,	Legal representatives of Zaccheus Tharp,	Zaccheus Tharp,	50	Bayou Pierre.

ABSTRACT FOR DECEMBER, 1806—Continued.

Commissioners' certificates.			Claim.			
When entered.	Number.	Date.	To whom granted.	Name of original setter.	Quantity allowed.	Situation.
1806.		1805.			Acres.	
December 20,	166	December 16,	David Sims, assignee of John King,	John King,	640	Cole's creek.
" 20,	168	December 16,	John Gibson,	John Gibson,	245	Bayou Pierre.
" 20,	171	December 16,	Buckner Dardin,	Buckner Dardin,	300	Cole's Creek.
" 20,	172	December 16,	Eli Crocket,	James Arbuthnot,	320	Bayou Pierre.
" 20,	173	December 16,	Thomas Parks,	Thomas Parks,	200	Bayou Pierre.
" 20,	161	December 16,	Landlot Porter,	Thomas Aldridge,	321	River Monochitto.
" 20,	164	December 16,	Samuel McCaleb,	Samuel McCaleb,	350	Bayou Pierre.
" 20,	175	December 17,	William Erwin,	William Erwin,	250	Buffalo creek.
" 20,	176	December 17,	Samuel Stocket,	Samuel Stocket,	500	Buffalo creek.
" 20,	177	December 17,	Legal representatives of William Dillahunter,	William Dillahunter,	100	Buffalo creek.
" 20,	179	December 17,	John Babcock,	John Babcock,	150	Buffalo creek.
" 20,	180	December 17,	William Jones,	William Jones,	190	Buffalo creek.
" 20,	181	December 17,	Joseph Johnson, assignee of Sylvester Stauts,	Sylvester Stauts,	105	Buffalo creek.
" 20,	182	December 17,	Daniel Leatherman,	Daniel Leatherman,	124	Bayou Sara.
" 20,	183	December 17,	Elijah Thearel,	Elijah Thearel,	390	Buffalo creek.
" 20,	184	December 17,	Rebecca Dove,	Rebecca Dove,	30	Buffalo creek.
" 20,	186	December 17,	Benjamin Rogers, Sen.	Benjamin Rogers,	134	Buffalo creek.
" 20,	187	December 17,	Robert Quine,	William West,	128	Buffalo creek.
" 30,	189	December 17,	Henry Quine,	Henry Quine,	130	Buffalo creek.
" 30,	195	December 17,	Gadi Gibson,	Gadi Gibson,	240	Bayou Pierre.
" 30,	196	December 17,	Gideon Gibson,	Gideon Gibson,	320	Bayou Pierre.
" 30,	197	December 17,	Eleazer Thorp,	James McElwee,	60	Bayou Pierre.
" 90,	199	December 17,	Jesse Griffin,	Jesse Griffin,	320	Bayou Pierre.
" 30,	200	December 17,	Westly W. Nealy, assignee of Lewis Coursey,	Lewis Coursey,	272	Bayou Pierre.
" 30,	203	December 17,	Joshua Matthews,	Joshua Mathiews,	100	Bayou Pierre.
" 30,	205	December 17,	Abijah Hunt, assignee of Asahel Oneal,	Thomas H. Woods,	403	Bayou Pierre.
" 30,	206	December 17,	Alexander Armstrong,	John Armstrong,	100	Bayou Pierre.
" 30,	207	December 17,	John Armstrong,	William Boyd,	100	Bayou Pierre.
" 22,	213	December 22,	James Bedsil, assignee of William Boyd,	Reuben Sutton,	250	Bayou Pierre.
" 22,	215	December 22,	Jesse Stephens,	Stephen Gibson,	390	River Big Black.
" 22,	217	December 22,	Stephen Gibson,	Nataniel Gibson,	180	River Mississippi.
" 22,	218	December 22,	Legal representatives of Nathaniel Gibson,	Tobias Gibson,	400	River Big Black.
" 22,	219	December 22,	Tobias Gibson,	William Lewis,	169	River Big Black.
" 22,	220	December 22,	William Lewis,	Jonas Griffin,	304	River Mississippi.
" 22,	221	December 22,	Jonas Griffin,	Jeremiah Jones,	650	River Mississippi.
" 22,	222	December 22,	Jeremiah Jones,	Ambrose McDonald,	334	River Mississippi.
" 22,	223	December 22,	Jonas Griffin, assignee of Ambrose McDonald,	Furney Griffin,	371	River Mississippi.
" 22,	225	December 22,	Legal representatives of Malachi Gibson,	Thomas Newman,	150	River Mississippi.
" 22,	230	December 29,	Thomas Newman,	Chileab Smith,	237	River Mississippi.
" 22,	231	December 22,	Chileab Smith,	Joseph Flannagan,	115	River Mississippi.
" 22,	235	December 22,	Elisha Flowers,		240	Bayou Pierre.

ABSTRACT FOR DECEMBER, 1806—Continued.

Commissioners' certificates.			Claim.			
When entered.	Number.	Date.	To whom granted.	Name of original settler.	Quantity allowed.	Situation.
1806.		1806.			Acres.	
December	246	December 22,	John D. Wilds, assignee of William Bovard,	William Bovard,	170	Bayou Sara.
"	248	December 22,	Benjamin Rawlins and J. D. Wilds,	Benjamin Rawlins,	200	Bayou Sara.
"	208	December 22,	Legal representatives of Gideon Matlock,	John Burnet,	240	River Mississippi.
"	209	December 22,	Daniel Burnet,	James Davenport,	300	Bayou Pierre.
"	214	December 22,	John and Samuel Cook,	John and Samuel Cook,	360	River Mississippi.
"	216	December 22,	Jeremiah Griffing,	Jeremiah Griffing,	560	River Mississippi.
"	224	December 22,	Thomas Arrananders,	Thomas Arrananders,	640	River Mississippi.
"	226	December 22,	William Hutchinson,	William Hutchinson,	640	River Mississippi.
"	229	December 22,	Shadrach Charvue,	Shadrach Charvue,	135	River Mississippi.
"	237	December 22,	Joseph Templeton and James Hyland,	Joseph Templeton,	300	River Big Black.
"	238	December 22,	James Lobdelle,	James Lobdelle,	125	River Big Black.
"	239	December 22,	Benjamin Steel,	Benjamin Steel,	55	River Mississippi.
"	242	December 22,	Lucius Smith,	Lucius Smith,	177	River Mississippi.
"	244	December 22,	Ezra Marble,	Ezra Marble,	106	River Mississippi.
"	245	December 22,	Thomas Hubbard,	Thomas Hubbard,	524	River Mississippi.
"	247	December 22,	Zachariah Walker,	David Lewis,	900	Bayou Sara.
"	249	December 22,	Pierson Nowland,	Pierson Nowland,	200	Thompson's creek.
"	250	December 24,	William Nowland,	William Nowland,	640	Thompson's creek.
"	251	December 24,	Joseph Dunham,	Joseph Dunham,	692	Thompson's creek.
"	252	December 24,	William Cain, assignee of Reuben Dunham,	Reuben Dunham,	400	Thompson's creek.
"	253	December 24,	Isaac Johnson,	Isaac Johnson,	1,250	Thompson's creek.
"	254	December 24,	Samuel Stockel, assignee of Francis Armstrong,	Francis Armstrong,	640	Thompson's creek.
"	255	December 24,	Moses Starnes,	Moses Starnes,	175	Thompson's creek.
"	256	December 24,	William West, Jun.	William West, Jun.	500	Thompson's creek.
"	257	December 24,	William West, Sen.	William West, Sen.	400	Thompson's creek.
"	258	December 24,	Micajah Frazier,	Micajah Frazier,	640	Bayou Sara.
"	261	December 24,	William Pharis,	William Pharis,	1,150	Thompson's creek.
"	262	December 24,	Henry Johnson, assignee of Hugh Dunham,	Hugh Dunham,	570	Thompson's creek.
"	263	December 24,	William Smith,	William Smith,	300	River Big Black.
"	264	December 24,	Samuel Ross,	Samuel Ross,	427	River Mississippi.
"	265	December 24,	Anthony Glass and Jesse Smith,	Jesse Smith,	640	River Mississippi.
"	268	December 24,	Joseph Ferguson, Jun,	Joseph Ferguson, Jun.	250	River Mississippi.
"	269	December 24,	George Ellis,	George Ellis,	640	Beaver creek.
"	274	December 24,	Robert Griffin,	Robert Griffin,	320	River Mississippi.
"	276	December 24,	Moses Floyd, assignee of John Calhoon,	John Calhoon,	320	River Big Black.
"	277	December 24,	Benjamin Hicks, assignee of George Marshall,	George Marshall,	351	River Big Black.
"	278	December 24,	S. B. Marshall,	S. B. Marshall,	378	River Big Black.
"	279	December 24,	Andrew Mundell,	Andrew Mundell,	410	Bayou Pierre.
"	280	December 24,	John Ellis,	John Ellis,	500	River Mississippi.
"	281	December 29,	Charles Collins,	Charles Collins,	640	River Mississippi.
"	282	December 29,	Seth Caston,	James Watkins,	258	River Mississippi.

ABSTRACT FOR DECEMBER, 1806—Continued.

Commissioners' certificates			Claim			
When entered.	Number.	Date.	To whom granted.	Name of original settler.	Quantity allowed.	Situation.
1806. December		1806. December			Acres.	
" 29,	283	December 29,	James Bolls,	James Bolls,	156	Cole's creek.
" 29,	284	December 29,	Anthony Glass,	Jacob Huffman,	320	River Mississippi.
" 29,	290	December 29,	Jonathan Mackey,	Jonathan Mackey,	341	Bayou Pierre.
" 29,	293	December 29,	William H. Wooldridge,	William H. Wooldridge,	458	Bayou Pierre.
" 29,	295	December 29,	Isaac A. B. Ross,	Samuel Jackson,	400	Cole's creek.
" 29,	297	December 29,	Gustavus Campbell,	Gustavus Campbell,	100	Cole's creek.
" 29,	302	December 29,	Jesse Cook,	Jesse Cook,	300	Cole's creek.
" 29,	304	December 29,	Lewis Humphreys, assignee of Robert Simmons,	Robert Simmons,	155	Cole's creek.
" 29,	305	December 29,	Jonathan Iones,	Jonathan Jones,	100	Cole's creek.
" 29,	306	December 29,	James Scartill, assignee of Ambrose Downs,	Ambrose Downs,	221	River Mississippi.
" 29,	307	December 29,	Andrew Glass,	Andrew Glass,	320	River Mississippi.
" 29,	309	December 29,	William Barland, assignee of Henry Platner,	Jesse Edwards,	640	River Mississippi.
" 29,	316	December 29,	Stephen Marble,	Stephen Marble,	113	Cole's creek.
" 29,	318	December 29,	James Melson, assignee of Thomas Owens,	Thomas Owens,	200	Cole's creek.
" 29,	380	December 29,	Richard Dardin, assignee of William Newman,	William Newman,	400	Cole's creek.
" 29,	322	December 29,	Abijah Hunt,	John Waddell,	640	Bayou Pierre.
" 29,	333	December 29,	Robert H. Morrow,	Darius Anderson,	100	River Homochitto.
" 29,	336	December 29,	Jacob Hyland,	Jacob Hyland,	300	River Mississippi.
" 29,	327	December 29,	William Cabean, assignee of Ire C. Kneeland,	Ire C. Kneeland,	409	River Comite.
" 29,	328	December 29,	James McCaleb, assignee of William Killcrease,	William Killcrease,	390	Bayou Pierre.
" 29,	329	December 29,	Legal representatives of Phillippina Beckley,	Phillippina Beckley,	900	Cole's creek.
" 29,	330	December 29,	Francis Blundell,	Francis Blundell,	400	Cole's Creek.
" 29,	331	December 29,	James Hyland, Jun.	James Hyland, Jun.	200	River Big Black.
" 29,	332	December 29,	John Gilbert,	John Gilbert,	50	Cole's creek.
" 29,	333	December 29,	John Gilbert,	Stephen Jett,	200	Cole's creek.
" 29,	334	December 29,	Isaac Fife,	Isaac Fife,	640	Bayou Pierre.
" 29,	335	December 29,	Abram Ellis,	Abram Ellis,	990	Cole's creek.
" 29,	336	December 29,	William Smith,	William Smith,	800	Bayou Pierre.
" 29,	337	December 29,	John B. Walback,	Joseph White,	204	Bayou Pierre.
" 29,	296	December 29,	Elisha Breazeale, assignee of Bartlet Shipp,	Bartlett Shipp,	120	Cole's creek.
" 29,	138	December 15,	Turner, Linton, & Co., assignees of Ephraim Bates,	Ephraim Bates,	400	River Amite.
" 29,	155	December 16,	John Callihan,	John Callihan,	640	River Homochitto.
" 29,	285	December 29,	Daniel McCaleb,	Daniel McCaleb,	157	Cole's creek.
" 29,	299	December 29,	Daniel Davis,	Daniel Davis,	130	Cole's creek.
" 29,	310	December 29,	William Fairbanks,	William Fairbanks,	200	River Mississippi.
" 29,	313	December 29,	Samuel Gibson, assignee of William Divine,	William Divine,	320	Bayou Pierre.
" 29,	210	December 22,	Samuel Bridges,	Robert Ashley,	150	Bayou Pierre.
" 29,	211	December 22,	James Smith,	James Smith,	289	Buffalo creek.
" 29,	271	December 24,	Micajah Davis, assignee of William Roach,	William Roach,	320	Beaver creek.
" 29,	116	December 15,	William Lea,	William Furlow,	261	River Amite.
" 29,	122	December 15,	Alexander McKay,	Alexander McKay,	84	Beaver creek.

ABSTRACT FOR DECEMBER, 1806—Continued.

Commissioners' certificates			Claim			
When entered.	Number.	Date.	To whom granted.	Name of original settler.	Quantity allowed.	Situation.
1806. December		1806.			Acres.	
29,	129	December 15,	John Francies, -	John Francies, -	176	Beaver creek.
29,	133	December 15,	Mark Cole, -	Mark Cole, -	336	Beaver creek.
29,	135	December 15,	Peter Haines, -	Peter Haines, -	260	River Amite.
29,	136	December 15,	Thomas Courtney,	Thomas Courtney,	320	Beaver creek.
29,	137	December 15,	Joseph Johnson, -	Joseph Johnson,	325	River Amite.
29,	139	December 15,	Owen Ellis, -	Owen Ellis, -	187	Beaver creek.
29,	143	December 16,	Caleb Worley, -	Caleb Worley,	238	Wells's creek.
29,	147	December 16,	George Davis, assignee of Andrew Ritchey,	Oliver Walton,	531	River Homochitto.
29,	148	December 16,	John McCoy, -	John McCoy,	50	River Homochitto.
29,	149	December 16,	Wylie Atkins, -	Wylie Atkins,	100	Wells's creek.
29,	150	December 16,	William R. Caston, assignee of John Caston;	John Caston,	230	River Homochitto.
29,	152	December 16,	Moses Miles, -	Luke Blount,	158	Sandy creek.
29,	153	December 16,	Absalom Wells, -	Absalom Wells,	178	Sandy creek.
29,	157	December 16,	Jesse Bryant,	Joseph Erwin,	160	Wells's creek.
29,	158	December 16,	Jeremiah Bass,	Jeremiah Bass,	184	River Homochitto.
29,	159	December 16,	John Hooser,	John Hooser,	640	River Homochitto.
29,	160	December 16,	John Wells, -	John Wells,	640	Sandy creek.
29,	163	December 16,	William Vardiman,	John Morgan,	380	River Amite.
29,	167	December 16,	James Norris,	James Norris,	400	Doul's creek.
29,	169	December 16,	Samuel Goodail,	Samuel Goodail,	200	Doul's creek.
29,	170	December 16,	Stephen Compton,	Stephen Compton,	245	Doul's creek.
29,	174	December 17,	John Hennington,	John Hennington,	31	Buffalo creek.
29,	178	December 17,	Joshua Baker,	John Nugent, -	320	Buffalo creek.
29,	185	December 17,	Benjamin Rogers, Jun,	Benjamin Rogers, Jun.	84	Buffalo creek.
29,	188	December 17,	Matthew Cole,	Matthew Cole,	61	Buffalo creek.
29,	190	December 17,	William Berry, assignee of Thomas Herren,	Thomas Herren,	500	Buffalo creek.
29,	191	December 17,	Reuben Jackson,	Reuben Jackson,	225	Buffalo creek.
29,	192	December 17,	Jacob Jones,	Jacob Jones,	500	Buffalo creek.
29,	193	December 17,	Augustine Roddy, -	Augustine Roddy,	90	Buffalo creek.
29,	194	December 17,	James Land, -	James Land,	57	Buffalo creek.
29,	198	December 17,	John Hannah,	John Hannah,	50	Buffalo creek.
29,	201	December 17,	Eli K. Ross,	Eli K. Ross,	640	Bayou Pierre.
29,	202	December 17,	David Sims,	David Sims,	200	Bayou Pierre.
29,	204	December 17,	William Pope,	William Pope,	100	Bayou Pierre.
29,	212	December 17,	John Murphree,	Lemuel Washburn,	102	Bayou Pierre.
29,	227	December 22,	William Downs,	William Downs,	500	Bayou Pierre.
29,	228	December 22,	Legal representatives of Sinclair Pruit,	Sinclair Pruit,	320	River Mississippi.
29,	232	December 22,	Mark Waters,	Mark Waters,	320	River Big Black.
29,	233	December 22,	Levi Norrell,	Levi Norrell,	500	Bayou Pierre.
29,	234	December 22,	George Cochran,	George Cochran,	172	Bayou Pierre.
29,	236	December 22,	Moses Jones,	John Thompson	105	Bayou Pierre.

ABSTRACT for DECEMBER, 1806—Continued.

Commissioners' certificates.			Claim.			
When entered.	Number.	Date.	To whom granted.	Name of original settler.	Quantity allowed.	Situation.
1806. December		1806. December			Acres.	
29,	240	22,	Simeon Holliday,	Simeon Holliday,	640	River Mississippi.
29,	241	22,	John Nailor,	John Nailor,	313	River Mississippi.
29,	259	24,	William Walker,	William Walker,	640	Bayou Sara.
29,	260	24,	James Collingsworth, William and George Brown,	James Collingsworth and Company,	1,600	Bayou Sara.
29,	266	24,	James Stansfield,	James Stansfield,	320	River Big Black.
29,	267	24,	Henry Parr,	Henry Parr, -	640	River Mississippi.
29,	270	24,	Thomas Holden, assignee of Matthew Robinson,	Matthew Robinson,	437	Tickfaw creek.
29,	272	24,	Benjamin Goodal,	Benjamin Goodal,	100	Petit Gulf creek.
29,	273	24,	Thomas Essex,	Thomas Essex,	320	River Mississippi.
29,	275	24,	Lemuel Hubbard,	Lemuel Hubbard,	640	River Mississippi.
29,	286	29,	Uriah Vining,	Uriah Vining,	130	Buffalo creek.
29,	287	29,	Stephen Terry,	Stephen Terry,	640	Cole's creek.
29,	288	29,	Michael Fake,	Michael Fake, -	152	Cole's creek.
29,	291	29,	Thomas Daniel,	Thomas Daniel,	330	Cole's creek.
29,	292	29,	James Corbet,	Lewis M. Talwood,	400	Cole's creek.
29,	294	29,	Joseph Bullen,	Joseph Bullen, -	640	Cole's creek.
29,	298	29,	Charles Trefore,	Charles Trefore,	100	Cole's creek.
29,	299	29,	Thomas Mosely, assignee of Henry Butcher,	Henry Butcher,	225	Cole's creek.
29,	300	29,	Edward Hinds, assignee of Major O'Dier,	William Gardner,	200	Cole's creek.
29,	303	29,	Joel Humphreys,	Joel Humphreys,	100	Cole's creek.
29,	308	29,	Rhoda Stanley,	Rhoda Stanley, -	269	Second creek.
29,	311	29,	Robert Moore,	Robert Moore,	640	Bayou Pierre.
29,	312	29,	Arthur Patton,	Briant Wheeler,	640	Bayou Pierre.
29,	314	29,	William Brocus, assignee of William Coursey,	William Coursey,	640	Bayou Pierre.
29,	315	29,	Joseph W. A. Lloyd,	Thomas Harrington,	320	Buffalo creek.
29,	317	29,	David R. Crosby,	David R. Crosby,	640	River Homochitto.
29,	319	29,	Daniel McNeely,	Daniel McNeely,	105	St. Catharine's.
29,	321	29,	William Atchinson,	William Atchinson,	130	Wella's creek.
29,	324	29,	Thomas J. Donaldson,	Thomas J. Donaldson,	183	Bayou Pierre.
29,	325	29,	Ezekiel Flower,	Ezekiel Flower,	250	Bayou Pierre.

LAND OFFICE WEST OF PEARL RIVER, *January* 1, 1807.

THOMAS H. WILLIAMS, *Register.*

REGISTER D—Continued.

Abstract of Pre-emption Certificates entered with the Register of the Land Office west of Pearl river, during the months of May and June, 1807.

Commissioners' certificates.			Claim.			
When entered.	Number.	Date.	To whom granted.	Name of original settler.	Quantity allowed.	Situation.
1807.		1807.			Acres.	
June 27,	338	May 16,	-	Daniel Harrigil,	100	Cole's creek.
" 27,	339	May 16,	-	Thomas Jordan,	100	Petit Gulf creek.
" 27,	340	May 16,	-	Hezekiah Harman,	130	Bayou Pierre.
" 27,	341	June 12,	-	Hugh Davis, -	800	Homochitto river.
" 27,	342	June 13,	-	Peter B. Bruin,	1,160	Bayou Pierre.
" 27,	343	June 13,	-	Adam Bingaman,	96	St. Catharine's river.
" 27,	344	June 13,	-	Moses Armstrong,	640	Bayou Pierre.
" 27,	345	June 13,	-	Elisha Eastes,	640	Wells's creek.

THOMAS H. WILLIAMS, *Register.*

LAND OFFICE, WEST OF PEARL RIVER, *January 1, 1807.*

REGISTER E.

Register of Pre-emption Certificates on which patents may not issue until a judicial decision shall have been obtained against the conflicting British claims.

Commissioners' certificates.			Claim.				Adverse British claim.	
When entered.	No.	Date.	To whom granted.	Name of original settler.	Quantity allowed.	Situation.	Name of claimant.	Name of original claimant.
1806.		1806.			Acres.			
Dec. 29,	1	Dec. 29,	Joseph Ferguson, sen.	Joseph Ferguson, sen.	598	Mississippi river,	Elihu Hall Bay, -	John Lorimer,
" 29,	2	Dec. 29,	James Chaney,	James Chaney, -	196	Cole's creek,	Augustine Provost, Ann Carr,	A. Provost, John Firby,
" 29,	3	Dec. 29,	Edward Turner,	Edward Turner,	160	Cole's creek,	Augustine Provost, -	A. Provost.
" 29,	4	Dec. 29,	Ed. Turner, assignee of D. W. Breazeale,	Drury W. Breazeale,	20	Cole's creek,	Augustine Provost, -	A. Provost.
" 29,	5	Dec. 29,	Washington Burch,	Washington Burch,	600	Cole's creek,	Ann Carr, -	John Firby.
" 29,	6	Dec. 29,	Zachariah Kirkland,	Z. Kirkland, -	640	Mississippi river,	Heirs of G. B. Rodney, -	Sir Geo. B. Rodney.
			John Burch,	John Burch, -	200	Cole's creek,	William Turpin, - -	William Marshall.

THOS. H. WILLIAMS, *Register.*

LAND OFFICE, WEST OF PEARL RIVER, *January 1, 1807.*

A List of Certificates granted by the Register and Receiver at the Land Office west of Pearl river, under act of June, 1812.

No. of certificate.	Register No.	Date	Names.	Where situated.	Quantity.
1	25	1812, Nov. 23,	Thomas Green,	In Adams county, near the city of Natchez,	100 arpents.
2	110	Nov. 23,	To the legal representatives of Joseph Benard,	In Wilkinson county, on the waters of Buffalo creek,	240 arpents.
3	161	Nov. 23,	Everard Green,	In Jefferson county, on the river Mississippi,	650 arpents.
4	259	Nov. 23,	Thomas Foster,	In Wilkinson county, on the waters of Buffalo creek,	640 acres.
5	347	Nov. 25,	Alexander Montgomery,	In Wilkinson county, on the waters of Buffalo creek,	640 acres.
6	368	Nov. 25,	David Corey,	In Claiborne county, on the waters of the river Homochitto,	500 arpents.
7	534	Nov. 25,	John Stampley,	In Claiborne county, on the waters of the river Big Black,	300 arpents.
8	739	Nov. 25,	John Henderson,	In Wilkinson county, on the waters of Thompson's creek,	640 acres.
9	714	Nov. 26,	Nehemiah Carter,	In Jefferson county, on the waters of Boyd's creek,	640 acres.
10	766	Nov. 26,	To the legal representatives of Garret Hapaige,	In Claiborne county, on the river Mississippi,	640 acres.
11	777	Nov. 26,	Joseph W. A. Loyd,	In Adams county, on the waters of Wells's creek,	500 arpents.
12	787	Nov. 26,	Thomas Percy,	In Wilkinson county, on the waters of the bayou Sara,	640 acres.
13	809	Nov. 26,	John Ellis,	In Wilkinson county, on the waters of Thompson's creek,	640 acres.
14	937	Nov. 26,	Catharine Surget,	In Wilkinson county, on the waters of Feliciana creek,	640 acres.
15	1,372	Nov. 26,	Charles Surget,	In Wilkinson county, on the waters of Feliciana creek,	500 arpents.
16	1,528	Nov. 30,	William Thomas,	In Claiborne county, on the bayou Pierre,	500 arpents.
17	1,568	Nov. 30,	Daniel Burnett,	In Claiborne county, on the waters of the bayou Pierre,	240 arpents.
18	1,926	Nov. 30,	Patrick McDermot,	In Wilkinson county, on the bayou Tunica,	440 arpents.
19	2,013	Nov. 30,	Solomon H. Wisdom,	In Adams county, lot No. 1, of square No. 13, city of Natchez.	
20	1,806	1813, Jan. 7,	Jacob Stampley,	In Adams county, on the river Homochitto,	200 arpents.
21	1,808	Jan. 7,	Ebenezer Rees,	In Claiborne county, on the waters of the bayou Pierre,	200 arpents.
22	813	Feb. 10,	Robert Dunbar, (duplicate issued July 26, 1819,)	In Claiborne county, on the waters of the bayou Pierre,	250 acres.
23	810	Feb. 10,	Robert Dunbar, (duplicate was granted, the original being lost,)	In Jefferson county, on the waters of Cole's creek,	400 arpents.
24	1,658	April 7,	James Cole,	Lot No. 4, in square No. 12, in the city of Natchez.	
25	1,367	Oct. 26,	To the legal representatives of Hiram Swayze,	Near the city of Natchez, in Adams county,	164 arpents.
26	285	1814, April 6,	Abraham Taylor,	Adams county, on the waters of the river Homochitto,	550 arpents.
27	442	May 31,	Prosper King, of Adams county,	Spanish order of survey to him, dated March 2, 1795, on the waters of Homochitto river, for 800 arpents,	
28	1,988	1815, Sept. 13,	John Girault, of Adams county,	Spanish warrant or order of survey to John St. German, dated December 16, 1785, situated in Warren county, near the mouth of the river Yaxe, for 1,000 arpents,	640 arpents.
29	1,989	Sept. 13,	John Girault, of Adams county,	Spanish warrant or order of survey to Henry Babikholst, dated March 22, 1785, situated in Warren county, 1¼ miles below the Walnut Hills,	640 arpents.
30	1,990	Sept. 13,	John Girault, of Adams county,	Spanish warrant or order of survey to Hugh Logan, dated April 7, 1791, situated on Cole's creek,	600 arpents.
31	1,001	Sept. 18,	John Ellis, of Wilkinson county	Spanish order of survey to him, dated April 15, 1789, for 800 arpents, on the waters of Thompson's creek,	240 arpents.
32	170	1818, June 9,	Daniel Burnett, of Claiborne county,	Spanish order of survey to James Davenport, dated August 18, 1789, for	640 acres.
33	468	June 9,	Daniel Burnett, of Claiborne county,	Spanish order of survey to James Stuart, dated November 16, 1794, for	300 arpents. 200 arpents.

SAMUEL L. WINSTON, *Register.*

LAND OFFICE WEST OF PEARL RIVER, *February 2, 1830.*

GILMER, R.H.,754
GILMORE, (Mr),664
GINDRAT, A.,746,747
GIRALT, Maria,783
GIRAULT, (Col),562, Francis,
777, John,563,565,566,570,
571,779,785,789,792,793,
797,802,811,824, Maria,781
GLASS, Andrew,820, Anthony,
905,812,819,820
GODLEY, Wm.,550
GOODAIL, Benjamin,822, Samuel,
821
GOODWIN, Phebe,808, Richard,
787, Thomas,582,587,588,
601,649,650,651,704,706,
716,718,725,770,772
GOODWN, Thomas,644
GORDON, J.,754,755, James,608,
616,617,624,625,650,670,
691,697,707,720,721,728,
748,762,763, John,581,587,
658,660,663,665,666,667,
671,725, Joseph,754
GORMAN, Wm.,779
GORMEZ, Salvador,627
GORMLEY, James,804
GOSSET, Ebenezer,812
GRAFTON, D.,780, Daniel,780,
Danl.Sr.,780, John,785
GRAHAM, Colin,547
GRANT, Allen,553,575,584,591,
760,761,768, Wm.,549
GRASS, Anthony,802, Antonic,
783
GRATON, Rebecca,809
GRAVES, Francis,817, John,817,
Richard,794,817
GRAY, Clinch,752, Ruffin,808
GREEN, Abner,775,777,791,794,
Abraham,778, Abram,777,
778, Everard,560,778,781,
785,796,824, Filmer,777,
778, Henry,563,786, Joseph,
777,814, Maria,777, Nathan,
704,R.,598 Raleigh,665,
671,699,723, Rawleigh,553,
587,666, Rawley,666,667
GREEN, Rawley,719,771, Rolley,
641, Rolly,597, Tho.M.,559,
Thomas,559,563,812,824,
Thos.M.,560,775,777,782,
Wm.,581,585,645,648,660,
708,719,771
GREENFIELD, Jesse,782
GREENLEAF, David,783,788,796
GRIFFIN, Absalom,785, Furney,
818, Gabriel,782, James,578,
585,596,597,654,690,702,
704,714,728,770, Jesse,818,
John,782, Jonas,818,
Robert,819, Samuel,657,
Wm.,805
GRIFFING, B.,786,787, Gabriel,
780,786, Jeremiah,819, John,
776,780,796
GRIMAREST, Henrique,616
GRIMBEAR, Simon,804
GRIMES, Dawson,627,654,660
GRINAGE, Aaron,696
GRUBB, Benjamin,568
GUICE, Abraham,775, Christop.,
780,785, Chrstop.,548,
Jacob,803, Jonath.,803,
Jonathan,765, Michael,780
GUION, Isaac,787,797, Sarah,
787
GULLETT, George,622,623
GURNET, Patrick,792
HACKLER, Martin,803, Samuel,
804
HAINES, Peter,821
HAINSWORTH, James,701, Levin,
581,585,588,660,662,663,
699,700,701,724
HALDERMAN, Anthony,557,
Fredr.,557
HALDERMAND, Fredr.,550
HALL, Charles,731, Edmund,803,
John,605,606, Sarah,731
HAMBERLIN, John,808, Wm.,811
HAMILTON, Cyrus,559, Jesse,
785, John,809
HANNA, Barton,619
HANNAH, John,821
HANNON, Barton,803, Philip,
778
HAPALGE, Garret,824
HAPER, Samuel,817
HARAULE, Charlott,625
HARDAWAY, Hartwell,598,599,
617,720
HARDESTY, Thomas,789
HARDING, Lyman,807
HARDY, Thomas,550
HARE, Andrew,796
HARGRAVE, (Capt),672, ,630,
671, Wm.,653, Wm.H.,581,
588,600,602,603,604,609,
612,632,644,647,649,651,
652,659,661,662,692,706,
714,719,724,726,727,772
HARGROVE, Wm.H.,599
HARMAN, Christ.,792,803,
Christian,807, Hezek.,571,
Hezekiah,780,823, Jacob,
560, James,570,810, Thomas,

800
HARPER, Jesse,813, Samuel,817
HARRIGIL, Daniel,823
HARRIGILL, Daniel,807
HARRINGTON, Thomas,822
HARRIS, George,705, Siddie,
705
HARRISON, Benj.,647,649,653,
Benjamin,578,589,601,609,
706,716,725,770,771,772,
Joseph,783,803, Patsey,800,
Rich.,784, Richard,564,
778,783,788,798,799,807
HARTLEY, John,777,781,783,
798, Michael,591,668,764,767
HARTLY, (Mrs),750, ,695, M.,
592, Michael,578,738,745,
749,750,751,752,753,767,
Rebecca,749, Wm.,749
HARWELL, R.,598,613,614,663,
688,690, Ransom,581,641,
642,643,667,671,704,719,
Ranson,587,771
HATLEY, Shered,649
HAURALE, Charlott,625,691
HAVARD, David,784
HAWKINS, John,589,698,701,
716,725,749, Richard,578,
589,651,668,688,692,695,
697,698,701,717,739
HAWLEY, Daniel,803
HAYES, James,809
HAYNSWORTH, Levin,670
HAZLETOP, James,817
HEADY, Samuel,807
HELVERSON, Godfrey,578,
Rachel,700
HELVERSTON, ,639, G.,585,
Godfrey,585,639,694,717,
718,724, Rachel,639
HENDERBRAND, David,805
HENDERSON, Alexr.,779,783,
784,785, Dorothy,787, John,
562,664,779,781,784,791,
824, Stephen,567,803, Wm.,
562,792,796
HENNINGTON, John,821
HENRY, John,749,750, Lemuel,
579,590,592,633,634,663,
668,692,693,695,710,720,
736,737,745,749,750,751,
754,763,764,767
HERAU, Charlott,650
HERAUL, Charlott,721
HERBERCEDER, Henry,787
HERREN, Thomas,821
HESTLER, Martin,793
HICKEY, Daniel,573
HICKMAN, Wm.,817
HICKS, Benjamin,819
HIGDON, Jephtha,568, Jeptha,
776,812
HILL, Henry,644,647, John,814,
Peter,784, Robert,815
HILLIS, Wm.,578,586,608,462,
715,748
HILLS, (Mr),672
HINDS, Edward,822, John,638
HINES, John,589,608,671,672,
709,713
HINSON, (Maj),711, J.,578,
John,620,621,642,643,711
HINSTON, ,609
HIORN, Wm.,775
HOCKET, Anthony,612, Wilford,
612
HODGE, David,549,550
HOGG, Stephen,769
HOGGATT, ,702, Anthony,580,
584,586,612,617,618,705,
710,769,781,782,789,812,
813, Antonia,618, James,555,
574,580,584,587,685,702,
709,778,788, Philip,807,
Wilford,584,587,612,629,
659,702,709,713,714,715,
716,769,772,782,803, Wm.,776
HOLBROOK, Austin,803
HOLCOMBE, John,786
HOLDEN, Joseph,806, Thomas,
822
HOLLAND, J.,809, John,807
HOLLAYDAY, Simeon,804,815
HOLLEWAY, John,619, Reuben,
653
HOLLIDAY, Samuel,550, Simeon,
822
HOLLINGER, ,703, A.,589,
Adam A.,628, Adam,578,579,
581,586,589,590,596,606,
607,608,627,628,629,638,
659,662,668,692,693,694,
698,702,709,713,716,718,
722,729,730,743,744,745,
746,747,748,749,750,751,
752,763,764,765,766,767,772
HOLLY, Nathanl.,804, Samuel,
805
HOLMES, Benjamin,782, Sarah,
775, Simpson,810
HOLT, David,776, John,566,813
HOOK, Benjamin,808, Simon,808,
812
HOOMAH, Alatala,773
HOOPER, Absalom,550, Innis,
802, Junis,547
HOOSER, John,821
HOOTER, Michael,778

HOOTSEL, Wm.,817
HOOVEN, Benjamin,578,734,740,
752,754,763,766
HOOVER, Benjamin,733
HOPKINS, Gideon,783, John,663,
796
HORNSBY, Leonard,817
HORTON, Abraham,783,787,806,
Enoch,802
HORTSUCK, Christ.,788
HOSTLER, John,780
HOUSE, John,817, Joseph,586,
619,689,715, Robert,619,655
HOVAN, Benj.,590
HOWARD, ,567, Charles,810,
James,782,808,810, Joshua,
563,568,574,584,587,606,
663,664,709,710,779,792,807
HOWEY, Wm.,806
HOYES, Wm.,799
HUBBA, Nanna,700,730
HUBBARD, ,571, Amos,814,
Lemuel,822, Thomas,807,
819, Wm.,570
HUCCABY, James,587
HUCKABY, James,582,648,651,
652,658,666,690,703,719,771
HUCKEBY, James,642
HUDSON, (Mr),669, Thomas,731
HUFFMAN, Jacob,820
HUGHES, Daniel,550, Felix,813,
James,549
HUMPHREY, Ralph,568
HUMPHREYS, Eustice,784,798,
812, Geo.W.,568,795,807,
Joel,822, Lewis,820, Ralph,
568, Sara,807
HUNT, A.,566,809, Abijah,558,
575,592,756,757,768,789,
792,794,796,807,810,811,
812,818,820, David,814, Wm.,
579,581,587,589,646,660,
662,663,667,714,724,727
HUNTER, Henry,783,789, Narsw.,
789, Narswor.,570,783
HUTCHINS, Anne,775, Anthony,
562,570,775,779,785,801,
Celeste,775,785, Eliz.,785,
John,775,798, Maria,785,
Samuel,567,779, Thomas,550,
798,801, Thos.Jr.,550,
Thos.Sr.,550
HUTCHINSON, Wm.,819
HUTSON, George,653, Kenith,
656, N.Kenner,584, Noah K.,
555,580,588,653,654,705,
714,715,769
HYLAND, Jacob,820, James Sr.,
810, James,819, Jas.Jr.,820
HYNUM, James,814
INGLES, Thomas,804
INNERARITY, James,748,755
IRVINE, Francis,571
ISINWOOD, Barnabas,804
ISRAEL, Philetus,783
IVERS, John,804, Wm.,551
IVY, Nathl.,779
JACKSON, Isaac,817, Joseph,
550,649,759,760, Reuben,821,
Samuel,820, Wm.,574,589,
705,706,709
JACOBS, Henry,808, Susanna,
549
JAMES, Barthol.,812, Benjamin,
703, John,649,806, Thomas,
549,564
JEFFERSON, Thomas,593
JELKS, Reuben,807
JETT, Stephen,820
JHNSON, Joseph,821
JOHNSON, D.,655, Daniel,578,
579,580,584,586,620,621,
630,631,632,642,643,646,
652,653,655,660,670,690,
708,711,712,713,714,715,
718, Edmund,808, George,689,
Henry,819, Isaac,565,566,
780,783,807,819, John,575,
578,580,584,590,592,621,624
JOHNSON, John,631,643,660,
689,711,712,724,732,747,
748,751,764,765, Joseph,818,
Moses,566, Solomon,578,
585,630,632,652,653,659,
670,690,713,715,726,727,
728, Wm.,550
JOHNSTON, Daniel,587,690,
George,605, John,553,587,
688, Solomon,587,772,773
JOICE, ,589
JOINER, Wm.,775
JONES, Charles,803, David,808,
Evan,573, Francis,563,816,
George,813, Harwood,816,
Jacob,821, James,550,573,
779, Jeremiah,818, John,777,
788, Jonath.,776, Jonathan,
820, Moses,821, Robert,588,
646,647,726,727,772,798,
Russel,811, Thomas,578
JONES, Thomas,587,656, Wm.,
818
JORDAN, Thomas,785,789,823
JOYCE, ,692,695, John,633,
641,659,668,669,702,703,
732,779, Maurice,779
JOYNER, Wm.,664
JURZAN, Peter,575, Pitagad,

www.ingramcontent.com/pod-product-compliance
Lightning Source LLC
Chambersburg PA
CBHW021852020426
42334CB00013B/300